Cutoff Points for the Student's *t* Distribution

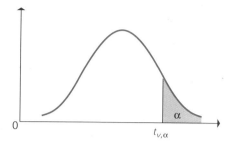

For selected probabilities, α, the table shows the values $t_{\nu,\alpha}$ such that $P(t_\nu > t_\alpha) = \alpha$, where t is a Student's t random variable with ν degrees of freedom. For example, the probability is .10 that a Student's t random variable with 10 degrees of freedom exceeds 1.372.

ν	α				
	0.100	0.050	0.025	0.010	0.005
1	3.078	6.314	12.706	31.821	63.657
2	1.886	2.920	4.303	6.965	9.925
3	1.638	2.353	3.182	4.541	5.841
4	1.533	2.132	2.776	3.747	4.604
5	1.476	2.015	2.571	3.365	4.032
6	1.440	1.943	2.447	3.143	3.707
7	1.415	1.895	2.365	2.998	3.499
8	1.397	1.860	2.306	2.896	3.355
9	1.383	1.833	2.262	2.821	3.250
10	1.372	1.812	2.228	2.764	3.169
11	1.363	1.796	2.201	2.718	3.106
12	1.356	1.782	2.179	2.681	3.055
13	1.350	1.771	2.160	2.650	3.012
14	1.345	1.761	2.145	2.624	2.977
15	1.341	1.753	2.131	2.602	2.947
16	1.337	1.746	2.120	2.583	2.921
17	1.333	1.740	2.110	2.567	2.898
18	1.330	1.734	2.101	2.552	2.878
19	1.328	1.729	2.093	2.539	2.861
20	1.325	1.725	2.086	2.528	2.845
21	1.323	1.721	2.080	2.518	2.831
22	1.321	1.717	2.074	2.508	2.819
23	1.319	1.714	2.069	2.500	2.807
24	1.318	1.711	2.064	2.492	2.797
25	1.316	1.708	2.060	2.485	2.787
26	1.315	1.706	2.056	2.479	2.779
27	1.314	1.703	2.052	2.473	2.771
28	1.313	1.701	2.048	2.467	2.763
29	1.311	1.699	2.045	2.462	2.756
30	1.310	1.697	2.042	2.457	2.750
40	1.303	1.684	2.021	2.423	2.704
60	1.296	1.671	2.000	2.390	2.660
∞	1.282	1.645	1.960	2.326	2.576

HAVE YOU THOUGHT ABOUT *Customizing* THIS BOOK?

The Prentice Hall Just-In-Time Program in Decision Science

You can combine chapters from this book with chapters from any of the Prentice Hall titles listed on the following page to create a text tailored to your specific course needs. You can add your own material or cases from our extensive case collection. By taking a few minutes to look at what is sitting on your bookshelf and the content available on our Web site, you can create your ideal textbook.

The Just-In-Time program offers:

➡ **Quality of Material to Choose From**—In addition to the books listed, you also have the option to include any of the cases from Prentice Hall Case Series and/or the Portfolio Custom Case Series which gives you access to cases (and teaching notes where available) from Darden, Harvard, Ivey, NACRA, and Thunderbird. Most cases can be viewed online at our Web site.

➡ **Flexibility**—Choose only that material you want, either from one title or several titles (plus cases) and sequence it in whatever way you wish.

➡ **Instructional Support**—You have access to all instructor's materials that accompany the traditional textbook and desk copies of your JIT book.

➡ **Outside Materials**—There is also the option to include up to 20% of the text from materials outside of Prentice Hall Custom Business Resources.

➡ **Cost Savings**—Students pay only for material you choose. The base price is $5.00, plus $2.00 for case material, plus $.08 per page. The text can be shrink-wrapped with other Pearson textbooks for a 10% discount. Outside material is priced at $.10 per page plus permission fees.

➡ **Quality of Finished Product**—Custom cover and title page—including your name, school, department, course title, and section number. Paperback, perfect bound, black-and-white printed text. Customized table of contents and index. Sequential pagination throughout the text. CD-ROMs can be included with the custom book if applicable.

Visit our Web site at http://www.prenhall.com/custombusiness

and download order forms online.

THE PRENTICE HALL
Just-In-Time program

BUSINESS STATISTICS

- Berenson/Levine, BASIC BUSINESS STATISTICS, 8/e
- Groebner/Shannon, BUSINESS STATISTICS, 5/e
- Levin/Rubin, STATISTICS FOR MANAGEMENT, 7/e
- Levine, et al., STATISTICS FOR MANAGERS USING MICROSOFT EXCEL 3/e
- Levine, et al., BUSINESS STATISTICS: A FIRST COURSE 3/e
- McClave/Benson/Sincich, STATISTICS FOR BUSINESS AND ECONOMICS, 8/e
- Newbold, STATISTICS FOR BUSINESS AND ECONOMICS, 5/e
- Shannon/Groebner, A COURSE IN BUSINESS STATISTICS, 3/e

PRODUCTION/OPERATIONS MANAGEMENT

- Anupindi, et al., MANAGING BUSINESS PROCESS FLOWS
- Chopra, SUPPLY CHAIN MANAGEMENT
- Foster, MANAGING QUALITY
- Handfield/Nichols, Jr., SUPPLY CHAIN MANAGEMENT
- Haksever/Render/Russell/Murdick, SERVICE MANAGEMENT AND OPERATIONS, 2/e
- Hanna/Newman, INTEGRATED OPERATIONS MANAGEMENT
- Heineke/Meile, GAMES AND EXERCISES IN OPERATIONS MANAGEMENT
- Heizer/Render, OPERATIONS MANAGEMENT, 6/e
- Heizer/Render, PRINCIPLES OF OPERATIONS MANAGEMENT, 4/e
- Krajewski/Ritzman, OPERATIONS MANAGEMENT, 6/e
- Latona/Nathan, CASES AND READINGS IN POM
- Russell/Taylor, OPERATIONS MANAGEMENT, 4/e
- Schmenner, PLANT AND SERVICE TOURS IN OPERATIONS MANAGEMENT, 5/e
- Nicholas, PROJECT MANAGEMENT, 2/e

MANAGEMENT SCIENCE/OPERATIONS RESEARCH

- Eppen/Gould, INTRODUCTORY MANAGEMENT SCIENCE, 5/e
- Moore/Weatherford, DECISION MODELING WITH MICROSOFT EXCEL, 6/e
- Render/Stair/Hanna, QUANTITATIVE ANALYSIS FOR MANAGEMENT, 8/e
- Render/Stair/Balakrishnan, MANAGERIAL DECISION MODELING WITH SPREADSHEETS
- Render, et al., CASES AND READINGS IN MANAGEMENT SCIENCE
- Taylor, INTRODUCTION TO MANAGEMENT SCIENCE, 7/e

For more information, or to speak to a customer service representative, contact us at 1-800-777-6872.

www.prenhall.com/custombusiness

5ᵀᴴ EDITION

STATISTICS FOR BUSINESS AND ECONOMICS

STATISTICS FOR BUSINESS AND ECONOMICS

PAUL NEWBOLD
UNIVERSITY OF NOTTINGHAM

WILLIAM L. CARLSON
ST. OLAF COLLEGE

BETTY M. THORNE
STETSON UNIVERSITY

Prentice
Hall

PRENTICE HALL, UPPER SADDLE RIVER, NEW JERSEY 07458

Library of Congress Cataloging-in-Publication Data

Newbold, Paul
    Statistics for business & economics / Paul Newbold, William L. Carlson, Betty
Thorne.—5th ed.
     p. cm.
    Includes bibliographical references and index
    ISBN 0-13-029320-2
    1. Commercial statistics. 2. Economics—Statistical methods. 3. Statistics. I. Title:
Statistics for business and economics. II. Carlson, William L. (William Lee), 1938– III.
Thorne, Betty. IV. Title
    HF1017.N48 2002
    519.5—dc21

2001059331

AVP/Executive Editor: Tom Tucker
Editor-in-Chief: PJ Boardman
Assistant Editor: Erika Rusnak
Editorial Assistant: Jisun Lee
Media Project Manager: Nancy Welcher
Marketing Manager: Debbie Clare
Managing Editor (Production): Cynthia Regan
Production Editor: Carol Samet
Production Assistant: Dianne Falcone
Permissions Coordinator: Suzanne Grappi
Associate Director, Manufacturing: Vincent Scelta
Production Manager: Arnold Vila
Manufacturing Buyer: Diane Peirano
Design Manager: Pat Smythe
Designer: Blair Brown
Interior Design: Blair Brown
Cover Design: Blair Brown
Manager, Print Production: Christy Mahon
Composition: UG / GGS Information Services, Inc.
Full-Service Project Management: UG / GGS Information Services, Inc.
Printer/Binder: Courier Kendallville

Credits and acknowledgments borrowed from other sources and reproduced, with permission, in this textbook appear on appropriate page within text.

Microsoft Excel, Solver, and Windows are registered trademarks of Microsoft Corporation in the U.S.A. and other countries. Screen shots and icons reprinted with permission from the Microsoft Corporation. This book is not sponsored or endorsed by or affiliated with Microsoft Corporation.

Pearson Education LTD.
Pearson Education Australia PTY, Limited
Pearson Education Singapore, Pte. Ltd
Pearson Education North Asia Ltd
Pearson Education, Canada, Ltd
Pearson Educación de Mexico, S.A. de C.V.
Pearson Education–Japan
Pearson Education Malaysia, Pte. Ltd

10 9 8 7 6 5 4 3 2 1
ISBN 0-13-029320-2

Bill Carlson is Professor of Economics and Department Chair of the Economics Department at St Olaf College, where he has taught for 29 years. His education includes engineering degrees from Michigan Technological University (BS) and Illinois Institute of Technology (MS) and a Ph.D. in Quantitative Management from the University of Michigan. His research includes numerous studies related to highway safety, management problems, and statistical education. He has previously published two statistics textbooks. He has led numerous student groups to study in various countries. He enjoys grandchildren, woodworking, travel, reading, and being on assignment in northern Wisconsin.

Author, researcher and award-winning teacher, Betty Thorne is Professor and Chair of the Department of Decision and Information Sciences in the School of Business Administration at Stetson University in DeLand, Florida. Winner of Stetson University's McEniry Award for Excellence in Teaching, the highest honor given to a Stetson University faculty member, Dr. Thorne also is the recipient of the Outstanding Teacher of the Year Award and Professor of the Year Award in the School of Business Administration at Stetson. She received her Bachelor of Science degree from Geneva College and the Master of Arts and Ph.D. degrees from Indiana University. She co-authored *Applied Statistical Methods for Business, Economics and the Social Sciences* (Prentice Hall, 1997) with Bill Carlson. Dr. Thorne is a member of the planning committee and serves as Secretary/Treasurer of the *Making Statistics More Effective in Schools and Business* conferences where she meets annually with fellow statisticians to discuss research and teaching issues. She also is a member of Decision Sciences Institute, the American Society for Quality, and the American Statistical Association.

She and her husband, Jim, have four children. They travel extensively, enjoy cruising, attend theological classes, and participate in international organizations dedicated to helping disadvantaged children.

BRIEF CONTENTS

CONTENTS

The fifth edition of *Statistics for Business and Economics* provides an understanding to support good statistical analysis and decision making. The importance of statistical analysis for business and economics has rapidly increased with the expansion of computer capabilities and electronic transfer of data. Data is collected routinely from all business, government, and non-profit activities. Keys to success in this fast paced and expanding world include correct statistical analysis, interpretation of output, an understanding of complex processes, and the use of computer resources.

FEATURES RETAINED FROM PREVIOUS EDITIONS

The previous editions of *Statistics for Business and Economics* were known for being unerring in accuracy and statistical precision as well as for their position at a mathematically higher level than most business statistics textbooks. The fifth edition of this book retains both the accuracy and level of previous editions. In addition, the authors have maintained the previous emphasis on care and clarity in explanations, reasons that various techniques are used, and the inclusion of a large number of examples and exercises involving real (or realistic) business and economic data.

CHANGES IN THE FIFTH EDITION

Building on the foundation of historical rigor and careful discussion of statistical concepts from previous editions, the fifth edition includes computer applications and interpretation as integral tools in the decision-making process and realistic examples and exercises with an accompanying CD-ROM that includes data files for all computer based exercises.

Computer Integration

Previous editions of this book did not include computer applications. One new feature of the fifth edition is the integration of computer applications with emphasis on statistical thinking and interpretation. You will find coverage of the Minitab Statistical System, Microsoft Excel and its Data Analysis ToolPak, and two add-ins to Excel: PHStat2, and TreePlan.

Our students use the computer with great success. We see an increase in student comprehension, a more positive attitude toward statistical analysis, and improved oral and written presentations. By using these tools, students are discovering the "fun" of statistics.

Minitab and Excel

Computer applications are integrated throughout the text on a need-to-know basis. We do not emphasize "how" to use a particular software package, but rather concentrate on the *interpretation of output* leaving instructions to screen shots and callouts. Figure 8.12 and Figure 2.3 illustrate computer output from Minitab and Excel respectively. Suppose that a student wants to estimate the mean fuel consumption for a particualr truck model. First, we develop an appropriate confidence interval. Then our approach turns to computer integration by obtaining Figure 8.12 with Minitab. Interpretation begins noting that no evidence of nonnormality exists (Anderson-Darling Normality Test). An icon in the margin with an arrow passsing through the word INTREPETATION indicates basic observations from the

FIGURE 8.12
Minitab Output for Trucks
Example

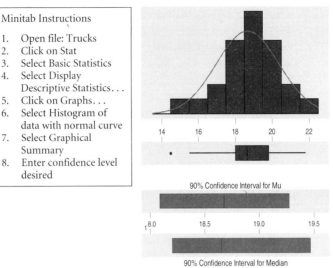

Descriptive Statistics

Variable: Example 8.5

Minitab Instructions

1. Open file: Trucks
2. Click on Stat
3. Select Basic Statistics
4. Select Display
   Descriptive Statistics...
5. Click on Graphs...
6. Select Histogram of
   data with normal curve
7. Select Graphical
   Summary
8. Enter confidence level
   desired

Anderson-Darling Normality Test
A-Squared: 0.286
P-Value: 0.594

Mean   18.6792
StDev   1.6953
Variance   2.87389
Skewness   -6.1E-01
Kurtosis   0.624798
N   24

Minimum   14.5000
1st Quartile   18.0000
Median   18.6500
3rd Quartile   19.8000
Maximum   21.8000

90% Confidence Interval for Mu
18.0861   19.2722

90% Confidence Interval for Sigma
1.3709   2.2471

90% Confidence Interval for Median
18.2000   19.4667

90% Confidence Interval for Mu

90% Confidence Interval for Median

graph. Figure 2.3, an Excel output, provides a histogram of the weights of a random sample of 100 bottles of a particular suntan lotion.

INTERPRETATION

If independent, random samples of 24 trucks are repeatedly selected from the population and confidence intervals for each of these samples are determined, then over a very large number of repeated trials, 90% of these intervals will contain the value of the true mean fuel consumption for this model truck. In practice, however, one does not repeatedly draw such independent samples.

Minitab 13.0 is used in this book. Academics and professionals respect the Minitab Statistical System for its power, ease-of-use, outstanding on-line help system, and excellent training opportunities. Minitab is widely used both in education and industry.

FIGURE 2.3
Cumulative Percentages for
Example 2.1 (Microsoft
Excel)

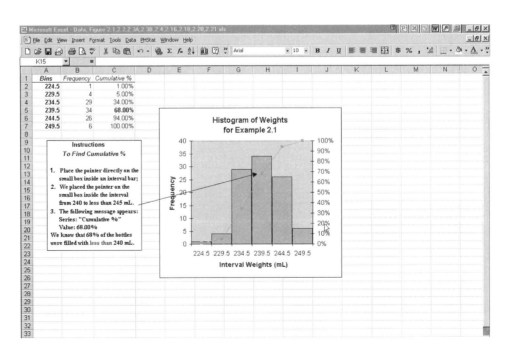

Most readers are already familiar with Microsoft Excel, the spreadsheet application from the Microsoft Office suite of programs. Keep in mind that Microsoft Excel is a spreadsheet package and not a statistical analysis package. The authors are well aware that many academics may question the use of Excel for statistical techniques. But many people wish to use Excel for some statistical analyses and in this book you will learn how and when to effectively use Excel. This text familiarizes students with Excel and the Data Analysis ToolPak, and discusses the positive features of Excel. Where appropriate, we also point out shortcomings in using Excel for statistical analysis purposes.

PHStat and TreePlan

The two add-ins to Microsoft Excel that are used in this book are PHStat2 and TreePlan. PHStat2 provides a custom menu of topics that supplement the Data Analysis Add-in Tools already included in Microsoft Excel. Between these two, the user is able to perform statistical analysis for most of the topics that would be covered in a business statistics course at the introductory level. TreePlan is useful with certain decision-making problems and is featured in Chapter 19 only.

Software and Data Files

PHStat2, TreePlan, and data files for both examples and exercises are included on a CD-ROM that accompanies this book.

Examples and Exercises

Examination of this book and the included CD-ROM reveals the importance that we place on working with real data. Problems that come to us in the business and economic world do not exactly fit the standard assumptions from mathematical statistics. Students need to learn how to interpret real problems and adapt them to standard models of analysis. In this way the great power of the standard analysis models can help you to unlock the important relationships contained in real processes and systems. Proper modeling, analyzing the data, and using the power of available computer procedures are the keys to understanding these important relationships. In this book you will see many examples of how statistical procedures are applied combined with discussions of why certain analyses were performed and how to interpret the results.

Suntan

A small CD icon in the margin next to an example indicates that the data for that example is stored in the CD-ROM that accompanies this book. The name of the data file is below the CD. For example, you will see a CD with the name **Suntan** in the margin next to Example 2.1.

In Example 2.1 the operations manager at a suntan lotion manufacturing plant wants to be sure that the process for filling 8 oz (237 mL) bottles of a particular suntan lotion is operating properly. The file **Suntan** contains weights of a random sample of 100 bottles of this particular suntan lotion. Files are saved in Minitab (with extensions .mtw and .mtp) and in Excel (with extension .xls). Students open the file corresponding to the software package that they intend to use. Here, a student can choose between Suntan.mtw, Suntan.mtp or Suntan.xls.

End-of-Chapter Bibliographies/Web Sites

Many of the chapters include bibliographic references and/or suggested Web sites that provide students with additional sources for more advanced information.

CHAPTER SUMMARIES

CHAPTERS 1–3: DATA ANALYSIS WITH EMPHASIS ON DESCRIPTIVE STATISTICS

Chapters 1 through 3 provide a strong data analysis foundation. Here you will learn basic computational procedures and how to examine data using statistical and graphical tools. The emphasis here is description of the data and how you can develop appropriate intuition as you examine data. Chapter 1 provides a foundation in systems thinking that helps us formulate problems. Chapter 2 provides extensive analysis procedures for single variables. Chapter 3 provides descriptive tools for beginning to explore the relationships between two variables—clearly an important requirement for business and economics problems. You will note the extensive use of examples and will learn how many computer based graphical procedures can be used to help gain insights.

CHAPTERS 4–6: PROBABILITY AND RANDOM VARIABLES

Chapters 4 through 6 provide a rigorous foundation in probability and random variables. This material provides the foundation for important decision making and for statistical analysis. We have included material that goes beyond most textbooks including extensive applications using Bayes Theorem and overinvolvment ratios. We show how to use the computer to obtain probabilities from standard distributions. We have included considerable discussion of joint random variables and linear combinations of independent and correlated random variables, to provide a foundation for applications in areas such as finance.

CHAPTERS 7–9: CLASSICAL STATISTICAL INFERENCE

Chapters 7 through 9 are a careful development of classical statistical inference that is basic to interpreting results and decision making. Sampling distributions are introduced and the central limit theorem is introduced using both practical discussion and Monte Carlo simulation. Confidence intervals and hypothesis tests are developed extensively for both single populations and comparisons between populations. You will learn the key modeling and analysis concepts and how to use the computer to perform the tedious calculations and to prepare clear displays of your results.

CHAPTERS 10–12: CORRELATION AND REGRESSION

Chapters 10 through 12 provide an extensive development of correlation and simple and multiple regression. In addition to development of both a clear understanding of regression analysis and its interpretation we have also included many important extensions such as transformations for non-linear models, dummy variables, lagged variables, effect of missing variables, time series data, and more. Many examples indicate how to interpret the various statistics. In addition there is discussion of the thinking required for developing regression models. An extended case example takes you through the various analysis procedures that would typically be used to develop a multiple regression model. This example illustrates how the computer can be used effectively in the model development process.

CHAPTER 13: NONPARAMETRIC STATISTICS

This chapter introduces the student to nonparametric statistics including the Sign Test, Wilcoxon Signed Rank Test, Mann-Whitney U Test, Wilcoxon Rank Sum Test, and the Spearman Rank Correlation. Confidence Intervals and computer applications are new in this edition.

CHAPTER 14: GOODNESS-OF-FIT TESTS AND CONTINGENCY TABLES

A test of the hypothesis that data are generated by a *fully specified* probability distribution is considered first. Next, we test the hypothesis that data are generated by some distribution, such as the binomial, the Poisson, or the normal, without assuming the parameters of that distribution to be known. The chi-square test can be extended to deal with a problem in which a sample is taken from a population, each of whose members can be uniquely cross classified according to a pair of attributes. Computer applications are included.

CHAPTER 15: ANALYSIS OF VARIANCE

Chapter 15 provides a good foundation for one-way and two-way analysis of variance. Clear computer based examples indicate how to implement the procedures.

CHAPTER 16: INTRODUCTION TO QUALITY

Control charts for means, standard deviations, proportions, number of occurrences, and ranges are included in this chapter. Process capabilities and computer applications are also discussed.

CHAPTER 17: TIME SERIES ANALYSIS AND FORECASTING

Chapter 17 provides an introduction to index numbers and to basic procedures for time series forecasting. With this chapter and the numerous examples you will be able to start developing some useful forecasting models.

CHAPTER 18: ADDITIONAL TOPICS IN SAMPLING

Students will study the basic steps of a sampling study, sampling and nonsampling errors, simple random sampling and stratified sampling, determination of sample size, and other sampling methods.

CHAPTER 19: STATISTICAL DECISION THEORY

Topics in this chapter include decision making under uncertainty, solutions not involving the specification of probabilities (maximin criterion and minimax regret criterion), expected monetary value, decision trees sampling information (Bayesian analysis and value), and allowing for risk (Utility Analysis). TreePlan and other computer applications are new to this edition.

SUPPLEMENT PACKAGE

This text is accompanied by many supplements for both students and instructors.

FOR THE STUDENT

Student Solutions Manual

A Student Solutions Manual, prepared by Steve Huchendorf, contains detailed solutions to all even-numbered exercises available with this text. These solutions provide feedback and allow you to check your answers to these exercises. The cycle of learning statistical procedures in depth followed by working with real problems followed by feedback on your solution has led to successful learning by thousands of students in our combined years of teaching statistics. Our teaching experience and shared discussion with many other strong teachers has provided the learning environment in this book that can also help you to be successful.

Companion Web Site

The Web site for this text found at **www.prenhall.com/newbold** includes: Interactive Study Guide, In the News articles, Internet Exercises, and the Instructor's Resources (password protected).

FOR THE INSTRUCTOR

Instructor's Solutions Manual

Prepared by Steve Huchendorf, the Instructor's Solutions Manual features detailed solutions and answers to all of the text exercises.

Test Item File

The test item file, prepared by Andrew Narwald of the University of San Diego, contains a variety of true/false, multiple choice, and essay questions for every chapter.

TestGen-EQ Software

New for this edition, the print Test Banks are designed for use with the TestGen-EQ test-generating software. This computerized package allows instructors to custom design, save and generate classroom tests. The test program permits instructors to edit, add, or delete questions from the test banks; edit existing graphics and create new graphics; analyze test results; and organize a database of tests and student results. This new software allows for greater flexibility and ease of use. It provides many options for organizing and displaying tests, along with a search and sort feature. The software can prepare 25 versions of a single test.

PowerPoint Presentations

Prepared by Mark Karscig of Central Missouri State University, the slides are oriented toward text learning objectives and build upon key concepts in the text. They are available for instructors to download from **www.prenhall.com.newbold**. They are also found on the Instructor's Resource CD-ROM.

Instructor's Resource CD-ROM

The Instructor's Resource CD-ROM provides the electronic files for the entire Instructor's Solutions Manual (in MS Word), PowerPoint presentations (in PowerPoint), Test Item File (in MS Word), and computerized test bank (TestGen-EQ).

WebCT, Blackboard, CourseCompass

Prentice Hall now makes its class-tested online course content available in WebCT, Blackboard, and CourseCompass. Instructors receive easy-to-use design templates, communication, testing, and course management tools. To learn more, contact your local Prentice Hall representative or go to **http://www.prenhall.com/demo** for a quick preview of our online solutions.

ACKNOWLEDGMENTS

Our sincere appreciation is extended to the many people who contributed to the development of this textbook.

We offer thanks to the following reviewers for their valuable input and suggestions for improvement:

Ken Alexander, *University of Southern California*

Eric Bentzen, *Copenhagen School of Business*

Myles J. Callan, *University of Virginia*

Gordon Fisher, *Concordia University*

Hans Geilenkirchen, *Erasmus University*

Paul Glasserman, *Columbia University*

William J. Hausman, *College of William and Mary*

Madhu S. Mohanty, *California State University at Los Angeles*

Andrew Narwold, *University of San Diego*

C. Barry Pfitzner, *Randolph-Macon College*

Peter C. Reiss, *Stanford School of Business*

Harold F. Williamson, *University of Illinois at Urbana-Champaign*

Sue Schou, *Idaho State University*

The outstanding staff at Prentice Hall deserves our highest compliments and thanks. A special note of appreciation is due to our Executive Editor Tom Tucker for his professional work, for keeping us on track, and for guidance during the development of this book. Thank you, Tom. And thanks to all the Prentice Hall staff who assisted with this project, including:

Executive Editor – Tom Tucker

Assistant Editor – Erika Rusnak

Editorial Assistant – Jisun Lee

Production Editor – Carol Samet

Media Project Manager – Nancy Welcher

Executive Marketing Manager – Debbie Clare

Special appreciation is extended to Sandra Gormley, UG Production Services, for her assistance and expertise.

From St. Olaf College we must thank Ms. Priscilla Hall, St. Olaf Administrative Assistant, for her work on various parts of the book and her management of the work of various student workers including Michael Loop, Holly Malcomson, Erin McMurtry, Terry Schwinghammer, and Catharina Zuber. Without their contributions this book would not have been possible.

From Stetson University, we extend appreciation to Paul Dascher, Shirley Ferguson, Marie Gilotti, Jan Pugh, Robert Saum, Jay Stryker, Sean A. Thomas, and John Tichenor. Also, a special thanks is given to Jennie Bishop (Computer Programmer Analyst II, State of Florida, Volusia County Health Department) and Jon Thorne (electronic business technology major at Stetson University).

In addition, we express special thanks to our families for support during many long hours devoted to this book. Bill Carlson extends special thanks to his wife Charlotte and to their adult children Andrea, Douglas, and Larry. Betty Thorne extends special thanks to her husband Jim and to their adult children Jennie Bishop, Ann Thorne, Renee Payne, and Jon Thorne.

WHY STUDY STATISTICS?

INTRODUCTION

In today's world we are surrounded on all sides by a veritable barrage of numbers. It seems that the world is afloat in data. Newspaper articles and television news reports include statements such as "the Dow-Jones average fell 6 points today," or "the Consumer Price Index rose by .8% last month," or "the latest survey indicates that the president's approval rating now stands at 53%." It is becoming the case that in order to obtain an intelligent appreciation of current developments, you need to absorb and interpret substantial amounts of numerical data. Government and businesses spend billions collecting data. Government has contributed to this development, both through its own collection efforts and through requirements for corporations to release information. The private sector, too, has played its part. The well-publicized Gallup surveys of voters' attitudes and Nielsen ratings of the week's television shows are merely the tip of a vast iceberg of market research studies. Certainly, the amount of such data that is collected has grown at a phenomenal rate over the past few years.

Somebody has to make sense of all the data. The computer age has given to us both the power to rapidly process, summarize, and analyze data and the encouragement to produce and store more data. Computers have brought data, such as stock quotes, to our fingertips. Proper interpretation of data is essential. If there has ever been a time that needs to understand statistics and to think statistically, it is now in the twenty first century. This text is designed to provide you with a foundation to understand, analyze, and interpret data in order to make wise decisions in the face of uncertainty.

1.1   DECISION MAKING IN AN UNCERTAIN ENVIRONMENT

Everyday decisions are made based on incomplete information. In any business, decisions are made regularly in an environment where decision makers cannot be certain of the future behavior of those factors that will eventually affect the outcome resulting from various options under consideration.

In submitting a bid for a contract, a manufacturer will not be completely certain of total future costs involved nor have knowledge about bids to be submitted by competitors. In spite of this uncertainty, a bid must be made. An investor, deciding how to balance a portfolio among stocks, bonds, and money market instruments, must make decisions when future market movements are unknown. This investor does not know with certainty whether the market will be buoyant, steady, or depressed.

Dealing with Uncertainty

Consider the following statements:

- "The price of IBM stock will be higher in six months than it is now."
- "If the federal budget deficit is as high as predicted, interest rates will remain high for the rest of the year."
- "The best opportunities for improvement in market share for this product lie in an advertising campaign aimed at the 18-to-25-year-old age group."

Each of these statements contains language suggesting a spurious amount of certainty. At the time the assertions were made, it would have been impossible to be *sure* of their truth. Although an analyst may believe that anticipated developments over the next few months are such that the price of IBM stock is likely to rise over the period, he or she will not be certain of this. Thus, from a purely semantic point of view, the statements should be modified, as indicated by the following examples:

- "The price of IBM stock is *likely* to be higher in six months than it is now."
- "If the federal budget deficit is as high as predicted, it is *probable* that interest rates will remain high for the rest of the year."
- "The best opportunities for improvement in market share for this product *probably* lie in an advertising campaign aimed at the 18-to-25-year-old age group."

However, our concern about uncertainty is not merely semantical. To replace unwarrantedly precise statements with unnecessarily vague statements is inadequate. After all, what is meant by "is likely to be" or "it is probable that"? Perhaps the modified statements could be interpreted as assertions that the events of interest are more likely than not to occur. But *how much* more likely is it? The English language is rich in words that describe uncertainty. Nevertheless, language alone is inadequate to provide a satisfactory description of the degree of uncertainty attached to the occurrence of a particular event. Rather, a more formal structure for this purpose is needed.

Sampling

Before bringing a new product to market, a manufacturer wants to arrive at some assessment of the likely level of demand, and a market research survey may be undertaken. The manufacturer is, in fact, interested in *all* potential buyers (the **population**). However, it is prohibitively expensive, if not impossible, for a typical market research survey to contact every potential buyer. Rather, a small subset (**sample**) of buyers will be contacted.

POPULATION AND SAMPLE

A **population** is the complete set of all items in which an investigator is interested. A population is the set of all of the outcomes from a system or process that is to be studied. *N* represents population size. A **sample** is an observed subset of population values with sample size given by *n*.

Other examples of populations might be:

1. Names of all the registered voters in the United States
2. Weights of the contents of all 24 oz (710 mL) bottles of natural spring water bottled by a particular company
3. Incomes of all families living in Daytona Beach
4. Annual returns of all stocks traded on the New York Stock Exchange
5. Costs of all claims for medical insurance coverage received by a company in a given year
6. Grade point averages (GPA) of all students in your university
7. Values of all accounts receivable for a corporation

Consider the population of all grade point averages for a small university of 2,000 students. You might conceivably obtain the GPA of every student. The data would then constitute the complete set, or population, of all student GPAs in this university. Or, depending on the problem to be studied, the population of interest might be the GPAs of only marketing majors, music majors, or senior accounting majors.

Population sizes are often so large that they are unwieldy to analyze. Collection of complete information for a population could be prohibitively expensive. Even in circumstances where sufficient resources seem available, time constraints make the examination of a subset, or sample, necessary.

If a sample is taken from a population, the analysis does not end at this point. The eventual aim is to make statements that have some validity about the population at large. Therefore, the sample must be representative of the population. Suppose, for instance, that a market researcher wants to estimate the income of Daytona Beach residents. It would be unwise to restrict the survey of incomes to the families living in the researcher's immediate neighborhood. Such incomes probably do not represent the incomes of all residents and may well be weighted toward one end of the income scale. To avoid errors of this type, it is important that the principle of *randomness* be embodied in the sample selection process. To obtain a random sample, the selection mechanism must be designed so that every sample of the same size is equally likely to be chosen. There are many types of random samples (some will be discussed in Chapter 18), but the most intuitively appealing and the type used throughout this book is the simple random sample.

RANDOM SAMPLE

Suppose a sample of *n* objects is to be selected from a population of *N* objects. **Simple random sampling** is a procedure in which every possible sample of *n* objects is equally likely to be chosen. This method is so common that the adjective *simple* is generally dropped, and the resulting sample is called a **random sample**.

It is important to mention that sometimes there are difficulties in obtaining simple random samples. It might be impossible, for example, to obtain a list of the population of all registered voters in the United States.

Sampling is vital in all functional areas of business. Sample output is selected to determine if a production process is operating correctly. An audit of accounts receivable will generally be based on a sample of all accounts. During presidential election years, estimates of voter preference are obtained from samples of registered voters, or perhaps an exit poll of voters may attempt to predict which candidate will obtain a state's electoral votes. Certainly, proper sampling is fundamental to any interpretation of data. Even the best of pollsters can make errors or have difficulties in obtaining random samples (for example, the 2000 U.S. Presidential election and subsequent debates concerning the Florida count).

However, taking a sample is merely a means to an end. The objective is not to make statements about the sample but, rather, to draw conclusions about the wider population. Statistics involve the extent to which it is possible to generalize about a population, based on results obtained from a sample. Some uncertainty will always remain.

Analyzing Relationships

- Does the rate of growth of the money supply influence the inflation rate?
- If General Motors increases the price of mid-size cars by 5%, what will be the effect on the sales of these cars?
- Does minimum wage legislation affect the level of unemployment?

Each of these questions is concerned with the possibility and nature of a relationship between two or more variables of interest. For example, how does one begin to answer the question about the effect on the demand for automobiles of a 5% increase in prices? Simple economic theory tells us that, all other things being equal, an increase in price will lead to a decrease in demand. However, such theory is purely qualitative. It does not tell us *by how much* demand will fall.

To proceed further, information must be collected in order to assess how demand has responded to price changes in the past. The study of statistics will help you to collect such information and to analyze relationships.

Forecasting

Reliable predictions are necessary in business. Investment decisions must be made well ahead of the time at which a new product can be brought to market, and forecasts of likely market conditions some years into the future would obviously be desirable. For established products, short-term sales forecasts are important in the setting of inventory levels and production schedules. Predictions of future interest rates are important to a company deciding whether to issue new debt. In formulating a coherent economic policy, the government requires forecasts of the likely outcomes for variables such as gross domestic product. Forecasts of future values are obtained through the discovery of regularities in past behavior. Thus, data are collected on the past behavior of the variable to be predicted, and on the behavior of other related variables. The analysis of this information may then suggest likely future trends.

EXERCISES

1.1 Find current articles in your local newspaper in which the reader must think about the numerical aspects of national or global issues of interest.

1.2 List several Web sites that contain government or business data.

1.3 Using the Web sites from Problem 1.2, identify specific situations or statements that indicate the use of data to make decisions dealing with uncertainty, forecasting, or analyzing relationships.

1.4 Select a business area of interest to you (such as accounting, marketing, management, finance, or information technology). Why is statistics valuable to this business area? (Hint: Begin by listing statements that deal with uncertainty, sampling, analyzing relationships, or forecasts. Throughout the book, continue to ask yourself this question as you study new statistical concepts.)

1.2   STATISTICAL THINKING

Decisions must be made in times of uncertainty. All functional areas of business use statistics to make such decisions. Accountants may need to select samples for auditing purposes. Financial investors use statistics to understand the market's fluctuations and to choose between various portfolio investments. Managers want to know if customers are satisfied with their company's products or services. To this end, surveys are used to collect data. Perhaps a marketing executive wants information concerning customers' taste preferences, shopping habits, or the demographics of Internet shoppers. For each of these situations, one must carefully define the problem, determine what data is needed, select a sample, gather data, summarize data, and then make inferences and decisions based on the data collected. Statistical thinking is essential from the initial problem definition to the final decisions.

The vision of the Statistics Division of the American Society for Quality (ASQ) is "Statistical Thinking Everywhere" (reference 8). What is statistical thinking? A tactical planning team of officers, past chairs, and committee chairs of the Statistics Division of

ASQ set forth three fundamental principles as the basis for statistical thinking (references 2, 8, and 9).

STATISTICAL THINKING

Statistical thinking is a philosophy of *learning* and *action* based on the following fundamental principles:

- All work occurs in a system of interconnected processes
- Variation exists in all processes
- Understanding and reducing variation are keys to success

The first principle of statistical thinking involves systems and processes.

SYSTEM AND PROCESS

A **system** is a number of components that are logically and sometimes physically linked together for some purpose. A **process** is a set of activities operating on a system that transforms inputs to outputs. A business (work) process consists of groups of logically related tasks and activities that when performed utilize the resources of the business to provide the definitive results required to achieve the business objectives.

Your computer system consists of a processor chip that performs simple tasks, other chips that store information, a keyboard, a screen, a disk storage drive, a printer, and/or connections to the world. A statistical computer program, such as Microsoft Excel or Minitab, is a system that contains a number of calculation modules that can be linked together. An automobile assembly line is a system that has many machine and human components that link together.

When you enter numbers into your statistical computer program, certain steps transform the entries into an output such as a graphical plot. Similarly, steel, plastic, paint, energy, and human efforts are part of the inputs to an automobile assembly line, and a process converts them to automobiles.

Statistical thinking is a thought process or a way of thinking; it is not "number crunching or calculations" (reference 9). The source of this concept, called statistical thinking, is generally thought to be in the management theory of Dr. W. Edwards Deming, whose thinking was influenced by the work of Walter Shewhart (references 1 and 7).

All "work" is not restricted to business or professional work. Think about your personal life: your study habits, the way you clean your room, or how you play tennis. As you begin to understand statistics and statistical thinking, you will notice that all of these activities occur through processes and that the processes act upon inputs and produce outputs (better grades, cleaner room, improved tennis match).

The second and third principles of statistical thinking refer to variation, a fundamental concept that will be addressed throughout this book. Since no two things are exactly alike, some variation will always exist. However, too much variation may result in product defects or inferior service. An understanding of the causes of variation is essential to reducing variation, reducing defective items, and increasing profits.

By understanding statistics you can measure and analyze outputs; improve systems and processes; reduce costs; increase customer satisfaction; and provide reliable service to your customers. You can begin to think statistically; to focus on a way of thinking, a thought process. Further study of systems and processes is included in later chapters and additional references.

EXERCISES

1.5 Discuss the benefits of statistical thinking.

1.6 The second principle of statistical thinking is that "variation exists in all processes." Discuss this principle in relation to daily processes in your own life.

1.7 Identify the processes and possible variations that could exist in:

(a) airline arrivals and departures
(b) spending habits
(c) weight loss programs

1.3 JOURNEY TO MAKING DECISIONS

To think statistically will involve a journey from problem definition to the transformation of data to information, and then the transformation of information to knowledge. Finally, knowledge should lead to better decision making.

DATA, INFORMATION, KNOWLEDGE

1. **Data:** specific observations of measured numbers.
2. **Information:** processed and summarized data yielding facts and ideas.
3. **Knowledge:** selected and organized information that provides understanding, recommendations, and the basis for decisions.

After a problem is identified and defined, data produced by various processes is collected according to a design. These data are analyzed by using one or more statistical procedures. From this analysis, information is obtained and converted to knowledge using understanding based on specific experience, theory, literature, and additional statistical procedures. Knowledge then leads to decision making. Both descriptive and inferential statistics are used to accomplish this transformation.

DESCRIPTIVE AND INFERENTIAL STATISTICS

Descriptive statistics include graphical and numerical procedures that summarize and process data and are used to transform data to information. **Inferential statistics** provide the bases for predictions, forecasts, and estimates that are used to transform information to knowledge.

Identification of a problem is an essential first step in the journey to making decisions. Throughout this book, you will study several ways to identify a problem and to discover root causes that need to be addressed. Once your problem is defined, you will proceed with data collection, descriptive statistics, and so forth until you reach the stage of decision making. Figure 1.1 describes the role of statistical analysis in this transformational process.

Figure 1.1 indicates that computers will play a role in both the transformation of data to information and the transformation of information to knowledge. Since statistical software packages are numerous and change quickly, emphasis throughout the book will be on *interpretation of computer output*. Limited computer instructions are included.

Minitab and Excel

People in government, industry, and academia are surrounded by data and often turn to software packages for a quick summary of the numbers. The selection of a software package for statistical analysis is important. Included in this book are interpretations of output

FIGURE 1.1
The Journey to Making
Decisions

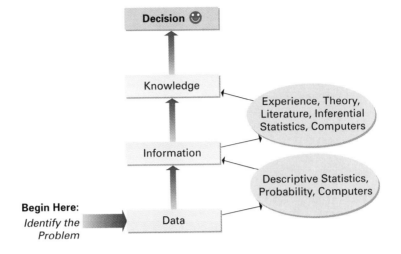

from Minitab and Microsoft Excel, the spreadsheet application from the Microsoft Office suite of programs. Because of its availability many businesses rely on Excel for at least some analysis. The authors recognize that students will use Microsoft Excel in other courses and in the workplace. Other excellent statistical software packages are available today, and new releases are frequently developed.

Some statisticians prefer the use of Minitab only, citing certain statistical errors that occur with Excel (references 4 and 5). Some of these errors are minor; others are more serious. When necessary, words of caution are included. PHStat, an add-in to Excel that accompanies this text, is also incorporated in this text. TreePlan, an Excel add-in developed by Michael Middleton (reference 6), is used with decision trees. For more serious research, Minitab or other statistical software such as SPSS or SAS are available.

In addition to possible errors generated with statistical programs, the Garbage In/Garbage Out problem remains.

> The mere fact that data analysis has been done by computer, however, doesn't guarantee that it's any good. The data may be bad, in that the variables aren't really relevant, the data collection is biased, or the assumptions are grossly violated. The choice of the data analysis method may have been a bad one. The results may be correctly calculated but wrongly interpreted. A human being must still decide what data to use, choose the method of analysis, check the assumptions, and interpret the results reasonably. Until artificial intelligence improves greatly, human intelligence will still be required (reference 3).

It has been said, "a graph is worth a thousand numbers." The basic graph in Example 1.1 provides a quick visualization of the production situation in a cereal manufacturing plant. Without any formal statistical procedures, the graph quickly identifies days of low production as well as days of increased production. Further discussion of graphs is included in Chapters 2 and 3.

EXAMPLE 1.1

CEREAL PRODUCTION (DESCRIPTIVE STATISTICS)

To better understand the cereal manufacturing process and to solve process problems, the production manager of Wheat Cereals formed a team of employees to determine if quality standards were being maintained and to find out if there were significant differences in the number of cereal packages produced each day. The first phase of the study included a random selection of packages that were weighed, and the density of the cereal product was measured. Next, the manager wanted to know if there were significant differences in the number of cereal packages produced each day. Production rates (in 1000s)

FIGURE 1.2
Daily Cereal Production at
Wheat Cereals

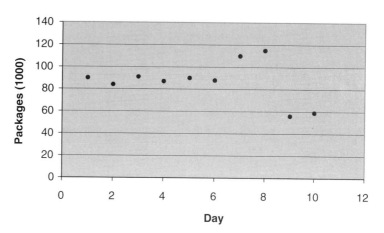

Daily Cereal Production

for a ten-day period were obtained. Show these results graphically and comment on your findings

Day	1	2	3	4	5	6	7	8	9	10
Packages (1000s)	84	81	85	82	85	84	109	110	60	63

SOLUTION

One possible graph of this small data set is given in Figure 1.2. There did not seem to be much difference in the number of packages produced on each of the first six days. There were variations from day to day, but all six points had numerical values that were very close. However, on days 7 and 8 the production level appeared to be higher. In contrast, on days 9 and 10 production appeared to be lower. Based on these observations, the team attempted to identify the conditions that resulted in higher and lower productivity. For example, perhaps key workers were absent on days 9 and 10, or maybe there had been a change in the method of production on those days, or perhaps there had been a change in raw materials on days 9 and 10. Similar efforts would lead to conditions that contributed to increased productivity. More sophisticated procedures will be developed throughout this book that will help the production manager to better understand the cereal manufacturing process.

Chapter Contributions

Chapters 2 and 3 present graphical and numerical methods to summarize data. The contributions of probability to understanding the patterns of data are considered in Chapters 4 through 6. Estimation and hypothesis testing will be considered in Chapters 7 through 9. Chapters 10 through 12 concentrate on important relationships between variables. Chapters 13 through 15 provide a look at procedures known as nonparametric statistics, goodness-of fit tests (frequently used in marketing studies), and analysis of variance. Chapter 16 is an introduction to process improvement procedures. Chapter 17 will discuss the use of time series analysis and forecasting. Sampling is the topic of Chapter

18. In Chapter 19, a Statistical Decision Theory, four criteria for decision making are discussed.

From problem definition to final decision or from process input to process output, statistical thinking is applied to make decisions in the face of uncertainty.

EXERCISES

1.8 Consider a process at your school that needs to be improved, perhaps registration for next semester's courses. Develop a possible process model.

1.9 You have been hired as the production manager of Wheat Cereals and decide to apply statistical thinking to better understand the cereal manufacturing process. One process problem of interest to you is to determine if quality standards are being maintained. How would you proceed with this problem? Develop a possible process model.

SUMMARY

The essential point in this chapter is that statistics provides business functional areas with tools to make decisions under conditions of uncertainty, such as making generalizations about a population based on a sample or analyzing relationships. Statistical thinking is important in business. Decisions based on statistics may lead to improved processes, reduced costs, and increased customer satisfaction.

KEY WORDS

data, 7
descriptive statistics, 7
inferential statistics, 7
information, 7

knowledge, 7
population, 3
process, 6
random sample, 4

sample, 3
simple random sampling, 4
statistical thinking, 6
system, 6

CHAPTER EXERCISES AND APPLICATIONS

1.10 Identify professional or personal situations in which an increase in variation may be desired.

1.11 Discuss the role of sampling in the Florida recount for the 2000 U.S. Presidential election.

REFERENCES

1. Deming, W.E. *Out of the Crisis* (Cambridge, MA: MIT Center for Advanced Engineering Study, 1986).
2. *Glossary and Tables for Statistical Quality Control*, 1996 Edition. Quality Press, 1996.
3. Hildebrand, David K. and Lyman Ott, *Statistical Thinking for Managers*, 4th ed. (Belmont, CA: Duxbury Press, 1998).
4. McCullough, B.D. and Berry Wilson, "On the Accuracy of statistical procedures in Microsoft Excel 97," Computational Statistics and Data Analysis 31 (1999), 27–37.
5. McKenzie, John D. and Ashok Rao, Making Statistics More Effective in Schools of Business: Report of the 1999 Conference. Babson Park, MA, Babson College, 1999.
6. Middleton, Michael. Professor, University of San Francisco. http://www.usaf.edu/~middleton.
7. Shewhart, W.A. *Economic Control of Quality of Manufactured Products* (New York: Van Norstrand and Company, 1931; reprinted by the American Society for Quality Control, Milwaukee, 1980).
8. "Statistical Thinking," *ASQ Statistics Division Newsletter* (Spring 1999), 3.
9. "Statistical Thinking." *ASQ Statistics Division Newsletter*, Special Publication, 1996.

DESCRIBING DATA

INTRODUCTION

Once a problem is carefully defined, data will need to be collected. Often the number of data collected is so large that the actual findings of the study are unclear. The statistician's objective is to summarize succinctly, bringing out the important characteristics of the numbers in such a way that a clear and accurate picture emerges. You will want to reduce the mass of data as far as possible, while guarding against the possibility of obscuring important features through too extreme a reduction. Unfortunately, there is no single "right way" to analyze data. Rather, the appropriate line of attack is typically problem-specific, depending on the characteristics of the data and the purposes of the analysis.

This chapter begins with a study of **tables** and **graphs** that are useful to summarize and describe data. This phase of analysis contributes to the transformation of data to information (see Chapter 1). It has been said that a picture is worth a thousand words. Likewise, a graph is worth a thousand numbers. Tables and graphs contribute to a better understanding of the meaning of data. Reports are enhanced with the inclusion of appropriate tables and graphs such as frequency distributions, bar charts, pie charts, Pareto diagrams, line charts, histograms, stem-and-leaf displays, ogives, or box-and-whisker plots. Visualization of statistical concepts is important. Always ask yourself, what does the graph suggest about the data? What is that you see?

In addition to graphical procedures, data can be summarized by **numerical measures**, such as the measures of central tendency and measures of variability. Additional tables, graphs, and numerical measures will be discussed throughout this book.

Proper analysis and interpretation of data is essential in order to communicate outcomes in a meaningful manner. To apply statistics to other courses and in your career requires the ability to write reports. As you learn new graphs, tables, and descriptive measures, consider how that information could be included in such reports. In subsequent chapters, you will study additional procedures that will lead to making decisions in an uncertain environment.

2.1 CLASSIFICATION OF VARIABLES

Systems and processes are studied in order to predict and/or modify their behavior. Process inputs and outputs are defined using variables. Variables can be classified in several ways. One method of classification refers to the type and amount of information contained in the data. Data are either numerical or categorical. Another method is to classify data by levels of measurement, giving either quantitative or qualitative variables.

Numerical or Categorical

Numerical variables include both discrete and continuous variables. A **discrete numerical variable** produces a response that comes from a counting process. A professor is asked the number of students that are enrolled in a class; a student is asked how many times a week an assignment is completed in the computer lab or the number of email messages sent each day; an investor is asked how many stocks of Microsoft are in the investor's portfolio. An insurance company wants to know how many claims were filed following a hurricane. Responses to each of these questions are 0, 1, 2, and so forth.

A **continuous numerical variable** produces a response that is the outcome of a measurement process. For example, you might tell someone that you are 6 feet (or 72 inches) tall, but your height could actually be 72.1 inches, 71.8 inches, or some other similar number depending on the accuracy of the instrument used to measure your height. You might state your age as "20 years," but you are constantly aging. You are actually 20 years, 3 months, 2 days, 5 hours, 4 minutes, 12 (now it's 13) seconds old. Sounds absurd. So you just say "20 years." The actual weight of packages could also deviate within a certain amount depending on the precision of the instrument used to weigh each package.

Categorical variables produce responses that belong to groups (sometimes called "classes") or categories. For example, responses to yes/no type questions belong in this category. "Do you own a cellular phone?" or "Do you have any homework tonight?" or "Have you ever been on a Mediterranean cruise?" are limited to yes or no answers. A health care insurance company may ask if a claim was incorrectly processed. The operations manager at a water bottling company asks if bottles are properly filled. Sometimes, categorical variables include a range of choices such as "strongly disagree" to "strongly agree."

Measurement Levels

Data could be described as **qualitative** (includes nominal and ordinal levels of measurement) or **quantitative** (includes interval and ratio levels of measurement).

Nominal and Ordinal Levels of Measurement refer to data obtained from categorical questions. A nominal scale indicates assignments to groups or classes such as gender, geographic region, political affiliation, the model of car you own, or simply the yes or no responses to questions such as the ownership of a cellular phone. Nominal data is considered the lowest or weakest type of data, since numerical identification is chosen strictly for convenience. Wes Moore, who was the starter point guard for the University of Tennessee at Chattanooga, wore uniform number "10." Although he was an outstanding athlete, the number "10" simply was a method of identification and not an indication of his skills.

Ordinal data indicates rank ordering of items. Examples include product quality ratings (poor, average, good) or satisfaction ratings with university food service, academic advising, or your new car (very unsatisfied, somewhat unsatisfied, neutral, somewhat satisfied, very satisfied). Marketing analysts may want to know the order in which consumers prefer three different types of soft drink. Studies may be conducted to determine preferences for long-distance carriers in a particular region of the country. You may be given a list of four places that deliver pizza late at night, a time when you study for final exams. Then you are asked to rank these four restaurants in order from your favorite ("1") to your least favorite ("4"). At the end of the semester you complete questionnaires about your course and your instructor. Often students are asked to respond to a statement such as "The instructor in this course was an effective teacher" with a number from 1 to 5 (with 1, strongly disagree; 2, slightly disagree; 3, neutral; 4, slightly agree; and 5, strongly agree). In these examples, the responses are ordinal, or put into a rank order. The difference between a beverage ranked your first and second choice may not be the same as the difference between the beverages ranked second and third place.

Interval and Ratio Levels of Measurement refer to data on an ordered scale where meaning is given to the difference between measurements. An interval scale indicates rank and distance from an arbitrary zero measured in unit intervals. Temperature is a classic example of this level of measurement where one could use either Fahrenheit or Celsius degrees. However, you cannot conclude that because it is 80 degrees Fahrenheit in Orlando, Florida, that it is four times as warm as 20 degrees Fahrenheit in St. Paul, Minnesota.

Ratio scale data does indicate both rank and the distance from a natural zero, with ratios of two measures having meaning. A person who weighs 200 pounds is twice the weight of a person who weighs only 100 pounds; a person who is 40 years old is twice as old as someone who is 20 years of age.

After you have defined the problem of interest, you will need to carefully design an instrument, such as a survey, to collect needed information. Or perhaps you will gather information from available data sources. In either case, before you can proceed to summarize or describe data, you will first need to classify responses as categorical or numerical, or by measurement scale. Certain graphs and descriptive measures are used for numerical variables. Analysts use different graphs and descriptive measures for categorical data.

EXERCISES

2.1 State whether each of the following variables is numerical or categorical. If numerical, is it discrete or continuous? Give the level of measurement.
  (a) Number of email messages you send daily
  (b) Actual cost of your textbooks for a given semester
  (c) Your monthly cellular phone bill
  (d) Faculty ranks (like Professor, Associate Professor, Assistant Professor)

2.2 A survey of students at a college in south Florida was conducted to provide information to address various concerns about the school library. For each question below, determine if the response is numerical or categorical. If numerical, is it discrete or continuous? Give the level of measurement.
  (a) Statement: There is an adequate variety of books in our library. Response: 1, Strongly agree; 2, Slightly agree; 3, Neutral; 4, Slightly disagree; 5, Strongly disagree
  (b) Do you think that the library hours should be extended? Response: Yes, No, or Uncertain
  (c) How many days per week do you use the library?
  (d) Response: Circle: 0   1   2   3   4   5   6   7

2.3 A questionnaire was distributed to students in a liberal arts college to find out the level of student satisfaction with various activities and services. For example, concerning the "method of registration for classes for the next semester," students were asked to check one of the following boxes:

  ☐ Very satisfied
  ☐ Somewhat satisfied
  ☐ Neutral
  ☐ Somewhat dissatisfied
  ☐ Very dissatisfied

Is a student's response to this question numerical or categorical? Explain.

2.4 The public relations office of an NBA team wants information about the fans who attend the postseason tournament games. A questionnaire is given to each fan upon entrance to the Arena. Are answers to the following questions numerical or categorical? Determine the level of measurement.
  (a) Are you a season-ticket holder?
  (b) Do you live in Orange County?
  (c) How much did you pay for your ticket to this postseason game?

Suntan

2.2   TABLES AND GRAPHS FOR NUMERICAL DATA

A first step in any study is to define a problem. Later, data is gathered and the need for analysis will be apparent. Appropriate statistical tools to convert data to information is the subject of this chapter; in later chapters, additional inferential procedures will be studied to transform information to knowledge that leads to decision making. Throughout this chapter reference will be made to Example 2.1.

EXAMPLE 2.1

CONTENT WEIGHTS (IN ML) OF SUNTAN LOTION BOTTLES (STATISTICAL THINKING)

Jennie Bishop, the operations manager at a suntan lotion manufacturing plant, wants to be sure that the process for filling 8 oz (237 mL) bottles of SunProtector is operating properly. You are asked to study the filling process for this product and to submit a report of your findings. Suppose that a random sample of 100 bottles of this lotion is selected, the contents are weighed, and the weights (in mL) are recorded in Table 2.1 (data are stored in file **Suntan**). What do the data indicate?

TABLE 2.1
Weights (in mL) of a Random Sample of Bottles of SunProtector

244	233	236	231	238	237	243	242	232	235
237	242	249	238	236	231	237	234	238	231
241	231	236	238	245	239	234	232	242	236
234	237	246	240	231	236	235	238	237	234
234	236	238	232	242	241	234	238	231	240
241	231	234	240	238	229	237	241	239	235
235	236	228	240	233	247	232	236	231	243
242	240	244	234	243	241	238	238	237	231
229	231	240	237	234	229	241	233	239	236
242	224	233	232	244	242	249	231	242	245

SOLUTION

Table 2.1 provides just a list of numbers that by itself does not provide direction or give answers to the problems that managers encounter.

Graphs, numerical descriptors, estimations, and other statistics are developed throughout this chapter and the remainder of the book to summarize data. To better understand what the data in Table 2.1 indicates, we will first study frequency distributions and histograms.

Frequency Distributions

In the preceding section, classification of data was discussed. Are the data in Table 2.1 categorical or numerical? For each bottle, the content weight in milliliters is given. The data are numerical and the level of measurement is ratio. One of the first analytical tools used to summarize numerical data is a frequency distribution. Data are classified into subgroups and the frequency, or number of observations, in each class is recorded.

FREQUENCY DISTRIBUTION

A **frequency distribution** is a table used to organize data. The left column (called classes or groups) includes numerical intervals on a variable being studied. The right column is a list of the frequencies, or number of observations, for each class. Intervals normally are of equal size, must cover the range of the sample observations, and be nonoverlapping.

Certain questions arise immediately in the construction of a frequency distribution. How many class intervals should be used? How wide is each interval? Where does the first interval begin? There are some general rules for preparing frequency distributions that make it easier to summarize data and to communicate results.

CONSTRUCTION OF A FREQUENCY DISTRIBUTION

Rule 1: Intervals (classes) must be inclusive and nonoverlapping.
Rule 2: Determine k, the number of classes.
Rule 3: Intervals should be the same width, w; the width is determined by the following:

$$w = \text{Interval Width} = \frac{(\text{Largest Number} - \text{Smallest Number})}{\text{Number of Intervals}} \qquad (2.1)$$

Both k and w should be rounded upward, possibly to the next largest integer.

RULE 1. INCLUSIVE AND NONOVERLAPPING INTERVALS

Interval classes must be inclusive and nonoverlapping. Each observation must belong to one and to only one class interval. Consider a frequency distribution for the ages (rounded to the nearest year) of a particular group of people. If the frequency distribution contains the intervals "age 20 to age 30" and "age 30 to age 40," to which of these two classes would a person age 30 belong?

The **boundaries**, or endpoints, of each class must be clearly defined. To avoid overlapping age intervals could be defined as "age 20 but *less than* age 30" followed by "age 30 but *less than* age 40," and so on. Another possibility is to define the age intervals as "19.5 to 29.5" and "29.5 to 39.5," and so forth. Since age is an integer, no overlapping occurs. Boundary selection is subjective. Simply be sure to define class boundaries that promote a clear understanding and interpretation of the data.

RULE 2. NUMBER OF INTERVALS

There are no absolute rules to determine the number of classes in a frequency distribution. Practitioners often use guidelines such as the one given here.

QUICK GUIDE TO NUMBER OF CLASSES FOR A FREQUENCY DISTRIBUTION

SAMPLE SIZE	NUMBER OF CLASSES	
Fewer than 50	5–6 classes	
50 to 100	6–8 classes	(2.2)
over 100	8–10 classes	

Practice and experience are the best guidelines. Larger data sets may require more class intervals.

As you gain experience in developing frequency distributions, you will see that if you select too few classes, the pattern and various characteristics of the data may be hidden. If you select too many classes, you will discover that some of your intervals may contain no observations or a very small number of frequencies.

RULE 3. INTERVAL WIDTH

After choosing the number of intervals, the next step is to choose the interval width:

$$w = \text{Interval Width} = \frac{(\text{Largest Number} - \text{Smallest Number})}{\text{Number of Intervals}}$$

The interval width is often rounded to a convenient whole number to provide for easy interpretation.

Two special frequency distributions are the cumulative frequency distribution and the relative cumulative frequency distribution.

CUMULATIVE AND RELATIVE CUMULATIVE FREQUENCY DISTRIBUTIONS

A **cumulative frequency distribution** contains the total number of observations whose values are less than the upper limit for each interval. It is constructed by adding the frequencies of all frequency distribution intervals up to and including the present interval. A **relative cumulative frequency distribution** converts all cumulative frequencies to cumulative percentages.

EXAMPLE 2.1

REVISITED (FREQUENCY DISTRIBUTIONS)

A frequency distribution with six classes (Equation 2.2) is developed for the data in Example 2.1. From Equation 2.1, the width of each class is

$$w = \frac{249 - 224}{6} = 5 \text{ mL (rounded up)}$$

Since the smallest value is 224, one choice for the first interval is "220 but less than 225." Subsequent intervals of equal width are added to the frequency distribution, as well as the number of bottles that belong to each class. Table 2.2 is a frequency distribution for the suntan lotion problem.

The manager may also be interested in the percentage of observations that fall below a certain value. For example, she may want to know the *percentage* of 8 oz. bottles of SunProtector that contain less than a specified amount, say 235 mL. Table 2.3 is a cumulative frequency distribution, from which cumulative percentages are obtained.

TABLE 2.2
A Frequency Distribution for the Suntan Lotion Example

WEIGHTS (IN ML)	NUMBER OF BOTTLES
220 less than 225	1
225 less than 230	4
230 less than 235	29
235 less than 240	34
240 less than 245	26
245 less than 250	6

TABLE 2.3
Cumulative Frequency Distribution for Suntan Lotion Example

WEIGHTS (IN ML)	CUMULATIVE NUMBER OF BOTTLES
less than 225	1
less than 230	5
less than 235	34
less than 240	68
less than 245	94
less than 250	100

Certainly these frequency distribution tables are an improvement over the original list of data in Table 2.1. You have at least summarized 100 weights into six categories. You are able to tell Jennie that slightly more than one-third (34%) of the bottles sampled contain less than 235 mL of lotion. You also observe that nearly one-third (32%) of the samples contain at least 240 mL of lotion (100% − 68%)!

Software can be used to produce these frequency distributions. Figure 2.1 is the output obtained with Microsoft Excel.

FIGURE 2.1
Frequency and Relative Cumulative Frequency Tables for Example 2.1 (Microsoft Excel)

Bins	Frequency	Cumulative %
224.5	1	1.00%
229.5	4	5.00%
234.5	29	34.00%
239.5	34	68.00%
244.5	26	94.00%
249.5	6	100.00%

Excel Instructions

1. Open file Suntan
2. Click on Tools
3. Click on Data Analysis
4. Select Histogram; click OK
5. Complete dialog box: Column A for the Input Range, Column B for the Bin Range
6. Select Labels and Cumulative Percentage
7. Delete (using Edit) last row called More

Notice that both the frequency distribution and the relative cumulative frequency distribution are combined in the same table. Also, notice that the far-left column, called **Bins**, includes only the upper class boundary of each interval. **Bins must be carefully defined**

when using Excel. In Figure 2.1, the first bin number is 224.5. What does this number mean? This bin number tells the reader that bottles with content weights between 219.5 mL to 224.5 mL *inclusive* are recorded in this class. The second class includes those bottles with content weights between 224.5 mL and 229.5 mL *inclusive*. In other words, a bottle is counted in the frequency for a certain class if the weight of the contents is *less than or equal* to the bin number. Since the weights in Table 2.1 are integers, no bottle will have a weight equal to the upper class boundaries (224.5, 229.5, and so forth).

Histograms and Ogives

Once you have developed the frequency and cumulative frequency distribution tables, you are ready to graph this information. Two graphs that summarize numerical data are histograms and ogives.

HISTOGRAM

A **histogram** is a graph that consists of vertical bars constructed on a horizontal line that is marked off with intervals for the variable being displayed. The intervals correspond to those in a frequency distribution table. The height of each bar is proportional to the number of observations in that interval. The number of observations can be displayed above the bars.

OGIVE

An **ogive**, sometimes called a *cumulative line graph*, is a line that connects points that are the cumulative percentage of observations below the upper limit of each class in a cumulative frequency distribution.

Figure 2.2 includes the histogram and ogive obtained with Microsoft Excel for the cumulative frequency distribution in Figure 2.1.

FIGURE 2.2
Histogram and Ogive for Example 2.1 (with Bins 224.5, 229.5, …)

Bins	Frequency	Cumulative %
224.5	1	1.00%
229.5	4	5.00%
234.5	**29**	**34.00%**
239.5	34	68.00%
244.5	26	94.00%
249.5	6	00.00%

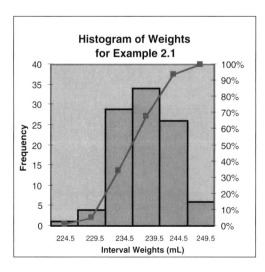

Comments
Understanding Bins

In Excel, the bin number is the upper boundary for the class.

- Look at the third bin "234.5"
- A bottle with content weight of 234 mL is counted in the frequency for this class. There are 29 bottles in this range (230 up to and including 234).
- A bottle with content weight of 235 mL is counted in the next bin "239.5."

FIGURE 2.3
Cumulative Percentages for
Example 2.1(Microsoft Excel)

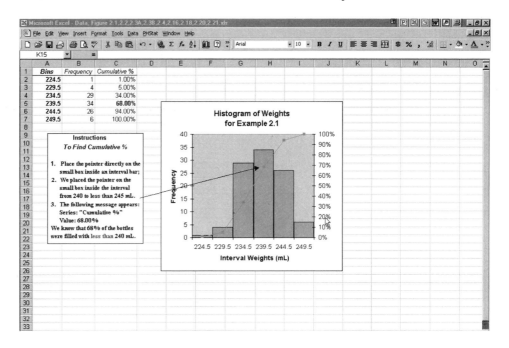

The right vertical axis in the histogram in Figure 2.2 gives percentages for the *ogive* that is placed on top of this histogram. To see the exact cumulative percentage for a particular class interval, place the pointer directly on the small box inside an interval. This is illustrated in Figure 2.3. You can see that the content of 68% of the bottles weighed less than 240 mL.

Recall that **Bins must be carefully defined when using Excel**. Suppose that the bins are defined as 225, 230 and so forth (see file **Suntan**, Column C) instead of 224.5, 229.5 and so forth. The frequency distribution, histogram, and ogive will be different from those in Figure 2.2 and Figure 2.3. This is illustrated in Figure 2.4 on page 20.

Stem-and-Leaf Display

Exploratory Data Analysis (EDA) consists of procedures to describe data in simple arithmetic terms with easy-to-draw pictures. One useful technique, the stem-and-leaf display, was developed by Professor John Tukey, a famous mathematical statistician, as a technique for summarizing data sets without losing the individual observations (reference 18). This technique was originally proposed as an easy pencil-and-paper procedure for quickly identifying the pattern of a newly acquired set of data. Subsequently, stem-and-leaf displays have become a standard component in most computer statistical software.

STEM-AND-LEAF DISPLAY

A **stem-and-leaf display** is an exploratory data analysis graph that is an alternative to the histogram. Data are grouped according to their leading digits (called the stem) while listing the final digits (called leaves) separately for each member of a class. The leaves are displayed individually in ascending order after each of the stems.

The number of digits in each class indicates the class frequency. The individual digits indicate the pattern of values within each class. Except for data with extreme **outliers** (values much larger or smaller than other values in the data set), all stems are included even if there are no observations in the corresponding subset. The number of digits in the stem varies according to the data set.

FIGURE 2.4
Frequency Distribution,
Histogram, and Ogive (with
Bins 225, 230 …)

Bins	Frequency	Cumulative %
225.0	1	1.00%
230.0	4	5.00%
235.0	**33**	**38.00%**
240.0	36	74.00%
245.0	22	96.00%
250.0	4	100.00%

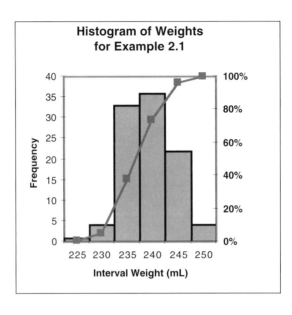

Comments
- Look at the third bin "235.0"
- A bottle that weighs 235 mL is counted in the frequency for this bin.
- The frequency is now "33" not "29" as in Figure 2.3A

The next three examples illustrate stem-and-leaf displays. Example 2.2 shows that a one-digit stem-and-leaf display can often be quickly constructed. Example 2.3 shows the use of Minitab to construct a two-digit stem-and-leaf display for a larger sample size. Example 2.4 was obtained using the PHStat add-in to Microsoft Excel.

EXAMPLE 2.2

TIME TO PREPARE A MEAL AT GILOTTI'S DELI (STEM-AND-LEAF)

Gilotti

Many of the customers at Gilotti's Deli order a cheese calzone for lunch. The owner is concerned about the time it takes the chefs to prepare this item. She asked help from some local university students who are her regular customers. The data are stored in the file **Gilotti**.

SOLUTION
The students agreed to conduct a study of preparation times. For one part of this study, they recorded the preparation times for a random sample of 25 calzones during a one-week period. The times (in minutes) necessary to prepare each of these 25 calzones were:

16	21	28	22	31
40	14	18	22	29
30	32	18	11	34
42	12	24	19	29
17	33	26	19	22

The students developed a quick stem-and-leaf display given in Figure 2.5 with a one-digit stem (the number in the ten's position).

The left column is a cumulative frequency of observations from the extremes to the center. Notice the "(9)" in the left column. This tells the reader that the middle of the data

FIGURE 2.5
Stem-and-Leaf Display for
Gilotti's Deli Example

```
Stem-and-leaf
Minutes   N  = 25
Leaf Unit = 1.0

    9      1 1 2 4 6 7 8 8 9 9
   (9)     2 1 2 2 2 4 6 8 9 9
    7      3 0 1 2 3 4
    2      4 0 2
```

is centered in the interval from 20 to 29 minutes. Numbers above the value in parenthesis indicate a "less than" cumulative frequency. For example, the top "9" in the left column tells us that 9 customers waited less than 20 minutes; The numbers below the value in parenthesis indicate an "at least" cumulative frequency. The "7" in the left column means that 7 customers waited at least 30 minutes. This information may help the owner to improve service time for lunch customers.

Two-digit stem-and-leaf displays are formed in different ways. Example 2.3 illustrates one way to handle a two-digit stem for the GPAs for a random sample of accounting majors at a university.

EXAMPLE 2.3

GRADE POINT AVERAGES (STEM-AND-LEAF)

Accounting GPAs

The accounting department chair at a large university wants information about the grade point averages of recent accounting majors. What information does the stem-and-leaf display in Figure 2.6 provide? The data are stored in the file **Accounting GPAs**.

SOLUTION

Data for a student's GPA was recorded to the nearest hundredths. Figure 2.6 is the output obtained using Minitab. A student with GPA of 3.25 is recorded as a stem of "32" and a leaf of "5." Several possible observations could be made from the stem-and-display in Figure 2.6.

FIGURE 2.6
Stem-and-Leaf for Grade
Point Averages (Minitab)

Cumulative Frequency	Stem	Leaf
1	21	2
3	22	2 9
7	23	3 4 5 9
13	24	0 1 3 4 7 9
19	25	1 2 3 5 5 7
24	26	1 1 1 2 6
30	27	1 2 3 5 6 8
40	28	0 2 3 4 4 4 5 6 9 9
51	29	0 1 2 2 4 4 4 5 7 7 7
(10)	30	1 1 1 2 6 7 8 8 8 9
51	31	0 1 1 1 2 4 5 6 8
42	32	1 1 4 5 6 8 9
35	33	1 2 3 5 7 8 8 9
27	34	0 0 1 1 1 3 3 3 4 6
17	35	1 6 7 7
13	36	0 1 2 5 5 6 6 8 8
4	37	2 3
2	38	0 7

Comments
• The stem 21 represents a GPA = 2.10
• The lowest GPA is 2.12
• The highest GPA is 3.87
• The middle of the data is centered in the interval form 3.00 to 3.09
• The number "42" in the left column tells us that 42 students had a GPA above 3.20

Sometimes, it is necessary to round data if more than one digit is used in the stem. Using the PHStat add-in to Microsoft Excel, Figure 2.7 was obtained. In Example 2.4, data with three digits are first rounded to the nearest tens column.

FIGURE 2.7
Stem-and-Leaf for Miles
Driven (Microsoft Excel,
PHStat Add-in)

Stem-and-Leaf Display for Miles	Comments
Stem unit: 100	• Excel auto-calculates the stem unit by rounding data to nearest tens. A stem of "2" and the leaf of "4" is used to round "242" miles. • A stem of 4 is included even though no observation was in the 400s.

```
1 | 5 6
2 | 4
3 | 1 6
4 |
5 | 6
```

EXAMPLE 2.4

MILES DRIVEN BY EMPLOYEE (STEM-AND-LEAF)

The owners of All Flow Plumbing want information about the number of miles driven by their employees during a given week. These data might be helpful to estimate insurance and gasoline costs. Suppose that the following number of miles were driven by a random sample of six employees during a given week: 357, 153, 156, 242, 310, 557 miles. Construct a stem-and-leaf display for this data.

SOLUTION
The stem-and-leaf display in Figure 2.7 is obtained using PHStat.

EXERCISES

2.5 ⬤ The demand for bottled water increases during the hurricane season in Florida. The operations manager at a plant that bottles drinking water wants to be sure that the filling process for one-gallon bottles is operating properly. Currently, the company is testing the weights of one-gallon (3.78 L) bottles. A random sample of 75 bottles are tested and the weights are:

3.93	3.79	3.67	3.89	3.75	3.71	3.87	3.69
3.78	3.72	3.74	3.87	3.73	3.77	3.84	3.71
3.98	3.77	3.77	3.85	3.99	3.82	4.06	3.69
3.82	3.91	3.63	3.79	3.94	3.74	3.96	3.81
3.77	3.96	3.88	3.81	3.84	3.79	3.94	3.74
3.94	3.77	3.81	3.75	3.67	3.86	3.72	
3.76	3.76	3.94	3.74	3.85	3.86	3.71	
4.11	3.75	3.64	3.82	3.71	3.57	3.65	
3.78	3.82	3.89	3.90	3.93	3.82	3.74	
3.67	3.81	3.77	3.79	3.95	3.81	3.80	

Study the filling process for this product and submit a report of your findings to the operations manager. Use Microsoft Excel to construct a frequency distribution, cumulative frequency distribution, histogram, ogive, and stem-and-leaf display. Incorporate these graphs into a well-written summary. How can you apply statistical thinking in this situation? The data is stored in the data file **Water**.

2.6 ⬤ The accompanying table shows test scores of 40 students. The data is stored in the data file **Scores**.

54	56	56	59	60
62	62	66	67	68
68	70	70	73	73
73	75	77	78	79
79	81	81	82	83
83	85	86	86	88
89	89	90	90	91
93	93	94	95	98

(a) Construct a frequency distribution of the data.
(b) Construct a cumulative frequency distribution of the data.
(c) Based on your answer to part (a), construct an appropriate histogram of the data.
(d) Construct a stem-and-leaf display of the data.

2.7 Construct a stem-and-leaf display for the hours that 20 students from a large class spent studying for a marketing test.

3.5	2.8	4.5	6.2	4.8	2.3	2.6	3.9	4.4	5.5
5.2	6.7	3.0	2.4	5.0	3.6	2.9	1.0	2.8	3.6

2.8 A sample of 20 financial analysts was asked to provide forecasts of earnings per share of a corporation for next year. The results are summarized in the following table.

FORECAST ($ per share)	9.95 < 10.45	10.45 < 10.95	10.95 <11.45	11.45 < 11.95	11.95 < 12.45
NUMBER OF ANALYSTS	2	8	6	3	1

(a) Draw the histogram.
(b) Find the relative frequencies.
(c) Find the cumulative frequencies.
(d) Find and interpret the cumulative relative frequencies.

2.9 The accompanying table shows percentage returns for the 25 largest U.S. common stock mutual funds for a particular day. The data are stored in the data file **Returns**.

38.0	24.5	21.5	30.8	20.3
24.0	29.6	19.4	25.6	39.5
13.3	28.0	30.8	32.9	30.3
19.9	24.6	32.3	24.7	18.7
36.8	31.2	50.9	30.7	20.3

(a) Construct a histogram to summarize these data.
(b) Draw a stem-and-leaf diagram to summarize these data.
(c) Use Minitab to obtain the histogram, ogive, and stem-and-leaf display.
(d) Use Microsoft Excel to obtain the histogram, ogive, and stem-and-leaf display.

2.3 TABLES AND GRAPHS FOR CATEGORICAL VARIABLES

Graphs that describe categorical variables include bar charts, pie charts, Pareto diagrams, and time plots. With continuous upgrades in software packages has come an increase in the use and misuse of graphics.

Edward Tufte and Howard Wainer are leaders in the area of data presentation (references 17 and 20). They have studied the proper design of graphs, as well as the causes and dangers of making inferences from graphs that are poorly drawn. Tufte points out that an excellent graph must "communicate complex ideas with clarity, precision and efficiency." Poorly designed graphs can easily distort the truth. With Chart Wizard or any software, be careful not to compress the horizontal or vertical axis so as to distort the truth.

Tables

As with numerical data, frequency distributions can be constructed for categorical data. However, by nature of the type of data, finding classes is not a problem as it was with numerical data.

EXAMPLE 2.5

CENTRAL FLORIDA'S TOP COMPANY EMPLOYERS IN 1999 (BAR AND PIE CHARTS)

Annual surveys are taken to determine the companies that employ the largest number of central Florida residents. Expansion of major attractions, increase in time-share resorts, and growth in the hotel industry are factors that contributed to tourism maintaining dominance in the employment of central Floridians. The information in this study is valuable to college students looking for part-time work or future employment; to companies and individuals who are considering moving into the central Florida region; and to retired individuals who may want to supplement their income or meet new people. Even if you are not in any of these groups, the concept is important. You should check in the area where you live or expect to work to obtain similar economic conditions. Often the chamber of commerce, the Internet, libraries, and local universities are helpful resources.

The companies are categorized as tourism, retail, health care, restaurants, communications, space, technology, and other (industries that each comprised no more than 5% of the work force). Information on public employers (such as school systems, utilities companies, postal service, and government agencies) is not included in this example. Disney, Universal, Central Florida Investments, and Sea World (Anheuser-Busch) are some of the companies in the tourism category. Retail includes Publix Super Markets, Wal-Mart, Winn-Dixie, J.C. Penney, Sears, Walgreens, and Kmart. Some of the companies included in the health care category are Adventist Health System, Orlando Regional Healthcare System, Health First Inc., and Memorial Health Systems. McDonald's, Darden (includes Red Lobster and Olive

TABLE 2.4
Frequency and Relative
Frequency Distribution for
Top Company Employers
Example

INDUSTRY	NUMBER OF EMPLOYEES	PERCENT
Tourism	85,287	0.35%
Retail	49,424	0.20
Health Care	39,588	0.16
Restaurants	16,050	0.06
Communications	11,750	0.05
Technology	11,144	0.05
Space	11,418	0.05
Other	21,336	0.08

Garden), and Burger King are the employers in the restaurant category. AT&T, Sprint, and BellSouth are companies in the communications category. Space includes Boeing, United Space Alliance and Space Gateway. Technology includes Harris, Siemens, and Lucent. Transportation, financial services, and defense constitute the "others" category.

The data in Table 2.4 represent the 35 companies by industry type that employs the highest number of central Florida residents (reference 7). Each company has at least 2500 employees. The employment numbers were provided by each company, with some companies, such as Disney, including seasonal help in the calculation of total employment figures. Four large companies declined participation in the study (two restaurants, a bakery, and an insurance company). A frequency distribution and a relative frequency distribution (Table 2.4), bar charts (Figures 2.8 and 2.9), and pie charts (Figures 2.10 and 2.11) are constructed with the available data.

FIGURE 2.8
Bar Chart for Top Company
Employers Example (Excel)

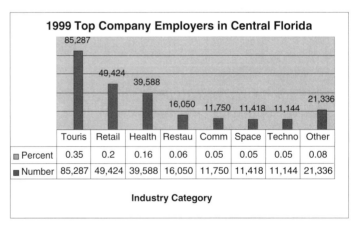

FIGURE 2.9
Bar Chart for Top Company
Employers Example (Excel)

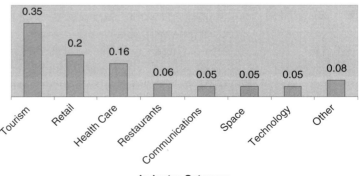

FIGURE 2.10
Pie Chart for Top Company
Employers Example

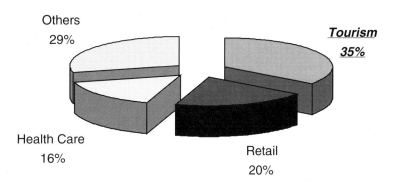

1999 Top Company Employers in Central Florida

Others
29%

***Tourism
35%***

Health Care
16%

Retail
20%

FIGURE 2.11
Is Y2K a Big Problem?
(Microsoft Excel)

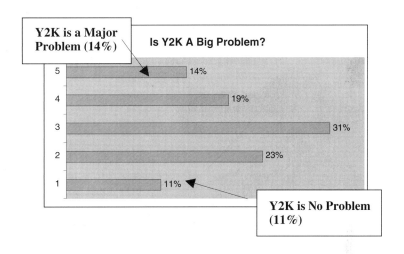

**Y2K is a Major
Problem (14%)**

Is Y2K A Big Problem?

5	14%
4	19%
3	31%
2	23%
1	11%

**Y2K is No Problem
(11%)**

INTERPRETATION

Notice from the frequency distributions that more than 1/3 of Central Florida residents work in tourism-related occupations. Also, one in every five Central Floridians works in a retail industry. Cumulative distributions do not make sense for categorical variables.

Bar Charts and Pie Charts

Two graphs that can be used for the categorical data in Table 2.4 are the bar chart and the pie chart. In a **bar chart**, the length or height of a rectangle represents the frequency or the percentage for a particular category. Unlike a histogram, there is no need for the bars to touch.

Recall that Tufte's criterion is that an excellent graph must "communicate complex ideas with clarity, precision and efficiency." Does the bar chart in Figure 2.8 meet that standard? Although this is a somewhat subjective question, notice that numbers appear twice—

both on top of every bar in the bar chart and in the table together with the percentages. This probably fails Tufte's precision and efficiency criterion. Figure 2.8 was obtained with Excel's Chart Wizard and can be modified to produce a more simple bar chart such as the bar chart in Figure 2.9.

Pie charts are used to depict the division of a whole into its constituent parts. The circle (or "pie") represents the total, and the segments (or "pieces of the pie") cut from its center depict shares of that total.

This example was selected for several reasons. First, to point out that with the availability of software, construction of graphs is quite simple and allows creativity. However, the chance of charting errors also increases. Figure 2.8 contains too much data. Now let's consider again the original employment data. Some companies included seasonal employment in the data. No doubt tourism would be more seasonal than technology or health care. Four large companies did not provide data. It is possible that the best graph could still be misleading.

A bar chart for ordinal data is illustrated in Example 2.6.

EXAMPLE 2.6

THE Y2K BUG (BAR CHART)

In the late 1990s the Y2K problem was greatly discussed. Studies and reports flourished about the implications of a possible Y2K crisis. In one on-line survey, respondents were asked, "How big a problem do you feel the Y2K issue will be?" Responses were on a scale from one to five, with five being a major problem and one being no problem (reference 10). The percent of respondents for the five-point scale (as of early Fall 1999) were: Scale of 5: 14% (The Y2K crisis is a major problem); Scale of 4: 19%; Scale of 3: 31%; Scale of 2: 23%; Scale of 1: 11% (The Y2K crisis is no problem). Construct a bar chart of this data.

SOLUTION

Using the Chart Wizard in Microsoft Excel, Figure 2.11 is easily obtained.

Pareto Diagrams

Quality control managers identify the major causes of problems and attempt to correct them quickly with a minimum cost. A statistical quality control tool that is frequently used to help with this task is called the Pareto diagram, named for the Italian economist, Vilfredo Pareto (1848–1923). Pareto identified the result that in most cases a small number of factors are responsible for most of the problems. In a Pareto chart, which is similar to the bar charts in Figure 2.8 and Figure 2.9, bars are arranged from left to right to emphasize the most frequent causes of defects.

PARETO DIAGRAM

A **Pareto diagram** is a bar chart that displays the frequency of defect causes. The bar at the left indicates the most frequent cause and bars to the right indicate causes in decreasing frequency. A **Pareto diagram** is used to separate the "vital few" from the "trivial many."

Pareto's result applies to a wide variety of behavior over many systems. It is sometimes referred to as the "80–20 Rule." A cereal manufacturer may find that most of the packaging errors are due to only a few causes. If you have participated in a fundraiser or worked on a group project, you may have thought that 80% of the work was done by only 20% of the people. The use of a Pareto chart can also improve communication with employees or management and within production teams. Example 2.7 illustrates the Pareto principle applied to a problem in a health insurance company.

EXAMPLE 2.7

INSURANCE CLAIMS
PROCESSING ERRORS
(PARETO DIAGRAM)

Insurance

Analysis and payment of health care insurance claims is a complex process that can result in a number of incorrectly processed claims. These errors lead to an increase in staff time to obtain the correct information and possibly errors in actual payment. Errors resulting in underpayment are usually detected by the payee. The recipient may often overlook overpayments. These errors can increase costs substantially in addition to having negative effects on customer relationships. Considerable effort is devoted to analyzing the reporting and claims-processing activity so that procedures for minimizing errors can be developed. A major health insurance company set a goal to reduce errors by 50%. Use Pareto analysis to help the company determine the significant factors contributing to process errors. The data are stored in the data file **Insurance.**

SOLUTION

The health insurance company asked Westley Moore to conduct an intensive investigation of the entire claims submission and payment process. Wes first organized a committee of key staff people including Ann Thorne from claims processing, Joseph Cadariu from provider relations and marketing, Norma Failer from internal audit, Jon Thorne from data processing, and Janice Stephenson from the medical review department. Under his leadership, the committee first prepared a list of the most common problems based on their experience and a review of the process. The committee finally agreed on a list of seven types of error. Three of these (procedure and diagnosis codes, provider information, and patient information) are related to the submission process and must be checked by reviewing patient medical records in clinics and hospitals. The other four (pricing schedules, contract applications, provider adjustments, and program and system errors) are related to the processing of claims for payment within the insurance company office. A random sample of 1,000 claims was selected for complete audit. Wes suggested that this audit should begin with checking the claim against medical records in clinics and hospitals, and proceed through the final payment stage. Claims with errors were separated and the total number of errors of each type was recorded. If a claim had multiple errors, then each error was recorded. In this process many decisions were made concerning error definition. If a child was coded for a procedure typically used for adults and the computer processing system did not detect this, then this error was recorded as error 7 (Program and System Errors) and also as error 3 (Patient Information Error). If treatment for a sprain was coded as a fracture, this was recorded as error 1 (Procedure Code). Table 2.5 is a frequency distribution of the categories and the number of errors in each code. Wes obtained the Pareto diagram in Figure 2.12 to identify the significant processing errors.

As the defect percentages for each type of error (from left to right) are added, the increase in the cumulative frequency line indicates the relative improvement that would result from correcting each of the most frequent problems. From the Pareto chart the analysts saw that error 1 (Procedure & Diagnosis Code) and error 5 (Contract Applications) were the major causes of error. The combination of errors 1, 5, and 4 (Pricing Schedules)

TABLE 2.5
Errors in Health Care
Claims Processing

CODE	CATEGORY	ERROR TYPE	FREQUENCY
A	1	Procedure & Diagnosis Codes	40
B	2	Provider Information	9
C	3	Patient Information	6
D	4	Pricing Schedules	17
E	5	Contract Applications	37
F	6	Provider Adjustments	7
G	7	Program & System Errors	4

FIGURE 2.12   Pareto Diagram: Errors in Health Care Claims Processing (Minitab)

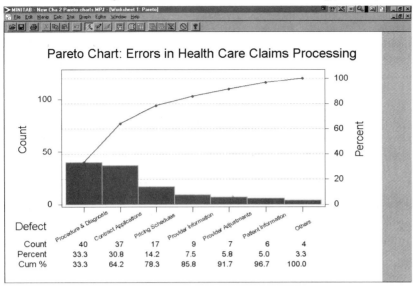

resulted in nearly 80 percent of the errors. By examining the Pareto chart, the analyst can quickly determine which causes should receive most of the problem correction effort. Pareto analysis separated the "vital few" causes from the "trivial many."

Armed with this information, Wes Moore and the task force made a number of recommendations to reduce errors and bring the process under control. These recommendations included:

1. Special training sessions for hospital and clinic claims' processors.
2. Surprise random audits to check for coding errors.
3. Monetary penalties for organizations with excessive errors.
4. Two people would each prepare the complete set of contract application tables separately. Next, all of the table entries would be compared using a computer program, and any differences would be resolved.
5. A master set of model claims would be prepared and used to test for correct contract applications.

Use of the Pareto chart and the subsequent recommendations resulted in substantially fewer errors. Overpayments on claims as well as the staff work required to correct the errors were reduced.

Line Charts (Time Plots)

The technology of the twenty-first century provides quick access to data that assist corporate decision making as well as personal decision making. E-commerce is important to all of us. Nation's retailers report to the government how much of their business is done on-line. The information is used in monthly government reports on the status of the economy. On-line shoppers can purchase just about anything: airline tickets, automobiles, electronics, books, flowers, stocks, and so on.

Numerous firms analyze and sell Internet surveys and statistical data. To develop marketing plans, many companies need demographics concerning on-line shoppers as well as off-line shoppers. A graph that is used to show trends over time is a line chart, also called a time plot.

> ## LINE CHART (TIME PLOT)
> A **line chart**, also called a **time plot**, is a series of data plotted at various time intervals. Measuring time along the horizontal axis and the numerical quantity of interest along the vertical axis yields a point on the graph for each observation. Joining points adjacent in time by straight lines produces a time plot.

EXAMPLE 2.8

TRENDS IN INTERNET USAGE (TIME PLOT)

The president of a major cruise agency plans to use the Internet to expand his business. He would like rapid answers to such critical questions as:

- How do on-line customers differ from off-line customers?
- Who is visiting my Web site?
- What products and services do my customers want and need?

Initially, he would like to see the *trend* in the ages of Internet users. This information might be beneficial in the development of his marketing plan. Can you help find this data?

SOLUTION

You make some inquiries and find that a leader in on-line market research is Cyber Dialogue, Inc. (reference 5). Beginning in 1993, Cyber Dialogue, Inc. offered one-to-one marketing, on-line database marketing, and on-line market research. From the company's Web site (*www.cyberdialogue.com*), you learn that Cyber Dialogue, Inc. conducts the American Internet User Survey annually during the second and fourth quarter. You also learn that in addition to the survey results and a management report, clients can purchase an "inquiry service" that provides "direct access to analysts for help with data interpretation, trends and daily marketing needs," (reference 5).

From the company's Web site you are able to obtain selected free data. You can find bar and pie charts that illustrate on-line shopping behaviors (such as the percent of males or females that seek on-line information and then order off-line), the content area preferences of males and females, or the percentage of adults who order various products or services.

To show the trend in age data over time intervals you could construct a line chart. With Microsoft Excel Chart Wizard and the free data from *www.cyberdialogue.com*, you produce a time plot (Figure 2.13) of recent growth trends in Internet usage for three age categories: age 18 to 29; age 30 to 49; and age 50 and over.

FIGURE 2.13
Growth Trends in Internet Usage by Age (Microsoft Excel)

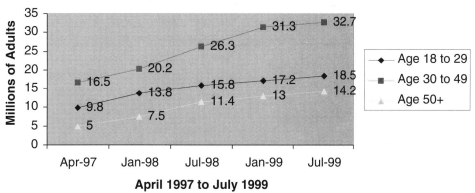

EXERCISES

2.10 The breakdown of total dollars spent on business trips in the United States is estimated as follows: 41% on air fares, 22% on lodging, 12% on meals, 8% on car rentals, and the remaining on other expenses (reference 3).

(a) Construct a pie chart to show this information.

(b) Construct a bar chart to show this information.

2.11 A recent estimate of U.S. federal budget spending showed that 46% was to entitlements, 18% was for defense, 15% was grants to states and localities, 14% was interest on debt, 6% was for other federal operations, and 1% was deposit insurance. Construct a pie chart to show this information.

2.12 In 1998, the global workforce reached 231 million people. The locations of the workforce were: 77.6 million in Northeast Asia, 33.7 million in South Asia, 22.2 million in Southeast Asia, 22 million in European Union, 20.8 million in North America, 15.2 million in Eastern Europe, and the remaining in other parts of the world. (reference 16).

(a) Illustrate this data in a pie chart.

(b) Illustrate this data in a bar chart.

2.13 In a recent study by Yochum and Agarwal (reference 2), the per-capita income levels in 212 of the nation's 300-plus metropolitan areas were found (adjustments for differences in prices between areas were made). The following table reflects the price-adjusted Florida metro income rankings that were above the national average:

NATIONAL RANK	METRO AREA	PER CAPITA INCOME	RATIO OF METRO INCOME TO NATIONAL AVERAGE
1	West Palm Beach	$35,358	1.58
3	Sarasota	$30,325	1.36
35	Fort Meyers	$25,553	1.14
37	Tampa	$25,434	1.14
49	Jacksonville	$24,666	1.10
97	Orlando	$22,560	1.01

Source: Reference 2

(a) Graphically display this data.

(b) What conclusions might you draw from this study?

2.14 What are the top overall internet sites (measured by the actual number of total users who visit the site once during a given month)? The following table indicates the top six sites during October 1999 (reference 9). Graphically display the data.

SITE	MONTHLY UNIQUE VISITORS (IN MILLIONS)
Yahoo.com	33.6
msn.com	30.3
aol.com	28.4
microsoft.com	21.8
netscape.com	20.8
geocities.com	20.3

2.15 What percent of undergraduate alumni made donations to their alma mater? The Institutional Research Office at one university reported the following percentages for the time period 1995 to 1999. Draw a time plot of this data. What action could the school take?

YEAR	PERCENT
1995	29.72%
1996	27.48%
1997	24.89%
1998	22.83%
1999	30.22%

2.16 The data in the following table indicate the number of first-time freshman and transfers entering a four-year private university during the time period from 1994 to 2002.

	1994	1995	1996	1997	1998	1999	2000	2001	2002
Freshmen	467	503	485	485	472	426	515	557	580
Transfers	168	168	171	150	150	132	147	120	160

Use a time plot to graphically portray this data. In Chapter 1 you learned that statistical thinking is a philosophy of learning and action. What possible conclusions or actions might the university consider? The data are stored in the data file **University.**

2.17 The data in the next table indicate the number of degrees awarded from 1994 to 2002 by degree type at a four-year private university. Data are stored in the data file **Degrees.**

TYPE/ YEAR	1995 TO 96	1996 TO 97	1997 TO 98	1998 TO 99	1999 TO 00	2000 TO 01	2001 TO 02
Bachelor	493	481	464	455	424	424	480
Graduate	68	68	77	93	76	102	150
Law	206	246	253	253	235	265	300

(a) Graph the data with a time plot.

(b) What possible conclusions or actions might the university consider?

2.18 Jon Payne, tennis coach, has kept a record of various types of errors made by each of his players during a one-week training camp. The type and number of errors for one of his students is given in the following frequency distribution:

ERROR	FREQUENCY
A	17
B	2
C	13
D	3
E	2
F	1
G	2

Use Minitab to construct a Pareto diagram of the data.

2.4 MEASURES OF CENTRAL TENDENCY

You are beginning to see that a collection of data attempts to tell a story. It is somewhat like solving a mystery. In the preceding sections you were introduced to graphical ways to summarize data. By doing so, you saw patterns emerge. Histograms often illustrate that data show a tendency to center or cluster around some value. In this section, you will study measures of central tendency including the mean, the median, the mode, and the geometric mean. You will also learn how the relationship between the mean and the median can give a visual picture of the pattern of the data.

Although formulas are given, manual computation is appropriate for only small data sets. There may be times that you need to quickly compute a particular measure. However, if you are to think statistically and apply statistics to other disciplines as well as to most business problems, computation will often require some type of statistical software such as Microsoft Excel and Minitab. No doubt there will be upgrades to current software, and new statistical packages are being and will be developed. By learning now to use existing sources you will find it easier to adapt to future improvements in technology. Factors such as time constraints and human errors also contribute to the use of statistical software packages. As mentioned earlier, errors do exist in software or in the manuals.

Measures of central tendency provide information about a "typical" observation in the data. Such measures are usually computed from sample data, rather than from population data.

STATISTIC AND PARAMETER

A **statistic** is a descriptive measure computed from a sample of data. A **parameter** is a descriptive measure computed from an entire population of data.

The Mean and the Median

The most common measure of central tendency is the arithmetic mean, usually referred to simply as the "mean" or the "average."

ARITHMETIC MEAN

The **arithmetic mean** of a set of data is the sum of the data values divided by the number of observations. If the data set is from a sample, then the **sample mean**, $\overline{X}$, is:

$$\overline{X} = \frac{\sum_{i=1}^{n} x_i}{n} = \frac{x_1 + x_2 + \cdots + x_n}{n} \tag{2.3}$$

n = sample size and Σ means "to add"

If the data set is from a population, then the **population mean**, μ, is:

$$\mu = \frac{\sum_{i=1}^{N} x_i}{N} = \frac{x_1 + x_2 + \cdots + x_N}{N} \qquad (2.4)$$

$N =$ population size.

$\overline{X}$ is a statistic and μ is a parameter.

Another measure of central tendency is the median.

ORDERED ARRAY AND MEDIAN (X_M)

An **ordered array** is an arrangement of data in either ascending or descending order. Once the data are arranged in order, the **median** is the value such that 50% of the observations are smaller and 50% of the observations are larger. If the sample size n is an odd number, the **median**, X_m, is the middle observation. If the sample size n is an even number, the **median**, X_m, is the average of the two middle observations. The median will be located in the

$$0.50(n + 1)\text{th ordered position.} \qquad (2.5)$$

Since outliers influence the mean, the median may be preferred when data contains extremely large or extremely small observations. In this case, the median may be a better representation of the center of the distribution. However, in Chapter 8 certain properties of the mean are discussed that make the sample mean more attractive than the median.

The mean is not an appropriate measure of central tendency for categorical data. If one person strongly agrees with a particular statement and another person strongly disagrees, is the mean "no opinion"?

EXAMPLE 2.9

TIMES TO WALK A 5K RACE (MEAN AND MEDIAN)

People across the country participate in various walks to raise funds for needed medical research. Recently, national and local businesses sponsored a Susan G. Komen Breast Cancer Foundation 5K "Race for the Cure" in Daytona Beach, Florida. Participants could either run or walk the race. The time to complete the race appeared on a large display as each participant enthusiastically crossed the finish line. The times (rounded to the nearest minute) for a random sample of 5 participants who walked this race are:

$$45 \quad 53 \quad 45 \quad 50 \quad 48$$

Compute the mean and median times for this random sample of participants.

SOLUTION

The mean and the median are very close. The sample mean time is easily found to be

$$\overline{X} = \frac{\sum_{i=1}^{n} x_i}{n} = \frac{45 + 53 + 45 + 50 + 48}{5} = 48.2 \text{ minutes}$$

The ordered array for these times to walk the 5K Race are:

$$45 \quad 45 \quad \mathbf{48} \quad 50 \quad 53$$

It is clear that "48" is the middle observation. The median time of X_m = **48** minutes indicates that at least half of the sample took at most 48 minutes. If the sample on page 32 included a sixth participant's time of 55 minutes, the median would be located in the 0.5(7)th position, or the 3.5th ordered observation, which would be 49 minutes.

The next example contains outliers. Notice the relationship between the mean and the median.

EXAMPLE 2.10

TYPICAL AMOUNT SPENT ON GROCERIES (MEAN VERSUS MEDIAN)

Bishop

The manager of Bishop's Supermarket wants information about the spending habits of the store's customers. Do these customers spend more money on groceries over the weekend than they spend on groceries during the week? How old are these customers? How many times a week do they shop at this store? What percentage of these shoppers use coupons? Since this supermarket recently decided to accept the American Express card for payment of groceries, the manager would like an estimate of the average amount billed to American Express. Questions like these will be answered in later chapters. For now, the manager would simply like to know the dollar amount that customers typically spend on a visit to this store. Find the mean and the median amounts spent on groceries for a random sample of 36 register receipts recorded in Table 2.6. Which measure is a better indicator of central tendency for this information? The data are stored in the data file **Bishop**.

SOLUTION

Construct the stem-and-leaf display in Figure 2.14 on page 34. Notice that the shape of the distribution has a long upper tail. The outliers of $250 and $254 influence the arithmetic mean.

You find the median amount is $39.50. X_m = 0.50(36 + 1)th ordered position = 18.5th ordered position. The 18th ordered position is $39 and the 19th ordered position is $40. Fifty percent of the customers in the sample spent less than $39.50, and the same percentage of the customers in the sample spent more than $39.50. The arithmetic mean is $55.11. The outliers $250 and $254 influence the mean. In this case, the median is a better indicator of the typical amount spent on groceries at this store.

TABLE 2.6
Amounts Spent on Groceries for a Random Sample of Customers at Bishop's Market

10	25	37	53	74	58
13	25	38	58	80	63
15	30	39	58	82	64
21	32	39	58	88	40
23	34	41	70	250	15
24	35	48	70	254	20

The Mode

MODE
The **mode**, if one exists, is the most frequently occurring observation.

From a stem-and-leaf display such as Figure 2.14, it is easy to see the value of the mode. Four customers spent $58 on groceries. This value occurred more often than any other amount.

FIGURE 2.14
Random Sample of Grocery
Bills (Minitab)

```
Stem-and-leaf of Amounts    N  = 36;   Leaf Unit = 1.0
 4      1 0 3 5 5
10      2 0 1 3 4 5 5
18      3 0 2 4 5 7 8 9 9
18      4 0 1 8
15      5 3 8 8 8 8
10      6 3 4
 8      7 0 0 4
 5      8 0 2 8
 2      9
 2     10
 2     11
 2     12
 2     13
 2     14
 2     15
 2     16
 2     17
 2     18
 2     19
 2     20
 2     21
 2     22
 2     23
 2     24
 2     25 0 4
```

Application to Suntan Lotion Example

Find the measures of central tendency for the weights given in the suntan lotion problem in Example 2.1 and Table 2.1. Microsoft Excel was used to obtain the summary of descriptive statistics in Figure 2.15. In addition to the mean, median, and mode, you see several measures (such as standard deviation and sample variance) that have not yet been discussed. These measures will be discussed later in the chapter.

INTERPRETATION

From the descriptive summary, several observations are made that you should include in your report. For example, you notice that the least amount of lotion in any bottle is 224 mL and the greatest amount of lotion in any bottle is 249 mL. However, you already knew this information. But now you see that more bottles are filled with 231 mL of lotion than any other amount. This is the mode of the data. The mean weight of the 100 bottles of suntan lotion is 236.99 mL and the median is 237 mL. Should the operations manager be concerned?

FIGURE 2.15
Descriptive Summary for
Suntan Lotion Example
(Microsoft Excel)

Weights	
Mean	**236.99**
Standard Error	0.487934
Median	**237**
Mode	**231**
Standard Deviation	4.879342
Sample Variance	23.80798
Kurtosis	-0.23268
Skewness	**0.1361**
Range	25
Minimum	**224**
Maximum	**249**
Sum	**23699**
Count	**100**

Excel Instructions
1. Open file Suntan
2. Click on Tools
3. Select Data Analysis...
4. Select Descriptive Statistics
5. Complete dialog box

Shape of the Distribution

An examination of the shape of a distribution will illustrate how the distribution is centered around the mean. Distributions are either symmetric or they are not symmetric, in which case the shape of the distribution is described as asymmetric or skewed.

SYMMETRY

The shape of a distribution is said to be **symmetric** if the observations are balanced, or evenly distributed, about the mean. In a symmetric distribution the mean and the median are equal.

SKEWNESS

A distribution is **skewed** if the observations are not symmetrically distributed above and below the mean.

A **positively skewed** (or skewed to the right) distribution has a tail that extends to the right in the direction of positive values. A **negatively skewed** (or skewed to the left) distribution has a tail that extends to the left in the direction of negative values.

One possible source for skewness is the presence of outliers that influence the mean. For example, if there are any unusually large observations in the data, the value of the mean is increased possibly resulting in positive skewness. Similarly, if there are any unusually small observations in the data, the value of the mean will decrease, possibly leading to negative skewness. Sometimes skewness is simply inherent in the distribution.

Consider the histograms of Figure 2.16. Figure 2.16A depicts a situation in which the data are symmetrically distributed about their central value. Extremely large observations are no more likely than extremely small ones. Here, the mean and the median are equal.

By contrast, the histogram of Figure 2.16B has a long tail to the right, with a far more abrupt cutoff to the left. This distribution is *skewed to the right*, or *positively skewed*. Distributions of incomes or wealth of households in a city, state, or country tend to contain a relatively small proportion of high values. A large proportion of the population have relatively modest incomes, but the incomes of, say, the highest 10% of all earners extend over a considerable range. As a result, the mean of such distributions is typically quite a bit higher than the median. The mean, which is pushed up by the very wealthy, gives a too optimistic view of the economic well-being of the community. The median is then preferred to the mean.

The distribution in Figure 2.16C is negatively skewed, with the lowest observations extending over a wide range to the left. The mean will be less than the median

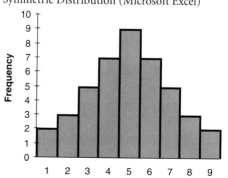

FIGURE 2.16A
Symmetric Distribution (Microsoft Excel)

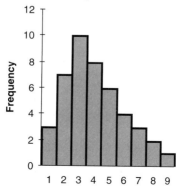

FIGURE 2.16B
Positively Skewed Distribution
(Microsoft Excel)

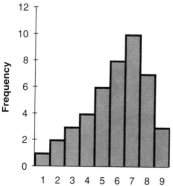

FIGURE 2.16C
Negatively Skewed Distribution
(Microsoft Excel)

in this type of distribution. Age at the time of death generally has a negative distribution.

EXAMPLE 2.11

CRUISE SPECIALS (OUTLIERS)

A cruise agency randomly sampled company records to find the number of weekly faxes received that announce cruise specials to Europe (reference 14). The results were: 20, 73, 75, 80, and 82 faxes. What do you notice about the data?

SOLUTION

The low number of "20" is an obvious outlier. The manager found the sample mean number of faxes was 66, smaller than the median of 75. This data appears to be skewed to the left. However, the manager should first check to see if the value "20" was incorrect.

Whenever there are outliers in the data, you need to look for possible causes. First, check to see if an error in data entry occurred. If not, check for some other cause; perhaps a hurricane delayed the companies from sending the cruise specials.

In spite of its advantage in discounting extreme observations, the median is used less frequently than the mean. The reason is that the theoretical development of inferential procedures based on the mean, and measures related to it, is considerably more straightforward than the development of procedures based on the median. Accordingly, most statisticians work with the mean and related measures, incorporating into their analysis special techniques to deal with those situations in which it is suspected that extreme outlying observations could exert undue influence. Another word of caution concerns missing values. See the Appendix to this chapter for a discussion of this issue.

The Geometric Mean

Another measure of central tendency that is important in business and economics is the *geometric mean.* Business analysts and economists who are interested in growth over a number of time periods use the geometric mean. You will no doubt find applications for the geometric mean in your finance classes as you study compound interest over several years, total sales growth, or population growth. An important question concerns the average growth each year that will result in a certain total growth over several years.

GEOMETRIC MEAN

The **Geometric Mean,** $\overline{X}_g$, is the nth root of the product of n numbers:

$$\overline{X}_g = \sqrt[n]{(x_1 \bullet x_2 \bullet \cdots \bullet x_n)} = (x_1 \bullet x_2 \bullet \cdots \bullet x_n)^{1/n} \qquad (2.6)$$

The Geometric Mean is used to obtain mean growth over several periods given compounded growth from each period.

The geometric mean of: 1.05, 1.02, 1.10, and 1.06 is:

$$\overline{X}_g = [(1.05)(1.02)(1.10)(1.06)]^{1/4} = 1.0571$$

EXAMPLE 2.12

ANNUAL GROWTH RATE
(GEOMETRIC MEAN)

Find the annual growth rate if sales have grown 25% over five years.

SOLUTION

The intuitive but naive temptation is simply to divide total growth, 25%, by the number of time periods, five, and conclude that the average annual growth rate is 5 percent. This result is incorrect because it ignores the compound effect of growth.

Suppose that the annual growth rate were actually 5%, then the total growth over five years would be:

$$(1.05)(1.05)(1.05)(1.05)(1.05) = 1.2763, \text{ or } 27.63\%$$

However, the annual growth rate, r, that would yield 25% over five years must satisfy the equation:

$$(1 + r)^5 = 1.25.$$

First, solve for the geometric mean,

$$\overline{X}_g = 1 + r = (1.25)^{1/5} = 1.046$$

The growth rate is $r = 0.046$, or 4.6%.

EXERCISES

2.19 ◉ Refer to the data in Exercise 2.5 and the data file **Water**.
(a) Find the mean fill of the one-gallon bottles of drinking water.
(b) Find the median fill of the one-gallon bottles of drinking water.
(c) Find the modal fill of the one-gallon bottles of drinking water.
(d) Be sure to add this information to your report.

2.20 A department store manager is interested in the number of complaints received by the customer service department about the quality of electrical products sold by the store. Records over a 10-week period yield the data shown in the table.

WEEK	1	2	3	4	5
NUMBER OF COMPLAINTS	13	15	8	16	8
WEEK	6	7	8	9	10
NUMBER OF COMPLAINTS	4	21	11	3	15

(a) Find the mean number of weekly complaints for this population.
(b) Find the median number of weekly complaints for this population.

2.21 ◉ The assessment rates (in percentages) assigned to a random sample of 40 commercially zoned parcels of land in the year 2000 are given as follows and contained in the data file **Rates**.

21	22	27	36	22	29	29	31	30	28
22	23	22	28	36	33	26	28	24	27
29	31	33	28	27	29	30	31	30	28
34	27	29	30	34	23	28	30	31	25

(a) Find the mean percentage assessment rate.
(b) Find the median of these percentage assessment rates.
(c) Find the mode of these percentage assessment rates.
(d) Describe the symmetry or skewness of the data.

2.22 A random sample of 22 business economists were asked to predict the percentage growth in the consumer price index over the next year. The forecasts were:

3.6 3.1 3.9 3.7 3.5 3.7 3.4 3.0 3.6 3.4 3.1
2.9 3.0 4.0 2.8 3.8 4.2 2.5 3.1 3.9 2.9 2.6

(a) Find the sample mean prediction.
(b) Find the sample median.

2.23 A department store chain randomly sampled 10 stores in a state. After a review of sales records, it was found that compared with the same period last year, the following percentage increases in dollar sales had been achieved over the Christmas period this year:

10.2 3.1 5.9 7.0 3.7 2.9 6.8 7.3 8.2 4.3

(a) Find the mean percentage increase in dollar sales.
(b) Find the median.

2.24 A sample of 12 senior executives found the following results for percentage of total compensation derived from bonus payments:

15.8   7.3 28.4 18.2 15.0 24.7
13.1 10.2 29.3 34.7 16.9 25.3

(a) Find the sample median.
(b) Find the sample mean.

2.25 ◉ A sample of 33 accounting students recorded the number of hours spent studying the course material in the week before the final exam.

The data is given below and contained in the data file **Study.**

```
12  7   4  16  21  5  6   8   9   7  6
 9  3  11  14  10  6  9  10  11   6  4
 8  2   9  11   8  9  4   7  10  11  9
```

(a) Find the sample mean.
(b) Find the sample median.
2.26 Sheila Newton, an investment counselor, has reported the following annual growth rates in the price of a particular stock: 4.3%, 6.0%, 3.5%, 8.2% and 7.0%.

(a) What is the mean growth rate over the five-year period?
(b) If this growth rate continued, how many years would be required for the price to double?
2.27 Inflation rates in a small country for the past five years have been 10%, 7%, 13%, 9% and 12%.
(a) What is the average annual rate of inflation?
(b) If this rate of inflation continues, how long will it take for prices to double?

2.5   MEASURES OF VARIABILITY

No two things are exactly alike. This is one of the basic principles of statistical quality control. Variation exists in all areas. In sports, the star basketball player might score five three-pointers in one game and none in the next; or he may play 40 minutes in one game and only 24 minutes in the next. Variation is obvious in the music industry. The weather varies greatly from day to day, or even from hour to hour; grades on a test differ for students taking the same course with the same instructor; your blood pressure, pulse, cholesterol level, and caloric intake vary daily.

It is possible that two data sets have the same mean, but the individual observations in one set could vary more from the mean than do the observations in the second set. It takes more than the mean alone to describe data. Measures of variability (also called measures of dispersion or spread) that you will study in this section include the range, the variance, the standard deviation, and the coefficient of variation.

The Range

> **RANGE**
> The **range** in a set of data is the difference between the largest and smallest observations.

The larger the range, the greater the spread of the data from the center. Since the range takes into account only the largest and smallest observations, it is susceptible to considerable distortion if there is an unusual extreme observation. If there is an outlier, the range should not be used to measure the deviation.

Variance and Standard Deviation

Although range gives a measure of the *total* spread of data, it only takes into account the two extreme values of the data. Statisticians searched for another measure that would consider each of the data values. Such a measure would *average* the total (Σ) distance between each observation and the mean. Since this distance would be negative for values smaller than the mean (and distance is not negative), each of these differences would need to be squared, $(x_i - \overline{X})^2$. Thus, each observation (both above and below the mean) contributes to the sum of the squared terms. The average of the sum of squared terms is called the variance.

VARIANCE

The **sample variance**, s^2, is the sum of the squared differences between each observation and the sample mean divided by the sample size minus 1.

$$s^2 = \frac{\sum_{i=1}^{n} (x_i - \overline{X})^2}{n-1} \tag{2.7}$$

The **population variance**, σ^2, is the sum of the squared differences between each observation and the population mean divided by the population size, N.

$$\sigma^2 = \frac{\sum_{i=1}^{N} (x_i - \mu)^2}{N} \tag{2.8}$$

Notice that for sample data, variance in Equation 2.7 is found by dividing the numerator by $(n-1)$ and not n. Since our goal to find an average of squared deviations about the mean, one would expect division by n. So why is sample variance found by division of $(n-1)$? If we were to take a very large number of samples, each of size n, from the population and compute the sample variance as given in Equation 2.7 for each of these samples, then the average of all of these sample variances would be the population variance, σ^2. In Chapter 8 you will learn that this means that Equation 2.7 is an "unbiased estimator" of the population variance, σ^2. For now, we rely on mathematical statisticians who have shown that if the population variance is unknown, a sample variance is a better estimator of the population variance if the denominator in sample variance is $(n-1)$ rather than n.

To compute the variance requires squaring the distances, which then changes the unit of measurement to square units. The standard deviation, which is the square root of variance, restores the data to its original measurement unit. If the original were in feet, the variance would be in feet squared, but the standard deviation would be in feet. The standard deviation measures the *average* spread around the mean.

STANDARD DEVIATION

The **sample standard deviation**, s, is the (positive) square root of the variance, and is defined as:

$$s = \sqrt{s^2} = \sqrt{\frac{\sum_{i=1}^{n} (x_i - \overline{X})^2}{n-1}} \tag{2.9}$$

The **population standard deviation** is

$$\sigma = \sqrt{\sigma^2} = \sqrt{\frac{\sum_{i=1}^{N} (x_i - \mu)^2}{N}} \tag{2.10}$$

TEST GRADES IN AN INTRODUCTORY MARKETING CLASS (MEASURES OF VARIABILITY)

A professor who teaches introductory marketing at a local university randomly selects test scores from two different sections of the same course (one taught at 8:00 A.M. and one taught at 1:00 P.M.) and reports that the average grade in both classes is 70. Look carefully at the data that follows:

| Class 1: | 50 | 60 | 70 | 80 | 90 |
| Class 2: | 72 | 68 | 70 | 74 | 66 |

Find the range, variance, and standard deviation for both classes.

SOLUTION

Although the average grade is 70 for both classes, you notice that the grades in Class 2 are closer to the mean, 70, than are the grades in Class 1. You expect the range of Class 2 to be smaller than the range of Class 1. The range for Class 1 is 40; for Class 2, the range is only $74 - 66 = 8$. You would also expect the standard deviation for Class 1 to be greater than the standard deviation for Class 2.

$$\textbf{For Class 1: } s_1^2 = \frac{(50-70)^2 + (60-70)^2 + (70-70)^2 + (80-70)^2 + (90-70)^2}{4} = 250$$

with a standard deviation, $s_1 = \sqrt{250} = 15.8$

$$\textbf{For Class 2: } s_2^2 = \frac{(66-70)^2 + (68-70)^2 + \cdots + (74-70)^2}{4} = 10; \quad \text{or } s_2 = \sqrt{10} = 3.16$$

The variance and standard deviations for each class could also be obtained with Excel (Figure 2.17) or Minitab.

FIGURE 2.17
Descriptive Summary for Marketing Example (Microsoft Excel)

Class 1	
Mean	70
Standard Error	7.071068
Median	70
Mode	
Standard Deviation	15.81139
Sample Variance	250
Kurtosis	-1.2
Skewness	0
Range	40
Minimum	50
Maximum	90
Sum	350
Count	5

Class 2	
Mean	70
Standard Error	1.414214
Median	70
Mode	
Standard Deviation	3.162278
Sample Variance	10
Kurtosis	-1.2
Skewness	0
Range	8
Minimum	66
Maximum	74
Sum	350
Count	5

Some people prefer either of the following two formulas (sometimes called shortcut formulas) to compute the variance and standard deviation. You can try these on your own.

SHORTCUT FORMULAS FOR SAMPLE VARIANCE

Shortcut formulas for the sample variance are:

$$s^2 = \frac{\sum x_i^2 - \frac{\left(\sum x_i\right)^2}{n}}{n-1} \quad \text{or} \quad s^2 = \frac{\sum x_i^2 - n\overline{X}^2}{n-1} \tag{2.11}$$

Example 2.14 illustrates an application of variance and standard deviation in the area of finance.

EXAMPLE 2.14

RISK OF A SINGLE ASSET (STANDARD DEVIATION)

Wes and Jennie Moore, owners of Moore's Foto Shop in western Pennsylvania, are considering one of two investment alternatives, Investment A or Investment B. They are not sure which of these two single assets is better, and they ask Sheila Newton, a financial planner, for some assistance.

SOLUTION

Sheila knows that the standard deviation, s, is the most common single indicator of the risk or variability of a single asset. In financial situations, the fluctuation around a stock's actual rate of return and its expected rate of return is called the risk of the stock. The standard deviation measures the variation of returns around an asset's average. Sheila obtained the rates of return on each asset for the last five years and calculated the means and standard deviations of each asset. The results are in Table 2.7. Notice that each asset had the same average rate of return of 12.2%. However, once Sheila obtained the standard deviations, it became apparent that Asset B was a more risky investment.

TABLE 2.7
Rates of Return: Investments A and B

YEAR	RATES OF RETURN	
	ASSET A	ASSET B
5 Years Ago	11.3%	9.4%
4 Years Ago	12.5	17.1
3 Years Ago	13.0	13.3
2 Years Ago	12.0	10.0
1 Year Ago	12.2	11.2
Total	61.0	61.0
Average Rate of Return	12.2%	12.2%
Standard Deviation	**0.63**	**3.12**

Empirical Rule

Consider a data set that is at least approximately symmetric and many of the data points cluster around the mean. Then "we can use the so-called *empirical rule* to examine the property of data variability and get a better sense of what the standard deviation is measuring" (reference 12). The Empirical Rule provides a way to approximate the percentage of observations that are contained within one, two, or three standard deviations around the mean.

EMPIRICAL RULE (THE 68%, 95%, OR ALMOST ALL RULE)

For a set of data with a mound-shaped histogram, the **Empirical Rule** is:

- approximately **68%** of the observations are contained with a distance of one standard deviation around the mean; $\mu \pm 1\sigma$

- approximately **95%** of the observations are contained with a distance of two standard deviations around the mean; $\mu \pm 2\sigma$

- **almost all** of the observations are contained with a distance of three standard deviations around the mean. $\mu \pm 3\sigma$

Coefficient of Variation

The coefficient of variation expresses the standard deviation as a percentage of the mean.

COEFFICIENT OF VARIATION

The **Coefficient of Variation, CV**, is a measure of relative dispersion that expresses the standard deviation as a percentage of the mean (provided the mean is positive).

The **sample coefficient of variation** is

$$CV = \frac{s}{X} \times 100\% \qquad \text{if } \overline{X} > 0 \tag{2.12}$$

The **population coefficient of variation** is

$$CV = \frac{\sigma}{\mu} \times 100\% \qquad \text{if } \mu > 0 \tag{2.13}$$

If the standard deviations in sales for large and small stores selling similar goods are compared, the standard deviation for large stores would almost always be bigger. A simple explanation is that a large store could be modeled as a number of small stores. Comparing variation using the standard deviation would be misleading. The coefficient of variation overcomes this problem by adjusting for the scale of units in the population.

EXAMPLE 2.15

COMPARISON OF CV FOR STOCK PURCHASE (COEFFICIENT OF VARIATION)

In Example 2.14 two different investments with the same mean rate of return were considered. Now, the owners are thinking about possibly purchasing shares of Stock A or shares of Stock B, both listed on the New York Stock Exchange. From the closing prices of both stocks over the last several months the standard deviations were found to be considerably different with

$$s_A = \$2.00 \quad \text{and} \quad s_B = \$8.00$$

Should Stock A be purchased since the standard deviation in Stock B is larger?

SOLUTION

You might think that Stock B is more volatile than Stock A. The mean closing prices for the two stocks are

$$\overline{X}_A = \$4.00 \quad \text{and} \quad \overline{X}_B = \$80.00$$

Next the coefficients of variation are computed to measure and compare the risk of these competing investment opportunities.

$$CV_A = \frac{\$2.00}{\$4.00} \times 100\% = 50\% \quad \text{and} \quad CV_B = \frac{\$8.00}{\$80.00} \times 100\% = 10\%$$

Notice that the market value of Stock A fluctuates more from period to period than does Stock B.

The Interquartile Range

To understand another measure of spread known as the interquartile range, it is first necessary to define percentiles and quartiles. It is often important to determine values that are not necessarily located in the *center* of the data. Individual observations are sometimes compared by use of their relative ranking. Percentiles and quartiles often describe large data sets, such as sales and survey data. Suppose that you scored in the 90th percentile on a college entrance exam. How did your score compare with those of other students who took the same test?

PERCENTILES AND QUARTILES

Data must first be in ascending order. **Percentiles** separate large ordered data sets into 100ths.
The **Pth percentile** is a number such that P percent of the observations are at or below that number.
Quartiles are descriptive measures that separate large ordered data sets into four quarters.

To score in the 90th percentile indicates 90% of the test scores were less than or equal to your score. You scored excellently! You scored in the upper 10% of all persons taking the test.

There are some special percentiles that you need to know.

FIRST QUARTILE, Q_1

The **first quartile, Q_1**, is another name for the **25th percentile**. The first quartile divides the ordered data such that 25% of the observations are at or below this value. Q_1 is located in the $.25(n+1)$st position when the data is in ascending order. That is,

$$Q_1 = \frac{(n+1)}{4} \text{ ordered observation} \tag{2.14}$$

THIRD QUARTILE, Q_3

The **third quartile, Q_3**, is another name for the **75th percentile**. The third quartile divides the ordered data such that 75% of the observations are at or below this value. Q_3 is located in the $0.75(n+1)$st position when the data is in ascending order. That is,

$$Q_3 = \frac{3(n+1)}{4} \text{ ordered observation} \tag{2.15}$$

The median is the 50th percentile, or the second quartile, Q_2.

Although the range measures the *total* spread of the data, the range may be an unsatisfactory measure of variability (spread) because it is influenced too much by an outlier, a single very high or very low observation. One way to avoid this difficulty is to arrange the data in ascending order, discard a few of the highest and a few of the lowest numbers, and find the range of those remaining.

INTERQUARTILE RANGE

The **Interquartile Range (IQR)** measures the spread in the *middle 50%* of the data; it is the difference between the observations at the 25th and the 75th percentiles:

$$\text{IQR} = Q_3 - Q_1 \tag{2.16}$$

The interquartile range has an easy and sometimes convenient interpretation. For large data sets, it is the range containing the middle 50% of all the observations. Sometimes the minimum value, the maximum value, the first and third quartiles, and the median are called the five-number summary.

FIVE-NUMBER SUMMARY

Five-number summary refers to the five descriptive measures: minimum, first quartile, median, third quartile, and maximum. Clearly, Minimum $< Q_1 <$ Median $< Q_3 <$ Maximum

---

Quartiles can be found in several ways. Graphically, you can construct a stem-and-leaf display to find the quartiles and the interquartile range. You also can use either Microsoft Excel PHStat or Minitab. Output from each of these software packages is illustrated.

EXAMPLE 2.16

FINDING QUARTILES FROM A STEM-AND-LEAF DISPLAY (IQR)

Using the data from Example 2.2, determine the interquartile range.

SOLUTION

Recall the stem-and-leaf display (obtained with Excel) for the times to prepare a cheese calzone at Gilotti's (Example 2.2)

Stem-and-Leaf Display

for Minutes

Stem unit: 10

```
1 | 1 2 4 6 7 8 8 9 9
2 | 1 2 2 2 4 6 8 9 9
3 | 0 1 2 3 4
4 | 0 2
```

The first and third quartiles must be computed to find the IQR.

- Q_1 is in the $.25(n + 1)$st position $= 0.25(26)$th position $=$ the value in the 6.5th position $= 18$ minutes
- Q_3 is in the $.75(n + 1)$st position $= 0.75(26)$th position $=$ the value in the 19.5th position $= 30.5$ minutes
- IQR $= 30.5 - 18 = 12.5$ minutes; that is, the *middle 50%* of the data has a spread of only 12.5 minutes

Minitab to Obtain Quartiles

For larger data sets, follow the command sequence Stat>Basic Statistics>Descriptive Statistics.

FIGURE 2.18
Descriptive Statistics for
Example 2.1 (Minitab)

Variable	N	Mean	Median	TrMean	StDev	SE Mean
Weights	100	236.99	237.00	236.93	4.88	0.49

Variable	Minimum	Maximum	Q1	Q3		
Weights	224.00	249.00	**233.25**	**241.00**		

FIGURE 2.19
Box-and-Whisker Plot
Dialogue Box (Microsoft
Excel, PHStat Add-in)

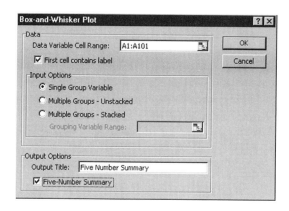

PHStat Instructions

1. Open file Suntan
2. Click on PHStat
3. Select Descriptive Statistics
4. Select Box-and-Whisker Plot...
5. Enter A1:A101 in Raw Data Cell Range:
6. Choose Five-Number Summary
7. Click OK

Output will look like Figure 2.20.

Microsoft Excel to Obtain Quartiles

Method 1 Syntax: =**QUARTILE(array,quart)** where array is the cell range of the numeric data and quart is a number from 0 to 4. Quart = 0 is the minimum value; quart = 1 is the first quartile; quart = 2 is the median (second quartile); quart = 3 is the third quartile; and quart = 4 is the maximum value. For the IQR, you would need to find both

$$=QUARTILE(array,3) \text{ and } =QUARTILE(array,1) \text{ and subtract.}$$

Method 2 PHStat: Figure 2.19 and the accompanying instructions illustrate finding the IQR with PHStat.

For Example 2.1 and the data file Suntan, you obtain different values for the first quartile if you use Minitab, Excel and the Syntax method, or PHStat.

Minitab	$Q_1 = 233.25$	**Figure 2.18**
Excel (Syntax)	$Q_1 = 233.75$	
PHStat	$Q_1 = 233$	**Figure 2.20**

In this case, the values of the third quartile were the same.

FIGURE 2.20
Five-Number Summary for
Suntan Lotion Example

Five-number Summary	
Minimum	224
First Quartile	**233**
Median	237
Third Quartile	**241**
Maximum	249

Box-and-Whisker Plots

One exploratory data analysis technique, the stem-and-leaf display, has already been introduced. The box-and-whisker plot, also called the boxplot, is another EDA technique introduced by Professor John Tukey as an easy-to-draw picture of data (reference 18). Box-and-whisker plots help you understand how the five-number summary is used to visualize the shape of a graph.

> ## BOX-AND-WHISKER PLOT
>
> A **box-and-whisker plot** is a graphical procedure that uses the five-number summary.
> A box-and-whisker plot consists of
>
> - an inner box that shows the numbers which span the range from Q_1 to Q_3
> - a line that is drawn through the box at the median
>
> The "whiskers" are lines from Q_1 to the minimum value, and from Q_3 to the maximum value.

EXAMPLE 2.17

ANALYSIS OF CONVENIENCE FOOD STORES (BOX-AND-WHISKER)

During the past three years Consolidated Oil Company has converted a number of its gasoline stations into Convenience Food Stores (CSF) to increase total sales revenue. Gasoline sales have not been increasing and therefore it was decided to expand into related business areas. Chris Bishop, the general manager of the CFS Division, asked a senior statistician, Renee Payne, to assist with this analysis. Renee obtained a random sample of ten weekdays from each of four stores. Store 1 and Store 4 are of particular interest to Chris. Compare the descriptive measures of these two stores and construct the box-and-whisker plots. Figure 2.21 is a Minitab printout for the daily sales data (in hundreds of dollars) for the four stores.

SOLUTION

Before you construct the box-and-whisker plots, you should be able to make some conclusions about store sales and the distribution of sales. What do the measures of central tendency tell you? Look at Store 1 and Store 4. Both have the same median daily sales of $1050, but the mean sales in Store 4 average $200 more per day. You should also notice that the mean and median sale for Store 1 are very close (suggesting that the graph is approximately symmetric). For Store 4, the mean is greater than the median, generally indicating positive skewness.

Look at the measures of dispersion for Store 1 and Store 4. Both the range and the standard deviation of Store 4 exceed that of Store 1. Clearly, the daily sales fluctuate more in Store 4. By quickly computing the IQR for Store 1 and Store 4, you find that the IQR for Store 1 = 4.5 and the IQR for Store 2 = 6.00. The range, the standard deviation, and the IQR tell you that the spread is bigger in Store 4. Although sales are higher on the average in Store 4 than in Store 1, the daily sales in Store 4 also vary more. Figure 2.22 obtained from Minitab shows the box-and-whisker plots for all four stores.

FIGURE 2.21
Descriptive Summary:
Convenience Food Store
Sales (Minitab)

	N	MEAN	MEDIAN	TRMEAN	STDEV	SEMEAN
Store 1	10	**10.10**	**10.50**	10.125	**2.601**	0.823
Store 2	10	10.10	10.00	10.120	7.250	2.290
Store 3	10	30.10	30.50	30.125	2.601	0.823
Store 4	10	**12.10**	**10.50**	11.370	**6.300**	1.990

	MIN	MAX	Q1	Q3
Store 1	6.00	14.00	7.75	12.25
Store 2	1.00	19.00	2.75	17.25
Store 3	26.00	34.00	27.75	32.25
Store 4	6.00	24.00	8.75	14.75

FIGURE 2.22
Box-and-Whisker Plots:
Stores 1, 2, 3, and 4 (Minitab)

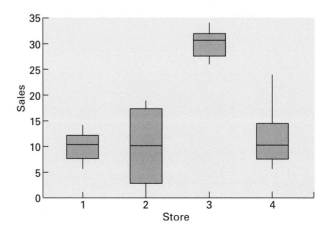

- The median sales (middle line of the boxes) are the same for Store 1 and Store 4.
- Notice the tails (whiskers) of Store 1. **Both whiskers in Store 1 are the same size.** Numerically,

$$Q_1 - X_{\text{Minimum}} = 7.75 - 6.00 = 1.75; X_{\text{Maximum}} - Q_3 = 14 - 12.25 = 1.75$$

  Store 1 is approximately symmetric.
- Notice the tails (whiskers) of Store 4. **The upper whisker in Store 4 is longer than the lower whisker.** Store 4 is positively skewed. Numerically,

$$Q_1 - X_{\text{Minimum}} = 8.75 - 6.00 = 2.75; X_{\text{Maximum}} - Q_3 = 24 - 14.75 = 9.25$$

By looking at the box-and-whisker plots, you also notice that Store 3 shows a similar pattern to Store 1 and that Store 2 shows wide dispersion for both its overall and interquartile range.

EXERCISES

2.28 ◐ Refer to the data in Exercise 2.5 and contained in the data file **Water**.
  (a) Find the range, variance, and standard deviation of the bottle weights.
  (b) Find the five-number summary of the weights.
  (c) Find and interpret the interquartile range for this data.
  (d) What is the value of the coefficient of variation?
  (e) Construct a box-and-whisker plot.
  (f) Use this data to write a report to the operations manager.

2.29 ◐ Refer to the test scores of the 40 students in a class given in Exercise 2.6 and stored in the data file **Scores**.

  (a) What is the mean grade on the test?
  (b) Find the standard deviation in test scores.
  (c) Find the coefficient of variation.
  (d) Find and interpret the interquartile range for this data.
  (e) Construct the box-and-whisker plot for test scores.

2.30 ◐ Refer to the assessment rates (in percentages) assigned to a random sample of 40 commercially zoned parcels of land in the year 2000 given in Exercise 2.21 and stored in the data file **Rates**. Find the standard deviation in the assessment rates.

2.6   NUMERICAL SUMMARY OF GROUPED DATA

Sometimes it is desirable to have methods to find numerical summary measures based on grouped data. For example, this type of scenario may exist for certain information collected by questionnaires or surveys where the respondent is simply asked to indicate his age from one of several categories. In these situations, it will not be possible to determine precisely the values of such quantities as the mean and variance. Instead, estimates of these measures are obtained from the recorded group frequencies.

Mean and Variance for Data With Multiple-Observation Values

Suppose that the data are such that only a few different observation values, which may occur repeatedly, are possible.

EXAMPLE 2.18

ERRORS PER PAGE (MEAN AND VARIANCE FOR MULTIPLE-OBSERVATION VALUES)

TABLE 2.8 Number of errors Found in a Textbook of 500 Pages

NUMBER OF ERRORS	NUMBER OF PAGES
0	102
1	138
2	140
3	79
4	33
5	8

A publisher receives from a printer a copy of a 500-page textbook. The page proofs are carefully read, and the number of errors on each page is recorded, producing the data shown in Table 2.8. Find the mean and variance of the number of errors per page for this data.

SOLUTION

The data presented here are simply a special case, in which there happens to be multiple-observation values, of the general data sets considered in this chapter. Thus, no new principles are involved in computing these numerical summary measures. On 102 pages there are zero errors; 138 days take the value of 1; 140 days take the value 2; and so on.

The mean number of errors per page is just the total number of errors divided by the number of pages. The total number of errors is

$$(102)(0) + (138)(1) + (140)(2) + (79)(3) + (33)(4) + (8)(5) = 827$$

Thus, the mean number of errors is

$$\mu = \frac{827}{500} = 1.654$$

Hence, the mean for this population is 1.654 errors per page.

The variance of the number of errors per page is the average of the squared discrepancies of all the observations from their mean. Now, there are 102 discrepancies of $(0 - 1.654)$, 138 discrepancies of $(1 - 1.654)$, and so on. Therefore, the sum of all squared discrepancies is

$$(102)(0 - 1.654)^2 + (138)(1 - 1.654)^2 + (140)(2 - 1.654)^2$$
$$+ (79)(3 - 1.654)^2 + (33)(4 - 1.654)^2 + (8)(5 - 1.654)^2 = 769.1420$$

Thus, the population variance is

$$\sigma^2 = \frac{769.142}{500} = 1.5383$$

The data have a standard deviation of 1.240 errors per page.

Consider the general case, in which there are K possible observation values, $m_1, m_2\ldots, m_k$ and the number of occurrences are, respectively, $f_1, f_2,\ldots, f_k$. The formulas for both the population case and the sample case are given in Equations 2.17 through 2.20.

MEAN AND VARIANCE FOR MULTIPLE-OBSERVATION VALUES

Suppose that a data set contains observation values $m_1, m_2,\ldots, m_k$ occurring with frequencies, $f_1, f_2,\ldots, f_k$, respectively.

(i) For a *population* of N observations, so that

$$N = \sum_{i=1}^{K} f_i$$

the mean is

$$\mu = \frac{\sum_{i=1}^{K} f_i m_i}{N} \tag{2.17}$$

and the variance is

$$\sigma^2 = \frac{\sum_{i=1}^{K} f_i (m_i - \mu)^2}{N} = \frac{\sum_{i=1}^{K} f_i m_i^2}{N} - \mu^2 \tag{2.18}$$

(ii) For a *sample* of n observations, so that

$$n = \sum_{i=1}^{K} f_i$$

the mean is

$$\overline{X} = \frac{\sum_{i=1}^{K} f_i m_i}{n} \tag{2.19}$$

and the variance is

$$s^2 = \frac{\sum_{i=1}^{K} f_i (m_i - \overline{X})^2}{n-1} = \frac{\sum_{i=1}^{K} f_i m_i^2 - n\overline{X}^2}{n-1} \tag{2.20}$$

The arithmetic is most conveniently set out in tabular form. For the data on errors in a textbook (Example 2.18), this is done in Table 2.9. The variance is found using the alternative, computationally efficient formula. Reading directly from the table,

$$\sum_{i=1}^{K} f_i = N = 500 \qquad \sum_{i=1}^{K} f_i m_i = 827 \qquad \sum_{i=1}^{K} f_i m_i^2 = 2{,}137$$

TABLE 2.9
Calculations for the Mean and Variance of Data on Errors Found in Textbook

m_i	f_i	$f_i m_i$	$f_i m_i^2$
0	102	0	0
1	138	138	138
2	140	280	560
3	79	237	711
4	33	132	528
5	8	40	200
Sums	500	827	2,137

Thus, the population mean is

$$\mu = \frac{\sum_{i=1}^{K} f_i m_i}{N} = \frac{827}{500} = 1.654$$

as before. For the variance,

$$\sigma^2 = \frac{\sum_{i=1}^{K} f_i m_i^2}{N} - \mu^2 = \frac{2,137}{500} - (1.654)^2 = 1.5383$$

confirming our previous calculations.

Mean and Variance for Grouped Data

Suppose that an investigator has available only data grouped into classes.

APPROXIMATE MEAN AND VARIANCE FOR GROUPED DATA

Suppose that data is grouped into K classes, with frequencies $f_1, f_2, \ldots, f_K$. If the midpoints of these classes are $m_1, m_2, \ldots, m_K$, then the mean and variance of the grouped data are estimated by using the formulas for multiple-observation values given in Equation 2.17 through Equation 2.20.

A word of caution is in order. If one or another of the extreme classes is much wider than the others, it is particularly important that the midpoint of that class be representative of its members' values, in order to obtain reasonably good estimates of the mean and variance.

EXAMPLE 2.19

CHEMICAL TESTED FOR CONCENTRATION OF IMPURITIES (MEAN AND VARIANCE FOR GROUPED VALUES)

A sample of 20 batches of a chemical was tested for concentration of impurities. The results obtained were

PERCENTAGE IMPURITIES	$0 < 2$	$2 < 4$	$4 < 6$	$6 < 8$	$8 < 10$
BATCHES	2	3	6	5	4

Find the sample mean and standard deviation of these percentage impurity levels.

SOLUTION

The computations are set out in the following table.

CLASSES	m_i	f_i	$f_i m_i$	$f_i m_i^2$
$0 < 2$	1	2	2	2
$2 < 4$	3	3	9	27
$4 < 6$	5	6	30	150
$6 < 8$	7	5	35	245
$8 < 10$	9	4	36	324
	Sums	20	112	748

From this table, then,

$$\sum_{i=1}^{K} f_i = n = 20 \qquad \sum_{i=1}^{K} f_i m_i = 112 \qquad \sum_{i=1}^{K} f_i m_i^2 = 748$$

The sample mean is estimated by

$$\overline{X} = \frac{\sum\limits_{i=1}^{K} f_i m_i}{n} = \frac{112}{20} = 5.6$$

Since these are sample data, the variance is estimated by

$$s^2 = \frac{\sum\limits_{i=1}^{K} f_i m_i^2 - n\overline{X}^2}{n-1} = \frac{748 - (20)(5.6)^2}{19} = 6.3579$$

Hence, the sample standard deviation is estimated as

$$s = \sqrt{s^2} = \sqrt{6.3579} = 2.52$$

Therefore, for this sample, the mean impurity concentration is estimated to be 5.6%, and the sample standard deviation is estimated to be 2.52%.

EXERCISES

2.31 A random sample of 50 personal property insurance policies found the following number of claims over the past two years.

Number of Claims	0	1	2	3	4	5	6
Number of Policies	21	13	5	4	2	3	2

  (a) Find the mean number of claims per day.
  (b) Find the sample variance and standard deviation.

2.32 For a random sample of 25 students from a large class, the accompanying table shows the amount of time spent studying for a test.

Study Time (Hours)	0 < 4	4 < 8	8 < 12	12 < 16	16 < 20
Number of Students	3	7	8	5	2

  (a) Estimate the sample mean study time.
  (b) Estimate the sample standard deviation.

2.33 A sample of 20 financial analysts was asked to provide forecasts of earnings per share of a corporation for next year. The results are summarized in the following table.

Forecast ($ per share)	9.95 < 10.45	10.45 < 10.95	10.95 < 11.45	11.45 < 11.95	11.95 < 12.45
Number of Analysts	2	8	6	3	1

  (a) Estimate the sample mean forecast.
  (b) Estimate the sample standard deviation of the forecasts.

SUMMARY

In this chapter you studied graphical and numerical procedures to summarize both numerical and qualitative variables. As you progress in this book, you will find that this information is the foundation for your continued statistical development. This chapter began with a problem set forth by the operations manager at a suntan lotion manufacturing plant. Throughout this chapter, various graphs and numerical descriptors of the data were developed. You should now gather the pertinent facts in this chapter and complete the report to the manager.

KEY WORDS

CHAPTER EXERCISES AND APPLICATIONS

2.34 According to a recent study (reference 19), 42% of men and 35% of women use the Internet. Another observation relates to Internet usage by income: 28% of people with incomes less than $50,000 use the Internet; these percentages increase to 48% of those in the income category from $50,000 to $74,999, and to 70% of those with incomes of at least $75,000.

(a) Use a pie chart to plot the gender percentages

(b) Use a pie chart or a bar chart to plot the income percentages.

2.35 Dr. James Mallet, Professor and Director of the Roland George Investment Institute at Stetson University reported in *USA Today* (reference 8) that the trend for student-managed funds is increasing. The following table gives the quarterly returns at the University of Texas MBA Investment Fund versus the S&P 500.

	Nov. '98	Feb. '99	May '99	Aug. '99	Nov. '99
MBA Investment Fund at University of Texas	16.1%	12.5%	2.5%	3.6%	7.0%
S&P 500	21.6%	6.4%	5.1%	1.4%	5.2%

Graph this data using a time plot.

2.36 What are the favorite countries for tourists to visit? According to a recent study (reference 21), more people (66.8 million) chose France as their choice of destination than any other country. Next was the United States with 48.9 million tourists; Spain with 43.4 million; Italy with 34 million; the United Kingdom with 26 million; China with 23.7 million; Poland with 19.5 million; Mexico with 18.6 million; Canada with 17.5 million, and then the Czech Republic with 17.4 million. Graph this data.

2.37 A major airport recently hired consultant John Cadariu to study the problem of air traffic delays. He recorded the number of minutes late for a sample of flights in the following table:

Minutes Late	0 < 10	10 < 20	20 < 30	30 < 40	40 < 50	50 < 60
Number of Flights	30	25	13	6	5	4

(a) Estimate the mean number of minutes late.

(b) Estimate the sample variance and standard deviation.

2.38 **Application Exercise: Statistical Thinking Consulting Case**

A team of undergraduate business students was challenged with the responsibility to study the County Appraiser's Office in order to recommend improvement to some process within the organization. These students began to understand that the first principle of statistical thinking, that "all work" in the process occurs in a system of interconnected processes, was relevant in this situation. The data entry process was selected for further study. Students spent time in the County Appraiser's Office and talked with employees performing different tasks. One noticeable concern was the small size of the monitors being used by the data-entry staff.

The team observed that all changes in real property (such as a change in the owner's name, increase in value of the property, and so forth) were recorded by individuals who had no knowledge of the data that they were entering. Numerous types of errors took place. For example, in posting the errors, an incorrect name or parcel number was entered. Another error that was observed was that sometimes deeds were received after tax bills had been printed.

Once the data were entered, they were sent to the deed's abstractors. In order to determine the number and types of defects, the deed's abstractors were asked to keep a record of the errors in data entry that were sent to them. The following table is a frequency distribution of errors:

Defects	Total
Posting error name	23
Posting error parcel	21
Property sold after tax bills were mailed	5
Inappropriate call transfer (not part of deeds/mapping)	18
Posting error legal description/incomplete legal description	4
Deeds received after tax bills printed	6
Correspondence — claimed property owner was deceased, but no death certificate was in the records	2
Miscellaneous errors	1

(a) Construct a Pareto diagram of these defects in data entry.

(b) What recommendations would you suggest to the County Appraiser?

REFERENCES

1. Blanchard, Peter. Smith-Barney, Inc.
2. Brown, Thomas S. "Low-end living: Cheap prices don't cut it." *News-Journal Focus*, Daytona Beach, FL. June 23, 1999, p. A1.
3. "Business Travel Expenses." Source: Runzheimer International reprinted in *Travel Agent*, October 14, 1996, p. 26.
4. Carlson, William and Betty Thorne, *Applied Statistical Methods for Business, Economics and the Social Sciences* (Upper Saddle River, NJ: Prentice Hall, 1997).
5. Cyber Dialogue, Inc. Web address: *www.cyberdialogue.com* September 21, 1999.
6. Dretzke, Beverly J. and Kenneth A. Heilman, *Statistics with Microsoft Excel* (Upper Saddle River, NJ: Prentice Hall, 1998).
7. Flynn, Barry. "Orlando's economy still turns on tourism." *CFB*, and *Orlando Sentinel* Special Supplement on Central Florida Business (*CFB*). September 6–12, 1999, p. 16–18.
8. Fogarty, Thomas A. "Student-run funds teach real skills with real cash." *USA Today*, December 13, 1999, p. 12B.
9. "Hit Parade." Source: mediametrix.com. Reprinted in *Access Internet Magazine*, Orlando Sentinel Special Supplement, December 19, 1999, p. 2.
10. "Is Y2K on your mind?" Reprinted from *www.Everything2000.com* in *Travel Weekly, Clipboard*, January 28, 1999, p. 61.
11. Lehmann, Millianne and Paul Zeitz, *Statistical Explorations with Microsoft Excel* (Pacific Grove, CA: Brooks/Cole Publishing Company, 1998).
12. Levine, David M. and Mark L. Berenson. *Basic Business Statistics: Concepts and Applications*, 7th ed. (Upper Saddle River, NJ: Prentice Hall), 1999.
13. Neufeld, John L, *Learning Business Statistics with Microsoft Excel 97* (Upper Saddle River, NJ: Prentice Hall, 1998).
14. Thorne, James R, MCC. Cruise Emporium of Ormond Beach.
15. Tichenor, John M. *Stetson University Fact Book 1998–1999 Academic Year.* (DeLand, FL: Stetson University Institutional Research Office, 1998).
16. "Travel and tourism jobs fuel the world economy." Source: 1998 World Travel and Tourism Council annual report. Reprinted in *Travel Weekly*, October 22, 1998, p. 32.
17. Tufte, E.R., *The Visual Display of Quantitative Information* (Cheshire, CT: Graphics Press, 1983).
18. Tukey, J. *Exploratory Data Analysis* (Reading: MA: Addison-Wesley, 1977).
19. "Use of Internet for travel plans or reservations." Source: Travel Industry Association of America, National Travel Survey. Reprinted in *Travel Weekly Clipboard*. March 25, 1999; p. 62.
20. Wainer, H., *Visual Revelations: Graphical Tales of Fate and Deception from Napoleon Bonaparte to Ross Perot* (New York: Copernicus/Springer-Verlag, 1997).
21. "World's top 10 tourist destinations." Source: Travel Industry Association of America. Reprinted in the *Orlando Sentinel*, September 25, 1999, p. C1.
22. Zavanelli, Max, "ZPR Investment Report: A Newsletter for ZPR Clients." Orange City, FL: January 2001.

APPENDIX

In many data files you will find that values for some variables may not be available for certain observations. That is, your data files will contain "missing values." For example, respondents to a questionnaire may choose not to answer certain questions about their age or income. Missing values require a special code in the data entry stage.

In Minitab an * is used for missing values in numeric columns. With this convention, Minitab generally interprets correctly missing values without further instructions from the user. In Excel, as in most spreadsheets, one method to code missing values is with blanks. Suppose that four students were asked to indicate their grade on a particular test. The responses were: 80, 70, No response, and 75. In Minitab you enter * for the third response; in Excel, you leave a blank for the third response. Using this convention, descriptive statistics are easily obtainable.

Sometimes missing values are coded with a number such as "−99" (provided that the value −99 is not a potential response to your question). However, a note of caution is important here. If you receive a data file with "−99" for missing data, some adjustments will need to be made since all −99 values will be treated as real values. In the above grade example, both Minitab and Excel would compute the descriptive measures using a score of "−99" for the student who did not respond. You will need to clear "−99" values from your data set. In Excel either use **Edit** > **Clear** > **All** or use **Data** > **Sort** (sort data column in descending order and omit all of the "−99" entries from your computation). There are options in Minitab to convert "−99" values to an *.

Missing values may occur in any data file. Unless missing values are properly handled, it is possible to obtain erroneous output for certain statistical procedures developed in later chapters in this book.

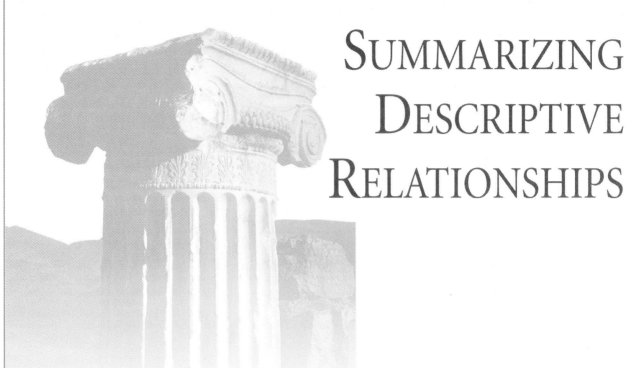

CHAPTER 3

SUMMARIZING DESCRIPTIVE RELATIONSHIPS

INTRODUCTION

In Chapter 2 we developed various procedures for summarizing data. These summaries include graphical procedures for providing "pictures" of data and descriptive statistics that measure central tendency and variation. By using these techniques you can help reveal and analyze the information contained in large data sets. Chapter 2 was concerned with descriptions of a single variable. However, in this chapter the idea of revealing and analyzing data will be extended to include the relationships between two variables.

Business and economic analyses are often concerned about relationships between variables. What is the change in quantity sold as the result of a change in price? How are total sales influenced by total disposable income in a geographic region? Does advertising increase sales? What is the change in infant mortality in developing countries as per capita income increases? To answer these questions we gather and analyze random samples of data collected from relevant populations. Here we will present some initial procedures for describing relationships using data. Later in the course we will extend these procedures and use them to develop more sophisticated procedures for extending initial descriptions into inferences about relationships between variables. Most of this chapter will emphasize relationships between quantitative variables, because these represent the major portion of statistical work in the fields of business and economics. In Section 3.4 two-way tables will be presented as a procedure for dealing with relationships between qualitative variables. Later, in Chapters 13 and 14 the analysis of qualitative variables will be expanded.

3.1 SCATTER PLOTS

As we begin to consider relationships between variables, the first step is to prepare a scatter plot picture of the relationship between two variables.

SCATTER PLOT

We can prepare a **scatter plot** by placing one point for each pair of two variables that represent an observation in the data set. The scatter plot—easily prepared using a computer—provides a picture of the data including the following:

1. Range of each variable
2. Pattern of values over the range
3. A suggestion as to a possible relationship between the two variables
4. Indication of outliers (extreme points)

You could prepare scatter plots by plotting individual points on graph paper. However, all modern statistical packages contain routines for preparing scatter plots directly from an electronic data file. Preparation of such a plot—as shown in Example 3.1—is a common task in any initial analysis of data that occurs at the beginning of economic and business studies. The following examples illustrate how to prepare and analyze scatter plots.

EXAMPLE 3.1

ENTRANCE SCORES AND COLLEGE GPA (SCATTER PLOTS)

Most of you have taken one or more academic aptitude tests as part of a college admission procedure. The results of these tests were used to help decide your admission to different colleges. An important question for college administrators and also for you is, Are these tests useful for deciding on college admissions? What information does the scatter plot in Figure 3.1 tell you about the two variables, a student's GPA at the time of graduation and the student's SAT Verbal score at the time of college admission?

FIGURE 3.1   Dialogue for Obtaining a Scatter Plot of GPA versus SAT Verbal Score for Graduating Seniors (Minitab)

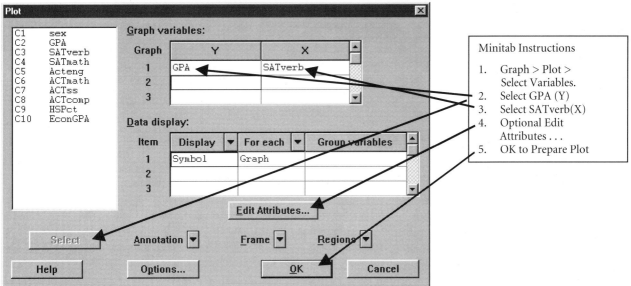

Student GPA

INTERPRETATION

SOLUTION

Data stored in **Student GPA** Figure 3.1 presents the Minitab dialogue screen for creating a scatter plot obtained using the command sequence

```
GRAPH > PLOT > SELECT VARIABLES
```

Figure 3.2 shows the resulting scatter plot of Grade Point Averages (GPA) at graduation and the SAT Verbal score from a test given before admission, for a sample of students at a selective midwestern liberal arts college.

We can make several observations from examining the scatter plot in Figure 3.2. GPA ranges from 2 to 4 (of course we knew that already because that is the required range for graduation—but this is a check on the accuracy of our original data). Similarly, the SAT Verbal score range is limited by the selection of students for admission to the college. In this example the ranges provide no new information, but in other examples the range is important. A much more interesting pattern is the positive upward trend—the central tendency of the GPA scores increases directly with increases in SAT Verbal scores. Note also that the relationship does not provide an exact prediction. Some students with low SAT Verbal scores have higher GPA scores than do students with higher SAT Verbal scores. We see that

FIGURE 3.2
GPA versus SAT Verbal Score
for Graduating Seniors

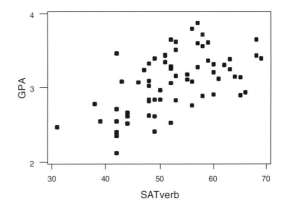

the basic pattern indicates that higher entrance scores predict higher grade point averages, but the results are not perfect.

EXAMPLE 3.2

FAMILY INCOME VERSUS EDUCATION (SCATTER PLOTS)

Income versus Education

A survey of residents included questions concerning personal and/or family information. Two questions on the survey were: (1) What is your family income? and (2) What is the educational level of the head of house? What information does the scatter plot in Figure 3.3 tell you about the relationship between the two variables, income and education level? Data stored in **Income versus Education**.

SOLUTION

The responses to educational level ranged from 1 to 8, where 1 indicated that the head of house completed no more than through the 9th grade, and 8 indicated that the head of house completed the most advanced graduate degree (such as MD, Ph.D. or JD). Income ranges from around $18,000 to around $90,000. Note that in this plot the educational level is an ordinal and not a quantitative variable. Thus the plot should be viewed as the distribution of income points at specific discrete educational level points and not as a scatter plot of the continuous relationship between income and education.

Several observations may be noted about this peculiar scatter plot. You would expect that as a person's education increased income would also increase. Although there appears to be a slight positive upward trend, the relationship is not overwhelmingly convincing. The researchers questioned the obvious outlier points at both the lower levels and the upper levels of education. That is, this scatter plot tells us that two respondents with educational levels of 1 and 2 (some high school, but did not finish high school) were earning between $75,000 and $85,000. This is the same amount as some of those with more advanced degrees. You will also note that one individual with education level "8" has an income around $25,000. Although these situations are quite possible, the researchers at least questioned the validity of this data. Perhaps data entry errors occurred. Another possibility is that the respondent did not answer the income question truthfully.

In this example we have seen how scatter plots can be used to compare a quantitative variable (income) with a qualitative ordinal variable (educational level).

FIGURE 3.3 Family Income versus Head of Household Education (Microsoft Excel)

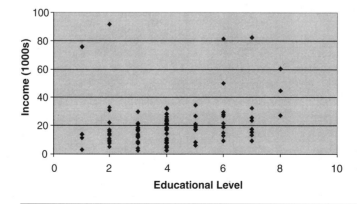

Excel Instructions

1. Highlight both Columns of data;
2. Select Insert>Chart> XY Scatter
3. Follow the dialogue sequence
4. Options are available to label and enhance the plot.

EXAMPLE 3.3

MUNICIPAL REVENUE AND COMMERCIAL PROPERTY (SCATTER PLOTS)

Another example comes from a study of municipal revenue generation capability. Many small cities make significant efforts to attract commercial property such as shopping centers and large retail stores. One of the arguments is that these facilities will contribute to the property that can be taxed and thus provide additional funds for local government needs. Figure 3.4 is a plot of "taxbase"—the assessed value of all city property in millions of dollars—versus "comper"—the percent of assessed property value that is commercial property. What does this scatter plot tell us about the assessable tax base versus the percent of commercial property in the city?

SOLUTION

We can see no relationship between the two variables and thus no evidence that emphasis on attracting a larger percentage of commercial property increases the tax base. The two outlier points on the right side of the plot might be used to argue that a very high amount of commercial property will provide a larger tax base. That argument, however, is contrary to the overall pattern of the data.

FIGURE 3.4
Tax Assessable Property versus % Commercial Property

Citydat

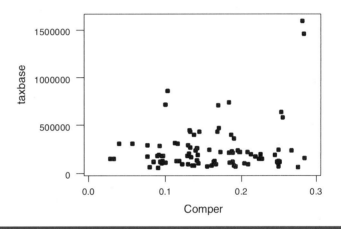

In the preceding examples we have indicated how scatter plots can be powerful analysis tools for studying economic relationships. Both Minitab and Microsoft Excel as well as other statistical packages can be used to obtain the scatter plots. The effort required is minimal—once the data is in an electronic data file—and the benefits from examining scatter plots are very high.

EXERCISES

3.1 Using the same data file **Citydat** used in Example 3.3, prepare a scatter plot for the variable tax rate versus the variable percent commercial property. What information does this scatter plot tell you about the two variables?

3.2 Bishop's supermarket (See Example 2.10) records the actual price for consumer food products and the weekly quantities sold. Use the data file **Bishop** to obtain the scatter plot for the actual price of a gallon of orange juice and the weekly quantities sold at that price. Does the scatter plot follow the pattern that you would expect from economic theory?

3.3 Rising Hills Manufacturing wishes to study the relationship between the number of workers, X, and the number of tables, Y, produced in its Redwood Falls plant. They have obtained a random sample of ten days of production. Prepare a scatter plot for the following (X, Y) combinations of points that were obtained:

(12,200)	(30,600)	(15,270)	(24,500)	(14,210)
(18,300)	(28,610)	(26,540)	(19,320)	(27,570)

Discuss briefly the relationship between the number of workers and the number of tables produced per day.

3.4 River Hills Hospital is interested in determining the effectiveness of a new drug for reducing the time required for complete recovery from knee surgery. Complete recovery is measured by a series of strength tests that compare the treated knee with the untreated knee. The drug was given in varying amounts to 18 patients over a six-month period. For each patient the number of drug units, X, and the days for complete recovery, Y, are given by the following (X, Y) data:

(5, 53) (21, 65) (14, 48) (11, 66) (9, 46) (4, 56)

(7, 53) (21, 57) (17, 49) (14, 66) (9, 54) (7, 56)

(9, 53) (21, 52) (13, 49) (14, 56) (9, 59) (4, 56)

(a) Prepare a scatter plot of the points.

(b) Briefly discuss the relationship between the number of drug units and the recovery time. What dosage would you recommend based on this initial analysis?

3.5 Acme Delivery offers three different shipping rates for packages under 5 pounds delivered from Maine to the west coast: regular, $3; fast, $5; and lightning, $10. To test the quality of these services, a major mail-order retailer shipped 15 packages at randomly selected times from Maine to Tacoma, Washington. The packages were shipped in groups of three by the three services at the same time to reduce variation resulting from the shipping day. The following data show the shipping cost, X, and the number of days, Y, in (X, Y) pairs:

(3, 7) (5, 5) (10, 2) (3, 9) (5, 6) (10, 5) (3, 6) (5, 6) (10, 1)

(3, 10) (5, 7) (10, 4) (3, 5) (5, 6) (10, 4)

Prepare a scatter plot of the points and comment on the relationship between shipping cost and the observed delivery times.

3.2 COVARIANCE AND CORRELATION COEFFICIENT

Next we will develop some summary statistical measures that provide greater precision for describing relationships. In this section we will learn about the covariance—a measure of joint variability for two variables. This will be followed by the correlation coefficient—a statistic that provides a standardized measure of the strength of the linear relationship between two variables.

Covariance

The sample covariance, defined by Equation 3.1, is a measure of the linearity of relationship between two paired variables. It provides an indication of the direction and strength of the relationship. Later we will also see that it plays an important role in determining the variance of linear combinations of variables. One important application of those results occurs in investment portfolio analysis.

SAMPLE COVARIANCE

The **covariance** is a measure of the linear relationship between two variables. A positive value indicates a direct or increasing linear relationship and a negative value indicates a decreasing linear relationship. The covariance calculation is defined by the equation

$$\text{Cov}(x, y) = S_{xy} = \frac{\sum_{i=1}^{n}(x_i - \overline{X})(y_i - \overline{Y})}{n - 1} \tag{3.1}$$

where x_i and y_i are the observed values, $\overline{X}$ and $\overline{Y}$ are the sample means, and n is the sample size.

The covariance computation equation is similar to the variance computation—the difference is that the product of the deviations of two variables is computed and summed instead of computing the square of a single deviation. The covariance is typically computed using a statistical package. The Minitab command sequence is:

```
STAT > BASIC STATISTICS > COVARIANCE > SELECT VARIABLES
```

The Excel command sequence is:

```
TOOLS > DATA ANALYSIS > COVARIANCE > SELECT VARIABLE COLUMNS
```

In Figures 3.5a and b we compare scatter plots for variables that have positive and negative covariances.

In Figure 3.5a we can see that the x and y deviations of points from the x and y means are both positive in the upper right quadrant and negative in the lower left quadrant. In this case the covariance would have a positive sign. Note that Figure 3.5a indicates a direct linear relationship—x and y both increase together. In contrast, in Figure 3.5b the x and y deviations of points from the x and y means in both the upper left and lower right quadrants have opposite signs—one is positive and the other is negative. In this case the covariance would have a negative sign. Figure 3.5b indicates a decreasing linear relationship. In most real data sets the data are not restricted to just two quadrants. But if the computed covariance has a positive sign, that indicates a tendency for a positive linear relationship, and if the computed covariance has a negative sign, that indicates a tendency for a negative linear relationship. If the data were symmetrically located in all four quadrants the covariance would be zero and indicate no linear relationship between the variables.

As the pattern of points approach a straight line, the absolute value of the covariance increases to a limit. For reference note that the covariance for Figure 3.2 is 1.79, indicating a direct linear relationship. The small value of the covariance could be the result of either a weak relationship or data scaling—in this case it is the latter given the scatter plot. Similarly the covariance for Figure 3.4 is 0.0000853. This is very small in spite of the data scaling—and we know from the scatter plot that the relationship is weak. Note that while the covariance has important uses in applied statistics it does not give us an indication of the strength of the relationship between two variables. For that reason we will consider a standardized version of the relationship called the correlation coefficient.

Correlation Coefficient

The sample correlation coefficient is a standardized measure of the linear relationship between two variables, which is defined by Equation 3.2. The correlation coefficient is computed by dividing the covariance by the standard deviations of the two variables, s_x and s_y. This division results in the correlation coefficient having a standardized range from -1 to $+1$. The corresponding correlation coefficients and covariances have the same signs. The correlation coefficient provides us with a better indication of relationship because it varies only in the range from -1 to $+1$ and its value directly indicates the strength of the relationship. The correlation coefficient is generally more useful as a descriptive statistic because there is a relationship between the correlation coefficient and the pattern of data points.

FIGURE 3.5
Scatter Plots of Idealized
Positive and Negative
Covariances

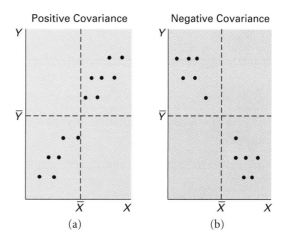

FIGURE 3.6   Scatter Plots and Correlation

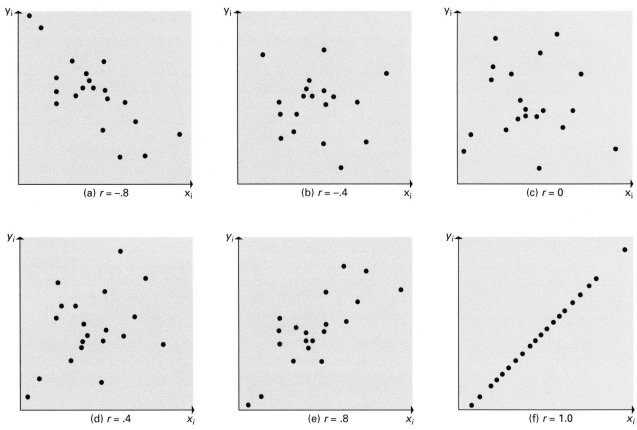

Figure 3.6 presents some examples of scatter plots and their corresponding correlation coefficients. As you work with various data sets you will develop experience that helps to relate particular sample correlation coefficients to various patterns of data.

SAMPLE CORRELATION COEFFICIENT

The **sample correlation coefficient**, r_{xy}, is computed by the equation

$$r_{xy} = \frac{\text{Cov}(x, y)}{s_x s_y} \qquad (3.2)$$

1. The correlation ranges from -1 to $+1$ with,

   - $r_{xy} = +1$ indicates a perfect positive linear relationship—the X and Y points would plot an increasing straight line
   - $r_{xy} = 0$ indicates no linear relationship between X and Y
   - $r_{xy} = -1$ indicates a perfect decreasing linear relationship—the X and Y points would plot a decreasing straight line.

2. **Positive correlations** indicate positive or increasing linear relationships with values closer to $+1$, indicating data points closer to a straight line, and closer to 0, indicating greater deviations from a straight line.

3. **Negative correlations** indicate decreasing linear relationships with values closer to -1, indicating points closer to a straight line, and closer to 0, indicating greater deviations from a straight line.

In Chapter 10 we will explore the statistical properties of the sample correlation coefficient and learn how it can be used for statistical inference.

ASSUMPTION

One question of importance concerns the minimum size of the correlation coefficient that is required to conclude that a relationship exists. In Chapter 10 we will develop a useful rule of thumb for initial analysis. If the absolute value of the sample correlation coefficient, r_{xy}, is greater than 2 divided by the square root of the sample size, n, then we can conclude that a relationship exists.

$$\left| r_{xy} \right| \geq \frac{2}{\sqrt{n}}$$

Using this rule when the sample size is $n = 36$, we see that the absolute value of the sample correlation coefficient should be greater than 0.33 (2/6) to conclude that a linear relationship exists between the two variables. With a sample size of, $n = 100$, the sample correlation coefficient should exceed 0.20 (2/10) to conclude that a relationship exists.

EXAMPLE 3.4

ANALYSIS OF STOCK PORTFOLIOS (CORRELATION COEFFICIENT ANALYSIS)

Alice Wong, Financial Analyst, for Integrated Securities is considering a number of different stocks for a new mutual fund she is developing. One of the questions concerns the correlation coefficients between prices of different stocks. To determine the patterns of stock prices she prepared a series of scatter plots and computed the sample correlation coefficients for each plot. These are shown in Figure 3.7. What information does Figure 3.7 provide Alice?

FIGURE 3.7
Relationships Between Various Stock Prices for Example 3.4

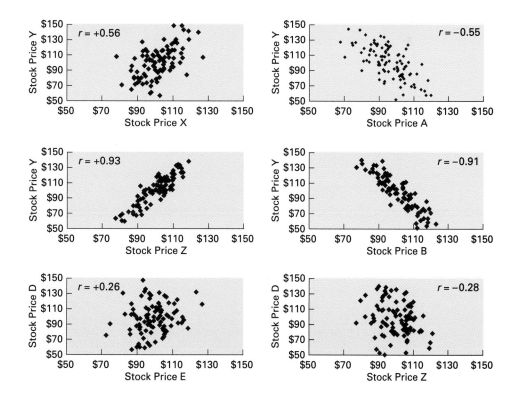

SOLUTION

INTERPRETATION

Alice sees that it is possible to control the variation in the average mutual fund price by combining various stocks into a portfolio. The portfolio variation is increased if stocks with positive correlation coefficients are included because the prices tend to increase together. In contrast, the portfolio variation is decreased if stocks with negative correlation coefficients are included. When the price of one stock increases the price of the other decreases and the combined price is stable. Experienced observers of stock prices might question the possibility of very large negative correlation coefficients. Our objective here is to illustrate graphically the correlation coefficients for certain patterns of observed data and not to accurately describe a particular market. After examining these correlation coefficients, Alice is ready to begin constructing her portfolio. In Chapter 5 we will show precisely how correlation coefficients between stock prices affect the variation of the entire portfolio.

The sample correlation coefficient provides us with a measure of the *linear* relationship between variable observations. A correlation coefficient of $r = 0$ indicates a lack of linear relationship but not necessarily a lack of relationship. For example, Figure 3.8 is a plot of average cost versus number of units produced. Typically average cost is initially reduced with increases in the number of units because fixed costs are spread over more units. At some point the number of units exceeds efficient facility size and the variable cost per unit begins to rise. This often results in a nonlinear relationship as shown in Figure 3.8. The correlation coefficient for the average cost versus number of units would be close to zero. But here we can see that there is an important nonlinear relationship.

Figure 3.9 is a plot of quarterly sales for a major retail company. Note that sales vary by quarter of the year, reflecting consumer purchasing patterns. The correlation coefficient between the time variable and quarterly sales would be zero. You can see a very definite seasonal relationship, but the relationship is not linear.

FIGURE 3.8
Mean Cost for Calculators

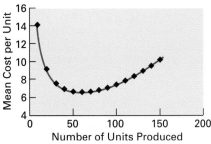

FIGURE 3.9
Retail Sales by Quarter Here

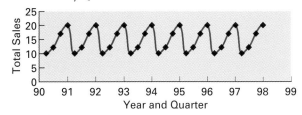

EXERCISES

3.6 ● Using the data file **Citydat** find
  (a) the covariance between tax rate and percent commercial property.
  (b) the correlation coefficient between tax rate and percent commercial property.
3.7 ● Refer to Exercise 3.2 and use the data file **Bishop**. Find:

  (a) the covariance between the price of a gallon of orange juice and the quantities sold.
  (b) the correlation coefficient between the price of a gallon of orange juice and the quantities sold.
3.8 Rising Hills Manufacturing wishes to study the relationship between the number of workers, X, and the number of tables, Y, produced in its Redwood Falls

plant. They have obtained a random sample of 10 days of production. The following (X, Y) combinations of points were obtained:

(12,200)   (30,600)   (15,270)   (24,500)   (14,210)

(18,300)   (28,610)   (26,540)   (19,320)   (27,570)

(a) Compute the covariance.
(b) Compute the correlation coefficient.
(c) Discuss briefly the relationship between the number of workers and the number of tables produced per day.

3.9 River Hills Hospital is interested in determining the effectiveness of a new drug for reducing the time required for complete recovery from knee surgery. Complete recovery is measured by a series of strength tests that compare the treated knee with the untreated knee. The drug was given in varying amounts to 18 patients over a six-month period. For each patient the number of drug units, X, and the days for complete recovery, Y, are given by the following (X, Y) data:

(5, 53)   (21, 65)   (14, 48)   (11, 66)   (9, 46)   (4, 56)

(7, 53)   (21, 57)   (17, 49)   (14, 66)   (9, 54)   (7, 56)

(9, 53)   (21, 52)   (13, 49)   (14, 56)   (9, 59)   (4, 56)

(a) Compute the covariance.
(b) Compute the correlation coefficient.
(c) Briefly discuss the relationship between the number of drug units and the recovery time. What dosage would you recommend based on this initial analysis?

3.10 Acme Delivery offers three different shipping rates for packages under 5 pounds delivered from Maine to the west coast: regular, $3; fast, $5; and lightning, $10. To test the quality of these services, a major mail-order retailer shipped 15 packages at randomly selected times from Maine to Tacoma, Washington. The packages were shipped in groups of three by the three services at the same time to reduce variation resulting from the shipping day. The following data show the shipping cost, X, and the number of days, Y, in (X, Y) pairs:

(3, 7)   (5, 5)   (10, 2)   (3, 9)   (5, 6)   (10, 5)   (3, 6)   (5, 6)   (10, 1)

(3, 10) (5, 7)   (10, 4)   (3, 5)   (5, 6)   (10, 4)

(a) Compute the covariance.
(b) Compute the correlation coefficient.
(c) Discuss the value of the higher-priced services in terms of quicker delivery.

3.3   OBTAINING LINEAR RELATIONSHIPS

We have now seen how the relationship between two variables can be described by using sample data. Scatter plots provide a picture of the relationship, and correlation coefficients provide a numerical measure. In many economic and business problems a specific functional relationship is desired. A manager would like to know what mean level of sales can be expected if the price is set at $10 per unit. If 250 workers are employed, how many units should be expected? If a developing country increases its fertilizer production by 1,000,000 tons, how much increase in grain production should be expected? Economic models use specific functional relationships to indicate the effect on endogenous variable outcomes that result from various changes in exogenous or input variables. In many cases we can adequately approximate the desired functional relationships by a linear equation.

LINEAR RELATIONSHIPS

Linear relationships can be represented by the basic equation

$$Y = \beta_0 + \beta_1 X \qquad (3.3)$$

where Y is the dependent or endogenous variable that is a function of X the independent or exogenous variable. The model contains two parameters, β_0 and β_1 that we will define as model coefficients. The coefficient β_0 is the intercept on the Y-axis and the coefficient β_1 is the change in Y for every unit change in X. The nominal assumption made in our applications is that different values of X can be set, and there will be a corresponding mean value of Y that results because of the underlying linear relationship in the process being studied. The linear equation model computes the mean of Y for every value of X. This idea is the basis for obtaining many economic and business relationships including demand functions, production functions, consumption functions, sales forecasts, and many other application areas.

We use regression to determine the best relationship between Y and X_1 for a particular application. This requires us to find the best values for the coefficients β_0 and β_1. Generally we use the data available from the process to compute "estimates" or numerical values for the coefficients, β_0, and β_1. These estimates—defined as b_0 and b_1—are generally computed by using **Least Squares Regression**, a technique widely implemented in statistical packages such as Minitab and in spreadsheets such as Excel. Least squares is a procedure that selects the best fit line given a set of data points. Consider a typical plot of points from a process that has a linear relationship as shown in Figure 3.10.

ASSUMPTION

The linear equation represented by the line is the best fit linear equation. We see that individual data points are above and below the line and that the line has points with both positive and negative deviations. The distance of each point (x_i, y_i) from the linear equation is defined as the residual, e_i. We would like to choose the equation so that some function of the positive and negative residuals is as small as possible. This implies finding estimates for the coefficients, β_0 and β_1. Equations to compute these estimates are developed using the least squares regression procedure that will be developed in Chapter 10. Least squares regression chooses b_0 and b_1 such that the sum of the squared residuals is minimized.

Early mathematicians struggled with the problem of developing a procedure for estimating the coefficients for the linear equation. Simply minimizing the deviations was not useful because the deviations have both positive and negative signs. Various procedures using absolute values have also been developed but none has proven as useful or as popular as least squares regression. We will learn later that coefficients developed using this procedure have very useful statistical properties. One important caution for least squares is that extreme outlier points can have such a strong influence on the regression line that the whole line is directed toward this point. Thus you should always examine scatter plots to be sure that the regression relationship is not based on just a few extreme points.

Computer Computation of Regression Coefficients

Next we will look at how we can use the computer to obtain regression equations and provide some initial understanding of the regression procedure. As with this entire chapter our objective is to learn how to describe data and not how to perform sophisticated statistical analysis of linear regression models. The latter will come as we move to Chapter 10 and beyond. Here we want to use a combination of scatter plots, correlation coefficients, and regression lines to describe relationships based on sample data. Consider the data showing the relationship between college GPA and SAT Verbal scores on the entrance examination.

FIGURE 3.10
Linear Function and Data Points

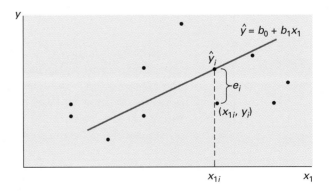

FIGURE 3.11
Graduation GPA versus
Entering SAT Verbal Score

Student GPA

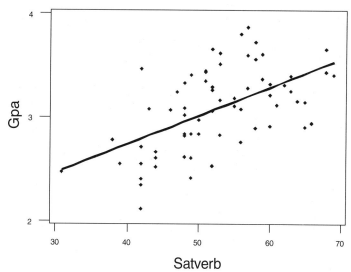

Y = 1.63837 + 2.74E-02X
R-Sq = 31.4 %

Figure 3.11 is a repeat of Figure 3.1 with a regression line drawn on the plot. This plot was prepared using the Minitab command sequence

```
STAT> REGRESSION> FITTED LINE PLOT
```

and selecting the variables Gpa and Satverb.

Here we see the regression line and its equation

$$\text{Gpa} = 1.64 + 0.0274 \text{ Satverb}$$

The line provides a good representation of the data points, and the distance of points from the line is about the same in the positive and negative direction and over the range of the independent variable, Satverb (X_1). The linear function intercepts the Y axis at 1.64, and each one point increase in the SAT Verbal score increases the mean GPA by 0.027. This is the kind of pattern that one anticipates when thinking about a regression derived equation. Note also that the SAT Verbal score does not extend beyond the range of 30 to 70. In most applications it is unwise to use the regression derived equation to predict a mean value of the dependent variable—Gpa—outside of the range of the independent variable—30 to 70—because there is simply no data to support extrapolation of the equation beyond the range of the data.

Minitab and other statistical packages will also provide a printed output that includes a number of statistics for analyzing the regression equation. The regression output prepared using Minitab for this example is shown in Figure 3.12. The Minitab Command Sequence is:

```
STAT>REGRESSION>REGRESSION
```

and then you can follow the dialogue box for variable selection.

The regression output in Figure 3.12 first presents the estimated linear equation with its coefficients. Next there is a tabular display that presents each coefficient in a row. The first column headed "Coef" contains the regression coefficients. The remainder of the line presents statistics that will be used later for statistical inference. The column headed "P" shows the "*p*-value"—the probability that the computed coefficient values would have resulted if

FIGURE 3.12
Regression Analysis for GPA
versus SAT Verbal Score

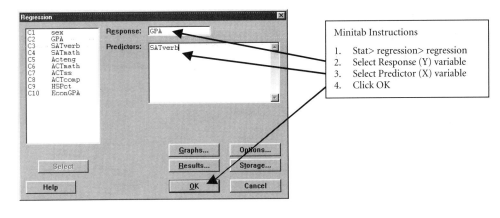

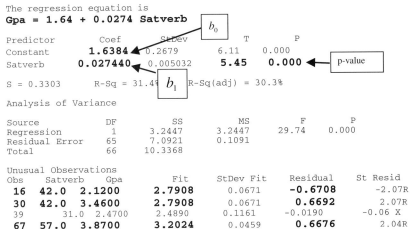

The regression equation is
Gpa = 1.64 + 0.0274 Satverb

Predictor	Coef	StDev	T	P
Constant	**1.6384**	0.2679	6.11	0.000
Satverb	**0.027440**	0.005032	**5.45**	**0.000**

S = 0.3303   R-Sq = 31.4%   R-Sq(adj) = 30.3%

Analysis of Variance

Source	DF	SS	MS	F	P
Regression	1	3.2447	3.2447	29.74	0.000
Residual Error	65	7.0921	0.1091		
Total	66	10.3368			

Unusual Observations

Obs	Satverb	Gpa	Fit	StDev Fit	Residual	St Resid
16	**42.0**	**2.1200**	**2.7908**	0.0671	**-0.6708**	-2.07R
30	**42.0**	**3.4600**	**2.7908**	0.0671	**0.6692**	2.07R
39	31.0	2.4700	2.4890	0.1161	-0.0190	-0.06 X
67	**57.0**	**3.8700**	**3.2024**	0.0459	**0.6676**	2.04R

R denotes an observation with a large standardized residual

X denotes an observation whose X value gives it large influence.

there were no relationship between the two variables. A very small *p*-value—say less than 0.05—would provide strong evidence that there is a relationship between the variables. Another "rule of thumb" for determining if there is a relationship uses the student *t* statistics for the coefficient estimate (in this example *t* = 5.45). If the coefficient student *t* has an absolute value greater than 2 we conclude that a relationship exists. The section titled Analysis of Variance will be discussed in Chapter 10.

At the bottom of the page there is a list of "unusual observations." Of particular interest are those with large residual values, indicating that the points are a great distance from the regression line. In many cases you can learn about unusual problems in the process being studied by examining these points. Note that in this regression analysis there were two students with an SAT Verbal score of 42. As indicated in the column labeled "Fit" this would predict an average GPA of 2.79. But one of the students ended with a GPA of 2.12—an underperformer—while the other had a GPA of 3.46—an overperformer. The residual values for these two students are $e = -0.6708$ (2.12 − 2.7908) and $e = 0.6692$ (3.46 − 2.7908). Another student with an SAT Verbal score of 57 had a GPA of 3.87 even though the predicted GPA given the test score was 3.20, resulting in a residual of $e = 0.6676$ (3.87 − 3.2024). Large residuals could of course be the result of data errors—regression analysis and scatter plots are good ways to screen for errors. In addition, by examining the records of these students and perhaps interviewing them one can determine factors other than test scores that help predict GPA. Exploratory analysis using the residuals could provide very important insights into the relationship between grades and entrance scores.

Using Microsoft Excel PHStat to Obtain Regression Output

One can also use PHStat in Excel to obtain the regression output. For this problem the results are shown in Figure 3.13. That regression output was generated in Excel using PHStat.

The lower portion of the Excel output contains a tabular presentation of the regression coefficients. The results are numerically the same and the interpretations from above apply equally to this output. Both Minitab and Excel also provide options for plotting residuals and performing other graphical analyses to gain further insights into the relationship.

As a final example we will consider the relationship between property tax rate and percent commercial property in small cities. The corresponding regression output is shown in Figure 3.14.

Note that the coefficient is very small, but more importantly we can see that the "P" value and the T statistic indicate that the data is insufficient to suggest a relationship between tax rate and percent commercial property. This provides a number to support the observed result from the scatter plot prepared for Exercise 3.1.

FIGURE 3.13
Excel Regression Output:
GPA versus SAT Verbal Score

Regression Analysis

Regression Statistics	
Multiple R	0.560264658
R Square	0.313896487
Adjusted R Square	0.303341048
Standard Error	0.330316589
Observations	67

PH STAT Instructions

1. Select the command sequence:
   PHSTAT>regression> simple linear
   regression > identify the data columns
2. Follow the dialogue sequence.

ANOVA

	df	SS	MS	F	Significance F
Regression	1	3.244673026	3.244673026	29.73789125	8.22036E-07
Residual	65	7.092088168	0.109109049		
Total	66	10.33676119			

	Coefficients	Standard Error	t Stat	P-value	Lower 95%	Upper 95%
Intercept	**1.6384**	0.2679	6.1147	0.0000	1.1033	2.1735
Satverb	**0.0274**	0.0050	**5.4532**	**0.0000**	0.0174	0.0375

b_0 b_1

FIGURE 3.14
Regression Analysis for Tax Rate versus Percent Commercial Property Obtained Using Minitab

Citydat

Regression Analysis

```
The regression equation is

Tax Rate = 0.0236 + 0.0213 Percent Commercial Property

Predictor        Coef        StDev          T          P
Constant     0.023622      0.002652       8.91      0.000
Commercial    0.02126      0.01525        1.39      0.167
```

EXERCISES

3.11 Refer to Exercise 3.8.
  (a) Compute the regression constant, b_0, and the slope coefficient, b_1.
  (b) What is the predicted number of tables when there are 20 workers?
  (c) Discuss briefly the relationship between the number of workers and the number of tables produced per day.

3.12 Refer to Exercise 3.9.
  (a) Compute the regression constant, b_0, and the slope coefficient, b_1.
  (b) What is the predicted recovery time when drug use is 6 units and when drug use is 15 units?

  (c) Discuss briefly the relationship between the number of drug units and the recovery time. What dosage would you recommend based on this initial analysis?

3.13 Refer to Exercise 3.10.
  (a) Compute the regression constant, b_0, and the slope coefficient, b_1.
  (b) Compute the predicted delivery time for each of the three delivery categories.
  (c) Discuss the value of the higher-priced services in terms of quicker delivery.

3.4   CROSS TABLES

In this chapter we have presented a number of techniques for describing relationships between variables. All of those techniques assume that we have interval variables. However, there are also a number of situations in which there is a need to describe relationships between categorical and/or ordinal variables. Market research organizations describe attitudes toward products, measured on an ordinal scale, as a function of educational levels, social status measures, geographic areas, and other ordinal or categorical variables. Personnel departments study employee evaluation levels versus job classifications, educational levels, or other employee variables. Production analysts study relationships between departments or production lines and performance measures, such as reason for product change, reason for interruption of production, and quality of output. These situations are usually described and analyzed using Cross Tables.

> ### CROSS TABLES
> **Cross Tables** present the number of observations that are defined by the joint occurrence of specific intervals for two variables. The combination of all possible intervals for the two variables defines the cells in a table.

EXAMPLE 3.5

PRODUCT DEMAND BY RESIDENTIAL AREA (CROSS TABLES)

A building products retailer has been working on a plan for new store locations as part of a regional expansion. In one city proposed for expansion there are three possible locations: north, east, or west. From past experience they know that the three major profit centers in her stores are tools, lumber, and paint. In selecting a location the demand patterns in the different parts of the city were important. Thus she requested help from the market research department to obtain and analyze relevant data.

SOLUTION

Table 3.1 is a cross table for the variables "residential location" versus "product purchased." This table was prepared by the market research personnel using data obtained from a random sample of households in the three major residential areas of the city. Each residential

TABLE 3.1

Cross Table of Household Demand for Products by Residential Area

AREA	TOOLS	LUMBER	PAINT	NONE	TOTAL
East	100	50	50	50	250
North	50	95	45	60	250
West	65	70	75	40	250
	215	215	170	150	750

area had a separate phone number prefix, and the last four digits were chosen using a computer random number generator. If the number was not a residence, another phone number was generated randomly. If the phone number was not answered, the number was called again up to a maximum of five times to ensure a high participation rate.

In each residential area 250 households were contacted by telephone and asked to indicate which of three categories of products they had purchased during their last trip to a building supply store. The survey was conducted to determine the demand for tools, lumber, and paint by people from the various neighborhoods. The three residential areas contain the same number of households, and thus the random sample of 750 represents the population of households in the entire city.

INTERPRETATION

Every cell in the table shows the number of sampled households in each of the residential areas that had purchased tools, lumber, or paint in the past month. If they had purchased from more than one category, they indicated the category with the largest sales value. For example, 100 sampled households in the east area had purchased tools, and 75 sampled households in the west area had purchased paint. At the right side of each row we see the total number of sampled households (250) in that row. Similarly, the number of sample households that have purchased from each product category are displayed at the bottom of each column. The displays at the right-hand side of the rows and the bottom of the columns are referred to as marginal distributions. These numbers are the frequency distributions for each of the two variables presented in the cross table.

The table provides a summary of the purchase patterns for households in the three neighborhoods. Based on this research the marketing staff now knows that people in the east area are more frequent purchasers of tools, whereas households in the north purchase more lumber. Demand for paint is highest in the west, and they also tend to purchase more from each product category.

In addition to store location information, these data indicate which products should be emphasized in advertisements directed toward each geographic area. The company decides to emphasize tools when distributing advertising material to the east and to emphasize lumber in the north. Advertising directed to the west will emphasize that all three product categories are in the same store. From the column marginal totals we see that tools and lumber will be purchased by about the same number of households in the city, while the demand for paint will be lower.

EXAMPLE 3.6

SOURCES OF DRINKING DRIVERS (CROSS TABLES)

A research team was assigned the task of determining the alcohol consumption sources of motor vehicle drivers who were at various levels of blood alcohol.

SOLUTION

A random sample of drivers was obtained, and the resulting data were used to prepare Table 3.2. This table displays the relationship between blood alcohol concentration and the location of the first drinking episode for night drivers who had been drinking. The data for this table were obtained from a random sample of drivers in Washtenaw County, Michigan, collected during the hours 7 P.M. to 3 A.M. The columns indicate the blood

TABLE 3.2
Cross Table of Driver BAC
by Location of First
Drinking Episode

LOCATION	≤ 0.02%	0.03% TO 0.04%	0.05% TO 0.09%	≥ 0.10%	TOTAL
Bar					
Number	22	25	17	14	78
Percent	28.2	32.1	21.8	17.9	100.0
Restaurant					
Number	11	3	9	1	24
Percent	45.8	12.5	37.5	4.2	100.0
Own Home					
Number	45	16	11	10	82
Percent	54.9	19.5	13.4	12.2	100.0
Another Home					
Number	42	10	6	0	58
Percent	72.5	17.2	10.3	0	100.0
Total					
Number	120	54	43	25	242
Percent	49.6	22.3	17.8	10.3	100.0

alcohol concentration (BAC) of the driver, obtained from a breath test. Common interpretations of these concentrations are: ≤0.02%, essentially no blood alcohol and no driving impairment; 0.03% to 0.04%, social drinking with no impairment for most drivers; 0.05% to 0.09%, almost all drivers will have noticeable impairment and could be convicted by a court; ≥0.10%, all drivers are seriously impaired and represent a threat to other vehicles and pedestrians. The table also includes the percentage of drivers in each intoxication category for each row. This makes it possible to compare the various sources of drinking drivers easily, even though the number of drivers from each drinking source is different.

INTERPRETATION

From Table 3.2 it was possible to obtain some important indications concerning drinking and driving behavior. The sample contained only drivers who had consumed at least one alcoholic beverage during the day. From the bottom row, which summarizes the entire set, over 70% did not have blood alcohol concentrations (BACs) that would seriously reduce their driving ability (e.g., ≤0.02% and 0.03% to 0.04%. The most likely source of seriously impaired drivers was bars. For the 78 people who drank first in a bar, 17.9% had BACs at or above 0.10%. For the 82 drivers who began drinking at home, 12.2% were at the highest BAC level. However, in this group of home drinkers almost 75% were in the lowest two BAC categories and thus not seriously impaired. Those people who had their first drink in another home were least likely to have high BAC levels. One important outcome of this analysis is that efforts to reduce the number of seriously impaired drivers should consider bars as a major source.[1]

Many statistical studies begin with an examination of two-way tables, and these tables provide important understandings of the relationships between variables. We have presented some examples that show how two-way tables can be used to study relationships between qualitative variables. Two-way tables are also used with quantitative variables when the relationships between variables are expected to be nonlinear and complex. In those cases quantitative variables are assigned to subgroups using defined subranges.

Most of these tables are prepared by statistical computer programs. Exercises will provide you with the opportunity to prepare two-way tables. Notice that two-way tables can-

[1] W. L. Carlson, "Alcohol Usage of the Nighttime Driver," *Journal of Safety Research* 4, no.14 (March 1972).

not be summarized by statistics such as the correlation coefficient or the regression line. In addition, they do not have the strong visual impact of a scatter plot. Many statistical computer packages provide graphical devices, such as three-dimensional histograms, which provide clear intuitive visual displays. Contact your local computer system for locally available procedures. In Chapter 14 more powerful statistical procedures for analyzing two-way tables will be presented.

EXERCISES

3.14 Refer to Example 3.5. Suppose that the market survey data had resulted in Table 3.3 instead of Table 3.1. Explain the conclusions from this survey in terms of the product strategy.

TABLE 3.3 Revised Cross Table of Household Demand for Products by Residential Area

AREA	TOOLS	LUMBER	PAINT	NONE	TOTAL
East	100	40	60	50	250
North	70	45	95	40	250
West	75	70	65	40	250
	245	155	220	130	750

3.15 You have been asked to study the patterns of daily sales in dollars by day of week for a sporting goods store. Sales by day of the week are contained in the **Stordata** data file. Using the computer, group the data by day of week and four different groups of sales data. The daily sales data should be divided into groups by quartile. Prepare a two-way table that contains the days of the week as rows and the four sales quartile intervals as columns.
(a) Compute the row percentages.
(b) What are the major differences in sales level by day of the week as indicated by the row percentages?
(c) Describe the expected sales volume patterns over the week based on this table.

SUMMARY

In this chapter we have provided you with tools for describing relationships between data including scatter plots, covariance and correlation coefficients, and least squares regression equations. These techniques provide important understandings of the relationships based on the pattern of the data points.

Scatter plots and correlation coefficients are often used by professional analysts at the beginning of every statistical analysis study. In Chapters 10 and 11 we will see how regression analysis is used for more sophisticated statistical inference.

KEY WORDS

cross tables, 70
least squares estimation procedure, 66

least squares regression, 65
sample correlation coefficient, 62

sample covariance, 60
scatter plot, 56

CHAPTER EXERCISES AND APPLICATIONS

3.16 Robert Johnson, Rice County solid waste director, wanted to establish a household garbage collection fee based on the weight of garbage collected at each household. Economic theory indicates that such a pricing strategy would encourage households to recycle and to reduce the total amount of waste generated. However, he wanted the rate to provide the same revenue for the garbage collectors as they earned with the old flat rate per household. He was also interested in developing a payment plan for haulers that would be consistent with neighboring counties. He obtained the annual garbage collection data from neighboring communities, which is shown in Table 3.4. To help with his planning, he wanted to know the relationship between total revenue and total number of households. In addition, he wanted to know the relationship between total revenue and total tons collected.

TABLE 3.4 Annual Solid Waste Collection Data

CITY	NUMBER OF HOUSEHOLDS	TOTAL TONS	REVENUE
A	2,200	3,080	$118,800
B	2,500	3,500	200,000
C	2,700	3,780	250,560
D	4,000	5,600	201,600
E	4,000	5,600	308,800
F	4,000	5,600	268,800
G	5,500	7,700	452,100
H	6,000	8,400	277,200
I	9,000	12,600	358,200

(a) Enter the observations for revenue, households, and tons into a computer data file and plot the relationship between revenue and households and between revenue and tons collected. Visually estimate the best-fit line and draw it on the graph.

(b) Use the computer to compute the correlation coefficients between revenue and number of households and between revenue and total tons collected. In addition, compute the regression equations for each relationship.

(c) Mr. Johnson is interested in estimating the annual revenue for a city that had 2900 households and 12,600 tons of solid waste. Estimate the revenue using both of the regression equations from part (b).

(d) What is the marginal revenue for haulers per ton of solid waste?

3.17 Ms. Agnes Larson wants you to study the demand for paint as a function of price. She has obtained (price, quantity) data for seven days of operation. These data are

(10, 100) (8, 120) (5, 200) (4, 200) (10, 90) (7, 110) (6, 150)

(a) Prepare a plot of quantity of paint versus price. Describe the relationship between quantity and price, with emphasis on any unusual observations.

(b) Compute the correlation coefficient for quantity versus price. Describe the relationship between quantity and price by interpreting the correlation coefficient.

3.18 George B. Smith, president of Forcasters, Inc., reported that the correlation coefficient between annual investment in the textile industry and the average temperature in Minnesota during January is −0.60. He then explains that investment in textiles is strongly influenced by the demand for clothing. He also visited Minnesota in January and discovered that people wear more clothing when the temperature is low. Explain the value of this forecast and either support or reject the reasoning.

3.19 A large consumer goods company has been studying the effect of advertising on total profits. As part of this study, data on advertising expenditures and total sales were collected for a six-month period and are as follows:

(10, 100) (15, 200) (7, 80) (12, 120) (14, 150)

The first number is advertising expenditures and the second is total sales.

(a) Plot the data and compute the correlation coefficient.

(b) Do these results provide evidence that advertising has a positive effect on sales?

(c) Present an alternative to the argument that advertising increases sales given the results from part (a).

3.20 In Exercise 3.17, recall that Ms. Agnes Larson wants you to study the demand for paint as a function of price. She had obtained (price, quantity) data for seven days of operation. These data are (10, 100) (8, 120) (5, 200) (4, 200) (10, 90) (7, 110) (6, 150)

(a) Compute the constant and slope coefficient for the least squares regression line of quantity on price.

(b) Compute the predicted values of quantity sold using the regression equation and the prices 5, 7, and 8. Compute the residual e for each of the three prices.

(c) Discuss the additional information about the demand for paint that you can obtain with results from parts (a) and (b), compared to the results obtained in Exercise 3.17.

3.21 Sam Kowalski, president of Floor Coverings Unlimited, has asked you to study the relationship between market price and the tons of rugs supplied by his competitor, Best Floor, Inc. He supplies you with the following observations of price per ton and number of tons, obtained from his secret files:

(2, 5) (4, 10) (3, 8) (6, 18) (3, 6) (5, 15) (6, 20) (2, 4)

The first number for each observation is price and the second is quantity.

(a) Prepare a graphical plot of quantity versus price, with price on the horizontal axis.

(b) Compute the covariance and correlation coefficient.

(c) Compute the constant and slope coefficients for the regression equation and draw the equation on the graph prepared in part (a).

(d) Write a short explanation of the regression equation that tells Sam how the equation can be used to describe his competition. Include an indication of the range over which the equation can be applied.

3.22 A random sample of 12 college baseball players participated in a special weight-training program in an attempt to improve their batting averages. The program lasted for 20 weeks immediately prior to the start of the baseball season. The average number of hours per week and the change in their batting averages from the preceding season are as follows:

(8.0, 10) (20.0, 100) (5.4, −10) (12.4, 79) (9.2, 50) (15.0, 89) (6.0, 34) (8.0, 30) (18.0, 68) (25.0, 110) (10.0, 34) (5.0, 10)

(a) Plot the data. Does it appear that the weight-training program was successful?

(b) Estimate the regression equation. What is the marginal value of each hour of weight training?

3.23 ⚫ You have been asked to estimate a demand function for the production of cotton fiber. The data file **Cotton**, which is on your data disk, contains data that can be used by your computer.

(a) Plot cotton production versus wholesale price. Sketch an approximate linear relationship.

(b) Use the computer program to compute the constant and slope for your regression equation. What is the marginal effect on quantity produced for each unit change in price?

3.24 ⚫ You have also been asked to estimate the relationship between exported cotton fabric and the production of cotton fiber.

The data file **Cotton**, which is on your data disk, contains data that can be used by your computer.

(a) Plot cotton production versus amount of exported cotton fabric. Sketch an approximate linear relationship.

(b) Compute the constant and slope for your regression equation. What is the marginal effect on quantity produced for each unit change in exported fabric?

3.25 ⚫ The production manager of Amalgamated Cereals Ltd. wishes to study the relationship between the amount of grits or broken cereal and the total cereal produced during a production run. These data are in the file **Cereal**, which is on your data disk. The four variables are C1, percent yield; C2, percent grits; C3, pounds of grits; and C4, pounds of cereal.

(a) Prepare a graph of total production (pounds) on the horizontal axis (abscissa) versus the amount of grits (pounds) on the vertical axis (ordinate).

(b) Label the graph so that it can easily be interpreted.

(c) Write a short description of the relationship between the total production and the amount of grits. Discuss the linear trend and the amount of variation about that trend.

3.26 ⚫ Refer to the cereal production situation discussed in Exercise 3.25.

(a) Use the computer program to compute the correlation coefficient between the amount of grits and total production.

(b) Compute the coefficients of the linear regression between total production and the amount of grits produced.

(c) What quantity of grits would be expected for each additional pound of cereal produced?

3.27 ⚫ Refer to the cereal production discussed in Exercise 3.25. The production manager also wished to determine the relationship between the percentage of grits produced and the percent yield of finished cereal product. The yield variable, which is included in the data file **Cereal**, is computed by dividing the pounds of finished cereal divided by the total weight of wet ingredients used in the production run.

(a) Plot the relationship between yield on the vertical axis and percent grits on the horizontal axis.

(b) Compute the regression coefficients for the regression of yield on percent grits—the relationship previously plotted.

(c) Draw the linear regression equation on the graphical plot.

(d) What change in yield do you expect for each percentage point increase in grits?

3.28 ⚫ Study the relationship between per capita personal income and the following variables: per capita health care expenditures, per capita retail sales, and per capita energy consumption using the data in the file **State**.

(a) Plot the relationships with per capita personal income on the horizontal axis and each of the other variables on the vertical axis.

(b) Compute the regression coefficients for each of the expenditure variables regressed on per capita personal income. Sketch the linear regression lines on the scatter plots.

(c) Briefly discuss the relationships based on your analysis.

3.29 ⚫ Study the relationship between per capita personal income and the following variables: per capita expenditures on education, per capita expenditures on highways, and per capita expenditures on public welfare using the data in the file **State**. When you examine the variables in the computer file you will discover that the government expenditures are expressed in totals for each state instead of per capita measures. Thus you will have to use your statistical computer package to compute the ratio of total expenditures divided by total state population for each expenditure category.

(a) Plot the relationships with per capita personal income on the horizontal axis and each of the other variables on the vertical axis.

(b) Compute the regression coefficients for each of the government expenditure variables regressed on per capita personal income. Sketch the linear regression lines on the graphical plots.

(c) Discuss briefly the relationships based on your analysis.

3.30 ⚫ Economists do not have uniform agreement concerning the effect of military spending on economic growth. This disagreement has been particularly important for analyses of economic growth in the Middle East. This region contains countries that have benefited from oil revenues and others that struggle greatly to improve conditions for their population but have limited resources. Alan Richards and John Waterbury discuss the issue of economic development in their book.[2]

---

[2] Alan Richards and John Waterbury. *A Political Economy of the Middle East: State Class and Economic Development.* (Boulder, CO: Westview Press, 1990).

Included in their analysis are the data shown in Table 3.5 and the data file **Middle East Expenditures**. The second column contains the annual percentage growth in gross domestic product (GDP), and the third column contains the annual military expenditure as a percentage of GDP. The data represent the period 1973 to 1984 except for Iran (1980 to 1985) and Iraq (1960 to 1980).

T A B L E   3 . 5 Middle Expenditures Growth

COUNTRY	GDP GROWTH RATE (%)	DEFENSE EXPENDITURE/GDP (%)
Algeria	6.4	2.0
Egypt	8.5	11.0
Iran	0.5	8.0
Iraq	5.3	51.0
Israel	3.1	17.0
Jordan	9.6	11.4
Libya	3.0	3.0
Morocco	4.5	4.3
Saudi Arabia	6.0	19.0
Sudan	5.5	3.0
Syria	7.0	18.0
Tunisia	5.5	5.0
Turkey	4.1	4.4
YAR	8.1	18.0

(a) Enter the data into your computer package and plot GDP growth rate versus military expenditures.

(b) Compute the correlation coefficient between growth rate and military expenditures.

(c) Compute the coefficients for the simple regression of GDP growth as a function of percent military expenditures.

(d) Based on your statistical analysis, what conclusion can you reach concerning the effect of military expenditures on economic growth in the Middle East?

(e) For the same time period the United States had a GDP growth rate of 2.3% and military expenditures of 6.5%, while Japan had a GDP growth rate of 4.3% and military expenditures of 1.0%. If you considered only these two countries, what would you conclude about military expenditures and growth?

(f) If you added these two countries to the graph of part (a) and the remaining statistical analysis, would your conclusion in part (d) change?

3.31 The following article appeared in **Status Report**, a publication of the Insurance Institute for Highway Safety.

Death Rates Higher in U.S. Than Germany Only Since 1987

"Despite longstanding claims about the safety of Germany's autobahns, the death rate on U.S. interstate high-

ways was lower until 1987. Then speed limits were raised to 65 mph on most rural interstates. And beginning in 1987, the death rate on U.S. interstates started exceeding the rate on autobahns. This pattern continued through 1989...."

The article implies that U.S. highway death rates have risen above autobahn death rates as a result of increasing the speed limit in 1987. Using the data in Table 3.6, and stored in a file named **autobahn**, plot U.S. interstate and German autobahn death rates versus time. Using your plot critically, evaluate the implication of the article.

T A B L E   3 . 6 Deaths per 100 Million Miles: U.S. Interstate versus German Autobahn

YEAR	U. S. INTERSTATE	AUTOBAHN
1975	1.24	2.75
1976	1.38	2.24
1977	1.55	2.13
1978	1.54	2.09
1979	1.51	1.75
1980	1.51	1.6
1981	1.48	1.57
1982	1.28	1.52
1983	1.2	1.59
1984	1.22	1.23
1985	1.12	1.14
1986	1.1	1.19
1987	1.11	1.01
1988	1.17	0.95
1989	1.08	0.97

3.32 The year 2000 United States presidential election generated considerable data and analyses designed to determine if there was any evidence of problems with the electoral process. In particular the state of Florida received considerable attention because the entire presidential outcome depended on the vote in Florida. One of the questions concerned the possibility of voter confusion as the result of the ballot design. After the election it is difficult to prove that voter confusion was an issue, but in many cases analytical models can be used to generate strong evidence of "unusual behavior" in some part of a system. In this problem you are asked to develop such a model.

The election involved two major candidates, Vice President Al Gore and Governor George W. Bush, and two minor candidates, Ralph Nader and Patrick Buchanan. Buchanan advocated positions to the right of Bush and Nader was to the left of Gore. Thus one might expect that counties that supported Bush would have more Buchanan supporters and those that supported Gore would have more Nader supporters.

(a) Using the data file **Florida Election 2000** prepare scatter plots of the county votes for the minor candidates versus those for the major candidates. Based on your examination of these plots, can you identify any counties where voter confusion may have occurred? Please explain your analysis and indicate support for your conclusion. (Data as of November 15, 2000 from abcnews.com and the Florida Secretary of State's office.)

(b) Using the data file prepare simple regression models for each of the scatter plots prepared in part (a). Using these regression models estimate the number of votes that might have been incorrectly cast for Patrick Buchanan in a particular county. Explain how you obtained your estimate.

C H A P T E R 4

PROBABILITY

INTRODUCTION

In this chapter we begin development of probability models that can be used to study business and economic problems for which future outcomes are unknown.

Consider the problem faced by George Smith, President of Advanced Systems Development, Inc. (ASD). The company has submitted five separate project proposals for the next year. George knows that the company will have to complete from up to five projects over the next year. At present the company staff can handle up to two projects and personnel could be hired to staff a third project. But if four or five projects are awarded to ASD there will be a need for subcontracting or major staff expansion. In this chapter we will develop probability concepts that can be used by George to determine the likely occurrence of the possible events—0, 1, 2, 3, 4, or 5 projects awarded. The probability of each event is a number from 0 to 1, such that the probabilities of all six events sum to exactly 1.0. The larger the probability of an event the more likely that event will occur compared to the others. If the probability of exactly two contracts being awarded is 0.80, then George will be more confident of that event, compared to the case where the probability is 0.20. But in either case George cannot be certain that the event will occur.

City Hospital knows from past experience that a mean of 1.0 emergency room admissions per hour occur on Saturday evenings. The emergency room has three acute-care rooms. If this pattern continues into the future, the hospital would like to know the probability that more than three people are admitted to the emergency room in any hour. If the probability of that event is high, then the hospital will need to provide additional acute-care rooms to meet patient demand. But if the probability of more than three admissions is low, then expensive care facilities would be idle most of the time and the resources could be better used for some other medical purpose. The probabilities of these events are thus very important for deciding how many rooms to provide.

We will show how probability models are used to study the variation in observed data so that inferences about the underlying process can be developed. Our objective, both in this chapter and in the next two chapters, is to understand probabilities and how they can be determined.

4.1   RANDOM EXPERIMENT, OUTCOMES, EVENTS

For the manager, the probability of a future event presents a level of knowledge. In contrast, the manager could know with certainty that the event will occur—e.g., a legal contract exists. Or the manager may have no idea if the event will occur—e.g., the event could occur or not occur as part of a new business opportunity. In most business situations we cannot be certain about the occurrence of a future event, but if the probability of the event is known, then we have a better chance of making the best possible decision, compared to having no idea about the likely occurrence of the event. Business decisions and policies are often based on an implicit or assumed set of probabilities.

In order to make probability statements about the uncertain problem environment, we need to develop definitions and concepts that provide language for a probability model. In this section we present the concepts of a sample space, outcomes, and events. These are the basic building blocks for defining and computing probabilities.

For our study of probability we will be concerned with processes that can have two or more outcomes, but there is uncertainty about which outcome will occur.

> **RANDOM EXPERIMENT**
>
> A **random experiment** is a process leading to two or more possible outcomes with uncertainty as to which outcome will occur.

Examples of random experiments include

1. A coin is tossed and the outcome is either a head or a tail.
2. The ASD example that has the possibility of 0 to 5 contract awards.
3. The number of admissions to a hospital emergency room during any hour.
4. A customer enters a store and either purchases a shirt or does not.
5. The daily change in an index of stock market prices is observed.
6. A bag of cereal is selected from a packaging line and weighed to determine if the weight is above or below the stated package weight.
7. A six-sided die is rolled.

In each of the random experiments listed we can specify the outcomes. A customer either purchases a shirt or does not. In each case, the different possible outcomes, defined as *basic outcomes*, have been listed.

> **SAMPLE SPACE**
>
> The possible outcomes of a random experiment are called the **basic outcomes**, and the set of all basic outcomes is called the **sample space**. The symbol S will be used to denote the sample space.

We have defined the basic outcomes in such a way that no two outcomes can occur simultaneously. In addition, the random experiment must necessarily lead to the occurrence of one of the basic outcomes.

EXAMPLE 4.1

ROLL OF A SINGLE DIE (SAMPLE SPACE)

What is the sample space for the roll of a single six-sided die?

SOLUTION

The basic outcomes are the six possible face numbers and the sample space is:

$$S = [1, 2, 3, 4, 5, 6]$$

The sample space contains six basic outcomes. No two outcomes can occur together, and one of the six must occur.

EXAMPLE 4.2

INVESTMENT OUTCOMES (SAMPLE SPACE)

An investor follows the Dow-Jones industrial index. What are the possible basic outcomes of the index at the close of the trading day?

SOLUTION

The sample space for this experiment is

$S = [\{1$. The index will be higher than at yesterday's close$\}, \{2$. The index will not be higher than yesterday's close$\}]$

One of these two outcomes must occur. They cannot occur simultaneously. Thus, these two outcomes constitute a sample space.

In many cases we are interested in some subset of the basic outcomes and not the individual outcomes. For example, for the roll of a die we might be interested in whether the outcome is even—that is, 2, 4, or 6.

EVENT

An **event**, *E*, is any subset of basic outcomes from the sample space. An event occurs if the random experiment results in one of its constituent basic outcomes. The null event represents the absence of a basic outcome and is denoted by $\emptyset$.

In some applications we are interested in the simultaneous occurrence of two or more events. For example, if a die is thrown, two events that might be considered are "Number resulting is even" and "Number resulting is at least 4." One possibility is that all the events of interest might occur. That will be the case if the basic outcome of the random experiment belongs to all these events. The set of basic outcomes belonging to every event in a group of events is called the *intersection* of these events.

INTERSECTION OF EVENTS

Let *A* and *B* be two events in the sample space *S*. Their **intersection**, denoted $A \cap B$, is the set of all basic outcomes in *S* that belong to both *A* and *B*. Hence, the intersection $A \cap B$ occurs if and only if both *A* and *B* occur.

More generally, given *K* events $E_1, E_2, \ldots, E_K$, their intersection $E_1 \cap E_2 \cap \ldots \cap E_K$ is the set of all basic outcomes that belong to every E_i ($i = 1, 2, \ldots K$).

It is possible that the intersection of two events is the empty set.

MUTUALLY EXCLUSIVE

If the events *A* and *B* have no common basic outcomes, they are called **mutually exclusive**, and their intersection $A \cap B$ is said to be the empty set indicating that $A \cap B$ cannot occur.

More generally, the *K* events $E_1, E_2, \ldots, E_K$ are said to be mutually exclusive if every pair (E_i, E_j) is a pair of mutually exclusive events.

Figure 4.1 presents a diagram illustrating intersections using a Venn diagram. In part (a) of Figure 4.1, the rectangle *S* represents the sample space and the two closed figures represent the events *A* and *B*. Basic outcomes belonging to *A* are within the circle labeled *A* and basic outcomes belonging to *B* are in the corresponding *B* circle. The intersection of *A* and *B*, $A \cap B$, is indicated by the shaded area where the figures intersect. We see that a basic outcome is in $A \cap B$ if and only if it is in both *A* and *B*. Thus, in rolling a die, the outcomes 4 and 6 both belong to the two events "Even number results" and "Number at least 4 results." In Figure 4.1(b) the figures do not intersect, indicating that events *A* and *B* are mutually exclu-

FIGURE 4.1
Venn Diagrams for the
Intersection of Events *A* and
B: (a) $A \cap B$ is the Shaded
Area; (b) *A* and *B* are
Mutually Exclusive

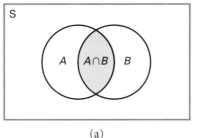

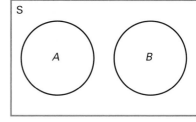

(a)   (b)

sive. For example, if a set of accounts is audited, the events "Less than 5% contain material errors" and "More than 10% contain material errors" are mutually exclusive.

When we consider jointly several events, another possibility of interest is that at least one of them will occur. This will happen if the basic outcome of the random experiment belongs to at least one of the events. The set of basic outcomes belonging to at least one of the events is called their *union*. For example, when throwing a die, the basic outcomes 2, 4, 5, and 6 all belong to at least one of the events "Even number results" or "Odd number results."

UNION

Let A and B be two events in the sample space S. Their **union**, denoted $A \cup B$, is the set of all basic outcomes in S that belong to at least one of these two events. Hence, the union $A \cup B$ occurs if and only if either A or B or both occur.

More generally, given the K events $E_1, E_2, \ldots, E_K$, their union $E_1 \cup E_2 \cup \ldots \cup E_K$ is the set of all basic outcomes belonging to at least one of these K events.

The Venn diagram in Figure 4.2 shows the union, from which it is clear that a basic outcome will be in $A \cup B$ if and only if it is in either A or B or both.

If the union of several events covers the entire sample space S we say that these events are *collectively exhaustive*. Since every basic outcome is in S, it follows that every outcome of the random experiment will be in at least one of these events. For example, if a die is thrown, the events "Result is at least 3" and "Result is at most 5" are together collectively exhaustive.

COLLECTIVELY EXHAUSTIVE

Given the K events $E_1, E_2, \ldots, E_K$ in the sample space S. If $E_1 \cup E_2 \cup \ldots \cup E_K = S$, these K events are said to be **collectively exhaustive**.

We can see that the set of all basic outcomes contained in a sample space is both mutually exclusive and collectively exhaustive. We have already noted that these outcomes are such that one must occur, but no more than one can simultaneously occur.

Next, let A be an event. Suppose that our interest is all of the basic outcomes not included in A.

COMPLEMENT

Let A be an event in the sample space S. The set of basic outcomes of a random experiment belonging to S but not to A is called the **complement** of A and is denoted by $\bar{A}$.

FIGURE 4.2
Venn Diagram for the Union of Events A and B

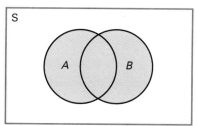

FIGURE 4.3
Venn Diagram for the Complement of Event A

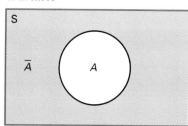

Clearly, the events A and $\overline{A}$ are mutually exclusive—no basic outcome can belong to both—and collectively exhaustive—every basic outcome must belong to one or the other. Figure 4.3 shows the complement of A using a Venn diagram.

We have now defined three important concepts—the intersection, the union, and the complement—that will be important in our development of probability. The following examples help to illustrate these concepts.

EXAMPLE 4.3

ROLL OF A SINGLE DIE (UNIONS, INTERSECTIONS, AND COMPLEMENTS)

A die is rolled. Let A be the event "Number resulting is even" and B the event "Number resulting is at least 4." Then

$$A = [2, 4, 6] \quad \text{and} \quad B = [4, 5, 6]$$

Find the complements of each event, the intersection, and the union of A and B, *and* $\overline{A} \cap B$.

SOLUTION

The complements of these events are respectively

$$\overline{A} = [1, 3, 5] \quad \text{and} \quad \overline{B} = [1, 2, 3]$$

The intersection of A and B is the event "Number resulting is both even and at least 4" and so

$$A \cap B = [4, 6]$$

The union of A and B is the event "Number resulting is either even or at least 4, or both" and so

$$A \cup B = [2, 4, 5, 6]$$

Note also that the events A and $\overline{A}$ are mutually exclusive, since their intersection is the empty set, and collectively exhaustive, since their union is the sample space S; that is

$$A \cup \overline{A} = [1, 2, 3, 4, 5, 6] = S$$

The same statements also apply for the events B and $\overline{B}$.

Consider another intersection of the two events $\overline{A}$ and B. Since the only outcome that is both "not even" and "at least 4" is 5, it follows that $\overline{A} \cap B = [5]$

EXAMPLE 4.4

DOW-JONES INDUSTRIAL AVERAGE (UNIONS, INTERSECTIONS, AND COMPLEMENTS)

We will designate four basic outcomes for the Dow-Jones industrial average over two consecutive days

O_1: Dow-Jones average rises on both days.

O_2: Dow-Jones average rises on the first day but does not rise on the second day.

O_3: Dow-Jones average does not rise on the first day but rises on the second day.

O_4: Dow-Jones average does not rise on either day.

Clearly, one of these outcomes must occur, but not more than one can occur at the same time. We can therefore write the sample space as $S = [O_1, O_2, O_3, O_4]$. Now, we will consider the two events

A: Dow-Jones average rises on the first day.

B: Dow-Jones average rises on the second day.

Find the intersection, union, and complement of A and B.

SOLUTION

We see that A occurs if either O_1 or O_2 occurs and thus

$$A = [O_1, O_2] \quad \text{and} \quad B = [O_1, O_3]$$

The intersection of A and B is the event "Dow-Jones average rises on the first day and rises on the second day." This is the set of all basic outcomes belonging to both A and B, $A \cap B = [O_1]$.

The union of A and B is the event "Dow-Jones average rises on at least one of the two days." This is the set of all outcomes belonging to either A or B, or both. Thus

$$A \cup B = [O_1, O_2, O_3]$$

Finally, the complement of A is the event "Dow-Jones average does not rise on the first day." This is the set of all basic outcomes in the sample space S that do not belong to A. Hence

$$\bar{A} = [O_3, O_4] \quad \text{and similarly,} \quad \bar{B} = [O_2, O_4].$$

Figure 4.4 shows the intersection of events $\bar{A}$ and B. This intersection contains all outcomes that belong in both $\bar{A}$ and B, and clearly $\bar{A} \cap B = [O_3]$.

FIGURE 4.4
Venn Diagram for the
Intersection of $\bar{A}$ and B

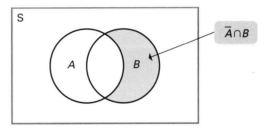

Three results involving unions and intersections of events are illustrated by Venn diagrams in Figures 4.5, 4.6 and 4.7.

FIGURE 4.5
Venn Diagram for Result 1:
$(A \cap B) \cup (\bar{A} \cap B) = B$

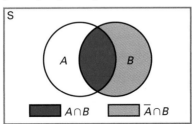

FIGURE 4.6
Venn Diagram for Result 2:
$A \cup (\bar{A} \cap B) = A \cup B$

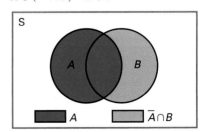

RESULT 1

Let A and B be two events. Then the events $A \cap B$ and $\overline{A} \cap B$ are mutually exclusive, and their union is B, as illustrated in the Venn diagram in Figure 4.5. Clearly,

$$(A \cap B) \cup (\overline{A} \cap B) = B \tag{4.1}$$

RESULT 2

Let A and B be two events. The events A and $\overline{A} \cap B$ are mutually exclusive, and their union is $A \cup B$. That is,

$$A \cup (\overline{A} \cap B) = A \cup B \tag{4.2}$$

RESULT 3

Let $E_1, E_2, \ldots, E_K$ be K mutually exclusive and collectively exhaustive events, and let A be some other event. Then the K events $E_1 \cap A, E_2 \cap A, \ldots, E_K \cap A$ are mutually exclusive, and their union is A. That is,

$$(E_1 \cap A) \cup (E_2 \cap A) \cup \ldots \cup (E_K \cap A) = A \tag{4.3}$$

FIGURE 4.7
Venn Diagram for Result 3:
$(E_1 \cap A) \cup (E_2 \cap A) \cup \ldots \cup (E_K \cap A) = A$

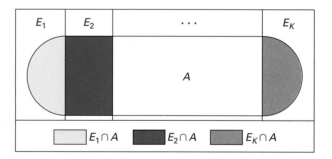

We can better understand the third statement by examining the Venn diagram in Figure 4.7. The large rectangle indicates the entire sample space and is divided into smaller rectangles depicting K mutually exclusive and collectively exhaustive events $E_1, E_2, \ldots, E_K$. The event A is represented by the closed figure. We see that the events comprised of the intersection of A and each of the E_1 are indeed exclusive and that their union is simply the event A. We can therefore write

$$(E_1 \cap A) \cup (E_2 \cap A) \cup \ldots \cup (E_K \cap A) = A$$

EXAMPLE 4.5

SINGLE DIE (RESULTS 4.1 AND 4.2)

Consider the die-rolling experiment in Example 4.3 with $A = [2, 4, 6]$ and $B = [4, 5, 6]$. Show

(a) $(A \cap B) \cup (\overline{A} \cap B) = B$
(b) $A \cup (\overline{A} \cap B) = A \cup B$

SOLUTION

We know that $\overline{A} = [1, 3, 5]$
It follows that $\overline{A} \cap B = [4, 6]$ and $\overline{A} \cap B = [5]$
Then $A \cap B$ and $\overline{A} \cap B$ are mutually exclusive and their union is $B = [4, 5, 6]$; that is,

$$(A \cap B) \cup (\overline{A} \cap B) = B \qquad \text{(result 1)}$$

Also A and $\overline{A} \cap B$ are mutually exclusive, and their union is

$$A \cup (\overline{A} \cap B) = [2, 4, 5, 6] = A \cup B \quad \text{(result 2)}$$

EXAMPLE 4.6

SINGLE DIE (RESULT 4.3)

Consider a die-rolling experiment with events A, E_1, E_2, E_3 given by

$$A = [2, 4, 6] \quad E_1 = [1, 2] \quad E_2 = [3, 4] \quad E_3 = [5, 6]$$

Show that $E_1 \cap A$, $E_2 \cap A$, $E_3 \cap A$ are mutually exclusive, and their union is A.

SOLUTION

First, we notice that E_1, E_2, and E_3 are mutually exclusive and collectively exhaustive. Then

$$E_1 \cap A = [2] \quad E_2 \cap A = [4] \quad E_3 \cap A = [6]$$

Clearly, these three events are mutually exclusive, and their union is

$$(E_1 \cap A) \cup (E_2 \cap A) \cup (E_3 \cap A) = [2, 4, 6] = A$$

EXAMPLE 4.7

SENSITIVE QUESTIONS (RESULT 4.3)

What should market researchers do if subjects are reluctant to answer sensitive questions? These subjects may either refuse to reply or answer the question dishonestly.

SOLUTION

One way of attacking this problem is through the method of randomized response. For instance, we might have the following pair of questions on a student survey:

(a) Have you cheated on an exam in the last six months?
(b) Have you made a purchase from the internet in the last six months?

Subjects are asked to flip a coin and then to answer question (a) if the result is "head" and (b) otherwise. Since the investigator cannot know which question is answered, it is hoped that honest responses will be obtained. The nonsensitive question is one for which the investigator already has information about the population under study. Thus, in this example, the investigator knows what proportion of the population made a purchase from the internet in the last six months. (Later in this chapter we will see how the responses can be analyzed to produce the proportion that answered question (a) positively.)

Now, we define the following events:

A: Subject answers "yes."
E_1:   Subject answers sensitive question.
E_2:   Subject answers nonsensitive question.

Clearly, the events E_1 and E_2 are mutually exclusive and collectively exhaustive. Thus, the conditions of result 3 are satisfied, and it follows that the events

    $A \cap E_1$: SUBJECT BOTH RESPONDS "YES" AND HAS ANSWERED THE
    SENSITIVE QUESTION

and

A ∩ E₂: SUBJECT BOTH RESPONDS "YES" AND HAS ANSWERED THE
NONSENSITIVE QUESTION

are mutually exclusive. Furthermore, their union must be the event A; that is

$$A = (A \cap E_1) \cup (A \cap E_2)$$

EXERCISES

4.1 A corporation takes delivery of some new machinery that must be installed and checked before it becomes available. The corporation is sure that it will take no more than seven days for this installation and check to take place. Let A be the event "It will be more than four days before the machinery becomes available" and B the event "It will be less than six days before the machinery becomes available."

(a) Describe the event that is the complement of event A.

(b) Describe the event that is the intersection of events A and B.

(c) Describe the event that is the union of events A and B.

(d) Are events A and B mutually exclusive?

(e) Are events A and B collectively exhaustive?

(f) Show that $(A \cap \underline{B}) \cup (\bar{A} \cap B) = B$

(g) Show that $A \cup (\bar{A} \cap B) = A \cup B$

4.2 Consider Example 4.4 with the four basic outcomes for the Dow-Jones industrial average over two consecutive days as

O_1: Dow-Jones average rises on both days.

O_2: Dow-Jones average rises on the first day but does not rise on the second day.

O_3: Dow-Jones average does not rise on the first day but rises on the second day.

O_4: Dow-Jones average does not rise on either day.

Let events A and B be given by

A: Dow-Jones average rises on the first day.

B: Dow-Jones average rises on the second day.

(a) Show that $(A \cap \underline{B}) \cup (\bar{A} \cap B) = B$

(b) Show that $A \cup (\bar{A} \cap B) = A \cup B$

4.3 Mark Thompson operates a small used car lot that has three Mercedes' (M_1, M_2, M_3) and two Toyotas (T_1, T_2). Two customers, Van Morris and Erika Delaney, come to his lot and each selects a car. The customers do not know each other and there is no communication between them. Let the events A and B be defined as:

A: The customers select at least one Toyota.

B: The customers select two cars of the same model.

(a) Identify the pairs of cars in the sample space.

(b) Describe event A.

(c) Describe event B.

(d) Describe the complement of A.

(e) Show that $(A \cap \underline{B}) \cup (\bar{A} \cap B) = B$

(f) Show that $A \cup (\bar{A} \cap B) = A \cup B$

4.2   PROBABILITY AND ITS POSTULATES

Now we are ready to use the language and concepts developed in the previous section to determine how to obtain an actual probability for a process of interest. Suppose that a random experiment is to be carried out and we want to determine the probability that a particular event occurs. Probability is measured over the range from 0 to 1. A probability of 0 indicates that the event will not occur and a probability of 1 indicates that the event is certain to occur. Neither of these extremes is typical in applied problems. Thus, we are interested in assigning probabilities between 0 and 1 to uncertain events. To do this, we need to utilize any information that might be available. For example, if incomes are high, then sales of luxury automobiles will occur more often. Alternatively, an experienced sales manager may be able to establish a probability that future sales will exceed the level for the company's profitability goal. In this section we will consider three definitions of probability:

1. Classical Probability
2. Relative Frequency Probability
3. Subjective Probability

Classical Probability

CLASSICAL DEFINITION OF PROBABILITY

The **classical definition of probability** is the proportion of times that an event will occur, assuming that all outcomes in a sample space are equally likely to occur. The probability of an event is determined by counting the number of outcomes in the sample space that satisfy the event and dividing by the total number of outcomes in the sample space. The probability of an event A is

$$P(A) = \frac{N_A}{N} \tag{4.4}$$

where N_A is the number of outcomes that satisfy the condition of event A and N is the total number of outcomes in the sample space. The important idea here is that one can develop a probability from fundamental reasoning about the process.

The classical statement of probability requires that we count outcomes in the sample space. Then we use the counts to determine the required probability. The following example indicates how classical probability can be used in a relatively simple problem.

EXAMPLE 4.8

COMPUTER PURCHASE SELECTION (CLASSICAL PROBABILITY)

Karlyn Akimoto operates a small computer store. On a particular day she has three Gateway and two Compaq computers in stock. Suppose that Susan Spencer comes into the store to purchase two computers. Susan is not concerned about which brand she purchases—they all have the same operating specifications—so Susan selects the computers purely by chance: any computer on the shelf is equally likely to be selected. What is the probability that Susan purchases one Gateway and one Compaq computer?

SOLUTION

The answer can be obtained using classical probability. To begin, the sample space will be defined as all possible pairs of two computers that can be selected from the store. The number of pairs will be counted followed by counting the number of outcomes that meet the condition—one Gateway and one Compaq. Define the three Gateway computers as, G_1, G_2, G_3, and the two Compaq computers as C_1, C_2. The sample space S contains the following pairs of computers,

$$S = \{G_1C_1, G_1C_2, G_2C_1, G_2C_2, G_3C_1, G_3C_2, G_1G_2, G_1G_3, G_2G_3, C_1C_2\}$$

The number of outcomes in the sample space is 10. If A is the event, one Gateway and one Compaq computer are chosen, then the number, N_A, of outcomes that have one Gateway and one Compaq computer is 6. Therefore the required probability of event A—one Gateway and one Compaq—is,

$$P(A) = \frac{N_A}{N} = \frac{6}{10} = 0.6$$

Counting all of the outcomes would be very time-consuming if we first had to identify every possible outcome. However, from previous courses many of you may have learned the basic formula to compute the number of combinations of *n* items taken *k* at a time.

> **FORMULA FOR DETERMINING THE NUMBER OF COMBINATIONS**
>
> The counting process can be generalized by using the following equation to compute the **number of combinations** of *n* items taken *k* at a time.
>
> $$C_k^n = \frac{n!}{k!(n-k)!} \qquad 0! = 1 \qquad\qquad (4.5)$$

The appendix at the end of this chapter develops combinations, and you should study that appendix if you need to learn about or review your understanding of combinations.

We illustrate the combination equation 4.5 by noting that in Example 4.8 the number of combinations of the five computers taken two at a time is the number of elements in the sample space

$$C_2^5 = \frac{5!}{2!(5-2)!} = \frac{5 \cdot 4 \cdot 3 \cdot 2 \cdot 1}{2 \cdot 1(3 \cdot 2 \cdot 1)} = 10$$

In Example 4.9 we will apply classical probability to a more difficult problem.

EXAMPLE 4.9

COMPUTER SELECTION REVISED (CLASSICAL PROBABILITY)

Suppose that Karlyn's store now contains ten Gateway Computers, five Compaq Computers and five Acer computers. Susan enters the store and wants to purchase three computers. The computers are selected purely by chance from the shelf. Now what is the probability that two Gateway and one Compaq computers are selected?

SOLUTION

The classical definition of probability will be used. But in this example, the counting formula will be used to determine the number of outcomes in the sample space and the number of outcomes that satisfy the condition, *A*: {2 Gateway and 1 Compaq}

The total number of outcomes in the sample space,

$$N = C_3^{20} = \frac{20!}{3!(20-3)!} = 1140$$

The number of ways that two Gateway computers out of the ten available can be assigned to a subgroup of three—or any other size subgroup—is computed by,

$$C_2^{10} = \frac{10!}{2!(10-2)!} = 45$$

Similarly the Compaq computer can be selected from any of the five available. Therefore the number of outcomes that satisfy event *A* is,

$$N_A = C_2^{10} \times C_1^5 = 45 \times 5 = 225$$

Finally the probability of *A* {exactly two Gateway and one Compaq computer} is,

$$P_A = \frac{N_A}{N} = \frac{C_2^{10} \times C_1^5}{C_3^{20}} = \frac{45 \times 5}{1140} = 0.197$$

Relative Frequency

We often use relative frequency to determine probabilities for a particular population. The relative frequency probability is the number of events in the population that meet the condition divided by the total number in the population. These probabilities indicate how often an event will occur compared to other events. For example, if event *A* has a probability of 0.40 we know that it will occur 40% of the time. This is more often than event *B* that has only a 0.30 probability of occurrence. But we do not know which event, *A* or *B*, will occur next.

RELATIVE FREQUENCY DEFINITION OF PROBABILITY

The **relative frequency definition of probability** is the limit of the proportion of times that an event *A* occurs in a large number of trials, *n*,

$$P(A) = \frac{n_A}{n} \qquad (4.6)$$

where n_A is the number of *A* outcomes and *n* is the total number of trials or outcomes in the population. The probability is the limit as *n* becomes large.

EXAMPLE 4.10

PROBABILITY OF INCOMES ABOVE $50,000 (RELATIVE PROBABILITY)

Sally Olson is considering an opportunity to establish a new car dealership in Dakota County, which has a population of 150,000 people. Experience from many other dealerships indicates that in similar areas a dealership will be successful if at least 40% of the households have annual incomes over $50,000. She has asked Paul Smith, a marketing consultant, to estimate the proportion of, or probability that, family incomes are above $50,000.

SOLUTION

After considering the problem, Paul decides that the probability should be based on the relative frequency. He first examines the most recent census data and finds that there were 54,345 households in Dakota County and that 31,496 had incomes above $50,000. Paul computed the probability for event *A*: Family income greater than $50,000 as,

$$P(A) = \frac{n_A}{n} = \frac{31,496}{54,345} = 0.580$$

Since Paul knows that there are various errors in census data, he also consulted similar data published by *Sales Management* magazine. From this source he found 55,100 households, with 32,047 having incomes above $50,000. Paul computed the probability of event *A* from this source as,

$$P(A) = \frac{n_A}{n} = \frac{32,047}{55,100} = 0.582$$

Since these numbers are close, he could report either. Paul chose to report the probability as 0.58.

This example shows that probabilities based on the relative frequency approach often can be obtained using existing data sources. It also indicates that different results can and do occur and that experienced analysts and managers will seek to verify their results by using more than one source. Experience and good judgment are needed to decide if confirming data is close enough.

Subjective Probability

> ### SUBJECTIVE DEFINITION OF PROBABILITY
> The **subjective definition of probability** expresses an individual's degree of belief about the chance that an event will occur. These subjective probabilities are used in certain management decision procedures.

We can understand the subjective probability concept by using the concept of fair bets. For example, if I assert that the probability of a stock price rising in the next week is 0.5, then I believe that the stock price is just as likely to increase as it is to decrease. In assessing this subjective probability I am not necessarily thinking in terms of repeated experimentation, but instead I am thinking about a stock price over the next week. My subjective probability assessment implies that I would view as fair a bet in which I paid $1 if the result were a price decrease and I would be paid $1 if the result were a price increase. If I were to receive more than $1 for a price increase, then I would regard the bet as being in my favor. Similarly, if I believe that the probability of a horse's winning a particular race is 0.4, I am asserting the personal view that there is a 40 to 60 chance of its winning. Given this belief, I would regard as fair a bet in which I gained $3 if the horse won and lost $2 if the horse lost.

We emphasize that subjective probabilities are personal. There is no requirement that different individuals should arrive at the same probabilities for the same event. In the stock price example, most people will conclude that the appropriate probability of a stock increase is 0.50. However, an individual with more information about the stock might believe otherwise. In the horse race example, it is likely that two bettors will reach different subjective probabilities. They may not have the same information, and even if they do, they may interpret the information differently. We know that individual investors do not all hold the same views on the future behavior of the stock market. Their subjective probabilities might be thought of as depending on the knowledge they have and the way they interpret it. Managers of different firms have different subjective probabilities about the potential sales opportunities in a given regional market and thus they make different decisions.

Probability Postulates

We need to develop a framework for assessing and manipulating probabilities. To do this, we will first set down three rules (or postulates) that probabilities will be required to obey and show that these requirements are "reasonable."

> ### PROBABILITY POSTULATES
> Let S denote the sample space of a random experiment, O_i are the basic outcomes, and A an event. For each event A of the sample space S, we assume that a number $P(A)$ is defined and we have the **postulates**
>
> 1. If A is any event in the sample space S
>
> $$0 \leq P(A) \leq 1$$
>
> 2. Let A be an event in S, and let O_i denote the basic outcomes. Then
>
> $$P(A) = \sum_A P(O_i)$$
>
> where the notation implies that the summation extends over all the basic outcomes in A.
> 3. $P(S) = 1$

The first postulate requires that the probability lies between 0 and 1. The second postulate can be motivated in terms of relative frequencies. Suppose that a random experiment is repeated N times. Let N_i be the number of times the basic outcome O_i occurs and let N_A be the number of times event A occurs. Then, since the basic outcomes are mutually exclusive, N_A is just the sum of N_i for all basic outcomes in A; that is

$$N_A = \sum_A N_i$$

and on dividing by the number of trials N, we obtain

$$\frac{N_A}{N} = \sum_A \frac{N_i}{N}$$

But under the relative frequency concept of probability, N_A/N tends to $P(A)$, and each N_i/N tends to $P(O_i)$ as N becomes infinitely large. Thus, the second postulate can be seen as a logical requirement when probability is viewed in this way. The third postulate can be paraphrased as "When a random experiment is carried out, something has to happen." Replacing A by the sample space S in the second postulate gives

$$P(S) = \sum_S P(O_i)$$

where the summation extends over all the basic outcomes in the sample space. But since $P(S) = 1$ by the third postulate, it follows that

$$\sum_S P(O_i) = 1$$

That is, the sum of the probabilities for all basic outcomes in the sample space is 1.

Consequences of the Postulates

We will now list and illustrate some immediate consequences of the three postulates.

1. If the sample space S consists of n equally likely basic outcomes, $E_1, E_2, \ldots, E_n$ then

$$P(O_i) = \frac{1}{n} \quad i = 1, 2, \ldots, n$$

This follows because the n outcomes cover the sample space and are equally likely. For example, if a fair die is rolled, the probability for each of the six basic outcomes is 1/6.

2. If the sample space S consists of n equally likely basic outcomes and the event A consists of n_A of these outcomes, then

$$P(A) = \frac{n_A}{n}$$

This follows from consequence 1 and the second postulate. Every basic outcome has probability $1/n$ and, by postulate 2, $P(A)$ is just the sum of the probabilities of the n_A basic outcomes in A. For example, if a fair die is rolled and A is the event "Even number results," there are $n = 6$ basic outcomes, and $n_A = 3$ of these are in A. Thus $P(A) = 3/6 = 1/2$.

3. Let A and B be mutually exclusive events. Then the probability of their union is the sum of their individual probabilities; that is

$$P(A \cup B) = P(A) + P(B)$$

In general, if $E_1, E_2, \ldots, E_K$ are mutually exclusive events

$$P(E_1 \cup E_2 \cup \ldots \cup E_K) = P(E_1) + P(E_2) + \cdots + P(E_K)$$

This result is a consequence of the second postulate. The probability of the union of A and B is

$$P(A \cup B) = \sum_{A \cup B} P(O_i)$$

where the summation extends over all basic outcomes in $A \cup B$. But since A and B are mutually exclusive, no basic outcome belongs to both, so

$$\sum_{A \cup B} P(O_i) = \sum_{A} P(O_i) + \sum_{B} P(O_i) = P(A) + P(B)$$

4. If $E_1, E_2, \ldots, E_K$ are collectively exhaustive events, the probability of their union is

$$P(E_1 \cup E_2 \cup \ldots \cup E_K) = 1$$

Since the events are collectively exhaustive, their union is the whole sample space S, and the result follows from the third postulate.

EXAMPLE 4.11

LOTTERY (PROBABILITY)

A charitable organization sells 1,000 lottery tickets. There are ten major prizes and 100 minor prizes, all of which must be won. The process of choosing winners is such that, at the outset, each ticket has an equal chance of winning a major prize, and each has an equal probability of winning a minor prize. No ticket can win more than one prize. What is the probability of winning a major prize with a single ticket? What is the probability of winning a minor prize? What is the probability of winning some prize?

SOLUTION

Of the 1,000 tickets, 10 will win major prizes, 100 will win minor prizes, and 890 will win no prize. Our single ticket is selected from the 1,000. Let A be the event "Selected ticket wins a major prize" and let B be the event "Selected ticket wins a minor prize." The probabilities are

$$P(A) = \frac{10}{1,000} = 0.01$$

$$P(B) = \frac{100}{1,000} = 0.10$$

The event "Ticket wins some prize" is the union of events A and B. Since only one prize is permitted, these events are mutually exclusive and

$$P(A \cup B) = P(A) + P(B) = 0.01 + 0.10 = 0.11$$

> **EXAMPLE 4.12**
>
> **DOW-JONES REVISITED (PROBABILITY)**

In Example 4.4, we considered the course of the Dow-Jones average over two days and defined four basic outcomes

O_1: Dow-Jones average rises on both days.

O_2: Dow-Jones average rises on the first day but does not rise on the second day.

O_3: Dow-Jones average does not rise on the first day but rises on the second day.

O_4: Dow-Jones average does not rise on either day.

Suppose we assume that these four basic outcomes are equally likely. In that case, what is the probability that the market will rise on at least one of the two days?

SOLUTION

The event of interest, "Market rises on at least one of the two days," contains three of the four basic outcomes—O_1, O_2, O_3. Since the basic outcomes are all equally likely, it follows that the probability of this event is 3/4.

> **EXAMPLE 4.13**
>
> **OIL WELL DRILLING (PROBABILITY)**

In the early stages of the development of the Hibernia oil site in the Atlantic Ocean, the Petroleum Directorate of Newfoundland estimated the probability to be 0.1 that economically recoverable reserves exceeded 2 billion barrels. The probability for reserves in excess of 1 billion barrels was estimated to be 0.5. Given this information, what is the estimated probability of reserves between 1 and 2 billion barrels?

SOLUTION

Let A be the event "reserves exceed 2 billion barrels," and B the event "reserves between 1 and 2 billion barrels." These are mutually exclusive, and their union, $A \cup B$, is the event "reserves exceed 1 billion barrels." We therefore have

$$P(A) = 0.1 \quad P(A \cup B) = 0.5$$

Then, since A and B are mutually exclusive

$$P(B) = P(A \cup B) - P(A) = 0.5 - 0.1 = 0.4$$

EXERCISES

4.4 Recall the corporation in Exercise 4-1. New machinery must be installed and checked before it becomes operational. The accompanying table shows a manager's probability assessment for the number of days required before the machinery becomes operational.

Number of Days	3	4	5	6	7
Probability	0.08	0.24	0.41	0.20	0.07

Let A be the event "It will be more than 4 days before the machinery becomes operational" and let B be the event "It will be less than 6 days before the machinery becomes available."
(a) Find the probability of event A.
(b) Find the probability of event B.

(c) Find the probability of the complement of event A.
(d) Find the probability of the intersection of events A and B.
(e) Find the probability of the union of events A and B.

4.5 A fund manager is considering investment in the stock of a health care provider. The manager's assessment of probabilities for rates of return on this stock over the next year is summarized in the accompanying table. Let A be the event "Rate of return will be more than 10%" and B the event "Rate of return will be negative."

Rate of Return	Less than −10%	−10% to 0%	0% to 10%	10% to 20%	More than 20%
Probability	0.04	0.14	0.28	0.33	0.21

(a) Find the probability of event A.
(b) Find the probability of event B.
(c) Describe the event that is the complement of A.
(d) Find the probability of the complement of A.
(e) Describe the event that is the intersection of A and B.
(f) Find the probability of the intersection of A and B.
(g) Describe the event that is the union of A and B.
(h) Find the probability of the union of A and B.
(i) Are A and B mutually exclusive?
(j) Are A and B collectively exhaustive?

4.6 A manager has available a pool of eight employees who could be assigned to a project-monitoring task. Four of the employees are women and four are men. Two of the men are brothers. The manager is to make the assignment at random, so that each of the eight employees is equally likely to be chosen. Let A be the event "Chosen employee is a man" and B the event "Chosen employee is one of the brothers."
(a) Find the probability of A.
(b) Find the probability of B.
(c) Find the probability of the intersection of A and B.
(d) Find the probability of the union of A and B.

4.7 If two events are mutually exclusive, we know that the probability of their union is the sum of their individual probabilities. However, this is *not* the case for events that are not mutually exclusive. Verify this assertion by considering the events A and B of Exercise 4-1.

4.8 A department store manager has monitored the number of complaints received per week about poor service. The probabilities for number of complaints in a week, established by this review, are shown in the table. Let A be the event "There will be at least one complaint in a week," and B the event "There will be less than 10 complaints in a week."

Number of Complaints	0	1 to 3	4 to 6	7 to 9	10 to 12	More than 12
Probability	0.14	0.39	0.23	0.15	0.06	0.03

(a) Find the probability of A.
(b) Find the probability of B.
(c) Find the probability of the complement of A.
(d) Find the probability of the union of A and B.
(e) Find the probability of the intersection of A and B.
(f) Are A and B mutually exclusive?
(g) Are A and B collectively exhaustive?

4.9 A corporation receives a particular part in shipments of 100. Research indicated the probabilities shown in the accompanying table for numbers of defective parts in a shipment.

Number Defective	0	1	2	3	More than 3
Probability	0.29	0.36	0.22	0.10	0.03

(a) What is the probability there will be less than three defective parts in a shipment?
(b) What is the probability there will be more than one defective part in a shipment?
(c) The five probabilities in the table sum to one. Why must this be so?

4.3   PROBABILITY RULES

We are now at the point where we can develop some important rules for computing probabilities for compound events for decision-making situations.

We begin with A as an event in the sample space S and with A and its complement $\overline{A}$ being mutually exclusive and collectively exhaustive.

$$P(A \cup \overline{A}) = P(A) + P(\overline{A}) = 1$$

and as a result we have the complement rule.

> **COMPLEMENT RULE**
> Let A be an event and $\overline{A}$ its complement. Then the **complement rule** is:
>
> $$P(\overline{A}) = 1 - P(A) \qquad (4.7)$$

For example, when a die is rolled the probability of obtaining a 1 is 1/6, and thus by the complement rule the probability of not getting a 1 is 5/6. This result is important because in some problems it may be easier to find $P(\overline{A})$ and then obtain $P(A)$, as seen in Example 4.14.

Fairselect Inc. is hiring candidates for four key positions in management. The candidates are five men and three women. Assuming that every combination of men and women is equally likely to be chosen, what is the probability that at least one woman will be selected?

SOLUTION

We will solve this problem by first computing the probability of the complement $\overline{A}$ "No woman is selected" and then using the complement rule to compute the probability of A "At least one woman is selected." This will be easier than computing the probabilities of one through four women being selected. Using the method of Classical Probability

$$P(\overline{A}) = \frac{C_4^5 C_0^3}{C_4^8} = \frac{1}{14}$$

and therefore the required probability is

$$P(A) = 1 - P(\overline{A}) = 1 - \frac{1}{14} = \frac{13}{14}$$

Previously, we showed that if two events are mutually exclusive, then the probability of their union is the sum of the probabilities of each event:

$$P(A \cup B) = P(A) + P(B)$$

Next, we want to determine the result when events A and B are not mutually exclusive. In Section 4.1 we noted that the events A and $\overline{A} \cap B$ are mutually exclusive and thus

$$P(A \cup B) = P(A) + P(\overline{A} \cap B)$$

In addition, the events $A \cap B$ and $\overline{A} \cap B$ are mutually exclusive, and their union is B. From this we can derive the result

$$P(\overline{A} \cap B) = P(B) - P(A \cap B)$$

Combining these two results we obtain the addition rule of probabilities.

> **THE ADDITION RULE OF PROBABILITIES**
> Let A and B be two events. The probability of their union is
> $$P(A \cup B) = P(A) + P(B) - P(A \cap B) \qquad (4.8)$$

The Venn diagram in Figure 4.8 on page 98 can motivate an intuitive understanding of the addition rule. The larger rectangle, S, represents the entire sample space. The smaller circles, A and B, represent the events A and B. You can see that the area where A and B overlap represents the intersection of the two probabilities $P(A \cap B)$. To compute the probability of the union of events A and B we first add the probabilities $P(A) + P(B)$. However, notice that the probability of the intersection $P(A \cap B)$ is counted twice and thus must be subtracted once.

A hamburger chain found that 75% of all customers use mustard, 80% use ketchup, and 65% use both. What is the probability that a customer will use at least one of these?

SOLUTION

Let A be the event "Customer uses mustard" and B the event "Customer uses ketchup." Thus we have

$$P(A) = 0.75 \quad P(B) = 0.80 \quad \text{and} \quad P(A \cap B) = 0.65$$

FIGURE 4.8
Venn Diagram for Addition Rule $P(A \cup B) = P(A) + P(B) - P(A \cap B)$

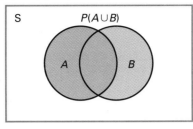

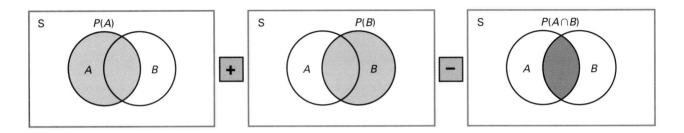

The required probability is

$$P(A \cup B) = P(A) + P(B) - P(A \cap B)$$
$$= 0.75 + 0.80 - 0.65 = 0.90$$

Conditional Probability

Consider a pair of events A and B. Suppose we are concerned about the probability of A given that B has occurred. This problem can be approached using the concept of conditional probability. The basic idea is that the probability of any event's occurring often depends on whether or not other events occurred. For example, a manufacturer planning to introduce a new brand may test-market the product in a few selected stores. This manufacturer will be much more confident about the brand's success in the wider market if it is well accepted in the test market than if it is not. The firms' assessment of the probability of high sales will therefore be conditioned by the test market outcome.

If I knew that interest rates were going to fall over the next year, I would be far more bullish about the stock market than if I believed they would rise. What I know, or believe, about interest rates conditions my probability assessment of the course of stock prices. Next, we give a formal statement of conditional probability that can be used to determine the effect of prior results on a probability.

CONDITIONAL PROBABILITY

Let A and B be two events. The **conditional probability** of event A, given that event B has occurred, is denoted by the symbol $P(A|B)$ and is found to be:

$$P(A \mid B) = \frac{P(A \cap B)}{P(B)} \text{ provided } P(B) > 0 \qquad (4.9)$$

Similarily

$$P(B \mid A) = \frac{P(A \cap B)}{P(A)}$$

provided that $P(A) > 0$

Relative frequencies can help us understand conditional probability. Suppose that we repeat a random experiment n times, with n_B occurrences of event B and $n_{A \cap B}$ occurrences of A and B together. Then the proportion of times that A occurs, when B has occurred, is $n_{A \cap B}/n_B$, and one can think of the conditional probability of A given B as the limit of this proportion as the number of replications of the experiment becomes infinitely large. But

$$\frac{n_{A \cap B}}{n_B} = \frac{n_{A \cap B}/n}{n_B/n}$$

and, as n becomes large, the numerator and denominator of the right-hand side of this expression approach $P(A \cap B)$ and $P(B)$, respectively.

EXAMPLE 4.16

PRODUCT CHOICE: KETCHUP AND MUSTARD (CONDITIONAL PROBABILITY)

In Example 4.15 we noted that 75% of the chain's customers use mustard, 80% use ketchup, and 65% use both. What are the probabilities that a ketchup user uses mustard and that a mustard user uses ketchup?

SOLUTION

From Example 4.15 we know that $P(A) = 0.75$, $P(B) = 0.80$, and $P(A \cap B) = 0.65$. The probability that a ketchup user uses mustard is the conditional probability of event A, given event B.

$$P(A \mid B) = \frac{P(A \cap B)}{P(B)} = \frac{0.65}{0.80} = 0.8125$$

In the same way, the probability that a mustard user uses ketchup is

$$P(B \mid A) = \frac{P(A \cap B)}{P(A)} = \frac{0.65}{0.75} = 0.8667$$

An immediate consequence of conditional probability is the multiplication rule of probabilities, which expresses the probability of an intersection in terms of probabilities for individual events and conditional probabilities.

THE MULTIPLICATION RULE OF PROBABILITIES

Let A and B be two events. The probability of their intersection can be derived from conditional probability as

$$P(A \cap B) = P(A \mid B)P(B) \tag{4.10}$$

Also,

$$P(A \cap B) = P(B \mid A)P(A)$$

In the following example we see an interesting application of the multiplication rule of probabilities. We also tie together some ideas introduced previously.

EXAMPLE 4.17

SENSITIVE QUESTIONS
(MULTIPLICATION RULE)

In Example 4.7, we introduced the randomized response approach for obtaining honest answers to sensitive questions in surveys. Suppose that a survey was carried out in New York, and each respondent was faced with the following two questions:

(a) Is the last digit of your Social Security number odd?
(b) Have you ever lied on an employment application?

Respondents were asked to flip a coin and then to answer question (a) if the result was "head" and (b) otherwise. A "yes" response was given by 37% of all respondents. What is the probability that a respondent who was answering the sensitive question (b) replied "yes"?

SOLUTION

We define the following events:

A: Respondent answers "yes."
E_1: Respondent answers question (a).
E_2: Respondent answers question (b).

From the problem discussion we know that $P(A) = 0.37$. We also know that the choice question was determined by a flip of a coin and $P(E_1) = 0.50$ and $P(E_2) = 0.50$. In addition we know the answers to question (a). Since half of all Social Security numbers have an odd last digit, it must be that the probability of a "yes" answer, given that question (a) has been answered, is 0.50—that is, $P(A|E_1) = 0.50$.

However, we require $P(A|E_2)$, the conditional probability of a "yes" response, given that question (b) was answered. We can obtain this probability by using two results from previous sections. We know that E_1 and E_2 are mutually exclusive and collectively exhaustive. We also know that the two intersections $E_1 \cap A$ and $E_2 \cap A$ are mutually exclusive and that their union is A. It therefore follows that the sum of the probabilities of these two intersections is the probability of A, so

$$P(A) = P(E_1 \cap A) + P(E_2 \cap A)$$

Next, we use the multiplication rule to obtain

$$P(E_1 \cap A) = P(A \mid E_1) P(E_1) = (0.50)(0.50) = 0.25$$

and

$$P(E_2 \cap A) = P(A) - P(E_1 \cap A) = 0.37 - 0.25 = 0.12$$

Then we can solve for the conditional probability

$$P(A \mid E_2) = \frac{P(E_2 \cap A)}{P(E_2)} = \frac{0.12}{0.50} = 0.24$$

From this result, we estimate that 24% of the surveyed population has lied on some employment application.

Statistical Independence

Statistical independence is a special case for which the conditional probability of A given B is the same as the unconditional probability of A. That is, $P(A|B) = P(A)$.

In general, this result is not true, but when it is we see that knowing that event B has occurred does not change the probability of event A.

STATISTICAL INDEPENDENCE

Let *A* and *B* be two events. These events are said to be **statistically independent** if and only if

$$P(A \cap B) = P(A)P(B)$$

From the multiplication rule it also follows that

$$P(A \mid B) = P(A) \quad (\text{if } P(B) > 0)$$
$$P(B \mid A) = P(B) \quad (\text{if } P(A) > 0)$$

More generally, the events $E_1, E_2, \ldots, E_K$ are mutually statistically independent if and only if

$$P(E_1 \cap E_2 \cap \ldots \cap E_K) = P(E_1)P(E_2)\ldots P(E_K)$$

The logical basis for the definition of statistical independence is best seen in terms of conditional probabilities and is most appealing from a subjective view of probability. Suppose I believe that the probability that event A will occur is $P(A)$. Then I am given the information that event B has occurred. If this new information does not change my view of the probability of A then $P(A) = P(A|B)$ and the information about the occurrence of B is of no value in determining $P(A)$. This definition of statistical independence agrees with a commonsense notion of "independence." In our following discussions we will refer to events being "independent." For example, the events "Dow-Jones will rise" and "Neckties are wider" are independent. Whatever I believe about the likelihood of the latter will not influence my judgment of the chances of the former. Example 4.18 illustrates a test for independence.

EXAMPLE 4.18

PROBABILITY OF COLLEGE
DEGREES (STATISTICAL
INDEPENDENCE)

Suppose that 48% of all bachelor degrees in a particular country are obtained by women and that 17.5% of all bachelor degrees are in business. Also, 6% of all bachelor degrees go to women majoring in business. Are the events "Bachelor degree holder is a woman" and "Bachelor degree is in business" statistically independent?

SOLUTION

Let A denote the event "Bachelor degree holder is a woman" and B the event "Bachelor degree is in business" and we have

$$P(A) = 0.48 \quad P(B) = 0.175 \quad P(A \cap B) = 0.06$$

Since

$$P(A)P(B) = (0.48)(0.175) = 0.084 \neq 0.06 = P(A \cap B)$$

these events are not independent. The dependence can be seen from the conditional probability

$$P(A \mid B) = \frac{P(A \cap B)}{P(B)} = \frac{0.06}{0.175} = 0.343 \neq 0.48 = P(A)$$

Thus, in the country of interest, only 34.3% of business degrees go to women, whereas women constitute 48% of all degree recipients.

It is important to distinguish between the terms *mutually exclusive* and *independence*. A pair of events are mutually exclusive if they cannot occur jointly; that is, the probability of their intersection is 0. For independent events the probability of their intersection is the product of their individual probabilities, and in general that probability is not 0 (unless the probability of one of the events is zero and that result is not very interesting). Also note that if we know two events are mutually exclusive, then if one occurs the other cannot and the events are not independent.

In some circumstances, independence can be deduced, or at least reasonably inferred, from the nature of a random experiment. Then the probability of the intersection can be computed from the product of individual probabilities. This is particularly useful in the case of repeated trials that are logically independent.

EXAMPLE 4.19

COMPUTER REPAIR
(INDEPENDENCE)

The experience for a particular model computer is that 90% of the computers will operate for at least one year before repair is required. A manager purchases three of these computers. What is the probability that all three will work for one year without requiring any repair?

SOLUTION

In this case it is reasonable to assume that computer failures are independent for the three computers. They were all produced on the same production line and their use in the company is likely to be similar. Given the assumption of independence, let E_i be "The ith computer works for one year without needing repair." The assumption of independence then leads to

$$P(E_1 \cap E_2 \cap E_3) = P(E_1)P(E_2)P(E_3) = 0.90^3 = 0.729$$

We must emphasize that events are not always independent. In Example 4.19 the computers might have their power supply from the same electrical circuit and that circuit may not be protected against electrical surges. In that case, a power surge that increases the probability of failure for one computer would result in an increase for all computers. Therefore the events are not independent. The condition that the events are independent is an assumption and should only be used after careful analysis of the process that is being analyzed.

The following two examples illustrate how we can often simplify the determination of the probability of an event by first computing the probability of the complement and then use the probability of the complement to obtain the probability of the event of interest.

EXAMPLE 4.20

THE BIRTHDAY PROBLEM
(COMPLEMENT RULE)

A great question for a party is, "What is the probability that at least two people in this room have the same birthday?" Unfortunately it will be difficult for you to share the solution procedure at the party.

To make the problem manageable, we assign all those born on February 29 to March 1 and assume that all 365 possible birthdays are equally likely in the population at large. We also assume that the people in the room are a random sample, with respect to birthdays, of the larger population. (These simplifications have only very small effects on the numerical results.)

SOLUTION

Let M be the number in the group and A the event "At least one pair has a common birthday." Now, to find the probability of A directly would be very tedious, since we would have to take into account the possibility of more than one pair of matching birthdays. It is easier to find the probability that "All M people have different birthdays." This is $\overline{A}$.

Since there are 365 possible birthdays for each person, and each can be associated with every possible birthday of other individuals, the total number of equally likely distinct arrangements for M people is 365^M. Next, we ask how many of these outcomes are contained in the event $\overline{A}$; that is, how many that involve the M individuals all have different birthdays. This is precisely the same as asking in how many ways M birthdays can be selected from 365 possible birthdays and arranged in order. The first person's birthday can occur on any of 365 days, the second on any of 364 days, the third on any of 363 days, and so forth. Thus, for M people the number of different birthdays is

$$(365)(364)(363)\cdots(365 - M + 1)$$

The number of possible birthdays for M people is 365^M. Hence, the probability that all M birthdays will be different is

$$P(\overline{A}) = \frac{(365)(364)\cdots(365 - M + 1)}{365^M}$$

The required probability of at least 2 persons is the complement

$$P(A) = 1 - P(\overline{A}) = 1 - \frac{(365)(364)\cdots(365 - M + 1)}{365^M}$$

Probabilities for selected numbers of people M are

M	10	20	22	23	30	40	60
P(A)	0.117	0.411	0.476	0.507	0.706	0.891	0.994

If at least 23 people are in the group, the probability of at least one pair with the same birthday exceeds 0.50. This probability rises sharply as the group size increases, until, with 60 people in the group, we are almost certain to find at least one pair. This result is surprising to most people. The probability that any given pair of people will have the same birthday is 1/365. But as the group size increases the number of possible matches increases until the probability of at least one match becomes quite large. Here, we have the union of events that are individually unlikely, but when the events are considered together the probability is quite large. Careful analysis using the rather simple probability rules sometimes leads to surprising results.

EXAMPLE 4.21

WINNING AIRLINE TICKETS (COMPLEMENT RULE)

In a promotion for a particular airline, customers and potential customers were given vouchers. A 1/325 proportion of these were worth a free round-trip ticket anywhere this airline flies. How many vouchers would an individual have needed to collect in order to have a 50% chance of winning at least one free trip?

SOLUTION

The event A of interest is "At least one free trip is won from M vouchers." Again it is easiest to find first the probability of the complement $\overline{A}$, where $\overline{A}$ is the event "No free trips are won with M vouchers." The probability of a win with one voucher is 1/325 and thus the probability of not winning is 324/325. If the individual has M vouchers, the event that none of these wins is just the intersection of the events "No win" for each of the M vouchers. Moreover, these events are independent and thus

$$P(\overline{A}) = \left(\frac{324}{325}\right)^M$$

and the probability of at least one win is

$$P(A) = 1 - P(\overline{A}) = 1 - \left(\frac{324}{325}\right)^M$$

In order for $P(A)$ to be at least 0.5, the individual needs at least $M = 225$ vouchers.

Again, this result is surprising. One might guess that if the probability of a win for a single voucher was 1/325, then 163 vouchers would be enough to insure a 50% chance of a win. However, in that case one would be implicitly assuming that the probability of a union was the sum of the individual probabilities, neglecting to subtract for double counting in the intersections (which in this case would involve more than one win from M vouchers).

EXERCISES

4.10 A company knows that a rival is about to bring out a competing product. It believes that this rival has three possible packaging plans (superior, normal, cheap) in mind and that all are equally likely. Also, there are three equally likely possible marketing strategies (intense media advertising, price discounts, and use of a coupon to reduce the price of future purchases). What is the probability that the rival will employ superior packaging in conjunction with an intense media advertising campaign? Assume that packaging plans and marketing strategies are determined independently.

4.11 A financial analyst was asked to evaluate earnings prospects for seven corporations over the next year and to rank them in order of predicted earnings growth rates.
   (a) How many different rankings are possible?
   (b) If, in fact, a specific ordering is simply guessed, what is the probability that this guess will turn out to be correct?

4.12 A company has 50 sales representatives. It decides that the most successful representative during the previous year will be awarded a January vacation in Hawaii, while the second most successful will win a vacation in Las Vegas. The other representatives will be required to attend a conference on modern sales methods in Buffalo. How many outcomes are possible?

4.13 A securities analyst claims that given a specific list of six common stocks, it is possible to predict, in the correct order, the three that will perform best during the coming year. What is the probability of making the correct selection by chance?

4.14 A student committee has six members—four undergraduates and two graduate students. A subcommittee of three members is to be chosen randomly, so that each possible combination of three of the six students is equally likely to be selected. What is the probability that there will be no graduate students on the subcommittee?

4.15 The Little League in one community has five teams. You are required to predict, in order, the top three teams at the end of the season. Ignoring the possibility of ties, calculate the number of different predictions you could make. What is the probability of making the correct prediction by chance?

4.16 A manager has four assistants—John, George, Mary, and Jean—to assign to four tasks. Each assistant will be assigned to one of the tasks, one assistant to each task.
   (a) How many different arrangements of assignments are possible?
   (b) If assignments are made at random, what is the probability that Mary will be assigned to a specific task?

4.17 The senior management of a corporation has decided that, in the future, it wishes to divide its advertising budget between two agencies. Eight agencies are currently being considered for this work. How many different choices of two agencies are possible?

4.18 You are one of seven female candidates auditioning for two parts—the heroine and her best friend—in a play. Before the auditions you know nothing of the other candidates, and you assume all candidates have equal chances for the part.
   (a) How many distinct choices are possible for casting the two parts?
   (b) In how many of the possibilities in (a) would you be chosen to play the heroine?
   (c) In how many of the possibilities in (a) would you be chosen to play the best friend?
   (d) Use the results in (a) and (b) to find the probability you will be chosen to play the heroine. Indicate a more direct way of finding this probability.

(e) Use the results in (a), (b), and (c) to find the probability you will be chosen to play one of the two parts. Indicate a more direct way of finding this probability.

4.19 A work crew for a building project is to be made up of two craftsmen and four laborers selected from a total of five craftsmen and six laborers available.
(a) How many different combinations are possible?
(b) The brother of one of the craftsmen is a laborer. If the crew is selected at random, what is the probability that both brothers will be selected?
(c) What is the probability that neither brother will be selected?

4.20 A mutual fund company has six funds that invest in the U.S. market and four that invest in international markets. A customer wants to invest in two U.S. funds and two international funds.
(a) How many different sets of funds from this company could the investor choose?
(b) Unknown to this investor, one of the U.S. funds and one of the international funds will seriously underperform next year. If the investor selects funds for purchase at random, what is the probability that at least one of the chosen funds will seriously underperform next year?

4.21 It was estimated that 30% of all seniors on a campus were seriously concerned about employment prospects, 25% were seriously concerned about grades, and 20% were seriously concerned about both. What is the probability that a randomly chosen senior from this campus is seriously concerned about at least one of these two things?

4.22 A music store owner finds that 30% of customers entering the store ask an assistant for help and that 20% of the customers make a purchase before leaving. It was also found that 15% of all customers both ask for assistance and make a purchase. What is the probability that a customer does at least one of these two things?

4.23 Refer to the information in Exercise 4-22, and consider the two events "Customer asks for assistance" and "Customer makes purchase." In answering the following questions, provide reasons expressed in terms of probabilities of relevant events.
(a) Are the two events mutually exclusive?
(b) Are the two events collectively exhaustive?
(c) Are the two events statistically independent?

4.24 A local public-action group solicits donations by telephone. For a particular list of prospects, it was estimated that for any individual, the probability was .05 of an immediate donation by credit card, .25 of no immediate donation but a request for further information through the mail, and .7 of no expression of interest. Mailed information is sent to all people requesting it, and it is estimated that 20% of these people will eventually donate. An operator makes a sequence of calls, the outcomes of which can be assumed to be independent.

(a) What is the probability that no immediate credit card donation will be received until at least four unsuccessful calls have been made?
(b) What is the probability that the first call leading to any donation (either immediately or eventually after a mailing) is preceded by at least four unsuccessful calls?

4.25 A mail-order firm considers three possible foul-ups in filling an order:
(a) The wrong item is sent.
(b) The item is lost in transit.
(c) The item is damaged in transit.
Assume that event A is independent of both B and C and that events B and C are mutually exclusive. The individual event probabilities are $P(A) = .02$, $P(B) = .01$, and $P(C) = .04$. Find the probability that at least one of these foul-ups occurs for a randomly chosen order.

4.26 A coach recruits for a college team a star player who is currently a high school senior. In order to play next year, the senior must both complete high school with adequate grades and pass a standardized test. The coach estimates that the probability the athlete will fail to obtain adequate high school grades is .02, the probability the athlete will not pass the standardized test is .15, and that these are independent events. According to these estimates, what is the probability this recruit will be eligible to play in college next year?

4.27 Market research in a particular city indicated that during a week 18% of all adults watch a television program oriented to business and financial issues, 12% read a publication oriented to these issues, and 10% do both.
(a) What is the probability that an adult in this city who watches a television program orientated to business and financial issues reads a publication oriented to these issues?
(b) What is the probability that an adult in this city who reads a publication orientated to business and financial issues watches a television program oriented to these issues?

4.28 An inspector examines items coming from an assembly line. A review of her record reveals that she accepts only 8% of all defective items. It was also found that 1% of all items from the assembly line are both defective and accepted by the inspector. What is the probability that a randomly chosen item from this assembly line is defective?

4.29 An analyst is presented with lists of four stocks and five bonds. He is asked to predict, in order, the two stocks that will yield the highest return over the next year and the two bonds that will have the highest return over the next year. Suppose that these predictions are made randomly and independently of each other. What is the probability that the analyst will be successful in at least one of the two tasks?

4.30 A bank classifies borrowers as high-risk or low-risk. Only 15% of its loans are made to those in the high-risk category. Of all its loans, 5% are in default, and 40% of those in default are to high-risk borrowers. What is the probability that a high-risk borrower will default?

4.31 A conference began at noon with two parallel sessions. The session on portfolio management was attended by 40% of the delegates, while the session on chartism was attended by 50%. The evening session consisted of a talk titled, "Is the random walk dead?" This was attended by 80% of all delegates.

(a) If attendance at the sessions on portfolio management and chartism are mutually exclusive, what is the probability that a randomly chosen delegate attended at least one of these sessions?

(b) If attendance at the portfolio management and evening sessions are statistically independent, what is the probability that a randomly chosen delegate attended at least one of these sessions?

(c) Of those attending the chartism session, 75% also attended the evening session. What is the probability that a randomly chosen delegate attended at least one of these two sessions?

4.32 A stock market analyst claims expertise in picking stocks that will outperform the corresponding industry norms. This analyst is presented with a list of five high-technology stocks and a list of five airline stocks, and she is invited to nominate, in order, the three stocks that will do best on each of these two lists over the next year. The analyst claims that success in just one of these two tasks would be a substantial accomplishment. If, in fact, the choices were made randomly and independently, what would be the probability of success in at least one of the two tasks merely by chance? Given this result, what do you think of the analyst's claim?

4.33 A quality control manager found that 30% of work-related problems occurred on Mondays, and that 20% occurred in the last hour of a day's shift. It was also found that 4% of worker-related problems occurred in the last hour of Monday's shift.

(a) What is the probability that a worker-related problem that occurs on a Monday does not occur in the last hour of the day's shift?

(b) Are the events "Problem occurs on Monday" and "Problem occurs in the last hour of the day's shift" statistically independent?

4.34 A corporation was concerned about the basic educational skills of its workers and decided to offer a selected group of them separate classes in reading and practical mathematics. Forty percent of these workers signed up for the reading classes, and 50% for the practical mathematics classes. Of those signing up for the reading classes, 30% signed up for the mathematics classes.

(a) What is the probability that a randomly selected worker signed up for both classes?

(b) What is the probability that a randomly selected worker who signed up for the mathematics classes also signed up for the reading classes?

(c) What is the probability that a randomly chosen worker signed up for at least one of these two classes?

(d) Are the events "Signs up for reading classes" and "Signs up for mathematics classes" statistically independent?

4.35 A lawn-care service makes telephone solicitations, seeking customers for the coming season. A review of the records indicated that 15% of these solicitations produced new customers, and that of these new customers, 80% had used some rival service in the previous year. It was also estimated that of all solicitation calls made, 60% were to people who had used a rival service the previous year. What is the probability that a call to a person who used a rival service the previous year will produce a new customer for the lawn-care service?

4.36 An editor may use all, some, or none of three possible strategies to enhance the sales of a book:

(a) An expensive prepublication promotion

(b) An expensive cover design

(c) A bonus for sales representatives who meet predetermined sales levels

In the past, these three strategies have been applied simultaneously to only 2% of the company's books. Twenty percent of the books have had expensive cover designs, and of these, 80% have had expensive prepublication promotion. A rival editor learns that a new book is to have both expensive prepublication promotion and cover design and now wants to know how likely it is that a bonus scheme for sales representatives will be introduced. Compute the probability of interest to the rival editor.

4.4   BIVARIATE PROBABILITIES

In this section we introduce a class of problems that involve two distinct sets of events that we label $A_1, A_2, \ldots, A_h$ and $B_1, B_2, \ldots, B_k$. These problems have broad application to a number of business and economics problems. They can be studied by constructing two-way tables that develop intuition for problem solutions. The events A_i and B_j are mutually exclusive and collectively exhaustive within their sets, but intersections $A_i \cap B_j$ can occur between all events from the two sets. These intersections can be regarded as basic outcomes

TABLE 4.1
Outcomes for Bivariate
Events

	B_1	B_2	$\ldots$	B_K
A_1	$P(A_1 \cap B_1)$	$P(A_1 \cap B_2)$	$\ldots$	$P(A_1 \cap B_k)$
A_2	$P(A_2 \cap B_1)$	$P(A_2 \cap B_2)$	$\ldots$	$P(A_2 \cap B_k)$
.	.	.	.	.
.	.	.	.	.
.	.	.	.	.
A_h	$P(A_h \cap B_1)$	$P(A_h \cap B_2)$	$\ldots$	$P(A_h \cap B_k)$

of a random experiment. Two sets of events, considered jointly in this way, are called *bivariate*, and the probabilities are called *bivariate probabilities*.

We will also consider situations where it is difficult to obtain desired conditional probabilities, but alternative conditional probabilities are available. It may be difficult to obtain probabilities because the costs of enumeration are high or because of some critical, ethical, or legal restriction that prevents direct collection of probabilities.

Table 4.1 illustrates the outcomes of bivariate events, labeled $A_1, A_2, \ldots, A_h$ and $B_1, B_2, \ldots, B_k$. If probabilities can be attached to all of the events $A_i \cap B_j$, then the whole probability structure of the random experiment is known and other probabilities of interest can be calculated.

As a discussion example, consider a potential advertiser who wants to know both the income and other relevant characteristics of the audience for a particular television show. Families may be categorized, using A_i, as to whether they regularly, occasionally, or never watch a particular series. In addition they can be categorized, using B_j, according to low, middle, or high-income subgroups. Then the nine possible cross-classifications can be set out in the form of Table 4.1 with $h = 3$ and $k = 3$. The subsetting of the population can also be displayed using a tree diagram, as shown in Figure 4.9. Beginning at the left we have the entire population of families. This population is separated into three branches depending upon their television viewing frequency. In turn each of these branches is separated into

FIGURE 4.9
Tree Diagram for Television
Viewing and Income Example

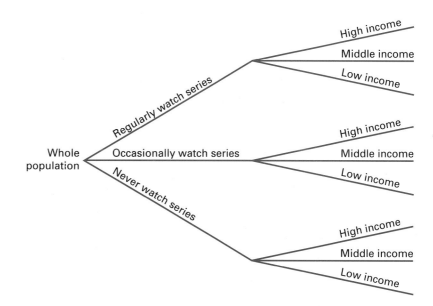

three sub-branches according to the family income level. As a result there are nine sub-branches corresponding to all combinations of viewing frequency and income level.

Now it is necessary to obtain the probabilities for each of the event intersections. These probabilities, as obtained from viewer surveys, are all presented in Table 4.2. For example 10% of the families have high incomes and occasionally watch the series. These probabilities are developed using the relative frequency concept of probability, assuming that the survey is sufficiently large that proportions can be approximated as probabilities. On this basis, the probability that a family chosen at random from the population has a high income and occasionally watches the show is 0.10.

JOINT AND MARGINAL PROBABILITIES

In the context of bivariate probabilities, the intersection probabilities $P(A_i \cap B_j)$ are called **joint probabilities**. The probabilities for individual events, $P(A_i)$ or $P(B_j)$, are called **marginal probabilities**. Marginal probabilities are at the margin of a table such as Table 4.2 and can be computed by summing the corresponding row or column.

To obtain the marginal probabilities for an event we merely sum the corresponding mutually exclusive joint probabilities

$$P(A_i) = P(A_i \cap B_1) + P(A_i \cap B_2) + \cdots + P(A_i \cap B_k)$$

Note that this would be equivalent to summing the probabilities for a particular row in Table 4.2. An analogous argument shows that the probabilities for B_j are the column totals.

Continuing with the example, define the television watching subgroups as A_1, "Regular"; A_2, "Occasional"; and A_3, "Never." Similarly define the income sub-groups as B_1, "High"; B_2, "Middle"; and B_3, "Low." Then the probability that a family is an occasional viewer is

$$P(A_2) = P(A_2 \cap B_1) + P(A_2 \cap B_2) + P(A_2 \cap B_3)$$
$$= 0.10 + 0.11 + 0.06 = 0.27$$

Similarly, we can add the other rows in Table 4.2 to obtain $P(A_1) = 0.21$ and $P(A_3) = 0.52$ We can also add the columns in Table 4.2 to obtain

$$P(B_1) = 0.27 \quad P(B_2) = 0.41 \quad \text{and} \quad P(B_3) = 0.32$$

Marginal probabilities can also be obtained from tree diagrams such as Figure 4.10, which has the same branches as Figure 4.9. The right hand side contains all of the joint probabilities, and the marginal probabilities for the three viewing frequency events are entered on the main branches by adding the probabilities on the corresponding sub-branches. The tree-branch model is particularly useful when there are more than two attributes of interest. In this case, for example, the advertiser might also be interested in the age of head of household or the number of children. The sum of marginal probabili-

TABLE 4.2
Probabilities for the Television Viewing and Income Example

VIEWING FREQUENCY	HIGH INCOME	MIDDLE INCOME	LOW INCOME	TOTALS
Regular	0.04	0.13	0.04	0.21
Occasional	0.10	0.11	0.06	0.27
Never	0.13	0.17	0.22	0.52
Totals	0.27	0.41	0.32	1.00

FIGURE 4.10
Tree Diagram for the
Television Viewing–Income
Example, Showing Joint and
Marginal Probabilities

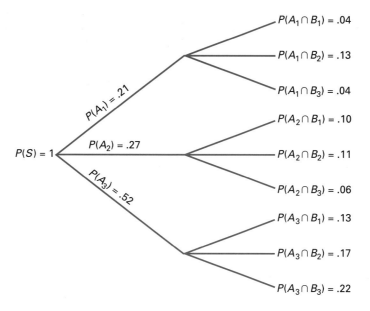

A_1: Regularly watch
A_2: Occasionally watch
A_3: Never watch
B_1: High income
B_2: Middle income
B_3: Low income
S : Sample space

ties for the various attributes all sum to 1 because those events are mutually exclusive and mutually exhaustive.

In many applications we find that the conditional probabilities are of more interest than the marginal probabilities. An advertiser may be more concerned about the probability that a high-income family is watching than the probability of any family watching. The conditional probability can be obtained easily from the table because we have all of the joint probabilities and the marginal probabilities. For example the probability of a high-income family regularly watching the show would be

$$P(A_1 \mid B_1) = \frac{P(A_1 \cap B_1)}{P(B_1)} = \frac{0.04}{0.27} = 0.15$$

Table 4.3 shows the conditional probability of the viewer groups conditional on income levels. Note that the conditional probabilities with respect to a particular income group always add up to 1, as seen for the three columns in Table 4.3. This will always be the case, as seen by the following

$$\sum_{i=1}^{h} P(A_i \mid B_j) = \sum_{i=1}^{h} \frac{P(A_i \cap B_j)}{P(B_j)} = \frac{P(B_j)}{P(B_j)} = 1$$

The conditional probabilities for the income groups given viewing frequencies can also be computed, as shown in Table 4.4, using the definition for conditional probability and the joint and marginal probabilities. To obtain the conditional probabilities with respect to

TABLE 4.3
Conditional Probabilities of
Viewing Frequencies Given
Income Levels

VIEWING FREQUENCY	HIGH INCOME	MIDDLE INCOME	LOW INCOME
Regular	0.15	0.32	0.12
Occasional	0.37	0.27	0.19
Never	0.48	0.41	0.69

TABLE 4.4
Conditional Probabilities of
Income Level Given Viewing
Frequencies

VIEWING FREQUENCY	HIGH INCOME	MIDDLE INCOME	LOW INCOME
Regular	0.19	0.62	0.19
Occasional	0.37	0.41	0.22
Never	0.25	0.33	0.42

income groups we would divide each of the joint probabilities in a row by the right side row marginal probability. For example

$$P(\text{Low Income} \mid \text{Occasional Viewer}) = \frac{0.06}{0.27} = 0.22$$

We can also check by using a two-way table whether or not a pair of events is statistically independent. Recall that the events A_i and B_j are independent if and only if their joint probability is the product of their marginal probabilities; that is if

$$P(A_i \cap B_j) = P(A_i)P(B_j)$$

In Table 4.2 joint events A_2 ("Occasionally Watch") and B_1 ("High Income") have a probability

$$P(A_2 \cap B_1) = 0.10$$

and

$$P(A_2) = 0.27 \qquad P(B_1) = 0.27$$

The product of these marginal probabilities is 0.0729 and thus not equal to the joint probability of 0.10. Hence, the two events A_2 and B_1 are not statistically independent.

INDEPENDENT ATTRIBUTES

Let A and B be a pair of attributes, each broken into mutually exclusive and collectively exhaustive event categories denoted by labels $A_1, A_2, \ldots, A_h$ and $B_1, B_2, \ldots, B_k$. If every event A_i is statistically independent of every event B_j, the A and B are **independent attributes.**

Since A_2 and B_1 are not statistically independent, it follows that the attributes viewing frequency and income are not independent.

In many practical applications, the joint probabilities will not be known precisely. A sample from a population is obtained, and estimates of the joint probabilities are made from the sample data. We would like to know based on this sample evidence if these attributes are independent of one another. We will develop a procedure for conducting such a test later in the book.

Odds

Odds are used to communicate probability information in some situations. For example, a sports analyst might report that the odds in favor of team A winning over team B is 2 to 1. The odds can be converted directly to probabilities, and probabilities can be converted to odds by the following equation.

ODDS

The **odds** in favor of a particular event are given by the ratio of the probability of the event divided by the probability of its complement. The odds in favor of *A* are

$$\text{odds} = \frac{P(A)}{1 - P(A)} = \frac{P(A)}{P(\overline{A})} \tag{4.11}$$

Therefore the odds of 2 to 1 can be converted to the probability of *A* winning

$$\frac{2}{1} = \frac{P(A)}{1 - P(A)}$$

and by basic algebra,

$$2 \times (1 - P(A)) = P(A)$$

giving,

$$P(A) = 0.67$$

Similarly if the odds in favor of winning are 3 to 2 then the probability of winning is 0.60. Note that 0.60/0.40 is equal to 3/2.

Overinvolvement Ratios

There are a number of situations where it is difficult to obtain desired conditional probabilities, but alternative conditional probabilities are available. It may be difficult to obtain probabilities because the costs of enumeration are high or because of some critical, ethical, or legal restriction that prevents direct collection of probabilities. In some of those cases it may be possible to use basic probability relationships to derive desired probabilities from available probabilities. In this section, we will develop one such approach based on the use of overinvolvement ratios (reference 3).

We will start by considering a simple example. Suppose we know that 60% of the purchasers of our product have seen our advertisement, but only 30% of the nonpurchasers have seen the advertisement. The ratio of 60% to 30% is the overinvolvement of the event "seen our advertisement" in the purchasers group compared to the nonpurchasers group. In the analysis to follow we will show how an overinvolvement ratio greater than one provides evidence that, for example, advertising influences purchase behavior.

An overinvolvement ratio, presented in Equation 4.12, is the ratio of the probability of an event—such as viewing an advertisement—that occurs under two mutually exclusive and complementary outcome conditions, such as a product sale or not a product sale. If the ratio of the conditional probabilities is not equal to 1.0 then the event has an influence on the outcome condition. These ratios have applications in a number of business situations, including marketing, production, and accounting. In this section we develop the theory and application of overinvolvement ratios.

OVERINVOLVEMENT RATIOS

The probability of event A_1 conditional on event B_1 divided by the probability of A_1 conditional on activity B_2 is defined as the **overinvolvement ratio**:

$$\frac{P(A_1 \mid B_1)}{P(A_1 \mid B_2)} \tag{4.12}$$

An overinvolvement ratio greater than 1,

$$\frac{P(A_1 \mid B_1)}{P(A_1 \mid B_2)} > 1.0$$

implies that event A_1 increases the conditional odds ratio in favor of B_1:

$$\frac{P(B_1 \mid A_1)}{P(B_2 \mid A_1)} > \frac{P(B_1)}{P(B_2)}$$

Consider a company that wishes to determine the effectiveness of a new advertisement. An experiment is conducted in which the advertisment is shown to one customer group and not to another, followed by observation of the purchase behavior of both groups. Studies of this type have a high probability of error; they can be biased because people who are watched closely often behave differently than they do when not being observed. It is possible, however, to measure the percentage of buyers who have seen an ad and to measure the percentage of nonbuyers who have seen the ad. Let us consider how that study data can be analyzed to determine the effectiveness of the new advertisement.

Advertising effectiveness will be determined using the following analysis. The population is divided into

B_1: Buyers

B_2: Nonbuyers

and into those who have and have not seen the advertising

A_1: those who have seen the advertisement

A_2: those who have not seen the advertisement

The odds in favor of the buyer in this problem are

$$\frac{P(B_1)}{P(B_2)}$$

Similarly, we can define the conditional odds, in which we use the ratio of the probabilities that are both conditional on the same event. For this problem the odds of a buyer conditional on "have seen an advertisement" are

$$\frac{P(B_1 \mid A_1)}{P(B_2 \mid A_1)}$$

If the conditional odds are greater than the unconditional odds, the conditioning event is said to have an influence on the event of interest. Thus advertising would be considered effective if

$$\frac{P(B_1 \mid A_1)}{P(B_2 \mid A_1)} > \frac{P(B_1)}{P(B_2)}$$

The left-side terms are equal to

$$P(B_1 \mid A_1) = \frac{P(A_1 \mid B_1)P(B_1)}{P(A_1)}$$

$$P(B_2 \mid A_1) = \frac{P(A_1 \mid B_2)P(B_2)}{P(A_1)}$$

By substituting these later terms, the first equation becomes

$$\frac{P(A_1 \mid B_1)P(B_1)}{P(A_1 \mid B_2)P(B_2)} > \frac{P(B_1)}{P(B_2)}$$

Dividing both sides by the right-side ratio, we obtain

$$\frac{P(A_1 \mid B_1)}{P(A_1 \mid B_2)} > 1.0$$

This result shows that if a larger percentage of buyers have seen the advertisement compared to nonbuyers then the odds in favor of purchasing conditional on having seen the advertisement is greater than the unconditional odds. Therefore we have evidence that the advertising is associated with an increased probability of purchase.

From the original problem, 60 percent of the purchasers and 30 percent of the nonpurchasers had seen the advertisement. The overinvolvement ratio is 2.0 (60/30) and thus we conclude that the advertisement increases the probability of purchase. Market researchers use this result to evaluate the effectiveness of advertising and other sales promotion activities. Purchasers of products are asked whether they have seen certain advertisements. This is combined with random sample surveys of households from which the percentage of nonpurchasers who have seen an advertisement is determined.

Consider another situation in which it is difficult, illegal, or unethical to obtain probability results.

EXAMPLE 4.22

ALCOHOL AND HIGHWAY CRASHES (OVERINVOLVEMENT RATIOS)

Researchers at the National Highway Traffic Safety Administration in the U. S. Department of Transportation wished to determine the effect of alcohol on highway crashes. Clearly it would be unethical to provide one group of drivers with alcohol and then compare their crash involvement with that of a group who did not have alcohol. However, researchers did find that 10.3% of the nighttime drivers in a specific county had been drinking and that 32.4% of the single-vehicle-accident drivers during the same time and in the same county had been drinking. Single-vehicle accidents were chosen to ensure that any driver error could be assigned to only one driver, whose alcohol usage had been measured. Based on these results they wanted to know if there was evidence to conclude that accidents increased at night when drivers had been drinking. Use this data to determine if alcohol usage leads to increased probability of crashes (reference 2).

SOLUTION

Using the overinvolvement ratios can solve this problem. First the events in the sample space need to be defined.

A_1: Driver had been drinking
A_2: Driver had not been drinking
C_1: Driver was involved in a crash
C_2: Driver was not involved in a crash

We know that alcohol, A_1 increases the probability of a crash if

$$\frac{P(A_1 \mid C_1)}{P(A_1 \mid C_2)} > 1.0$$

From the research the conditional probabilities are

$$P(A_1 \mid C_1) = 0.324$$
$$P(A_1 \mid C_2) = 0.103$$

Using these results the over-involvement ratio is

$$\frac{P(A_1 \mid C_1)}{P(A_1 \mid C_2)} = \frac{0.324}{0.103} = 3.15$$

Based on this analysis there is evidence to conclude that alcohol increases the probability of automobile crashes.

The overinvolvement ratio is a good example of how mathematical manipulations of probabilities can be used to obtain useful results for business decisions. The wide usage of automated data collection using bar code scanners, audience segmentation, and census data on tapes and disks provides the possibility to compute many different probabilities, conditional probabilities, and overinvolvement ratios. As a result, analyses similar to those presented in this chapter become part of the daily routine for marketing analysts and product managers.

EXERCISES

4.37 A survey carried out for a supermarket classified customers according to whether their visits to the store are frequent or infrequent and to whether they often, sometimes, or never purchase generic products. The accompanying table gives the proportions of people surveyed in each of the six joint classifications.

FREQUENCY OF VISIT	PURCHASE OF GENERIC PRODUCTS		
	Often	*Sometimes*	*Never*
Frequent	0.12	0.48	0.19
Infrequent	0.07	0.06	0.08

(a) What is the probability that a customer is both a frequent shopper and often purchases generic products?
(b) What is the probability that a customer who never buys generic products visits the store frequently?
(c) Are the events "Never buys generic products" and "Visits the store frequently" independent?
(d) What is the probability that a customer who infrequently visits the store often buys generic products?
(e) Are the events "Often buys generic products" and "Visits the store infrequently" independent?
(f) What is the probability that a customer frequently visits the store?
(g) What is the probability that a customer never buys generic products?
(h) What is the probability that a customer either frequently visits the store or never buys generic products, or both?

4.38 A consulting organization predicts whether corporations' earnings for the coming year will be unusually low, unusually high, or normal. Before deciding whether to continue purchasing these forecasts, a stockbroker compares past predictions with actual outcomes.

The accompanying table shows proportions in the nine joint classifications.

OUTCOME	PREDICTION		
	Unusually High	*Normal*	*Unusually Low*
Unusually high	0.23	0.12	0.03
Normal	0.06	0.22	0.08
Unusually low	0.01	0.06	0.19

(a) What proportion of predictions have been for unusually high earnings?
(b) What proportion of outcomes were for unusually high earnings?
(c) If a firm were to have unusually high earnings, what is the probability that the consulting organization would correctly predict this event?
(d) If the organization predicted unusually high earnings for a corporation, what is the probability that these would materialize?
(e) What is the probability that a corporation for which unusually high earnings had been predicted will have unusually low earnings?

4.39 Subscribers to a local newspaper were asked whether they regularly, occasionally, or never read the business section, and also whether they had traded common stocks (or shares in a mutual fund) over the last year. The table given here shows proportions of subscribers in six joint classifications.

TRADED STOCKS	READ BUSINESS SECTION		
	Regularly	*Occasionally*	*Never*
Yes	0.18	0.10	0.04
No	0.16	0.31	0.21

(a) What is the probability that a randomly chosen subscriber never reads the business section?

(b) What is the probability that a randomly chosen subscriber has traded stocks over the last year?

(c) What is the probability that a subscriber who never reads the business section has traded stocks over the last year?

(d) What is the probability that a subscriber who traded stocks over the last year never reads the business section?

(e) What is the probability that a subscriber who does not regularly read the business section traded stocks over the last year?

4.40 A corporation regularly takes deliveries of a particular sensitive part from three subcontractors. It found that the proportion of parts that are good or defective from the total received were as shown in the following table.

PART	SUBCONTRACTOR		
	A	B	C
Good	0.27	0.30	0.33
Defective	0.02	0.05	0.03

(a) If a part is chosen randomly from all those received, what is the probability that it is defective?

(b) If a part is chosen randomly from all those received, what is the probability it is from subcontractor B?

(c) What is the probability that a part from subcontractor B is defective?

(d) What is the probability that a randomly chosen defective part is from subcontractor B?

(e) Is the quality of a part independent of the source of supply?

(f) In terms of quality, which of the three subcontractors is most reliable?

4.41 Students in a business statistics class were asked what grade they expected in the course and whether they worked additional problems beyond those assigned by the instructor. The table gives proportions of students in each of eight joint classifications.

WORKED PROBLEMS	EXPECTED GRADE			
	A	B	C	Below C
Yes	0.12	0.06	0.12	0.02
No	0.13	0.21	0.26	0.08

(a) Find the probability that a randomly chosen student from this class worked additional problems.

(b) Find the probability that a randomly chosen student from this class expects an A.

(c) Find the probability that a randomly chosen student who worked additional problems expects an A.

(d) Find the probability that a randomly chosen student who expects an A worked additional problems.

(e) Find the probability that a randomly chosen student who worked additional problems expects a grade below B.

(f) Are working additional problems and expected grade statistically independent?

4.42 The accompanying table shows proportions of computer salespeople classified according to marital status and whether they left their jobs or stayed over a period of one year.

MARITAL STATUS	STAYED	LEFT
Married	0.64	0.13
Single	0.17	0.06

(a) What is the probability that a randomly chosen salesperson was married?

(b) What is the probability that a randomly chosen salesperson left the job within the year?

(c) What is the probability that a randomly chosen single salesperson left the job within the year?

(d) What is the probability that a randomly chosen salesperson who stayed in the job over the year was married?

4.43 The accompanying table shows proportions of adults in nonmetropolitan areas, categorized as to whether they were readers or nonreaders of newspapers and whether or not they voted in the last election.

VOTED	READERS	NONREADERS
Yes	0.63	0.13
No	0.14	0.10

(a) What is the probability that a randomly chosen adult from this population voted?

(b) What is the probability that a randomly chosen adult from this population read newspapers?

(c) What is the probability that a randomly chosen adult from this population who did not read newspapers did not vote?

4.44 A campus student club distributed material about membership to new students attending an orientation meeting. Of those receiving this material, 40% were men and 60% were women. Subsequently, it was found that 7% of the men and 9% of the women who received this material joined the club.

(a) Find the probability that a randomly chosen new student who receives the membership material will join the club.

(b) Find the probability that a randomly chosen new student who joins the club after receiving the membership material is a woman.

4.45 An analyst attempting to predict a corporation's earnings next year believes that the corporation's business is quite sensitive to the level of interest rates. She believes that if average rates in the next year are more than 1% higher than this year, the probability of significant earnings growth is 0.1. If average rates next year are more than 1% lower than this year, the probability of significant earnings growth is estimated to be 0.8. Finally, if average interest rates next year are within 1% of this year's rates, the probability for significant earnings growth is put at 0.5. The analyst estimates that the probability is 0.25 that rates next year will be more than 1% higher than this year, and 0.15 that they will be more than 1% lower than this year.

(a) What is the estimated probability that both interest rates will be 1% higher and significant earnings growth will result?

(b) What is the probability that this corporation will experience significant earnings growth?

(c) If the corporation exhibits significant earnings growth, what is the probability that interest rates will have been more than 1% lower than in the current year?

4.46 Forty-two percent of blue-collar employees in a corporation were in favor of a modified health care plan, and 22% of the corporation's blue-collar employees favored a proposal to change the work schedule. Thirty-four percent of those favoring the health plan modification favored the work schedule change.

(a) What is the probability that a randomly selected blue-collar employee is in favor of both the modified health care plan and the changed work schedule?

(b) What is the probability that a randomly chosen blue-collar employee is in favor of at least one of the two changes?

(c) What is the probability that a blue-collar employee favoring the work schedule change also favors the modified health plan?

4.47 The grades of a freshman college class, obtained at the end of their first year of college, were analyzed. Seventy percent of the students in the top quarter of the college class had graduated in the upper 10% of their high school class, as had 50% of the students in the middle half of the college class and 20% of the students in the bottom quarter of the college class.

(a) What is the probability that a randomly chosen freshman graduated in the upper 10% of his or her high school class?

(b) What is the probability that a randomly chosen freshman who graduated in the upper 10% of his or her high school class will be in the top quarter of the college class?

(c) What is the probability that a randomly chosen freshman who did not graduate in the upper 10% of his or her high school class will not be in the top quarter of the college class?

4.48 Before books aimed at preschool children are marketed, reactions are obtained from a panel of preschool children. These reactions are categorized as "favorable," "neutral," or "unfavorable." Subsequently, book sales are categorized as "high," "moderate," or "low," according to the norms of this market. Similar panels have evaluated 1,000 books in the past. The accompanying table shows their reactions and the resulting market performance of the books.

	PANEL REACTION		
SALES	*Favorable*	*Neutral*	*Unfavorable*
High	173	101	61
Moderate	88	211	70
Low	42	113	141

(a) If the panel reaction is favorable, what is the probability that sales will be high?

(b) If the panel reaction is unfavorable, what is the probability that sales will be low?

(c) If the panel reaction is neutral or better, what is the probability that sales will be low?

(d) If sales are low, what is the probability that the panel reaction was neutral or better?

4.49 A manufacturer produces boxes of candy, each containing 10 pieces. Two machines are used for this purpose. After a large batch has been produced, it is discovered that one of the machines, which produces 40% of the total output, has a fault that has led to the introduction of an impurity into 10% of the pieces of candy it makes. From a single box of candy, one piece is selected at random and tested. If that piece contains no impurity, what is the probability that the faulty machine produced the box from which it came?

4.50 A student feels that 70% of his college courses have been enjoyable and the remainder have been boring. This student has access to student evaluations of professors and finds out that 60% of his enjoyable courses and 25% of his boring courses have been taught by professors who had previously received strong positive evaluations from their students. Next semester the student decides to take three courses, all from professors who have received strongly positive student evaluations. Assume that this student's reactions to the three courses are independent of one another.

(a) What is the probability that this student will find all three courses enjoyable?

(b) What is the probability that this student will find at least one of the courses enjoyable?

4.5 BAYES' THEOREM

In this section we will introduce an important result that has many applications to management decision making. Bayes' theorem provides a way of revising conditional probabilities by using available information. It also provides a procedure for determining how probability statements should be adjusted given additional information.

Reverend Thomas Bayes (1702–1761) developed Bayes' Theorem, originally published after his death in 1763 and published again in 1958 (reference 1). Because games of chance and hence probability were considered to be works of the devil, the results were not widely publicized. Since World War II, a major area of statistics and a major area of management decision theory have developed, based on the original works of Thomas Bayes. We will begin our development with an example problem followed by a more formal development.

EXAMPLE 4.23

DRUG SCREENING (BAYES' THEOREM)

A number of corporations use routine screening tests to determine if prospective employees are drug users or have various medical conditions or both. Jennifer Smith, President of Fairweather Industries Inc., has requested an analysis to determine the feasibility of screening prospective employees to determine if they are HIV positive. The potential future medical costs for such persons can dramatically raise the cost of health insurance for employees of the company, and Jennifer would like to minimize the chances of such costs. Suppose that 10% of the potential job applicants are HIV positive. In addition, a test is available that identifies correctly a person's condition 90% of the time. If a person is HIV positive the probability is 0.90 that the person is correctly identified by the test as HIV positive. Similarly, if the person is not HIV positive the probability is 0.90 that the person is correctly identified as not HIV positive.

We should note that there is a potential ethical and possible legal question concerning the denial of employment based on a person's medical condition. Of course such concerns are a very important part of the decision concerning the use of a testing procedure. Here we are concerned about the feasibility of using such a test if one had decided that such a test was proper given the legal and value system.

SOLUTION

The first step in the analysis is to identify the events in the sample space.

H_1: The person is HIV positive.

H_2: The person is not HIV positive

The proposed test indicates positive or negative results

T_1: Test says that the person is HIV positive

T_2: Test says that the person is not HIV positive.

From the information provided the following probabilities can be defined:

$$P(H_1) = 0.10 \qquad P(H_2) = 0.90$$
$$P(T_1 \mid H_1) = 0.90 \qquad P(T_2 \mid H_1) = 0.10$$
$$P(T_1 \mid H_2) = 0.10 \qquad P(T_2 \mid H_2) = 0.90$$

Using these probabilities a two-way table containing the joint probabilities can be constructed

$$P(H_1 \cap T_1) = P(T_1 \mid H_1)P(H_1) = 0.90 \times 0.10 = 0.09$$
$$P(H_1 \cap T_2) = P(T_2 \mid H_1)P(H_1) = 0.10 \times 0.10 = 0.01$$
$$P(H_2 \cap T_1) = P(T_1 \mid H_2)P(H_2) = 0.10 \times 0.90 = 0.09$$
$$P(H_2 \cap T_2) = P(T_2 \mid H_2)P(H_2) = 0.90 \times 0.90 = 0.81$$

From Table 4.5 we can easily determine the conditional probability of HIV positive given that the test says HIV positive by dividing the joint probability of T_1 and H_1 (0.09) by the marginal probability of T_1 (0.18)

$$P(H_1 \mid T_1) = \frac{P(H_1 \cap T_1)}{P(T_1)} = \frac{0.09}{0.18} = 0.50$$

TABLE 4.5
Drug Test Sub-groups

	T_1 (TEST SAYS HIV)	T_2 (TEST SAYS NOT HIV)	TOTAL
H_1 (HIV positive)	0.09	0.01	0.10
H_2 (not HIV positive)	0.09	0.81	0.90
Total	0.18	0.82	1.0

Similarly the probability of not HIV positive given that the test says not HIV positive can be obtained from the second column of Table 4.5

$$P(H_2 \mid T_2) = \frac{P(H_2 \cap T_2)}{P(T_2)} = \frac{0.81}{0.82} = 0.988$$

From these results we see that if the test says a person is not HIV positive the probability is very high that the test result is correct. However, if the test says that the person is HIV positive the probability is only 0.50 that the person is HIV positive. This is a large increase over a probability of 0.10 for a randomly selected person. However, it is clear that the company would not want to reject prospective employees merely on the results of this screening test. The potential for unethical hiring procedures and serious legal action would be too great. The best strategy would be to use a second independent test to further screen the people identified as HIV positive by the first test. We stress again that there may be serious ethical and medical concerns if people are rejected for employment because they are HIV positive.

Given this background, we will now provide a more formal development of Bayes' theorem. To begin, we first review the multiplication rule, Equation 4.10

$$P(A \cap B) = P(A \mid B)P(B) = P(B \mid A)P(A)$$

Bayes' theorem follows from this rule.

BAYES' THEOREM

Let *A* and *B* be two events. Then **Bayes' Theorem** states that:

$$P(B \mid A) = \frac{P(A \mid B)P(B)}{P(A)} \tag{4.13}$$

and

$$P(A \mid B) = \frac{P(B \mid A)P(A)}{P(B)}$$

An interesting interpretation of Bayes' theorem is in terms of subjective probabilities. Suppose that an individual is interested in the event *B* and forms a subjective view of the probability that *B* will occur; in this context, the probability $P(B)$ is called a *prior* probability. If then the individual acquires an additional piece of information—namely, that the event *A* has occurred—this may cause a modification of the initial judgment as to the likelihood of the occurrence of *B*. Since *A* is known to have happened, the relevant probability for *B* is now the conditional probability of *B* given *A* and is termed the *posterior* probability. Viewed in this way, Bayes' theorem can be thought of as a mechanism for updating a prior probability to a posterior probability when the information that *A* has occurred becomes available. The theorem then states that the updating is accomplished through the multiplication of the prior probability by $P(A|B)/P(A)$.

We know that people commonly form and subsequently modify subjective probability assessments. For example, an important part of an auditor's work is to determine whether or not the account balances are correct. Before examining a particular account, the auditor will have formed an opinion, based on previous audits, of the probability that there is an error. However, if the balance is found to be substantially different from what might be expected on the basis of the last few years' figures, the auditor will believe that the probability of an error is higher and therefore give the account particularly close attention. Here, the prior probability has been updated in the light of additional information.

EXAMPLE 4.24

AUDITING BUSINESS RECORDS (BAYES' THEOREM)

Based on an examination of past records of a corporation's account balances, an auditor finds that 15% have contained errors. Of those balances in error, 60% were regarded as unusual values based on historical figures. Of all the account balances, 20% were unusual values. If the figure for a particular balance appears unusual on this basis, what is the probability that it is in error?

SOLUTION

Let A be "Error in account balance" and B "Unusual values based on historical figures." Then from the available information

$$P(A) = 0.15 \quad P(B) = 0.20 \quad P(B \mid A) = 0.60$$

Using Bayes' theorem

$$P(A \mid B) = \frac{P(B \mid A)P(A)}{P(B)} = \frac{(0.60)(0.15)}{0.20} = 0.45$$

Thus, given the information that the account balance appears unusual, the probability that it is in error is modified from the prior 0.15 to the posterior 0.45.

Bayes' theorem is often expressed in a different but equivalent form that uses more detailed information. Let $E_1, E_2, \ldots, E_K$ be K mutually exclusive and collectively exhaustive events and let A be some other event. We can find the probability of E_i, given A by using Bayes' theorem

$$P(E_i \mid A) = \frac{P(A \mid E_i)P(E_i)}{P(A)}$$

The denominator can be expressed in terms of the probabilities of A given the various E_i's by using the intersections and multiplication rule

$$P(A) = P(A \cap E_1) + P(A \cap E_2) + \cdots + P(A \cap E_K)$$
$$= P(A \mid E_1)P(E_1) + P(A \mid E_2)P(E_2) + \cdots + P(A \mid E_K)P(E_K)$$

These results can be combined to provide a second form of Bayes' theorem.

BAYES' THEOREM (ALTERNATIVE STATEMENT)

Let $E_1, E_2, \ldots, E_K$ be K mutually exclusive and collectively exhaustive events and let A be some other event. The conditional probability of E_i given A can be expressed as **Bayes' Theorem:**

$$P(E_i \mid A) = \frac{P(A \mid E_i)P(E_i)}{P(A \mid E_1)P(E_1) + P(A \mid E_2)P(E_2) + \cdots + P(A \mid E_K)P(E_K)} \tag{4.14}$$

The advantage of this restatement of the theorem lies in the fact that the probabilities it involves are often precisely those that are directly available.

Application of Bayes' theorem requires a careful analysis of the problem. The first task is to identify the events in the sample space. The sample space in Example 4.23 consists of prospective employees separated into H_1, HIV positive, and H_2, not HIV positive. This required an independent judgment of which people were actually HIV positive and which were not. These events cover the sample space. Events were also identified by their test classification. Events are: T_1, the test indicates HIV positive, and T_2, the test indicates non-HIV positive. These events also cover the sample space. Note that a test result T_1 which indicates HIV positive, does not guarantee that the person is HIV positive, H_1.

After the events have been defined we need to determine the capability of the procedure to predict using the data. Thus in the preceding example the test was given to a group of known HIV positives and to a group of non-HIV positives. These test results provided the conditional probabilities of the test results given either HIV positive or not. This data was converted to information concerning the quality of the screening test predictions by using Bayes' theorem. The final task is to express one or more questions in the form of Bayes' theorem. In the previous example we were interested in the probability that a prospective employee was HIV positive, given that the person obtained a positive result on the test. We also realized that it was important to know the probability that a person was not HIV positive given a positive test result.

This process can be summarized as follows:

SOLUTION STEPS: BAYES' THEOREM

1. Define the subset events from the problem.
2. Define the probabilities for the events defined in Step 1.
3. Compute the complements of the probabilities.
4. Apply Bayes' theorem to compute the probability for the problem solution.

EXAMPLE 4.25

AUTOMOBILE SALES INCENTIVE (BAYES' THEOREM)

A car dealership knows from past experience that 10% of the people who come into the showroom and talk to a salesperson will eventually purchase a car. To increase the chances of success, you propose to offer a free dinner with a salesperson for all people who agree to listen to a complete sales presentation. You know that some people will do anything for a free dinner even if they do not intend to purchase a car. However, some people would rather not spend a dinner with a car salesperson. Thus you wish to test the effectiveness of this sales promotion incentive. The project is conducted for six months, and 40% of the people who purchased cars had a free dinner. In addition, 10% of the people who did not purchase cars had a free dinner.

The specific questions to be answered are:

(a) Do people who accept the dinner have a higher probability of purchasing a new car?
(b) What is the probability that a person who does not accept a free dinner will purchase a car?

SOLUTION

Step 1. Define the subset events from the problem.

D_1: Customer has dinner with the salesperson.
D_2: Customer does not have dinner with the salesperson.
P_1: Customer purchases a car.
P_2: Customer does not purchase a car.

Step 2. Define the probabilities for the events defined in Step 1.

$$P(P_1) = 0.10 \quad P(D_1 \mid P_1) = 0.40 \quad P(D_1 \mid P_2) = 0.10$$

Step 3. Compute the complements of the probabilities.

$$P(P_2) = 0.90 \quad P(D_2 \mid P_1) = 0.60 \quad P(D_2 \mid P_2) = 0.90$$

Step 4. Apply Bayes' theorem to compute the probability for the problem solution.

(**a**) We know that the sales promotion plan increased the probability of a car purchase if more than 10% of those that had dinner purchased a car. Specifically we ask if

$$P(P_1 \mid D_1) > P(P_1)$$
$$P(P_1 \mid D_1) > 0.10$$

Using Bayes' theorem we find that

$$\begin{aligned}
P(P_1 \mid D_1) &= \frac{P(D_1 \mid P_1)P(P_1)}{P(D_1 \mid P_1)P(P_1) + P(D_1 \mid P_2)P(P_2)} \\
&= \frac{0.40 \times 0.10}{0.40 \times 0.10 + 0.10 \times 0.90} \\
&= 0.308
\end{aligned}$$

Therefore the probability of purchase is higher given the dinner with the salesperson.

(**b**) This question asks that we compute the probability of purchase, P_1, given that the customer does not have dinner with the sales person, D_2. We again apply Bayes' theorem to compute

$$\begin{aligned}
P(P_1 \mid D_2) &= \frac{P(D_2 \mid P_1)P(P_1)}{P(D_2 \mid P_1)P(P_1) + P(D_2 \mid P_2)P(P_2)} \\
&= \frac{0.60 \times 0.10}{0.60 \times 0.10 + 0.90 \times 0.90} \\
&= 0.069
\end{aligned}$$

We see that those who refuse the dinner have a lower probability of purchase. To provide additional evaluation of the sales program we might also wish to compare the six-months sales experience with that of other dealers and with previous sales experience given similar economic conditions.

We have presented a logical step-by-step or linear procedure for solving Bayes' problems. This procedure works very well for persons experienced in solving this type of problem. The procedure can also help you to organize Bayes' problems. However, most real problem solving in new situations does not follow a step-by-step or linear procedure. Thus, you are likely to move back to previous steps and revise your initial definitions. In some cases you may find it useful to write out Bayes' theorem before you define the probabilities. The mathematical form defines the probabilities that must be obtained from the problem description. Alternatively, you may want to construct a two-way table as we did in Example 4.23. As you are learning to solve these problems use the structure, but learn to be creative and willing to go back to previous steps.

EXERCISES

4.51 A publisher sends advertising materials for an accounting text to 80% of all professors teaching the appropriate accounting course. Thirty percent of the professors who received this material adopted the book, as did 10% of the professors who did not receive the material. What is the probability that a professor who adopts the book has received the advertising material?

4.52 A stock market analyst examined the prospects of the shares of a large number of corporations. When the performance of these stocks was investigated one year later, it turned out that 25% performed much better than the market average, 25% much worse, and the remaining 50% about the same as the average. Forty percent of the stocks that turned out to do much better than the market were rated "good buys" by the analyst, as were 20% of those that did about as well as the market and 10% of those that did much worse. What is the probability that a stock rated a "good buy" by the analyst performed much better than the average?

SUMMARY

In this chapter we introduced the basic ideas of probability. A rigorous set of definitions and rules provide the capability to develop procedures for solving the core of probability problems that occur in economic and business settings. We developed these problem solving procedures using joint probabilities, marginal probabilities, independence, conditional probabilities, overinvolvement ratios, and Bayes' theorem.

KEY WORDS

addition rule of probabilities, 97
basic outcomes, 81
Bayes' Theorem, 118
Bayes' Theorem (alternative statement), 119
classical probability, 89
collectively exhaustive, 83
combination 128
complement, 83
complement rule, 96

conditional probability, 98
event, 82
independence for attributes, 110
intersection, 82
joint probabilities, 108
marginal probabilities, 108
multiplication rule of probabilities, 99
mutually exclusive, 82
number of combinations, 90
odds, 111

overinvolvement ratios, 111
permutations, 127
probability postulates, 92
random experiment, 81
relative frequency probability, 91
sample space, 81
solution steps: Bayes' Theorem, 120
statistical independence, 101
subjective probability, 92
union, 83

CHAPTER EXERCISES AND APPLICATIONS

4.53 Suppose that you have an intelligent friend who has not studied probability. How would you explain to your friend the distinction between mutually exclusive events and independent events? Illustrate your answer with suitable examples.

4.54 State, with reasons, whether each of the following statements is true or false:

(a) The complement of the union of two events is the intersection of their complements.

(b) The sum of the probabilities of collectively exhaustive events must equal 1.

(c) The number of combinations of x objects chosen from n is equal to the number of combinations of $(n - x)$ objects chosen from n, where $1 \leq x \leq (n - 1)$.

(d) If A and B are two events, the probability of A given B is the same as the probability of B given A if the probability of A is the same as the probability of B.

(e) If an event and its complement are equally likely to occur, the probability of that event must be 0.5.

(f) If A and B are independent, then $\overline{A}$ and $\overline{B}$ must be independent.

(g) If A and B are mutually exclusive, then $\overline{A}$ and $\overline{B}$ must be mutually exclusive.

4.55 Explain carefully the meaning of conditional probability. Why is this concept important in discussing the chance of an event's occurrence?

4.56 "Bayes' theorem is important, as it provides a rule for moving from a prior probability to a posterior probability." Elaborate on this statement so that it would be well understood by a fellow student who has not yet studied probability.

4.57 State, with reasons, whether each of the following statements is true or false:
  (**a**) The probability of the union of two events cannot be less than the probability of their intersection.
  (**b**) The probability of the union of two events cannot be more than the sum of their individual probabilities.
  (**c**) The probability of the intersection of two events cannot be greater than either of their individual probabilities.
  (**d**) An event and its complement are mutually exclusive.
  (**e**) The individual probabilities of a pair of events cannot sum to more than 1.
  (**f**) If two events are mutually exclusive, they must also be collectively exhaustive.
  (**g**) If two events are collectively exhaustive, they must also be mutually exhaustive.

4.58 Distinguish among joint probability, marginal probability, and conditional probability. Provide some examples to make the distinctions clear.

4.59 State, giving reasons, whether each of the following claims is true or false:
  (**a**) The conditional probability of A given B must be at least as large as the probability of A.
  (**b**) An event must be independent of its complement.
  (**c**) The probability of A given B must be at least as large as the probability of the intersection of A and B.
  (**d**) The probability of the intersection of two events cannot exceed the product of their individual probabilities.
  (**e**) The posterior probability of any event must be at least as large as its prior probability.

4.60 Show that the probability of the union of the events A and B can be written

$$P(A \cup B) = P(A) + P(B)[1 - P(A \mid B)]$$

4.61 An insurance company estimated that 30% of all automobile accidents were partly caused by weather conditions and that 20% of all automobile accidents involved bodily injury. Further, of those accidents that involved bodily injury, 40% were partly caused by weather conditions.
  (**a**) What is the probability that a randomly chosen accident both was partly caused by weather conditions and involved bodily injury?
  (**b**) Are the events "partly caused by weather conditions" and "involved in bodily injury" independent?
  (**c**) If a randomly chosen accident was partly caused by weather conditions, what is the probability that it involved bodily injury?
  (**d**) What is the probability that a randomly chosen accident both was not partly caused by weather conditions and did not involve bodily injury?

4.62 A company places a rush order for wire of two thicknesses. Consignments of each thickness are to be sent immediately when they are available. Previous experience suggests that the probability is 0.8 that at least one of these consignments will arrive within a week. It is also estimated that if the thinner wire arrives within a week, the probability is 0.4 that the thicker wire will also arrive within a week. Further, it is estimated that if the thicker wire arrives within a week, the probability is 0.6 that the thinner wire will also arrive within a week.
  (**a**) What is the probability that the thicker wire will arrive within a week?
  (**b**) What is the probability that the thinner wire will arrive within a week?
  (**c**) What is the probability that both consignments will arrive within a week?

4.63 Based on a survey of students on a large campus, it was estimated that 35% of the students drink at least once a week in campus bars and that 40% of all students have grade-point averages of B or better. Further, of those who drink at least once a week in campus bars, 30% have a B average or better.
  (**a**) What is the probability that a randomly chosen student both drinks at least once a week in campus bars and has a B average or better?
  (**b**) What is the probability that a randomly chosen student who has a B average or better drinks at least once a week in campus bars?
  (**c**) What is the probability that a randomly chosen student has at least one of the characteristics "drinks at least once a week in campus bars" or "B average or better"?
  (**d**) What is the probability that a randomly chosen student who does not have a B average or better does not drink at least once a week in campus bars?
  (**e**) Are the events "drinks at least once a week in campus bars" and "B average or better" independent?
  (**f**) Are the events "drinks at least once a week in campus bars" and "B average or better" mutually exclusive?
  (**g**) Are the events "drinks at least once a week in campus bars" and "B average or better" collectively exhaustive?

4.64 In a campus restaurant, it was found that 35% of all customers order hot meals and that 50% of all customers are students. Further, 25% of all customers who are students order hot meals.
  (**a**) What is the probability that a randomly chosen customer is both a student and orders a hot meal?
  (**b**) If a randomly chosen customer orders a hot meal, what is the probability that the customer is a student?
  (**c**) What is the probability that a randomly chosen customer both does not order a hot meal and is not a student?
  (**d**) Are the events "customer orders a hot meal" and "customer is a student" independent?

(e) Are the events "customer orders a hot meal" and "customer is a student" mutually exclusive?

(f) Are the events "customer orders a hot meal" and "customer is a student" collectively exhaustive?

4.65 It is known that 20% of all farms in a state exceed 160 acres and that 60% of all farms in that state are owned by persons over 50 years old. Of all farms in the state exceeding 160 acres, 55% are owned by persons over 50 years old.

(a) What is the probability that a randomly chosen farm in this state both exceeds 160 acres and is owned by a person over 50 years old?

(b) What is the probability that a farm in this state is either bigger than 160 acres or is owned by a person over 50 years old (or both)?

(c) What is the probability that a farm in this state, owned by a person over 50 years old, exceeds 160 acres?

(d) Are size of farm and age of owners in this state statistically independent?

4.66 In a large corporation, 80% of the employees are men and 20% are women. The highest levels of education obtained by the employees are graduate training for 10% of the men, undergraduate training for 30% of the men, and high school training for 60% of the men. The highest levels of education obtained are also graduate training for 15% of the women, undergraduate training for 40% of the women, and high school training for 45% of the women.

(a) What is the probability that a randomly chosen employee will be a man with only a high school education?

(b) What is the probability that a randomly chosen employee will have graduate training?

(c) What is the probability that a randomly chosen employee who has graduate training is a man?

(d) Are gender and level of education of employees in this corporation statistically independent?

(e) What is the probability that a randomly chosen employee who has not had graduate training is a woman?

4.67 A large corporation organized a ballot for all its workers on a new bonus plan. It was found that 65% of all night-shift workers favored the plan and that 40% of all female workers favored the plan. Also, 50% of all employees are night-shift workers and 30% of all employees are women. Finally, 20% of the night-shift workers are women.

(a) What is the probability that a randomly chosen employee is a woman in favor of the plan?

(b) What is the probability that a randomly chosen employee is either a woman or a night-shift worker (or both)?

(c) Is employee gender independent of whether the night-shift is worked?

(d) What is the probability that a female employee is a night-shift worker?

(e) If 50% of all male employees favor the plan, what is the probability that a randomly chosen employee both does not work the night shift and does not favor the plan?

4.68 A jury of twelve members is to be selected from a panel consisting of eight men and eight women.

(a) How many different jury selections are possible?

(b) If the choice is made randomly, what is the probability that a majority of the jury members will be men?

4.69 A consignment of twelve electronic components contains one component that is faulty. Two components are chosen randomly from this consignment for testing.

(a) How many different combinations of two components could be chosen?

(b) What is the probability that the faulty component will be one of the two components chosen for testing?

4.70 Of 100 patients with a certain disease, 10 were chosen at random to undergo a drug treatment that increases the cure rate from 50% for those not given the treatment to 75% for those given the drug treatment.

(a) What is the probability that a randomly chosen patient both was cured and was given the drug treatment?

(b) What is the probability that a patient who was cured had been given the drug treatment?

(c) What is the probability that a specific group of 10 patients was chosen to undergo the drug treatment? (Leave your answer in terms of factorials)

4.71 Subscriptions to a particular magazine are classified as gift, previous renewal, direct mail, or subscription service. In January, 8% of expiring subscriptions were gift; 41%, previous renewal; 6%, direct mail; and 45%, subscription service. The percentages of renewals in these four categories were 81%, 79%, 60%, and 21% respectively. In February of the same year, 10% of expiring subscriptions were gift; 57%, previous renewal; 24%, direct mail; and 9%, subscription service. The percentages of renewals were 80%, 76%, 51%, and 14%, respectively.

(a) Find the probability that a randomly chosen subscription expiring in January was renewed.

(b) Find the probability that a randomly chosen subscription expiring in February was renewed.

(c) Verify that the probability in part (b) is higher than that in part (a). Do you believe that the editors of this magazine should view the change from January to February as a positive or negative development?

4.72 In a large city, 8% of the inhabitants have contracted a particular disease. A test for this disease is positive in 80% of people who have the disease and is negative in 80% of people who do not have the disease. What is the probability that a person for whom the test result is positive has the disease?

4.73 A life insurance salesman finds that of all the sales he makes, 70% are to people who already own policies. He also finds that of all contacts for which no sale is made, 50% already own life insurance policies. Furthermore, 40% of all contacts result in sales. What is the probability that a sale will be made to a contact who already owns a policy?

4.74 A professor finds that she awards a final grade of A to 20% of the students. Of those who obtain a final grade of A, 70% obtained an A on the midterm examination. Also, 10% of students who failed to obtain a final grade of A earned an A the midterm exam. What is the probability that a student with an A on the midterm examination will obtain a final grade of A?

4.75 The accompanying table shows, for 1,000 forecasts of earnings per share made by financial analysts, the numbers of forecasts and outcomes in particular categories (compared with the previous year).

OUTCOME	FORECAST		
	Improvement	*About The Same*	*Worse*
Improvement	210	82	66
About the Same	106	153	75
Worse	75	84	149

(a) Find the probability that if the forecast is for a worse performance in earnings, this outcome will result.

(b) If the forecast is for an improvement in earnings, find the probability that this outcome fails to result.

4.76 A dean has found that 62% of entering freshmen and 78% of community college transfers eventually graduate. Of all entering students, 73% are freshmen and the remainder are community college transfers.

(a) What is the probability that a randomly chosen entering student is a freshman who will eventually graduate?

(b) Find the probability that a randomly chosen entering student will eventually graduate.

(c) What is the probability that a randomly chosen entering student is either a freshmen or will eventually graduate, or both?

(d) Are the events "Eventually graduates" and "Enters as junior college transfer" statistically independent?

4.77 A market research group specializes in providing assessments of the prospects of sites for new clothing stores in shopping centers. The group assesses prospects as either good, fair, or poor. The records of requests for assessments made to this group were examined, and it was found that for all stores that turned out to be successful, the assessment was good for 70%, fair for 20%, and poor for 10%. For all stores that turned out to be unsuccessful, the assessment was good for 20%, fair for 30%, and poor for 50%. It is

known that 60% of new clothing stores are successful and 40% are unsuccessful.

(a) For a randomly chosen store, what is the probability that prospects will be assessed as good?

(b) If prospects for a store are assessed as good, what is the probability that it will be successful?

(c) Are the events "Prospects assessed as good" and "Store is successful" statistically independent?

(d) Suppose that five stores are chosen at random. What is the probability that at least one of them will be successful?

4.78 A restaurant manager classifies customers as well dressed, moderately dressed, or poorly dressed, and finds 50%, 40%, and 10% respectively of all customers fall into these categories. The manager found that wine was ordered by 70% of the well dressed, by 50% of the moderately dressed, and by 30% of the poorly dressed customers.

(a) What is the probability that a randomly chosen customer orders wine?

(b) If wine is ordered, what is the probability that the person ordering was well dressed?

(c) If wine is ordered, what is the probability that the person ordering was not well dressed?

4.79 A record store owner assesses customers entering the store as high school age, college age, or older, and finds 30%, 50%, and 20% respectively of all customers fall into these categories. The owner also found that purchases were made by 20% of high school age customers, by 60% of college age customers, and by 80% of older customers.

(a) What is the probability that a randomly chosen customer entering the store will make a purchase?

(b) If a randomly chosen customer makes a purchase, what is the probability that this customer is high school age?

4.80 Note that the following question represents a completely imaginary situation. Suppose that a statistics class contained exactly 8 men and 8 women. You have discovered that the teacher decided to assign 5 F's on this exam by randomly selecting names from a hat. He concluded that this would be easier than actually grading all those papers and that you are all equally skilled in statistics—but someone has to have an F. What is the probability that all five F's were given to male students?

4.81 A robbery has been committed and McGuff the crime-fighting dog has been called in to investigate. He discovers that Sally Coldhands was seen wearing gloves in the neighborhood shortly after the crime, and thus he concludes that she should be arrested. From past experience you know that 50 percent of the people that McGuff says should be arrested for robbery are actually guilty. Before making the arrest you order some additional investigation. From a large population of convicted robbers you find that 60% wore gloves at the time of the crime and continued to wear them for an interval after the crime. Further investigation reveals that 80% of the people in the neighborhood of the crime were wearing gloves around the time of the crime.

(a) Based on the fact that Sally was wearing gloves, what is the probability that Sally actually committed the crime?

(b) If you did charge her with the crime, do you think a jury would convict her based on the glove evidence? Explain why or why not.

4.82 You are responsible for detecting the source of the error when the computer system fails. From your analysis you know that the source of error is either the disk drive, the computer memory, or the operating system. You know that 50% of the errors are disk errors, 30% are computer memory errors, and the remainder are operating system errors. From the component performance standards you know that when a disk error occurs the probability of failure is 0.60, when a computer memory

error occurs the probability of failure is 0.7, and when an operating system error occurs the probability of failure is 0.4. Given the information from the component performance standards, what is the probability of a disk error given that a failure occurred?

4.83 After meeting with the regional sales managers, Lauretta Anderson, President of Cowpie Computers Inc., believes that the probability that sales will grow by 10% in the next year is 0.70. After coming to this conclusion she receives a report that John Cadariu of Minihard Software Inc. has just announced a new operating system that will be available for customers in 8 months. From past history she knows that in situations where growth has eventually occurred new operating systems have been announced 30% of the time. However, in situations where growth has not eventually occurred new operating systems have been announced 10% of the time. Based on all of these facts what is the probability that sales will grow by 10%?

APPENDIX: PERMUTATIONS AND COMBINATIONS

A practical difficulty that sometimes arises in computing the probability of an event is counting the numbers of basic outcomes in the sample space and the event of interest. For some problems, the use of *permutations* or *combinations* can be helpful.

1) NUMBER OF ORDERINGS

We begin with the problem of ordering. Suppose that we have some number *x* of objects that are to be placed in order. Each object may be used only once. How many different sequences are possible? We can view this problem as a requirement to place one of the objects in each of *x* boxes arranged in a row.

Beginning with the left box in Figure 4.11, there are *x* different ways to fill it. Once an object is put in that box, there are $(x - 1)$ objects remaining, and so $(x - 1)$ ways to fill the second box. That is, for each of the *x* ways to place an object in the first box, there are $(x - 1)$ possible ways to fill the second box, so the first two boxes can be filled in a total of $x \times (x - 1)$ ways. Given that the first two boxes are filled, there are now $(x - 2)$ ways of filling the third box, so the first three boxes can be filled in a total of $x \times (x - 1) \times (x - 2)$ ways. Finally, when we arrive at the last box there is only one object left to put in it. Finally, we arrive at the number of possible orderings.

> **NUMBER OF POSSIBLE ORDERINGS**
>
> The total number of possible ways of arranging *x* objects in order is given by,
>
> $$x(x - 1)(x - 2)\cdots(2)(1) = x! \qquad (4.15)$$
>
> where x! is read "x factorial."

FIGURE 4.11
The Orderings of *x* Objects

| X | $(X-1)$ | $(X-2)$ | $\cdots$ | 2 | 1 |

FIGURE 4.12
The Permutations of x
Objects Chosen From n

| n | $(n-1)$ | $(n-2)$ | $\cdots$ | $(n-X+2)$ | $(n-X+1)$ |

$(n-X)$ objects left over

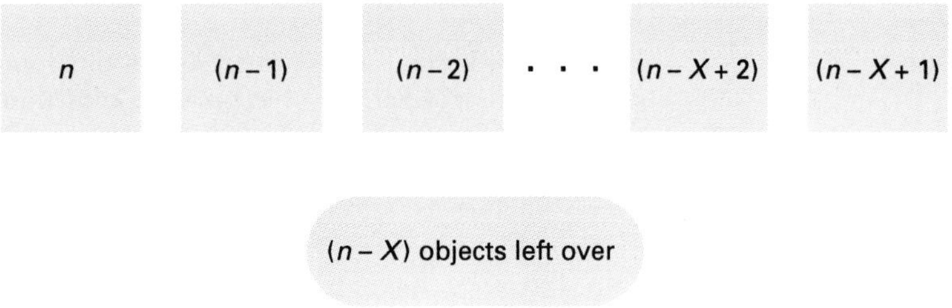

2)   PERMUTATIONS

Suppose now that we have a number n of objects with which the x *ordered* boxes could be filled (with $n > x$). Each object may be used only once. The number of possible orderings is called the number of *permutations* of x objects chosen from n and is denoted by the symbol, P_x^n.

Now, we can argue precisely as before, except that there will be n ways to fill the first box, $(n-1)$ ways to fill the second box, and so on, until we come to the final box. At this point there will be $(n-x+1)$ objects left, each of which could be placed in that box, as illustrated in Figure 4.12.

PERMUTATIONS

The total number of **permutations** of x objects chosen from n, P_x^n, is the number of possible arrangements when x objects are to be selected from a total of n and arranged in order.

$$P_x^n = n(n-1)(n-2)\cdots(n-x+1) \tag{4.16}$$

Multiplying and dividing Equation 4.16 by

$$(n-x)(n-x-1)\cdots(2)(1) = (n-x)!$$

gives

$$P_x^n = \frac{n(n-1)(n-2)\cdots(n-x+1)(n-x)(n-x-1)\cdots(2)(1)}{(n-x)(n-x-1)\cdots(2)(1)}$$

or

$$P_x^n = \frac{n!}{(n-x)!} \tag{4.17}$$

EXAMPLE 4.26

FIVE LETTERS (PERMUTATIONS)

Suppose that two letters are to be selected from A, B, C, D, E and arranged in order. How many permutations are possible?

SOLUTION

The number of permutations, with $n = 5$ and $x = 2$, is

$$P_2^5 = \frac{5!}{3!} = 20$$

These are:

AB	AC	AD	AE	BC
BA	CA	DA	EA	CB
BD	BE	CD	CE	DE
DB	EB	DC	EC	ED

3)   COMBINATIONS

Finally, suppose that we are interested in the number of different ways that x objects can be selected from n (where no object may be chosen more than once) but are *not concerned about the order*. Notice in Example 4.26 that the entries in the second and fourth rows are just rearrangements of those directly above them and may therefore be ignored. Thus, there are only ten possibilities for selecting two objects from a group of five, if order is not important. The number of possible selections is called the number of combinations and is denoted C_x^n where x objects are to be chosen from n. To find this number, note first that the number of possible permutations is P_x^n. However, many of these will be rearrangements of the same x objects and so are irrelevant. In fact, since x objects can be ordered in $x!$ ways, we are concerned with only a proportion $1/x!$ of the permutations. This leads us to a previously stated outcome, namely Equation 4.5 in Section 4.2, which we repeat here for completeness.

COMBINATIONS

The number of **combinations**, C_x^n, of x objects chosen from n is the number of possible selections that can be made. This number is,

$$C_x^n = \frac{P_x^n}{x!}$$

or simply,

$$C_x^n = \frac{n!}{x!\,(n-x)!} \qquad (4.18)$$

EXAMPLE 4.27

PROBABILITY OF EMPLOYEE
SELECTION (COMBINATIONS)

A personnel officer has eight candidates to fill four similar positions. Five candidates are men, and three are women. If, in fact, every combination of candidates is equally likely to be chosen, what is the probability that no women will be hired?

SOLUTION

First, the total number of possible combinations of four candidates chosen from eight is

$$C_4^8 = \frac{8!}{4!\,4!} = 70$$

Now, in order for no women to be hired, it follows that the four successful candidates must come from the available five men. The number of such combinations is

$$C_4^5 = \frac{5!}{4!\,1!} = 5$$

Therefore, if at the outset each of the seventy possible combinations was equally likely to be chosen, the probability that one of the five all-male combinations would be selected is 5/70 = 1/14.

REFERENCES

1. Bayes, Thomas, "Essay towards solving a problem in the doctrine of chance," *Biometrika*, Vol. 45, 1958, pp. 293–315 (reproduction of 1763 paper).

2. Carlson, William L. "Alcohol Usage of the Night Driver," *Journal of Safety Research*, March 1972, Vol. 4, No. I.

3. Carlson, William L. and Betty Thorne. *Applied Statistical Methods for Business and Economics* (Upper Saddle, NJ: Prentice Hall), 1997.

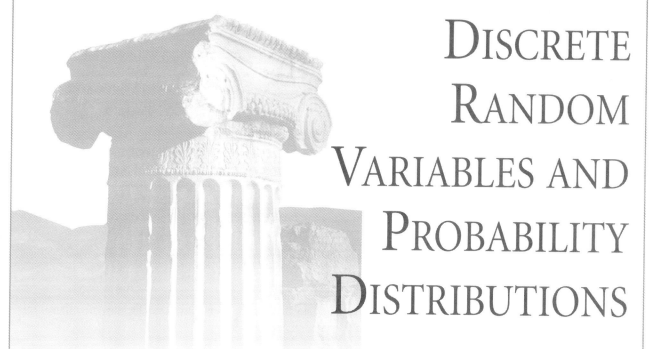

CHAPTER 5

DISCRETE RANDOM VARIABLES AND PROBABILITY DISTRIBUTIONS

INTRODUCTION

In Chapter 4 we began our development of probability to represent situations with uncertain outcomes. In this chapter, we extend those ideas to develop probability models with emphasis on discrete random variables. Chapter 6 will develop probability models for continuous random variables.

Probability models have extensive application to a number of business problems, and some of these applications will be developed here. Suppose you have a business that rents a variety of equipment. From past experience—relative frequency—you know that 30% of the people who enter your store want to rent a trailer. Today you have three trailers available. Five completely unrelated people enter your store (the probability of one of them renting a trailer is independent of the others). What is the probability that these five people are seeking to rent a total of four or five trailers? If that happens, rental opportunities will be missed and customers will be disappointed. The probability of the events (number of trailers desired) can be computed using the Binomial model that will be developed in this chapter.

5.1   RANDOM VARIABLES

When the outcomes are numerical values, these probabilities can be conveniently summarized through the notion of a *random variable*.

> ### RANDOM VARIABLE
> A **random variable** is a variable that takes on numerical values determined by the outcome of a random experiment.

It is important to distinguish between a random variable and the possible values that it can take. Notationally, we do this by using capital letters, such as X, to denote the random variable and the corresponding lowercase, x, to denote a possible value. For example, prior to the result's being observed in the throw of a die, the random variable X can be used to denote the outcome. This random variable can take the specific values $x = 1$, $x = 2$, ..., $x = 6$, each with probability $\frac{1}{6}$.

A further important distinction is between *discrete* and *continuous* random variables. The die throw provides an example of the former; there are only six possible outcomes, and a probability can be attached to each.

> ### DISCRETE RANDOM VARIABLE
> A random variable is **discrete** if it can take on no more than a countable number of values.

It follows from the definition that any random variable that can take on only a finite number of values is discrete. For example, the number of heads resulting from 10 throws of a coin is a discrete random variable. Even if the number of possible outcomes is infinite but countable, the random variable is discrete. An example is the number of throws of a coin needed before a head first appears. The possible outcomes are 1, 2, 3, ..., and a probability can be attached to each. (A discrete random variable that can take a countably infinite number of values will be discussed in Section 5.6.) Some other examples of discrete random variables are:

1. The number of defective items in a sample of 20 items from a large shipment
2. The number of customers arriving at a check-out counter in an hour
3. The number of errors detected in a corporation's accounts
4. The number of claims on a medical insurance policy in a particular year

By contrast, suppose that we are interested in the day's high temperature. The random variable, temperature, is measured on a continuum and so is said to be *continuous*.

CONTINUOUS RANDOM VARIABLE

A random variable is **continuous** if it can take any value in an interval.

For continuous random variables, one cannot attach probabilities to specific values. For example, the probability that today's high temperature will be precisely 77.236° Fahrenheit is 0. It will certainly not be *precisely* that figure. However, probabilities may be determined for ranges, so that one could attach a probability to the event "Today's high temperature will be between 75 and 80°." Some other examples of continuous random variables include:

1. The yearly income for a family
2. The amount of oil imported into the United States in a particular month
3. The change in the price of a share of IBM common stock in a month
4. The time that elapses between the installation of a new component and its failure
5. The percentage of impurity in a batch of chemicals

The distinction that has been made between discrete and continuous random variables may appear rather artificial. After all, rarely is anything actually measured on a continuum. For example, the day's high temperature cannot be reported more precisely than the measuring instrument allows. Moreover, a family's income in a year will be some integer number of cents. However, when measurements can be made on such a fine scale that differences between adjacent values are of no significance, it is convenient to act as if they had truly been made on a continuum. The difference between a family's income of $35,276.21 and $35,276.22 is of very little significance, and the attachment of probabilities to each would be a tedious and worthless exercise.

For practical purposes, we will treat as discrete all random variables for which probability statements about the individual possible outcomes have worthwhile meaning; all other random variables will be regarded as continuous. Because of this distinction, it is convenient to treat these two classes separately. Discrete random variables are discussed in this chapter; continuous random variables will be treated in Chapter 6.

EXERCISES

5.1 For each of the following indicate if a discrete or a continuous random variable provides the best definition.
  (a) The number of cars that arrive each day for repair in a two-person repair shop
  (b) The number of cars produced annually by General Motors
  (c) Total daily e-commerce sales in dollars

  (d) The number of passengers that are bumped from a specific airline flight three days before Christmas

5.2 An Equity actor auditions 100 times a year. Is her work schedule (number of plays) a discrete or random variable?

5.3 List four examples of discrete random variables that could be observed in a new consulting business.

5.4 Define three continuous random variables that a Marketing vice president should regularly examine.

5.2   PROBABILITY DISTRIBUTIONS FOR DISCRETE RANDOM VARIABLES

Suppose that X is a discrete random variable and that x is one of its possible values. The probability that the random variable X takes the specific value x is denoted $P(X = x)$. The *probability distribution* of a random variable is a representation of the probabilities for all the possible outcomes. This representation might be algebraic, graphical, or tabular. For discrete random variables, one simple procedure is to list the probabilities of all possible outcomes, according to the values of x.

PROBABILITY DISTRIBUTION FUNCTION (PDF)

The **probability distribution function,** $P(x)$, of a discrete random variable X expresses the probability that X takes the value x, as a function of x. That is

$$P(x) = P(X = x), \text{ for all values of } x. \tag{5.1}$$

Because the probability function takes nonzero values only at discrete points x, it is sometimes called a *probability mass function*. Once the probabilities have been calculated, the function can be graphed.

Graph the probability distribution function for the roll of a single six-sided balanced die.

EXAMPLE 5.1

ROLLING A DIE (PROBABILITY FUNCTION GRAPH)

SOLUTION

Let the random variable X denote the number resulting from a single roll of a six-sided balanced die. Since

$$P(X = 1) = P(X = 2) = \cdots = P(X = 6) = \frac{1}{6}, \text{ the probability function is}$$

$$P(x) = P(X = x) = \frac{1}{6} \text{ for } x = 1, 2, 3, \ldots, 6$$

The function takes the value 0 for all other values of x, which cannot occur. The probability distribution function is graphed in Figure 5.1, where spikes of height $\frac{1}{6}$ represent probability masses at the points $x = 1, x = 2, \ldots, x = 6$.

FIGURE 5.1
Graph of PDF for
Example 5.1

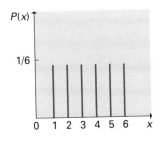

The probability distribution function of a discrete random variable must satisfy the following two properties.

REQUIRED PROPERTIES OF PROBABILITY DISTRIBUTION FUNCTIONS OF DISCRETE RANDOM VARIABLES

Let X be a discrete random variable with probability distribution function, $P(x)$. Then

i. $P(x) \geq 0$ for any value x.
ii. The individual probabilities sum to 1; that is

$$\sum_x P(x) = 1$$

where the notation indicates summation over all possible values x.

Property (i) merely states that probabilities cannot be negative. Property (ii) follows from the fact that the events "$X = x$," for all possible values x, are mutually exclusive and collectively exhaustive. The probabilities for these events must therefore sum to 1. That this is in fact so can be verified directly. It is simply a way of saying that when a random experiment is to be carried out, something must happen.

Another representation of discrete probability distributions is also useful.

CUMULATIVE PROBABILITY FUNCTION $F(x_0)$

The **cumulative probability function,** $F(x_0)$ of a random variable X expresses the probability that X does not exceed the value x_0, as a function of x_0. That is

$$F(x_0) = P(X \leq x_0) \tag{5.2}$$

where the function is evaluated at all values x_0.

For discrete random variables, the cumulative probability function is sometimes called the *cumulative mass function*. It can be seen from the definition that as x_0 increases, the cumulative probability function will change values only at those points x_0 that can be taken by the random variable with positive probability. Its evaluation at these points can be carried out in terms of the probability function.

DERIVED RELATIONSHIP BETWEEN PROBABILITY FUNCTION AND CUMULATIVE PROBABILITY FUNCTION

Let X be a random variable with probability function $P(x)$ and cumulative probability function $F(x_0)$. Then we can show that

$$F(x_0) = \sum_{x \leq x_0} P(x) \tag{5.3}$$

where the notation implies that summation is over all possible values x that are less than or equal to x_0.

The result in Equation 5.3 follows since the event "$X \leq x_0$" is the union of the mutually exclusive events "$X = x$" for every x less than or equal to x_0. The probability of the union is then the sum of these individual event probabilities.

DERIVED PROPERTIES OF CUMULATIVE PROBABILITY FUNCTIONS FOR DISCRETE RANDOM VARIABLES

Let X be a discrete random variable with cumulative probability function $F(x_0)$. Then we can show that

i. $0 \leq F(x_0) \leq 1$ for every number x_0
ii. If x_0 and x_1 are two numbers with $x_0 < x_1$, then $F(x_0) \leq F(x_1)$

Property (i) simply states that a probability cannot be less than 0 or greater than 1. Property (ii) implies that the probability that a random variable does not exceed some number cannot be more than the probability that it does not exceed any larger number.

EXAMPLE 5.2

AUTOMOBILE SALES (COMPUTE PROBABILITIES)

TABLE 5.1
Probability Distribution Function for Automobile Sales

x	P(x)	F(x)
0	0.15	0.15
1	0.30	0.45
2	0.20	0.65
3	0.20	0.85
4	0.10	0.95
5	0.05	1.00

Stetson Motors, Inc. is a car dealer in a small Midwestern town. Based on an analysis of their sales history they know that on any single day the number of Vertigo A cars sold can vary from 0 to 5. How can the probability distribution function shown in Table 5.1 be used for inventory planning?

SOLUTION

The random variable, X, takes on the values, x, indicated in the first column, and the probability function, $P(x)$, is defined in the second column. The third column contains the cumulative distribution, $F(x)$. This model could be used for planning the inventory of cars. For example, if there are only four cars in stock, Stetson Motors could satisfy customers' need for a car 95% of the time. But if only two cars are in stock, then 35% $[(1-0.65) \times 100]$ of the customers would not have their needs satisfied.

EXERCISES

5.5 Let the random variable represent the number of times that you will miss class this semester. Prepare a table that shows the probability function and the cumulative probability function.

5.6 The number of computers sold per day in Dan's Computer Works is defined by the following probability distribution.

x	0	1	2	3	4	5	6
P(x)	.05	.10	.20	.20	.20	.15	.10

(a) $P(3 \le x < 6) = ?$
(b) $P(x > 3) = ?$
(c) $P(x \le 4) = ?$
(d) $P(2 < x \le 5) = ?$

5.7 American Travel Air has asked you to study flight delays during the week before Christmas at Midway Airport. The random variable x is the number of flights delayed per hour.

X	0	1	2	3	4	5	6	7	8	9
P(x)	.10	.08	.07	.15	.12	.08	.10	.12	.08	.10

(a) What is the cumulative probability distribution?
(b) What is the probability of five or more delayed flights?
(c) What is the probability of three through seven (inclusive) delayed flights?

5.3 DESCRIPTIVE MEASURES FOR DISCRETE RANDOM VARIABLES

The probability distribution contains all the information about the probability properties of a random variable, and graphical inspection of this distribution can certainly be valuable. However, it is frequently desirable to have some summary measures of the distribution's characteristics.

Expected Value of a Discrete Random Variable

In order to obtain a measure of the center of a probability distribution, we introduce here the notion of the *expectation* of a random variable. In Chapter 2 we found it convenient to compute the mean as a measure of central location. The *expected value* is the corresponding measure of central location for a random variable. Before introducing its definition, it is convenient to dismiss a superficially attractive alternative measure.

Consider the following example: A review of textbooks in a segment of the business area found that 81% of all pages of text were error-free, 17% of all pages contained one error, and the remaining 2% contained two errors. If we let the random variable X denote the number of errors on a page chosen at random from one of these books, we see that its possible values are 0, 1, and 2, with probability function

$$P(0) = 0.81 \qquad P(l) = 0.17 \qquad P(2) = 0.02$$

Now, one possible measure of the central location of a random variable might be the simple average of the values it can take. In our example, the possible numbers of errors on a page are 0, 1, and 2. Their average is, then, one error. However, a moment's reflection will convince the reader that this is an absurd measure of central location. In calculating this average, we have paid no attention to the fact that 81% of all pages contain no errors, while only 2% contain two errors. In order to obtain a sensible measure of central location, it is desirable to *weight* the various possible outcomes by the probabilities of their occurrence.

FIGURE 5.2
Probability Function for Number of Errors Per Page in Business Textbooks; Location of Population Mean, μ_x, for Example 5.3

EXPECTED VALUE

The **expected value**, $E(X)$, of a discrete random variable X is defined as

$$E(X) = \sum_x xP(x) \tag{5.4}$$

where the notation indicates that summation extends over all possible values x.
The expected value of a random variable is also called its **mean** and is denoted μ_x.

The definition of expected value can be motivated in terms of long-run relative frequencies. Suppose that a random experiment is repeated N times and that the event "$X = x$" occurs in N_x of these trials. The average of the values taken by the random variable over all N trials will then be the sum of xN_x/N over all possible values x. Now, as the number of replications N becomes infinitely large, the ratio N_x/N tends to the probability of the occurrence of the event "$X = x$"—that is, to $P(x)$. Hence, the quantity xN_x/N tends to $xP(x)$. Thus, the expected value can be viewed as the long-run average value that a random variable would take over a large number of trials. Recall that in Chapter 2, we used the word *mean* for the average of a set of numerical observations. The foregoing justifies the use of the same term for the expectation of a random variable.

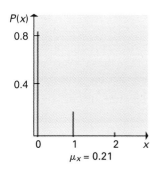

$P(x)$
0.8
0.4
0   1   2 x
$\mu_x = 0.21$

EXAMPLE 5.3

ERRORS IN TEXTBOOKS (COMPUTE EXPECTED VALUE)

Suppose that the probability function for the number of errors, X, on pages from business textbooks is

$$P(0) = 0.81 \quad P(1) = 0.17 \quad \text{and} \quad P(2) = 0.02.$$

Find the mean number of errors per page.

SOLUTION
We have

$$\mu_x = E(X) = \sum_x xP(x) = (0)(0.81) + (1)(0.17) + (2)(0.02) = 0.21$$

We thus conclude that over a large number of pages, we would expect to find an average of 0.21 error per page. Figure 5.2 above shows the probability function, with the location of the mean indicated.

The notion of expectation is not restricted to the random variable itself but can be applied to any function of the random variable. For example, a contractor may be uncertain of the time required to complete a contract. This uncertainty could be represented by a random variable whose possible values are the number of days elapsing from the beginning to the completion of work on the contract. However, the contractor's primary concern is not with the time taken but rather with the cost of fulfilling the contract. This cost will be a function of the time taken, so in determining expected cost, it is necessary to find the expectation of a function of the random variable "Time to completion."

EXPECTED VALUE: FUNCTIONS OF RANDOM VARIABLES

Let X be a discrete random variable with probability function $P(x)$ and let $g(X)$ be some function of X. Then the **expected value**, $E[g(X)]$, of that function is defined as

$$E[g(X)] = \sum_x g(x)P(x) \tag{5.5}$$

The definition of $E[g(X)]$ can be motivated in precisely the same way as the previous one. That is, the expectation can be thought of as the average value that $g(X)$ would take over a very large number of repeated trials.

Variance of a Discrete Random Variable

In Chapter 2, one useful measure of the spread of a set of numerical observations was found to be the *variance*, the average of the squared discrepancies of the observations from their mean. In the same way, this notion can be used to measure dispersion in the probability distribution of a random variable. In defining the variance of a random variable, a weighted average of the squares of its possible discrepancies about the mean is formed; the weight associated with $(x - \mu_x)^2$ is the probability that the random variable takes the value x. The variance can then be viewed as the average value that will be taken by the function $(X - \mu_x)^2$ over a very large number of repeated trials as defined by Equation 5.6.

VARIANCE AND STANDARD DEVIATION OF A DISCRETE RANDOM VARIABLE

Let X be a discrete random variable. The expectation of the squared discrepancies about the mean, $(X - \mu_X)^2$, is called the **variance**, denoted σ_X^2 and given by

$$\sigma_X^2 = E[(X - \mu_X)^2] = \sum_x (x - \mu_X)^2 P(x) \tag{5.6}$$

The **standard deviation**, σ_X, is the positive square root of the variance.

ASSUMPTION

The concept of variance can be very useful in comparing the dispersions of probability distributions. Consider, for example, viewing as a random variable the return over a year on an investment. Two investments may have the same expected returns but will still differ in an important way if the variances of these returns are substantially different. A higher variance indicates that returns substantially different from the mean are more likely than if the variance of returns is small. In this context, then, variance of the return can be associated with the concept of the risk of an investment—the higher the variance, the greater the risk.

Taking the square root of the variance to obtain the standard deviation yields a quantity in the original units of measurement, as noted in Chapter 2.

In some practical applications, an alternative but equivalent formula for the variance is preferable for computational purposes. That alternative formula is defined by Equation 5.7, which can be verified algebraically (See Appendix 5.1).

VARIANCE OF A DISCRETE RANDOM VARIABLE (ALTERNATIVE FORMULA)

The **variance** of a discrete random variable X can be expressed as

$$\sigma_X^2 = E(X^2) - \mu_X^2$$
$$= \sum_x x^2 P(x) - \mu_X^2 \qquad (5.7)$$

EXAMPLE 5.4

EXPECTED VALUE AND VARIANCE OF AUTOMOBILE SALES (COMPUTE EXPECTED VALUE AND VARIANCE)

In Example 5.2, Stetson Motors, Inc. determined that the number of Vertigo A cars sold daily could vary from 0 to 5, with the probabilities given in Table 5.1. Find the expected value and variance for this probability distribution.

SOLUTION

Using Equation 5.4, the expected value is

$$\mu_X = E(X) = \sum_x xP(x) = 0(0.15) + 1(0.30) + \cdots + 5(0.05) = 1.95$$

Using Equation 5.6, the variance is

$$\sigma_X^2 = (0 - 1.95)^2(0.15) + (1 - 1.95)^2(0.3) + \cdots + (5 - 1.95)^2(0.05) = 1.9475$$

For more complex probability distributions, you might want to use Excel for these computations. Figure 5.3 and Figure 5.4 illustrate how to obtain the expected value and variance for the distribution in Table 5.1.

FIGURE 5.3
Expected Value for the Discrete Random Variable in Table 5.1 Obtained Using Microsoft Excel 97

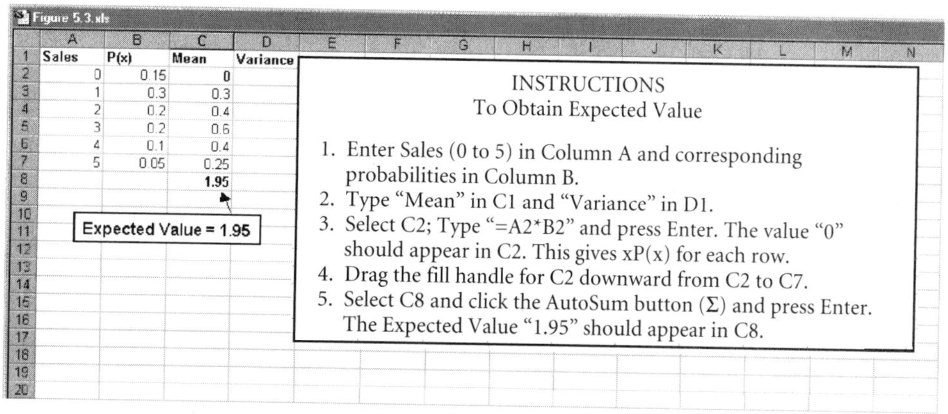

INSTRUCTIONS
To Obtain Expected Value

1. Enter Sales (0 to 5) in Column A and corresponding probabilities in Column B.
2. Type "Mean" in C1 and "Variance" in D1.
3. Select C2; Type "=A2*B2" and press Enter. The value "0" should appear in C2. This gives xP(x) for each row.
4. Drag the fill handle for C2 downward from C2 to C7.
5. Select C8 and click the AutoSum button (Σ) and press Enter. The Expected Value "1.95" should appear in C8.

FIGURE 5.4
Variance for Discrete
Random Variable in Table 5.1
Obtained Using Microsoft
Excel 97

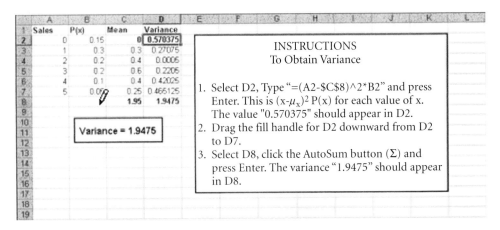

TABLE 5.2
Probability Distribution
Function for Automobile
Sales Revised

SALES	P(X)
0	0.3
1	0.2
2	0.1
3	0.05
4	0.15
5	0.2

Suppose that the Probability Distribution Function (PDF) in Table 5.1 is changed to reflect a higher probability of both low and high sales. The new probabilities are in Table 5.2 Figure 5.5 indicates the change in mean and variance.

COMMENTS

- In Table 5.2 there is a higher probability of 0 sales (0.30 rather than 0.15 in Table 5.1). Also there is a higher probability of selling all 5 cars (0.20 rather than 0.05 from Table 5.1).
- The variance should increase because the probability of extreme values 0 and increases.

FIGURE 5.5
Comparison of Means and
Variances Obtained Using
Microsoft Excel 97

	Table 5.1					Table 5.2		
Sales	P(x)	Mean	Variance		Sales	P(x)	Mean	Variance
0	0.15	0	0.570375		0	0.3	0	1.38675
1	0.3	0.3	0.27075		1	0.2	0.2	0.2645
2	0.2	0.4	0.0005		2	0.1	0.2	0.00225
3	0.2	0.6	0.2205		3	0.05	0.15	0.036125
4	0.1	0.4	0.42025		4	0.15	0.6	0.513375
5	0.05	0.25	0.465125		5	0.2	1	1.6245
		1.95	1.9475				2.15	3.8275

COMMENTS			
	Table 5.1	Table 5.2	Statement
Expected Value	1.95	2.15	A modest change in the means
Variance	1.9475	3.8275	Larger change in the variances

Since the variance uses the squared deviations from the mean, extreme values of the random variable have a greater effect than the values closer to the mean.

Sample Observations of a Random Variable

Now that we have developed the basic definitions and properties of random variables and probability distributions, let us consider the behavior of a random variable as we obtain sample observations from the probability distribution. We can study the behavior by making use of the capability of Minitab or some other statistical package to draw random samples from a discrete probability distribution. Figure 5.6 provides the instructions for obtaining random samples from a probability distribution. We will use this procedure to obtain random samples of different sizes and discuss the outcome. However, you can also use this procedure to obtain your own random sample from any discrete probability distribution.

Random samples can be obtained by following the steps in Figure 5.6. First we define the sample space in column C1 of the spreadsheet. We have assigned the variable name X to these values. In column C1 we have three 1s, four 2s, and three 3s. This corresponds to a discrete probability distribution defined as, $P(1) = 0.3$, $P(2) = 0.4$, and $P(3) = 0.3$. Then we use the command sequence,

```
CALC > RANDOM DATA > SAMPLE FROM COLUMNS
```

to bring up the indicated screen. Following the sequence we requested a random sample of size $n = 20$ to be stored in a variable named "Sample20." Note that we selected "Sample with replacement" to indicate that we are sampling from an infinite population.

FIGURE 5.6
Obtaining Sample Observations of a Random Variable Using Minitab

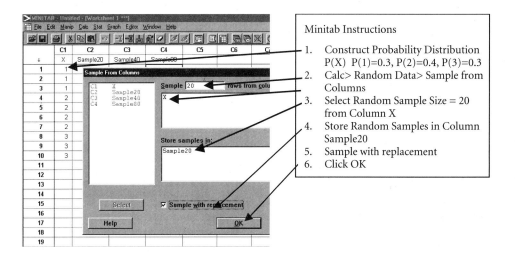

Minitab Instructions

1. Construct Probability Distribution P(X) P(1)=0.3, P(2)=0.4, P(3)=0.3
2. Calc> Random Data> Sample from Columns
3. Select Random Sample Size = 20 from Column X
4. Store Random Samples in Column Sample20
5. Sample with replacement
6. Click OK

INTERPRETATION

Figure 5.7 presents a description of the random sample obtained using the procedure in Figure 5.6. In addition we selected additional samples of size $n = 40$, $n = 80$, and $n = 1000$ for comparison. We have described each sample by using a Histogram and computing the sample mean and standard deviation. For comparison we have the mean and standard deviation of the actual probability distribution defined as variable X. Note that the population standard deviation is actually 0.775 instead of the reported sample standard deviation shown as 0.816. (From Chapter 2 we recall that the population standard deviation is computed by dividing by N and the sample standard deviation uses $n - 1$.) Examining Figure 5.7 we note that as the sample size becomes larger the histogram percentages approach the actual probabilities in the probability distribution. In addition the sample means become closer to the population mean of 2.0. If we drew a second set of samples of the same size we would find slightly different patterns in the histogram. The probability model defined by a random variable and its probability distribution function indicates the comparative frequencies of observations for all possible sample draws from a population. Larger samples will more closely approximate the probability distribution function, but in general the sample will not exactly duplicate the distribution function and each sample will have a dif-

FIGURE 5.7
Descriptions of Random
Samples from a Discrete
Probability Distribution

Descriptive Statistics: X, Sample20, Sample40, Sample80, Sample1000

Variable	N	Mean	Median	TrMean	StDev	SE Mean
X	10	2.000	2.000	2.000	0.816	0.258
Sample20	20	2.100	2.000	2.111	0.641	0.143
Sample40	40	2.025	2.000	2.028	0.800	0.127
Sample80	80	1.9875	2.0000	1.9861	0.8190	0.0916
Sample10	1000	2.0270	2.0000	2.0300	0.7752	0.0245

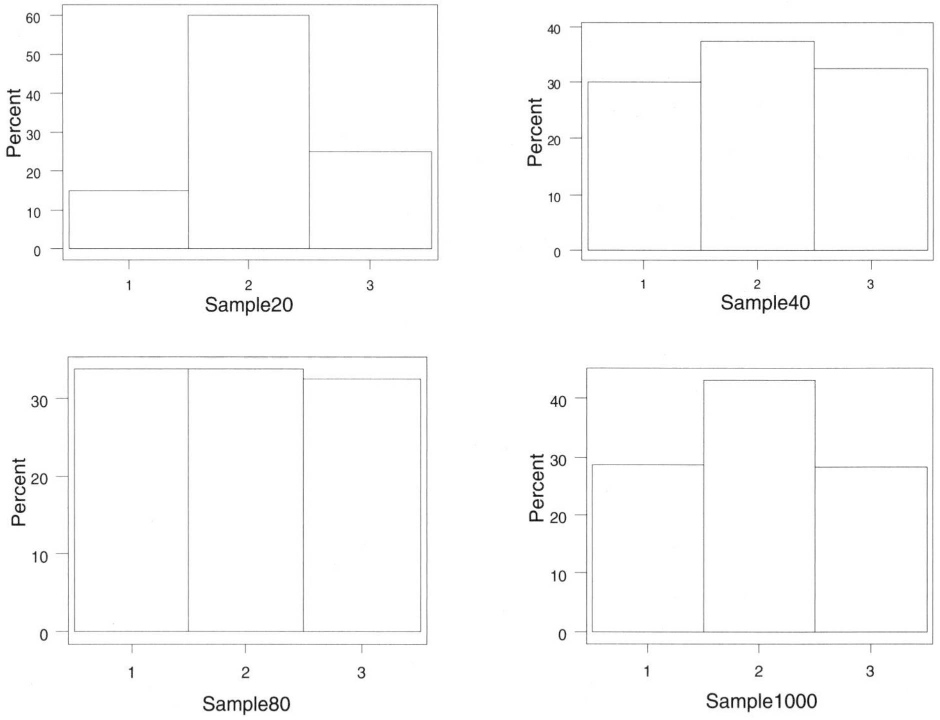

ferent frequency for the random variable values. You can obtain a better appreciation for this variability by actually running the procedure in Figure 5.6 a number of times with different sample sizes. In that way you can obtain valuable experience with random samples. We will examine this idea more completely in our discussion of Sampling Distributions in Chapter 7.

Mean and Variance of Linear Functions of a Random Variable

The expectation of a function of a random variable X is defined by Equation 5.5. In this section we develop the expected value and variance for linear functions of a random variable. First, consider the linear function $a + bX$, where a and b are constant fixed numbers. Let X be a random variable that takes the value x with probability $P(x)$ and consider a new random variable Y, defined by

$$Y = a + bX$$

When the random variable X takes the specific value x, Y must take the value $a + bx$. We frequently require the mean and variance of such variables. The mean, variance and standard deviation for a linear function of a random variable are derived in the Chapter Appendix. The results are summarized in Equations 5.8 and 5.9.

SUMMARY OF PROPERTIES FOR LINEAR FUNCTION OF A RANDOM VARIABLE

Let X be a random variable with mean, μ_X, and variance σ_X^2; and let a and b be any constant fixed numbers. Define the random variable $Y = a + bX$. Then, the **mean and variance of Y** are

$$\mu_Y = E(a + bX) = a + b\mu_X \tag{5.8}$$

and

$$\sigma_Y^2 = \text{Var}(a + bX) = b^2\sigma_X^2 \tag{5.9}$$

so that the **standard deviation of Z** is

$$\sigma_Y = |b|\sigma_X \tag{5.10}$$

EXAMPLE 5.5

TOTAL PROJECT COST (COMPUTATIONS FOR FUNCTIONS OF RANDOM VARIABLES)

A contractor is interested in the total cost of a project on which he intends to bid. He estimates that materials will cost $25,000 and that his labor will be $900 per day. If the project takes X days to complete, the total labor cost will be $900X$ dollars, and the total cost of the project (in dollars) will be:

$$C = 25,000 + 900X$$

The contractor forms subjective probabilities (Table 5.3) of likely completion times for the project.

(a) Find the mean and variance for completion time X.
(b) Find the mean, variance, and standard deviation for total cost C.

TABLE 5.3
Probability Distribution for Completion Times

Completion Time X (Days)	10	11	12	13	14
Probability	0.1	0.3	0.3	0.2	0.1

SOLUTION

(a) The mean and variance for completion time X can be found using Equations 5.4 and 5.6.

$$\mu_X = E(X) = \sum_x xP(x)$$
$$= (10)(0.1) + (11)(0.3) + (12)(0.3) + (13)(0.2) + (14)(0.1) = 11.9 \text{ days}$$

and

$$\sigma_X^2 = E[(X - \mu_X)^2] = \sum_x (x - \mu_X)^2 P(x)$$
$$= (10 - 11.9)^2(0.1) + (11 - 11.9)^2(0.3) + \cdots + (14 - 11.9)^2(0.1) = 1.29$$

(b) The mean, variance, and standard deviation of total cost C is obtained using Equations 5.8, 5.9 and 5.10.
The mean is:

$$\mu_C = E(25,000 + 900X) = (25,000 + 900\mu_X)$$
$$= 25,000 + (900)(11.9) = \$35,710$$

the variance is:

$$\sigma_C^2 = \text{Var}(25{,}000 + 900X) = (900)^2\,\sigma_X^2$$
$$= (810{,}000)(1.29) = 1{,}044{,}900$$

the standard deviation is:

$$\sigma_C = \sqrt{\sigma_C^2} = \$1{,}022.20$$

Three special examples of the linear function $W = a + bX$ are important. The first example considers a constant function, $W = a$, for any constant a. In this situation, the slope $b = 0$. In the second example, $a = 0$, giving $W = bX$. The expected value and the variance for these functions are defined by Equations 5.11 and 5.12. The third example is significant in later chapters. The mean and variance of this special linear function are defined by Equations 5.13 and 5.14.

SUMMARY RESULTS FOR THE MEAN AND VARIANCE OF SPECIAL LINEAR FUNCTIONS

(a) Let $b = 0$ in the linear function, $W = a + bX$. Then $W = a$ (for any constant a).

$$E(a) = a \quad \text{and} \quad \text{Var}(a) = 0 \tag{5.11}$$

If a random variable always takes the value a, it will have a mean a and a variance 0.

(b) Let $a = 0$ in the linear function, $W = a + bX$. Then $W = bX$.

$$E(bX) = b\mu_X \quad \text{and} \quad \text{Var}(bX) = b^2\sigma_X^2 \tag{5.12}$$

THE MEAN AND VARIANCE OF $Z = \dfrac{X - \mu_X}{\sigma_X}$

Let $a = -\mu_X/\sigma_X$ and $b = 1/\sigma_X$ in the linear function $Z = a + bX$. Then,

$$Z = a + bX = \frac{X - \mu_X}{\sigma_X}$$

so that

$$E\left(\frac{X - \mu_X}{\sigma_X}\right) = -\frac{\mu_X}{\sigma_X} + \frac{1}{\sigma_X}\mu_X = 0 \tag{5.13}$$

and

$$\text{Var}\left(\frac{X - \mu_X}{\sigma_X}\right) = \frac{1}{\sigma_X^2}\sigma_X^2 = 1 \tag{5.14}$$

Thus, subtracting from a random variable its mean and dividing by its standard deviation yields a random variable with mean 0 and standard deviation 1.

EXERCISES

5.8 An automobile dealer calculates the proportion of new cars sold that have been returned various numbers of times for the correction of defects during the warranty period. The results are shown in the table.

Number of Returns	0	1	2	3	4
Proportion	.28	.36	.23	.09	.04

  (a) Draw the probability function.
  (b) Calculate and draw the cumulative probability function.
  (c) Find the mean of the number of returns of an automobile for corrections for defects during the warranty period.
  (d) Find the variance of the number of returns of an automobile for corrections for defects during the warranty period.
  (e) Use Microsoft Excel to verify your answers to parts (c) and (d).

5.9 A company specializes in installing and servicing central heating furnaces. In the prewinter period, service calls may result in an order for a new furnace. The table shows estimated probabilities for numbers of new furnace orders generated in this way in the last two weeks of September.

Number of Orders	0	1	2	3	4	5
Probability	.10	.14	.26	.28	.15	.07

  (a) Draw the probability function.
  (b) Calculate and draw the cumulative probability function.
  (c) Find the probability that at least three orders will be generated in this period.
  (d) Find the mean of the number of orders for new furnaces in this period of two weeks.
  (e) Find the standard deviation of the number of orders for new furnaces in this period of two weeks.
  (f) Use Microsoft Excel to verify your answers to parts (d) and (e).

5.10 A corporation produces packages of paper clips. The number of clips per package varies, as indicated in the accompanying table.

Number of Clips	47	48	49	50	51	52	53
Proportion of Packages	.04	.13	.21	.29	.20	.10	.03

  (a) Draw the probability function.
  (b) Calculate and draw the cumulative probability function.
  (c) What is the probability that a randomly chosen package will contain between 49 and 51 clips (inclusive)?
  (d) Two packages are chosen at random. What is the probability that at least one of them contains at least 50 clips?
  (e) Use Microsoft Excel to find the mean and standard deviation of the number of paper clips per package.
  (f) The cost (in cents) of producing a package of clips is $16 + 2X$, where X is the number of clips in the package. The revenue from selling the package, however many clips it contains, is $1.50. If profit is defined as the difference between revenue and cost, find the mean and standard deviation of profit per package.

5.11 A municipal bus company has started operations in a new subdivision. Records were kept on the numbers of riders from this subdivision during the early-morning service. The accompanying table shows proportions over all weekdays.

Number of Riders	0	1	2	3	4	5	6	7
Proportion	.02	.12	.23	.31	.19	.08	.03	.02

  (a) Draw the probability function.
  (b) Calculate and draw the cumulative probability function.
  (c) What is the probability that on a randomly chosen weekday, there will be at least four riders from the subdivision on this service?
  (d) Two weekdays are chosen at random. What is the probability that on both if these days there will be fewer than three riders from the subdivision on this service?
  (e) Find the mean and standard deviation of the number of riders from this subdivision on this service on a weekday.
  (f) If the cost of a ride is 50 cents, find the mean and standard deviation of the total payments of riders from this subdivision on this service on a weekday.

5.12 (a) A very large shipment of parts contains 10% defectives. Two parts are chosen at random from the shipment and checked. Let the random variable X denote the number of defectives found. Find the probability function of this random variable.
  (b) A shipment of twenty parts contains two defectives. Two parts are chosen at random from the shipment and checked. Let the random variable Y denote the number of defectives found. Find the probability function of this random variable. Explain why your answer is different from that of part (a).
  (c) Find the mean and variance of the random variable X in part (a).

(d) Find the mean and variance of the random variable Y in part (b).

5.13 A student needs to know details of a class assignment that is due the next day and decides to call fellow class members for this information. She believes that, for any particular call, the probability of obtaining the necessary information is .40. She decides to continue calling class members until the information is obtained. Let the random variable X denote the number of calls needed to obtain the information.

(a) Find the probability function of X.

(b) Find the cumulative probability function of X.

(c) Find the probability that at least three calls are required.

5.14 A college basketball player who sinks 75% of his free throws comes to the line to shoot a "one and one" (if the first shot is successful, he is allowed a second shot, but no second shot is taken if the first is missed; one point is scored for each successful shot). Assume that the outcome of the second shot, if any, is independent of that of the first. Find the expected number of points resulting from the "one and one." Compare this with the expected number of points from a "two-shot foul," where a second shot is allowed irrespective of the outcome of the first.

5.15 A professor teaches a large class and has scheduled an examination for 7:00 P.M. in a different classroom. She estimates the probabilities in the table for the number of students who will call her at home, in the hour before the examination, asking in which classroom it will be held.

Number of Calls	0	1	2	3	4	5
Probability	.10	.15	.19	.26	.19	.11

Find the mean and standard deviation of the number of calls.

5.16 Students in a large accounting class were asked to rate the course by assigning a score of 1, 2, 3, 4 or 5 to the course. A higher score indicates that the students received greater value from the course. The accompanying table shows proportions of students rating the course in each category.

Rating	1	2	3	4	5
Proportion	.07	.19	.28	.30	.16

Find the mean and standard deviation of the ratings.

5.17 A store owner stocks an out-of-town newspaper, which is sometimes requested by a small number of customers. Each copy of this newspaper costs him 70 cents, and he sells them for 90 cents each. Any copies left over at the end of the day have no value and are destroyed. Any requests for copies that cannot be met because stocks have been exhausted are considered by the store owner as a loss of 5 cents in goodwill. The probability distribution of the number of requests for the newspaper in a day is shown in the accompanying table. If the store owner defines total daily profit as total revenue from newspaper sales, less total cost of newspapers ordered, less goodwill loss from unsatisfied demand, how many copies per day should he order to maximize expected profit?

Number of Requests	0	1	2	3	4	5
Probability	.12	.16	.18	.32	.14	.08

5.18 A factory manager is considering whether to replace a temperamental machine. A review of past records indicates the following probability distribution for the number of breakdowns of this machine in a week.

Number of Breakdowns	0	1	2	3	4
Probability	.10	.26	.42	.16	.06

(a) Find the mean and standard deviation of the number of weekly breakdowns.

(b) It is estimated that each breakdown costs the company $1,500 in lost output. Find the mean and standard deviation of the weekly cost to the company from breakdowns of this machine.

5.19 An investor is considering three strategies for a $1,000 investment. The probable returns are estimated as follows:

STRATEGY 1 A profit of $10,000 with probability .15 and a loss of $1,000 with probability .85

STRATEGY 2 A profit of $1,000 with probability .50, a profit of $500 with probability .30, and a loss of $500 with probability .20

STRATEGY 3 A certain profit of $400

Which strategy has the highest expected profit? Would you necessarily advise the investor to adopt this strategy?

5.4 BINOMIAL DISTRIBUTION

Suppose that a random experiment can give rise to just two possible mutually exclusive and collectively exhaustive outcomes, which for convenience we will label "success" and "failure." Let π denote the probability of success, so that the probability of failure is

$(1 - \pi)$. Now define the random variable X so that X takes the value 1 if the outcome of the experiment is success and 0 otherwise. The probability function of this random variable is then

$$P(0) = (1 - \pi) \qquad \text{and} \qquad P(1) = \pi$$

This distribution is known as the *Bernoulli distribution*. Its mean and variance can be found by direct application of the equations in Section 5.3.

DEVIATION OF THE MEAN AND VARIANCE OF A BERNOULLI RANDOM VARIABLE

The **mean** is:

$$\mu_X = E(X) = \sum_X xP(x) = (0)(1 - \pi) + (1)\pi = \pi \qquad (5.15)$$

and the **variance** is:

$$\sigma_X^2 = E[(X - \mu_X)^2] = \sum_X (x - \mu_X)^2 P(x) \qquad (5.16)$$

$$= (0 - \pi)^2(1 - \pi) + (1 - \pi)^2\pi = \pi(1 - \pi)$$

EXAMPLE 5.6

CONTRACT SALE (COMPUTE BERNOULLI MEAN AND VARIANCE)

Shirley Ferguson, an insurance broker, believes that for a particular contact, the probability of making a sale is 0.4. If the random variable X is defined to take the value 1 if a sale is made and 0 otherwise, then X has a Bernoulli distribution with probability of success π equal to 0.4. Find the mean and the variance of the distribution.

SOLUTION

The probability function of X is $P(0) = 0.6$ and $P(1) = 0.4$. The mean of the distribution is $\pi = 0.40$ and the variance is $\sigma_X^2 = \pi(1 - \pi) = (0.4)(0.6) = 0.24$.

An important generalization of the Bernoulli distribution concerns the case where a random experiment, with two possible outcomes, is repeated several times and the repetitions are independent. Suppose again that the probability of a success resulting in a single trial is π and that n independent trials are carried out, so that the result of any one trial has no influence on the outcome of any other. The number of successes X resulting from these n trials could be any whole number from 0 to n, and we are interested in the probability of obtaining exactly $X = x$ successes in n trials.

We develop the result in two stages. First, observe that the n trials will result in a sequence of n outcomes, each of which must be either success (S) or failure (F). One sequence with x successes and

$(n - x)$ failures is: S, S, ... , S   F, F, ... , F
                           (x times)   ($n - x$) times

In words, the first x trials result in success, while the remainder result in failure. Now, the probability of success in a single trial is π, and the probability of failure is $(1 - \pi)$. Since the n trials are independent of one another, the probability of any particular sequence of outcomes is, by the multiplication rule of probabilities (Chapter 4), equal to the product of the probabilities for the individual outcomes. Thus, the probability of observing the specific sequence of outcomes just described is:

$$[\pi \times \pi \times \cdots \times \pi] \quad \times \quad [(1-\pi) \times (1-\pi) \times \cdots \times (1-\pi)] = \pi^x(1-\pi)^{(n-x)}$$
$$(x \text{ times}) \qquad\qquad\qquad (n - x) \text{ times}$$

This line of argument establishes that the probability of observing *any specific sequence* involving x successes and $(n - x)$ failures is $\pi^x(1 - \pi)^{(n-x)}$. For example, suppose we have five independent trials each with probability of success $\pi = 0.6$ and we are interested in the probability of exactly three successes. Using + to designate a success and 0 to indicate a nonsuccess, we could designate possible desired outcomes such as

$$+ + + 0\, 0 \qquad \text{or} \qquad + 0 + 0 +$$

The probability of either of these specific outcomes would be $(0.6)^3(0.4)^2 = 0.03456$.

Our original interest concerned the determination not of the probability of occurrence of a particular sequence but of the probability of precisely x successes, regardless of the order of the outcomes. There are several sequences in which x successes could be arranged among $(n - x)$ failures. In fact, the number of such possibilities is just the number of combinations of x objects chosen from n, since we can select any x locations from a total of n in which to place the successes and the total number of successes can be computed using Equation 5.17. Returning to our example of three successes in five trials ($\pi = 0.6$) we see that the number of different sequences with three successes would be

$$C_3^5 = \frac{5!}{3!(5-3)!} = 10$$

The probability of three successes in five independent Bernouli trials is thus ten times the probability of each of the sequences that have three successes and thus

$$P(X = 3) = (10)(0.03456) = 0.3456$$

Next we will generalize this result for any combination of n and x.

NUMBER OF SEQUENCES WITH X SUCCESSES IN N TRIALS
The **number of sequences with x successes in n independent trials** is:

$$C_x^n = \frac{n!}{x!\,(n-x)!} \tag{5.17}$$

where $n! = n \times (n - 1) \times (n - 2) \times \cdots \times 1$ and $0! = 1$.
   These C_x^n sequences are mutually exclusive, since no two of them can occur at the same time. This result was developed in the Chapter 4 Appendix.

We have now shown that the event "x successes result from n trials" can occur in C_x^n mutually exclusive ways, each with probability $\pi^x(1 - \pi)^{(n-x)}$. Therefore, by the addition rule of probabilities (Chapter 4), the probability required is the sum of these C_x^n individual probabilities. The result is given by Equation 5.18.

THE BINOMIAL DISTRIBUTION

Suppose that a random experiment can result in two possible mutually exclusive and collectively exhaustive outcomes, "success" and "failure," and that π is the probability of a success resulting in a single trial. If n independent trials are carried out, the distribution of the number of successes "x" resulting is called the **binomial distribution**. Its probability distribution function for the binomial random variable $X = x$ is:

$$P(x \text{ successes in } n \text{ independent trials}) = P(x) = \frac{n!}{x!\,(n-x)!}\,\pi^x (1-\pi)^{(n-x)} \quad \text{for} \quad x = 0, 1, 2, \ldots, n$$

(5.18)

The mean and variance are derived in Appendix 5.1, and the results are given by Equations 5.19 and 5.20.

DERIVED MEAN AND VARIANCE OF A BINOMIAL PROBABILITY DISTRIBUTION

Let X be the number of successes in n independent trials, each with probability of success π. Then X follows a binomial distribution with **mean**,

$$\mu_X = E(X) = n\pi$$

(5.19)

and **variance**,

$$\sigma_X^2 = E[(X - \mu_X)^2] = n\pi(1-\pi)$$

(5.20)

Binominal Application

The Binomial distribution is widely used in business and economic applications involving the probability of discrete occurrences. Before using the binomial we must carefully analyze the specific situation to determine if:

1. The application involves several trials each of which has only two outcomes: yes or no, on or off, success or failure.
2. The probability of the outcome is the same for each trial.
3. The probability of the outcome on one trial does not affect the probability on other trials.

In the following examples we will provide typical applications. Discuss the sequence assumption and possible problems in this example.

Binomial distribution probabilities can be obtained in a variety of ways. We illustrate how you can obtain binomial probabilities using:

1. Equation 5.18 (good for small values of n); see Example 5.7
2. Tables in the Appendix (good for selected n and π); see Example 5.8
3. Microsoft Excel; see Example 5.9
4. Minitab; see Example 5.10

EXAMPLE 5.7

MULTIPLE CONTRACT SALES (BINOMIAL CALCULATIONS)

Suppose that the insurance broker, Shirley Ferguson, in Example 5.6 has five contracts, and she believes that for each contract, the probability of making a sale is 0.40. Use Equation 5.18 to find:

(a) The probability that she makes at most one sale.

(b) The probability that she makes between two and four sales (inclusive).

(c) Graph the probability distribution function.

SOLUTION

(a) $P(\text{at most one sale}) = P(X \leq 1) = P(X = 0) + P(X = 1) = 0.078 + 0.259 = 0.337$ since

$$P(\text{no sales}) = P(0) = \frac{5!}{0!5!}(0.4)^0(0.6)^5 = (0.6)^5 = 0.078$$

$$P(1 \text{ sales}) = P(1) = \frac{5!}{1!4!}(0.4)^1(0.6)^4 = 5(0.4)(0.6)^4 = 0.259$$

(b) $P(2 \leq X \leq 4) = P(2) + P(3) + P(4) = 0.346 + 0.230 + 0.077 = 0.653$ since

$$P(2) = \frac{5!}{2!3!}(0.4)^2(0.6)^3 = 10(0.4)^2(0.6)^3 = 0.346$$

$$P(3) = \frac{5!}{3!2!}(0.4)^0(0.6)^2 = 10(0.4)^3(0.6)^2 = 0.230$$

$$P(4) = \frac{5!}{4!1!}(0.4)^4(0.6)^1 = 5(0.4)^4(0.6)^1 = 0.077$$

(c) The probability distribution function (PDF) is in Figure 5.8.

FIGURE 5.8
Graph of Binomial
Probability Function for
Example 5.7 ($n = 5$, $\pi = 0.4$)

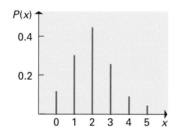

Comments
- This shape is typical for binomial probabilities when π is neither very large nor very small.
- At the extremes (0 or 5 sales), the probabilities are quite small.

Unless the number of trials n is very small, the calculations of binomial probabilities is likely to be extremely cumbersome. Binomial probabilities can also be obtained from tables in the Appendix.

EXAMPLE 5.8

COLLEGE ADMISSIONS (SOLVING A BINOMIAL USING TABLES)

Early in August an undergraduate college discovers that it can accommodate a few extra students. Enrolling those additional students would provide a substantial increase in revenue without increasing the operating costs of the college; that is, no new classes would have to be added. From past experience, the college knows that 40% of those students admitted will actually enroll.

(a) What is the probability that at most six students will enroll if the college offers admission to ten more students?

(b) What is the probability that more than 12 will actually enroll if admission is offered to 20 students?

(c) If 70% of those students admitted actually enroll, what is the probability that at least 12 out of 15 students will actually enroll?

SOLUTION

(a) This probability can be obtained using the cumulative binomial probability distribution from Table 2 in the Appendix. The probability of at most 6 students enrolling if $n = 10$ and $\pi = 0.40$ is

$$P(X \leq 6 \,|\, n = 10, \pi = 0.40) = 0.945$$

(b) $P(X > 12 \mid n = 20, \pi = 0.40) = 1 - P(X \le 12) = 1 - 0.979 = 0.021$

(c)   The probability that at least 12 out of 15 students enroll is the same as the probability that at most 3 out of 15 students do not enroll (the probability of a student not enrolling is $1 - 0.70 = 0.30$).

$$P(X \ge 12 \mid n = 15, \pi = 0.70) = P(X \le 3 \mid n = 15, \pi = 0.30) = 0.297$$

Both Microsoft Excel and Minitab can be used to solve binomial problems.

EXAMPLE 5.9

INSURANCE CLAIMS PROCESSING SYSTEM (COMPUTE BINOMIAL PROBABILITIES)

Suppose that a new computerized claims processing system has been installed by a major health insurance company. Only 40% of the claims require work by a human claims processor when this system is used. On a particular day 100 claims arrived for processing. Assume that the number of claims requiring work by a human follows a binomial distribution. What is the probability that:

(a)   there are between 37 and 43 (inclusive) claims that require work by a human?

(b)   there are at most 38 claims that need the attention of a human?

(c)   there are more than 42 claims that require work by a human?

SOLUTION

To solve these problems without a computer would be very tedious. Open a new Excel spreadsheet and follow these steps to get to the Binomial Probability Distribution dialog box in Figure 5.9:

    PHStat > PROBABILITY & PROB. DISTRIBUTION > BINOMIAL . . .

Now follow the Instruction Box to enter data.

FIGURE 5.9
Binomial Dialog Box in
Microsoft Excel PHStat

Binomial Probability Distribution	PHStat Instructions
Data Sample Size: `100` Probability of Success: `0.4` Outcomes From: `36` To: `43` OK Cancel **Output Options** Output Title: `Figure 5.7` ☑ Cumulative Probabilities ☐ Histogram	1. Enter the sample size "100", the probability of success "0.4" and the outcomes "36" T and "40" in the Data edit boxes. 2. Select "Cumulative Probabilities" under the Output Option. 3. Click OK.

Notice that we entered 36 to 43, rather than 37 to 43. You will see the reason for this in the solution to part (a). An Output Title is optional. By selecting the "Cumulative Probabilities" under the Output Options, you will get the results in Figure 5.10 (notice all the columns that are included).

(a) $P(37 \le X \le 43) = P(37) + P(38) + P(39) + P(40) + P(41) + P(42) + P(43)$
$$= 0.068199 + 0.075378 + 0.079888 + \cdots + 0.066729$$
$$= 0.524858$$

FIGURE 5.10
Binomial Probabilities,
$n =100$, $\pi = 0.40$, Microsoft
Excel PHStat

3	**Sample size**	100				
4	**Probability of success**	0.4				
5	**Mean**	40				
6	**Variance**	24				
7	**Standard deviation**	4.899				
8						
9	**Binomial Probabilities Table**					
10		**X**	**P(X)**	**P(<=X)**	**P(<X)**	**P(>X)**	**P(>=X)**
11		36	0.059141	0.2386107	0.179469	0.76139	0.820531
12		37	0.068199	0.3068098	0.238611	0.69319	0.761389
13		38	0.075378	0.3821877	0.30681	0.61781	0.69319
14		39	0.079888	0.4620753	0.382188	0.53792	0.617812
15		40	0.081219	0.5432945	0.462075	0.45671	0.537925
16		41	0.079238	0.6225327	0.543294	0.37747	0.456706
17		42	0.074207	0.6967399	0.622533	0.30326	0.377467
18		43	0.066729	0.7634688	0.69674	0.23653	0.30326
19							

Alternatively,

$$P(37 \leq X \leq 43) = P(X \leq 43) - P(X \leq 36)$$
$$= 0.7634688 - 0.2386107$$
$$= 0.5248581$$

(b) The probability that there are at most 38 claims that need the attention of a human is:

$$P(X \leq 38) = 0.3821877$$

Here, the answer is read directly from the second column from the left, labeled $P(<=X)$.

(c) The probability that there are more than 42 claims is:

$$P(X > 42) = 0.30326$$

where the answer is read directly from the second column from the right, labeled $P(>X)$. Alternatively, using the complement rule of probability,

$$P(X > 42) = 1 - P(X \leq 42) = 1 - 0.6967399 = 0.3032601.$$

EXAMPLE 5.10

**SALES OF AIRLINE SEATS
(COMPUTE BINOMIAL
PROBABILITIES)**

Have you ever agreed to give up your airplane ticket in return for a free ticket? Have you ever searched for the cheapest flight so that you could visit a special friend? The following example provides some of the analysis that leads to results such as overbooked flights or reduced fares on certain flights.

Suppose that you are in charge of marketing airline seats for a major carrier. Four days before the flight date you have 16 seats remaining on the plane. You know from past experience data that 80% of the people that purchase tickets in this time period will actually show up for the flight.

(a) If you sell 20 extra tickets, what is the probability that (a) you will overbook the flight or (b) have at least one empty seat?

(b) If you sell 18 extra tickets, what is the probability that you will (a) overbook the flight or (b) have at least one empty seat?

SOLUTION

(a) To find $P(X > 16)$ given $n = 20$ and $\pi = 0.80$, we use Minitab. With Minitab the user must select *either* Probability [such as $P(X = 16)$] *or* Cumulative Probability [$P(X = 16)$], but not both simultaneously. Open a new Minitab worksheet. To obtain the Minitab Dialog Box in Figure 5.11 follow the sequence of menu selections given by:

```
CALC > PROBABILITY DISTRIBUTIONS > BINOMIAL . . .
```

Now follow the Instruction Box to enter data.

FIGURE 5.11
Binomial Probability Dialog Box for $n = 20$, $\pi = 0.8$ Using Minitab

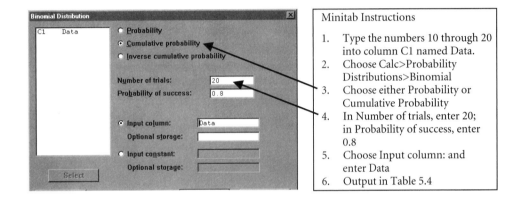

Minitab Instructions

1. Type the numbers 10 through 20 into column C1 named Data.
2. Choose Calc>Probability Distributions>Binomial
3. Choose either Probability or Cumulative Probability
4. In Number of trials, enter 20; in Probability of success, enter 0.8
5. Choose Input column: and enter Data
6. Output in Table 5.4

TABLE 5.4
Binomial Probabilities Obtained from Minitab for $n = 20$, $\pi = 0.8$

X	$P(X \le X)$
10.00	0.0026
11.00	0.0100
12.00	0.0321
13.00	0.0867
14.00	0.1958
15.00	0.3704
16.00	0.5886
17.00	0.7939
18.00	0.9308
19.00	0.9885
20.00	1.0000

COMMENTS
- To find the probability of overbooking:
  $P(X > 16) = 1 - P(X \le 16) = 1 - 0.589 = 0.411$
- If 20 tickets are sold, this also means that the probability of 15 or fewer people will arrive is:
  $P(X \le 15) = 0.37$. That is, there is a 37% chance that selling 20 tickets results in at least one empty seat!

(b) To find the chance that you overbook the flight by selling 18 tickets, follow the same steps as above. The chance that you overbook the flight will only be 10%, but the probability of at least one empty seat will increase to 72.9%!

The airline management then must evaluate the cost of overbooking (providing free tickets) versus the cost of empty seats that generate no revenue. Airlines analyze data to determine the number of seats that should be sold at reduced rates to maximize the ticket revenue from each flight. This analysis is complex, but it has its starting point in analyses such as the example presented here.

EXERCISES

5.20 A production manager knows that 5% of components produced by a particular manufacturing process have some defect. Six of these components, whose characteristics can be assumed to be independent of each other, were examined.
  (a) What is the probability that none of these components has a defect?
  (b) What is the probability that one of these components has a defect?
  (c) What is the probability that at least two of these components have a defect?

5.21 A politician believes that 25% of all macroeconomists in senior positions would strongly support a proposal he wishes to advance. Suppose that this belief is correct and that five senior macroeconomists are approached at random.
  (a) What is the probability that at least one of the five would strongly support the proposal?
  (b) What is the probability that a majority of the five would strongly support the proposal?

5.22 A public interest group hires students to solicit donations by telephone. After a brief training period, students make calls to potential donors and are paid on a commission basis. Experience indicates that early on, these students tend to have only modest success, and that 70% of them give up their jobs in their first two weeks of employment. The group hires six students, who can be viewed as a random sample.
  (a) What is the probability that at least two of the six will give up in the first two weeks?
  (b) What is the probability that at least two of the six will not give up in the first two weeks?

5.23 Suppose that the probability is .5 that the value of the U.S. dollar will rise against the Japanese yen over any given week, and that the outcome in one week is independent of that in any other week. What is the probability that the value of the U.S. Dollar will rise against the Japanese yen in a majority of weeks over a period of seven weeks?

5.24 A company installs new central heating furnaces and has found that for 15% of all installations a return visit is needed to make some modifications. Six installations were made in a particular week. Assume independence of outcomes for these installations.
  (a) What is the probability that a return visit was needed in all of these cases?
  (b) What is the probability that a return visit was needed in none of these cases?
  (c) What is the probability that a return visit was needed in more than one of these cases?

5.25 The Cubs are to play a series of five games in St. Louis against the Cardinals. For any one game, it is estimated that the probability of a Cubs win is .4. The outcomes of the five games are independent of one another.
  (a) What is the probability that the Cubs will win all five games?
  (b) What is the probability that the Cubs will win a majority of the five games?
  (c) If the Cubs win the first game, what is the probability that they will win a majority of the five games?
  (d) Before the series begins, what is the expected number of cubs' wins in these five games?
  (e) If the Cubs win the first game, what is the expected number of Cubs' wins in the five games?

5.26 A small commuter airline flies planes that can seat up to eight passengers. The airline has determined that the probability that a ticketed passenger will not show up for a flight is .2. For each flight, the airline sells tickets to the first ten people placing orders. The probability distribution for the number of tickets sold per flight is shown in the accompanying table. For what proportion of the airline's flights does the number of ticketed passengers showing up exceed the number of available seats? (Assume independence between number of tickets sold and the probability that a ticketed passenger will show up.)

Number of Tickets	6	7	8	9	10
Probability	.25	.35	.25	.10	.05

5.27 Following a touchdown, a college football coach has the option to elect to attempt a "2-point conversion"; that is, 2 additional points are scored if the attempt is successful, and none if it is unsuccessful. The coach believes that the probability is .4 that his team will be successful in any attempt, and that outcomes of different attempts are independent of each other. In a particular game, the team scored four touchdowns and 2-point conversion attempts were made each time.
  (a) What is the probability that at least two of these attempts were successful?
  (b) Find the mean and standard deviation of the total number of points resulting from these four attempts.

5.28 An automobile dealer mounts a new promotional campaign, in which it is promised that purchasers of new automobiles may, if dissatisfied for any reason, return them within two days of purchase and receive a full refund. It is estimated that the cost to the dealer of such a refund is $250. The dealer estimates that 15% of all purchasers will indeed return automobiles and obtain refunds. Suppose that fifty automobiles are purchased during the campaign period.
  (a) Find the mean and standard deviation of the num-

ber of these automobiles that will be returned for refunds.

(b) Find the mean and standard deviation of the total refund costs that will accrue as a result of these fifty purchases.

5.29 A family of mutual funds maintains a service that allows clients to switch money among accounts through a telephone call. It was estimated that 3.2% of callers either got a busy signal or were kept on hold so long that they hung up. Fund management assesses any failure of this sort as a $10 goodwill loss. Suppose that 2,000 calls were attempted over a particular period.

(a) Find the mean and standard deviation of the number of callers who either got a busy signal or hung up after being kept on hold.

(b) Find the mean and standard deviation of the total goodwill loss to the mutual fund company from these 2,000 calls.

5.30 We have seen that, for a binomial distribution with n trials, each with probability of success π, the mean is

$$\mu_X = E(X) = n\pi$$

Verify this result for the data of Example 5.7 by calculating the mean direct from

$$\mu_X = \sum xP(x)$$

Showing that, for the binomial distribution, the two formulas produce the same answer.

5.31 A campus finance officer finds that for all parking tickets issued, fines of 78% are paid. The fine is $2. In the most recent week, 620 parking tickets have been issued.

(a) Find the mean and standard deviation of the number of these tickets for which the fines will be paid.

(b) Find the mean and standard deviation of the amount of money that will be obtained from the payment of these fines.

5.32 A company receives a very large shipment of components. A random sample of sixteen of these components are checked, and the shipment is accepted if fewer than two of these components are defective. What is the probability of accepting a shipment containing:

(a) 5% defectives?

(b) 15% defectives?

(c) 25% defectives?

5.33 The following two acceptance rules are being considered for determining whether to take delivery of a large shipment of components:

(i) A random sample of ten components is checked, and the shipment is accepted only if none of them is defective.

(ii) A random sample of twenty components is checked, and the shipment is accepted only if not more than one of them is defective.

Which of these acceptance rules has the smaller probability of accepting a shipment containing 20% defectives?

5.34 A company receives large shipments of parts from two sources. Seventy percent of the shipments come from a supplier whose shipments typically contain 10% defectives, while the remainder are from a supplier whose shipments typically contain 20% defectives. A manager receives a shipment but does not know the source. A random sample of twenty items from this shipment is tested, and one of the parts is found to be defective. What is the probability that this shipment came from the more reliable supplier? [*Hint:* Use Bayes's theorem.]

5.5 HYPERGEOMETRIC DISTRIBUTION

In Section 5.4 we learned that the binomial distribution assumes that the items are drawn independently with the probability of selecting an item being constant. In many applied problems these assumptions can be met if a small sample is drawn from a large population. But here we will consider a situation where it is necessary to select 5 employees from a group of 15 equally qualified applicants—a small population. In the group of 15 there are 9 women and 6 men. Suppose that in the group of 5 selected employees 3 are men and 2 are women. What is the probability of selecting that particular group if the selections are made randomly without bias. In the initial group of 15 the probability of selecting a woman is 9/15. If a woman is not selected in the first draw then the probability of selecting a woman in the second draw is 9/14. Thus the probabilities change with each selection. We see that the assumptions for the binomial are not met and thus a different probability model must be selected. This probability distribution is the *Hypergeometric Probability Distribution*.

We can use the binomial distribution in situations that are defined as "sampling with replacement." If we replaced the selected item in the population then the probability of selecting that type of item would remain the same and the binomial assumptions would be met. In contrast, if we did not replace the items—"sampling without replacement"—the probabilities change with each selection and thus the appropriate probability model is the hypergeometric. If the population is large ($N > 10,000$) and the sample size is small (<1%) then the change in probability after each draw is very small. In those situations the binomial is a very good approximation and is typically used. The hypergeometric probability model is given in Equation 5.21.

HYPERGEOMETRIC DISTRIBUTION

Suppose that a random sample of n objects is chosen from a group of N objects, S of which are successes. The distribution of the number of successes X in the sample is called the **hypergeometric distribution**. Its probability function is:

$$P(x) = \frac{C_x^S C_{n-x}^{N-S}}{C_n^N} = \frac{\dfrac{S!}{x!(S-x)!} \times \dfrac{(N-S)!}{(n-x)!(N-S-n+x)!}}{\dfrac{N!}{n!(N-n)!}} \qquad (5.21)$$

where x can take integer values ranging from the larger of 0 and $[n - (N - S)]$ to the smaller of n and S.

The logic for the hypergeometric distribution was developed in Section 4.3 using the Classic definition of probability and the counting formulas for combinations. In Equation 5.21 the individual components are:

1. The number of possible ways that x successes can be selected for the sample out of S successes contained in the population.

$$C_x^S = \frac{S!}{x!(S-x)!}$$

2. The number of possible ways that $n - x$ non-successes can be selected from the population that contains $N - S$ non-successes.

$$C_{n-x}^{N-S} = \frac{(N-S)!}{(n-x)!(N-S-n+x)!}$$

3. And finally the total number of different samples of size n that can be obtained from a population of size N.

$$C_n^N = \frac{N!}{n!(N-n)!}$$

By combining these components together using the classical definition of probability we obtain the hypergeometric probability distribution.

<hr>

EXAMPLE 5.11

SHIPMENT OF ITEMS (COMPUTE HYPERGEOMETRIC PROBABILITY)

A company receives a shipment of twenty items. Because inspection of each individual item is expensive, it has a policy of checking a random sample of six items from such a shipment, accepting delivery if no more than one sampled item is defective. What is the probability that a shipment of five defective items will be accepted?

SOLUTION

If we identify "defective" with "success" in this example, the shipment contains $N = 20$ items, and $S = 5$ of which are successes. A sample of $n = 6$ items is selected. Then the number of successes X in the sample has a hypergeometric distribution with probability function:

$$P(x) = \frac{C_x^S C_{n-x}^S}{C_n^N} = \frac{C_x^5 C_{6-x}^{15}}{C_6^{20}} = \frac{\dfrac{5!}{x!(5-x)!} \times \dfrac{15!}{(6-x)!(9+x)!}}{\dfrac{20!}{6!14!}}$$

The shipment is accepted if the sample contains either zero or one success (defective), so that the probability of its acceptance is:

$$P(\text{Shipment accepted}) = P(0) + P(1)$$

The probability of no defectives in the sample is:

$$P(0) = \frac{\dfrac{5!}{0!5!} \times \dfrac{15!}{6!9!}}{\dfrac{20!}{6!14!}} = 0.129$$

The probability of one defective item in the sample is:

$$P(1) = \frac{\dfrac{5!}{1!4!} \times \dfrac{15!}{5!10!}}{\dfrac{20!}{6!14!}} = 0.387$$

Therefore, the probability that the shipment of twenty items containing five defectives is accepted using this procedure is $P(\text{Shipment accepted}) = P(0) + P(1) = 0.129 + 0.387 = 0.516$. This is a high error rate, which indicates a need for process improvement.

Hypergeometric problems are easily solved with PHStat. Figure 5.12 is the dialog box for a hypergeometric distribution.

FIGURE 5.12
Hypergeometric Dialog Box
Using PHStat

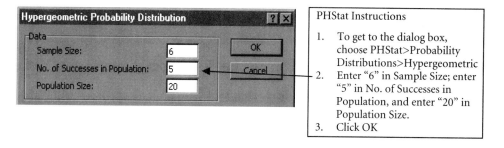

PHStat Instructions

1. To get to the dialog box, choose PHStat>Probability Distributions>Hypergeometric
2. Enter "6" in Sample Size; enter "5" in No. of Successes in Population, and enter "20" in Population Size.
3. Click OK

From the output in Figure 5.13, we can quickly and easily obtain the probability that the shipment will be accepted.

FIGURE 5.13
Hypergeometric Output for
Example 5. 11 Obtained
Using PHStat

Hypergeometric Probabilities		
Sample size	6	
No. of successes in population	5	
Population size	20	
Hypergeometric Probabilities Table		
	X	P(x)
	0	0.129
	1	0.387
	2	0.352
	3	0.117
	4	0.014
	5	4E-04

EXERCISES

5.35 A company receives a shipment of sixteen items. A random sample of four items is selected, and the shipment is rejected if any of these items proves to be defective.
  (a) What is the probability of accepting a shipment containing four defective items?
  (b) What is the probability of accepting a shipment containing one defective item?
  (c) What is the probability of rejecting a shipment containing one defective item?

5.36 A committee of eight members is to be formed from a group of eight men and eight women. If the choice of committee members is made randomly, what is the probability that precisely half of these members will be women?

5.37 A bond analyst was given a list of twelve corporate bonds. From that list, she selected three whose ratings she felt were in danger of being downgraded in the next year. In actuality, a total of four of the twelve bonds on the list had their ratings downgraded in the next year. Suppose that the analyst had simply chosen three bonds randomly from this list. What is the probability that at least two of the chosen bonds would be among those whose ratings were to be downgraded in the next year?

5.38 A bank executive is presented with loan applications from ten people. The profiles of the applicants are similar, except that five are minorities and five are nonminorities. In the end, the executive approved six of the applications. If these six approvals had been chosen at random from the ten applications, what is the probability that less than half the approvals would be of applications involving minorities?

5.6 THE POISSON PROBABILITY DISTRIBUTION

The Poisson probability distribution was first proposed by Simeon Poisson (1781–1840) in a book published in 1837. The number of applications began to increase early in the twentieth century, and the availability of the computer has brought about further applications in the twenty-first century. The Poisson probability distribution is an important discrete probability distribution for a number of applications, including:

1. The number of failures in a large computer system during a given day
2. The number of replacement orders for a part received by a firm in a given month
3. The number of ships arriving at a loading facility during a six-hour loading period
4. The number of delivery trucks to arrive at a central warehouse in an hour
5. The number of dents, scratches, or other defects in a large roll of sheet metal used to manufacture filters
6. The number of customers to arrive for flights during each 15-minute time interval from 3:00 P.M. to 6:00 P.M. on weekdays
7. The number of customers to arrive at a checkout aisle in your local grocery store during a particular time interval

Each of these random variables, characterized as the number of occurrences or successes of a certain event in a given continuous interval (such as time, surface area, or length), are represented by the Poisson probability distribution.

A Poisson probability distribution is modeled according to certain assumptions.

ASSUMPTIONS OF THE POISSON PROBABILITY DISTRIBUTION

Assume that an interval is divided into a very large number of subintervals so that the probability of the occurrence of an event in any subinterval is very small. The **assumptions of a Poisson probability distribution** are:

1. The probability of the occurrence of an event is constant for all subintervals.
2. There can be no more than one occurrence in each subinterval.
3. Occurrences are independent; that is, the number of occurrences in any nonoverlapping intervals is independent of one another.

The equation for computing Poisson probabilities can be derived directly from the binomial probability distribution by taking the mathematical limits as $\pi \to 0$ and $n \to \infty$. With this limit the parameter, $\lambda = n\pi$, is a constant that specifies the average number of occurrences (successes) for a particular time and/or space. The Poisson probability distribution function is given in Equation 5.22.

THE POISSON PROBABILITY DISTRIBUTION FUNCTION, MEAN AND VARIANCE

The random variable X is said to follow the **Poisson probability distribution** if it has the probability function:

$$P(x) = \frac{e^{-\lambda}\lambda^x}{x!}, \text{ for } x = 0, 1, 2... \tag{5.22}$$

where

$P(x) =$ the probability of x successes over a given time or space, given λ
λ = the expected number of successes per time or space unit; $\lambda > 0$.
$e \cong 2.71828$ (the base for natural logarithms)

The **mean and variance of the Poisson probability distribution** are:

$$\mu_x = E(X) = \lambda \qquad \text{and} \qquad \sigma_x^2 = E[(X - \mu_x)^2] = \lambda$$

The sum of Poisson random variables is also a Poisson random variable. Thus the sum of K Poisson random variables, each with mean λ, is a Poisson random variable with mean $K\lambda$.

EXAMPLE 5.12

SYSTEM COMPONENT FAILURE (COMPUTE POISSON PROBABILITIES)

Andrew Whittaker, computer center manager, reports that his computer system experienced three component failures during the past 100 days.

(a) What is the probability of no failures in a given day?
(b) What is the probability of one or more component failures on a given day?
(c) What is the probability of at least two failures in a three day period?

SOLUTION

A modern computer system has a very large number of components, each of which could fail and thus result in a computer system failure. To compute the probability of failures using the Poisson distribution, assume that each of the millions of components has the same very small probability of failure. Also, assume that the first failure does not affect the probability of a second failure (in some cases, these assumptions may not hold and more complex distributions would be used).

From past experience, the expected number of failures per day is 3/100 or $\lambda = 0.03$. To obtain the needed probabilities, we can use the Microsoft Excel PHStat.

```
PHStat > PROBABILITY DISTRIBUTION > POISSON > FOLLOW THE
DIALOG BOX
```

A partial table of the Poisson probabilities is given in Figure 5.14.

(a) P(no failures in a given day) $= P(X = 0 \mid \lambda = 0.03) = \dfrac{e^{-0.03}\lambda^0}{0!} = 0.970446$

(b) From the table in Figure 5.14, P(at least one component failure in a given day, assuming $\lambda = 0.03$) $= 0.029554$. The same answer is found using Equation 5.22:

$$P(X \geq 1) = 1 - P(X = 0)$$
$$= 1 - \left[\frac{e^{-\lambda}\lambda^x}{x!}\right] = 1 - \left[\frac{e^{-0.03}\lambda^0}{0!}\right]$$
$$= 1 - e^{-0.03} = 1 - 0.970446 = 0.029554$$

FIGURE 5.14
Partial Poisson Probabilities
for $\lambda = 0.03$ Obtained Using
Microsoft Excel PHStat

Poisson Probabilities Table

X	P(X)	P(<=X)	P(<X)	P(>X)	P(>=X)
0	0.970446	0.970446	0.000000	0.029554	1.000000
1	0.029113	0.999559	0.970446	0.000441	0.029554
2	0.000437	0.999996	0.999559	0.000004	0.000441
3	0.000004	1.000000	0.999996	0.000000	0.000004
4	0.000000	1.000000	1.000000	0.000000	0.000000

(c) P(at least 2 failures in a three-day period) $= P(X \geq 2 | \lambda = 0.09)$ where the average over a three-day period is $\lambda = 3(0.03) = 0.09$.

$$P(X \geq 2 \,|\, \lambda = 0.09) = 1 - P(X \leq 1) = 1 - \left[P(X = 0) + P(X = 1)\right] = 1 - [0.913931 + 0.082254]$$
$$= 0.996185$$

and thus,

$$P(X \geq 2 \,|\, \lambda = 0.09) = 1 - 0.996185 = 0.003815.$$

The Poisson distribution has been found to be particularly useful in *waiting line*, or *queuing*, problems. Examples include the number of customers to arrive at a checkout aisle in a grocery store, the number of delivery trucks to arrive at a central warehouse, the number of people to arrive for flights, the number of students waiting to purchase texts in the university bookstore, and so forth. In practice, it is often possible to represent arrival processes of this sort by a Poisson distribution.

EXAMPLE 5.13

CUSTOMERS AT A
PHOTOCOPYING MACHINE
(COMPUTE POISSON
PROBABILITY)

Customers arrive at a photocopying machine at an average rate of two every five minutes. We assume that these arrivals are independent, with a constant arrival rate, and this problem follows a Poisson model with X denoting the number of arriving customers in a five-minute period and mean $\lambda = 2$. Find the probability that more than two customers arrive in a five-minute period.

SOLUTION

Since the mean number of arrivals in five minutes is two we see that $\lambda = 2$. To find the probability that more than two customers arrive we will first compute the probability of at most two arrivals in a five-minute period, and then use the complement rule.

You can find these probabilities in the Appendix Table or by using a computer. Use PHStat or Minitab.

$$P(X = 0) = \frac{e^{-2} 2^0}{0!} = e^{-2} = 0.135335$$

$$P(X = 1) = \frac{e^{-2} 2^1}{1!} = 2e^{-2} = 0.27067$$

$$P(X = 2) = \frac{e^{-2} 2^2}{2!} = 2e^{-2} = 0.27067$$

Thus, the probability of more than two arrivals in a five-minute period is:

$$P(X > 2) = 1 - P(X \leq 2) = 1 - [0.135335 + 0.27067 + 0.27067] = 0.323325$$

Poisson Approximation to the Binomial Distribution

The computation of probabilities for a binomial distribution could be tedious if the number of trials n is large. Of course, such probabilities are easily obtained using PHStat, Minitab, or some other statistical software package. In this section we note that the Poisson distribution can be used to approximate the binomial probabilities when the number of trials n is large and at the same time the probability π is small (generally such that $\lambda = n\pi \leq 7$). Examples of situations that would satisfy these conditions include:

- An insurance company will hold a large number of life policies on individuals of any particular age, and the probability that a single policy will result in a claim during the year is very low. Here we have a binomial distribution with large n and small π.
- A company may have a large number of machines working on a process simultaneously. If the proability that any one of them will break down in a single day is small, the distribution of the number of daily breakdowns is binomial with large n and small π.

POISSON APPROXIMATION TO THE BINOMIAL DISTRIBUTION

Let X be the number of successes resulting from n independent trials, each with probability of success, π. The distribution of the number of successes X is binomial, with mean $n\pi$. If the number of trials n is large and $n\pi$ is of only moderate size (preferably $n\pi \leq 7$), this distribution can be **approximated by the Poisson distribution** with $\lambda = n\pi$. The probability function of the approximating distribution is then:

$$P(x) = \frac{e^{-n\pi}(n\pi)^x}{x!} \text{ for } x = 0, 1, 2, \ldots \tag{5.23}$$

EXAMPLE 5.14

PROBABILITY OF BANKRUPTCY (COMPUTE POISSON PROBABILITY)

An analyst predicted that 3.5% of all small corporations would file for bankruptcy in the coming year. For a random sample of 100 small corporations, estimate the probability that at least three will file for bankruptcy in the next year, assuming that the analyst's prediction is correct.

SOLUTION

The distribution of the number X of filings for bankruptcy is binomial with $n = 100$ and $\pi = 0.035$, so that the mean of the distribution is $\mu_x = n\pi = 3.5$. Using the Poisson distribution to approximate the probability of at least three bankruptcies, we find

$$P(X \geq 3) = 1 - P(X \leq 2)$$
$$P(0) = \frac{e^{-3.5}(3.5)^0}{0!} = e^{-3.5} = 0.030197$$
$$P(1) = \frac{e^{-3.5}(3.5)^1}{1!} = (3.5)(0.030197) = 0.1056895$$
$$P(2) = \frac{e^{-3.5}(3.5)^2}{2!} = (6.125)(0.030197) = 0.1849566$$

Thus, $P(X \leq 2) = P(0) + P(1) + P(2) = 0.030197 + 0.1056895 + 0.1849566 = 0.3208431$

$$P(X \geq 3) = 1 - 0.3208431 = 0.6791569$$

The binomial probability of $X \geq 3$, is

$$P(X \geq 3) = 0.684093$$

The Poisson probability is simply an estimate of the actual binomial probability.

EXERCISES

5.39 Customers arrive at a busy check-out counter at an average rate of three per minute. If the distribution of arrivals is Poisson, find the probability that in any given minute there will be two or fewer arrivals.

5.40 The number of accidents in a production facility has a Poisson distribution with mean 2.6 per month.
  (a) For a given month, what is the probability there will be fewer than two accidents?
  (b) For a given month, what is the probability there will be more than three accidents?

5.41 A professor receives, on average, 4.2 telephone calls from students the day before a final examination. If the distribution of calls is Poisson, what is the probability of receiving at least three of these calls on such a day?

5.42 Records indicate that on average, 3.2 breakdowns per day occur on an urban highway during the morning rush hour. Assume that the distribution is Poisson.
  (a) Find the probability that on any given day, there will be fewer than two breakdowns on this highway during the early morning rush hour.
  (b) Find the probability that on any given day, there will be more than four breakdowns on this highway during the early morning rush hour.

5.43 The Internal Revenue Service reported that 5.5% of all taxpayers filling out the 1040 short form make mistakes.

If 100 of these forms are chosen at random, what is the probability that fewer than three of them contain errors? Use the Poisson approximation to the binomial distribution.

5.44 A corporation has 250 personal computers. The probability that any one of them will require repair in a given week is .01. Find the probability that fewer than four of the personal computers will require repair in a particular week. Use the Poisson approximation to the binomial distribution.

5.45 An insurance company holds fraud insurance policies on 6,000 firms. In any given year, the probability that any single policy will result in a claim is .001. Find the probability that at least three claims are made in a given year. Use the Poisson approximation to the binomial distribution.

5.46 A state has a law requiring motorists to carry insurance. It was estimated that, despite this law, 7.5% of all motorists in the state are uninsured. A random sample of 60 motorists was taken. Use the Poisson approximation to the binomial distribution to estimate the probability that at least three of the motorists in this sample are uninsured. Also, indicate what calculations would be needed to find this probability exactly if the Poisson approximation was not used.

5.7 JOINTLY DISTRIBUTED DISCRETE RANDOM VARIABLES

Business and economic applications of statistics are often concerned about the relationships between variables. Products at different quality levels are priced at different price intervals. Age groups have different preferences for clothing, for automobiles, and for music. The percent returns on two different stocks will tend to be related. For example, the probability of higher returns for both may increase when the market is growing. Alternatively, when the return on one stock is growing the return on the other might be decreasing. When we work with probability models for problems involving relationships between variables it is important that the effect of these relationships are included in the probability model. For example, the probability distribution for purchasing one of the following automobiles, (1) red two-door compact, (2) blue minivan, (3) silver full-size sedan, would not be the same for women whose ages are in the 20s, 30s, and 50s. Thus it is important that probability models reflect the joint affect of variables on probabilities.

In Section 4.6 we discussed joint probabilities. We now consider the case where we wish to examine two or more, possibly related, discrete random variables. As for a single random variable, the probabilities for all possible outcomes can be summarized in a probability function, where we now need to define the probabilities that the random variables of interest simultaneously take specific values. Consider the following example involving the use of jointly distributed discrete random variables.

EXAMPLE 5.15

MARKET RESEARCH (COMPUTE JOINT PROBABILITIES)

Adrian Peterson, a marketing analyst, has been asked to develop a probability model for the relationship between the sale of luxury cookware and age group. This model will be important for developing a marketing campaign for a new line of chef-grade cookware. She believes that purchasing patterns for luxury cookware are different for different age groups.

SOLUTION

To represent the market Adrian proposes to use three age groups, 16 to 25, 26 to 45, 46 to 65, and two purchasing patterns, "buy" versus "not buy." Next, she collects a random sample of persons for the age range 16 to 65 and records their age group and desire to purchase. The results of this data collection is a joint probability distribution contained in Table 5.5.

TABLE 5.5
Joint Probability Distribution of Age Group (X) Versus Purchase Decision (Y)

	AGE, X			
DECISION, Y	**1 (16 TO 25)**	**2 (26 TO 45)**	**3 (46 TO 65)**	**$P(y)$**
1 (Buy)	0.10	0.20	0.10	0.40
2 (Not Buy)	0.25	0.25	0.10	0.60
$P(x)$	0.35	0.45	0.20	1.00

Table 5.5 thus provides a summary of the probability of purchase and age group that will provide a valuable resource for marketing analysis.

JOINT PROBABILITY FUNCTION

Let X and Y be a pair of discrete random variables. Their **joint probability function** expresses the probability that simultaneously X takes the specific value x and Y takes the value y, as a function of x and y. The notation used is $P(x, y)$ so,

$$P(x, y) = P(X = x \cap Y = y)$$

When dealing with jointly distributed random variables, we are frequently interested in the probability functions for the individual random variables.

DERIVATION OF THE MARGINAL PROBABILITY FUNCTION

Let X and Y be a pair of jointly distributed random variables. In this context the probability function of the random variable X is called its **marginal probability function** and is obtained by summing the joint probabilities over all possible values; that is,

$$P(x) = \sum_y P(x, y) \tag{5.24}$$

Similarly, the **marginal probability function** of the random variable Y is

$$P(y) = \sum_x P(x, y) \qquad (5.25)$$

An example of these marginal probability functions is shown in the lower row and the right column in Table 5.5.

Marginal probabilities must sum to 1. Joint probability functions must have the following properties.

PROPERTIES OF JOINT PROBABILITY FUNCTIONS OF DISCRETE RANDOM VARIABLES

Let X and Y be discrete random variables with joint probability function $P(x, y)$. Then

1. $P(x, y) \geq 0$ for any pair of values x and y
2. The sum of the joint probabilities $P(x, y)$ over all possible pairs of values must be 1.

The conditional probability function of one random variable, given specified values of another, is the collection of conditional probabilities.

CONDITIONAL PROBABILITY FUNCTION

Let X and Y be a pair of jointly distributed discrete random variables. The **conditional probability function** of the random variable Y, given that the random variable X takes the value x, expresses the probability that Y takes the value y, as a function of y, when the value x is specified for X. This is denoted $P(y|x)$, and so by the definition of conditional probability:

$$P(y \mid x) = \frac{P(x, y)}{P(x)} \qquad (5.26)$$

Similarly, the **conditional probability function** of X, given $Y = y$ is:

$$P(x \mid y) = \frac{P(x, y)}{P(y)} \qquad (5.27)$$

For example, using the probabilities in Table 5.5 we can compute the conditional probability of purchase ($y = 1$) given age group 26 to 45 ($x = 2$) as

$$P(1 \mid 2) = \frac{P(2, 1)}{P(2)} = \frac{0.20}{0.45} = 0.44$$

In Chapter 4 we discussed independence of events. This concept extends directly to random variables.

INDEPENDENCE OF JOINTLY DISTRIBUTED RANDOM VARIABLES

The jointly distributed random variables X and Y are said to be **independent** if and only if their joint probability function is the product of their marginal probability functions, that is, if and only if

$$P(x, y) = P(x)P(y) \qquad \text{for all possible pairs of values } x \text{ and } y.$$

And k random variables are independent if and only if

$$P(X_1, X_2,..., X_k) = P(X_1)P(X_2) \cdots P(X_k) \qquad \textbf{(5.28)}$$

From the definition of conditional probability functions, it follows that if the random variables X and Y are independent, then the conditional probability function of Y given X is the same as the marginal probability function of Y; that is:

$$P(y|x) = P(y) \qquad \text{Similarly, it follows that:} \qquad P(x|y) = P(x)$$

Previously we defined the expectation of a function of a single random variable. This definition can be extended to functions of several random variables.

EXPECTED VALUE: FUNCTION OF JOINTLY DISTRIBUTED RANDOM VARIABLES

Let X and Y be a pair of discrete random variables with joint probability function $P(x, y)$. The **expectation of any function $g(X, Y)$** of these random variables is defined as:

$$E[g(X, Y)] = \sum_x \sum_y g(x, y)P(x, y) \qquad \textbf{(5.29)}$$

Example 5.16 considers the possible percent returns for two stocks, A and B, and illustrates the computation of marginal probabilities, tests for independence, and finds the means and variances of two jointly distributed random variables.

EXAMPLE 5.16

STOCK RETURNS, MARGINAL PROBABILITY, MEAN, VARIANCE (COMPUTE JOINT PROBABILITIES)

Suppose that Charlotte King has two stocks, A and B. Let X and Y be random variables of possible percent returns (0%, 5%, 10%, and 15%) for each of these two stocks with joint probability distribution given in Table 5.6.

(a) Find the marginal probabilities;
(b) Determine if X and Y are independent;
(c) Find the means and variances of both X and Y.

SOLUTION

(a) We solve this problem using the definitions developed in this chapter. Note that for every combination of values for X and Y, that $P(x, y) = 0.0625$. That is, there is a 6.25% probability for each possible combination of x and y returns. To find the marginal probability that X has a 0% return:

$$P(X = 0) = \sum_y P(0, y) = 0.0625 + 0.0625 + 0.0625 + 0.0625 = 0.25$$

TABLE 5.6
Joint Probability Distribution for Random Variables X and Y

X RETURN	Y RETURN			
	0%	5%	10%	15%
0%	0.0625	0.0625	0.0625	0.0625
5%	0.0625	0.0625	0.0625	0.0625
10%	0.0625	0.0625	0.0625	0.0625
15%	0.0625	0.0625	0.0625	0.0625

Here all the marginal probabilities of X are 25%. Notice that the sum of the marginal probabilities is 1. Similar results are true for the marginal probabilities of Y.

(b) To test for independence, we need to check if $P(x, y) = P(x)P(y)$ for all possible pairs of values x and y.

$P(x, y) = 0.0625$ for all possible pairs of values x and y.
$P(x) = 0.25$ and $P(y) = 0.25$ for all possible pairs of values x and y.
$P(x, y) = 0.0625 = (0.25)(0.25) = P(x)P(y)$ for all possible pairs of values x and y.

Therefore, X and Y are independent.

(c) The mean of X is:

$$\mu_X = E(X) = \sum_X xP(x)$$
$$= 0(0.25) + 0.05(0.25) + 0.10(0.25) + 0.15(0.25) = 0.075$$

Similarly, the mean of Y is $\mu_Y = E(y) = 0.075$.
The variance and standard deviation of X are:

$$\sigma_X^2 = \sum_X (x - \mu_X)^2 P(x) = P(x)\sum_X (x - \mu_X)^2 = (0.25)\sum_x (x - \mu_x)^2$$
$$= (0.25)[(0 - 0.075)^2 + (0.05 - 0.075)^2 + (0.10 - 0.075)^2 + (0.15 - 0.075)^2]$$
$$= 0.003125$$

and the standard deviation of X is $\sigma_X = \sqrt{0.003125} = 0.0559016$, or 5.59%.

Follow similar steps to find the marginal probabilities, mean, and variance of Y.

Computer Applications

There is no add-in currently available to make the computations of marginal probabilities, means, and variances of jointly distributed random variables easy to find. However, we can develop formulas in Excel to simplify our efforts. To find marginal probabilities, means, and variances of jointly distributed random variables X and Y using Microsoft Excel, follow the instruction box in Figure 5.15 on page 165.

Covariance

The covariance is a measure of the joint variability for two random variables. We will see that the covariance can be used to compute the variance of linear combinations of random variables—such as the variance for the total value for the combination of two stocks in a portfolio. In addition, the covariance is used to compute a standardized measure of joint variability called the *correlation*. We will first develop the definition of the covariance and then present some important applications. Suppose that X and Y are a pair of random variables that are not statistically independent. We would like some measure of the nature and strength of the relationship between them. This is rather difficult to achieve, since they could conceivably be related in any number of ways. To simplify matters, we restrict attention to the possibility of linear association. For example, a high value of X might be associated on the average with a high value of Y, and a low value of X with a low value of Y in such a way that, to a good approximation, a straight line might be drawn through the associated values when plotted on a graph.

Suppose that the random variable X has mean μ_x and Y has mean μ_Y, and consider the product $(X - \mu_X)(Y - \mu_Y)$. If high values of X tend to be associated with high values of Y

FIGURE 5.15
Marginal Probabilities, Means and Variances of X and Y

	A	B	C	D	E	F	G	H	I
1			Y Return						
2	X Return	0%	5%	10%	15%	P(x)	Mean of X	Var of X	StDev of X
3	0%	0.0625	0.0625	0.0625	0.0625	0.25	0	0.00140625	
4	5%	0.0625	0.0625	0.0625	0.0625	0.25	0.0125	0.00015625	
5	10%	0.0625	0.0625	0.0625	0.0625	0.25	0.025	0.00015625	
6	15%	0.0625	0.0625	0.0625	0.0625	0.25	0.0375	0.00140625	
7	P(y)	0.25	0.25	0.25	0.25		0.075	0.003125	0.055902
8									
9	Mean of Y	0	0.0125	0.025	0.0375	0.075			
10	Var of Y	0.00140625	0.00015625	0.00015625	0.00140625	0.003125			
11	StDev of Y					0.055902			

Excel Instructions

1. Enter Table 5.6 in Excel
2. Enter appropriate names in cells F2, G2, H2, I2, A7, A9, A10, and A11.
3. To obtain P(x), the Marginal Probability of X
   - Use the AutoSum (Σ) button to obtain the marginal probabilities in F3-F6 and B7 to E7. Example, F3 = B3+C3+D3+E3 = 0.25.

4. To Obtain Mean of X
   - Type "=A3*F3" in cell G3
   - Drag the fill handle for G3 downward from G3 to G6. Select G7 and click the AutoSum button (Σ).
5. To Obtain Variance of X
   - Type "=(A3-G7)^2*F3" in cell H3
   - Drag the fill handle for H3 downward from H3 to H6. Select H7 and click the AutoSum button (Σ).
6. To Obtain the StDev of X
   - Select cell I7 and Type "=SQRT(H7)"
   - Press Enter

and low values of X with low values of Y, we would expect this product to be positive, and the stronger the association, the larger the expectation of $(X - \mu_X)(Y - \mu_Y)$. By contrast, if high values of X are associated with low values of Y and low X with high Y, the expected value for this product would be negative. An expectation of 0 for $(X - \mu_X)(Y - \mu_Y)$ would imply an absence of linear association between X and Y. Thus, as a measure of linear association in the population, we are led to an examination of the expected value of $(X - \mu_X)(Y - \mu_Y)$.

COVARIANCE

Let X be a random variable with mean μ_X, and let Y be a random variable with mean μ_Y. The expected value of $(X - \mu_X)(Y - \mu_Y)$ is called the **covariance** between X and Y, denoted Cov(X, Y). For discrete random variables

$$\text{Cov}(X, Y) = E[(X - \mu_X)(Y - \mu_Y)] = \sum_x \sum_y (x - \mu_x)(y - \mu_Y)P(x, y) \quad (5.30)$$

An equivalent expression is:

$$\text{Cov}(X, Y) = E(XY) - \mu_x \mu_Y = \sum_x \sum_y xy P(x, y) - \mu_x \mu_Y$$

Correlation

Although the covariance provides us with an indication of the direction of the relationship between random variables, the covariance does not have an upper or lower bound and its size is greatly influenced by the scaling of the numbers. We define a strong linear relationship as a condition where the individual observation points are close to a straight line. It is difficult to use the covariance to provide a measure of the strength of a linear relationship because it is unbounded. A related measure, the correlation coefficient, gives us a measure of the strength of the linear relationship between two random variables, with the measure being limited to the range from −1 to +1.

CORRELATION

Let X and Y be jointly distributed random variables. The **correlation** between X and Y is:

$$\rho = \text{Corr}(X, Y) = \frac{\text{Cov}(X, Y)}{\sigma_X \sigma_Y} \tag{5.31}$$

The correlation is the covariance divided by the standard deviations of the two random variables. This results in a standardized measure of relationship that varies from −1 to +1. The following interpretations are important:

1. A correlation of 0 indicates that there is no linear relationship between the two random variables. If the two random variables are independent the correlation is equal to 0.
2. A positive correlation indicates that if one random variable is high (low) then the other random variable has a higher probability of being high (low). We say that the variables are positively dependent. Perfect positive linear dependency is indicated by a correlation of +1.0.
3. A negative correlation indicates that if one random variable is high (low) then the other random variable has a higher probability of being low (high). The variables are negatively dependent. Perfect negative linear dependency is indicated by a correlation of −1.0.

ASSUMPTION

We will find that the correlation is more useful for describing relationships than the covariance. With a correlation of +1 we know that the two random variables have a perfect positive linear relationship and therefore a specific value of one variable, X, predicts the other variable, Y, exactly. A correlation of −1 indicates a perfect negative linear relationship between two variables with one variable, X, predicting the negative of the other variable, Y. A correlation of 0 indicates no linear relationship between the two variables. Intermediate values indicate that variables tend to be related with stronger relationships occurring as the absolute value of the correlation approaches 1.

We also know that correlation is a term that has moved into common usage. We find that in many cases correlation is used to indicate that a relationship exists. However, variables that have nonlinear relationships will not have a correlation coefficient close to 1.0. This distinction is important for us so that we avoid confusion between correlated random variables and those with nonlinear relationships.

EXAMPLE 5.17

JOINT DISTRIBUTION OF STOCK PRICES (COMPUTE COVARIANCE AND CORRELATION)

Find covariance and correlation for the stocks A and B from Example 5.16 with the joint probability distribution in Table 5.6.

SOLUTION

The computation of covariance is tedious for even a problem such as Example 5.16, which is simplified so that all of the joint probabilities, $P(x, y) = 0.0625$ for all pairs of values x and y. By definition, you need to find:

$$\text{Cov}\,(X, Y) = \sum_x \sum_y xyP(x, y) - \mu_x\mu_y$$
$$= 0[(0)(0.0625) + (0.05)(0.0625) + (0.10)(0.0625) + (0.15)(0.0625)]$$
$$+ \cdots + (0.15)\,[(0)(0.0625) + (0.05)(0.0625) + (0.10)(0.0625)$$
$$+ (0.15)(0.0625)] - (0.075)(0.075)$$
$$= 0.005625 - 0.005625$$

Thus,

$$\rho = \text{Corr}(X, Y) = \frac{\text{Cov}(X, Y)}{\sigma_X\sigma_Y} = 0$$

To use Microsoft Excel, you will need to follow carefully the steps in the Instruction box to Figure 5.16.

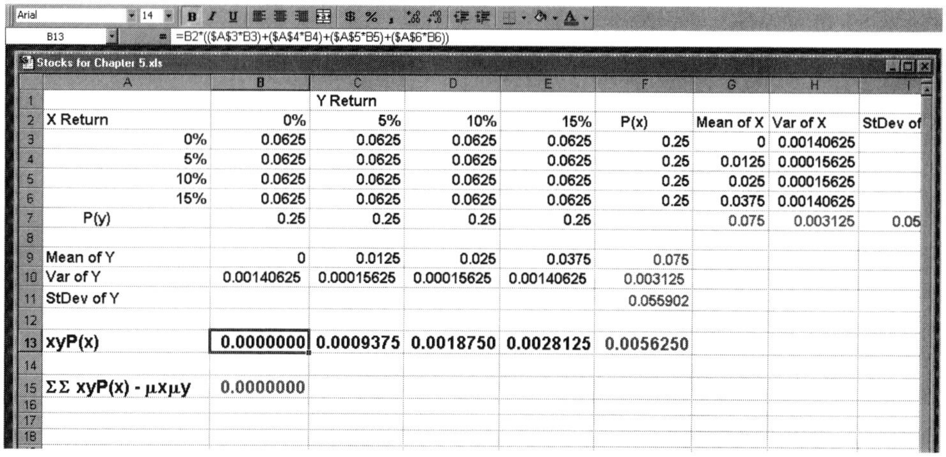

FIGURE 5.16
Covariance and Correlation

Excel Instructions

1. Enter the names given to cells A13 and A15 in your Excel Spreadsheet from Figure 5.15.
2. Type: "=B2*((A3*B3)+(A4*B4)+(A5*B5)+($A6*B6))" in cell B13. Press Enter and the value "0" will appear in B13.
3. Drag cell B13 across C13, D13 and E13.
4. Use the AutoSum button (Σ) to add B13+C13+D13+E13 = 0.005625 appears in cell F13.
5. Finally, subtract the product of the expectations of X and Y from cell F13. To do this, type "=F13-(G7*F9)" in cell B15. Press Enter and the value "0" will appear in B15. This is the Covariance between X and Y. Thus, COV(X, Y) = 0
6. It follows that the correlation between X and Y is also 0.

COVARIANCE AND STATISTICAL INDEPENDENCE

If two random variables are **statistically independent**, the **covariance** between them is 0. However, the converse is not necessarily true.

The reason a covariance of 0 does not necessarily imply statistical independence is that covariance is designed to measure linear association, and it is possible that this quantity may not detect other types of dependency. Suppose that the random variable X has probability function:

$$P(-1) = 1/4 \qquad P(0) = 1/2 \qquad P(1) = 1/4$$

and let the random variable Y be defined as

$$Y = X^2$$

Thus, knowledge of the value taken by X implies knowledge of the value taken by Y, and hence, these two random variables are certainly not independent. We know that whenever $X = 0$, then $Y = 0$, and that if X is either -1 or 1, then $Y = 1$. The joint probability function of X and Y is

$$P(-1, 1) = 1/4 \qquad P(0, 0) = 1/2 \qquad P(1, 1) = 1/4$$

with the probability of any other combination of values being equal to 0. It is then straightforward to verify that

$$E(X) = 0 \qquad E(Y) = 1/2 \qquad E(XY) = 0$$

The covariance between X and Y is 0.

To conclude our discussion of joint distributions, we consider the mean and variance of a random variable that can be written as the sum or difference of other random variables. These results are summarized below and can be derived using Equation 5.29.

SUMMARY RESULTS FOR SUMS AND DIFFERENCES OF RANDOM VARIABLES

Let X and Y be a pair of random variables with means μ_X and μ_Y and variances σ_X^2 and σ_Y^2. The following properties hold:

1. The **expected value of their sum** is the sum of their expected values:

$$E(X + Y) = \mu_X + \mu_Y \tag{5.32}$$

2. The **expected value of their differences** is the difference between their expected values:

$$E(X - Y) = \mu_X - \mu_Y \tag{5.33}$$

3. If the covariance between X and Y is 0, the **variance of their sum** is the sum of their variances:

$$\text{Var}(X + Y) = \sigma_X^2 + \sigma_Y^2 \tag{5.34}$$

   but if the covariance is not 0 then

$$\text{Var}(X + Y) = \sigma_X^2 + \sigma_Y^2 + 2\,\text{cov}(X, Y)$$

4. If the covariance between X and Y is 0, the **variance of their differences** is the *sum* of their variances:

$$\text{Var}(X - Y) = \sigma_X^2 + \sigma_Y^2 \tag{5.35}$$

   but if the covariance is not 0 then

$$\text{Var}(X + Y) = \sigma_X^2 + \sigma_Y^2 - 2\,\text{cov}(X, Y)$$

> Let $X_1, X_2, \ldots X_K$ be K random variables with means $\mu_1, \mu_2, \ldots, \mu_K$ and variances $\sigma_1^2, \sigma_2^2, \ldots, \sigma$. The following properties hold:
>
> 5. The expected value of their sum is:
>
> $$E(X_1 + X_2 + \cdots + X_K) = \mu_1 + \mu_2 + \cdots + \mu_K \qquad (5.36)$$
>
> 6. If the covariance between every pair of these random variables is 0, the variance of their sum is:
>
> $$\mathrm{Var}(X_1 + X_2 + \cdots + X_K) = \sigma_1^2 + \sigma_2^2 + \cdots + \sigma_K^2 \qquad (5.37)$$

EXAMPLE 5.18

SIMPLE INVESTMENT
PORTFOLIO (COMPUTE MEANS
AND VARIANCES. FUNCTIONS
OF RANDOM VARIABLES)

An investor has \$1,000 to invest and two investment opportunities, each requiring a minimum of \$500. The profit per \$100 from the first can be represented by a random variable X, having the following probability function:

$$P(X = -5) = 0.4 \quad \text{and} \quad P(X = 20) = 0.6$$

The profit per \$100 from the second is given by the random variable Y, whose probability function is:

$$P(Y = 0) = 0.6 \qquad \text{and} \qquad P(Y = 25) = 0.4$$

The random variable X and Y are independent. The investor has the following possible strategies:

(a) \$1,000 in the first investment
(b) \$1,000 in the second investment

Find the mean and variance of the profit from each strategy.

SOLUTION
The random variable X has mean

$$\mu_X = E(X) = \sum_x xP(x) = (-5)(0.4) + (20)(0.6) = \$10$$

and variance

$$\sigma_X^2 = E[(X - \mu_x)^2] = \sum_x (x - \mu_x)^2 P(x)$$
$$= (-5 - 10)^2(0.4) + (20 - 10)^2(0.6) = 150$$

Strategy (a) has mean profit of: $E(10X) = 10E(X) = \$100$ and variance of:

$$\mathrm{Var}(10X) = 100\mathrm{Var}(X) = 15,000$$

The random variable Y has mean:

$$\mu_Y = E(Y) = \sum_y yP(y) = (0)(0.6) + (25)(0.4) = \$10$$

and variance

$$\sigma_Y^2 = E[(Y - \mu_Y)^2] = \sum_Y (y - \mu_Y)^2 P(y)$$
$$= (0 - 10)^2 (0.6) + (25 - 10)^2 (0.4) = 150$$

Strategy (b) has mean profit: $E(10Y) = 10E(Y) = \$100$ and variance

$$\mathrm{Var}(10Y) = 100\mathrm{Var}(Y) = 15{,}000$$

Later we consider another possible strategy available to the investor: Strategy (c): $500 in each investment.

Portfolio Analysis

Investment managers spend considerable effort developing investment portfolios that consist of a set of financial instruments that each have returns defined by a probability distribution model. Portfolios are used to obtain a combined investment that has a given expected return and risk. Stock portfolios with a high risk can be constructed by combining several individual stocks whose values tend to increase or decrease together. With such a portfolio an investor will have either large gains or large losses. Stocks whose values move in opposite directions could be combined to create a portfolio with a more stable value, implying less risk. Decreases in one stock price would be balanced by increases in another stock price.

This process of portfolio construction and analysis is conducted using probability models defined by random variables and probability distribution functions. The mean value of the portfolio is the linear combination of the mean values of the two stocks in the portfolio. The variance of the portfolio value is computed using the sum of the variances and the covariance of the joint distribution of the stock values. We will develop the method using an example with a portfolio consisting of two stocks.

Consider a portfolio that consists of a shares of Stock A and b shares of Stock B. It is important to be able to find the mean and variance for the market value, W, of a portfolio, where W is the linear function $W = aX + bY$. The mean and variance are derived in Appendix 5.1.

THE MEAN AND VARIANCE FOR THE MARKET VALUE OF A PORTFOLIO

The random variable X is the price for stock A and the random variable Y is the price for stock B. The **market value**, W, for the portfolio is given by the linear function,

$$W = aX + bY$$

where, a, is the number of shares of stock A and, b, is the number of shares of stock B.
   The **mean value for W** is,

$$\mu_W = E[W] = E[aX + bY] \atop = a\mu_X + b\mu_Y \tag{5.39}$$

The **variance for W** is,

$$\sigma_W^2 = a^2\sigma_X^2 + b^2\sigma_Y^2 + 2ab\mathrm{Cov}(X, Y) \tag{5.40}$$

or using the correlation,

$$\sigma_W^2 = a^2 \sigma_X^2 + b^2 \sigma_Y^2 + 2ab\text{Corr}(X, Y)\sigma_X \sigma_Y$$

EXAMPLE 5.19

ANALYSIS OF STOCK PORTFOLIOS (COMPUTE MEANS AND VARIANCES. FUNCTIONS OF RANDOM VARIABLES)

George Tiao has five shares of Stock A and ten shares of Stock B, whose price variation is modeled by the probability distribution in Table 5.7. Find the mean and variance of the portfolio.

SOLUTION

The value, W, of the portfolio can be represented by the linear combination, $W = 5X + 10Y$. The mean and variance for Stock A are \$53 and 31.3, while for Stock B they are \$55 and 125. The covariance is 59.17 and the correlation is 0.947. These results were obtained using Microsoft Excel in steps similar to Figure 5.16.

The mean value for the portfolio is thus,

$$\mu_W = E[W] = E[5X + 10Y] = 5(53) + 10(55) = 815$$

The variance for the portfolio is,

$$\begin{aligned}\sigma_W^2 &= 5^2 \sigma_X^2 + 10^2 \sigma_Y^2 + 2 \times 5 \times 10 \times \text{Cov}(X, Y) \\ &= 5^2 \times 31.3 + 10^2 \times 125 + 2 \times 5 \times 10 \times 59.17 = 19{,}199.5\end{aligned}$$

George knows that high variance implies high risk. He believes that the risk for this portfolio is too high. Thus, he asks you to prepare a portfolio that has lower risk. After some investigation you discover a different pair of stocks whose prices follow the probability model in Table 5.8.

The mean for Stock C is \$53, the same as Stock A. Similarly, the mean for Stock D is \$55, the same as previous Stock B. Thus, the mean value of the portfolio is not changed.

The variances for each stock is also the same, but the covariance is -59.17. The variance for the portfolio now includes the *negative covariance* term and is

$$\begin{aligned}\sigma_W^2 &= 5^2 \sigma_X^2 + 10^2 \sigma_Y^2 + 2 \times 5 \times 10 \times \text{Cov}(X, Y) \\ &= 5^2 \times 31.3 + 10^2 \times 125 + 2 \times 5 \times 10 \times (-59.17) = 7{,}365.5\end{aligned}$$

We see that the effect of the negative covariance is to reduce the variance and hence reduce the risk of the portfolio.

TABLE 5.7
Stock A and Stock B Prices

STOCK A PRICE	STOCK B PRICE			
	$40	**$50**	**$60**	**$70**
$45	0.24	0.003333	0.003333	0.003333
$50	0.003333	0.24	0.003333	0.003333
$55	0.003333	0.003333	0.24	0.003333
$60	0.003333	0.003333	0.003333	0.24

TABLE 5.8
New Portfolio of Stock C and
Stock D

STOCK C PRICE	STOCK D PRICE			
	$40	$50	$60	$70
$45	0.003333	0.003333	0.003333	0.24
$50	0.003333	0.003333	0.24	0.003333
$55	0.003333	0.24	0.003333	0.003333
$60	0.24	0.003333	0.003333	0.003333

Figure 5.17 shows us how portfolio variance and hence risk changes with different cor-relation between stock prices. Thus to help control risk, designers of stock portfolios will select stocks based on the correlation between prices.

FIGURE 5.17
Portfolio Variance versus
Correlation of Stock Price

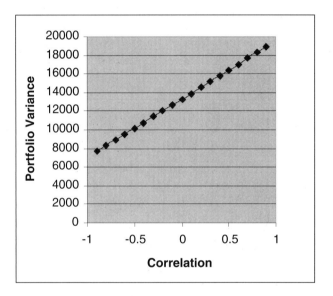

ASSUMPTION

As seen in Example 5.19 the correlation between stock prices, or any two random variables, has important effects on the portfolio value random variable. A positive correlation indi-cates that both prices, X and Y, increase or decrease together. Thus large or small values of the portfolio are magnified resulting in greater range and variance compared to a zero cor-relation. Conversely, a negative correlation leads to price increases for X matched by price decreases for Y. As a result the range and variance of the portfolio are decreased compared to a zero correlation. By selecting stocks with particular combinations of correlations, fund managers can control the variance and the risk for portfolios.

EXAMPLE 5.20

**SIMPLE INVESTMENT
PORTFOLIO REVISITED
(COMPUTE MEANS AND
VARIANCES. INVESTMENT
PORTFOLIOS)**

Recall Example 5.18 where an investor has $1,000 to invest and two investment opportuni-ties, each requiring a minimum of $500. The profit per $100 from the first can be repre-sented by a random variable X, having the following probability function:

$$P(X = -5) = 0.4 \qquad \text{and} \qquad P(X = 20) = 0.6$$

The profit per $100 from the second is given by the random variable Y, whose probability function is

$$P(Y = 0) = 0.6 \qquad \text{and} \qquad P(Y = 25) = 0.4$$

The random variables X and Y are independent. In Example 5.17 we consider strategies (a) and (b). Now let's consider strategy (c): $500 in each investment. Find the mean and variance of the profit for this strategy.

SOLUTION

Now the return from strategy (c) is $5X + 5Y$, which has mean

$$E(5X + 5Y) = E(5X) + E(5Y) = 5E(X) + 5E(Y) = \$100$$

Thus, all three strategies have the same expected profit. However, since X and Y are independent and covariance 0, the variance of the return from strategy (c) is

$$\text{Var}(5X + 5Y) = \text{Var}(5X) + \text{Var}(5Y) = 25\text{Var}(X) + 25\,\text{Var}(Y) = 7{,}500$$

This is smaller than the variances of the other strategies, reflecting the decrease in risk that follows from diversification in an investment portfolio. This investor should certainly prefer strategy (c), since it yields the same expected return as the other two, but with lower risk.

EXERCISES

5.47 A researcher suspected that the number of between-meal snacks eaten by students in a day during final examinations week might depend on the number of tests a student had to take on that day. The accompanying table shows joint probabilities, estimated from a survey.

NUMBER OF SNACKS (Y)	NUMBER OF TESTS (X)			
	0	1	2	3
0	.07	.09	.06	.01
1	.07	.06	.07	.01
2	.06	.07	.14	.03
3	.02	.04	.16	.04

(a) Find the probability function of X and hence the mean number of tests taken by students on that day.
(b) Find the probability function of Y and hence the mean number of snacks eaten by students on that day.
(c) Find, and interpret, the conditional probability function of Y, given $X = 3$.
(d) Find the covariance between X and Y.
(e) Are number of snacks and number of tests independent of each other?

5.48 A real estate agent is interested in the relationship between the number of lines in a newspaper advertisement for an apartment and the volume of inquiries from potential renters. Let volume of inquiries be denoted by the random variable X, with the value 0 for little interest, 1 for moderate interest, and 2 for heavy interest. The real estate agent estimated the joint probability function shown in the accompanying table.

NUMBER OF LINES (Y)	NUMBER OF ENQUIRIES (X)		
	0	1	2
3	.09	.14	.07
4	.07	.23	.16
5	.03	.10	.11

(a) Find the joint cumulative probability function at $X = 1$, $Y = 4$, and interpret your result.
(b) Find and interpret the conditional probability function for Y, given $X = 0$.
(c) Find and interpret the conditional probability function for X, given $Y = 5$.
(d) Find and interpret the covariance between X and Y.
(e) Are number of lines in the advertisement and volume of inquiries independent of one another?

5.49 The accompanying table shows, for credit card holders with one to three cards, the joint probabilities for number of cards owned (X) and number of credit purchases made in a week (Y).

NUMBER OF CARDS (X)	NUMBER OF PURCHASES IN WEEK (Y)				
	0	1	2	3	4
1	.08	.13	.09	.06	.03
2	.03	.08	.08	.09	.07
3	.01	.03	.06	.08	.08

(a) For a randomly chosen person from this group, what is the probability function for number of purchases made in a week?

(b) For a person in this group who has three cards, what is the probability function for number of purchases made in the week?

(c) Are the number of cards owned and number of purchases made statistically independent?

5.50 A market researcher wants to determine whether a new model of a personal computer, which had been advertised on a late-night talk show, had achieved more brand-name recognition among people who watched the show regularly than among people who did not. After conducting a survey, it was found that 15% of all people both watched the show regularly and could correctly identify the product. Also, 16% of all people regularly watched the show and 45% of all people could correctly identify the product. Define a pair of random variables as follows:

$X = 1$ if regularly watch the show $X = 0$ otherwise

$Y = 1$ if product correctly identified $Y = 0$ otherwise

(a) Find the joint probability function of X and Y.

(b) Find the conditional probability function of Y, given $X = 1$.

(c) Find and interpret the covariance between X and Y.

5.51 A college bookseller makes calls at the offices of professors and forms the impression that professors are more likely to be away from their offices on Friday than any other working day. A review of the records of calls, one-fifth of which are on Fridays, indicates that for 16% of Friday calls, the professor is away from the office, while this occurs for only 12% of calls on every other working day. Define the random variables as follows:

$X = 1$ if call is made on a Friday $X = 0$ otherwise

$Y = 1$ if professor is away from the office $Y = 0$ otherwise

(a) Find the joint probability function of X and Y.

(b) Find the conditional probability function of Y, given $X = 0$.

(c) Find the marginal probability functions of X and Y.

(d) Find and interpret the covariance between X and Y.

5.52 A restaurant manager receives occasional complaints about the quality of both the food and the service. The marginal probability functions for the number of weekly complaints in each category are shown in the accompanying table. If complaints about food and service are independent of each other, find the joint probability function.

NUMBER OF FOOD COMPLAINTS	PROBABILITY	NUMBER OF SERVICE COMPLAINTS	PROBABILITY
0	.12	0	.18
1	.29	1	.38
2	.42	2	.34
3	.17	3	.10

5.53 Refer to the information in Exercise 5.52. Find the mean and standard deviation of the total number of complaints received in a week. Having reached this point, you are concerned that numbers of food and service complaints may not be independent of each other. However, you have no information about the nature of their dependence. What can you now say about the mean and standard deviation of the total number of complaints received in a week?

5.54 A company has five representatives covering large territories and ten representatives covering smaller territories. The probability distributions for the numbers of orders received by each of these types of representatives in a day are shown in the accompanying table. Assuming that the number of orders received by any representative is independent of the number received by any other, find the mean and standard deviation of the total number of orders received by the company in a day.

NUMBERS OF ORDERS (LARGE TERRITORY)	PROBABILITY	NUMBERS OF ORDERS (SMALLER TERRITORY)	PROBABILITY
0	.08	0	.18
1	.16	1	.26
2	.28	2	.36
3	.32	3	.13
4	.10	4	.07
5	.06		

SUMMARY

In this chapter we have presented discrete probability models. These models are defined by a random variable and by a probability distribution function. We also developed expected values and variances for these models. Three important discrete probability models—the Binomial, the Poisson, and the Hypergeometric—were developed along with potential applications. Finally, we developed joint discrete probability distributions and indicated how to compute the covariance for these models. We showed how joint probability models can be used to determine the mean and variance for linear combinations of random variables, with particular application to stock portfolios.

KEY WORDS

CHAPTER EXERCISES AND APPLICATIONS

5.55 As an investment advisor, you tell a client that an investment in a mutual fund has (over the next year) a higher expected return than an investment in the money market. The client then asks the following questions:

(**a**) Does that imply that the mutual fund will certainly yield a higher return than the money market?

(**b**) Does it follow that I should invest in the mutual fund rather than in the money market?

How would you reply?

5.56 A contractor estimates the probabilities for the number of days required to complete a certain type of construction project as follows:

Time (Days)	1	2	3	4	5
Probability	.05	.20	.35	.30	.10

(**a**) What is the probability that a randomly chosen project will take less than three days to complete?

(**b**) Find the expected time to complete a project.

(**c**) Find the standard deviation of time required to complete a project.

(**d**) The contractor's project cost is made up of two parts—a fixed cost of $20,000, plus $2,000 for each day taken to complete the project. Find the mean and standard deviation of total project cost.

(**e**) If three projects are undertaken, what is the probability that at least two of them will take at least four days to complete, assuming independence of individual project completion times?

5.57 A car salesman estimates the following probabilities for the number of cars that he will sell in the next week.

Number of Cars	0	1	2	3	4	5
Probability	.10	.20	.35	.16	.12	.07

(**a**) Find the expected number of cars that will be sold in the week.

(**b**) Find the standard deviation of the number of cars that will be sold in the week.

(**c**) The salesman receives for the week a salary of $250, plus an additional $300 for each car sold. Find the mean and standard deviation of his total salary for the week.

(**d**) What is the probability that the salesman's salary for the week will be more than $1,000?

5.58 A multiple-choice test has nine questions. For each question, there are four possible answers from which to select. One point is awarded for each correct answer, and points are not subtracted for incorrect answers. The instructor awards a bonus point if the student spells his or her name correctly. A student who has not studied for this test decides to choose at random an answer for each question.

(**a**) Find the expected number of correct answers for the student on these nine questions.

(**b**) Find the standard deviation of the number of correct answers for the student on these nine questions.

(**c**) The student spells his name correctly.

(**i**) Find the expected total score on the test for this student.

(**ii**) Find the standard deviation of his total score on the test.

5.59 Develop realistic examples of pairs of random variables for which you would expect to find:

(**a**) Positive covariance

(**b**) Negative covariance

(**c**) Zero covariance

5.60 A long-distance taxi service owns four vehicles. These are of different ages and have different repair records. The probabilities that on any given day, each vehicle will be available for use are .95, .90, .90, and .80. Whether one vehicle is available is independent of whether any other vehicle is available.

(**a**) Find the probability function for the number of vehicles available for use on a given day.

(**b**) Find the expected number of vehicles available for use on a given day.

(**c**) Find the standard deviation of the number of vehicles available for use on a given day.

5.61 Students in a college were classified according to years in school (X) and number of visits to a museum in the last year ($Y = 0$ for no visits, 1 for one visit, 2 for more than one visit). The joint probabilities in the accompanying table were estimated for these random variables.

NUMBER OF VISITS (Y)	YEARS IN SCHOOL (X)			
	1	2	3	4
0	.07	.05	.03	.02
1	.13	.11	.17	.15
2	.04	.04	.09	.10

(**a**) Find the probability that a randomly chosen student has not visited a museum in the last year.

(**b**) Find the means of the random variables X and Y.

(**c**) Find and interpret the covariance between the random variables X and Y.

5.62 A basketball team's star 3-point shooter takes six 3-point shots in a game. Historically, he makes 40% of all 3-point shots taken in a game. State at the outset what assumptions you have made.

(**a**) Find the probability that at least two shots were made.

(**b**) Find the probability that exactly three shots were made.

(**c**) Find the mean and standard deviation of the number of shots made.

(**d**) Find the mean and standard deviation of the total number of points scored as a result of these shots.

5.63 It is estimated that 55% of the freshmen entering a particular college will graduate from that college in four years.

(**a**) For a random sample of five entering freshmen, what is the probability that exactly three will graduate in four years?

(**b**) For a random sample of five entering freshmen, what is the probability that a majority will graduate in four years?

(**c**) Eighty entering freshmen are chosen at random. Find the mean and standard deviation of the proportion of these eighty who will graduate in four years.

5.64 The World Series of baseball is to be played by team A and team B. The first team to win four games wins the series. Suppose that team A is the better team, in the sense that the probability is .6 that team A will win any specific game. Assume also that the result of any game is independent of that of any other.

(**a**) What is the probability that team A will win the series?

(**b**) What is the probability that a seventh game will be needed to determine the winner?

(**c**) Suppose that, in fact, each team wins two of the first four games.

(**i**) What is the probability that team A will win the series?

(**ii**) What is the probability that a seventh game will be needed to determine the winner?

5.65 Using detailed cash flow information, a financial analyst claims to be able to spot companies that are likely candidates for bankruptcy. The analyst is presented with information on the past records of fifteen companies and told that in fact five of these have failed. He selects as candidates for failure five companies from the group of fifteen. In fact, three of the five companies selected by the analyst were among those that failed. Evaluate the financial analyst's performance on this test of his ability to detect failed companies.

5.66 A team of five analysts is about to examine the earnings prospects of twenty corporations. Each of the five analysts will study four of the corporations. These analysts are not equally competent. In fact, one of them is a star, having an excellent record of anticipating changing trends. Ideally, management would like to allocate to this analyst the four corporations whose earnings will deviate most from past trends. However, lacking this information, management allocates corporations to analysts randomly. What is the probability that at least two of the four corporations whose earnings will deviate most from past trends are allocated to the star analyst?

5.67 On the average, 2.4 customers per minute arrive at an airline check-in desk during the peak period. Assume that the distribution of arrivals is Poisson.

(**a**) What is the probability that there will be no arrivals in a minute?

(**b**) What is the probability that there will be more than three arrivals in a minute?

5.68 A recent estimate suggested that of all individuals and couples reporting income in excess of $200,000, 6.5% either paid no federal tax or paid tax at an effective rate of less than 15%. A random sample of 100 of those reporting income in excess of $200,000 was taken. What is the probability that more than two of the sample members either paid no federal tax or paid tax at an effective rate of less than 15%.

5.69 A company has two assembly lines, each of which stalls an average of 2.4 times per week according to a Poisson distribution. Assume that the performances of these assembly lines are independent of one another. What is the probability that at least one line stalls at least once in any given week?

APPENDIX: VERIFICATIONS

In this part of the chapter appendix, we verify the following:

(a) Alternative Formula for the Variance of a Discrete Random Variable (Equation 5.7)
(b) Mean and Variance of a Linear Function of a Random Variable (Equations 5.8 and 5.9)
(c) Mean and Variance of the Binomial Distribution (Equations 5.19 and 5.20)
(d) Mean and Variance of the Market Value, W, of a Portfolio (Equations 5.38 and 5.39)

1) VERIFICATION OF A: ALTERNATIVE FORMULA FOR THE VARIANCE OF A DISCRETE RANDOM VARIABLE (EQUATION 5.7)

Begin with the original definition of variance:

$$\sigma_X^2 = \sum_x (x - \mu_X)^2 P(x) = \sum_x (x^2 - 2\mu_X x + \mu_X^2)P(x)$$
$$= \sum_x x^2 P(x) - 2\mu_X \sum_x xP(x) + \mu_X^2 \sum_x P(x)$$

But, we have seen that:

$$\sum_x xP(x) = \mu_X \qquad \text{and} \qquad \sum_x P(x) = 1$$

Thus,

$$\sigma_X^2 = \sum_x x^2 P(x) - 2\mu_X^2 + \mu_X^2$$

and finally,

$$\sigma_X^2 = \sum_x x^2 P(x) - \mu_X^2$$

2) VERIFICATION OF B: MEAN AND VARIANCE OF A LINEAR FUNCTION OF A RANDOM VARIABLE (EQUATIONS 5.8 AND 5.9)

It follows from the definition of expectation that if W takes values $a + bx$ with probabilities $P_X(x)$, its mean is:

$$E(W) = \mu_W = \sum_x (a + bx)P(x)$$

$$= a \sum_x P(x) + b \sum_x xP(x)$$

Then, since the first summation on the right-hand side of this equation is 1, and the second summation is the mean of X, we have:

$$E(W) = a + b\mu_X \quad \text{as in Equation 5.8.}$$

Further, the variance of W is, by definition:

$$\sigma_W^2 = E[(W - \mu_W)^2] = \sum_X [(a + bx) - \mu_W]^2 P(x)$$

Substituting $a + b\mu_X$ for μ_W then gives:

$$\sigma_W^2 = \sum_X (bx - b\mu_X)^2 P(x) = b^2 \sum_X (x - \mu_X)^2 P(x)$$

Since the summation on the right-hand side of this equation is, by definition, the variance of X, the result in Equation 5.9 follows:

$$\sigma_W^2 = \text{Var}(a + bX) = b^2 \sigma_X^2$$

3)   VERIFICATION OF C: MEAN AND VARIANCE OF THE BINOMIAL DISTRIBUTION (EQUATIONS 5.19 AND 5.20)

To find the mean and variance of the binomial distribution, it is convenient to return to the Bernoulli distribution. Consider n independent trials, each with probability of success, π, and let $X_i = 1$ if the ith trial results in success and 0 otherwise. The random variables $X_1, X_2, \ldots, X_n$ are therefore n independent Bernoulli variables, each with probability of success π. Moreover, the total number of successes X is:

$$X = X_1 + X_2 + \cdots X_n$$

Thus, the binomial random variable can be expressed as the sum of independent Bernoulli random variables.

The mean and the variance for Bernoulli random variables can be used to find the mean and variance of the binomial distribution. Using Equation 5.15, we know that:

$$E(X_i) = \pi \qquad \text{and that } \sigma_{xi}^2 = \pi(1 - \pi) \quad \text{for all } i = 1, 2, \ldots, n$$

Then, for the binomial distribution:

$$E(X) = E(X_1 + X_2 + \cdots + X_n) = $$
$$E(X_1) + E(X_2) + \cdots E(X_n) = n\pi$$

Since the Bernoulli random variables are independent, the covariance between any pair of them is zero, and

$$\sigma_X^2 = \sigma^2(X_1 + X_2 + \cdots X_n)$$
$$= \sigma^2(X_1) + \sigma^2(X_2) + \cdots \sigma^2(X_n)$$
$$= n\pi(1 - \pi)$$

4)   VERIFICATION OF D: MEAN AND VARIANCE OF THE MARKET VALUE, W, OF A PORTFOLIO (EQUATIONS 5.38 AND 5.39)

You are given a linear combination, W, of random variables X and Y, where

$$W = aX + bY \quad \text{and} \quad a \text{ and } b \text{ are constants.}$$

The mean of W is:

$$\mu_W = E[W] = E[aX + bY]$$
$$= a\mu_X + b\mu_Y$$

and, the variance of W is:

$$\sigma_W^2 = E[(W - \mu_W)^2\}$$

$$= E[(aX + bY - (a\mu_X + b\mu_Y))^2]$$
$$= E[(a(X - \mu_X) + b(Y - \mu_Y))^2]$$
$$= E[a^2(X - \mu_X)^2 + b^2(Y - \mu_Y)^2 + 2ab(X - \mu_X)(Y - \mu_Y)]$$
$$= a^2 E[(X - \mu_X)^2] + b^2 E[(Y - \mu_Y)^2] + 2ab E[(X - \mu_X)(Y - \mu_Y)]$$
$$= a^2 \sigma_X^2 + b^2 \sigma_Y^2 + 2ab\text{Cov}(X, Y)$$

CHAPTER 6

CONTINUOUS RANDOM VARIABLES AND PROBABILITY DISTRIBUTIONS

INTRODUCTION

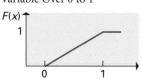

In Chapter 5 we developed discrete random variables and probability distributions. Here we will extend the probability concepts to continuous random variables and probability distributions. The concepts and insights for discrete random variables also apply to continuous random variables, so we are building directly on the previous chapter. Many economic and business measures such as sales, investment, consumption, costs, and revenues can be represented by continuous random variables. In addition, measures of time, distance, temperature, and weight also fit into this category. Probability statements for continuous random variables are specified over ranges. The probability that sales are between 140 and 190 or greater than 200 are typical examples. Mathematical theory leads us to conclude that in reality random variables for all applied problems are discrete because measurements are rounded to some value. But for us the important fact is that continuous random variables and probability distributions provide good approximations for many applied problems. Thus these models are very important and provide excellent tools for business and economic applications.

6.1   CONTINUOUS RANDOM VARIABLES

Here we will again define X as a random variable and x as a specific value of the random variable. We begin by defining the *cumulative distribution function*.

> **CUMULATIVE DISTRIBUTION FUNCTION**
> The **cumulative distribution function**, $F(x)$, for a continuous random variable X expresses the probability that X does not exceed the value of x, as a function of x
>
> $$F(x) = P(X \leq x) \qquad (6.1)$$

We will illustrate the cumulative distribution function by using a simple probability structure. Consider a tunnel that is exactly one mile long. The random variable X indicates the distance into the tunnel measured in miles from the beginning. We are concerned with the probability of breakdowns at various distances into the tunnel, where the probability of a breakdown is the same for all stretches of the same length. The distribution of X is said to follow a *uniform probability distribution* and the cumulative distribution is

$$F(x) = \begin{cases} 0 \to \text{if} \cdots x < 0 \\ x \to \text{if} \cdots 0 \leq x \leq 1 \\ 1 \to \text{if} \cdots x > 1 \end{cases}$$

FIGURE 6.1
Cumulative Distribution Function for a Random Variable Over 0 to 1

This function is graphed as a straight line between 0 and 1 as shown in Figure 6.1. From this we see that the probability of a breakdown during the first 0.40 distance in the tunnel is

$$P(X \leq 0.40) = F(0.40) = 0.40$$

To obtain the probability that a continuous random variable X falls in a specified range we find the difference between the cumulative probability at the upper end of the range and the cumulative probability at the lower end of the range.

PROBABILITY OF A RANGE USING A CUMULATIVE DISTRIBUTION FUNCTION

Let X be a continuous random variable with a cumulative distribution function $F(x)$, and let a and b be two possible values of X, with $a < b$. The **probability that X lies between a and b** is

$$P(a < X < b) = F(b) - F(a) \qquad \textbf{(6.2)}$$

For continuous random variables, it does not matter whether we write "less than" or "less than or equal to" because the probability that X is precisely equal to b is 0.

For the random variable that is distributed uniformly in the range 0 to 1, the cumulative distribution function in that range is $F(x) = x$. Therefore if a and b are two numbers between 0 and 1, with $a < b$

$$P(a < X < b) = F(b) - F(a) = b - a$$

For example, if a breakdown occurs, the probability that it happens between 0.25 mile and 0.75 mile is

$$P(0.25 < X < 0.75) = 0.75 - 0.25 = 0.50$$

We have seen that the probability that a continuous random variable that lies between any two values can be expressed in terms of its cumulative distribution function. This function therefore contains all the information about the probability structure of the random variable. However, for many purposes a different function is more useful. In Chapter 5 we discussed the probability function for discrete random variables, which expresses the probability that a discrete random variable takes any specific value. Since the probability of a specific value is 0 for continuous random variables, that concept is not directly relevant here. However, a related function, called the *probability density function*, as defined in the box can be constructed for continuous random variables, allowing for graphical interpretation of their probability structure.

PROBABILITY DENSITY FUNCTION

Let X be a continuous random variable, and let x be any number lying in the range of values this random variable can take. The **probability density function**, $f(x)$, of the random variable is a function with the following properties:

1. $f(x) > 0$ for all values of x.
2. The area under the probability density function $f(x)$ over all values of the random variable X is equal to 1.0.
3. Suppose this density function is graphed. Let a and b be two possible values of the random variable X, with $a < b$. Then the probability that X lies between a and b is the area under the density function between these points.
4. The cumulative distribution function $F(x_0)$ is the area under the probability density function $f(x)$ up to x_0

$$F\left(x_0\right) = \int_{x_m}^{x_0} f(x)\,dx$$

where x_m is the minimum value of the random variable x.

The probability density function can be approximated by a discrete probability distribution with many discrete values close together, as seen in Figure 6.2.

FIGURE 6.2
Approximation of a
Probability Density Function
by a Discrete Probability
Distribution

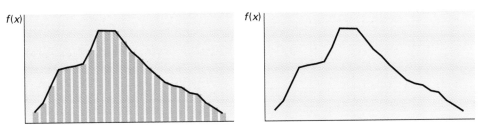

Figure 6.3 shows the plot of an arbitrary probability density function for some continuous random variable. Two possible values, *a* and *b*, are shown, and the shaded area under the curve between these points is the probability that the random variable lies in the interval between them (Appendix 1).

Now we will consider a probability density function that represents a probability distribution over the range of 0 to 1. Figure 6.4 is a graph of the probability density function. This is the probability density function for the vehicle breakdown in a tunnel example. Since the probability is the same for any interval of the same length in the one-mile tunnel, we deduce that the probability density function is constant over the range from 0 to 1 and can be defined as the uniform probability density function, which can be written as

$$f(x) = \begin{cases} 1 \rightarrow 0 \le x \le 1 \\ 0 \rightarrow \text{else} \end{cases}$$

This probability density function can be used to find the probability that the random variable falls within a specific range. For example, the probability that a breakdown occurs between 0.25 miles and 0.75 miles is shown in Figure 6.5. Since the height of the density function is $f(x) = 1$, the area under the curve between 0.25 and 0.75 is equal to 0.50, which is the required probability. Note that this is the same result obtained previously using the cumulative probability function.

We have seen that the probability that a random variable that lies between a pair of values is the area under the probability density function between these two values. There are two important results worth noting. The area under the entire probability density function is 1 and the cumulative probability $F(x_0)$ is the area under the density function to the left of x_0.

AREAS UNDER CONTINUOUS PROBABILITY DENSITY FUNCTIONS

Let X be a continuous random variable with probability density function $f(x)$ and cumulative distribution function $F(x)$. Then the following properties hold:

1. The total area under the curve $f(x)$ is 1.
2. The area under the curve $f(x)$ to the left of x_0 is $F(x_0)$, where x_0 is any value that the random variable can take.

FIGURE 6.3
Shaded Area Is the Probability That X is
Between *a* and *b*

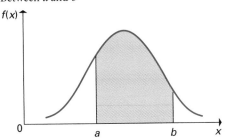

FIGURE 6.4
Probability Density Function
for a Uniform 0 to 1 Random
Variable

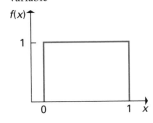

FIGURE 6.5
Density Function Showing
the Probability That X is
Between 0.25 and 0.75

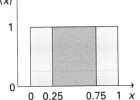

FIGURE 6.6
Properties of the Probability
Density Function

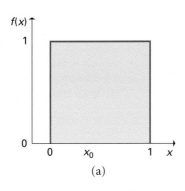
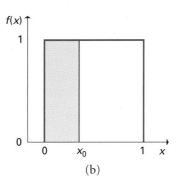

(a)   (b)

These results are shown in Figure 6.6 for the uniform distribution, with Figure 6.6a showing that the entire area under the probability density function is equal to 1 and Figure 6.6b indicating the area to the left of x_0.

EXAMPLE 6.1

PROBABILITY OF PIPELINE FAILURE (CUMULATIVE DISTRIBUTION FUNCTION)

A repair team is responsible for a stretch of oil pipeline 2 miles long. The distance (in miles) at which any fracture arrives can be represented by a uniformly distributed random variable, with probability density function

$$f(x) = 0.5$$

Find the cumulative distribution function and the probability that any given fracture occurs between 0.5 miles and 1.5 miles along this stretch of pipeline.

SOLUTION

FIGURE 6.7
Probability Density Function
for Example 6.1

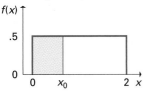

Figure 6.7 shows a plot of the probability density function with the shaded area indicating the cumulative distribution function evaluated at x_0, $F(x_0)$. Thus we see that

$$F(x_0) = 0.5x_0 \qquad\qquad \text{for } 0 < x_0 < 2$$

The probability that a fracture occurs between 0.5 mile and 1.5 miles along the pipe is

$$P(0.5 < X < 1.5) = F(1.5) - F(0.5)$$
$$= (0.5)(1.5) - (0.5)(0.5) = 0.5$$

This is the area under the probability density function from $x = 0.5$ to $x = 1.5$.

EXERCISES

6.1 An analyst has available two forecasts, F_1 and F_2, of earnings per share of a corporation next year. He intends to form a compromise forecast as a weighted average of the two individual forecasts. In forming the compromise forecast, weight X will be given to the first forecast and weight $(1 - X)$ to the second, so that the compromise forecast is $XF_1 + (1 - X)F_2$. The analyst wants to choose a value between 0 and 1 for the weight X, but he is quite uncertain of what will be the best choice. Suppose that what eventually emerges as the best possible choice of the weight X can be viewed as a random variable uniformly distributed between 0 and 1, having probability density function

$$f(x) = \begin{cases} 1 & \text{for } 0 \leq x \leq 1 \\ 0 & \text{for all other values of } x \end{cases}$$

(a) Draw the probability density function.
(b) Find and draw the cumulative distribution function.
(c) Find the probability that the best choice of the weight X is less than .25.
(d) Find the probability that the best choice of the weight X is more than .75.
(e) Find the probability that the best choice of the weight X is between .2 and .8.

6.2 The jurisdiction of a rescue team includes emergencies occurring on a stretch of river that is 4 miles long.

Experience has shown that the distance along this stretch, measured in miles from its northernmost point, at which an emergency occurs can be represented by a uniformly distributed random variable over the range 0 to 4 miles. Then, if X denotes the distance (in miles) of an emergency from the northernmost point of this stretch of river, its probability density function is

$$f(x) = \begin{cases} .25 & \text{for } 0 < x < 4 \\ 0 & \text{for all other } x \end{cases}$$

(a) Draw the probability density function.
(b) Find and draw the cumulative distribution function.
(c) Find the probability that a given emergency arises within 1 mile of the northernmost point of this stretch of river.
(d) The rescue team's base is at the midpoint of this stretch of river. Find the probability that a given emergency arises more than 1.5 miles from this base.

6.3 The incomes of all families in a particular suburb can be represented by a continuous random variable. It is known that the median income for all families in this suburb is $60,000 and that 40% of all families in the suburb have incomes above $72,000.
(a) For a randomly chosen family, what is the probability that income will be between $60,000 and $72,000?
(b) Given no further information, what can be said about the probability that a randomly chosen family has income below $65,000?

6.4 At the beginning of winter, a homeowner estimates that the probability is .4 that her total heating bill for the three winter months will be less than $380. She also estimates that the probability is .6 that the total bill will be less than $460.
(a) What is the probability that the total bill will be between $380 and $460?
(b) Given no further information, what can be said about the probability that the total bill will be less than $400?

6.2   EXPECTATIONS FOR CONTINUOUS RANDOM VARIABLES

In Section 5.2, we presented the concept of expected value for a discrete random variable and the expected value of a function of that random variable. Here we will extend those ideas to continuous random variables. Because the probability of any specific value is 0 for a continuous random variable we need to use Equation 6.3.

RATIONALE FOR EXPECTATIONS OF CONTINUOUS RANDOM VARIABLES

Suppose that a random experiment leads to an outcome that can be represented by a continuous random variable. If N independent replications of this experiment are carried out, then the **expected value** of the random variable is the average of the values taken, as the number of replications becomes infinitely large. The expected value of a random variable is denoted by $E(X)$.

Similarly, if $g(X)$ is any function of the random variable, X, then the expected value of this function is the average value taken by the function over repeated independent trials, as the number of trials becomes infinitely large. This expectation is denoted $E[g(X)]$.

By using calculus we can define expected values for continuous random variables similarly to that used for discrete random variables.

$$E\big[g(x)\big] = \int_x g(x)f(x)\,dx \qquad (6.3)$$

These concepts can be clearly presented if one understands integral calculus as shown in the chapter Appendix. Using Equation 6.3 we can obtain the mean and variance for continuous random variables. Equations 6.4 and 6.5 present the mean and variance for continuous random variables.

MEAN, VARIANCE, AND STANDARD DEVIATION

Let X be a continuous random variable. There are two important expected values that are used routinely to define continuous probability distributions.

1. The **mean of X**, denoted by μ_X, is defined as the expected value of X,

$$\mu_X = E(X) \tag{6.4}$$

2. The **variance of X**, denoted by σ_X^2, is defined as the expectation of the squared deviation, $(X - \mu_X)^2$, of the random variable from its mean

$$\sigma_X^2 = E[(X - \mu_X)^2] \tag{6.5}$$

or an alternative expression can be derived

$$\sigma_X^2 = E(X^2) - \mu_X^2 \tag{6.6}$$

3. The **standard deviation of X**, σ_X, is the square root of the variance.

ASSUMPTION

The mean and variance provide two important pieces of summary information about a probability distribution. The mean provides a measure of the center of the distribution. Consider a physical interpretation as follows: Cut out the graph of a probability density function. The point along the x-axis at which the figure exactly balances on one's finger is the mean of the distribution. For example, in Figure 6.4 the uniform distribution is symmetric about $x = 0.5$ and thus $\mu_X = 0.5$ is the mean of the random variable. In the example about vehicle breakdowns in a one-mile-long tunnel, a mean breakdown distance of 0.5 indicates that over a very large number of breakdowns the average distance into the tunnel is 0.5 mile.

The variance—or its square root, the standard deviation—provides a measure of the dispersion or spread of a distribution. Thus if we compare two uniform distributions with the same mean $\mu_X = 1$, one over the range 0.5 to 1.5 and the other over the range 0 to 2, we will find that the later has a larger variance because it is spread over a greater range.

In Section 5.3 we showed how to obtain the means and variances of linear functions of discrete random variables. The results are the same for continuous random variables, because the derivations make use of the expected value operator. The summary results from Chapter 5 are repeated in the box.

LINEAR FUNCTIONS OF RANDOM VARIABLES

Let X be a continuous random variable with mean μ_X and variance σ_X^2, and let a and b be any constant fixed numbers. Define the random variable W as

$$W = a + bX$$

Then the mean and variance of W are

$$\mu_W = E(a + bX) = a + b\mu_X \tag{6.7}$$

and

$$\sigma_W^2 = \text{Var}(a + bX) = b^2\sigma_X^2 \tag{6.8}$$

and the standard deviation of W is

$$\sigma_W = |b|\sigma_X \tag{6.9}$$

An important special case of these results is the, standardized random variable

$$Z = \frac{X - \mu_X}{\sigma_X} \tag{6.10}$$

which has mean 0 and variance 1.

EXAMPLE 6.2

HOME HEATING COSTS
(COMPUTE MEAN AND
STANDARD DEVIATION)

A homeowner estimates that within the range of likely temperatures, her January heating bill Y, in dollars, will be

$$Y = 290 - 5T$$

Where T is the average temperature in the month, in degrees Fahrenheit. If the average January temperature can be represented by a random variable with mean 24 and standard deviation 4, find the mean and standard deviation of this homeowner's January heating bill.

SOLUTION
The random variable T has mean, $\mu_T = 24$, and standard deviation, $\sigma_T = 4$. Therefore the expected heating bill is

$$\mu_Y = 290 - 5\mu_T$$
$$= 290 - (5)(24) = \$170.$$

The standard deviation is

$$\sigma_Y = |-5|\sigma_T = (5)(4) = \$20$$

EXERCISES

6.5 An author receives from a publisher a contract, according to which she is to be paid a fixed sum of $10,000, plus $1.50 for each copy of her book sold. Her uncertainty about total sales of the book can be represented by a random variable with mean 30,000 and standard deviation 8,000. Find the mean and standard deviation of the total payments she will receive.

6.6 A contractor submits a bid on a project, for which more research and development work needs to be done. It is estimated that the total cost of satisfying the project specifications will be $20 million, plus the cost of the further research and development work. The contractor views the cost of this work as a random variable with a mean $4 million and standard deviation $1 million. The contractor wishes to submit a bid such that his expected profit will be 10% of his expected

costs. What should be the bid? If this bid is accepted, what will be the standard deviation of the profit made by the project?

6.7 A charitable organization solicits donations by telephone. Employees are paid $60 plus 20% of the money their calls generate each week. The amount of money generated in a week can be viewed as a random variable with mean $700 and standard deviation $130. Find the mean and standard deviation of an employee's total pay in a week.

6.8 A salesman receives an annual salary of $6,000, plus 8% of the value of the orders he takes. The annual value of these orders can be represented by a random variable with the mean $600,000 and standard deviation $180,000. Find the mean and standard deviation of the salesman's annual income.

6.3   THE NORMAL DISTRIBUTION

In this section we present the normal probability distribution, which is the most used continuous random variable probability distribution for Economics and Business applications. An example of the normal probability density function is shown in Figure 6.8.

There are many reasons for its wide application.

1. The normal distribution closely approximates the probability distributions of a wide range of random variables. For example, the dimensions of parts or the weights of food packages often follow a normal distribution. This leads to Quality Control applications. Total sales or production often follow a normal distribution that leads us to a large family of applications in marketing and production management. The patterns of stock and bond prices are often modeled using the normal distribution in large computer-based financial trading models. Economic models use the normal distribution for a number of economic measures.

2. Distributions of sample means approach a normal distribution given a "large" sample size.

3. Computation of probabilities is direct and elegant.

4. The most important reason is that the normal probability distribution has led to good business decisions for a number of applications.

A formal definition of the normal probability density function is given by Equation 6.11.

PROBABILITY DENSITY FUNCTION OF THE NORMAL DISTRIBUTION

The **probability density function for a normally distributed random variable X** is

$$f(x) = \frac{1}{\sqrt{2\pi\sigma^2}} e^{-(x-\mu)^2/2\sigma^2} \qquad \text{for} \quad -\infty < x < \infty \qquad (6.11)$$

where μ and σ^2 are any number such that $-\infty < \mu < \infty$ and $0 < \sigma^2 < \infty$ and where e and π are physical constants, $e = 2.71828\ldots$ and $\pi = 3.14159\ldots.$

The normal probability distribution represents a large family of distributions, each with a unique specification for the parameters μ and σ^2. These parameters have a very convenient interpretation.

FIGURE 6.8
Probability Density Function for a Normal Distribution

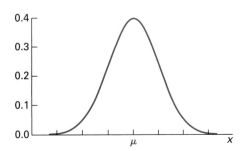

PROPERTIES OF THE NORMAL DISTRIBUTION

Suppose that the random variable X follows a normal distribution with parameters μ and σ^2. Then the following properties hold:

1. The mean of the random variable is μ,

$$E(X) = \mu$$

2. The variance of the random variable is σ^2,

$$\text{Var}(X) = E[(X - \mu)^2] = \sigma^2$$

3. The shape of the probability density function is a symmetric bell-shaped curve centered on the mean μ as shown in Figure 6.8.
4. By knowing the mean and variance we can define the normal distribution by using the notation

$$X \sim N(\mu, \sigma^2)$$

For our applied statistical analyses the normal distribution has a number of important characteristics. It is symmetric. Different central tendencies are indicated by differences in μ. In contrast, differences in σ^2 results in density functions of different width. By selecting values for μ and σ^2 we can define a large family of normal probability density functions. Differences in the means result in shifts of the entire distribution. In contrast, differences in the variance result in distributions with different widths.

Recall from Chapter 2 that we presented the empirical rule that states as a rough guide $\mu \pm \sigma$ covers about 68% of the range, while $\mu \pm 2\sigma$ covers about 95% of the range. For all practical purposes almost none of the range is outside $\mu \pm 3\sigma$. This useful approximation tool for interpretations based on descriptive statistics is based on the normal distribution.

The distribution mean provides a measure of central location, and the variance gives a measure of dispersion about the mean. Thus the parameters μ and σ^2 have different effects on the probability density function of a normal random variable. Figure 6.9(a) shows probability density functions for two normal distributions with a common variance and different means. We see that increases in the mean shift the distribution without changing its shape. In Figure 6.9(b), the two density functions have the same mean but different variances. Each is symmetric about the common mean, but the larger variance results in a wider distribution.

Our next task is to learn how to obtain probabilities for a specified normal distribution. First we will introduce the cumulative distribution function.

FIGURE 6.9
Effects of μ and σ^2 on the Probability Density Function of a Normal Random Variable
a. Two Normal Distributions with Different Means
b. Two Normal Distributions with Different Variances and Mean = 5

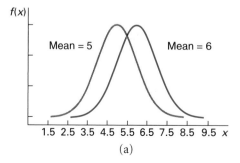

(a)

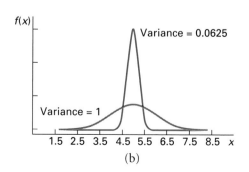

(b)

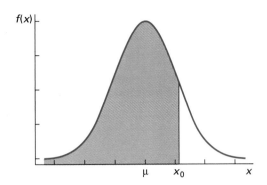

FIGURE 6.10
The Shaded Area is the Probability That X Does Not Exceed x_0 for a Normal Random Variable

---

CUMULATIVE DISTRIBUTION FUNCTION OF THE NORMAL DISTRIBUTION

Suppose that X is a normal random variable with mean μ and variance σ^2; that is $X \sim N(\mu, \sigma^2)$. Then the cumulative distribution function

$$F(x_0) = P(X \le x_0)$$

This is the area under the normal probability density function to the left of x_0, as illustrated in Figure 6.10. As for any proper density function, the total area under the curve is 1; that is

$$F(\infty) = 1$$

FIGURE 6.11
Cumulative Distribution for a Normal Random Variable

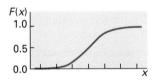

We do not have a simple algebraic expression for calculating the cumulative distribution function for a normally distributed random variable (chapter Appendix). The general shape of the cumulative distribution function is shown in Figure 6.11. Equation 6.12 is used to compute normal probabilities using the cumulative distribution function.

RANGE PROBABILITIES FOR NORMAL RANDOM VARIABLES

Let X be a normal random variable with cumulative distribution function $F(x)$, and let a and b be two possible values of X, with $a < b$. Then

$$P(a < X < b) = F(b) - F(a) \qquad \textbf{(6.12)}$$

The probability is the area under the corresponding probability density function between a and b as shown in Figure 6.12.

Any probability can be obtained from the cumulative distribution function. However, we do not have a convenient way to directly compute the probability for any normal distribution with a specific mean and variance. We could use numerical integration procedures

FIGURE 6.12
Normal Density Function with the Shaded Area Indicating the Probability That X Is Between a and b

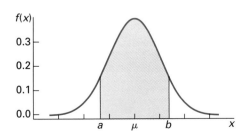

with a computer, but that approach would be tedious and cumbersome. Fortunately we can convert any normal distribution to a standard normal distribution with mean 0 and variance 1.

THE STANDARD NORMAL DISTRIBUTION

Let Z be a normal random variable with mean 0 and variance 1; that is

$$Z \sim N(0, 1)$$

We say that Z follows the **standard normal distribution**.
Denote the cumulative distribution function as $F(z)$, and a and b as two numbers with $a < b$, then

$$P(a < Z < b) = F(b) - F(a) \qquad \qquad \textbf{(6.13)}$$

We can obtain probabilities for any normally distributed random variable by first converting the random variable to a standard normally distributed random variable, Z. There is always a direct relationship between any normally distributed random variable and the standard normally distributed random variable, Z. That relationship uses the transformation

$$Z = \frac{X - \mu}{\sigma}$$

where X is a normally distributed random variable

$$X \sim N(\mu, \sigma^2)$$

This important result allows us to use the standard normal table to compute probabilities associated with any normally distributed random variable. Now let us see how probabilities can be computed for the standard normal Z.

The cumulative distribution function of the standard normal distribution is tabulated in Table 1 in the Appendix. This table gives values of

$$F(z) = P(Z \leq z)$$

for nonnegative values of z. For example the cumulative probability for a Z value of 1.25 from Table 1

$$F(1.25) = 0.8944$$

This is the area , designated in Figure 6.13, for Z less than 1.25. Because of the symmetry of the normal distribution the probability that $Z > -1.25$ is also equal to 0.8944. In general

FIGURE 6.13
Standard Normal
Distribution with Probability
for $Z = 1.25$

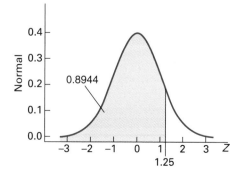

FIGURE 6.14
Standard Normal
Distribution for Negative *Z*
Equal to –1

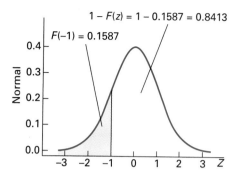

values of the cumulative distribution function for negative values of *z* can be inferred using the symmetry of the probability density function.

To find the cumulative probability for a negative *z* (for example $Z = -1.0$) defined as

$$F(-Z_0) = P(Z \leq -Z_0) = F(-1.0)$$

we use the complement of the probability for $Z = +1$ as shown in Figure 6.14.

From the symmetry we can state that

$$F(-Z) = 1 - P(Z \leq +Z) = 1 - F(Z)$$
$$F(-1) = 1 - P(Z \leq +1) = 1 - F(1)$$

Figure 6.15 indicates the symmetry for the corresponding positive values of *Z*.

FIGURE 6.15
Normal Distribution for
Positive *Z* = +1

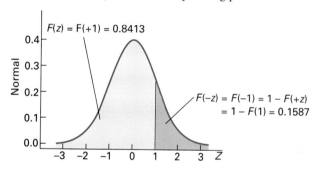

In Figure 6.16 we can see that the area under the curve to the left of $Z = -1$ is equal to the area to the right of $Z = +1$ because of the symmetry of the normal distribution. The area substantially below $-Z$ is often called the "lower tail" and the area substantially above $+z$ is called the "upper tail."

FIGURE 6.16
Normal Density Function
with Symmetric Upper and
Lower Values

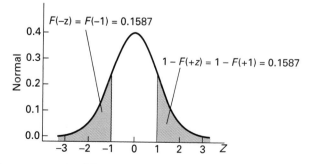

EXAMPLE 6.3

INVESTMENT PORTFOLIO VALUE PROBABILITIES (COMPUTE NORMAL PROBABILITIES)

A client has an investment portfolio whose mean value is equal to $500,000 with a standard deviation of $15,000. She has asked you to determine the probability that the value of her portfolio is between $485,000 and $530,000.

SOLUTION

The problem is illustrated in Figure 6.17. To solve the problem we must first determine the corresponding Z values for the portfolio limits. For \$485,000 the corresponding Z value is

$$Z_{485} = \frac{485,000 - 500,000}{15,000} = -1.0$$

And for the upper value, \$530,000, the Z value is

$$Z_{530} = \frac{530,000 - 500,000}{15,000} = +2.0$$

As shown in Figure 6.17 the probability that the portfolio value, X, is between \$485,000 and \$530,000 is equal to the probability that Z is between -1 and $+2$. To obtain the probability we first compute the probabilities for the lower and the upper tail and subtract these probabilities from 1. Algebraically the result is

$$P(485,000 \leq X \leq 530,000) = P(-1 \leq Z \leq +2) = 1 - P(Z \leq -1) - P(Z \geq +2)$$
$$= 1 - 0.1587 - 0.0228 = 0.8185$$

The probability for the indicated range is thus 0.8185.

FIGURE 6.17
Normal Distribution for
Example 6.3

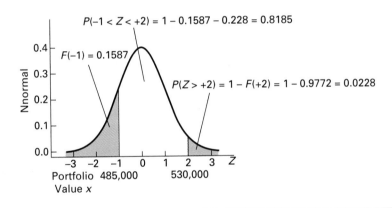

The probabilities can also be computed by using Equation 6.14.

FINDING RANGE PROBABILITIES FOR NORMALLY DISTRIBUTED RANDOM VARIABLES

Let X be a normally distributed random variable with mean μ and variance σ^2. Then random variable $Z = (X - \mu)/\sigma$ has a standard normal distribution: $Z \sim N(0, 1)$
    It follows that if a and b are any numbers with $a < b$, then

$$P(a < X < b) = P\left(\frac{a - \mu}{\sigma} < Z < \frac{b - \mu}{\sigma}\right) \tag{6.14}$$
$$= F\left(\frac{b - \mu}{\sigma}\right) - F\left(\frac{a - \mu}{\sigma}\right)$$

where Z is the standard normal random variable and $F(z)$ denotes its cumulative distribution function.

EXAMPLE 6.4

NORMAL PROBABILITY
DISTRIBUTION (COMPUTE
NORMAL PROBABILITIES)

If $X \sim N(15, 16)$, find the probability that X is larger than 18.

SOLUTION

This probability can be computed as follows

$$
\begin{aligned}
P(X > 18) &= P\left(Z > \frac{18 - \mu}{\sigma}\right) \\
&= P\left(Z > \frac{18 - 15}{4}\right) \\
&= P(Z > 0.75) \\
&= 1 - P(Z < 0.75) \\
&= 1 - F(0.75)
\end{aligned}
$$

From Table 3 in the Appendix, $F(0.75)$ is 0.7734 and therefore

$$
P(X > 18) = 1 - 0.7734 = 0.2266
$$

EXAMPLE 6.5

LIGHTBULB LIFE (COMPUTE
NORMAL PROBABILITIES)

A company produces lightbulbs whose life follows a normal distribution with mean 1,200 hours and standard deviation 250 hours. If we choose a lightbulb at random, what is the probability that its lifetime will be between 900 and 1,300 hours?

SOLUTION

Let X represent lifetime in hours. Then

$$
\begin{aligned}
P(900 < X < 1,300) &= P\left(\frac{900 - 1,200}{250} < Z < \frac{1,300 - 1,200}{250}\right) \\
&= P(-1.2 < Z < 0.4) \\
&= F(0.4) - F(-1.2) \\
&= 0.6554 - (1 - 0.8849) = 0.5403
\end{aligned}
$$

Hence the probability is approximately 0.54 that a lightbulb will last between 900 and 1,300 hours.

EXAMPLE 6.6

STUDENT TEST SCORES
(COMPUTE NORMAL
PROBABILITIES)

A very large group of students obtains test scores that are normally distributed with mean 60 and standard deviation 15. What proportion of the students obtained scores between 85 and 95?

SOLUTION

Let X denote the test score. Then the probability can be computed as follows.

$$
\begin{aligned}
P(85 < X < 95) &= P\left(\frac{85 - 60}{15} < Z < \frac{95 - 60}{15}\right) \\
&= P(1.67 < Z < 2.33) \\
&= F(2.33) - F(1.67) \\
&= 0.9901 - 0.9525 = 0.0376
\end{aligned}
$$

That is, 3.76% of the students obtained scores in the range 85 to 95.

EXAMPLE 6.7

CUTOFF POINTS FOR STUDENT
TEST SCORES (COMPUTE
NORMAL RANDOM VARIABLES)

For the test scores of Example 6.6 find the cutoff point for the top 10% of all students.

SOLUTION

Define b as the cutoff point. To determine the numerical value of the cutoff point we first note that the probability of exceeding b is 0.10 and thus the probability of being less than b is 0.90. The upper tail value of 0.10 is shown in Figure 6.18. We can now state the probability from the cumulative distribution as

$$0.90 = P\left(Z < \frac{b - 60}{15}\right)$$

$$= F\left(\frac{b - 60}{15}\right)$$

FIGURE 6.18
Normal Distribution with
Mean 60 and Standard
Deviation 15 Showing Upper
Tail Probability Equal to 0.10

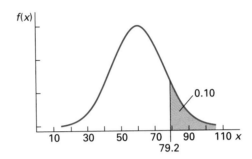

From Table 3 of the Appendix, we find that $Z = 1.28$ when $F(Z) = 0.90$. Therefore we have

$$\frac{b - 60}{15} = 1.28$$
$$b = 79.2$$

Thus we conclude that 10% of the students obtain scores above 79.2.

In Examples 6.6 and 6.7 we note that test scores are typically given as integer values and thus the distribution of test scores is discrete. However, because of the large number of possible outcomes the normal distribution provides a very good approximation for the discrete distribution. In most applied business and economic problems we are in fact using the normal distribution to approximate a discrete distribution that has many different outcomes.

Normal Probability Plots

The normal probability model is the most used probability model for the reasons previously noted. In most applied problems we cannot be sure that the data comes from a normal distribution. Thus we are assuming that the normal distribution is a close approximation to the actual unknown distribution. Normal probability plots provide a good way to test this assumption and determine if the normal model can be used. Usage is simple. If the data follows a normal distribution the plot will be a straight line. Figure 6.19 is a normal probability plot for a random sample of $n = 1,000$ observations from a normal distribution with $\mu = 100$ and $\sigma = 25$. The plot was generated using Minitab with the command

```
GRAPH>PROBABILITY PLOT>NORMAL
```

FIGURE 6.19
Minitab Output: Normal
Probability Plot for a Normal
Distribution

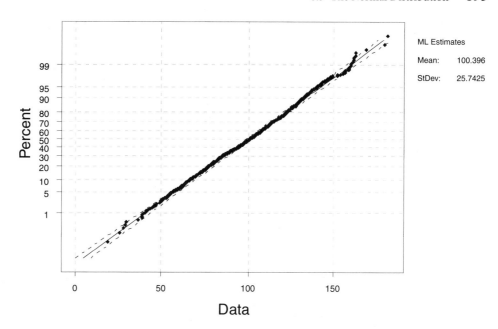

The horizontal axis indicates the data points ranked in order from the smallest to the largest. The vertical axis indicates the cumulative normal probabilities of the ranked data values if the sample data was obtained from a population whose random variables follow a normal distribution. We see that the vertical axis has a transformed normal scale. The data plots in Figure 6.19 are close to a straight line even at the upper and lower limits, and that result provides solid evidence that the data has a normal distribution. The dotted lines provide an interval within which data points from a normally distributed random variable would occur in most cases. Thus if the plotted points are within the boundaries established by the dotted lines we can conclude that the data points represent a normally distributed random variable.

Uniform Distribution

Next consider a random sample of $n = 1,000$ observations drawn from a *uniform distribution* with limits 25 to 175. Figure 6.20 shows the normal probability plot. In this case the data plot has an S shape that clearly deviates from a straight line, and the sample data does not follow a normal distribution. Large deviations at the extreme high and low values are a major concern because statistical inference is often based on small probabilities of extreme values.

Skewed Distribution

Next let us consider a highly skewed discrete distribution as shown in Figure 6.21.
In Figure 6.22 we see the normal probability plot for this highly skewed distribution.

Again we see that the data plot is not a straight line but has considerable deviation at the extreme high and low values. This plot clearly indicates that the data does not come from a normal distribution.

The previous examples provide us with an indication of possible results from a normal probability plot. If the plot from your problem is similar to Figure 6.19, then you are safe in assuming that the normal model is a good approximation. Note, however, that if your plot deviates from a straight line, as do those in Figures 6.20 and 6.22, then the normal probability distribution should not be used.

FIGURE 6.20
Minitab Output: Normal
Probability Plot for a
Uniform Distribution

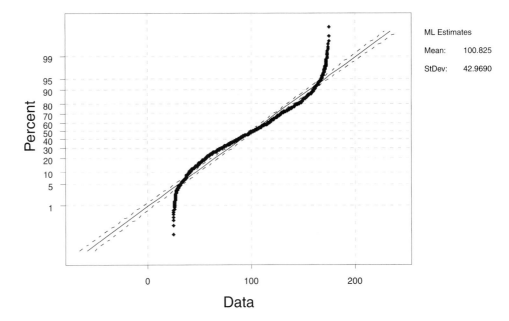

FIGURE 6.21
Skewed Discrete Probability
Distribution Function

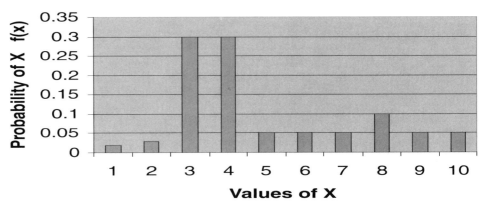

FIGURE 6.22
Minitab Output: Normal
Probability Plot for a Highly
Skewed Distribution

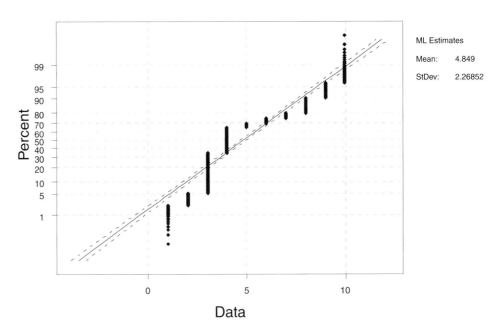

EXERCISES

6.9 Let the random variable Z follow a standard normal distribution.
(a) Find $P(Z < 1.20)$
(b) Find $P(Z > 1.33)$
(c) Find $P(Z < -1.70)$
(d) Find $P(Z > -1.00)$
(e) Find $P(1.20 < Z < 1.33)$
(f) Find $P(-1.70 < Z < 1.20)$
(g) Find $P(-1.70 < Z < -1.00)$

6.10 Let the random variable Z follow a standard normal distribution.
(a) The probability is .70 that Z is less than what number?
(b) The probability is .25 that Z is less than what number?
(c) The probability is .2 that Z is greater than what number?
(d) The probability is .6 that Z is greater than what number?

6.11 It is known that amounts of money spent on textbooks in a year by students on a particular campus follow a normal distribution with mean $380 and standard deviation $50.
(a) What is the probability that a randomly chosen student will spend less than $400 on textbooks in a year?
(b) What is the probability that a randomly chosen student will spend more than $360 on textbooks in a year?
(c) Draw a graph to illustrate why the answers to parts (a) and (b) are the same.
(d) What is the probability that a randomly chosen student will spend between $300 and $400 on textbooks in a year?
(e) You want to find a range of dollar spending on textbooks in a year that includes 80% of all students on this campus. Explain why any number of such ranges could be found, and find the shortest one.

6.12 Anticipated consumer demand for a product next month can be represented by a normal random variable with mean 1,200 units and standard deviation 100 units.
(a) What is the probability that sales will exceed 1,000 units?
(b) What is the probability that sales will be between 1,100 and 1,300 units?
(c) The probability is .10 that sales will be more than how many units?

6.13 The tread life of a particular brand of tire has a normal distribution with mean 35,000 miles and standard deviation 4,000 miles.
(a) What proportion of these tires have tread lives of more than 38,000 miles?

(b) What proportion of these tires have tread lives of less than 32,000 miles?
(c) What proportion of these tires have tread lives of between 32,000 and 38,000 miles?
(d) Draw a graph of the probability density function of tread lives, illustrating
    (i) Why the answers to (a) and (b) are the same.
    (ii) Why the answers to (a), (b), and (c) sum to one.

6.14 An investment portfolio contains stocks of a large number of corporations. Over the last year the rates of return on these corporate stocks followed a normal distribution, with mean 12.2%, and standard deviation 7.2%.
(a) For what proportion of these corporations was the rate of return higher than 20%?
(b) For what proportion of these corporations was the rate of return negative?
(c) For what proportion of these corporations was the rate of return between 5% and 15%?

6.15 A company produces bags of a chemical, and it is concerned about impurity content. It is believed that the weights of impurities per bag are normally distributed, with mean 12.2 grams, and standard deviation 2.8 grams. A bag is chosen at random.
(a) What is the probability that it contains less than 10 grams of impurities?
(b) What is the probability that it contains more than 15 grams of impurities?
(c) What is the probability that it contains between 12 and 15 grams of impurities?
(d) It is possible, without doing the detailed calculations, to deduce which of the answers to (a) and (b) will be the larger. How?

6.16 A contractor regards the cost of fulfilling a particular contract as a normally distributed random variable with mean $500,000 and standard deviation $50,000.
(a) What is the probability that the cost of fulfilling the contract will be between $460,000 and $540,000?
(b) The probability is .2 that the contract will cost less than how much to fulfill?
(c) Find the shortest range such that the probability is .95 that the cost of fulfilling the contract will fall in this range.

6.17 Scores on a test follow a normal distribution. What is the probability that a randomly selected student will achieve a score that exceeds the mean score by more than 1.5 standard deviations?

6.18 A new television series is to be shown. A broadcasting executive feels that his uncertainty about the rating which the show will receive in its first month can be represented by a normal distribution with mean 18.2 and standard deviation 1.6. According to this executive, the probability is .1 that the rating will be less than what number?

6.19 A broadcasting executive is reviewing the prospects for a new television series. According to her judgment, the probability is .25 that the show will achieve a rating higher than 17.8, and the probability is .15 that it will achieve a rating higher than 19.2. If the executive's uncertainty about the rating can be represented by a normal distribution, what are the mean and variance of that distribution?

6.20 Scores on an examination taken by a very large group of students are normally distributed with mean 700 and standard deviation 120.
  (a) An A is awarded for a score higher than 820. What proportion of all students obtain an A?
  (b) A B is awarded for scores between 730 and 820. An instructor has a section of 100 students who can be viewed as a random sample of all students in the large group. Find the expected number of students in this section who will obtain a B.
  (c) It is decided to give a failing grade to 5% of students with the lowest scores. What is the minimum score needed to avoid a failing grade?

6.21 I am considering two alternative investments. In both cases, I am unsure about the percentage return but believe that my uncertainty can be represented by normal distributions with the means and standard deviations shown in the accompanying table. I want to make the investment that is more likely to produce a return of at least 10%. Which should I choose?

	MEAN	STANDARD DEVIATION
Investment A	10.4	1.2
Investment B	11.0	4.0

6.22 A company can purchase raw material from either of two suppliers and is concerned about the amounts of impurity the material contains. A review of the records for each supplier indicates that the percentage impurity levels in consignments of the raw material follow normal distributions with the means and standard deviations given in the table. The company is particularly anxious that the impurity level in a consignment not exceed 5% and wants to purchase from the supplier more likely to meet that specification. Which supplier should be chosen?

	MEAN	STANDARD DEVIATION
Supplier A	4.4	0.4
Supplier B	4.2	0.6

6.23 An instructor has found that times spent by students on a particular homework assignment follow a normal distribution with mean 150 minutes and standard deviation 40 minutes.

  (a) The probability is .9 that a randomly chosen student spends more than how many minutes on this assignment?
  (b) The probability is .8 that a randomly chosen student spends less than how many minutes on this assignment?
  (c) Two students are chosen at random. What is the probability that at least one of them spends at least two hours on this assignment?

6.24 A company services copiers. A review of its records shows that the time taken for a service call can be represented by a normal random variable with mean 75 minutes and standard deviation 20 minutes.
  (a) What proportion of service calls take less than one hour?
  (b) What proportion of service calls take more than 90 minutes?
  (c) Sketch a graph to show why the answers to parts (a) and (b) are the same.
  (d) The probability is .1 that a service call takes more than how many minutes?

6.25 Scores on an achievement test are known to be normally distributed, with mean 420 and standard deviation 80.
  (a) For a randomly chosen person taking this test, what is the probability of a score between 400 and 480?
  (b) What is the minimum test score needed in order to be in the top 10% of all people taking the test?
  (c) For a randomly chosen individual, state, without doing the calculations, in which of the following ranges his or her score is most likely to be: 400–440, 440–480, 480–520, 520–560.
  (d) In which of the ranges listed in (c) is the individual's score least likely to be?
  (e) Two people taking the test are chosen at random. What is the probability that at least one of them scores more than 500 points?

6.26 It is estimated that the times a well-known rock band, the Living Ingrates, spends on-stage at their concerts follow a normal distribution with mean 200 minutes and standard deviation 20 minutes.
  (a) What proportion of concerts played by this band last between 180 and 200 minutes?
  (b) An audience member smuggles a tape recorder with reel-to-reel tapes with capacity 245 minutes into a Living Ingrates concert. What is the probability that this capacity will be insufficient to record the entire concert?
  (c) If the standard deviation of concert time was only 15 minutes, state, without doing the calculations, whether the probability that a concert would last more than 245 minutes would be larger than, smaller than, or the same as that found in (b). Sketch a graph to illustrate your answer.
  (d) The probability is .1 that a Living Ingrates concert will last less than how many minutes? (Assume, as

originally, that the population standard deviation is 20 minutes.)

6.27 An economics test is taken by a large group of students. The test scores are normally distributed with mean 70, and the probability that a randomly chosen student receives a score less than 85 is .9332. Four students are chosen at random. What is the probability that at least one of them scores more than 80 points on this test?

6.4 NORMAL DISTRIBUTION APPROXIMATION FOR BINOMIAL DISTRIBUTION

In this section we will show how the normal distribution can be used to approximate the discrete binomial and proportion random variables that are used extensively in business and economics. This approximation can be used to compute probabilities for larger sample sizes when tables are not readily available. The normal distribution approximation of the binomial distribution also provides a benefit for applied problem solving. We will learn that procedures based on the normal distribution can also be applied in problems involving binomial and proportion random variables. Thus you can reduce the number of different procedures that you need to know for business statistical problem solving.

Let us consider a problem with n independent trials, each with probability of success π. In Section 5.4 we saw that the binomial random variable X could be written as the sum of n independent Bernoulli random variables

$$X = X_1 + X_2 + \cdots + X_n$$

where the random variable X_i takes the value 1 if the outcome of the ith trial is "success" and 0 otherwise, with respective probabilities π and $1 - \pi$. The number X of successes that result has a binomial distribution with mean and variance

$$E(X) = n\pi \qquad\qquad \mathrm{Var}(X) = n\pi(1 - \pi)$$

The plot of a binomial distribution with $\pi = 0.5$ and $n = 100$, in Figure 6.23, shows us that the binomial has the same shape as the normal. This visual evidence that the binomial

FIGURE 6.23
Binomial Distribution with $n = 100$ and $\pi = 0.5$

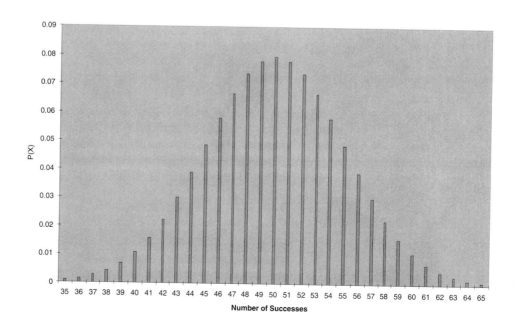

can be approximated by a normal distribution with the same mean and variance is also established in work done by mathematical statisticians. A good rule for us is that the normal distribution provides a good approximation for the binomial distribution when $n\pi(1-\pi) > 9$.

In order to better understand the normal distribution approximation for the binomial distribution consider Figure 6.24 a and b. In both a and b we have shown points from a normal probability density function compared to the corresponding probabilities from a binomial distribution. In part a we note that the approximation rule value is

$$n\pi(1-\pi) = 100(0.5)(1-0.5) = 25 > 9$$

and that the normal distribution provides a very close approximation to the binomial distribution. In contrast the example in part b has an approximation rule value

$$n\pi(1-\pi) = 25(0.2)(1-0.2) = 4 < 9$$

and the normal distribution does not provide a good approximation for the binomial distribution. You can develop other similar examples using Minitab and the commands,

```
CALC> PROBABILITY DISTRIBUTIONS> BINOMIAL
```

and

```
CALC> PROBABILITY DISTRIBUTIONS> NORMAL
```

and then using the command,

```
GRAPH> PLOT.
```

Evidence such as that contained in Figure 6.24 has provided the rationale for widespread application of the normal approximation for the Binomial. We will now proceed to develop the procedure for its application.

FIGURE 6.24
Comparison of Binomial and Normal Approximation

a. Binomial with $\pi = 0.5$ and $n = 100$ and Normal with $\mu = 50$ and $\sigma = 5$

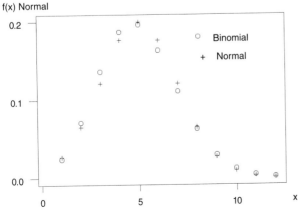

b. Binomial with $\pi = 0.2$ and $n = 25$ and Normal with $\mu = 5$ and $\sigma = 2$

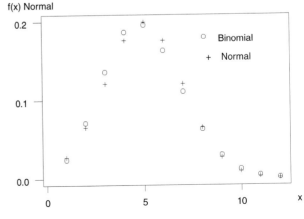

By using the mean and the variance from the Binomial distribution we find that if the number of trials n is large—such that $n\pi(1-\pi) > 9$—then the distribution of the random variable

$$Z = \frac{X - E(X)}{\sqrt{\mathrm{Var}(X)}} = \frac{X - n\pi}{\sqrt{n\pi(1-\pi)}}$$

is approximately standard normal.

This result is very important because it allows us to find, for large n, the probability that the number of successes lies in a given range. If we want to determine the probability that the number of successes will be between a and b, inclusive, we have

$$P(a \le X \le b) = P\left(\frac{a - n\pi}{\sqrt{n\pi(1-\pi)}} \le \frac{X - n\pi}{\sqrt{n\pi(1-\pi)}} \le \frac{b - n\pi}{\sqrt{n\pi(1-\pi)}}\right)$$

$$= P\left(\frac{a - n\pi}{\sqrt{n\pi(1-\pi)}} \le Z \le \frac{b - n\pi}{\sqrt{n\pi(1-\pi)}}\right)$$

With n large Z is well approximated by the standard normal and we can find the probability using the methods from Section 6.3.

If the number of trials is only of moderate size we can improve the approximation by using a *continuity correction factor*. Since we are approximating a discrete random variable by using a continuous random variable we need to adjust for the differences between the discrete values. We can do this by replacing a and b by $(a - 0.5)$ and $(b + 0.5)$, respectively. Then we have

$$P(a \le X \le b) \cong P\left(\frac{a - 0.5 - n\pi}{\sqrt{n\pi(1-\pi)}} \le Z \le \frac{b + 0.5 - n\pi}{\sqrt{n\pi(1-\pi)}}\right)$$

The continuity correction factor can be used when, $5 < n\pi(1-\pi) < 9$.

To see the rationale for this modification, suppose that we seek the probability that the number of successes is greater than or equal to 15 and less than or equal to 19. Figure 6.25 shows the upper end of this interval approximation. The actual number of successes must be an integer. The integer 19 includes the continuous normal distribution interval from 18.5 to 19.5. Thus if 19 is included—$X \le 19$—at the upper end of the interval we use the continuous value 19.5 for the normal approximation. But if 19 is excluded—$X < 19$—at the upper end of the interval we use the continuous value 18.5 for the normal approximation.

FIGURE 6.25
Continuity Correction for
Normal Approximation of
the Binomial

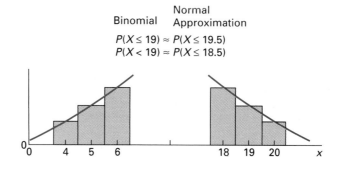

RESULTS FOR APPROXIMATING BINOMIAL PROBABILITIES USING THE NORMAL DISTRIBUTION

Let X be the number of successes from n independent Bernoulli trials, each with probability of success π. The number of successes, X, is a Binomial random variable and if $n\pi(1-\pi) > 9$ a good approximation is

$$P(a \leq X \leq b) \cong P\left(\frac{a - n\pi}{\sqrt{n\pi(1-\pi)}} \leq Z \leq \frac{b - n\pi}{\sqrt{n\pi(1-\pi)}}\right) \qquad (6.15)$$

or if $5 < n\pi(1-\pi) < 9$ we can use the **continuity correction factor** to obtain

$$P(a \leq X \leq b) \cong P\left(\frac{a - 0.5 - n\pi}{\sqrt{n\pi(1-\pi)}} \leq Z \leq \frac{b + 0.5 - n\pi}{\sqrt{n\pi(1-\pi)}}\right) \qquad (6.16)$$

where Z is a standard normal random variable.

EXAMPLE 6.8

CUSTOMER SALES (COMPUTE NORMAL PROBABILITIES)

A salesman makes initial telephone contact with potential customers in an effort to assess whether a follow-up visit to their homes is likely to be worthwhile. His experience suggests that 40% of the initial contacts lead to follow-up visits. If he contacts 100 people by telephone, what is the probability that between 45 and 50 home visits will result?

SOLUTION

Let X be the number of follow-up visits. Then X has a binomial distribution with $n = 100$ and $\pi = 0.40$. Approximating the required probability without using the continuity correction factor gives

$$
\begin{aligned}
P(45 \leq X \leq 50) &\cong P\left(\frac{45 - (100)(0.4)}{\sqrt{(100)(0.4)(0.6)}} \leq Z \leq \frac{50 - (100)(0.4)}{\sqrt{(100)(0.4)(0.6)}}\right) \\
&= P(1.02 \leq Z \leq 2.04) \\
&= F(2.04) - F(1.02) \\
&= 0.9793 - 0.8461 = 0.1332
\end{aligned}
$$

This probability is shown as an area under the standard normal curve in Figure 6.26.

FIGURE 6.26
Probability of 45 to 50 Successes for a Binomial Distribution with $n = 100$ and $\pi = 0.4$

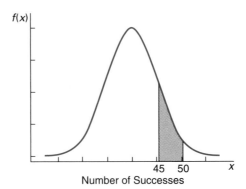

Proportion Random Variable

In a number of applied problems we have a need to compute probabilities for proportion intervals. We can do this by using a direct extension of the normal distribution approximation for the binomial distribution. A proportion random variable P can be computed by dividing the number of successes, X, by the sample size n.

$$P = \frac{X}{n}$$

Then using the linear transformation of random variables the mean and the variance of P can be computed as

$$\mu = \pi$$
$$\sigma^2 = \frac{\pi(1 - \pi)}{n}$$

We can use the resulting mean and variance with the normal to compute the desired probability.

EXAMPLE 6.9

ELECTION FORECASTING (COMPUTE PROPORTION PROBABILITIES)

We have often observed the success in forecasting elections by television networks. This is a good example of the success of probability methods in applied problems. Consider how elections can be predicted by using relatively small samples in a simplified example. An election forecaster has obtained a random sample of 900 voters, in which 500 indicate that they will vote for Susan Chung. Should Susan anticipate winning the election?

SOLUTION

In this problem we assume only two candidates and thus if more than 50% of the population supports Susan she will win the election. We will compute the probability that 500 or more voters out of a sample 900 support Susan under the assumption that exactly 50%, $\pi = 0.50$, of the entire population supports Susan.

$$P(X \geq 500 \mid n = 900, \pi = 0.50) \approx P(X \geq 500 \mid \mu = 450, \sigma^2 = 225)$$
$$= P\left(Z \geq \frac{500 - 450}{\sqrt{225}}\right)$$
$$= P(Z \geq 3.33)$$
$$= 0.001$$

The probability of 500 successes out of 900 trials if $\pi = 0.50$ is very small and therefore we conclude that π must be greater than 0.50. Hence we predict that Susan Chung will win the election.

We could also compute the probability that more than 55.6% (500/900) of the sample indicate support for Susan if the population proportion is $\pi = 0.50$. Using the mean and variance for proportion random variables

$$\mu = \pi = 0.50$$
$$\sigma^2 = \frac{\pi(1 - \pi)}{n} = \frac{.50(1 - .50)}{900}$$
$$\sigma = 0.0167$$
$$P(P \geq 0.556 \mid n = 900, \pi = 0.50) \approx P(P \geq 0.556 \mid \mu = 0.50, \sigma = 0.0167)$$
$$= P\left(Z \geq \frac{0.556 - 0.50}{0.0167}\right)$$
$$= P(Z \geq 3.33)$$
$$= 0.001$$

Note that the probability is exactly the same as that for the corresponding binomial random variable. This is always the case because each proportion value is directly related to a specific number of successes.

EXERCISES

6.28 A car rental company has determined that the probability a car will need service work in any given month is .2. The company has 900 cars.
  (a) What is the probability that more than 200 cars will require service work in a particular month?
  (b) What is the probability that fewer than 175 cars will need service work in a given month?
  (Use the normal approximation to the binomial distribution, without the continuity correction.)

6.29 It is known that 10% of all the items produced by a particular manufacturing process are defective. From the very large output of a single day, 400 items are selected at random.
  (a) What is the probability that at least 35 of the selected items are defective?
  (b) What is the probability that between 40 and 50 of the selected items are defective?
  (c) What is the probability that between 34 and 48 of the selected items are defective?
  (d) Without doing the calculations, state which of the following ranges of defectives has the highest probability: 37–39, 39–41, 41–43, 43–45, 45–47.
  (Use the normal approximation to the binomial distribution, without the continuity correction.)

6.30 A sample of 100 blue-collar employees at a large corporation is taken to assess their attitudes on a proposed new work schedule. If 60% of all blue-collar employees at this corporation favor the new schedule, what is the probability that less than 50 of the sample members will be in favor?
  (Use the normal approximation to the binomial distribution, without the continuity correction.)

6.31 Suppose that half of all students in campus dormitories are dissatisfied with the food service. A random sample of 40 students was taken.
  (a) What is the probability that more than 15 students in the sample were dissatisfied with the food service?
  (b) What is the probability that the number of students who were dissatisfied with the food service was between 18 and 22 (inclusive)?
  (Use the normal approximation to the binomial distribution, with the continuity correction.)

6.32 A hospital finds that 25% of its bills are at least one month in arrears. A random sample of 45 bills was taken.
  (a) What is the probability that less than 10 bills in the sample were at least one month in arrears?
  (b) What is the probability that the number of bills in the sample at least one month in arrears was between 12 and 15 (inclusive)?
  (Use the normal approximation to the binomial distribution, with the continuity correction.)

6.33 The tread life of a brand of tire can be represented (as in Exercise 20) by a normal distribution with mean 35,000 miles and standard deviation 4,000 miles. A sample of 100 of these tires is taken. What is the probability that more than 25 of them have tread lives of more than 38,000 miles?
  (Use the normal approximation to the binomial distribution, without the continuity correction.)

6.34 Bags of a chemical produced by a company have impurity weights that can be represented by a normal distribution with mean 12.2 grams, and standard deviation 2.8 grams. A random sample of 400 of these bags is taken. What is the probability that at least 100 of them contain less than 10 grams of impurities?

6.5 THE EXPONENTIAL DISTRIBUTION

We will now introduce a continuous distribution, the *exponential distribution*, that has been found to be particularly useful for waiting line, or queuing, problems. In many service time problems the service times can be modeled by using the exponential distribution. We should note that the exponential distribution differs from the normal in two important ways: It is restricted to random variables with positive values, and its distribution is not symmetric.

THE EXPONENTIAL DISTRIBUTION

The exponential random variable $T(t > 0)$ has a probability density function

$$f(t) = \lambda e^{-\lambda t} \qquad \text{for } t > 0 \tag{6.17}$$

where λ is the mean number of occurrences per unit time, t is the number of time units until the next occurrence, and $e = 2.71828....$ Then T is said to follow an **exponential probability distribution.** It can be shown that λ is the same parameter used for the Poisson distribution in Section 5.6 and that the mean time between occurrences is $1/\lambda$.

The cumulative distribution function is

$$F(t) = 1 - e^{-\lambda t} \qquad \text{for } t > 0 \tag{6.18}$$

The distribution has mean $1/\lambda$ and variance $1/\lambda^2$.

The random variable T can be used to represent the length of time until the end of a service time or the time until the next arrival to a queuing process, beginning at an arbitrary time 0. The model assumptions are the same as those for the Poisson distribution. Note that the Poisson distribution provides the probability of X successes or arrivals during a unit time. In contrast the exponential distribution provides the probability that a success or arrival will occur during an interval of time t. Figure 6.27 shows the probability density function for an exponential distribution with $\lambda = 0.2$. The area to the left of 10 gives the probability that a task will be completed before time 10. This area can be obtained by evaluating the function $1 - e^{-\lambda t}$ for the given value of $t = 10$. The function can be computed either by using your hand electronic calculator or by using Table 2 of the Appendix. Now let us consider an example problem to demonstrate the application of the exponential distribution.

FIGURE 6.27
Probability Density Function for an Exponential Distribution with $\lambda = 0.2$

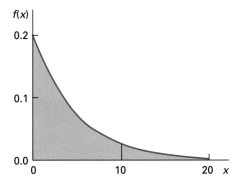

EXAMPLE 6.10

SERVICE TIME AT LIBRARY INFORMATION DESK (COMPUTE EXPONENTIAL PROBABILITIES)

Service times for customers at a library information desk can be modeled by an exponential distribution with a mean service time of 5 minutes. What is the probability that a customer service time will take longer than 10 minutes?

SOLUTION

Let t denote the service time in minutes. The service rate is $\lambda = 1/5 = 0.2$ per minute and the probability density function is

$$f(t) = \lambda e^{-\lambda t}$$

which is shown in Figure 6.27. The required probability can be computed as follows:

$$P(T > 10) = 1 - P(T < 10)$$
$$= 1 - F(10)$$
$$= 1 - (1 - e^{-(0.20)(10)})$$
$$= e^{-2.0} = 0.1353$$

Thus the probability that a service time exceeds 10 minutes is 0.1353.

EXAMPLE 6.11

TIME BETWEEN STRIKES IN TYPICAL BRITISH INDUSTRIAL PLANTS (COMPUTE EXPONENTIAL PROBABILITIES)

An industrial plant in Britain with 2,000 employees has a mean number of lost-time accidents per week equal to $\lambda = 0.4$, and the number of accidents follows a Poisson distribution. What is the probability that the time between accidents is less than two weeks?

SOLUTION

In this problem we note that the time interval is measured in weeks and our rate is $\lambda = 0.4$ per week or a mean time between accidents of $\mu = 1/(0.4) = 2.5$ weeks. Then the probability that the time between accidents is less than two weeks is

$$P(T < 2) = F(2) = 1 - e^{-(0.4)(2)}$$
$$= 1 - e^{-0.8}$$
$$= 1 - 0.4493 = 0.5507$$

and thus the probability of less than two weeks between accidents is about 55%.

EXERCISES

6.35 A professor sees students during regular office hours. Times spent with students follow an exponential distribution with mean 10 minutes.
 (a) Find the probability that a given student spends less than 20 minutes with the professor.
 (b) Find the probability that a given student spends more than 5 minutes with the professor.
 (c) Find the probability that a given student spends between 10 and 15 minutes with the professor.

6.36 Times to gather preliminary information from arrivals at an outpatients clinic follow an exponential distribution with mean 15 minutes. Find the probability, for a randomly chosen arrival, that more than 18 minutes will be required.

6.37 It is known that for a laboratory computing system, the number of system failures during a month has a

Poisson distribution with mean .8. The system has just failed. Find the probability that at least two months will elapse before a further failure.

6.38 Suppose that the time between successive occurrences of an event follows an exponential distribution with mean $1/\lambda$ minutes. Assume that an event occurs.
 (a) Show that the probability that more than 3 minutes elapses before the occurrence of the next event is $e^{-3\lambda}$.
 (b) Show that the probability that more than six minutes elapses before the occurrence of the next event is $e^{-6\lambda}$.
 (c) Using the results of (a) and (b), show that if three minutes has already elapsed, the probability that a further three minutes will elapse before the next occurrence is $e^{-3\lambda}$. Explain your answer in words.

6.6   JOINTLY DISTRIBUTED CONTINUOUS RANDOM VARIABLES

In Section 5.7 we introduced joint distributions for discrete random variables. Here we will show that many of the concepts and results from discrete random variables also apply for continuous random variables. Many continuous random variables can be modeled using jointly distributed random variables. The market values of various stock prices are regularly modeled as joint random variables. Studies of the production and sales patterns for various companies and industries use jointly distributed continuous random variables. The number of units sold by a large retail store during a particular week and the price per unit can be modeled by joint random variables. Studies of import and export behavior for various countries regularly use joint random variables as part of the analysis.

After we have developed some basic concepts we present a number of application examples to show the importance of the procedures and how to analyze jointly distributed continuous random variables.

JOINT CUMULATIVE DISTRIBUTION FUNCTION

Let X_1, X_2, ..., X_k be continuous random variables

1. Their **joint cumulative distribution function**, $F(x_1, x_2, ..., x_k)$ defines the probability that simultaneously X_1 is less than x_1, X_2 is less than x_2, and so on; that is

$$F(x_1, x_2, ..., x_k) = P\left(X_1 < x_1 \cap X_2 < x_2 \cap \cdots X_k < x_k\right) \qquad (6.19)$$

2. The cumulative distribution functions $F(x_1)$, $F(x_2)$, ..., $F(x_k)$ of the individual random variables are called their **marginal distribution functions**. For any i, $F(x_i)$ is the probability that the random variable X_i does not exceed the specific value x_i.
3. The random variables are *independent* if and only if

$$F(x_1, x_2, ..., x_k) = F(x_1)F(x_2) \cdots F(x_k) \qquad (6.20)$$

We note that the notion of independence here is precisely the same as in the discrete case. Independence of a set of random variables implies that the probability distribution of any one of them is unaffected by the values taken by the others. Thus, for example, the assertion that consecutive daily changes in the price of a share of common stock are independent of one another implies that information about the past price changes is of no value in assessing what is likely to happen tomorrow.

The notion of expectation extends to functions of jointly distributed continuous random variables. As in the case of discrete random variables we have the concept of covariance, which is used in assessing linear relationships between pairs of random variables.

COVARIANCE

Let X and Y be a pair of continuous random variables, with respective means μ_x and μ_y. The expected value of $(X - \mu_x)(Y - \mu_y)$ is called the **covariance** between X and Y. That is

$$\text{Cov}(X, Y) = E\left[(X - \mu_x)(Y - \mu_y)\right] \qquad (6.21)$$

An alternative but equivalent expression can be derived as

$$\text{Cov}(X, Y) = E(XY) - \mu_x \mu_y \qquad (6.22)$$

If the random variables X and Y are independent, then the covariance between them is 0. However, the converse is not necessarily true.

In Section 5.7 we also presented the correlation as a standardized measure of the relationship between two discrete random variables. The same results hold for continuous random variables.

CORRELATION

Let X and Y be jointly distributed random variables. The **correlation** between X and Y is

$$\rho = \text{Corr}(X, Y) = \frac{\text{Cov}(X, Y)}{\sigma_X \sigma_Y}$$

(6.23)

In Section 5.7 we presented the means and variances for sums and differences of discrete random variables. The same results apply for continuous random variables, because the results are established using expectations and thus are not affected by the condition of discrete or continuous random variables.

SUMS OF RANDOM VARIABLES

Let $X_1, X_2, \ldots, X_K$ be K random variables with means $\mu_1, \mu_2, \ldots, \mu_K$ and variances $\sigma_1^2, \sigma_2^2, \ldots, \sigma_K^2$. The following properties hold:

1. The mean of their sum is the sum of their means; that is

$$E\big(X_1 + X_2 + \cdots + X_K\big) = \mu_1 + \mu_2 + \cdots + \mu_K$$

(6.24)

2. If the covariance between every pair of these random variables is 0, then the variance of their sum is the sum of their variances; that is

$$\text{Var}(X_1 + X_2 + \cdots + X_K) = \sigma_1^2 + \sigma_2^2 + \cdots + \sigma_K^2$$

(6.25)

However, if the covariances between pairs of random variables are not 0, the variance of their sum is

$$\text{Var}(X_1 + X_2 + \cdots + X_K) = \sigma_1^2 + \sigma_2^2 + \cdots + \sigma_K^2 + 2\sum_{i=1}^{K-1}\sum_{j=i+1}^{K} \text{Cov}(X_i, X_j)$$

(6.26)

DIFFERENCES BETWEEN A PAIR OF RANDOM VARIABLES

Let X and Y be a pair of random variables with means μ_X and μ_Y and variances σ_X^2 and σ_Y^2. The following properties hold:

1. The mean of their difference is the difference of their means; that is

$$E\big(X - Y\big) = \mu_X - \mu_Y$$

(6.27)

2. If the covariance between X and Y is 0 then the variance of their difference is

$$\text{Var}(X - Y) = \sigma_X^2 + \sigma_Y^2$$

(6.28)

3. If the covariance between X and Y is not 0 then the variance of their difference is

$$\text{Var}(X - Y) = \sigma_X^2 + \sigma_Y^2 - 2\,\text{Cov}(X, Y)$$

(6.29)

EXAMPLE 6.12

TOTAL PROJECT COSTS (COMPUTE MEAN AND STANDARD DEVIATION)

A contractor is uncertain of the precise total costs for either materials or labor for a project. It is believed that material costs can be represented by a random variable with mean $100,000 and standard deviation $10,000. Labor costs are $1,500 a day, and the number of days needed to complete the project can be represented by a random variable with mean 80 and standard deviation 12. Assuming that material and labor costs are independent, what are the mean and standard deviation of total project cost (materials plus labor)?

SOLUTION

Let the random variables X_1 and X_2 denote, respectively, materials and labor costs. Then X_1 has mean $\mu_1 = 100,000$ and standard deviation $\sigma_1 = 10,000$. For the random variable X_2

$$\mu_2 = (1,500)(80) = 120,000 \qquad \text{and} \qquad \sigma_2 = (1,500)(12) = 18,000$$

The total project cost is $X_1 + X_2$, we have mean cost

$$\mu_1 + \mu_2 = 100,000 + 120,000 = \$220,000$$

and since X_1 and X_2 are independent, the variance of their sum is

$$\sigma_1^2 + \sigma_2^2 = (10,000)^2 + (18,000)^2 = 424,000,000$$

Taking the square root, we find that the standard deviation is $20,591.

EXAMPLE 6.13

INVESTMENT PORTFOLIO RISK (COMPUTE LINEAR FUNCTION MEAN AND VARIANCE)

Henry Chang has asked for your assistance in establishing a portfolio containing two stocks. Henry has $1,000, which can be allocated in any proportion to two alternative stocks. The returns per dollar from these investments will be designated as random variables X and Y. Both of these random variables are independent and have the same mean and variance. Henry wishes to know the risk for various allocation options. You point out that risk is directly related to variance and thus that his question would be answered if he knew the variance of various allocation options.

SOLUTION

The amount of money allocated to the first investment will be designated as α and hence the remaining $1,000 - \alpha$ will be allocated to the second investment. The total return on the investment is

$$R = \alpha X + (1,000 - \alpha)Y$$

This random variable has expected value

$$E(R) = \alpha E(X) + (1,000 - \alpha)E(Y)$$
$$= \alpha\mu + (1,000 - \alpha)\mu = \$1,000\mu$$

Thus we see that the expected return is the same for any allocation. However, the risk or variance is a different story.

$$\text{Var}(R) = \alpha^2 \, \text{Var}(X) + (1,000 - \alpha)^2 \, \text{Var}(Y)$$
$$= \alpha^2\sigma^2 + (1,000 - \alpha)^2 \sigma^2$$
$$= (2\alpha^2 - 2,000\,\alpha + 1,000,000)\sigma^2$$

If α is equal to either 0 or 1,000, so that the entire portfolio is allocated to just one of the stocks, the variance of the total return is 1,000,000 σ^2. However, if $500 is allocated to each investment the variance of the total return is 500,000 σ^2, which is the smallest possible variance. By spreading his investment over two stocks Henry is able to mitigate the effect of either high or low returns from one of the shares. Thus it is possible to obtain the same expected return with a variety of risk levels.

Linear Combinations of Random Variables

In Chapter 5 we developed the mean and variance for linear combinations of discrete random variables. These results also apply for continuous random variables because their development is based on operations with expected values and do not depend on the particular probability distributions. Equations 6.30 through 6.33 indicate the important properties of linear combinations.

LINEAR COMBINATIONS OF RANDOM VARIABLES

The linear combination of two random variables, X and Y, is

$$W = aX + bY \tag{6.30}$$

where a and b are constant numbers.
  The mean value for W is

$$\mu_W = E[W] = E[aX + bY] \tag{6.31}$$
$$= a\mu_X + b\mu_Y$$

The variance for W is

$$\sigma_W^2 = a^2\sigma_X^2 + b^2\sigma_Y^2 + 2ab\,\text{Cov}(X, Y) \tag{6.32}$$

or, using the correlation,

$$\sigma_W^2 = a^2\sigma_X^2 + b^2\sigma_Y^2 + 2ab\,\text{Corr}(X, Y)\sigma_X\sigma_Y \tag{6.33}$$

If both X and Y are joint normally distributed random variables then the resulting random variable, W, is also normally distributed with mean and variance derived as shown.

This result enables us to determine the probability that the linear combination W is within a specific interval.

EXAMPLE 6.14

PORTFOLIO ANALYSIS (COMPUTE PROBABILITY OF A PORTFOLIO)

Kirsten Judge, the account manager for Northern Securities, has a portfolio that includes 20 shares of Albertine Information Systems and 30 shares of Beta Cyber Analytics. Both firms provide Web access devices that compete in the consumer market. The price of Albertine stock is normally distributed with mean $\mu_X = 25$ and variance $\sigma_X^2 = 81$. The price of Beta stock is also normally distributed with mean, $\mu_Y = 40$ and variance $\sigma_Y^2 = 121$. The stock prices have a negative correlation $\rho_{XY} = -0.40$. Kirsten has asked you to determine the probability that the portfolio value exceeds 2,000.

SOLUTION

The value of Kirsten's portfolio W is defined by the linear combination,

$$W = 20X + 30Y$$

and W is normally distributed. The mean value for her stock portfolio is

$$\mu_W = 20\mu_X + 30\mu_Y$$
$$= 20 \times 25 + 30 \times 40 = 1{,}700$$

The variance for the portfolio value is

$$\sigma_W^2 = 20^2\,\sigma_X^2 + 30^2\,\sigma_Y^2 + 2 \times 20 \times 30\;\text{Corr}(X,Y)\sigma_X\sigma_Y$$
$$= 20^2 \times 81 + 30^2 \times 121 + 2 \times 20 \times 30 \times (-0.40) \times 9 \times 11 = 93{,}780$$

and the standard deviation of the portfolio value is

$$\sigma_W = 306.24$$

The Standard normal Z for 2,000 is

$$Z_W = \frac{2{,}000 - 1{,}700}{306.24} = 0.980$$

And the probability that the portfolio value exceeds 2,000 is 0.1635. From the symmetry of the normal distribution it follows that the probability that the portfolio value is less than 1,400 is also 0.1635.

If the two stock prices had a positive correlation $\rho = +0.40$ the mean would be the same but the variance and standard deviation would be

$$\sigma_W^2 = 20^2\,\sigma_X^2 + 30^2\,\sigma_Y^2 + 2 \times 20 \times 30\;\text{Corr}(X,Y)\sigma_X\sigma_Y$$
$$= 20^2 \times 81 + 30^2 \times 121 + 2 \times 20 \times 30 \times (+0.40) \times 9 \times 11 = 188{,}820$$
$$\sigma_W = 434.53$$

The Standard normal Z for 2,000 is

$$Z_W = \frac{2{,}000 - 1{,}700}{434.53} = 0.690$$

The probability that her portfolio value exceeds 2,000 is 0.2451, and the probability that it is less than 1,400 is also 0.2451.

Thus we see that a positive correlation between stock prices leads to a higher variance and higher risk. The risk in this example increases the probability that the portfolio exceeds 2,000, from 0.1635 to 0.2451. This also implies a similar change in the probability that the portfolio value is less than 1,400. The higher risk implies that there is a higher probability that the portfolio has higher or lower values compared to the lower risk option.

EXERCISES

6.39 An investor plans to divide $200,000 between two investments. The first yields a certain profit of 10%, while the second yields a profit with expected value 18% and standard deviation 6%. If the investor divides the money equally between these two investments, find the mean and standard deviation of the total profit.

6.40 A homeowner has installed a new energy-efficient furnace. It is estimated that, over a year, the new furnace will reduce energy costs by an amount that can be regarded as a random variable with mean $200 and standard deviation $60. Stating any assumptions you need to make, find the mean and standard deviation of total energy cost reductions over a period of five years.

6.41 A consultant is beginning work on three projects. The expected profits from these projects are $50,000, $72,000, and $40,000. The associated standard deviations are $10,000, $12,000, and $9,000. Assuming independence of outcomes, find the mean and standard deviation of the consultant's total profit from these three projects.

6.42 Continuing Example 6.13, assume the same specifications as that example, except that now we no longer assume that the random variables X and Y are independent of one another. Denote by C the covariance between these random variables. Show now that the variance of total return is

$$\text{Var}(R) = (2\alpha^2 - 2{,}000\,\alpha + 1{,}000{,}000)\,\sigma^2 + 2\alpha(1{,}000 - \alpha)C$$

Show that the choice of $\alpha = 500$ is less risky than the choice of $\alpha = 0$, provided $C < \sigma^2$ (as it must be). For what values of C does diversification most reduce risk?

6.43 A consultant has three sources of income—from teaching short courses, from selling computer software, and from advising on projects. His expected annual incomes from these sources are $20,000, $25,000, $15,000, and the respective standard deviations are $2,000, $5,000, $4,000. Assuming independence, find the mean and standard deviation of his total annual income.

6.44 Five inspectors are employed to check the quality of components produced on an assembly line. For each inspector, the number of components that can be checked in a shift can be represented by a random variable with mean 120 and standard deviation 16. Let X represent the number of components checked by an inspector in a shift. Then the total number checked is $5X$, which has mean 600 and standard deviation 80. What is wrong with this argument? Assuming that inspectors' performances are independent of one another, find the mean and standard deviation of the total number of components checked in a shift.

6.45 It is estimated that in normal highway driving, the number of miles that can be covered by automobiles of a particular model on 1 gallon of gasoline can be represented by a random variable with mean 28 and standard deviation 2.4. Sixteen of these cars, each with 1 gallon of gasoline, are driven independently under highway conditions. Find the mean and standard deviation of the average number of miles that will be achieved by these cars.

SUMMARY

In Chapter 6 we have developed continuous random variable probability models following a pattern similar to that used for discrete random variable probability models in Chapter 5. We developed two parametric probability distribution models, the normal and the exponential. In addition, we showed how the normal can be used as an approximation for the binomial when the sample size is large. Finally, we developed joint distributions for continuous random variables. We extended the linear combinations of random variable models to show how we can use the mean and variance to compute the probability that total portfolio is in a specific range, based on the normal probability model. These and other extensive applications provide a solid foundation for using continuous random variables.

KEY WORDS

approximating binomial probabilities using the normal distribution, 202
areas under continuous probability density functions, 182
continuity correction factor, 202
correlation, 208
covariance, 207
cumulative distribution function, 180
cumulative distribution function of the normal distribution, 189
differences between pairs of random variables, 208
expectations of continuous random variables, 184

exponential probability distribution, 205
finding range probabilities for normal random variables, 192
joint cumulative distribution function, 207
linear combinations of random variables, 210
linear functions of random variables, 185
marginal distribution functions, 207
mean of a continuous random variable, 185
probability density function, 181

probability density function of the normal distribution, 187
properties of the normal distribution, 188
range probabilities for normal random variables, 189
range probabilities Using a cumulative distribution function, 181
standard deviation: continuous random variable, 185
standard normal distribution, 190
sums of random variables, 208
uniform distribution, 182
variance, 185

CHAPTER EXERCISES AND APPLICATIONS

6.46 Explain verbally what can be learned from doing each of the following:

(a) The cumulative distribution function of a continuous random variable

(b) The probability density function of a continuous random variable

(c) The mean of a continuous random variable

(d) The standard deviation of a continuous random variable

(e) The covariance between a pair of continuous random variables

6.47 "In the real world, measurements on any quantity of interest are almost invariably made on a discrete scale. Therefore, the study of continuous random variables is only of academic interest and has no practical value." Comment on this statement.

6.48 Answer the following questions:

(a) Why is it necessary to use tables to find probabilities for the normal distribution?

(b) Why is it necessary to tabulate probabilities for only one of the infinite number of normal distributions?

(c) Why is the normal distribution important in the study of statistics?

6.49 In practice, we find probabilities for any normal distribution based on probabilities for the standard normal distribution. Suppose that you had available tables of probabilities for the normal distribution with mean 1 and standard deviation 10, rather than tables for the standard normal distribution. Could these tables be used to find probabilities for any other normal distribution? If so, explain how.

6.50 A consultant knows that it will cost her $10,000 to fulfill a particular contract. The contract is to be put out for bids, and she believes that the lowest bid, excluding her own, can be represented by a distribution that is uniform between $8,000 and $20,000. Therefore, if the random variable X denotes the lowest of all other bids (in thousands of dollars), its probability density function is

$$f_X(x) = \begin{cases} 1/12 & \text{for } 8 < x < 20 \\ 0 & \text{for all other values of } x \end{cases}$$

(a) What is the probability that the lowest of the other bids will be less than the consultant's cost estimate of $10,000?

(b) If the consultant submits a bid of $12,000, what is the probability that she will secure the contract?

(c) The consultant decides to submit a bid of $12,000. What is her expected profit from this strategy?

(d) If the consultant wants to submit a bid so that her expected profit is as high as possible, discuss how she should go about making this choice.

6.51 The ages of a group of executives attending a convention are uniformly distributed between 35 and 65 years.

If X denotes ages in years, the probability density function is

$$f_X(x) = \begin{cases} 1/30 & \text{for } 35 < x < 65 \\ 0 & \text{for all other values of } x \end{cases}$$

(a) Draw the probability density function for this random variable X.

(b) Find and draw the cumulative distribution function for this random variable.

(c) Find the probability that the age of a randomly chosen executive in this group is between 40 and 50 years.

(d) Find the mean age of the executives in the group.

6.52 The random variable X has probability density function

$$f_X(x) = \begin{cases} x & \text{for } 0 < x < 1 \\ 2 - x & \text{for } 1 < x < 2 \\ 0 & \text{for all other values of } x \end{cases}$$

(a) Draw the probability density function for this random variable.

(b) Show that the density has the properties of a proper probability density function.

(c) Find the probability that this random variable takes a value between .5 and 1.5.

6.53 An investor puts $2,000 into a deposit account with a fixed rate of return of 10% per annum. A second sum of $1,000 is invested in a fund with expected rate of return of 16% and standard deviation of 8% per annum.

(a) Find the expected value of the total amount of money this investor will have after a year.

(b) Find the standard deviation of the total amount after a year.

6.54 A hamburger stand sells burgers for $1.45 each. Daily sales have a distribution with mean 530 and standard deviation 69.

(a) Find the mean daily total revenues from the sale of hamburgers.

(b) Find the standard deviation of total revenues from the sale of hamburgers.

(c) Daily costs (in dollars) are given by

$$C = 100 + .95X$$

where X is the number of hamburgers sold. Find the mean and standard deviation of daily profits from sales.

6.55 An analyst forecasts corporate earnings, and her record is evaluated by comparing actual earnings with predicted earnings. Define

```
ACTUAL EARNINGS = PREDICTED EARNINGS
+ FORECAST ERROR
```

If the predicted earnings and forecast error are independent of each other, show that the variance of predicted earnings is less than the variance of actual earnings.

6.56 Let X_1 and X_2 be a pair of random variables. Show that the covariance between the random variables $(X_1 + X_2)$ and $(X_1 - X_2)$ is 0 if and only if X_1 and X_2 have the same variance.

6.57 Grade point averages of students on a large campus follow a normal distribution with mean 2.6 and standard deviation .5.

  (a) One student is chosen at random from this campus. What is the probability that student has a grade point average higher than 3.0?

  (b) One student is chosen at random from this campus. What is the probability that student has a grade point average between 2.25 and 2.75?

  (c) What is the minimum grade point average needed for a student's grade point average to be among the highest 10% on this campus?

  (d) A random sample of 400 students is chosen from this campus. What is the probability that at least 80 of these students have grade point averages higher than 3.0?

  (e) Two students are chosen at random from this campus. What is the probability that at least one of them has a grade point average higher than 3.0?

6.58 A company services home air conditioners. It is known that times for service calls follow a normal distribution with mean 60 minutes and standard deviation 10 minutes.

  (a) What is the probability that a single service call takes more than 65 minutes?

  (b) What is the probability that a single service call takes between 50 and 70 minutes?

  (c) The probability is .025 that a single service call takes more than how many minutes?

  (d) Find the shortest range of times that includes 50% of all service calls.

  (e) A random sample of four service calls is taken. What is the probability that exactly two of them take more than 65 minutes?

6.59 It has been found that times taken by people to complete a particular tax form follow a normal distribution with mean 100 minutes and standard deviation 30 minutes.

  (a) What is the probability that a randomly chosen person takes less than 85 minutes to complete this form?

  (b) What is the probability that a randomly chosen person takes between 70 and 130 minutes to complete this form?

  (c) Five percent of all people take more than how many minutes to complete this form?

  (d) Two people are chosen at random. What is the probability that at least one of them takes more than an hour to complete this form?

  (e) Four people are chosen at random. What is the probability that exactly two of them take longer than an hour to complete this form?

  (f) For a randomly chosen person, state in which of the following ranges (expressed in minutes) time to complete the form is most likely to lie.

  70–90   90–110   110–130   130–150

  (g) For a randomly chosen person, state in which of the following ranges (expressed in minutes) time to complete the form is least likely to lie.

  70–90   90–110   110–130   130–150

6.60 A pizza delivery service delivers to a campus dormitory. Delivery times follow a normal distribution with mean 20 minutes and standard deviation 4 minutes.

  (a) What is the probability that a delivery will take between 15 and 25 minutes?

  (b) The service does not charge for the pizza if delivery takes more than 30 minutes. What is the probability of getting a free pizza from a single order?

  (c) During final exams week, a student plans to order pizza five consecutive evenings. Assume that these delivery times are independent of each other. What is the probability that the student will get at least one free pizza?

  (d) Find the shortest range of times that includes 40% of all deliveries from this service.

  (e) For a single delivery, state in which of the following ranges (expressed in minutes) delivery time is most likely to lie.

  18–20   19–21   20–22   21–23

  (f) For a single delivery, state in which of the following ranges (expressed in minutes) delivery time is least likely to lie.

  18–20   19–21   20–22   21–23

6.61 A video rental chain estimates that annual expenditures of members on rentals follow a normal distribution with mean $100. It was also found that 10% of all members spend more than $130 in a year. What percentage of members spend more than $140 in a year?

6.62 It is estimated that amounts of money spent on gasoline by customers at a gas station follow a normal distribution with standard deviation $2.50. It was also found that 10% of all customers spend more than $15. What percentage of customers spend less than $10?

6.63 A market research organization has found that 40% of all supermarket shoppers refuse to cooperate when questioned by its pollsters. If 1,000 shoppers are approached, what is the probability that less than 500 will refuse to cooperate?

6.64 An organization that gives regular seminars on sales motivation methods determines that 60% of its clients have attended previous seminars. From a sample of 400 clients, what is the probability that more than half have attended previous seminars?

6.65 An emergency towing service receives an average of 70 calls per day for assistance. For any given day, what is the probability that fewer than 50 calls will be received?

6.66 In a large department store, a customer complaints office handles an average of six complaints per hour about quality of service. The distribution is Poisson.

(a) What is the probability that in any hour exactly six complaints will be received?

(b) What is the probability that more than 20 minutes will elapse between successive complaints?

(c) What is the probability that less than 5 minutes will elapse between successive complaints?

(d) The store manager observes the complaints office for a 30-minute period, during which no complaints are received. She concludes that a talk she gave to her staff on the theme "the customer is always right" has obviously had a beneficial effect. Suppose that in fact the talk had no effect. What is the probability of the manager's observing a period of 30 minutes or longer with no complaints?

6.67 A Chicago radio station believes that 40% of its listeners are younger than 25 years of age. Six hundred listeners are chosen at random.

(a) If the station's belief is correct, what is the probability that more than 260 of these listeners are younger than 25?

(b) If the station's belief is correct, the probability is .6 that more than how many of these 600 listeners are younger than 25?

6.68 It is estimated that major league baseball game times-to-completion follow a normal distribution with mean 132 minutes and standard deviation 12 minutes.

(a) What proportion of all games last between 120 minutes and 150 minutes?

(b) Thirty-three percent of all games last longer than how many minutes?

(c) What proportion of games last less than 120 minutes?

(d) If 100 games are chosen at random, what is the probability that at least 25 of these games last less than 120 minutes?

6.69 A management consultant found that the amount of time per day spent by executives performing tasks that could equally well be done by subordinates followed a normal distribution with mean 2.4 hours. It was also found that 10% of executives spent over 3.5 hours per day on tasks of this type. For a random sample of 400 executives, find the probability that more than 80 spend more than 3 hours per day on tasks of this type.

APPENDIX

1. Readers with a knowledge of calculus will recognize that the probability that a random variable lies in a given range is the integral of the probability density function between the endpoints of the range; that is

$$P(a < X < b) = \int_{a}^{b} f(x)\,dx$$

2. Formally, in integral calculus notation

$$\int_{-\infty}^{\infty} f(x)\,dx = 1$$

The cumulative distribution function is thus the integral

$$F(x_0) = \int_{-\infty}^{x_0} f(x)\,dx$$

It therefore follows that the probability density function is the derivative of the cumulative distribution function; that is

$$f(x) = \frac{dF(x)}{dx}$$

3. Formally, using integral calculus, we express the expected value of the random variable X by

$$E(X) = \int_{-\infty}^{\infty} x\,f(x)\,dx$$

and the expected value of the function $g(X)$ by

$$E[g(X)] = \int_{-\infty}^{\infty} g(x)f(x)\,dx$$

Notice that in forming these expectations the integral plays the same role as the summation operator in the discrete case.

4. The integral

$$F(x_0) = \int_{-\infty}^{x_0} \frac{1}{\sqrt{2\pi\sigma^2}}\, e^{-(x-\mu)^2/2\sigma^2}\,dx$$

does not have a simple algebraic form.

5. By using integral calculus we see that:

$$P(t \le T) = \int_0^T \lambda e^{-\lambda t}\,dt$$
$$= 1 - e^{-\lambda T}$$

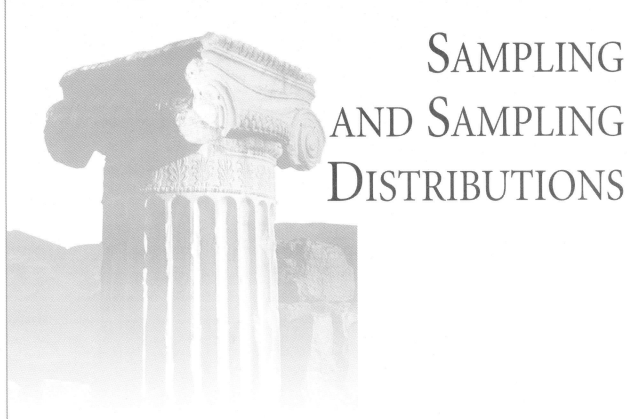

CHAPTER 7

SAMPLING AND SAMPLING DISTRIBUTIONS

INTRODUCTION

In the past three chapters we developed probability models that can be used to represent the underlying variability of various business and economic processes. In Chapters 2 and 3 descriptive statistics were developed that can be used to summarize samples of data obtained from these various processes. In this chapter these concepts will be linked together. This combination will enable us to construct probability models for various statistics computed from sample data. These probability models are called *sampling distributions* and will be used to develop various procedures for statistical inference throughout the remainder of this book.

Statistical procedures focus on drawing inferences about large populations of items by using a small sample of the items. Typical examples of populations include

1. The incomes of all families living in the city of Chicago
2. The annual yields of all stocks traded on the New York Stock Exchange
3. The set of all claims for automobile accident insurance coverage received during a year
4. The annual repair costs for all cars of a particular model
5. The errors in a large collection of accounts receivable

We might be interested in learning about specific characteristics, or attributes, of these populations. For example, we might want to make an inference about the mean or variance of the population distribution of family incomes in Chicago or about the proportion of all families in the city with annual incomes below $15,000.

7.1 SAMPLING FROM A POPULATION

Samples are used instead of the entire population because the cost of measuring every item in the population would be prohibitive. In general we achieve greater accuracy by carefully obtaining a random sample of the population instead of spending the resources to measure every item. It is well known among statistical professionals that the census conducted every 10 years produces an undercount in which certain groups are seriously underrepresented (Hogan, 90).

We obtain a sample from a population so that valid statements can be made about the population as a whole. The ideal sample is a *simple random sample*.

> **SIMPLE RANDOM SAMPLE**
>
> Suppose that we want to select a sample of *n* objects from a population of *N* objects. A **simple random sample** is selected such that every object has an equal probability of being selected and the objects are selected independently—the selection of one object does not change the probability of selecting any other objects.
>
> Simple random samples are the ideal sample. In a number of real world sampling studies analysts develop alternative sampling procedures to lower the costs of sampling. But the basis for determining if these strategies are acceptable is to determine how closely the results approximate a simple random sample.

It is important that a sample represents the population as a whole. If a marketing manager wants to assess reactions to a new food product she would not sample only her friends and neighbors. Those groups are unlikely to have views that represent the entire population and are likely to be concentrated over a narrower range. To avoid these problems items are selected randomly and independently. Random selection is our insurance policy against allowing personal biases to influence the selection.

Simple random sampling can be implemented in many ways. We could place the N items in a population—for example colored balls—in a large barrel and mix them thoroughly. Then from this well-mixed barrel we select individual balls from different parts of the barrel. In practice we often use random numbers to select objects that can be assigned some numerical value. For example, market research groups may use random numbers to select telephone numbers to call and ask about preferences for a product. Various statistical computer packages and spreadsheets have routines for obtaining random numbers and these are generally used for most sampling studies. These computer-generated random numbers have the required properties to develop random samples.

We will focus on methods for analyzing sample results to gain information about the population. This process, which will extend through the next three chapters, is known as classical inference. These methods generally assume that simple random samples are being used. However, there are other sampling procedures, and in some applied circumstances alternative sampling schemes may be preferred.

Random samples provide protection against the sample's being unrepresentative of the population. If a population were repeatedly sampled using random sampling procedures, no particular subgroup would be overrepresented in the samples. Moreover, the concept of a sampling distribution allows us to determine the probability of obtaining a particular sample.

We use sample information to make inferences about the parent population. The distribution of all values of interest in this population can be represented by a random variable. It would be too ambitious to attempt to describe the entire population distribution based on a small random sample of observations. However, we may well be able to make quite firm inferences about important characteristics of the population distribution, such as the population mean and variance. For example, given a random sample of the fuel consumption for 20 cars of a particular model, we can make inferential statements about the mean and variance of fuel consumption for the population of all cars of that model. This inference will be based on the sample information. We could ask questions such as "If the fuel consumption, in miles per gallon, of the population of all cars of a particular model has a mean of 25 and a standard deviation of 2, what is the probability that for a random sample of 20 such cars, the average fuel consumption will be less than 24 miles per gallon?" To answer that question, we could use the sampling distribution of the sample mean.

We need to be sure that we distinguish between population attributes and the corresponding sample quantities. In the preceding paragraph the population of fuel consumption for all automobiles of a particular model has a distribution with a specific mean. This mean, an attribute of the population, is a fixed (but unknown) number. We make inferences about this attribute by drawing a random sample from the population and computing the sample mean. For each sample we draw there will be a different sample mean, and the sample mean can be regarded as a random variable, with a probability distribution. The distribution of possible sample outcomes provides a basis for inferential statements about the sample. In this chapter we will examine the properties of *sampling distributions*.

SAMPLING DISTRIBUTIONS

Consider a random sample selected from a population to make an inference about some population characteristic, such as the population mean, by using a sample statistic such as the sample mean, $\overline{X}$. The inference is based on the realization that every random sample would have a different number for $\overline{X}$ and thus $\overline{X}$. is a random variable. The **sampling distribution** of this statistic is the probability distribution of the values it could take over all possible samples of the same number of observations drawn from the population.

We will illustrate the concept of a sampling distribution by considering the position of a supervisor with six employees, whose years of experience are

$$2 \quad 4 \quad 6 \quad 6 \quad 7 \quad 8$$

Four of these employees are to be chosen randomly for a particular work group. The mean years of experience for this population of six employees is

$$\mu = \frac{2 + 4 + 6 + 6 + 7 + 8}{6} = 5.5$$

Now let us consider the mean number of years of experience of the four employees chosen from the population of six. Fifteen possible different random samples could be selected. Table 7.1 shows all of the possible samples and associated sample means. Note that some samples (such as 2, 4, 6, 7) occur twice because there are two employees with six years of experience in the population.

Each of the 15 samples in Table 7.1 has the same probability, 1/15, of being selected. Note that there are several occurrences of the same sample mean. For example the sample mean 5.75 occurs three times and thus the probability of obtaining a sample mean of 5.75 is, 3/15. Table 7.2 presents the sampling distribution for the various sample means from the population.

The probability function is graphed in Figure 7.1. We see that while the number of years of experience for the six workers range from 2 to 8, the possible values of the sample mean have a range from only 4.50 to 6.75. In addition, most of the values lie in the central portion of the range.

ASSUMPTION

Table 7.3 presents similar results for a sample size of $n = 5$. Notice that the means are concentrated over a narrower range. These sample means are all closer to the population mean, $\mu = 5.5$. We will always find this to be true—**the sampling distribution becomes concentrated closer to the population mean as the sample size increases.** This important result provides an important foundation for statistical inference. In the following sections and chapters we will build a set of rigorous analysis tools on this foundation.

TABLE 7.1
Samples and Sample Means from the Worker Population
Sample Size $n = 4$

SAMPLE	SAMPLE MEAN	SAMPLE	SAMPLE MEAN
2, 4, 6, 6	4.50	2, 6, 7, 8	5.75
2, 4, 6, 7	4.75	2, 6, 7, 8	5.75
2, 4, 6, 8	5.00	4, 6, 6, 7	5.75
2, 4, 6, 7	4.75	4, 6, 6, 8	6.00
2, 4, 6, 8	5.00	4, 6, 7, 8	6.25
2, 4, 7, 8	5.25	4, 6, 7, 8	6.25
2, 6, 6, 7	5.25	6, 6, 7, 8	6.75
2, 6, 6, 8	5.50		

TABLE 7.2
Sampling Distribution of the Sample Means from the Worker Population
Sample Size $n = 4$

SAMPLE MEAN $\overline{X}$	PROBABILITY OF $\overline{X}$
4.50	1/15
4.75	2/15
5.00	2/15
5.25	2/15
5.50	1/15
5.75	3/15
6.00	1/15
6.25	2/15
6.75	1/15

FIGURE 7.1
Probability Function for the
Sampling Distribution of
Sample Means
Sample Size $n = 4$

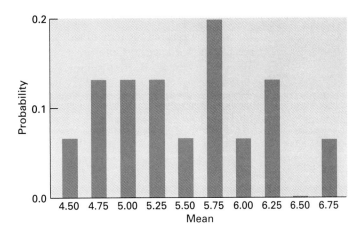

TABLE 7.3
Sampling Distribution of the
Sample Means from the
Worker Population
Sample Size $n = 5$

SAMPLE	$\overline{X}$	PROBABILITY
2, 4, 6, 6, 7	5.0	1/6
2, 4, 6, 6, 8	5.2	1/6
2, 4, 6, 7, 8	5.4	2/6
2, 4, 6, 7, 8	5.4	2/6
2, 6, 6, 7, 8	5.8	1/6
4, 6, 6, 7, 8	6.2	1/6

EXERCISES

7.1 Suppose you toss a pair of dice and write down the mean of the faces from each die.
   (a) What is the population distribution for one die?
   (b) Determine the sampling distribution of these sample means.

7.2 A population contains 6 million 0's and 4 million 1's. What is the approximate sampling distribution of the sample mean when
   (a) The sample size is $n = 5$.
   (b) The sample size is $n = 100$.

Note: There is a hard and an easy way to answer this question. We recommend the latter.

7.3 Suppose that a mathematician said that it would be impossible to obtain a simple random sample from a real world population. Therefore the whole basis for applying statistical procedures to real problems is useless. How would you respond?

7.2   SAMPLING DISTRIBUTION OF THE SAMPLE MEAN

We will now develop important properties of the sampling distribution of the sample mean. Our analysis begins with a random sample of n observations from a population with mean μ_X and variance σ^2 and the sample observations are denoted $X_1, X_2, \ldots, X_n$. Before the sample is observed, there will be uncertainty about the outcomes. This uncertainty is characterized by viewing the individual observations as random variables with the population mean μ and variance σ^2. Our primary interest is in making inferences about the population mean μ. An obvious starting point is the *sample mean.*

SAMPLE MEAN

Let $X_1, X_2, \ldots, X_n$ be a random sample from a population. The **sample mean** value of these observations is defined as

$$\overline{X} = \frac{1}{n} \sum_{i=1}^{n} X_i$$

Let us now consider the sampling distribution of the random variable $\overline{X}$. First we determine the mean of the distribution. In Chapters 5 and 6 we saw that the expectation of a linear combination of random variables is the linear combination of the expectations.

$$E(\overline{X}) = E\left(\frac{1}{n}(X_1 + X_2 + \cdots + X_n)\right) = \frac{n\mu}{n} = \mu$$

Thus the mean of the sampling distribution of the sample mean is the population mean. If samples of n random and independent observations are repeatedly and independently drawn from a population, then as the number of samples becomes very large, the mean of the sample means approaches the true population mean. This result is an important result of random sampling and indicates the protection that random samples provide against unrepresentative samples. A single sample mean could be larger or smaller than the population mean. However, on average, there is no reason for us to expect a sample mean that is either higher or lower than the population mean. In section 7.3 we will demonstrate this result by using computer generated random samples.

EXAMPLE 7.1

EXPECTED VALUE OF THE SAMPLE MEAN (EXPECTED VALUE)

We are asked to compute the expected value of the sample mean for the employee group example previously discussed.

SOLUTION

The sampling distribution of the sample mean is shown in Table 7.2 and Figure 7.1. From this distribution we can compute the expected value of the sample mean as

$$E(\overline{X}) = \sum \overline{x}P(\overline{x}) = (4.50)\left(\frac{1}{15}\right) + (4.75)\left(\frac{2}{15}\right) + \cdots + (6.75)\left(\frac{1}{15}\right) = 5.5$$

which is the population mean, μ.

Now that we have established that the distribution of sample means is centered about the population means we need to determine the variance of the distribution of sample means. Suppose that a random sample of 20 cars yielded an average fuel consumption of 24 miles per gallon. The sample mean would be used as an estimate of the population mean. But we would also wish to know how good $\overline{X} = 24$ is as the approximation of the population mean. We use the variance of the sampling distribution of the sample means to provide the answer.

If the population is very large compared to the sample size, then the distributions of the individual sample members from random samples are independent of each other. In Chapters 5 and 6 we saw that the variance of a linear combination of independent random variables is the sum of the linear coefficients squared times the variance of the random variables. It follows that

$$\operatorname{Var}(\overline{X}) = \operatorname{Var}\left(\frac{1}{n}X_1 + \frac{1}{n}X_2 + \cdots + \frac{1}{n}X_n\right) = \sum_{i=1}^{n}\left(\frac{1}{n}\right)^2 \sigma_i^2 = \frac{n\sigma^2}{n^2} = \frac{\sigma^2}{n}$$

The variance of the sampling distribution of $\overline{X}$ decreases as the sample size n increases. In effect, this says that larger sample sizes result in the more concentrated sampling distributions. The simple example in the previous section demonstrated this result. Thus larger samples result in greater certainty about our inference of the population mean. This is to be expected. As we obtain more information from a population—from a larger sample—we are able to learn more about population characteristics such as the population mean. The variance of the sample mean is denoted as $\sigma_{\overline{X}}^2$, and the corresponding standard deviation, called the standard error of $\overline{X}$, is given by

$$\sigma_{\overline{X}} = \frac{\sigma}{\sqrt{n}}$$

If the sample size n is not a small fraction of the population size, N, then the individual sample members are not distributed independently of one another. Since a population member cannot be included more than once in a sample, the probability of a specific sample member being the second observation depends on the sample member chosen as the first observation. Thus the observations are not selected independently. It can be shown in this case that the variance of the sample mean is

$$\operatorname{Var}(\overline{X}) = \frac{\sigma^2}{n} \cdot \frac{N-n}{N-1}$$

The term $(N - n)/(N - 1)$ is often called a *finite population correction factor*. We saw this result in Chapter 5. The variance of the hypergeometric distribution is $(N - n)/(N - 1)$ times the variance of the binomial distribution.

We have now developed expressions for the mean and variance of the sampling distribution of $\overline{X}$. For most applications the mean and the variance will define the distribution. If the parent population is a normal distribution, then we can compute the standard normal Z for the sample mean. In Chapter 6 we saw that we can use the standard normal, Z, to compute probabilities for any normally distributed random variable. That result also applies for the sample mean.

STANDARD NORMAL DISTRIBUTION FOR THE SAMPLE MEAN

Whenever the sampling distribution of the sample mean is a normal distribution we can compute a **standardized normal random variable, Z,** that has mean 0 and variance 1

$$Z = \frac{\overline{X} - \mu}{\sigma_{\overline{X}}} = \frac{\overline{X} - \mu}{\dfrac{\sigma}{\sqrt{n}}} \tag{7.1}$$

Finally, the results of this section are summarized.

RESULTS FOR THE SAMPLING DISTRIBUTION OF THE SAMPLE MEAN

Let $\overline{X}$ denote the sample mean of a random sample of n observations from a population with mean μ_X and variance σ^2. Then

1. The sampling distribution of $\overline{X}$ has mean

$$E(\overline{X}) = \mu \qquad (7.2)$$

2. The sampling distribution of $\overline{X}$ has standard deviation

$$\sigma_{\overline{X}} = \frac{\sigma}{\sqrt{n}} \qquad (7.3)$$

This is called the standard error of $\overline{X}$.

3. If the sample size n is not small compared to the population size N, then the standard error of $\overline{X}$ is

$$\sigma_{\overline{X}} = \frac{\sigma}{\sqrt{n}} \cdot \sqrt{\frac{N - n}{N - 1}} \qquad (7.4)$$

4. If the population distribution is normal, then the random variable

$$Z = \frac{\overline{X} - \mu}{\sigma_{\overline{X}}} \qquad (7.5)$$

has a standard normal distribution with mean 0 and variance 1.

Figure 7.2 shows the sampling distribution of the sample mean for sample sizes $n = 25$ and $n = 100$ from a normal distribution. Each distribution is centered on the mean, but as the sample size increases the distribution becomes concentrated more closely around the population mean because the standard error of the sample mean decreases as the sample size increases. Thus the probability that a sample mean is a fixed distance from the population mean decreases with increased sample size.

FIGURE 7.2
Probability Density Functions for Sample Means from a Population with $\mu = 100$ and $\sigma = 5$

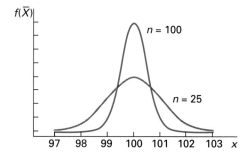

EXAMPLE 7.2

EXECUTIVE SALARY DISTRIBUTIONS (NORMAL PROBABILITY CALCULATION)

Suppose that the annual percentage salary increases for the chief executive officers of all mid-size corporations are normally distributed with mean 12.2% and standard deviation 3.6%. A random sample of nine observations is obtained from this population and the sample mean computed. What is the probability that the sample mean will be less than 10%?

SOLUTION

We know that

$$\mu = 12.2 \qquad \sigma = 3.6 \qquad n = 9$$

Let $\overline{X}$ denote the sample mean and compute the standard error of the sample mean

$$\sigma_{\overline{X}} = \frac{\sigma}{\sqrt{n}} = \frac{3.6}{\sqrt{9}} = 1.2$$

Then we can compute

$$P(\overline{X} < 10) = P\left(\frac{\overline{X} - \mu}{\sigma_{\overline{X}}} < \frac{10 - 12.2}{1.2}\right) = P(Z < -1.83) = 0.0336$$

where Z has a standard normal distribution and the resulting probability is obtained from Table 1 of the Appendix using the procedures developed in Chapter 6.

From this analysis we conclude that the probability that the sample mean will be less than 10% is only 0.0336. If a sample mean of less than 10% actually occurred we might begin to suspect that the population mean is less than 12.2%.

EXAMPLE 7.3

SPARK PLUG LIFE (NORMAL PROBABILITY CALCULATION)

A spark plug manufacturer claims that the life of its plugs is normally distributed with mean 36,000 miles and standard deviation 4,000 miles. A random sample of 16 plugs had an average life of 34,500 miles. If the manufacturer's claim is correct, what is the probability of finding this sample mean or smaller?

SOLUTION

To compute the probability we need to first obtain the standard error of the sample mean

$$\sigma_{\overline{X}} = \frac{\sigma}{\sqrt{n}} = \frac{4,000}{\sqrt{16}} = 1,000$$

The desired probability is

$$P(\overline{X} < 34,500) = P\left(\frac{\overline{X} - \mu}{\sigma_{\overline{X}}} < \frac{34,500 - 36,000}{1,000}\right) = P(Z < -1.50) = 0.0668$$

Figure 7.3a shows the probability density function of $\overline{X}$ with the shaded portion indicating the probability that the sample mean is less than 34,500. In Figure 7.3b we see the

FIGURE 7.3
a. Probability that Sample Mean is Less Than 34,500
b. Probability That a Standard Normal Random Variable is Less Than -1.5

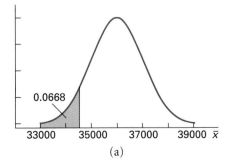
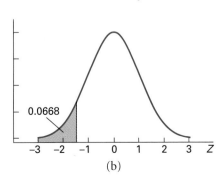

(a)   (b)

standard normal density function and the shaded area indicates the probability that Z is less than -1.5. Note that in comparing these figures we see that every value of $\overline{X}$ has a corresponding value of Z and the comparable probability statements provide the same result.

Using the standard normal Z, the normal probability values from Table 1 of the appendix, and the procedures from Chapter 6 we find that the probability that $\overline{X}$ is less than 34,500 is 0.0668. This probability suggests that if the manufacturers claim—$\mu = 36{,}000$ and $\sigma = 4{,}000$—is true, then a sample mean of 34,500 or less has a small probability. As a result we are skeptical about the manufacturers claim. This important concept—using the probability of sample statistics to question the original assumption—will be developed more fully in Chapter 9.

Central Limit Theorem

In the previous section we learned that the sample mean, $\overline{X}$, for a random sample of size n drawn from a population with a normal distribution with mean, μ, and variance, σ^2, is also normally distributed with mean, μ, and variance, σ^2/n. In this section we present the *central limit theorem*, which states that the mean of a random sample, drawn from a population with any probability distribution, will be approximately normally distributed with mean, μ, and variance, σ^2/n given a large enough sample size.

This important result enables us to use the normal distribution to compute probabilities for sample means obtained from many different populations. In applied statistics the probability distribution for the population being sampled is often not known, and in particular there is no way to conclude that the underlying distribution is normal.

In applied statistical analysis many of the random variables used can be characterized as the sum or mean of a large number of random variables. For example, total daily sales in a store is the result of a number of sales to individual customers—each of which can be modeled as a random variable. Total national investment spending in a month is the sum of many individual investment decisions by specific firms. Thus if X_1, X_2, ..., X_n represent the result of individual random events the observed random variable

$$X = X_1 + X_2 + \cdots + X_n$$

and from Chapter 5

$$E(X) = n\mu \qquad\qquad \mathrm{Var}(X) = n\sigma^2$$

The central limit theorem states that the resulting sum X is normally distributed and can be used to compute a random variable, Z, with mean 0 and variance 1

$$Z = \frac{X - E(X)}{\sqrt{\mathrm{Var}(X)}} = \frac{X - n\mu}{\sqrt{n\sigma^2}}$$

In addition, if X is divided by n to obtain a mean $\overline{X}$, then a corresponding Z with mean 0 and variance 1 can also be computed.

$$Z = \frac{\overline{X} - \mu_X}{\sigma_{\overline{X}}} = \frac{\overline{X} - \mu_X}{\dfrac{\sigma_X}{\sqrt{n}}}$$

Using these results we have the central limit theorem.

STATEMENT OF THE CENTRAL LIMIT THEOREM

Let $X_1, X_2, \ldots, X_n$ be a set of n independent random variables having identical distributions with mean μ and variance σ^2, with X as the sum and $\overline{X}$ as the mean of these random variables. As n becomes large, the **central limit theorem** states that the distribution of

$$Z = \frac{\overline{X} - \mu_X}{\sigma_{\overline{X}}} = \frac{X - n\mu_X}{\sqrt{n\sigma^2}} \qquad (7.6)$$

approaches the standard normal distribution.

ASSUMPTION

The central limit theorem provides the basis for considerable work in applied statistical analysis. As indicated, many random variables can be modeled as sums or means of independent random variables. By this theorem the normal distribution very often provides a good approximation of the true distribution. Thus the standard normal distribution can be used to obtain probability values for many observed sample means or sums.

The central limit theorem can be applied to both discrete and continuous random variables. In Section 7.3 we will use this result for discrete random variables to develop probabilities for proportion random variables, using procedures similar to those used for sample means.

The central limit theorem results from a formal mathematical proof that is beyond the scope of this book. This theorem is a key result that supports many statistical applications. Results from random sample simulations can also be used to demonstrate the central limit theorem. In addition, there are homework problems that enable you to conduct further experimental analysis. We will now present some results using Monte Carlo sample simulations to obtain sampling distributions. To obtain each of these results we selected 1000 random samples of size n and displayed the sampling distributions in histograms and normal probability plots. The chapter appendix presents the procedure for obtaining sampling distributions for the sample mean from any probability distribution. In this appendix and on the data disk we include a Minitab Computer Macro for easily obtaining your own sampling distributions.

Symmetrically Distributed Random Variable (0 to 10)

First let us consider a symmetric probability distribution over the range 0 to 10. The probability distribution is shown in Figure 7.4.

FIGURE 7.4
Probability Distribution for a
Symmetric Random Variable

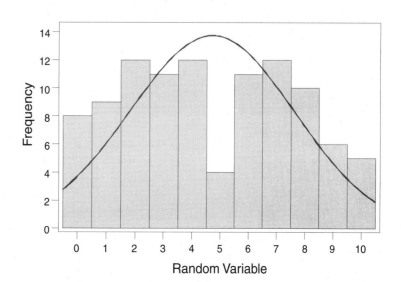

FIGURE 7.5
Sampling Distributions
of the Sample Mean from
a Symmetric Distribution
with $n = 5$

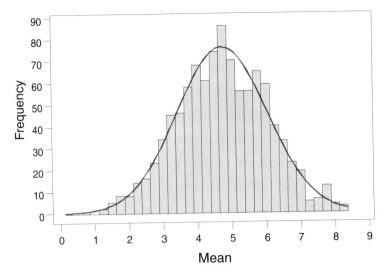

Clearly the values of the random variable are not normally distributed since the values are balanced over the range from 0 to 10. Next we will use the computer simulation to generate random samples of various sizes from this probability distribution, compute the sample mean for each sample, and analyze the distribution of those means. In that process we are constructing empirical sampling distributions of the sample means. Look at the histograms in Figures 7.5 and 7.6 using 1,000 samples first with a sample size, $n = 5$, and then with a sample size, $n = 20$. A normal probability density function with the same mean and variance is sketched over the histogram to provide a comparison.

We can see from the histograms that the means from samples of size 5 tend toward central values. With samples of size 20 the histogram is symmetric and is similar to sample histograms that would be obtained from a normal distribution. Generally the distribution of sample means from symmetric distributions can be closely approximated by the normal distribution, even with small sample sizes.

Skewed Distribution

In Chapter 2 we saw that the distribution of observations for many business and economic processes are skewed. For example, family incomes and housing prices in a city, state, or country are often skewed to the right or high. There are typically a small percentage of fam-

FIGURE 7.6
Sampling Distributions
of the Sample Mean from
a Symmetric Distribution
with $n = 20$

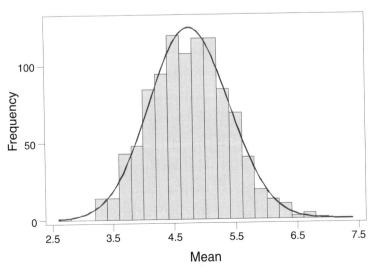

FIGURE 7.7
Probability Distribution for a
Skewed Distribution

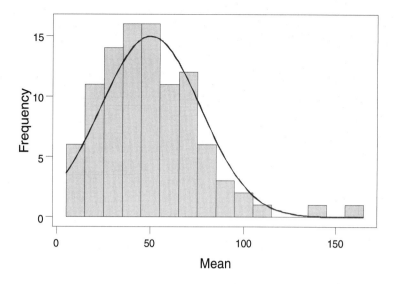

ilies with very high incomes and these families tend to live in expensive houses. Next we will consider a probability distribution that is skewed. Consider the discrete probability distribution shown in Figure 7.7. This could be a distribution of family incomes for a developing country. Suppose you wanted to compare mean incomes for that country against a development standard.

Mean incomes are compared using a random sample from the probability distribution shown in Figure 7.7. Figure 7.8 shows a histogram for 1000 samples of size $n = 10$ and Figure 7.9 a histogram for samples of size $n = 25$. If you had used a random sample of size $n = 10$ and assumed that the sample mean was normally distributed, the chances for estimating incorrect probabilities would be great. These mistakes in probability estimates would be particularly large for sample means in the upper tail of the distribution. Note that the histogram is different from one that would be obtained from a normal distribution. But if you had used a random sample of size 25 your results would be much better. Note that the second histogram—$n = 25$—is much closer to a normal distribution. If we had obtained sampling distributions for larger samples the results would have been even better. Thus, even when the distribution of individual observations is highly skewed the distribution of sample means closely approximates a normal distribution.

FIGURE 7.8
Sampling Distribution of
Sample Means: Skewed
Distribution with Sample Size
$n = 10$

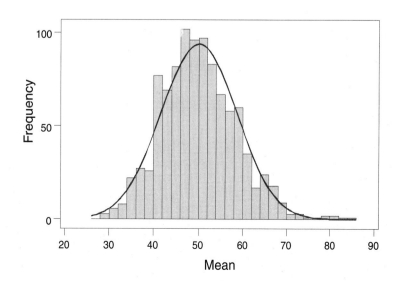

FIGURE 7.9
Sampling Distribution
of Sample Means: Skewed
Distribution with Sample
Size *n* = 25

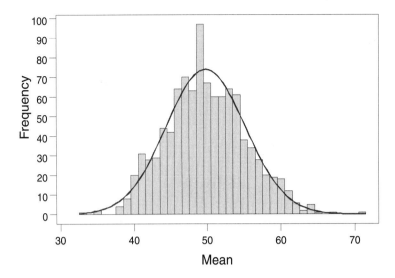

In Chapter 6 we learned that the binomial random variable has an approximate normal distribution as the sample size becomes large. From the random sampling studies in this chapter and our previous study of the binomial distribution we have evidence to demonstrate the central limit theorem. Similar demonstrations have been produced numerous times by many statisticians. As a result, there is a large body of empirical evidence that supports the application of central limit theorem to realistic statistical applications.

The only question for applied analysis concerns the sample size required to ensure that sample means have a normal distribution. Based on considerable research and experience we know that if the distributions are symmetric then means from sample sizes of *n* = 20 to 25 are well approximated by the normal distribution. For skewed distributions the required sample sizes are generally somewhat larger. But note that in the previous examples using a skewed distribution, a sample size of *n* = 25 produced a sampling distribution of sample means that closely followed a normal distribution.

ASSUMPTION

In this chapter we have begun our discussion of the important statistical problem of making inferences about a population based on results from a sample. The sample mean or sample proportion is often computed to make inferences about population means or proportions. By using the central limit theorem we have a rationale for applying the techniques we will develop in future chapters to a wide range of problems. The following examples show important applications of the central limit theorem.

Acceptance Intervals

In many statistical applications we would like to determine the range within which sample means are likely to occur. Determining such ranges is a direct application of the sampling distribution concepts we have developed. Acceptance intervals based on the normal distribution are defined by the distribution mean and variance. From the central limit theorem we know that the sampling distributions of sample means are often approximately normal, and thus acceptance intervals based on the normal distribution have wide applications. A symmetric acceptance interval would be

$$\mu \pm Z_{\alpha/2}\sigma_{\overline{X}}$$

provided that $\overline{X}$ has a normal distribution and $Z_{\alpha/2}$ is the standard normal when the upper tail probability is $\alpha/2$. The probability that the sample mean $\overline{X}$ is included in the interval is $1 - \alpha$.

EXAMPLE 7.4

MARKETING STUDY FOR ANTELOPE COFFEE. (NORMAL PROBABILITY CALCULATION)

Antelope Coffee Inc. is considering the possibility of opening a gourmet coffee shop in Big Rock, Montana. Previous research has indicated that their shops will be successful in cities of this size if the per capita annual income is above $60,000. It is also known that the standard deviation of income is $5,000.

A random sample of 36 people was obtained and the mean income was $62,300. Does this sample provide evidence to conclude that a shop should be opened?

SOLUTION

The distribution of incomes is known to be skewed, but the central limit theorem enables us to conclude that the sample mean is approximately normally distributed. To answer the question we need to determine the probability of obtaining a sample mean at least as high as $\overline{X} = 62,300$ if the population mean is $\mu = 60,000$.

First compute the standardized normal Z statistic

$$Z = \frac{\overline{X} - \mu}{\sigma/\sqrt{n}} = \frac{62,300 - 60,000}{5,000/\sqrt{36}} = 2.76$$

From the standard normal table we find that the probability of obtaining a Z value of 2.76 or larger is 0.0029. Because this probability is very small we can conclude that it is likely that the population mean income is not 60,000 but is a larger value. This result provides strong evidence that the population mean income is higher than $60,000 and that the coffee shop is likely to be a success. In this example we can see the importance of sampling distributions and the central limit theorem for problem solving.

Quality Control Charts

Acceptance intervals are widely used for quality control monitoring of various production and service processes. The interval

$$\mu \pm Z_{\alpha/2}\sigma_{\overline{X}}$$

(called an X-bar chart) provides limits for the value of $\overline{X}$ given that the population mean is μ. Typically α is very small ($\alpha < .01$), standard practice in the United States industries is to use $Z = 3$. If sample mean is outside the acceptance interval then we suspect that the population mean is not μ. In Chapter 16 we will develop control charts much more extensively.

EXAMPLE 7.5

MONITORING HEALTH INSURANCE CLAIMS (COMPUTING ACCEPTANCE INTERVAL)

Charlotte King, Vice President of Financial Underwriting, for a large health insurance company wishes to monitor daily insurance claims payments to determine if average claims per subscriber are stable or if claims are increasing or decreasing. Individual claims vary up and down from one day to the next, and it would be naive to draw conclusions or change operations based on these daily variations. But at some point the changes are substantial and should be noted. She has asked you to develop a procedure for monitoring the level of claims.

SOLUTION

Your initial investigation indicates that health insurance claims are highly skewed, with a small number of very large claims for major medical procedures. To determine changes we first need to determine the historical or standard mean and variance for individual claims.

After some investigation you also find that the mean for random samples of $n = 100$ claims is normally distributed. Based on past history the mean, μ, level for individual claims is $4,000 with a standard deviation, $\sigma = 2,000$.

Using this information you proceed to develop a claims monitoring system that obtains a random sample of 100 claims each day and computes the sample mean. The company has established a 95% acceptance interval for monitoring claims. An interval defined for the standard normal using $Z = \pm 1.96$ includes 95% of the values. From this you compute the 95% acceptance interval for insurance claims as

$$4,000 \pm 1.96 \frac{2,000}{\sqrt{100}}$$
$$4,000 \pm 392$$

FIGURE 7.10
Ninety-Five Percent Acceptance Interval for Health Insurance Claims

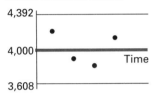

Each day the sample mean for 100 randomly selected claims is computed and compared to the acceptance interval. If the sample mean is outside the interval, 3,608 to 4,392, Ms. King can conclude that claims are deviating from the historical standard. You explain to her that this conclusion will be correct 95% of the time. The sample mean could be outside the interval even with a population mean of 4,000 with probability 0.05. In those cases Ms. King's conclusion would be wrong. To simplify the analysis you instruct the analysts to plot the daily claims mean on a control chart, shown in Figure 7.10.

Using this control chart Charlotte King and her staff can study the patterns of the sample means and determine if there are trends and if means are outside of the boundaries that indicate standard claims behavior.

EXAMPLE 7.6

PRAIRIE VIEW CEREAL PACKAGE WEIGHTS (COMPUTING ACCEPTANCE INTERVALS)

Cereal Package Weight

Prairie View Cereals, Inc. is concerned about maintaining correct package weights for its cereal packaging facility. The package label weight is 440 grams, and company officials are interested in monitoring the process to ensure that package weights are stable.

SOLUTION

A random sample of 5 packages is collected every 30 minutes and each package is weighed electronically. The mean weight is then plotted on an "X-bar" control chart such as the one in Figure 7.11. When the X-bar chart is used for monitoring limits on product quality—and numerous highly successful firms do—the central limit theorem provides the rationale for using the normal distribution to establish limits for the small sample means. Thus a fundamentally important statistical theory drives a key management process.

FIGURE 7.11
X-bar Chart for Cereal Package Weight

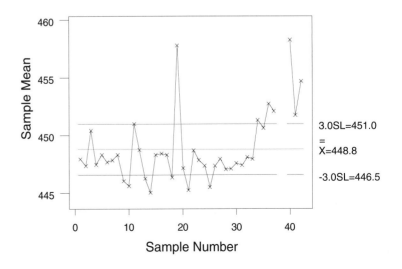

INTERPRETATION

In this chart "SL" is the standard deviation for the sample mean. The upper and lower limits are set at $\pm 3\sigma_{\bar{X}}$ instead of the $\pm 1.96\sigma_{\bar{X}}$, or 95%, acceptance interval used in the previous example. The interval $\bar{X} \pm 3\sigma_{\bar{X}}$ (Minitab labels the mean for the entire sample as $\bar{X}$) includes almost all of the sample means under the normal distribution given a stable mean and variance. Thus a sample mean outside of the control limits indicates that something has changed and corrections should be made. Given the number of points outside the acceptance interval we recommend that the process be stopped and adjusted.

EXERCISES

7.4 When a production process is operating correctly, the number of units produced per hour has a normal distribution with mean 92.0 and standard deviation 3.6. A random sample of four components was taken.
(a) Find the mean of the sampling distribution of the sample mean resistance.
(b) Find the variance of the sample mean.
(c) Find the standard error of the sample mean.
(d) What is the probability that the sample mean exceeds 93.0 units?

7.5 The lifetimes of light bulbs produced by a particular manufacturer have mean 1,200 hours and standard deviation 400 hours. The population distribution is normal. Suppose that you purchase nine bulbs, which can be regarded as a random sample from the manufacturer's output.
(a) What is the mean of the sample mean lifetime?
(b) What is the variance of the sample mean?
(c) What is the standard error of the sample mean?
(d) What is the probability that, on average, those nine lightbulbs have lives of less than 1,050 hours?

7.6 The fuel consumption, in miles per gallon, of all cars of a particular model has mean 25 and standard deviation 2. The population distribution can be assumed to be normal. A random sample of these cars is taken.
(a) Find the probability that sample mean fuel consumption will be less than 24 miles per gallon if
(i)   a sample of one observation is taken
(ii) a sample of four observations is taken
(iii) a sample of sixteen observations is taken.
(b) Explain why the three answers in (a) differ in the way they do. Draw a graph to illustrate your reasoning.

7.7 The mean selling price of new homes in a city over a year was $115,000. The population standard deviation was $25,000. A random sample of 100 new home sales from this city was taken.
(a) What is the probability that the sample mean selling price was more than $110,000?
(b) What is the probability that the sample mean selling price was between $113,000 and $117,000?
(c) What is the probability that the sample mean selling price was between $114,000 and $116,000?

(d) Without doing the calculations, state in which of the following ranges the sample mean selling price is most likely to lie:

$113,000 to $115,000, $114,000 to $116,000,
$115,000 to $117,000, $116,000 to $118,000

(e) Suppose that, after you had done these calculations, a friend asserted that the population distribution of selling prices of new homes in this city was almost certainly not normal. How would you respond?

7.8 Candidates for employment at a city fire department are required to take a written aptitude test. Scores on this test are normally distributed with mean 280 and standard deviation 60. A random sample of nine test scores was taken.
(a) What is the standard error of the sample mean score?
(b) What is the probability that the sample mean score is less than 270?
(c) What is the probability that the sample mean score is more than 250?
(d) Suppose that the populations standard deviation is in fact 40 rather than 60. Without doing the calculations, state how this would change your answers to (a), (b), and (c). Illustrate your conclusions with appropriate graphs.

7.9 A random sample of 16 junior managers in the offices of corporations in a large city center was taken to estimate average daily commuting times for all such managers. Suppose that the population times have a normal distribution with mean 87 minutes and standard deviation 22 minutes.
(a) What is the standard error of the sample mean commuting time?
(b) What is the probability that the sample mean is less than 100 minutes?
(c) What is the probability that the sample mean is more than 80 minutes?
(d) What is the probability that the sample mean is outside the range 85 to 95 minutes?
(e) Suppose that a second (independent) random sample, of 50 junior managers, is taken. Without doing

the calculations, state whether the probabilities in parts (b), (c), and (d) would be higher, lower, or the same for the second sample. Sketch graphs to illustrate your answers.

7.10 A company produces breakfast cereal. The true mean weight of the content of the boxes of its cereal is 20 ounces, and the standard deviation is .6 ounce. The population distribution of weights is normal. Suppose that you purchase four boxes, which can be regarded as a random sample of all those produced.
  (a) What is the standard error of the sample mean weight?
  (b) What is the probability that, on average, the contents of these four boxes will weigh less than 19.7 ounces?
  (c) What is the probability that, on average, the contents of these four boxes will weigh more than 20.6 ounces?
  (d) What is the probability that, on average, the contents of these four boxes will weigh between 19.5 and 20.5 ounces?
  (e) Two of the four boxes are chosen at random. What is the probability that, on average, the contents of these two boxes will weigh between 19.5 and 20.5 ounces?

7.11 Assume that the standard deviation of monthly rents paid by students in a particular town is $40. A random sample of 100 students was taken to estimate the mean monthly rent paid by the whole student population.
  (a) What is the standard error of the sample mean monthly rent?
  (b) What is the probability that the sample mean exceeds the population mean by more than $5?
  (c) What is the probability that the sample mean is more than $4 below the population mean?
  (d) What is the probability that the sample mean differs from the population mean by more than $3?

7.12 Times spent studying by students in the week before final exams follow a normal distribution with standard deviation eight hours. A random sample of four students was taken in order to estimate the mean study time for the population of all students.
  (a) What is the probability that the sample mean exceeds the population mean by more than two hours?
  (b) What is the probability that the sample mean is more than three hours below the population mean?
  (c) What is the probability that the sample mean differs from the population mean by more than four hours?
  (d) Suppose that a second (independent) random sample of ten students was taken. Without doing the calculation, state whether the probabilities in (a), (b), and (c) would be higher, lower, or the same for the second sample.

7.13 An industrial process produces batches of a chemical whose impurity levels follow a normal distribution with standard deviation 1.6 grams per hundred grams of

chemical. A random sample of 100 batches is selected in order to estimate the population mean impurity level.
  (a) The probability is .05 that the sample mean impurity level exceeds the population mean by how much?
  (b) The probability is .10 that the sample mean impurity level is below the population mean by how much?
  (c) The probability is .15 that the sample mean impurity level differs from the population mean by how much?

7.14 The price-earnings ratios for all companies whose shares are traded on the New York Stock Exchange follow a normal distribution with a standard deviation 3.8. A random sample of these companies is selected in order to estimate the population mean price-earnings ratio.
  (a) How large a sample is necessary in order to ensure that the probability that the sample mean differs from the population mean by more than 1.0 is less than .10?
  (b) Without doing the calculations, state whether a larger or smaller sample than that in part (a) would be required to guarantee that the probability that the sample mean differs from the population mean by more than 1.0 is less than .05.
  (c) Without doing the calculations, state whether a larger or smaller sample than that in part (a) would be required to guarantee that the probability that the sample mean differs from the population mean by more than 1.5 hours is less than .05.

7.15 The number of hours spent studying by students on a large campus in the week before final exams follows a normal distribution with standard deviation 8.4 hours. A random sample of these students is taken to estimate the population mean number of hours studying.
  (a) How large a sample is needed to ensure that the probability that the sample mean differs from the population mean by more than 2.0 hours is less than .05?
  (b) Without doing the calculations, state whether a larger or smaller sample than that in part (a) would be required to guarantee that the probability that the sample mean differs from the population mean by more than 2.0 hours is less than .10.
  (c) Without doing the calculations, state whether a larger or smaller sample than that in part (a) would be required to guarantee that the probability that the sample mean differs from the population mean by more than 1.5 hours is less than .05.

7.16 In Table 7.1 and Example 7.1, we considered samples of $n = 4$ observations from a population of $N = 6$ values of years on the job for employees. The population mean is $\mu_x = 5.5$ years.
  (a) Confirm from the six population values that the population variance is

$$\sigma_x^2 = \frac{47}{12}$$

(b) Confirm, following the approach of Example 6.1, that the variance of the sampling distribution of the sample mean is

$$\sigma_{\bar{x}}^2 = \Sigma(\bar{x} - \mu_x)^2 P_{\bar{x}}(\bar{x}) = \frac{47}{20}$$

(c) Verify for this example that

$$\sigma_{\bar{x}}^2 = \frac{\sigma_x^2}{n} \cdot \frac{N-n}{N-1}$$

7.17 In taking a sample of n observations from a population of N members, the variance of the sampling distribution of the sample mean is

$$\sigma_{\bar{x}}^2 = \frac{\sigma_x^2}{n} \cdot \frac{N-n}{N-1}$$

The quantity $\frac{(N-n)}{(N-1)}$ is called the "finite population correction factor."

(a) To get some feeling for possible magnitudes of the finite population correction factor, calculate it for samples of $n = 20$ observations from populations of $N = 20, 40, 100, 1,000,$ and $10,000$ members.

(b) Explain why the result for $N = 20$, found in part (a), is precisely what one should expect on intuitive grounds.

(c) Given the results in part (a), discuss the practical significance of using the finite population correction factor for samples of 20 observations from populations of different sizes.

7.18 A town has 500 real estate agents. The mean value of the properties sold in a year by these agents is $800,000, and the standard deviation is $300,000. A random sample of 100 agents is selected, and the value of the properties they sold in a year is recorded.

(a) What is the standard error of the sample mean?

(b) What is the probability that the sample mean exceeds $825,000?

(c) What is the probability that the sample mean exceeds $780,000?

(d) What is the probability that the sample mean is between $790,000 and $820,000?

7.19 An economics course was taken by 250 students. Each member of a random sample of 50 of these students was asked to estimate the amount of time he or she spent on the previous week's assignment. Suppose that the population standard deviation is 30 minutes.

(a) What is the probability that the sample mean exceeds the population mean by more than 2.5 minutes?

(b) What is the probability that the sample mean is more than 5 minutes below the population mean?

(c) What is the probability that the sample mean differs from the population mean by more than 10 minutes?

7.20 For an audience of 600 people attending a concert, the average time on the journey to the concert was 32 minutes, and the standard deviation was 10 minutes. A random sample of 150 audience members was taken.

(a) What is the probability that the sample mean journey time was more than 31 minutes?

(b) What is the probability that the sample mean journey time was less than 33 minutes?

(c) Draw a graph to illustrate why the answers to (a) and (b) are the same.

(d) What is the probability that the sample mean journey time was not between 31 and 33 minutes?

7.3 SAMPLING DISTRIBUTION OF A SAMPLE PROPORTION

In Section 5.4 we developed the binomial distribution as the sum of n independent Bernoulli random variables, each with probability of success π. To characterize the distribution we need a value for π. Here we will indicate how we can use the sample proportion to obtain inferences about the population proportion. The proportion random variable has many applications including studying percent market share, percent successful business investments, and outcomes of elections.

> ### SAMPLE PROPORTION
>
> Let X be the number of successes in a binomial sample of n observations, with parameter π. The parameter is the proportion of the population members that have a characteristic of interest. We define the **sample proportion** as
>
> $$p = \frac{X}{n} \tag{7.7}$$

> The sum X is the sum of a set of n independent Bernoulli random variables each with probability of success π. As a result p is the mean of a set of independent random variables, and the results we developed in the previous sections for sample means apply. In addition, the central limit theorem can be used to argue that the probability distribution for p can be modeled as a normal.

The mean and variance of the sampling distribution of the sample proportion p can be obtained from the mean and variance of the number of successes X.

$$E(X) = n\pi \qquad\qquad \text{Var}(X) = n\pi(1 - \pi)$$

and thus

$$E(p) = E\left(\frac{X}{n}\right) = \frac{1}{n} E(X) = \pi$$

We see that the mean of the distribution of p is the population proportion π

$$\text{Var}(p) = \text{Var}\left(\frac{X}{n}\right) = \frac{1}{n^2} \text{Var}(X) = \frac{\pi(1 - \pi)}{n}$$

The variance of p is the variance of the population distribution of the Bernoulli random variables divided by n. The standard deviation of p, which is the square root of the variance, is called its standard error.

Similar to the result for the variance of the sample mean we can use the finite population correction when the population is not large compared to the sample size

$$\text{Var}(p) = \frac{\pi(1 - \pi)}{n}\frac{N - n}{N - 1}$$

We have seen that the distribution of the number of successes and of the sample proportion is approximately normal for large sample sizes. As a result we can obtain a standard normal random variable by subtracting π from p and dividing by the standard error.

SAMPLING DISTRIBUTION OF THE SAMPLE PROPORTION

Let p be the sample proportion of successes in a random sample from a population with proportion success π. Then

1. The sampling distribution of p has mean π

$$E(p) = \pi \tag{7.8}$$

2. The sampling distribution of p has standard deviation

$$\sigma_p = \sqrt{\frac{\pi(1 - \pi)}{n}} \tag{7.9}$$

3. If the sample size is large, the random variable

$$Z = \frac{p - \pi}{\sigma_p} \tag{7.10}$$

is approximately distributed as a standard normal. This approximation is good if

$$n\pi(1 - \pi) > 9.$$

FIGURE 7.12
Probability Density Functions
for the Sample Proportions

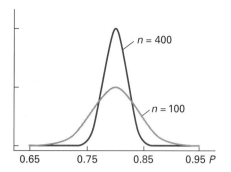

Similar to the results from the previous section we see that the standard error of the sample proportion, p, decreases as the sample size increases and the distribution becomes more concentrated, as seen in Figure 7.12. This is expected because the sample proportion is a sample mean. With larger sample sizes our inferences about the population proportion for a particular characteristic improve. From the central limit theorem we know that the binomial distribution can be approximated by the normal distribution with corresponding mean and variance. We see this result in the following examples.

EXAMPLE 7.7

EVALUATION OF HOME ELECTRIC WIRING (COMPUTING PROBABILITY OF SAMPLE PROPORTION)

A random sample of 250 homes was taken from a large population of older homes to esti-mate the proportion of homes with unsafe wiring. If, in fact, 30% of the homes have unsafe wiring, what is the probability that the sample proportion will be between 25% and 35%?

SOLUTION
For this problem we have

$$\pi = 0.30 \qquad n = 250$$

We can compute the standard deviation of the sample proportion p as

$$\sigma_p = \sqrt{\frac{\pi(1-\pi)}{n}} = \sqrt{\frac{0.30(1-0.30)}{250}} = 0.029$$

The required probability is

$$P(0.25 < p < 0.35) = P\left(\frac{0.25 - \pi}{\sigma_p} < \frac{\hat{p} - \pi}{\sigma_p} < \frac{0.35 - \pi}{\sigma_p}\right)$$
$$= P\left(\frac{0.25 - 0.30}{0.029} < Z < \frac{0.35 - 0.30}{0.029}\right)$$
$$= P(-1.72 < Z < 1.72)$$
$$= 0.9146$$

where the probability for the Z interval is obtained using Table 1 in the Appendix.

Thus we see that the probability that the sample proportion is within the interval 0.25 to 0.35, given $\pi = 0.30$, is 0.9146. This interval can be called a 91.46% acceptance interval. We can also note that if the sample proportion was actually outside this interval we might begin to suspect that the population proportion π was not 0.30.

EXAMPLE 7.8

BUSINESS COURSE SELECTION (COMPUTING PROBABILITY OF SAMPLE PROPORTION)

It has been estimated that 43% of business graduates believe that a course in business ethics is very important for imparting ethical values to students (David et al. 90). Find the probability that more than one-half of a random sample of 80 business graduates have this belief.

SOLUTION

We are given that

$$\pi = 0.43 \qquad n = 80$$

We will first compute the standard deviation of the sample proportion

$$\sigma_p = \sqrt{\frac{\pi(1-\pi)}{n}} = \sqrt{\frac{0.43(1-0.43)}{80}} = 0.055$$

Then the required probability can be computed as

$$
\begin{aligned}
P(p > 0.50) &= P\left(\frac{p - \pi}{\sigma_p} > \frac{0.50 - \pi}{\sigma_p}\right) \\
&= P\left(Z > \frac{0.50 - 0.43}{0.055}\right) \\
&= P(Z > 1.27) \\
&= 0.1020
\end{aligned}
$$

This probability as shown in Figure 7.13 was computed using probabilities from Table 1 in the Appendix.

The probability of having one-half of the sample believing in the value of business ethics courses is approximately 0.1.

FIGURE 7.13
The Probability that a Standard Normal Random Variable Exceeds 1.27

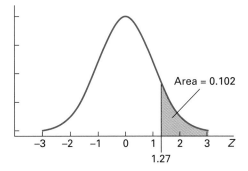

EXERCISES

7.21 In 1992, Canadians voted in a referendum on a new constitution. In the province of Quebec, 42.4% of those who voted were in favor of the new constitution. A random sample of 100 voters from the province was taken.
   (a) What is the mean of the sample proportion in favor of a new constitution?

   (b) What is the variance of the sample proportion?
   (c) What is the standard error of the sample proportion?
   (d) What is the probability that the sample proportion is bigger than .5?

7.22 According to the Internal Revenue Service, 75% of all

tax returns lead to a refund. A random sample of 100 tax returns is taken.
- (a) What is the mean of the sample proportion of returns leading to refunds?
- (b) What is the variance of the sample proportion?
- (c) What is the standard error of the sample proportion?
- (d) What is the probability that the sample proportion exceeds .8?

7.23 A record store owner finds that 20% of customers entering her store make a purchase. One morning 180 people, who can be regarded as a random sample of all customers, enter the store.
- (a) What is the mean of the sample proportion of customers making a purchase?
- (b) What is the variance of the sample proportion?
- (c) What is the standard error of the sample proportion?
- (d) What is the probability that the sample proportion is less than .15?

7.24 An administrator for a large group of hospitals believes that of all patients, 30% will generate bills that become at least two months overdue. A random sample of 200 patients is taken.
- (a) What is the standard error of the sample proportion that will generate bills that become at least two months overdue?
- (b) What is the probability that the sample proportion is less than .25?
- (c) What is the probability that the sample proportion is more than .33?
- (d) What is the probability that the sample proportion is between .27 and .33?

7.25 A corporation receives 120 applications for positions from recent college graduates in business. Assuming that these applicants can be viewed as a random sample of all such graduates, what is the probability that between 35% and 45% of them are women if 40% of all recent college graduates in business are women?

7.26 A charity has found that 42% of all donors from last year will donate again this year. A random sample of 300 donors from last year was taken.
- (a) What is the standard error of the sample proportion who will donate again this year?
- (b) What is the probability that more than half of these sample members will donate again this year?
- (c) What is the probability that the sample proportion is between .40 and .45?
- (d) Without doing the calculations, state in which of the following ranges the sample proportion is more likely to lie: .39 to .41, .41 to .43, .43 to .45, .45 to .47.

7.27 A corporation is considering a new issue of convertible bonds. Management believes that the offer terms will be found attractive by 20% of all its current stockholders. Suppose that the belief is correct. A random sample of 130 current stockholders is taken.
- (a) What is the standard error of the sample proportion who find this offer attractive?
- (b) What is the probability that the sample proportion is more than .15?
- (c) What is the probability that the sample proportion is between .18 and .22?
- (d) Suppose that a sample of 500 current stockholders had been taken. Without doing the calculations, state whether the probabilities in (b) and (c) would have been higher, lower, or the same as those found.

7.28 A store has determined that 30% of all lawn mower purchasers will also purchase a service agreement. In one month 280 lawn mowers are sold to customers who can be regarded as a random sample of all purchasers.
- (a) What is the standard error of the sample proportion of those who will purchase a service agreement?
- (b) What is the probability that the sample proportion will be less than .32?
- (c) Without doing the calculations, state in which of the following ranges the sample proportion is most likely to be: .29 to .31, .30 to .32, .31 to .33, .32 to .34.

7.29 A random sample of 100 voters is taken to estimate the proportion of a state's electorate in favor of an increase in the level of gasoline tax to provide additional revenue for highway repairs. What is the largest value that the standard error of the sample proportion in favor of this measure can take?

7.30 In Exercise 29, suppose that it is decided that a sample of 100 voters is too small to provide a sufficiently reliable estimate of the population proportion. It is required instead that the probability that the sample proportion differs from the population proportion (whatever its value) by more than .03 should not exceed .05. How large a sample is needed to guarantee that this requirement is met?

7.31 A company wants to estimate the proportion of people who are likely purchasers of electric shavers, and who watch the nationally telecast baseball playoffs. A random sample obtained information from 120 people who were identified as likely purchasers of electric shavers. Suppose that the proportion of likely purchasers of electric shavers in the population who watch the telecast is .25.
- (a) The probability is .10 that the sample proportion watching the telecast exceeds population proportion by how much?
- (b) The probability is .05 that the sample proportion is lower than the population proportion by how much?
- (c) The probability is .30 that the sample proportion differs from the population proportion by how much?

7.32 Suppose that 50% of all adult Americans believe that a major overhaul of the nation's health care delivery system is essential. What is the probability that more than 56% of a random sample of 150 adult Americans would hold this belief?

7.33   Suppose that 50% of all adult Americans believe that federal budget deficits at recent levels cause long-term harm to the nation's economy. What is the probability that more than 58% of a random sample of 250 adult Americans would hold this belief.

7.34   A journalist wanted to learn the views of the chief executive officers of the 500 largest U.S. corporations on program trading of stocks. In the time available, it was only possible to contact a random sample of 81 of these chief executive officers. If 55% of all the population members believe that program trading should be banned, what is the probability that less than half the sample members hold this view?

7.35   A small college has an entering freshmen class of 528 students. Of these, 211 have brought their own personal computers to campus. A random sample of 120 entering freshmen was taken.
   (a)   What is the standard error of the sample proportion bringing their own personal computers to campus?

(b)   What is the probability that the sample proportion is less than .33?
   (c)   What is the probability that the sample proportion is between .5 and .6?

7.36   A manufacturing plant has 438 blue-collar employees. Of this group, 239 are concerned about future health care benefits. A random sample of 80 of these employees was questioned to estimate the population proportion concerned about future health care benefits.
   (a)   What is the standard error of the sample proportion who are concerned?
   (b)   What is the probability that the sample proportion is less than .5?
   (c)   What is the probability that the sample proportion is between .5 and .6?

7.37   The annual percentage salary increases for the chief executive officers of all midsize corporations are normally distributed with mean 12.2% and standard deviation 3.6%. A random sample of 81 of these chief executive officers was taken. What is the probability that more than half the sample members had salary increases of less than 10%?

7.4   SAMPLING DISTRIBUTION OF THE SAMPLE VARIANCE

Now that we have considered the inferences about population means and proportions we will next consider inferences about population variances. As business and industry increases its emphasis on producing products that provide customer satisfaction there is an increased need to measure and reduce population variance. High variance for a process implies a wider acceptance interval and thus a wider range of possible outcomes. This wider range of outcomes will result in more individual products that perform below an acceptable standard. After all, a customer does not care if a product performs well "on average." She is concerned that the particular item that she purchased works. Thus if we seek high-quality products from a manufacturing process, we want a low population variance for the unit outputs so that fewer units are below the desired quality standard. By understanding the sampling distribution of the sample variance we will be able to make inferences about the population variance. From these inferences we can identify processes that have low variance and recommend their use. We can also identify processes with high variance and either improve the process or eliminate its use. In addition, a smaller population variance improves our capability to make inferences about population means by using sample means.

We begin by considering a random sample of n observations drawn from a population with unknown mean μ and unknown variance σ^2. Denote the sample members as $X_1, X_2, \ldots, X_n$. The population variance is the expectation

$$\sigma^2 = E[(X - \mu)^2]$$

which suggests that we consider the mean of $(X_i - \overline{X})^2$ over n observations. Since μ_x is unknown we will use the sample mean $\overline{X}$ to compute a sample variance.

SAMPLE VARIANCE

Let $X_1, X_2, \ldots, X_n$ be a random sample from a population. The quantity

$$s^2 = \frac{1}{n-1} \sum_{i=1}^{n} (X_i - \overline{X})^2$$

is called the **sample variance** and its square root s is called the sample standard deviation. Given a specific random sample we would compute the sample variance, and the sample variance would be different for each random sample because of differences in sample observations.

We might be initially surprised by the use of $(n - 1)$ as the divisor in the above definition. One simple explanation is that in a random sample of n observations we have n different values or degrees of freedom. But after we know the computed sample mean there are only $n - 1$ different values that can be uniquely defined. In addition it can be shown that the expected value of the sample variance computed in this way is the population variance. This result is established in Appendix 7.2 at the end of this chapter and holds when the actual sample size n is a small proportion of the population size N.

$$E(s^2) = \sigma^2$$

The conclusion that the expected value of the sample variance is the population variance is quite general. But, for statistical inference we would like to know more about the underlying population distribution. If we can assume that the underlying population distribution is normal, then it can be shown that the sample variance and the population variance are related through a probability distribution known as the *chi-square distribution*.

CHI-SQUARE DISTRIBUTION OF SAMPLE AND POPULATION VARIANCES

Given a random sample of n observations from a normally distributed population whose population variance is σ^2 and the resulting sample variance is s^2, then it can be shown that

$$\frac{(n-1)s^2}{\sigma^2} = \frac{\sum_{i=1}^{n} (X_i - \overline{X})^2}{\sigma^2}$$

has a distribution known as the χ^2 **distribution (chi-square)** with $n - 1$ degrees of freedom.

We frequently use the chi-square family of distributions in applied statistical analysis because it provides a relationship between the sample and the population variances. The chi-square distribution with $n - 1$ degrees of freedom is the distribution of the sum of squares of $n - 1$ independent standard normal random variables. The relationship between the sample and population variances indicated by the chi-square distribution and the resulting computed probabilities for various values of s^2 requires that the population distribution is normal.

The distribution is defined for only positive values since variances are all positive values. An example of the probability density function is shown in Figure 7.14. The density function is asymmetric with a long positive tail. We can characterize a particular member of the family of chi-square distributions by a single parameter referred to as the degrees of freedom, denoted as ν. A χ^2 distribution with ν degrees of freedom will be denoted as χ^2_ν.

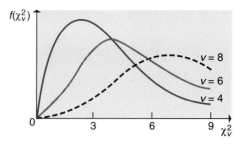

The mean and variance of this distribution are equal to the number of degrees and twice the number of degrees of freedom.

$$E\left(\chi_v^2\right) = v \quad \text{and} \quad \text{Var}\left(\chi_v^2\right) = 2v$$

Using these results for the mean and variance of the chi-square distribution we find that

$$E\left[\frac{(n-1)s^2}{\sigma^2}\right] = (n-1)$$

$$\frac{(n-1)}{\sigma^2} E(s^2) = (n-1)$$

$$E(s^2) = \sigma^2$$

To obtain the variance of s^2 we have

$$\text{Var}\left[\frac{(n-1)s^2}{\sigma^2}\right] = 2(n-1)$$

$$\frac{(n-1)^2}{\sigma^4} \text{Var}(s^2) = 2(n-1)$$

$$\text{Var}(s^2) = \frac{2\sigma^4}{(n-1)}$$

We can use the properties of the χ^2 distribution to find the variance of the sampling distribution of the sample variance, when the parent population is normal.

The parameter v of the χ^2 distribution is called the degrees of freedom. To help understand the degrees of freedom concept consider first that the sample variance is the sum of squares for n values of the form $(X_i - \overline{X})$. These n values are not independent because their sum is zero (as we can show using the definition of the mean). Thus if we know any $n - 1$ of the values $(X_i - \overline{X})$

$$\sum_{i=1}^{n} (X_i - \overline{X}) = 0$$

$$X_n - \overline{X} = \sum_{i=1}^{n-1} (X_i$$

Since we can determine the nth quantity if we know the remaining $n - 1$ quantities, we say that there are $n - 1$ degrees of freedom for computing s^2. In contrast if μ_X were known we could compute an estimate of σ^2 by using the quantities

$$(X_1 - \mu_X),\ (X_2 - \mu_X),\ldots,(X_n - \mu_X)$$

each of which are independent. In that case we would have n degrees of freedom from the n independent sample observations, X_i. However, μ_X is not known and we must use its estimate $\bar{X}$ to compute the estimate of σ^2. As a result one degree of freedom is lost in computing the sample mean and we have $n - 1$ degrees of freedom for s^2.

For many applications involving the population variance we need to find values for the cumulative distribution of χ^2, especially the upper and lower tails of the distribution, for example

$$P(\chi_{10}^2 < K) = 0.05$$
$$P(\chi_{10}^2 > K) = 0.05$$

For this purpose we have the distribution of the chi-square random variable tabulated in Table 7 in the Appendix. In Table 5 the degrees of freedom are noted in the left column and the critical values of K for various probability levels are indicated in the other columns. Thus for 10 degrees of freedom the value of K for the lower interval is 3.94 and for the upper interval is 18.31

$$P(\chi_{10}^2 < 3.94) = 0.05$$
$$P(\chi_{10}^2 > 18.31) = 0.05$$

These probabilities are shown in Figure 7.15.

A summary of the results concerning population and sample variances.

SAMPLING DISTRIBUTION OF THE SAMPLE VARIANCE

Let s_X^2 denote the sample variance for a random sample of n observations from a population with a variance σ^2. Then

1. The sampling distribution of s^2 has mean σ^2

$$E(s^2) = \sigma^2 \tag{7.11}$$

2. The variance of the sampling distribution of s_X^2 depends on the underlying population distribution. If that distribution is normal, then

$$\text{Var}(s^2) = \frac{2\sigma^4}{n-1} \tag{7.12}$$

3. If the population distribution is normal then $\dfrac{(n-1)s^2}{\sigma^2}$ is distributed as $\chi_{(n-1)}^2$.

FIGURE 7.15
Upper and Lower χ_{10}^2 Probabilities with 10 Degrees of Freedom

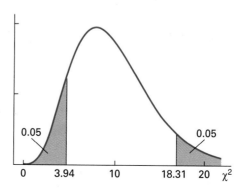

Thus if we have a random sample from a population with a normal distribution we can make inferences about the sample variance σ^2 by using s^2 and the chi-square distribution. We illustrate the process in the following examples.

EXAMPLE 7.9

PROCESS MONITORING FOR INTEGRATED ELECTRONICS (COMPUTING PROBABILITY OF SAMPLE VARIANCE)

George Samson is responsible for quality assurance at Integrated Electronics. He has asked you to establish a quality monitoring process for the manufacture of control device A. The variability of the electrical resistance, measured in ohms, is critical for this device. Manufacturing standards specify a standard deviation of 3.6 and the population distribution of resistance measures is normal. The monitoring process requires that a random sample of $n = 6$ observations is obtained from the population of devices and the sample variance is computed. Determine an upper limit for the sample variance such that the probability of exceeding this limit, given a population standard deviation of 3.6, is less than 0.05.

SOLUTION

For this problem we have $n = 6$ and $\sigma^2 = (3.6)^2 = 12.96$. Using the chi-square distribution we can state that

$$P(s^2 > K) = P\left(\frac{(n-1)s^2}{12.96} > 11.07\right) = 0.05$$

where K is the desired upper limit and $\chi_5^2 = 11.07$ is the upper 0.05 critical value of the chi-square distribution with 5 degrees of freedom (see Figure 7.16). The required upper limit for s_X^2—labeled as K—can be obtained by solving

$$\frac{(n-1)K}{12.96} = 11.07$$

$$K = \frac{(11.07)(12.96)}{(6-1)} = 28.69$$

FIGURE 7.16
Computation of Chi-square Critical Value Using Minitab

Inverse Cumulative Distribution Function	
Chi-Square with 5 DF	
$P(X \le X)$	x
0.9500	11.0705

If the sample variance s^2 from a random sample of size $n = 6$ exceeds 28.69 there is strong evidence to suspect that the population variance exceeds 12.96 and that the manufacturing process should be halted and that appropriate adjustments be performed.

The required upper limit for the chi-square distribution can also be obtained using a computer package. For example, using Minitab we would use the command sequence:

```
CALC > PROBABILITY DISTRIBUTION > CHI-SQUARE
```

to obtain the Chi-square dialog box. Next, follow the steps in the dialog box.

EXAMPLE 7.10

PROCESS ANALYSIS FOR GREEN VALLEY FOODS (COMPUTING PROBABILITY OF SAMPLE VARIANCE)

Shirley Mendez is the manager of quality assurance for Green Valley Foods, Inc., a packer of frozen vegetable products. Shirley wants to be sure that the variation of package weights is small so that the company does not produce a large proportion of packages that are under the stated package weight. She has asked you to obtain upper and lower limits for the ratio of the sample variance divided by the population variance for a random sample of $n = 20$ observations. The limits are such that the probability that the ratio is below the lower limit is 0.025 and the probability that the ratio is above the upper limit is 0.025. Thus 95% of the ratios will be between these limits. The population distribution can be assumed to be normal.

SOLUTION

We are asked to obtain values K_L and K_U such that

$$P\left(\frac{s^2}{\sigma^2} < K_L\right) = 0.025 \qquad \text{and} \qquad P\left(\frac{s^2}{\sigma^2} > K_U\right) = 0.025$$

given a random sample of size $n = 20$ is used to compute the sample variance. For the lower limit we can state

$$0.025 = P\left[\frac{(n-1)s^2}{\sigma^2} < (n-1)K_L\right] = P\left[\chi_{19}^2 < (n-1)K_L\right]$$

For the upper limit we can state

$$0.975 = P\left[\frac{(n-1)s^2}{\sigma^2} > (n-1)K_U\right] = P\left[\chi_{19}^2 > (n-1)K_U\right]$$

FIGURE 7.17
Upper and Lower Chi-square Values for 95% Acceptance Interval with 19 Degrees of Freedom

Inverse Cumulative Distribution Function	
Chi-Square with 19 DF	
$P(X \le x)$	x
0.0250	8.9065
0.9750	32.8523

These upper and lower limits of chi-square define an interval such that if the computed chi-square is within that interval we accept the assumption that the process variance is at the assumed value. This interval is defined as an *Acceptance Interval*.

The upper and lower values for the chi-square distribution can be found from Table 7 or by using the Minitab command Calc > Probability Distribution > Chi-square. Place the lower limit probability—0.025—in row 1 of column 1 and the upper limit probability—0.975—in row 2 of column 1 and specify the computation of inverse probabilities with 19 degrees of freedom. The resulting display is shown in Figure 7.17.

From the above lower and upper bounds for the chi-square acceptance interval we can compute the acceptance interval limits, K_L and K_U, for the ratio of sample to population variance.

$$0.025 = P\left[\chi_{19L}^2 < (n-1)K_L\right] = P\left[8.9065 < (19)K_L\right]$$

and thus

$$K_L = 0.469$$

For the upper limit we have

$$0.975 = P\left[\chi_{19U}^2 > (n-1)K_U\right] = P\left[32.8523 > (19)K_U\right]$$

and thus

$$K_U = 1.729$$

The 95% acceptance interval for the ratio of sample variance divided by population variance is

$$P\left(0.469 \le \frac{s^2}{\sigma^2} \le 1.729\right) = 0.95$$

Thus the sample variance is between 46.9% and 172.9% of the population variance with probability 0.95.

ASSUMPTION

At this point it is important that we emphasize that the procedures used to make inferences about the population variance are substantially influenced by the assumption of a normal population distribution. Inferences concerning the population mean based on the sample mean are not substantially affected by departures from a normal distribution. In addition, inferences based on the sample mean can also make use of the central limit theorem, which states that sample means will typically be normally distributed if the sample size is reasonably large. Thus we state that inferences based on the sample mean are robust with respect to the assumption of normality. Unfortunately, inferences based on sample variances are not robust with respect to the assumption of normality.

We know that in many applications the population variance is of direct interest to an investigator. But when using the procedures we have demonstrated we must keep in mind that if only a moderate number of sample observations are available, serious departures from normality in the parent population can severely invalidate the conclusions of analyses. The cautious analyst will therefore be rather tentative in making inferences in these circumstances.

EXERCISES

7.38 A process produces batches of a chemical whose impurity concentrations follow a normal distribution with variance 1.75. A random sample of 20 of these batches is chosen. Find the probability that the sample variance exceeds 3.10.

7.39 Monthly rates of return on the shares of a particular common stock are independent of one another and normally distributed with a standard deviation of 1.7. A sample of 12 months is taken.
  (a) Find the probability that the sample standard deviation is less than 2.5.
  (b) Find the probability that the sample standard deviation is bigger than 1.0.

7.40 It is believed that first-year salaries for newly qualified accountants follow a normal distribution with standard deviation $2,500. A random sample of 16 observations was taken.
  (a) Find the probability that the sample standard deviation is more than $3,000.
  (b) Find the probability that the sample standard deviation is less than $1,500.

7.41 A mathematics test of 100 multiple choice questions is to be given to all freshmen entering a large university. Initially, in a pilot study, the test was given to a random sample of 20 freshmen. Suppose that, for the population of all entering freshmen, the distribution of number of correct answers would be normal with variance 250.
  (a) What is the probability that the sample variance would be less than 100?
  (b) What is the probability that the sample variance would be more than 500?

7.42 In a large city it was found that summer electricity bills for single-family homes followed a normal distribution with standard deviation $100. A random sample of 25 bills was taken.
  (a) Find the probability that the sample standard deviation is less than $75.
  (b) Find the probability that the sample standard deviation is more than $150.

7.43 Numbers of hours spent watching television by students in the week before final exams have a normal distribution with standard deviation 4.5 hours. A random sample of 30 students was taken.
  (a) Is the probability more than .95 that the sample standard deviation exceeds 3.5 hours?
  (b) Is the probability more than .95 that the sample standard deviation is less than 6 hours?

7.44 In Table 7.1, we considered the fifteen possible samples of four observations from a population of $N = 6$ values of years on the job for employees. The population variance for these six values is

$$\sigma_X^2 = \frac{47}{12}$$

For each of the fifteen possible samples, calculate the sample variance. Find the average of these fifteen sample variances, thus confirming that the expected value of the sample variance is not equal to the population variance when the number of sample members is not a small proportion of the number of population members. [In fact, as you can verify here, $E(s_x^2) = N\sigma_x^2 / (N - 1)$.]

7.45 A production process manufactures electronic components with timing signals whose duration follows a normal distribution. A random sample of six components was taken, and the durations of their timing signals were measured.
  (a) The probability is .05 that the sample variance is bigger than what percentage of the population variance?
  (b) The probability is .10 that the sample variance is less than what percentage of the population variance?

7.46 A random sample of 10 stock market mutual funds was taken. Suppose that rates of returns on the population of all stock market mutual funds follow a normal distribution.
  (a) The probability is .10 that sample variance is bigger than what percentage of the population variance?
  (b) Find any pair of numbers, a and b, to complete the following sentence. The probability is .95 that the sample variance is between $a\%$ and $b\%$ of the population variance.
  (c) Suppose that a sample of 20 mutual funds had been

taken. Without doing the calculations, indicate how this would change your answer to part (b).

7.47 Each member of a random sample of 15 business economists was asked to predict the rate of inflation for the coming year. Assume that the predictions for the whole population of business economists follow a normal distribution with the standard deviation 1.8%.

   (a) The probability is .01 that the sample standard deviation is bigger than what number?

   (b) The probability is .025 that the sample standard deviation is smaller than what number?

   (c) Find any pair of numbers such that the probability that the sample standard deviation lies between these numbers is .90.

7.48 A precision instrument is checked by making 12 readings on the same quantity. The population distribution of readings is normal.

   (a) The probability is .95 that the sample variance is more than what percentage of the population variance?

   (b) The probability is .90 that the sample variance is more than what percentage of the population variance?

   (c) Determine any pair of appropriate numbers a and b to complete the following sentence: The probability is .95 that the sample variance is between a% and b% of the population variance.

7.49 A drug company produces pills containing an active ingredient. The company is concerned about the mean weight of this ingredient per pill, but it also requires that the variance (in squared milligrams) be no more than 1.5. A random sample of 20 pills is selected, and the sample variance is found to be 2.05. How likely is it that a sample variance this high or higher would be found if the population variance is in fact 1.5? Assume that the population distribution is normal.

7.50 A manufacturer has been purchasing raw materials from a supplier whose consignments have a variance of 15.4 (in squared pounds) in impurity levels. A rival supplier claims that he can supply consignments of this raw material with the same mean impurity level but with lower variance. For a random sample of 25 consignments from the second supplier, the variance in impurity levels was found to be 12.2. What is the probability of observing a value this low or lower for the sample variance if, in fact, the true population variance is 15.4? Assume that the population distribution is normal.

SUMMARY

In Chapter 7 we have presented the concept of sampling distributions defined as the probability distribution for sample statistics. Sampling distributions enable us to determine the probability of a particular sample statistic given a specific probability distribution model for the sampling distribution. We are thus linking the sample statistics developed in Chapter 2 with the probability distributions developed in Chapters 5 and 6. We will see in future chapters how this link allows us to use our sample statistics to obtain certain conclusions or inferences about the system and process that develops a population of data from which our sample was obtained. This is the basis for objective decisions based on sample data. In our discussion we included the important concept of acceptance intervals. Acceptance intervals define a range, with a given probability, for sample statistics based on an assumed probability distribution function. If the sample statistic is within that range then we "accept" the assumed probability model as being correct.

KEY WORDS

central limit theorem, 227
chi-square distribution, 241
sample mean, 222
sample proportion, 235
sample variance, 241
sampling distributions, 219
sampling distribution of the sample mean, 224
sampling distribution of the sample proportion, 236
sampling distribution of the sample variance, 243
simple random sample, 218
standard normal distribution for sample mean, 223

CHAPTER EXERCISES AND APPLICATIONS

7.51 What is meant by the statement that the sample mean has a sampling distribution?

7.52 An investor is considering six different money market funds. The average number of days to maturity for these funds is

    41   39   35   35   33   38

Two of these funds are to be chosen at random.

   (a) How many possible samples of two funds are there?

   (b) List all possible samples.

   (c) Find the probability function of the sampling distribution of the sample mean.

   (d) Verify directly that the mean of the sampling distribution of the sample mean is equal to the population mean.

7.53 Of what relevance is the central limit theorem to the sampling distribution of the sample mean?

7.54 Refer to Exercise 7.52. Find the probability function of the sampling distribution of the sample proportion of funds with average maturity more than 36 days for samples of two observations. Also verify directly that the mean of the sampling distribution of the sample proportion is equal to the population proportion.

7.55 The scores of all applicants taking an aptitude test required by a law school have a normal distribution with mean 420 and standard deviation 100. A random sample of 25 scores is taken.
   (a) Find the probability that the sample mean score is bigger than 450.
   (b) Find the probability that the sample mean score is between 400 and 450.
   (c) The probability is .10 that the sample mean score is bigger than what number?
   (d) The probability is .10 that the sample mean score is less than what number?
   (e) The probability is .05 that the sample standard deviation of the scores is bigger than what number?
   (f) The probability is .05 that the sample standard deviation of the scores is less than what number?
   (g) If a sample of 50 test scores had been taken, would the probability of a sample mean score bigger than 450 be smaller than, larger than, or the same as the correct answer to part (a)? It is not necessary to do the detailed calculations here. Sketch a graph to illustrate your reasoning.

7.56 A company services home air conditioners. It has been found that times for service calls follow a normal distribution with mean 60 minutes and standard deviation 10 minutes. A random sample of four service calls was taken.
   (a) What is the probability that the sample mean service time is more than 65 minutes?
   (b) The probability is .10 that the sample mean service time is less than how many minutes?
   (c) The probability is .10 that the sample standard deviation of service times is more than how many minutes?
   (d) The probability is .10 that the sample standard deviation of service times is less than how many minutes?
   (e) What is the probability that more than two of these calls take more than 65 minutes?

7.57 In a particular year, the percentage rates of returns of U.S. common stock mutual funds had a normal distribution with mean 14.8 and standard deviation 6.3. A random sample of nine of these mutual funds was taken.
   (a) What is the probability that the sample mean percentage rate of return is more than 19.0?
   (b) What is the probability that the sample mean percentage rate of return is between 10.6 and 19.0?

   (c) The probability is .25 that the sample mean percentage return is less than what number?
   (d) The probability is .10 that the sample standard deviation of percentage return is more than what number?
   (e) If a sample of 20 of these funds was taken, state whether the probability of a sample mean percentage rate of return of more than 19.0 wold be smaller than, bigger than, or the same as the correct answer to (a). Sketch a graph to illustrate your reasoning.

7.58 The lifetimes of a certain electronic component are known to be normally distributed with a mean of 1,600 hours and a standard deviation of 400 hours.
   (a) For a random sample of 16 components, find the probability that the sample mean is more than 1,500 hours.
   (b) For a random sample of 16 components, the probability is .15 that the sample mean lifetime is more than how many hours?
   (c) For a random sample of 16 components, the probability is .10 that the sample standard deviation lifetime is more than how many hours?
   (d) For a random sample of 121 components, find the probability that less than half the sampled components have lifetimes of more than 1,500 hours.

7.59 Refer to Appendix A6.1 in order to derive the mean of the sampling distribution of the sample variance for a sample of n observations from a population of N members, when the population variance is σ_x^2. By appropriately modifying the argument in Appendix A7.2 show that

$$E\left(S_x^2\right) = N\sigma_x^2 \Big/ \left(N-1\right)$$

Note the intuitive plausibility of this result when $n = N$.

7.60 It has been found that times taken by people to complete a particular tax form follow a normal distribution with mean 100 minutes and standard deviation 30 minutes. A random sample of nine people who have completed this tax form was taken.
   (a) What is the probability that the sample mean time taken is more than two hours?
   (b) The probability is .20 that the sample mean time taken is less than how many minutes?
   (c) The probability is .05 that the sample standard deviation of time taken is less than how many minutes?

7.61 It was found that 80% of seniors at a particular college had accepted a job offer before graduation. For those accepting offers, salary distribution was normal with mean $29,000 and standard deviation $4,000.
   (a) For a random sample of sixty seniors, what is the probability that less than 70% have accepted job offers?
   (b) For a random sample of six seniors, what is the probability that less than 70% have accepted job offers?

(**c**) For a random sample of six seniors who have accepted job offers, what is the probability that the average salary is more than $30,000?

(**d**) A senior is chosen at random. What is the probability that he or she has accepted a job offer with a salary of more than $30,000?

7.62 Plastic bags used for packaging produce are manufactured so that the breaking strengths of the bags are normally distributed with a standard deviation of 1.8 pounds per square inch. A random sample of 16 bags is selected.

(**a**) The probability is .01 that the sample standard deviation of breaking strengths exceeds what number?

(**b**) The probability is .15 that the sample mean exceeds the population mean by how much?

(**c**) The probability is .05 that the sample mean differs from the population mean by how much?

7.63 A quality control manager was concerned about variability in the amount of active ingredient in pills produced by a particular process. A random sample of 21 pills was taken. What is the probability that the sample variance of the amount of active ingredient was more than twice the population variance?

7.64 A sample of 100 students is to be taken to determine which of two brands of beer is preferred in a blind taste test. Suppose that, in the whole population of students, 50% would prefer brand A.

(**a**) What is the probability that more than 60% of the sample members prefer brand A?

(**b**) What is the probability that between 45% and 55% of the sample members prefer brand A?

(**c**) Suppose that a sample of only 10 students was available. Indicate how the method of calculation of probabilities would differ, compared with your solutions to (a) and (b)?

7.65 Scores on a particular test, taken by a large group of students, follow a normal distribution with standard deviation 40 points. A random sample of 16 scores was taken to estimate the population mean score. Let $\overline{X}$ denote the sample mean. What is the probability that the interval $(\overline{X} - 10)$ to $(\overline{X} + 10)$ contains the true population mean?

7.66 A manufacturer of liquid detergent claims that the mean weight of liquid in containers sold is at least 30 ounces. It is known that the population distribution of weights is normal with standard deviation 1.3 ounces. In order to check the manufacturer's claim, a random sample of 16 containers of detergent is examined. The claim will be questioned if the sample mean weight is less than 29.5 ounces. What is the probability that the claim will be questioned if in fact the population mean weight is 30 ounces?

7.67 In a particular year, 40% of home sales were partially financed by the seller. A random sample of 250 sales is examined.

(**a**) The probability is .8 that the sample proportion is bigger than what amount?

(**b**) The probability is .9 that the sample proportion is smaller than what amount?

(**c**) The probability is .7 that the sample proportion differs from the population proportion by how much?

7.68 A candidate for office intends to campaign in a state if her initial support level exceeds 30% of the voters. A random sample of 300 voters is taken, and it is decided to campaign if the sample proportion supporting the candidate exceeds .28.

(**a**) What is the probability of a decision not to campaign if in fact the initial support level is 20%?

(**b**) What is the probability of a decision not to campaign if in fact the initial support level is 40%?

7.69 It is known that the incomes of subscribers to a particular magazine have a normal distribution with standard deviation $6,600. A random sample of 25 subscribers is taken.

(**a**) What is the probability that the sample standard deviation of their incomes is bigger than $4,000?

(**b**) What is the probability that the sample standard deviation of their incomes is less than $8,000?

7.70 Batches of chemical are manufactured by a production process. Samples of 20 batches from a production run are selected for testing. If the standard deviation of the percentage impurity contents in the sample batches exceeds 2.5%, the production process is thoroughly checked. Assume that the population distribution of percentage impurity concentrations is normal. What is the probability that the production process will be thoroughly checked if the population standard deviation of percentage impurity concentrations is 2%?

APPENDIX 7.1
MONTE CARLO SAMPLE SIMULATIONS USING MINITAB

In Section 7.2 we presented results from Monte Carlo sampling simulations to demonstrate the central limit theorem. In this Appendix we will indicate how you can construct similar simulations for a probability distribution. The simulation can be performed by using a Minitab macro named "Centlimit.mac" that is contained on the disk supplied with the textbook. To use this macro copy it to the directory

MTBWIN\MACROS\

FIGURE 7.18
Monte Carlo Sampling
Simulation in Minitab

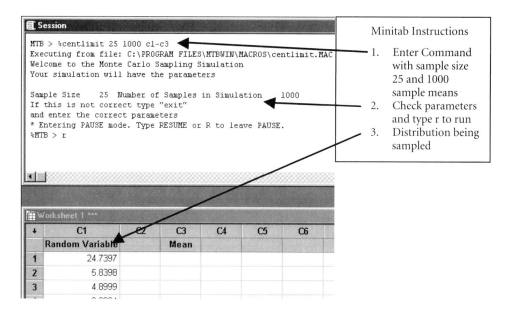

using the Windows Explorer. This macro will then be stored with other macros supplied with the Minitab package. When the macro is stored in this directory it can be run directly in Minitab. Alternatively the macro can be stored in another directory and the entire path is supplied to run the macro. To run the sampling simulation use the following steps

1. Store a set of values in column 1 that have the frequency indicated by the probability distribution that you are interested in simulating. Typically we store 100 values, but any number could be stored. For example, to store a binomial distribution with $\pi = 0.40$ you

FIGURE 7.19
Results of the Monte Carlo
Sampling Simulation

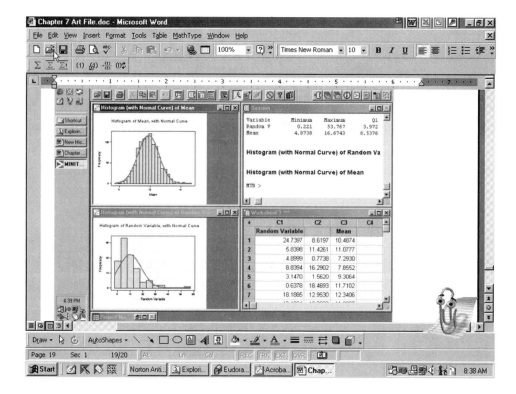

would store 40 1's and 60 0's in column 1. You could also store an empirical distribution of numbers from a population being studied. Another procedure for obtaining the sample values is to use the command

CALC > RANDOM DATA > "SELECT PROBABILITY DISTRIBUTION"

This would provide you with a random sample from one of a number of common probability distributions.

FIGURE 7.20
Copy of the Minitab Macro "Centlim.Mac"

```
Macro
Centlimit n1,n2,Dist,Samp,Xbar
#   Dr.William L. Carlson
#   Professor of Economics
#   St Olaf College
#   Northfield MN   55057
#   Carlson@Stolaf.edu
#   To Execute this Macro in Minitab  Type
#   %Centlimit "sample size"  "Number of Samples"  C1 C2 C3
#
#The output includes a histogram and a normal probability plot for the
original #distribution and a histogram and normal probability plot for the
sampling #distribution of sample means
#Macro is Stored as a text file in C:\program
files\mtbwin\macros\centlimit.mac
#
#Definition of Variables
#
# n1   Sample size obtained from probability distribution
# n2   Number of samples of size n1 obtained in this simulation
# Dist        Column that contains an empirical distribution from which the
random #       sample is obtained.
# Xbar        Column that contains the sample means from each of the n2 samples
#             obtained in the simulation
# Samp        Column that will be used to generate each of the samples.
#
#
Mconstant  n1 n2 k1 k2
Mcolumn Dist Xbar Samp c11 c12 c13 c14
Name Dist 'Random Variable' Xbar 'Mean'
Let c11="Sample Size"
Let c12= n1
Let c13="Number of Samples in Simulation"
Let c14=n2
Note Welcome to the Monte Carlo Sampling Simulation
Note Your simulation will have the parameters
Write 'Terminal' c11-c14
Note If this is not correct type "exit"
Note and enter the correct parameters
Pause
Brief 0
Do k1=1:n2
Sample n1 Dist Samp;
Replace.
Mean Samp k2
Let xbar(k1)=k2
Enddo
Brief
Describe Dist Xbar;
GNHist.
Endmacro
```

2. In the Minitab Session Window type the command

```
MTB > %CENTLIMIT N1 N2 C1-C3
```

Where

n1 is the sample size for the individual samples being simulated.

n2 is the number of samples whose means are to be obtained from the simulation. Generally 500 to 1,000 samples will provide a good sampling distribution, but you can select any reasonable value. Recognize that the greater the number of samples the longer it will take to run the simulation.

c1 to c3 are the columns used by Minitab for the simulation, with your probability distribution of interest in column 1. You could use any columns as long as your probability distribution is in column 1

Figure 7.18, on page 250, shows a run of the sampling simulation.

The simulation will generate samples in column 2 and compute the sample mean. The mean for each sample will be stored in column 3 titled "Mean." Descriptive statistics and histograms will be computed for the "random variable" values in column 1 and for the sample "Means" in column 3. By clicking on the menu command

```
WINDOWS > TILE
```

You can obtain the screen in Figure 7.19, on page 250, that is useful for comparing the original distribution and the sampling distribution with a comparable normal.

In Figure 7.19 we see that the distribution of the Random Variable is definitely not normal but is highly skewed to the right. In contrast, the sampling distribution of the mean closely approximates a normal distribution. Figure 7.20, on page 251, presents a copy of the "Centlim.Mac" Minitab macro, which is also stored on the data disk for the textbook. Users familiar with Minitab macros could modify this macro to obtain different outputs.

APPENDIX 7.2

In this Appendix, we will show that the mean of the sampling distribution of the sample variance is the population variance. We begin by finding the expectation of the sum of squares of the sample members about their mean; that is, the expectation of

$$
\begin{aligned}
\sum_{i=1}^{n}\left(X_i - \overline{X}\right)^2 &= \sum_{i=1}^{n}\left[\left(X_i - \mu\right) - \left(\overline{X} - \mu\right)\right]^2 \\
&= \sum_{i=1}^{n}\left[\left(X_i - \mu\right)^2 - 2\left(\overline{X} - \mu\right)\left(X_i - \mu\right) + \left(\overline{X} - \mu\right)^2\right] \\
&= \sum_{i=1}^{n}\left(X_i - \mu\right)^2 - 2\left(\overline{X} - \mu\right)\sum_{i=1}^{n}\left(X_i - \mu\right) + \sum_{i=1}^{n}\left(\overline{X} - \mu\right)^2 \\
&= \sum_{i=1}^{n}\left(X_i - \mu\right)^2 - 2n\left(\overline{X} - \mu\right)^2 + n\left(\overline{X} - \mu\right)^2 \\
&= \sum\left(X_i - \mu\right)^2 - n\left(\overline{X} - \mu\right)^2
\end{aligned}
$$

Taking expectations then gives

$$
\begin{aligned}
E\left[\sum_{i=1}^{n}\left(X_i - \overline{X}\right)^2\right] &= E\left[\sum_{i=1}^{n}\left(X_i - \mu\right)^2\right] - nE\left[\left(\overline{X} - \mu\right)^2\right] \\
&= \sum_{i=1}^{n}E\left[\left(X_i - \mu\right)^2\right] - nE\left[\left(\overline{X} - \mu\right)^2\right]
\end{aligned}
$$

Now, the expectation of each $(X_i - \mu)^2$ is the population variance σ^2, and the expectation of $(\overline{X} - \mu)^2$ is the variance of the sample mean—that is, σ^2/n. Hence, we have

$$E\left[\sum_{i=1}^{n}\left(X_i - \overline{X}\right)^2\right] = n\sigma^2 - \frac{n\sigma^2}{n} = (n-1)\sigma^2$$

Finally, for the expected value of the sample variance, we have

$$E\left(S^2\right) = E\left[\frac{1}{n-1}\sum_{i=1}^{n}\left(X_i - \overline{X}\right)^2\right]$$
$$= \frac{1}{n-1}E\left[\sum_{i=1}^{n}\left(X_i - \overline{X}\right)^2\right]$$
$$= \frac{1}{n-1}(n-1)\sigma^2 = \sigma^2$$

This is the result we set out to establish.

REFERENCES

1. F. R. David, L. M. Anderson, and K. W. Lawrimore, "Perspectives on Business Ethics in Management Education," *S. A. M. Advanced Management Journal*, 55, no. 4 (1990), 26–32.

2. H. Hogan, "The 1990 Post-enumeration Survey: An Overview," *American Statistician*, 46 (1992), 261–269.

CHAPTER 8

ESTIMATION

INTRODUCTION

This chapter emphasizes inferential statements about a population, based on the information contained in one or more random samples. The population mean, variance, and the proportion of population members possessing some specific attribute are characteristics, or *parameters*, of the population upon our attention is focused. Examples of such statements include

1. The average weekly demand for a particular brand of orange juice
2. The average weight of 18-oz. boxes of cereal packaged by a particular machine
3. The proportion of a corporation's employees favoring the introduction of a modified bonus plan
4. The proportion of counties in the United States that use a particular voting system, such as the punch card system, the optical scan system, or any of several other methods (*USA Today*, November 14, 2000; see reference 9)
5. The proportion of blank or spoiled ballots in a precinct, county, or state during a presidential election (*Orlando Sentinel*, November 12, 2000; reference 10)
6. The variance in impurity levels in batches of a manufactured chemical

8.1 POINT ESTIMATORS

Any inference drawn about the population will be based on sample statistics. The choice of appropriate statistics will depend on which population parameter is of interest. The value of the population parameter will be unknown, and one objective of sampling could be to estimate its value. A distinction must be made between the two terms, *estimator* and *estimate*.

ESTIMATOR AND ESTIMATE

An **estimator** of a population parameter is a random variable that depends on the sample information and whose value provides approximations to this unknown parameter. A specific value of that random variable is called an **estimate.**

Hildebrand (reference 8) points out that there is "a technical distinction between an *estimator* as a function of random variables and an *estimate* as a single number. It is the distinction between a process (the estimator) and the result of that process (the estimate)." To clarify this distinction between estimator and estimate, consider the estimation of the mean weekly sales of a particular brand of orange juice. One possible *estimator* of the population mean is the sample mean, $\overline{X}$. If the sample mean weekly sales of this particular brand of orange juice is found to be 3,280 gallons, then 3,280 is an *estimate* of the population mean weekly sales. Another possible *estimator* of the mean weekly sales could be the sample median.

Other estimators were studied in early chapters of this book, such as the sample variance, s^2, which is an estimator of the population variance, σ^2 (Chapter 2). If the value of the sample variance for the weekly demand of orange juice is 300 gallons, then s^2 is the estimator and 300 is the estimate. In Chapter 3, other estimators were introduced, including the sample correlation coefficient, the least-squares coefficient for slope, and the least-squares coefficient for the *y*-intercept of the regression line.

In discussing the estimation of an unknown parameter, two possibilities must be considered. First, a *single number* could be computed from the sample as "most representative" of the unknown population parameter. This is called a point estimate. The estimate of 3,280 gallons of orange juice is an example of a *point estimate*. Alternatively, it might be possible to find an interval or range that most likely contains the value of the population parameter. For example, the mean weekly demand in this store for this particular brand of orange juice is, with some specified degree of confidence, between 2500 and 3500 gallons. This interval estimate is called a *confidence interval* and will be discussed later in this chapter.

POINT ESTIMATOR AND POINT ESTIMATE

Let θ represent a population parameter (such as the population mean μ or the population proportion π). A **point estimator,** $\hat{\theta}$, of a population parameter, θ, is a function of the sample information that yields a single number called a **point estimate**. For example, the sample mean $\bar{X}$ is a point estimator of the population mean μ, and the value that $\bar{X}$ assumes for a given set of data is called the point estimate.

At the outset it must be pointed out that no single mechanism exists for the determination of a uniquely "best" point estimator in all circumstances. What is available instead is a set of criteria under which particular estimators can be evaluated. You may be thinking that the sample median also gives a point estimate of the population mean μ. The median, as discussed later in this chapter, is not the best estimator for the mean of some distributions.

Two important properties to evaluate estimators are unbiasedness and efficiency.

Unbiasedness

In searching for an estimator of a population parameter, the first property an estimator should possess is unbiasedness.

UNBIASED ESTIMATOR

The point estimator $\hat{\theta}$ is said to be an **unbiased estimator** of the parameter θ if the expected value, or mean, of the sampling distribution of $\hat{\theta}$ is θ; that is,

$$E(\hat{\theta}) = \theta$$

Notice that unbiasedness does not state that a *particular* value of $\hat{\theta}$ is exactly the correct value of θ. Rather, an unbiased estimator has "the capability of estimating the population parameter correctly on the average ... An unbiased estimator is correct on the average. We can think of the expected value of $\hat{\theta}$ as the average of $\hat{\theta}$ values for all possible samples, or alternatively, as the long-run average of $\hat{\theta}$ values for repeated samples. The condition that the estimator $\hat{\theta}$ should be unbiased says that the *average* $\hat{\theta}$ value is exactly correct. It does not state that a particular $\hat{\theta}$ value is exactly correct," (reference 8).

Sometimes $\hat{\theta}$ will overestimate and other times underestimate the parameter, but it follows from the notion of expectation that if the sampling procedure is repeated many times, then on the average, the value obtained for an unbiased estimator will be equal to the population parameter. It seems reasonable to assert that, all other things being equal, unbiasedness is a desirable property in a point estimator. Figure 8.1 illustrates the probability density functions for two estimators, $\hat{\theta}_1$ and $\hat{\theta}_2$ of the parameter θ. It should be obvious that $\hat{\theta}_1$ is an unbiased estimator of θ and $\hat{\theta}_2$ is not an unbiased estimator.

FIGURE 8.1
Probability Density Functions
for Estimators $\hat{\theta}_1$ (Unbiased)
and $\hat{\theta}_2$(Biased)

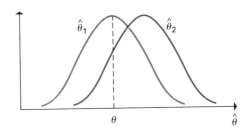

The sample mean, sample variance, and sample proportion are unbiased estimators of their corresponding population parameters:

1. the sample mean is an unbiased estimator of μ; ($E(\overline{X} = \mu)$
2. the sample variance is an unbiased estimator of σ^2; ($E(s^2) = \sigma^2$)
3. the sample proportion is an unbiased estimator of π; ($E(p) = \pi$)

An estimator that is not unbiased is *biased*. The extent of the bias is the difference between the mean of the estimator and the true parameter.

BIAS

Let $\hat{\theta}$ be an estimator of θ. The **bias** in $\hat{\theta}$ is defined as the difference between its mean and θ; that is

$$\text{Bias}(\hat{\theta}) = E(\hat{\theta}) - \theta$$

It follows that the bias of an unbiased estimator is 0.

Unbiasedness is not the only desirable characteristic of an estimator, since there may be several unbiased estimators for any population parameter. For example, if the population is normally distributed, the median is also an unbiased estimator of the population mean.

Efficiency

In many practical problems, different unbiased estimators can be obtained, and some method of choosing among them needs to be found. In this situation, it is natural to prefer the estimator whose distribution is most closely concentrated about the population parameter being estimated. Values of such an estimator are less likely to differ, by any fixed amount, from the parameter being estimated than are those of its competitors. Using variance as a measure of concentration, the *efficiency* of an estimator as a criterion for preferring one estimator to another estimator is introduced.

MOST EFFICIENT ESTIMATOR AND RELATIVE EFFICIENCY

Suppose there are several unbiased estimators of θ. Then the unbiased estimator with the **smallest variance** is said to be the **most efficient estimator** or to be the **minimum variance unbiased estimator** of θ. Let $\hat{\theta}_1$ and $\hat{\theta}_2$ be two unbiased estimators of θ, based on the same number of sample observations. Then,

(a) $\hat{\theta}_1$ is said to be **more efficient** than $\hat{\theta}_2$ if $\text{Var}(\hat{\theta}_1) < \text{Var}(\hat{\theta}_2)$
(b) The **relative efficiency** of $\hat{\theta}_1$ with respect to $\hat{\theta}_2$ is the **ratio of their variances**; that is,

$$\text{Relative Efficiency} = \frac{\text{Var}(\hat{\theta}_2)}{\text{Var}(\hat{\theta}_1)}$$

EXAMPLE 8.1

SELECTION FROM COMPETING
UNBIASED ESTIMATORS
(RELATIVE EFFICIENCY)

Let $X_1, X_2, \ldots, X_n$ be a random sample from a normally distributed population with mean μ and variance σ^2. Should the sample mean or the sample median be used to estimate the population mean?

SOLUTION

Assuming a population that is normally distributed with a very large population size compared to the sample size, the sample mean, $\overline{X}$, is an unbiased estimator of the population mean with variance:

$$\text{Var}(\overline{X}) = \frac{\sigma^2}{n}$$

As an alternative estimator, the median of the sample observations could be used. It can be shown that this estimator is also unbiased for μ and that when n is large, its variance is:

$$\text{Var(Median)} = \frac{\pi}{2} \times \frac{\sigma^2}{n} = \frac{1.57\sigma^2}{n}$$

The sample mean is more efficient than the median; the relative efficiency of the mean with respect to the median being:

$$\text{Relative Efficiency} = \frac{\text{Var(Median)}}{\text{Var}(\overline{X})} = 1.57$$

The variance of the sample median is 57% higher than that of the sample mean. Here, in order for the sample median to have as small a variance as the sample mean, it would have to be based on 57% more observations. One advantage of the median over the mean is that it gives less weight to extreme observations. A potential disadvantage in using the sample median as a measure of central location is in terms of its relative efficiency.

It should be noted that if the population is not normally distributed, the sample mean may not be the most efficient estimator of the population mean. In particular, if outliers heavily affect the population distribution, the sample mean is less efficient than other estimators (such as the median, or a trimmed mean). Table 8.1 is a summary of some properties for selected point estimators. It is neither an exhaustive list of estimators nor an exhaustive list of properties that an estimator possesses.

TABLE 8.1
Point Estimators of Selected
Population Parameters

POPULATION PARAMETER	POINT ESTIMATOR	PROPERTIES
Mean, μ	$\overline{X}$	Unbiased, most efficient (assuming normality)
Mean, μ	X_m	Unbiased (assuming normality), but not most efficient
Proportion, π	p	Unbiased, most efficient
Variance, σ^2	s^2	Unbiased, most efficient (assuming normality)

EXAMPLE 8.2

PRICE-EARNINGS RATIOS
(ESTIMATORS)

Suppose that you randomly sampled stocks traded on the New York Stock Exchange on a particular day and found the price-earnings ratios of these stocks to be:

$$\begin{array}{ccccccc} 10 & 16 & 13 & 11 & 12 & 14 & 12 \\ 15 & 14 & 14 & 13 & 13 & 13 & \end{array}$$

Find point estimates of the mean and variance. Discuss the properties of these estimators.

FIGURE 8.2
Minitab Output for Price-
Earnings Ratios Example

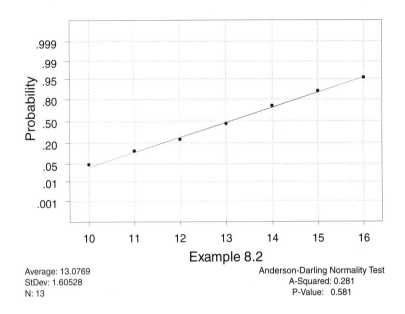

Normal Probability Plot

Example 8.2

Average: 13.0769
StDev: 1.60528
N: 13

Anderson-Darling Normality Test
A-Squared: 0.281
P-Value: 0.581

SOLUTION

From the normal probability plot in Figure 8.2 there appears to be no evidence of nonnormality. Assuming a normal distribution, an estimate of the mean price earnings ratios is the sample mean, 13.1, and an estimate of the variance is $s^2 = 2.58$. Both $\bar{X}$ and s^2 are unbiased and efficient point estimators of μ and σ^2 respectively.

A problem that often arises in practice is how to choose an appropriate point estimator for a population parameter. An attractive possibility is to choose the most efficient of all unbiased estimators. However, sometimes there are estimation problems for which no unbiased estimator is very satisfactory; or there may be situations in which it is not always possible to find a minimum variance unbiased estimator. It is also possible that data may not be normally distributed. In these situations, selecting the best point estimator is not straightforward and involves considerable mathematical intricacy beyond the scope of this book.

EXERCISES

8.1 Prairie Flower Cereal Inc. is a small but growing producer of hot and ready-to-eat breakfast cereals (reference 5). Gordon Thorson, a successful grain farmer started the company in 1910. One machine that packages 18-ounce (510-gram) boxes of sugar-coated wheat cereal is being studied. The weights for a random sample of 100 boxes of cereal packaged by this machine are contained in the data file **Sugar**.
  (a) Find an unbiased point estimate of the population mean package weight.

(b) Is there evidence that the data is not normally distributed?
(c) Use an unbiased estimation procedure to find a point estimate of the variance of the sample mean.

8.2 A random sample of eight homes in a particular suburb had the following selling prices (in thousands of dollars):

| 92 | 83 | 112 | 127 | 109 | 96 | 102 | 90 |

(a) Is there evidence that the data is not normally distributed?

(b) Find a minimum variance unbiased point estimate of the population mean.

(c) Use an unbiased estimation procedure to find a point estimate of the variance of the sample mean.

(d) Use an unbiased estimator to estimate the proportion of homes in this suburb selling for less than $92,500.

8.3 Project Romanian Rescue (PRR) is a registered Romanian foundation ministering to the needs of the tragically disadvantaged children in Constanta, Romania (reference 16). As an interdenominational Christian mission, PRR's services include street outreach, a day center (Casa Charis), a boys' group home, a girls' group home (Casa Chara) and individualized educational assistance for children from poor families. PRR intends to open soon a village center in nearby Kogalniceanu to house additional street children. Suppose that Daniel Mercado, the project founder, and Camelia Vilcoci, the managing director of the project, maintain records such as the number of meals delivered daily to street children, the number of children who attend the day center, the ages of the children, and suppose that a random sample of such records is contained in the data file **PRR**.

(a) Check each variable to determine if the data is normally distributed.

(b) Find unbiased estimates of the population mean and population variance.

8.4 Let X_1 and X_2 be a random sample of observations from a population with mean μ and variance σ^2. Consider the following three point estimators, X, Y, Z, of μ:

$$X = \frac{1}{2}X_1 + \frac{1}{2}X_2 \quad Y = \frac{1}{4}X_1 + \frac{3}{4}X_2 \quad Z = \frac{1}{3}X_1 + \frac{2}{3}X_2$$

(a) Show that all three estimators are unbiased.

(b) Which of the estimators is the most efficient?

(c) Find the relative efficiency of X with respect to each of the other two estimators.

8.5 On a college campus, 480 men and 370 women live in residence halls. Of a random sample of 60 men, 24 were satisfied with campus food. Of a random sample of 60 women, 32 were satisfied with campus food. Using an unbiased estimation procedure, find a point estimate of the proportion of all students living in the residence halls on this campus who are satisfied with campus food.

8.6 Al Fiedler, the plant manager at LDS Vacuum Products, Altamonte Springs, FL, applies statistical thinking in his workplace. As a major supplier to automobile manufacturers, LDS wants to be sure that the leak rate (in cubic centimeters per second) of transmission oil coolers (TOC) meets the established specification limits. A random sample of 50 TOCs are tested, and the leak rates are recorded in the file named **Toc** (reference 7).

(a) Is there evidence that the data is not normally distributed?

(b) Find a minimum variance unbiased point estimate of the population mean.

(c) Use an unbiased estimation procedure to find a point estimate of the variance of the sample mean.

8.7 The demand for bottled water increases during the hurricane season in Florida. The operations manager at a plant that bottles drinking water wants to be sure that the filling process for one-gallon bottles is operating properly. Currently, the company is testing the weights of one-gallon (3.78 L) bottles. Suppose that a random sample of 75 bottles is tested, and the weights are recorded in the data file **Water**.

(a) Is there evidence that the data is not normally distributed?

(b) Find a minimum variance unbiased point estimate of the population mean.

(c) Find a minimum variance unbiased point estimate of the population variance.

8.2 CONFIDENCE INTERVALS FOR THE MEAN OF A NORMAL DISTRIBUTION: POPULATION VARIANCE KNOWN

In the preceding section, the production of a single number (a point estimate) that in some sense is a "good guess" of the unknown population parameter of interest was discussed. For most practical problems, a point estimate alone is not adequate. A more complete understanding of the process that generated the population also requires a measure of variability. For example, the average number of cars produced per day in a factory is an important measure. Wide variation above and below the mean might result in excessive inventory costs or lost sales. An estimator and an estimate that takes into account this variation are needed, giving a range of values in which the quantity to be estimated appears likely to lie. In this section, the general format of such estimators is established.

In sampling from a population, with all other things being equal, a more secure *knowledge* about that population is obtained with a relatively large sample than would be obtained from a smaller sample. However, this factor is not reflected in point estimates. For example, a point estimate of the proportion of defective parts in a shipment would be the same if 1 defective part in a sample of 10 parts is observed or if 100 defective parts in a sample of 1,000 parts are observed. Increased precision in our information about population parameters is reflected in *confidence interval estimates*; specifically, the larger the sample size, the shorter, all other things being equal, will be the interval estimates that reflect our uncertainty about a parameter's true value.

CONFIDENCE INTERVAL ESTIMATOR

A **confidence interval estimator** for a population parameter θ is a rule for determining (based on sample information) a range, or interval that is likely to include the parameter. The corresponding estimate is called a **confidence interval estimate**.

So far, interval estimators have been described as being "likely" or "very likely" to include the true, but unknown, value of the population parameter. To make our discussion more precise, it is necessary to phrase such terms as probability statements. Suppose that a random sample has been taken and that based on the sample information, it is possible to find two random variables, *A* and *B*, with *A* less than *B*. If the specific sample values of the random variables *A* and *B* are *a* and *b*, then the interval extending from *a* to *b* either includes the parameter θ or it doesn't. We really don't know for sure. However, suppose that random samples are repeatedly taken from the population and in this same fashion similar intervals are found. In the long run, a certain percentage of these intervals (say 95% or 98%) will contain the unknown value. According to the frequency concept of probability, an interpretation of such intervals follows: *If the population is repeatedly sampled and intervals calculated in this fashion, then in the long run 95% (or some other percentage) of the intervals would contain the true value of the unknown parameter.* The interval from *A* to *B* is then said to be a 95% confidence interval estimator for θ. The general case follows.

CONFIDENCE INTERVAL AND CONFIDENCE LEVEL

Let θ be an unknown parameter. Suppose that on the basis of sample information, random variables *A* and *B* are found such that $P(A < \theta < B) = 1 - \alpha$, where α is any number between 0 and 1. If the specific sample values of *A* and *B* are *a* and *b*, then the interval from *a* to *b* is called a $100(1 - \alpha)\%$ **confidence interval** of θ. The quantity $(1 - \alpha)$ is called the **confidence level** of the interval.

If the population were repeatedly sampled a very large number of times, the true value of the parameter θ would be contained in $100(1 - \alpha)\%$ of intervals calculated this way. The confidence interval calculated in this manner is written as $a < \theta < b$ with $100(1 - \alpha)\%$ confidence.

Keep in mind that any time sampling occurs, one expects the possibility of a difference between the particular value of even the best point estimator and the parameter's true value. The true value of an unknown parameter might be somewhat greater or somewhat less than the value determined by even the best point estimator. It is not surprising that for many estimation problems, a confidence interval estimate of the unknown parameter takes on the form, point estimate ± some error factor.

Assume that a random sample is taken from a population that is normally distributed with unknown mean and *known* variance, and that the objective is to find a confidence interval for the population mean. This problem is somewhat unrealistic, since rarely will a population variance be precisely known and yet the mean be unknown. It does sometimes happen, however, that similar populations have been sampled so often in the past that the variance of the population of interest can be assumed known to a very close approximation on the basis of past experience. If the sample size n is large enough, the procedures developed for the case where the population variance is known can be used if that variance has to be estimated from the sample. Nevertheless, the chief virtue in beginning with this problem is that it allows a fairly straightforward exposition of the procedures involved in finding confidence intervals.

Let $X_1, X_2, \ldots, X_n$ be a random sample of n observations from a normally distributed population with unknown mean μ and known variance σ^2. Confidence intervals for the population mean are based on the result that the random variable, $Z = \dfrac{\overline{X} - \mu}{\sigma / \sqrt{n}}$ has a standard normal distribution.

Suppose that a 95% confidence interval of the population mean is to be found. From the standard normal distribution table:

$$P(0 < Z < 1.96) = 0.475 \quad \text{and} \quad P(-1.96 < Z < 0) = 0.475$$

Figure 8.3 shows that the probability is 0.95 that a standard normal random variable falls between the numbers -1.96 and 1.96.

Converting this probability statement into a confidence interval for the population mean is as follows:

$$\begin{aligned}
0.95 &= P(-1.96 < Z < 1.96) \\
&= P\left(-1.96 < \frac{\overline{X} - \mu}{\sigma / \sqrt{n}} < 1.96\right) \\
&= P\left(\frac{-1.96\sigma}{\sqrt{n}} < \overline{X} - \mu < \frac{1.96\sigma}{\sqrt{n}}\right) \\
&= P\left(\overline{X} - \frac{1.96\sigma}{\sqrt{n}} < \mu < \overline{X} + \frac{1.96\sigma}{\sqrt{n}}\right)
\end{aligned}$$

Therefore, the probability is 0.95 that the random interval from

$$\left(\overline{X} - 1.96\frac{\sigma}{\sqrt{n}}\right) \text{ to } \left(\overline{X} + 1.96\frac{\sigma}{\sqrt{n}}\right)$$

contains the population mean μ.

FIGURE 8.3
$P(-1.96 < Z < 1.96) = 0.95$,
Where Z Is a Standard
Normal Random Variable

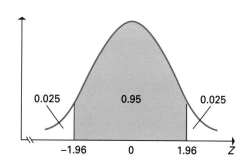

EXAMPLE 8.3

TIME AT THE GROCERY STORE (CONFIDENCE INTERVAL)

Suppose that shopping times for customers at a local grocery store are normally distributed. A random sample of 16 shoppers in the local grocery store had a mean time of 25 minutes. Assume $\sigma = 6$ minutes. Find a 95% confidence interval for the population mean, μ.

SOLUTION

The 95% confidence interval is given by

$$\overline{X} - \frac{1.96\sigma}{\sqrt{n}} < \mu < \overline{X} + \frac{1.96\sigma}{\sqrt{n}}$$

$$25 - \frac{(1.96)(6)}{\sqrt{16}} < \mu < 25 + \frac{(1.96)(6)}{\sqrt{16}}$$

$$25 \pm 2.94$$

$$22.06 < \mu < 27.94$$

How is such a confidence interval interpreted? Based on a sample of 16 observations, a 95% confidence interval for the unknown population mean ranges from approximately 22 minutes to approximately 28 minutes. Now, this particular sample is just one of many that might have been drawn from the population. Starting over again, take a second sample of 16 shoppers. It is virtually certain that the mean of the second sample will differ from that of the first. Accordingly, if a 95% confidence interval is calculated from the results of the second sample, it probably will differ from the interval just found. Imagine taking a very large number of independent random samples of sixteen observations from this population and, from each sample result, calculating a 95% confidence interval. *The confidence level of the interval implies that in the long run 95% of intervals found in this manner contain the true value of the population mean.* It is in this sense that it is reported that there is 95% confidence in our interval estimate. However, it is not known whether our interval is one of the good 95% or bad 5% without knowing μ.

Figure 8.4 shows the sampling distribution of the sample mean of n observations from a population that is normally distributed with mean μ and standard deviation σ. This sampling distribution is normally distributed with mean μ and standard deviation $\sigma/\sqrt{n}$. A confidence interval for the population mean will be based on the observed value of the sample mean—that is, on an observation drawn from our sampling distribution.

Figure 8.5 shows a schematic description of a sequence of 95% confidence intervals, obtained from independent samples taken from the population. The centers of these inter-

FIGURE 8.4
Sampling Distribution of Sample Mean of n Observations from a Normal Distribution with Mean μ, Variance σ^2, and 95% Confidence Level

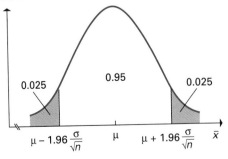

FIGURE 8.5
Schematic Description of 95% Confidence Intervals

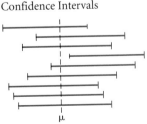

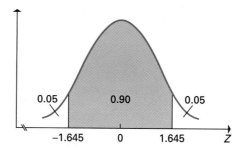

vals, which are just the observed sample means, will often be quite close to the population mean, μ. However, some may differ quite substantially from μ. It follows that 95% of a large number of these intervals will contain the population mean.

The general case of finding confidence intervals with any required confidence level $(1 - \alpha)$ where α is any number such that $0 < \alpha < 1$ follows. A new notation $Z_{\alpha/2}$ indicates the value in the standard normal table that cuts off a right tail area of $\alpha/2$.

NOTATION

Let $Z_{\alpha/2}$ be the number for which

$$P(Z > Z_{\alpha/2}) = \frac{\alpha}{2}$$

where the random variable Z follows a standard normal distribution.

For example, if $\alpha = 0.10$, then $Z_{\alpha/2} = Z_{0.05} = 1.645$ as illustrated in Figure 8.6.

Selected values of $Z_{\alpha/2}$ found from the standard normal distribution table are summarized in Table 8.2.

For any $100(1 - \alpha)\%$ confidence interval for the population mean, it follows that

$P(Z > Z_{\alpha/2}) = \dfrac{\alpha}{2}$ and so, by the symmetry of the standard normal density function about its mean of zero

$$P(Z < -Z_{\alpha/2}) = \frac{\alpha}{2}$$

Thus,

$$P(-Z_{\alpha/2} < Z < Z_{\alpha/2}) = 1 - \frac{\alpha}{2} - \frac{\alpha}{2} = 1 - \alpha$$

TABLE 8.2
Selected Values $Z_{\alpha/2}$ from the Standard Normal Distribution Table

α	0.01	0.02	0.05	0.10
$Z_{\alpha/2}$	2.58	2.33	1.96	1.645
Confidence Level	99%	98%	95%	90%

Using exactly the same line of argument as employed in developing the 95% interval, the derivation of the confidence interval for the mean of a population with known population variance and confidence level $1 - \alpha$ is

$$1 - \alpha = P(-Z_{\alpha/2} < Z < Z_{\alpha/2})$$

$$= P\left(-Z_{\alpha/2} < \frac{\overline{X} - \mu}{\sigma/\sqrt{n}} < Z_{\alpha/2}\right)$$

$$= P\left(\frac{-Z_{\alpha/2}\sigma}{\sqrt{n}} < \overline{X} - \mu < \frac{Z_{\alpha/2}\sigma}{\sqrt{n}}\right)$$

$$= P\left(\overline{X} - \frac{Z_{\alpha/2}\sigma}{\sqrt{n}} < \mu < \overline{X} + \frac{Z_{\alpha/2}\sigma}{\sqrt{n}}\right)$$

CONFIDENCE INTERVALS FOR THE MEAN OF A POPULATION THAT IS NORMALLY DISTRIBUTED: POPULATION VARIANCE KNOWN

Consider a random sample of n observations from a normal distribution with mean μ and known variance σ^2. If the sample mean is $\overline{X}$, then a $100(1 - \alpha)\%$ **confidence interval for the population mean with known variance** is given by

$$\overline{X} - \frac{Z_{\alpha/2}\sigma}{\sqrt{n}} < \mu < \overline{X} + \frac{Z_{\alpha/2}\sigma}{\sqrt{n}} \tag{8.1}$$

or equivalently,

$$\overline{X} \pm B$$

where the **margin of error** (also called **the sampling error, the bound,** or **the interval half width**) is given by

$$B = Z_{\alpha/2}\frac{\sigma}{\sqrt{n}} \tag{8.2}$$

INTERPRETATION

The interpretation of this general confidence interval corresponds to that for the specific 95% interval. If random samples of n observations are drawn repeatedly and independently from the population and $100(1 - \alpha)\%$ confidence intervals are calculated by Equation 8-1, then over a very large number of repeated trials, $100(1 - \alpha)\%$ of these intervals will contain the true value of the population mean.

EXAMPLE 8.4

REFINED SUGAR (CONFIDENCE INTERVAL)

A process produces bags of refined sugar. The weights of the contents of these bags are normally distributed with standard deviation 1.2 ounces. The contents of a random sample of 25 bags had mean weight of 19.8 ounces. Find and interpret a 99% confidence interval for the true mean weight for all bags of sugar produced by the process.

SOLUTION

Since a 99% confidence interval is required, it follows that $\alpha = 0.01$. This means that $Z_{\alpha/2} = Z_{0.005}$ and that the number $Z_{0.005}$, for which $P(Z > Z_{0.005}) = 0.005$ is required. From the standard normal distribution table, it follows that

$$Z_{0.005} = 2.58$$

Using Equation 8-1, the confidence interval for the population mean μ with known variance is

$$\overline{X} - \frac{Z_{\alpha/2}\sigma}{\sqrt{n}} < \mu < \overline{X} + \frac{Z_{\alpha/2}\sigma}{\sqrt{n}}$$

where the sample mean is 19.8 and

$$Z_{\alpha/2} = 2.58 \qquad \sigma = 1.2 \qquad n = 25$$

The required 99% confidence interval is

$$19.8 - \frac{(2.58)(1.2)}{\sqrt{25}} < \mu < 19.8 + \frac{(2.58)(1.2)}{\sqrt{25}}$$

or

$$19.18 < \mu < 20.42$$

Strictly speaking, what do these numbers mean? How is the processor of refined sugar to interpret these numbers? If samples of $n = 25$ observations are drawn repeatedly and independently from the population, then over a very large number of repeated trials, 99% of these intervals will contain the value of the true population mean weight.

PHStat

Let's turn to the use of PHStat.

From the output in Figure 8.7, he same confidence interval is obtained: $19.18 < \mu < 20.42$. Since no interpretation is given with computer output, it is important that you provide the correct interpretation. As stated earlier, if samples of $n = 25$ observations are drawn repeatedly and independently from the population, then over a very large number of repeated trials, 99% of these intervals will contain the value of the true population mean. The term *Interval Half Width* in the PHStat output is simply another phrase for the margin of error.

Minitab could also be used to find this confidence interval. This will be done in a later example. The margin of error for this type of confidence interval can be found by use of the function CONFIDENCE in Excel (see Chapter Appendix).

Table 8.3 is a brief summary of terms that are often used with respect to confidence interval estimation problems. In this chapter confidence intervals for several different population parameters are presented. The basic terms will remain the same.

FIGURE 8.7
PHStat Output for Refined Sugar Example

Mean Weights of Refined Sugar Bags		PHStat Instructions
Population Standard Deviation	**1.2**	1. Click on PHStat
Sample Mean	**19.8**	2. Select Confidence Intervals
Sample Size	**25**	
Confidence Level	**99%**	3. Select Estimate of the mean, sigma known
Standard Error of the Mean	0.24	
Z Value	-2.57583451	
Interval Half Width	0.618200283	4. Complete dialog box
Interval Lower Limit	19.18179972	
Interval Upper Limit	20.41820028	

TABLE 8.3
Basic Terminology for
Confidence Interval for a
Population Mean with
Known Population Variance

TERMS	SYMBOL	TO OBTAIN
Standard Error of the Mean	$\sigma_{\overline{X}}$	$\sigma/\sqrt{n}$
Z Value (also called **reliability factor**)	$Z_{\alpha/2}$	Use standard normal distribution table
Margin of Error (also called the bound, sampling error, or interval half width, in PHStat)	B	$B = Z_{\alpha/2}\dfrac{\sigma}{\sqrt{n}}$
Lower Confidence Limit (called the interval lower limit in PHStat)	LCL	$LCL = \overline{X} - Z_{\alpha/2}\dfrac{\sigma}{\sqrt{n}}$
Upper Confidence Limit (called the interval upper limit in PHStat)	UCL	$UCL = \overline{X} + Z_{\alpha/2}\dfrac{\sigma}{\sqrt{n}}$
Width (width is twice the bound; or twice the margin of error)	w	$w = 2B = 2Z_{\alpha/2}\dfrac{\sigma}{\sqrt{n}}$

Reducing the Margin of Error

Can the margin of error (and consequently the width) of a confidence interval be reduced? Consider the factors that affect the margin of error: the population standard deviation, the sample size n, and the confidence level.

Keeping all other factors constant, the more that the population standard deviation σ can be reduced, the smaller the margin of error will be. Corporations strive to reduce variability in product measurements (Chapter 16). When possible, this should be the first step to decrease width. However, sometimes the population standard deviation cannot be reduced.

Another way to reduce the margin of error is to increase the sample size. This will reduce the standard deviation of the sampling distribution of the sample mean and hence the margin of error. That is, keeping all other factors constant, an increase in the sample size n will decrease the margin of error. The more information obtained from a population, the more precise should be our inference about its mean. By looking at the equation for the margin of error, notice that the interval width is directly proportional to $1/\sqrt{n}$. For example, if the sample size is increased by a factor of 4, the interval width will be reduced by half. If the original sample size were 100, an increase to a sample size of 400 would lead to an interval half the width of the original confidence interval (keeping all other factors constant). The disadvantage to an increased sample size is increased costs.

Finally, keeping all other factors constant, if the confidence level $(1 - \alpha)$ is decreased, the margin of error will be reduced. For example, a 95% confidence interval will be shorter

FIGURE 8.8
Effects of Sample Size,
Population Standard
Deviation, and Confidence
Level on Confidence Intervals

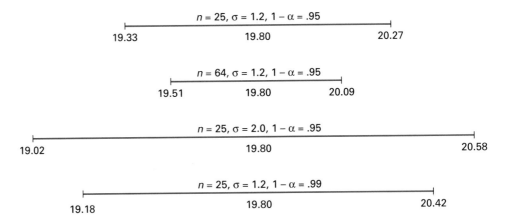

than a 99% confidence interval based on the same information. Caution: the reduction of the confidence level reduces the probability that the interval includes the value of the true population parameter. Figure 8.8 illustrates some of the effects of sample size n, population standard deviation σ, and confidence level $(1 - \alpha)$ on confidence intervals for the mean of a population that has a normal distribution; in each case the sample mean is 19.80.

EXERCISES

8.8 A college admissions officer for an M.B.A. program has determined that historically, applicants have undergraduate grade point averages that are normally distributed with standard deviation 0.45. From a random sample of 25 applications from the current year, the sample mean grade point average is 2.90.
  (a) Find a 95% confidence interval for the population mean. Check your answer using PHStat.
  (b) Based on these sample results, a statistician computes for the population mean a confidence interval extending from 2.81 to 2.99. Find the confidence level associated with this interval.

8.9 A process producing bricks is known to give output whose weights are normally distributed with standard deviation of 0.12 lb. A random sample of 16 bricks from today's output had mean weight of 4.07 lb.
  (a) Find a 99% confidence interval for the mean weight of all bricks produced this day.
  (b) Without doing the calculations, explain whether a 95% confidence interval for the population mean would be wider than, narrower than, or the same width as that found in (a).
  (c) It is decided that tomorrow a sample of 20 bricks will be taken. Without doing the calculations,

explain whether a correctly calculated 99% confidence interval for the mean weight of tomorrow's output would be wider than, narrower than, or the same width as that found in (a).
  (d) Suppose that the population standard deviation for today's output is 0.15 pound (not 0.12 pound). Without doing the calculations, explain whether a correctly calculated 99% confidence interval for the mean weight of today's output would be wider than, narrower than, or the same width as that found in (a).

8.10 A personnel manager has found that, historically, the scores on aptitude tests given to applicants for entry-level positions follow a normal distribution with standard deviation of 32.4 points. A random sample of nine test scores from the current group of applicants had a mean score of 187.9 points.
  (a) Find an 80% confidence interval for the population mean score of the current group of applicants.
  (b) Based on these sample results, a statistician found for the population mean a confidence interval extending from 165.8 to 210.0 points. Find the confidence level of this interval.

8.3 CONFIDENCE INTERVALS FOR THE MEAN OF A NORMAL DISTRIBUTION: POPULATION VARIANCE UNKNOWN

In the preceding section, confidence intervals for the mean of a normal population when the population variance was known were derived. Now we study the case of considerable practical importance where the value of the population variance is unknown. For example,

1. Corporate executives employed by retail distributors may want to estimate mean daily sales for their retail stores.
2. Manufacturers may want to estimate the average productivity, in units per hour, for workers using a particular manufacturing process.
3. Automobile/ truck manufacturers may want to estimate the average fuel consumption, measured in miles per gallon, for a particular vehicle model.

In these types of situations, there probably is no historical information concerning either the population mean or the population variance. To proceed further, it is necessary to introduce a new class of probability distributions that were developed by William Sealy

Gosset, an Irish statistician, who was employed by the Guinness Brewery in Dublin in the early 1900s (reference 14).

Student's *t* Distribution

Gosset sought to develop a probability distribution, when the population variance σ^2 is not known, for a normally distributed random variable. At this time, laboratory tests and the scientific method were beginning to be applied to the brewing industry. Gosset, whose works appeared under the pseudonym "Student," was influential in the development of modern statistical thinking and process variation. "The circumstances of brewing work, with its variable materials and susceptibility to temperature change … emphasize the necessity for a correct method of treating small samples. It was thus no accident, but the circumstances of his work, that directed Student's attention to this problem, and led to his discovery of the distribution of the sample standard deviation.…" (reference 15). Gosset showed the connection between statistical research and practical problems. Today, the distribution is still known as the "Student's *t* distribution." The *t*-distribution developed by Gosset is the ratio of two distributions (see Chapter Appendix).

The development of Section 8.2 was based on the fact that the random variable Z, given by

$$Z = \frac{\overline{X} - \mu}{\sigma/\sqrt{n}}$$

has a standard normal distribution. In the case where the population standard deviation is unknown, this result cannot be used directly. It is natural in such circumstances to consider the random variable obtained by replacing the unknown σ by the sample standard deviation s, giving

$$t = \frac{\overline{X} - \mu}{s/\sqrt{n}}$$

This random variable does not follow a standard normal distribution. However, its distribution is known and is in fact a member of a family of distributions called **Student's *t*.**

STUDENT'S *t* DISTRIBUTION

Given a random sample of n observations, with mean $\overline{X}$ and standard deviation s, from a normally distributed population with mean μ, the random variable t follows the **Student's *t* distribution** with $(n - 1)$ degrees of freedom and is given by

$$t = \frac{\overline{X} - \mu}{s/\sqrt{n}}$$

A specific member of the family of Student's *t* distributions is characterized by the number of degrees of freedom. The parameter v is used to represent the degrees of freedom and a Student's *t* random variable with v degrees of freedom will be denoted t_v. The shape of the Student's *t* distribution is rather similar to that of the standard normal distribution. Both distributions have mean 0, and the probability density functions of both are symmetric about their means. However, the density function of the Student's *t* distribution has a larger dispersion (reflected in a larger variance) than the standard normal distribution. This can be seen in Figure 8.9, which shows density functions for the standard normal distribution and the Student's *t* distribution with 3 degrees of freedom.

FIGURE 8.9
Probability Density Functions of the Standard Normal and the Student's t Distribution with 3 Degrees of Freedom

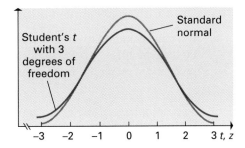

The additional dispersion in the Student's t distribution arises as a result of the extra uncertainty caused by replacing the known population standard deviation by its sample estimator. As the number of degrees of freedom increases, the Student's t distribution becomes increasingly similar to the standard normal distribution. For large degrees of freedom, the two distributions are virtually identical. This is intuitively reasonable and follows from the fact that for a large sample, the sample standard deviation is a very precise estimator of the population standard deviation.

In order to base inferences about a population mean on the Student's t distribution, critical values analogous to $Z_{\alpha/2}$ are needed. To describe these probabilities, some further notation is required, as presented in the box that follows and illustrated in Figure 8.10.

NOTATION

A random variable having the Student's t distribution with v degrees of freedom will be denoted t_v. Then $t_{v,\alpha/2}$ is defined as the number for which

$$P(t_v > t_{v,\alpha/2}) = \alpha/2$$

In the typical application, the value $t_{v,\alpha/2}$ that corresponds to v degrees of freedom and a specified confidence level α needs to be found. These quantities can be read directly from the Student's t table. To illustrate, suppose that the number that is exceeded with probability 0.10 by a Student's t random variable with 15 degrees of freedom is required. That is,

$$P(t_{15} > t_{15,0.10}) = 0.10$$

Reading directly from the table,

$$t_{15,0.10} = 1.341$$

Many computer programs can be used to obtain these values as well.

FIGURE 8.10
$P(t_v > t_{v,\alpha/2}) = \alpha/2$, Where t_v is a Student's t Random Variable with v Degrees of Freedom

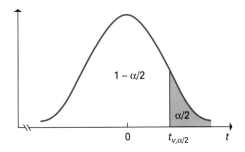

Population Variance Unknown

It is more common to encounter situations in which the population variance is not known. Finding the $100(1 - \alpha)\%$ confidence interval for this type of problem follows precisely the same line of reasoning as in Section 8.2.

CONFIDENCE INTERVALS FOR THE MEAN OF A NORMAL POPULATION: POPULATION VARIANCE UNKNOWN

Suppose there is a random sample of n observations from a *normal distribution* with mean μ and unknown variance. If the sample mean and standard deviation are, respectively, $\overline{X}$ and s, then a **100(1 − α)% confidence interval for the population mean, variance unknown,** is given by

$$\overline{X} - t_{n-1,\alpha/2} \frac{s}{\sqrt{n}} < \mu < \overline{X} + t_{n-1,\alpha/2} \frac{s}{\sqrt{n}} \qquad (8.3)$$

or equivalently,

$$\overline{X} \pm B$$

where the **margin of error**, the sampling error, or the bound, B, is given by

$$B = t_{n-1,\alpha/2} \frac{s}{\sqrt{n}} \qquad (8.4)$$

and $t_{n-1,\alpha/2}$ is the number for which

$$P(t_{n-1} > t_{n-1,\alpha/2}) = \frac{\alpha}{2}$$

The random variable t_{n-1} has a Student's t distribution with $v = (n - 1)$ degrees of freedom.

ASSUMPTION

The Student's t distribution assumes that a random sample of n observations is normally distributed. The normal probability plot obtained with Minitab is one method to test if the data is not normally distributed. Chapter 14 introduces another way to test whether the sample data could have come from a normally distributed population. Although normality is assumed throughout this chapter, you should always check this assumption first.

EXAMPLE 8.5

TRUCKS: GASOLINE CONSUMPTION (CONFIDENCE INTERVAL)

Trucks

Gasoline prices rose drastically during the early years of this century. Suppose that a recent study was conducted using truck drivers with equivalent years of experience to test run 24 trucks of a particular model over the same highway. Estimate the population mean fuel consumption for this model of trucks with 90% confidence if the fuel consumption, in miles per gallon, for these 24 trucks were:

15.5	21.0	18.5	19.3	19.7	16.9	20.2	14.5
16.5	19.2	18.7	18.2	18.0	17.5	18.5	20.5
18.6	19.1	19.8	18.0	19.8	18.2	20.3	21.8

SOLUTION

The normal probability plot in Figure 8.11 does not provide evidence of nonnormality (see Chapter 6).

FIGURE 8.11
Normal Probability Plot

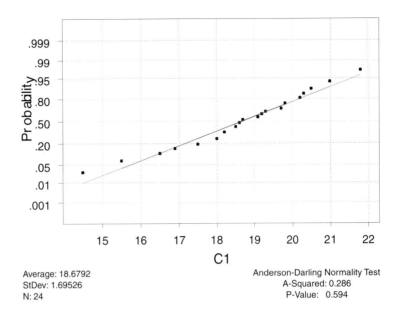

Normal Probability Plot

Average: 18.6792
StDev: 1.69526
N: 24

Anderson-Darling Normality Test
A-Squared: 0.286
P-Value: 0.594

The 90% confidence interval using Equation 8.3 is:

$$\overline{X} \pm t_{n-1,\alpha/2}\ \frac{s}{\sqrt{n}} = 18.68 \pm t_{23,0.05}\ \frac{1.69526}{\sqrt{24}} = 18.68 \pm (1.714) \times (0.3460)$$

$$= 18.68 \pm 0.5930$$
$$18.1 < \mu < 19.3$$

Figure 8.12 illustrates the Minitab output for this example.

FIGURE 8.12
Minitab Output for Trucks
Example

Descriptive Statistics

Minitab Instructions

1. Open file: Trucks
2. Click on Stat
3. Select Basic Statistics
4. Select Display
   Descriptive Statistics. . .
5. Click on Graphs. . .
6. Select Histogram of
   data with normal curve
7. Select Graphical
   Summary
8. Enter confidence level
   desired

90% Confidence Interval for Mu

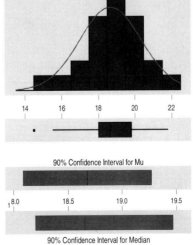

90% Confidence Interval for Median

Variable: Example 8.5

Anderson-Darling Normality Test

A-Squared: 0.286
P-Value: 0.594

Mean   18.6792
StDev   1.6953
Variance   2.87389
Skewness   -6.1E-01
Kurtosis   0.624798
N   24

Minimum   14.5000
1st Quartile 18.0000
Median   18.6500
3rd Quartile 19.8000
Maximum   21.8000

90% Confidence Interval for Mu

18.0861   19.2722

90% Confidence Interval for Sigma

1.3709   2.2471

90% Confidence Interval for Median

18.2000   19.4667

INTERPRETATION

The interpretation of the confidence interval is important. If independent, random samples of 24 trucks are repeatedly selected from the population and confidence intervals for each of these samples are determined, then over a very large number of repeated trails, 90% of these intervals will contain the value of the true mean fuel consumption for this model truck. In practice, however, one does not repeatedly draw such independent samples. (See the appendix to this chapter for an alternate way to find confidence intervals using Minitab.)

A word of caution is in order concerning the use of function CONFIDENCE in Excel. It was mentioned in Section 8.2 that this function could be used to find the margin of error to estimate the population mean when the variance is known (see Appendix to this chapter). However, you cannot find the margin of error by use of the function CONFIDENCE in Excel when the variance is unknown. Either PHStat or Minitab are available for this type of confidence interval.

EXERCISES

8.11 🖙 Al Fiedler, Plant Manager at LDS Vacuum Products, Altamonte Springs, FL, applies statistical thinking in his workplace. As a major supplier to automobile manufacturers, LDS wants to be sure that the leak rate (in cubic centimeters per second) of transmission oil coolers (TOC) meets the established specification limits. A random sample of 50 TOCs are tested and the leak rates are recorded in the data file named **Toc** (reference 7).
   (a) Estimate with 95% confidence the mean leak rate for this particular product.
   (b) Estimate with 98% confidence the mean leak rate for this particular product.

8.12 🖙 A machine that packages 18-ounce (510-gram) boxes of sugar-coated wheat cereal is being studied. The weights for a random sample of 100 boxes of cereal packaged by this machine are contained in the data file **Sugar**.
   (a) Find a 90% confidence interval for the population mean cereal weight.
   (b) Without doing the calculations, state whether an 80% confidence interval for the population mean would be wider than, narrower than, or the same as the answer to (a).

8.13 A marketing research assistant for a veterinary hospital surveyed a random sample of 457 pet owners. One question that respondents were asked was to indicate the number of times that they visit their veterinarian each year. The sample mean response was 3.59 and the sample standard deviation was 1.045. Based on these results, a confidence interval from 3.49 to 3.69 was calculated for the population mean. Find the probability content for this interval.

8.14 A random sample of 174 college students were asked to indicate the number of hours per week that they surf

the net for either personal information or material for a class assignment. The sample mean response was 6.06 hours and the sample standard deviation was 1.43 hours. Based on these results, a confidence interval extending from 5.96 to 6.16 was calculated for the population mean. Find the confidence level of this interval.

8.15 A clothing store is interested in how much college students spend on clothing during the first month of the school year. For a random sample of nine students, the mean expenditure was $157.82, and the sample standard deviation was $38.89. Assuming that the population is normally distributed, find the margin of error of a 95% confidence interval for the population mean.

8.16 There is concern about the speed of automobiles traveling over a particular stretch of highway. For a random sample of seven automobiles, radar indicated the following speeds, in miles per hour:

79	73	68	77	86	71	69

Assuming a normal population distribution, find the margin of error of a 95% confidence interval for the mean speed of all automobiles traveling over this stretch of highway.

8.17 A clinic offers a weight-reduction program. A review of its records found the following weight losses, in pounds, for a random sample of 10 of its clients at the conclusion of the program:

18.2	25.9	6.3	11.8	15.4	20.3	16.8	19.5	12.3	17.2

   (a) Find a 99% confidence interval for the population mean.
   (b) Without doing the calculations, explain whether a 90% confidence interval for the population mean would be wider than, narrower than, or the same as that found in (a).

8.18 A business school placement officer wants to estimate the mean annual salaries of the school's former students 5 years after graduation. A random sample of 25 such graduates found a sample mean of $42,740 and a sample standard deviation of $4,780. Assuming that the population distribution is normal, find a 90% confidence interval for the population mean.

8.19 A car rental company is interested in the amount of time its vehicles are out of operation for repair work.

Stating any assumptions you need to make, find a 90% confidence interval for the mean number of days in a year that all vehicles in the company's fleet are out of operation, if a random sample of nine cars showed the following number of days that each had been inoperative:

16	10	21	22	8	17	19	14	19

8.4 CONFIDENCE INTERVALS FOR POPULATION PROPORTION (LARGE SAMPLES)

Suppose that the proportion of population members possessing some specific attribute is of interest. For example, suppose that an estimate of the proportion of all adult Americans in favor of handgun control legislation is desired. If a random sample is taken from the population, the sample proportion provides a natural point estimator of the population proportion. In this section, confidence intervals for the population proportion are established.

Using the binomial set up, let p denote the proportion of "successes" in n independent trials, each with probability of success π. It was seen earlier in this book that if the number n of sample members is large, then the random variable

$$Z = \frac{p - \pi}{\sqrt{\pi(1 - \pi)/n}}$$

has, to a close approximation, a standard normal distribution. If the sample size is large enough that $(n)(\pi)(1 - \pi) > 9$, then a good approximation is obtained if π replaces the point estimator p in the denominator; that is

$$\sqrt{\frac{\pi(1 - \pi)}{n}} \approx \sqrt{\frac{p(1 - p)}{n}}$$

Hence, for large sample sizes, the distribution of the random variable

$$Z = \frac{p - \pi}{\sqrt{p(1 - p)/n}}$$

is approximately standard normal. This result can now be used to obtain confidence intervals for the population proportion. The derivation is similar to the preceding examples.

$$1 - \alpha = P(-Z_{\alpha/2} < Z < Z_{\alpha/2})$$

$$= P\left(-Z_{\alpha/2} < \frac{p - \pi}{\sqrt{\dfrac{p(1 - p)}{n}}} < Z_{\alpha/2}\right)$$

$$= P\left(-Z_{\alpha/2}\sqrt{\frac{p(1 - p)}{n}} < p - \pi < Z_{\alpha/2}\sqrt{\frac{p(1 - p)}{n}}\right)$$

$$= P\left(p - Z_{\alpha/2}\sqrt{\frac{p(1 - p)}{n}} < \pi < p + Z_{\alpha/2}\sqrt{\frac{p(1 - p)}{n}}\right)$$

Therefore, if the observed sample proportion is p, an approximate $100(1 - \alpha)\%$ confidence interval for the population proportion is given, as seen in the box that follows:

CONFIDENCE INTERVALS FOR POPULATION PROPORTION (LARGE SAMPLES)

Let p denote the observed proportion of "successes" in a random sample of n observations from a population with a proportion π of successes. Then, if n is large enough that $(n)(\pi)(1 - \pi) > 9$, then a $100(1 - \alpha)\%$ **confidence interval for the population proportion** is given by

$$p - Z_{\alpha/2} \sqrt{\frac{p(1 - p)}{n}} < \pi < p + Z_{\alpha/2} \sqrt{\frac{p(1 - p)}{n}} \qquad (8.5)$$

or equivalently,

$$p \pm B$$

where the **margin of error**, the sampling error or the bound, B, is given by

$$B = Z_{\alpha/2} \sqrt{\frac{p(1 - p)}{n}} \qquad (8.6)$$

and $Z_{\alpha/2}$, is the number for which a standard normal variable Z satisfies

$$P(Z > Z_{\alpha/2}) = \frac{\alpha}{2}$$

Recent research suggests the possibility of other intervals as alternatives to the confidence interval stated in Equation 8.5. Such adjusted intervals avoid sample size guidelines and are useful with both large and small samples (references 1 and 2). These readings are recommended for more advanced studies.

Confidence intervals for the population proportion are centered on the sample proportion. Also, it can be seen that all other things being equal, the larger the sample size, n, the narrower the confidence interval. This reflects the increasing precision of the information about the population proportion obtained as the sample size becomes larger.

EXAMPLE 8.6

UNITED STATES 2000 PRESIDENTIAL ELECTION: FLORIDA PROCESS(CONFIDENCE INTERVAL)

There is no doubt that after the 2000 presidential election in the United States, American voters at least agree that the election process needs improvement. Suppose that a random sample of 344 registered voters in a Florida county was asked: "Do you think that Florida should have a uniform system of county ballots?" Currently, 65 of the 67 counties in Florida use one of the following primary methods: 1) Optical Precinct (ballot is tabulated by machine at the precinct level and again at the central elections office); 2) Optical Central (ballot is tabulated by machine only at the central elections office); and 3) Punch Cards (reference 10). Each of the other 2 counties uses some other method. In the sample of registered voters from the county sampled, suppose that 261 voters think that the state should have a uniform voting process. Find a 90% confidence interval for the population proportion of all voters who agree with a change to a uniform process.

SOLUTION

If π denotes the true population proportion and p the sample proportion, then confidence intervals for the population proportion are obtained from

$$p - Z_{\alpha/2} \sqrt{\frac{p(1 - p)}{n}} < \pi < p + Z_{\alpha/2} \sqrt{\frac{p(1 - p)}{n}}$$

where, for a 90% confidence interval, $\alpha = 0.10$, so that

$$\alpha/2 = 0.05 \qquad \text{and} \qquad Z_{\alpha/2} = Z_{0.05} = 1.645$$

from the standard normal distribution. It follows that

$$n = 344 \qquad p = 261/344 = 0.759$$

and

$$Z_{\alpha/2} = 1.645$$

Therefore, a 90% confidence interval for the population proportion is

$$0.759 - 1.645\sqrt{\frac{(0.759)(0.241)}{344}} < \pi < 0.759 + 1.645\sqrt{\frac{(0.759)(0.241)}{344}}$$

or $0.721 < \pi < 0.797$. Strictly speaking, what do these numbers mean? You could say that, in the long run, approximately 76% (with a 4% margin of error at the 90% confidence level) of the population of all registered voters in this county favor a uniform counting process.

Minitab

Follow the Minitab Instructions and then complete the 1 Proportion–options dialog box as illustrated in Figure 8.13. The Minitab output appears in Figure 8.14.

INTERPRETATION

Remember that Minitab uses the letter "p" and we use the letter "π." Although confidence intervals are easily found with various software packages, the interpretation of the output is not provided. The user is responsible for a correct understanding of the data. In the long run, approximately 76% of the population of all registered voters in this county favor a uniform counting process. The margin of error is about 4%.

FIGURE 8.13
Options Dialog Box

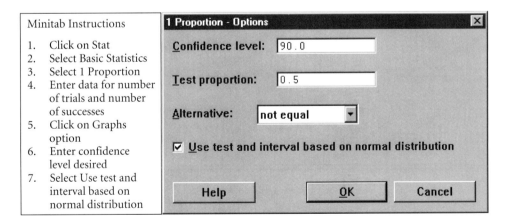

FIGURE 8.14
Minitab Output for the 2000
Presidential Election Example

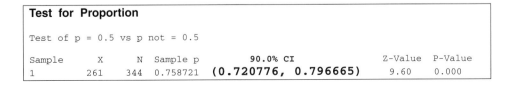

FIGURE 8.15
PHStat Output for the 2000
Presidential Election Example
(90%)

Sample Size	344
Number of Successes	261
Confidence Level	90%
Sample Proportion	0.75872093
Z Value	-1.644853
Standard Error of the Proportion	0.023068621
Interval Half Width	0.037944491
Interval Lower Limit	0.72077644
Interval Upper Limit	0.796665421

PHStat

Follow the command sequence **PHStat > Confidence Intervals > Estimate for the Proportion ...** and complete the dialog box with sample size, number of successes and the confidence level desired. The output is given in Figure 8.15.

A nice feature in PHStat is that the user can quickly obtain results for different confidence levels by simply entering the new confidence level in the output box given in Figure 8.15. By increasing the confidence level to 99%, you quickly notice the wider confidence interval given in Figure 8.16.

Compare the 90% and the 99% confidence intervals. By increasing the confidence level from 90% to 99%, the margin of error (and the width) also increased. For the 90% confidence interval, the range was from approximately 72.1% to 79.7% giving a 3.8% margin of error; whereas, for the 99% confidence interval, the range was from approximately 69.9% to 81.8% giving a 5.95% margin of error.

FIGURE 8.16
PHStat Output for the 2000
Presidential Election Example
(99%)

Sample Size	344
Number of Successes	261
Confidence Level	99%
Sample Proportion	0.75872093
Z Value	-2.57583451
Standard Error of the Proportion	0.023068621
Interval Half Width	0.05942095
Interval Lower Limit	0.69929998
Interval Upper Limit	0.818141881

EXAMPLE 8.7

GRADUATE ADMISSIONS (CONFIDENCE INTERVAL)

Suppose that a random sample of 142 graduate admissions personnel was asked what role standardized test scores (such as GMAT or GRE) play in the consideration of a candidate for graduate school. Of these sample members, 87 answered "very important." Find a 95% confidence interval for the population proportion of graduate admissions personnel with this view.

SOLUTION

For a 95% confidence interval, $\alpha = .05$, so $Z_{\alpha/2} = Z_{0.025} = 1.96$ from the standard normal distribution table. Also note that

$$n = 142 \qquad p = 87/142 = 0.613 \qquad Z_{\alpha/2} = 1.96$$

Substituting these values into the general formula gives the 95% confidence interval

$$0.613 - 1.96\sqrt{\frac{(0.613)(0.387)}{142}} < \pi < 0.613 + 1.96\sqrt{\frac{(0.613)(0.387)}{142}}$$

or

$$0.533 < \pi < 0.693$$

Therefore, a 95% confidence interval for the percentage of graduate admissions personnel viewing scores on standardized tests as very important runs from 53.3% to 69.3%.

Wide intervals for a given α reflect imprecision in our knowledge about the population proportion. Narrower confidence intervals can be obtained by taking larger samples. Later in this chapter, the sample size to achieve a confidence interval of specific width is considered.

EXERCISES

8.20 In a recent study of a university library, students were asked if they thought that the school's library had an adequate collection of books. The survey results are stored in a data file called **Library**.
   (a) Find an unbiased point estimate of the proportion of students who think that the collection is adequate (coded as 1-yes, 2-no).
   (b) Find a 90% confidence interval for the proportion of students who think that the school's library collection is adequate.

8.21 Consider the 2000 United States Presidential Election. Suppose that in one state a random sample of 189 absentee ballots was examined and 57 ballots were not accepted in the final count. These unaccepted ballots lacked a proper signature, were postmarked after the deadline date, had no postmark date, or had some other error. Estimate with 95% confidence the proportion of all unacceptable absentee ballots in that state.

8.22 Suppose that in a random sample of 600 registered voters in one Florida county, 87.9% strongly agreed with the statement: "The State of Florida should have only one method of reading and counting ballots." Based on this information, a statistician calculated, for the percentage of all registered voters with this view, a confidence interval extending from 85.8% to 90.0%. Find the confidence level associated with this interval.

8.23 The University of Michigan School of Business publishes the American Customer Satisfaction Index (ACSI) four times a year (reference 3). Started in 1994 and based on thousands of customer interviews, customer satisfaction ratings based on a scale from 0 to 100 are gathered for retailers, supermarkets, financial services, parcel-delivery express mail, airlines, and so forth. "Understaffed stores, clueless sales clerks, automated phone lines that lead you in circles" are a few reasons why the scores for most companies declined between 1995 and 2000 (*Orlando Sentinel*, November 24, 2000; reference 17). Suppose that, concerned about this report, Moises Cohen, the manager of a national retail

store in one community, surveyed a random sample of 320 customers and found that 80 customers thought that customer service in his store was also on the decline. What conclusions can you draw from this data? State your level of confidence in your response.

8.24 In a random sample of 95 manufacturing firms, 67 indicated that their company attained ISO certification within the last two years. Find a 99% confidence interval for the population proportion of companies that have been certified within the last two years.

8.25 "Hoping to protect wildlife and the natural sights and sounds of Yellowstone and Grand Teton, the National Park Service has decided to phase out the use of snowmobiles in both parks" (*Orlando Sentinel*, November 24, 2000; reference 13). Business owners in Montana and Wyoming are concerned about the economic impact of this phase-out that is to be completed by winter 2003. Assume that in a random sample of 320 visitors to these parks that 240 agree with this plan to phase out the snowmobiles. Estimate the population proportion of visitors who support this phase out.

8.26 Of a random sample of 198 marketing students, 98 rated a case of resume inflation as unethical. Based on this information (reference 6), a statistician computed for the population proportion a confidence interval extending from 0.445 to 0.545. What is the confidence level of this interval?

8.27 In a presidential election year, candidates want to know the percentage of voters in various parts of the country who will vote for them. Suppose that 420 registered voters in the northeast are asked if they would vote for a particular candidate if the election were held today, and 223 indicated that they would vote for this particular candidate. Estimate, with 95% confidence, this candidate's support in the northeast. What is the margin of error?

8.28 It was reported by the U.S. Center for Disease Control and Prevention (CDC) that "influenza activity in the United States has been low and is lower than the same period last year," (reference 4, Minneapolis *Star Tribune*, December 14, 2000). Suppose that a random sample of 246 residents in the Twin Cities (Minneapolis/St. Paul) were asked if this news by the CDC would persuade them to not take the flu vaccine. If only 40 people stated that they now would not take the flu vaccine, estimate with 98% confidence the proportion of all residents in the twin cities who now consider the flu vaccine unnecessary.

8.29 It is important for airlines to follow the published scheduled departure times of flights. Suppose that one

airline that recently sampled the records of 246 flights originating in Orlando found that 10 flights were delayed for severe weather; 4 flights were delayed for maintenance concerns, and all the other flights were on time.

(a) Estimate the percentage of on-time departures using a 98% confidence level.

(b) Estimate the percentage of flights delayed for severe weather using a 98% confidence level.

8.5 CONFIDENCE INTERVALS FOR THE VARIANCE OF A NORMAL DISTRIBUTION

On occasion, interval estimates are required for the variance of a population. As might be expected, such estimates are based on the sample variance.

Suppose a random sample of n observations from a normally distributed population with variance σ^2 and sample variance s^2 is taken. The random variable

$$\chi^2_{n-1} = \frac{(n-1)s^2}{\sigma^2}$$

follows a chi-square distribution with $(n-1)$ degrees of freedom. This result forms the basis for the derivation of confidence intervals for the population variance when sampling from a normal distribution.

In order to develop the formula for calculating confidence intervals for the variance, an additional notation is needed, as described in the box and illustrated in Figure 8.17.

NOTATION

A random variable having the chi-square distribution with $v = n - 1$ degrees of freedom will be denoted by χ^2_v or simply χ^2_{n-1}. Define as $\chi^2_{n-1,\alpha}$ the number for which

$$P(\chi^2_{n-1} > \chi^2_{n-1,\alpha}) = \alpha$$

For a specified probability α, a chi-square number for $n - 1$ degrees of freedom is needed; that is, $\chi^2_{n-1,\alpha}$. This can be achieved from values of the cumulative distribution

FIGURE 8.17
Chi-Square Distribution

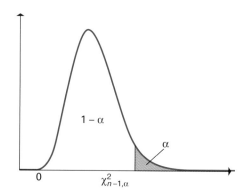

function of a chi-square random variable. For instance, suppose the number that is exceeded with probability 0.05 by a chi-square random variable with 6 degrees of freedom is needed; that is

$$P(\chi_6^2 > \chi_{6,0.05}^2) = 0.05$$

From the Chi-Square Distribution Table, $\chi_{6,0.05}^2 = 12.59$. Similarly,

$$P(\chi_{n-1}^2 > \chi_{n-1,\alpha/2}^2) = \frac{\alpha}{2}$$

It follows that $\chi_{n-1,1-\alpha/2}^2$ is given by,

$$P(\chi_{n-1}^2 > \chi_{n-1,1-\alpha/2}^2) = 1 - \frac{\alpha}{2}$$

and hence,

$$P(\chi_{n-1}^2 < \chi_{n-1,1-\alpha/2}^2) = \frac{\alpha}{2}$$

Finally,

$$P(\chi_{n-1,1-\alpha/2}^2 < \chi_{n-1}^2 < \chi_{n-1,\alpha/2}^2) = 1 - \frac{\alpha}{2} - \frac{\alpha}{2} = 1 - \alpha$$

This probability is illustrated in Figure 8.18.

Suppose a pair of numbers is needed such that the probability that a chi-square random variable with 6 degrees of freedom lying between these numbers is 0.90. Then $\alpha = 0.10$ and

$$P(\chi_{6,0.95}^2 < \chi_6^2 < \chi_{6,0.05}^2) = 0.90$$

Previously, it was found that $\chi_{6,0.05}^2 = 12.59$. From the Chi-Square Distribution Table, you find that $\chi_{6,0.95}^2 = 1.64$. The probability is 0.90 that this chi-square random variable falls between 1.64 and 12.59.

To find confidence intervals for the population variance,

$$1 - \alpha = P(\chi_{n-1,1-\alpha/2}^2 < \chi_{n-1}^2 < \chi_{n-1,\alpha/2}^2)$$

$$= P\left(\chi_{n-1,1-\alpha/2}^2 < \frac{(n-1)s^2}{\sigma^2} < \chi_{n-1,\alpha/2}^2 \right)$$

$$= P\left(\frac{(n-1)s^2}{\chi_{n-1,\alpha/2}^2} < \sigma^2 < \frac{(n-1)s^2}{\chi_{n-1,1-\alpha/2}^2} \right)$$

FIGURE 8.18
Chi-Square Distribution for $n - 1$ and $(1 - \alpha)\%$ Confidence Level

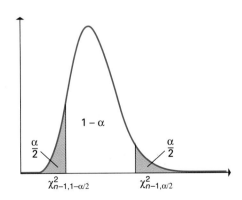

CONFIDENCE INTERVALS FOR THE VARIANCE OF A NORMAL POPULATION

Suppose that there is a random sample of n observations from a normally distributed population with variance σ^2. If the observed sample variance is s^2, then a $100(1 - \alpha)\%$ **confidence interval for the population variance** is given by

$$\frac{(n-1)s^2}{\chi^2_{n-1,\alpha/2}} < \sigma^2 < \frac{(n-1)s^2}{\chi^2_{n-1,1-\alpha/2}} \qquad (8.7)$$

where $\chi^2_{n-1,\alpha/2}$ is the number for which

$$P(\chi^2_{n-1} > \chi^2_{n-1,\alpha/2}) = \frac{\alpha}{2}$$

and $\chi^2_{n-1,1-\alpha/2}$ is the number for which

$$P(\chi^2_{n-1} < \chi^2_{n-1,1-\alpha/2}) = \frac{\alpha}{2}$$

and the random variable χ^2_{n-1} follows a chi-square distribution with $(n - 1)$ degrees of freedom.

ASSUMPTION

Although it is assumed throughout this section that the population is normally distributed, you should always check for any evidence that this assumption fails. Notice that the confidence interval in Equation 8.7 is not of the usual form, sample estimator ± bound.

EXAMPLE 8.8

COMPARING TEMPERATURE VARIANCES (CONFIDENCE INTERVAL)

The manager of Northern Steel, Inc. wants to assess the temperature variation in the firm's new electric furnace. A random sample of 25 temperatures over a one-week period is obtained and the sample variance is found to be $s^2 = 100$. Find a 95% confidence interval for the population variance temperature.

SOLUTION

Here, $n = 25$ and $s^2 = 100$, and for a 95% confidence interval, $\alpha = 0.05$. It follows from the Chi-Square Table that (see Figure 8.19)

$$\chi^2_{n-1,1-\alpha/2} = \chi^2_{24,0.975} = 12.401 \qquad \text{and} \qquad \chi^2_{n-1,\alpha/2} = \chi^2_{24,0.025} = 39.364$$

FIGURE 8.19
Chi-Square Distribution for $n = 25$ and 95% Confidence Level

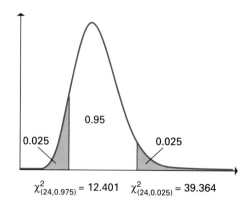

$\chi^2_{(24,0.975)} = 12.401$ $\chi^2_{(24,0.025)} = 39.364$

The 95% confidence interval for the population variance is given by

$$\frac{(n-1)s^2}{\chi^2_{n-1,\alpha/2}} < \sigma^2 < \frac{(n-1)s^2}{\chi^2_{n-1,1-\alpha/2}}$$

Substitution yields

$$\frac{(24)(100)}{39.364} < \sigma^2 < \frac{(24)(100)}{12.401}$$
$$60.97 < \sigma^2 < 193.53$$

It is dangerous to follow the procedure just demonstrated when the population distribution is not normal. The validity of the interval estimator for the variance depends far more critically on the assumption of normality than does that of the interval estimator for the population mean.

EXERCISES

8.30 LDS wants to be sure that the leak rate (in cubic centimeters per second) of transmission oil coolers (TOC) meets the established specification limits. A random sample 50 TOCs are tested and the leak rates are recorded in the data file **Toc** (reference 7). Estimate the variance in leak rate with a 95% confidence level (check normality).

8.31 A clinic offers a weight-reduction program. A review of its records found the following weight losses, in pounds, for a random sample of 10 clients at the conclusion of the program:

18.2   25.9   6.3   11.8   15.4   20.3   16.8   19.5   12.3   17.2

Find a 90% confidence interval for the population variance of weight losses for clients of this weight reduction program.

8.32 The Quality Control Manager of a chemical company randomly sampled twenty 100-pound bags of fertilizer to estimate the variance in the pounds of impurities. The sample variance was found to be 6.62. Find a 95% confidence interval for the population variance in the pounds of impurities.

8.33 A psychologist wants to estimate the variance of employee test scores. A random sample of 18 scores had sample standard deviation 10.4. Find a 90% confidence interval for the population variance. What assumption, if any, have you made in calculating this interval estimate?

8.34 A manufacturer is concerned about the variability of the levels of impurity contained in consignments of raw material from a supplier. A random sample of 15 consignments showed a standard deviation of 2.36 in the concentration of impurity levels. Assume normality.

(a) Find a 95% confidence interval for the population variance.

(b) Would a 99% confidence interval for this variance be wider or narrower than that found in (a)?

8.35 A manufacturer bonds a plastic coating to a metal surface. A random sample of nine observations on the thickness of this coating is taken from a week's output and the thickness (in millimeters) of each observation is as follows:

19.8   21.2   18.6   20.4   21.6   19.8   19.9   20.3   20.8

Assuming normality, find a 90% confidence interval for the population variance.

8.6 CONFIDENCE INTERVALS FOR THE DIFFERENCE BETWEEN MEANS OF TWO NORMAL POPULATIONS

An important problem in statistical inference deals with the comparison of two means from normally distributed populations. A company might receive shipments of a chemical from two suppliers and be concerned about the difference between the mean levels of impurity present in the chemicals from the two sources of supply. A farmer may consider the use of two alternative fertilizers. His interest is in the difference between the resulting mean crop yields per acre.

To compare population means, random samples are drawn from the two populations, and an inference about the difference between population means is based on the sample results. The appropriate method for analyzing this information depends on the procedure used in selecting the samples. Two very common sampling schemes are considered in this section.

1. **MATCHED PAIRS/DEPENDENT SAMPLES.** In this scheme, the sample members are chosen in pairs, one from each population. The idea is that, apart from the factor under study, the members of these pairs should resemble one another as closely as possible so that the comparison of interest can be made directly. For instance, consider a medical study to compare the difference in effectiveness of two particular drugs to lower cholesterol levels or, perhaps, blood pressure. For each person randomly selected to test the first drug, a person similar to this individual in factors such as age, weight, or whatever conditions the medical profession deems necessary is selected to test the second drug. Or, suppose that the effectiveness of a speed-reading course is to be measured. One possible approach would be to record the number of words per minute read by a sample of students before taking the course and compare with results *for the same students* after completing the course. In this case, each pair of observations consists of "before" and "after" measurements on a single student.

2. **INDEPENDENT SAMPLES.** In this scheme, samples are drawn independently from the two populations of interest so that the membership of one sample is not influenced by the membership of the other sample. Suppose that in the chemical company example where shipments are received from two suppliers, independent random samples of batches from each supplier are selected and the impurity levels of each batch sampled are measured. Three situations of independent samples are discussed: (1) when the variances of both populations are known; (2) when the variances of both populations are not known, but are assumed to be equal; and (3) when the variances of both populations are not known, but are *not* assumed to be equal.

Two Means, Matched Pairs

Consider a study to compare the effectiveness of two cholesterol-lowering drugs. The research team would use a paired sample approach to control variation in reduction that might be due to factors other than the drug itself. For example, suppose that a random sample of eight pairs of patients with known cholesterol problems is selected. Each member of a pair is matched by age, weight, lifestyle, cholesterol range, or other pertinent factors. Drug A is given to one person randomly selected in each pair, and Drug B is given to the other individual in the pair. After a specified amount of time, each person's cholesterol levels were measured again. Table 8.4A gives the number of points by which each person's cholesterol level was reduced. A confidence interval for paired or matched data is needed to determine if there is a difference in the effectiveness of these two drugs.

An interval estimate for the general case of n matched pairs of observations, denoted $(x_1, y_1), (x_2, y_2), \ldots , (x_n, y_n)$, selected from populations with means μ_X and μ_Y follows. Consider the n differences $d_i = x_i - y_i$ and let $\overline{d}$ and s_d denote the observed sample mean and standard deviation for the n differences. Also let $\mu_d = \mu_A - \mu_B$. Now there is only one variable D, and Equations 8.3 and 8.4 are applied to obtain Equations 8.8 and 8.9.

TABLE 8.4A
Comparison of Two
Cholesterol-reducing Drugs

PAIR	DRUG A	DRUG B
1	29	26
2	32	27
3	31	28
4	32	27
5	32	30
6	29	26
7	31	33
8	30	36

CONFIDENCE INTERVALS FOR TWO MEANS: MATCHED PAIRS

Suppose that there is a random sample of n matched pairs of observations from normal distributions with means μ_X and μ_Y. That is, let $x_1, x_2, \ldots, x_n$ denotes the values of the observations from the population with mean μ_X; and $y_1, y_2, \ldots, y_n$ the matched sampled values from the population with the mean μ_Y. Let $\bar{d}$ and s_d denote the observed sample mean and standard deviation for the n differences $d_i = x_i - y_i$. If the population distribution of the differences is assumed to be normal, then a $100(1 - \alpha)\%$ **confidence interval for the difference between means** $(\mu_d = \mu_X - \mu_Y)$ is given by

$$\bar{d} - t_{n-1,\alpha/2}\,\frac{s_d}{\sqrt{n}} < \mu_d < \bar{d} + t_{n-1,\alpha/2}\,\frac{s_d}{\sqrt{n}} \qquad (8.8)$$

or equivalently,

$$\bar{d} \pm B$$

where the **margin of error**, the sampling error or the bound, B, is given by

$$B = t_{n-1,\alpha/2}\,\frac{s_d}{\sqrt{n}} \qquad (8.9)$$

and $t_{n-1,\alpha/2}$ is the number for which

$$P(t_{n-1} > t_{n-1,\alpha/2}) = \frac{\alpha}{2}$$

The random variable t_{n-1}, has a Student's t distribution with $(n - 1)$ degrees of freedom.

EXAMPLE 8.9

CHOLESTEROL REDUCTION
STUDY (CONFIDENCE INTERVAL)

Using the data from Table 8.4A, estimate with a 99% confidence the mean difference in the effectiveness of the two drugs, A and B, to lower cholesterol.

SOLUTION
Table 8.4B includes the difference, $d_i = x_i - y_i$, and the squared differences for each pair. From the information in the table, the sample mean and sample variance of the differences in cholesterol reduction can be calculated. For the sample mean.

$$\bar{d} = 1.625$$

and the observed sample standard deviation is

$$s_d = 3.777$$
$$t_{n-1,\alpha/2} = t_{7,0.005} = 3.499$$

TABLE 8.4B
Cholesterol Reduction

PAIR	DRUG A	DRUG B	DIFFERENCE $d_I = x_I - y_I$	d_i^2
1	29	26	3	9
2	32	27	5	25
3	31	28	3	9
4	32	27	5	25
5	32	30	2	4
6	29	26	3	9
7	31	33	−2	4
8	30	36	−6	36

from the Student's t distribution table. Hence, the 99% confidence interval is obtained for the difference between the population means by Equation 8.8:

$$\bar{d} - \frac{t_{n-1,\alpha/2} s_d}{\sqrt{n}} < \mu_X - \mu_Y < \bar{d} + \frac{t_{n-1,\alpha/2} s_d}{\sqrt{n}}$$

$$1.625 - \frac{(3.499)(3.777)}{\sqrt{8}} < \mu_X - \mu_Y < 1.625 + \frac{(3.499)(3.777)}{\sqrt{8}}$$

$$-3.05 < \mu_X - \mu_Y < 6.30$$

INTERPRETATION

This confidence interval can be obtained using PHStat or Minitab. The interpretation of the output in Figure 8.20 is important. Since the confidence interval contains the value of zero, it is not possible to determine if either drug is more effective in reducing one's cholesterol level. A brief discussion of matched pairs with missing values is in the Chapter Appendix.

FIGURE 8.20
PHStat Output for
Cholesterol Reduction
Example

Confidence Interval Estimate for the Mean	
Sample Standard Deviation	3.777281713
Sample Mean	1.625
Sample Size	8
Confidence Level	99%
Standard Error of the Mean	1.335470757
Degrees of Freedom	7
t Value	3.499480954
Interval Half Width	4.673454479
Interval Lower Limit	**-3.05**
Interval Upper Limit	**6.30**

Two Means, Independent Samples, Known Population Variances

Consider the case where independent samples, not necessarily of equal size, are taken from the two populations of interest. Suppose that there is a random sample of n_X observations from a population with mean μ_X and variance σ_X^2 and an independent random sample of n_Y observations from a population with mean μ_Y and variance σ_Y^2. Let the respective sample means be $\bar{X}$ and $\bar{Y}$.

As a first step, examine the situation where the two population distributions are normal with known variances. Since the object of interest is the difference between the two population means, it is natural to base an inference on the difference between the corresponding sample means. This random variable has mean

$$E(\bar{X} - \bar{Y}) = E(\bar{X}) - E(\bar{Y}) = \mu_X - \mu_Y$$

and, since the samples are independent,

$$\text{Var}\,(\overline{X} - \overline{Y}) = \text{Var}\,(\overline{X}) + \text{Var}\,(\overline{Y}) = \frac{\sigma_X^2}{n_X} + \frac{\sigma_Y^2}{n_Y}$$

Furthermore, it can be shown that its distribution is normal. It therefore follows that the random variable

$$Z = \frac{(\overline{X} - \overline{Y}) - (\mu_X - \mu_Y)}{\sqrt{\dfrac{\sigma_X^2}{n_X} + \dfrac{\sigma_Y^2}{n_Y}}}$$

has a standard normal distribution. An argument parallel to that of Section 8.2 can then be used to obtain confidence intervals for the difference between the population means. Since this interval requires knowledge of the true population variances, it is rarely of much direct use.

CONFIDENCE INTERVALS FOR DIFFERENCE BETWEEN MEANS: INDEPENDENT SAMPLES (NORMAL DISTRIBUTIONS AND KNOWN POPULATION VARIANCES)

Suppose that there are two **independent random samples** of n_x and n_y observations from normally distributed populations with means μ_X and μ_Y and variances σ_X^2 and σ_Y^2. If the observed sample means are $\overline{X}$ and $\overline{Y}$, then a $100(1 - \alpha)\%$ confidence interval for $(\mu_X - \mu_Y)$ is given by

$$(\overline{X} - \overline{Y}) - Z_{\alpha/2}\sqrt{\frac{\sigma_X^2}{n_x} + \frac{\sigma_Y^2}{n_y}} < \mu_X - \mu_Y < (\overline{X} - \overline{Y}) + Z_{\alpha/2}\sqrt{\frac{\sigma_X^2}{n_x} + \frac{\sigma_Y^2}{n_y}} \qquad (8.10)$$

or equivalently,

$$(\overline{X} - \overline{Y}) \pm B$$

where the **margin of error** is given by

$$B = Z_{\alpha/2}\sqrt{\frac{\sigma_X^2}{n_X} + \frac{\sigma_Y^2}{n_Y}} \qquad (8.11)$$

In some applications, use of the historical variances from similar studies can be used as the true population variances.

EXAMPLE 8.10

RELEVANCE OF STRATEGIC MANAGEMENT RESEARCH (CONFIDENCE INTERVAL)

Independent random samples of accounting professors and information systems (IS) professors were asked to provide the number of hours they spend in preparation for each class. The sample of 321 information systems professors had a mean time of 3.01 preparation hours and the sample of 94 accounting professors had a mean rating of 2.88 hours. From similar past studies the population standard deviation for the information systems professors is assumed to be 1.09, and similarly, the population standard deviation for the accounting professors is 1.01. Denoting by μ_X the population mean for IS professors and by μ_Y the population mean for accounting professors, find a 95% confidence interval for $(\mu_X - \mu_Y)$.

SOLUTION

The confidence interval equation

$$(\overline{X} - \overline{Y}) - Z_{\alpha/2}\sqrt{\frac{\sigma_X^2}{n_x} + \frac{\sigma_Y^2}{n_y}} < \mu_X - \mu_Y < (\overline{X} - \overline{Y}) + Z_{\alpha/2}\sqrt{\frac{\sigma_X^2}{n_x} + \frac{\sigma_Y^2}{n_y}}$$

with

$$n_x = 321 \qquad \overline{X} = 3.01 \qquad \sigma_x = 1.09$$
$$n_y = 94 \qquad \overline{Y} = 2.88 \qquad \sigma_y = 1.01$$

and for a 95% confidence interval

$$Z_{\alpha/2} = Z_{0.025} = 1.96$$

The interval is then

$$(3.01 - 2.88) - 1.96\sqrt{\frac{(1.09)^2}{321} + \frac{(1.01)^2}{94}} < \mu_X - \mu_Y < (3.01 - 2.88) + 1.96\sqrt{\frac{(1.09)^2}{321} + \frac{(1.01)^2}{94}}$$

or

$$-0.11 < \mu_X - \mu_Y < 0.37$$

This interval includes zero, indicating an absence of strong evidence that the population means are different.

Two Means, Independent Samples, Unknown Population Variances Assumed to be Equal

Consider estimating the difference between means of two populations with normal distributions and unknown population variances. Independent random samples from these two populations are chosen. First, consider the special case where it is assumed that the two population variances, although unknown, are equal. In this situation, a fairly straightforward method is available. Next, the case of unknown population variances that are *not* assumed to be equal is addressed.

Suppose again that there are two independent random samples of n_X and n_Y observations from normally distributed populations with means μ_X and μ_Y and that the populations have a common (unknown) variance σ^2, that is, $\sigma_X^2 = \sigma_Y^2 = \sigma^2$. Inference about the population means is based on the difference $(\overline{X} - \overline{Y})$ between the two sample means. This random variable has a normal distribution with mean $(\mu_X - \mu_Y)$ and variance

$$\text{Var}(\overline{X} - \overline{Y}) = \text{Var}(\overline{X}) + \text{Var}(\overline{Y})$$
$$= \frac{\sigma^2}{n_X} + \frac{\sigma^2}{n_Y}$$

It therefore follows that the random variable,

$$Z = \frac{(\overline{X} - \overline{Y}) - (\mu_X - \mu_Y)}{\sqrt{\dfrac{\sigma^2}{n_X} + \dfrac{\sigma^2}{n_Y}}}$$

has a standard normal distribution. However, this result cannot be used as it stands because the unknown population variance is involved.

Since $\sigma_X^2 = \sigma_Y^2 = \sigma^2$, then both s_X^2 and s_Y^2 are estimators of the common population variance σ^2. To use only s_X^2 or only s_Y^2 to estimate the common variance would ignore information from the other sample. If the sample sizes are the same $(n_X = n_Y)$, then the average of s_X^2 and s_Y^2 could be used to estimate the common variance. However, in the more general situation of unequal sample sizes, an estimate is needed that acknowledges the fact that more information about the common variance is obtained from the sample with the larger sample size. Thus, a weighted average of s_X^2 and s_Y^2 is used. This estimator, s_p^2, that pools together the two sets of sample information is given in Equation 8.14 (see Chapter Appendix).

CONFIDENCE INTERVALS FOR TWO MEANS: UNKNOWN POPULATION VARIANCES THAT ARE ASSUMED TO BE EQUAL

Suppose that there are two independent random samples with n_X and n_Y observations from **normally** distributed populations with means μ_x and μ_y and a **common, but unknown population variance**. If the observed sample means are $\overline{X}$ and $\overline{Y}$, and the observed sample variances are s_X^2 and s_Y^2, then a $100(1-\alpha)\%$ confidence interval for $(\mu_X - \mu_y)$ is given by

$$(\overline{X} - \overline{Y}) - t_{n_x+n_y-2,\alpha/2}\sqrt{\frac{s_p^2}{n_X} + \frac{s_p^2}{n_Y}} < \mu_x - \mu_y < (\overline{X} - \overline{Y}) + t_{n_x+n_y-2,\alpha/2}\sqrt{\frac{s_p^2}{n_X} + \frac{s_p^2}{n_Y}} \quad (8.12)$$

or equivalently,

$$(\overline{X} - \overline{Y}) \pm B$$

where the **margin of error** is

$$B = t_{n_x+n_y-2,\alpha/2}\sqrt{\frac{s_p^2}{n_X} + \frac{s_p^2}{n_Y}} \quad (8.13)$$

and the **pooled sample variance**, s_p^2, is given by

$$s_p^2 = \frac{(n_x - 1)s_X^2 + (n_y - 1)s_Y^2}{n_x + n_y - 2} \quad (8.14)$$

$t_{n_x+n_y-2,\alpha/2}$ is the number for which

$$P(t_{n_x+n_y-2} > t_{n_x+n_y-2,\alpha/2}) = \frac{\alpha}{2}$$

The random variable, T, is approximately a Student's t distribution with $n_X + n_Y - 2$ degrees of freedom and T is given by,

$$T = \frac{(\overline{X} - \overline{Y}) - (\mu_x - \mu_y)}{s_p\sqrt{\frac{1}{n_X} + \frac{1}{n_Y}}}$$

EXAMPLE 8.11

TRAFFIC FINES (CONFIDENCE INTERVAL)

The residents of Orange City complain that traffic speeding fines given in their city are higher than the traffic speeding fines that are given in nearby DeLand. The assistant to the county manager agreed to study the problem and to indicate if the complaints were reasonable. Independent random samples of the amounts paid by residents for speeding tickets in each of two cities over the last three months were obtained. These amounts were:

Orange City:	100	125	135	128	140	142	128	137	156	142
DeLand:	95	87	100	75	110	105	85	95		

Assuming an equal population variance, find a 95% confidence interval for the difference in the mean cost of speeding tickets in these two cities.

SOLUTION

Let the X-population be Orange City and the Y-population be DeLand. A check of the normal probability plots for both samples does not indicate evidence of nonnormality (Use Minitab to verify).

$$n_X = 10 \qquad \overline{X} = \$133.30 \qquad s_x^2 = 218.0111$$
$$n_Y = 8 \qquad \overline{Y} = \$94.00 \qquad s_y^2 = 129.4286$$

The pooled sample variance is found by Equation 8.14 to be:

$$s_p^2 = \frac{(n_x - 1)s_X^2 + (n_y - 1)s_Y^2}{n_x + n_y - 2} = \frac{(10 - 1)(218.011) + (8 - 1)(129.4286)}{10 + 8 - 2} = 179.2562$$

and

$$(\overline{X} - \overline{Y}) = (133.30 - 94.00) = \$39.30$$

The degrees of freedom is $n_X + n_Y - 2 = 16$ and $t_{(16, 0.025)} = 2.12$
The confidence interval is obtained by Equation 8.12:

$$(\overline{X} - \overline{Y}) - t_{n_x + n_y - 2, \alpha/2} \sqrt{\frac{s_p^2}{n_X} + \frac{s_p^2}{n_Y}} < \mu_x - \mu_y < (\overline{X} - \overline{Y}) + t_{n_x + n_y - 2, \alpha/2} \sqrt{\frac{s_p^2}{n_X} + \frac{s_p^2}{n_Y}}$$

$$39.3 - (2.12)\sqrt{\frac{179.2562}{10} + \frac{179.2562}{8}} < \mu_x - \mu_y < 39.3 + (2.12)\sqrt{\frac{179.2562}{10} + \frac{179.2562}{8}}$$

$$39.3 \pm 13.46$$

In the long run there is a difference in the cost of speeding tickets given in Orange City and those tickets given in DeLand. The mean cost of a speeding ticket in Orange City is as little as $25.84 or as much as $52.76 higher than the mean cost of a similar ticket in DeLand.

Minitab: Two Means (Unknown Variances that are Assumed to be Equal)

To use Minitab, follow the command sequence:

```
STAT > BASIC STATISTICS > 2- SAMPLE T
```

and complete the dialog box. Be sure to select "Assume equal variances" and then click on Options. The Minitab output is given in Figure 8.21.

Remember that no interpretation is given with either the Minitab output or Excel output. Be careful to include the interpretation if you use these or any other computer software. As previously stated, it is determined that *in the long run* (that is, with repeated samples) there is a difference in the cost of speeding tickets given in Orange City and those tickets given in DeLand. The mean cost of a speeding ticket in Orange City is as little as $25.84 or as much as $52.76 higher than the mean cost of a similar ticket in DeLand.

INTERPRETATION

FIGURE 8.21
Minitab Output for Traffic Fines Example

	N	Mean	StDev	SE Mean
Orange City	10	133.3	14.8	4.7
DeLand	8	94.0	11.4	4.0

Difference = mu Orange City - mu DeLand
Estimate for difference: 39.30
95% CI for difference: (25.84, 52.76)

Two Means, Independent Samples, Unknown Population Variances Assumed To Be Not Equal

The case where the population variances are assumed to be unequal involves distribution theory problems that are beyond the scope of this book. Only a brief discussion for completeness is included here.

CONFIDENCE INTERVALS FOR TWO MEANS: UNKNOWN POPULATION VARIANCES, ASSUMED NOT EQUAL

Suppose that there are two **independent random samples** of n_X and n_Y observations from **normally** distributed populations with means μ_X and μ_Y, and it is assumed that the population variances are not equal. If the observed sample means and variances are $\overline{X}$, $\overline{Y}$, and s_X^2, s_Y^2, then a $100(1-\alpha)\%$ confidence interval for $(\mu_X - \mu_Y)$ is given by

$$(\overline{X} - \overline{Y}) - t_{(v,\alpha/2)}\sqrt{\frac{s_X^2}{n_X} + \frac{s_Y^2}{n_Y}} < \mu_x - \mu_y < (\overline{X} - \overline{Y}) + t_{(v,\alpha/2)}\sqrt{\frac{s_X^2}{n_X} + \frac{s_Y^2}{n_Y}} \quad (8.15)$$

where the **margin of error** is

$$B = t_{(v,\alpha/2)}\sqrt{\frac{s_X^2}{n_X} + \frac{s_Y^2}{n_Y}} \quad (8.16)$$

and the degrees of freedom, v, is given by

$$v = \frac{\left[\left(\frac{s_X^2}{n_X}\right) + \left(\frac{s_Y^2}{n_Y}\right)\right]^2}{\left(\frac{s_X^2}{n_X}\right)^2 / (n_X - 1) + \left(\frac{s_Y^2}{n_Y}\right)^2 / (n_Y - 1)} \quad (8.17)$$

If the sample sizes are equal, then the degrees of freedom reduces to

$$v = \left(1 + \frac{2}{\frac{s_X^2}{s_Y^2} + \frac{s_Y^2}{s_X^2}}\right) \times (n - 1) \quad (8.18)$$

EXAMPLE 8.12

AUDITORS (CONFIDENCE INTERVAL)

Master's Accounting Firm conducted a random sample of the accounts payable for the east and the west offices of Amalgamated Distributors. From these two independent samples, they wanted to estimate the difference between the population mean values of the payables. The sample statistics obtained were:

	EAST OFFICE (POPULATION X)	WEST OFFICE (POPULATION Y)
Sample Mean	$290	$250
Sample Size	16	11
Sample Standard Deviation	15	50

Assume that the population variances, which are unknown, are unequal. A procedure to determine if the variances are equal is developed in Chapter 9. Estimate the difference between the mean values of the payables for the two offices. Use a 95% confidence level.

SOLUTION

Before the margin of error is found, first calculate the degrees of freedom by use of Equation 8.17:

$$v = \frac{\left[\left(\frac{s_X^2}{n_X}\right) + \left(\frac{s_Y^2}{n_Y}\right)\right]^2}{\left(\frac{s_X^2}{n_X}\right)^2 / (n_X - 1) + \left(\frac{s_Y^2}{n_Y}\right)^2 / (n_Y - 1)} = \frac{\left[(225/16 + 2500/11\right]^2}{\left(\frac{225}{16}\right)^2 / 15 + \left(\frac{2500}{11}\right)^2 / 10}$$

The bound is now found by use of Equation 8.16:

$$B = t_{(v,\alpha/2)}\sqrt{\frac{s_X^2}{n_X} + \frac{s_Y^2}{n_Y}} = t_{(12,0.025)}\sqrt{\frac{225}{16} + \frac{2500}{11}} = 2.179(15.534967) = 33.85$$

Using Equation 8.15, the 95% confidence interval is

$$(290 - 250) \pm 33.85$$

or

$$6.15 < \mu_X - \mu_Y < 73.85$$

EXERCISES

8.36 A random sample of ten pairs of identical houses was chosen in a large midwestern city, and a passive solar heating system was installed in one member of each pair. The total fuel bills (in dollars) for three winter months for these homes were then determined as shown in the accompanying table. Assuming normal population distributions, find a 90% confidence interval for the difference between the two population means.

PAIR	WITHOUT PASSIVE SOLAR	WITH PASSIVE SOLAR	PAIR	WITHOUT PASSIVE SOLAR	WITH PASSIVE SOLAR
1	485	452	6	386	380
2	423	386	7	426	395
3	515	502	8	473	411
4	425	376	9	454	415
5	653	605	10	496	441

8.37 A random sample of six salespersons that attended a motivational course on sales techniques was monitored in the three months before and the three months after the course. The table shows the values of sales, in thousands of dollars, generated by these six salespersons in the two periods. Assuming that the population distributions are normal, find an 80% confidence interval for the difference between the two population means.

SALESPERSON	BEFORE COURSE	AFTER COURSE
1	212	237
2	282	291
3	203	191
4	327	341
5	165	192
6	198	180

8.38 From a random sample of six students in an introductory finance class that uses group-learning techniques, the mean examination score was found to be 76.12 and the sample standard deviation was 2.53. For an independent random sample of nine students in another introductory finance class that does not use group-learning techniques, the sample mean and standard deviation of exam scores were 74.61 and 8.61, respectively.

Use Equations 8.15 and 8.17 to estimate with 95% confidence the difference between the two population mean scores, assuming that the unknown population variances are not equal.

8.39 Prairie Flower Cereal Inc. is a small but growing producer of hot and ready-to-eat breakfast cereals. Gordon Thorson, a successful grain farmer, started the company in 1910 (reference 5). Two machines are used for packaging 18-oz. (510-gram) boxes of sugar-coated wheat cereal. Estimate the difference in the mean weights of boxes of this type of cereal packaged by the two machines. Use a 95% confidence level and the data file **Sugar Coated Wheat.** Explain your findings.

8.40 Recent business graduates currently employed in full-time positions were surveyed. Family backgrounds were self-classified as relatively high or low socioeconomic status. For a random sample of 138 high socioeconomic status recent business graduates, mean total compensation was $36,558 and the sample standard deviation was $11,624. For an independent random sample of 266 low socioeconomic status recent business graduates, mean total compensation was $37,499 and the sample standard deviation was $16,521 (reference 18). Find a 90% confidence interval for the difference between the two population means.

8.41 Suppose, for a random sample of 200 firms that revalued their fixed assets, the mean ratio of debt to tangible assets was 0.517 and the sample standard deviation was 0.148. For an independent random sample of 400 firms that did not revalue their fixed assets, the mean ratio of debt to tangible assets was 0.489 and the sample stan-

dard deviation was 0.159. Find a 99% confidence interval for the difference between the two population means.

8.42 A researcher intends to estimate the effect of a drug on the scores of human subjects performing a task of psychomotor coordination. The members of a random sample of nine subjects were given the drug prior to testing. Their mean score was 9.78, and the sample variance was 17.64. An independent random sample of ten subjects was used as a control group and given a placebo prior to testing. The mean score in this control group was 15.10, and the sample variance was 27.01. Assuming that the population distributions are normal with equal variances, find a 90% confidence interval for the difference between the population mean scores.

8.43 A company sends a random sample of 12 of its salespeople to a course designed to increase their motivation and hence, presumably, their effectiveness. In the following year, these people generated sales with an average value of $435,000 and a sample standard deviation of $56,000. During the same period, an independently chosen random sample of 15 salespeople who had not attended the course obtained sales with an average value of $408,000 and standard deviation $43,000. Assume that the two population distributions are normal and have the same variance. Find a 95% confidence interval for the difference between their means.

8.44 Students in an introductory economics class are assigned to quiz sections conducted by teaching assistants. For one teaching assistant, the 21 students in the quiz section obtained a mean score of 72.1 on the final examination, and a standard deviation of 11.3. For a second teaching assistant, the 18 students in the section obtained a mean score on the final exam of 73.8, and a standard deviation of 10.6. Assuming that these data can be regarded as independent random samples from normally distributed populations with a common variance, find an 80% confidence interval for the difference between the population means.

8.7 CONFIDENCE INTERVALS FOR THE DIFFERENCE BETWEEN TWO POPULATION PROPORTIONS (LARGE SAMPLES)

Confidence intervals for a single population proportion were derived in Section 8.4. Often, a comparison of two population proportions is of interest. For instance, one might want to compare the proportion of residents in one city who indicate that they will vote for a particular presidential candidate with the proportion of residents in another city who indicate the same candidate preference. Confidence intervals for the difference between two population proportions with independent large samples taken from these two populations is considered in this section.

Suppose that a random sample of n_X observations from a population with proportion π_X of "successes" yields sample proportion p_X, and that an independent random sample of

n_Y observations from a population with proportion π_Y of "successes" produces sample proportion p_Y. Since our concern is with the population difference $(\pi_X - \pi_Y)$, it is natural to examine the random variable $(p_X - p_Y)$. This has mean

$$E(p_X - p_Y) = E(p_X) - E(p_Y) = \pi_X - \pi_Y$$

and, since the samples are taken independently, variance

$$\text{Var}(p_X - p_Y) = \text{Var}(p_X) + \text{Var}(p_Y)$$
$$= \frac{\pi_X(1 - \pi_X)}{n_x} + \frac{\pi_Y(1 - \pi_Y)}{n_y}$$

Furthermore, if the sample sizes are large, the distribution of this random variable is approximately normal, so subtracting its mean and dividing by its standard deviation gives a standard normally distributed random variable. Moreover, for large sample sizes, this approximation remains valid when the unknown population proportions π_X and π_Y are replaced by the corresponding sample quantities. Thus, to a good approximation, the random variable

$$Z = \frac{(p_X - p_Y) - (\pi_X - \pi_Y)}{\sqrt{\dfrac{p_X(1 - p_X)}{n_x} + \dfrac{p_Y(1 - p_Y)}{n_y}}}$$

has a standard normal distribution. This result allows the derivation of confidence intervals for the difference between the two population proportions when the same sample sizes are large.

CONFIDENCE INTERVALS FOR THE DIFFERENCE BETWEEN POPULATION PROPORTIONS (LARGE SAMPLES)

Let p_X denote the observed proportion of successes in a random sample of n_X observations from a population with proportion π_X successes, and let p_Y denote the proportion of successes observed in an independent random sample from a population with proportion π_Y successes. Then, if the sample sizes are large (generally at least 40 observations in each sample), a $100(1 - \alpha)\%$ **confidence interval for the difference between population proportions**, $(\pi_X - \pi_Y)$ is given by

$$(p_X - p_Y) \pm B \tag{8.19}$$

where the **margin of error** is

$$B = Z_{\alpha/2} \sqrt{\frac{p_X(1 - p_X)}{n_X} + \frac{p_Y(1 - p_Y)}{n_Y}} \tag{8.20}$$

EXAMPLE 8.13

PRECINCT PREFERENCE (CONFIDENCE INTERVAL)

During a presidential election year, many forecasts are made to determine how voters perceive a particular candidate. In a random sample of 120 registered voters in Precinct A, 107 indicated that they supported the candidate in question. In an independent random sample of 141 registered voters in Precinct B, only 73 indicated support for the same candidate. If the respective population proportions are denoted π_A and π_B, find a 95% confidence interval for the population difference $(\pi_A - \pi_B)$.

SOLUTION

From the sample information, it follows that

$$n_A = 120 \quad \text{and} \quad p_A = 107/120 = 0.892; \qquad n_B = 141 \quad \text{and} \quad p_B = 73/141 = 0.518$$

FIGURE 8.22
Minitab Output for Precinct
Preference Example

Sample	X	N	Sample p
1	107	120	0.891667
2	73	141	0.517730

Estimate for p(1) - p(2): 0.373936
95% CI for p(1) - p(2): **(0.274463, 0.473409)**

For a 95% confidence interval, $\alpha = .05$, and so

$$z_{\alpha/2} = z_{.025} = 1.96$$

The required interval is therefore

$$(0.892 - 0.518) - 1.96\sqrt{\frac{(0.892)(0.108)}{120} + \frac{(0.518)(0.482)}{141}}$$
$$< \pi_A - \pi_B < (0.892 - 0.518) + 1.96\sqrt{\frac{(0.892)(0.108)}{120} + \frac{(0.518)(0.482)}{141}}$$
$$0.275 < \pi_A - \pi_B < 0.473$$

The fact that zero is well outside this range suggests that there is a difference in the population proportion of registered voters in Precinct A and Precinct B who support this presidential candidate. In the long run, the difference is estimated to be as little as 27.5% or as high as 47.3% .

Minitab

Obtaining the confidence interval for the difference in two population proportions for large samples is easily accomplished with Minitab. Follow the command sequence:

```
STAT > BASIC STATISTICS > 2 PROPORTIONS…
```

 **INTERPRETATION**

and complete the dialog box. Figure 8.22 is the Minitab output for Example 8.13. The data suggests that there is a difference in the population proportion of registered voters in Precinct A and Precinct B who support this presidential candidate. In the long run, about 95% of all such intervals would contain the true value of the difference.

EXERCISES

8.45 In a random sample of 120 large retailers, 85 used regression as a method of forecasting. In an independent random sample of 163 small retailers, 78 used regression as a method of forecasting. Find a 98% confidence interval for the difference between the two population proportions.

8.46 🌐 Do seniors and freshmen have different views concerning the university's library collection? Using the data file **Library**, estimate the difference in proportion of seniors and freshmen who think that the school's library has an adequate collection of books. Use a confidence level of 90%.

8.47 🌐 "Would you use the library more if the hours were extended?" From a random sample of 138 fresh-

men, 80 indicated that they would use the school's library more if the hours were extended. In an independent random sample of 96 sophomores, 73 responded that they would use the library more if the hours were extended. Estimate the difference in proportion of first year and second year students responding affirmatively to this question. Use a 95% confidence level.

8.48 A random sample of 100 men contained 61 in favor of a state constitutional amendment to retard the rate of growth of property taxes. An independent random sample of 100 women contained 54 in favor of this amendment. The confidence interval

$$0.04 < \pi_X - \pi_Y < 0.10$$

was calculated for the difference between the population proportions. What is the confidence level of this interval?

8.49 Supermarket shoppers were observed and questioned immediately after putting an item in the cart. Of a random sample of 510 choosing a product at the regular price, 320 claimed to check price at the point of choice. Of an independent random sample of 332 choosing a product at a special price, 200 made this claim. Find a 90% confidence interval for the difference between the two population proportions.

8.8   SAMPLE SIZE DETERMINATION

Methods for finding confidence intervals have been developed for a population parameter on the basis of the information contained in a given sample. Following such a process, an investigator may believe that the resulting confidence interval is too wide, reflecting an undesirable amount of uncertainty about the parameter being estimated. Typically, one way to obtain a narrower interval with a given confidence level is to take a larger sample.

In some circumstances, the investigator may be able to fix in advance the width of the confidence interval, choosing a sample size big enough to guarantee that width. In this section, consideration of how sample size can be chosen in this way for two interval estimation problems is given. Similar procedures can be employed to solve other problems.

Chapter 18 concentrates on the problem of a researcher who wants to discover something about a population that is not necessarily large. The investigator intends to collect information on only a subset of the population members and requires guidance as to how to proceed.

Sample Size Determination for Mean of a Normally Distributed Population with Known Population Variances

If a random sample of n observations is taken from a normally distributed population with mean μ and known variance σ^2, it was seen in Section 8.4 that a $100(1 - \alpha)\%$ confidence interval for the population mean is provided by

$$\overline{X} - \frac{Z_{\alpha/2}\sigma}{\sqrt{n}} < \mu < \overline{X} + \frac{Z_{\alpha/2}\sigma}{\sqrt{n}}$$

where $\overline{X}$ is the observed sample mean and $Z_{\alpha/2}$ is the appropriate cutoff point of the standard normal distribution. This interval is centered on the sample mean and extends a distance of B, the margin of error as given in Equation 8.2,

$$B = \frac{Z_{\alpha/2}\sigma}{\sqrt{n}}$$

on each side of the sample mean, so that B is half the width of the interval. Suppose, now, that the investigator wants to fix B in advance. From basic algebra, it follows that if,

$$B = \frac{Z_{\alpha/2}\sigma}{\sqrt{n}}$$

then,

$$\sqrt{n} = \frac{Z_{\alpha/2}\sigma}{B}$$

and by squaring both sides of the equation, the sample size n is

$$n = \frac{Z_{\alpha/2}^2 \sigma^2}{B^2}$$

This choice of the sample size ensures that the confidence interval extends a distance B on each side of the sample mean.

SAMPLE SIZE FOR THE MEAN OF A NORMALLY DISTRIBUTED POPULATION WITH KNOWN POPULATION VARIANCE

Suppose that a random sample from a normally distributed population with known variance σ^2 is selected. Then a $100(1 - \alpha)\%$ confidence interval for the population mean extends a distance B (sometimes called the bound, sampling error, or the margin of error) on each side of the sample mean, if the sample size, n, is

$$n = \frac{Z_{\alpha/2}^2 \sigma^2}{B^2} \tag{8.21}$$

Of course, the number of sample observations must necessarily be an integer, if the number n resulting from the sample size formula is not an integer, then *round up* to the next whole number in order to guarantee that our confidence interval does not exceed the required width.

EXAMPLE 8.14

LENGTH OF METAL RODS(SAMPLE SIZE)

The lengths of metal rods produced by an industrial process are normally distributed with standard deviation of 1.8 millimeters. Based on a random sample of nine observations from this population, the 99% confidence interval

$$194.65 < \mu < 197.75$$

was found for the population mean length. Suppose that a production manager believes that the interval is too wide for practical use and instead requires a 99% confidence interval extending no further than 0.50 mm on each side of the sample mean. How large a sample is needed to achieve such an interval?

SOLUTION

Since

$$B = 0.50 \qquad \sigma = 1.8 \qquad \text{and} \qquad Z_{\alpha/2} = Z_{0.005} = 2.576$$

the required sample size is

$$\begin{aligned}
n &= \frac{Z_{\alpha/2}^2 \sigma^2}{B^2} \\
&= \frac{(2.576)^2 (1.8)^2}{(0.5)^2} \approx 86
\end{aligned}$$

Therefore, to satisfy the manager's requirement, a sample of at least eighty-six observations is needed. This large increase in the sample size represents the additional cost of achieving the higher precision in the estimate of the true value of the population mean, reflected in a narrower confidence interval. The value 2.576 rather than 2.58 was used to determine the sample size needed.

PHStat

Follow the command sequence

```
PHSTAT > SAMPLE SIZE > DETERMINATION FOR THE MEAN...
```

and complete the dialog box. The output appears in Figure 8.23.

Sample Size Determination for Population Proportion

Section 8.4 considered that for a random sample of n observations, a $100(1 - \alpha)\%$ confidence interval for the population proportion π is

$$p - Z_{\alpha/2}\sqrt{\frac{p(1-p)}{n}} < \pi < p + Z_{\alpha/2}\sqrt{\frac{p(1-p)}{n}}$$

where p is the observed sample proportion. This interval is centered on the sample proportion and extends a distance (Equation 8.6):

$$B = Z_{\alpha/2}\sqrt{\frac{p(1-p)}{n}}$$

on each side of the sample proportion. Now, this result *cannot* be used directly to determine the sample size necessary to obtain a confidence interval of some specific width, since it involves the sample proportion, which will not be known at the outset. However, whatever the outcome, $p(1 - p)$ cannot be bigger than 0.25, its value when the sample proportion is 0.5. Thus, the largest possible value for B is given by

$$B = Z_{\alpha/2}\sqrt{\frac{0.25}{n}} = \frac{(0.5)Z_{\alpha/2}}{\sqrt{n}}$$

Suppose, then, that a sufficiently large sample size is chosen to *guarantee* that the confidence interval extends no more than "B" on each side of the sample proportion. Again using basic algebra,

$$\sqrt{n} = \frac{0.5Z_{\alpha/2}}{B}$$

and squaring yields

$$n = \frac{0.25(Z_{\alpha/2})^2}{(B)^2}$$

FIGURE 8.23
PHStat Output for Metal
Rods Example

		Comments
Population Standard Deviation	1.8	It is easy to find the sample size
Sampling Error	0.5	
Confidence Level	99%	for different confidence levels
Z Value	-2.57583451	and/or different sampling errors
Calculated Sample Size	85.98860787	by simply changing the values in
Sample Size Needed	86	this PHStat output box.

SAMPLE SIZE FOR POPULATION PROPORTION

Suppose that a random sample is selected from a population. Then a $100(1 - \alpha)\%$ confidence interval for the population proportion, extending a distance of at most B on each side of the sample proportion, can be guaranteed if the sample size is

$$n = \frac{0.25(Z_{\alpha/2})^2}{B^2} \tag{8.22}$$

EXAMPLE 8.15

GRADUATE ADMISSIONS PERSONNEL (SAMPLE SIZE)

In Example 8.7, a 95% confidence interval was calculated for the proportion of graduate admissions personnel who viewed scores on standardized exams as very important in the consideration of a candidate. Based on 142 observations, the interval obtained was

$$0.533 < \pi < 0.693$$

Suppose, instead, it is desired to ensure that a 95% confidence interval for the population proportion extends no further than 0.06 on each side of the sample proportion. How large a sample must be taken?

SOLUTION

It is given that

$$B = 0.06 \qquad \text{and} \qquad Z_{\alpha/2} = Z_{0.025} = 1.96$$

Thus, the number of sample observations needed is

$$n = \frac{0.25Z_{\alpha/2}^2}{(B)^2} = \frac{0.25(1.96)^2}{(.06)^2} = 266.78$$

To achieve this narrower confidence interval, a minimum of 267 sample observations is required (a significant increase over the original 142 observations).

PHStat

Turning again to Microsoft Excel PHStat, you can easily determine the sample size required for a specified confidence interval for the population proportion by following the command sequence,

```
PHSTAT > SAMPLE SIZE > DETERMINATION FOR THE PROPORTION...
```

Complete the dialog box giving the "Estimate of the True Proportion," the sampling error, and the desired confidence level. If no estimate of the true proportion is known, use 0.50. PHStat output for Example 8.15 is given in Figure 8.24.

FIGURE 8.24
PHStat Output for Graduate Admissions Personnel Example

Estimate of True Proportion	0.5
Sampling Error	0.06
Confidence Level	95%
Z Value	-1.95996108
Calculated Sample Size	266.7671836
Sample Size Needed	**267**

Again, you can simply change the estimate of the true proportion, the sampling error, or the confidence level in the output to obtain new sample sizes.

Media Reports of Opinion Surveys

The media frequently report the results of surveys of the opinions of the population, or some subset of the population, on issues of current interest. Typically these reports give estimates of the percentage of population members holding particular views. These reports often end with a statement like: "There is a plus or minus 3% sampling error," or "The poll has a 3% margin of error." As you know, the margin of error is the same as the sampling error or the bound of confidence intervals. Specifically, these intervals are the sample percentage, plus or minus the advertised sampling error or margin of error.

EXAMPLE 8.16

ELECTORAL COLLEGE(SAMPLE SIZE)

Suppose that an opinion survey following a presidential election reported the views of a sample of U.S. citizens of voting age concerning changing the electoral college process. The poll was said to have "a 3% margin of error." The implication is that a 95% confidence interval for the population proportion holding a particular opinion is the sample proportion plus or minus at most 3%. How many citizens of voting age need to be sampled to obtain this 3% margin of error?

SOLUTION
Using Equation 8.22,

$$n = \frac{0.25 Z_{\alpha/2}^2}{(B)^2} = \frac{(0.25)(1.96)^2}{(0.03)^2} = 1067.111$$

Therefore, 1068 U.S. citizens of voting age need to be sampled to achieve the desired result.

EXERCISES

8.50 A research group wants to estimate the proportion of consumers who plan to buy a scanner for their PC during the next three months.
  (a) How many people should be sampled so that the sampling error is at most 0.04 with a 90% confidence interval?
  (b) What is the sample size required if the confidence is increased to 95%, keeping the sampling error the same?
  (c) What is the required sample size if the research group extends the sampling error to 0.05 and wants a 98% confidence level?

8.51 A politician wants to estimate the proportion of con-

stituents favoring a controversial piece of proposed legislation. Suppose that a 99% confidence interval that extends at most 0.05 on each side of the sample proportion is required. How many sample observations are needed?

8.52 The student government association at a university wants to estimate the percentage of the student body that support a change being considered in the academic calendar of the university for the next academic year. How many students should be surveyed if a 90% confidence interval is desired and the margin of error is to be only 3%?

SUMMARY

This chapter emphasized estimators and confidence intervals. In particular, interval estimates were developed for such parameters as (1) the population mean of a normally distributed

population when the population variance is either known or unknown; (2) the population proportion for large samples; (3) the variance of a normally distributed population; (4) the difference between means of two normally distributed populations for both matched pairs and independent samples; and (5) the difference between two population proportions for large samples.

Generally, adding and subtracting the sampling error from the point estimator forms confidence intervals. This was not the case for the population variance, however. Three tables, the standard normal Z table, the student's t table, and the chi-square table were used in the development of the confidence intervals in this chapter. Finally, an introduction to determining the sample size for two particular interval estimates was considered. Additional sampling is discussed in Chapter 18.

KEY WORDS

bias, 258
bound, 266
confidence interval, 266
   for mean, known variance, 266
   for mean, unknown variance, 272
   for proportion, 276
   for two means, independent, 287
   for two means, matched, 285
   for two means, variances equal, 289
   for two means, variances not equal, 291

for two proportions, 294
   for variance, 282
confidence level, 262
estimate, 256
estimator, 256
interval half width, 266
lower confidence limit, LCL, 268
margin of error, 266
minimum variance unbiased estimator, 258
most efficient estimator, 258

point estimate, 257
point estimator, 257
relative efficiency, 258
reliability factor, 268
sample size for mean, known variance, 296
sample size for proportion, 299
sampling error, 266
Student's t, 270
unbiased estimator, 257
upper confidence limit, UCL, 268
width, 268

CHAPTER EXERCISES AND APPLICATIONS

8.53 Several drugs are used to treat diabetes. A sales specialist for a leading pharmaceutical company randomly sampled the records of 10 sales districts to estimate the number of new prescriptions that had been written during a particular month for his company's new diabetes drug. The number of new prescriptions were:

210   240   190   275   290   265   312   284   261   243

(**a**) Find a 90% confidence interval for the average number of new prescriptions written for this new drug among all the sales districts. What are your assumptions?

(**b**) Use Microsoft Excel to find the widths for 85% and 98% confidence intervals.

(**c**) Assuming that the confidence level remains constant, what sample size is needed to reduce by half the bound of the confidence interval in part (a)?

8.54 Suppose that the manager of a Sam's Club in Chattanooga, TN, wants to estimate the mean number of gallons of milk that are sold during a typical weekday. Brent checked the sales records for a random sample of 16 days and found the mean number of gallons sold is 150 gallons per day; the sample standard deviation is 12 gallons. With 95% confidence, estimate the number of gallons that Brent should stock daily.

8.55 Everyone knows that exercise is important. Recently, residents in one community were surveyed and asked, "How many minutes do you spend daily on some form of rigorous exercise?" From a random sample of 50 residents, the mean time spent on vigorous daily exercise was half an hour. The standard deviation was found to be 4.2 minutes. Find a 90% interval estimate of the time spent daily on rigorous exercise by these residents.

8.56 The following data represent the number of passengers per flight for a random sample of 50 flights from Jacksonville, FL, to Baltimore, MD, on one particular airline.

163	165	94	137	123	95	170	96	117	129
152	138	147	119	166	125	148	180	152	149
167	120	129	159	150	119	113	147	169	151
116	150	110	110	143	90	134	145	156	165
174	133	128	100	86	148	139	150	145	100

Estimate the average number of passengers per flight with a 95% interval estimate. Use PHStat.

8.57 The supervisor of a bottle-filling plant randomly sampled bottles to determine if any of the following defects were present: dents, missing labels; incorrect labels; or a wrong color. The types of defects (see table) are in the data file **Defects**.

Dent	Missing label	Wrong color	Dent	Wrong color	Wrong color	Missing label	Wrong color
Wrong color	Incorrect label	Dent	Missing label	Dent	Dent	Wrong color	Incorrect label
Dent	Missing label	Wrong color	Dent	Wrong color	Incorrect label	Dent	Missing label
Dent	Incorrect label	Missing label	Missing label	Dent	Missing label	Dent	Incorrect label
Incorrect label	Missing label	Missing label	Incorrect label	Incorrect label	Missing label	Dent	Dent
Wrong color	Missing label	Missing label	Wrong color	Wrong color	Wrong color	Wrong color	Missing label

(a) Estimate the proportion of defects due to an incorrect label. Use an 88% confidence level.

(b) Estimate the percentage of defects due to a missing label. Use a 92% confidence level.

8.58 A proposal for a new 1-cent tax increase to support cancer research is to appear on the ballot in one county's next election. The residents in two cities were questioned as to their level of support. In Sterling Heights, a recent survey of 225 residents showed that 140 people supported the proposal, 35 were undecided, and the remainder was opposed to the new proposal. In another nearby community, Harrison Township, the results of a random sample of 210 residents found that 120 people supported the tax, 30 were opposed, and the remainder was undecided.

(a) Estimate the difference in the percentage of residents from these two communities who support this proposal. Use a 95% confidence level.

(b) Use Minitab to check your results in part (a).

8.59 Is the average amount spent on textbooks per semester by accounting majors significantly different than the average amount spent on textbooks per semester by management majors? Answer this question with a 90% confidence interval using the following data from random samples of students majoring in accounting or management. Discuss assumptions.

	ACCOUNTING MAJORS	MANAGEMENT MAJORS
Mean	$340	$285
Standard Dev.	20	30
Sample Size	40	50

8.60 The supervisor of an orange juice bottling company is considering the purchase of a new machine to bottle 16 fl. oz. (473 mL) bottles of 100% pure orange juice and wants an estimate of the difference in the filling weights between the new machine and the old machine. Random samples of bottles of orange juice that had been filled by both machines were obtained. Do the following data indicate that there is a difference in the mean filling weights between the new and the old machine? Discuss assumptions.

	NEW MACHINE	OLD MACHINE
Mean	470 mL	460 mL
Standard Dev.	5 mL	7 mL
Sample Size	15	12

8.61 Renee Payne, who is employed by a major investment firm in West Palm Beach, FL, would like to estimate the percentage of new clients who will make a certain type of investment. If she wants a sampling error no greater than 2.5% and a confidence level of 90%, how many clients should she sample? What sample size is required for an 85% confidence level?

8.62 Eight randomly selected batches of a chemical were tested for impurity concentration. The percentage impurity levels found in this sample were:

3.2   4.3   2.1   2.8   3.2   3.6   4.0   3.8

(a) Find the most efficient estimates of the population mean and variance.

(b) Estimate the proportion of batches with impurity levels greater than 3.75%.

8.63 An agency offers students preparation courses for a graduate school admissions test. As part of an experiment to evaluate the merits of the course, twelve students were chosen and divided into six pairs, in such a way that the two members of any pair had similar academic records. Before taking the test, one member of each pair was assigned at random to take the preparation course, while the other member took no course. The achievement test scores are contained in the **Student Pair** data file. Assuming that the differences in scores are normally distributed, find a 98% confidence interval for the difference in means scores between those who took the course and those who did not.

APPENDIX

1. **Confidence Interval for Population Mean, Variance Unknown: Minitab**

Example 8.5 illustrated one way to find the confidence intervals for a normally distributed population mean when the population variance is unknown by use of Minitab. Here is another way to use Minitab to accomplish the same purpose. Follow the Minitab command sequence

```
STAT > BASIC STATISTICS > 1-SAMPLE T > OPTIONS...
```

Consider again Example 8.5, fuel consumption measured in miles per gallon for 24 trucks. Minitab output is in Figure 8.25.

FIGURE 8.25
Minitab Output for Trucks
Example

One-Sample T:

N	Mean	StDev	SE Mean	90.0% CI
24	18.679	1.695	0.346	(18.086, 19.272)

Minitab Instructions

1. Open file: Trucks
2. Click on Stat
3. Select Basic Statistics option
4. Select 1-Sample t
5. Click Options...
6. Enter Confidence level desired

2. **Confidence Interval for Population Mean, Variance Known: Function CONFIDENCE in Excel**

   The function CONFIDENCE can be used in Excel to find the margin of error for a confidence interval for the population mean when the population variance, σ^2, is known (Section 8.2). Consider again the process that produces bags of refined sugar in Example 8.4. The population standard deviation was given as 1.2 ounces, and the mean weight for a sample of 25 bags was 19.8 ounces. Simply enter the following in the formula bar: =CONFIDENCE(0.01,1.2,25). Notice that the first entry is α (0.01 for a 99% confidence level); the second entry is the value of the population standard deviation (1.2); and the third entry is the sample size (25). The only output is the value of the bound, 0.6182.

   The function CONFIDENCE cannot be used for the other confidence intervals in this chapter. In addition, the output does not provide as much information as output from PHStat (see Figure 8.7) or output from Minitab.

3. **Student's t Distribution**

   Gosset sought to develop a probability distribution for normally distributed random variables that did not include the population variance σ^2. As a result, he took the ratio of Z, a standard normal random variable and the square root of χ^2 divided by its degrees of freedom, v. In mathematical notation,

   $$t = \frac{Z}{\sqrt{\chi^2/v}}$$

   $$t = \frac{(X - \mu)/\sigma}{\sqrt{s^2(n-1)/\sigma^2(n-1)}} = \frac{(X - \mu)}{s}$$

   The resulting t statistic has $n - 1$ degrees of freedom. Notice that the t probability distribution is based on normally distributed random variables. For applications, the normal Z is used when the population variance σ^2 is available and the Student's t when only the sample variance s^2 is available. Statistical research using computer-generated random samples has shown that t can be used to study the distribution of sample means even if the distribution of the individual random variables is not normal.

4. **Student's t-Test For Two Means with Unknown Population Variances Assumed to Be Not Equal**

   For the difference between two populations,

   $$Z = \frac{(\overline{X} - \overline{Y}) - (\mu_X - \mu_Y)}{\sqrt{\dfrac{\sigma_X^2}{n_X} + \dfrac{\sigma_Y^2}{n_Y}}} \qquad \text{and} \qquad \chi^2 = \chi_X^2 + \chi_Y^2$$

   is the sum of two independent chi-square random variables from the two independent random samples

   $$\chi_X^2 = \frac{(n_X - 1)s_X^2}{\sigma_X^2}$$

   $$\chi_Y^2 = \frac{(n_Y - 1)s_Y^2}{\sigma_Y^2}$$

with $(n_X - 1)$ and $(n_Y - 1)$ degrees of freedom respectively. The degrees of freedom for χ^2 is the sum of the component degrees of freedom, $v = (n_x - 1) + (n_y - 1) = n_x + n_y - 2$. Bringing these pieces together,

$$t = \frac{\left[(\overline{X} - \overline{Y}) - (\mu_X - \mu_Y)\right] / \sqrt{\sigma_X^2 / n_X + \sigma_Y^2 / n_Y}}{\sqrt{\left[(n_X - 1)s_X^2 / \sigma_X^2 + (n_Y - 1)s_Y^2 / \sigma_Y^2\right] / (n_X + n_Y - 2)}}$$

If $\sigma_X^2 = \sigma_Y^2$, then this reduces to

$$t = \frac{(\overline{X} - \overline{Y}) - (\mu_X - \mu_Y)}{\sqrt{\dfrac{s_p^2}{n_X} + \dfrac{s_p^2}{n_Y}}}$$

5. **Matched Pairs with Missing Values**

Consider matched pairs with missing values. Suppose that at least one value from the first sample is missing and *exactly* the same number of missing values occurs in the second sample (not from the same observations). In this one case, Excel will perform the calculations giving incorrect results. You must first follow the procedure in the Appendix to Chapter 2 to remove all those cases from both samples that contain missing values. This will also apply in Chapter 9 when hypothesis tests of matched pairs are considered.

REFERENCES

1. Agresti, A. and Coull, B. A. "Approximate is Better than 'Exact' for Interval Estimation of Binomial Proportions." *The American Statistician* 52 (1998): 119–126.

2. Agresti, A., and Caffo, B., "Simple and Effective Confidence Intervals for Proportions and Differences of Proportions Result from Adding Two Successes and Two Failures." *The American Statistician* 54 (2000): 280–288.

3. *American Customer Satisfaction Index*, published by University of Michigan Business School, 2000.

4. Burcum, Jill, "Flu Season's here: 2 cases confirmed," *Minneapolis Star Tribune*, December, 14, 2000, B1.

5. Carlson, William L., *Cases in Managerial Data Analysis*. (Belmont, CA: Wadsworth Publishing Company, 1997).

6. Dabholkar, P. A. and J. J. Kellaris, "Toward Understanding Marketing Students' Ethical Judgment of Controversial Personal Selling Practices." *Journal of Business Research* 24 (1992): 313–329.

7. Fiedler, Alfred W., Plant Manager. Machine reading leak rate repeatability studies conducted at LDS Vacuum Products, Altamonte Springs, FL, February 1999.

8. Hildebrand, David and A. L. Ott, *Statistical Thinking for Managers*. (New York: Brooks/Cole, 1998).

9. Lawrence, Jill, "Think election was a mess? Look at system," *USA Today*, November 14, 2000, 21A.

10. "Lost Votes?" *Orlando Sentinel*, November 12, 2000, A11.

11. Neufeld, John L., *Learning Business Statistics with Microsoft Excel 97*. (Upper Saddle River, NJ: Prentice Hall, 1998).

12. Neufeld, John L., *Learning Business Statistics with Microsoft Excel 2000*. (Upper Saddle River, NJ: Prentice Hall, 1998).

13. "New park signs will read: No snowmobiles," Associated Press article in *Orlando Sentinel*, November 24, 2000, A18.

14. Pearson, Egon Sharpe, R. L. Plackett (ed.), *Student: A Statistical Biography of William Sealy Gosset*. (Oxford: Clarendon Press, 1990).

15. Pearson, Egon Sharpe and John Wishart (eds.), *Development of Statistics: Student's Collected Papers*." (Cambridge: 1958). Forward by Launce McMullen. Materials provided to the authors by Teresa O'Donnell, Guiness (GIG) Archivist, September 13, 2000.

16. *Project Romanian Rescue: Headline News*, October 2000.

17. Wessel, Harry, "Lousy service? Get used to it," *Orlando Sentinel*, November 24, 2000, A1.

18. Whitely, O. W., T. W. Dougherty, and G. F. Dreher, "Relationship of Career Mentoring and Socioeconomic Origin to Managers' and Professionals' Early Career Progress." *Academy of Management Journal* 34 (1991): 331–351.

HYPOTHESIS TESTING

INTRODUCTION

In this chapter we will develop hypothesis testing procedures that enable us to test the validity of some conjecture or claim by using sample data. This form of inference contrasts and complements the estimation procedures developed in Chapter 8. The process begins with an investigator forming a hypothesis about the nature of some population. This hypothesis is stated clearly as involving two options, and then one option is selected based on the results of a statistic computed from a random sample of data. Examples of typical problems include

1. Malt O Meal Inc., a producer of ready-to-eat cereal claims that on average its cereal packages weigh at least 16 ounces. We can test this claim by collecting a random sample of cereal packages, determining the weight of each one, and computing the sample mean package weight from the data.

2. A company receiving a large shipment of parts may want to accept delivery only if no more than 5% of the parts are defective. The decision on whether to accept the shipment might be based on a random sample of the parts.

3. An instructor is interested in determining if assigning case studies increases the student test scores in the course. She could assign cases in one section and not in the other. Then by collecting data from each class she could determine if there is strong evidence that the use of case studies increases exam scores.

4. A news reporter wants to know if a tax reform appeals equally to men and women. To test this he obtains the opinions of randomly selected men and women. That data is used to provide an answer.

These examples are based on a common theme. We form a hypothesis about some population and then use sample data to test the validity of that hypothesis.

9.1   CONCEPTS OF HYPOTHESIS TESTING

Here we will introduce a general framework for testing hypotheses given that we are using statistics computed from random samples. Given that these statistics have a sampling distribution, we know that our decision is made in the face of random variation. This requires that we have clear decision rules for choosing between the alternatives. The process we will develop here is analogous to a jury trial. In a jury trial we begin by assuming that the person is innocent and will only be convicted if there is strong evidence against the presumption of innocence. That process has rigorous procedures for presenting and evaluating evidence, a judge to enforce the rules, and a decision mechanism—the jury. A person found guilty has a high likelihood of being guilty because of the initial presumption of innocence. However, the initial presumption or hypothesis also has the possibility that a number of guilty people will be acquitted.

We will begin our general discussion by using θ to denote a population probability distribution parameter of interest, such as the mean, variance, or proportion. Our discussion begins with a hypothesis about the parameter that will be maintained unless there is strong contrary evidence. This hypothesis can be thought of as a maintained hypothesis. In statistical language it is called the **null hypothesis**. For example we might initially accept the cereal manufacturer's claim that, on average, the contents of the packages weigh at least 16 ounces. Then after collecting sample data this hypothesis can be tested. If the null hypothesis is not true then some alternative must be true. In carrying out a hypothesis test the investigator defines an **alternative hypothesis** against which the null hypothesis is tested.

For this cereal example a likely alternative is that on average package weights are less than 16 ounces. These hypotheses are chosen such that one or the other must be true. The null hypothesis will be denoted as H_0 and the alternative hypothesis as H_1.

Our analysis will be designed with the objective of seeking strong evidence to reject the null hypothesis and accept the alternative hypothesis. We will only reject the null hypothesis when there is a small probability that the null hypothesis is true. Thus rejection will provide strong evidence against H_0 and in favor of the alternative hypothesis, H_1. If we fail to reject H_0 then either H_0 is true or our evidence is not sufficient to reject H_0 and hence accept H_1. When we fail to reject there is often a high probability of error and we do not have strong evidence to accept H_0. Thus we will be more comfortable with our decision if we reject H_0 and accept H_1.

A hypothesis, whether null or alternative, might specify a single value, say θ_0, for the population parameter θ. In that case, the hypothesis is said to be a simple hypothesis designated as

$$H_0 : \theta = \theta_0$$

that is read as, "The null hypothesis is that the population parameter θ is equal to the specific value θ_0." For example, a cereal production manager might begin his study of the packaging process with the null hypothesis that the mean package weight is 16 ounces.

Alternatively, a range of values might be specified for the unknown parameter. We define such a hypothesis as a composite hypothesis, and it will hold true for more than one value of the population parameter. For example, if we define the null hypothesis as the average weight is greater than 16 ounces, then we have a composite hypothesis. This hypothesis would be true for any population mean weight greater than 16 ounces.

In many applications, a simple null hypothesis, say

$$H_0 : \theta = \theta_0$$

is tested against a composite alternative. One possibility would be to test the null hypothesis against the general two-sided composite hypothesis

$$H_1 : \theta \neq \theta_0$$

In other cases, only alternatives on one side of the null hypothesis are of interest. For example, a consumer protection inspector would be perfectly happy if the mean cereal package weight were greater than 16 ounces. Then we could write the null hypothesis as

$$H_0 : \theta \geq \theta_0$$

and the alternative hypothesis of interest might be

$$H_1 : \theta < \theta_0$$

We call these hypotheses one-sided composite alternatives

The specification of null and alternative hypotheses depends on the problem as indicated in the following examples:

1. Let θ denote the population mean weight (in ounces) of cereal per box. The null hypothesis is that this mean is at least 16 ounces

$$H_0 : \theta \geq 16$$

and the obvious alternative is that the weight is less than 16 ounces

$$H_1 : \theta < 16$$

For this problem we would be seeking strong evidence that the mean weight of packages is less than 16 ounces. For example, a regulatory agency might be considering legal action against a company that is believed to have low package weights. The agency would only take action if it had strong evidence that results from rejecting H_0.

2. A company intends to accept delivery of parts unless it has evidence to suspect that more than 5% are defective. Let θ denote the population proportion of defectives. The null hypothesis is that the proportion is less than 0.05, that is

$$H_0: \theta \leq 0.05$$

and the alternative hypothesis is

$$H_1: \theta > 0.05$$

The null hypothesis is that the shipment of parts is of adequate quality overall, while the alternative is that the shipment is not of adequate quality. In this case the shipment would only be rejected if there is strong evidence that there are more than 5% defectives.

3. Suppose an instructor conjectures that completing assigned cases does not change overall examination scores. Let θ denote the difference between mean final examination scores in two classes with and without case studies. The null hypothesis is the simple hypothesis

$$H_0: \theta = 0$$

The alternative of interest is that the use of cases actually increases average examination scores and thus the alternative hypothesis is

$$H_1: \theta > 0$$

In this problem the instructor would only decide to assign cases if there is strong evidence that using cases increases mean examination scores. Strong evidence would result from rejecting H_0 and accepting H_1.

4. A reporter might hold, as a working hypothesis, that a new tax proposal is equally appealing to men and women. Using θ as the difference—proportion of men favoring minus the proportion of women favoring—between the two population proportions in favor of the proposal, then the null hypothesis is

$$H_0: \theta = 0$$

If the reporter has no good reason to suspect that the bulk of support comes from either men or women, then this null hypothesis would be tested against the two-sided composite alternative hypothesis

$$H_1: \theta \neq 0$$

In this example, rejection of H_0 would provide strong evidence that there is a difference between men and women in their reponse to the tax proposal.

Once we have specified a null and alternative hypothesis and collected sample data, a decision concerning the null hypothesis must be made. We can either accept the null hypothesis or reject it in favor of the alternative. For good reasons many statisticians prefer not to use the term "accept the null hypothesis" and instead say "fail to reject." When we accept or fail to reject the null hypothesis, then either the hypothesis is true or our test procedure was not strong enough to reject and we have committed an error. **When we use the** term "accept a null hypothesis" in this book that statement can be considered shorthand for failure to reject and should be interpreted in that way. To select the hypothesis—null or alternative—a decision rule based on sample evidence needs to be developed. Further on in this chapter we will present specific decision rules for various problems. In many cases the form of the rule is fairly obvious. If we wanted to test the null hypothesis that the average weight of cereal boxes is greater than 16 ounces, we would take a random sample of boxes and compute the sample mean. If the sample mean was substantially below 16 ounces, that could lead us to reject the null hypothesis and accept the alternative hypothesis. In general, the lower the sample mean is below 16 the greater the chance of rejecting the null hypothesis.

From our discussion of sampling distributions in Chapter 7 we know that the sample mean is different from the population mean. With only a sample mean we cannot be certain of the value of the population mean. Thus the decision rule we adopt will have some chance of reaching an erroneous conclusion. Table 9.1 summarizes the possible types of error. One error we call Type I error. **Type I error** is defined as the rejection of the null hypothesis when the null hypothesis is true. We will see that our decision rules will be defined so that the probability of rejecting a true null hypothesis, denoted as α, is "small." The probability, α, is defined as the significance level of the test. Since the null hypothesis is either accepted or rejected, it follows that the probability of accepting the null hypothesis when it is true is $(1 - \alpha)$. The other possible error, called a **Type II error,** arises when a false null hypothesis is accepted. We say that for a particular decision rule, the probability of making such an error when the null hypothesis is false is denoted β. Then, the probability of rejecting a false null hypothesis is $(1 - \beta)$, which is called the power of the test.

We will illustrate these ideas by reference to one of our earlier examples. Our news reporter is trying to determine if a tax reform proposal appeals equally to men and women. The null hypothesis is that in the population the proportion of men favoring the proposal is equal to the proportion of women favoring the proposal. This null hypothesis is tested against the alternative that the two proportions differ. To test the hypothesis, independent random samples of men and women are obtained and the sample proportions favoring the proposal are computed. Then we compute the difference—proportion men favoring minus proportion women favoring—between the two sample proportions. If this difference in the sample proportions is large we would reject the null hypothesis that the population proportions are equal, otherwise the null hypothesis would be accepted. Let p_x denote the sample proportion of men and p_y the sample proportion of women in favor of the tax reform proposal. Then a possible decision rule is

$$\text{Reject } H_0 \text{ if } \quad (p_x - p_y) > 0.038 \quad \text{or} \quad (p_x - p_y) < -0.038$$

Now, suppose that the null hypothesis is true. We could still find that the sample proportions differ by more than 0.038 and, according to our decision rule, the null hypothesis would be rejected. In that case, a Type I error would have occurred. The probability of rejec-

TABLE 9.1
States of Nature and Decisions on Null Hypothesis, with Probabilities of Making the Decisions, Given the States of Nature

	STATES OF NATURE	
Decisions on Null Hypothesis	**Null Hypothesis is True**	**Null Hypothesis is False**
Accept (Fail to Reject)	Correct Decision Probability $= 1 - \alpha$	Type II error Probability $= \beta$
Reject	Type I error Probability $= \alpha$ (α is called the significance level)	Correct decision Probability $= 1 - \beta$ ($1 - \beta$ is called power)

tion when the null hypothesis is true is the significance level α. By contrast, suppose that the null hypothesis is false—the population proportions of men and women favoring the proposal are not equal. The sample proportions could differ by less than 0.038 and, according to our decision rule, the null hypothesis would be accepted. Thus a Type II error would have occurred. The probability of making such an error will depend on just how different the two population proportions are. We would be less likely to accept the null hypothesis for a given sample size if in the population 80% of men and 20% of women favored the proposal compared to the case where the population proportions are 55% and 45%.

Ideally we would like to have the probabilities of both types of error be as small as possible. However, there is a trade-off between the probabilities of the two types of error. Given a particular sample, any reduction in the probability of Type I error, α, will result in an increase in the probability of Type II error, β, and vice versa. We should emphasize that in general there is not a direct linear substitution—e.g., a reduction of 0.02 in α does not usually result in an increase of 0.02 in β. Thus in the above example we could reduce the probability of Type I error, α, by changing the decision rule to

$$\text{Reject } H_0 \text{ if} \quad (p_x - p_y) > 0.07 \quad \text{or} \quad (p_x - p_y) < -0.07$$

But we would be more likely to accept the null hypothesis even if the null hypothesis is false. As a result the probability of Type II error, β, would be increased. In practice we typically select a small (e.g., less than 0.10) probability of Type I error, and use that probability to set the decision rule. The probability of Type II error is then determined, as shown in Figure 9.1.

Suppose we want to test whether the true mean weight of cereal boxes is at least 16 ounces. We would begin our analysis by first fixing the probability of Type I error. In a sense this is like deciding the rules for a baseball or soccer game before the game starts instead of making up the rules as we go along. After analyzing the nature of the decision process we decide that our decision rule should have a probability of 0.05 or less of rejecting the null hypothesis when it is true. We do this by selecting an appropriate number, K, in the decision rule "Reject the null hypothesis if the sample mean is less than K ounces." In the following sections we will indicate how to choose K. Once the number K has been chosen, the probability of Type II error can be computed—for a particular value of θ included in H_1—using the procedures to be developed in Section 9.9.

Another concept used in hypothesis testing is the **power** of the test, defined as the probability of rejecting H_0 when H_1 is true. The power is computed for particular values of θ that satisfy the null hypothesis. The power is typically different for every different value of θ. Consider the cereal problem with

$$H_0 : \theta = 16$$
$$H_1 : \theta > 16$$

Thus for any value of θ contained in the null hypothesis H_1

$$\text{Power} = P\left(\text{Reject } H_0 \mid \theta, (\theta \subset H_1)\right)$$

Since the decision rule is determined by the significance level chosen for the test, the concept of power does not directly affect the decision to accept or reject a null hypothesis. However, by computing the power of the test for particular significance levels and values of

FIGURE 9.1
Consequences of Fixing the Significance Level of a Test

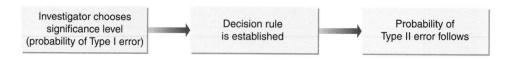

θ included in H_1 the investigator obtains valuable information about the properties of the decision rule. For example, we will see that by taking a larger sample size we can increase the power of the test for a given significance level, α. Thus an investigator will balance the increased costs of a larger sample size against the benefits of increasing the power of the test. Another important use of power calculations occurs when we have a choice between two or more possible tests that each have the same significance level, for a given sample size. Then it would be appropriate to choose the test that has the smallest probability of Type II error—that is, the test with the highest power.

In Sections 9.2 to 9.8, we show how, for given significance levels, decision rules can be formulated for some important classes of hypothesis-testing problems. We will return in Section 9.9 to consider the power of a test. A summary of the important terms and ideas we have developed thus far is included in the box.

SUMMARY OF HYPOTHESIS-TESTING TERMINOLOGY

Null Hypothesis (H_0): A maintained hypothesis that is held to be true unless sufficient evidence to the contrary is obtained.

Alternative Hypothesis (H_1): A hypothesis against which the null hypothesis is tested and which will be held to be true if the null is held false.

Simple Hypothesis: A hypothesis that specifies a single value for a population parameter of interest.

Composite Hypothesis: A hypothesis that specifies a range of values for a population parameter.

One-Sided Alternative: An alternative hypothesis involving all possible values of a population parameter on either one side or the other of (that is, either greater than or less than) the value specified by a simple null hypothesis.

Two-Sided Alternative: An alternative hypothesis involving all possible values of a population parameter other than the value specified by a simple null hypothesis.

Hypothesis Test Decisions: A decision rule is formulated, leading the investigator to either accept or reject the null hypothesis on the basis of sample evidence.

Type I Error: The rejection of a true null hypothesis.

Type II Error: The acceptance of a false null hypothesis.

Significance Level: The probability of rejecting a null hypothesis that is true. This probability is sometimes expressed as a percentage, so a test of significance level α is referred to as a $100\alpha\%$-level test.

Power: The probability of rejecting a null hypothesis that is false.

We use the terms accept—or failure to reject—and reject for possible decisions about a null hypothesis in formal summaries of the outcomes of tests. As we have noted, these terms do not adequately reflect the asymmetry of the status of null and alternative hypotheses or the consequences of a procedure in which the significance level is fixed and the probability of a Type II error is not controlled. The null hypothesis has the status of a maintained hypothesis—held to be true—unless the data contain strong evidence to reject the hypothesis. By setting the significance level, α, at a low level we ensure that the probability of rejecting a true null hypothesis is small. When we reject we know the probability of error is the significance level, α. But if we have only a small sample then we are likely to reject the null hypothesis only when it is wildly in error. As we increase the sample size we increase the probability of rejecting a false null hypothesis. But if we "accept" a null hypothesis, we have much greater uncertainty because we do not know the probability of Type II error. Thus if we fail to reject we know either that the null hypothesis is true or that our procedure for detecting a false null hypothesis does not have sufficient power—for example, the sample size is too small. Thus many analysts use the phrase "The null hypothesis is not rejected" rather than "The null hypothesis is accepted." We will use the term "accept" as an efficient way of expressing this idea, but it is important that the interpretation of this term be kept in mind.

When we reject the null hypothesis we have strong evidence that the null hypothesis is not true and therefore the alternative hypothesis is true. If we seek strong evidence in favor of a particular outcome we define that outcome as the alternative hypothesis, H_1, and the other outcome as the null hypothesis. This is called a counterfactual argument. When we reject H_0 there is strong evidence in favor of H_1 and we are confident that our decision is correct. But failing to reject leads to great uncertainty. We will see many applications of this idea in the following sections.

The analogy to a criminal trial is apparent. An accused defendant is presumed innocent—the null hypothesis—unless sufficient strong evidence is produced to indicate guilt beyond a reasonable doubt—rejection of the null hypothesis. The defendant may be found innocent either because he is innocent or because the evidence was not strong enough to convict. The burden of proof rests on the sample data.

EXERCISES

9.1 During the years 2000 and 2001 many people in Europe objected to purchasing food that was genetically modified, produced by farmers in the United States. The U.S. farmers argued that there was no scientific evidence to conclude that these products were not healthy. The Europeans argued that there still might be a problem with these foods.
(a) State the null and alternative hypotheses from the perspective of the Europeans.
(b) State the null and alternative hypotheses from the perspective of the U.S. farmers.

9.2 The 2000 presidential election in the United States was very close, and the decision came down to the results of the presidential voting in the state of Florida. The election was finally decided in favor of George W. Bush over Al Gore by a United States Supreme Court decision that stated that it was not appropriate to hand-count ballots that had been rejected by the voting machines in vari-

ous counties. At that time Bush had a small lead based on the ballots that had been counted. Imagine that you were a lawyer for George W. Bush. State your null and alternative hypothesis concerning the population vote totals for each candidate. Given your hypotheses, what would you argue about the results of the proposed recount—if it had actually occurred?

9.3 The Federal Reserve Board is meeting and attempting to decide if they should reduce interest rates in order to stimulate economic growth. State the null and alternative hypotheses regarding economic growth that the Board would formulate to guide their decision.

9.4 John Stull, Senior Vice President of Manufacturing, is seeking strong evidence to support his hope that the new operating procedures have reduced the percentage of underfilled cereal packages from the Ames production line. State his null and alternative hypotheses and indicate the results that would provide strong evidence.

9.2   TESTS OF THE MEAN OF A NORMAL DISTRIBUTION: POPULATION VARIANCE KNOWN

In this and the following sections we will present specific procedures for developing and implementing hypothesis test procedures with applications to business and economic problems. In this section our procedure will use a random sample of n normally distributed observations $x_1, x_2, \ldots, x_n$ obtained from a population with mean μ and variance σ^2 known. We will test a hypothesis concerning the unknown population mean. Later we will see that the assumption of normality can be relaxed in many cases because of the central limit theorem.

In our discussion of hypothesis testing in Section 9.1 we noted that if we reject a null hypothesis using a test with significance level α, then we know the probability of error. In this case we are either correct or we have committed a Type I error. But if we accept a null hypothesis we do not know the probability of error. Thus if we want strong evidence to support a specific position we would choose our null and alternative hypotheses such that rejecting the null hypothesis and accepting the alternative hypothesis leads to the support of our specific position. We will demonstrate this in the following example.

Consider our previous example concerning the filling of cereal boxes. Suppose that the industry regulations state that if the population mean package weight is 15.9 ounces or less for a population of packages with label weight 16 ounces then the manufacturer will be prosecuted. Thus our objective is to prove that the mean package weight μ is greater than 15.9 ounces. In this case we would state our null hypothesis as

$$H_0 : \mu = \mu_0 = 15.9$$

and the alternative hypothesis would be

$$H_1 : \mu > \mu_0 = 15.9$$

By designing our testing rule with significance level α we know that if we reject the null hypothesis then we have great confidence that the mean weight is greater than 15.9 ounces, because the probability of error is a small value α.

Our test of the population mean would use the sample mean $\overline{X}$. If the sample mean is substantially greater than $\mu_0 = 15.9$ then we would reject the null hypothesis. In order to obtain the appropriate decision value we will use the fact that the standard random variable

$$Z = \frac{\overline{X} - \mu_0}{\sigma / \sqrt{n}}$$

has a standard normal distribution mean 0 and variance 1 given that H_0 is true. Then if α is the probability of Type I error and Z is large such that

$$P(Z > Z_\alpha) = \alpha$$

then to test the null hypothesis we can use the decision rule

$$\text{Reject } H_0 \text{ if} \quad \frac{\overline{X} - \mu_0}{\sigma / \sqrt{n}} > Z_\alpha$$

It follows that the probability of rejecting the null hypothesis H_0 when it is true is the significance level α. Note also that by simple algebraic manipulation we could also state the decision rule as

$$\text{Reject } H_0 \text{ if} \quad \overline{X} > \overline{X}_c = \mu_0 + Z_\alpha \sigma / \sqrt{n}$$

This value $\overline{X}_c$ is often called the "critical value" for the decision. Note that for every value Z obtained from the standard normal distribution there is also a value $\overline{X}_c$ and either of the above decision rules provides exactly the same result.

Suppose that for this problem the population standard deviation $\sigma = 0.4$ and we obtain a random sample of size 25. For a hypothesis test with significance level $\alpha = 0.05$ the value of $Z_\alpha = 1.645$ from the standard normal table. In this case our decision rule would be

$$\text{Reject } H_0 \text{ if} \quad \frac{\overline{X} - \mu_0}{\sigma / \sqrt{n}} = \frac{\overline{X} - 15.9}{0.4 / \sqrt{25}} > 1.645$$

Equivalently the rule

$$\text{Reject } H_0 \text{ if} \quad \overline{X} > \overline{X}_c = \mu_0 + Z_\alpha \sigma / \sqrt{n} = 15.9 + 1.645 \times (0.4 / \sqrt{25}) = 16.032$$

If we rejected H_0 using this rule then we would accept the alternative hypothesis that the mean weight is greater than 15.9 ounces and know that the probability of Type I error is 0.05 or less. This would provide strong evidence to support our conclusion. The decision rules are illustrated in Figure 9.2. The hypothesis test for testing a simple null hypothesis concerning the population mean is summarized next.

A TEST OF THE MEAN OF A NORMAL POPULATION: POPULATION VARIANCE KNOWN

Given that we have a random sample of n observations from a normal population with mean μ and known variance σ^2. If the observed sample mean is $\overline{X}$, then a test with significance level α of the null hypothesis

$$H_0 : \mu = \mu_0$$

against the alternative

$$H_1 : \mu > \mu_0$$

is obtained from the decision rule

$$\text{Reject } H_0 \text{ if} \quad Z = \frac{\overline{X} - \mu_0}{\sigma / \sqrt{n}} > Z_\alpha \qquad (9.1)$$

Or equivalently

$$\text{Reject } H_0 \text{ if} \quad \overline{X} > \mu_0 + Z_\alpha \sigma / \sqrt{n}$$

where Z_α is the number for which

$$P(Z > Z_\alpha) = \alpha$$

and Z is the standard normal random variable.

FIGURE 9.2
Normal Probability Density Function Showing Both Z and X Values for the Decision Rule to Test the Null Hypothesis $H_0 : \mu = 15.9$ versus $H_1 : \mu > 15.9$

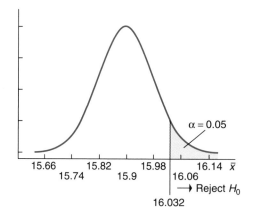
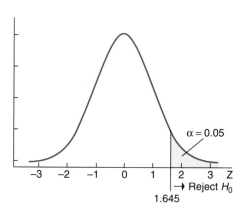

INTERPRETATION

Let us pause to consider what is meant by the rejection of a null hypothesis. In the cereal-box problem, the hypothesis that the population mean is 15.9 was rejected with significance level 0.05. This certainly does not mean that we have proved that the population mean weight exceeds 15.9 units. Given only sample information, it will never be possible to be certain about a population parameter. Rather, we might view the data as having cast some doubt on the truth of the null hypothesis. If that hypothesis were true, then if the observed value of the sample mean was 16.1 then

$$\overline{X} = 16.1$$

would represent a single observation drawn from a normal distribution with mean 15.9 and standard deviation

$$\frac{\sigma}{\sqrt{n}} = \frac{0.4}{\sqrt{25}} = 0.08$$

In testing hypotheses, we are really asking how likely it would be to observe such an extreme value if the null hypothesis were in fact true. We saw that the probability of observing a mean value greater than 16.032 is 0.05. Hence, in rejecting the null hypothesis, we are saying either that the null hypothesis is false or that we have observed an unlikely event—one that would occur only with the probability of less than specified by the significance level. This is the sense in which the sample information has aroused doubt about the null hypothesis.

p-Value

There is another popular procedure for considering the test of the null hypothesis. Notice that in our cereal problem, the null hypothesis was rejected at significance level 0.05 but would not have been rejected at the lower 0.01 level. If we lowered the significance level, we would reduce the probability of rejecting a true null hypothesis and therefore modify the decision rule to make it less likely that the null hypothesis would be rejected whether or not it is true. Obviously, the lower the significance level at which a null hypothesis can be rejected, the greater the doubt cast on its truth. Rather than testing hypotheses at preassigned levels of significance, investigators often determine the smallest level of significance at which a null hypothesis can be rejected.

We define the *p*-value as the probability of obtaining a value of the test statistic as extreme as, or more extreme than, the actual value obtained when the null hypothesis is true. Thus the *p*-value is the smallest significance level at which a null hypothesis can be rejected given the observed sample statistic. For example, suppose that in the cereal-box problem with the population mean equal to 15.9, $\sigma = 0.4$, $n = 25$ and under the null hypothesis, and we had obtained a sample mean of 16.1 ounces. Then the *p*-value would be

$$P(\overline{X} > 16.1 \mid H_0 : \mu = 15.9) = P\left(Z > \frac{16.1 - 15.9}{0.08} = 2.5\right)$$
$$= 0.0062$$

From the normal probability table we find that the probability of obtaining a sample mean of 16.1 from a normal distribution with population mean 15.9 and standard deviation of the sample mean 0.08 is equal to 0.0062. Thus the *p*-value for this test is 0.0062. Now the *p*-value (0.0062) represents the smallest significance level, α, that would lead to rejection of the null hypothesis. When the *p*-value is calculated we could test the null hypothesis by using the rule

Reject H_0: if *p*-value $< \alpha$

This rule will result in the same conclusion as obtained using Equation 9.1. There is another more important reason for the popularity of the *p*-value. The *p*-value provides more precise information about the strength of the rejection of the null hypothesis that results from the observed sample mean. Suppose that in the test of the cereal-box weight we had set the significance level at $\alpha = 0.05$—a popular choice. Then with a sample mean equal to 16.1 we would state the null hypothesis was rejected at significance level 0.05. However, in fact, that sample result points to a much stronger conclusion. We could have rejected the null hypothesis at a significance level of $\alpha = 0.0063$. Alternatively suppose that the computed *p*-value based on a different sample mean had been 0.07. In that case we could not reject the null hypothesis, but we would also know that we were quite close to rejecting the null hypothesis. In contrast a *p*-value of 0.30 would tell us that we were quite far from rejecting the null hypothesis. The popularity of the *p*-value is that it provides more information than merely stating that the null hypothesis was accepted or rejected at a particular significance level. The *p*-value is summarized next.

INTERPRETATION OF THE PROBABILITY VALUE OR *p*-VALUE

The probability value or *p*-value is the smallest significance level at which the null hypothesis can be rejected. Consider a random sample of size *n* observations from a population that has a normal distribution with mean *μ* and standard deviation *σ*, and the resulting computed sample mean, $\overline{X}$. We are asked to test the null hypothesis

$$H_0: \mu = \mu_0$$

against the alternative hypothesis

$$H_1: \mu > \mu_0$$

The *p*-value for the test is

$$p\text{-value} = P\left(\frac{\overline{X} - \mu_0}{\sigma/\sqrt{n}} \geq Z_p \mid H_0: \mu = \mu_0 \right) \tag{9.2}$$

where Z_p is the standard normal value associated with the smallest significance level at which the null hypothesis can be rejected. The *p*-value is regularly computed by most statistical computer programs and provides more information about the test, based on the observed sample mean. Thus it is a popular tool for many statistical applications.

EXAMPLE 9.1

EVALUATING A NEW PRODUCTION PROCESS (HYPOTHESIS TEST)

The production manager of Northern Windows Inc., has asked you to evaluate a proposed new procedure for producing its Regal Line of double-hung windows. The present process has a mean production of 80 units per hour with a population standard deviation of $\sigma = 8$. The manager indicates that she does not want to change to a new procedure unless there is strong evidence that the mean production level is higher with the new process.

SOLUTION

The manager will only change to the new process if there is strong evidence in its favor. Therefore, we will define the null hypothesis as

$$H_0: \mu \leq 80$$

and the alternative hypothesis as

$$H_0: \mu > 80$$

We see that if we define the significance level $\alpha = 0.05$, then if we reject the null hypothesis and conclude that the new process has higher productivity, our probability of error would be 0.05 or less. This would imply strong evidence in favor of our recommendation.

We will obtain a random sample of $n = 25$ production hours using the proposed new process and compute the sample mean $\overline{X}$. With a significance level of $\alpha = 0.05$ the decision rule would be

$$\text{Reject } H_0 \text{ if } \quad Z = \frac{\overline{X} - 80}{8/\sqrt{25}} > 1.645$$

where $z_{0.05} = 1.645$ is obtained from the standard normal table. Alternatively we could use the rule

$$\text{Reject } H_0 \text{ if } \quad \overline{X} > \mu_0 + z_\alpha \sigma / \sqrt{n} = 80 + 1.645 \times (8/\sqrt{25}) = 82.63$$

The sample mean would typically be computed using a computer package as discussed in Chapter 2.

Suppose that the resulting sample mean was $\overline{X} = 83$. Based on that result

$$Z = \frac{83 - 80}{8/\sqrt{25}} = 1.875 > 1.645$$

and we would reject the null hypothesis and conclude that there was strong evidence to support the conclusion that the new process resulted in higher productivity. Given this sample mean we could also determine the p-value for this test by determining the smallest significance value for which H_0 could be rejected, which in this case would be

$$p\text{ - value} = P(Z > 1.875) = 0.03$$

Thus we would recommend the new process to the production manager.

These computations could be made directly from the sample data in Minitab by using the command sequence

```
STAT > BASIC STATISTICS > 1-SAMPLE Z
```

and then following the dialogue box.

These computations could also be made with PHStat in Excel using the commands

```
PHStat > ONE-SAMPLE TESTS > Z TEST FOR MEAN SIGMA KNOWN
```

Suppose that in place of the simple null hypothesis, $H_0 : \mu = \mu_0$, we had wanted to test the composite null hypothesis

$$H_0 : \mu \leq \mu_0$$

against the alternative hypothesis

$$H_1 : \mu > \mu_0$$

at significance level α. The resulting test would have the same decision rule as presented in Equation 9.1 and the p-value results would also be the same. Essentially we use the value of the parameter in the composite null hypothesis that is closest to the alternative hypothesis mean and proceed as we would using the simple hypothesis. In this case any value of the mean less than μ_0 would have a smaller significance value and p-value and thus our test is conservative.

A TEST OF THE MEAN OF A NORMAL DISTRIBUTION (VARIANCE KNOWN): COMPOSITE NULL AND ALTERNATIVE HYPOTHESIS

The appropriate procedure for testing, at significance level α, the null hypothesis

$$H_0: \mu \leq \mu_0$$

against the alternative hypothesis

$$H_1: \mu > \mu_0$$

is precisely the same as when the null hypothesis is $H_0: \mu = \mu_0$. In addition, the p-values are also computed in exactly the same way.

Consider our previous example concerning the filling of cereal boxes. Suppose that the industry regulations state that if the mean package weight is not 16 ounces or more for a population of packages with label weight 16 ounces then the company will be prosecuted. In this situation, we as the regulators could only prosecute if we found strong evidence that the mean package weight was less than 16 ounces. Thus our objective is to prove that the mean package weight μ is not 16.0 ounces or more. In this case we would state the simple null hypothesis as

$$H_0: \mu = \mu_0 = 16.0$$

or using the composite hypothesis

$$H_0: \mu \geq \mu_0 = 16.0$$

and the alternative hypothesis would be

$$H_1: \mu < \mu_0 = 16.0$$

for either the simple or composite hypothesis. By designing our testing rule with significance level α we know that if we reject the null hypothesis then we have great confidence that the mean weight is less than 16.0 ounces, because the probability of a Type I error is a small value α.

Our test of the population mean would use the sample mean $\overline{X}$. If the sample mean is substantially less than $\mu_0 = 16.0$ then we would reject the null hypothesis. In order to obtain the appropriate decision value we will use the fact that the standard random variable

$$Z = \frac{\overline{X} - \mu_0}{\sigma/\sqrt{n}}$$

has a standard normal distribution mean 0 and variance 1 when the population mean is μ_0. Then if Z has a large negative value such that

$$P(Z < -Z_\alpha) = \alpha$$

then to test the null hypothesis we can use the decision rule

$$\text{Reject } H_0 \text{ if } \quad \frac{\overline{X} - \mu_0}{\sigma/\sqrt{n}} < -Z_\alpha$$

It follows that the probability of rejecting the null hypothesis H_0 when it is true is the significance level α. Note also that by simple algebraic manipulation we could also state the decision rule as

$$\text{Reject } H_0 \text{ if } \quad \overline{X} < \overline{X}_c = \mu_0 - Z_\alpha \sigma/\sqrt{n}$$

This value $\overline{X}_c$ is often called the "critical value" for the decision. Note that for every value $-Z_\alpha$ obtained from the standard normal distribution there is also a value $\overline{X}_c$ and either of the preceding decision rules provides exactly the same result.

Suppose that for this problem the population standard deviation $\sigma = 0.4$ and we obtain a random sample of size 25. For a hypothesis test with significance level $\alpha = 0.05$ the value of $Z_\alpha = 1.645$ from the standard normal table. In this case our decision rule would be

$$\text{Reject } H_0 \text{ if } \quad \frac{\overline{X} - \mu_0}{\sigma/\sqrt{n}} = \frac{\overline{X} - 16.0}{0.4/\sqrt{25}} < -1.645$$

or we could use the rule

$$\text{Reject } H_0 \text{ if } \quad \overline{X} < \overline{X}_c = \mu_0 - Z_\alpha \sigma / \sqrt{n} = 16.0 - 1.645 \times (0.4 / \sqrt{25}) = 15.868$$

If we rejected H_0 using this rule, then we would accept the alternative hypothesis that the mean weight is less than 16.0 ounces and know that the probability of error is 0.05 or less. This would provide strong evidence to support our conclusion. This decision rule is illustrated in Figure 9.3.

Note that this hypothesis test is the complement of the first example. The hypothesis testing rules for alternative hypotheses dealing with the lower tail are mirror images of those dealing with the upper tail of the distribution. Computation of p-values would also follow using the lower tail instead of the upper tail probabilities. This result is summarized in Equation 9.3.

The cereal examples presented us with two different objectives. In the first case we wanted strong evidence that the mean weight was greater than 16 ounces and thus the null hypothesis was

$$H_0 : \mu \leq 16$$

FIGURE 9.3

Normal Probability Density Function Showing X Values for the Decision Rule to Test the Null Hypothesis $H_0 : \mu \geq 16.0$ versus $H_0 : \mu < 16.0$

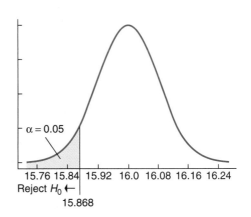

In the second case we wanted strong evidence that the mean was less than 16 ounces and therefore we defined the null hypothesis as

$$H_0: \mu \geq 16$$

Possibilities of this type are present in many decision situations and the decision maker is required to determine which option should be used in the particular problem being considered.

A TEST OF THE MEAN OF A NORMAL DISTRIBUTION (VARIANCE KNOWN): COMPOSITE OR SIMPLE NULL AND ALTERNATIVE HYPOTHESIS

The appropriate procedure for testing, at significance level α, the null hypothesis

$$H_0: \mu = \mu_0 \quad \text{or} \quad H_0: \mu \geq \mu_0$$

against the alternative hypothesis

$$H_1: \mu < \mu_0$$

uses the decision rule

$$\text{Reject } H_0 \text{ if} \quad Z = \frac{\overline{X} - \mu_0}{\sigma/\sqrt{n}} < -Z_\alpha$$

Or equivalently

$$\text{Reject } H_0 \text{ if} \quad \overline{X} < \overline{X}_c = \mu_0 - Z_\alpha \sigma/\sqrt{n} \tag{9.3}$$

Where $-Z_\alpha$ is the number for which

$$P(Z < -Z_\alpha) = \alpha$$

and Z is the standard normal random variable.
   In addition the p-values can also be computed by using the lower tail probabilities.

EXAMPLE 9.2

BALL BEARING PRODUCTION (HYPOTHESIS TEST)

The production manager of Twin Forks Ball Bearing Inc. has asked your assistance in evaluating a modified ball bearing production process. When the process is operating properly the process produces ball bearings whose weights are normally distributed with population mean 5 ounces and population standard deviation of 0.1 ounce. A new raw material supplier was used for a recent production run, and the manager wants to know if that change has resulted in a lowering of the mean weight of the ball bearings. There is no reason to suspect a problem with the new supplier and the manager will continue to use the new supplier unless there is strong evidence that underweight ball bearings are being produced.

SOLUTION

In this case we are interested in knowing if there is strong evidence to conclude that lower weight bearings are being produced. Therefore we will test the null hypothesis

$$H_0: \mu = \mu_0 = 5$$

against the alternative hypothesis

$$H_1: \mu < 5$$

Note how the notion of strong evidence leads us to choose the null and alternative hypotheses. We will only take action if we reject the null and accept the alternative because we can specify the significance level. We will specify our significance level at $\alpha = 0.05$ and thus the corresponding lower tail value for the standard normal random variable is $Z_\alpha = 1.645$ from the normal distribution table. For this problem we have taken a random sample of $n = 16$ observations and found that the sample mean was $\bar{X} = 4.962$. Now our decision rule for this problem is

$$\text{Reject } H_0: \text{ if } \quad Z = \frac{\bar{X} - \mu_0}{\sigma/\sqrt{n}} = \frac{4.962 - 5.0}{0.1/\sqrt{16}} = -1.52 < -1.645$$

We see that we cannot reject the null hypothesis H_0 and thus we conclude that we do not have strong evidence that the production process is producing underweight ball bearings.

We could also determine the p-value for this sample result by noting that for the standard normal distribution

$$p\text{-value} = P(Z < -1.52) = 0.0643$$

And of course we could use a computer to compute the p-value and the result of the hypothesis test as we did in Example 9.1.

Two-Sided Alternative Hypothesis

There are some problems where deviations either too high or too low are of equal importance. For example the diameter of an automobile engine piston cannot be too large or too small. In those situations we consider the test of the null hypothesis

$$H_0: \mu = \mu_0$$

against the alternative hypothesis

$$H_1: \mu \neq \mu_0$$

Here we assume no strong reason for suspecting departures either above or below the hypothesized population mean, μ_0. The null hypothesis would be doubted if the sample mean were much greater or much smaller than μ_0. Again if the random variable has a normal distribution with known variance, σ, we would obtain a test with significance level α by using the result that under the null hypothesis

$$P(Z > Z_{\alpha/2}) = \frac{\alpha}{2} \quad \text{and} \quad P(Z < -Z_{\alpha/2}) = \frac{\alpha}{2}$$

In this case we have divided the significance level α equally between the two tails of the normal distribution. Hence, the probability that Z either exceeds $Z_{\alpha/2}$ or is less than $-Z_{\alpha/2}$ is α. The decision rule for a test with significance level α is

$$\text{Reject } H_0: \text{ if } \quad \frac{\bar{X} - \mu_0}{\sigma/\sqrt{n}} \text{ is either bigger than } Z_{\alpha/2} \text{ or less than } -Z_{\alpha/2}$$

These results are summarized in Equation 9.4.

A TEST OF THE MEAN OF A NORMAL DISTRIBUTION AGAINST TWO-SIDED ALTERNATIVE: σ KNOWN

The appropriate procedure for testing, at significance level α, the null hypothesis

$$H_0 : \mu = \mu_0$$

against the alternative hypothesis

$$H_1 : \mu \neq \mu_0$$

is obtained from the decision rule

$$\text{Reject } H_0 \text{ if } \quad Z = \frac{\overline{X} - \mu_0}{\sigma/\sqrt{n}} < -Z_{\alpha/2} \quad \text{or} \quad \text{Reject } H_0 \text{ if } \quad Z = \frac{\overline{X} - \mu_0}{\sigma/\sqrt{n}} > Z_{\alpha/2} \quad (9.4)$$

equivalently

$$\text{Reject } H_0 \text{ if } \quad \overline{X} < \mu_0 - Z_{\alpha/2}\sigma/\sqrt{n} \quad \text{or} \quad \text{Reject } H_0 \text{ if } \quad \overline{X} > \mu_0 + Z_{a/2}\sigma/\sqrt{n}$$

In addition the p-values can also be computed by noting that the corresponding tail probability would be doubled to reflect a p-value that refers to the sum of the upper and lower tail probabilities for the positive and negative values of Z. The p-value for the two tailed test is

$$p\text{-value} = 2P\left(\left| \frac{\overline{X} - \mu_0}{\sigma/\sqrt{n}} \right| > Z_{p/2} \mid H_0 : \mu = \mu_0 \right) \quad (9.5)$$

where $Z_{p/2}$ is the standard normal value associated with the smallest probability of rejecting the null hypothesis at either tail of the probability distribution.

EXAMPLE 9.3

ANALYSIS OF DRILL HOLE DIAMETERS (HYPOTHESIS TEST)

The production manager of Circuits Unlimited has asked for your assistance in analyzing a production process. This process involves drilling holes whose diameters are normally distributed with population mean 2 inches and population standard deviation 0.06 inches. A random sample of 9 measurements had a sample mean of 1.95 inches. Use a significance level of $\alpha = 0.05$ to determine if the observed sample mean is unusual and suggests that the drilling machine should be adjusted.

SOLUTION

In this case the diameter could be either too large or too small. Therefore we would do a two-tailed hypothesis test with the null hypothesis

$$H_0 : \mu = 2.0$$

and the alternative hypothesis

$$H_1 : \mu \neq 2.0$$

The decision rule is to reject H_0 in favor of H_1 if

$$Z = \frac{\overline{X} - \mu_0}{\sigma/\sqrt{n}} < -Z_{\alpha/2} \quad \text{or} \quad Z = \frac{\overline{X} - \mu_0}{\sigma/\sqrt{n}} > Z_{\alpha/2}$$

and for this problem

$$\frac{\overline{X} - \mu_0}{\sigma/\sqrt{n}} = \frac{1.95 - 2.0}{0.06/\sqrt{9}} = -2.50$$

for a 5%-level test $\alpha = 0.05$ and $Z_{\alpha/2} = Z_{0.05/2} = 1.96$. Thus since -2.50 is less than -1.96, we reject the null hypothesis and conclude that the drilling machine requires adjustment.

To compute the p-value we first find that the probability of obtaining Z less than -2.50 from the normal table is 0.0062. Here we want the p-value for a two-tailed test and we must double the one-tail value. Thus the p-value for this test is 0.0124, and the null hypothesis would have been rejected for a significance level above 1.24%.

EXERCISES

9.5 A manufacturer of detergent claims that the contents of boxes sold weigh on average at least 16 ounces. The distribution of weight is known to be normal, with standard deviation .4 ounce. A random sample of 16 boxes yielded a sample mean weight of 15.84 ounces. Test at the 10% significance level the null hypothesis that the population mean weight is at least 16 ounces.

9.6 A company which receives shipments of batteries tests a random sample of nine of them before agreeing to take a shipment. The company is concerned that the true mean lifetime for all batteries in the shipment should be at least 50 hours. From past experience, it is safe to conclude that the population distribution of lifetimes is normal, with standard deviation 3 hours. For one particular shipment, the mean lifetime for a sample of nine batteries was 48.2 hours. Test at the 10% level the null hypothesis that the population mean lifetime is at least 50 hours.

9.7 A pharmaceutical manufacturer is concerned about the impurity concentration in pills, and it is anxious that this concentration does not exceed 3%. It is known that from a particular production run, impurity concentrations follow a normal distribution with standard deviation .4%. A random sample of 64 pills from a production run was checked, and the sample mean impurity concentration was found to be 3.07%.

(a) Test at the 5% level the null hypothesis that the population mean impurity concentration is 3% against the alternative that it is more than 3%.

(b) Find the p-value for this test.

(c) Suppose that the alternative hypothesis had been two-sided rather than one-sided (with null hypothesis $H_0 : \mu = 3$). State, without doing the calculations, whether the p-value of the test would be higher than, lower than, or the same as that found in (b). Sketch a graph to illustrate your reasoning.

(d) In the context of this problem, explain why a one-sided alternative hypothesis is more appropriate than a two-sided alternative.

9.3 TESTS OF THE MEAN OF A NORMAL DISTRIBUTION: POPULATION VARIANCE UNKNOWN

In this section we consider the same set of hypothesis tests we discussed in Section 9.2. The only difference is that the population variance is unknown, and thus we must use tests based on the student t distribution. We introduced the Student's t distribution in Section 8.3 and showed its application for developing confidence intervals. Recall that the Student's t distribution depends on the degrees of freedom for computing the sample variance, $n - 1$. In addition, the Student's t distribution becomes close to the normal distribution as the sample size increases. Thus for sample sizes over 100 the normal can be used to approximate the Student's t distribution. Using the sample mean and variance we know that the random variable

$$t_{n-1} = \frac{\overline{X} - \mu}{s/\sqrt{n}}$$

follows a Student's t distribution. The procedures for performing hypothesis tests using the sample variance are defined in Equations 9.6 and 9.7.

TESTS OF THE MEAN OF A NORMAL DISTRIBUTION: POPULATION VARIANCE UNKNOWN

We are given a random sample of n observations from a normal population with mean μ. Using the sample mean and sample standard deviation $\overline{X}$ and s, we can use the following tests with significance level α.

i. To test either null hypothesis

$$H_0: \mu = \mu_0 \quad \text{or} \quad H_0: \mu \leq \mu_0$$

against the alternative

$$H_1: \mu > \mu_0$$

the decision rule is

$$\text{Reject } H_0 \text{ if} \quad t = \frac{\overline{X} - \mu_0}{s/\sqrt{n}} > t_{n-1,\alpha}$$

Or equivalently

$$\text{Reject } H_0 \text{ if} \quad \overline{X} > \overline{X}_c = \mu_0 + t_{n-1,\alpha}\, s/\sqrt{n} \tag{9.6}$$

ii. To test either the null hypothesis

$$H_0: \mu = \mu_0 \quad \text{or} \quad H_0: \mu \geq \mu_0$$

against the alternative

$$H_1: \mu < \mu_0$$

the decision rule is

$$\text{Reject } H_0 \text{ if} \quad t = \frac{\overline{X} - \mu_0}{s/\sqrt{n}} < -t_{n-1,\alpha} \tag{9.7}$$

Or equivalently

$$\text{Reject } H_0 \text{ if} \quad \overline{X} < \overline{X}_c = \mu_0 - t_{n-1,\alpha}\, s/\sqrt{n}$$

iii. To test the null hypothesis

$$H_0: \mu = \mu_0$$

against the alternative hypothesis

$$H_1 : \mu \neq \mu_0$$

the decision rule is

Reject H_0 if $\quad t = \dfrac{\overline{X} - \mu_0}{s/\sqrt{n}} < -t_{n-1,\alpha/2} \quad$ or $\quad$ Reject H_0 if $\quad t = \dfrac{\overline{X} - \mu_0}{s/\sqrt{n}} > t_{n-1,\alpha/2}$

$$(9.8)$$

equivalently

Reject H_0 if $\quad \overline{X} < \mu_0 - t_{n-1,\alpha/2} s/\sqrt{n} \quad$ or $\quad$ Reject H_0 if $\quad \overline{X} > \mu_0 + t_{n-1,\alpha/2} s/\sqrt{n}$

where $t_{n-1,\alpha/2}$ is the student t value for $n-1$ degrees of freedom and upper tail probability $\alpha/2$.

The p-values for these tests are computed in the same way as we did for tests with known variance except that the Student's t value is substituted for the normal Z value.

EXAMPLE 9.4

ANALYSIS OF WEEKLY SALES OF FROZEN BROCCOLI (HYPOTHESIS TEST)

Broccoli

Grand Junction Vegetables is a producer of a wide variety of frozen vegetables. The company president has asked you to determine if the weekly sales of 16-ounce packages of frozen broccoli has increased. The weekly sales per store has had a mean of 2,400 packages over the past 6 months. You have obtained a random sample of sales data from 134 stores for your study. The data is stored in the file **Broccoli**.

SOLUTION

Given the project objectives you decide that you will test the hypothesis that population mean sales are 2,400 versus the alternative that sales have increased using a significance level $\alpha = 0.05$. The null hypothesis is

$$H_0 : \mu = 2,400$$

versus the alternative hypothesis

$$H_1 : \mu > 2,400$$

We are interested in the sales of broccoli. Figure 9.4 shows the Minitab output containing the sample mean and variance. This result was created using the Minitab command sequence

```
STAT > BASIC STATISTICS > DISPLAY DESCRIPTIVE STATISTICS >
SELECT 'BROCCOLI'
```

FIGURE 9.4
Minitab Output for Broccoli Sales

Descriptive Statistics: Broccoli

Variable	N	Mean	Median	TrMean	StDev	SE Mean
Broccoli	134	3593	2181	2792	4919	425

Variable	Minimum	Maximum	Q1	Q3
Broccoli	156	27254	707	3300

INTERPRETATION

From the Minitab output we see that the sample mean is much larger than the median and that the upper quartile has a very wide range. Thus it is clear that the distribution of the individual observations is not a normal distribution. But the sample size is large, and thus by applying the central limit theorem from Chapter 7 we can assume that the sampling distribution for the sample mean is normal; therefore, a Student's t test would be appropriate for the hypothesis test. We see that the sample mean is 3,593 and the sample standard deviation is 4,919. The t statistic for the test is

$$t = \frac{3,593 - 2,400}{4,919/\sqrt{134}} = 2.81$$

The value of t for $n - 1 = 133$ degrees of freedom and $\alpha = 0.05$ for the upper tail is—from the t distribution table—1.645. Based on this result we would reject the null hypothesis and conclude that mean sales had increased.

We could also use the Minitab commands

```
STAT > BASIC STATISTICS > 1-SAMPLE T
```

and the instructions in the dialog box to compute all of the results directly without first using Descriptive Statistics.

EXERCISES

9.8 An engineering research center claims that through the use of a new computer control system, automobiles should achieve on average an additional 3 miles per gallon of gas. A random sample of 100 automobiles was used to evaluate this product. The sample mean increase in miles per gallon achieved was 2.4 and the sample standard deviation was 1.8 miles per gallon. Test the null hypothesis that the population mean is at least 3 miles per gallon. Find the p-value of this test, and interpret your findings.

9.9 A random sample of 1,562 undergraduates enrolled in management ethics courses was asked to respond on a scale from one (strongly disagree) to seven (strongly agree) to the proposition: "Senior corporate executives are interested in social justice." The sample mean response was 4.27 and the sample standard deviation was 1.32. Test at the 1% level, against a two-sided alternative, the null hypothesis that the population mean is 4.

9.10 A random sample of 76 percentage changes in promised health benefits of single employer plans after the establishment of the Health Benefit Guarantee Corporation was observed. The sample mean percentage change was .078 and the sample standard deviation was .201. Find and interpret the p-value of a test of the null hypothesis that the populations mean percentage change is 0, against a two-sided alternative.

9.11 A random sample of 172 marketing students was asked to rate on a scale from one (not important) to five (extremely important) health benefits as a job characteris-

tic. The sample mean rating was 3.31 and the sample standard deviation was .70. Test at the 1% significance level the null hypothesis that the population mean rating is at most 3.0 against the alternative that it is bigger than 3.0.

9.12 A random sample of 170 people was provided with a forecasting problem. Each sample member was given, in two ways, the task of forecasting the next value of a retail sales variable. The previous 20 values were presented both as numbers and as points on a graph. Subjects were asked to predict the next value. The absolute forecasting errors were measured. The sample then consisted of 170 differences in absolute forecast errors (numerical minus graphical). The sample mean of these differences was −2.91 and the sample standard deviation was 11.33. Find and interpret the p-value of a test of the null hypothesis that the population mean difference is 0, against the alternative that it is negative. (The alternative can be viewed as the hypothesis that, in the aggregate, people are more successful at graphical than numerical prediction.)

9.13 The accounts of a corporation show that, on average, accounts payable are $125.32. An auditor checked a random sample of 16 of these accounts. The sample mean was $131.78 and the sample standard deviation was $25.41. Assume that the population distribution is normal. Test as the 5% significance level against a two-sided alternative the null hypothesis that the population mean is $125.32.

9.14 On the basis of a random sample, the null hypothesis

$$H_0 : \mu = \mu_0$$

is tested against the alternative

$$H_1 : \mu > \mu_0$$

and the null hypothesis is not rejected at the 5% significance level.

(a) Does this necessarily imply that μ_0 is contained in the 95% confidence interval for μ?

(b) Does this necessarily imply that μ_0 is contained in the 90% confidence interval for μ, if the observed sample mean is bigger than μ_0?

9.15 A company selling licenses for new e-commerce computer software advertises that firms using this software obtain, on average during the first year, a yield of 10% on their initial investments. A random sample of 10 of these franchises produced the following yields for the first year of operation:

6.1   9.2   11.5   8.6   12.1   3.9   8.4   10.1   9.4   8.9

Assuming that population yields are normally distributed, test the company's claim.

9.16 A process that produces bottles of shampoo, when operating correctly, produces bottles whose contents weigh, on average, 20 ounces. A random sample of nine bottles from a single production run yielded the following content weights (in ounces):

21.4   19.7   19.7   20.6   20.8   20.1   19.7   20.3   20.9

Assuming that the population distribution is normal, test at the 5% level against a two-sided alternative the null hypothesis that the process is operating correctly.

9.17 A statistics instructor is interested in the ability of students to assess the difficulty of a test they have taken. This test was taken by a large group of students, and the average score was 78.5. A random sample of eight students was asked to predict this average score. Their predictions were:

72   83   78   65   69   77   81   71

Assuming a normal distribution, test the null hypothesis that the population mean prediction would be 78.5. Use a two-sided alternative and a 10% significance level.

9.18 A beer distributor claims that a new display, featuring a life-size picture of a well-known rock singer, will increase product sales in supermarkets by an average of 50 cases in a week. For a random sample of 20 high-volume liquor outlets, the average sales increase was 41.3 cases and the sample standard deviation was 12.2 cases. Test at the 5% level the null hypothesis that the population mean sales increase is at least 50 cases, stating any assumption you make.

9.19 In contract negotiations, a company claims that a new incentive scheme has resulted in average weekly earnings of at least $400 for all customer service workers. A union representative takes a random sample of 15 workers and finds that their weekly earnings have an average of $381.35 and a standard deviation of $48.60. Assume a normal distribution.

(a) Test the company's claim.

(b) If the same sample results had been obtained from a random sample of 50 employees, could the company's claim be rejected at a lower significance level than in part (a)?

9.4   TESTS FOR THE POPULATION PROPORTION (LARGE SAMPLES)

Another important set of business and economics problems involve population proportions. Business executives are interested in the percent market share for their products and government officials are interested in the percentage of people that support a proposed new program. Thus inference about the population proportion based on sample proportions is an important application of hypothesis testing.

From our work in Chapter 6 we know that the distribution of the sample proportion can be approximated quite accurately by using the normal distribution. In this approximation we denote π as the population proportion and p as the sample proportion. Thus the sample proportion p estimated from a random sample of size n has an approximate normal distribution with mean π and variance $\pi(1 - \pi)/n$. Then the standard normal statistic is

$$Z = \frac{p - \pi}{\sqrt{\pi(1 - \pi)/n}}$$

If the null hypothesis is that the population proportion is

$$H_0: \pi = \pi_0$$

it follows that when this hypothesis is true, the random variable

$$Z = \frac{p - \pi_0}{\sqrt{\pi_0(1 - \pi_0)/n}}$$

approximately follows a standard normal distribution. Using that result we can define the tests.

TESTS OF THE POPULATION PROPORTION (LARGE SAMPLE SIZES)

We begin by assuming a random sample of n observations from a population, that has a proportion π whose members possess a particular attribute. If $n\pi(1 - \pi) > 9$ and the sample proportion is p the following tests have significance level α:

i. To test either the null hypothesis

$$H_0: \pi = \pi_0 \quad \text{or} \quad H_0: \pi \leq \pi_0$$

against the alternative

$$H_1: \pi > \pi_0$$

the decision rule is

$$\text{Reject } H_0 \text{ if } \quad \frac{p - \pi_0}{\sqrt{\pi_0(1 - \pi_0)/n}} > Z_\alpha \qquad \textbf{(9.9)}$$

ii. To test either the null hypothesis

$$H_0: \pi = \pi_0 \quad \text{or} \quad H_0: \pi \geq \pi_0$$

against the alternative

$$H_1: \pi < \pi_0$$

the decision rule is

$$\text{Reject } H_0 \text{ if } \quad \frac{p - \pi_0}{\sqrt{\pi_0(1 - \pi_0)/n}} < -Z_\alpha \qquad \textbf{(9.10)}$$

iii. To test the null hypothesis

$$H_0: \pi = \pi_0$$

against the two-sided alternative

$$H_1: \pi \neq \pi_0$$

the decision rule is

$$\text{Reject } H_0 \text{ if } \quad \frac{p - \pi_0}{\sqrt{\pi_0(1 - \pi_0)/n}} > Z_{\alpha/2} \quad \text{or} \quad \frac{p - \pi_0}{\sqrt{\pi_0(1 - \pi_0)/n}} < -Z_{\alpha/2} \qquad \textbf{(9.11)}$$

For all of these tests the p-value is the smallest significance level at which the null hypothesis can be rejected.

EXAMPLE 9.5

SUPERMARKET SHOPPERS PRICE KNOWLEDGE (HYPOTHESIS TEST USING PROPORTIONS)

Market Research Inc. wants to know if shoppers are sensitive to the prices of items produced in a supermarket. They obtained a random sample of 802 shoppers and found that 378 supermarket shoppers were able to state the correct price of an item immediately after putting it into the cart. Test at the 7% level the null hypothesis that at least one-half of all shoppers are able to state the correct price.

SOLUTION

We will let π denote the population proportion of supermarket shoppers able to state the correct price in these circumstances. Test the null hypothesis

$$H_0: \pi \geq \pi_0 = 0.50$$

against the alternative

$$H_1: \pi < 0.50$$

The decision rule is to reject the null hypothesis in favor of the alternative if

$$\frac{p - \pi_0}{\sqrt{\pi_0(1 - \pi_0)/n}} < -Z_\alpha$$

For this example $n = 802$ and $p = 378/802 = 0.471$.
For a 7% level test $\alpha = 0.07$ and $Z_\alpha = -1.474$ from the normal distribution table.
The test statistic is

$$\frac{p - \pi_0}{\sqrt{\pi_0(1 - \pi_0)/n}} = \frac{0.471 - 0.50}{\sqrt{0.50(1 - 0.50)/802}} = -1.62$$

Since -1.62 is less than -1.474, we reject the null hypothesis and conclude that less than one-half of the shoppers can correctly state the price immediately after putting an item into their supermarket cart. Using the calculated Z value of 1.62 we also find that the p-value for the test is 0.052.

EXERCISES

9.20 Of a random sample of 361 owners of small businesses that had gone into bankruptcy, 105 reported conducting no marketing studies prior to opening the business. Test the null hypothesis that at most 25% of all members of this population conducted no marketing studies before opening the business.

9.21 In a random sample of 998 adults in the United States, 17.3% of the sample members indicated some measure of disagreement with the statement: "Globalization is more than an economic trade system—instead it includes institutions and culture." Test at the 5% level the null hypothesis that at least 25% of all U.S. adults would disagree with this statement.

9.22 In a random sample of 160 business school students, 72 sample members indicated some measure of agreement with the statement: "Scores on a standardized entrance exam are less important for a student's chance to suc-

ceed academically than is the student's high school GPA." Test the null hypothesis that one-half of all business school graduates would agree with this statement against a two-sided alternative. Find and interpret the p-value of the test.

9.23 Of a random sample of 199 auditors, 104 indicated some measure of agreement with the statement: "Cash flow is an important indication of profitability." Test at the 10% significance level against a two-sided alternative the null hypothesis that one-half of the members of this population would agree with this statement. Also, find and interpret the p-value of this test.

9.24 A random sample of 50 university admissions officers was asked about expectations in application interviews. Of these sample members, 28 agreed that the interviewer usually expects the interviewee to have volunteer experience doing community projects. Test the null hypothesis that one-half of all interviewers have this expectation against the alternative that population proportion is bigger than one-half.

9.25 Of a random sample of 172 elementary school educators, 118 said that parental support was the most important source of a child's success. Test the null hypothesis that parental support is the most important source of a child's success for at least 75% of elementary school educators against the alternative that the population percentage is less than 75%.

9.26 A random sample of 202 business faculty members was asked if there should be a required foreign language course for business majors. Of these sample members, 140 felt there was a need for a foreign language course. Test the null hypothesis that at least 75% of all business faculty members hold this view.

9.5 TESTS OF THE VARIANCE OF A NORMAL DISTRIBUTION

In addition to the need for tests based on the sample mean there are a number of situations where we want to determine if the population variance is a particular value or set of values. In modern quality control work this need is particularly important because a process that, for example, has an excessively large variance can produce many defective items. Here we will develop procedures for testing the population variance σ^2, based on a random sample of n observations from a normally distributed population, by using the sample variance s_x^2. The basis for developing particular tests lies in the fact that the random variable

$$\chi_{n-1}^2 = \frac{(n-1)s_x^2}{\sigma^2}$$

follows a chi-square distribution with $(n-1)$ degrees of freedom. If the null hypothesis is that the population variance is equal to some specified value σ_0^2, that is

$$H_0 : \sigma^2 = \sigma_0^2$$

then when this hypothesis is true, the random variable

$$\chi_{n-1}^2 = \frac{(n-1)s_x^2}{\sigma_0^2}$$

obeys a chi-square distribution with $(n-1)$ degrees of freedom. Hypothesis tests are based on computed values of this statistic. If the alternative hypothesis is that the population variance is larger than σ_0^2, we would be suspicious of the null hypothesis if the sample variance greatly exceeded σ_0^2. A high computed value of χ_{n-1}^2 would result in the rejection of the null hypothesis. Conversely an alternative hypothesis that the population variance was less than σ_0^2 would be accepted if the value of χ_{n-1}^2 was small. For a two-sided alternative that the population variance differs from σ_0^2 we would reject the null hypothesis if the value was either unusually high or unusually low. The chi-square distribution tests are more sensitive to the assumption of normality in the underlying distribution compared to the standard normal distribution tests. Thus if the underlying population deviates considerably from the normal, the significance levels computed using the chi-square distribution may deviate from the correct significance levels based on the exact distribution.

The rationale for the development of appropriate tests follows the logic developed in Section 9.2 and uses the chi-square distribution notation developed in Section 8.5. We denote $\chi_{v,\alpha}^2$ as the number that is exceeded with probability α by a chi-square random variable with v degrees of freedom. That is

$$P(\chi_v^2 > \chi_{v,\alpha}^2) = \alpha$$

FIGURE 9.5
Some Probabilities for the
Chi-Square Distribution

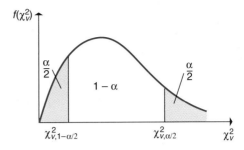

and in addition that

$$P(\chi_v^2 < \chi_{v,1-\alpha}^2) = \alpha$$

and for two-tailed tests

$$P(\chi_v^2 > \chi_{v,\alpha/2}^2 \quad \text{or} \quad \chi_v^2 < \chi_{v,1-\alpha/2}^2) = \alpha$$

These probabilities are shown in Figure 9.5 and the various tests are summarized in Equations 9.12, 9.13, and 9.14.

It is also possible to determine p-values for the chi-square test for variances. From the general result just stated, the p-value for the chi-square test is the smallest significance level at which the null hypothesis can be rejected.

TESTS OF VARIANCE OF A NORMAL POPULATION

We are given a random sample of n observations from a normally distributed population with variance σ^2. If we observe the sample variance s_x^2, then the following tests have significance level α.

i. To test either the null hypothesis

$$H_0: \sigma^2 = \sigma_0^2 \quad \text{or} \quad H_0: \sigma^2 \leq \sigma_0^2$$

against the alternative

$$H_1: \sigma^2 > \sigma_0^2$$

the decision rule is

$$\text{Reject } H_0 \text{ if } \quad \frac{(n-1)s_x^2}{\sigma_0^2} > \chi_{n-1,\alpha}^2 \qquad \textbf{(9.12)}$$

ii. To test either null hypothesis

$$H_0: \sigma^2 = \sigma_0^2 \quad \text{or} \quad H_0: \sigma^2 \geq \sigma_0^2$$

against the alternative

$$H_1: \sigma^2 < \sigma_0^2$$

the decision rule is

$$\text{Reject } H_0 \text{ if } \quad \frac{(n-1)s_x^2}{\sigma_0^2} < \chi_{n-1,1-\alpha}^2 \qquad \textbf{(9.13)}$$

iii. To test the null hypothesis

$$H_0 : \sigma^2 = \sigma_0^2$$

against the two-sided alternative

$$H_1 : \sigma^2 \neq \sigma_0^2$$

the decision rule is

$$\text{Reject } H_0 \text{ if } \quad \frac{(n-1)s_x^2}{\sigma_0^2} > \chi_{n-1,\alpha/2}^2 \quad \text{or} \quad \frac{(n-1)s_x^2}{\sigma_0^2} < \chi_{n-1,1-\alpha/2}^2 \qquad \textbf{(9.14)}$$

Where χ_{n-1}^2 is a chi-square random variable and $P(\chi_{n-1}^2 > \chi_{n-1,\alpha}^2) = \alpha$

The p-value for these tests is the smallest significance level at which the null hypothesis can be rejected given the sample variance.

EXAMPLE 9.6

VARIANCE OF CHEMICAL IMPURITIES (HYPOTHESIS TESTS FOR POPULATION VARIANCES)

The quality control manager of Stonehead Chemicals has asked you to determine if the variance of impurities in its shipments of fertilizer is within the established standard. This standard states that for 100-pound bags of fertilizer the variance in the pounds of impurities cannot exceed 4.

SOLUTION

A random sample of 20 bags is obtained and the pounds of impurities are measured for each bag. The sample variance was computed to be 6.62. In this problem we are testing the null hypothesis

$$H_0 : \sigma^2 \leq \sigma_0^2 = 4$$

against the alternative

$$H_1 : \sigma^2 > 4$$

Based on the assumption that the population distribution is a normal distribution, the decision rule, for a test of significance level α, is to reject H_0 in favor of H_1 if

$$\frac{(n-1)s_x^2}{\sigma_0^2} > \chi_{n-1,\alpha}^2$$

For this test, with $\alpha = 0.05$ and 19 degrees of freedom, the critical value of the chi-square variable is, from the Chi-Square Table in the Appendix, 30.14. There, using the test data we find that

$$\frac{(n-1)s_x^2}{\sigma_0^2} = \frac{(20-1)(6.62)}{4} = 31.45 > \chi_{n-1,\alpha}^2 = 30.14$$

Therefore we reject the null hypothesis and conclude that the variability of the impurities exceeds the standard. As a result we recommend that the production process be studied and improvements made to reduce the variability of the product components.

The p-value for this test is the probability of obtaining a chi-square statistic with 19 degrees of freedom that is greater than the observed 31.45

$$p\text{-value} = P\left(\frac{(19)s_x^2}{\sigma_0^2} > \chi_{19}^2 = 31.45\right) = 0.036$$

The p-value of 0.036 was computed using the Minitab command sequence

```
CALC > PROBABILITY DISTRIBUTIONS > CHI-SQUARE
```

and entering 19 degrees of freedom and 31.45 as the input constant in the dialog box.

EXERCISES

9.27 At the insistence of a government inspector, a new safety device is installed in an assembly-line operation. After the installation of this device, a random sample of eight days output gave the following results for numbers of finished components produced:

    618   660   638   625   571   598   639   582

Management is concerned about the variability of daily output and views as undesirable any variance above 500. Test at the 10% significance level the null hypothesis that the population variance for daily output does not exceed 500.

9.28 Plastic sheets produced by a machine are periodically monitored for possible fluctuations in thickness. If the true variance in thicknesses exceeds 2.25 square millimeters, there is cause for concern about product quality. Thickness measurements for a random sample of ten sheets produced in a particular shift were taken, giving the following results (in millimeters):

    226   226   232   227   225
    228   225   228   229   230

(a) Find the sample variance.
(b) Test at the 5% significance level the null hypothesis that the population variance is at most 2.25.

9.29 One way to evaluate the effectiveness of a teaching assistant is to examine the scores achieved by his or her students in an examination at the end of the course. Obviously, the mean score is of interest. However, the variance also contains useful information—some teachers have a style that works very well with more able students but is unsuccessful with less able or poorly motivated students. A professor sets a standard examination at the end of each semester for all sections of a course. The variance of the scores on this test is typically very close to 300. A new teaching assistant has a class of 30 students, whose test scores had a variance of 480. Regarding these students' test scores as a random sample from a normal population, test against a two-sided alternative the null hypothesis that the population variance of their scores is 300.

9.30 A company produces electric devices operated by a thermostatic control. The standard deviation of the temperature at which these controls actually operate should not exceed 2.0 degrees Fahrenheit. For a random sample of 20 of these controls, the sample standard deviation of operating temperatures was 2.36 degrees Fahrenheit. Stating any assumptions you need to make, test at the 5% level the null hypothesis that the population standard deviation is 2.0 against the alternative that it is bigger.

9.31 An instructor has decided to introduce a greater component of independent study into an intermediate microeconomics course, as a way of motivating students to work independently and think more carefully about the course material. A colleague cautions that a possible consequence may be increased variability in student performance. However, the instructor responds that she would expect less variability. From her records, she found that, in the past, student scores on the final exam for this course followed a normal distribution with standard deviation 18.2 points. For a class of 25 students using the new approach, the standard deviation of scores on the final exam was 15.3 points. Assuming that these 25 students can be viewed as a random sample of all those who might be subjected to the new approach, test the null hypothesis that the population standard deviation is at least 18.2 points against the alternative that is lower.

9.6   TESTS FOR THE DIFFERENCE BETWEEN TWO POPULATION MEANS

There are a number of applications where we wish to make conclusions about the differences between population means instead of the absolute levels of the means. For example, we might want to compare the output between two different production processes for which we do not know either population mean. Similarly we might want to know if one marketing strategy results in higher sales than another without having the population mean sales for either. These questions can be handled effectively by hypothesis testing procedures. As we saw in Section 8.6, there are several different assumptions that can be made when confidence intervals are computed for the differences between two population means. These assumptions generally deal with the procedures for obtaining the population variance for the difference between sample means or for obtaining an estimate of the difference between sample means. There are parallel hypothesis tests that involve similar procedures for obtaining the variance. We will organize our discussion of the various hypothesis testing procedures parallel with the confidence interval estimates in Section 8.6.

Two Means, Matched Pairs

Here we assume that a random sample of n matched pairs of observations is obtained from populations with means μ_x and μ_y. The observations will be denoted (x_1, y_1), (x_2, y_2), ..., (x_n, y_n). When we have matched pairs and the pairs are positively correlated the variance of the difference between the means

$$\overline{D} = \overline{X} - \overline{Y}$$

will be reduced compared to using independent samples. This results because some of the characteristics of the pairs are similar, and thus that portion of the variability is removed from the total variability of the differences between the means. For example when we consider measures of human behavior the differences between twins will usually be less than the differences between two randomly selected people. In general the dimensions for two parts produced on the same specific machine will be closer than the dimensions for parts produced on two different randomly selected machines. Thus whenever possible we would prefer to use matched pairs of observations when comparing two populations, because the variance of the difference will be smaller. With a smaller variance there is a greater probability that we will reject H_0 when the null hypothesis is not true. This principle will be developed in Section 9.9 in the discussion of the power of a test. The specific decision rules for different forms of the hypothesis test are summarized in Equations 9.15, 9.16, and 9.17.

TESTS OF THE DIFFERENCE BETWEEN POPULATION MEANS: MATCHED PAIRS

Suppose that we have a random sample of n matched pairs of observations from distributions with means μ_x and μ_y. Let $\overline{D}$ and S_D denote the observed sample mean and standard deviation for the n differences $(x_i - y_i)$. If the population distribution of the differences is a normal distribution, then the following tests have significance level α.

i.   To test either null hypothesis

$$H_0 : \mu_x - \mu_y = D_0 \quad \text{or} \quad H_0 : \mu_x - \mu_y \le D_0$$

against the alternative

$$H_1 : \mu_x - \mu_y > D_0$$

the decision rule is

$$\text{Reject } H_0 \text{ if } \quad \frac{\overline{D} - D_0}{s_D/\sqrt{n}} > t_{n-1,\alpha} \tag{9.15}$$

ii. To test either null hypothesis

$$H_0: \mu_x - \mu_y = D_0 \quad \text{ or } \quad H_0: \mu_x - \mu_y \geq D_0$$

against the alternative

$$H_1: \mu_x - \mu_y < D_0$$

the decision rule is

$$\text{Reject } H_0 \text{ if } \quad \frac{\overline{D} - D_0}{s_D/\sqrt{n}} < -t_{n-1,\alpha} \tag{9.16}$$

iii. To test the null hypothesis

$$H_0: \mu_x - \mu_y = D_0$$

against the two-sided alternative

$$H_1: \mu_x - \mu_y \neq D_0$$

the decision rule is

$$\text{Reject } H_0 \text{ if } \quad \frac{\overline{D} - D_0}{s_D/\sqrt{n}} < -t_{n-1,\alpha/2} \quad \text{ or } \quad \frac{\overline{D} - D_0}{s_D/\sqrt{n}} > t_{n-1,\alpha/2} \tag{9.17}$$

Here $t_{n-1,\alpha}$ is the number for which

$$P(t_{n-1} > t_{n-1,\alpha}) = \alpha$$

where the random variable t_{n-1} follows a Student's t distribution with $(n-1)$ degrees of freedom.

When we want to test the null hypothesis that the two population means are equal, we set $D_0 = 0$ in the formulas.

   P-values for all of these tests are interpreted as the smallest significance level at which the null hypothesis can be rejected given the test statistic.

EXAMPLE 9.7

BRAIN ACTIVITY AND RECALL OF TV ADVERTISING

Brain Wave Measurements

Researchers conducted a study to estimate the relationship between a subject's brain activity while watching a television commercial and the subject's subsequent ability to recall the contents of the commercial. Subjects were shown two commercials for each of ten products. For each commercial, the ability to recall 24 hours later was measured, and each member of a pair of commercials viewed by a specific subject was then designated "high-recall" or "low-recall." Table 9.2 shows an index of the total amount of brain activity of subjects while watching these commercials. Researchers wanted to know if brain wave activity was higher for high-recall ads compared to low-recall ads (see file **Brain Wave Measurements**).

SOLUTION

Denote μ_x the population mean for high-recall commercials and μ_y the population mean of low-recall commercials, and then the differences $D_i(i = 1, \ldots, 10)$ are a random sample of

TABLE 9.2
Brain Activities of Subjects Watching Ten Pairs of Television

| Product Observation | COMMERCIALS | |
	High Recall X	Low Recall Y
1	141	55
2	139	116
3	87	83
4	129	88
5	51	36
6	50	68
7	118	91
8	161	115
9	61	90
10	148	113

10 observations from a population with mean $(\mu_x - \mu_y)$. Using these assumptions we can define the null hypothesis of no difference in brain activity levels

$$H_0: \mu_x - \mu_y = 0$$

against the alternative that, on average brain activity is greater for the high-recall commercials, that is

$$H_1: \mu_x - \mu_y > 0$$

In this testing we compute the sample standard deviation of the differences, and thus we will use the Student's t distribution for the test.

The pattern of paired data is illustrated in Table 9.2. Each subject was given a high-recall and low-recall ad, and these are paired by observation number. Minitab can be used to calculate the required output using the command

```
STAT > BASIC STATISTICS > PAIRED T
```

The output for this problem is shown in Figure 9.6. The test is based on the statistic

$$t = \frac{\overline{D} - D_0}{s_d/\sqrt{n}} = \frac{23}{33.0/\sqrt{10}} = 2.21$$

From Table 6 in the Appendix we find that the value $t_{9,0.05} = 1.833$. Since 2.21 exceeds this value we reject the null hypothesis and accept the alternative hypothesis. Thus we conclude that there is substantial evidence to conclude that brain activity is higher for the high-recall compared to the low-recall group. We also note that the p-value for this test is 0.027 as shown in the Minitab output.

FIGURE 9.6
Minitab Hypothesis Testing for Differences Between Brain Waves

```
Paired T for X - Y

               N      Mean     StDev    SE Mean
X              10     108.5     42.5      13.4
Y              10      85.5     26.5       8.4
Difference     10      23.0     33.0      10.4

95% lower bound for mean difference: 3.9
T-Test of mean difference = 0 (vs > 0): T-Value = 2.21   P-Value = 0.027
```

Finally we note the affect of missing data, a problem that often occurs in applied statistical work. For example, suppose that the brain wave measurement was lost for one of the two ads for a particular subject. Standard procedure would argue that the entire observation should be removed and the analysis carried out with nine paired observations. Minitab and most statistical packages do this properly, but Excel does not. Therefore all observations containing missing data should be removed before using Excel to compute paired t test statistics.

Two Means, Independent Samples, Known Population Variances

Now we will consider the case where we have independent random samples from two normally distributed populations. The first population has mean μ_x and variance σ_x^2 and we obtain a random sample of size n_x. The second population has mean μ_y and variance σ_y^2 and we obtain a random sample of size n_y.

In Section 8.6, we saw that if the sample means are denoted $\overline{X}$ and $\overline{Y}$, then the random variable

$$Z = \frac{(\overline{X} - \overline{Y}) - (\mu_x - \mu_y)}{\sqrt{\dfrac{\sigma_x^2}{n_x} + \dfrac{\sigma_y^2}{n_y}}}$$

has a standard normal distribution. If the two population variances are known, tests for the difference between the population means can be based on this result, using the same arguments as before. Generally we are comfortable using known population variances if the process being studied has been stable over some time and we have obtained similar variance measurements over this time. Of course we can also perform a hypothesis test of the variance as shown in Section 9.5. And because of the central limit theorem the results hold for large sample sizes even if the populations are not normal. For large sample sizes the approximation is quite satisfactory when sample variances replace population variances. This allows the derivation of tests of wide applicability, as summarized in Equations 9.18, 9.19, and 9.20.

TESTS FOR DIFFERENCE BETWEEN POPULATION MEANS: INDEPENDENT SAMPLES (KNOWN VARIANCES)

Suppose that we have independent random samples of n_x and n_y observations from normal distributions with means μ_x and μ_y and variances σ_x^2 and σ_y^2. If the observed sample means are $\overline{X}$ and $\overline{Y}$ then the following tests have significance level α.

i. To test either null hypothesis

$$H_0 : \mu_x - \mu_y = D_0 \quad \text{or} \quad H_0 : \mu_x - \mu_y \leq D_0$$

against the alternative

$$H_1 : \mu_x - \mu_y > D_0$$

the decision rule is

$$\text{Reject } H_0 \text{ if } \quad \frac{\overline{X} - \overline{Y} - D_0}{\sqrt{\dfrac{\sigma_x^2}{n_x} + \dfrac{\sigma_y^2}{n_y}}} > Z_\alpha \tag{9.18}$$

ii. To test either null hypothesis

$$H_0 : \mu_x - \mu_y = D_0 \quad \text{or} \quad H_0 : \mu_x - \mu_y \geq D_0$$

against the alternative

$$H_1 : \mu_x - \mu_y < D_0$$

the decision rule is

$$\text{Reject } H_0 \text{ if} \quad \frac{\overline{X} - \overline{Y} - D_0}{\sqrt{\dfrac{\sigma_x^2}{n_x} + \dfrac{\sigma_y^2}{n_y}}} < -Z_\alpha \tag{9.19}$$

iii. To test the null hypothesis

$$H_0 : \mu_x - \mu_y = D_0$$

against the alternative

$$H_1 : \mu_x - \mu_y \neq D_0$$

the decision rule is

$$\text{Reject } H_0 \text{ if} \quad \frac{\overline{X} - \overline{Y} - D_0}{\sqrt{\dfrac{\sigma_x^2}{n_x} + \dfrac{\sigma_y^2}{n_y}}} < -Z_{\alpha/2} \quad \text{or} \quad \frac{\overline{X} - \overline{Y} - D_0}{\sqrt{\dfrac{\sigma_x^2}{n_x} + \dfrac{\sigma_y^2}{n_y}}} > Z_{\alpha/2} \tag{9.20}$$

If the sample sizes are large ($n > 100$) then a good approximation at significance level α can be made if the population variances are replaced by the sample variances. In addition the central limit leads to good approximations even if the populations are not normally distributed.

p-values for all of these tests are interpreted as the smallest significance level at which the null hypothesis can be rejected given the test statistic.

EXAMPLE 9.8

COMPARISON OF ALTERNATIVE FERTILIZERS (HYPOTHESIS TEST FOR DIFFERENCES BETWEEN MEANS)

Shirley Brown, an agricultural economist, wants to compare cow manure and turkey dung as fertilizers. Historically, farmers had used cow manure on their cornfields. Recently a major turkey farmer offered to sell composted turkey dung at a favorable price. The farm association decided that it would use this new fertilizer only if there was strong evidence that productivity increased over the productivity that occurred with cow manure. Shirley was asked to conduct the research and statistical analysis in order to develop a recommendation for the farm.

SOLUTION

To begin the study Shirley specified a hypothesis test

$$H_0 : \mu_x - \mu_y \leq 0$$

versus the alternative that

$$H_1 : \mu_x - \mu_y > 0$$

where μ_x is the population mean productivity turkey dung and μ_y is the population mean productivity using cow manure. H_1 indicates that turkey dung results in higher productivity. The farmers will not change their fertilizer unless there is strong evidence in favor of increased productivity. She decided before collecting the data that a significance level of $\alpha = 0.05$ would be used for this test.

Using this design Shirley implemented an experiment to test the hypothesis. Cow manure was applied to one set of $n_y = 25$ randomly selected fields. The sample mean productivity was $\overline{Y} = 100$. From past experience, the variance in productivity for these fields was assumed to be $\sigma_y^2 = 400$. Turkey dung was applied to a second random sample of $n_x = 25$ fields and the sample mean productivity was $\overline{X} = 115$. Based on published research reports, the variance for these fields was assumed to be $\sigma_X^2 = 625$. The two sets of random samples were independent. The decision rule is to reject H_0 in favor of H_1 if

$$\frac{\overline{X} - \overline{Y}}{\sqrt{\dfrac{\sigma_x^2}{n_x} + \dfrac{\sigma_y^2}{n_y}}} > z_\alpha$$

The computed statistics for this problem are:

$$
\begin{array}{lll}
n_x = 25 & \overline{X} = 115 & \sigma_X^2 = 625 \\
n_y = 25 & \overline{Y} = 100 & \sigma_y^2 = 400
\end{array}
$$

$$Z = \frac{115 - 100}{\sqrt{\dfrac{625}{25} + \dfrac{400}{25}}} = 2.34$$

Comparing the computed value of $Z = 2.34$ with $z_{0.05} = 1.645$ we find that the null hypothesis is clearly rejected. In fact we find that the p-value for this test is 0.0096. As a result we conclude that there is overwhelming evidence that turkey dung results in higher productivity than cow manure.

Two Means, Independent Populations, Unknown Variances Assumed to be Equal

In those cases where the population variance is not known and sample sizes are under 100, we need to use the Student's t distribution. There are some theoretical problems when we use the Student's t distribution for differences between sample means. However, these problems can be solved using the procedure that follows if we can assume that the population variances are equal. This assumption is realistic in many cases where we are comparing groups. In Section 9.8 we will present a procedure for testing the equality of variances from two normal populations.

The major difference is that this procedure uses a common pooled estimator of the equal population variance. This estimator is

$$s_p^2 = \frac{(n_x - 1)s_x^2 + (n_y - 1)s_y^2}{(n_x + n_y - 2)}$$

The hypothesis test is performed using the Student's t statistic for the difference between two means

$$t = \frac{(\overline{X} - \overline{Y}) - (\mu_x - \mu_y)}{\sqrt{\dfrac{s_p^2}{n_x} + \dfrac{s_p^2}{n_y}}}$$

Note that the form for the test statistic is similar to the one used for the Z statistic when the population variances are known. The various tests using this procedure are summarized in the following box.

TESTS FOR THE DIFFERENCE BETWEEN SAMPLE MEANS: POPULATION VARIANCES UNKNOWN AND EQUAL

These tests assume that we have independent random samples of size n_x and n_y observations from normally distributed populations with means μ_x and μ_y and a common variance. The sample variances s_x^2 and s_y^2 are used to compute a pooled variance estimator

$$s_p^2 = \frac{(n_x - 1)s_x^2 + (n_y - 1)s_y^2}{(n_x + n_y - 2)} \tag{9.21}$$

Then using the observed sample means $\overline{X}$ and $\overline{Y}$, the following tests have significance level α:

i. To test either null hypothesis

$$H_0: \mu_x - \mu_y = D_0 \quad \text{or} \quad H_0: \mu_x - \mu_y \leq D_0$$

against the alternative

$$H_1: \mu_x - \mu_y > D_0$$

the decision rule is

$$\text{Reject } H_0 \text{ if} \quad \frac{\overline{X} - \overline{Y} - D_0}{\sqrt{\dfrac{s_p^2}{n_x} + \dfrac{s_p^2}{n_y}}} > t_{n_x + n_y - 2, \alpha} \tag{9.22}$$

ii. To test either null hypothesis

$$H_0: \mu_x - \mu_y = D_0 \quad \text{or} \quad H_0: \mu_x - \mu_y \geq D_0$$

against the alternative

$$H_1: \mu_x - \mu_y < D_0$$

the decision rule is

$$\text{Reject } H_0 \text{ if } \quad \frac{\overline{X} - \overline{Y} - D_0}{\sqrt{\dfrac{s_p^2}{n_x} + \dfrac{s_p^2}{n_y}}} < -t_{n_x + n_y - 2, \alpha} \qquad \text{(9.23)}$$

iii. To test the null hypothesis

$$H_0: \mu_x - \mu_y = D_0$$

against the alternative

$$H_1: \mu_x - \mu_y \neq D_0$$

the decision rule is

$$\text{Reject } H_0 \text{ if } \quad \frac{\overline{X} - \overline{Y} - D_0}{\sqrt{\dfrac{s_p^2}{n_x} + \dfrac{s_p^2}{n_y}}} < -t_{n_x + n_y - 2, \alpha/2} \quad \text{or} \quad \frac{\overline{X} - \overline{Y} - D_0}{\sqrt{\dfrac{s_p^2}{n_x} + \dfrac{s_p^2}{n_y}}} > t_{n_x + n_y - 2, \alpha/2} \qquad \text{(9.24)}$$

Here $t_{n_x + n_y - 2, \alpha}$ is the number for which

$$P(t_{n_x + n_y - 2} > t_{n_x + n_y - 2, \alpha}) = \alpha$$

p-values for all of these tests are interpreted as the smallest significance level at which the null hypothesis can be rejected given the test statistic.

EXAMPLE 9.9

RETAIL SALES PATTERNS (HYPOTHESIS TEST FOR DIFFERENCES BETWEEN MEANS)

A sporting goods store is operated in a medium-sized shopping mall. In order to plan staffing levels the manager has asked for your assistance to determine whether Saturday or Monday are the days with highest sales. She wants to know if there is strong evidence that Monday sales are higher than Saturday sales.

SOLUTION

To answer the question you decide to gather random samples of 25 Saturdays and of 25 Mondays from a population of several years of data. The samples were drawn independently. Minitab was used to compute the sample mean and standard deviation. You decide to test the null hypothesis

$$H_0: \mu_M - \mu_S \leq 0$$

against the alternative hypothesis

$$H_1: \mu_M - \mu_S > 0$$

where the subscripts M and S refer to Monday and Saturday sales. From the Minitab statistical output you found the following sample statistics

$$\overline{X}_M = 1078 \qquad s_M = 633 \qquad n_M = 25$$
$$\overline{Y}_S = 908.2 \qquad s_S = 469.8 \qquad n_S = 25$$

The pooled variance estimate is

$$s_p^2 = \frac{(25-1)(633)^2 + (25-1)(469.8)^2}{25+25-2} = 310,700$$

The test statistic is then computed as

$$t = \frac{\overline{X} - \overline{Y}}{\sqrt{\dfrac{s_p^2}{n_x} + \dfrac{s_p^2}{n_y}}} = \frac{1078 - 908.2}{\sqrt{\dfrac{310,700}{25} + \dfrac{310,700}{25}}} = 1.08$$

Using a significance level of $\alpha = 0.05$ and 48 degrees of freedom we find that the critical value of t is 1.677. Therefore we conclude that there is not sufficient evidence to reject the null hypothesis, and thus there is no reason to conclude that mean sales on Monday are higher.

EXAMPLE 9.10

BRAIN ACTIVITY STUDY (HYPOTHESIS TEST FOR DIFFERENCES BETWEEN MEANS)

Brain Wave Measurements

In this example we will examine the affect of using different assumptions for Student's t tests for differences between population means. Recall that in Example 9.7 we prepared the analysis assuming that the sample observations were paired and found that there was evidence to reject the hypothesis that there was no difference between the population means and to accept the hypothesis that the high-recall ads had a higher population mean brain activity (use data file **Brain Wave Measurements**).

SOLUTION

First we will drop the assumption that the sample observations are matched pairs and correlated. We will, however, assume that the two population variances are the same. Again we are testing the same hypothesis that we tested in Example 9.7. Using Minitab, the commands to produce the analysis are

```
STAT > BASIC STATISTICS > 2-SAMPLE T
```

In the dialog box we chose the same sample data and indicated that the population variances were equal. The Minitab results are shown in Figure 9.7.

FIGURE 9.7
Minitab Output for Brain Wave Study; Independent Samples Population Variances Equal

Variances Equal

```
MTB > TwoSample 'X' 'Y';
SUBC>    Pooled;
SUBC>    Alternative 1.
```

Two-Sample T-Test and CI: X, Y

```
Two-sample T for X vs Y

      N      Mean      StDev    SE Mean
X    10     108.5      42.5        13
Y    10      85.5      26.5       8.4

Difference = mu X - mu Y
Estimate for difference:   23.0
95% lower bound for difference: -4.5
T-Test of difference = 0 (vs >): T-Value = 1.45   P-Value = 0.082   DF = 18
Both use Pooled StDev = 35.4
```

We see that the Student's t value is 1.45 and the p-value is 0.082 and the degrees of freedom are 18. Thus with a significance level of 0.05 we cannot reject the null hypothesis and conclude that there was a difference in brain wave activity. Without the assumption of paired and positively correlated samples the variance of the difference is too large to conclude that the difference is significant.

Two Means, Independent Samples, Unknown Population Variances Assumed to be Not Equal

Hypothesis tests for differences between population means when the individual variances are unknown and not equal require modification of the variance computation and the degrees of freedom. These add complexities to the computation and to the determination of degrees of freedom for the critical value of the Student's t statistic. The specific computational forms were presented in Section 8.6 and Equations 8.15 through 8.18. The procedures are summarized in the following box.

TESTS FOR THE DIFFERENCE BETWEEN SAMPLE MEANS: POPULATION VARIANCES UNKNOWN AND NOT EQUAL

These tests assume that we have independent random samples of size n_x and n_y observations from normal populations with means μ_x and μ_y and a common variance. The sample variances s_x^2 and s_y^2 are used. The degrees of freedom, v, for the student t statistic is given by

$$v = \frac{\left[\left(\frac{s_X^2}{n_X}\right) + \left(\frac{s_Y^2}{n_Y}\right)\right]^2}{\left(\frac{s_X^2}{n_X}\right)^2 / (n_X - 1) + \left(\frac{s_Y^2}{n_Y}\right)^2 / (n_Y - 1)} \tag{9.25}$$

Then using the observed sample means $\overline{X}$ and $\overline{Y}$, the following tests have significance level α:

i. To test either null hypothesis

$$H_0: \mu_x - \mu_y = D_0 \quad \text{or} \quad H_0: \mu_x - \mu_y \leq D_0$$

against the alternative

$$H_1: \mu_x - \mu_y > D_0$$

the decision rule is

$$\text{Reject } H_0 \text{ if } \quad \frac{\overline{X} - \overline{Y} - D_0}{\sqrt{\frac{s_x^2}{n_x} + \frac{s_y^2}{n_y}}} > t_{v,\alpha} \tag{9.26}$$

ii. To test either null hypothesis

$$H_0: \mu_x - \mu_y = D_0 \quad \text{or} \quad H_0: \mu_x - \mu_y \geq D_0$$

against the alternative

$$H_1 : \mu_x - \mu_y < D_0$$

the decision rule is

$$\text{Reject } H_0 \text{ if} \quad \frac{\overline{X} - \overline{Y} - D_0}{\sqrt{\dfrac{s_x^2}{n_x} + \dfrac{s_y^2}{n_y}}} < -t_{v,\alpha} \qquad (9.27)$$

iii. To test the null hypothesis

$$H_0 : \mu_x - \mu_y = D_0$$

against the alternative

$$H_1 : \mu_x - \mu_y \neq D_0$$

the decision rule is

$$\text{Reject } H_0 \text{ if} \quad \frac{\overline{X} - \overline{Y} - D_0}{\sqrt{\dfrac{s_x^2}{n_x} + \dfrac{s_y^2}{n_y}}} < -t_{v,\alpha/2} \quad \text{or} \quad \frac{\overline{X} - \overline{Y} - D_0}{\sqrt{\dfrac{s_x^2}{n_x} + \dfrac{s_y^2}{n_y}}} > t_{v,\alpha/2} \qquad (9.28)$$

Here $t_{n_x+n_y-2,\alpha}$ is the number for which

$$P(t_{n_x+n_y-2} > t_{n_x+n_y-2,\alpha}) = \alpha$$

The analysis for Example 9.10 will be run without assuming equal population variances. The Minitab results are shown in Figure 9.8. Here the only important change is that the degrees of freedom are lower, resulting in a slightly higher *p*-value.

FIGURE 9.8
Minitab Output for Brain Wave Study; Independent Samples

Population Variances Not Assumed Equal

```
MTB > TwoSample 'X' 'Y';
SUBC>    Alternative 1.
```

Two-Sample T-Test and CI: X, Y

```
Two-sample T for X vs Y

      N      Mean     StDev    SE Mean
X    10     108.5      42.5        13
Y    10      85.5      26.5       8.4

Difference = mu X - mu Y
Estimate for difference:  23.0
95% lower bound for difference: -4.8
T-Test of difference = 0 (vs >): T-Value = 1.45   P-Value = 0.083   DF = 15
```

EXERCISES

9.32 🌐 A college placement office wants to determine whether male and female economics graduates receive, on average, different salary offers for their first position after graduation. The placement officer randomly selected eight pairs of business graduates in such a way that the qualifications, interests, and backgrounds of members of any pair were as similar as possible. The data file **Salary Pair** contains the highest salary offer received by each sample member at the end of the recruiting round. Assuming that the distributions are normal, test the null hypothesis that the population means are equal against the alternative that the true mean for males is higher than for females.

9.33 🌐 An agency offers students preparation courses for a graduate school admissions test. As part of an experiment to evaluate the merits of the course, twelve students were chosen and divided into six pairs, in such a way that the two members of any pair had similar academic records. Before taking the test, one member of each pair was assigned at random to take the preparation course, while the other member took no course. The achievement test scores are contained in the **Student Pair** data file. Assuming that the differences in scores follow a normal distribution, test at the 5% level the null hypothesis that the two population means are equal against the alternative that the true mean is higher for students taking the preparation course.

9.34 In a study comparing banks in Germany and Great Britain, a sample of 145 matched pairs of banks was formed. Each pair contained one German and one Great Britain bank. The pairings were made in such a way that the two members were as similar as possible in regard to such factors as size and age. The ratio of total loans outstanding to total assets was calculated for each of the banks. For this ratio, the sample mean difference (German—Great Britain) was .0518, and the sample standard deviation of the differences was .3055. Test against a two-sided alternative the null hypothesis that the two population means are equal.

9.35 A screening procedure was designed to measure attitudes toward minorities as managers. High scores indicate negative attitudes and low scores indicate positive attitudes. Independent random samples were taken of 151 male financial analysts and 108 female financial analysts. For the former group, the sample mean and standard deviation scores were 85.8 and 19.13, while the corresponding statistics for the latter group were 71.5 and 12.2. Test the null hypothesis that the two population means are equal against the alternative that the true mean score is higher for male than for female financial analysts.

9.36 For a random sample of 125 British entrepreneurs, the mean number of job changes was 1.91 and the sample standard deviation was 1.32. For an independent random sample of 86 British corporate managers, the mean number of job changes was .21 and the sample standard deviation was .53. Test the null hypothesis that the population means are equal against the alternative that the mean number of job changes is higher for British entrepreneurs than for British corporate managers.

9.37 A political science professor is interested in comparing the characteristics of students who do and do not vote in national elections. For a random sample of 114 students who claimed to have voted in the last presidential election, she found a mean grade point average of 2.71 and standard deviation .64. For an independent random sample of 123 students who did not vote, the mean grade point average was 2.79, and the standard deviation was .56. Test against a two-sided alternative the null hypothesis that the population means are equal.

9.38 In light of a recent large corporation bankruptcy, auditors are becoming increasingly concerned about the possibility of fraud. Auditors might be helped in evaluation of the chances of fraud by carefully measuring cash flow. To evaluate this possibility, samples of midlevel auditors from C.P.A. firms were presented with cash-flow information from a fraud case, and they were asked to evaluate the chance of material fraud, on a scale from zero to 100. A random sample of 36 auditors used the cash flow information. Their mean assessment was 36.21, and the sample standard deviation was 22.93. For an independent random sample of 36 auditors not using the cash flow information, the sample mean and standard deviation were respectively 47.56 and 27.56. Assuming that the two population distributions are normal with equal variances, test against a two-sided alternative the null hypothesis that the population means are equal.

9.39 Initial public offerings prospectuses were examined. In a random sample of 70 prospectuses in which sales forecasts were disclosed, the mean debt-to-equity ratio prior to the offering issue was 3.97, and the sample standard deviation was 6.14. For an independent random sample of 51 prospectuses in which sales earnings forecasts were not disclosed, the mean debt-to-equity ratio was 2.86, and the sample standard deviation was 4.29. Test against a two-sided alternative the null hypothesis that population mean debt-to-equity ratios are the same for disclosers and nondisclosers of earnings forecasts.

9.40 A publisher is interested in the effects on sales of college texts that include more than 100 data files. The publisher plans to produce 20 texts in the business area and randomly chooses 10 to have more than 100 data files. The remaining 10 are produced with at most 100 data files. For those with more than 100, first-year sales averaged 9,254, and the sample standard deviation was 2,107. For the books with at most 100, average first-year sales were 8,167, and the sample standard deviation was 1,681. Assuming that the two population distributions are normal with the same variance, test the null hypothesis that the population means are equal against the alternative that the true mean is higher for books with more than 100 data files.

9.7 TESTS FOR THE DIFFERENCE BETWEEN TWO POPULATION PROPORTIONS (LARGE SAMPLES)

Next we will develop procedures for comparing two population proportions. We will consider a standard model with a random sample of n_x observations with a proportion p_x "successes" and an independent random sample of n_y observations from a population with a proportion p_y "successes".

In Section 8.7 we saw that for large samples, proportions can be approximated as normally distributed random variables and as a result

$$Z = \frac{(p_x - p_y) - (\pi_x - \pi_y)}{\sqrt{\dfrac{\pi_x(1 - \pi_x)}{n_x} + \dfrac{\pi_y(1 - \pi_y)}{n_y}}}$$

has a standard normal distribution.

We want to test the hypothesis that the population proportions π_x and π_y are equal. Denote their common value by π_0, then we have under this hypothesis

$$Z = \frac{(p_x - p_y)}{\sqrt{\dfrac{\pi_0(1 - \pi_0)}{n_x} + \dfrac{\pi_0(1 - \pi_0)}{n_y}}}$$

follows to a good approximation a standard normal distribution.

Finally, the unknown proportion π_0 can be estimated by a pooled estimator defined as

$$p_0 = \frac{n_x p_x + n_y p_y}{n_x + n_y}$$

The null hypothesis in these tests assumes that the population proportions are equal. If the null hypothesis is true then the unbiased estimator and efficient estimator for π_0 can be obtained by combining the two random samples and as a result p_0 is computed using this equation. Then we can replace the unknown π_0 by p_0 to obtain a random variable that has a distribution close to the standard normal, for large sample sizes.

The tests are summarized as follows

TESTING THE EQUALITY OF TWO POPULATION PROPORTIONS (LARGE SAMPLES)

We are given independent random samples of size n_x and n_y with proportion successes p_x and p_y. When we assume that the population proportions are equal, an estimate of the common proportion is

$$p_0 = \frac{n_x p_x + n_y p_y}{n_x + n_y}$$

For large sample sizes — $n\pi(1 - \pi) > 9$— the following tests have significance level α:

i. To test either null hypothesis

$$H_0: \pi_x - \pi_y = 0 \quad \text{or} \quad H_0: \pi_x - \pi_y \leq 0$$

against the alternative

$$H_1: \pi_x - \pi_y > 0$$

the decision rule is

$$\text{Reject } H_0 \text{ if } \quad \frac{(p_x - p_y)}{\sqrt{\dfrac{p_0(1 - p_0)}{n_x} + \dfrac{p_0(1 - p_0)}{n_y}}} > Z_\alpha \qquad (9.29)$$

ii. To test either null hypothesis

$$H_0: \pi_x - \pi_y = 0 \quad \text{or} \quad H_0: \pi_x - \pi_y \geq 0$$

against the alternative

$$H_1: \pi_x - \pi_y < 0$$

the decision rule is

$$\text{Reject } H_0 \text{ if } \quad \frac{(p_x - p_y)}{\sqrt{\dfrac{p_0(1 - p_0)}{n_x} + \dfrac{p_0(1 - p_0)}{n_y}}} < -Z_\alpha \qquad (9.30)$$

iii. To test the null hypothesis

$$H_0: \pi_x - \pi_y = 0$$

against the alternative

$$H_1: \pi_x - \pi_y \neq 0$$

the decision rule is

$$\text{Reject } H_0 \text{ if } \quad \frac{(p_x - p_y)}{\sqrt{\dfrac{p_0(1 - p_0)}{n_x} + \dfrac{p_0(1 - p_0)}{n_y}}} < -Z_{\alpha/2} \quad \text{or} \quad \frac{(p_x - p_y)}{\sqrt{\dfrac{p_0(1 - p_0)}{n_x} + \dfrac{p_0(1 - p_0)}{n_y}}} > Z_{\alpha/2}$$

$$(9.31)$$

It is also possible to compute and interpret p-values for these tests by calculating the minimum significance level at which the null hypothesis can be rejected.

EXAMPLE 9.11

HUMOR IN BRITISH AND
AMERICAN TRADE MAGAZINE
ADVERTISEMENTS (HYPOTHESIS
TESTS FOR DIFFERENCES
BETWEEN PROPORTIONS)

A study was conducted to determine if there was a difference in humor content in British and American trade magazine advertisements. In an independent random sample of 270 American trade magazine advertisements, 56 were humorous. An independent random sample of 203 British trade magazine advertisements contained 52 humorous ads. Does this data provide evidence that there is a difference in the proportion of humorous ads in British versus American trade magazines?

SOLUTION

Define π_x and π_y as the population proportions of humorous British and American advertisements, respectively. The null hypothesis is

$$H_0 : \pi_x - \pi_y = 0$$

and the alternative hypothesis is

$$H_1 : \pi_x - \pi_y \neq 0$$

The decision rule is to reject H_0 in favor of H_1 if

$$\frac{(p_x - p_y)}{\sqrt{\dfrac{\pi_0(1-\pi_0)}{n_x} + \dfrac{\pi_0(1-\pi_0)}{n_y}}} < -Z_{\alpha/2} \quad \text{or} \quad > Z_{\alpha/2}$$

The data for this problem is

$$n_x = 203 \qquad p_x = 52/203 = 0.256 \qquad n_y = 270 \qquad p_y = 56/270 = 0.207$$

The estimate of the common variance π_0 under the null hypothesis is

$$p_0 = \frac{n_x p_x + n_y p_y}{n_x + n_y} = \frac{(203)(0.256) + (270)(0.207)}{203 + 270} = 0.228$$

The test statistic is

$$\frac{(p_x - p_y)}{\sqrt{\dfrac{p_0(1-p_0)}{n_x} + \dfrac{p_0(1-p_0)}{n_y}}} = \frac{0.256 - 0.207}{\sqrt{\dfrac{(0.228)(1-0.228)}{203} + \dfrac{(0.228)(1-0.228)}{270}}} = 1.26$$

For a two-tailed test with $\alpha = 0.10$ the $z_{0.05}$ value is 1.645. Thus it is not possible to reject the null hypothesis and we have little evidence that there is a difference in humorous ads in the two countries.

The test calculations can also be carried out by using PHStat in Excel

```
PHStat > TWO-SAMPLE TESTS > Z TEST FOR DIFFERENCES IN
PROPORTIONS > FOLLOW DIAGLOG BOX
```

The results are shown in Figure 9.9. In Figure 9.9 we see all of the intermediate computations and the test statistic. In addition the p-value for this test is 0.211. There is no evidence of a difference between the population proportions.

FIGURE 9.9
PHStat Output Comparison
of Population Proportions

Z Test for Differences in Two Proportions

Hypothesized Difference	**0**
Level of Significance	**0.05**
Group 1	
Number of Successes	**52**
Sample Size	**203**
Group 2	
Number of Successes	**56**
Sample Size	**270**
Group 1 Proportion	0.256157635
Group 2 Proportion	0.207407407
Difference in Two Proportions	0.048750228
Average Proportion	0.22832981
Z Test Statistic	1.250198038

1. Z Test Statistic
2. p-value

Two-Tailed Test	
Lower Critical Value	**-1.959961082**
Upper Critical Value	**1.959961082**
p-**Value**	**0.211227344**
Do not reject the null hypothesis	

EXERCISES

9.41 A random sample of 1,556 people in country A were asked to respond to the statement: "Increased world trade can increase our per capita prosperity." Of these sample members, 38.4% agreed with the statement. When the same statement was presented to a random sample of 1,108 people in country B, 52.0% agreed. Test the null hypothesis that the population proportions agreeing with this statement were the same in the two countries against the alternative that a higher proportion agreed in country B.

9.42 Small business phone users were surveyed six months after access to carriers other than ATT became available for wide-area phone service. Of a random sample of 368 users, 92 said they were attempting to learn more about their options, as did 37 of an independent random sample of 116 users of alternate carriers. Test at the 5% significance level, against a two-sided alternative, the null hypothesis that the two population proportions are the same.

9.43 Employees of a building materials chain, facing a shutdown, were surveyed on a prospective employee ownership plan. Some employees pledged $10,000 to this plan, putting up $800 immediately, while others indicated that they did not intend to pledge. Of a random sample of 175 pledgers, 78 had already been laid off, while 208 of a random sample of 604 nonpledgers had already been laid off. Test at the 5% level, against a two-sided alternative, the null hypothesis that the population proportions already laid off were the same for pledgers as for nonpledgers.

9.44 Of a random sample of 381 high quality investment equity options, 191 had less than 30% debt. Of an independent random sample of 166 high risk investment equity options, 145 had less than 30% debt. Test against a two-sided alternative the null hypothesis that the two population proportions are equal.

9.45 Independent random samples of consumers were asked about satisfaction with their computer system in two slightly different ways. The options available for answer were the same in the two cases. When asked how *satisfied* they were with their computer system, 138 of 240 sample members opted for "very satisfied." When asked how *dissatisfied* they were with their computer system, 128 of 240 sample members opted for "very satisfied." Test at the 5% level, against the obvious one-sided alternative, the null hypothesis that the two population proportions are equal.

9.46 Of a random sample of 1,200 people in Denmark, 480 had a positive attitude toward car salesmen. Of an independent random sample of 1,000 people in France, 790 had a positive attitude toward car salesmen. Test at the 1% significance level the null hypothesis that the population proportions are equal, against the alternative that a higher proportion of French have a positive attitude toward car salesmen.

9.8 TESTING OF THE EQUALITY OF THE VARIANCES BETWEEN TWO NORMALLY DISTRIBUTED POPULATIONS

There are a number of situations where we are interested in comparing the variances from two normally distributed populations. The Students's t test in Section 9.6 assumed equal variances and used the two sample variances to compute a pooled estimator for the common variances. We will see that comparisons of variances are important inferential procedures for regression analysis—see Chapters 10 and 11—and for analysis of variance—see Chapter 15. Quality control studies are often concerned with the question of which process has the smaller variance.

In this section we will develop a procedure for testing the assumption that population variances from independent samples are equal. To perform such tests we will introduce the F probability distribution. We begin by letting s_x^2 be the sample variance for a random sample of n_x observations from a normally distributed population with population variance σ_x^2. A second independent random sample of size n_y provides a sample variance of s_y^2 from a normal population with population variance σ_y^2. Then the random variable

$$F = \frac{s_x^2 / \sigma_x^2}{s_y^2 / \sigma_y^2}$$

follows a distribution known as the F distribution. This family of distributions, which is widely used in statistical analysis, is identified by the degrees of freedom for the numerator and the degrees of freedom for the denominator. Degrees of freedom for the numerator are associated with the sample variance s_x^2 and equal to $(n_x - 1)$. Similarly the degrees of freedom for the denominator are associated with the sample variance s_y^2 and equal to $(n_y - 1)$.

The F distribution is constructed as the ratio of two chi-square random variables, each divided by their degrees of freedom. The chi-square distribution relates the sample and population variances for a normally distributed population. Hypothesis tests that use the F distribution depend on the assumption of a normal distribution. The characteristics of the F distribution are summarized in the box.

THE *F* DISTRIBUTION

Given that we have two independent random samples with n_x and n_y observations from two normal populations with variances σ_x^2 and σ_y^2. If the sample variances are s_x^2 and s_y^2 then the random variable

$$F = \frac{s_x^2 / \sigma_x^2}{s_y^2 / \sigma_y^2} \tag{9.32}$$

has an *F* distribution with numerator degrees of freedom $(n_x - 1)$ and denominator degrees of freedom $(n_y - 1)$.

An *F* distribution with numerator degrees of freedom ν_1 and denominator degrees of freedom ν_2 will be denoted F_{ν_1, ν_2}. We denote $F_{\nu_1, \nu_2, \alpha}$ the number for which

$$P(F_{\nu_1, \nu_2} > F_{\nu_1, \nu_2, \alpha}) = \alpha$$

We need to emphasize that this test is quite sensitive to the assumption of normality.

FIGURE 9.10
F Probability Density
Function with 10 Numerator
Degrees of Freedom and 20
Denominator Degrees of
Freedom

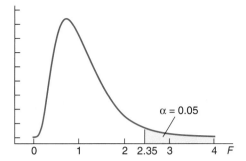

The cutoff points $F_{v_1, v_2, \alpha}$, for α equal to 0.05 and 0.01, are provided in Table 9 of the Appendix. For example, for 10 numerator degrees of freedom and 20 denominator degrees of freedom, we see from the table

$$F_{10,20,0.05} = 2.35 \quad \text{and} \quad F_{10,20,0.01} = 3.37$$

Hence

$$P(F_{10,20} > 2.35) = 0.05 \quad \text{and} \quad P(F_{10,20} > 3.37) = 0.01$$

Figure 9.10 presents a schematic description of the *F* distribution for this example.

In practical applications we usually arrange the *F* ratio so that the larger sample variance is in the numerator and the smaller in the denominator. Thus we only need to use the upper cutoff points to test the hypothesis of equality of variances. When the population variances are equal, the *F* random variable becomes

$$F = \frac{s_x^2}{s_y^2}$$

and this ratio of sample variances becomes the test statistic. The intuition for this test is quite simple: If one of the sample variances greatly exceeds the other then we must conclude that the population variances are not equal. The hypothesis tests for equality of variances are summarized as follows.

TESTS FOR EQUALITY OF VARIANCES FROM TWO NORMAL POPULATIONS

Let s_x^2 and s_y^2 be observed sample variances from independent random samples of size n_x and n_y from normally distributed populations with variances σ_x^2 and σ_y^2. Use s_x^2 to denote the larger variance, then the following tests have significance level α:

i. To test either null hypothesis

$$H_0: \sigma_x^2 = \sigma_y^2 \quad \text{or} \quad H_0: \sigma_x^2 \leq \sigma_y^2$$

against the alternative

$$H_1: \sigma_x^2 > \sigma_y^2$$

the decision rule is

$$\text{Reject } H_0 \text{ if} \quad F = \frac{s_x^2}{s_y^2} > F_{n_x - 1, n_y - 1, \alpha} \tag{9.33}$$

ii. To test the null hypothesis

$$H_0: \sigma_x^2 = \sigma_y^2$$

against the alternative

$$H_1: \sigma_x^2 \neq \sigma_y^2$$

the decision rule is

$$\text{Reject } H_0 \text{ if } F = \frac{s_x^2}{s_y^2} > F_{n_x-1, n_y-1, \alpha/2} \qquad (9.34)$$

where s_x^2 is the larger of the two sample variances. Since either sample variance could be larger, this rule is actually based on a two-tailed test, and hence we use $\alpha/2$ as the upper tail probability.

Here, F_{n_x-1, n_y-1} is the number for which

$$P(F_{n_x-1, n_y-1} > F_{n_x-1, n_y-1, \alpha}) = \alpha$$

where F_{n_x-1, n_y-1} has an F distribution with $(n_x - 1)$ numerator degrees of freedom and $(n_y - 1)$ denominator degrees of freedom.

For all of these tests a p-value is defined as the smallest significance level at which the null hypothesis can be rejected. Because of the complexity of the F distribution, critical values are computed for only a few special cases. Thus p-values will be typically computed using a statistical package such as Minitab or by using Excel with PHStat.

EXAMPLE 9.12

STUDY OF MATURITY
VARIANCES BY INVESTORS NOW
(HYPOTHESIS TESTS FOR TWO
VARIANCES)

The research staff of Investors Now, an on-line financial trading firm, was interested in determining if there is a difference in the variance of the maturities of AAA-rated industrial bonds compared to CCC-rated industrial bonds.

SOLUTION

This question requires that we design a study that compares the population variances of maturities for the two different bonds. We will test the null hypothesis

$$H_0: \sigma_x^2 = \sigma_y^2$$

against the alternative hypothesis

$$H_1: \sigma_x^2 \neq \sigma_y^2$$

where σ_x^2 is the variance in maturities for AAA-rated bonds and σ_y^2 is the variance in maturities for CCC-rated bonds. The significance level of the test was chosen as $\alpha = 0.02$.

The decision rule is to reject H_0 in favor of H_1 if

$$\frac{s_x^2}{s_y^2} > F_{n_x-1, n_y-1, \alpha/2}$$

Note here that either sample variance could be larger and thus in the denominator. Hence the probability for this upper tail is $\alpha/2$. A random sample of 17 AAA-rated bonds resulted in a sample variance $s_x^2 = 123.35$, and an independent random sample of 11 CCC-rated bonds resulted in a sample variance $s_y^2 = 8.02$. The test statistic is thus

$$\frac{s_x^2}{s_y^2} = \frac{123.35}{8.02} = 15.38$$

Given a significance level of $\alpha = 0.02$ we find that the critical value of F, from interpolation in Table 7 of the Appendix is

$$F_{16,10,0.01} = 4.53.$$

Clearly the computed value of F (15.38) exceeds the critical value (4.53) and we reject H_0 in favor of H_1. Thus there is strong evidence that variances in maturities are different for these two types of bonds.

The computations for this test can also be performed using PHStat in Excel using the command sequence

```
PHSTAT > TWO SAMPLE TESTS > F TEST FOR DIFFERENCES IN
VARIANCES
```

and then following the dialog box. The results of this procedure are shown in Figure 9.11. Note the p-value is 0.0001, indicating strong evidence for a difference.

FIGURE 9.11
Comparison of Variance in Bond Maturities: F Test Using PHStat

F Test for Differences in Two Variances

Level of Significance	0.02
Population 1 Sample	
Sample Size	17
Sample Standard Deviation	11.113
Population 2 Sample	
Sample Size	11
Sample Standard Deviation	2.832
F-Test Statistic	15.39842
Population 1 Sample Degrees of Freedom	16
Population 2 Sample Degrees of Freedom	10
Two-Tailed Test	
Lower Critical Value	0.270933
Upper Critical Value	4.520416
p-Value	0.000114
Reject the null hypothesis	

1. F-test Statistic
2. Critical Value
3. P-Value

EXERCISES

9.47 It is hypothesized that the more expert a group of people examining personal income tax filings, the more variable will be their judgments about its accuracy. Independent random samples, each of 30 individuals, from groups of different levels of expertise were chosen. The "low-expertise" group consisted of people who had just completed their first intermediate accounting course. Members of the "high-expertise" group had completed undergraduate studies and were employed by reputable C.P.A. firms. The sample members were asked to judge the accuracy of personal income tax filings. For the low-expertise group, the sample variance was 451.770, while for the high-expertise group it was 1,614.208. Test the null hypothesis that the two population variances are equal against the alternative that the true variance is higher for the high-expertise group.

9.48 It is hypothesized that the total sales of a corporation should vary more in an industry with active price competition than in one with duopoly and tacit collusion. In a study of the merchant ship production industry, it was found that in four years of active price competition, the variance of Company A's total sales was 114.09. In the following seven years, in which there was duopoly and tacit collusion, this variance was 16.08. Assume that the data can be regarded as an independent random sample from two normal distributions.

Test at the 5% level the null hypothesis that the two population variances are equal against the alternative that the variance of total sales is higher in years of active price competition.

9.49 In Exercise 9.38, it was assumed that population variances for assessments of the chance of material fraud were the same for auditors using cash flow information as for auditors not using cash flow information. Test this assumption against a two-sided alternative hypothesis.

9.50 In Exercise 9.40, it was assumed that population variances were equal for first-year sales of textbooks with more than 100 data files and those with at most 100 data files. Test this assumption against a two-sided alternative.

9.51 A university research team was studying the relationship between idea generation by groups with and without a moderator. For a random sample of four groups with a moderator, the mean number of ideas generated per group was 78.0, and the standard deviation was 24.4. For a random sample of four groups without a moderator the mean number of ideas generated was 63.5 and the standard deviation was 20.2 Test the assumption that the two population variances were equal against the alternative that the population variance is higher for groups with a moderator.

9.9 ASSESSING THE POWER OF A TEST

In Sections 9.2 to 9.8 we have developed various hypothesis tests with significance level α. In all of these tests we developed decision rules for rejecting the null hypothesis in favor of an alternative hypothesis. In carrying out these various tests we know that the probability of committing a Type I error when we reject the null hypothesis is a small value α or less. In addition, we may also compute the p-value for the test and thus know the smallest significance level at which the null hypothesis can be rejected. When we reject the null hypothesis we conclude that we have strong evidence to support our conclusion. But if we fail to reject the null hypothesis we know that either the null hypothesis is true or that we have committed a Type II error by failing to reject the null hypothesis when the alternative is true.

In this section we will consider the characteristics of some of our tests when the null hypothesis is not true. We will learn how to compute the probability of Type II error and also how to determine the power of the hypothesis test. Of course a Type II error can only occur if the alternative hypothesis is true.

Thus we will consider Type II error and Power for specific values of the population parameter that are included in the alternative hypothesis.

Tests of the Mean of a Normal Distribution: Population Variance Known

Following the procedures of Section 9.2 we want to test the null hypothesis that the mean of a normal population is equal to a specific value μ_0. Specifically we want to test

$$H_0 : \mu = \mu_0$$

against the alternative

$$H_1 : \mu > \mu_0$$

Using a decision rule

$$\text{Reject } H_0 \text{ if } \quad \frac{\overline{X} - \mu_0}{\sigma / \sqrt{n}} > Z_\alpha \quad \text{or} \quad \overline{X} > \mu_0 + Z_\alpha \sigma / \sqrt{n}$$

The probability of a Type II error, β, can be computed for every value of μ that is greater than μ_0.

DETERMINING THE PROBABILITY OF TYPE II ERROR

Consider the test

$$H_0 : \mu = \mu_0$$

against the alternative

$$H_1 : \mu > \mu_0$$

Using a decision rule

$$\text{Reject } H_0 \text{ if } \quad \frac{\overline{X} - \mu_0}{\sigma / \sqrt{n}} > Z_\alpha \quad \text{or} \quad \overline{X} > \mu_0 + Z_\alpha \sigma / \sqrt{n} = \overline{X}_c$$

Using the decision rule, determine the values of the sample mean that result in accepting the null hypothesis. Now for any value of the population mean defined by the alternative hypothesis H_1 find the probability that the sample mean will be in the acceptance region for the null hypothesis. This is the probability of Type II error. Thus we consider a $\mu = \mu^*$ such that $\mu^* > \mu_0$. Then for μ^* the probability of Type II error is

$$\begin{aligned} \beta &= P(\overline{X} < \overline{X}_c \mid \mu = \mu^*) \\ &= P\left(Z < \frac{\overline{X}_c - \mu^*}{\sigma / \sqrt{n}} \right) \end{aligned} \tag{9.35}$$

and

$$\text{Power} = 1 - \beta$$

The value of β and the Power will be different for every μ^*.

Consider an example where we are testing the null hypothesis that the population mean weight of ball bearings from a production process is 5 ounces versus the alternative hypothesis that the population mean weight is greater than 5 ounces. We will conduct the test with a random sample of 16 observations and a significance level of 0.05. The population distribution is assumed to be a normal distribution with a standard deviation of 0.1 ounce. Thus the null hypothesis is

$$H_0 : \mu = 5$$

versus the alternative hypothesis

$$H_0 : \mu > 5$$

and the decision rule is

$$\text{Reject } H_0 \text{ if } \quad \frac{\overline{X} - 5}{0.1/\sqrt{16}} > 1.645 \quad \text{ or } \quad \overline{X} > 5 + 1.645(0.1/\sqrt{16} = 5.041$$

Now if the sample mean is less than 5.041 then, using our rule, we will accept the null hypothesis.

Suppose that we want to determine the probability that the null hypothesis will be accepted if the true mean weight is 5.05 ounces. Clearly the alternative hypothesis is correct, and we want to determine the probability that we will accept the null hypothesis and thus commit a Type II error. That is, we want to determine the probability that the sample mean is less than 5.041 if the population mean is actually 5.05. Using the 16 observations we will compute the probability of Type II error as

$$\beta = P(\overline{X} \le 5.041 \mid \mu = 5.05) = P\left(Z \le \frac{5.041 - 5.05}{0.1/\sqrt{16}} \right)$$
$$= P(Z \le -0.36)$$
$$= 1 - 0.6406 = 0.3594$$

Thus, using the preceding decision rule, we find that the probability, β, of Type II error when the population mean is 5.05 ounces is 0.3594. Since the power of a test is one minus the probability of Type II error we have, when the population mean is 5.05,

$$\text{Power} = 1 - \beta = 1 - 0.3594 = 0.6406$$

These power calculations are shown in Figure 9.12. In part (a), we see that when the population mean is 5, the probability that the sample mean exceeds 5.041 is 0.05, the significance level of the test. Part (b) of the figure shows the density function of the sampling distribution of the sample mean when the population mean is 5.05. The shaded area in this figure shows the probability that the sample mean exceeds 5.041 when the population mean is 5.05—the power of the test. Similar calculations could be made to determine the power and probability of a Type II error for any value of μ greater than 5.0.

By computing the power of a test for all values of μ included in the null hypothesis we can generate the power function as shown in Figure 9.13.

FIGURE 9.12
Sampling Distribution of Sample Mean for Sixteen Observations with $\sigma = 0.1$

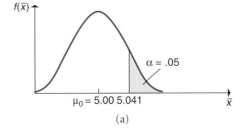

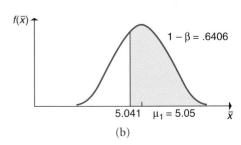

FIGURE 9.13
Power Function for Test
$H_0 : \mu = 5$ Against $H_1 : \mu > 5$
$(\alpha = 0.05, \sigma = 0.1, n = 16)$

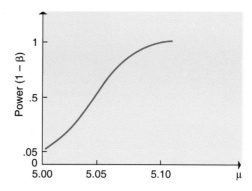

The power function has the following features

1. The farther the true mean is from the hypothesized mean μ_0, the greater is the power of the test, everything else being equal. Figure 9.13 illustrates this result.
2. The smaller the significance level of the test, the smaller the power, everything else being equal. Thus reducing the probability of Type I error increases the probability of Type II error, but reducing β by 0.01 does not generally increase β by 0.01—the changes are not linear.
3. The larger the population variance, the lower the power of the test, everything else being equal.
4. The larger the sample size, the greater the power of the test, everything else being equal. Note that larger sample sizes reduce the variance of the sample mean and thus provide a greater chance that we will reject H_0 when it is not correct. Figure 9.14 presents a set of power curves at sample sizes of 4, 9, and 16 that illustrate the effect.
5. The power of the test at μ_0 equals α, and the power of the test at the critical value equals 0.5.

FIGURE 9.14
Power Functions for Test H_0:
$\mu = 5$ Against $H_1 : \mu > 5$
$(\alpha = 0.05, \sigma = 0.1)$ for Sample
Sizes 4, 9, 16

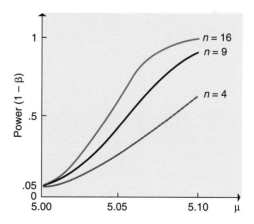

Computer Computation of the Power for a Specific Test Option

Many statistical computer packages have computational routines to compute the power of a test. For example, in Minitab the command sequence

```
STAT > POWER AND SAMPLE SIZE
```

provides a number of different test options. Figure 9.15 shows the dialog box and computer output for a two-sample Student's *t* test. Notice that you are required to enter the sample size, standard deviation, and difference between sample means. Several other options are available in the dialog boxes.

FIGURE 9.15
Minitab Computation of the
Power

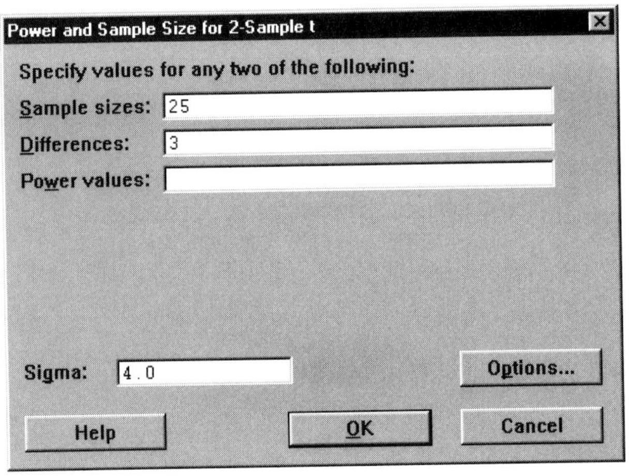

```
2-Sample t Test

Testing mean 1 = mean 2 (versus >)
Calculating power for mean 1 = mean 2 + difference
Alpha = 0.05   Sigma = 4

                Sample
Difference       Size    Power
        3          25   0.8338
```

Power for Population Proportion Tests (Large Samples)

In Section 9.6 we developed hypothesis tests and decision rules for testing if the population proportion had certain values. Using methods similar to those in the previous section we can also develop the probability of Type II error for proportion tests. The probability, β, of making a Type II error for any given population proportion π_1 included in H_1 is found as follows:

1. From the test decision rule, find the range of values of the sample proportion leading to acceptance of the null hypothesis.
2. Using the value π_1 for the population proportion—where π_1 is included in the alternative hypothesis—find the probability that the sample proportion will be in the acceptance range determined in (1) for samples of n observations when the population proportion is π_1.

We demonstrate this procedure in the following example.

EXAMPLE 9.13

FORECASTS OF CORPORATE
EARNINGS FOR ELECTRONIC
INVESTORS INC. (POWER AND
TYPE II ERROR)

The President of Electronic Investors Inc. has asked you to prepare an analysis of the forecasts of corporate earnings per share that were made by a group of financial analysts. Researchers were equally interested in the proportion of forecasts that exceeded the actual level of earnings and the proportion of forecasts that were less than the actual level of earnings.

SOLUTION

Begin your analysis by constructing a hypothesis test to determine if there was strong evidence to conclude that the proportion of forecasts that were above actual earnings was different from 50%. Using π to denote the proportion of forecasts that exceeded the actual level, the null hypothesis is

$$H_0 : \pi = \pi_0 = 0.50$$

and the alternative hypothesis is

$$H_1: \pi \neq 0.50$$

The decision rule is

$$\text{Reject if} \quad \frac{p_x - \pi_0}{\sqrt{\dfrac{\pi_0(1 - \pi_0)}{n}}} > Z_{\alpha/2} \quad \text{or} \quad \frac{p_x - \pi_0}{\sqrt{\dfrac{\pi_0(1 - \pi_0)}{n}}} < -Z_{\alpha/2}$$

A random sample of $n = 600$ forecasts was obtained, and it was determined that 382 exceeded actual earnings. Using a significance level of $\alpha = 0.05$, the decision rule is to reject the null hypothesis if

$$\frac{p_x - 0.50}{\sqrt{\dfrac{(0.50)(0.50)}{600}}} > 1.96 \quad \text{or} \quad \frac{p_x - 0.50}{\sqrt{\dfrac{(0.50)(0.50)}{600}}} < -1.96$$

Also H_0 is rejected if

$$p_x > 0.50 + 1.96\sqrt{\frac{(0.50)(0.50)}{600}} = 0.50 + 0.04 = 0.54$$

or

$$p_x < 0.50 - 0.04 = 0.46$$

The observed sample proportion is

$$p_x = \frac{382}{600} = 0.637$$

and thus the null hypothesis is rejected at the 5% level.

Now we want to determine the probability of a Type II error when this decision rule is used. Suppose that the true population proportion was $\pi_1 = 0.55$. We want to determine the probability that the sample proportion is between 0.46 and 0.54 if the population proportion is 0.55. Thus the probability of Type II error is

$$P(0.46 \leq p_x \leq 0.54) = P\left[\frac{0.46 - \pi_1}{\sqrt{\dfrac{\pi_1(1 - \pi_1)}{n}}} \leq Z \leq \frac{0.54 - \pi_1}{\sqrt{\dfrac{\pi_1(1 - \pi_1)}{n}}}\right]$$

$$= P\left[\frac{0.46 - 0.55}{\sqrt{\dfrac{(0.55)(0.45)}{600}}} \leq Z \leq \frac{0.54 - 0.55}{\sqrt{\dfrac{(0.55)(0.45)}{600}}}\right]$$

$$= P(-4.43 \leq Z \leq -0.49) = 0.3121$$

Given the decision rule, the probability of a Type II error involved in accepting the null hypothesis when the true proportion is 0.55 is $\beta = 0.3121$. The power of the test for this value of the population proportion is

$$\text{Power} = 1 - \beta = 0.6879$$

FIGURE 9.16
Power Function for Test of H_0
: $\pi = 0.50$ Against $H_1 : \pi \neq$
0.50 ($\alpha = 0.05$, $n = 600$)

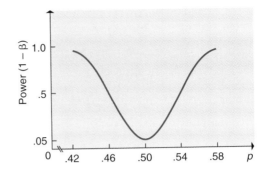

This probability can be calculated for any proportion π_1. Figure 9.16 shows the power function for this example. Because the alternative hypothesis is two-sided, the power function differs in shape from that of Figure 9.15. Here we are considering possible values of the population proportion on either side of the hypothesized value, 0.50. As we see, the probability of rejecting the null hypothesis when it is false increases the farther the true population proportion is from the hypothesized value.

EXERCISES

9.52 Refer to Exercise 9.6. Find the power of a 10%-level test when the true mean lifetime of batteries is 49 hours.

9.53 Refer to Exercise 9.7(a). Find the probability of a 5%-level test rejecting the null hypothesis when the true mean impurity concentration is 3.10%.

9.54 Refer to Exercise 9.9. Find the probability of a 1%-level test accepting the null hypothesis when the true mean response is 3.95.

9.55 A random sample of 802 supermarket shoppers had 378 shoppers that preferred generic brand items if the price was lower. Test at the 10% level the null hypothesis that at least one-half of all shoppers preferred generic brand items, against the alternative that the population proportion is less than one-half. Find the power of a 10%-level test if in fact 45% of the supermarket shoppers are able to state the correct price of an item immediately after putting it into the cart.

9.56 Refer to Exercise 9.21. Find the probability of rejecting the null hypothesis with a 5%-level test if in fact 20% of all U.S. adults would disagree with the statement.

9.57 Refer to Exercise 9.23. Find the probability of accepting the null hypothesis with a 10%-level test if in fact 60% of all auditors agree that cash flow is an important indicator of profitability.

9.58 A fast-food chain tests each day that the average weight of its "two-pounders" is at least 32 ounces. The alternative hypothesis is that the average weight is less than 32 ounces, indicating that new processing procedures are needed. The weights of two-pounders can be assumed to be normally distributed, with a standard deviation of 3 ounces. The decision rule adopted is to reject the null hypothesis if the sample mean weight is less than 30.8 ounces.

(a) If random samples of $n = 36$ two-pounders are selected, what is the probability of a Type I error, using this decision rule?

(b) If random samples of $n = 9$ two-pounders are selected, what is the probability of a Type I error, using this decision rule? Explain why your answer differs from that in part (a).

(c) Suppose that the true mean weight is 31 ounces. If random samples of 36 two-pounders are selected, what is the probability of a Type II error, using this decision rule?

9.59 A wine producer claims that the proportion of its customers who cannot distinguish its product from frozen grape juice is at most .10. The producer decides to test this null hypothesis against the alternative that the true proportion is more than .10. The decision rule adopted is to reject the null hypothesis if the sample proportion who cannot distinguish between these two flavors exceeds .14.

(a) If a random sample of 100 customers is chosen, what is the probability of a Type I error, using this decision rule?

(b) If a random sample of 400 customers is selected, what is the probability of a Type I error, using this decision rule? Explain, in words and graphically, why your answer differs from that in part (a).

(c) Suppose that the true proportion of customers who cannot distinguish between these flavors is .20. If a random sample of 100 customers is selected, what is the probability of a Type II error?

(d) Suppose that instead of the given decision rule, it is decided to reject the null hypothesis if the sample proportion of customers who cannot distinguish between the two flavors exceeds .16. A random sample of 100 customers is selected.

    (i) Without doing the calculations, state whether the probability of a Type I error will be higher than, lower than, or the same as in part (a).

    (ii) If the true proportion is .20, will the probability of a Type II error be higher than, lower than, or the same as in part (c)?

9.10 SOME COMMENTS ON HYPOTHESIS TESTING

In this chapter we have presented several important applications of hypothesis-testing methodology. In an important sense, the methodology is fundamental to decision making and analysis in the face of random variability. As a result, the procedures have great applicability to a number of research and management decisions. The procedures are relatively easy to use and various computer processes minimize the computational effort. Thus we have a tool that is appealing and quite easy to use. However, there are some subtle problems and areas of concern that we need to consider in order to avoid serious mistakes.

The null hypothesis plays a crucial role in the hypothesis-testing framework. In a typical investigation we set the significance level, α, at a small probability value. Then we obtain a random sample and use the data to compute a test statistic. If the test statistic is outside of the acceptance region (depending on the direction of the test) the null hypothesis is rejected and the alternative hypothesis is accepted. When we do reject we have strong evidence—small probability of error—in favor of the alternative hypothesis. In some cases we may fail to reject a drastically false null hypothesis simply because of limited sample information or because the test has low power. There may be important cases where this outcome is appropriate. For example, we would not change an existing process that is working effectively unless we had strong evidence that a new process clearly would be even better. In other cases, however, the special status of the null hypothesis is neither warranted nor appropriate. In those cases we might consider the costs of making both Type I and Type II errors in a decision process. We might also consider a different specification of the null hypothesis—noting that rejection of the null provides strong evidence in favor of the alternative. When we have two alternatives we could initially choose either as the null hypothesis. In the cereal-package weight example at the beginning of this chapter the null hypothesis could be either that

$$H_0 : \mu \geq 16$$

or

$$H_0 : \mu \leq 16$$

In the first case, rejection would provide strong evidence that the population mean package is less than 16. In the latter case, rejection would provide strong evidence that the population mean weight is greater than 16. As we have indicated, accepting either of these null hypotheses would not provide strong evidence. There are also procedures for controlling both Type I and Type II errors simultaneously—for example, see Carlson and Thorne (1997).[1]

On some occasions, very large amounts of sample information are available and we reject the null hypothesis even when differences are not practically important. Thus we need to contrast statistical significance with a broader definition of significance. Suppose that very large samples are used to compare annual mean family incomes in two cities. One result might be that the sample means differ by $2.67, and that difference might lead to rejecting a null hypothesis and thus concluding that one city has a higher mean family income than the other. While that result might be statistically significant, it clearly has no practical significance with respect to consumption or quality of life.

In specifying a null hypothesis and a testing rule we are defining the rules before we look at the sample data that was generated by a process that includes a random component. Thus if we look at the data before defining the null and alternative hypothesis we no longer have the stated probability of error, and the concept of "strong evidence" resulting from rejecting the null hypothesis is not valid. For example, if we were to decide on the significance level of our test after we have seen the p-values, then we cannot interpret our results in probability terms. Suppose that an economist compares each of five different income-enhancing programs against a standard minimal level using a hypothesis test. After collecting the data and computing p-values he determines that the null hypothesis—income not above the standard minimal level—can be rejected for one of the five programs with a significance level of $\alpha = 0.20$. Clearly this result violates the proper use of hypothesis testing. But we have seen this done.

As statistical computing tools have become more powerful there are a number of new ways of violating the principle of pre-specifying the null hypothesis before seeing the data. The recent popularity of data mining—using a computer program to search for relationships between variables in a very large data set—introduces new possibilities for abuse. Data mining can provide a description of subsets and differences in a particularly large sample of data. However, after seeing the results from a data mining operation, analysts may be tempted to define hypothesis tests based on the same data. This clearly violates the principle of defining the hypothesis test before seeing the data. A drug company may screen large numbers of medical treatment cases and discover that 5 out of 100 drugs have significant effects for the treatment of previously unintended diseases. Such a result might legitimately be used to identify potential research questions for a new research study with new random samples. However, if the original data is then used to test a hypothesis concerning the treatment benefits of the 5 drugs, we have a serious violation of the proper application of hypothesis testing and none of the probabilities of error are correct.

Defining the null and alternative hypothesis requires a careful consideration of the objectives of the analysis. For example, we might be faced with a proposal to introduce a specific new production process. In one case the present process might include considerable new equipment, well-trained workers, and a belief that the process performs very well. In that case we would define the productivity for the present process using the null hypothesis and the new process as the alternative. Then we would only adopt the new process if there is strong evidence—rejecting the null with a small α—that the new process has higher productivity. Alternatively the present process might be old and include equipment that needs to be replaced and a number of workers that require supplementary training. In that case we might choose to assign the new process productivity as the null hypothesis. Thus we would only continue with the old process if there is strong evidence that the old process productivity is higher.

---

[1] W. L. Carlson, and B. Thorne, "Applied Statistical Methods", 539–547, (Upper Saddle River, NJ: Prentice Hall 1997).

When we establish control charts for monitoring process quality, as we will see in Chapter 16, we set the desired process level as the null hypothesis and also set a very small significance level—$\alpha < 0.01$. Thus we only reject when there is very strong evidence that the process is no longer performing properly. However, these control chart hypothesis tests are established only after there has been considerable work to bring the process under control and minimize its variability. Therefore we are quite confident that the process is working properly and we do not wish to change in response to small variations in the sample data. But if we do find sample data outside the acceptance interval and hence reject the null hypothesis, we can be quite confident that something has gone wrong and we need to fix the process immediately.

The tests developed in this chapter are based on the assumption of an underlying normal distribution or that the central limit theorem applies for the distribution of sample means or proportions. When the normality assumption no longer holds, those probabilities of error may not be valid. Since we cannot be sure that most populations are precisely normal we might have some serious concerns for the validity of our tests. Considerable research has shown that tests involving means do not strongly depend on the normality assumption. These tests are said to be "robust" with respect to normality. However, tests involving variances are not robust. Thus greater caution is required when using hypothesis tests based on variances.

SUMMARY

In this chapter we have developed the methodology for classical hypothesis testing. We began with the rationale for making decisions in the face of uncertainty. We define decisions that involve the choice between two options. Decisions are made by rejecting a null hypothesis and thus providing strong evidence in favor of the alternative hypothesis. There are two possible errors, Type I, rejecting the null hypothesis when it is true, and Type II, failing to reject the null hypothesis when it is not true.

A variety of specific test procedures and decision rules were presented. These involve tests of the mean both when the variances are known and unknown, tests of proportions, and tests involving differences between means and differences between proportions. We also developed hypothesis tests for comparing sample variances against a single population variance and tests involving the comparison of sample variances from two independent samples. Finally, we considered characteristics of the problem-solving environment and noted appropriate and inappropriate applications of hypothesis testing.

KEY WORDS

CHAPTER EXERCISES AND APPLICATIONS

9.60 Explain carefully the distinction between each of the following pairs of terms:
  (a) Null and alternative hypotheses
  (b) Simple and composite hypotheses
  (c) One-sided and two-sided alternatives
  (d) Type I and Type II errors
  (e) Significance level and power

9.61 A statistician tests the null hypothesis that the proportion of men favoring a tax reform proposal is the same as the proportion of women. Based on sample data, the null hypothesis is rejected at the 5% significance level. Does this imply that the probability is at least .95 that the null hypothesis is false? If not, provide a valid probability statement.

9.62 Carefully explain what is meant by the p-value of a test, and discuss the use of this concept in hypothesis testing.

9.63 A random sample of 10 students found the following observations, in hours, for time spent studying in the week before final exams.

$$28 \quad 57 \quad 42 \quad 35 \quad 61 \quad 39 \quad 55 \quad 46 \quad 49 \quad 38$$

Assume that the population distribution is normal.
  (a) Find the sample mean and standard deviation.
  (b) Test at the 5% significance level the null hypothesis that the population mean is 40 hours against the alternative that it is higher.
  (c) Test at the 5% significance level against a two-sided alternative the null hypothesis that the population standard deviation is 10 hours.

9.64 State whether each of the following is true or false.
  (a) The significance level of a test is the probability that the null hypothesis is false.
  (b) A Type I error occurs when a true null hypothesis is rejected.
  (c) A null hypothesis is rejected at the .025 level, but is accepted at the .01 level. This means that the p-value of the test is between .01 and .025
  (d) The power of a test is the probability of accepting a null hypothesis that is true.
  (e) If a null hypothesis is rejected against an alternative at the 5% level, then using the same data, it must be rejected against that alternative at the 1% level.
  (f) If a null hypothesis is rejected against an alternative at the 1%-level, then using the same data must be rejected against the alternative at the 5% level.
  (g) The p-value of a test is the probability that the null hypothesis is true.

9.65 A process produces cable for the local telephone company. When the process is operating correctly, cable diameter follows a normal distribution with mean 1.6 inches and standard deviation .05 inch. A random sample of 16 pieces of cable found diameters with mean 1.615 inches and sample standard deviation .086 inches.
  (a) Assuming that the population standard deviation is .05 inch, test at the 10% level against a two-sided alternative the null hypothesis that the population mean is 1.6 inches. Find also the lowest level of significance at which this null hypothesis can be rejected against the two-sided alternative.
  (b) Test at the 10% level the null hypothesis that the population standard deviation is .05 inch against the alternative that it is bigger.

9.66 When operating normally, a manufacturing process produces tablets for which the mean weight of the active ingredient is 5 grams, and the standard deviation is .025 gram. For a random sample of 12 tablets, the following weights of active ingredient (in grams) were found:

5.01	4.69	5.03	4.98	4.98	4.95
5.00	5.00	5.03	5.01	5.04	4.95

  (a) without assuming that the population variance is known, test the null hypothesis that the population mean weight of active ingredient per tablet is 5 grams. Use a two-sided alternative and a 5% significance level. State any assumptions that you make.
  (b) Stating any assumptions that you make, test the null hypothesis that the population standard deviation is .025 gram against the alternative hypothesis that the population standard deviation exceeds .025 gram. Use a 5% significance level.

9.67 An insurance company employs agents on a commission basis. It claims that in their first year, agents will earn a mean commission of at least $40,000 and that the population standard deviation is no more than $6,000. A random sample of nine agents found, for commission in the first year,

$$\sum_{i=1}^{9} x_i = 333 \quad \text{and} \quad \sum_{i=1}^{9} \left(x_i - \bar{x} \right)^2 = 312$$

where x_i are measured in thousands of dollars and the population distribution can be assumed to be normal.

(a) Test at the 5% level the null hypothesis that the population mean is at least $40,000.

(b) Test at the 10% significance level the null hypothesis that the population standard deviation is at most $6,000.

9.68 Supporters claim that a new windmill can generate an average of at least 800 kilowatts of power per day. Daily power generation for the windmill is assumed to be normally distributed with a standard deviation of 120 kilowatts. A random sample of 100 days is taken to test this claim against the alternative hypothesis that the true mean is less than 800 kilowatts. The claim will be accepted if the sample mean is 776 kilowatts or more and rejected otherwise.

(a) What is the probability α of a Type I error using the decision rule if the population mean is in fact 800 kilowatts per day?

(b) What is the probability β of a Type II error using this decision rule if the population mean is in fact 740 kilowatts per day?

(c) Suppose that the same decision rule is used, but with a sample of 200 days rather than 100 days.

   (i) Would the value of α be larger than, smaller than, or the same as that found in (a)?

   (ii) Would the value of β be larger than, smaller than, or the same as that found in (b)?

(d) Suppose that a sample of 100 observations was taken, but that the decision rule was changed so that the claim would be accepted if the sample mean was at least 765 kilowatts.

   (i) Would the value of α be larger than, smaller than, or the same as that found in (a)?

   (ii) Would the value of β be larger than, smaller than, or the same as that found in (b)?

9.69 Of a random sample of 545 accountants engaged in preparing county operating budgets for use in planning and control, 117 indicated that estimates of cash flow were the most difficult element of the budget to derive.

(a) Test at the 5% level the null hypothesis that at least 25% of all accountants find cash flow the most difficult estimates to derive.

(b) Based on the procedure used in (a), what is the probability that the null hypothesis would be rejected if the true percentage of those finding cash flow estimates most difficult was:

   (i) 20%

   (ii) 25%

   (iii) 30%

9.70 A random sample of 104 marketing vice presidents from large Fortune 500 corporations was questioned on future developments in the business environment. Of those sample members, 50 indicated some measurement of agreement with the statement: "Firms will concen-

trate their efforts more on cash flow than on profits." What is the lowest level of significance at which the null hypothesis, which states that the true proportion of all such executives who would agree with this statement is one-half, can be rejected against a two-sided alternative?

9.71 In a random sample of 99 National Basketball Association games, the home team won 57 games. Test the null hypothesis that the home team wins one-half of all games against the alternative that the home team wins a majority of games.

9.72 Of a random sample of 150 business graduates, fifty agreed or strongly agreed that businesses should focus their efforts on innovative e-commerce strategies. Test at the 5% level the null hypothesis that at most 25% of all business graduates would be in agreement with this assertion.

9.73 Of a random sample of 142 admissions counselors on college campuses, 39 indicated that on average they spent 15 minutes or less studying each resume. Test the null hypothesis that at most 20% of all admissions counselors spend this little time studying resumes.

9.74 💿 In an agricultural experiment, two expensive high-yield varieties of corn are to be tested and the yield improvements measured. The experiment is arranged so that each variety is planted in ten pairs of similar plots. The data contained in data file '**Corn Yield**' are the percentage yield increases obtained for these two varieties. Stating any assumptions you make, test at the 10% significance level the null hypothesis that the two population mean percentage yield increases are the same. Use a two-sided alternative hypothesis.

9.75 💿 Two financial analysts were asked to predict earnings per share for a random sample of 12 corporations over the coming year. The quality of their forecasts was evaluated in terms of absolute percentage forecast error, defined as

$$100 \cdot \frac{|Actual - Predicted|}{Actual}$$

The absolute percentage forecast errors made are shown in the data file '**Analyst Prediction**'. Stating any assumptions you make, test against a two-sided alternative the null hypothesis that the population mean absolute percentage forecast errors are the same for these two financial analysts.

9.76 In a study of performance ratings of ex-smokers, a random sample of 34 ex-smokers had a mean absenteeism of 2.21 days per month and a sample standard deviation of 2.21 days per month. For an independent random sample of 86 long-term ex-smokers, the mean rating was 1.47 days per month and the sample standard deviation was 1.69 days per month. Find the lowest level of significance at which the null hypothesis of equality of the two population means can be rejected against a two-sided alternative.

9.77 Independent random samples of business managers and college economics faculty were asked to respond on a scale from one (strongly disagree) to seven (strongly agree) to the statement: "Grades in advanced economics are good indicators of students' analytical skills." For a sample of 70 business managers, the mean response was 4.4 and the sample standard deviation was 1.3. For a sample of 106 economics faculty, the mean response was 5.3 and the sample standard deviation was 1.4.

(a) Test at the 5% significance level the null hypothesis that the population mean response for business managers would be at most 4.0.

(b) Test at the 5% significance level the null hypothesis that the population means are equal, against the alternative that the population mean response is higher for economics faculty than for business managers.

9.78 Independent random samples of bachelors and masters degree holders in statistics, whose initial job was with a major actuarial firm, and who subsequently moved to an insurance company, were questioned. For a sample of 44 bachelor degree holders, the mean number of months before the first job change was 35.02 and the sample standard deviation was 18.20. For a sample of 68 master degree holders, the mean number of months before the first job change was 36.34 and the sample standard deviation was 18.94. Test at the 10% significance level, against a two-sided alternative, the null hypothesis that the population mean number of months before the first job change are the same for the two groups.

9.79 A study was aimed at assessing the effects of group size and characteristics of groups on the generation of advertising concepts. To assess the influence of group size, groups of four and eight members were compared. For a random sample of four 4-member groups, the mean number of advertising concepts generated per group was 78.0 and the sample standard deviation was 24.4. For an independent random sample of four 8-member groups, the mean number of advertising concepts generated per group was 114.7 and the sample standard deviation was 14.6. (In each case, the groups had a moderator.) Stating any assumptions that you need to make, test at the 1% level the null hypothesis that the population means are the same against the alternative that the mean is higher for 8-member groups.

9.80 An index of reading difficulty of a written text is calculated through the following steps:

(i) Find the average number of words per sentence.

(ii) Find the percentage of words with four or more syllables.

(iii) The index is 40% of the sum of (i) and (ii).

A random sample of six advertisements taken from Magazine A had the following fog indices:

15.75   11.55   11.16   9.92   9.23   8.20

An independent random sample of six advertisements from Magazine B had the following fog indices:

9.17   8.44   6.10   5.78   5.58   5.36

Stating any assumptions you need to make, test at the 5% level the null hypothesis that the population mean fog indices are the same against the alternative that the true mean is higher for Magazine A than for Magazine B.

9.81 From Exercise 9.80, the fog indices for a random sample of six advertisements in Magazine C were as follows:

9.50   8.60   8.59   6.50   4.79   4.29

For an independent random sample of six advertisements in Magazine D, the indices were as follows:

10.21   9.66   7.67   5.12   4.88   3.12

Stating any assumptions you need to make, test against a two-sided alternative the null hypothesis that the two population mean fog indices are the same.

9.82 Independent random samples of business and economics faculty were asked to respond on a scale from one (strongly disagree) to four (strongly agree) to the statement: "The threat and actuality of takeovers of publicly held companies provide discipline for boards and managers to maximize the value of the company to shareholders." For a sample of 202 business faculty, the mean response was 2.83 and the sample standard deviation was .89. For a sample of 291 economics faculty, the mean response was 3.00 and the sample standard deviation was .67. Test the null hypothesis that the population means are equal against the alternative that the mean is higher for economics faculty.

9.83 Independent random samples of knee and hip replacement patients were asked to assess the quality of service on a scale from one (low) to seven (high). (These patients had received breast implants.) For a sample of 83 knee patients, the mean rating was 6.543 and the sample standard deviation was .649. For a sample of 54 hip replacement patients, the mean rating was 6.733 and the sample standard deviation was .425. Test against a two-sided alternative the null hypothesis that the population mean ratings for these two types of patients are the same.

9.84 Of a random sample of 148 accounting majors, 75 rated a sense of humor as a very important trait to their career performance. This same view was held by 81 of an independent random sample of 178 finance majors.

(a) Test at the 5% level of significance the null hypothesis that at least one-half of all finance majors rate a sense of humor as very important.

(b) Test at the 5% level of significance against a two-sided alternative the null hypothesis that the population proportions of accounting and finance majors who rate a sense of humor as very important are the same.

9.85 Aimed at finding substantial earnings decrease, a random sample of 23 firms with substantial earnings decrease showed mean returns on assets three years previously was .058 and sample standard deviation .055. An independent random sample of 23 firms without a substantial earnings decrease showed mean return of .146 and standard deviation .058 for the same period. Assume that the two population distributions are normal with equal standard deviations. Test at the 5% significance level the null hypothesis that the population mean returns on assets are the same against the alternative that the true mean is higher for firms without substantial earnings decrease.

9.86 Random samples of employees in fast-food restaurants where the employer provides a training program were drawn. Of a sample of 67 employees who had not completed high school, 11 had participated in a training program provided by their current employer. Of an independent random sample of 113 employees who had completed high school but had not attended college, 27 had participated. Test at the 1% significance level the null hypothesis that the participation rates are the same for the two groups, against the alternative that the rate is lower for those who have not completed high school.

9.87 Of a random sample of 69 health insurance firms, 47 did public relations in-house, as did 40 of an independent random sample of 69 casualty insurance firms. Find and interpret the *p*-value of a test of equality of the population proportions against a two-sided alternative.

9.88 Independent random samples were taken of male and female clients of University Entrepreneurship Centers. These clients were considering starting a business. Of 94 male clients, 53 actually started a business venture, as did 47 of 68 female clients. Find and interpret the *p*-value of a test of equality of the population proportions against the alternative that the proportion of female clients actually starting a business is higher than the proportion of male clients.

9.89 Using the data of Exercise 9.80, test against a two-sided alternative the null hypothesis that the population standard deviation of the index of advertisements in Magazine A is the same as the population standard deviation of the index of advertisements in Magazine B.

9.90 Based on the material of Section 9.8, can you use the data of Exercise 9.75 to test the null hypothesis of equality of population variances for absolute percentage forecast errors for the two analysts?

9.91 🖰 You are the product manager for Brand 4 in a large food company. The company president has complained that a competing brand, called Brand 2, has higher average sales. The data services group has stored the latest product sales and price data in a file named **Storet** which is contained on your data disk or local computer system and described in the Appendix.

(a) Based on a statistical hypothesis test, does the president have strong evidence to support his complaint? Show all statistical work and reasoning.

(b) After analyzing the data you note that a large outlier of value 971 is contained in the sample for Brand 2. Repeat part (a) with this extreme observation removed. What do you now conclude about the president's complaint?

9.92 🖰 BBW Ltd. does quality control work on the final loaves of bread produced. The data file named **BBWltd**, which is stored on your data disk or local computer system, contains data collected as part of its analysis of the market. The variables in the file are:

1. "Dbread," which contains a random sample of weights, in grams, of their dark bread collected from supermarket shelves.

2. "Sbread," which contains a random sample of weights, in grams, of their specialty bread collected from supermarket shelves.

3. "Csbread," which contains a random sample of weights, in grams, of their competitor's specialty bread collected from supermarket shelves.

The company guarantees that its dark bread will have a weight of 100 grams or more. Based on the sample do they have strong evidence, $\alpha = 0.05$, that the guarantee is being met? Provide an appropriate hypothesis test result as evidence.

9.93 You are in charge of rural economic development in a rapidly developing country that is using its new-found oil wealth to develop the entire country. As part of your responsibility you have been asked to determine if there is evidence that the new rice growing procedures have increased output per hectare. A random sample of 27 fields was planted using the old procedure, and the sample mean output was 60 per hectare with a sample variance of 100. During the second year the new procedure was applied to the same fields and the sample mean output was 64 per hectare, with a sample variance of 150. The sample correlation between the two fields was 0.38. The population variances are assumed to be equal and that assumption should be used for the problem analysis.

(a) Use a hypothesis test, with a probability of Type I error = 0.05, to determine if there is strong evidence to support the conclusion that the new process leads to higher output per hectare and interpret the results..

(b) Under the assumption that the population variances are equal, construct a 95% acceptance interval for the ratio of the sample variances. Do the observed sample variances lead us to conclude that the population variances are the same? Please explain.

9.94 🖰 Joe Ortega is the Product Manager for Ole ice cream. You have been asked to determine if Ole ice cream has greater sales than Carl's ice cream, which is a strong competitor. The data file "**Ole** " contains weekly sales and price data for the competing brands over the year in three different supermarket chains. This sample data represents a random sample of all ice cream sales for the two brands.

(a) Design and implement an analysis to determine if there is strong evidence to conclude that Ole ice cream has higher mean sales than Carl's ice cream ($\alpha = 0.05$). Explain your procedure and show all computations. You may include Minitab output if appropriate to support your analysis. Explain your conclusions.

(b) Design and implement an analysis to determine if the prices charged for the two brands are different ($\alpha = 0.05$). Carefully explain your analysis, show all computations, and interpret your results.

9.95 Mary Peterson is in charge of preparing blended flour for exotic bread making. The process is to take two different types of flour and mix them together in order to achieve high quality breads. For one of the products, flour A and flour B are mixed together. The package of flour A comes from a packing process that has a population mean weight of 8 ounces with a population variance of 0.04. The package of flour B has a population mean weight of 8 ounces and a population variance of 0.06. The package weights have a correlation of 0.40. The A and B packages are mixed together to obtain a 16-ounce package of special exotic flour. Every 60 minutes a random sample of four packages of exotic flour are selected from the process and the mean weight for the four packages is computed. Prepare a 99% acceptance interval for a quality control chart for the sample means from the sample of four packages. Show all of your work and explain your reasoning. Explain how this acceptance chart would be used to ensure that the package weights maintain their standard.

9.96 Northeastern Franchisers Ltd. has a number of clients that use their process for producing exotic Norwegian dinners for customers throughout New England. The operating cost for the franchised process has a fixed cost of $1,000 per week plus $5 for every unit produced. Recently a number of restaurant owners using the process have complained that the cost model is no longer valid and in fact the weekly costs are higher. Your job is to determine if there is strong evidence to support their claim. You obtain a random sample of $n = 25$ restaurants and determine their costs. You also know

that the number of units produced in each restaurant is normally distributed with mean, $\mu = 400$ and variance $\sigma^2 = 625$. The random sample mean ($n = 25$) for weekly costs was $3,050. Prepare and implement an analysis to determine if there is strong evidence to conclude that costs are greater than those predicted by the cost model.

9.97 The president of Amalgamated Retailers International, Samiha Peterson, has asked for your assistance in studying the market penetration for their new cell phone. You are asked to study two markets and determine if the difference in market share remains the same. Historically Market 1, in Western Poland, has had a 30% market share for Amalgamated. Similarly Market 2, in Southern Austria, has had a 35% market share for Amalgamated. You obtain a random sample of potential customers from each area. From Market 1, 258 out of a total sample of 800 indicate they will purchase from Amalgamated. From Market 2, 260 out of 700 indicate they will purchase from Amalgamated.

(a) Using a probability of error $\alpha = 0.03$ test the hypothesis that the market shares are equal versus the hypothesis that they are not equal. (Market 2 − Market 1)

(b) Using a probability of error $\alpha = 0.03$ test the hypothesis that the market shares are equal versus the hypothesis that the share in Market 2 is larger.

9.98 Big River Inc., a major Alaskan fish processor, is attempting to determine the weight of salmon in the Northwest Green River. A random sample of salmon was obtained and weighed. The data is stored in the file labeled **Bigfish**. Use a classical hypothesis test to determine if there is strong evidence to conclude that the population mean weight for the fish is greater than 40, using a probability of Type I Error $\alpha = 0.05$.

Prepare a power curve for the test. Hint, Determine the population mean values for $\beta = 0.50$, $\beta = 0.25$, $\beta = 0.10$, and $\beta = 0.05$ and plot those means versus the power of the test.

9.99 Prairie Flower Cereal Inc. has asked you to study the variability of the weights of cereal bags produced in Plant 2 located in rural Malaysia. The package weights are known to be normally distributed. Using a random sample of size $n = 71$ you find that the sample mean weight is 40 and the sample variance is 50.

The marketing vice president claims that there is a very small probability that the population mean weight is less than 39. Using an appropriate statistical analysis comment on his claim.

CHAPTER 10

SIMPLE REGRESSION

INTRODUCTION

The discussion to this point has focused on analysis and inference related to a single variable. In this chapter we will extend our analysis to relationships between variables. First there will be a brief introduction to correlation analysis, followed by the development of simple regression analysis. Our discussion here follows Chapter 3, where we emphasized descriptive relationships including the use of scatter plots, correlation coefficients, and linear regression as tools to describe the relationships between variables. We assume that the reader is familiar with that material.

The analysis of business and economic processes makes extensive use of relationships between variables. These relationships are expressed mathematically as

$$Y = f(X)$$

where the function can follow many linear and nonlinear forms. In some of those cases the form of the relationship is not precisely known. Here we will develop analyses that are based on linear relationships. In many cases linear relationships provide a good model of the process. In other cases we are interested in a limited portion of a nonlinear relationship that can be approximated by a linear relationship. In Section 11.7 we will show how some important nonlinear relationships can also be analyzed using the procedures for regression analysis. Thus the correlation and regression procedures will be shown to have wide application to a broad range of problems.

Linear relationships are very useful for many business and economic applications as indicated in the following examples. The president of Amalgamated Materials, a manufacturer of sheetrock building material, believes that the mean annual quantity of sheetrock sold in her region is a linear function of the total value of building permits issued during the previous year. A grain dealer wants to know the effect of total output on price per ton. He is working on a prediction model that uses historical data. The marketing department needs to know how gasoline price affects total sales of gasoline. By using weekly price and sales data, they plan to develop a linear model that will tell them how much sales change as the result of price changes.

With the advent of many high-quality statistical packages and spreadsheets such as Excel it is now possible for almost anyone to compute correlation and regression statistics. Unfortunately we also know that it is not possible for everyone to interpret and use these computer results correctly. Here you will learn key insights that will guide your use of regression analysis. We will begin with a discussion of correlation analysis that directly follows the material in Chapter 3.

10.1 CORRELATION ANALYSIS

In this section we will use correlation coefficients to study relationships between variables. In Chapter 3 the sample correlation coefficient was developed to describe the relationship between variables indicated in the data. In Chapters 5 and 6 we learned about the population correlation. Here we develop inference procedures that use the correlation coefficient for studying linear relationships between variables.

In principle, there are any number of ways in which a pair of random variables might be related to each other. As we begin our analysis it is helpful to postulate some functional form for their relationship. It is often reasonable to conjecture, as a good approximation, that the association is linear. Thus, if the pair of linearly related random variables X and Y

is being considered, a scatter plot of the joint observations on this pair will tend to be clustered around a straight line. Conversely, if a linear relationship does not exist then the scatter plot will not follow a straight line. Not all of the relationships that we will study will be tightly clustered about a straight line. Many important relationships will have scatter plots that show a tendency toward a linear relationship, but with considerable deviation from a straight line. We saw a number of such examples in Chapter 3 scatter plots.

Correlations have wide applications in business and economics. In many applied economic problems we argue that there is an independent or exogenous variable X, whose values are "fixed" by activities outside of the economic system being modeled, and that there is a dependent or endogenous variable Y, whose value depends on the value of X. If we ask if sales increase when prices are reduced we are thinking about a situation in which a seller deliberately and independently adjusts prices up or down and observes changes in sales. Now suppose that prices and quantities sold result from equilibriums of supply and demand as proposed by the basic economic model. Then we could model prices and quantities as random variables and ask if these two random variables are related to each other. The correlation coefficient can be used to determine if there is a relationship between variables in either of these situations.

In such cases both X and Y may be determined simultaneously by factors that are outside of the economic system being modeled. Therefore a model in which both X and Y are random variables is often more realistic. In Chapter 5 the correlation coefficient ρ_{xy} was developed as a measure of the relationship between two random variables X and Y. In those cases the correlation coefficient, ρ_{xy}, is used to indicate a linear relationship without implying that one variable is independent and the other is dependent. In situations where one variable is logically dependent on a second variable we can use regression analysis to develop a linear model as a logical next step after correlation analysis. This will be the topic of the next section. Here we will develop statistical inference procedures that use sample correlations to determine characteristics of population correlations.

Hypothesis Test for Correlation

The sample correlation coefficient

$$r = \frac{S_{xy}}{S_x S_y}$$

$$S_{xy} = \frac{\sum \left(x_i - \overline{X}\right)\left(y_i - \overline{Y}\right)}{n - 1}$$

is useful as a descriptive measure of the strength of linear association in a sample. We can also use the correlation to test the hypothesis that there is no linear association in the population between a pair of random variables; that is

$$H_0 : \rho = 0$$

This particular null hypothesis of no linear relationship between a pair of random variables is of great interest in a number of applications. When we compute the sample correlation from data the result is likely to be different from 0 even if the population correlation is 0. Thus we would like to know how large a difference from zero is required for a sample correlation to provide evidence that the population correlation is not 0.

We can show that when the null hypothesis is true and the random variables have a joint normal distribution then the random variable

$$t = \frac{r\sqrt{(n-2)}}{\sqrt{(1-r^2)}}$$

follows a Student's t distribution with $(n-2)$ degrees of freedom. The appropriate hypothesis tests are shown in Equations 10.1 through 10.3.

TESTS FOR ZERO POPULATION CORRELATION

Let r be the sample correlation coefficient, calculated from a random sample of n pairs of observations from a joint normal distribution. The following tests of the null hypothesis

$$H_0: \rho = 0$$

have a significance value α:

i.   To test H_0 against the alternative

$$H_1: \rho > 0$$

the decision rule is

$$\text{Reject } H_0 \text{ if} \qquad \frac{r\sqrt{(n-2)}}{\sqrt{(1-r^2)}} > t_{n-2,\alpha} \qquad\qquad (10.1)$$

ii. To test H_0 against the alternative

$$H_1: \rho < 0$$

the decision rule is

$$\text{Reject } H_0 \text{ if} \qquad \frac{r\sqrt{(n-2)}}{\sqrt{(1-r^2)}} < -t_{n-2,\alpha} \qquad\qquad (10.2)$$

iii. To test H_0 against the two-sided alternative

$$H_1: \rho \neq 0$$

the decision rule is

$$\text{Reject } H_0 \text{ if} \quad \frac{r\sqrt{(n-2)}}{\sqrt{(1-r^2)}} < -t_{n-2,\alpha/2} \quad \text{or} \quad \frac{r\sqrt{(n-2)}}{\sqrt{(1-r^2)}} > t_{n-2,\alpha/2} \quad (10.3)$$

Here, $t_{n-2,\alpha}$ is the number for which

$$P(t_{n-2} > t_{n-2,\alpha}) = \alpha$$

where the random variable t_{n-2} follows a Student's t distribution with $(n-2)$ degrees of freedom.

EXAMPLE 10.1

**POLITICAL RISK
SCORE(HYPOTHESIS TEST FOR
CORRELATION)**

A research team was attempting to determine if political risk in countries is related to inflation for these countries. In this research a survey of political risk analysts produced a mean political risk score for each of 49 countries.[1]

SOLUTION

The political risk score is scaled such that the higher the score the greater the political risk. The sample correlation between political risk score and inflation for these countries was 0.43.

We wish to determine if the population correlation, ρ, between these measures is different from 0. Specifically we want to test

$$H_0: \rho = 0$$

against

$$H_1: \rho > 0$$

using the sample information

$$n = 49 \qquad r = 0.43$$

The test is based on the statistic

$$t = \frac{r\sqrt{(n-2)}}{\sqrt{(1-r^2)}} = \frac{0.43\sqrt{(49-2)}}{\sqrt{1-(0.43)^2}} = 3.265$$

Since there are $(n - 2) = 47$ degrees of freedom, we have from the Student's t table in the Appendix

$$t_{47,0.005} < 2.704$$

Therefore we can reject the null hypothesis at the 0.5% significance level. As a result we have strong evidence of a positive linear relationship between inflation and experts' judgements of political riskiness of countries. Note that from this result we cannot conclude that one variable led to the other, but only that they are related.

EXERCISES

10.1 An instructor in a statistics course set a final examination and also required the students to do a data analysis project. For a random sample of 10 students, the scores obtained are shown in the table. Find the sample correlation between the examination and project scores.

EXAMINATION	81	62	74	78	93	69	72	83	90	84
PROJECT		76	71	69	76	87	62	80	75	92	79

10.2 ● The accompanying table and the data file **Dow Jones** shows percentage changes (x_i) in the Dow-Jones index over the first five trading days of each of thirteen years, and also the corresponding percentage changes (y_i) in the index over the whole year.

X	Y
1.5	14.9
0.2	−9.2
−0.1	19.6
2.8	20.3
2.2	−3.7
−1.6	27.7
−1.3	22.6
5.6	2.3
−1.4	11.9
1.4	27
1.5	−4.3
−4.7	20.3
1.1	4.2

[1]Data from J. L. Mumpower, S. Livingston, and T. J. Lee, "Expert judgements of political riskiness," *Journal of Forecasting*, 6 (1987), 51–65.

(a) Calculate the sample correlation.

(b) Test at the 10% significance level, against a two-sided alternative, the null hypothesis that the population correlation is 0.

10.3 A college administers for all its courses a student evaluation questionnaire. For a random sample of 12 courses, the accompanying table and the data file **Student Evaluation** shows both the average student ratings of the instructor (on a scale from 1 to 5), and average expected grades of the students (on a scale from A = 4 to E = 0).

INSTRUCTOR RATING	2.8	3.7	4.4	3.6	4.7	3.5
EXPECTED GRADE	2.6	2.9	3.3	3.2	3.1	2.8
INSTRUCTOR RATING	4.1	3.2	4.9	4.2	3.8	3.3
EXPECTED GRADE	2.7	2.4	3.5	3.0	3.4	2.5

(a) Find the sample correlation between the instructor ratings and expected grades.

(b) Test at the 10% significance level the hypothesis that the population correlation coefficient is zero against the alternative that it is positive.

10.4 In an advertising study, the following results, also shown in the data file, **Advertising Revenue** were found:

X	Y
7.7	141.77
4.17	96.97
1.52	163.92
10.04	154.7
6.02	151.61
4.81	147.82
1.57	98.61
3.63	179.18
1.57	125.19

X	Y
4.65	171.81
2.97	200.23
0.98	120.49
4.18	95.83
6.09	196.67
3.09	275.97
3.08	289.59
1.76	105.71

x_i = Cost of advertisement ÷ Number of inquiries received

y_i = Revenue from inquiries ÷ Number of inquiries received

Find the sample correlation, and test against a two-sided alternative the null hypothesis that the population correlation is 0.

10.5 In the study of 49 countries discussed in Example 10.1, the sample correlation between the experts' political riskiness score and the infant mortality rate in these countries was .75. Test the null hypothesis of no correlation between these quantities against the alternative of positive correlation.

10.6 For a random sample of 353 high school teachers, the correlation between annual raises and teaching evaluations was found to be .11. Test the null hypothesis that these quantities are uncorrelated in the population against the alternative that the population correlation is positive.

10.7 The sample correlation for 68 pairs of annual returns on common stocks in Country A and Country B was found to be .51. Test the null hypothesis that the population correlation is 0, against the alternative that it is positive.

10.2 LINEAR REGRESSION MODEL

We use correlation to provide a measure of the strength of any linear association between a pair of random variables. The random variables are treated perfectly symmetrically, and it is a matter of indifference whether we speak of "the correlation between X and Y" or "the correlation between Y and X." In the remainder of this chapter, we will continue to discuss the linear relationship between a pair of variables, but in terms of dependency of one or the other. The symmetry of our previous discussion is now removed. Rather, the concept here is that, given that the random variable X takes a specific value, we expect a response in the random variable Y. That is, the value taken by X influences the value of Y. This can be thought of as a dependence of Y on X. Endogenous—Y—variables have values that depend on exogenous—X—variables whose values are in turn manipulated or influenced by factors external to a specific economic process.

Linear models are not as restrictive as they might seem for applied business and economic analysis. First, we will often find that linear models provide a very good approximation of a relationship over the range being considered. Second, we will see in Chapters 11 and 12 that a number of nonlinear functions can be converted to implicit linear functions for regression analysis.

In this chapter we will focus on a formal study of regression analysis and related statistical inference for simple linear models. In Chapter 3 we introduced scatter plots, correlation, and simple regression as tools for describing data. In Chapter 11 we will apply these ideas to multiple regression models that have more than one predictor variable. Then in Chapter 12 we will develop advanced procedures and applications that extend our capabilities for analyzing business and economic problems.

Our discussion will begin with an example that indicates a typical application of regression analysis and the kind of results that can be obtained.

EXAMPLE 10.2

SALES PREDICTION FOR KNOX RETAILERS (REGRESSION MODEL ESTIMATION)

Retail Sales

The president of Knox Retailers has asked you to develop a model that will predict total sales for proposed new retail store locations. Knox is a rapidly expanding general retailer, and they need a rational strategy for determining where new stores should be located. As part of the model project you need to estimate a linear equation that predicts retail sales per household as a function of household disposable income. They have obtained data from a national sampling survey of households and the variables, retail sales (Y), and income (X) per household will be used to develop the model (reference 1).

SOLUTION

In Figure 10.1 we have a scatter plot showing the relationship between retail sales and disposable income for families. The actual data are shown in Table 10.1 and stored in a data file named **Retail Sales**. From economic theory we know that sales should increase with increases in disposable income and the plot strongly supports that theory. Regression

FIGURE 10.1
Retail Sales per Household versus Per Capita Disposable Income

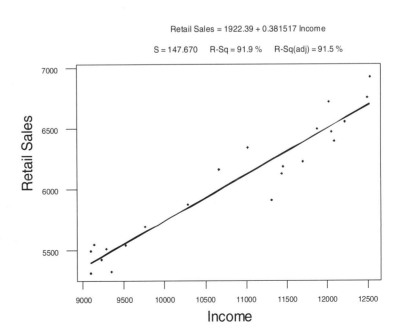

TABLE 10.1
Data on Disposable Income
per Household (*x*) and Retail
Sales per Household (*y*)

YEAR	INCOME (X)	RETAIL SALES (Y)	YEAR	INCOME (X)	RETAIL SALES (Y)
1	9098	5492	12	11307	5907
2	9138	5540	13	11432	6124
3	9094	5305	14	11449	6186
4	9282	5507	15	11697	6224
5	9229	5418	16	11871	6496
6	9347	5320	17	12018	6718
7	9525	5538	18	12523	6921
8	9756	5692	19	12053	6471
9	10282	5871	20	12088	6394
10	10662	6157	21	12215	6555
11	11019	6342	22	12494	6755

analysis, as shown in Section 3.3, provides us with a linear model that can be used to compute retail sales per household for various levels of disposable income. A line drawn on the graph represents the simple regression model

$$Y = 1,922.39 + 0.381517X$$

where Y is retail sales per household and X is disposable income per household. Thus the regression equation provides us with the best model for predicting sales for a given disposable income. Notice that this model tells us that every \$1 increase in per capita disposable family income, X, is associated with an increase in the expected value of retail sales, Y, by \$0.38. Clearly that result is important for forecasting retail sales. For example, we find that a family income of \$10,000 would predict retail sales at \$5,737 (1,922 + 10,000 × 0.3815).

At this point we need to emphasize that the regression results summarize the information contained in the data and do not "prove" that increased income "causes" increased sales. Economic theory suggests that there is causation and these results support that theory. Scatter plots, correlations, or regression equations cannot prove causation, but they can provide supporting evidence. Thus in order to establish conclusions we need a combination of theory—experience in business management and economics—and good statistical analysis.

From our study of economics we know that the quantity of goods purchased, Y, in a specific market can be modeled as a linear function of the disposable income, X. If income is a specific level, x_i, purchasers respond by purchasing a quantity, y_i. In the real world we know there are other factors that influence the actual quantity purchased. These include identifiable factors such as price of the goods in question, advertising, and prices of competing goods. In addition there are other unknown factors that can influence the actual quantity purchased. In a simple linear equation we model the effect of these factors, other than income, by the error term, ε. Figure 10.2 presents an example of one set of observations that were generated by the underlying model of the process. The mean level of Y, for every X, is represented by the population equation

$$Y = \beta_0 + \beta_1 x$$

We are concerned with the expected value of the random variable Y when X takes on a specific value. The assumption of linearity then implies that this expectation can be written

$$E\left(Y \mid X = x\right) = \beta_0 + \beta_1 x$$

FIGURE 10.2
Population Model for Linear
Regression

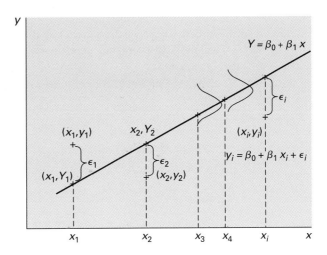

where β_0 represents the Y intercept of the equation and β_1 is the slope. The actual observed value of Y for a given value of X is modeled as being equal to the expected value or population mean plus a random error, ε, that has mean 0 and variance σ^2

$$y_i = \beta_0 + \beta_1 x_i + \varepsilon_i$$

Least squares regression provides us with an estimated model of the linear relationship between an independent or exogenous variable and a dependent or endogenous variable. We begin the process of regression modeling by assuming a population model that has predetermined X values, and for every X there is a mean value of Y plus a random error term. We use the estimated regression equation—as shown in Figure 10.1—to estimate the mean value of Y for every value of X. Individual points vary about this line because of a random error term that has mean zero and a common variance for all values of X. The random error represents all of the influences on Y that are not represented by the linear relationship between Y and X. Effects of these factors, which are assumed to be independent of X, behave like a random variable whose population mean is 0.

LINEAR REGRESSION POPULATION EQUATION MODEL

In the application of regression analysis the process being studied is represented by a population model, and an estimated model, utilizing available data, is computed using least squares regression. The population model is specified as

$$y_i = \beta_0 + \beta_1 x_i + \varepsilon_i \tag{10.4}$$

where β_0 and β_1 are the population model coefficients and ε is a random error term. For every observed value, x_i, an observed value, y_i, is generated by the population model. For purposes of statistical inference, as we will develop in Section 10.4, ε is assumed to have a normal distribution with mean 0 and variance σ^2. Later we will see how the central limit theorem can be used to relax the assumption of a normal distribution. The model of the linear relationship between Y and X is defined by the two coefficients, β_0 and β_1. Figure 10.2 represents the model schematically.

INTERPRETATION

In the least squares regression model we assume that values of the independent variable, x_i, are selected and for each x_i there is a population mean of Y. The observed values of y_i contain the mean and the random deviation ε_i. A set of n (x_i, y_i) points are observed and used to obtain estimates of the model coefficients using the least squares procedure. We will use the concepts of classical inference developed in Chapters 8 and 9 to make inferences about the underlying population model by using the estimated regression model. In Chapter 11 we will see how several independent variables can be considered simultaneously using multiple regression.

The estimated regression model as shown schematically in Figure 10.3 is given by the equation

$$y_i = b_0 + b_1 x_i + e_i$$

where b_0 and b_1 are the estimated values of the coefficients and e is the difference between the predicted value of Y on the regression line, defined as

$$\hat{y}_i = b_0 + b_1 x_i$$

and the observed value y_i. The difference between y_i and $\hat{y}_i$ for each value of X is defined as the residual

$$e_i = y_i - \hat{y}_i = y_i - (b_0 + b_1 x_i)$$

Thus for each observed value of X there is a predicted value of Y from the estimated model and an observed value. The difference between the observed and predicted values of Y is defined as the residual. The residual, e_i, is not the model error, ε, but is the combined measure of the model error and errors in estimating, b_0 and b_1, and in turn the errors in estimating the predicted value.

We determine the estimated regression model by obtaining estimates, b_0 and b_1, of the population coefficients using the process called least squares analysis that we will develop below. And these coefficients are in turn used to obtain predicted values of Y for every value of X.

LINEAR REGRESSION OUTCOMES

Linear regression provides two important results:

1. Predicted values of the dependent or endogenous variable as a function of an independent or exogenous variable.
2. Estimated marginal change in the endogenous variable that results from a one unit change in the independent or exogenous variable.

FIGURE 10.3
Estimated Regression Model

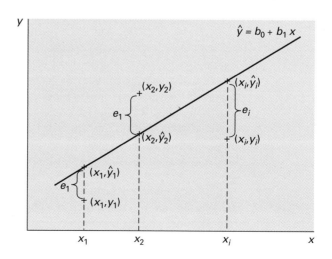

EXERCISES

10.8 What is the difference between a population linear model and an estimated linear regression model?

10.9 Explain the difference between the residual e_i and the model error ε_i.

10.10 Suppose that we obtained an estimated equation for the regression of weekly sales of "palm pilots" and the price

charged during the week. Interpret the constant b_0 for the product brand manager.

10.11 A regression model of total grocery sales on disposable income was estimated using data from small isolated towns in the western United States. Prepare a list of factors that might contribute to the random error term.

10.3 LEAST SQUARES COEFFICIENT ESTIMATORS

The population regression line is a useful theoretical construct, but for applications we need to determine an estimate of the model using available data. Suppose that we have n pairs of observations $(x_1, y_1), (x_2, y_2), \ldots, (x_n, y_n)$. We would like to find the straight line that best fits these points. To do this we need to find estimators of the unknown coefficients β_0 and β_1 of the population regression line.

We obtain the coefficient estimators, b_0 and b_1 using equations derived by using the least squares procedure. As shown in Figure 10.3 there is a deviation, e_i between the observed, y_i, and the predicted value, $\hat{y}_i$, on the estimated regression equation for each value of X, where $e_i = y_i - \hat{y}_i$. We then compute a mathematical function that represents the effect of squaring all of the residuals and computing the sum of the squared residuals. This function—whose left side is labeled *SSE*—includes the coefficients, b_0 and b_1. The quantity *SSE* is defined as the "Error Sum of Squares." The coefficient estimators b_0 and b_1 are selected as the estimators that minimize the Error Sum of Squares.

LEAST SQUARES PROCEDURE

The least squares procedure obtains estimates of the linear equation coefficients, b_0 and b_1, in the model

$$\hat{y}_i = b_0 + b_1 x_i \tag{10.5}$$

by minimizing the sum of the squared residuals e_i

$$SSE = \sum e_i^2 = \sum \left(y_i - \hat{y}_i\right)^2 \tag{10.6}$$

The coefficients b_0 and b_1 are chosen so that the quantity

$$SSE = \sum_{i=1}^{n} e_i^2 = \sum_{i=1}^{n} (y_i - (b_0 + b_1 x_i))^2 \tag{10.7}$$

is minimized. We use differential calculus to obtain the coefficient estimators that minimize SSE. The derivation of the estimators using calculus is presented in the chapter Appendix.

The resulting coefficient estimator is

$$b_1 = \frac{\sum_{i=1}^{n}(x_i - \overline{X})(y_i - \overline{Y})}{\sum_{i=1}^{n}(x_i - \overline{X})^2} = \frac{\sum_{i=1}^{n}(x_i - \overline{X})y_i}{\sum_{i=1}^{n}(x_i - \overline{X})x_i} = \frac{\sum_{i=1}^{n} x_i y_i - n\overline{X}\overline{Y}}{\sum_{i=1}^{n} x_i^2 - n\overline{X}^2}$$

Note that the numerator of the estimator is the sample covariance of X and Y multiplied by $n - 1$ and the denominator is the sample variance of X multiplied by $n - 1$. Then with some algebraic manipulations we can show that the coefficient estimator is also equal to

$$b_1 = r_{xy} \frac{S_Y}{S_X}$$

where r_{xy} is the sample correlation and S_Y and S_X are the sample standard deviations for X and Y. This is an important result because it indicates how the standardized relationship between X and Y, the correlation r_{xy}, is directly related to the slope coefficient. In the chapter Appendix we also show that the constant estimator is

$$b_0 = \overline{Y} - b_1 \overline{X}$$

Substituting this value for b_0 into the linear equation we have

$$y = \overline{Y} - b_1 \overline{X} + b_1 x$$
$$y - \overline{Y} = b_1\left(x - \overline{X}\right)$$

From this equation we see that when $x = \overline{X}$ then $y = \overline{Y}$ and that regression equation always passes through the point $(\overline{X}, \overline{Y})$. The estimated value of the dependent variable, $\hat{Y}$, is then obtained by using the equation

$$\hat{y}_i = b_0 + b_1 x_i$$

and the model equation can also be written as

$$\hat{y}_i = \overline{Y} + b_1(x_i - \overline{X})$$

This form emphasizes that the regression line goes through the means of X and Y.

LEAST SQUARES DERIVED COEFFICIENT ESTIMATORS

The slope coefficient estimator is

$$b_1 = \frac{\sum_{i=1}^{n}(x_i - \overline{X})(y_i - \overline{Y})}{\sum_{i=1}^{n}(x_i - \overline{X})^2} = r_{xy}\frac{S_Y}{S_X}$$

and the constant or intercept estimator is

$$b_0 = \overline{Y} - b_1 \overline{X}$$

We also note that the regression line always goes through the mean $\overline{X}, \overline{Y}$.

Assumptions for Inference Using the Linear Regression Model

The least squares procedure could be used to compute coefficient estimates, b_0 and b_1, using any set of paired data. However, in most applications we want to make inferences about the underlying population model that is part of our economic or business problem. In order to make inferences it is necessary that we agree on certain assumptions. Given these assumptions it can be shown that the least squares coefficient estimators are unbiased and have minimum variance.

STANDARD ASSUMPTIONS FOR THE LINEAR REGRESSION MODEL

The following assumptions are used to make inferences about the population linear model by using the estimated model coefficients.

1. The x's are fixed numbers, or they are realizations of random variable, X that are independent of the error terms, ε_i's. In the later case, inference is carried out conditionally on the observed values of the, x's.
2. The error terms are random variables with mean 0 and the same variance, σ^2. The latter is called homoscedasticity or uniform variance.

$$E[\varepsilon_i] = 0 \quad \text{and} \quad E[\varepsilon_i^2] = \sigma^2 \quad \text{for} \quad (i = 1, \ldots, n)$$

3. The random error terms, ε_i, are not correlated with one another, so that

$$E[\varepsilon_i \varepsilon_j] = 0 \quad \text{for all } i \neq j$$

The first of these assumptions is generally, with justification, taken to be true, although in some advanced econometric work it is untenable. (The assumption fails to hold, for example, when the x_i cannot be measured precisely or when the regression is part of a system of interdependent equations.) Here, however, we will take this assumption as given.

Assumptions 2 and 3 concern the error terms ε_i in the regression equation. The expected discrepancy is 0 and all discrepancies have the same variance. Thus, we do not expect the variances of the error terms to be higher for some observations than for others. Figure 10.2 shows this pattern with the errors for all X values being sampled from populations with the same variance. Finally, it is assumed that the discrepancies are not correlated with one another. Thus, for example, the occurrence of a large positive discrepancy at one observation point does not help us predict the values of any of the other error terms. Assumptions 2 and 3 will be satisfied if the error terms ε_i can be viewed as a random sample from a population with mean zero.

In the remainder of this chapter, it will be taken that these assumptions hold. The possibility for relaxing some of these assumptions will be considered in Chapter 12.

Computer Computation of Regression Coefficient

Extensive application of regression analysis has been made possible by statistical computer packages. As you might suspect, the computations to obtain the regression coefficient estimates are tedious. The estimator equations and other important statistical computations are included in computer packages and are used to compute the coefficient estimates for specific problems. Since we are primarily interested in applications, our most important task is proper analysis of the regression computations for these applications. This analysis should be guided by knowing the estimator equations and the related discussion. We will

FIGURE 10.4
Screen for Entering Minitab
Instructions for Regression
Analysis

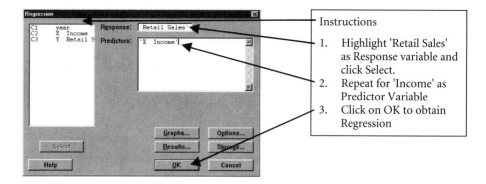

not, however, use these equations to actually compute the estimates or other regression statistics. **We will assign the computation to computers—our task is to think, to analyze, and to make recommendations.**

Here we will prepare a regression analysis for the retail sales versus income problem using Minitab. First you enter the data file into Minitab and then use the command sequence

```
STAT > REGRESSION > REGRESSION
```

to obtain the screen shown in Figure 10.4.

Figure 10.5 presents a portion of the Minitab output for the retail sales example. Note the location of the constant, b_0, and the slope coefficient, b_1, estimates in the computer output. The remaining items on each line help interpret the quality of the estimates and will be developed in subsequent sections.

In this regression the estimated constant, $b_0 = 1922$, and the estimated slope coefficient, $b_1 = 0.382$. These values were computed using the coefficient estimator equations previously developed. The estimated equation can be written as

$$\hat{y} = 1,922 + 0.382x$$

or by using the means $\overline{X} = 10,799$ and $\overline{Y} = 6,042$

$$\hat{y} = 6,042 + 0.382(x - 10,799)$$

INTERPRETATION

Typically regression models should only be used over the range of the observed X values where we have information about the relationship, because the relationship may not be linear outside this range. The second form of the regression model is centered on the data means with a rate of change equal to b_1. By using this form we focus on the mean location of the regression model and not on the intercept with the Y axis. Naïve users of regression analysis will sometimes attempt interpretations of the constant b_0, claiming certain conclusions about the endogenous variable when the exogenous variable has a value of zero. Consider the example regression of retail sales on disposable income. Would we really claim that retail sales are $1,922 when disposable income is zero? In fact we simply do not

FIGURE 10.5
Regression Analysis for Retail
Sales Example

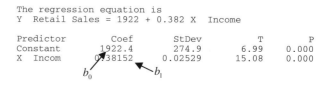

```
The regression equation is
Y  Retail Sales = 1922 + 0.382 X  Income

Predictor        Coef        StDev          T          P
Constant        1922.4       274.9        6.99      0.000
X  Incom       0.38152      0.02529      15.08      0.000
```

have data to support any sales amount when disposable income is zero. This is another example of the importance of good analysis instead of silly interpretations. As professional analysts we must be careful not to claim results that simply do not exist.

EXERCISES

10.12 A company sets different prices for a particular DVD system in eight different regions of the country. The accompanying table shows the numbers of units sold and the corresponding prices (in hundreds of dollars).

SALES	420	380	350	400	440	380	450	420
PRICE	5.5	6.0	6.5	6.0	5.0	6.5	4.5	5.0

   (a) Plot these data, and estimate the linear regression of sales on price.
   (b) What effect would you expect a $100 increase in price to have on sales?

10.13 Refer to the data of Exercise 2 on percentage change (x) in the Dow-Jones index over the first five trading days of the year, and percentage change (y) in the index over the whole year.
   (a) Estimate the linear regression of y on x.
   (b) Provide interpretations of the intercept and slope of the sample regression line.

10.14 🌐 On Friday, November 13, 1989, prices on the New York Stock Exchange fell steeply; the Standard and Poors 500-share index was down 6.1% on that day. The accompanying table and the data file **New York Stock Exchange Gains and Losses** shows the percentage *losses* (y) of the 25 largest mutual funds on November 13, 1989. Also shown are the percentage *gains* (x), assuming reinvested dividends and capital gains, for these same funds for 1989, through November 12. This data is stored in a data file.

y	x	y	x	y	x
4.7	38.0	6.4	39.5	4.2	24.7
4.7	24.5	3.3	23.3	3.3	18.7
4.0	21.5	3.6	28.0	4.1	36.8
4.7	30.8	4.7	30.8	6.0	31.2
3.0	20.3	4.4	32.9	5.8	50.9
4.4	24.0	5.4	30.3	4.9	30.7
5.0	29.6	3.0	19.9	3.8	20.3
3.3	19.4	4.9	24.6		
3.8	25.6	5.2	32.3		

   (a) Estimate the linear regression of November 13 losses on pre-November 13, 1989, gains.
   (b) Interpret the slope of the sample regression line.

10.15 🌐 Ace Manufacturing is studying worker abscence. The figures in the accompanying table and the data file **Employee Absence** were found for annual change in overall absentee rate and annual change in mean employee absence rate due to own illness.

YEAR	CHANGE IN ABSENTEE RATE	CHANGE IN MEAN EMPLOYEE ABSENCE RATE DUE TO OWN ILLNESS
1	−.2	+.2
2	−.1	+.2
3	+1.4	+.2
4	+1.0	−.4
5	−.3	−.1
6	−.7	+.2
7	+.7	−.1
8	+2.9	−.8
9	−.8	+.2
10	−.7	+.2
11	−1.0	+.2

   (a) Estimate the linear regression of change in mean employee absence rate due to own illness on change in absentee rate.
   (b) Interpret the estimated slope of the regression line.

10.16 For a sample of 20 monthly observations, a financial analyst wants to regress the percentage rate of return (Y) of the common stock of a corporation on the percentage rate of return (X) of the Standard and Poor's 500 Index. The following information is available:

$$\sum_{i=1}^{20} y_i = 22.6 \quad \sum_{i=1}^{20} x_i = 25.4 \quad \sum_{i=1}^{20} x_i^2 = 145.7 \quad \sum_{i=1}^{20} x_i y_i = 150.5$$

   (a) Estimate the linear regression of Y on X.
   (b) Interpret the slope of the sample regression line.
   (c) Interpret the intercept of the sample regression line.

10.17 A corporation administers an aptitude test to all new sales representatives. Management is interested in the extent to which this test is able to predict their eventual success. The accompanying table records average weekly sales (in thousands of dollars) and aptitude test scores for a random sample of eight representatives.

WEEKLY SALES	10	12	28	24	18	16	15	12
TEST SCORE	55	60	85	75	80	85	65	60

   (a) Estimate the linear regression of weekly sales on aptitude test scores.
   (b) Interpret the estimated slope of the regression line.

10.18 It was hypothesized that the number of bottles of an imported premium beer sold per evening in the restaurants of a city depends linearly on the average costs of meals in the restaurants. The following results were obtained for a sample of $n = 17$ restaurants, of approximately equal size, where

y = Number of bottles sold per evening

x = Average cost, in dollars, of a meal

$$\bar{x} = 25.5 \quad \bar{y} = 16.0 \quad \frac{\sum_{i=1}^{n}(x_i - \bar{x})^2}{n - 1} = 350 \quad \frac{\sum_{i=1}^{n}(x_i - \bar{x})(y_i - \bar{y})}{n - 1} = 180$$

(a) Find the sample regression line.

(b) Interpret the slope of the sample regression line.

(c) Is it possible to provide a meaningful interpretation of the intercept of the sample regression line? Explain.

10.4   THE EXPLANATORY POWER OF A LINEAR REGRESSION EQUATION

The estimated regression model that we have developed can be viewed as an attempt to explain the variation in a dependent variable Y that results from changes in an independent variable X. If we only had observations of the dependent variable Y then the central tendency of Y would be represented by the mean, $\bar{Y}$, and the total variability about Y would be represented by the numerator of the sample variance estimator, $\Sigma(y_i - \bar{Y})^2$. When we also have measures of X we have shown that the central tendency of Y can now be expressed as a function of X. We expect that the linear equation would be closer to the individual values of Y, and thus the variability about the linear equation would be smaller than the variability about the mean.

Now we are ready to develop measures that indicate how effectively the variable X explains the behavior of Y. In our retail sales example shown in Figure 10.1, retail sales, Y, tends to increase with disposable income, X, and thus disposable income explains some of the differences in retail sales. The points, however, are not all on the line and so the explanation is not perfect. Here we will develop measures, based on the partitioning of variability, that measure the capability of X to explain Y in a specific regression application.

ANALYSIS OF VARIANCE

The total variability in a regression analysis, SST, can be partitioned into a component explained by the regression, SSR, and a component due to unexplained error, SSE,

$$SST = SSR + SSE \tag{10.8}$$

with the components defined as:
Total sum of squares

$$SST = \sum_{i=1}^{n}(y_i - \bar{Y})^2 \tag{10.9}$$

Error sum of squares

$$SSE = \sum_{i=1}^{n}(y_i - (b_0 + b_1 x_i))^2 = \sum_{i=1}^{n}(y_i - \hat{y}_i)^2 = \sum_{i=1}^{n}e_i^2 \tag{10.10}$$

Regression sum of squares

$$SSR = \sum_{i=1}^{n}(\hat{y}_i - \bar{Y})^2 = b_1^2 \sum_{i=1}^{n}(x_i - \bar{X})^2 \tag{10.11}$$

FIGURE 10.6
Partitioning of Variability

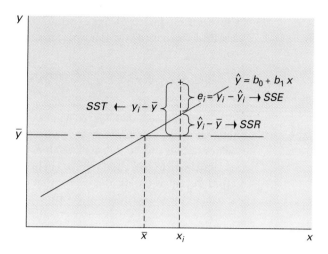

The analysis of variance, ANOVA, for least squares regression is developed by partitioning the total variability of Y into an explained and an error component. In Figure 10.6 we show that the deviation of an individual Y value from its mean can be partitioned into a deviation of the predicted value from the mean and the deviation of the observed value from the predicted value

$$y_i - \overline{Y} = (y_i - \hat{y}_i) + (\hat{y}_i - \overline{Y})$$

We square each side of the equation—because the sum of deviations about the mean is equal to 0—and sum the result over all n points

$$\sum_{i=1}^{n} (y_i - \overline{Y})^2 = \sum_{i=1}^{n} (y_i - \hat{y})^2 + \sum_{i=1}^{n} (\hat{y}_i - \overline{Y})^2$$

Some of you may note the squaring of the right-hand side should include the cross product of the two terms in addition to their squared quantities. It can be shown that the cross product term goes to zero. This equation is expressed as

$$SST = SSR + SSE$$

Here we see that the total variability—SST—can be partitioned into a component—SSR—that represents variability that is explained by the slope of the regression equation. (The mean of Y is different at different levels of X.) The second component—SSE—results from the random or unexplained deviation of points from the regression line. This variability provides an indication of the uncertainty that is associated with the regression model. We define the left side as the "Total Sum of Squares."

$$SST = \sum_{i=1}^{n} (y_i - \overline{Y})^2$$

The amount of variability explained by the regression equation is defined as the "Regression Sum of Squares" and computed as

$$SSR = \sum_{i=1}^{n} (\hat{y}_i - \overline{Y})^2 = b_1^2 \sum_{i=1}^{n} (x_i - \overline{X})^2$$

We see that the variability explained by the regression depends directly on the size of the coefficient, b_1, and on the spread of the independent, X, variable data. The deviations about the regression line, e_i, that are used to compute the unexplained or "Error Sum of Squares" can be defined using the following algebraic forms

$$SSE = \sum_{i=1}^{n} (y_i - (b_0 + b_1 x_i))^2 = \sum_{i=1}^{n} (y_i - \hat{y}_i)^2 = \sum_{i=1}^{n} e_i^2$$

For a given set of observed values of the dependent variables, Y, the SST is fixed as the total variability of all observations from the mean. We see that in this partitioning larger values of SSR and hence smaller values of SSE indicate a regression equation that "fits" or comes closer to the observed data. This partitioning is shown graphically in Figure 10.6. From the equation for SSR we see that explained variability, SSR, is directly related to the spread of the independent or X variable. Thus as we are thinking about regression applications we know that we should try to obtain data that has a large range for the independent variable so that the resulting regression model will have a smaller unexplained variability.

With this background let us return to our retail sales example and look at how we use the partitioned variability to determine how well our model explains the process being studied. Table 10.2 shows the detailed calculations of residuals, e_i, deviations of Y from the mean, and deviations of predicted values of Y from the mean. These provide us with the components to compute SSE, SST, and SSR. The sum of squared deviations for column 5 is $SSE = 436,127$. The sum of squared deviations for column 6 is $SST = 5,397,561$. Finally, the sum of squared deviations for column 7 is $SSR = 4,961,434$. Figure 10.7 is a copy of the regression output with the Analysis of Variance section included.

TABLE 10.2
Actual and Predicted Values for Retail Sales per Household and Residuals from its Linear Regression on Income per Household

YEAR	X INCOME	Y RETAIL SALES	PREDICTED RETAIL SALES	RESIDUAL	OBSERVED DEVIATION FROM THE MEAN	PREDICTED DEVIATION FROM THE MEAN
1	9,098	5,492	5,394	98	−550	−649
2	9,138	5,540	5,409	131	−502	−633
3	9,094	5,305	5,392	−87	−737	−650
4	9,282	5,507	5,464	43	−535	−578
5	9,229	5,418	5,444	−26	−624	−599
6	9,347	5,320	5,489	−169	−722	−554
7	9,525	5,538	5,557	−19	−504	−486
8	9,756	5,692	5,645	47	−350	−397
9	10,282	5,871	5,846	25	−171	−197
10	10,662	6,157	5,991	166	115	−52
11	11,019	6,342	6,127	215	300	84
12	11,307	5,907	6,237	−330	−135	194
13	11,432	6,124	6,284	−160	82	242
14	11,449	6,186	6,291	−105	144	248
15	11,697	6,224	6,385	−161	182	343
16	11,871	6,496	6,452	44	454	409
17	12,018	6,718	6,508	210	676	465
18	12,523	6,921	6,701	220	879	658
19	12,053	6,471	6,521	−50	429	479
20	12,088	6,394	6,535	−141	352	492
21	12,215	6,555	6,583	−28	513	541
22	12,494	6,755	6,689	66	713	647
		Sum of squared values		436,127	5,397,561	4,961,434

FIGURE 10.7
Regression Analysis for Retail
Sales on Disposable Income

```
The regression equation is
Y  Retail Sales = 1922 + 0.382 X   Income

Predictor         Coef      SE Coef          T        P
Constant        1922.4        274.9       6.99    0.000
X  Incom       0.38152      0.02529      15.08    0.000

S = 147.7       R-Sq = 91.9%       R-Sq(adj) = 91.5%

Analysis of Variance

Source            DF          SS          MS        F        P
Regression         1     4961434     4961434   227.52    0.000
Residual Error    20      436127       21806
Total             21     5397561

Unusual Observations
Obs    X   Incom    Y  Retai         Fit      SE Fit     Residual     St Resid
12        11307      5907.0       6236.2        34.0       -329.2       -2.29R

R denotes an observation with a large standardized residual
```

Coefficient of Determination R^2

We have seen that the fit of the regression equation to the data is improved as SSR increases and SSE decreases. The ratio of the regression sum of squares, SSR, divided by the total sum of squares, SST, provides a descriptive measure of the proportion or percent of the total variability that is explained by the regression model. This measure is called the *coefficient of determination*—or more generally, R^2.

$$R^2 = \frac{SSR}{SST} = 1 - \frac{SSE}{SST}$$

The coefficient of determination is often interpreted as the percent of variability in Y that is explained by the regression equation. Previously we showed that SSR increases directly with the spread of the independent variable X

$$SSR = \sum_{i=1}^{n}(\hat{y}_i - \overline{Y})^2 = b_1^2 \sum_{i=1}^{n}(x_i - \overline{X})^2$$

Thus we see that R^2 also increases directly with the spread of the independent variable. When you are seeking data to estimate a regression model, one important criteria is to choose the observations of the independent variable to obtain the largest possible spread in X so that we obtain a regression model with the highest R^2.

COEFFICIENT OF DETERMINATION, R^2

The coefficient of determination for a regression equation is defined as

$$R^2 = \frac{SSR}{SST} = 1 - \frac{SSE}{SST} \qquad (10.12)$$

This quantity varies from 0 to 1, and higher values indicate a better regression. Caution should be used in making general interpretations of R^2 because a high value can result from either a small SSE or a large SST or both.

R^2 can vary from 0 to 1 since SST is fixed and $0 < SSE < SST$. Thus a larger R^2 implies a better regression, everything else being equal. In the regression output—Figure 10.7— we see that the R^2 for the retail sales regression is 0.919 or 91.9%. One popular interpretation is that R^2 is the "percent explained variability."

INTERPRETATION

The second form of the equation emphasizes that R^2 depends on the ratio of SSE divided by SST. We can have a high R^2 because one has a small SSE—the desired goal—or because there is a large SST or both. General interpretations of R^2 that apply to all regression equations are dangerous. Two regression models with the same set of observed y_i's can always be compared using R^2, and the model with the larger R^2 provides a better explanation of Y. But global comparisons of R^2—stating that a model is good because its R^2 is above a particular value—are misleading. Generally experienced analysts have found that R^2 is 0.80 and above for models based on time series data. Cross section data models (e.g., cities, states, firms) have values in the 0.40 to 0.60 range, and models based on data from individual people often have R^2 in the 0.10 to 0.20 range.

To illustrate the problem of global interpretations of R^2 consider two regression models—whose plots are shown in Figure 10.8—each of which is based on a total of 25 observations. Both models have SSE equal to 17.89 and so the fit of the regression equation to the data points is the same. But the first model has a total sum of squares equal to 5,201.05 while the second has $SST = 68.22$. The R^2 values for the two models are

Model 1

$$R^2 = 1 - \frac{SSE}{SST} = 1 - \frac{17.89}{5,201.05} = 0.997$$

Model 2

$$R^2 = 1 - \frac{SSE}{SST} = 1 - \frac{17.89}{68.22} = 0.738$$

Since both models have the same SSE and thus the same goodness of fit, one cannot claim that model 1 fits the data better. Yet model 1 has a substantially higher R^2 compared to model 2. As we see here, one should be very careful about global interpretations of R^2. Note the two different vertical axis intervals in Figure 10.8 that result from different values for SST.

FIGURE 10.8
Comparison of R^2 for Two Regression Models

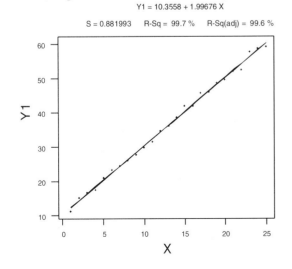

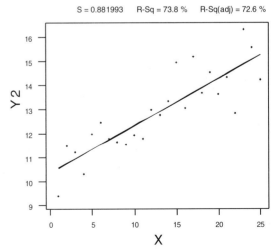

Correlation and R^2

We can also link the correlation coefficient with R^2 as shown by noting that the correlation squared is equal to coefficient of determination. Another interpretation of the correlation is that it is the square root of the percent explained variability.

CORRELATION AND R^2

The coefficient of determination, R^2, for simple regression is equal to the simple correlation squared:

$$R^2 = r_{xy}^2 \qquad \text{(10.13)}$$

This provides an important link between correlation and the regression model.

The error sum of squares can also be used to obtain an estimate of the variance of the model error ε_i. As we will see, the estimator for the variance of the model error will be used for regression model statistical inference. Recall that we have assumed that ε_i has mean zero and variance σ^2. The estimator for σ^2 is computed as follows.

ESTIMATION OF MODEL ERROR VARIANCE

The quantity SSE is a measure of the total squared deviation about the estimated regression line and e_i is the residual. An estimator for the variance of the population model error is

$$\hat{\sigma}^2 = S_e^2 = \frac{\sum_{i=1}^{n} e_i^2}{n-2} = \frac{SSE}{n-2} \qquad \text{(10.14)}$$

Division by $n-2$ instead of $n-1$ results because the simple regression model uses two estimated parameters, b_0 and b_1, instead of one. In the next section we will see that this variance estimator is the basis for statistical inference in the regression model.

EXERCISES

10.19 Let the sample regression line be

$$y_i = b_0 + b_1 x_i + e_i = \hat{y}_i + e_i \qquad (i = 1, 2, \ldots, n)$$

and let $\bar{x}$ and $\bar{y}$ denote the sample means for the independent and dependent variables, respectively.

(a) Show that

$$e_i = y_i - \bar{y} - b\left(x_i - \bar{x}\right)$$

(b) Using the result in part (a), show that

$$\sum_{i=1}^{n} e_i = 0$$

(c) Using the result in part (a), show that

$$\sum_{i=1}^{n} e_i^2 = \sum_{i=1}^{n} (y_i - \bar{y})^2 - b^2 \sum_{i=1}^{n} (x_i - \bar{x})^2$$

(d) Show that

$$\hat{y}_i - \bar{y} = b_i (x_i - \bar{x})$$

(e) Using the results in parts (c) and (d), show that

$$SST = SSR + SSE$$

(f) Using the result in part (a), show that

$$\sum_{i=1}^{n} e_i (x_i - \bar{x}) = 0$$

10.20 Let

$$R^2 = \frac{SSR}{SST}$$

denote the coefficient of determination for the sample regression line.

(a) Using part (d) of Exercise 8, show that

$$R^2 = b_1^2 \frac{\sum_{i=1}^{n} (x_i - \bar{x})^2}{\sum_{i=1}^{n} (y_i - \bar{y})^2}$$

(b) Using the result in part (a), show that the coefficient of determination is equal to the square of the sample correlation between X and Y.

(c) Let b_1 be the slope of the least squares regression of Y on X, b_1^* the slope of the least squares regression of X on Y, and r the sample correlation between X and Y. Show that

$$b_1 \cdot b_1^* = r^2$$

10.21 Find and interpret the coefficient of determination for the regression of stereo system sales on price, using the following data.

SALES	420	380	350	400	440	380	450	420
PRICE	5.5	6.0	6.5	6.0	5.0	6.5	4.5	5.0

10.22 Find and interpret the coefficient of determination for the regression of the percentage change in the Dow-Jones index in a year on the percentage change in the index over the first five trading days of the year, continuing the analysis of Exercise 10.2. Compare your answer with the sample correlation found for these data in Exercise 10.2.

10.23 Find the proportion of the sample variability in mutual fund percentage losses on November 13, 1989, explained by their linear dependence on 1989 percent-

age gains through November 12, based on the data of Exercise 10.14 in the data file **New York Stock Exchange Gains and Losses**.

10.24 Refer to the data on unemployment rate and employee absence rate in Exercise 10.15.

(a) Find the predicted values, $\hat{Y}_i$, and the residuals, e_i, for the least squares regression of change in mean employee absence rate due to own illness on change in unemployment rate.

(b) Find the sums of squares SST, SSR, and SSE, and verify that

$$SST = SSR + SSE$$

(c) Using the results in part (b), find and interpret the coefficient of determination.

10.25 For the problem in Exercise 10.16, use

$$\sum_{i=1}^{20} y_i^2 = 196.2$$

to find the coefficient of determination for the regression of the rate of return of the corporation's common stock on the rate of return of the $S.$ and $P.$ 500 index. [*Hint*: Use the result in part (a) of Exercise 10.9.]

10.26 Refer to the data on weekly sales and aptitude test scores achieved by sales representatives given in Exercise 10.17.

(a) Find the predicted values, $\hat{Y}_i$, and residuals, e_i, for the least squares regression of weekly sales on aptitude test scores.

(b) Find the sums of squares SST, SSR, and SSE, and verify that

$$SST = SSR + SSE$$

(c) Using the results in part (b), find and interpret the coefficient of determination.

(d) Find directly the sample correlation coefficient between sales and aptitude test scores, and verify that its square is equal to the coefficient of determination.

10.27 In a study it was shown that for a sample of 353 college faculty, the correlation was .11 between annual raises and teaching evaluations. What would be the coefficient of determination of a regression of annual raises on teaching evaluations for this sample? Interpret your result.

10.5   STATISTICAL INFERENCE: HYPOTHESIS TESTS AND CONFIDENCE INTERVALS

Now that we have developed the coefficient estimators and an estimator for σ^2 we are ready to make population model inferences. The basic approach will follow that developed in Chapters 8 and 9. We will develop variance estimators for the coefficient estimators, b_0 and b_1 and then use the estimated parameters and variances to test hypotheses and compute confidence intervals using the Student's t distribution. Inferences from regression analysis will help us understand the process being modeled and make decisions about the process. Initially we assume that random model errors, ε, are normally distributed. Later this assumption will be replaced by the central limit theorem assumption. We begin by developing variance estimators and useful test forms. Then these will be applied using our retail sales data.

In Section 10.2 we defined the population model for simple regression as

$$y_i = \beta_0 + \beta_1 x_i + \varepsilon_i$$

with the x_i's being predetermined values and not random variables. From our work in Chapters 5 and 6 on linear functions of random variables we know that if ε_i is a normally distributed random variable with variance σ^2 then y_i is also normally distributed with the same variance. The right-hand side is a linear function of X except for the random variable ε_i. If we add a function of X to a random variable we do not change the variance. In Section 10.3 we found that the estimator for the slope coefficient, b_1, is

$$b_1 = \frac{\sum_{i=1}^{n}(x_i - \overline{X})(y_i - \overline{Y})}{\sum_{i=1}^{n}(x_i - \overline{X})^2} = \frac{\sum_{i=1}^{n}(x_i - \overline{X})y_i}{\sum_{i=1}^{n}(x_i - \overline{X})^2} = \sum\left(\frac{(x_i - \overline{X})}{\sum(x_i - \overline{X})^2}\right)y_i = \sum a_i y_i$$

where

$$a_i = \frac{(x_i - \overline{X})}{\sum_{i=1}^{n}(x_i - \overline{X})^2}$$

In this estimator we see that b_1 is a linear function of the random variable y_i whose variance is σ^2. The y_i's include independent random variables. Thus the variance of b_1 is a simple transformation of the variance of Y. Using the results from Chapter 6 the linear function can be written as

$$b_1 = \sum_{i=1}^{n} a_i y_i$$

$$a_i = \frac{(x_i - \overline{X})}{\sum_{i=1}^{n}(x_i - \overline{X})^2}$$

$$\sigma_{b_1}^2 = \sum_{i=1}^{n} a_i^2 \sigma^2$$

$$\sigma_{b_1}^2 = \sum_{i=1}^{n}\left(\frac{(x_i - \overline{X})}{\sum_{i=1}^{n}(x_i - \overline{X})^2}\right)^2 \sigma^2 = \frac{\sum_{i=1}^{n}(x_i - \overline{X})^2}{\left(\sum_{i=1}^{n}(x_i - \overline{X})^2\right)^2}\sigma^2 = \frac{\sigma^2}{\sum_{i=1}^{n}(x_i - \overline{X})^2}$$

Since y_i is normally distributed and b_1 is a linear function of independent normal variables, this linear function implies that b_1 is also normally distributed. From this analysis we can derive the population and sample variances.

SAMPLING DISTRIBUTION OF THE LEAST SQUARES COEFFICIENT ESTIMATOR

If the standard least squares assumptions hold, then b_1 is an unbiased estimator for β_1 and has a population variance

$$\sigma^2_{b_1} = \frac{\sigma^2}{\sum_{i=1}^{n}(x_i - \overline{X})^2} = \frac{\sigma^2}{(n-1)S_X^2} \tag{10.15}$$

and an unbiased sample variance estimator

$$S^2_{b_1} = \frac{S_e^2}{\sum_{i=1}^{n}(x_i - \overline{X})^2} = \frac{S_e^2}{(n-1)S_X^2} \tag{10.16}$$

The regression constant estimator, b_0, is also a linear function of the random variable y_i and thus it can be shown to be normally distributed and its variance estimator can be derived as

$$S^2_{b_0} = \left(\frac{1}{n} + \frac{\overline{X}^2}{(n-1)S_X^2} \right) S_e^2$$

It is important to observe that the variance of the slope coefficient, b_1, depends on two important quantities

1. The distance of the points from the regression line measured by S_e^2. Higher values imply greater variance for b_1.
2. The total deviation of the X values from the mean measured by $(n - 1)S_X^2$. Greater spread in the X values implies smaller variance for the slope coefficient.

INTERPRETATION

These two results are very important as one is thinking about choices of data for a regression model. Previously we noted that a wider spread in the independent, X, variable resulted in a higher R^2 indicating a stronger relationship. Now we see that a wider spread in the independent variable—measured by S_X^2—results in a smaller variance for the estimated slope coefficient, b_1. It follows that smaller variance slope coefficient estimators imply a better regression model. We need to also add that many research conclusions and policy decisions are based on the change in Y that results from a change in X, as estimated by b_1. Thus we would like to have the variance of this important decision variable, b_1, be as small as possible.

In applied regression analysis we first would like to know if there is a relationship. In the regression model we see that if β_1 is zero then there is no linear relationship—Y would not continuously increase or decrease with increases in X. To determine if there is a linear relationship we can test the hypothesis

$$H_0: \beta_1 = 0$$
$$H_1: \beta_1 \neq 0$$

This hypothesis can be tested using the estimator b_1 that is normally distributed with sample variance $S_{b_1}^2$. We can test this hypothesis by using the Student's t statistic

$$t = \frac{b_1 - \beta_1}{S_{b_1}} = \frac{b_1 - 0}{S_{b_1}} = \frac{b_1}{S_{b_1}}$$

that is distributed as Student's t with $n - 2$ degrees of freedom. The hypothesis test can also be performed for values of β_1 other than zero. One rule of thumb is to conclude that a relationship exists if the absolute value of the t statistic is greater than 2. This result holds exactly for a two-tailed test with $\alpha = 0.05$ and 60 degrees of freedom and provides a close approximation for $n > 30$.

BASIS FOR INFERENCE ABOUT THE POPULATION REGRESSION SLOPE

Let β_1 be a population regression slope and b_1 its least squares estimate based on n pairs of sample observations. Then if the standard regression assumptions hold and it can also be assumed that the errors ε_i are normally distributed, the random variable

$$t = \frac{b_1 - \beta_1}{S_{b_1}} \qquad (10.17)$$

is distributed as Student's t with $(n - 2)$ degrees of freedom. In addition, the central limit theorem enables us to conclude that this result is approximately valid for a wide range of non-normal distributions and large enough sample sizes, n.

The coefficient standard deviation and Student's t statistic—for $\beta_1 = 0$—are routinely computed in most regression programs. An example output from Minitab is shown in Figure 10.9.

For the retail sales model the slope coefficient, $b_1 = 0.382$, with a standard deviation, $s_{b_1} = 0.02529$. To decide if there is a relationship between retail sales, Y, and disposable income, X, we can test the hypothesis

$$H_0: \beta_1 = 0$$
$$H_1: \beta_1 \neq 0$$

FIGURE 10.9
Minitab Output for Retail
Sales Model: Coefficient
Variance Estimators

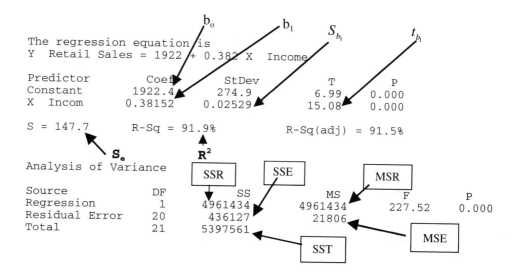

Under the null hypothesis the ratio of the coefficient estimator, b_1, to its standard deviation has a Student's t distribution. For the retail sales example we find that the computed Student's t statistic is

$$t = \frac{b_1 - \beta_1}{s_{b_1}} = \frac{b_1 - 0}{s_{b_1}} = \frac{0.38152 - 0}{0.02529} = 15.09$$

The resulting Student's t statistic, $t = 15.08$, as shown in the regression output, provides strong evidence to reject the null hypothesis and conclude that there is a strong relationship between retail sales and disposable income. We also note that the p-value for b_1 is 0.000 providing alternative evidence that β_1 is not equal to 0. Recall from Chapter 8 that the p-value is the smallest significance level at which the null hypothesis can be rejected.

Hypothesis tests could also be performed on the equation constant, b_0, using the standard deviation previously developed and shown in the Minitab output. However, because we are usually interested in rates of change—measured by b_1—tests involving the constant are generally less important.

If the sample size is large enough for the central limit theorem to apply then we can perform such hypothesis tests even if the errors, ε_i, are not normally distributed. The key question concerns the distribution of b_1. If b_1 has an approximate normal distribution then the hypothesis test can be performed.

TESTS OF THE POPULATION REGRESSION SLOPE

If the regression errors ε_i are normally distributed and the standard least squares assumptions hold (or if the distribution of b_1 is approximately normal), the following tests have significance level α:

i. To test either null hypothesis

$$H_0: \beta_1 = \beta_1^* \qquad \text{or} \qquad H_0: \beta_1 \leq \beta_1^*$$

Against the alternative

$$H_1: \beta_1 > \beta_1^*$$

the decision rule is

$$\text{Reject } H_0 \text{ if } \frac{b_1 - \beta_1^*}{s_{b_1}} \geq t_{n-2,\alpha} \qquad \textbf{(10.18)}$$

ii. To test either null hypothesis

$$H_0: \beta_1 = \beta_1^* \qquad \text{or} \qquad H_0: \beta_1 \geq \beta_1^*$$

Against the alternative

$$H_1: \beta_1 < \beta_1^*$$

the decision rule is

$$\text{Reject } H_0 \text{ if } \frac{b_1 - \beta_1^*}{s_b} \leq -t_{n-2,\alpha} \qquad \textbf{(10.19)}$$

iii. To test the null hypothesis

$$H_0 : \beta_1 = \beta_1^*$$

Against the two-sided alternative

$$H_1 : \beta_1 \neq \beta_1^*$$

the decision rule is

$$\text{Reject } H_0 \text{ if } \frac{b_1 - \beta_1^*}{s_{b_1}} \geq t_{n-2, \alpha/2} \qquad \text{or} \qquad \frac{b_1 - \beta_1^*}{s_{b_1}} \leq -t_{n-2, \alpha/2} \qquad \textbf{(10.20)}$$

We can derive confidence intervals for the slope β_1 of the population regression line by using the coefficient and variance estimators we have developed and the rationale presented in Chapter 8.

CONFIDENCE INTERVALS FOR THE POPULATION REGRESSION SLOPE β_1

If the regression errors, ε_i, are normally distributed and the standard regression assumptions hold, a $100(1 - \alpha)\%$ confidence interval for the population regression slope β_1 is given by

$$b_1 - t_{(n-2, \alpha/2)} s_{b_1} < \beta_1 < b_1 + t_{(n-2, \alpha/2)} s_{b_1} \qquad \textbf{(10.21)}$$

where $t_{(n-2, \alpha/2)}$ is the number for which

$$P(t_{(n-2)} > t_{(n-2, \alpha/2)}) = \alpha/2$$

and the random variable $t_{(n-2)}$ follows a Student's t distribution with $(n - 2)$ degrees of freedom.

From the regression output for the retail sales on disposable income regression in Figure 10.9 we know that

$$n = 22 \quad b_1 = 0.3815 \quad S_{b_1} = 0.0253$$

For a 99% confidence interval for β_1, we have $1 - \alpha = 0.99$, and $n - 2 = 20$ degrees of freedom and thus from Table 8 of the Appendix

$$t_{(n-2, a/2)} = t_{(20, 0.005)} = 2.845$$

and therefore we have the 99% confidence interval

$$0.3815 - (2.845)(0.0253) < \beta_1 < 0.3815 + (2.845)(0.0253)$$

or

$$0.3095 < \beta_1 < 0.4535$$

We see that the 99% confidence interval for the expected increase in retail sales per household associated with a $1 increase in disposable income per household covers the range from $0.3095 to $0.4353. Figure 10.10 also shows the 90% and 95% confidence intervals for the population regression slope.

FIGURE 10.10
Confidence Intervals for the
Retail Sales Population
Regression Slope at
Confidence Levels, 90%, 95%,
and 99%

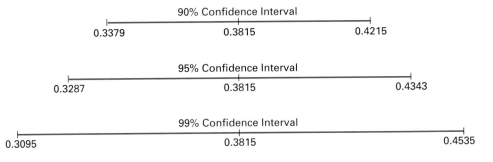

Hypothesis Test for Population Slope Coefficient Using the F Distribution

There is an alternative test for the hypothesis that the slope coefficient β_1 is equal to zero.

$$H_0: \beta_1 = 0$$
$$H_1: \beta_1 \neq 0$$

This test is based on the partitioning of variability that we developed in Section 10.4. The assumption for this test is that if the null hypothesis is true then both SSE and SSR can be used to obtain independent estimators of the model error variance σ^2. To perform this test we obtain two sample estimates of the population standard deviation σ. These are defined as mean square terms. The regression sum of squares SSR has one degree of freedom since it refers to the single slope coefficient, and the mean square for regression, MSR, is

$$MSR = \frac{RSS}{1} = RSS$$

If the null hypothesis—no relationship—is true then MSR is an estimate of the overall model variance, σ^2. We also use the error sum of squares as before to obtain the mean square for error, MSE

$$MSE = \frac{ESS}{n-2} = s_e^2$$

In Section 9.8 we introduced the F distribution as the ratio of independent sample estimates of variance given equal population variances. It can be shown that MSR and MSE are independent and under H_0 both are estimates of the population variance, σ^2. Thus if H_0 is true then we can show that the ratio

$$F = \frac{MSR}{MSE} = \frac{RSS}{s_e^2}$$

has an F distribution with 1 degree of freedom for the numerator and $n - 2$ degrees of freedom for the denominator. It should also be noted that the F statistic is equal to the squared t statistic for the slope coefficient. This can be shown algebraically. From distribution theory we can show that a squared Student's t with $n - 2$ degrees of freedom and the F with 1 degree of freedom for the numerator and $n - 2$ degrees of freedom for the denominator are equal.

$$F_{\alpha,1,n-2} = t_{\alpha/2,n-2}^2$$

The analysis of variance for the retail sales regression from the Minitab output is shown in Figure 10.9. In our retail sales example the error sum of squares is divided by the 20 degrees for freedom to compute the MSE

$$MSE = \frac{436,127}{20} = 21,806$$

Then the F ratio is computed as the ratio of the two mean squares

$$F = \frac{MSR}{MSE} = \frac{4,961,434}{21,806} = 227.52$$

This F ratio is substantially larger than the critical value for $\alpha < 0.01$ with 1 degree of freedom for the numerator and 20 degrees of freedom for the denominator ($F_{1,20,0.01} = 8.10$) from the Appendix. The Minitab output—Figure 10.9—for the retail sales regression shows the p-value for this computed F as 0.00 providing alternative evidence to reject H_0. Also note that the F statistic is equal to t^2 where the Student's t statistic is computed for the slope coefficient b_1

$$F = t^2$$
$$227.52 \neq 15.08^2$$

F TEST FOR SIMPLE REGRESSION COEFFICIENT

We can test the hypothesis

$$H_0: \beta_1 = 0$$

against the alternative

$$H_1: \beta_1 \neq 0$$

By using the F statistic

$$F = \frac{MSR}{MSE} = \frac{SSR}{S_e^2} \qquad (10.22)$$

The decision rule is

$$\text{Reject } H_0 \text{ if } F \geq F_{1,n-2,\alpha} \qquad (10.23)$$

We can also show that the F statistic is

$$F = t_{b_1}^2 \qquad (10.24)$$

for any simple regression analysis.

From this result we see that hypothesis tests relating to the population slope coefficient will provide exactly the same result when using either the Student's t or the F distribution. We will learn in Chapter 11 that the F distribution—when used in a multiple regression analysis—also provides the opportunity for testing the hypothesis that several population slope coefficients are simultaneously equal to zero.

EXERCISES

10.28 Consider the linear regression of DVD system sales on price, based on the data of Exercise 10.21.
   (a) Use an unbiased estimation procedure to find an estimate of the variance of the error terms in the population regression.
   (b) Use an unbiased estimation procedure to find an estimate of the variance of the least squares estimator of the slope of the population regression line.
   (c) Find a 90% confidence interval for the slope of the population regression line.

10.29 Continue the analysis of Exercise 10.22 of the regression of the percentage change in the Dow-Jones index in a year on the percentage change in the index over the first five trading days of the year.
  (a) Use an unbiased estimation procedure to find a point estimate of the variance of the error terms in the population regression.
  (b) Use an unbiased estimation procedure to find a point estimate of the variance of the least squares estimator of the slope of the population regression line.
  (c) Find and interpret a 95% confidence interval for the slope of the population regression line.
  (d) Test at the 10% significance level, against a two-sided alternative, the null hypothesis that the slope of the population regression line is 0.

10.30 Consider the model for mutual fund losses on November 13, 1989, based on the data of Exercise 10.14 in the data file **New York Stock Exchange Gains and Losses**.
  (a) Use an unbiased estimation procedure to obtain a point estimate of the variance of the error terms in the population regression.
  (b) Use an unbiased estimation procedure to obtain a point estimate of the variance of the least squares estimator of the slope of the population regression line.
  (c) Find 90%, 95%, and 99% confidence intervals for the slope of the population regression line.

10.31 A fast-food chain decided to carry out an experiment to assess the influence of advertising expenditure on sales. Different relative changes in advertising expenditure, compared to the previous year, were made in eight regions of the country, and resulting changes in sales levels were observed. The accompanying table shows the results.

Increase In Advertising Expenditure (%)	0	4	14	10	9	8	6	1
Increase In Sales (%)	2.4	7.2	10.3	9.1	10.2	4.1	7.6	3.5

  (a) Estimate by least squares the linear regression of increase in sales on increase in advertising expenditure.
  (b) Find a 90% confidence interval for the slope of the population regression line.

10.32 A liquor wholesaler is interested in assessing the effect of the price of a premium scotch whiskey on the quantity sold. The results in the accompanying table on price, in dollars, and sales, in cases, were obtained from a sample of eight weeks of sales records.

PRICE	19.2	20.5	19.7	21.3	20.8	19.9	17.8	17.2
SALES	25.4	14.7	18.6	12.4	11.1	15.7	29.2	35.2

Find a 95% confidence interval for the expected change in sales resulting from a $1 increase in price.

10.6 PREDICTION

Regression models can also be used to compute predictions or forecasts, for the dependent variable given an assumed future value for the independent variable. Suppose that we are interested in forecasting the value of the dependent variable given that the independent variable is equal to a specified value, x_{n+1}, and that the linear relationship between dependent and independent variables continues to hold. The corresponding value of the dependent variable will then be

$$y_{n+1} = \beta_0 + \beta_1 x_{n+1} + \varepsilon_{n+1}$$

which, given x_{n+1}, has expectation

$$E[y_{n+1}|x_{n+1}] = \beta_0 + \beta_1 x_{n+1}$$

Two distinct options are of interest:

  1. We may want to estimate the actual value that will result for a single observation y_{n+1}. This option is shown in Figure 10.11.
  2. We might want to estimate the conditional expected value $E[y_{n+1}|x_{n+1}]$, that is, the average value of the dependent variable when the independent variable is fixed at x_{n+1}. This option is shown in Figure 10.12.

FIGURE 10.11
Least Squares Estimated
Regression Line of Retail
Sales on Disposable Income
for a Single Observed Value

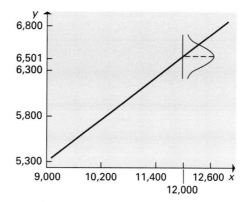

Given that the standard regression assumptions continue to hold, the same point estimate results for either option. We simply replace the unknown β_0 and β_1 by their least squares estimates, b_0 and b_1. That is $(\beta_0 + \beta_1 x_{n+1})$ is estimated by $(b_0 + b_1 x_{n+1})$. We know that the corresponding estimator is the best linear unbiased estimator for Y given X. With the first option we are interested in the best forecast for a single occurrence of the process. But for the second option we are interested in the expected value or long-term average for the process. For both options, an appropriate point estimate under our assumptions is

$$\hat{y}_{n+1} = b_0 + b_1 x_{n+1}$$

This follows since we do not know anything useful about the random variable ε_{n+1} except that its mean is 0. Thus without other information we will use 0 as its point estimate.

However, we usually want intervals in addition to point estimates, and for that purpose the two options are different. This is because the variance estimators are different for the two different quantities being estimated. The results for these different variance estimators lead to the two different intervals. The interval for the first option is generally defined as a prediction interval because we are predicting the value for a single point. The interval for the second option is referred to as a confidence interval because it is the interval for the expected value.

FIGURE 10.12
Least Squares Estimated
Regression Line of Retail
Sales on Disposable Income
for the Expected Value

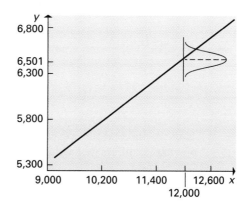

FORECAST CONFIDENCE INTERVALS AND PREDICTION INTERVALS

Suppose that the population regression model is

$$y_i = \beta_0 + \beta_1 x_i + \varepsilon_i \quad (i = 1, \ldots, n+1)$$

and that the standard regression assumptions hold, and that the ε_i are normally distributed. Let b_0 and b_1 be the least squares estimates of β_0 and β_1, based on $(x_1, y_1), (x_2, y_2), \ldots, (x_n, y_n)$. Then it can be shown that the following are $100(1 - \alpha)\%$ intervals;

i. For the forecast of the actual value resulting for Y_{n+1}, the prediction interval is

$$\hat{y}_{n+1} \pm t_{n-2,\alpha/2} \sqrt{\left[1 + \frac{1}{n} + \frac{(x_{n+1} - \overline{X})^2}{\displaystyle\sum_{i=1}^{n}(x_i - \overline{X})^2} \right]} S_e \qquad (10.25)$$

ii. For the forecast of the conditional expectation, $E(Y_{n+1} \mid x_{n+1})$, the confidence interval is

$$\hat{y}_{n+1} \pm t_{n-2,\alpha/2} \sqrt{\left[\frac{1}{n} + \frac{(x_{n+1} - \overline{X})^2}{\displaystyle\sum_{i=1}^{n}(x_i - \overline{X})^2} \right]} S_e \qquad (10.26)$$

Where

$$\overline{X} = \frac{\displaystyle\sum_{i=1}^{n} x_i}{n} \qquad \text{and} \qquad \hat{y}_{n+1} = b_0 + b_1 x_{n+1}$$

EXAMPLE 10.3

FORECASTING RETAIL SALES (REGRESSION MODEL FORECASTING)

We will illustrate the interval computation by using the retail sales and disposable income from Example 10.1. We have been asked to determine the forecast value for retail sales per household for both next year and for the long-run expected value when disposable income per household is $12,000. In addition we have been asked to compute prediction intervals and confidence intervals for these forecasts.

SOLUTION

The forecast value for both next year and for the long-run average is,

$$\hat{y}_{n+1} = b_0 + b_1 x_{n+1}$$
$$= 1{,}923 + (0.3815)(12{,}000) = 6{,}501$$

Thus we find that the estimated sales is $6,501 when disposable income is $12,000. From previous examples we have also found that

$$n = 22 \qquad \overline{X} = 10{,}799 \qquad \sum (x_i - \overline{X})^2 = 34{,}110{,}178 \qquad s_e^2 = 21{,}789.95$$

Hence the standard error for a predicted single observation of Y is,

$$\sqrt{\left[1 + \frac{1}{n} + \frac{(x_{n+1} - \overline{X})^2}{\displaystyle\sum_{i=1}^{n} (x_i - \overline{X})^2}\right]} s_e = \sqrt{\left[1 + \frac{1}{22} + \frac{(12{,}000 - 10{,}799)^2}{34{,}110{,}178}\right]} \sqrt{21{,}789.95} = 153.954$$

Similarly, we find that the standard error for the expected value of Y is,

$$\sqrt{\left[\frac{1}{n} + \frac{(x_{n+1} - \overline{X})^2}{\displaystyle\sum_{i=1}^{n} (x_i - \overline{X})^2}\right]} s_e = \sqrt{\left[\frac{1}{22} + \frac{(12{,}000 - 10{,}799)^2}{34{,}110{,}178}\right]} \sqrt{21{,}789.95} = 43.725$$

Suppose that 95% intervals are required for the forecasts, with $\alpha = 0.05$ and

$$t_{n-2, \alpha/2} = t_{20, 0.025} = 2.086$$

Using these results we find that the 95% prediction interval for next year's retail sales when disposable income is $12,000 is computed as

$$6{,}501 \pm (2.086)(153.954)$$
$$6{,}501 \pm 321$$

Thus, the 95% prediction interval for sales in a single year in which income is $12,000 runs from $6,180 to $6,822.

For the confidence interval for the expected value of retail sales when disposable income is $12,000, we have

$$6{,}501 \pm (2.086)(43.725)$$
$$6{,}501 \pm 91$$

Hence, the 95% confidence interval for the expected value runs from $6,410 to $6,592.

INTERPRETATION

The distinction between these two interval estimation problems is illustrated in Figures 10.11 and 10.12. We see in each figure the estimated regression line for our retail sales–disposable income data. Also, in Figure 10.11 we see a probability density function representing our uncertainty about the value that retail sales will take in any specific year in which the disposable income is $12,000. The probability density function in Figure 10.12 represents our uncertainty about expected, or average, retail sales in years when disposable income is $12,000. Of course we would be less certain about sales in a single specific year than about average sales, and this is reflected in the shapes of the two density functions. We see that both are centered on retail sales of $6,501, but that the density function in Figure 10.11 has greater dispersion. As a result, the prediction interval for a specific value is wider than the confidence interval for expected retail sales.

We can obtain some further insights by studying the general forms of the prediction and confidence intervals. As we have seen, the wider the interval, the greater the uncertainty surrounding the point forecast. From these formulas we make four observations:

1. All other things being equal, the larger the sample size n, the narrower the confidence interval. Thus we see that the more sample information we have available the more sure will be our inference.
2. All other things being equal, the larger s_e^2, is the wider is the confidence interval. Again this is to be expected, since s_e^2 is an estimate of σ_ε^2, the variance of the regression errors ε_i. Since these errors

$$\varepsilon_i = y_i - \beta_0 - \beta_1 x_i$$

represent the discrepancy between the observed values of the dependent variables and their expectations given the independent variables, the bigger the magnitude of this discrepancy, the more imprecise will be our inference.
3. Consider now the quantity $\left(\sum_{i=1}^{n} (x_i - \overline{X})^2 \right)$. This is simply a multiple of the sample variance of the observations on the independent variable. A large variance implies that we have information for a wide range of values of this variable, which allows more precise estimates of the population regression line and correspondingly narrower confidence intervals.
4. We also see that larger values of the quantity $(x_{n+1} - \overline{X})^2$ result in wider confidence intervals for the predictions. Thus confidence intervals become wider as we move from the mean of the independent variable, X. Since our sample data are centered at the mean $\overline{X}$, we would expect to be more definitive about our inference when the independent variable is relatively close to this central value than when it is some distance away.

INTERPRETATION

Extrapolation of the regression equation outside the range of the data used for estimation is not recommended. Suppose that you are asked to predict retail sales per household in a year when disposable income is $30,000. Referring to the data in Table 10.1 and the regression line in Figure 10.12 we see that $30,000 is well outside the range of the data used to develop the regression model. An inexperienced analyst might use the procedures previously developed to estimate a prediction or a confidence interval. From the equations we can see that the resulting intervals would be very wide and thus the forecast would be of limited value. There is a more fundamental problem with forecasts made outside the range of the original data. The problem is that we simply have no evidence to indicate the nature of the relationship outside of the range of the data. There is no reason in economic theory that requires absolutely that the relationship will remain linear with the same rate of change when we move outside of the range of the data used to estimate the regression model coefficients. Any extrapolation of the model outside of the range of the data to obtain predicted values must be based on knowledge or evidence beyond that contained in the regression analysis on the available data. Major errors can result when analysts have attempted this kind of extrapolation.

EXERCISES

10.33 A sample of 25 blue-collar employees at a production plant was taken. Each employee was asked to assess his or her own job satisfaction (x), on a scale from 1 to 10. In addition, the number of days absent (y) from work during the last year were found for these employee's. The sample regression line

$$y = 12.6 - 1.2x$$

was estimated by least squares for these data. Also found were

$$\bar{x} = 6.0 \quad \sum_{i=1}^{25}(x_i - \bar{x})^2 = 130.0 \quad SSE = 80.6$$

(a) Test at the 1% significance level against the appropriate one-sided alternative the null hypothesis that job satisfaction has no linear effect on absenteeism.
(b) A particular employee has job satisfaction level 4. Find a 90% interval for the number of days this employee would be absent from work in a year.

10.34 Doctors are interested in the relationship between the dosage of a medicine and the time required for a patient's recovery. The following table shows, for a sample of five patients, dosage levels (in grams) and recovery times (in hours). These patients have similar characteristics except for medicine dosages.

DOSAGE LEVEL	1.2	1.0	1.5	1.2	1.4
RECOVERY TIME	25	40	10	27	16

(a) Estimate the linear regression of recovery time on dosage level.
(b) Find and interpret a 90% confidence interval for the slope of the population regression line.
(c) Would the sample regression derived in part (a) be useful in predicting recovery time for a patient given 2.5 grams of this drug? Explain your answer.

10.35 For the stock rate-of-return problem of Exercise 10.16 it was found that

$$\sum_{i=1}^{20} y_i^2 = 196.2$$

(a) Test the null hypothesis that the slope of the population regression line is 0 against the alternative that it is positive.
(b) Test against the two-sided alternative the null hypothesis that the slope of the population regression line is 1.

10.36 Using the data of Exercise 10.17 , test the null hypothesis that representatives' weekly sales are not linearly related to their aptitude test scores against the alternative that there is positive association.

10.37 Refer to the data of Exercise 30. Test against a two-sided alternative the null hypothesis that mutual fund losses on Friday, November 13, 1989, did not depend linearly on previous gains in 1989.

10.38 Denote by r the sample correlation between a pair of random variables.
(a) Show that

$$\frac{1 - r^2}{n - 2} = \frac{s_e^2}{SST}$$

(b) Using the result in part (a), show that

$$\frac{r}{\sqrt{(1 - r^2)/(n - 2)}} = \frac{b}{s_e / \sqrt{\sum (x_i - \bar{x})^2}}$$

(c) Using the result in part (b), deduce that the test of the null hypothesis of 0 population correlation, given in Section 10.1, is the same as the test of 0 population regression slope, given in Section 10.5.

10.39 For the problem of Exercise 10.18, on sales of premium beer in restaurants, it was found that

$$\frac{\sum (y_i - \bar{y})^2}{n - 1} = 250$$

Test against a two-sided alternative the null hypothesis that the slope of the population regression line is 0.

10.40 For a sample of 74 monthly observations, the regression of the percentage return on gold (y) against the percentage change in the consumer price index (x) was estimated. The sample regression line, obtained through least squares, was

$$y = -.003 + 1.11x$$

The estimated standard deviation of the slope of the population regression line was 2.31. Test the null hypothesis that the slope of the population regression line is 0 against the alternative that the slope is positive.

10.41 Refer to the data of Exercise 10.32. Test at the 5% level against the appropriate one-sided alternative the null hypothesis that sales do not depend linearly on price for this premium scotch whiskey.

10.42 Refer to the data of Exercise 10.21.
(a) Find a point estimate for the volume of sales when the price of the stereo system is $480 in a given region.
(b) If the price of the system is set at $480, find 95% confidence intervals for the actual volume of sales in a particular region and the expected number of sales in that region.

10.43 Continue the analysis of Exercise 2. If the Dow-Jones index increases by 1.0% in the first five trading days of a year, find 90% confidence intervals for the *actual*, and also for the *expected*, percentage changes in the index over the whole year. Discuss the distinction between these intervals.

10.44 Refer to the data in Exercise 10.15. For a year in which there is no change in the unemployment rate, find a 90% confidence interval for the *actual*, and also for the *expected*, change in mean employee absence rate due to own illness.

10.45 Use the data of Exercise 10.16 to find 90% and 95% confidence intervals for the expected return on the corporation's stock when the rate of return on the Standard and Poor's 500 Index is 1%.

10.46 A new sales representative for the corporation of Exercise 10.17 scores 70 on the aptitude test. Find 80% and 90% confidence intervals for the value of weekly sales he will achieve.

10.7   GRAPHICAL ANALYSIS

We have developed the theory and analysis procedures that provide a strong basis for performing regression analysis and building linear models. By using hypothesis tests and confidence intervals we can determine the quality of our model and identify certain important relationships. These inferential procedures initially assume that the model errors are normally distributed. But we also know that the central limit theorem will help us perform hypothesis tests and construct confidence intervals as long as the sampling distributions of the coefficient estimators and predicted values are approximately normal. The regression model is also based on a set of assumptions. However, there are many ways that regression analysis applications can go wrong, either because assumptions are not satisfied or because the data does not follow the patterns that we assumed. Here we will talk about how you can detect some of the problems.

The example of retail sales regressed on disposable income—Figure 10.1—that we have used in this chapter has a scatter plot that follows the pattern assumed in regression analysis. That pattern, however, does not always occur when new data are studied. One of the best ways to detect potential problems for simple regression analysis is to prepare scatter plots of the data and observe the pattern. Here we will consider some examples.

EXAMPLE 10.4

THE EFFECT OF EXTREME *X* VALUES (SCATTER PLOT ANALYSIS)

Here we are interested in determining the effect of extreme x values on the regression.

SOLUTION

Figure 10.13 is a scatter plot with a regression line drawn on the points, and Figure 10.14 is the output from the regression analysis computed with the data. Note that the regression slope is not zero and $R^2 = .632$. But note that two extreme points seem to determine the regression relationship.

FIGURE 10.13
Scatter Plot with Two Extreme Points: Positive Slope

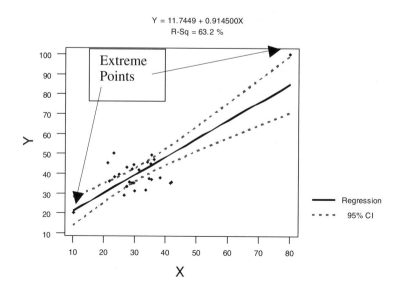

FIGURE 10.14
Minitab Output for
Regression Analysis with Two
Extreme Points: Positive
Slope

```
The regression equation is
y = 11.7 + 0.915 x
Predictor        Coef      StDev         T        P
Constant       11.745      4.717      2.49    0.020
x              0.9145     0.1397      6.55    0.000

S = 8.415      R-Sq = 63.2%      R-Sq(adj) = 61.7%
```

Now let us consider the effect of changing the two extreme data points as shown in Figures 10.15 and 10.16.

FIGURE 10.15
Scatter Plot with Extreme X
Points: Negative Slope

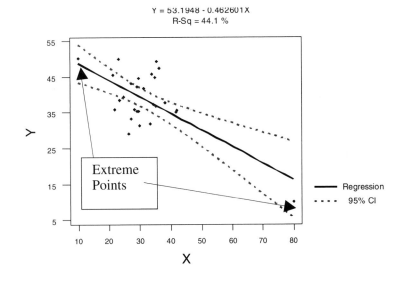

FIGURE 10.16
Minitab Output for
Regression with Extreme X
Points: Negative Slope

```
The regression equation is
y = 53.2 - 0.463 x

Predictor        Coef      StDev         T        P
Constant       53.195      3.518     15.12    0.000
x             -0.4626     0.1042     -4.44    0.000

S = 6.276      R-Sq = 44.1%      R-Sq(adj) = 41.9%
```

As the result of changing only two data points, the relationship now has a statistically significant negative slope and the predictions would be substantially different. Without examining the scatter plots we would not know why we had either a positive or negative slope. We might have thought that our results represented a standard regression situation such as we saw in the retail sales scatter plot.

INTERPRETATION

This situation demonstrates a common problem when historical data are used. Suppose that X is the number of workers employed on a production shift and Y is the number of units produced on that shift. Most of the time the factory operates with a relatively stable workforce, and output depends in large part on the amount of raw materials available and the sales requirements. The operation adjusts up or down over a narrow range in response to demands and to the available work force, x. Thus we see that the scatter plot covers a narrow range for the X variable. But occasionally there is a very large or small work force—or the number of workers has been recorded incorrectly. On those days the production might be unusually high or low—or might be recorded incorrectly. As a result we have extreme points—either a positive or a negative slope. These few days determine the regression results. Without the extreme points the regression would indicate no relationship. If these extreme points represent extensions of the relationship then the estimated model is useful. But if these points result from unusual conditions the model is misleading.

In a particular application we may find that these outlier points are correct and should be used to determine the regression line. But the analyst needs to make that decision knowing that all of the other data points do not support a significant relationship. In fact, you do need to think carefully, understand the system and process that generated the data, and evaluate the available data.

EXAMPLE 10.5

THE EFFECT OF OUTLIERS IN THE Y VARIABLE (SCATTER PLOT ANALYSIS)

In this example we consider the effect of outliers in the Y or vertical direction. Recall that the regression analysis model assumes that all of the variation is in the Y direction. Thus we know that outliers in the Y direction will have large residuals and these will result in a higher estimate of the model error. In this example we will see that the effects can be even more extreme.

SOLUTION

To begin, please observe the scatter plot and regression analysis in Figures 10.17 and 10.18. In this example we have a strong relationship between the X and Y variables. The scatter plot clearly supports a linear relationship. In addition, the regression model R^2 is close to 1 and the Student's t statistic for the slope coefficient is very large. Clearly we have strong evidence to support a linear model.

FIGURE 10.17
Scatter Plot With Anticipated Pattern

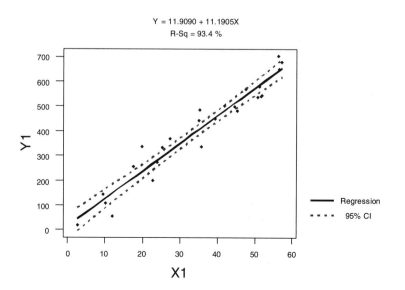

Y = 11.9090 + 11.1905X
R-Sq = 93.4 %

FIGURE 10.18
Minitab Output for
Regression with Anticipated
Pattern

```
              y = 11.9 + 11.2 x

Predictor        Coef        StDev           T          P
Constant        11.91        23.90        0.50      0.623
x             11.1905       0.6193       18.07      0.000

S = 50.83       R-Sq = 93.4%      R-Sq(adj) = 93.1%
```

Now let us consider the effect of changing two observations to outlier data points as shown in Figure 10.19. This could occur because of a data recording error or because of a very unusual condition in the process being studied.

The regression slope is still positive, but now $b_1 = 6.842$ and the slope estimate has a larger standard error as shown in Figure 10.20. The confidence interval is much wider and the predicted value from the regression line is not as accurate. The correct regression model is now not as clear. If the two outlier points actually occurred in the normal operation of the process then you must include them in your analysis. But the fact that they deviate so strongly from the pattern indicates that you should carefully investigate the data situations that generated those points and study the process that you are modeling.

FIGURE 10.19
Scatter Plot with Y Outlier
Points

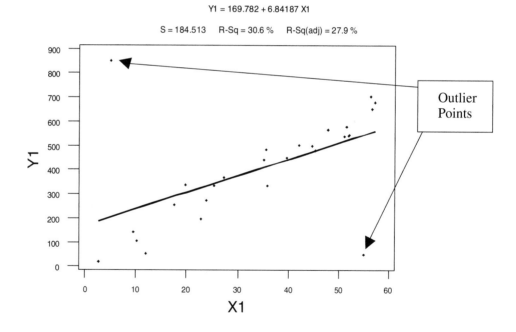

FIGURE 10.20
Minitab Output for
Regression with Y Outlier
Points

```
              y = 170 + 6.84 x

Predictor        Coef        StDev           T          P
Constant       169.78        79.53        2.13      0.043
x               6.842        2.059        3.32      0.003

S = 184.5       R-Sq = 30.6%      R-Sq(adj) = 27.9%
```

There are many other examples that could be generated. You might find that a non-linear relationship is suggested by the scatter plot and thus would provide a better model for a particular application problem. In Chapters 11 and 12 we will learn how we can use regression to model nonlinear relationships. You will see many different data patterns as you proceed with various applications of regression. The important point is that you must regularly follow analysis procedures—including the preparation of scatter plots—that can provide as much insight as possible. A good analyst must **"Know Thy Data!"**

EXERCISES

10.47 🌐   Frank Anscombe, Senior Research Executive, has asked you to analyze the following four linear models using data contained in the data file **Anscombe.**

$$Y_1 = \beta_0 + \beta_1 X_1$$
$$Y_2 = \beta_0 + \beta_1 X_1$$
$$Y_3 = \beta_0 + \beta_1 X_1$$
$$Y_4 = \beta_0 + \beta_1 X_2$$

Use your computer package to obtain linear regression estimates for each of the models. Prepare scatter plots for the data used in each of the four models. Write a report, including regression and graphical outputs, that compares and contrasts the four models.

10.48 🌐   John Foster, president of Public Research Inc., has asked for your assistance in a study of the occurrence of crimes in different states before and after a large Federal Government expenditure to reduce crime. As part of this study he wants to know if the crime rate for selected crimes after the expenditure can be predicted using the crime rate before the expenditure. He has asked you to test the hypothesis that crime before predicts crime after for Total Crime rate, Murder, Rape, and Robbery. The data for your analysis is contained in the data file **Crime Study**. Perform appropriate analysis and write a report that summarizes your results.

SUMMARY

In this chapter we have developed the two variable or simple least squares models. We have built on some of the initial descriptive concepts developed in Chapter 3. The simple regression model assumes that a set of exogenous or independent variables have a linear relationship to the expected value of an endogenous or dependent random variable. By developing estimates of the coefficients of this model we can better understand business and economic processes and can predict values of the endogenous variable as a function of the exogenous variable. Our study has included the development of

estimator's for coefficients and for dependent variables. We have also developed measures of regression goodness of fit—Analysis of Variance and R^2.

Following that study we have developed statistical inference procedures—hypothesis testing and confidence intervals for the key regression estimators. We also considered correlation analysis —simply examining the relationship between two variables. Finally, we discussed the importance of scatter plots and graphical analysis in the development and testing of regression models.

KEY WORDS

analysis of variance, 384
assumptions for the least squares coefficient estimators, 381
basis for inference about the population regression slope, 393
coefficient of determination, R^2, 387
coefficient estimators, 380
confidence intervals for predictions, 400

confidence intervals for the population regression slope b_1, 395
correlation and R^2, 389
estimation of model error variance, 389
F test for simple regression coefficient, 397
least squares procedure, 379
linear regression outcomes, 378

linear regression population equation model, 377
sampling distribution of the least squares coefficient estimator, 392
tests for zero population correlation, 372
tests of the population regression slope, 394

CHAPTER EXERCISES

10.49 What is meant by the statement that a pair of random variables are positively correlated? Give examples of pairs of random variables for which you would expect the following:
   (a) Positive correlation
   (b) Negative correlation
   (c) Zero correlation

10.50 A random sample of five sets of observations on a pair of random variables yielded the results given in the table.

X	4	1	0	1	4
Y	−2	−1	0	1	2

   (a) Find the sample correlation coefficient.
   (b) In light of the fact that each y_i value is the square of the corresponding x_i value, comment on your answer in part (a).

10.51 For a random sample of 53 building supply stores in a chain, the correlation between annual euro sales per square meter of floor space and annual euro rent per square meter of floor space was found to be .37. Test the null hypothesis that these two quantities are uncorrelated in the population against the alternative that the population correlation is positive.

10.52 For a random sample of 526 firms, the sample correlation between the proportion of a firm's officers who are directors and a risk-adjusted measure of return on the firm's stock was found to be .1398. Test against a two-sided alternative the null hypothesis that the population correlation is zero.

10.53 For a sample of 66 months, the correlation between the returns on Canadian and Hong Kong 10-year bonds was found to be .293. Test the null hypothesis that the population correlation is 0 against the alternative that it is positive.

10.54 For a random sample of 192 female employees, a sample correlation of −.18 was found between age and a measure of willingness to relocate. Given only this information, derive all the conclusions you can about the regression of willingness to relocate on age.

10.55 Based on a sample on n observations, (x_1, y_1), (x_2, y_2), ..., (x_n, y_n), the sample regression of y on x is calculated. Show that the sample regression line passes through the point $(x = \bar{x}, y = \bar{y})$, where $\bar{x}$ and $\bar{y}$ are the sample means.

10.56 🔵 A company routinely administers an aptitude test to all new management trainees. At the end of the first year with the company, these trainees are graded by their immediate supervisors. For a random sample of 12 trainees, the results shown in the data file **Employee Test** were obtained.
   (a) Estimate the regression of supervisor's grade on aptitude score.

   (b) Interpret the slope of the sample regression line.
   (c) Is it possible to give a useful interpretation of the intercept of the sample regression line? Explain.
   (d) Find and interpret the coefficient of determination for this regression.
   (e) Test against the obvious one-sided alternative the null hypothesis that the slope of the population regression line is 0.
   (f) Find a 95% confidence interval for the supervisor's grade that would be obtained by a particular trainee who had an aptitude score of 70.

10.57 An attempt was made to evaluate the inflation rate as a predictor of the spot rate in the German treasury bill market. For a sample of 79 quarterly observations, the estimated linear regression

$$y = .0027 + .7916x$$

was obtained, where

   y = Actual change in the spot rate
   x = Change in the spot rate predicted by the inflation rate

The coefficient of determination was .097, and the estimated standard deviation of the estimator of the slope of the population regression line was .2759.
   (a) Interpret the slope of the estimated regression line.
   (b) Interpret the coefficent of determination.
   (c) Test the null hypothesis that the slope of the population regression line is 0 against the alternative that the true slope is positive, and interpret your result.
   (d) Test against a two-sided alternative the null hypothesis that the slope of the population regression line is 1, and interpret your result.

10.58 The table shows, for eight vintages of select wine, purchases per buyer (y) and the wine buyer's rating in a year (x).

x	3.6	3.3	2.8	2.6	2.7	2.9	2.0	2.6
y	24	21	22	22	18	13	9	6

   (a) Estimate the regression of purchases per buyer on the buyer's rating.
   (b) Interpret the slope of the estimated regression line.
   (c) Find and interpret the coefficent of determination.
   (d) Find and interpret a 90% confidence interval for the slope of the population regression line.
   (e) Find a 90% confidence interval for expected purchases per buyer for a vintage for which the buyer's rating is 2.0.

10.59 For a sample of 306 students in a basic business statistics course, the sample regression line

$$y = 58.813 + .2875x$$

was obtained. Here

$y =$ Final student score at the end of the course

$x =$ Score on a diagnostic statistics test given at the beginning of the course

The coefficient of determination was .1158, and the estimated standard deviation of the estimator of the slope of the population regression line was .04566.

(a) Interpret the slope of the sample regression line.
(b) Interpret the coefficient of determination.
(c) The information given allows the null hypothesis that the slope of the population regression line is 0 to be tested against the alternative that it is positive in two different ways. Carry out these tests and show that they reach the same conclusion.

10.60 Based on a sample of 30 observations, the population regression model

$$Y_i = \beta_0 + \beta_1 x_i + \varepsilon_i$$

was estimated. The least squares estimates obtained were

$$b_0 = 10.1 \quad \text{and} \quad b_1 = 8.4$$

The regression and error sums of squares were

$$SSR = 128 \quad \text{and} \quad SSE = 286$$

(a) Find and interpret the coefficient of determination.
(b) Test at the 10% significance level against a two-sided alternative the null hypothesis that β_1 is 0.
(c) Find

$$\sum_{i=1}^{30} \left(x_i - \overline{X} \right)^2$$

10.61 Based on a sample of 25 observations, the population regression model

$$Y_i = \beta_0 + \beta_1 x_i + \varepsilon_i$$

was estimated. The least squares estimates obtained were

$$b_0 = 15.6 \quad \text{and} \quad b_1 = 1.3$$

The total and error sums of squares were

$$SST = 268 \quad \text{and} \quad SSE = 204$$

(a) Find and interpret the coefficient of determination.
(b) Test against a two-sided alternative at the 5% significance level the null hypothesis that the slope of the population regression line is 0.
(c) Find a 95% confidence interval for β_1.

10.62 An analyst believes that the only important determinant of banks' return on assets (Y) is the ratio of loans to deposits (x). For a random sample of twenty banks, the sample regression line

$$Y = .97 + .47x$$

was obtained, with coefficient of determination .720.

(a) Find the sample correlation between return on assets and the ratio of loans to deposits.
(b) Test against a two-sided alternative at the 5% level the null hypothesis of no linear association between.
(c) Find

$$\frac{S_e}{\sqrt{\sum \left(x_i - \overline{X} \right)^2}}$$

10.63 Comment on the following statement:
If a regression of the yield per acre of corn on the quantity of fertilizer used were estimated, using fertilizer quantities in the range typically used by farmers, the slope of the estimated regression line would certainly be positive. However, it is well known that if an enormously high amount of fertilizer were to be used, corn yield would be very low. Therefore, regression equations are not of much use in forecasting.

10.64 ⬤ A college Economics Department is attempting to determine if verbal or mathematical proficiency is more important for predicting academic success in the study of economics. They have decided to use the grade-point average in economics courses for graduates as a measure of success. Measurement of verbal proficiency is available in the SAT verbal and the ACT English entrance examination test scores. Mathematical proficiency is measured by the SAT mathematics and the ACT mathematics entrance examination scores. The data for 112 students are available in a data file named **Student GPA**, which is available on your data disk. The designation of the variable columns is presented at the beginning of the data file. You should use your local statistical computer program to perform the analysis for this problem.

(a) Prepare a graphical plot of economics GPA versus each of the two verbal proficiency scores and each of the two mathematical proficiency scores. Which variable is a better predictor? Note any unusual patterns in the data.
(b) Compute the linear model coefficients and the regression analysis statistics for the models that predict economics GPA as a function of each verbal and each mathematical score. Using both the SAT mathematics and verbal measures and the ACT measures, determine whether mathematical or verbal proficiency is the best predictor of economics GPA.
(c) Compare the descriptive statistics—mean, standard deviation, upper and lower quartiles, range—for the predictor variables. Note the differences and indicate how these differences affect the capability of the linear model to predict.

10.65 ⬤ The administrator of the National Highway Traffic Safety Administration (NHTSA) wants to know if the different types of vehicles in a state have a relationship to the highway death rate in the state. She has asked you to perform several regression analyses to determine if average vehicle weight, percentage imported cars, percentage light trucks, or average car age are related to "crash deaths in automobiles and pickups." The data for the analysis is located in the data file named **Crash**, which is located on your data disk. The variable descriptions and locations are contained in the data file catalog in the Appendix.

(a) Prepare graphical plots of crash deaths versus each of the potential predictor variables. Note the relationship and any unusual patterns in the data points.

(b) Prepare a simple regression analysis of crash deaths on the potential predictor variables. Determine which, if any, of the regressions indicate a significant relationship.

(c) State the results of your analysis and rank the predictor variables in terms of their relationship to crash deaths.

10.66 The department of transportation wishes to know if states with a larger percentage of urban population have higher automobile and pickup crash death rates. In addition, they want to know if the average speed on rural roads or the percentage of rural roads that are surfaced are related to crash death rates. Data for this study is included in the file **Crash** stored on your data disk. Prepare graphical plots of crash deaths versus each of the potential predictor variables. Note the relationship and any unusual patterns in the data points.

(a) Prepare a simple regression analysis of crash deaths on the potential predictor variables. Determine which, if any, of the regressions indicate a significant relationship.

(b) State the results of your analysis and rank the predictor variables in terms of their relationship to crash deaths.

10.67 An economist wishes to predict the market value of owner-occupied homes in small Midwestern cities. He has collected a set of data from 45 small cities for a two-year period and wants you to use this as the data source for the analysis. The data is stored in the file **Citydat**, which is stored on your data disk and described in the data file catalog in the Appendix. He wants you to develop two prediction equations: one that uses the size of the house as a predictor and a second that uses tax rate as a predictor.

(a) Plot the market value of houses versus size of house and tax rate. Note any unusual patterns in the data.

(b) Prepare regression analyses for the two predictor variables. Which variable is the stronger predictor of the value of houses?

(c) A business developer in a Midwestern state has stated that local property tax rates in small towns need to be lowered because if they are not, no one will purchase a house in these towns. Based on your analysis in this problem, evaluate the business developer's claim.

10.68 Stuart Wainwright, the vice president of purchasing for a large national retailer, has asked you to prepare an analysis of retail sales by state. He wants to know if either the percent unemployment or the per capita personal income are related to per capita retail sales. Data for this study is stored in the data file named **Retail**, which is stored on your data disk and described in the data file catalog in the Appendix.

(a) Prepare graphical plots and regression analyses to determine the relationships between per capita retail sales and unemployment and personal income. Compute 95% confidence intervals for the slope coefficients in each regression equation.

(b) What is the effect of a $1,000 decrease in per capita income on per capita sales?

(c) For the per capita income regression equation, what is the 95% confidence interval for retail sales at the mean per capita income and at $1,000 above the mean per capita income?

10.69 A major national supplier of building materials for residential construction is concerned about total sales for next year. It is well known that the company's sales are directly related to the total national residential investment. Several New York bankers are predicting that interest rates will rise about 2 percentage points next year. You have been asked to develop a regression analysis that can be used to predict the effect of Interest rate changes on residential investment. The time series data for this study are contained in the data file named **Macro2000**, which is stored on your data disk.

(a) Develop two regression models to predict residential investment using prime interest rate for one and federal funds interest rate for the other. Analyze the regression statistics and indicate which equation provides the best predictions.

(b) Determine the 95% confidence interval for the slope coefficient in both regression equations.

(c) Based on each model, predict the effect of a 2-percentage-point increase in interest rates on residential investment.

(d) Using both models, compute 95% confidence intervals for the change in residential investment that results from a 2-percentage-point increase in interest rates.

APPENDIX

In this Appendix, we derive the least squares estimates of the population regression parameters. We want to find the values b_0 and b_1 for which the sum of squared discrepancies

$$SSE = \sum_{i=1}^{n} e_i^2 = \sum_{i=1}^{n} (y_i - b_0 - b_1 x_i)^2$$

is as small as possible.

As a first step, we keep b_1 constant and differentiate[2] with respect to b_0, giving

$$\frac{\partial SSE}{\partial b_0} = -2 \sum_{i=1}^{n} (y_i - b_0 - b_1 x_i)$$

$$= -2 \left(\sum y_i - n b_0 - b_1 \sum x_i \right)$$

Since this derivative must be 0 for a minimum, we have

$$\sum y_i - n b_0 - b_1 \sum x_i = 0$$

Hence, dividing through by n yields

$$b_0 = \bar{y} - b_1 \bar{x}$$

Substituting this expression for b_0 gives

$$SSE = \sum_{i=1}^{n} [(y_i - \bar{y}) - b_1 (x_i - \bar{x})]^2$$

Differentiating this expression with respect to b_1 then gives

$$\frac{\partial SSE}{\partial b_1} = -2 \sum_{i=1}^{n} (x_i - \bar{x})[(y_i - \bar{y}) - b_1 (x_i - \bar{x})]$$

$$= -2 \left(\sum (x_i - \bar{x})(y_i - \bar{y}) - b_1 \sum (x_i - \bar{x})^2 \right)$$

This derivative must be 0 for a minimum, and so we have

$$\sum (x_i - \bar{x})(y_i - \bar{y}) = b_1 \sum (x_i - \bar{x})^2$$

Hence,

$$b_1 = \frac{\sum (x_i - \bar{x})(y_i - \bar{y})}{\sum (x_i - \bar{x})^2}$$

[2] Here we are using the concept of **partial differentiation.** The partial derivative of SSE with respect to b_0 is denoted $\partial SS / \partial b_0$ and is obtained by differentiating SSE with respect to b_0, treating other variables as constant. The sum of squares SSE is a minimum with respect to b_0 and b_1 when both partial derivatives, $\partial SSE / \partial b_0$ and $\partial SSE / \partial b_1$, are 0.

REFERENCE

1. Dhalla, N.K., "Short-Term Forecasts of Advertising Expenditures," *Journal of Advertising Research*, *19*, no. 1 (1979), 7–14.

MULTIPLE REGRESSION

INTRODUCTION

In Chapter 10 we developed simple regression as a procedure for obtaining a linear equation that predicts a dependent or endogenous variable as a function of a single independent or exogenous variable—for example, total number of items sold as a function of price. However, in many situations several independent variables jointly influence a dependent variable. Multiple regression enables us to determine the simultaneous effect of several independent variables on a dependent variable using the least squares principle.

Many important applications of multiple regression occur in business and economics. These applications include the following:

1. The quantity of goods sold is a function of price, income, advertising, price of substitute goods, and other variables.
2. Capital investment occurs when a business person believes that a profit can be made. Thus capital investment is a function of variables related to the potential for profit, including interest rate, gross domestic product, consumer expectations, disposable income, and technological level.
3. Salary is a function of experience, education, age, and job rank.

Business and economic analysis has some unique characteristics compared to analysis in other disciplines. Natural scientists work in a laboratory where many—but not all—variables can be controlled. In contrast, the economist's and manager's laboratory is the world and conditions cannot be controlled. Thus we need tools such as multiple regression to estimate the simultaneous effect of several variables. Multiple regression as a "lab tool" is very important for the work of managers and economists. In this chapter we will see many specific applications in discussion examples and problem exercises.

The methods for fitting multiple regression models are based on the same least squares principle learned in Chapter 10, and thus the insights gained there will extend directly to multiple regression. However, there are complexities introduced because of the relationships between the various exogenous variables. These require additional insights that will be developed in this chapter.

11.1 THE MULTIPLE REGRESSION MODEL

Our objective here is to learn how to use multiple regression for creating and analyzing models. We will learn how multiple regression works and some guidelines for interpretation. A good understanding provides the capability for solving a wide range of applied problems. This study of multiple regression methods will parallel the study of simple regression. First we will study the least squares process, followed by an analysis of variability to identify the effects of each predictor variable. Then we will study estimation, confidence intervals, and hypothesis testing. Computer applications will be used extensively to indicate how the theory is applied to realistic problems. Your study of this material will be aided if you relate the ideas in this chapter to those presented in Chapter 10.

We begin with an application that illustrates the important task of regression model specification. Model specification includes selection of the exogenous variables and the functional form of the model.

EXAMPLE 11.1

PROCESS MANUFACTURING (REGRESSION MODEL SPECIFICATION)

The production manager for Flexible Circuits Inc. has asked for your assistance in studying a manufacturing process. Flexible circuits are produced from a continuous roll of flexible resin with a thin film of copper conducting material bonded to its surface. Copper is bonded to the resin by passing the resin through a copper-based solution. The thickness of the copper is critical for high-quality circuits. Copper thickness depends in part upon the temperature of the copper solution, speed of the production line, density of the solution, and thickness of the flexible resin. To control the thickness of the bonded copper the production manager needs to know the effect of each of these variables. You have been asked for assistance to develop a multiple regression model.

SOLUTION

Multiple regression can be used to provide estimates of the effect of each variable in combination with the other variables. In this example the dependent variable, Y, is the copper thickness. Independent variables include temperature of the copper solution, x_1, speed of the production line, x_2, density of the solution, x_3, and thickness of the flexible resin, x_4. These variables were identified as potential predictors of copper thickness, Y, by engineers and scientists that understand the technology of the plating process. The resulting model is

$$Y = \beta_0 + \beta_1 x_1 + \beta_2 x_2 + \beta_3 x_3 + \beta_4 x_4$$

EXAMPLE 11.2

STORE LOCATION MODEL SPECIFICATION (REGRESSION MODEL DEVELOPMENT)

The director of planning for a large retailer was dissatisfied with their new store development experience. In the past four years 25% of new stores failed to obtain their projected sales within the two-year trial period and were closed with substantial economic losses. The director wanted to develop better criteria for choosing store locations and decided that the historical experience of successful and unsuccessful stores should be studied.

SOLUTION

Discussion with a consultant indicated that data from stores that met and that did not meet anticipated sales should be used to develop a multiple regression model. The consultant suggested that the second year's sales should be used as the dependent variable, Y. A regression model would be used to predict second-year sales as a function of several independent variables that define the area surrounding the store. Stores would only be located where the predicted sales exceeded a minimum level. The model would also indicate the effect of various independent variables on sales.

After considerable discussion with people in the company the consultant recommended the following independent variables;

1. X_1 Size of store.
2. X_2 Traffic volume on highway in front of store.
3. X_3 Stand-alone store versus shopping mall location.
4. X_4 Location of competing store within one quarter mile.
5. X_5 Per capita income of population within five miles.
6. X_6 Total number of people within five miles.
7. X_7 Per capita income of population within ten miles.
8. X_8 Total number of people within ten miles.

Multiple regression was used to obtain estimates of the sales prediction model coefficients using data collected for all stores opened during the past eight years. The data set included both stores that were still operating and those that were closed. A model was developed that could be used to predict second-year sales. To apply the model

$$\hat{y}_i = b_0 + \sum_{j=1}^{8} b_j x_{ji}$$

measurements of the independent variables were collected for each proposed new store location and the predicted sales were computed for that location. Predicted sales level was used along with the judgement of marketing analysts and a committee of successful store managers as inputs to the store location decision process.

The strategy for model development will be influenced by the model objectives. One objective is prediction of a dependent or outcome variable. Applications include predicting or forecasting sales, output, total consumption, total investment, and many other business and economic performance criteria. A second objective is estimating the marginal effect of each independent variable. Economists and managers need to know how changes of independent variables, X_j, $j = 1, \ldots K$, change performance measures, Y. For example:

1. How do sales change as a result of a price increase and advertising expenditures?
2. How does output change when the amount of labor and capital are changed?
3. Does infant mortality become lower when health care expenditures and local sanitation are increased?

REGRESSION OBJECTIVES

Multiple regression provides two important results:

1. A linear equation that predicts the dependent variable, Y, as a function of "K" independent variables, x_{ji}, $j = 1, \ldots K$.

$$\hat{y}_1 = b_0 + b_1 x_{1i} + b_2 x_{2i} + \cdots + b_K x_{Ki}$$

Where $i = 1, \ldots, n$ observations.

2. The marginal change in the dependent variable, Y, that is related to changes in the independent variables — measured by the partial coefficients, b_j's. In multiple regression these partial coefficients depend on what other variables are included in the model. The coefficient b_j indicates the change in Y given a unit change in x_j while controlling for the simultaneous effect of the other independent variables.

In some problems both results are equally important. However, usually one will predominate (e.g., prediction of store sales, Y, in the store location example).

Marginal change is more difficult to estimate because the independent variables are not only related to the dependent variables but also to each other. If two or more independent variables change in a direct linear relationship with each other it is difficult to determine the individual effect of each independent variable on the dependent variable.

When applying multiple regression we construct a model to explain variability in the dependent variable. In order to do this we want to include the simultaneous and individual influences of several independent variables. For example, suppose we wanted to develop a model that would predict the annual profit margin for savings and loan associations using data collected over a period of years. An initial model specification indicated that the annual profit margin was related to net revenues per deposit dollar and the number of savings and loan offices. Net revenues are expected to increase annual profit margins, and the number of savings and loan offices are anticipated to decrease profit margins because of increased competition. This would lead us to specify a population regression model

$$y = \beta_0 + \beta_1 X_1 + \beta_2 X_2 + \varepsilon$$

where

y is the annual profit margin

X_1 is the net annual revenues per deposit dollar

X_2 is the number of savings and loan offices for that year

Savings and Loan

Table 11.1 and the data file named **Savings and Loan** contains 25 observations of annual sets of observations for these variables. This data will be used to develop a linear model that predicts annual profit margin as a function of revenue per deposit dollar and number of offices (reference 2).

But before we can estimate the model we need to develop and understand the multiple regression procedure.

To begin, let us consider the general multiple regression model and note the differences from the simple regression model. The population model for multiple regression is

$$y_i = \beta_0 + \beta_1 x_{1i} + \beta_2 x_{2i} + \cdots + \beta_K x_{Ki} + \varepsilon_i$$

where ε_i is the random error term with mean 0 and variance σ^2, the β_j's are the coefficients or marginal effects of the independent or exogenous variables, X_j, $j = 1, \ldots, K$, given the effects of the other independent variables. The i's indicate the observations with $i = 1, \ldots, n$. We use lower case x_{ji}'s to denote specific values of variable X_j at observation i. We assume that the ε_i's are independent of the X_j's and of each other to ensure proper estimates of the coefficients and their variances. In Chapter 12 we will indicate the effect of relaxing these assumptions.

The sample estimated model is

$$y_i = b_0 + b_1 x_{1i} + b_2 x_{2i} + \cdots + b_K x_{Ki} + e_i$$

where e_i is the residual or difference between the observed value of Y and the estimated value of Y obtained by using the estimated coefficients, b_j, $j = 1, \ldots, K$. The regression pro-

TABLE 11.1
Savings and Loan
Associations Operating Data

YEAR	REVENUE PER DOLLAR	NO. OF OFFICES	PROFIT MARGIN	YEAR	REVENUE PER DOLLAR	NO. OF OFFICES	PROFIT MARGIN
1	3.92	7298	0.75	14	3.78	6672	0.84
2	3.61	6855	0.71	15	3.82	6890	0.79
3	3.32	6636	0.66	16	3.97	7115	0.7
4	3.07	6506	0.61	17	4.07	7327	0.68
5	3.06	6450	0.7	18	4.25	7546	0.72
6	3.11	6402	0.72	19	4.41	7931	0.55
7	3.21	6368	0.77	20	4.49	8097	0.63
8	3.26	6340	0.74	21	4.7	8468	0.56
9	3.42	6349	0.9	22	4.58	8717	0.41
10	3.42	6352	0.82	23	4.69	8991	0.51
11	3.45	6361	0.75	24	4.71	9179	0.47
12	3.58	6369	0.77	25	4.78	9318	0.32
13	3.66	6546	0.78				

FIGURE 11.1
The Plane Is the Expected
Value of Y as a Function of X_1
and X_2

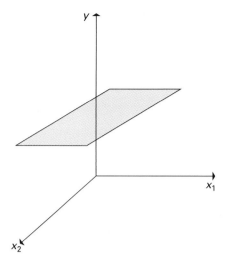

cedure obtains simultaneous estimates, b_j, of the population model coefficients, β_j, using the least squares procedure.

In our savings and loan associations example the population model for individual data points is

$$y_i = \beta_0 + \beta_1 x_{1i} + \beta_2 x_{2i} + \varepsilon_i$$

This reduced model with only two predictor variables provides the opportunity for developing additional insights into the regression procedure. The regression function can be depicted graphically in three dimensions as shown in Figure 11.1. The regression function is shown as a plane whose Y values are a function of the independent variable values of X_1 and X_2. For each possible pair, x_{1i}, x_{2i}, the expected value of the dependent variable, y_i, is on the plane. Figure 11.1 specifically illustrates the savings and loan example. An increase in X_1 leads to an increase in the expected value of Y, conditional on the effect of X_2. Similarly an increase in X_2 leads to a decrease in the expected value of the dependent variable Y, conditional on the effect of X_1.

To complete our model we add an error term defined as ε. This error term recognizes that no postulated relationship will hold exactly and that there are likely to be additional variables that also affect the observed value of Y. Thus in the application setting we observe the expected value of the dependent variable, Y,—as depicted by the plane in Figure 11.1— plus a random error term ε that represents the portion of Y not included in the expected value. As a result the general model has the form

$$y_i = \beta_0 + \beta_1 x_{1i} + \beta_2 x_{2i} + \cdots + \beta_K x_{Ki} + \varepsilon_i$$

THE POPULATION MULTIPLE REGRESSION MODEL

The **population multiple regression model** defines the relationship between a dependent or endogenous variable, Y, and a set of independent or exogenous variables, X_j, $j = 1, \ldots, K$. The x_{ji}'s are assumed to be fixed numbers and Y is a random variable, defined for each observation, i, where, $i = 1, \ldots, n$, and n is the number of observations. The model is defined as

$$y_i = \beta_0 + \beta_1 x_{1i} + \beta_2 x_{2i} + \cdots + \beta_K x_{Ki} + \varepsilon_i \qquad (11.1)$$

where the β_j's are constant coefficients and the ε's are random variables with mean 0 and variance σ^2.

FIGURE 11.2
Comparison of the Observed and Expected Values of Y as a Function of Two Independent Variables

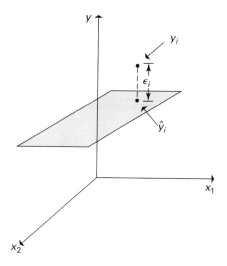

For the savings and loan example, with two independent variables, the population regression model is

$$y_i = \beta_0 + \beta_1 x_{1i} + \beta_2 x_{2i} + \varepsilon_i$$

Given particular values of net revenue, x_{1i}, and the number of savings and loan offices, x_{2i}, the observed profit margin, y_i, is the sum of two parts, the expected value, $\beta_0 + \beta_1 x_{1i} + \beta_2 x_{2i}$, and the random error term, ε_i. The random error term can be regarded as the combination of the effects of numerous other unidentified factors that affect profit margins. Figure 11.2 illustrates the model, with the plane indicating the expected value for various combinations of the independent variables, and the ε_i, shown as the deviation between the plane—expected value—and the observed value of Y—marked by a large dot—for a particular data point. In general the observed values of Y will not lie on the plane but instead will be above or below the plane because of the positive or negative error terms, ε.

Simple regression, developed in the previous chapter, is merely a special case of multiple regression with only one predictor variable, and hence the plane is reduced to a line. Thus the theory and analyses developed there also applies to multiple regression. However, there are some additional interpretations that we will develop in our study of multiple regression. One of the important interpretations is illustrated in the following discussion of three-dimensional graphing.

Three-Dimensional Graphing

Your understanding of the multiple regression procedure might be helped by considering a simplified graphical image. Look at the corner of the room in which you are sitting. The lines formed by the two walls and the floor represent the axis for two independent variables X_1 and X_2. The corner between the two walls is the dependent variable Y axis. To estimate a regression line we collect sets of points; $(x_{1i}, x_{2i}, $ and $y_i)$. Now picture these points plotted in your room using the wall and floor corners as the three axes. With these points hanging in your room, we find a plane in space that comes close to all of them. This plane is the geometric form of the least squares equation.

Geometric interpretations of multiple regression become increasingly complex as the number of independent variables increases. However, the analogy to simple regression is extremely useful. We estimate the coefficients by minimizing the sum of squared deviations in the Y dimension about a linear function of the independent variables. In simple regression the function is a straight line on a two dimensional graph. With two independent variables the function is a plane in three-dimensional space. Beyond two independent variables we have various complex hyperplanes that are impossible to visualize.

EXERCISES

11.1 An aircraft company wanted to predict the number of worker-hours necessary to finish the design of a new plane. Relevant explanatory variables were thought to be the plane's top speed, its weight, and the number of parts it had in common with other models built by the company. A sample of 27 of the company's planes was taken, and the following model estimated:

$$y_i = \beta_0 + \beta_1 x_{1i} + \beta_2 x_{2i} + \beta_3 x_{3i} + \varepsilon_i$$

where

y_i = Design effort, in millions of worker-hours
x_{1i} = Plane's top speed, in miles per hour
x_{2i} = Plane's weight, in tons
x_{3i} = Percentage number of parts in common with other models

The estimated partial regression coefficients were

$$b_1 = .661 \quad b_2 = .065 \quad b_3 = -.018$$

Interpret these estimates.

11.2 In a study of the influence of financial institutions on bond interest rates in Germany, quarterly data over a period of 12 years were analyzed. The postulated model was

$$y_i = \beta_0 + \beta_1 x_{1i} + \beta_2 x_{2i} + \varepsilon_i$$

where

y_i = Change over the quarter in the bond interest rates
x_{1i} = Change over the quarter in bond purchases by financial institutions
x_{2i} = Change over the quarter in bond sales by financial institutions

The estimated partial regression coefficients were

$$b_1 = .057 \quad b_2 = -.065$$

Interpret these estimates.

11.3 The following model was fitted to a sample of 30 families in order to explain household milk consumption:

$$y_i = \beta_0 + \beta_1 x_{1i} + \beta_2 x_{2i} + \varepsilon_i$$

where

y_i = Milk consumption, in quarts per week
x_i = Weekly income, in hundreds of dollars
x_i = Family size

The least squares estimates of the regression parameters were

$$b_0 = -.025 \quad b_1 = .052 \quad b_2 = 1.14$$

(a) Interpret the estimates b_1 and b_2
(b) Is it possible to provide a meaningful interpretation of the estimate b_0?

11.4 The following model was fitted to a sample of 25 students using data obtained at the end of their freshman year in college. The aim was to explain students' weight gains.

$$y_i = \beta_0 + \beta_1 x_{1i} + \beta_2 x_{2i} + \beta_3 x_{3i} + \varepsilon_i$$

where

y_i = Weight gained, in pounds, during freshman year
x_{1i} = Average number of meals eaten per week
x_{2i} = Average number of hours exercise per week
x_{3i} = Average number of beers consumed per week

The least squares estimates of the regression parameters were

$$b_0 = 7.35 \quad b_1 = .653 \quad b_2 = -1.345 \quad b_3 = .613$$

(a) Interpret the estimates b_1, b_2, and b_3
(b) Is it possible to provide a meaningful interpretation of the estimate b_0?

11.2 ESTIMATION OF COEFFICIENTS

Multiple regression coefficients are computed using estimators obtained by the least squares procedure. This least squares procedure is similar to that presented in Chapter 10 for simple regression. However, the estimators are complicated by the relationship between the independent x_j variables that occur simultaneously with the relationships between the independent and dependent variables. For example, if two independent variables increase or decrease linearly with each other—positive or negative correlation—while at the same time there are increases or decreases in the dependent variable, we cannot identify which independent variable is actually related to the change in the dependent variable. As a result we will find that the estimated regression coefficients are less reliable if there are high correlations between two or more independent variables. The estimates of coefficients and their variances are always obtained using a computer. However, we will spend considerable effort studying the algebra and computational forms in least squares regression. This effort will provide you with the background to understand the procedure and to determine how different data patterns influence the results. We begin with the standard assumptions for the multiple regression model.

STANDARD MULTIPLE REGRESSION ASSUMPTIONS

The population multiple regression model is

$$y_i = \beta_0 + \beta_1 X_{1i} + \beta_2 X_{2i} + \cdots + \beta_K X_{Ki} + \varepsilon_i$$

and we assume that n sets of observations are available. The following standard assumptions are made for the model.

1. The x_{ji}'s are fixed numbers, or they are realizations of random variables, X_{ji}'s that are independent of the error terms, ε_i's. In the later case, inference is carried out conditionally on the observed values of the, x_{ji}'s.
2. The error terms are random variables with mean 0 and the same variance, σ^2. The later is called homoscedasticity or uniform variance.

$$E[\varepsilon_i] = 0 \text{ and } E[\varepsilon_i^2] = \sigma^2 \text{ for } (i = 1, \ldots, n)$$

3. The random error terms, ε_i, are not correlated with one another, so that

$$E[\varepsilon_i \varepsilon_j] = 0 \text{ for all } i \neq j$$

4. It is not possible to find a set of non-zero numbers, $c_0, c_1, \ldots, c_K$, such that

$$c_0 + c_1 x_{1i} + c_2 x_{2i} + \cdots + c_K x_{Ki} = 0$$

This is the property of no linear relation for the X_j's.

The first three assumptions are essentially the same as those made for simple regression. However, Assumption 4 excludes certain cases in which there are linear relationships between the predictor variables. For example, suppose we are interested in explaining the variability in rates charged for shipping corn. One obvious explanatory variable would be the distance the corn is shipped. Distance could be measured in several different units such as miles or kilometers. But it would not make sense to use both distance in miles and distance in kilometers as predictor variables. These two measures are linear functions of each other and would not satisfy Assumption 4. In addition it would be foolish to try to assess their separate effects. As we shall see, the equations to compute the coefficient estimates and the computer programs will not work if Assumption 4 is not satisfied. In most cases proper model specification will avoid violating Assumption 4.

Least Squares Procedure

The least squares procedure for multiple regression computes the estimated coefficients to minimize the sum of the residuals squared. Recall that the residual is defined as

$$e_i = y_i - \hat{y}_i$$

where y_i is the observed value of Y and $\hat{y}_i$ is the value of Y predicted from the regression. Formally we

```
MINIMIZE SSE
```

$$SSE = \sum_{i=1}^{n} e_i^2 = \sum_{i=1}^{n} (y_i - \hat{y}_i)^2 = \sum_{i=1}^{n} (y_i - (b_0 + b_1 x_{1i} + \cdots + b_K x_{Ki}))^2$$

This minimization requires the use of partial derivatives to develop a set of simultaneous normal equations that are then solved to obtain the coefficient estimators. The chapter Appendix presents some of the details of the process. We assume here that the computations are performed using a statistical computer package such as Minitab, *SAS*, *SPSS*, or Excel supported by PHStat. Our objective here is to understand how to interpret the regression results and use them to solve problems. We will do this by examining some of the intermediate algebraic results to help understand the effects of various data patterns on the coefficient estimators.

LEAST SQUARES ESTIMATION AND THE SAMPLE MULTIPLE REGRESSION

We begin with a sample of n observations denoted as $(x_{1i}, x_{2i}, \ldots, x_{Ki}, y_i, i = 1, \ldots, n)$ measured for a process whose population multiple regression model is

$$y_i = \beta_0 + \beta_1 x_{1i} + \beta_2 x_{2i} + \cdots + \beta_K x_{Ki} + \varepsilon_i$$

The least squares estimates of the coefficients, $\beta_1, \beta_2, \ldots, \beta_K$ are the values $b_0, b_1, \ldots, b_K$ for which the sum of the squared deviations

$$SSE = \sum_{i=1}^{n} (y_i - b_0 - b_1 x_{1i} - b_2 x_{2i} - \cdots b_K x_{Ki})^2 \qquad (11.2)$$

is a minimum.

The resulting equation

$$\hat{y} = b_0 + b_1 x_1 + b_2 x_2 + \cdots + b_K x_K \qquad (11.3)$$

is the sample multiple regression of Y on $X_1, X_2, \ldots, X_K$.

Let us consider again the regression model with only two predictor variables.

$$\hat{y}_i = b_0 + b_1 x_{1i} + b_2 x_{2i}$$

The coefficient estimators can be solved for the following forms

$$b_1 = \frac{S_Y(r_{x_1 y} - r_{x_1 x_2} r_{x_2 y})}{S_{X_1}(1 - r_{x_1 x_2}^2)}$$

(11.4)

$$b_2 = \frac{S_Y(r_{x_2 y} - r_{x_1 x_2} r_{x_1 y})}{S_{X_2}(1 - r_{x_1 x_2}^2)}$$

(11.5)

$$b_0 = \overline{Y} - b_1 \overline{X}_1 - b_2 \overline{X}_2$$

(11.6)

where

$r_{x_1 y}$ is the sample correlation between x_1 and y

$r_{x_2 y}$ is the sample correlation between x_2 and y

$r_{x_1 x_2}$ is the sample correlation between x_1 and x_2

S_{X_1} is the sample standard deviation for x_1

S_{X_2} is the sample standard deviation for x_2

S_Y is the sample standard deviation for y

INTERPRETATION

In the equations for the coefficient estimators we see that the slope coefficient estimate, b_1, depends not only on the correlation between Y and X_1 but is also affected by the correlation between X_1 and X_2 and the correlation between X_2 and Y. If the correlation between X_1 and X_2 is equal to 0 then the coefficient estimators b_1 and b_2 would be the same as the coefficient estimator for simple regression—we should note that this hardly ever happens in business and economic analysis. Conversely, if the correlation between the independent variables were equal to 1 the coefficient estimators would be undefined. If the independent variables are perfectly correlated then they both experience simultaneous relative changes. We see that in that case it is not possible to tell which variable predicts the change in Y. In example 11.3 we will see the effect of the correlations between independent variables by considering the savings and loan association problem, whose data is shown in Table 11.1.

EXAMPLE 11.3

PROFIT MARGINS OF SAVINGS AND LOAN ASSOCIATIONS (ESTIMATING REGRESSION COEFFICIENTS)

Savings and Loan

The Director of the savings and loan association has asked you to identify variables that affect the percent profit margin.

SOLUTION

As a first step we develop a multiple regression model that predicts profit as a function of the percent net revenue per deposit dollar and the number of offices. Using the data in Table 11.1 that is stored in the **Savings and Loan** data file, we have estimated a multiple regression model as seen in the Minitab output in Figure 11.3. The computer instructions are

```
STAT > REGRESSION > REGRESSION > SELECT VARIABLES & FOLLOW
DIALOG BOX
```

FIGURE 11.3
Regression Equation for
Savings and Loan
Associations Profit

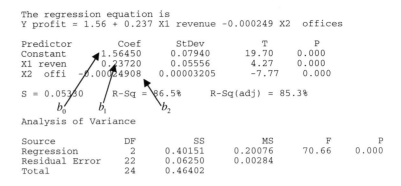

The estimated coefficients are identified in the computer output. We see that each unit increase in revenue, X_1, results in a 0.237 increase in percent profit—if the other variable did not change—and a unit increase in the number of offices decreases profit by 0.000249. Now consider the two simple regression models in Figures 11.4 and 11.5 with Y regressed on each independent variable by itself. First consider Y regressed on revenue, X_1, in Figure 11.4. In this simple regression the coefficient for X_1 is −0.169 which is clearly different from +0.237 in multiple regression. We will see that the correlation between X_1 and X_2 is 0.941. This large correlation has a major impact on the coefficient of X_1 in the multiple regression equation.

Next consider the regression of Y on X_2 alone in Figure 11.5. In this simple regression the slope coefficient for number of offices, X_2, is −0.000130 in contrast to −0.000249 for the multiple regression coefficient. This change in coefficients, while not quite as dramatic compared to the coefficient for X_1, also results from the high correlation between the independent variables.

The correlations between the three variables are

	$X1$ revenue	$X2$ offices
$X2$ offices	0.941	
Y profit	−0.704	−0.868

We see that the correlation between X_1 and X_2 is 0.941. Thus the two variables tend to move together and it is not surprising that the multiple regression coefficients are different from the simple regression coefficients. We should note that the multiple regression coefficients are "conditional coefficients"; that is, the estimated coefficient b_1 depends on the other variables included in the model. This will always be the case in

FIGURE 11.4
Savings and Loan Profit
Regressed on Revenue

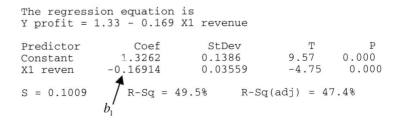

FIGURE 11.5
Savings and Loan Profit
Regressed on Number of
Offices

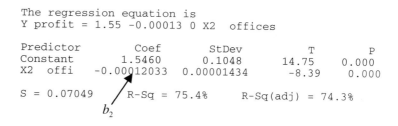

```
The regression equation is
Y profit = 1.55 -0.00013 0 X2  offices

Predictor          Coef         StDev          T          P
Constant         1.5460        0.1048       14.75      0.000
X2  offi    -0.00012033   0.00001434       -8.39      0.000

S = 0.07049        R-Sq = 75.4%      R-Sq(adj) = 74.3%
```
b_2

multiple regression unless two independent variables have a sample correlation of zero—a very unlikely event.

These relationships can also be studied by using a "matrix plot" from Minitab as shown in Figure 11.6. To obtain the plot use the Minitab instructions

```
GRAPH > MATRIX PLOTS > OPTIONS > MATRIX DISPLAY > LOWER
LEFT
```

Note that the simple relationship between Y and X_2 is clearly linear, while the simple relationship between Y and X_1 is somewhat curvilinear. This nonlinear relationship between X_1 and Y explains in part why the coefficient of X_1 changed so dramatically from simple to multiple regression. We see from this example that correlations between independent variables can have a major influence on the estimated coefficients. Thus if one has a choice highly correlated independent variables should be avoided. But in many cases we do not have that choice. Regression coefficient estimates are always conditional on the other predictor variables in the model. In this example profit increases as a function of percent revenue per deposit dollar. However, the simultaneous increase in number of offices—that reduced profit—would hide the profit increase if a simple regression analysis were used. Thus proper model specification—choice of predictor variables—is very important. Model specification requires an understanding of the problem context and appropriate theory.

FIGURE 11.6
Matrix Plots For Savings and
Loan Variables

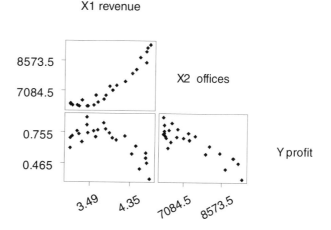

EXERCISES

11.5 Consider the estimated linear regression equations

$$Y = a_0 + a_1 X_1$$

$$Y = b_0 + b_1 X_1 + b_2 X_2$$

(a) Show in detail the coefficient estimators for a_1 and b_1 when the correlation between X_1 and X_2 are equal to 0.

(b) Show in detail the coefficient estimators for a_1 and b_1 when the correlation between X_1 and X_2 are equal to 1.

11.6 Amalgamated Power Inc. has asked you to estimate a regression equation to determine the effect of various predictor variables on the demand for electricity sales. You will prepare a series of regression estimates and discuss their results using the quarterly data for electrical sales during the past 17 years in the data file **Power Demand**.

(a) Estimate a regression equation with electricity sales as the dependent variable using number of customers and price as predictor variables. Interpret the coefficients.

(b) Estimate a regression equation (electricity sales) using only number of customers as a predictor variable. Interpret the coefficient and compare the result to the results from (a).

(c) Estimate a regression equation (electricity sales) using price and degree days as predictor variables. Interpret the coefficients. Compare the coefficient for price with that obtained in (a).

(d) Estimate a regression equation (electricity sales) using disposable income and degree days as predictor variables. Interpret the coefficients.

11.7 Transportation Research Inc. has asked you to prepare some multiple regression equations to estimate the effect of variables on fuel economy. The data for this study is contained in the data file **Motors**, and the dependent variable is miles per gallon—milpgal— as established by the Department of Transportation certification.

(a) Prepare a regression equation that uses vehicle horsepower—horsepower—and vehicle weight—weight—as independent variables. Interpret the coefficients.

(b) Prepare a second regression equation that adds the number of cylinders—cylinder—as an independent variable to the equation from part (a). Interpret the coefficients.

(c) Prepare a regression equation that uses number of cylinders and vehicle weight as independent variables. Interpret the coefficients and compare the results with those from parts (a) and (b).

(d) Prepare a regression equation that uses vehicle horsepower, vehicle weight, and price as predictor variables. Interpret the coefficients.

(e) Write a short report that summarizes your results.

11.8 Transportation Research Inc. has asked you to prepare some multiple regression equations to estimate the effect of variables on vehicle horsepower. The data for this study is contained in the data file **Motors** and the dependent variable is vehicle horsepower—horsepower— as established by the Department of Transportation certification.

(a) Prepare a regression equation that uses vehicle weight—weight—and cubic inches of cylinder displacement—displacement—as predictor variables. Interpret the coefficients.

(b) Prepare a regression equation that uses vehicle weight, cylinder displacement, and number of cylinders—cylinder—as predictor variables. Interpret the coefficients and compare the results with those in part (a).

(c) Prepare a regression equation that uses vehicle weight, cylinder displacement, and miles per gallon—milpgal—as predictor variables. Interpret the coefficients and compare the results with those in part (a).

(d) Prepare a regression equation that uses vehicle weight, cylinder displacement, miles per gallon, and price as predictor variables. Interpret the coefficients and compare the results with those in part (c).

(e) Write a short report that presents the results of your analysis of this problem.

11.3   EXPLANATORY POWER OF A MULTIPLE REGRESSION EQUATION

Multiple regression uses independent variables to explain the behavior of the dependent variable. We find that variability in the dependent variable can, in part, be explained by the linear function of the independent variables. In this section we will develop a measure of the proportion of the variability in the dependent variable that can be explained by the multiple regression model.

The estimated regression model from the sample is

$$y_i = b_0 + b_1 x_{1i} + b_2 x_{2i} + \cdots + b_K x_{Ki} + e_i$$

Alternatively, we can write

$$y_i = \hat{y}_i + e_i$$

where

$$\hat{y}_i = b_0 + b_1 x_{1i} + b_2 x_{2i} + \cdots + b_K x_{Ki}$$

is the predicted value of the dependent variable and the residual, e_i, is the difference between the observed and the predicted value. Table 11.2 contains these quantities for the savings and loan example in the first three columns.

We can subtract the sample mean of the dependent variable from both sides giving

$$(y_i - \bar{y}) = (\hat{y}_i - \bar{y}) + e_i$$

which can be stated as

OBSERVED DEVIATION FROM THE SAMPLE MEAN = PREDICTED DEVIATION FROM THE SAMPLE MEAN + RESIDUAL

TABLE 11.2
Actual Values, Predicted Values, and Residuals for Savings and Loan Regression

y_i	$\hat{y}_i$	$e_i = y_i - \hat{y}_i$	$y_i - \bar{y}$	$\hat{y}_i - \bar{y}$
0.75	0.677	0.073	0.076	0.003
0.71	0.713	−0.003	0.036	0.039
0.66	0.699	−0.039	−0.014	0.025
0.61	0.672	−0.062	−0.064	−0.002
0.7	0.684	0.016	0.026	0.010
0.72	0.708	0.012	0.046	0.034
0.77	0.740	0.030	0.096	0.066
0.74	0.759	−0.019	0.066	0.085
0.9	0.794	0.106	0.226	0.120
0.82	0.794	0.026	0.146	0.120
0.75	0.798	−0.048	0.076	0.124
0.77	0.827	−0.057	0.096	0.153
0.78	0.802	−0.022	0.106	0.128
0.84	0.799	0.041	0.166	0.125
0.79	0.754	0.036	0.116	0.080
0.7	0.734	−0.034	0.026	0.060
0.68	0.705	−0.025	0.006	0.031
0.72	0.693	0.027	0.046	0.019
0.55	0.635	−0.085	−0.124	−0.039
0.63	0.613	0.017	−0.044	−0.061
0.56	0.570	−0.010	−0.114	−0.104
0.41	0.480	−0.070	−0.264	−0.194
0.51	0.437	0.073	−0.164	−0.237
0.47	0.395	0.075	−0.204	−0.279
0.32	0.377	−0.057	−0.354	−0.297
Sum of squares:		0.0625 (SSE)	0.4640 (SST)	0.4015 (SSR)

Then by squaring both sides and summing over the index, i, we have

$$\sum_{i=1}^{n}(y_i - \bar{y})^2 = \sum_{i=1}^{n}(y_i - \hat{y}_1 + \hat{y}_1 - \bar{y})^2$$

$$= \sum_{i=1}^{n}(\hat{y}_i - \bar{y})^2 + \sum_{i=1}^{n}e_i^2$$

which is the sum of squares decomposition presented in Chapter 10.

```
SST = SSE + SSR
```

```
TOTAL SUM OF SQUARES = ERROR SUM OF SQUARES + REGRESSION SUM
OF SQUARES
```

SUM OF SQUARES DECOMPOSITION AND THE COEFFICIENT OF DETERMINATION

Given the multiple regression model fitted by least squares

$$y_i = b_0 + b_1 x_{1i} + b_2 x_{2i} + \cdots + b_K x_{Ki} + e_i = \hat{y}_i + e_i$$

where the b_j's are the least squares estimates of the coefficients of the population regression model and e's are the residuals from the estimated regression model.

The model variability can be partitioned into the components

$$SST = SSR + SSE \tag{11.7}$$

where
Total Sum of Squares:

$$SST = \sum_{i=1}^{n}(y_i - \bar{y})^2 \tag{11.8}$$

$$= \sum(\hat{y}_i - \bar{y})^2 + \sum_{i=1}^{n}(y_i - \hat{y}_i)^2 \tag{11.9}$$

Error Sum of Squares:

$$SSE = \sum_{i=1}^{n}(y_i - \hat{y}_i)^2 = \sum_{i=1}^{n}e_i^2 \tag{11.10}$$

Regression Sum of Squares:

$$SSR = \sum_{i=1}^{n}(\hat{y}_i - \bar{y})^2 \tag{11.11}$$

This decomposition can be interpreted as

Total sample variability = Explained variability + Unexplained variability

The coefficient of determination, R^2, of the fitted regression is defined as the proportion of the total sample variability explained by the regression

$$R^2 = \frac{SSR}{SST} = 1 - \frac{SSE}{SST} \tag{11.12}$$

and it follows that

$$0 \le R^2 \le 1$$

The sum of squared errors is also used to compute the estimation for the variance of population model errors as shown in Equation 11.13. As with simple regression the variance of population errors is used for multiple regression statistical inference.

ESTIMATION OF ERROR VARIANCE

Given the population multiple regression model

$$y_i = \beta_0 + \beta_1 X_{1i} + \beta_2 X_{2i} + \cdots + \beta_K X_{Ki} + \varepsilon_i$$

and the standard regression assumptions, let σ_ε^2 denote the common variance of the error term ε_i. Then an unbiased estimate of that variance is

$$S_e^2 = \frac{\sum\limits_{i=1}^{n} e_i^2}{n - K - 1} = \frac{SSE}{n - K - 1} \tag{11.13}$$

The square root of the variance, S_e is also called the **standard error of the estimate.**

The sample mean for the savings and loan profit dependent variable is $\bar{y} = 0.674$, and we have used this value to compute the last two columns of Table 11.2. Using the data in Table 11.2 and the components we can show that

$$SSE = 0.0625, \quad SST = 0.4640 \quad \text{and that} \quad R^2 = 0.87.$$

From these results we find that for this sample 87% of the variability in the savings and loan association's profit is explained by the linear relationship with net revenues and number of offices. Note that we could also compute the regression sum of squares from the identity

$$SSR = SST - SSE = 0.4640 - 0.0625 = 0.4015$$

We can also compute an estimate for the error variance σ^2 by using Equation 11.13

$$S_e^2 = \frac{\sum\limits_{i=1}^{n} e_i^2}{n - K - 1} = \frac{SSE}{n - K - 1} = \frac{0.0625}{25 - 1 - 2} = 0.0284$$

Figure 11.7 is the regression output from Minitab for the savings and loan association problem, with the various computed sums of squares indicated. These quantities are routinely computed by statistical computer packages, and the detail in Table 11.2 is included only to indicate how the sums of squares are computed. In all of the work that follows we assume that the sums of squares are calculated by a computer package.

The components of variability have associated degrees of freedom. The SST quantity has $n - 1$ degrees of freedom because the mean of Y is required for its computation. The SSR component has K degrees of freedom because K coefficients are required for its computation. Finally the SSE component has $n - 1 - K$ degrees of freedom because K coefficients and the mean are required for its computation. Note that in Figure 11.7 the degrees of freedom (DF) associated with each component are included in the output.

FIGURE 11.7
Regression Output for the
Savings and Loan Association
Problem

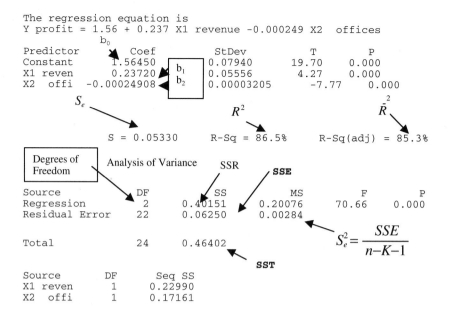

We use the coefficient of determination, R^2, routinely as a descriptive statistic to describe the strength of the linear relationship between the independent variables and the dependent variable, Y. It is important to emphasize that R^2 can only be used to compare regression models that have the same set of sample observations of y_i, $i = 1, \ldots, n$. This result is seen from the equation form

$$1 - \frac{SSE}{SST}$$

Thus we see that R^2 can be large either because SSE is small—indicating that the observed points are close to the predicted points—or because SST is large. We have seen that SSE and S_e^2 indicate the closeness of the observed points to the predicted points. With the same SST for two or more regression equations R^2 provides a comparable measure of the goodness of fit for the equations.

There is a potential problem with using R^2 as an overall measure of the quality of a fitted equation. As additional independent variables are added to a multiple regression model—in essentially all applied situations—the explained sum of squares, SSR, will increase even if the additional independent variable is not an important predictor variable. Thus we might find that R^2 has increased spuriously after one or more nonsignificant predictor variables are added to the multiple regression model. In such a case the increased value of R^2 would be misleading. To avoid this problem the adjusted coefficient of determination can be computed as shown in Equation 11.14.

ADJUSTED COEFFICIENT OF DETERMINATION

The **adjusted coefficient of determination** $\bar{R}^2$ is defined as

$$\bar{R}^2 = 1 - \frac{SSE/(n - K - 1)}{SST/(n - 1)} \tag{11.14}$$

We use this measure to correct for the fact that nonrelevant independent variables will result in some small reduction in the error sum of squares. Thus the adjusted $\bar{R}^2$ provides a better comparison between multiple regression models with different numbers of independent variables.

Returning to our savings and loan example we see that

$$n = 25 \quad K = 2 \quad SSE = 0.0625 \quad SST = 0.4640$$

and thus the adjusted coefficient of determination is

$$\overline{R}^2 = 1 - \frac{0.0625/22}{0.4640/24} = 0.853$$

In this example the difference between R^2 and $\overline{R}^2$ is not very large. However, if the regression model had contained a number of independent variables that were not important conditional predictors then the difference would be substantial. Another measure of relationship in multiple regression is the coefficient of multiple correlation.

COEFFICIENT OF MULTIPLE CORRELATION

The **coefficient of multiple correlation** is the correlation between the predicted value and the observed value of the dependent variable

$$R = \text{Corr}(\hat{y}, y) = \sqrt{R^2} \tag{11.15}$$

and is equal to the square root of the multiple coefficient of determination. We use R as another measure of the strength of the relationship between the dependent variable and the independent variables. Thus it is comparable to the correlation between Y and X in simple regression.

EXERCISES

11.9 In the study of Exercise 11.1, where the least squares estimates were based on 27 sets of sample observations, the total sum of squares and regression sum of squares were found to be

$$SST = 3.881 \quad \text{and} \quad SSR = 3.549$$

(a) Find and interpret the coefficient of determination.
(b) Find the error sum of squares.
(c) Find the adjusted coefficient of determination.
(d) Find and interpret the coefficient of multiple correlation.

11.10 In the study of Exercise 11.3, where the least squares estimates were based on 30 sets of sample observations, the total sum of squares regression sum of squares were found to be

$$SST = 162.1 \quad \text{and} \quad SSE = 88.2$$

(a) Find and interpret the coefficient of determination.
(b) Find the adjusted coefficient of determination.
(c) Find and interpret the coefficient of multiple correlation.

11.11 In the study of Exercise 11.4, 25 observations were used to calculate the least squares estimates. The regression sum of squares and error sum of squares were found to be

$$SSR = 79.2 \quad \text{and} \quad SSE = 45.9$$

(a) Find and interpret the coefficient of determination.
(b) Find the adjusted coefficient of determination.
(c) Find and interpret the coefficient of multiple correlation.

11.12 Refer to the savings and loan association data given in Table 11.1.

(a) Estimate by least squares the regression of profit margin on number of offices.
(b) Estimate by least squares the regression of net revenues on number of offices.
(c) Esitimate by least squares the regression of profit margin on net revenues.
(d) Estimate by least squares the regression of number of offices on net revenues.
(e) Based on the results in parts (a) and (b), verify that the sample partial correlation between profit margin and net revenues for a given number of offices is .67.
(f) Based on the results in parts (c) and (d), verify that the sample partial correlation between profit margin and number of offices for a given level of net revenues is −.86.

11.4 CONFIDENCE INTERVALS AND HYPOTHESIS TESTS FOR INDIVIDUAL REGRESSION COEFFICIENTS

In Section 11.2 we developed and discussed the point estimators for the parameters of the multiple regression model

$$y_i = \beta_0 + \beta_1 x_{1i} + \beta_2 x_{2i} + \cdots + \beta_K x_{Ki} + \varepsilon_i$$

Now we will develop confidence intervals and tests of hypotheses for the model.

In Chapter 10 the relationship between the model error, ε, and the various coefficient estimators was presented. We showed that the dependent variable Y is a conditional random variable with the same variance, σ^2, as the model error, because Y is a linear function of fixed coefficients and the X variables with a random error term added. If ε is normally distributed, then Y will also be a conditionally normal distributed random variable with variance σ^2 because the random variable ε is added to the linear function. In the regression model the mean of Y depends on the value of X. In turn there is also a linear relationship between the coefficient estimator, b_1, and the random variable Y. Thus b_1 is also normally distributed with a variance that is a function of σ^2. The predicted value of Y is a linear function of the coefficient estimators and is also normally distributed with a variance that is a function of σ^2. These results provide the basis for hypothesis testing and confidence intervals in multiple regression.

Based on the linear relationship between the coefficients and Y we know that the coefficient estimates are normally distributed if the model error ε is normally distributed. Because of the central limit theorem we generally find that the coefficient estimates are approximately normally distributed even if ε is not normally distributed. Thus the hypothesis tests and confidence intervals we will develop are not seriously affected by departures from normality in the distribution of the error terms.

We might think of the error term in the population regression model as including the combined influences on the dependent variable of a multitude of factors not included in the list of independent variables. These factors individually may not have an important influence, but in combination their effect can be important. The fact that the error term is made up of a large number of components whose effects are random provides a further basis for assuming that the coefficient errors are normally distributed.

Fortunately the same basic logic holds for multiple regression. Y is still a conditionally normal distributed random variable with variance, σ^2. The coefficient estimators, b_j, are also linear functions of Y, but the linear function is more complex. And of course the predicted value of Y is a linear function of the regression coefficient estimators. The computer does the computations resulting from the complex relationships. However, these relationships can sometimes cause interpretation problems. Thus we will spend time gaining important insights into the variance computations. If we do not understand how the variances are determined we will not be able to adequately understand hypothesis tests and confidence intervals.

The variance of a coefficient estimate is affected by the relationships between the independent variables in addition to the effect of the model error term. Thus it is important to understand how these correlations affect both confidence intervals and tests of hypotheses. Previously we saw how the correlations between the independent variables influence the coefficient estimators. These correlations between independent variables also increase the variance of the coefficient estimators. An important conclusion is that the **variance** of the coefficient estimators, in addition to the coefficient estimators, are conditional on the entire set of independent variables in the regression model.

To gain some understanding of the effect of independent variable correlations we will consider the variance estimators from the multiple regression model with two predictor variables

$$\hat{y} = b_0 + b_1 X_1 + b_2 X_2$$

The coefficient variance estimators are,

$$S_{b_1}^2 = \frac{S_e^2}{(n-1)S_{X_1}^2 (1 - r_{x_1 x_2}^2)} \tag{11.16}$$

$$S_{b_2}^2 = \frac{S_e^2}{(n-1)S_{X_2}^2 (1 - r_{x_1 x_2}^2)} \tag{11.17}$$

and the square roots of these variance estimators S_{b_1} and S_{b_2} are called the *coefficient standard errors.*

INTERPRETATION

The variance of the coefficient estimators increases directly with the distance the points are from the line, measured by S_e^2, the estimated model variance. In addition, a wider spread of the independent variable values—measured by $S_{X_1}^2$ or by $S_{X_2}^2$—decreases the coefficient variance. Recall that these results also applied for simple regression coefficient estimators. We also see that the variance of the coefficient estimators increases with increases in the correlation between the independent variables in the model. As the correlation increases between two independent variables it becomes more difficult to separate the effect of the individual variables for predicting the dependent variables. As the number of independent variables in a model increase, the influences on the coefficient variance continue to be important, but the algebraic structure becomes very complex and will not be presented here. The correlation effect leads to the result that coefficient variance estimators are conditional on the other independent variables in the model. Recall that the actual coefficient estimators are also conditional on the other independent variables in the model, again because of the effect of correlations between the independent variables.

The basis for inference about population regression coefficients is summarized below. We are typically more interested in the partial regression coefficients β_j than in the constant or intercept β_0. Thus we will concentrate on the former, noting that inference about the latter proceeds along similar lines.

BASIS FOR INFERENCE ABOUT THE POPULATION REGRESSION PARAMETERS

Let the population regression model be

$$y_i = \beta_0 + \beta_1 x_{1i} + \beta_2 x_{2i} + \cdots + \beta_K x_{Ki} + \varepsilon_i$$

Let $b_0, b_1, \ldots, b_K$ be the least squares estimates of the population parameters and $s_{b_0}, s_{b_1}, \ldots, s_{b_K}$ be the estimated standard deviations of the least squares estimators. Then if the standard regression assumptions hold and if the error terms, ε_i, are normally distributed, the random variables corresponding to

$$t_{b_j} = \frac{b_j - \beta_j}{s_{b_j}} \quad (j = 1, 2, \ldots, K) \tag{11.18}$$

are distributed as Student's t with $(n - K - 1)$ degrees of freedom.

Confidence intervals for the β_j can be derived by using Equation 11.19.

CONFIDENCE INTERVALS FOR PARTIAL REGRESSION COEFFICIENTS

If the population regression errors, ε_i, are normally distributed and the standard regression assumptions hold, the $100(1 - \alpha)\%$ confidence intervals for the partial regression coefficients, β_j, are given by

$$b_j - t_{n-K-1,\alpha/2}s_{b_j} < \beta_j < b_j + t_{n-K-1,\alpha/2}s_{b_j} \tag{11.19}$$

where $t_{n-K-1,\alpha/2}$ is the number for which

$$P(t_{n-K-1} > t_{n-K-1,\alpha/2}) = \frac{\alpha}{2}$$

and the random variable t_{n-K-1} follows a Student's t distribution with $(n - K - 1)$ degrees of freedom.

EXAMPLE 11.4

DEVELOPING THE SAVINGS AND LOAN MODEL (CONFIDENCE INTERVAL ESTIMATION)

Savings and Loan

We have been asked to determine confidence intervals for the coefficients of the savings and loan regression model developed in Example 11.3.

SOLUTION

The Minitab regression output for the savings and loan regression model is shown in Figure 11.8. The coefficient estimators and their standard deviations for the revenue, b_1, and number of offices, b_2, predictor variables are computed as

$$b_1 = 0.2372, \quad S_{b_1} = 0.0556; \quad b_2 = -0.000249 \text{ and } S_{b_2} = 0.00003205$$

Thus, we see that the standard deviation of the sampling distribution of the least squares estimator for β_1 is estimated as 0.0556 and for β_2 is estimated as 0.0003205.

FIGURE 11.8
Savings and Loan Regression:
Minitab Output

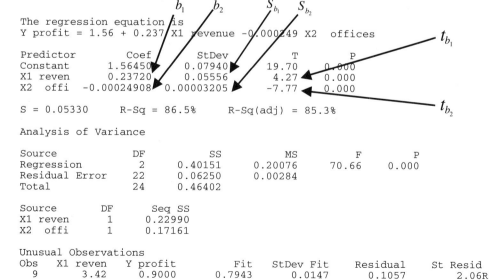

```
Regression Analysis

The regression equation is
Y profit = 1.56 + 0.237 X1 revenue -0.000249 X2  offices

Predictor        Coef        StDev          T        P
Constant      1.56450      0.07940      19.70    0.000
X1 reven      0.23720      0.05556       4.27    0.000
X2  offi   -0.00024908    0.00003205     -7.77    0.000

S = 0.05330      R-Sq = 86.5%       R-Sq(adj) = 85.3%

Analysis of Variance

Source            DF          SS          MS          F        P
Regression         2      0.40151     0.20076      70.66    0.000
Residual Error    22      0.06250     0.00284
Total             24      0.46402

Source            DF      Seq SS
X1 reven           1     0.22990
X2  offi           1     0.17161

Unusual Observations
Obs   X1 reven   Y profit        Fit   StDev Fit    Residual    St Resid
  9       3.42     0.9000     0.7943      0.0147      0.1057        2.06R

R denotes an observation with a large standardized residual
```

To obtain the 99% confidence intervals for β_1 and β_2 we use the Student's t value from the Appendix.

$$t_{n-k-1,\alpha/2} = t_{22,0.005} = 2.819$$

Using these results we find that the 99% coefficient confidence interval for β_1 is

$$0.237 - (2.819)(0.0556) < \beta_1 < 0.237 + (2.819)(0.0556)$$

or

$$0.0810 < \beta_1 < 0.394$$

Thus, the 99% confidence interval for the expected increase in savings and loan profit margins resulting from a 1-unit increase in net revenues, given a fixed number of offices, runs from 0.080 to 0.394. The 99% coefficient confidence interval for β_2 is

$$-0.000249 - (2.819)(0.0000320) < \beta_2 < -0.000249 + (2.819)(0.0000320)$$

or

$$-0.000339 < \beta_2 < -0.000159$$

Therefore we see that the 99% confidence interval for the expected decrease in profit margins resulting from an increase of 1,000 offices, for a fixed level of net revenue, runs from 0.159 to 0.339.

INTERPRETATION

Tests of hypotheses for partial regression coefficients can also be developed using the coefficient variance estimates. Of particular interest is the hypothesis test

$$H_0 : \beta_j = 0$$

that is frequently used to determine if a specific independent variable is conditionally important in a multiple regression model. Many analysts argue that if we cannot reject the conditional hypothesis that the coefficient is 0 then we conclude that the variable should not be included in the regression model. The Student's t statistic for this test is typically computed in most regression programs and is printed next to the coefficient variance estimate, and in addition the p-value for the hypothesis test is also typically included. These are shown in the Minitab output in Figure 11.8. By using the printed Student's t statistic or the p-value we can immediately conclude whether or not a particular predictor variable is conditionally significant, given the other variables in the regression model.

There are clearly other procedures for deciding if an independent variable should be included in a regression model. We see that the preceding selection procedure ignores Type II error—the coefficient is not equal to zero but we fail to conclude that it is not equal to zero. This is a particular problem when a model based on economic or other theory is carefully specified to include certain independent variables. Then because of a large error ε and/or correlations between independent variables we cannot reject the hypothesis that the coefficient is 0. In this case, many analysts will include the independent variable in the model because the original model specification is believed to dominate. This is a difficult issue and requires good judgement based on both statistical results and theory concerning the underlying relationship being modeled.

TESTS OF HYPOTHESES FOR THE PARTIAL REGRESSION COEFFICIENTS

If the regression errors, ε_i, are normally distributed and the standard regression assumptions hold, then the following hypothesis tests have significance level α:

1. To test either the null hypothesis

$$H_0 : \beta_j = \beta_* \qquad \text{or} \qquad H_0 : \beta_j \leq \beta_*$$

against the alternative

$$H_1 : \beta_j > \beta_*$$

the decision rule is

$$\text{Reject } H_0 \text{ if} \qquad \frac{b_j - \beta_*}{s_{b_j}} > t_{n-K-1,\alpha} \tag{11.20}$$

2. To test either the null hypothesis

$$H_0 : \beta_j = \beta_* \qquad \text{or} \qquad H_0 : \beta_j \geq \beta_*$$

against the alternative

$$H_1 : \beta_j < \beta_*$$

the decision rule is

$$\text{Reject } H_0 \text{ if} \qquad \frac{b_j - \beta_*}{s_{b_j}} < -t_{n-K-1,\alpha} \tag{11.21}$$

3. To test the null hypothesis

$$H_0 : \beta_j = \beta_*$$

against the two-sided alternative

$$H_1 : \beta_j \neq \beta_*$$

the decision rule is

$$\text{Reject } H_0 \text{ if} \qquad \frac{b_j - \beta_*}{s_{b_j}} > t_{n-K-1,\alpha/2} \qquad \text{or} \qquad \frac{b_j - \beta_*}{s_{b_j}} < -t_{n-K-1,\alpha/2} \tag{11.22}$$

EXAMPLE 11.5

DEVELOPING THE SAVINGS AND LOAN MODEL (COEFFICIENT HYPOTHESIS TESTS)

Savings and Loan

We have been asked to determine if the coefficients in the savings and loan regression model are conditionally significant predictors of profit.

SOLUTION

The hypothesis test for this question will use the Minitab regression results shown in Figure 11.8. First we wish to determine if total revenue has a significant effect on increasing profit conditional on or controlling for the effect of the number of offices. The null hypothesis is

$$H_0 : \beta_1 = 0$$

versus the alternative hypothesis

$$H_1 : \beta_1 > 0$$

The test can be performed by computing the Student's t statistic associated with the coefficient given H_0

$$t_{b_1} = \frac{b_1 - \beta_1}{s_{b_1}} = \frac{0.237 - 0}{0.0555} = 4.27$$

From the Student's t table in the Appendix we can determine that the critical value for the Student's t statistic is

$$t_{22, 0.005} = 2.819$$

which also indicates that the p-value for the hypothesis test is less than 0.005. Based on this evidence, we reject H_0 and accept H_1 and conclude that total revenue is a statistically significant predictor of increased profit for savings and loans given that we have also controlled for the effect of the number of offices.

Similarly, we can determine if the total number of offices has a significant effect on reducing profit margins. The null hypothesis is

$$H_0 : \beta_2 = 0$$

versus the alternative hypothesis

$$H_1 : \beta_2 < 0$$

The test can be performed by computing the Student's t statistic associated with the coefficient given H_0

$$t_{b_2} = \frac{b_2 - \beta_2}{s_{b_2}} = \frac{-0.000249 - 0}{0.0000320} = -7.77$$

From Table 6 of the Appendix we can find that the critical value for the Student's t statistic is

$$t_{22, 0.005} = 2.819$$

which also indicates that the p-value for the hypothesis test is less than 0.005. Based on this evidence we reject H_0 and accept H_1 and conclude that number of offices is a statistically significant predictor of lower profit for savings and loans given that we have controlled for the effect of total revenue.

It is important to emphasize that both of the hypothesis tests are based on the particular set of variables included in the regression model. If, for example, additional predictor variables were included then these tests would no longer be valid. With additional variables in the model the coefficient estimates and their estimated standard deviations computed by Minitab would be different and thus the Student's t statistics would also be different.

Note that in the Minitab regression output for this problem, shown in Figure 11.8, the Student's t statistic for the null hypothesis that a coefficient is equal to 0 is computed as the ratio of the estimated coefficient divided by the estimated coefficient standard error—contained in the two columns to the left of the Student's t. The probability or p-value for the two-tailed hypothesis test is also displayed. Thus an analyst can perform these hypothesis tests directly by examining the multiple regression output. The computed Student's t and the p-value are computed in every modern statistical package, including PHStat and Excel. Most analysts routinely look for these test results as they examine regression output from a computer statistical package.

EXAMPLE 11.6

FACTORS AFFECTING PROPERTY TAX RATE (ANALYSIS OF REGRESSION COEFFICIENTS)

A group of City Managers commissioned a study to determine the factors that influence urban property tax rates for cities with populations between 100,000 and 200,000.

SOLUTION

Using a sample of 20 U.S. cities the following regression model was estimated

$$\hat{y} = 1.79 + 0.000567x_1 + 0.0183x_2 - 0.000191x_3$$
$$\quad\quad\quad\quad (0.000139)\quad\quad (0.0082)\quad\quad (0.000446)$$
$$R^2 = 0.71 \quad\quad\quad\quad n = 20$$

where

> y is the effective property tax rate (actual levies divided by market value of the tax base)
>
> x_1 is the number of housing units per square mile
>
> x_2 is the percentage of total city revenue represented by grants from state and federal governments
>
> x_3 is the median per capita personal income, in dollars

(The numbers under the coefficients are the estimated coefficient standard errors.)

INTERPRETATION

The results indicate that the conditional estimates of the effects of the three predictor variables are

1. An increase of one housing unit per square mile increases the effective property tax rate by 0.000567. Note that property tax rates are typically expressed in terms of dollars per $1,000 of assessed property value. Thus an increase of 0.000567 indicates that property tax rates are higher by $0.567 per $1,000 of assessed property value.
2. An increase of 1% of the total city revenue from state and federal grants increases the effective tax rate by 0.0183.
3. An increase of $1 in median per capita personal income leads to an expected decrease in the effective tax rate by 0.000191.

We emphasize again that these coefficient estimates are only valid for a model with all three of the above predictor variables included.

To better understand the accuracy of these effects we will construct conditional 95% confidence intervals. For the estimated regression model there are $(20 - 3 - 1) = 16$

degrees of freedom for error. Thus the Student's t statistic for computing confidence intervals is, from the Appendix, $t_{16,0.025} = 2.12$. The format for confidence intervals is

$$b_j - t_{n-K-1,\alpha/2}s_{b_j} < \beta_j < b_j + t_{n-K-1,\alpha/2}s_{b_j}$$

Thus the coefficient for the number of housing units per square mile has a 95% confidence interval

$$0.000567 - (2.12)(0.000139) < \beta_1 < 0.000567 + (2.12)(0.000139)$$
$$0.000272 < \beta_1 < 0.000862$$

The coefficient for the percentage of revenue represented by grants has a 95% confidence interval

$$0.0183 - (2.12)(0.0082) < \beta_2 < 0.0183 + (2.12)(0.0082)$$
$$0.0009 < \beta_2 < 0.0357$$

Finally the coefficient for median per capita personal income has a 95% confidence interval

$$-0.000191 - (2.12)(0.000446) < \beta_3 < -0.000191 + (2.12)(0.000446)$$
$$-0.001137 < \beta_3 < 0.000755$$

Again we emphasize that these intervals are conditional on all three predictor variables being included in the model.

We see that the 95% confidence interval for β_3 includes 0, and thus we could not reject the two-tailed hypothesis that this coefficient is 0. Based on this confidence interval we conclude that X_3 is not a statistically significant predictor variable in the multiple regression model. However, the confidence intervals for the other two variables do not include 0 and thus we conclude that they are statistically significant.

EXAMPLE 11.7

EFFECT OF FISCAL FACTORS ON HOUSING PRICES (ESTIMATING REGRESSION MODEL COEFFICIENTS)

Citydat

INTERPRETATION

Northern City, MN, was interested in the effect of local property development on the market price of houses in the city. Northern City is one of many small, non-metropolitan, midwestern cities with populations in the range from 6,000 to 40,000. One of the objectives was to determine how increased commercial property development would influence the value of local housing. Data stored in file **Citydat**.

SOLUTION

To answer this question, data was collected from a number of cities and used to construct a regression model that estimates the effect of key variables on housing price. For this study the following variables were obtained for each city.

y (hseval) is the mean market price for houses in the city
x_1 (sizehse) is the mean number of rooms in houses
x_2 (incom72) is the mean household income
x_3 (taxrate) is the tax rate per thousand dollars of assessed value for houses
x_4 (comper) is the percentage of taxable property that is commercial property

The multiple regression output, prepared using Minitab, is shown in Figure 11.9. The coefficient for the mean number of rooms in city houses is 7.878 with a coefficient standard deviation of 1.809. In this study housing values are in units of $1,000 with a mean of $21,000 over all cities. Thus if the mean number of rooms in a city's houses were

FIGURE 11.9
Housing Price Regression
Model (Minitab Output)

Regression Analysis

```
The regression equation is
hseval = - 28.1 + 7.88 sizehse + 0.00367 incom72 - 172 taxrate - 10.6 Comper

Predictor        Coef       StDev          T          P
Constant      -28.075       9.766      -2.87      0.005
sizehse         7.878       1.809       4.35      0.000
incom72      0.003666    0.001344       2.73      0.008
taxrate       -171.80       43.09      -3.99      0.000
Comper        -10.614       6.491      -1.64      0.106

S = 3.677       R-Sq = 47.4%      R-Sq(adj) = 45.0%

Analysis of Variance

Source            DF          SS          MS          F          P
Regression         4     1037.49      259.37      19.19      0.000
Residual Error    85     1149.14       13.52
Total             89     2186.63
```

larger by 1.0 then the mean price would be larger by $7,878. The resulting Student's t statistic is 4.35 and the p-value is 0.000. Thus the conditional hypothesis that this coefficient is equal to zero is rejected. The same result occurs for the income and tax rate variables. The incom72 variable is in units of dollars, and thus if a city's mean income is higher by $1,000 then the coefficient of 0.003666 indicates that mean housing prices will be $3,666 higher. We see that the regression analysis leads to the conclusion that each of these three variables are significant predictors of the mean house price in the cities included in this study. However, we see that the coefficient for the percent commercial property, "comper" is -10.614 with a coefficient standard deviation of 6.491, resulting in a Student's t statistic equal to -1.64. Note that here is an important area for judgment. The coefficient would have a single tail p-value of 0.053 or a two-tailed p-value of 0.106. Thus it appears to have some effect in reducing the mean price of houses. Given that the effect of house size, income, and tax rate on the market price for houses have been included, we see that the percent commercial property does not increase housing prices. Thus the argument that the market value of houses will increase if more commercial property is developed is not supported by this analysis. That conclusion is only true for a model that includes these four predictor variables.

Note also the values of $R^2 = 47.4\%$ and the standard error of the regression, $S_e = 3.677$, are also included in the regression output.

The advocates of increased commercial development also claimed that increasing the amount of commercial property would decrease the taxes paid on owner occupied houses. This claim was tested using the regression output in Figure 11.10 prepared using Excel. The coefficient estimators and their standard errors are indicated. The Student's t statistics for the size of house and the tax rate coefficients are 2.65 and 6.36, indicating that these variables are important predictors. The Student's t statistic for income is 1.83 with a p-value of 0.07 for a two-tailed test. Thus income has some influence as a predictor, but its effect is not as strong as the previous two variables. Again we see a place for good judgment that considers the problem context. The conditional hypothesis that increased commercial property decreases taxes on owner occupied houses can be tested by using the conditional Student's t statistic for the variable "comper" in the regression output. The conditional Student's t statistics is -1.03 with a p-value of 0.308. Thus the hypothesis that increased commercial property does not decrease house taxes cannot be rejected. There is no evidence from this analysis that house taxes would be lowered if there was additional commercial development.

FIGURE 11.10
House Tax Regression Model
(Excel Output)

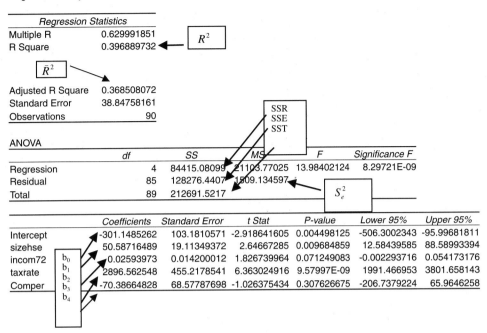

Regression Analysis

Regression Statistics	
Multiple R	0.629991851
R Square	0.396889732
Adjusted R Square	0.368508072
Standard Error	38.84758161
Observations	90

ANOVA

	df	SS	MS	F	Significance F
Regression	4	84415.08099	21103.77025	13.98402124	8.29721E-09
Residual	85	128276.4407	1509.134597		
Total	89	212691.5217			

	Coefficients	Standard Error	t Stat	P-value	Lower 95%	Upper 95%
Intercept	-301.1485262	103.1810571	-2.918641605	0.004498125	-506.3002343	-95.99681811
sizehse	50.58716489	19.11349372	2.64667285	0.009684859	12.58439585	88.58993394
incom72	0.02593973	0.014200012	1.826739964	0.071249083	-0.002293716	0.054173176
taxrate	2896.562548	455.2178541	6.363024916	9.57997E-09	1991.466953	3801.658143
Comper	-70.38664828	68.57787698	-1.026375434	0.307626675	-206.7379224	65.9646258

Based on the regression analyses performed in this study the consultants concluded that there was no evidence that increased commercial property would either increase the market value of houses or lower the property taxes for a house.

EXERCISES

11.13 In the study of Exercise 11.1, the estimated standard errors were

$$S_{b_1} = .099 \quad S_{b_2} = .032 \quad S_{b_3} = .0023$$

(a) Find 90% and 95% confidence intervals for β_1.
(b) Find 95% and 99% confidence intervals for β_2.
(c) Test against a two-sided alternative the null hypothesis that, all else being equal, the plane's weight has no linear influence on its design effort.
(d) The error sum of squares for this regression was .332. Using the same data, a simple linear regression of design effort on percentage number of common parts was fitted, yielding error sum of squares 3.311. Test at the 1% level the null hypothesis that, taken together, top speed and weight contribute nothing in a linear sense to explanation of design effort, given that percentage number of common parts is also used as an explanatory variable.

11.14 In the study of Exercise 11.3, where the sample regression was based on 30 observations, the estimated standard errors were

$$S_{b_1} = .023 \quad S_{b_2} = .35$$

(a) Test against the appropriate one-sided alternative the null hypothesis that for fixed family size, milk consumption does not depend linearly on income.
(b) Find 90%, 95%, and 99% confidence intervals for β_2.

11.15 In the study of Exercise 11.4, where the sample regression was based on 25 observations, the estimated standard errors were

$$S_{b_1} = .189 \quad S_{b_2} = .565 \quad S_{b_3} = .243$$

(a) Test against the appropriate one-sided alternative the null hypothesis that, all else being equal, hours of exercise do not linearly influence weight gain.

(b) Test against the appropriate one-sided alternative the null hypothesis that, all else being equal, beer consumption does not linearly influence weight gain.

(c) Find 90%, 95%, and 99% confidence intervals for β_1.

11.16 Refer to the data of Example 11.6.

(a) Test against a two-sided alternative the null hypothesis that, all else being equal, median per capita personal income has no influence on the effective property tax rate.

(b) Test the null hypothesis that, taken together, the three independent variables do not linearly influence the effective property tax rate.

11.17 Refer to the data of Example 11.7.

(a) Find 95% and 99% confidence intervals for the expected change in the market price for houses resulting from a 1-unit increase in the mean number of rooms, as a percentage of closing market price, when the values of all other independent variables remain unchanged.

(b) Test the null hypothesis that, all else being equal, mean household income does not influence the market price, against the alternative that the higher is the mean household income, the higher is the market price.

11.18 In a study of revenue generated by national lotteries, the following regression equation was fitted to data from 29 countries with lotteries:

$$y = -31.323 + .04045x_1 + .8772x_2 - 365.01x_3 - 9.9298x_4$$
$$\quad\quad\quad (.00755)\quad\quad (.3107)\quad\quad (263.88)\quad\quad (3.4520)$$

$R^2 = .51$

where

y = Dollars of net revenue per capita per year generated by the lottery

x_1 = Mean per capita personal income of the country

x_2 = Number of hotel, motel, inn, and resort rooms per thousand of population

x_3 = Spendable revenue per capita per year generated by parimutual betting, racing, and other legalized gambling

x_4 = Percentage of the nation's border contiguous with a state or states with a lottery

The numbers in parentheses below the coefficient estimates are the corresponding estimated standard errors.

(a) Interpret the estimated coefficient on x_1.

(b) Find and interpret a 95% confidence interval for the coefficient on x_2, in the population regression.

(c) Test the null hypothesis that the coefficient on x_3 if the population regression is 0, against the alternative that this coefficient is negative. Interpret your findings.

11.19 A study was conducted to determine whether certain features could be used to explain variability in the prices of furnaces. For a sample of 19 furnaces, the following regression was estimated:

$$y = -68.236 + .0023x_1 + 19.729x_2 + 7.653x_3 \quad R^2 = .84$$
$$\quad\quad\quad\quad (.005)\quad\quad (8.992)\quad\quad (3.082)$$

where

y = Price (in dollars)

x_1 = Rating of furnaces, in BTU per hour

x_2 = Energy efficiency ratio

x_3 = Number of settings

The figures in parentheses beneath the coefficient estimates are the corresponding estimated standard errors.

(a) Find a 95% confidence interval for the expected increase in price resulting from an additional setting when the values of the rating and the energy efficient ratio remain fixed.

(b) Test the null hypothesis that, all else being equal, the energy efficiency ratio of furnaces does not affect their price against the alternative that the higher the energy efficiency ratio, the higher the price.

11.20 In a study of the demand for imports in Nigeria, the following model was fitted to 19 years of data:

$$y = -58.9 + .20x_1 - .10x_2 \quad \bar{R}^2 = .96$$
$$\quad\quad\quad (.0092)\quad (.084)$$

where

y = Quantity of imports

x_1 = Personal consumption expenditures

x_2 = Price of imports ÷ Domestic prices

The figures in parentheses beneath the coefficient estimates are their estimated standard errors.

(a) Find a 95% confidence interval for β_1.

(b) Test against the appropriate one-sided alternative the null hypothesis that $\beta_2 = 0$.

11.21 In a study of foreign holdings in British banks, the following sample regression was obtained, based on 14 annual observations.

$$y = -3.248 + .101x_1 - .244x_2 + .057x_3 \quad R^2 = .93$$
$$\quad\quad\quad\quad (.023)\quad\quad (.080)\quad\quad (.00925)$$

where

y = Year-end share of assets in British bank subsidiaries held by foreigners, as a percentage of total assets

x_1 = Annual change, in billions of pounds, in foreign direct investment in Great Britain (excluding finance, insurance, and real estate)

x_2 = Bank price-earnings ratio

x_3 = Index of the exchange value of the pounds

The figures in brackets beneath coefficient estimates are estimated standard errors.

(a) Find a 90% confidence interval for β_1 and interpret your result.

(b) Test the null hypothesis that β_2 is zero, against the alternative that it is negative, and interpret your result.

(c) Test the null hypothesis that β_3 is zero, against the alternative that it is positive, and interpret your result.

11.22 In a study of differences in levels of community demand for firefighters, the following sample regression was obtained, based on data from 39 towns in Maryland.

$$y = -.00232 - .00024x_1 - .00002x_2 + .00034x_3 + .48122x_4$$
$$\quad\;\;(.00010)\quad\;(.000018)\quad\;(.00012)\quad\;(.77954)$$
$$\quad + .04950x_5 - .00010x_6 + .00645x_7 \quad \overline{R}^2 = ..3572$$
$$\quad\;\;(.01172)\quad\;(.00005)\quad\;(.00306)$$

where

y = Number of full-time firefighters per capita

x_1 = Maximum base salary of firefighters, in thousands of dollars

x_2 = Percentage of population

x_3 = Estimated per capita income, in thousands of dollars

x_4 = Population density

x_5 = Amount of intergovernmental grants per capita, in thousands of dollars

x_6 = Number of miles from the regional city

x_7 = Percentage of population that is male and between 12 and 21 years of age

The figures in brackets beneath the coefficient estimates are estimated standard errors.

(a) Find and interpret a 99% confidence interval for β_5.

(b) Test against a two-sided alternative the null hypothesis that β_4 is 0, and interpret your result.

(c) Test against a two-sided alternative the null hypothesis that β_7 is 0, and interpret your result.

11.5 TESTS ON SETS OF REGRESSION PARAMETERS

In the previous section we showed how a conditional hypothesis test can be conducted to determine if a specific variable coefficient is conditionally significant in a regression model. There are, however, situations where we are interested in the effect of the combination of several variables. For example, in a model that predicts quantity sold we might be interested in the combined effect of both the seller's price and the competitor's price. In other cases we might be interested in knowing if the combination of all variables are useful predictors of the dependent variable. In this section we will present hypothesis tests to determine if sets of several coefficients are all simultaneously equal to zero. Consider again the model

$$y_i = \beta_0 + \beta_1 X_{1i} + \beta_2 X_{2i} + \cdots + \beta_K X_{Ki} + \varepsilon_i$$

First we will consider the null hypothesis that all of the coefficients are simultaneously equal to zero

$$H_0: \beta_1 = \beta_2 = \cdots = \beta_K = 0$$

Accepting this hypothesis would lead us to conclude that none of the predictor variables in the regression model are statistically significant and thus they provide no useful information. If this were to occur, then we would need to go back to the model specification process and develop a new set of predictor variables. Fortunately in most applied regression situations this hypothesis is rejected, because the specification process usually leads to identifying at least one significant predictor variable.

To test the above hypothesis we can use the partitioning of variability developed in Section 11.3

```
SST = SSR + SSE
```

Recall that *SSR* is the amount of variability explained by the regression and *SSE* is the amount of unexplained variability. We recall that the variance of the regression model can be estimated using

$$S_e^2 = \frac{SSE}{(n - K - 1)}$$

If the null hypothesis that all coefficients are equal to zero is true, then SSR is also a measure of error with K degrees of freedom. As a result the ratio of

$$F = \frac{SSR/K}{SSE/(n - K - 1)}$$

has an F distribution with K degrees of freedom for the numerator and $n - K - 1$ degrees of freedom for the denominator. The computed value of F is compared with the critical value of F from Table 7 in the Appendix at a significance level α. If the computed value exceeds the critical value from the table we reject the null hypothesis and conclude that at least one coefficient is not equal to zero. This test procedure is summarized in Equation 11.23.

TEST ON ALL THE PARAMETERS OF A REGRESSION MODEL

Consider the multiple regression model

$$y_i = \beta_0 + \beta_1 X_{1i} + \beta_2 X_{2i} + \cdots + \beta_K X_{Ki} + \varepsilon_i$$

To test the null hypothesis

$$H_0 : \beta_1 = \beta_2 = \cdots = \beta_K = 0$$

against the alternative hypothesis

$$H_1 : \text{At least one } \beta_j \neq 0$$

at a significance level α we use the decision rule

$$\text{Reject } H_0 : \text{ if } \quad F_{K,n-K-1} = \frac{SSR/K}{s_e^2} > F_{K,n-K-1,\alpha} \qquad (11.23)$$

Where $F_{K,n-K-1,\alpha}$ is the critical value of F from Table 7 in the Appendix for which

$$P(F_{K,n-K-1} > F_{K,n-K-1,\alpha}) = \alpha$$

The computed random variable $F_{K,n-K-1}$ follows an F distribution with numerator degrees of freedom K and denominator degrees of freedom $(n - K - 1)$.

EXAMPLE 11.8

HOUSING PRICE PREDICTION MODEL (SIMULTANEOUS COEFFICIENT TESTING)

Citydat

During the development of the housing price prediction model for Northern City the analysts wanted to know if there was evidence that the combination of four predictor variables were not significant predictors of housing price. That is, they wanted to test the hypothesis

$$H_0 : \beta_1 = \beta_2 = \beta_3 = \beta_4 = 0$$

SOLUTION

This testing procedure can be illustrated by the housing price regression in Figure 11.9. In the analysis of variance table the computed F statistic is 19.19 with 4 degrees of freedom for the numerator and 85 degrees of freedom for the denominator. This exceeds the critical value of $F = 3.6$ for $\alpha = 0.01$ from Table 7 in the Appendix. In addition note that Minitab—and most statistics packages—compute the p-value, which is in this example equal to 0.000. Thus we would reject the hypothesis that all coefficients are equal to zero.

Test On A Subset of the Regression Parameters

In the previous sections we have developed hypothesis tests for individual regression parameters and for all regression parameters taken together. Next we will develop a hypothesis test for a subset of regression parameters, such as the combined price example previously discussed. We use this test to determine if the combined effect of several independent variables is significant in a regression model.

Consider a regression model that contains independent variables designated as X_j's and Z_j's

$$y_i = \beta_0 + \beta_1 X_{1i} + \cdots + \beta_K X_{Ki} + \alpha_1 Z_{1i} + \cdots + \alpha_r Z_{ri} + \varepsilon_i$$

and the null hypothesis to be tested is

$$H_0: \alpha_1 = \alpha_2 = \cdots = \alpha_r = 0 \quad \text{given} \quad \beta_j \neq 0, j = 1, \ldots K$$

If H_0 is true then the Z_j variables should not be included in the regression model because they provide nothing further for explaining the behavior of the dependent variable beyond that explained by the X_j variables. The procedure for performing this test is summarized in Equation 11.24, following a detailed discussion of the testing procedure that follows.

The test is conducted by comparing the error sum of squares SSE from the complete regression model, that includes both the X and Z variables, with the $SSE(r)$ from a restricted model that includes only the X variables. First we run a regression on the complete regression model above and obtain the error sum of squares designated as "SSE". Next we run the restricted regression that excludes the Z variables. (Note that the coefficients α_j are all restricted to values of 0 in this regression.)

$$y_i = \beta_0 + \beta_1 X_{1i} + \cdots + \beta_K X_{Ki} + \varepsilon_i^*$$

From this regression obtain the restricted error sum of squares designated as "SSE(r)." Then we compute the F statistic with r degrees of freedom for the numerator—r is the number of variables removed simultaneously from the restricted model—and $n - K - r - 1$ degrees of freedom for the denominator—the degrees of freedom for error in the model that includes both the X and the Z independent variables. The F statistic is

$$F = \frac{(SSE(r) - SSE)/r}{S_e^2}$$

where s_e^2 is the estimated variance of the error for the complete model. This statistic follows an F distribution with r degrees of freedom in the numerator and $n - K - r - 1$

degrees of freedom in the denominator. If the computed F is greater than the critical value of F then the null hypothesis is rejected and we conclude that the Z variables as a set should be included in the model. Note that this test does not imply that individual Z variables should not be excluded by, for example, using the Student's t test discussed previously. In addition, the test for all Z's does not imply that a subset of the Z variables cannot be excluded by using this test procedure with a different subset of Z variables.

TEST ON A SUBSET OF THE REGRESSION PARAMETERS

Given a regression model with the independent variables partitioned into X and Z subsets

$$y_i = \beta_0 + \beta_1 X_{1i} + \cdots + \beta_K X_{Ki} + \alpha_1 Z_{1i} \cdots + \alpha_r Z_{ri} + \varepsilon_i$$

To test the null hypothesis

$$H_0: \alpha_1 = \alpha_2 = \cdots = \alpha_r = 0$$

that a subset of regression parameters are simultaneously equal to 0 against the alternative hypothesis

$$H_1: \text{At least one } \alpha_j \neq 0 \quad (j = 1, \ldots, r)$$

we compare the error sum of squares for the complete model with the error sum of squares for the restricted model. First run a regression for the complete model that includes all independent variables and obtain the error sum of squares SSE. Next run a restricted regression that excludes the Z variables whose coefficients are the α's—the number of variables excluded is r. From this regression obtain the restricted error sum of squares $SSE(r)$. Then compute the F statistic and apply the decision rule for a significance level α

$$\text{Reject } H_0 \text{ if } F = \frac{(SSE(r) - SSE)/r}{S_e^2} > F_{r, n-K-r-1, \alpha} \qquad (11.24)$$

EXAMPLE 11.9

HOUSING PRICE PREDICTION
FOR SMALL CITIES (HYPOTHESIS
TESTS FOR COEFFICIENT
SUBSETS)

Citydat

The developers of the housing price prediction model wanted to determine if the combined effect of tax rate and percent commercial property contributes to the prediction after the effect of house size and income have been previously included.

SOLUTION

Continuing with the problem from Example 11.7 we have a conditional test of the hypothesis that two variables are not significant predictors given that the other two are significant predictors.

$$H_0: \beta_3 = \beta_4 = 0 \mid \beta_1, \beta_2 \neq 0$$

This test will be conducted using the procedure in Equation 11.24. Figure 11.9 presents the regression for the complete model with all four predictor variables. In that regression $SSE = 1149.13$. In Figure 11.11 we have the reduced regression with only house size and income as predictor variables. In that regression $SSE = 1426.93$. The hypothesis is tested by first com-

FIGURE 11.11
Minitab Output for Housing
Price Regression: Reduced
Model

Regression Analysis

```
The regression equation is
hseval = - 42.2 + 9.14 sizehse + 0.00393 incom72

Predictor         Coef       StDev         T        P
Constant       -42.208       9.810     -4.30    0.000
sizehse          9.135       1.940      4.71    0.000
incom72       0.003927    0.001473      2.67    0.009

S = 4.050      R-Sq = 34.7%      R-Sq(adj) = 33.2%

Analysis of Variance
                                              SSE(r)
Source             DF          SS         MS         F        P
Regression          2      759.70     379.85     23.16    0.000
Residual Error     87     1426.93      16.40
Total              89     2186.63
```

puting the *F* statistic whose numerator is the difference in Error Sum of Squares (*SSE*) for the reduced model minus the *SSE* for the complete model.

$$F = \frac{(1426.93 - 1149.14)/2}{13.52} = 10.27$$

The *F* statistic has 2 degrees of freedom—for the two variables being tested simultaneously—for the numerator and 85 degrees of freedom for the numerator. Note that the variance estimator, $S^2(Y|X)$, is obtained from the complete model in Figure 11.9, which has 85 degrees of freedom for error. The critical value for *F* with $\alpha = 0.01$, from Table 7 in the Appendix, is approximately 7.00. Since the computed value of *F* exceeds the critical value, we reject the null hypothesis that tax rate and percent commercial property are not conditionally significant. The combined effect of these two variables does improve the model that predicts housing price. Therefore tax rate and percent commercial property should be included in the model.

EXERCISES

11.23 Suppose that a dependent variable is related to *K* independent variables through a multiple regression model. Let R^2 denote the coefficient of determination and $\overline{R}^2$ the corrected coefficient. Suppose that *n* sets of observation are used to fit the regression.

(a) Show that

$$\overline{R}^2 = \frac{(n-1)R^2 - K}{n - K - 1}$$

(b) Show that

$$R^2 = \frac{(n - K - 1)\overline{R}^2 + K}{n - 1}$$

(c) Show that the statistic for testing the null hypothesis that all the partial regression coefficients are 0 can be written

$$\frac{SSR/K}{SSE/(n - K - 1)} = \frac{n - K - 1}{K} \cdot \frac{\overline{R}^2 + A}{1 - \overline{R}^2}$$

where

$$A = \frac{K}{n - K - 1}$$

11.24 Refer to the study on aircraft design effort of Exercises 11.1 and 11.9.

(a) Test the null hypothesis

$$H_0: \beta_1 = \beta_2 = \beta_3 = 0$$

(b) Set out the analysis of variance table.

11.25 For the study on the influence of financial institutions on share prices of Exercise 11.2, 48 quarterly observations were used, and the corrected coefficient of determination was found to be $R^2 = .463$. Test the null hypothesis.

$$H_0: \beta_1 = \beta_2 = 0$$

11.26 Refer to the study on milk consumption, described in Exercises 11.3, 11.10, and 11.14.
   (a) Test the null hypothesis

$$H_0: \beta_1 = \beta_2 = 0$$

   (b) Set out the analysis of variance table.

11.27 Refer to the study on weight gains, described in Exercises 11.4, 11.11 and 11.15.
   (a) Test the null hypothesis

$$H_0: \beta_1 = \beta_2 = \beta_3 = 0$$

   (b) Set out the analysis of variance table.

11.28 Refer to Exercise 11.18. Test the null hypothesis that, taken together, the four independent variables do not linearly influence revenue generated by state lotteries.

11.29 Refer to Exercise 11.19. Test the null hypothesis that, taken together, the three independent variables do not linearly influence the price of air conditioners.

11.30 Refer to the study of Exercise 11.20. Test the null hypothesis that taken together, consumption expenditures and the relative price of imports do not linearly affect the demand for imports in Jamaica.

11.31 Refer to the study on the determinants of community demand for police officers discussed in Exercise 11.22. Test the null hypothesis

$$H_0: \beta_1 = \beta_2 = \beta_3 = \beta_4 = \beta_5 = \beta_6 = \beta_7 = 0$$

and interpret your findings.

11.32 A dependent variable is regressed on K independent variables, using n sets of sample observations. We denote by SSE the error sum of squares and by R^2 the coefficient of determination for this estimated regression. We want to test the null hypothesis that K_1 of these independent variables, taken together, do not linearly affect the dependent variable, given that the other ($K - K_1$) independent variables are also to be used. Suppose that the regression is reestimated, with the K_1 independent variables of interest excluded. Let SSE^* denote the error sum of squares and R^{*2} the coefficient of determination for this regression. Show that the statistic for testing our null hypothesis, introduced in Section 11.5, can be expressed as

$$\frac{(SSE^* - SSE)/K_1}{SSE/(n - K - 1)} = \frac{R^2 - R^{*2}}{1 - R^2} \cdot \frac{n - K - 1}{K_1}$$

11.33 In the study of Exercises 11.3, 11.10, and 11.14 on milk consumption, a third independent variable—number of preschool children in the household—was added to the regression model. The sum of squared errors when this augmented model was estimated by least squares was found to be 83.7. Test the null hypothesis that, all other things being equal, the number of preschool children in the household does not linearly affect milk consumption.

11.6   PREDICTION

An important application of regression models is to predict or forecast values of the dependent variable given values for independent variables. Forecasts can be computed directly from the estimated regression model using the coefficient estimates in that model, as shown in Equation 11.25.

PREDICTIONS FROM THE MULTIPLE REGRESSION MODELS

Given that the population regression model

$$y_i = \beta_0 + \beta_1 x_{1i} + \beta_2 x_{2i} + \cdots + \beta_K x_{Ki} + \varepsilon_i \quad (i = 1, 2, \ldots, n)$$

holds and that the standard regression assumptions are valid, let $b_0, b_1, \ldots, b_K$ be the least squares estimates of the model coefficients, $\beta_j, j = 1, 2, \ldots, K$, based on the $x_{1i}, x_{2i}, \ldots, x_{Ki}, y_i$ ($i = 1, 2, \ldots, n$) data points. Then given a new observation of a data point, $x_{1,n+1}, x_{2,n+1}, \ldots, x_{K,n+1}$ the best linear unbiased forecast of $\hat{Y}_{n+1}$ is

$$\hat{y}_{n+1} = b_0 + b_1 x_{1,n+1} + b_{2,n+1} + \cdots + b_K x_{K,n+1} \tag{11.25}$$

It is very risky to obtain forecasts that are based on X values outside the range of the data used to estimate the model coefficients, because we do not have data evidence to support the linear model at those points.

In addition to the predicted value of Y for a particular set of x's we are often interested in a confidence interval or a prediction interval associated with the prediction. As we discussed in Section 10.6, the confidence interval includes the expected value of Y with probability $1 - \alpha$. In contrast the prediction interval includes individual predicted values—expected value of Y plus the random error term. To obtain these intervals we need to compute estimates of the standard deviations for the expected value of Y and for the individual points. These computations are similar in form to those used in simple regression, but the estimator equations are much more complicated. The standard deviations for predicted values, $S_{\hat{y}}$, are a function of the standard error of the estimate, S_e, the standard deviation of the predictor variables, and the square of the distance between the mean of the independent variables and the X's for the prediction. This standard deviation is similar to the standard deviation for simple regression predictions in Chapter 10. However the equations for multiple regression are very complex and will not be presented here—instead we will use the computed values from Minitab. The standard deviations for the prediction interval and for the confidence intervals and the corresponding intervals are computed by most good statistics packages.

EXAMPLE 11.10

FORECAST OF SAVINGS AND LOAN PROFIT MARGINS (REGRESSION MODEL FORECASTS)

Savings and Loan

You have been asked to forecast the savings and loan profit margin for a year in which the percentage net revenue is 4.50 and there are 9,000 offices, using the Savings and Loan regression model. Data stored in file **Savings and Loan**.

SOLUTION

Using the notation from Equation 11.25 we have the variables

$$x_{1,n+1} = 4.50 \qquad\qquad x_{2,n+1} = 9,000$$

Using these values we find that our point predictor of profit margin is

$$\hat{y}_{n+1} = b_0 + b_1 x_{1,n+1} + b_{2,n+1}$$
$$= 1.565 + (0.237)(4.50) - (0.000249)(9,000) = 0.39$$

Thus for a year with percentage net revenues per deposit dollar are 4.50 and the number of offices is 9,000, we predict that the percentage profit margin for savings and loan associations will be 0.39.

Predicted values, confidence intervals, and prediction intervals can be computed directly in the Minitab regression routine using the instructions

```
STAT > REGRESSION > REGRESSION > OPTIONS
```

Then type the required X predictor values in the dialog box labeled "Prediction Intervals for New Observations."

The regression output is shown in Figure 11.12. The predicted value, $\hat{Y} = 0.39$, and its standard deviation, 0.0277, is presented along with the confidence interval and the prediction interval. The confidence interval—CI—provides an interval for the expected value of Y on the linear function defined by the values of the independent variables. This interval is a function of the standard error of the regression model, the distance that the x_j values are from their individual sample means, and the correlation between the x_j variables used to fit the model. The prediction interval—PI—provides an interval for a single observed value. Thus it includes the variability associated with the expected value plus the variability of a single point about the predicted value.

FIGURE 11.12
Minitab Output Forecasts
and Forecast Intervals for
Multiple Regression

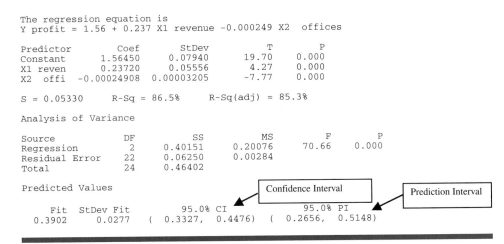

```
The regression equation is
Y profit = 1.56 + 0.237 X1 revenue -0.000249 X2  offices

Predictor         Coef        StDev         T         P
Constant       1.56450      0.07940     19.70     0.000
X1 reven       0.23720      0.05556      4.27     0.000
X2  offi   -0.00024908   0.00003205     -7.77     0.000

S = 0.05330      R-Sq = 86.5%      R-Sq(adj) = 85.3%

Analysis of Variance

Source           DF          SS          MS         F        P
Regression        2      0.40151     0.20076     70.66     0.000
Residual Error   22      0.06250     0.00284
Total            24      0.46402

Predicted Values                        ┌─────────────────┐              ┌─────────────────┐
                                        │ Confidence Interval │           │ Prediction Interval │
                                        └─────────────────┘              └─────────────────┘
    Fit   StDev Fit         95.0% CI               95.0% PI
  0.3902     0.0277    ( 0.3327,  0.4476)    ( 0.2656,  0.5148)
```

EXERCISES

11.34 Using the information in Exercise 11.4, predict the weight gain for a freshman who eats an average of 20 meals per week, exercises an average of 10 hours per week, and consumes an average of 6 beers per week.

11.35 Using the information in Exercise 11.3, predict the weekly milk consumption of a family of four with an income of $600 per week.

11.36 For the regression on aircraft design effort of Exercise 1, the estimated intercept was

$$b_0 = .578$$

Predict design effort for a plane with top speed Mach 1.0, weighing 7 tons, and having 50% of its parts in common with other models.

11.37 A real estate agent hypothesizes that in her town, the selling price of a house in dollars (y) depends on its size in square feet of floor space (x_1), the lot size in square feet (x_2), the number of bedrooms (x_3), and the number of bathrooms (x_4). For a random sample of 20 house

sales, the following least squares estimated model was obtained:

$$y = 1998.5 + 22.352x_1 + 1.4686x_2 + 6767.3x_3 + 2701.1x_4$$
$$\quad\quad\quad (2.5543)\quad\quad (1.4492)\quad\quad (1820.8)\quad\quad (1996.2)$$

$$R^2 = .9843$$

The figures in parentheses are estimated standard errors.

(a) Interpret in the context of this model the estimated coefficient on x_2.

(b) Interpret the coefficient of determination.

(c) Assuming that the model is correctly specified, test at the 5% level against the appropriate one-sided alternative the null hypothesis that, all else being equal, selling price does not depend on number of bathrooms.

(d) Estimate the selling price of a house with 1,250 square feet of floor space, on a lot of 4,700 square feet, with 3 bedrooms and 1½ bathrooms.

11.7 TRANSFORMATIONS FOR NONLINEAR REGRESSION MODELS

We have seen how regression analysis can be used to estimate linear relationships that predict a dependent variable as a function of one or more independent variables. These applications are very important. However, in addition there are a number of economic and business relationships that are not strictly linear. In this section we will develop procedures for modifying certain nonlinear model formats so that multiple regression procedures can be used to estimate the model coefficients.

By examining the least squares algorithm we can see that by careful manipulation of nonlinear models it is possible to use least squares for a broader set of applied problems. The assumptions concerning independent variables in multiple regression are not very restrictive. Independent variables define points at which we measure a random variable Y. We assume that there is a linear relationship between the levels of the independent variables $X_j, j = 1,\ldots, K$ and the expected value of the dependent variable Y. We can take advantage of this freedom to expand the set of models that can be estimated. Thus we can move beyond linear models in our multiple regression applications. Three examples are shown in Figure 11.13:

1. Supply functions may be nonlinear.
2. The increase in total output with increases in the number of workers may become flatter as more workers are added.
3. Average costs per unit produced are often minimized at an intermediate level of production.

Quadratic Transformations

We have spent considerable time developing regression analysis to estimate linear equations that represent various business and economic processes. There are also many processes that can best be represented by nonlinear equations. Total revenue has a quadratic relationship with price with maximum revenue occurring at an intermediate price level if the demand function has a negative slope. In many cases the minimum production cost per unit occurs at an intermediate level of output, with cost per unit decreasing as we approach the minimum cost per unit and then increasing after passing the minimum unit cost level. We can model a number of these economic and business relationships by using a quadratic model

$$Y = \beta_0 + \beta_1 X_1 + \beta_2 X_1^2 + \varepsilon$$

To estimate the coefficients of a quadratic model for applications such as these we can transform or modify the variables as shown in Equations 11.26 and 11.27. In this way a nonlinear quadratic model is converted to a model that is linear in a modified set of variables.

FIGURE 11.13
Examples of Quadratic Functions

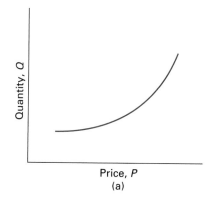

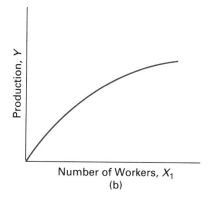

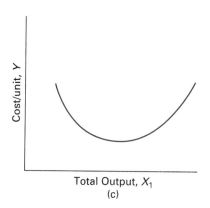

QUADRATIC MODEL TRANSFORMATIONS

The quadratic function

$$Y = \beta_0 + \beta_1 X_1 + \beta_2 X_1^2 + \varepsilon \tag{11.26}$$

can be transformed into a linear multiple regression model by defining new variables.

$$z_1 = x_1$$
$$z_2 = x_1^2$$

and then specifying the model as

$$y_i = \beta_0 + \beta_1 z_{1i} + \beta_2 z_{2i} + \varepsilon_i \tag{11.27}$$

which is linear in the transformed variables. Transformed quadratic variables can be combined with other variables in a multiple regression model. Thus we could fit a multiple quadratic regression using transformed variables.

INTERPRETATION

By transforming the variables we can estimate a linear multiple regression model and use the results as a nonlinear model. Inference procedures on transformed quadratic models are the same as those that we have previously developed for linear models. In this way we avoid confusion that would result if different statistical procedures were used for linear versus quadratic models. The coefficients must be combined together for interpretation. Thus if we have a quadratic model then the effect of a variable X is indicated by both the coefficients of the linear and quadratic terms. We can also perform a simple hypothesis test to determine if a quadratic model is an improvement over a linear model. The Z_2 or X_1^2 variable is merely an additional variable whose coefficient can be tested—$H_0 : \beta_2 = 0$—using the conditional Student's t or F statistic. If a quadratic model fits the data better than a linear model then the coefficient of the quadratic variable—$Z_2 = X_1^2$—will be significantly different from 0.

EXAMPLE 11.11

PRODUCTION COSTS (QUADRATIC MODEL ESTIMATION)

Production Cost

Arnold Sorenson, production manager of New Frontiers Instruments Inc., was interested in estimating the mathematical relationship between the number of electronic assemblies produced during an eight-hour shift and the average cost per assembly. This function would then be used to estimate cost for various production order bids and to determine the production level that would minimize average cost. Data are found in the data file **Production Cost**.

SOLUTION

Arnold collected data from nine shifts during which the number of assemblies ranged from 100 to 900. In addition he obtained the average cost per unit for those days from the accounting department. This data and a scatter plot prepared using Excel is shown in Figure 11.14. As a result of his study of economics and his experience George suspected that the function might be quadratic with an intermediate minimum average cost. He designed his analysis to consider both a linear and quadratic average production cost function.

Figure 11.15 (on page 453) presents the PHStat output for a simple regression of cost as a linear function of the number of units. We see that the linear relationship is almost flat, indicating no linear relationship between average cost and number of units produced. If Arnold had simply used this relationship he would have been led to serious errors in his cost estimation procedures.

FIGURE 11.14
Mean Production Costs as a
Function of Number of Units

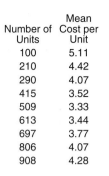

Number of Units	Mean Cost per Unit
100	5.11
210	4.42
290	4.07
415	3.52
509	3.33
613	3.44
697	3.77
806	4.07
908	4.28

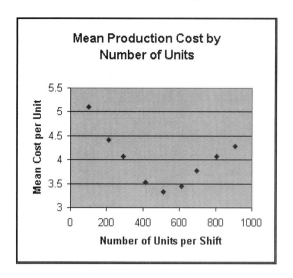

Figure 11.16 (on page 454) presents the PHStat output for a quadratic regression that shows mean cost per unit as a nonlinear function of the number of units produced. The lower portion of Figure 11.16 indicates the format of the data for the regression model. Note that b_2 is different from zero and thus should be included in the model. In addition, note that the R^2 for the quadratic model is 0.949 compared to 0.174 for the linear model. By using the quadratic model prepared using the transformation Arnold has produced a substantially more useful mean cost model.

Logarithmic Transformations

A number of economic relationships can be modeled by exponential functions. For example if the percent change in quantity of goods sold changes linearly in response to percent changes in the price then the demand function will have an exponential form

$$Q = \beta_0 P^{\beta_1}$$

where Q is the quantity demanded and P is the price per unit. Exponential demand functions have constant elasticity and thus a 1% change in price results in the same percent

FIGURE 11.15
Linear Regression Using
PHStat: Average Cost on
Number of Units

Regression Analysis

Regression Statistics	
Multiple R	0.418
R Square	0.174
Adjusted R Square	0.056
Standard Error	0.548
Observations	9

ANOVA

	df	SS	MS	F	Significance F
Regression	1	0.443	0.443	1.478	0.263
Residual	7	2.099	0.300		
Total	8	2.542			

	Coefficients	Standard Error	t Stat	P-value	Lower 95%	Upper 95%
Intercept	4.433	0.399	11.100	0.000	3.489	5.377
Number of Units	-0.001	0.001	-1.216	0.263	-0.003	0.001

b_1

FIGURE 11.16
PHStat Regression Analysis
Using Quadratic Model

Regression Analysis

Regression Statistics	
Multiple R	0.981
R Square	0.962
Adjusted R Square	
Standard Error	0.127
Observations	9

ANOVA

	df	SS	MS	F	Significance F
Regression	2	2.446	1.223	75.973	0.000
Residual	6	0.097	0.016		
Total	8	2.542			

	Coefficients	Standard Error	t Stat	P-value	Lower 95%	Upper 95%
Intercept	5.9084143891	0.1614294134	36.601	0.000	5.5134105554	6.3034182228
Number of Units	-0.0088415125	0.0007343565	-12.040	0.000	-0.0106384194	-0.0070446056
Units Squared	0.0000079325	0.0000007112	11.154	0.000	0.0000061923	0.0000096728

b_1 b_2

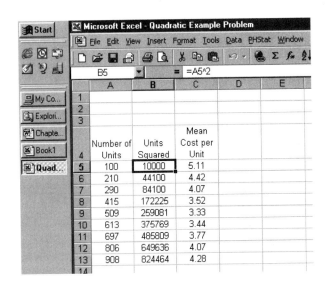

Comment

The values in column B
-- $x_2 = x_1^2$ --
Are computed by
squaring the values in
column A

change in quantity demanded for all price levels. In contrast, linear demand models indicate that a unit change in the price variable will result in the same change in quantity demanded for all price levels. Exponential demand models are widely used in the analysis of market behavior. One important feature of exponential models is that the coefficient β_1 is the constant elasticity, e, of demand Q with respect to price P.

$$e = \frac{\partial Q/Q}{\partial P/P} = \beta_j$$

This result is developed in most microeconomics textbooks. Exponential model coefficients are estimated by using logarithmic transformations as shown in Equation 11.29.

The logarithmic transformation assumes that the random error term multiplies the true value of Y to obtain the observed value. Thus in the exponential model the error is a percentage of the true value and the variance of the error distribution increases with increases in Y. If this result is not true, the log transformation is not correct. In that case a much more complex nonlinear estimation technique must be used. Those techniques are considerably beyond the scope of this book.

EXPONENTIAL MODEL TRANSFORMATIONS

Coefficients for exponential models of the form

$$Y = \beta_0 X_1^{\beta_1} X_2^{\beta_2} \varepsilon \tag{11.28}$$

can be estimated by first taking the logarithm of both sides to obtain an equation that is linear in the logarithms of the variables.

$$\log(Y) = \log(\beta_0) + \beta_1 \log(X_1) + \beta_2 \log(X_2) + \log(\varepsilon) \tag{11.29}$$

Using this form we can regress the logarithm of Y on the logarithms of the two X variables and obtain estimates for the coefficients β_1, β_2 directly from the regression analysis. Note that this estimation procedure requires that the random errors are multiplicative in the original exponential model. Thus the error term, ε, is expressed as a percentage increase or decrease instead of the addition or subtraction of a random error as we have seen for linear regression models.

Another important application of exponential models is the Cobb-Douglas production function that has the form

$$Q = \beta_0 L^{\beta_1} K^{\beta_2}$$

where Q is the quantity produced, L is the amount of labor used, and K is the amount of capital. β_1 and β_2 are the relative contributions of changes in labor and changes in capital to changes in quantity produced. In one special case, the sum of the coefficients are restricted to equal 1 and we have constant returns to scale. In that case, β_1 and β_2 are the percent contributions of labor and capital to productivity increase.

INTERPRETATION

Estimation of the coefficients when their sum is equal to 1 is one example of restricted estimation in regression models. Equation 11.29 is modified by the restriction

$$\beta_1 + \beta_2 = 1$$

and therefore substitution of the form

$$\beta_2 = 1 - \beta_1$$

is included and the new estimation equation becomes

$$\log(Y) = \log(\beta_0) + \beta_1 \log(X_1) + (1 - \beta_1) \log(X_2) + \log(\varepsilon)$$
$$\log(Y) - \log(X_2) = \log(\beta_0) + \beta_1 \big[\log(X_1) - \log(X_2)\big] + \log(\varepsilon)$$

$$\log\left(\frac{Y}{X_2}\right) = \log(\beta_0) + \beta_1 \log\left(\frac{X_1}{X_2}\right) + \log(\varepsilon) \tag{11.30}$$

Thus we see that the β_1 coefficient is obtained by regressing $\log(Y/X_2)$ on $\log(X_1/X_2)$. Then β_2 is computed by subtracting β_1 from 1.0.

EXAMPLE 11.12

PRODUCTION FUNCTION FOR MINONG BOAT WORKS (EXPONENTIAL MODEL ESTIMATION)

Boat Production

The Minong Boat Works began producing small fishing boats in the early 1970s for northern Wisconsin fishermen. The owners developed a low-cost production method for producing quality boats. As a result they have experienced increased demand over the years. The production method uses a workstation with a set of jigs and power tools that can be operated by a varying number of workers. Over the years the number of workstations (units of capital) have grown from 1 to 20 to meet the demand for boats. At the same time the workforce has grown from 2 person years to 25. They are now considering expanding their sales to potential markets in Michigan and Minnesota. Therefore, they need to decide how much to increase the number of workstations and number of workers to achieve various levels of increased production.

SOLUTION

Their daughter, a senior economics major, suggested that they should estimate a restricted Cobb-Douglas production function using data from previous years of operation. She explains that this production function would enable them to predict the number of boats produced for different levels of workstations and workers. The owners agree that such an analysis would be a good idea and ask their daughter to prepare the analysis. She begins the analysis by collecting the production data, contained in the data file **Boat Production** from old company records. To obtain the coefficient estimates she first must transform the original model specification to a form that can be estimated by least squares regression. The Cobb-Douglas production function model is

$$Y = \beta_0 K^{\beta_1} L^{\beta_2}$$

with the restriction

$$\beta_2 = 1 - \beta_1$$

where Y is the number of boats produced each year, K is the number of production stations (units of capital) used each year, and L is the number of workers used each year.

The restricted Cobb-Douglas production function was transformed to the estimation form

$$\log\left(\frac{Y}{K}\right) = \log(\beta_0) + \beta_2 \log\left(\frac{L}{K}\right)$$

for least squares estimation. The Minitab procedure for obtaining the transformations is shown in Figure 11.17.

FIGURE 11.17
Logarithmic Transformation Using Minitab

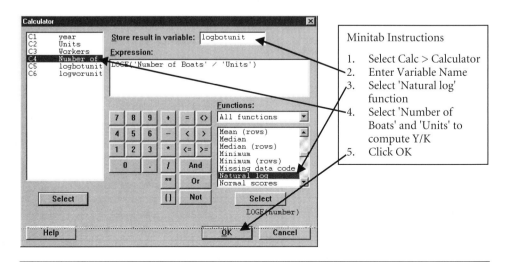

FIGURE 11.18
Minitab Output for
Restricted Production
Function Regression Analysis

```
The regression equation is
logbotunit = 3.02 + 0.845 logworunit

Predictor          Coef      SE Coef          T          P
Constant        3.02325      0.04387      68.92      0.000
logworun        0.84479      0.09062       9.32      0.000

S = 0.1105      R-Sq = 79.8%      R-Sq(adj) = 78.9%

Analysis of Variance

Source              DF          SS          MS          F          P
Regression           1      1.0618      1.0618      86.90      0.000
Residual Error      22      0.2688      0.0122
Total               23      1.3306
```

The regression model estimate is shown in Figure 11.18 with the resulting equation

$$\log\left(\frac{Y}{K}\right) = 3.02 + 0.845\log\left(\frac{L}{K}\right) \tag{11.31}$$

After applying the appropriate algebraic transformations the production function model is

$$Y = 20.49K^{0.845}L^{0.155} \tag{11.32}$$

This production function can be used as a tool for predicting the expected output obtained by using various levels of capital and labor. The estimated model coefficients $\beta_1 = 0.845$ and $\beta_2 = 0.155$ indicate that 84.5% of the value of production comes from labor and 15.5% from capital.

Figure 11.19 presents a comparison of the observed number of boats and the forecast number of boats from the transformed regression equation. The forecast number of boats was computed using Equation 11.31. That analysis also indicates that the R^2 for the regression of the number of boats on the predicted number of boats is 0.987. This R^2 can be interpreted just as you would an R^2 for any linear regression model and thus we see that this transformed exponential equation provides a good fit for the observed boat production data. The R^2 for the transformed regression data in Figure 11.18 cannot be easily interpreted as an indicator of the relationship between the number of boats produced and the independent variables labor and capital because the units are in logarithms of ratios.

FIGURE 11.19
Comparison of Observed and
Predicted Production

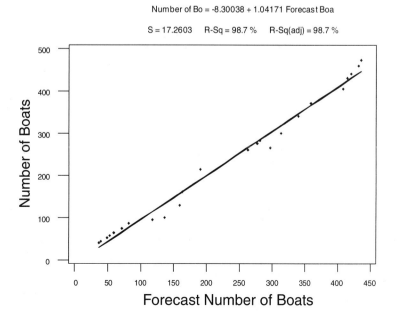

Number of Bo = -8.30038 + 1.04171 Forecast Boa

S = 17.2603   R-Sq = 98.7 %   R-Sq(adj) = 98.7 %

EXERCISES

11.38 Describe an example from your experience in which a quadratic model would be better than a linear model.

11.39 John Swanson, president of Market Research Inc., has asked you to estimate the coefficients of the model

$$Y = \beta_0 + \beta_1 X_1 + \beta_2 X_1^2 + \beta_3 X_2$$

Where Y is the expected sales of office supplies in a large retail distributor of office supplies, X_1 is the total disposable income of residents within five miles of the store, and X_2 is the total number of employment in information-based businesses within five miles of the store. Recent work by a national consulting firm has concluded that the coefficients in the model must have the following restriction

$$\beta_1 + \beta_2 = 2$$

Describe how you would estimate the model coefficients using least squares.

11.40 🌐 Angelica Chandra, president of Benefits Research Inc., has asked you to study the salary structure of her firm. Benefits Research provides consulting and management for employee health care and retirement programs. Their clients are mid- to large-size firms. As a first step you are asked to estimate a regression model that estimates the expected salary as a function of years of experience in the firm. You are to consider linear, quadratic, and cubic models and determine which one would be most suitable. Estimate appropriate regression models and write a short report that recommends the best model. Use the data contained in the file **Benefits Research.**

11.41 In a study of the determinants of household expenditures on vacation travel, data were obtained from a sample of 2,246 households.[1] The model estimated was

$$\log y = -4.054 + 1.1556 \log x_1 - .4408 \log x_2$$
$$\underset{(.0546)}{} \qquad \underset{(.0490)}{}$$

$$R^2 = .168$$

where

$$y = \text{Expenditure on vacation travel}$$
$$x_1 = \text{Total annual consumption expenditure}$$
$$x_2 = \text{Number of members in household}$$

The figures in parentheses beneath the coefficient estimates are the corresponding estimated standard errors.

(a) Interpret the estimated partial regression coefficients.

(b) Interpret the coefficient of determination.

(c) All else being equal, find a 95% confidence interval for the percentage increase in expenditure on vacation travel resulting from a 1% increase in total annual consumption expenditure.

(d) Assuming that the model is correctly specified, test at the 1% significance level the null hypothesis that, all else being equal, number of members in household does not affect expenditure on vacation travel against the alternative that the greater the number of household members, the lower vacation travel expenditure.

11.42 The following model was estimated for a sample of 322 supermarkets in large metropolitan areas.[2]

$$\text{Log } y = 2.921 + .680 \log x \qquad R^2 = .19$$
$$\underset{(.077)}{}$$

where

$$y = \text{Store size}$$
$$x = \text{Median income in zip code area in which store is located}$$

(a) Interpret the estimated coefficient on log x.

(b) Test the null hypothesis that income has no impact on store size against the alternative that higher income tends to be associated with larger store size.

11.43 An agricultural economist believes that the amount of beef consumed (y) in tons in a year in the United States depends on the price of beef (x_1) in dollars per pound, the price of pork (x_2) in dollars per pound, the price of chicken (x_3), and income per household (x_4) in thousands of dollars. The following sample regression was obtained through least squares, using 30 annual observations:

$$\text{Log } y = -.024 - .529 \log x_1 + .217 \log x_2 + .193 \log x_3$$
$$\underset{(.168)}{} \qquad \underset{(.103)}{} \qquad \underset{(.106)}{}$$

$$+ .416 \log x_4 \qquad R^2 = .683$$
$$\underset{(.163)}{}$$

(a) Interpret the coefficient on log x_1.

(b) Interpret the coefficient on log x_2.

(c) Test at the 1% significance level the null hypothesis that the coefficient on log x_4 in the population regression is 0, against the alternative that it is positive.

(d) Test the null hypothesis that the four variables (log x_1, log x_2, log x_3, log x_4) do not, as a set, have any linear influence on log y.

(e) The economist is also concerned that over the years, increasing awareness of the effects of heavy red

[1] R.P. Hagermann, "The determinants of household vacation travel: Some empirical evidence," *Applied Economics,* 13 (1981), 225–34.
[2] J.M. MacDonald and P.E. Nelson, "Do the poor still pay more? Food price variations in large metropolitan areas," *Journal of Urban Economics,* 30 (1991), 344-59.

meat consumption on health may have influenced the demand for beef. If this is indeed the case, how would this influence your view of the original estimated regression?

11.44 The data file **German Imports** shows German real imports (y), real private consumption (x_1), and real exchange rate (x_2), in terms of U.S. dollars per mark, over a period of 31 years. Estimate the model

$$\log Y_t = \beta_0 + \beta_1 \log x_{1t} + \beta_2 \log x_{2t} + \varepsilon_t$$

and write a report on your findings.

11.45 You have been asked to develop an exponential production function—Cobb-Douglas form—that will predict the number of microprocessors produced by a manufacturer, Y, as a function of the units of capital, X_1, the units of labor, X_2, and the number of computer science staff involved in basic research, X_3. Specify the model form and then carefully and completely indicate how you would estimate the coefficients. Do this first using an unrestricted model and then a second time including the restriction that the coefficients of the three variables should sum to 1.

11.46 Consider the following nonlinear model with multiplicative errors.

$$Y = B_0 X_1^{B_1} X_2^{B_2} X_3^{B_3} X_4^{B_4} \varepsilon$$

$$B_1 + B_2 = 1$$
$$B_3 + B_4 = 1$$

(a) Show how you would obtain the coefficient estimates. Coefficient restrictions must be satisfied. Show all work and explain what you are doing.

(b) What is the constant elasticity for Y versus X_4? Show all work.

11.8 DUMMY VARIABLES FOR REGRESSION MODELS

In the discussion of multiple regression up to this point we have assumed that the independent variables, x_j, have existed over a range and contained many different values. However, in the multiple regression assumptions the only restriction on the independent variables is that they are fixed values. Thus we could have an independent variable that took on only two values, $x_j = 0$, $x_j = 1$. This structure is commonly defined as a "dummy variable," and we will see that it provides a valuable tool for applying multiple regression to situations involving categorical variables. One important example is a linear function that shifts in response to some influence. Consider first a simple regression equation

$$Y = \beta_0 + \beta_1 X_1$$

Now suppose that we introduce a dummy variable, X_2, that has values 0 and 1 and the resulting equation is

$$Y = \beta_0 + \beta_1 X_1 + \beta_2 X_2$$

When $X_2 = 0$ in this equation the constant is β_0, but when $X_2 = 1$ the constant is $\beta_0 + \beta_2$. Thus we see that the dummy variable shifts the linear relationship between Y and X_1 by the value of the coefficient β_2. In this way we can represent the effect of shifts in our regression equation. We will begin our discussion with an example of an important application.

EXAMPLE 11.13

WAGE DISCRIMINATION ANALYSIS (DUMMY VARIABLE MODEL ESTIMATION)

Gender and Salary

The president of Investors Ltd. wants to determine if there is any evidence of wage discrimination in the salaries of male and female financial analysts. Figure 11.20 presents an example of annual wages versus years of experience for the analysts. See the data file **Gender and Salary**.

SOLUTION
Examining the data and the graph we see two different subsets of salaries, and those for males appear to be uniformly higher across the years of experience.

This problem can be analyzed by estimating a multiple regression model of salary, Y, versus years of experience, X_1, and a second variable, X_2, that is coded as

0	Female Employees
1	Male Employees

FIGURE 11.20
Example of Data Pattern
Indicating Wage
Discrimination

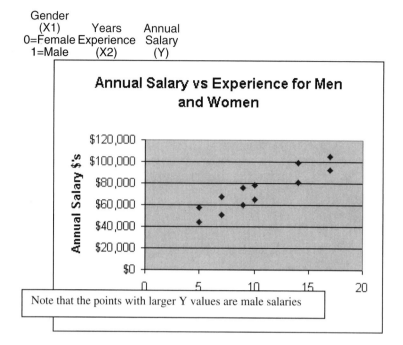

The resulting multiple regression model

$$\hat{y} = b_0 + b_1 x_1 + b_2 x_2$$

can be analyzed using the procedures we have learned, noting that the coefficient, b_1, is an estimate of the expected annual increase in salary per year of experience and, b_2, is the shift in mean salary from male to female employees. If b_2 is positive we have an indication that male salaries are uniformly higher.

Figure 11.21 presents the multiple regression analysis from Minitab for this problem. From this analysis we see that the coefficient of x_1—gender—has a Student's t statistic equal to 14.88 and a p value of 0, which leads us to reject the null hypothesis that the coefficient is equal to 0. This result indicates that male salaries are significantly higher. We also see that $b_2 = 4076.5$, indicating that the expected value for the annual increase is \$4,076.5, and that the coefficient $b_1 = 14683.7$, indicating that the male salaries are on average \$14,683.7 higher. Analyses such as these have been used successfully in a number of wage discrimination law suits. As a result most companies will perform an analysis similar to this to determine if there is any evidence of salary discrimination.

FIGURE 11.21
Regression Analysis for Wage
Discrimination Example
Regression Analysis: Annual
Salary versus Gender (X2),
Years Experience

Regression Analysis: Annual Salary versus Gender (X2), Years Experience

```
The regression equation is
Annual Salary (Y) = 23608 + 14684 Gender (X1) 0=Female 1=Male
               + 4076 Years Experience (X2)

Predictor        Coef      SE Coef         T        P
Constant        23608         1434     16.46    0.000
Gender (     14683.7          987.0    14.88    0.000
Years Ex      4076.5          121.3    33.61    0.000

S = 1709       R-Sq = 99.3%      R-Sq(adj) = 99.2%

Analysis of Variance

Source           DF           SS           MS         F        P
Regression        2   3948240796   1974120398    675.53    0.000
Residual Error    9     26300913      2922324
Total            11   3974541710
```

Examples such as the previous one have wide application to a number of problems including the following:

1. The relationship between the number of units produced and the number of employees is likely to shift if new technology is added to the process.
2. The relationship between aggregate consumption and aggregate disposable income may shift in time of war or other major national event.
3. The relationship between total output and number of workers may shift as the result of the introduction of new production technology.
4. The demand function for a product may shift because of a new advertising campaign or a news release relating to the product.

This discussion has introduced the concept of dummy variable regression as a procedure for extending our analysis capability. The procedure is summarized in the following box.

DUMMY VARIABLE REGRESSION ANALYSIS

The relationship between Y and X_1

$$Y = \beta_0 + \beta_1 X_1 + \varepsilon$$

can shift in response to a changed condition. The shift effect can be estimated by using a dummy variable which has values of 0 (condition not present) and 1 (condition present). As shown in Figure 11.20, all of the observations from the upper set of data points have dummy variable $X_2 = 1$, and the observations for the lower points have $X_2 = 0$. In these cases the relationship between Y and X_1 is specified by the multiple regression model

$$\hat{y} = b_0 + b_2 x_2 + b_1 x_1 \qquad (11.33)$$

The coefficient b_2 represents the shift of the function between the upper set of points and the lower set in Figure 11.20. The functions for each set of points are

$$\hat{y} = b_0 + b x_1 \qquad \text{when} \quad x_2 = 0$$

and

$$\hat{y} = (b_0 + b_2 x_2) + b_1 x_1 \qquad \text{when} \quad x_2 = 1$$

In the first function the constant is b_0, while in the second the constant is $b_0 + b_2$. Dummy variables are also called *indicator variables*.

This simple specification of the regression model is a very powerful tool for problems that involve a shift of the linear function by identifiable discrete factors. In addition the multiple regression structure provides a direct procedure for performing a hypothesis test as we did in Example 11.13. The hypothesis test is

$$H_0: \beta_2 = 0 \mid \beta_1 \neq 0$$
$$H_1: \beta_2 \neq 0 \mid \beta_1 \neq 0$$

Rejection of the null hypothesis H_0 leads to the conclusion that the constant is different between the two subsets of data. In Example 11.13 we saw that there was a significant shift in wages between the male and female subgroups.

Differences in Slope

We can also use dummy variables to model and test for differences in the slope coefficient by adding an interaction variable. Figure 11.22 presents a typical example. To test for both differences in the constant and differences in slope we use a more complex regression model.

DUMMY VARIABLE REGRESSION FOR DIFFERENCES IN SLOPE

To determine if there are significant differences in slopes between two discrete conditions we need to expand our regression model to a more complex form

$$\hat{y} = b_0 + b_2 x_2 + (b_1 + b_3 x_2) x_1 \qquad (11.34)$$

Now we see that the slope coefficient of x_1 contains two components, b_1 and $b_3 x_2$. When x_2 equals 0, the slope estimate is the usual b_1. However, when x_2 equals 1, the slope is equal to the algebraic sum of $b_1 + b_3$. To estimate the model we actually need to multiply the variables to create a new set of transformed variables that are linear. Therefore the model actually used for estimation is

$$\hat{y} = b_0 + b_2 x_2 + b_1 x_1 + b_3 x_2 x_1 \qquad (11.35)$$

The resulting regression model is now linear with three variables. The new variable $x_1 x_2$ is often called an *interaction variable*. Note that when the dummy variable $x_2 = 0$ this variable has a value of 0, but when $x_2 = 1$ this variable has the value of x_1. The coefficient b_3 is an estimate of the difference in the coefficient of x_1 when $x_2 = 1$ compared to $x_2 = 0$. Thus the Student's t statistic for b_3 can be used to test the hypothesis

$$H_0: \beta_3 = 0 \mid \beta_1 \neq 0, \beta_2 \neq 0$$
$$H_1: \beta_3 \neq 0 \mid \beta_1 \neq 0, \beta_2 \neq 0$$

If we reject the null hypothesis, we conclude that there is a difference in the slope coefficient for the two subgroups. In many cases we will be interested in both the difference in the constant and difference in the slope and will test both of the hypotheses presented in this section.

EXAMPLE 11.14

SALARY MODEL FOR SYSTEMS INC. (DUMMY VARIABLE MODEL ESTIMATION)

The president of Systems Inc. is interested in knowing if the annual salary increases for the women engineers in the company has maintained the same level as those for the male engineers. There have been some complaints from both men and women engineers that the increases for women engineers has not been at the same rate.

SOLUTION

The data for the company and a scatter plot is shown in Figure 11.22. The scatter plot suggests that the slope is higher for the upper subgroup representing male engineers. In Figure 11.23 we present the multiple regression analysis from Excel that can be used to test the

FIGURE 11.22
Annual Salary Data for Systems Inc.

Gender (X2) 0=Female 1=Male	Experience times Gender	Years Experience (X1)	Annual Salary (Y)
0	0.00	5	$36,730
0	0.00	7	$40,650
0	0.00	9	$46,820
0	0.00	10	$50,149
0	0.00	14	$59,679
0	0.00	17	$67,360
1	5.00	5	$51,535
1	7.00	7	$62,289
1	9.00	9	$72,486
1	10.00	10	$75,022
1	14.00	14	$93,379
1	17.00	17	$105,979

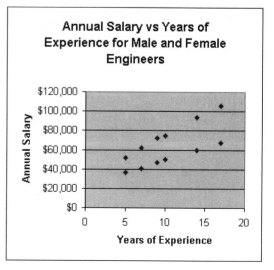

FIGURE 11.23
Regression Analysis for
Annual Salary versus
Experience and Gender

Regression Analysis

Regression Statistics	
Multiple R	0.9993
R Square	0.9985
Adjusted R Square	0.9980
Standard Error	936.4916
Observations	12

ANOVA

	df	SS	MS	F	Significance F
Regression	3	4773033949	1591011316	1814.12	0.00
Residual	8	7016132	877016		
Total	11	4780050081			

	Coefficients	Standard Error	t Stat	P-value	Lower 95%	Upper 95%
Intercept	23459.68	1043.51	22.48	0.00	21053.34	25866.02
Gender (X2) 0=Female 1=Male	7053.21	1475.75	4.78	0.00	3650.14	10456.29
Experience times Gender	1886.82	132.88	14.20	0.00	1580.39	2193.25
Years Experience (X1)	2590.79	93.96	27.57	0.00	2374.11	2807.47

b_3 b_1 b_2

**Gender and Salary
Increase**

hypothesis that the rates of increase are the same for both subgroups of engineers. From this analysis we see that the experience times gender variable has a Student's t statistic of 14.20 and a p value of 0. We reject the hypothesis that both male and female engineers have had the same rate of salary increase with increases in experience. Thus it will be important to take steps to deal with the salary discrimination that is evident in the data. The data is stored in the file **Gender and Salary Increase**.

EXERCISES

11.47 The following model was fitted to observations from 1972 to 1979, in an attempt to explain pricing behavior.

$$y = 37x_1 + 5.22x_2$$
$$\quad (.029) \quad (.50)$$

where
  y = Difference between price in the current year and price in the previous year, in dollars per barrel
  x_1 = Difference between spot price in the current year and price in the previous year
  x_2 = Dummy variable taking the value 1 in 1974 and 0 otherwise, to represent the specific effect of the oil embargo of that year

Interpret verbally and graphically the estimated coefficient on the dummy variable.

11.48 The following model was fitted, to explain the selling prices of condo, to a sample of 815 sales.

$$y = -1264 + 48.18x_1 + 3382x_2 - 1859x_3 + 3219x_4 + 2005x_5$$
$$\qquad\qquad (0.91) \quad\ (515) \quad\ (488) \quad\ (947) \quad\ (768)$$
$$\bar{R}^2 = .86$$

where
  y = Selling price of condo, in dollars
  x_1 = Square footage of living area
  x_2 = Size of garage, in number of cars
  x_3 = Age of condo, in years
  x_4 = Dummy variable taking the value 1 if the house has a fireplace, and 0 otherwise
  x_5 = Dummy variable taking the value 1 if the condo has wood floors and 0 if it has vinyl floors

(a) Interpret the estimated coefficient of x_4.
(b) Interpret the estimated coefficient of x_5.
(c) Find a 95% confidence interval for the impact of a fireplace on selling price, all other things equal.
(d) Test the null hypothesis that type of flooring has no impact on selling price, against the alternative that, all other things equal, condo with wood floors have a higher selling price than houses with vinyl flooring.

11.49 The following model was fitted to data on 32 insurance companies.

$$y = 7.62 - 0.16x_1 + 1.23x_2 \qquad R^2 = .37$$
$$\qquad\quad (.008) \qquad (.496)$$

where

y = Price-earnings ratio

x_1 = Size of insurance company assets, in billions of dollars

x_2 = Dummy variable, taking the value 1 for regional companies and 0 for national companies

(a) Interpret the estimated coefficient on the dummy variable.

(b) Test against a two-sided alternative the null hypothesis that the true coefficient on the dummy variable is 0.

(c) Test at the 5% significance level the null hypothesis $\beta_1 = \beta_2 = 0$, and interpret your result.

11.50 A business school dean wanted to assess the importance of factors that might help in predicting success in law school. For a random sample of 50 students, data were obtained when they graduated from law school, and the following model was fitted:

$$Y_i = \alpha + \beta_1 x_{1i} + \beta_2 x_{2i} + \beta_3 x_{3i} + \varepsilon_i$$

where

Y_i = Score reflecting overall performance while in law school

x_{1i} = Undergraduate grade point average

x_{2i} = Score on GMAT

x_{3i} = Dummy variable taking the value 1 if the student's letters of recommendation are unusually strong and 0 otherwise

Use the portion of the computer output from the estimated regression shown here to write a report summarizing the findings of this study.

SOURCE	DF	SUM OF SQUARES	MEAN SQUARE	F VALUE	R-SQUARE
MODEL	3	641.04	213.68	8.48	.356
ERROR	46	1159.66	25.21		
CORRECTED TOTAL	49	1800.70			

PARAMETER	ESTIMATE	T FOR H0: PARAMETER = 0	STD. ERROR OF ESTIMATE
INTERCEPT	6.512		
X1	3.502	1.45	2.419
X2	.491	4.59	.107
X3	10.327	2.45	4.213

11.51 The following model was fitted to data on 50 states.

$$y = 13{,}472 + 547x_1 + 5.48x_2 + 493x_3 + 32.7x_4 + 5{,}793x_5$$
$$\quad\quad\quad\;\;(124.3)\quad(1.858)\quad(208.9)\quad(234)\quad(2{,}897)$$
$$-\,3{,}100x_6 \quad\quad R^2 = .54$$
$$\;\;(1{,}761)$$

where

y = Annual salary of the attorney general of the state

x_1 = Average annual salary of lawyers, in thousands of dollars

x_2 = Number of bills enacted in previous legislative session

x_3 = Number of due process reviews by state courts that resulted in overturn of legislation in previous 40 years

x_4 = Length of term of the attorney general of the state

x_5 = Dummy variable, taking value 1 if justices of the state supreme court can be removed from office by the governor, judicial review board, or majority vote of the supreme court, and 0 otherwise

x_6 = Dummy variable, taking value 1 if supreme court justices are elected on partisan ballots, and 0 otherwise

(a) Interpret the estimated coefficient on the dummy variable x_5.

(b) Interpret the estimated coefficient on the dummy variable x_6.

(c) Test at the 5% level the null hypothesis that the true coefficient on the dummy variable x_5 is 0, against the alternative that it is positive.

(d) Test at the 5% level the null hypothesis that the true coefficient on the dummy variable x_6 is 0, against the alternative that it is negative.

(e) Find and interpret a 95% confidence level for the parameter β_1.

11.52 In a student survey of 27 undergraduates at the University of Illinois, the accompanying results were obtained on grade point average (y), number of hours per week spent on studying (x_1), average number of hours spent preparing for tests (x_2), number of hours per week spent in bars (x_3), whether students take notes or mark highlights when reading tests ($x_4 = 1$ if yes, 0 if no), and average number of credit hours taken per semester (x_5). Estimate the regression of grade point average using the data file on the five independent variables, and write a report on your findings. The data is in the data file **Student Performance** on your data disk.

11.53 A consulting group offers courses in financial management for executives. At the end of these courses, participants are asked to provide overall ratings of the value of the course. For a sample of 25 courses, the following regression was estimated by least squares.

$$y = 42.97 + .38x_1 + .52x_2 - .08x_3 + 6.21x_4 \quad\quad R^2 = .569$$
$$\quad\quad\;\;(.29)\quad\;(.21)\quad\;(.11)\quad\;(.359)$$

where

y = Average rating by participants of the course

x_1 = Percentage of course time spent in group discussion sessions

x_2 = Money, in dollars, per course member spent on preparing course material

x_3 = Money, in dollars, per course member spent on food and drinks

x_4 = Dummy variable, taking the value 1 if a visiting guest lecturer is brought in, and 0 otherwise

(a) Interpret the estimated coefficient on x_4.

(b) Test against the alternative that it is positive the null hypothesis that the true coefficient on x_4 is 0.

(c) Interpret the coefficient of determination, and use it to test the null hypothesis that, taken as a group, the four independent variables do not linearly influence the dependent variable.

(d) Find and interpret a 95% confidence interval for β_2.

11.54 A regression model was estimated to compare performance of students taking a business statistics course—either as a standard fourteen-week course, or as an intensive three-week course. The following model was estimated from observations on 350 students.[3]

$$y = -.7052 + 1.4170x_1 + 2.1624x_2 + .8680x_3 + 1.0845x_4$$
$$\quad\quad\quad (0.4568)\quad\quad (0.3287)\quad\quad (.4393)\quad\quad (0.3766)$$
$$+ .4694x_5 + .0038x_6 + .0484x_7 \quad\quad R^2 = .344$$
$$\quad (0.0628)\quad\quad (0.0094)\quad\quad (0.0776)$$

where

y = Score on a standardized test of understanding of statistics after taking the course

x_1 = Dummy variable taking the value 1 if the three-week course was taken, and 0 if the fourteen-week course was taken

x_2 = Student's grade point average

x_3 = Dummy variable taking the value 0 or 1, depending on which of two teachers had taught the course

x_4 = Dummy variable taking the value 1 if the student is male and 0 if female

x_5 = Score on a standardized test of understanding of mathematics before taking the course

x_6 = Number of semester credit hours the student had completed

x_7 = Age of student

Write a report discussing what can be learned from this fitted regression.

11.55 💿 You have been asked to develop a model to analyze salary in a large business organization. The data for this model is stored in a file named **Salorg** which is stored in the class account.

(a) Using the data in the file, develop a regression model which predicts salary as a function of the variables you select. Compute the conditional F and conditional t statistics for the coefficient of each predictor variable included in the model. Show all work and carefully explain your analysis process.

(b) Test the hypothesis that female employees have a lower annual salary conditional on the variables in your model. The variable "Gender_1F" is coded 1 for female employees and 0 for male employees.

(c) Test the hypothesis that the female employees have had a lower rate of salary increase conditional on the variables in the model developed for part (b).

11.56 Sharon Parsons, president of Gourmet Box Mini Pizza, has asked for your assistance in developing a model that predicts the demand for the new snack lunch pizza named Pizza1. This product competes in a market with three other brands that are named B2, B3, and B4 for identification. At present the products are sold by three major distribution chains identified as 1, 2, and 3. These three chains have a different market size, and thus sales for each distributor are likely to be different. The data file **Market** contains weekly data collected over the past 52 weeks from the three distribution chains. The variables in the data file are defined below.

You are to use multiple regression to develop a model that predicts the quantity of Pizza1 sold per week by each distributor. The model should contain only important predictor variables.

Distributor	Numerical identifier of the distributor 1, 2, 3
Weeknum	Sequential number of the week in which data was collected
Sales Pizza1	Number of units of Pizza1 sold during the week by the distributor
Price Pizza1	Retail price for Pizza1 during that week by the distributor
Promotion	Level of promotion for the week designated as 0, 1, 2, or 3
	0 No promotion 1 Television ad, 2 Store display 3 Both television and store display
Sales B2	Number of units of brand 2 sold during the week by the distributor
Price B2	Retail price for brand 2 during that week by the distributor
Sales B3	Number of units of brand 3 sold during the week by the distributor
Price B3	Retail price for brand 3 during that week by the distributor
Sales B4	Number of units of brand 4 sold during the week by the distributor
Price B4	Retail price of brand 4 during that week by the distributor

---

[3] L.J. Van Scyoc and J. Gleason, "Traditional or intensive course lengths? A comparison of outcomes in economics learning," *Journal of Economic Education*, 24 (1993), 15-22.

11.9   MULTIPLE REGRESSION ANALYSIS APPLICATION PROCEDURE

Cotton

In this section we will present an extended case study that indicates how a statistical study would be conducted. Careful study of this example can provide guidance in using many of the analysis procedures developed in this chapter and previous chapters.

The objective in this study is to produce a multiple regression model to predict sales of cotton fabric. Data for the project is obtained from the data file **Cotton** that is included on the data disk for this textbook. The variables in the data file are,

Quarter	Quarter of year
Year	Year of observation
Cottonq	Quantity of Cotton Fabric Produced
Whopri	Wholesale Price Index
Impfab	Quantity of Imported Fabric
Expfab	Quantity of Exported Fabric

Model Specification

The first step in model development is an examination of appropriate economic theory that provides a rationale for the model analysis. This process of identifying a set of likely predictor variables and the mathematical form of the model is known as "Model Specification." In this case the appropriate theory is based on that of economic demand models. Economic theory indicates that price should have an important effect—increased price reduces the quantity demanded. In addition there are likely to be other variables that influence the quantity of cotton demanded. We would anticipate that the quantity of cotton fabric imported is likely to reduce the demand for domestic fabric and the quantity of cotton fabric exported is likely to increase the demand for domestic fabric. In economic language, imports and exports of fabric shift the demand function. Based on this analysis our original specification would include price with a negative coefficient, exported fabric with a positive coefficient, and imported fabric with a negative coefficient. All coefficients will be initially specified as having linear effects. The model would have the form

$$Y_i = \beta_0 + \beta_1 x_{1i} + \beta_2 x_{2i} + \beta_3 x_{3i} + \varepsilon_i$$

where, x_1 is the wholesale price, x_2 is the quantity of imported fabric, and x_3 is the quantity of exported fabric.

There is also the possibility that the quantity demanded varies over time, and thus the model should include the possibility of a time variable to reduce unexplained variability. For this analysis we wish to use a variable which represents time, but time is indicated by a combination of year and quarter. Using the transformation option in Minitab we will create a continuous time variable. Use the command sequence

```
CALC > CALCULATOR
```

Then enter the transformation

```
TIME = YEAR + 0.25* QUARTER
```

in the display box. This will produce a new variable for time that is continuously increasing.

The first task in the analysis will be to prepare a statistical description of the variables and their relationships. We will exclude year and quarter from this analysis because they have been replaced by time and their inclusion would only add confusion to the analysis.

FIGURE 11.24
Minitab Output for
Descriptive Statistics for
Cotton Market Variables

Variable	N	Mean	Median	TrMean	StDev	SE Mean
cottonq	28	1779.8	1762.5	1779.6	290.5	54.9
whoprice	28	106.81	107.40	106.81	6.11	1.16
impfab	28	7.52	4.85	7.02	7.33	1.38
expfab	28	274.0	277.1	273.7	107.7	20.3
Time	28	69.625	69.625	69.625	2.056	0.389

Variable	Minimum	Maximum	Q1	Q3
cottonq	1277.0	2287.0	1535.2	2035.0
whoprice	98.00	115.80	100.45	112.20
impfab	1.30	27.00	2.78	9.05
expfab	80.0	477.0	190.5	358.1
Time	66.250	73.000	67.812	71.438

We will use the "Descriptive Statistics" option in Minitab to produce measures of central tendency and dispersion and also obtain some understanding of the pattern of the observations. Descriptive statistics as shown in Figure 11.24 are prepared in Minitab by using the command sequence

    STAT > BASIC STATISTICS > DISPLAY DESCRIPTIVE STATISTICS

Examination of the mean, standard deviation, and the minimum and maximum indicate the potential application region for the model. The estimated regression model always passes through the mean of the model variables. Predicted values of the dependent variable, cottonq, are useable over the range of the independent variables.

The next step is to examine the simple relationships between the variables, using both the correlation matrix and the matrix plots option. These should be examined together to determine the strength of the linear relationships (correlations) and to determine the form of the relationships (matrix plot)

    STAT > BASIC STATISTICS > CORRELATION

Figure 11.25 contains the Minitab correlation matrix for the variables in the study.

The p-value shown with each correlation indicates the probability that the hypothesis of zero correlation between the two variables is true. Using our screening rule based on hypothesis testing we could conclude that a p-value less than 0.05 provides evidence for a strong linear relationship between the two variables. Examining the first column we see that there are strong linear relationships between Cottonq and both whoprice and time. The variable expfab has a possible marginally significant simple relationship. A good rule of thumb, as shown in Section 10.1, for examining correlation coefficients is that the absolute value of the correlation should be greater than 2 divided by the square root of the sample size, n. For this problem the screening value is $2\sqrt{28} = 0.38$.

The second task is to determine if there are strong simple relationships between the pairs of possible predictor variables. We see a very high correlation between time and whoprice and significant relationships between impfab and both time and whoprice. Thus there is a possible multicolinearity problem if both time and whoprice are included as predictor variables.

FIGURE 11.25
Minitab Output: Correlations
for Cotton Variables

```
Correlations (Pearson)

               Cottonq       whoprice      impfab        expfab
whoprice       -0.950
               0.000

impfab          0.291        -0.439
                0.133         0.019

expfab          0.370        -0.285        0.181
                0.052         0.142        0.357

Time           -0.950         0.992       -0.392        0.238
0.238
                0.000         0.000        0.039        0.222

Cell Contents: Correlation
               P-Value
```

We can also examine the relationships between variables by using Minitab to generate matrix plots shown in Figure 11.26. These scatter plots show the relationships between a number of different variables simultaneously. Thus they provide a display format that is similar to a correlation matrix. The advantage of the scatter plot is that it includes all of the data points. Thus one can also see if there is a simple nonlinear relationship between variables or if there is some strange grouping of observations, in addition to determining if there is a linear correlation between the variables. All variables except year and quarter were included in the same order as the correlation matrix. This provides a direct comparison between the correlations and the scatter plots. Matrix plots can be generated in Minitab using the command sequence

```
GRAPH > MATRIX PLOTS > OPTIONS > MATRIX DISPLAY > LOWER LEFT
```

Note the correspondence between the correlations and the scatter plots. Both whoprice and time have strong negative linear relationships with cottonq. However the strong positive linear relationship between whoprice and time will have a major influence on the estimated coefficients as shown in Section 11.2 and on the coefficient standard errors as shown in Section 11.4. There are no other strong simple relationships between the potential predictor variables. Neither imports nor exports are correlated with wholesale price, time, or each other.

Multiple Regression

The next step is to estimate the first multiple regression model. The economic theory for this analysis suggests that the quantity of cotton fabric produced should be inversely related to price and to the amount of fabric imported and directly related to the amount of fabric exported. In addition the strong correlation between time and cotton fabric production indicates that production declined linearly over time, but wholesale price also increased linearly over time. The resulting very high negative correlation between time and wholesale price influences both coefficients in a multiple regression equation. We selected cottonq as the dependent variable and the selected independent variables were whoprice, impfab, expfab, and time, in that order. The first multiple regression model shown in Figure 11.27 was computed by Minitab. The command to initiate the regression was

```
STAT > REGRESSION > REGRESSION
```

Analysis of the regression statistics indicates a high R-squared, and the standard error of the estimate (S) equals 78.91 compared to the standard deviation of 290.5 for cottonq by itself. The variables, impfab and expfab are both conditionally significant with signs corre-

FIGURE 11.26
Matrix Plots for Variables in the Study

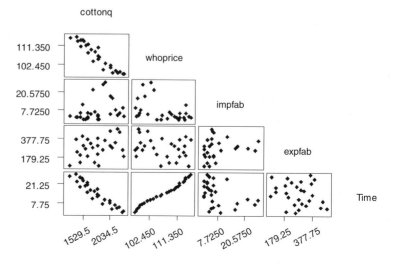

FIGURE 11.27
Minitab Output: Initial
Multiple Regression Model

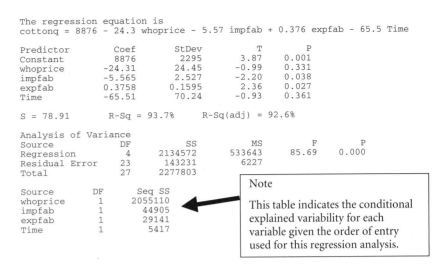

```
The regression equation is
cottonq = 8876 - 24.3 whoprice - 5.57 impfab + 0.376 expfab - 65.5 Time

Predictor        Coef       StDev         T         P
Constant         8876        2295      3.87     0.001
whoprice       -24.31       24.45     -0.99     0.331
impfab         -5.565       2.527     -2.20     0.038
expfab         0.3758      0.1595      2.36     0.027
Time           -65.51       70.24     -0.93     0.361

S = 78.91       R-Sq = 93.7%     R-Sq(adj) = 92.6%

Analysis of Variance
Source          DF          SS         MS         F        P
Regression       4     2134572     533643     85.69    0.000
Residual Error  23      143231       6227
Total           27     2277803

Source      DF     Seq SS
whoprice     1    2055110
impfab       1      44905
expfab       1      29141
Time         1       5417
```

Note

This table indicates the conditional explained variability for each variable given the order of entry used for this regression analysis.

sponding to economic theory. The small Student's *t* statistics for both whoprice and time indicate that in fact there is a serious problem. Both variables cannot be included as predictors because they both represent the same effect. The rules for dropping variables are based on a combination of both theories for the model and statistical indicators. The statistical rule would be to drop the variable with the smallest absolute Student's *t*, that is time. Economic theory would argue for including a price variable in a model to predict quantity produced or quantity demanded. We see that in this case both rules lead to the same conclusion. This will not always be the case, and thus good judgment and clear thinking about model objectives are very important. We emphasize that it is important that one clearly state the rationale for variable selection before examining the statistical output. In economic demand or supply models such as the one considered here we would have a very strong desire to follow economic theory and include price, unless the statistical results were very strong against that prior judgment. For example if the absolute value of the Student's *t* for time was above 2.5 or 3 and the absolute value of the Student's *t* for wholesale price was less than 1 there would be strong evidence against the theory that price is an important variable. Based on this analysis we estimated a second regression model, shown in Figure 11.28, with time excluded as a predictor variable.

FIGURE 11.28
Minitab Output: Final
Regression Analysis Model

```
The regression equation is
cottonq = 6757 - 47.0 whoprice - 6.52 impfab + 0.319 expfab

Predictor        Coef       StDev         T         P
Constant       6757.0       322.2     20.97     0.000
whoprice      -46.956       2.835    -16.56     0.000
impfab         -6.517       2.306     -2.83     0.009
expfab         0.3190      0.1471      2.17     0.040

S = 78.70       R-Sq = 93.5%     R-Sq(adj) = 92.7%

Analysis of Variance
Source          DF          SS         MS         F        P
Regression       3     2129156     709719    114.59    0.000
Residual Error  24      148648       6194
Total           27     2277803

Source      DF     Seq SS
whoprice     1    2055110
impfab       1      44905
expfab       1      29141
```

Note

This sequential conditional explained sums of squares are the same as those for the regression in Figure 11.27, that included time as a predictor variable

```
Unusual Observations
Obs    whoprice    cottonq      Fit   StDev Fit   Residual   St Resid
 18         110     1810.0    1642.0       18.7      168.0      2.20R
R denotes an observation with a large standardized residual
```

INTERPRETATION

We see that whoprice is now highly significant and that the S and R-Sq statistics are essentially the same as those in the first regression analysis (Figure 11.27). Note also that the explained regression sum of squares (SSR) and the residual error sum of squares (SSE) are essentially the same. The standard deviation for the whoprice coefficient has dropped from 24.44 to 2.834, and as a result the Student's t is substantially larger. As we saw in Section 11.4, high correlations between independent variables result in much larger variances for the coefficient estimator. We see that effect here. Note also that for this regression model the wholesale price coefficient estimate changed from -24.20 to -46.948. In Section 11.2 we saw that correlations between predictor variables have a complex effect on coefficient estimates and so there will not always be a difference that is this large. However, correlations between independent variables always increases the coefficient standard error. The standard errors for the other two coefficients have not changed substantially because the correlations with time were not large.

Minitab also provides a list of observations with extreme residuals. We see in Observation 18 that the observed value of cottonq is substantially above the value predicted by the equation. In this case we might decide to go back to the original data and try to determine if there was an error in the reported data. Such an investigation might also provide some important insights into the process being studied using multiple regression.

Effect of Dropping a Statistically Significant Variable from a Regression Model

In this section we will consider the effect of removing a conditionally significant variable from the regression model. The regression analysis in Figure 11.29 has expfab removed from the regression model in Figure 11.28. We saw in Figure 11.28 that expfab was a statistically significant predictor of the quantity of cotton produced.

Note that as a result of removing expfab the standard error of the estimate increased from 78.65 to 84.33 and the R-Sq decreased from 93.5% to 92.2%. These results indicate that model error term is now larger and thus that the quality of the model has been reduced.

INTERPRETATION

The conditional F statistics for expfab can be computed using the analysis of variance tables from the models in Figures 11.28 and 11.29. In the following equation we define the final regression from Figure 11.28 as Model 1 and the regression from Figure 11.29, with expfab removed, as Model 2. Using these conventions, the conditional F statistic for the variable expfab, X_3, under the null hypothesis that its coefficient is 0, can be computed as follows

$$F_{x_3} = \frac{SSR_1 - SSR_2}{S_e^2} = \frac{(2{,}129{,}156 - 2{,}100{,}015)}{6{,}194} = 4.705$$

FIGURE 11.29
Minitab Output: Regression
Analysis with Exported Fabric
Eliminated

```
The regression equation is
cottonq = 6995 - 48.4 whoprice - 6.20 impfab

Predictor        Coef       StDev          T          P
Constant       6994.8       324.6      21.55      0.000
whoprice      -48.388       2.955     -16.38      0.000
impfab         -6.195       2.465      -2.51      0.019

S = 84.33      R-Sq = 92.2%      R-Sq(adj) = 91.6%

Analysis of Variance
Source            DF          SS         MS         F         P
Regression         2     2100015    1050007    147.65     0.000
Residual Error    25      177788       7112
Total             27     2277803
```

We can also compute the conditional Student's t statistic for variable x_3 by taking the square root of the conditional F_{x_3}

$$t_{x_3} = \sqrt{4.705} = 2.169$$

and of course we see that this is the same as the Student's t statistic for the expfab (x_3) variable in Figure 11.27. The conditional F test for a single independent variable is always exactly the same as the conditional F because an F with one degree of freedom for the numerator is exactly equal to t^2.

Analysis of Residuals

After fitting the regression model it is valuable to examine the residuals to determine how the model actually fits the data and the regression assumptions. Recall that the residuals are computed as

$$\hat{e}_i = y_i - \hat{y}_i$$

A variable that contains the residuals for a particular regression analysis can be computed in Minitab by using the command

```
REGRESSION > REGRESSION > STORAGE
```

and then checking the box that indicates residuals are to be saved as a new variable. This was done for the final regression model in Figure 11.28. In the following analysis we will use the variable named 'resl1' that contains the residuals from the final regression model. The first step was to examine the pattern of the residuals by constructing a histogram using the Minitab command

```
GRAPH > HISTOGRAM
```

Using this command the histogram of the residuals was prepared as shown in Figure 11.30. We see that the distribution of the residuals is approximately symmetric. The distribution also appears to be somewhat uniform over its range. Note that this in part results from the small sample size used to construct the histogram.

Another useful analysis to determine the pattern of the residuals is to prepare a normal probability plot as shown in Figure 11.31. The plot indicates an approximate linear relationship, and thus it is not possible to reject the assumption of normally distributed residuals.

It is also a good practice to plot the residuals against each of the independent variables that were included in the analysis. This provides a check that there were not a few unusual

FIGURE 11.30
Histogram for Residuals from Final Regression Model

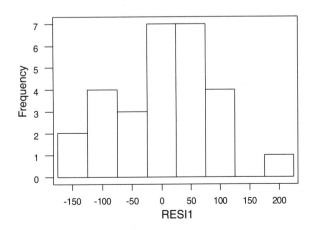

FIGURE 11.31
Normal Probability Plot for
Model Residuals

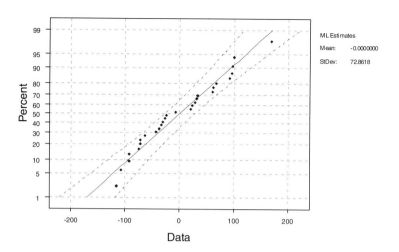

data points or a complex conditional nonlinear relationship for one of the independent variables. If the model has been correctly specified and estimated we would expect that there would be no pattern of relationship between the independent variables and the residuals. One efficient way to produce residual plots is to use the "draftsmen plot" option under graphics, such as shown in Figure 11.32. Generally preparing two plots at a time is recommended. This places two plots side by side. With more than two the horizontal scale becomes too small and relationships might be hard to detect. In some cases you might wish to consider preparing only one graph at a time in order to spread independent variable effects over a wider range. To obtain the draftsman plot in Minitab use the command sequence

```
GRAPH > DRAFTSMEN PLOT > SELECT RESI1 AND THEN WHOPRICE,
TIME
```

Based on an examination of these plots we see that there is no indication of a relationship between the residuals and either wholesale price or time.

FIGURE 11.32
Draftsmen Plot: Residuals
Versus Wholesale Price and
Time

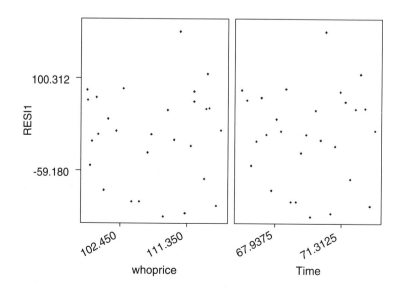

FIGURE 11.33
Draftsmen Plot: Residuals versus Exported Fabric and Imported Fabric

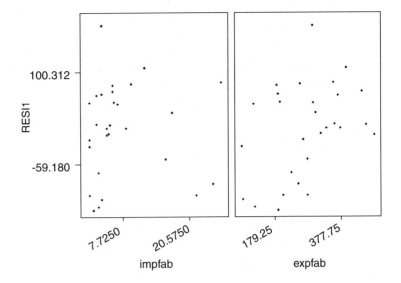

A second draftsmen plot showing the relationship between the residuals and exported fabric and imported fabric is shown in Figure 11.33. From our examination of these plots we see that there is no indication of a relationship between the residuals and either imported fabric or exported fabric.

INTERPRETATION

The final residuals analysis will examine the relationship between the residuals and the dependent variable. We will consider a plot of the residuals versus the observed value of the dependent variable (Figure 11.34) and versus the predicted value of the dependent variable (Figure 11.35). We can see that—Figure 11.34—there is a positive relationship between the residuals and the observed value of cottonq. There are more negative residuals at low values of cottonq and more positive residuals at high values of cottonq. It is possible to show mathematically that there is always a positive correlation between the residuals and the observed values of the dependent variable. Therefore a plot of the residuals versus the observed value does not provide any useful information. However, one should always plot the residuals versus the predicted or fitted values of the dependent variable. This will provide a way to determine if the model errors are stable over the range of predicted values. In this example, note that there is not a relationship between the residuals and the predicted values. Thus the model errors are stable over the range.

FIGURE 11.34
Residuals versus Observed Cotton Production

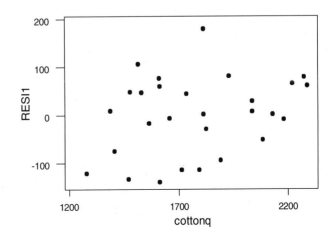

FIGURE 11.35
Residuals versus Predicted
Cotton Production

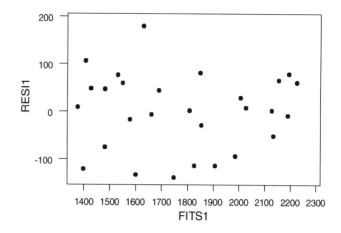

EXERCISES

11.57 In order to assess the effect in a state of casualty insurance company's economic power on their political power, the following model was hypothesized and fitted to data from all 50 states.

$$Y = \beta_0 + \beta_1 x_1 + \beta_2 x_2 + \beta_3 x_3 + \beta_4 x_4 + \beta_5 x_5 + \varepsilon$$

where

Y = Ratio of company's provisions for state and local taxes (in thousands of dollars) to total state and local tax revenues (in millions of dollars)

x_1 = Insurance company state concentration ratio (a measure of the concentration of banking resources)

x_2 = Per capita income in the state (in thousands of dollars)

x_3 = Ratio of nonfarm income to the sum of farm and nonfarm income

x_4 = Ratio of insurance company's net after-tax income to insurance reserves (multiplied by 1,000)

x_5 = Average of insurance reserves (divided by 10,000)

Part of the computer output from the estimated regression is shown here. Write a report summarizing the findings of this study.

R-SQUARE = 0.515

PARAMETER	ESTIMATE	STUDENT'S t FOR HO: PARAMETER = 0	STD. ERROR OF ESTIMATE
INTERCEPT	10.60	2.41	4.40
X1	−.90	−.69	1.31
X2	.14	.50	.28
X3	−11.85	−2.83	4.18
X4	.080	.50	.160
X5	.100	5.00	.020

11.58 The subjects of a random sample of 93 freshmen at the University of Illinois were asked to rate on a scale from 1 (low) to 10 (high) their overall opinion of residence hall life. They were also asked to rate their levels of satisfaction with roommates, with the floor, with the hall, and with the resident adviser. (Information on satisfaction with the room itself was obtained, but this was later discarded as it provided no useful additional power in explaining overall opinion.) The following model was estimated:

where

$$Y = \beta_0 + \beta_1 x_1 + \beta_2 x_2 + \beta_3 x_3 + \beta_4 x_4 + \varepsilon$$

Y = Overall opinion of residence hall

x_1 = Satisfaction with roommates

x_2 = Satisfaction with floor

x_3 = Satisfaction with hall

x_4 = Satisfaction with resident adviser

Use the accompanying portion of the computer output from the estimated regression to write a report summarizing the findings of this study.

DEPENDENT VARIABLE: Y OVERALL OPINION

SOURCE	DF	SUM OF SQUARES	MEAN SQUARE	F VALUE	R-SQUARE
MODEL	4	37.016	9.2540	9.958	.312
ERROR	88	81.780	.9293		
TOTAL	92	118.79			

PARAMETER	ESTIMATE	STUDENT'S t FOR HO: PARAMETER = 0	STD. ERROR OF ESTIMATE
INTERCEPT	3.950	5.84	.676
X1	.106	1.69	.063
X2	.122	1.70	.072
X3	.092	1.75	.053
X4	.169	2.64	.064

11.59 The following model was fitted to 47 monthly observations in an attempt to explain the difference between certificate of deposit rates and commercial paper rates:

$$Y = \beta_0 + \beta_1 x_1 + \beta_2 x_2 + \varepsilon$$

where

Y = Commercial paper certificate of deposit rate less commercial paper rate

x_1 = Commercial paper rate

x_2 = Ratio of loans and investments to capital

Use the part of the computer output from the estimated regression shown here to write a report summarizing the findings of this analysis.

R-SQUARE = 0.730

PARAMETER	ESTIMATE	STUDENT'S t FOR HO: PARAMETER = 0	STD. ERROR OF ESTIMATE
INTERCEPT	−5.559	−4.14	1.343
X1	.186	5.64	.033
X2	.450	2.08	.216

11.60 You have been asked to develop a multiple regression model to predict annual number of traffic death rates in the United States as a function of total miles traveled and average travel speed. The data file **Traffic Death Rate** contains 10 years of annual data on death rates per 100 million vehicle miles (y), total travel in billion vehicle miles (x_1), and the average speed in miles per hour of all vehicles (x_2). Compute the multiple regression of y on x_1 and x_2, and write a report discussing your findings.

11.61 The data file **Household Income** contains data for 50 states in the United States. The variables included in the data file are percentage of females that are in the labor force (y), median household personal income (x_1), mean years of education completed by females (x_2), and the unemployment rate of women (x_3). Compute the multiple regression of y on x_1, x_2, and x_3, and write a report on your findings.

11.62 You have been asked to develop a multiple regression model that predicts real money supply in Germany as a function of income and interest rate. The data file **Real Money** contains 12 annual observations on real money per capita (y), real income per capita (x_1), and interest rates (x_2) in Germany. Use this data to develop a model that predicts per capita real money as a function of per capita income and interest rate, and write a report on your findings.

11.63 The United Nations has hired you as a consultant to help identify factors that predict manufacturing growth in developing countries. You have decided to use multiple regression to develop a model and identify important variables that predict growth. You have collected the data in the data file **Developing Country** from 48 countries. The variables included are percentage manufacturing growth (y), percentage agricultural growth (x_1), percentage exports growth (x_2), and percentage rate of inflation (x_3) in 48 developing countries. Develop the multiple regression model and write a report on your findings.

SUMMARY

In this chapter we have developed the necessary background for understanding and applying multiple regression procedures. This work began with a detailed discussion of the model assumptions and the implications of those assumptions. From this we presented the least squares procedure and the methods for obtaining coefficient estimates. With that background we developed procedures for determining how well the regression model fits the observed data. This in turn led to developing classical inference procedures for testing hypotheses about the coefficients and for constructing confidence intervals. Then we were led to methods for obtaining predictions of the dependent variable from the model and inferences concerning the predicted values.

With this background and understanding of the basic model we proceeded to examine some important application techniques. We developed procedures for transforming quadratic models into linear functions. Transformations were also developed for log linear models. Finally, we began the development of procedures for using dummy variables to represent categorical predictor variables. The chapter ends with an extended application model that shows how an analyst would carry out the entire process of regression model development. This process begins with simple descriptive statistics and graphical techniques, application of regression procedures, and ends with residuals analysis to examine model compatibility with the data and model assumptions.

KEY WORDS

CHAPTER EXERCISES AND APPLICATIONS

11.64 The method of least squares is used far more often than any alternative procedure to estimate the parameters of a multiple regression model. Explain the basis for this method of estimation, and discuss why its use is so widespread.

11.65 It is common practice to compute an analysis of variance table in conjunction with an estimated multiple regression. Carefully explain what can be learned from such a table.

11.66 State whether each of the following statements is true or false.
(a) The error sum of squares must be smaller than the regression sum of squares.
(b) Instead of carrying out a multiple regression, we can get the same information from simple linear regressions of the dependent variable on each independent variable.
(c) The coefficient of determination cannot be negative.
(d) The adjusted coefficient of determination cannot be negative.
(e) The coefficient of multiple correlation is the square root of the coefficient of determination.

11.67 If an additional independent variable, however irrelevant, is added to a multiple regression model, a smaller sum of squared errors will result. Explain why this is so, and discuss the consequences for the interpretation of the coefficient of determination.

11.68 A dependent is regressed on two independent variables. It is possible that the hypothesis $H_0: \beta_1 = 0$ and $H_0: \beta_2 = 0$ cannot be rejected at low significance levels, yet the hypothesis $H_0: \beta_1 = \beta_2 = 0$ can be rejected at a very low significance level. In what circumstances might this result arise?

11.69 [*This exercise requires the material in the Chapter Appendix.*] Suppose that the regression model

$$Y_1 = \beta_0 + \beta_1 x_{1i} + \beta_2 x_{2i} + \varepsilon_i$$

is estimated by least squares. Show that the residuals, e_i, from the fitted model sum to 0.

11.70 A study was conducted to assess the influence of various factors on the start of new firms in the computer chip industry. For a sample of 70 countries, the following model was estimated:

$$y = -59.31 + 4.983x_1 + 2.198x_2 + 3.816x_3 - .310x_4$$
$$ {}_{(1.156)} \quad\quad {}_{(.210)} \quad\quad {}_{(2.063)} \quad\quad {}_{(.330)}$$
$$-.886x_5 + 3.215x_6 + .085x_7 \quad R^2 = .766$$
$${}_{(3.055)} \quad\quad {}_{(1.568)} \quad\quad {}_{(.354)}$$

where

y = New business starts in the industry
x_1 = Population in millions
x_2 = Industry size
x_3 = Measure of economic quality of life
x_4 = Measure of political quality of life
x_5 = Measure of environmental quality of life
x_6 = Measure of health and educational quality of life
x_7 = Measure of social quality of life

The figures in parentheses beneath the coefficient estimates are their estimated standard errors.
(a) Interpret the estimated partial regression coefficients.
(b) Interpret the coefficient of determination.
(c) Find a 90% confidence interval for the increase in new business starts resulting from a 1-unit increase in the economic quality of life, with all other variables unchanged.
(d) Test against a two-sided alternative at the 5% significance level the null hypothesis that, all else remaining equal, the environmental quality of life does not influence new business starts.
(e) Test against a two-sided alternative at the 5% significance level the null hypothesis that, all else remaining equal, the health and educational quality of life does not influence new business starts.
(f) Test the null hypothesis that taken together, these seven independent variables do not influence new business starts.

11.71 A survey research group conducts regular studies of households through mail questionnaires and is concerned about the factors influencing the response rate. In an experiment, 30 sets of questionnaires were mailed to potential respondents. The regression model fitted to the resulting data set was

$$Y = \beta_0 + \beta_1 x_1 + \beta_2 x_2 + \varepsilon$$

where

Y = Percentage of responses received

x_1 = Number of questions asked

x_2 = Length of questionnaire, in number of words

Part of the SAS computer output from the estimate regression is shown here.

PARAMETER	ESTIMATE	STUDENT'S t FOR HO: PARAMETER = 0	STD. ERROR OF ESTIMATE
INTERCEPT	74.3652		
X1	−1.8345	−2.89	.6349
X2	−.0162	−1.78	.0091

R-SQUARE = 0.637

(a) Interpret the estimated partial regression coefficients.
(b) Interpret the coefficient of determination.
(c) Test at the 1% significance level the null hypothesis that, taken together, the two independent variables do not linearly influence the response rate.
(d) Find and interpret a 99% confidence interval for β_1.
(e) Test the null hypothesis

$$H_0: \beta_2 = 0$$

against the alternative

$$H_1: \beta_2 < 0$$

and interpret your findings

11.72 A consulting group offers courses in financial management for executives. At the end of these courses, participants are asked to provide overall ratings of the value of the course. To assess the impact of various factors on ratings, the model

$$Y = \beta_0 + \beta_1 x_1 + \beta_2 x_2 + \beta_3 x_3 + \varepsilon$$

was fitted for 25 such courses, where

Y = Average rating by participants of the course

x_1 = Percentage of course time spent in group discussion sessions

x_2 = Amount of money (in dollars) per course member spent on the preparation subject matter material

x_3 = Amount of money per course member spent on the provision of non-course-related material (food, drinks, and so forth.)

Part of the SAS computer output for the fitted regression is shown here.

PARAMETER	ESTIMATE	T FOR HO: PARAMETER = 0	STD. ERROR OF ESTIMATE
INTERCEPT	42.9712		
X1	.3817	1.89	.2018
X2	.5172	2.64	.1957
X3	.0753	1.09	.0693

R-SQUARE = .579

(a) Interpret the estimated partial regression coefficients.
(b) Interpret the coefficient of determination.
(c) Test at the 5% level the null hypothesis that taken together, the three independent variables do not linearly influence the course rating.
(d) Find and interpret a 90% confidence interval for β_1.
(e) Test the null hypothesis

$$H_0: \beta_2 = 0$$

against the alternative

$$H_1: \beta_2 > 0$$

and interpret your result.
(f) Test at the 10% significance level the null hypothesis

$$H_0: \beta_3 = 0$$

against the alternative

$$H_1: \beta_3 \neq 0$$

and interpret your result.

11.73 At the end of classes, professors are rated by their students on a scale from 1 (poor) to 5 (excellent). Students are also asked what course grades they expect, and these are coded as A = 4, B = 3, and so on. The data file **Teacher Rating** contains, for a random sample of 20 classes, ratings of professors, average expected grades, and the numbers of students in the classes. Compute the multiple regression of rating on expected grade and number of students, and write a report on your findings.

11.74 Flyer Computer Inc. wishes to know the effect of various variables on labor efficiency. Based on a sample of 64 observations, the following model was estimated by least squares:

$$y = -16.528 + 28.729x_1 + .022x_2 - .023x_3 - .054x_4$$
$$- .077x_5 + .411x_6 + .349x_7 + .028x_8 \quad R^2 = .467$$

where

y = Index of direct labor efficiency in production plant

x_1 = Ratio of overtime hours to straight-time hours worked by all production workers

x_2 = Average number of hourly workers in the plant

x_3 = Percentage of employees involved in some quality-of-worklife program

x_4 = Number of grievances filed per 100 workers

x_5 = Disciplinary action rate

x_6 = Absenteeism rate for hourly workers

x_7 = Salaried workers' attitudes, from low (dissatisfied) to high, as measured by questionnaire

x_8 = Percentage of hourly employees submitting at least one suggestion in a year to the plant's suggestion program

Also obtained by least squares from these data was the fitted model

$$y = 9.062 - 10.944x_1 - .320x_2 + .019x_3 \qquad R^2 = .242$$

The variables x_4, x_5, x_6, x_7, x_8 are measures of the performance of a plant's industrial relations system. Test at the 1% level the null hypothesis that they do not contribute to explaining direct labor efficiency, given that x_1, x_2, x_3 are also to be used.

11.75 Based on 107 students' scores on the first examination in a course on business statistics, the following model was estimated by least squares:

$$y = 2.178 + .469x_1 + 3.369x_2 + 3.054x_3 \qquad R^2 = .686$$
$${\scriptstyle(.090)}{\scriptstyle(.456)}{\scriptstyle(1.457)}$$

where

y = Student's actual score on the examination

x_1 = Student's expected score on the examination

x_2 = Hours per week spent working on the course

x_3 = Student's grade point average

(a) Interpret the estimate of β_1.
(b) Find and interpret a 95% confidence interval for β_2.
(c) Test against a two-sided alternative the null hypothesis that β_3 is 0, and interpret your result.
(d) Interpret the coefficient of determination.
(e) Test the null hypothesis $\beta_1 = \beta_2 = \beta_3 = 0$.
(f) Find and interpret the coefficient of multiple correlation.
(g) Predict the score of a student who expects a score of 80, works 8 hours per week on the course, and has a grade point average of 3.0.

11.76 Based on 25 years of annual data, an attempt was made to explain savings in India. The model fitted was

$$Y = \beta_0 + \beta_1 x_{1i} + \beta_2 x_{2i} + \varepsilon_i$$

where

Y = Change in real deposit rate

x_1 = Change in real per capita income

x_2 = Change in real interest rate

The least squares parameter estimates (with standard errors in parentheses) were (reference 1)

$$b_1 = .0974(.0215) \qquad b_2 = .374(.209)$$

The corrected coefficient of determination was

$$\overline{R}^2 = .91$$

(a) Find and interpret a 99% confidence interval for β_1.
(b) Test against the alternative that it is positive the null hypothesis that β_2 is 0.
(c) Find the coefficient of determination.
(d) Test the null hypothesis $\beta_1 = \beta_2 = 0$.
(e) Find and interpret the coefficient of multiple correlation.

11.77 Based on data on 2,679 high school basketball players, the following model was fitted:

$$Y_i = \beta_0 + \beta_1 x_{1i} + \beta_2 x_{2i} + \cdots + \beta_9 x_{9i} + \varepsilon_i$$

where

Y = Minutes played in season

x_1 = Field goal percentage

x_2 = Free throw percentage

x_3 = Rebounds per minute

x_4 = Points per minute

x_5 = Fouls per minute

x_6 = Steals per minute

x_7 = Blocked shots per minute

x_8 = Turnovers per minute

x_9 = Assists per minute

The least squares parameter estimates (with standard errors in parentheses) were:

$b_0 = 358.848\ (44.695)$ $b_1 = .6742\ (.0639)$ $b_2 = .2855\ (.0388)$
$b_3 = 303.81\ (77.73)$ $b_4 = 504.95\ (43.26)$ $b_5 = -3923.5\ (120.6)$
$b_6 = 480.04\ (224.9)$ $b_7 = 1350.3\ (212.3)$ $b_8 = -891.67\ (180.87)$
$b_9 = 722.95\ (110.98)$

The coefficient of determination was

$$R^2 = .5239$$

(a) Find and interpret a 90% confidence interval for β_6.
(b) Find and interpret a 99% confidence interval for β_7.
(c) Test against the alternative that it is negative the null hypothesis that β_8 is 0. Interpret your result.
(d) Test against the alternative that it is positive the null hypothesis that β_9 is 0. Interpret your result.
(e) Interpret the coefficient of determination.
(f) Find and interpret the coefficient of multiple correlation.

11.78 Based on data from 63 counties, the following model was estimated by least squares:

$$y = .058 - .052x_1 - .005x_2 \qquad R^2 = .17$$
$$(.019) (.042)$$

where

$\quad y$ = Growth rate in real gross domestic product

$\quad x_1$ = Real income per capita

$\quad x_2$ = Average tax rate, as a proportion of gross national product

(a) Test against a two-sided alternative the null hypothesis that β_1 is 0. Interpret your result.

(b) Test against a two-sided alternative the null hypothesis that β_2 is 0. Interpret your result.

(c) Interpret the coefficient of determination.

(d) Find and interpret the coefficient of multiple correlation.

11.79 The following regression model was fitted to data on 60 U.S. female amateur golfers:

$$y = 164{,}683 + 341.10x_1 + 170.02x_2 + 495.19x_3 - 4.23x_4$$
$$\phantom{y = 164{,}683 +}(100.59) (167.18) (305.48) (90.0)$$
$$- 136{,}040x_5 - 35{,}549x_6 + 202.52x_7$$
$$(25{,}634) (16{,}240) (106.20)$$

$$\overline{R}^2 = .516$$

where figures in brackets are estimated standard errors and

$\quad y$ = Winnings per tournament, in dollars

$\quad x_1$ = Average length of drive, in yards

$\quad x_2$ = Percentage times drive ends in fairway

$\quad x_3$ = Percentage times green reached in regulation

$\quad x_4$ = Percentage times par saved after hitting into sandtrap

$\quad x_5$ = Average number of putts taken on greens reached in regulation

$\quad x_6$ = Average number of putts taken on greens not reached in regulation

$\quad x_7$ = Number of years golfer has played

Write a report summarizing what can be learned from these results.

11.80 The economics department wishes to develop a multiple regression model to predict student GPA for economics courses. They have collected data for 112 graduates, which includes the variables economics GPA, SAT verbal, SAT mathematics, ACT English, ACT social science, and high school percentile rank. The data are stored in a file named **Student GPA** on your data disk. The appendix contains a description of the variables.

(a) Use the SAT variables and class rank to determine the best prediction model. Remove any independent variables that are not significant. What are the coefficients, their Student's t statistics, and the model?

(b) Use the ACT variables and class rank to determine the best prediction model. Remove any independent variables that are not significant. What are the coefficients, their Student's t statistics and the model?

(c) Which model predicts Economics GPA better? Present the evidence to support your conclusion.

11.81 The data file **Salary Model** contains a dependent variable and seven independent variables. You are to obtain the "best" regression model that predicts Y as a function of the seven independent variables. The data are stored on your data disk.

The dependent variable is named "Y" in the file and the independent variables are also appropriately labeled. Use regression analysis to determine which variables should be in the final model and to estimate the coefficients. Show the conditional F test and the conditional t test for any variables removed. Analyze the model residuals using plots. Show your results and discuss your conclusions. Transform variables if the residuals indicate a nonlinear relationship. Present your final model clearly, showing the coefficients and the coefficient Student's t statistics.

11.82 Use the data in the file **Citydat** to estimate a regression equation that can be used to determine the marginal effect of the percent commercial property on the market value per owner-occupied residence. Include percent owner-occupied residences, percent industrial property, the median rooms per residence, and per capita income as additional predictor variables in your multiple regression equation. The variables are included on your data disk and described in the appendix. Indicate which of the variables are conditionally significant. Your final equation should include only significant variables. Discuss and interpret your final regression model, including an indication of how you would select a community for your house.

11.83 The administrator of the National Highway Traffic Safety Administration (NHTSA) wants to know if the different types of vehicles in a state have a relationship to the highway death rate in the state. She has asked you to develop multiple regression analyses to determine if average vehicle weight, percentage imported cars, percentage light trucks, and average car age are related to "crash deaths in automobiles and pickups." The data for the analysis are located in the data file named **Crash**, which is located on your data disk. The variable descriptions and locations are contained in the data file catalog in the Appendix.

(a) Prepare a correlation matrix for crash deaths and the predictor variables. Note the simple relationships between crash deaths and the predictor variables. In addition, indicate any potential multicollinearity problems between the predictor variables.

(b) Prepare a multiple regression analysis of crash deaths on the potential predictor variables. Remove any nonsignificant predictor variables, one at a time, from the regression model. Indicate your best final model.

(c) State the conclusions from your analysis and discuss the conditional importance of the variables in terms of their relationship to crash deaths.

11.84 The Department of Transportation wishes to know if "states with a larger percentage of urban population" is related to "higher automobile and pickup crash death rates." In addition, they want to know if the average speed on rural roads or the percentage of rural roads that are surfaced are conditionally related to crash death rates given percentage of urban population. Data for this study are included in the file **Crash**, which is stored on your data disk.

(a) Prepare a correlation matrix and descriptive statistics for crash deaths and the potential predictor variables. Note the relationships and any potential problems of multicolinearity.

(b) Prepare a multiple regression analysis of crash deaths on the potential predictor variables. Determine which of the variables should be retained in the regression model because they have a conditionally significant relationship.

(c) State the results of your analysis in terms of your final regression model. Indicate which variables are conditionally significant.

11.85 An economist wishes to predict the market value of owner-occupied homes in small Midwestern cities. He has collected a set of data from 45 small cities for a two-year period and wants you to use this as the data source for the analysis. The data are stored in the file **Citydat**, which is stored on your data disk. He wants you to develop a multiple regression prediction equation. The potential predictor variables include the size of the house, tax rate, percent commercial property, per capita income, and total city government expenditures.

(a) Compute the correlation matrix and descriptive statistics for the market value of residences and the potential predictor variables. Note any potential problems of multicollinearity. Define the approximate range for your regression model by the variable means ±2 standard deviations.

(b) Prepare multiple regression analyses using the predictor variables. Remove any variables that are not conditionally significant. Which variable, size of house or tax rate, has the stronger conditional relationship to the value of houses?

(c) A business developer in a Midwestern state has stated that local property tax rates in small towns need to be lowered because if they are not, no one will purchase a house in these towns. Based on your analysis in this problem, evaluate the business developer's claim.

11.86 Stuart Wainwright, the vice-president of purchasing for a large national retailer, has asked you to prepare

an analysis of retail sales by state. He wants to know if the percent unemployment and the per capita personal income are jointly related to per capita retail sales. Data for this study are stored in the data file named **Retail**, which is stored on your data disk.

(a) Prepare a correlation matrix, compute descriptive statistics, and obtain a regression analysis of per capita retail sales on unemployment and personal income. Compute 95% confidence intervals for the slope coefficients in each regression equation.

(b) What is the conditional effect of a $1,000 decrease in per capita income on per capita sales?

(c) Would the prediction equation be improved by adding the state population as an additional predictor variable?

11.87 A major national supplier of building materials for residential construction is concerned about total sales for next year. It is well known that the company's sales are directly related to the total national residential investment. Several New York bankers are predicting that interest rates will rise about 2 percentage points next year. You have been asked to develop a regression analysis that can be used to predict the effect of interest rate changes on residential investment. In addition to interest rate, you also believe that GNP, money supply, government spending, and the price index for finished goods might also be predictors of residential investment. Therefore you decide that two multiple regression models will be needed. One will include prime interest rate and important additional variables. The second will include federal funds interest rate and important additional variables. The time-series data for this study are contained in the data file named **Macro2000**, which is stored on your data disk.

(a) Develop two multiple regression models to predict residential investment using prime interest rate for one and federal funds interest rate for the other. The final regression models should include only predictor variables that have a significant conditional effect. Analyze the regression statistics and indicate which equation provides the best predictions.

(b) Determine the 95% confidence interval for the interest rate conditional slope coefficient in both regression equations.

11.88 The Congressional Budget Office (CBO) is interested in determining if state-level infant death rates are related to the level of medical resources available in the state. Data for the study are contained in the data file named **State**, which is stored on your data disk. The measure of infant deaths is infant deaths under 1 year per 100 live births. The set of possible predictor variables includes physicians per 100,000 population, per capita personal income, and total expenditures for hospitals (this variable should be expressed on a per capita base by dividing by the state population).

(a) Prepare the multiple regression analysis and determine which of the predictor variables should be included in the multiple regression model. Interpret your final regression model including a discussion of the coefficients, their Student's ts, the standard error of the estimate, and R^2.

(b) Identify two additional variables that might be additional predictors if added to the multiple regression model. Test their effect in a multiple regression analysis and indicate if your initial suspicions were correct.

11.89 ● Develop a multiple regression model to predict salary as a function of other independent variables, using the data in the file **Salary Model**, which is stored on your data disk. For this problem, do not use years of experience; instead, use age as a surrogate for experience.

(a) Describe the steps used to obtain the final regression model.

(b) Test the hypothesis that the rate of change in female salaries as a function of age is less than the rate of change for male salaries as a function of age. Your hypothesis test should be set up to provide strong evidence of discrimination against females if it exists. [*Note*: Females are indicated by a "1" for the variable "sex" in column 5. The test should be made conditional on the other significant predictor variables from part (a).]

11.90 ● A group of activists in Peaceful, MT, are seeking increased development for this pristine enclave that has received some national recognition on the television program, "Four Dirty Old Men." They claim that increased commercial and industrial development will bring new prosperity and lower taxes to Peaceful. Specifically, they claim that an increased percentage of commercial and industrial development will decrease the property tax rate and increase the market value for owner-occupied residences.

You have been hired to analyze their claims. For this purpose you have obtained the data file **Citydat**, which contains data from 45 small Montana cities. From these data you will first develop regression models that predict average value of owner-occupied housing and the property tax rate. Then you will determine if and how the addition of percent commercial property and then percent industrial property affects the variability in these regression models. The basic model for predicting market value of houses (c10) includes size of house (c4), tax rate (c7), per capita income (c9), and percent owner-occupied residence (c12) as independent variables. The basic model for predicting tax rate (c7) includes the tax assessment base (c6), current city expenditures per capita (c5/c8), and percent owner-occupied residence (c12) as independent variables.

Determine if the percent commercial (c14) and the percent industrial (c15) variables improve the explained variability in each of the two models. Perform conditional F tests for each of these additional variables. First estimate the conditional effect of percent commercial property by itself and next the conditional effect of percent industrial property by itself. Carefully explain the results of your analysis. Include in your report an explanation of why it was important to include all of the other variables in the regression model instead of just examining the effect of the direct and simple relationship between percent commercial property and percent industrial property on the tax rate and market value of housing.

11.91 ● Use the data in the data file named **Student GPA**, which is stored on your data disk and described in the Appendix, to develop a model to predict a student's grade-point average in economics. Begin with the variables ACT scores, gender, HSpct.

(a) Use appropriate statistical procedures to choose a subset of statistically significant predictor variables. Describe your strategy and carefully define your final model.

(b) Discuss how this model might be used as part of the colleges decision process to select students for admission.

11.92 For a random sample of 50 observations, an economist estimated the regression model

$$\text{Log } Y_i = \alpha + \beta_1 \log x_{1i} + \beta_2 \log x_{2i} + \beta_3 \log x_{3i} + \beta_4 \log x_{4i} + \varepsilon_i$$

where

Y_i = Gross revenue from a medical practice

x_{1i} = Average number of hours worked by physicians in the practice

x_{2i} = Number of physicians in the practice

x_{3i} = Number of allied health personnel (such as nurses) employed in the practice

x_{4i} = Number of rooms used in the practice

Use the portion of the computer output shown here to write a report on these results.

R-SQUARE = 0.927			
		STUDENT'S t FOR H0:	STD. ERROR OF
PARAMETER	ESTIMATE	PARAMETER = 0	ESTIMATE
INTERCEPT	2.347		
LOG X1	.239	3.27	.073
LOG X2	.673	8.31	.081
LOG X3	.279	6.64	.042
LOG X4	.082	1.61	.051

APPENDIX

Least-Squares Derivation of Estimators

The derivation of coefficient estimators for a model with two predictor variables is as follows:

$$\hat{y}_1 = b_0 + b_1 x_{1i} + b_2 x_{2i}$$

Minimize

$$SSE = \sum_{i=1}^{n} \left[y_i - (b_0 + b_1 x_{1i} + b_2 x_{2i}) \right]^2$$

Applying differential calculus, we obtain a set of three normal equations that can be solved for the coefficient estimators

$$\frac{\partial SSE}{\partial b_0} = 0$$

$$2 \sum_{i=1}^{n} \left[y_i - (b_0 + b_1 x_{1i} + b_2 x_{2i}) \right](-1) = 0$$

$$\sum_{i=1}^{n} y_i - n b_0 - b_1 \sum_{i=1}^{n} x_{1i} - b_2 \sum_{i=1}^{n} x_{2i} = 0$$

$$n b_0 + b_1 \sum_{i=1}^{n} x_{1i} + b_2 \sum_{i=1}^{n} x_{2i} = \sum_{i=1}^{n} y_i$$

$$\frac{\partial SSE}{\partial b_1} = 0$$

$$2 \sum_{i=1}^{n} \left[y_i - (b_0 + b_1 x_{1i} + b_2 x_{2i}) \right](-x_{1i}) = 0$$

$$\sum_{i=1}^{n} x_{1i} y_i - b_0 \sum_{i=1}^{n} x_{1i} - b_1 \sum_{i=1}^{n} x_{1i}^2 - b_2 \sum_{i=1}^{n} x_{1i} x_{2i} = 0$$

$$b_0 \sum_{i=1}^{n} x_{1i} + b_1 \sum_{i=1}^{n} x_{1i}^2 + b_2 \sum_{i=1}^{n} x_{1i} x_{2i} = \sum_{i=1}^{n} x_{2i} y_i$$

$$\frac{\partial SSE}{\partial b_2} = 0$$

$$2 \sum_{i=1}^{n} \left[y_1 - (b_0 + b_1 x_{1i} + b_2 x_{2i}) \right](-x_{2i}) = 0$$

$$\sum_{i=1}^{n} x_{2i} y_1 - b_0 \sum_{i=1}^{n} x_{2i} - b_1 \sum_{i=1}^{n} x_{1i} x_{2i} - b_2 \sum_{i=1}^{n} x_{2i}^2 = 0$$

$$b_0 \sum_{i=1}^{n} x_{2i} + b_1 \sum_{i=1}^{n} x_{1i} x_{2i} + b_2 \sum_{i=1}^{n} x_{2i}^2 = \sum_{i=1}^{n} x_{2i} y_i$$

As a result of applying the least squares algorithm, we have a system of three linear equations in three unknowns:

$$b_0, b_1, b_2$$

$$nb_0 + b_1 \sum_{i=1}^{n} x_{1i} + b_2 \sum_{i=1}^{n} x_{2i} = \sum_{i=1}^{n} y_i$$

$$b_0 \sum_{i=1}^{n} x_{1i} + b_1 \sum_{i=1}^{n} x_{1i}^2 + b_2 \sum_{i=1}^{n} x_{1i} x_{2i} = \sum_{i=1}^{n} x_{1i} y_i$$

$$b_0 \sum_{i=1}^{n} x_{2i} + b_1 \sum_{i=1}^{n} x_{1i} x_{2i} + b_2 \sum_{i=1}^{n} x_{2i}^2 = \sum_{i=1}^{n} x_{2i} y_i$$

The normal equations are solved for the desired coefficients by first computing the various X and Y squared and cross-product terms.

The intercept term is estimated by

$$b_0 = \bar{y} - b_1 \bar{x}_1 - b_2 \bar{x}_2$$

Total Explained Variability

The explained variability SSR term in multiple regression is more complex than the term in simple regression.

For the two-independent-variable regression model

$$Y = \beta_0 + \beta_1 X_1 + \beta_2 X_2$$

we find that

$$\begin{aligned}
SSR &= \sum_{i=1}^{n} \left(\hat{y}_i - \bar{Y} \right)^2 \\
&= \sum_{i=1}^{n} \left[b_0 + b_1 x_{1i} + b_2 x_{2i} - \left(b_0 + b_1 \bar{X}_1 + b_2 \bar{X}_2 \right) \right]^2 \\
&= \sum_{i=1}^{n} \left[b_1^2 \left(x_{1i} - \bar{X}_1 \right)^2 + b_2^2 \left(x_{2i} - \bar{X}_1 \right)^2 + 2b_1 b_2 \left(x_{1i} - \bar{X}_1 \right) \left(x_{2i} - \bar{X}_2 \right) \right] \\
&= (n-1) \left(b_1^2 S_{x_1}^2 + b_2^2 S_{x_2}^2 + 2r_{x_1 x_2} b_1 b_2 S_{x_1} S_{x_2} \right)
\end{aligned}$$

We see that the explained variability has a portion directly associated with each of the independent variables and a portion associated with the correlation between the two variables.

REFERENCES

1. Ghatak, S. and D. Deadman, "Money, Prices and Stabilization Policies in Some Developing Countries." *Applied Economics*, 21 (1989), 853–865.

2. Spellman, L. J., "Entry and Profitability in a Rate-free Savings and Loan Market." *Quarterly Review of Economics and Business*, 18, no. 2 (1978), 87–95.

C H A P T E R 12

ADDITIONAL TOPICS IN REGRESSION ANALYSIS

INTRODUCTION

In Chapters 10 and 11 we developed simple and multiple regression as a tool to estimate the coefficients for linear models for business and economic applications. We now understand that the purpose of fitting a regression equation is to use information about the independent variables to explain the behavior of the dependent variables and to derive predictions of the dependent variable. The model coefficients can also be used to estimate the rate of change of the dependent variable as the result of changes in an independent variable, conditional on the particular set of other independent variables included in the model remaining fixed. In this chapter we will study a set of alternative specifications. In addition, we will consider situations in which the basic regression assumptions are violated.

The topics in this chapter can be selected individually to supplement your study of regression analysis. Most everyone will be interested in the model-building discussion in the next section. The process of model building is fundamental to all regression applications, and thus we begin with those ideas. The section dealing with dummy variables and experimental design provides methods for extending the model applications. Sections such as those dealing with heteroscedasticity and autocorrelations indicate how to deal with violations of assumptions.

Regression models are developed in business and economic applications to increase understanding and guide decisions. Developing these models requires a good understanding of the system and process being studied. Statistical theory provides a link between the underlying process and the data observed from that process. This linking of the problem context and good statistical analysis usually requires an interdisciplinary team that can provide expertise on all aspects of the problem. In the authors' experience, success of these teams requires that all team members learn from each other—production specialists need to have a basic understanding of statistical procedures and statisticians need to understand the production process.

12.1   MODEL-BUILDING METHODOLOGY

Here a general strategy for constructing regression models is developed. We live in a complex world, and no one believes that we can capture precisely the complexities of economic and business behavior in one or more equations. Our goal is to use a relatively simple model that provides a sufficiently close approximation of the complex reality, to provide useful insights. The art of model building recognizes the impossibility of representing the many individual influences on a variable of interest and tries to pick out the most influential factors. Next, it is necessary to formulate a model to depict relationships between these factors. We want to build a simple model that is easy to interpret but not so oversimplified that important influences are ignored.

The process of statistical model building is problem-specific. Our approach will depend on what is known about the behavior of the quantities under study and what data are available. However, various stages of model building as presented in Figure 12.1 are discussed.

Model Specification

Analysis begins with the development of the model specification. This includes selection of the dependent and independent variables and the algebraic form of the model. We seek a specification that provides an adequate representation of the system and process under study. The

FIGURE 12.1
The Stages of Statistical
Model Building

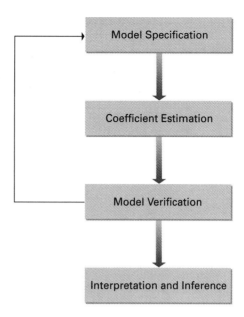

examples in Chapters 10 and 11 that dealt with retail sales, profitability of savings and loan associations, and cotton production all postulated a linear relationship between the dependent variable and the independent variables. Often this specification will provide a good approximation for the problem of interest. But we will not always find this to be true.

Model specification typically requires considerable thinking about a problem and the process that underlies the problem. When we have complex problems involving a number of factors, it is important that the interdisciplinary team carefully analyzes all aspects of the problem. It may be necessary to do additional research and perhaps include others that have important insights. Specification requires serious study and analysis. If not done properly, the entire model development will be seriously compromised. This is also the time where we need to determine the required data for the study. In many cases this may involve deciding if the available data—or data that could be obtained—will be adequate for model estimation. If we do not know what we want to do or understand the context of the problem, then our best analysis tools and skills will not give us the best possible answer. Inexperienced analysts often leap to running computer-based computations before thinking carefully about the problem. Professional analysts know that such an approach leads to inferior results.

Coefficient Estimation

A statistical model, once specified, typically involves a number of unknown coefficients, or parameters. The next stage of the model-building exercise is to employ available data in the estimation of these coefficients. Both point estimates and interval estimates should be obtained for the multiple regression model

$$y_i = \beta_0 + \beta_1 x_{1i} + \beta_2 x_{2i} + \cdots + \beta_k x_{Ki} + \varepsilon_i$$

From a statistical perspective, regression model objectives can be divided into either estimation of the mean of the dependent variable y or estimation of one or more of the individual coefficients, β_j. In many cases the objectives are not completely separate, but these alternatives identify important options.

If the objective is prediction, we want a model that has a small standard error of the estimate, S_e. We are not as concerned about correlated independent variables because we know that a number of different combinations of correlated variables will result in the same prediction precision. However, we do need to know that the correlations between independent variables will continue to hold in future populations. We also need to have a wide spread for the independent variables to ensure a small prediction variance over the desired range of the model application.

Alternatively, estimation of the slope coefficients leads us to consider a wider range of issues. The estimated standard deviation, S_{β_j}, of the slope coefficients is influenced directly by the standard error of the model and inversely by the spread of the independent variables and the correlations between independent variables, as seen in Section 11.4. Multicollinearity—correlations between independent variables—is a critical issue as we will discuss in Section 12.5. Also, we will see in Section 12.4 that failure to include important predictor variables results in a biased estimator of the coefficients for predictor variables included in the model. These two results lead to a classic statistical problem. Do we include a predictor variable that is highly correlated with the other predictor variables and thus avoid a biased coefficient estimate but also substantially increase the variance of the coefficient estimator? Or do we exclude a correlated predictor variable to reduce the coefficient estimator variance and increase the bias by excluding a predictor variable? Selecting the proper balance of estimator bias and variance is often a problem in applied model building.

Model Verification

When developing the model specification, an investigator incorporates insights concerning the behavior of the underlying system and process. Certain simplifications and assumptions occur when translating these insights into algebraic forms and when selecting data for model estimation. Since some of these might prove untenable, it is important to check the adequacy of the model.

After estimating a regression equation we may find that the estimates do not make sense, given what we know about the process. For example, suppose the model indicates that the demand for cars increases as prices increase. This runs counter to basic economic theory. This result may have occurred because of inadequate data or because of some high correlations between price and other predictor variables. These are likely causes of the wrong sign for coefficients. But the problem may also result from faulty model specification. Failure to include the proper set of predictor variables can lead to bias and incorrect signs for the coefficients.

We also need to check the assumptions made about the statistical properties of the random variables in the model. For example, the basic regression assumptions state that the error terms all have the same variance and are uncorrelated with one another. In Sections 12.6 and 12.7 we will see how these assumptions can be checked by using the available data.

If we find implausible results, then it is necessary to examine our assumptions, model specification, and the data. This may lead us to consider a different model specification. Thus in Figure 12.1 we indicate a feedback loop in the model-building process. As we develop experience with model building and other difficult problem solving we will discover that these processes tend to be iterative, with considerable cycling back to earlier stages until a satisfactory model and problem solution are developed.

Model Interpretation and Inference

Once a model has been constructed, it can be used to learn something about the system and process being studied. In regression analysis, this may involve finding confidence intervals for the model parameters, testing hypotheses of interest, or forecasting future values of the dependent variable, given assumed values of the independent variables. It is important to recognize that inference of this sort is based on the assumption of an appropriate model specification and estimation. The more severe are any specification or estimation errors, the less reliable, in general, is any inference derived from the estimated model.

12.2 DUMMY VARIABLES AND EXPERIMENTAL DESIGN

Dummy variables were introduced in Section 11.8 in applications involving regression models applied to two different subsets of data. We saw how they could be used to test for gender discrimination in the salary example.

In this section we will expand the potential applications of dummy variables. First we will present an application in which a regression model is applied to more than two subsets of data. Next we will show how dummy variables can be used to estimate the seasonal effects on a regression model applied to time series data. Finally, we will show how dummy variables can be used to analyze data from experimental situations which are defined by multiple-level categorical variables.

EXAMPLE 12.1

DEMAND FOR WOOL PRODUCTS (DUMMY VARIABLE MODEL ANALYSIS)

A senior marketing analyst for the American Wool Producers Association is interested in estimating the demand for wool products in various cities as a function of total disposable income in the city. Data were gathered from 30 randomly selected Standard Metropolitan Statistical Areas (SMSAs). As a first step the analyst estimates a regression model for the relationship between sales and disposable income:

$$\hat{y} = b_0 + b_1 x_1$$

where x_1 is the per capita annual disposable income for a city and Y is the per capita sales of wool products in the city. After some additional discussions, the analyst wonders if overall sales level differs between different geographic regions: north, central, and south.

SOLUTION

The analysis began by placing each of the cities in one of the three regions. Figure 12.2 is a scatter plot of per capita sales versus disposable income. The data appear to be separated into three distinct subgroups corresponding to geographic regions. Two dummy variables were used to identify each of the three regions. The identifications are:

North: $X_2 = 0, \quad X_3 = 1$
Central: $X_2 = 1, \quad X_3 = 0$
South: $X_2 = 0, \quad X_3 = 0$

FIGURE 12.2
Per Capita Wool Sales versus
Per Capita Disposable
Income

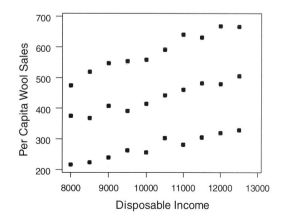

In general, k distinct regions or subsets can be identified uniquely with $k - 1$ dummy variables. If we try to use k dummy variables to represent k distinct subsets then perfect multicollinearity will result. This is sometimes referred to as the "dummy variable trap."

Shifts in the model constant could be estimated using the model

$$Y = \beta_0 + \beta_2 X_2 + \beta_3 X_3 + \beta_1 X_1 + \varepsilon$$

Applying this model to the north it becomes

$$\begin{aligned} Y &= \beta_0 + \beta_2(0) + \beta_3(1) + \beta_1 X_1 + \varepsilon \\ &= (\beta_0 + \beta_3) + \beta_1 X_1 + \varepsilon \end{aligned}$$

In the central states we find

$$\begin{aligned} Y &= \beta_0 + \beta_2(1) + \beta_3(0) + \beta_1 X_1 + \varepsilon \\ &= (\beta_0 + \beta_2) + \beta_1 X_1 + \varepsilon \end{aligned}$$

Finally, for the southern states the model is

$$\begin{aligned} Y &= \beta_0 + \beta_2(0) + \beta_3(0) + \beta_1 X_1 + \varepsilon \\ &= \beta_0 + \beta_1 X_1 + \varepsilon \end{aligned}$$

Summarizing these results, the constants for the various regions are

North: $\beta_0 + \beta_3$
Central: $\beta_0 + \beta_2$
South: β_0

This formulation defines the south as the "base" constant, with β_3 and β_2 defining the shift of the function for northern and central cities respectively. Hypothesis tests, using the coefficient Student's t statistic, could be used to determine if there are significant differences between the constants for the different regions, compared in this case to the constant for the south region. For additional regions, constants could be modeled by using dummy variables that continued this pattern. The dummy variables could be specified so that any level could be the base level to which the other levels are compared. In this problem, specifying the south as the base condition is natural given the problem objectives.

The model with differences in slope coefficients and constants is

$$\begin{aligned} Y &= \beta_0 + \beta_2 X_2 + \beta_3 X_3 + (\beta_1 + \beta_4 X_2 + \beta_5 X_3) X_1 + \varepsilon \\ &= \beta_0 + \beta_2 X_2 + \beta_3 X_3 + \beta_1 X_1 + \beta_4 X_2 X_1 + \beta_5 X_3 X_1 + \varepsilon \end{aligned}$$

Applying this model to the northern states, we see that

$$\begin{aligned} Y &= \beta_0 + \beta_2(0) + \beta_3(1) + (\beta_1 + \beta_4(0) + \beta_5(1)) X_1 + \varepsilon \\ &= (\beta_0 + \beta_3) + (\beta_1 + \beta_5) X_1 + \varepsilon \end{aligned}$$

For the central states the model is

$$\begin{aligned} Y &= \beta_0 + \beta_2(1) + \beta_3(0) + (\beta_1 + \beta_4(1) + \beta_5(0)) X_1 + \varepsilon \\ &= (\beta_0 + \beta_2) + (\beta_1 + \beta_4) X_1 + \varepsilon \end{aligned}$$

Finally, for the southern states,

$$Y = \beta_0 + \beta_2(0) + \beta_3(0) + (\beta_1 + \beta_4(0) + \beta_5(0))X_1 + \varepsilon$$
$$= \beta_0 + \beta_1 X_1 + \varepsilon$$

The X_1 slope coefficient for cities in different regions are

North: $\beta_1 + \beta_5$
Central: $\beta_1 + \beta_4$
South: β_1

Again the south is the base condition with slope, β_1. Hypothesis tests can be used to determine the statistical significance of slope coefficient differences compared to the base condition—in this case the south region. Using this dummy variable regression model the analyst can estimate the relationship between sales and disposable income by region of the country.

INTERPRETATION

Using the sample of 30 SMSAs divided equally between the three geographic regions, a dummy variable multiple regression model was estimated using Minitab. The results are contained in Figure 12.3. From the regression model we can determine characteristics of the wool purchase patterns. Conditional hypothesis tests of the form

$$H_0: \beta_j = 0 \mid \beta_l \neq 0, l = 1,\dots, K, l \neq j$$
$$H_1: \beta_j \neq 0 \mid \beta_l \neq 0, l = 1,\dots, K, l \neq j$$

can be used to determine the conditional effects of the various factors on the demand for wool. The coefficient for the X_3 dummy variable $\beta_3 = 138.46$, indicates that people in the north spend an average of \$138.46 more than people in the south. Similarly, people in the central region spend an average of \$96.33 more than people in the south. These coefficients are each conditionally significant, different from 0 with the p-value equal to 0.022. The coefficient for disposable income was 0.0252, indicating that for people in the south each dollar of increased per capita income increases the purchase of wool products by 0.025, and this result is conditionally significant. For people in the north each dollar of increased income increases expenditure for wool products by 0.042 (0.0252 + 0.0168), and the difference in the increased slope is conditionally significant. The estimated rate of increase in

FIGURE 12.3
Dummy Variable Multiple Regression Model to Estimate Per Capita Wool Consumption

```
The regression equation is
Per Capita Wool Sales = 12.7 + 138 North X3 + 96.3 Central X2
            + 0.0252 Disposable Income + 0.0168 NorX3Inc + 0.00608 CentX2Inc

Predictor       Coef       StDev          T        P
Constant       12.73       27.74       0.53    0.600
North X3      138.46       39.22       3.53    0.002
Central X2     96.33       39.22       2.46    0.022
Disposab    0.025231    0.002680       9.42    0.000
NorX3Inc    0.016839    0.003790       4.44    0.000
CentX2In    0.006085    0.003790       1.61    0.121

S = 12.17       R-Sq = 99.4%      R-Sq(adj) = 99.2%

Analysis of Variance

Source          DF          SS          MS         F        P
Regression       5      553704      110741    747.71    0.000
Residual Error  24        3555         148
Total           29      557259
```

purchase per dollar of increased income is also greater for people in the central region compared to the south. However, that difference is not conditionally significant. By using these results, sales by region can be predicted more precisely compared to a model that combined all regions and used only per capita income.

EXAMPLE 12.2

FORECASTING SALE OF WOOL PRODUCTS (SEASONAL DUMMY VARIABLES)

After finishing the regional sales analysis, the analyst decided to study the relationship between sales and disposable income using time-series data. After some discussion it was realized that sales are different for each quarter of the year. For example, during the fourth quarter sales were high in anticipation of holiday-season gifts and colder weather. Assistance with the study is requested.

SOLUTION

After discussing the problem you recommend that the four quarters for each year be represented by three dummy variables. In this way the multiple regression model can be used to estimate differences in sales between the different quarters. Specifically, you propose a structure that is similar to the regional dummy variable model

First quarter: $X_2 = 0, X_3 = 0, X_4 = 0$
Second quarter: $X_2 = 1, X_3 = 0, X_4 = 0$
Third quarter: $X_2 = 0, X_3 = 1, X_4 = 0$
Fourth quarter: $X_2 = 0, X_3 = 0, X_4 = 1$

The dummy variable coefficients are estimates of shifts in the wool consumption function between quarters in the model

$$Y = \beta_0 + \beta_2 X_2 + \beta_3 X_3 + \beta_4 X_4 + \beta_1 X_1 + \varepsilon$$

where Y is the total sales of wool products and X_1 is disposable income. The constants for the various quarters are as follows:

First quarter: β_0
Second quarter: $\beta_0 + \beta_2$
Third quarter: $\beta_0 + \beta_3$
Fourth quarter: $\beta_0 + \beta_4$

Experimental Design Models

Experimental design procedures have been a major area of statistical research and practice for a number of years. Early work dealt with agricultural research. The efforts of statisticians such as R. A. Fisher and O. L. Davies in England during the 1920's provided the foundation for experimental design methodology and for statistical practice in general. Agricultural experiments require an entire growing season to obtain data. Thus it was important to develop procedures that could answer a number of questions and ensure great precision. In addition, most of the experiments defined activity using variables with discrete as opposed to continuous levels. Experimental design methods have also been used extensively in the study of human behavior and in various industrial experiments. The recent emphasis on improving quality and productivity has spawned increased activity in this area of statistics, with important contributions from groups such as the Center for Quality and Productivity led by George Box at the University of Wisconsin.

EXPERIMENTAL DESIGN

Dummy variable regression can be used as a tool in experimental design work. The experiments have a single outcome variable, which contains all of the random error. Each experimental outcome is measured at discrete combinations of experimental (independent) variables, X_j.

There is an important difference in philosophy for experimental designs in comparison to most of the problems we have considered. Experimental design attempts to identify causes for the changes in the dependent variable. This is done by prespecifying combinations of discrete independent variables at which the dependent variable will be measured. An important objective is to choose experimental points, defined by independent variables that provide minimum variance estimators. The order in which the experiments are performed is chosen randomly to avoid biases from variables not included in the experiment.

Experimental outcomes, Y, are measured at specific combinations of levels for treatment and blocking variables. A treatment variable represents a variable whose effect we are interested in estimating with minimum variance. For example, we might wish to know which of four different production machines will provide the highest productivity per hour. In that case the treatment is the production machines represented by a four-level categorical variable, Z_j. A blocking variable represents a variable that is part of the environment and we cannot control the variable level. But we want to include the level of the blocking variable in our model so that we can remove the variability in the outcome variable, Y, that is associated with different levels of the blocking variables. We can represent a K level treatment or blocking variable by using $K - 1$ dummy variables. Let us consider a simple example that has one four-level treatment variable, Z_1, and one three-level blocking variable, Z_2. These variables could be represented by dummy variables, as shown in Table 12.1. Then by using these dummy variables the experimental design model could be estimated by the multiple regression model

$$Y = \beta_0 + \beta_1 X_1 + \beta_2 X_2 + \beta_3 X_3 + \beta_4 X_4 + \beta_5 X_5 + \varepsilon$$

In this model, for example, the coefficient, β_3, provides an estimate of the amount of higher productivity for treatment level 4 compared to treatment level 1, for categorical treatment variable, Z_1. Of course if β_3 were negative, we would know that treatment level 1 has a higher productivity than treatment level 4. Following the logic of multiple regression we know that variables X_4 and X_5 will have the effect of explaining some of the variability in Y and hence result in a smaller variance estimator. This model could easily be expanded to include several treatment variables simultaneously with several other blocking variables.

TABLE 12.1
Example of Dummy Variable Specification for Treatment and Blocking Variables

Z_1	X_1	X_2	X_3
1	0	0	0
2	1	0	0
3	0	1	0
4	0	0	1

Z_2	X_4	X_5
1	0	0
2	1	0
3	0	1

In addition if there were a continuous variable, for example ambient temperature, that affected the productivity, then that variable could be added directly to the regression model. In many cases several replications of the basic design are conducted to provide sufficient degrees of freedom for error. This process is demonstrated in Example 12.3.

EXAMPLE 12.3

WORKER TRAINING PROGRAM (DUMMY VARIABLE MODEL SPECIFICATION)

Mary Cruz is the production manager for a large auto parts factory. She is interested in determining the effect of a new training program on worker productivity. Considerable research supports the conclusion that productivity is also influenced by the machine type and by the amount of education a worker has received.

SOLUTION

Mary defines the following variables for the experiment;

Y The number of units produced per eight-hour shift

Z_1 The type of training
1. Traditional classroom lecture and film presentation
2. Interactive Computer Assisted Instruction (CAI)

Z_2 Machine type
1. Machine Type 1
2. Machine Type 2
3. Machine Type 3

Z_3 Workers educational level
1. High school education
2. At least one year of post-high school education

The variable Z_1 is called a treatment variable because the major study objective is an evaluation of the training program. The variables Z_2 and Z_3 are called *blocking variables* because they are included to help reduce or block out some of the unexplained variability. In this way the variance is reduced and the test for the main treatment effects has greater power. The term *blocking variable* is a carryover from the agricultural experiments where fields were separated into small blocks, each of which had different soil conditions. It is also possible to estimate the effect of these blocking variables. Thus one does not lose information by calling certain variables blocking variables instead of treatment variables.

Experimental design observations are predefined using the independent variables. Table 12.2 presents a listing of the observations with each observation designated using lev-

TABLE 12.2
Experimental Design for
Productivity Study

PRODUCTION Y	TRAINING Z_1	MACHINE Z_2	EDUCATION Z_3
Y_1	1	1	1
Y_2	1	1	2
Y_3	1	2	1
Y_4	1	2	2
Y_5	1	3	1
Y_6	1	3	2
Y_7	2	1	1
Y_8	2	1	2
Y_9	2	2	1
Y_{10}	2	2	2
Y_{11}	2	3	1
Y_{12}	2	3	2

els of the Z variables. In this design, which is called a full factorial design, there are twelve observations, one for each combination of the treatment and blocking variables. The y_i observations represent the measured responses at each of the experimental conditions. In the data, model y_i contains the effect of the treatment and blocking variables plus random error. In many experimental designs this pattern of twelve observations would be replicated (repeated) to provide more degrees of freedom for error and lower variance estimates of the effects of the design variables. This design could also be analyzed using analysis of variance procedures. However, we will show here how the analysis can be performed using dummy variable regression.

The levels for each of the three design variables, Z_1, Z_2, and Z_3, can be expressed as a set of dummy variables. Define the following dummy variables:

$$Z_1 = 1 \rightarrow X_1 = 0$$
$$Z_1 = 2 \rightarrow X_1 = 1$$
$$Z_2 = 1 \rightarrow X_2 = 0 \ \& \ X_3 = 0$$
$$Z_2 = 2 \rightarrow X_2 = 1 \ \& \ X_3 = 0$$
$$Z_2 = 3 \rightarrow X_2 = 0 \ \& \ X_3 = 1$$
$$Z_3 = 1 \rightarrow X_4 = 0$$
$$Z_3 = 2 \rightarrow X_4 = 1$$

By using these relationships, the experimental design model in Table 12.2, which uses the Z variables, can be represented by dummy variables, as shown in Table 12.3. Using these dummy variables we can define a multiple regression model:

$$Y_i = \beta_0 + \beta_1 X_{1i} + \beta_2 X_{2i} + \beta_3 X_{3i} + \beta_4 X_{4i} + \varepsilon_i$$

INTERPRETATION

The regression coefficients would be estimated using the variables as previously specified. The twelve experiments or observations defined in Tables 12.2 and 12.3 are defined as one replication of the experimental design. A replication contains all of the individual experiments that are included in the experimental design. Often several replications of the design would be made to provide greater accuracy for the coefficient estimates and to provide sufficient degrees of freedom for estimating the variance. In the dummy variable model we estimate four coefficients and a constant, leaving $n - 4 - 1$ degrees of freedom for estimating the variance. With one replication $n = 12$ and we have 7 degrees of freedom for estimating the variance. With two replications of the design, $n = 24$ leaving 19 degrees of freedom for estimating the variance, and with three replications we have 31 degrees of

TABLE 12.3
Experimental Design for Productivity Study Using Dummy Variables

PRODUCTIVITY Y	X_1	X_2	X_3	X_4
Y_1	0	0	0	0
Y_2	0	0	0	1
Y_3	0	1	0	0
Y_4	0	1	0	1
Y_5	0	0	1	0
Y_6	0	0	1	1
Y_7	1	0	0	0
Y_8	1	0	0	1
Y_9	1	1	0	0
Y_{10}	1	1	0	1
Y_{11}	1	0	1	0
Y_{12}	1	0	1	1

freedom. Usually at least 15 or 20 degrees of freedom are required to obtain stable estimates of variance. Using the definitions of the dummy variables we find that the estimated regression coefficients would be interpreted as follows:

1. b_1 is the productivity increase for the new CAI training compared to the standard classroom training.
2. b_2 is the productivity increase for machine type 2 compared to machine type 1.
3. b_3 is the productivity increase for machine type 3 compared to machine type 1.
4. b_4 is the productivity increase for the post-high school education compared to high school alone.

Any of these "increases" could be negative, implying a decrease.

The significance of each of these effects can be tested using our standard hypothesis testing procedures. Note that if an experimental observation were lost or failed the same regression model could still be used to estimate the coefficients. However, we would have a larger variance and hence the hypothesis tests would have lower power.

It is also possible to add continuous variables or covariates to the model. Suppose that Mary suspects that the number of years of worker experience and the ambient temperature also influence productivity. These two continuous variables could be measured for each experiment and added to the dummy variable regression model. The regression model would then become:

$$Y_i = \beta_0 + \beta_1 X_{1i} + \beta_2 X_{2i} + \beta_3 X_{3i} + \beta_4 X_{4i} + \beta_5 X_{5i} + \beta_6 X_{6i} + \varepsilon_i$$

where X_5 is the years of experience and X_6 is the ambient temperature. If these later variables are important they will reduce the variance and increase the power of the hypothesis tests for the effects of other variables.

INTERPRETATION

Another possible extension is the inclusion of interaction effects. Suppose that Mary suspects that the CAI training would provide greater benefits for workers working with machine type 3. To test for this effect she could include an interaction variable $X_7 = X_1 X_3$. The values for X_7 would be merely the product of the X_1 and the X_3 variables. Thus in Table 12.3 we would have a column for X_7 which had 1s for the 11th and 12th observations and 0s for the remaining observations. If she also suspected that the CAI training would benefit workers with more education she could define another interaction variable $X_8 = X_1 X_4$. This variable would add another column to Table 12.3 with 1s for the 8th, 10th, and 12th observations and 0s for the remaining observations. It is possible to add other variables and interaction terms. Thus the number of options with these experimental designs is very large.

With all of these additions, the regression model would be:

$$Y_i = \beta_0 + \beta_1 X_{1i} + \beta_2 X_{2i} + \beta_3 X_{3i} + \beta_4 X_{4i} + \beta_5 X_{5i} + \beta_6 X_{6i} + \beta_7 X_{7i} + \beta_8 X_{8i} + \varepsilon_i$$

In this equation there are eight coefficients and a constant to estimate, leaving only three degrees of freedom for estimating the variance if only one replication of the design was performed. In situations where measurements can be made accurately and the various effects are large, this design with even one replication could provide useful information about the factors which influence productivity. In most cases more than one replication would be desirable. More observations provide better coefficient estimates and a smaller coefficient variance. However, in an industrial situation experiments may involve the entire factory and thus can be very expensive. Analysts try to maximize the understanding gained from each set of experiments.

In this section we introduced experimental designs and their analysis using dummy variables. Experimental design is a major area for applied statistics which can be studied in many other courses and books. Statistical software, such as Minitab, typically contain an extensive set of routines for developing various sophisticated experimental design models. These should only be used after you have learned about their specific details and interpretations. However, even with the introduction presented here you have a powerful tool for handling some important productivity problems.

Applications of experimental design have become increasingly important in manufacturing and other business operations. Experiments to identify variables related to increased production and decreased number of defects are important in efforts to improve production operations. The use of dummy variables and multiple regression for experimental design analysis extends the problem types that you can handle without learning additional analysis techniques. This is an important additional advantage for dummy variable procedures.

EXERCISES

12.1 Write the model specification and define the variables for a multiple regression model to predict college GPA as a function of entering SAT scores and the year in college: First Year, Sophomore, Junior, and Senior.

12.2 Write the model specification and define the variables for a multiple regression model to predict wages in U.S. dollars as a function of years of experience and country of employment indicated as Germany, Great Britain, Japan, United States, and Turkey.

12.3 Write the model specification and define the variables for a multiple regression model to predict the cost per unit produced as a function of factory type indicated as classic technology, computer controlled machines, and computer controlled material handling, and a function of country indicated as Colombia, South Africa, and Japan.

12.4 An economist wants to estimate a regression equation relating demand for a product (y) to its price (x_1) and income (x_2). It is to be based on 12 years of quarterly data. However, it is known that demand for this product is seasonal—that is, it is higher at certain times of the year than others.

(a) One possibility for accounting for seasonality is to estimate the model

$$y_t = \alpha + \beta_1 x_{1t} + \beta_2 x_{2t} + \beta_3 x_{3t} + \beta_4 x_{4t} + \beta_5 x_{5t} + \beta_6 x_{6t} + \varepsilon_t$$

where $x_{3t}, x_{4t}, x_{5t}, x_{6t}$ are dummy variables, with

> $x_{3t} = 1$ in first quarter of each year, 0 otherwise
>
> $x_{4t} = 1$ in second quarter of each year, 0 otherwise
>
> $x_{5t} = 1$ in third quarter of each year, 0 otherwise
>
> $x_{6t} = 1$ in fourth quarter of each year, 0 otherwise

Explain why this model cannot be estimated by least squares.

(b) A model that can be estimated is

$$y_t = \alpha + \beta_1 x_{1t} + \beta_2 x_{2t} + \beta_3 x_{3t} + \beta_4 x_{4t} + \beta_5 x_{5t} + \varepsilon_t$$

Interpret the coefficients on the dummy variables in this model.

12.3 LAGGED VALUES OF THE DEPENDENT VARIABLES AS REGRESSORS

In this section we will consider lagged dependent variables, an important topic when time series data are analyzed—that is, when measurements on the quantities of interest are taken over time. For example, we might have monthly observations, quarterly observations, or annual observations. Economists regularly use time series variables such as interest rates, inflation measures, aggregate investment, aggregate consumption, and many others for various analysis and modeling projects. We will specify time series observations by using the subscript t to denote time instead of the i used to denote cross section data. Thus a multiple regression model would be

$$Y_t = \beta_0 + \beta_1 x_{1t} + \beta_2 x_{2t} + \cdots + \beta_K x_{Kt} + \varepsilon_t$$

In many time series applications the dependent variable in time period t is often related also to the value taken by this variable in the previous time period—that is, to Y_{t-1}. The value of the dependent variable in an earlier time period is called a *lagged dependent variable*.

REGRESSIONS INVOLVING LAGGED DEPENDENT VARIABLES

Consider the following regression model linking a dependent variable, Y, and K independent variables

$$y_t = \beta_0 + \beta_1 x_{1t} + \beta_2 x_{2t} + \cdots + \beta_K x_{Kt} + \gamma Y_{t-1} + \varepsilon_t \tag{12.1}$$

where $\beta_0, \beta_1, \ldots, \beta_K, \gamma$ are fixed coefficients. If data are generated by this model:

1. An increase of 1 unit in the independent variable x_j in time period t, with all other independent variables held fixed, leads to an expected increase in the dependent variable of β_j in period t, $\beta_j\gamma$ in period $(t+1)$, $\beta_j\gamma^2$ in period $(t+2)$, $\beta_j\gamma^3$ in period $(t+3)$, and so on. The total expected increase over all current and future time periods is $\dfrac{\beta_j}{(1-\gamma)}$.

2. The coefficients $\beta_0, \beta_1, \ldots, \beta_K, \gamma$ can be estimated by least squares in the usual manner.

3. Confidence intervals and hypothesis tests for the regression coefficients can be computed precisely the same as for the ordinary multiple regression model. (Strictly speaking, when the regression equation contains lagged dependent variables, these procedures are only approximately valid. The quality of the approximation improves, all other things being equal, as the number of sample observations increases.)

4. Caution should be used when using confidence intervals and hypothesis tests with time series data. There is the possibility that the equation errors, ε_i, are no longer independent from one to another. We will consider this in Section 12.7 under autocorrelations. In particular, when the errors are correlated the coefficient estimates are unbiased, but not efficient. Thus confidence intervals and hypothesis tests are no longer valid. Econometricians have developed procedures for obtaining estimates under these conditions, and these will be introduced in Section 12.7.

To illustrate the calculation of regression estimates and inference based on the fitted regression equation when the model includes lagged dependent variables, we consider extended Example 12.4 (reference 1).

EXAMPLE 12.4

ADVERTISING EXPENDITURE AS A FUNCTION OF RETAIL SALES (LAGGED VARIABLE REGRESSION MODEL)

Advertising Retail

A researcher was interested in forecasting advertising expenditures as a function of retail sales, while knowing that the previous year's advertising also had an influence.

SOLUTION

It was believed that local advertising per household would depend on retail sales per household. Also, since advertisers may be unwilling or unable to adjust their plans to sudden changes in the level of retail sales, the value of local advertising expenditures per household in the previous year was added to the model. Thus, advertising expenditures in the current year are related to retail sales (x_t) in the current year and advertising expenditures (Y_{t-1}) in the previous year. The model to be fitted is, then

$$y_t = \beta_0 + \beta_1 x_t + \gamma Y_{t-1} + \varepsilon_t$$

where

y_t is the local advertising per household in year t

x_t is the retail sales per household in year t

The data for advertising and retail sales are stored in a Minitab data file labeled **Advertising Retail**. To obtain the lagged value of the dependent variable, Y_{t-1}, use the option

```
CALC > CALCULATOR
```

In the resulting screen you can scroll to the "lag" option , click select, and then choose the advertising variable to be lagged. The screen with appropriate entries is shown in Figure 12.4.

After completing the lag transformation the Minitab data file will include the lagged variable. A portion of the Minitab spreadsheet with the data is shown in Figure 12.5. Note the relationship of the lagged variable to the unknown variable. We also see that observation 1 for the lagged variable has a missing data symbol. As a result, the data set available for the regression has only 21 observations. This will always be the case when lagged variables are created. Of course you might have access to data from the previous year—year 0 in this example—and that value could replace the missing value. The data is now ready to run multiple regression using the conventional Minitab commands. The resulting regression output is shown in Figure 12.6.

FIGURE 12.4
Minitab Entry Box to Obtain Lagged Variables

FIGURE 12.5
Minitab Spreadsheet with Advertising, Retail Sales, and Lagged Advertising

↓	C1 year	C2 Advertising Y(t)	C3 Retail Sales X(t)	C4 lag advertising	C5	C6	C7	C8
1	1	117.66	5492	*				
2	2	115.62	5540	117.66				
3	3	110.79	5305	115.62				
4	4	119.22	5507	110.79				
5	5	120.78	5418	119.22				
6	6	110.20	5320	120.78				
7	7	110.86	5538	110.20				
8	8	114.06	5692	110.86				

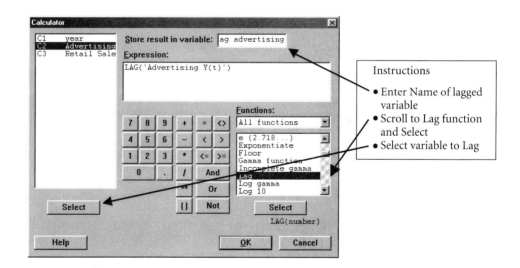

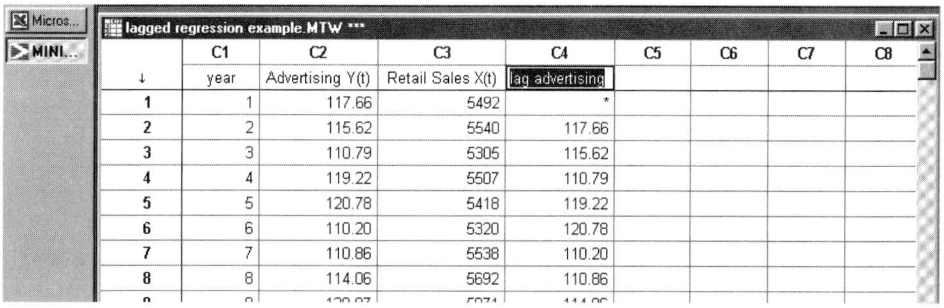

FIGURE 12.6
Minitab Output for
Advertising Expenditure as a
Function of Retail Sales and
Lagged Advertising
Expenditure

Regression Analysis

```
The regression equation is
Advertising Y(t) = - 43.8 + 0.0188 Retail Sales X(t) + 0.479 lag advertising

21 cases used 1 cases contain missing values

Predictor        Coef       StDev          T        P
Constant       -43.766       9.843      -4.45    0.000
Retail S      0.018777    0.002855       6.58    0.000
lag adve       0.47906     0.08732       5.49    0.000

S = 3.451        R-Sq = 96.3%       R-Sq(adj) = 95.9%

Analysis of Variance

Source             DF           SS          MS         F        P
Regression          2       5559.1      2779.5    233.43    0.000
Residual Error     18        212.3        11.9
Total              20       5773.4

Source          DF     Seq SS
Retail S         1     5200.7
lag adve         1      358.4

Unusual Observations
Obs    Retail S   Advertis        Fit   StDev Fit    Residual    St Resid
  4        5507    119.220    112.716      1.222       6.504       2.02R
 20        6394    145.370    151.853      1.774      -6.483      -2.19R

R denotes an observation with a large standardized residual
```

The resulting regression for this problem (with the first observation missing) is

$$y_t = -43.8 + 0.0188x_t + 0.479y_{t-1}$$
$${}_{(0.0029)}{}_{(0.087)}$$

The numbers below the regression coefficients are the coefficient standard deviations. The Student's t statistics for each coefficient are quite large and the resulting p-values are 0.00, indicating that we can reject the null hypothesis that the coefficients are 0. With 18 degrees of freedom for error the critical value for a Student's t statistic for a two-tailed hypothesis with $\alpha = 0.05$ is $t = 2.101$.

INTERPRETATION

In time series models the coefficient of determination R^2 can be somewhat misleading. For example, the high value for $R^2 = 96.3\%$ in the present problem would not necessarily indicate a strong relationship between local advertising and retail sales. Rather, it is a well-known empirical fact that the time plots of many business and economic time series exhibit a rather smooth evolutionary pattern over time. This fact alone is enough to ensure a high value for the coefficient of determination when a lagged dependent variable is included in the regression model. As a practical matter, the reader is advised to pay relatively little attention to the value of R^2 for such models.

The estimated regression for this problem can be interpreted as follows. Suppose that retail sales per household increase by $1 in the current year. The expected impact on local advertising per household is an increase of 0.0188 in the current year, a further increase of

$$(0.479)(0.0188) = \$0.0090$$

next year, a further increase of

$$(0.479)^2(0.0188) = \$0.0043$$

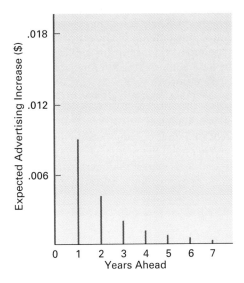

FIGURE 12.7
Expected Future Increases in Local Advertising per Household

in two years, and so on. The total effect on all future advertising expenditure per household is an expected increase of

$$\frac{0.0188}{1 - 0.479} = \$0.0361$$

Thus, we see that the expected effect of an increase in sales is an immediate increase in advertising expenditure, a further smaller increase in the following year, a yet smaller increase two years ahead, and so on. Figure 12.7 illustrates this geometrically decreasing effect of an increase in sales in the current year on advertising in future years.

EXERCISES

12.5 A market researcher is interested in the average amount of money per year spent by college students on clothing. From 25 years of annual data the following estimated regression was obtained through least squares.

$$y_t = 50.72 + .142x_{1t} + .027x_{2t} + .432y_{t-1}$$
$$\quad\quad\quad\;\; (.047) \quad\quad (.021) \quad\quad (.136)$$

where

y = Expenditure per student, in dollars, on clothes

x_1 = Disposable income per student, in dollars, after the payment of tuition, fees, and room and board

x_2 = Index of advertising, aimed at the student market, on clothes

(a) Test at the 5% level, against the obvious one-sided alternative, the null hypothesis that, all else being equal, advertising does not affect expenditures on clothes in this market.

(b) Find a 95% confidence interval for the coefficient on x_1 in the population regression.

(c) With advertising held fixed, what would be the expected impact over time of a \$1 increase in disposable income per student in clothing expenditure?

12.6 In Chapter 10, using the data of Table 10.1, we estimated the regression model

$$y_t = \beta_0 + \beta_1 x_t + \varepsilon_t$$

where

y_t = Retail sales per household

x_t = Disposable income per household

Use the data from the **Retail Sales** file to estimate the regression model

$$y_t = \beta_0 + \beta_1 x_t + \gamma Y_{t-1} + \varepsilon_t$$

and test the null hypothesis that $\gamma = 0$.

12.7 Use the data file **Money UK**, which contains observations from the United Kingdom on the quantity of money in million pounds (y), income in million pounds (x_1), and the local authority interest rate (x_2). Estimate the model (reference 5)

$$y_t = \beta_0 + \beta_1 x_{1t} + \beta_2 x_{2t} + \gamma Y_{t-1} + \varepsilon_t$$

and write a report on your findings.

y	x	y	x	y	x
1103	339	2637	1145	1896	964
1266	562	2177	1012	1684	811
1473	745	1920	836	1633	789
1423	749	1910	941	1657	802
1767	862	1984	981	1569	770
2161	1034	1787	974	1390	639
2336	1054	1689	766	1387	644
2602	1164	1866	920	1289	564
2518	1102				

12.8 The data file **Pension Funds** contains data on the market return (x) of stocks and the percentage (y) of portfolios in common stocks at market value at the end of the year for private pension funds. Estimate the regression model

$$y_t = \beta_0 + \beta_1 x_t + \gamma Y_{t-1} + \varepsilon_t$$

and write a report on your findings.

12.9 The data file **Income Canada** shows quarterly observations on income (y) and money supply (x) in Canada. Estimate the model (reference 3)

$$y_t = \beta_0 + \beta_1 x_t + \gamma Y_{t-1} + \varepsilon_t$$

and write a report on your findings.

12.10 The data file **Births Australia** shows annual observations on the first confinement resulting in a live birth of the current marriage (y) and the number of first marriages (for females) in the previous year (x) in Australia. Estimate the model (reference 4)

$$y_t = \beta_0 + \beta_1 x_t + \gamma Y_{t-1} + \varepsilon_t$$

and write a report on your findings.

12.11 The accompanying table shows annual observations on unit sales (y) and advertising expenditure (x), both in thousands of dollars, of Lydia E. Pinkham. Using the data file **PinkhamSales** estimate the model

$$\log y_t = \beta_0 + \beta_1 \log x_t + \gamma \log y_{t-1} + \varepsilon_t$$

and write a report on your findings (reference 2)

12.12 The accompanying table and the data file **Thailand Consumption** shows 29 annual observations on private consumption (y) and disposable income (x) in Thailand. Fit the regression model

$$\mathrm{Log}(y_t) = \beta_0 + \beta_1\,\mathrm{Log}(X_{1t}) + \gamma_2\,\mathrm{Log}(y_{t-1})$$

and write a report on your findings.

y_t	x_t	y_t	x_t	y_t	x_t
170	179	360	377	580	731
181	195	394	421	618	773
196	204	404	434	652	827
213	216	427	453	663	856
233	247	462	495	693	901
252	264	491	541	761	978
267	285	527	596	831	1093
278	307	554	623	919	1206
333	343	557	656	1003	1296
336	359	564	695		

12.4 SPECIFICATION BIAS

The specification of a statistical model that adequately depicts real-world behavior is a delicate and difficult task. We know that no simple model can describe perfectly the nature of a process and the determinants of process outcomes. Our objective in model building is to discover a straightforward formulation that adequately models the underlying process for the questions of interest. However, we should also note that there are certain cases where substantial divergence of the model from reality can result in conclusions that are seriously in error.

We have seen previously some techniques for specifying a model that more appropriately models the process. Our use of dummy variables in Sections 11.8 and 12.2 and transformations of nonlinear models to linear forms in Section 11.7 are important examples. In this section we will consider the implications of not including important predictor variables in our regression model.

In formulating a regression model, an investigator attempts to relate the dependent variable of interest to all of its important determinants. Thus, if we adopt a linear model, we want to include as independent variables all variables that might markedly influence the dependent variable of interest. In formulating the regression model

$$y_t = \beta_0 + \beta_1 x_{1t} + \beta_2 x_{2t} + \cdots + \beta_K x_{Kt} + \varepsilon_t$$

we implicitly assume that the set of independent variables, $X_1, X_2, \ldots, X_K$ contains all quantities that significantly affect the behavior of the dependent variable, Y. We know that in any real applied problem there will be other factors that also affect the dependent variable. The joint influence of these factors is absorbed within the error term ε_i. A serious problem can occur if an important variable is omitted from the list of independent variables.

BIAS FROM EXCLUDING SIGNIFICANT PREDICTOR VARIABLES

When significant predictor variables are omitted from the model, the least squares estimates will usually be biased, and the usual inferential statements from hypothesis tests or confidence intervals can be seriously misleading. In addition, the estimated model error will include the effect of the missing variables and thus will be larger. In the rare case where omitted variables are uncorrelated with the independent variables included in the regression model, this will not occur.

We will illustrate how the bias in estimating regression coefficients results by showing the effect of omitting a variable from a model with two independent variables

$$y_i = \beta_0 + \beta_1 x_{1i} + \beta_2 x_{2i} + \varepsilon_i$$

Suppose that in this situation the analyst leaves out variable x_2 and instead estimates the regression model

$$y_i = \alpha_0 + \alpha_1 x_{1i} + \mu_i$$

Note that we have used two different symbols to emphasize the fact that the coefficient estimators will be different. For the simple regression model the estimator for the coefficient of x_1 is

$$\hat{\alpha}_1 = \frac{\sum_{i=1}^{n} (x_{1i} - \overline{X})y_i}{\sum_{i=1}^{n} (x_{1i} - \overline{X})^2}$$

By substituting the correct model with two predictor variables and determining the expected value we find that

$$E[\hat{\alpha}_1] = E\left[\frac{\sum_{i=1}^{n} (x_{1i} - \overline{X})Y_i}{\sum_{i=1}^{n} (x_{1i} - \overline{X})^2} \right] = E\left[\frac{\sum_{i=1}^{n} (x_{1i} - \overline{X})(\beta_0 + \beta_1 x_{1i} + \beta_2 x_{2i} + \varepsilon_i)}{\sum_{i=1}^{n} (x_{1i} - \overline{X})^2} \right]$$

When we compute the expected value we find that

$$E[\hat{\alpha}_1] = \beta_1 + \beta_2 \left[\frac{\sum_{i=1}^{n} (x_{1i} - \overline{X})x_{2i}}{\sum_{i=1}^{n} (x_{1i} - \overline{X})^2} \right]$$

Thus we see that the coefficient of the X_1 variable is biased unless the correlation between X_1 and X_2 is 0.

We will also show this bias in Example 12.5.

EXAMPLE 12.5

SAVINGS AND LOAN REGRESSION MODEL WITH OMITTED VARIABLE (MODEL SPECIFICATION ERROR)

Savings and Loan

Consider the savings and loan example used in Chapter 11. In that example the annual percentage profit margin (y) of savings and loan associations was regressed on their percentage net revenues per deposit dollar (x_1), and the number of offices (x_2). In Figure 11.3 we estimated the regression coefficients and found that the model was

$$\hat{y} = 1.565 + 0.237x_1 - 0.000249x_2 \qquad R^2 = 0.865$$
$$\phantom{\hat{y} = 1.565 + } {\scriptstyle (0.0555)} {\scriptstyle (0.0000320)}$$

One conclusion that follows from this analysis is that for a fixed number of offices, a 1-unit increase in net revenues per deposit dollar leads to an expected increase of 0.237 unit in profit margin. What would happen if we regressed profit margin on only the net revenues per deposit dollar? Data stored in file **Savings and Loan**.

SOLUTION

Using the data, we ran the regression of profit margin (y) on net revenues per deposit dollar (x_1) and found the model was

$$\hat{y} = 1.326 - 0.169x_1 \qquad R^2 = 0.50$$
$$\phantom{\hat{y} = 1.326 - } {\scriptstyle (0.036)}$$

Comparing the two fitted models we notice that one consequence of ignoring x_2 is that the percent explained variability R^2 is substantially reduced.

INTERPRETATION

There is, however, a more serious effect on the coefficient of net revenue. In the multiple regression model a 1-unit increase in net revenue increased profit by 0.237, while in the simple regression model the effect was a decrease of 0.169. In both models we would reject the null hypothesis that there is not a relationship. This result is clearly counterintuitive—we should not expect an increase in net revenue to decrease profit margin. Here we see the result of the biased estimator for the coefficient that occurs when a significant variable x_2 is not included in the model. Without including the conditional effect of the number of offices we obtain a biased estimator.

This example rather nicely illustrates the point. If an important explanatory variable is not included in the regression model, any conclusions drawn about the effects of other independent variables can be seriously misleading. In this particular case, we have seen that adding a relevant variable could well alter the impression of a significant negative association to the conclusion of significant positive association. Further insight can be gained from casual inspection of the data in Table 11.1. Over the latter part of the period, at least, profit margins fell and net revenues rose, suggesting a negative association between these variables. However, a further look at the data reveals an increase in the number of offices over this same period, suggesting the possibility that this factor could be the cause of the declining profit margins. The only legitimate way to disentangle the separate effects of the two independent variables on the dependent variable is to model them jointly in a regression equation. This example illustrates the importance of using the multiple regression model rather than simple linear regression equations when there is more than one relevant independent variable.

EXERCISES

12.13 Transportation Research Inc. has asked you to prepare some multiple regression equations to estimate the effect of variables on fuel economy. The data for this study are contained in the data file **Motors**, and the dependent variable is miles per gallon—milpgal—as established by the Department of Transportation certification.

    (a) Prepare a regression equation that uses vehicle horsepower—horspwer—and vehicle weight—weight—as independent variables. Interpret the coefficients.

    (b) Prepare a second biased regression with vehicle weight not included. What can you conclude about the coefficient of horsepower?

12.14 Use the data in the file **Citydat** to estimate a regression equation that can be used to determine the marginal effect of the percent commercial property on the market value per owner-occupied residence. Include percent owner-occupied residences, percent industrial property, the median rooms per residence, and per capita income as additional predictor variables in your multiple regression equation. The variables are included on your data disk and described in the appendix. Indicate which of the variables are conditionally significant. Your final equation should include only sig-

nificant variables. Run a second regression with median rooms per residence excluded. Interpret the new coefficient for percent commercial property that results from the second regression. Compare the two coefficients.

12.15 Suppose that the true linear model for a process was

$$Y = \beta_0 + \beta_1 X_1 + \beta_2 X_2 + \beta_3 X_3$$

and you incorrectly estimated the model

$$Y = \alpha_0 + \alpha_1 X_2$$

Interpret and contrast the coefficients for X_2 in the two models. Show the bias that results from using the second model.

12.16 Suppose that a regression relationship is given by

$$Y = \beta_0 + \beta_1 X_1 + \beta_2 X_2 + \varepsilon$$

If the simple linear regression of Y on X_1 is estimated from a sample of n observations, the resulting slope estimate will generally be biased for β_1. However, in the special case where the sample correlation between the X_{1i} and X_{2i} is 0, this will not be so. In fact, in that case, the same estimate results whether or not X_{2i} is included in the regression equation.

    (a) Explain verbally why this sentence is true.

    (b) Show algebraically that this statement is true.

12.5 MULTICOLLINEARITY

If a regression model is correctly specified and the assumptions are satisfied, the least squares estimates are the best that can be achieved. Nevertheless, in some circumstances they may not be very good!

    To illustrate, consider again the savings and loan association example of Chapter 11. In this particular study, we observed 25 pairs of annual values of the model variables. These data were then used to estimate, through a multiple regression model, the separate effects of the two independent variables on profit margins. Imagine, now, that you wanted to study this problem but were in the fortunate position of the laboratory scientist, able to design the experiment. The best choice for selecting observations depends somewhat on the objectives of the analysis, but there are best strategies. There are, however, choices that we would not make. For example, we would not choose the same values of the independent variables for all of the observations.

Another bad choice would be to choose independent variables that are highly correlated. In Section 11.2 we saw that it would be impossible to estimate the coefficients if the independent variables were perfectly correlated. And in Section 11.4 we saw that the variance of coefficient estimators increase as the correlation moves away from 0. In Figure 12.8 we see examples of perfect correlation between the variables x_1 and x_2. From these plots we see that changes in one variable are directly related to changes in the other variable. Now suppose we were attempting to use independent variable values such as these to estimate the coefficients of the regression model

$$y_i = \beta_0 + \beta_1 x_{1i} + \beta_2 x_{2i} + \varepsilon_i$$

The futility of such a task is apparent. If a change in x_1 occurs simultaneously with a change in x_2 then we cannot tell which of the independent variables actually is related to the change in Y. If we want to assess the separate effects of the independent variables, it is essential that they do not move in unison through the experiment. The standard assumptions for multiple regression analysis exclude cases of this sort.

The use of these two correlated independent variables was clearly a bad design choice. A slightly less extreme case is illustrated in Figure 12.9. Here, the design points do not lie on single straight lines but are very close to doing so. In this situation, the results are able to provide some information about the separate influences of the independent variables, but not very much. It will be possible to calculate least squares estimates of the coefficients, but these coefficient estimates will have high variance. As a result the estimated coefficients will not be statistically significant even when the relationships might be quite strong. This phenomenon is referred to as **multicollinearity**.

In the vast majority of practical cases involving business and economic applications we are not able to control the choice of variable observations. Rather, we are constrained to work with the particular data set that fate has given us. In this context, then, multicollinearity is a problem arising not from bad choice of data but from the data that are available for our analysis. More generally, in regression equations involving several independent variables, the multicollinearity problem arises from patterns of strong intercorre-

FIGURE 12.8
Two Designs with Perfect Multicollinearity

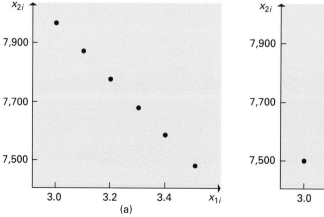
(a)

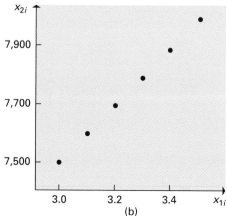
(b)

FIGURE 12.9
Illustrations of Designs with Multicollinearity

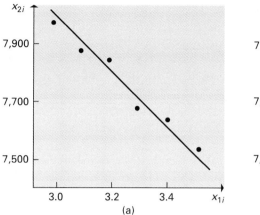 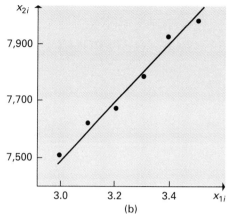

(a)   (b)

lations among the independent variables. Perhaps the most frustrating aspect of the problem, which can by summarized as having data that are not very informative about the parameters of interest, is that typically little can be done about it. It is, however, still important to be aware of the problem and watch for its occurrence.

There are a number of indicators of multicollinearity. First, of course, you should always examine a simple correlation matrix of the independent variables to determine if any of the independent variables are individually correlated. We did this in the extended application example in Section 11.9. Another indication of the likely presence of multicollinearity occurs when, taken as a group, a set of independent variables appears to exert considerable influence on the dependent variable, but when looked at separately, through tests of hypotheses, all appear individually to be insignificant. In this case a linear function of the several variables might be used to compute a new variable to replace several correlated variables. Another strategy is to regress individual independent variables on all of the other independent variables in the model. This can indicate complex examples of multicollinearity. Given multicollinearity, it would be unwise in these circumstances to jump to the conclusion that a particular independent variable did not affect the dependent variable. Rather, it is preferable to acknowledge that the group as a whole is clearly influential, but the data are not sufficiently informative to allow the disentangling, with any precision, of its members' separate effects.

EXERCISES

12.17 In the regression model

$$y = \beta_0 + \beta_1 X_1 + \beta_2 X_2 + \varepsilon$$

the extent of any multicollinearity can be evaluated by finding the correlation between X_1 and X_2 in the sample. Explain why this is so.

12.18 An economist estimates the regression model

$$y_i = \alpha + \beta_1 x_{1i} + \beta_2 x_{2i} + \varepsilon_i$$

The estimates of the parameters β_1 and β_2 are not very large, compared with their respective standard errors. But the size of the coefficient of determination indicates quite a strong relationship between the dependent variable and the pair of independent variables. Having

obtained these results, the economist strongly suspects the presence of multicollinearity. Since his chief interest is in the influence of x_1 on the dependent variable, he decides that he will avoid the problem of multicollinearity by regressing Y on x_1 alone. Comment on this strategy.

12.19 Refer to Exercise 11.78 of Chapter 11. The independent variable x_1, real income per capita, was dropped from the model, and the regression of growth rate in real gross domestic product on x_1, average tax rate, was estimated. This yielded the fitted model

$$y = .060 - .074x_2 \qquad R^2 = .072$$
$$\quad\;\; (0.34)$$

Comment on this result.

12.6   HETEROSCEDASTICITY

The least squares estimation method and its inferential procedures are based on the standard regression assumptions. When these assumptions hold, least squares regression provides a powerful set of analysis tools. However, when one or more of these assumptions are violated the estimated coefficients can be inefficient and the inferences drawn could be misleading.

For example, in Section 12.4 we saw the problems associated with specification bias. If important explanatory variables are omitted from a regression model, then the estimated coefficients of the remaining variables may be biased if the omitted variables are correlated with those in the estimated regression model.

In the next two sections we will consider the problems associated when the assumptions concerning the distribution of error terms, ε_i, in the model

$$y_i = \beta_0 + \beta_1 x_{1i} + \beta_2 x_{2i} + \cdots + \beta_K x_{Ki} + \varepsilon_i.$$

Specifically, we have assumed that these errors have uniform variance and are uncorrelated with each other. In the following section we will examine the possibility of correlated errors. Here we consider the assumption of uniform variance.

There are many examples that suggest the possibility of nonuniform variance. Consider a situation in which we are interested in factors affecting output from a particular industry. We collect data from several different firms that include measures of output and likely predictor variables. If these firms have different sizes then total output will vary. In addition, it is likely that the larger firms have greater variance in their output measure compared to small firms. This results from the observation that there are more factors that affect the error terms in a large firm than there are in a small firm. Hence the error terms will be larger in both positive and negative terms.

Models in which the error terms do not all have the same variance are said to exhibit **heteroscedasticity**. When this phenomenon is present, least squares is not the most efficient procedure for estimating the coefficients of the regression model. Moreover, the usual procedures for deriving confidence intervals and tests of hypotheses for these coefficients are no longer valid. Thus we need procedures that test for heteroscedasticity. Most of the common procedures check the assumption of constant error variance against some plausible alternative. We may find that the size of the error variance is directly related to one of the independent predictor variables. Another possibility is that the variance increases with the expected value of the dependent variable.

In our estimated regression model we can obtain estimates of the expected values of the dependent variable by using

$$\hat{y}_i = b_0 + b_1 x_{1i} + b_2 x_{2i} + \cdots + b_K x_{Ki}$$

And in turn we can estimate the error terms, ε_i, by the residuals

$$e_i = y_i - \hat{y}_i$$

We often find that graphical techniques are useful for detecting heteroscedasticity. In practice we prepare scatter plots of the residuals versus the independent variables and the predicted values, $\hat{Y}_i$, from the regression. For example consider Figure 12.10, which shows possible plots of the residual, e_i, against the independent variable x_{1i}. In part (a) of the figure, we see that the magnitude of the errors tend to increase with increasing values of x_1,

FIGURE 12.10
Plots of Residuals Against an
Independent Variable

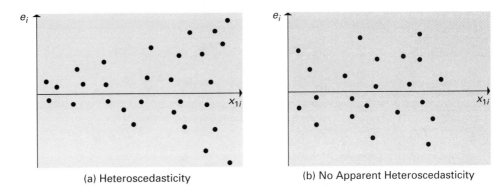

(a) Heteroscedasticity   (b) No Apparent Heteroscedasticity

indicating that the error variances are not constant. In contrast, part (b) of the figure shows no systematic relationship between the errors and x_1. Thus in part (b) there is no evidence of nonuniform variance.

In Chapter 11, we developed a least squares regression model to estimate the relationship between savings and loan profit margins (y) and the net revenue per deposit dollar (x_1) and the number of offices (x_2) through the model

$$\hat{y}_i = b_0 + b_1 x_{1i} + b_2 x_{2i}$$

We will use the estimated regression model from Figure 11.3 to compute the residuals from all observations. Using Minitab we can compute the residuals as a new variable as part of the regression analysis using the command sequence

```
STAT > REGRESSION > REGRESSION > STORAGE
```

This procedure was demonstrated in the extended example problem in Section 11.9. In Figures 12.11 and 12.12 we present scatter plots of the residuals versus the revenues per deposit dollar and versus the number of offices. Examination of these plots indicates that there does not appear to be any relationship between the magnitude of the residuals and

FIGURE 12.11
Plot of residuals versus
Revenues per deposit dollar

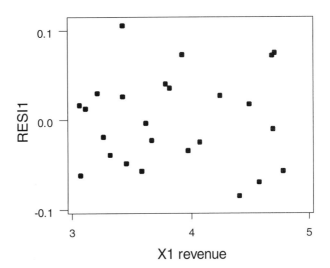

FIGURE 12.12
Plot of Residuals versus
Number of Offices

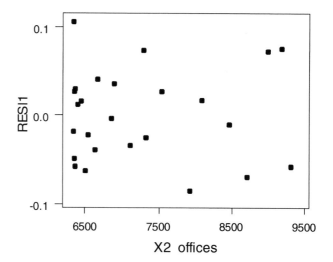

either of the independent variables. Figure 12.13 presents a scatter plot of the residuals versus the predicted value of the dependent variable. Again there does not appear to be any relationship between the predicted value of Y and the magnitude of the residuals. Recall from Section 11.9 that residuals are linearly related to the observed value of the dependent variable, and thus it would not be useful to plot the residuals versus the observed value of Y. Based on an examination of the residual plots we find no evidence of heteroscedasticity.

We will now consider a more formal procedure for detecting heteroscedasticity and for estimating the coefficients of regression models when it is strongly suspected that the assumption of constant error variance is violated. There are many possible forms for heteroscedasticity that can be detected with a variety of procedures. We will consider one such procedure that can be used to detect heteroscedasticity when the variance of the error term has a linear relationship with the predicted value of the dependent variable.

FIGURE 12.13
Plot of Residuals versus
Predicted Profit Margin

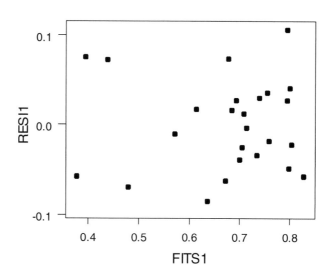

TEST FOR HETEROSCEDASTICITY

Consider a regression model

$$y_i = \beta_0 + \beta_1 x_{1i} + \beta_2 x_{2i} + \cdots + \beta_K x_{Ki} + \varepsilon_i$$

linking a dependent variable to K independent variables and based on n sets of observations. Let $b_0, b_1, \ldots, b_K$ be the least squares estimates of the model coefficients, with the predicted values

$$\hat{y}_i = b_0 + b_1 x_{1i} + b_2 x_{2i} + \cdots + b_K x_{Ki}$$

and the residuals from the fitted model are

$$e_i = y_i - \hat{y}_i$$

To test the null hypothesis that the error terms, ε_i, all have the same variance against the alternative that their variances depend on the expected values

$$\hat{y}_i = b_0 + b_1 x_{1i} + b_2 x_{2i} + \cdots + b_K x_{Ki}$$

we estimate a simple regression. In this regression, the dependent variable is the square of the residuals—that is e_i^2—and the independent variable is the predicted value, $\hat{y}_i$.

$$e_i^2 = a_0 + a_1 \hat{y}_i \tag{12.2}$$

Let R^2 be the coefficient of determination of this auxiliary regression. Then for a test of significance level α, the null hypothesis is rejected if nR^2 is bigger than $\chi^2_{1,\alpha}$ where $\chi^2_{1,\alpha}$ is the critical value of the chi-square random variable with 1 degree of freedom and probability of error α.

We will provide an example of this test using the savings and loan example. A subset of the regression output from Minitab and a partial screen shot of the data are shown in Figure 12.14. The Calc function was used to compute the residuals squared, which were then regressed on the predicted value.

From the regression of the squared residuals on the predicted values we obtain the estimated model

$$e^2 = 0.00621 + \underset{(0.00433)}{0.00550} \hat{y} \qquad R^2 = 0.066$$

The regression includes $n = 25$ observations and thus the test statistic is

$$nR^2 = (25)(0.066) = 1.65$$

From the Appendix, we find, for a 10% level test

$$\chi^2_{1,0.10} = 2.71$$

Therefore we cannot reject the null hypothesis that the regression model has uniform variance over the predicted values. This confirms our initial conclusions based on examining the scatter plots of residuals in Figures 12.11, 12.12, and 12.13.

Now suppose that we had rejected the null hypothesis that the variance was uniform. Then ordinary least squares would not be the appropriate estimation procedure for the initial model. There are a number of estimation strategies depending on the nature of the

FIGURE 12.14

Minitab Output Regression of Residual Squared on Predicted Value

Regression Analysis

```
The regression equation is
ResSquared = 0.00621 - 0.00550 FITS1

Predictor        Coef        StDev          T         P
Constant     0.006211     0.002970       2.09     0.048
FITS1       -0.005503     0.004327      -1.27     0.216

S = 0.002742    R-Sq = 6.6%       R-Sq(adj) = 2.5%
```

	C1	C2	C3	C4	C5	C6	C7	C8	C9
↓	year	X1 revenue	X2 offices	Y profit	FITS1	RESI1	ResSquared		
1	1	3.92	7298	0.75	0.676530	0.073470	0.0053978		
2	2	3.61	6855	0.71	0.713341	-0.003341	0.0000112		
3	3	3.32	6636	0.66	0.699102	-0.039102	0.0015290		
4	4	3.07	6506	0.61	0.672183	-0.062183	0.0038667		
5	5	3.06	6450	0.70	0.683760	0.016240	0.0002637		
6	6	3.11	6402	0.72	0.707575	0.012425	0.0001544		

nonuniform error. Most procedures involve transforming the model variables so that the error terms have a uniform magnitude over the range of the model. Consider the example where the variance of the error terms is directly proportional to the square of the expected value of the dependent variable. In this case we could approximate the model error term as

$$\varepsilon_i = \hat{y}_i \delta_i$$

where δ_i is a random variable with uniform variance over the range of the regression model. Using this error term the regression model would be

$$y_i = \beta_0 + \beta_1 x_{1i} + \beta_2 x_{2i} + \cdots + \beta_k x_{ki} + \hat{y}_i \delta_i$$

In this approximation the error term increases linearly with the expected value—implying that the variance increases with the square of the expected value. Here we could obtain an error term whose magnitude was uniform over the model by dividing every term on both sides of the equation by $\hat{y}_i$. When this particular form is assumed, a simple two-stage procedure is used to estimate the parameters of the regression model. At the first stage, the model is estimated by least squares in the usual way, and the predicted values, $\hat{y}_i$, of the dependent variable are recorded. At the second stage, we estimate the regression equation.

$$\frac{y_i}{\hat{y}_i} = \beta_0 \frac{1}{\hat{y}_i} + \beta_1 \frac{x_{1i}}{\hat{y}_i} + \beta_2 \frac{x_{2i}}{\hat{y}_i} + \cdots + \beta_K \frac{x_{Ki}}{\hat{y}_i} + \delta_i$$

with an error term that meets the standard regression assumptions. In this model we would regress $y_i / \hat{y}_i$ on the independent variables $1/\hat{y}_i, x_{1i}/\hat{y}_i, x_{2i}/\hat{y}_i, \ldots, x_{ki}/\hat{y}_i$. This model does not include a constant or Y intercept term, but most statistical packages have an option that provides for coefficient estimates with the constant term excluded. The estimated coefficients are the estimates for the original model coefficients.

The appearance of heteroscedastic errors can also result if a linear regression model is estimated in circumstances where a log linear model is appropriate. When the process is such that a log linear model is appropriate we should make the transformations and estimate a log linear model. Taking logarithms will dampen the influence of large observations, especially if the large observations result from percentage growth from previous states—an exponential growth pattern. The resulting model will often appear to be free from heteroscedasticity. Log linear models are often appropriate when the data under study are time series of economic variables, such as consumption, income, and money, that tend to grow exponentially over time.

EXERCISES

12.20 In Chapter 10, the regression of retail sales per household on disposable income per household was estimated by least squares. The data are given in Table 10.1, and Table 10.2 shows the residuals and the predicted values of the dependent variable.
   (a) Graphically check for heteroscedasticity in the regression errors.
   (b) Check for heteroscedasticity by using a formal test.
12.21 Refer to Exercise 11.50 that uses 48 observations. Let e_i denote the residuals from the fitted regression and $\hat{y}_i$ the in-sample predicted values of the dependent vari-

able. The least squares regression of e_i^2 on $\hat{y}_i$ has coefficient of determination .032. What can you conclude from this finding?
12.22 In Exercise 11.61 (Chapter 11), a regression explaining the percentage of females in the labor force was fitted to data from 50 states using the data file **Household Income**.
   (a) Graphically check for heteroscedasticity in the regression errors.
   (b) Use a formal test to check for heteroscedasticity.

12.7 AUTOCORRELATED ERRORS

In this section we will examine the effects on the regression model if the error terms in a regression model are correlated with one another. Up to this point we have assumed that the random errors for our model are independent. However, in many business and economic problems we use time series data. When time series data are analyzed, the error term represents the effect of all factors, other than the independent variables, that influence the dependent variable. In time series data the behavior of many of these factors might be quite similar over several time periods and the result would be a correlation between the error terms that are close together in time.

To emphasize time series observations we will subscript the observations by t and write the regression model as

$$y_t = \beta_0 + \beta_1 x_{1t} + \beta_2 x_{2t} + \cdots + \beta_K x_{Kt} + \varepsilon_t$$

The hypothesis tests and confidence intervals in multiple regression assume that the errors are independent. If the errors are not independent then the estimated standard errors for the coefficients are biased. For example, it can be shown that if there is a positive correlation between the error terms from adjacent time series observations then the least squares estimate of the coefficient standard error is too small. As a result the computed Student's t statistics for the coefficient will be too large. This could lead us to conclude that certain coefficients are significantly different from 0—by rejecting the null hypothesis $\beta_j = 0$—when in fact the null should not be rejected. In addition, estimated confidence intervals would be too narrow.

It is therefore critically important in regressions with time series data to test the hypothesis that the error terms are not correlated with one another. Correlations between first-order errors through time are defined as **autocorrelated errors**. As we study this problem it is useful to have in mind some autocorrelation structure. One appealing model is that the error in time, t, ε_t, is highly correlated with the error in the previous time period, ε_{t-1}, but less correlated with errors two or more periods previous in the time series. We will define

$$\text{Corr}(\varepsilon_t, \varepsilon_{t-1}) = \rho$$

where ρ is a correlation coefficient and thus exists over the range from -1 to $+1$, as discussed in Chapter 10. In most applications we are most concerned about positive values of the correlation coefficient. For errors that are separated by j periods the autocorrelation can be modeled as

$$\text{Corr}(\varepsilon_t, \varepsilon_{t-j}) = \rho^j$$

As a result the correlation decays rapidly as the number of periods of separation grow. We see then that the correlation between errors far apart in time is relatively weak, while that between errors closer to one another in time is possibly quite strong.

Now, if we assume that the errors ε_t all have the same variance, it is possible to show that the autocorrelation structure corresponds to the model

$$\varepsilon_t = \rho \varepsilon_{t-1} + u_t$$

where the random variable u_t has mean 0 and a constant variance σ^2 and is not autocorrelated. This is defined as the first order autoregressive model of autocorrelated behavior. Looking at this equation, we see that the value taken by the error at time t, ε_t depends on its value in the previous time period (the strength of that dependence being determined by the correlation coefficient ρ) and on a second random term μ_t. This model is illustrated in Figure 12.15, which shows time plots of errors generated by the model for values of $\rho = 0$, 0.3, 0.6, 0.9. The case $\rho = 0$ corresponds to no autocorrelation in the errors. In part (a) of the figure, it can be seen that there is no apparent pattern in the progression through time of the errors. The value taken by one does not influence the values of the others. As we move from relatively weak autocorrelation ($\rho = 0.3$) to quite strong autocorrelation ($\rho = 0.9$), in parts (b), (c), and (d), it emerges that the pattern through time of the errors becomes increasingly less jagged, so that in part (d), of the figure, it is quite clear that an error is likely to be relatively close in value to its immediate neighbor.

Examination of Figure 12.15 suggests that graphical methods might be useful in detecting the presence of autocorrelated errors. Ideally we would like to plot the model errors, ε_t, but these are unknown and so we typically examine the plot of residuals from the regression model. In particular we could examine a time plot of residuals such as shown in Figure 12.16 for the savings and loan regression. This time series plot was prepared using the Minitab command sequence

    GRAPH > TIME SERIES PLOT

(Note that after generating the plot we clicked on the Minitab Editor and used the command **Edit** to draw the horizontal line representing the zero value for the residuals.)

Examining the time series plot in Figure 12.16, we do not see any autocorrelation in the residuals but instead have the jagged pattern seen in Figure 12.15(a). This evidence would argue against autocorrelation. However, since the problem is so important, it is desirable to have a more formal test of hypothesis of no autocorrelation in the errors of a regression model.

FIGURE 12.15
Time Plots of Residuals from
Regressions Whose Error
Terms Follow a First Order
Autoregressive Process

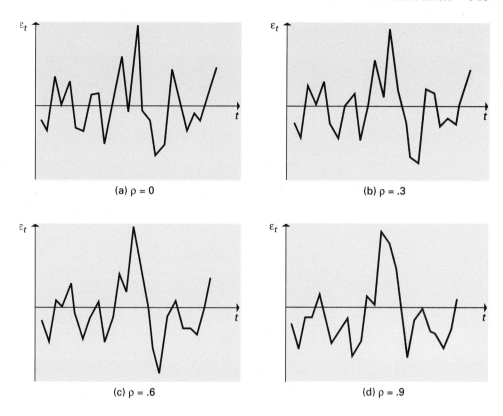

(a) ρ = 0

(b) ρ = .3

(c) ρ = .6

(d) ρ = .9

The test that is most often used is the *Durbin-Watson test,* based on the model residuals, e_t. The test statistic, d, is calculated by

$$d = \frac{\sum_{t=2}^{n} (e_t - e_{t-1})^2}{\sum_{t=1}^{n} e_t^2}$$

and the test procedure is described in the box.

We can show that the Durbin-Watson statistic can be written approximately as

$$d = 2(1 - r)$$

FIGURE 12.16
Time Series Plot of Residuals
from Savings and Loan
Regression

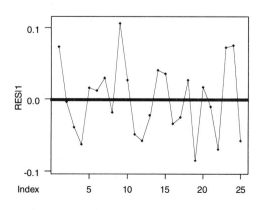

FIGURE 12.17
Decision Rule for The
Durbin-Watson Test

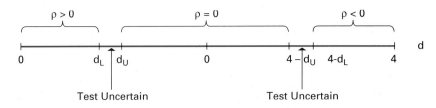

where, r, is the sample estimate of the population correlation, ρ, between adjacent errors. If the errors are not autocorrelated then r is approximately 0 and d is approximately 2. In contrast, positive correlation would lead to small values of d with 0 being the lower limit and negative correlation would lead to large values of d with 4 being the upper limit. There is a theoretical difficulty involved in basing tests for autocorrelated errors on the Durbin-Watson statistic. The problem is that the actual sampling distribution of d, even when the hypothesis of no autocorrelation is true, depends on the particular values of the independent variables. It is obviously infeasible to tabulate the distribution for every possible set of values of the independent variables. Fortunately, it is known that whatever the independent variables, the distribution of d lies between that of two other random variables, whose percentage points can be tabulated. For tests of significance levels 1% and 5%, cutoff points for these random variables are tabulated in Table 10 of the Appendix. For various combinations of n and K, these tables give values of d_L and d_U. The null hypothesis of no autocorrelation is rejected against the alternative of positive autocorrelation if the calculated d is less than d_L. The null hypothesis is accepted if d is larger than d_U and less than $4 - d_U$, while if d lies between d_L and d_U, the test is inconclusive. Finally, if the d statistic is greater than $4 - d_L$ we would conclude that there is negative autocorrelation. This complex pattern is illustrated in Figure 12.17.

THE DURBIN-WATSON TEST

Consider the regression model

$$y_t = \beta_0 + \beta_1 x_{1t} + \beta_2 x_{2t} + \cdots + \beta_k x_{kt} + \varepsilon_t$$

based on sets of n observations. We are interested in determining if the error terms are autocorrelated and follow a first-order autoregressive model

$$\varepsilon_t = \rho \varepsilon_{t-1} + u_t$$

where u_t is not autocorrelated.
   The test of the null hypothesis of no autocorrelation

$$H_0 : \rho = 0$$

is based on the Durbin-Watson statistic

$$d = \frac{\sum_{t=2}^{n} (e_t - e_{t-1})^2}{\sum_{t=1}^{n} e_t^2} \tag{12.3}$$

where the e_t are the residuals when the regression equation is estimated by least squares. When the alternative hypothesis is of positive autocorrelation in errors, that is

$$H_1: \rho > 0$$

the decision rule is as follows:

Reject H_0 if $d < d_L$
Accept H_0 if $d > d_U$
Test inconclusive if $d_L < d < d_U$

Where d_L and d_U are tabulated for values of n and K and for significance levels of 1% and 5% in Table 10 of the Appendix.

Occasionally, one wants to test against the alternative of negative autocorrelation that is

$$H_1: \rho < 0$$

the decision rule is as follows:

Reject H_0 if $d > 4 - d_L$
Accept H_0 if $d < 4 - d_U$
Test inconclusive if $4 - d_L > d > 4 - d_U$

The Durbin-Watson d statistic can be computed by most computer programs by request. Figure 12.18 shows the Minitab computation window and the resulting output for the savings and loan example. The Durbin-Watson d statistic can be obtained by using the command sequence

REGRESSION > REGRESSION > OPTIONS > DURBIN-WATSON STATISTIC

FIGURE 12.18
Minitab Output . Durbin-
Watson d Statistic Calculation

Regression Analysis

```
The regression equation is
Y profit = 1.56 + 0.237 X1 revenue -0.000249 X2  offices

Predictor        Coef        StDev           T        P
Constant      1.56450      0.07940       19.70    0.000
X1 reven      0.23720      0.05556        4.27    0.000
X2 offi    -0.00024908  0.00003205       -7.77    0.000

S = 0.05330     R-Sq = 86.5%      R-Sq(adj) = 85.3%

Analysis of Variance

Source          DF          SS           MS         F        P
Regression       2      0.40151      0.20076     70.66    0.000
Residual Error  22      0.06250      0.00284
Total           24      0.46402

Durbin-Watson statistic = 1.95
```

INTERPRETATION

The computed Durbin-Watson d statistic is 1.95 and from the Appendix with $\alpha = 0.01$, $k = 2$, and $n = 25$ the critical values are $d_L = 0.98$ and $d_U = 1.30$. Thus $H_0: \rho = 0$ cannot be rejected and we conclude that the error terms are not autocorrelated.

Estimation of Regressions with Autocorrelated Errors

When we conclude, based on the Durbin-Watson test, that we do have autocorrelated errors, we need to modify the regression procedure to remove the effect of the autocorrelated errors. Typically this is done by an appropriate transformation of the variables used in the regression estimation procedure. We will develop the basic method in the steps that follow. First consider a multiple regression model with autocorrelated errors

$$y_t = \beta_0 + \beta_1 x_{1t} + \beta_2 x_{2t} + \cdots + \beta_k x_{kt} + \varepsilon_t$$

and the same regression model at time $t - 1$ is

$$y_{t-1} = \beta_0 + \beta_1 x_{1,t-1} + \beta_2 x_{2,t-1} + \cdots + \beta_k x_{k,t-1} + \varepsilon_{t-1}$$

Multiplying both sides of this equation by ρ, the correlation between adjacent errors gives

$$\rho y_{t-1} = \beta_0 + \beta_1 \rho x_{1,t-1} + \beta_2 \rho x_{2,t-1} + \cdots + \beta_k \rho x_{k,t-1} + \rho \varepsilon_{t-1}$$

Then we subtract this equation from the first equation to obtain

$$y - \rho y_{t-1} = \beta_0 (1 - \rho) + \beta_1 (x_{1t} - \rho x_{1,t-1}) + \beta_2 (x_{2t} - \rho x_{2,t-1}) + \cdots$$
$$+ \beta_k (x_{kt} - \rho x_{k,t-1}) + u_t$$

where

$$u_t = \varepsilon_t - \rho \varepsilon_{t-1}$$

and the random variable δ_t has uniform variance and is not autocorrelated. We see that now we have a regression model linking the dependent variable $(Y_t - \rho Y_{t-1})$ and the independent variables $(x_{1t} - \rho x_{1,t-1})$, $(x_{2t} - \rho x_{2,t-1})$,..., $(x_{k1t} - \rho x_{k,t-1})$. The parameters of this model are precisely the same as those of the original model except that the constant term is $\beta_0 (1 - \rho)$ instead of β_0. More important is the fact that in this model the errors are not autocorrelated and thus least squares multiple regression can be used to estimate the model coefficients. The least squares inferential procedures for confidence intervals and hypothesis tests are appropriate for this transformed model.

Based on this analysis we see that the problem of autocorrelated errors can be avoided by estimating the least squares regression using the dependent variable $(y_t - \rho y_{t-1})$ and the independent variables $(x_{1t} - \rho x_{1,t-1})$, $(x_{2t} - \rho x_{2,t-1})$,..., $(x_{k1t} - \rho x_{k,t-1})$. Unfortunately this approach faces a problem in practice because we do not know the value of ρ. Various procedures for obtaining an estimate for ρ are used in different computer programs. Here we will demonstrate a simple procedure where we use

$$r = 1 - \frac{d}{2}$$

to estimate ρ.

ESTIMATION OF REGRESSION MODELS WITH AUTOCORRELATED ERRORS

Suppose that we want to estimate the coefficients of the regression model

$$y_t = \beta_0 + \beta_1 x_{1t} + \beta_2 x_{2t} + \cdots + \beta_k x_{kt} + \varepsilon_t$$

when the error term ε_t is autocorrelated.

This can be accomplished in two stages, as follows:

i. Estimate the model by least squares, obtaining the Durbin-Watson statistic, *d*, and hence the estimate

$$r = 1 - \frac{d}{2} \tag{12.4}$$

of the autocorrelation parameter

ii. Estimate by least squares a second regression in which the dependent variable is $(y_t - ry_{t-1})$ and the independent variables are $(x_{1t} - rx_{1,t-1})$, $(x_{2t} - rx_{2,t-1})$,..., $(x_{k1t} - rx_{k,t-1})$.

The parameters $\beta_1, \beta_2, \ldots, \beta_k$ are estimated regression coefficients from this second model. An estimate of β_0 is obtained by dividing the estimated intercept for the second model by $(1 - r)$. Hypothesis tests and confidence intervals for the regression coefficients can be carried out using the output from the second regression.

EXAMPLE 12.6

TIME SERIES REGRESSION MODEL (REGRESSION ANALYSIS WITH CORRELATED ERRORS)

Macro2000

In this extended example we will demonstrate how to carry out a regression analysis, using Minitab, when the errors are autocorrelated. In this example we wish to develop a model that predicts the aggregate consumption of durable goods as a function of disposable income and the federal funds interest rate.

SOLUTION

The data for this project are contained in a file named **Macro2000**. The variables for this data file are described in the chapter Appendix. We will use the variables

CDH   Personal Consumption Expenditures: Durable Goods (1996 real dollars)
YPDH   Disposable Personal Income (1996 real dollars)
FFED   Federal Funds Effective rate

The data file contains quarterly data from 1946.1 (1st quarter) through 2000.2 (2nd quarter), but we wished to estimate the model using data from 1980.1 through 2000.2. Therefore our first task was to obtain a subset of the larger data. This can be accomplished in Minitab using the commands

```
MANIP > SUBSET WORKSHEET
```

Figure 12.19 indicates the procedure for obtaining a subset of a Minitab data file.

We then ran the multiple regression and obtained the output in Figure 12.20.

The Durbin-Watson statistic for this model was 0.23, indicating severe autocorrelation. Thus it was necessary to use transformations to obtain appropriate variables for running the regression. An estimated value for serial correlation, r, was computed using the relationship in Equation 12.4:

$$r = 1 - \frac{d}{2} = 1 - \frac{0.23}{2} = 0.885$$

Figure 12.21 presents the procedure for obtaining the transformed variables in Minitab using the estimated value $r = 0.885$. Since the transformation uses a lagged value of each variable, we lose the first observation in the data set. That was the reason we chose to include the fourth quarter of 1979 in the selection in Figure 12.19.

Figure 12.22 presents the regression model prepared using the modified variables.

Comparing the regression outputs in Figures 12.20 and 12.22 clearly indicates the problems associated with regression models that have autocorrelated errors. The first regression analysis was

$$CDH = -562 + 0.205 \underset{(0.00706)}{YPDH} + 6.38 \underset{(1.660)}{FFED}$$
$$R^2 = 0.953 \qquad\qquad d = 0.23$$

(Note that the numbers below the coefficients are the coefficient standard errors.)

The first regression had a Durbin-Watson statistic $d = 0.23$ indicating strong autocorrelation. Based on the regression statistics for the estimated coefficients we would have con-

FIGURE 12.19
Procedure for Obtaining a
Subset of a Minitab Data File

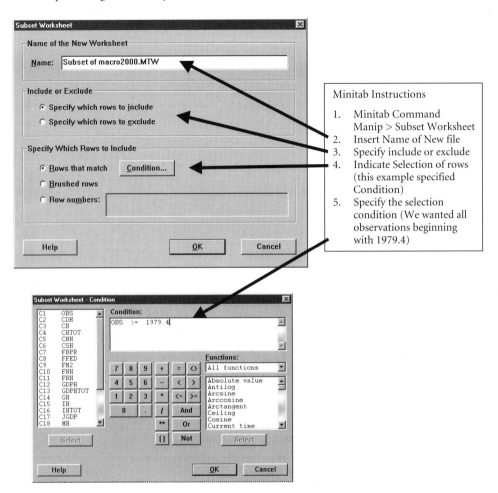

Minitab Instructions

1. Minitab Command
   Manip > Subset Worksheet
2. Insert Name of New file
3. Specify include or exclude
4. Indicate Selection of rows
   (this example specified
   Condition)
5. Specify the selection
   condition (We wanted all
   observations beginning
   with 1979.4)

FIGURE 12.20
Multiple Regression to
Predict Consumption of
Durables: Original Data

Regression Analysis

```
The regression equation is
CDH = - 562 + 0.205 YPDH + 6.38 FFED

Predictor        Coef      SE Coef          T        P
Constant       -561.76       45.20      -12.43    0.000
YPDH          0.204966     0.007063       29.02    0.000
FFED             6.375        1.660        3.84    0.000

S = 34.12       R-Sq = 95.3%      R-Sq(adj) = 95.2%

Analysis of Variance

Source            DF          SS          MS         F       P
Regression         2     1895460      947730    814.25   0.000
Residual Error    80       93115        1164
Total             82     1988574


Durbin-Watson statistic = 0.23
```

FIGURE 12.21
Procedure for Obtaining Transformed Variables Without Autocorrelation

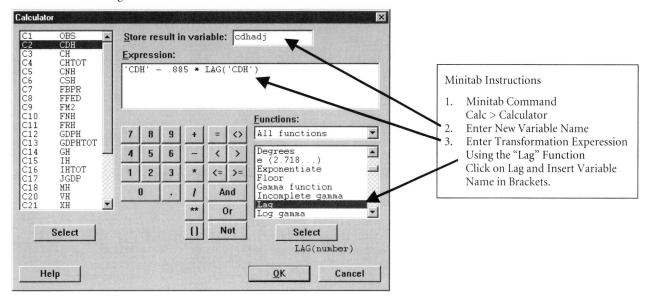

cluded that both disposable income ($\beta_1 = 0.205$) and federal funds interest rate ($\beta_2 = 6.38$) were statistically significant predictors of consumption expenditures for durable goods.

However, the second regression analysis—using data for the model without autocorrelated errors—provides a different conclusion

$$\text{CDHadj} = -56.8 + 0.201 \text{ ypdhadj} + 0.044 \text{ ffedadj}$$
$$\qquad\qquad\qquad\quad {\scriptstyle(0.0152)} \qquad\qquad {\scriptstyle(1.438)}$$
$$R^2 = 0.690 \qquad\qquad\qquad d = 2.16$$

INTERPRETATION

Notice that the variable names have been modified to reflect the fact that they have been transformed to variables that will produce a model that does not have autocorrelation. In addition, note that the Durbin-Watson statistic is $d = 2.16$ indicating that autocorrelation does not exist. We see that the estimated coefficient for disposable income ($\beta_1 = 0.201$) is similar to that from the first regression and that the coefficient standard error is 0.0152.

FIGURE 12.22
Regression Analysis Using
Transformed Variables
Without Autocorrelation

```
The regression equation is
cdhadj = - 56.8 + 0.201 ypdhadj + 0.04 ffedadj

82 cases used 1 cases contain missing values

Predictor       Coef      SE Coef          T        P
Constant     -56.796        9.434      -6.02    0.000
ypdhadj      0.20114      0.01525      13.19    0.000
ffedadj        0.044        1.438       0.03    0.975

S = 14.44      R-Sq = 69.0%      R-Sq(adj) = 68.2%

Analysis of Variance

Source           DF          SS          MS        F        P
Regression        2       36650       18325    87.87    0.000
Residual Error    79       16476         209
Total             81       53126


Durbin-Watson statistic = 2.16
```

The resulting Student's t statistic, 13.19, would lead us to conclude that disposable income is a significant predictor of durable goods consumption. In contrast, the coefficient of federal funds interest is $\beta_2 = 0.044$ with a Student's t statistic of 0.03. Thus we cannot reject the null hypothesis that the coefficient for federal funds interest is 0 and that we should eliminate that variable as a predictor in the regression model.

In this example we have seen that the autocorrelation led to an incorrect conclusion concerning the importance of federal funds interest rate. Without adjusting the data to remove the correlation we would have used the Student's t statistic from the model with the original data, and that Student's t statistic from the unadjusted regression overestimated the Student's t statistic from the adjusted regression. The Student's t for the disposable income coefficient in the first regression was also overestimated. However, after adjustment to the correct estimator we found that the coefficient was still substantially different from 0.

A number of statistical packages such as Eviews3 and SAS, which are designed for working with time series data, have built in routines for automatically estimating the autocorrelation coefficient and adjusting for autocorrelation. Many of these routines have iterative computational routines and as a result generate improved estimates of model coefficients and variances compared to the routine demonstrated here. Thus if you have access to such a package you would find the estimation easier than using Minitab or using PHStat with Excel in a parallel procedure. In general, those other computer packages would provide more efficient estimates of the coefficients.

Autocorrelated Errors in Models with Lagged Dependent Variables

When we have a regression model with lagged dependent variables on the right hand and also have autocorrelated errors, the usual least squares procedures can result in even more severe problems. In addition to the usual problems concerning the estimation of coefficient errors we also know that the coefficient estimators are not consistent. This occurs because there is a correlation between the model error and a predictor variable, and that introduces a bias in the coefficient estimate. Unfortunately, in this situation of lagged dependent variables, the previously discussed procedures for testing for autocorrelated errors are not valid. So we will briefly introduce an appropriate procedure.

Consider the model

$$y_t = \beta_0 + \beta_1 x_{1t} + \beta_2 x_{2t} + \cdots + \beta_k x_{kt} + \gamma y_{t-1} + \varepsilon_t$$

Suppose that this model is fitted to n sets of sample observations by least squares. Let d be the usual Durbin-Watson statistics with

$$r = 1 - \frac{d}{2}$$

and let s_c denote the estimated standard deviation of the estimated coefficient γ for the lagged dependent variable. Our null hypothesis is that the autoregressive parameter ρ is 0. A test of this hypothesis, approximately valid in large samples, is based on Durbin's h statistic

$$h = r\sqrt{n/(1 - ns_e^2)}$$

Under the null hypothesis, this statistic has a distribution that is well approximated in large samples by the standard normal. Thus, for example, the null hypothesis of no autocorrelation is rejected against the alternative that ρ is positive at the 5% level if the h statistic exceeds 1.645.

If the autoregressive error is

$$u_t = \varepsilon_t - \rho\varepsilon_{t-1}$$

then using a modification of the procedure previously developed for autocorrelation adjustment we can develop the following model

$$y_t - \rho y_{t-1} = \beta_0(1-\rho) + \beta_1(x_{1t} - \rho x_{1,t-1}) + \beta_2(x_{2t} - \rho x_{2,t-1}) + \cdots$$
$$+ \beta_k(x_{kt} - \rho x_{k,t-1}) + \gamma(y_{t-1} - \rho y_{t-2}) + \delta_t$$

One possible approach to parameter estimation, which requires only an ordinary least squares estimation program, is to substitute in turn possible values of ρ—say, 0.1, 0.3, 0.5, 0.7, and 0.9 in the preceding equation. Then the regression of dependent variable $(y_t - \rho y_{t-1}$ and the independent variables $(x_{1t} - \rho x_{1,t-1})$, $(x_{2t} - \rho x_{2,t-1})$,..., $(x_{k1t} - \rho x_{k,t-1})$, $(y_{t-1} - \rho y_{t-2})$ is fitted by least squares for each possible ρ value. The value of ρ chosen is that for which the resulting sum of squared errors is smallest. Inference about the β_j is then based on the corresponding fitted regression.

EXERCISES

12.23 In a regression based on 30 annual observations, U.S. farm income was related to four independent variables—grain exports, federal government subsidies, population, and a dummy variable for bad weather years. The model was fitted by least squares, resulting in a Durbin-Watson statistic of 1.29. The regression of e_i^2 on $\hat{y}_i$ yielded a coefficient of determination of .043.
(a) Test for heteroscedasticity.
(b) Test for autocorrelated errors.

12.24 Consider the regression model

$$y_i = \beta_0 + \beta_1 x_{1i} + \beta_2 x_{2i} + \ldots + \beta_K x_{Ki} + \varepsilon_i$$

Show that if

$$\text{Var}(\varepsilon_i) = Kx_i^2 \quad (K > 0)$$

then

$$\text{Var}\left(\frac{\varepsilon_i}{x_i}\right) = K$$

Discuss the possible relevance of this result in treating a form of heteroscedasticity.

12.25 Refer to Exercise 12.7. Let e_i denote the residuals from the fitted regression and $\hat{y}_i$ the in-sample predicted values. The least squares regression of e_i^2 on $\hat{y}_i$ has coefficient of determination .087. What can you conclude from this finding?

12.26 Refer to Exercise 11.76 of Chapter 11 explaining the change in the real deposit rate in India. The Durbin-Watson statistic for the fitted regression model was 1.71. Test the null hypothesis of no autocorrelated errors against the alternative of positive autocorrelation.

12.27 Refer to Exercise 12.7 on Money Supply in the United Kingdom. What can be concluded from the Durbin-Watson statistic for the fitted regression?

12.28 Refer to Exercise 12.12 on Thailand consumption. Test the null hypothesis of no autocorrelated errors against the alternative of positive autocorrelation.

12.29 Refer to the regression, in Chapter 10, of retail sales per household on disposable income per household.
(a) Calculate the Durbin-Watson d statistic.
(b) Test the null hypothesis of no autocorrelation in the regression errors.
(c) If necessary, reestimate the model allowing for autocorrelated errors.

12.30 A factory operator hypothesizes that her unit output costs (y) depend on wage rate (x_1), other input costs (x_2), overhead costs (x_3), and advertising expenditures (x_4). A series of 24 monthly observations were obtained, and a least squares estimate of the model yielded the following results:

$$y_t = .75 + .24x_{1t} + .56x_{2t} - .32x_{3t} + .23x_{4t}$$
$$\quad\quad\;\; (.07) \quad\;\; (.12) \quad\;\; (.23) \quad\;\; (.05)$$
$$R^2 = .79 \quad d = .85$$

The figures in parentheses below the estimated coefficients are their estimated standard errors. What can you conclude from these results?

12.31 ⬤ The data file, **Advertising Retail**, shows, for a consumer goods corporation, 22 consecutive years of data on sales (y) and advertising (x).
(a) Estimate the regression

$$y_t = \beta_0 + \beta_1 x_t + \varepsilon_t$$

(b) Check for autocorrelated errors in this model.

(c) If necessary, reestimate the model, allowing for autocorrelated errors.

12.32 The omission of an important independent variable from a time series regression model can result in the appearance of autocorrelated errors. In Example 12.5, we estimated the model

$$y_t = \beta_0 + \beta_1 x_{1t} + \varepsilon_t$$

Relating profit margins to net revenues for our savings and loan data. Carry out a Durbin-Watson test on the residuals from this model. What can you infer from the results?

12.33 Refer to Exercise 12.5 on money spent by students on clothing. The Durbin-Watson statistic for the fitted regression model was 1.82. Test the null hypothesis of no autocorrelated errors against the alternative of positive autocorrelation.

SUMMARY

In this chapter we have shown that regression modeling involves more than the basic procedures presented in Chapters 10 and 11. In practice, much art is involved in successful model building, and careful analysis must be practiced. In particular, important explanatory variables should not be ignored. A number of problems require the use of dummy variables or lagged independent variables. Recall that in Chapter 11 we showed how we might also use transformed models including quadratic and log linear forms.

As we have seen, we should also check, as far as possible, any assumptions made about the behavior of the error terms. Tests for heteroscedasticity and autocorrelated errors can be carried out if one suspects either of these problems. And if these problems do occur we would need to reestimate the model using appropriate procedures developed in this chapter and in advanced texts.

Here we have explored some of the possible circumstances in which a departure from the standard regression treatment is desirable. There are many other procedures that are included in econometric textbooks. If you have uncertainties about the assumptions concerning a particular approach you should consult an advanced text or better an econometrician familiar with those advanced procedures.

KEY WORDS

autocorrelated errors, 514
autocorrelated errors with lagged dependent variables, 522
bias from excluding significant predictor variables, 503
coefficient estimation, 487
dummy variables, 489
durbin-watson test, 516
estimation of regression models with autocorrelated errors, 518
experimental design, 493
heteroscedasticity, 508
model interpretation and inference, 488
model specification, 486
model verification, 488
multicollinearity, 506
regressions involving lagged dependent variables, 498
test for heteroscedasticity, 511

CHAPTER EXERCISES AND APPLICATIONS

12.34 Write brief reports, including examples, explaining the use of each of the following in specifying regression models:

(a) Dummy variables
(b) Lagged dependent variables
(c) The logarithmic transformation

12.35 In Section 12.2, we discussed the fitting of the model

$$y = \beta_0 + \beta_1 x_1 + \beta_2 x_2 + \beta_2 x_2 + \varepsilon$$

where

$y =$ Tax revenues as a percentage of gross national product in a country

$x_1 =$ Exports as a percentage of gross national product in the country

$x_2 =$ Income per capita in the country

$x_3 =$ Dummy variable taking the value 1 if the country participates in some form of economic integration, 0 otherwise.

This provides a means of allowing for the effects on tax revenue of participation in some form of economic integration. Another possibility would be to estimate the regression

$$y = \beta_0 + \beta_1 x_1 + \beta_2 x_2 + \varepsilon$$

separately for countries that did and did not participate in some form of economic integration. Explain how these approaches to the problem differ.

12.36 Discuss the following statement: "In many practical regression problems, multicollinearity is so severe that it would be best to run separate simple linear regressions of the dependent variable on each independent variable."

12.37 Explain the nature of and the difficulties caused by each of the following:
(**a**) Heteroscedasticity
(**b**) Autocorrelated errors

12.38 The following model was fitted to data on 90 German chemical companies.

$$y = .819 + 2.11x_1 + .96x_2 - .059x_3 + 5.87x_4 + .00226x_5$$
$$\qquad\quad (1.79) \quad (1.94) \quad (.144) \quad (4.08) \quad (.00115)$$

$$\overline{R}^2 = .410$$

where numbers in brackets are estimated standard errors, and

$$y = \text{Share price}$$
$$x_1 = \text{Earnings per share}$$
$$x_2 = \text{Funds flow per share}$$
$$x_3 = \text{Dividends per share}$$
$$x_4 = \text{Book value per share}$$
$$x_5 = \text{A measure of growth}$$

(**a**) Test at the 10% level the null hypothesis that the coefficient on x_1 is zero in the population regression, against the alternative that the true coefficient is positive.

(**b**) Test at the 10% level the null hypothesis that the coefficient on x_2 is zero in the population regression, against the alternative that the true coefficient is positive.

(**c**) The variable x_1 was dropped from the model, and the regression of y on (x_2, x_3, x_4, x_5) was estimated. The estimated coefficient on x_2 was dropped from the original model, and the regression of y on (x_1, x_3, x_4, x_5) was estimated. The estimated coefficient on x_1 was 2.95, with standard error .63. How can these results be reconciled with the conclusions of parts (a) and (b)?

12.39 The following model was fitted to data from 28 countries in 1989 in order to explain the market value of their debt at that time.

$$y = 77.2 - 9.6\,x_1 - 17.2\,x_2 - .15\,x_3 + 2.2\,x_4 \qquad R^2 = .84$$
$$\qquad\quad (8.0) \quad (2.73) \quad (.056) \quad (1.0)$$

where

$$y = \text{Secondary market price, in dollars, in 1989}$$
$$\text{of \$100 of country's debt}$$

$x_1 = 1$ if U.S. bank regulators have mandated write-down for the country's assets on books of U.S. banks, 0 otherwise

$x_2 = 1$ if country suspended interest payments in 1989, 2 if the country suspended interest payments before 1989 and was still in suspension, and 0 otherwise

$x_3 = $ Debt to gross national product ratio

$x_4 = $ Rate of real gross national product growth, 1980–85.

(**a**) Interpret the estimated coefficient on x_1.

(**b**) Test the null hypothesis that, all else being equal, debt to gross national product ratio does not linearly influence the market value of a country's debt against the alternative that the higher this ratio the lower is the value of the debt.

(**c**) Interpret the coefficient of determination.

(**d**) The specification of the dummy variable x_2 is unorthodox. An alternative would be to replace x_2 by the pair of variables (x_5, x_6), defined as:

$x_5 = 1$ if country suspended interest payments in 1987, 0 otherwise

$x_6 = 1$ if country suspended interest payments before 1987 and was still in suspension, 0 otherwise

Compare the implications of these two alternative specifications.

12.40 An attempt was made to construct a regression model explaining student scores in intermediate economics courses (reference 6). The population regression model assumed was where

$$y = \text{Total student score in intermediate economics courses}$$

$$x_1 = \text{Mathematics score on scholastic aptitude test}$$

$$x_2 = \text{Verbal score on scholastic aptitude test}$$

$$x_3 = \text{Grade in college algebra (A = 4, B = 3, C = 2, D = 1)}$$

$$x_4 = \text{Grade in college principles of economics course}$$

$$x_5 = \text{Dummy variable taking the value 1 if the student is female, and 0 if male}$$

$$x_6 = \text{Dummy variable taking the value 1 if instructor is male, and 0 if female}$$

$$x_7 = \text{Dummy variable taking the value 1 if student and instructor are the same gender, and 0 otherwise.}$$

This model was fitted to data on 262 students. Below we report t-ratios, so that t_i is the ratio of the estimate of $\beta_{,i}$

to its associated estimated standard error. These ratios are

$$t_1 = 4.69 \quad t_2 = 2.89 \quad t_3 = .46 \quad t_4 = 4.90$$
$$t_5 = .13 \quad t_6 = -1.08 \quad t_7 = .88$$

The objective of this study was to assess the impact of the gender of student and instructor on performance. Write a brief report outlining what has been learned about this issue.

12.41 The following regression was fitted by least squares to 32 annual observations on time series data:

$$\log y_t = 4.52 - .62 \log x_{1t} + .92 \log x_{2t} + .61 \log x_{3t} + .16 \log x_{4t}$$
$$\qquad\quad (.28) \qquad\quad (.38) \qquad\quad (.21) \qquad\quad (.12)$$
$$\overline{R}^2 = .638 \qquad d = .61$$

where

y_t = Quantity of U.S. wheat exported

x_{1t} = Price of U.S. wheat on world market

x_{2t} = Quantity of U.S. wheat harvested

x_{3t} = Measure of income in countries importing U.S. wheat

x_{4t} = Price of barley on world market

(a) Interpret the estimated coefficient on $\log x_{1t}$ in the context of the assumed model.

(b) Test at the 5% level the null hypothesis that, all else being equal, income in importing countries has no effect on U.S. wheat exports against the alternative that higher income leads to higher expected exports. (Ignore, for now, the Durbin-Watson d statistic.)

(c) What null hypothesis can be tested by the d statistic? Carry out this test for the present problem, using a 1% significant level.

(d) In view of your finding in part (c), comment on your conclusion in part (b). How might you proceed to test the null hypothesis of part (b)?

12.42 The following regression was fitted by least squares to 30 annual observations on time series data:

$$\log y_t = 4.31 + .27 \log x_{1t} + .53 \log x_{2t} - .82 \log x_{3t}$$
$$\qquad\qquad (.17) \qquad\quad (.21) \qquad\quad (.30)$$
$$\overline{R}^2 = .615 \qquad d = .49$$

where

y_t = Number of business failures

x_{1t} = Rate of unemployment

x_{2t} = Short-term interest rate

x_{3t} = Value of new business orders placed

(a) Interpret the estimated coefficient on $\log x_{3t}$ in the context of the assumed model.

(b) What null hypothesis can be tested by the d statistic? Carry out this test for the present problem, using a 1% significance level.

(c) Given your results in part (b), is it possible to test, with the information given, the null hypothesis that, all else being equal, short-term interest rates do not influence business failures?

(d) Estimate the correlation between adjacent error terms in the regression model.

12.43 A stockbroker is interested in the factors influencing the rate of return on the common stock of banks. For a sample of 30 banks the following regression was estimated by least squares:

$$y = 2.37 + .84x_1 + .15x_2 - .13x_3 + 1.67x_4 \qquad R^2 = .317$$
$$\qquad\quad (.39) \quad (.12) \quad (.09) \quad (1.97)$$

where

y = Percentage rate of return on common stock of bank

x_1 = Percentage rate of growth of bank's earnings

x_2 = Percentage rate of growth of bank's assets

x_3 = Loan losses as percentage of bank's assets

x_4 = 1 if bank head office is in New York City, and 0 otherwise

(a) Interpret the estimated coefficient on x_4.

(b) Interpret the coefficient of determination and use it to test the null hypothesis that, taken as a group, the four independent variables do not linearly influence the dependent variable.

(c) Let e_i denote the residuals from the fitted regression and $\hat{y}^1$ the in-sample predicted values of the dependent variable. The least square regression of e_i^2 on $\hat{y}^1$ yielded coefficient of determination .082. What can be concluded from this finding?

12.44 A market researcher is interested in the average amount of money per year spent by students on entertainment. From 30 years of annual data, the following regression was estimated by least squares:

$$y_t = 40.93 + .253x_t + .546y_{t-1} \qquad d = 1.86$$
$$\qquad\qquad (.106) \qquad (.134)$$

where

y_t = Expenditure per student, in dollars, on entertainment

x_t = Disposable income per student, in dollars, after payment of tuition, fees, room, and board

(a) Find a 95% confidence interval for the coefficient on x_t in the population regression.

(b) What would be the expected impact over time of a $1 increase in disposable income per student on entertainment expenditure?

(c) Test the null hypothesis of no autocorrelation in the errors against the alternative of positive autocorrelation.

12.45 A local public utility would like to be able to predict a dwelling unit's average monthly electricity bill. The company statistician estimated by least squares the following regression model:

$$y_i = \beta_0 + \beta_1 x_{1i} + \beta_2 x_{2i} + \varepsilon_i$$

where

y = Average monthly electricity bill, in dollars

x_1 = Average bimonthly automobile gasoline bill, in dollars

x_2 = Number of rooms in dwelling unit

From a sample of 25 dwelling units, the statistician obtained the following output from the SAS program:

PARAMETER	ESTIMATE	T FOR HO: PARAMETER = 0	STD. ERROR OF ESTIMATE
INTERCEPT	−10.8030		
X1	−.0247	−.956	.0259
X2	10.9409	18.517	.5909

(a) Interpret, in the context of the problem, the least squares estimate of β_2.

(b) Test against a two-sided alternative the null hypothesis

$$H_0: \beta_1 = 0$$

(c) The statistician is concerned about the possibility of multicollinearity. What information is needed to assess the potential severity of this problem?

(d) It is suggested that household income is an important determinant of size of electricity bill. If this is so, what can you say about the regression estimated by the statistician?

(e) Given the fitted model, the statistician obtains the predicted electricity bills, $\hat{y}$ and the residuals, e. He then regresses e^2 on $\hat{y}$, finding that the regression has a coefficient of determination of .0470. Interpret this finding.

12.46 The data file **Indonesia Revenue** shows 15 annual observations from Indonesia on total government tax revenues, other than from oil (y), national income (x_1), and the value added by oil as a percentage of gross domestic product (x_2). Estimate by least squares regression

$$\log y_t = \beta_0 + \beta_1 \log x_{1t} + \beta_2 \log x_{2t} + \varepsilon_t$$

Write a report summarizing your findings, including a test for autocorrelated errors.

12.47 The data file **German Income** shows 22 annual observations from the Federal Republic of Germany on percentage change in wages and salaries (y), productivity growth (x_1), and the rate of inflation (x_2) as measured by the gross national product price deflator. Estimate by least squares the regression

$$y_t = \beta_0 + \beta_1 x_{1t} + \beta_2 x_{2t} + \varepsilon_t$$

Write a report summarizing your findings, including a test for heteroscedasticity and a test for autocorrelated errors.

12.48 The data file **Japan Imports** shows 35 quarterly observations from Japan on quantity of imports (y), ratio of import prices to domestic prices (x_1), and real gross national product (x_2). Estimate by least squares the regression

$$\log y_t = \beta_0 + \beta_1 \log x_{1t} + \beta_2 \log x_{2t} + \gamma \log y_{t-1} + \varepsilon_t$$

Write a report summarizing your findings, including a test for autocorrelated errors.

12.49 A study was conducted on the labor-hour costs of Federal Deposit Insurance Corporation (FDIC) audits of banks. Data were obtained on 91 such audits. Some of these were conducted by the FDIC alone, some jointly with state auditors. Auditors rated banks' management as good, satisfactory, fair, or unsatisfactory. The model estimated was

$$\log y = 2.41 + .3674 \log x_1 + .2217 \log x_2 + .0803 \log x_3$$
$$\quad\quad\quad\;\, (.0477) \quad\quad\;\; (.0628) \quad\quad\;\; (.0287)$$
$$\quad -.1755 x_4 + .2799 x_5 + .5634 x_6 - .2572 x_7$$
$$\quad\;\; (.2905) \quad\;\; (.1044) \quad\; (.1657) \quad\;\; (.0787)$$
$$R^2 = .766$$

where

y = FDIC auditor labor-hours

x_1 = Total assets of bank

x_2 = Total number of offices in bank

x_3 = Ratio of classified loans to total loans for bank

x_4 = 1 if management rating was "good," 0 otherwise

x_5 = 1 if management rating was "fair," 0 otherwise

x_6 = 1 if management rating was "unsatisfactory," 0 otherwise

x_7 = 1 if audit was conducted jointly with the state, 0 otherwise

The numbers in parentheses beneath coefficient estimates are the associated standard errors.

Write a report on these results.

12.50 The data file **Britain Sick Leave** shows data from Great Britain on days of sick absence per person (y), the unemployment rate (x_1), the ratio of benefits to earnings (x_2), and the real wage rate (x_3). Estimate the model

$$\log y_t = \beta_0 + \beta_1 \log x_{1t} + \beta_2 \log x_{2t} + \beta_3 \log x_{3t} + \varepsilon_t$$

and write a report on your findings. Include in your analysis a check on the possibility of autocorrelated errors and, if necessary, a correction for this problem.

12.51 The U.S. Department of Commerce has asked you to develop a regression model to predict quarterly investment in production and durable equipment. The suggested predictor variables include GDP, prime interest rate, price index for industrial commodities, and government spending. The data for your analysis is found in the data file **Macro2000**, which is stored on your data disk and described in the data dictionary in the chapter Appendix.

(a) Estimate a regression model using only interest rate to predict the investment. Use the Durbin-Watson statistic to test for autocorrelation.

(b) Find the best multiple regression equation to predict investment using the predictor variables previously indicated. Use the Durbin-Watson statistic to test for autocorrelation.

(c) What are the differences between the regression models in (a) and (b) in terms of goodness of fit, prediction capability, autocorrelation, and contributions to understanding the investment problem?

12.52 🌐   An Economist has asked you to develop a regression model to predict consumption of service goods as a function of GNP and other important variables. The data for your analysis is found in the data file **Macro2000**, which is stored on your data disk and described in the data dictionary in the chapter Appendix.

(a) Estimate a regression model using only GDP to predict consumption of service goods. Test for autocorrelation using the Durbin-Watson test.

(b) Estimate a multiple regression model using GNP, total consumption lagged 1 period, and prime interest rate as additional predictors. Test for autocorrelation. Does this multiple regression model reduce the problem of autocorrelation?

12.53 🌐   Jack Wong, a Tokyo investor, is considering plans to develop a primary steel plant in Japan. After reviewing the initial design proposal he is concerned about the proposed mix of capital and labor. He has asked you to prepare several production functions using some historical data from the United States. The data file, **Metals**, contains 27 observations of value-added output, labor input, and the gross value of plant and equipment per factory.

(a) Use multiple regression to estimate a linear production function with value added regressed on labor and capital.

(b) Plot the residuals versus labor and equipment. Note any unusual patterns

(c) Use multiple regression with transformed variables to estimate a Cobb-Douglas production function of the form

$$y = \beta_0 L^{\beta_1} K^{\beta_2}$$

where y is the value added, L is the labor input, and K is the capital input.

(d) Use multiple regression transformed variables to estimate a Cobb-Douglas production function with constant returns to scale. Note that this production function has the same form as the function estimated in part (c), but it has the additional restriction that $\beta_1 + \beta_2 = 1$. To develop the transformed regression model, substitute β_2 as a function of β_1 and convert to a regression format.

(e) Compare the three production functions using residual plots and a standard error of the estimate that is expressed in the same scale. You will need to convert the predicted values from parts (c) and (d) (which are in logarithms) back to the original units. Then you can subtract the predicted values from the original values of Y to obtain the residuals. Use the residuals to compute comparable standard errors of the estimate.

12.54 🌐   The administrator of a small city has asked you to identify variables that influence the mean market value of houses in small Midwestern cities. You have obtained data from a number of small cities, which is stored in the data file **Citydat**. The candidate predictor variables are median size of house, property tax rate (tax levy divided by total assessment), total expenditures for city services, and the percent commercial property.

(a) Estimate the multiple regression model using all of the indicated predictor variables. Select only statistically significant variables for your final equation.

(b) An economist stated that since the data came from cities of different population, your model is likely to contain heteroscedasticity. He argued that mean housing prices from larger cities would have a smaller variance because the number of houses used to compute the mean housing prices would be larger. Test for heteroscedasticity.

(c) Estimate the multiple regression equation using weighted least squares with population as the weighting variable. Compare the coefficients for the weighted and the unweighted multiple regression model.

APPENDIX

DATA DICTIONARY FOR DATA FILE MACRO2000

This quarterly data is available from the first quarter 1946 through the second quarter 2000. Except where indicated the data is in 1996 dollars using the new chain-type price index. A few of the series do not begin in 1946, and they are indicated as having fewer than 218 observations.

FM2	series	M	Money Stock: M2 (SA, Bil.$)
FFED	series	M	Federal Funds [effective] Rate (% p.a.)
FBPR	series	M	Bank Prime Loan Rate (% p.a.)
CDH	series	Q	Personal Consumption Expenditures: Durable Goods (SAAR, Bil.Chn.1996$)
CNH	series	Q	Personal Consumption Expenditures: Nondurable Goods (SAAR, Bil.Chn.1996$)
CSH	series	Q	Personal Consumption Expenditures: Services (SAAR, Bil.Ch.1996$)
CH	series	Q	Personal Consumption Expenditures (SAAR, Bil.Chn.1996$)
Chtot		Q	CDH + CNH + CSH
FNH	series	Q	Fixed Private Nonresidential Investment (SAAR, Bil.Chn.1996$)
FRH	series	Q	Fixed Private Residential Investment (SAAR, Bil.Chn.1996$)
VH	series	Q	Change in Business Inventories (SAAR, Bil.Chn.1996$)
IH	series	Q	Gross Private Domestic Investment (SAAR, Bil.Chn.1996$)
IHTOT		Q	IHTOT = FNH + FRH + VH
XH	series	Q	Exports of Goods and Services (SAAR, Bil.Chn.1996$)
MH	series	Q	Imports of Goods and Services (SAAR, Bil.Chn.1996$)
GH	series	Q	Government Consumption Expenditures/Gross Investment (SAAR, Bil.Chn.96$)
GDPH	series	Q	Gross Domestic Product (SAAR, Bil.Chn.1996$)
Gdphtot		Q	CHTOT + IHTOT + GH + XH − MH
JGDP	series	Q	Gross Domestic Product: Chain-type Price Index (SA, 1996 = 100)
YP	series	Q	Personal Income (SAAR, Bil.$)
YPD	series	Q	Disposable Personal Income (SAAR, Bil.$)
YPDH	series	Q	Disposable Personal Income (SAAR, Bil.Chn.1996$)
YPSV	series	Q	Personal Saving (SAAR, Bil.$)
YPO	series	Q	Personal Outlays (SAAR, Bil.$)

REFERENCES

1. Dhalla, N.K., "Short-Term Forecasts of Advertising Expenditures." *Journal of Advertising Research, 19*, no. 1 (1979), 7–14.

2. Erikson, G.M., "Using Ridge Regression to Estimate Directly Lagged Effects in Marketing." *Journal of American Statistical Association, 76* (1981), 766–773.

3. Hsiao, C., "Autoregressive Modeling of Canadian Money and Income Data." *Journal of American Statistical Association, 74* (1979), 553–560.

4. McDonald, J., "Modeling Demographic Relationships: An Analysis of Forecast Functions for Australian Births." *Journal of the American Statistical Association, 76* (1981), 782–792.

5. Mills, T.C., "The Functional Form of the UK Demand for Money." *Applied Statistics, 27* (1978), 52–57.

6. Waldauer, C., V.G. Duggal, and M.L. Willliams, "Gender Differences in Economic Knowledge: A Further Extension of the Analysis." *Quarterly Review of Economics and Finance, 32*, no. 4 (1992), 138–43.

NONPARAMETRIC
STATISTICS

INTRODUCTION

In Chapter 2, we learned that data is classified as numerical or qualitative. The statistical procedures we have studied up to now require the use of numerical data. For such data, the means, variances, and standard deviations are meaningful. However, for qualitative data (nominal or ordinal), parametric methods are not applicable. In this chapter, you will be introduced to *nonparametric* tests that are often the appropriate procedure needed to make statistical conclusions about nominal or ordinal data. Such data are frequently obtained in many settings including marketing research studies, business surveys, and questionnaires.

In Chapter 9, several hypothesis tests that depended on the assumption of normality for population distributions were introduced. Frequently, the assumption of normality is reasonable. Moreover, by virtue of the central limit theorem, many of these test procedures remain approximately valid when applied to large samples even if the population distribution is not normal. However, it may be the case that in practical applications the normality assumption is not tenable. In these circumstances, it is desirable to base inferences on *nonparametric* tests that are valid over a wide range of distributions of the parent population. Such tests are often referred to as *distribution-free* tests.

In this chapter, we describe some of the nonparametric tests that are appropriate for analyzing nominal data, ordinal data, or numerical data when the normality assumption cannot be made about the probability distribution of the population. Other nonparametric tests will be discussed in subsequent chapters. It is not our intention here to attempt to describe the entire wide array of such nonparametric procedures that are available. Rather, our objective is the more modest one of providing a flavor of selected nonparametric procedures including the Sign Test, the Wilcoxon Signed Rank Test, the Mann-Whitney *U* Test, the Wilcoxon Rank Sum Test, and the Spearman Rank Correlation Test. These are nonparametric alternatives to various procedures introduced earlier in the book.

13.1 SIGN TEST AND CONFIDENCE INTERVAL

The simplest nonparametric test to carry out is the **sign test** It is most frequently employed in testing hypotheses about the central location (median) of a population distribution or analyzing data from paired samples. The sign test is used in market research studies to identify if consumer preference exists for one of two products. Since respondents simply name their preference, the data is nominal and lends itself to nonparametric procedures.

Sign Test for Paired or Matched Samples

Suppose that paired or matched samples are taken from a population, and the differences equal to 0 are discarded, leaving n observations. The sign test can be used to test the null hypothesis that the population median of the differences is 0 (which would be true, for example, if the differences came from a population whose distribution was symmetric about a mean of 0). Let + indicate a positive difference and – indicate a negative difference. If the null hypothesis were true, our sequence of + and – differences could be regarded as a random sample from a population in which the probabilities for + and – were each 0.5. In that case, the observations would constitute a random sample from a binomial population in which the probability of + was 0.5. Thus, if π denotes the true proportion of +'s in the population (that is, the true proportion of positive differences), the null hypothesis is simply

$$H_0: \pi = 0.5.$$

The sign test is then based on the fact that the number of positive observations, S, in the sample has a binomial distribution (with $\pi = 0.5$ under the null hypothesis).

SIGN TEST FOR PAIRED SAMPLES

Suppose that paired or matched random samples are taken from a population and the differences equal to 0 are discarded, leaving n observations. Calculate the difference for each pair of observations and record the sign of this difference. The sign test is used to test:

$$H_0 : \pi = 0.5$$

where π is the proportion of nonzero observations in the population that are positive. The **test-statistic S** for the **sign test for paired samples** is simply,

$$S = \text{the number of pairs with a } \textbf{positive} \text{ difference}$$

and S has a binomial distribution with $\pi = 0.5$ and n = the number of nonzero differences.

After determining the null and alternative hypotheses and finding a test-statistic, the next step is to determine the p-value and to draw conclusions based on a decision rule.

DETERMINING *P*-VALUE FOR A SIGN TEST

The **p-value for a Sign Test** is found using the binomial distribution with n = number of nonzero differences, S = number of positive differences, and $\pi = 0.5$.

(a) For an upper-tail test,

$$H_1 : \pi > 0.5, \quad p\text{-value} = P(x \geq S) \tag{13.1}$$

(b) For a lower-tail test,

$$H_1 : \pi < 0.5, \quad p\text{-value} = P(x \leq S) \tag{13.2}$$

(c) For a two-tail test,

$$H_1 : \pi \neq 0.5, \quad 2(p\text{-value}) \tag{13.3}$$

EXAMPLE 13.1

PRODUCT PREFERENCE (SIGN TEST)

An Italian restaurant, close to a college campus, contemplated a new recipe for the sauce used in its pizza. A random sample of eight students was chosen, and each was asked to rate on a scale from 1 to 10 the taste of the original and the proposed new product. The scores of the taste comparison are shown in Table 13.1, with higher numbers indicating a greater liking of the product.

Do the data indicate an overall tendency to prefer the new pizza sauce to the original pizza sauce?

SOLUTION

Also shown in Table 13.1 are the differences in the scores for every taster and the signs of these differences. Thus, a + is assigned if the original product is preferred, a − if the new product is preferred, and 0 if the two products are rated equally. In this particular experiment, two tasters preferred the original pizza sauce and five the new; one rated them equal.

The null hypothesis of interest is that in the population at large, there is no overall tendency to prefer one product to the other. In assessing this hypothesis, we compare the

TABLE 13.1
Taster Ratings for Pizza Sauce

| TASTER | RATING | | DIFFERENCE | SIGN OF DIFFERENCE |
	Original Product	*New Product*	*(Original - New)*	
A	6	8	−2	−
B	4	9	−5	−
C	5	4	1	+
D	8	7	1	+
E	3	9	−6	−
F	6	9	−3	−
G	7	7	0	0
H	5	9	−4	−

numbers expressing a preference for each product, discarding those who rated the products equally. In the present example then, the values for Taster G are omitted in further analysis and the effective sample size is reduced to $n = 7$. The only sample information on which our test is based is that two of the seven tasters preferred the original product. Hence, the test-statistic is $S = 2$.

The null hypothesis can be viewed as the hypothesis that the population median of the differences is 0. If the null hypothesis were true, our sequence of + and − differences could be regarded as a random sample from a population in which the probabilities for + and − were each 0.5. In that case, the observations would constitute a random sample from a binomial population in which the probability of + was 0.5. Thus, if π denotes the true proportion of +'s in the population (that is, the true proportion of the population who prefer the original pizza sauce), the null hypothesis is simply

$H_0: \pi = 0.5$ There is no overall tendency to prefer one product to the other

A one-tailed test is used to determine if there is an overall tendency to prefer the new pizza sauce to the original pizza sauce. The alternative of interest is that in the population, the majority of preferences are for the new product. This alternative is expressed as

$H_1: \pi < 0.5$ Majority preferred new product (or, fewer than 50% prefer the old sauce)

Next we find the probability of observing a sample result as extreme as or more extreme than that found if the null hypothesis were in fact true. This value is the p-value of the test. If we denote by $P(x)$ the probability of observing x "successes" (+'s) in $n = 7$ binomial trials, each with probability of success 0.5, then the cumulative binomial probability of observing two or fewer +'s can be obtained using the binomial formula, a binomial table, or from computer software such as Microsoft Excel PHStat. The p-value is found with Equation 13.3 to be

$$p\text{-value} = P(x \le 2) = P(x = 0) + P(x = 1) + P(x = 2)$$
$$= 0.0078 + 0.0547 + 0.1641 = 0.2266$$

With a p-value this large, we are unable to reject the null hypothesis and conclude the data is not sufficient to suggest that the students have a preference for the new sauce. Similarly, we could have said that if we adopt the decision rule "Reject H_0 if two or fewer +'s occur in the sample," then the probability is 0.2266 that the null hypothesis will be rejected when it is in fact true. Hence, such a test has a p-value of 22.66%. Since the p-value is the smallest significance level at which the null hypothesis can be rejected, for the present example, the null hypothesis can be rejected at 22.66% or higher. It is unlikely that one would be willing to accept such a high significance level. Again, we conclude that the data is not statistically significant to recommend a change in the pizza sauce. Perhaps, our decision is a consequence of our having such a small number of sample observations.

To illustrate a two-tailed test procedure, suppose that you had been asked to determine if there is an overall preference in the population for either one of the products. Then, $H_1: \pi \neq 0.5$ and by Equation 13.3 the p-value = $2P(x \leq 2) = 2(0.2266) = 0.4532$.

Also, note that

$$p\text{-value} = P(x \leq 2) + P(x \geq 5) = P(0) + P(1) + P(2) + P(5) + P(6) + P(7) = 0.4532.$$

Such a large p-value would suggest that the data is not sufficient to think that the students prefer one of the pizza sauces to the other. Only with a significance level of 45.32% or higher could we reject the null hypothesis and conclude that such a preference for pizza sauce exists.

Normal Approximation

As a consequence of the central limit theorem, the normal distribution can be used to approximate the binomial distribution if the sample size is large. Experts differ on the exact definition of "large." We suggest that the normal approximation is acceptable if the sample size exceeds 20. A continuity correction factor in the test-statistic compensates for estimating discrete data with a continuous distribution and provides a closer approximation to the p-value.

THE SIGN TEST: NORMAL APPROXIMATION (LARGE SAMPLES)

If the number n of nonzero sample observations is large, then the sign test is based on **the normal approximation** to the binomial with mean and standard deviation

Mean: $\mu = n\pi = 0.5n$; Standard Deviation: $\sigma = \sqrt{n\pi(1 - \pi)} = \sqrt{0.25n} = 0.5\sqrt{n}$

The test-statistic is:

$$Z = \frac{S^* - \mu}{\sigma} = \frac{S^* - 0.5n}{0.5\sqrt{n}} \qquad (13.4)$$

where S^* is the test-statistic corrected for continuity defined as:

(a) For a two-tail test,

$$S^* = S + 0.5, \text{ if } S < \mu \qquad \text{or} \qquad S^* = S - 0.5, \text{ if } S > \mu \qquad (13.5)$$

(b) For an upper-tail test,

$$S^* = S - 0.5 \qquad (13.6)$$

(c) For a lower-tail test,

$$S^* = S + 0.5 \qquad (13.7)$$

EXAMPLE 13.2

ICE CREAM (SIGN: NORMAL APPROXIMATION)

A random sample of one hundred children was asked to compare two new ice cream flavors—peanut butter ripple and bubblegum surprise. Fifty-six sample members preferred peanut butter ripple, forty preferred bubblegum surprise, and four expressed no preference. Use the *normal approximation* to determine if there is an overall preference for either flavor. Compare your result to the binomial probabilities obtained using both PHStat and Minitab.

SOLUTION

To test if there is an overall preference in this population for one flavor over the other, the hypotheses are

$$H_0: \pi = 0.5 \quad \text{Children have no preference for either flavor}$$
$$H_1: \pi \neq 0.5 \quad \text{Children have a preference for one flavor}$$

Let π be the population proportion that prefer bubblegum surprise giving $S = 40$ (we could just as well have chosen π to be the population proportion who prefer peanut butter ripple with $S = 56$). Using Equations 13.4 and 13.5,

$$\mu = n\pi = 0.5n = 0.5(96) = 48$$
$$\sigma = 0.5\sqrt{96} = 4.899$$
$$Z = \frac{S^* - \mu}{\sigma} = \frac{40.5 - 48}{4.899} = -1.53 \quad \text{since} \quad 40 < 48, \ S^* = 40.5$$

From the standard normal distribution, it follows that the approximate p-value $= 2(0.0630) = 0.126$. Hence, the null hypothesis can be rejected at all significance levels greater than 12.6%. If no continuity correction factor is used, the value Z becomes $Z = -1.633$, giving a slightly smaller p-value of 0.1024.

Minitab and PHStat (Sign Test)

Since the sign test relies on the binomial probability distribution, use of either Minitab or PHStat (see Chapter 5) is straightforward.

INTERPRETATION

From the Minitab output (Figure 13.1A), the p-value $= 2(0.0627) = 0.1254$, and from the PHStat output (Figure 13.1B), the p-value $= P(x \leq 40) + P(x \geq 56) = 0.062673 + 0.062673 = 0.125346$. Both of the p-values are close to the p-value of 0.126 found using Equations 13.4 and 13.5. The data is not sufficient to suggest that children have an overall preference for either flavor of ice cream.

FIGURE 13.1A
Minitab Output for Ice Cream Example; $n = 96$, $\pi = 0.5$, $S = 40$

x	P (x <= x)
40.0	0.0627

FIGURE 13.1B
PHStat Output for Ice Cream Example; $n = 96$, $\pi = 0.5$, $S = 40$

X	P(X)	P(<=X)	P(<X)	P(>X)	P(>=X)
40	0.021576	**0.062673**	0.041097	0.937327	0.958903
56	0.021576	0.958903	0.937327	0.041097	**0.062673**

Sign Test for Single Population Median

The sign test can also be used for a single sample to test the hypothesis that the median is a given value.

EXAMPLE 13.3

STARTING INCOMES OF RECENT COLLEGE GRADUATES (SIGN TEST)

Income

The dean of the School of Business Administration at a particular university would like information about the starting income of recent college graduates. A random sample of 23 recent graduates indicated the following starting salaries:

29250	29900	28070	31400	31100	29000	33000	50000	28500	31000
34800	42100	33200	36000	65800	34000	29900	32000	31500	29900
32890	36000	35000

Do the data indicate that the median starting income differs from $35,000? The data for this problem can be found in the data file **Income**.

SOLUTION

Since the distribution of incomes is often skewed, the sign test will be used. The null and alternative hypotheses are:

$$H_0 : Median = \$35,000$$
$$H_1 : Median \neq \$35,000$$

Here we test the null hypothesis using a binomial distribution with $\pi = 0.50$. First, we approximate the answer using Equations 13.4 and 13.5. Notice that there are 17 students who indicated a starting income greater than \$35,000; 5 with starting incomes less than \$35,000 and one student with a starting income of \$35,000. The sample size is reduced to $n = 22$ and $S = 17$. The mean and the standard deviation are found to be

$$\mu = n\pi = 0.5n = 0.5(22) = 11$$
$$\sigma = 0.5\sqrt{22} = 2.345$$

Since $S = 17 > \mu = 11$, the test-statistic for the normal approximation is:

$$Z = \frac{16.5 - 11}{2.345} = 2.35$$

Using the table for the standard normal distribution, the *approximate* p-value is $2(0.0094) = 0.0188$. Figure 13.2 is a partial output obtained using Microsoft Excel PHStat to solve this problem.

$P(X \leq 5 \mid n = 22, \pi = 0.5) = P(X \geq 17 \mid n = 22, \pi = 0.5) = 0.00845$. For this example, which is two-tailed, the p-value $= 2(0.00845) = 0.0169$ (slightly smaller than 0.0188 found by the method of normal approximation).

FIGURE 13.2
PHStat Output for Starting Income Example

Binomial Probabilities Table

X	P(X)	P(<=X)
0	2.38E-07	2.38E-07
1	5.25E-06	5.48E-06
2	5.51E-05	6.06E-05
3	0.000367	0.000428
4	0.001744	0.002172
5	0.006279	0.00845

Minitab (Sign Test)

Figure 13.3 gives the Minitab instructions and output for this example.

Both PHStat and Minitab compute p-value using the binomial probabilities. If $n > 50$, Minitab calculates the p-value using the normal approximation.

FIGURE 13.3
Minitab Output for Starting Income Example

```
Sign test of median = 35000 versus not = 35000
```

N	Below	Equal	Above	P	Median
23	17	1	5	**0.0169**	32000

Minitab Instructions

1. Open file Income
2. Click on Stat
3. Select Nonparametrics
4. Select 1-Sample Sign...
5. Choose Test median
6. Complete dialog box

Confidence Interval for the Median

Minitab can be used to determine confidence intervals for the median based on the sign test. Consider the starting incomes given in Example 13.3 and found in the data file **Income**. Notice that three confidence intervals are included in the Minitab output in Figure 13.4. Follow the Minitab instructions for Figure 13.3 with one exception: In step 5, choose "Confidence interval" rather than "Test median." Be sure to indicate the desired confidence level.

Income

FIGURE 13.4
Minitab Output, Confidence
Interval for Starting Incomes
Example

```
Sign confidence interval for median

                                 Achieved
                      N    Median   Confidence    Confidence interval    Position
        Incomes      23     32000    0.9069     (  31000,   34000)          8
                                      0.9500     (  30393,   34442)        NLI
                                      0.9653     (  29900,   34800)          7
```

INTERPRETATION

The first row gives the achievable confidence level (0.9069) just below the requested confidence level (0.95); the third row gives the achievable confidence level (0.9653) just above the requested level (0.95). "The calculation of the first and third intervals uses a method similar to the sign method used when doing a hypothesis test of the median. Observations are first ordered. The interval that goes from the dth smallest observation to the dth largest observation has confidence $1 - 2P(X < d)$ using the binomial distribution with $\pi = 0.5$. The intervals with confidence coefficients just above and below the requested level are those selected. Only rarely can you achieve the requested confidence with these intervals (reference 7)." In our example, the interval that goes from the 8th smallest observation to the 8th largest observation has a confidence level of 0.9069, where X has a binomial distribution with $n = 23$ and $\pi = 0.5$. The middle interval states that the median income is between $30,393 and $34,442 with 95% confidence. Similarly, the interval that goes from the 7th smallest observation to the 7th largest observation has a confidence level of 0.9653, where X has a binomial distribution with $n = 23$ and $\pi = 0.5$.

Hettmansperger and Sheather developed the nonlinear interpolation procedure used by Minitab to find the middle confidence interval (reference 3). Other confidence intervals for nonparametric procedures discussed in this chapter are found in a similar manner.

EXERCISES

13.1 A random sample of twelve financial analysts was asked to predict the percentage increases in the prices of two common stocks over the next year. The results obtained are shown in the table. Use the sign test to test the null hypothesis that for the population of analysts, there is no overall preference for one stock over the other.

ANALYST	STOCK 1	STOCK 2	ANALYST	STOCK 1	STOCK 2
A	6.8	7.2	G	9.3	10.1
B	9.8	12.3	H	1.0	2.7
C	2.1	5.3	I	−.2	1.3
D	6.2	6.8	J	9.6	9.8
E	7.1	7.2	K	12.0	12.0
F	6.5	6.2	L	6.3	8.9

13.2 An organization offers a program designed to increase the level of comprehension achieved by students when reading technical material quickly. Each member of a random sample of 10 students was given 30 minutes to read an article. A test of the level of comprehension achieved was then administered. This process was repeated after these students had completed the program. The accompanying table shows comprehension scores before and after completion of the program. Use the sign test to test the null hypothesis that for this population, there is no overall improvement in comprehension levels following completion of the program.

STUDENT	BEFORE	AFTER	STUDENT	BEFORE	AFTER
A	62	69	F	53	61
B	63	72	G	49	63
C	84	80	H	58	59
D	70	70	I	83	87
E	60	69	J	92	98

13.3 A sample of 11 managers in retail stores having self check out were asked if their customers have a positive attitude about the scanning process. Seven managers answered "yes," and four answered "no." Test against a two-sided alternative the null hypothesis that, for the population of managers, responses would be equally divided between "yes" and "no."

13.4 A sample of 60 corporations buying back franchises was examined. Of these cases, returns on common stock around the buy-back announcement date were positive 39 times, negative 18 times, and zero 3 times. Test the null hypothesis that positive and negative returns are equally likely against the alternative that positive returns are more likely (reference 2).

13.5 Of a random sample of 130 voters, 44 favored a state tax increase to raise funding for education, 68 opposed the tax increase, and 18 expressed no opinion. Test against a two-sided alternative the null hypothesis that voters in the state are evenly divided on the issue of this tax increase.

13.6 A random sample of 60 professional economists was asked to predict whether next year's inflation rate would be higher than, lower than, or about the same as in the current year. The results are shown in the following table. Test the null hypothesis that the profession is evenly divided on the question.

PREDICTION	NUMBER
Higher	20
Lower	29
About the same	11

13.2   WILCOXON SIGNED RANK TEST

One disadvantage of the sign test is that it takes into account only a very limited amount of information—namely, the signs of the differences. For example, in Table 13.1 the sign test simply records which product is preferred, *ignoring the strengths of the preferences*. When the sample size is small, it might be suspected therefore that the test would not be very powerful. The **Wilcoxon Signed Rank Test** provides a method to incorporate information about the magnitude of the differences between matched pairs. It is still a distribution-free test. Like many nonparametric tests, it is based on *ranks*.

THE WILCOXON SIGNED RANK TEST FOR PAIRED SAMPLES

The **Wilcoxon Signed Rank Test** can be employed when a random sample of matched pairs of observations is available. Assume that the population distribution of the differences in these **paired samples** is symmetric, and we want to test the null hypothesis that this distribution is centered at 0. Discarding pairs for which the difference is 0, we rank the remaining n absolute differences in ascending order with ties assigned the average of the ranks they occupy. The sums of the ranks corresponding to positive and negative differences are calculated, and the smaller of these sums is the Wilcoxon Signed Rank Statistic T, that is

$$T = \min(T_+, T_-) \tag{13.8}$$

where

T_+ = the sum of the positive ranks
T_- = the sum of the negative ranks
n = the number of nonzero differences

The null hypothesis is rejected if T is less than or equal to the value in the Appendix table.

EXAMPLE 13.4

PRODUCT PREFERENCE (WILCOXON SIGNED RANK TEST)

Solve Example 13.1, the taster ratings for pizza sauce, using the Wilcoxon Signed-Rank Test.

SOLUTION

As with the Sign Test, we ignore any difference of "0," so that Taster G is removed from the study and the sample size is reduced to $n = 7$. The nonzero absolute differences are then ranked in ascending order of magnitude. That is, the smallest absolute value is given a rank of "1." If two or more values are equal, they are assigned the average of the next available ranks. In our example, the two smallest absolute differences are equal. The rank assigned to

TABLE 13.2
Calculation of Wilcoxon Test Statistic for Taste Preference Data

TASTER	DIFFERENCE	RANK (+)	RANK (−)
A	−2		3
B	−5		6
C	1	1.5	
D	1	1.5	
E	−6		7
F	−3		4
G	0		
H	−4		5

Sums 3   **25**

Wilcoxon Signed Rank Statistic T = minimum (3, 25) = 3

them is therefore the average of ranks 1 and 2—that is, 1.5. The next absolute value is assigned rank 3, and so on. We rank all differences and obtain Table 13.2.

The ranks for positive and negative differences are summed separately. The smaller of these sums is the Wilcoxon Signed Rank Statistic T. Here $T = 3$.

We will now suppose that the population distribution of the paired differences is symmetric. The null hypothesis to be tested is that the center of this distribution is 0. In our example, then, we are assuming that differences in the ratings of the two products have a symmetric distribution, and we want to test whether that distribution is centered on 0—that is, no difference between ratings. We would be suspicious of the null hypothesis if the sum of the ranks for positive differences was very different from that for negative differences. Hence, the null hypothesis will be rejected for low values of the statistic T.

Cutoff points for the distribution of this random variable are given in the Appendix for tests against a one-sided alternative that the population distribution of the paired differences is specified either to be centered on some number bigger than 0 or to be centered on some number less than 0. For sample size, n, the table shows, for selected probabilities α, the number T_α such that $P(T < T_\alpha) = \alpha$. For example, let $\alpha = 0.05$, we read in the table for $n = 7$ that $P(T \le 4) = 0.05$. Since the Wilcoxon Signed Rank Test Statistic is $T = 3$, the null hypothesis is rejected against the one-sided alternative at the 5% level. It appears likely that overall, ratings are higher for the new product.

Minitab (Wilcoxon Signed Rank Test)

Minitab can be used for a Wilcoxon Signed Rank Test. Consider again the taster ratings for pizza sauce given in Table 13.1 (Example 13.1) and repeated here:

Taster:	A	B	C	D	E	F	G	H
Rating (Original):	6	4	5	8	3	6	7	5
Rating (New):	8	9	4	7	9	9	7	9

For paired samples, enter the data for each pair in separate columns in a Minitab worksheet and use Calc to obtain column differences, or simply enter the differences of the two columns if readily available. Minitab instructions for the Wilcoxon Signed Rank Test are similar to those for a sign test (see Figure 13.5).

INTERPRETATION

Here, the p-value is 0.038 for the one-sided lower tail test. Notice that the additional information provided by the ranks allows the rejection of the null hypothesis at a much lower level of significance than was possible for the sign test. We know that although computer software provides information such as the p-value, the correct interpretation is the responsibility of the reader. This is frequently the case for studies reported in research journals

FIGURE 13.5
Minitab Output for Pizza
Sauce Example

Wilcoxon Signed Rank Test for Pizza Sauce Example

Test of median = 0.000000 versus median < 0.000000

	N	N for Test	Wilcoxon Statistic	P	Estimated Median
Pizza Sauce	8	7	3.0	**0.038**	-2.250

Minitab Instructions
1. Enter data
2. Click on Stat
3. Select Nonparametrics
4. Select 1-Sample Wilcoxon
5. Enter Column number of differences in the Variables edit box
6. Choose Test median
7. Select appropriate alternative hypothesis

(See, for example, Exercise 13.7 taken from *Financial Management*, Summer 2000). Proper interpretation is a must.

Normal Approximation: Wilcoxon Signed Rank Test

When the number n of nonzero differences in the sample is large ($n > 20$), the normal distribution provides a good approximation to the distribution of the Wilcoxon statistic T under the null hypothesis that the population differences are centered on 0. When this hypothesis is true, the mean and variance of this distribution are given in equations.

THE WILCOXON SIGNED RANK TEST: NORMAL APPROXIMATION (LARGE SAMPLES)

Under the null hypothesis that the population differences are centered on 0, the Wilcoxon Signed Rank Test has mean and variance given by

$$E(T) = \mu_T = \frac{n(n+1)}{4} \tag{13.9}$$

and

$$\text{Var}(T) = \sigma_T^2 = \frac{n(n+1)(2n+1)}{24} \tag{13.10}$$

Then, for large n, the distribution of the random variable, Z, is approximately standard normal where

$$Z = \frac{T - \mu_T}{\sigma_T} \tag{13.11}$$

If the number n of nonzero differences is large and T is the observed value of the Wilcoxon statistic, then the following tests have significance level α,

i.   If the alternative hypothesis is one sided, reject the null hypothesis if

$$\frac{T - \mu_T}{\sigma_T} < -Z_\alpha$$

ii. If the alternative hypothesis is two-sided, reject the null hypothesis if

$$\frac{T - \mu_T}{\sigma_T} < -Z_{\alpha/2}$$

EXAMPLE 13.5

POSTAUDIT PROCEDURES (WILCOXON SIGNED RANK)

A study compared firms with and without sophisticated postaudit procedures. A sample of thirty-one matched pairs of firms was examined. For each firm the ratio of market valuation to replacement cost of assets was computed as a measure of firm performance. In each of the thirty-one pairs, one firm employed sophisticated postaudit procedures and the other did not. The thirty-one differences in ratios were calculated, and the absolute differences were ranked. The smaller of the rank sums, 189, was for those pairs where the ratio was higher for the firm without sophisticated postaudit procedures. Test the null hypothesis that the distribution of differences in ratios is centered on 0 against the alternative that the ratio of market valuation to replacement cost of assets tends to be lower for firms without sophisticated postaudit procedures (reference 8).

SOLUTION

Given a sample of $n = 31$ pairs, the Wilcoxon statistic has, under the null hypothesis, the mean

$$\mu_T = \frac{n(n+1)}{4} = \frac{(31)(32)}{4} = 248$$

and variance

$$\text{Var}(T) = \sigma_T^2 = \frac{n(n+1)(2n+1)}{24} = \frac{(31)(32)(63)}{24} = 2{,}604$$

so that the standard deviation is

$$\sigma_T = 51.03$$

The observed value of the statistic is $T = 189$. It follows from Equations 13.9 – 13.11 that the null hypothesis is rejected against the one-sided alternative if

$$Z = \frac{T - \mu_T}{\sigma_T} = \frac{189 - 248}{51.03} = \frac{-59}{51.03} = -1.16 < z_\alpha$$

For $\alpha = 0.05$,

$$z_\alpha = -1.645$$

The test result is not sufficient to reject the null hypothesis. Using the standard normal distribution, the null hypothesis can be rejected at all significance levels 12.3% or higher.

EXERCISES

13.7 Irvine and Rosenfeld (*Financial Management*, Summer 2000) studied the "impact of selling Monthly Income Preferred Stock (MIPS) on the common share prices of the issuing firms." The IRS has allowed dividends in MIPS to be tax deductible, from the time that Goldman Sachs first introduced them in 1993. Thus, "issuing MIPS enables the firm to increase its equity base at an after-tax cost nearly equal to that of long-term debt," (reference 4). One aspect of their study concerned a comparison of selected financial characteristics of firms that had issued MIPS (a total of 185) with comparable firms that had not issued MIPS before January 1, 1999. The MIPS issuing firms were also divided between publicly traded industrials and public utilities, such as telephone, electric, gas, and water. The following table is a partial listing of selected findings of this study:

	MIPS FIRMS N	MIPS FIRMS MEAN	COMPARABLE FIRMS	SIGN TEST	SIGN RANK TEST
Total Assets (billions)					
All firms issuing MIPS	185	26.47	19.42	0.01	0.01
Utilities	83	10.45	8.65	0.01	0.01
Industrials	102	39.60	28.26	0.01	0.01
Interest Coverage					
All firms issuing MIPS	164	5.53	7.71	0.04	0.01
Utilities	83	4.44	5.15	0.01	0.01
Industrials	81	6.63	10.25	0.06	0.01
Long Term Debt to Total Assets (%)					
All firms issuing MIPS	185	23.5	21.4	0.06	0.03
Utilities	83	32.6	29.3	0.03	0.01
Industrials	102	16.1	14.9	0.19	0.28

Discuss the findings of this portion of the study.

13.8 A random sample of ten students were asked to rate, in a blind taste test, the quality of two brands of beer, one domestic and one imported. Ratings were on a scale from one (poor) to ten (excellent). The accompanying table gives the results. Use the Wilcoxon test to test the null hypothesis that the distribution of the paired differences is centered on 0 against the alternative that the population of all student beer drinkers prefers the imported brand.

STUDENT	DOMESTIC	IMPORTED	STUDENT	DOMESTIC	IMPORTED
A	2	6	F	4	8
B	3	5	G	3	9
C	7	6	H	4	6
D	8	8	I	5	4
E	7	5	J	6	9

13.9 Sixteen freshmen on a college campus were grouped into eight pairs, in such a way that the two members of any pair were as similar as possible in academic backgrounds—as measured by high school class rank and achievement test scores—and also in social backgrounds. The major difference within pairs was that one student was from in state and the other from out of state. At the end of the first year of college, grade point averages of these students were recorded, yielding the results shown in the table. Use the Wilcoxon test to analyze the data. Discuss the implications of the test results.

PAIR	IN-STATE	OUT-OF-STATE	PAIR	IN-STATE	OUT-OF-STATE
A	3.4	2.8	E	3.9	3.7
B	3.0	3.1	F	2.3	2.8
C	2.4	2.7	G	2.6	2.6
D	3.8	3.3	H	3.7	3.3

13.10 A random sample of 40 business majors who had just completed introductory courses in both statistics and accounting was asked to rate each in terms of level of interest, on a scale from one (very uninteresting) to ten (very interesting). The 40 differences in the pairs of ratings were calculated and the absolute differences ranked. The smaller of the rank sums, which was for those finding accounting the more interesting, was 281. Test the null hypothesis that the population of business majors would rate these courses equally against the alternative that the statistics course is viewed as the more interesting.

13.11 A consultant is interested in the impact of the introduction of a total quality management program on job satisfaction of employees. A random sample of 30 employees was asked to assess level of satisfaction on a scale from one (very dissatisfied) to ten (very satisfied) three months before the introduction of the program. These same sample members were asked to make this assessment again three months after the introduction of the program. The 30 differences in the pairs of ratings were calculated and the absolute differences ranked. The smaller of the rank sums, which was for those more satisfied before the introduction of the program, was 169. What can be concluded from these findings?

13.12 A random sample of 80 owners of videocassette recorders was taken. Each sample member was asked to assess the amounts of time in a month spent watching material he or she had recorded from television broadcasts and on watching purchased or rented commercially recorded tapes. The 80 differences in times spent were then calculated and their absolute values ranked. The smaller of the rank sums, for material recorded from television, was 1,502. Discuss the implications of these sample results.

13.3 MANN-WHITNEY *U* TEST

In Section 10.3, we saw how the central locations of two population distributions could be compared when a random sample of matched pairs was available. In this section, we introduce a test for the same problem when *independent random samples* are taken from the two populations. This first test is the **Mann-Whitney *U* Test**. The distribution of the Mann-Whitney statistic, *U*, approaches the normal distribution quite rapidly as the number of sample observations increases. The approximation is adequate if each sample contains at least 10 observations. Thus, we will only consider here samples with $n_1 \geq 10$ and $n_2 \geq 10$. In testing the null hypothesis that the central locations of the two population distributions are the same, we assume that apart from any possible differences in central location, the two population distributions are identical.

THE MANN-WHITNEY U STATISTIC

Assume that apart from any possible differences in central location, that the two population distributions are identical. Suppose that n_1 observations are available from the first population and n_2 observations from the second. The two samples are pooled and the observations are ranked in ascending order, with ties assigned the average of the next available ranks. Let R_1 denote the sum of the ranks of the observations from the first population. The **Mann-Whitney U statistic** is then defined as

$$U = n_1 n_2 + \frac{n_1(n_1 + 1)}{2} - R_1 \qquad (13.12)$$

It can be shown, then, that if the null hypothesis is true, the random variable U has mean and variance as defined in Equations 13.13 and 13.14.

MANN-WHITNEY U TEST: NORMAL APPROXIMATION

Assuming that the null hypothesis that the central locations of the two population distributions are the same, the **Mann-Whitney U**, has mean and variance

$$E(U) = \mu_U = \frac{n_1 n_2}{2} \qquad (13.13)$$

$$\text{Var}(U) = \sigma_U^2 = \frac{n_1 n_2 (n_1 + n_2 + 1)}{12} \qquad (13.14)$$

Then for large sample sizes (both at least 10), the distribution of the random variable,

$$Z = \frac{U - \mu_U}{\sigma_U} \qquad (13.15)$$

is approximated by the normal distribution.

The decision rules for the Mann-Whitney Test Statistic, U, are given in Equations 13.16 through 13.18.

DECISION RULES FOR THE MANN-WHITNEY TEST

It is assumed that the two population distributions are identical, apart from any possible differences in central location. In testing the null hypothesis that the two population distributions have the same central location, the decision rule for a given significance level is

1. For a one-sided upper-tailed alternative hypothesis, the decision rule is:

$$\text{Reject } H_0 \text{ if } Z = \frac{U - \mu_U}{\sigma_U} < -z_\alpha \qquad (13.16)$$

2. For a one-sided lower-tailed hypothesis, the decision rule is

$$\text{Reject } H_0 \text{ if } Z = \frac{U - \mu_U}{\sigma_U} > z_\alpha \qquad (13.17)$$

3. For a two-sided alternative hypothesis, the decision rule is

$$\text{Reject } H_0 \text{ if } Z = \frac{U - \mu_U}{\sigma_U} < -z_{\alpha/2} \quad \text{or} \quad \text{Reject } H_0 \text{ if } Z = \frac{U - \mu_U}{\sigma_U} > z_{\alpha/2} \quad (13.18)$$

EXAMPLE 13.6

HOURS OF STUDY (MANN-WHITNEY *U* TEST)

Hours

TABLE 13.3
Number of Hours per Week
Spent Studying for
Introductory Finance and
Accounting Courses

Table 13.3 shows the numbers of hours per week students claim to spend studying for introductory finance and accounting courses. The data are from independent random samples of 10 finance students and 12 accounting students.

Do the data indicate a difference in the median number of hours per week that students spend studying for introductory finance and accounting courses? The name of the data file is **Hours**.

| Finance | 10 | 6 | 8 | 10 | 12 | 13 | 11 | 9 | 5 | 11 | | |
| Accounting | 13 | 17 | 14 | 12 | 10 | 9 | 15 | 16 | 11 | 8 | 9 | 7 |

SOLUTION

Our null hypothesis is that the central locations (medians) of the two population distributions are identical.

H_0 : *MEDIAN(1) = MEDIAN(2)* STUDENTS SPEND THE SAME AMOUNT OF TIME STUDYING INTRODUCTORY FINANCE AND ACCOUNTING COURSES

The two samples are pooled and the observations are ranked in ascending order, ties being treated in the same way as previously. These ranks are shown in Table 13.4.

Now, if the null hypothesis were true, we would expect the average ranks for the two samples to be quite close. In the particular example, the average rank for the finance students is 9.35, while that for the accounting students is 13.29. As usual, when testing hypotheses, we want to know how likely a discrepancy of this magnitude would be if the null hypothesis were true.

It is not necessary to calculate both rank sums, for if we know one, we can deduce the other. In this example, for instance, the ranks must sum to the sum of the integers 1 through 22—that is, to 253. Thus, any test of the hypothesis can be based on just one of the rank sums. If Finance is the first sample, then

$$n_1 = 10 \qquad n_2 = 12 \qquad R_1 = 93.5$$

so that the value observed for the Mann-Whitney statistic, *U*, is by Equation 13.12,

_U_ STATISTIC (EQUATION 13.12)

$$U = n_1 n_2 + \frac{n_1(n_1 + 1)}{2} - R_1 = (10)(12) + \frac{(10)(11)}{2} - 93.5 = 81.5$$

TABLE 13.4
Number of Hours per Week
Spent Studying for
Introductory Finance and
Accounting Courses

FINANCE	(RANK)	ACCOUNTING	(RANK)
10	(10)	13	(17.5)
6	(2)	17	(22)
8	(4.5)	14	(19)
10	(10)	12	(15.5)
12	(15.5)	10	(10)
13	(17.5)	9	(7)
11	(13)	15	(20)
9	(7)	16	(21)
5	(1)	11	(13)
11	(13)	8	(4.5)
		9	(7)
		7	(3)
Rank sum	**93.5**	**Rank sum**	**159.5**

Under the null hypothesis that the central locations of the two population distributions are the same, and using Equation 13.13, the distribution of the statistic has mean

MEAN OF THE U STATISTIC (EQUATION 13.13)

$$E(U) = \mu_U = \frac{n_1 n_2}{2} = \frac{(10)(12)}{2} = 60$$

and variance

VARIANCE OF THE U STATISTIC (EQUATION 13.14)

$$\text{Var}(U) = \sigma_U^2 = \frac{n_1 n_2 (n_1 + n_2 + 1)}{12} = \frac{(10)(12)(23)}{12} = 230$$

It follows that:

$$Z = \frac{U - \mu_U}{\sigma_U} = \frac{81.5 - 60}{\sqrt{230}} = 1.42 \quad \text{and} \quad p\text{-value} = 0.1556.$$

Hence, the null hypothesis can be rejected at significance levels higher than 15.56%. With the usual 0.05 significance level, the test result is not sufficient to conclude that students spend more time studying for one of these subjects than the other. We could have used a continuity correction factor in the normal approximation. The p-value will be slightly higher than 0.1556.

If Accounting is population 1 with $n_1 = 12$ and $R_1 = 159.5$, the outcome will be the same since the value for Z will now be $Z = -1.42$. The p-value will still be 0.1556.

Minitab (Mann-Whitney U Test)

Minitab instructions (see Figure 13.6) are similar to those for both the Sign and Wilcoxon Signed Rank Tests.

Minitab computes the Z value using a continuity correction factor. Notice that the p-value is slightly higher.

FIGURE 13.6
Minitab Output for Study Hours Example

Mann-Whitney Test: Finance, Accounting

```
Finance   N =  10     Median =        10.000
Accounti  N =  12     Median =        11.500

Point estimate for ETA1-ETA2 is      -2.000
95.6 Percent CI for ETA1-ETA2 is (-5.001,1.000)

W = 93.5

Test of ETA1 = ETA2   vs   ETA1 not = ETA2 is significant at 0.1661
The test is significant at 0.1643 (adjusted for ties)

Cannot reject at alpha = 0.05
```

Minitab Instructions
1. Open file Hours
2. Click on Stat
3. Select Nonparametrics
4. Select Mann-Whitney
5. Complete dialog box

EXERCISES

13.13 A study compared firms with and without an audit committee. For samples of firms of each type, the extent of directors' ownership was measured as number of shares owned by the board as a proportion of the total number of shares issued. In the sample, directors' ownership was, overall, higher for firms without an audit committee. To test for statistical significance, the Mann-Whitney U statistic was calculated. Then, $(U - \mu_U)/\sigma_U$ was found to be 2.01. What can you conclude from this result? (reference 1)

13.14 A stock market analyst produced at the beginning of the year a list of stocks to buy and another list of stocks to sell. For a random sample of 10 stocks from the "buy list," percentage returns over the year were as follows:

| 9.6 | 5.8 | 13.8 | 17.2 | 11.6 |
| 4.2 | 3.1 | 11.7 | 13.9 | 12.3 |

For an independent random sample of 10 stocks from the "sell list," percentage returns over the year were as follows:

| -2.7 | 6.2 | 8.9 | 11.3 | 2.1 |
| 3.9 | -2.4 | 1.3 | 7.9 | 10.2 |

Use the Mann-Whitney test to interpret these data.

13.15 For a random sample of 12 business graduates from a technical college, the starting salaries accepted for employment on graduation (in thousands of dollars) were the following:

| 26.2 | 29.3 | 31.3 | 28.7 | 27.4 | 25.1 |
| 26.0 | 27.2 | 27.5 | 29.8 | 32.6 | 34.6 |

For an independent random sample of 10 graduates from a state university, the corresponding figures were as follows:

| 25.3 | 28.2 | 29.2 | 27.1 | 26.8 |
| 26.5 | 30.7 | 31.3 | 26.3 | 24.9 |

Analyze the data using the Mann-Whitney test, and comment on the results.

13.4 WILCOXON RANK SUM TEST

The **Wilcoxon Rank Sum Test** is similar to the Mann-Whitney U Test. The results will be the same for both tests. We include it here for completeness since the Wilcoxon Rank Sum Test can be performed using **Microsoft Excel PHStat**. Some statisticians prefer The Wilcoxon Rank Sum Test for its ease.

> ## WILCOXON RANK SUM STATISTIC T
>
> Suppose that n_1 observations are available from the first population and n_2 observations from the second. The two samples are pooled and the observations are ranked in ascending order, with ties assigned the average of the next available ranks. Let T denote the sum of the ranks of the observations from the first population (T in the Wilcoxon Rank Sum Test is the same as R_1 in the Mann-Whitney U Test). Assuming that the null hypothesis to be true, the **Wilcoxon Rank Sum Statistic T** has
>
> $$E(T) = \mu_T = \frac{n_1(n_1 + n_2 + 1)}{2} \qquad (13.19)$$
>
> and variance
>
> $$\text{Var}(T) = \sigma_T^2 = \frac{n_1 n_2 (n_1 + n_2 + 1)}{12} \qquad (13.20)$$
>
> Then for large samples ($n_1 \geq 10$ and $n_2 \geq 10$), the distribution of the random variable,
>
> $$Z = \frac{T - \mu_T}{\sigma_T} \qquad (13.21)$$
>
> is approximated by the normal distribution. For a large number of ties, Equation 13.20 may not be correct (reference 6).

For the data in Table 13.4, $T = R_1 = 93.5$ with

$$E(T) = \mu_T = \frac{n_1(n_1 + n_2 + 1)}{2} = \frac{10(23)}{2} = 115$$

and

$$\text{Var}(T) = \sigma_T^2 = \frac{n_1 n_2 (n_1 + n_2 + 1)}{12} = 230$$

Notice that the variance of the sampling distribution of the Wilcoxon Rank Sum Statistic T is the same as the variance of the sampling distribution of the Mann-Whitney Statistic U. It follows that

$$Z = \frac{T - \mu_T}{\sigma_T} = \frac{93.5 - 115}{\sqrt{230}} = -1.42 \quad \Rightarrow \quad p\text{-value} = 0.1556.$$

PHStat (Wilcoxon Rank Sum Test)

The output from PHStat appears in Figure 13.7.

EXAMPLE 13.7

EARNINGS FOR TWO FIRMS (WILCOXON RANK SUM TEST)

In a study designed to compare the performance of firms that give management forecasts of earnings with those that do not, independent random samples of 80 firms from each of the populations were taken. The variability of the growth rate of earnings over the previous 10 periods was measured for each of the 160 firms, and these variabilities were ranked. The sum of the ranks for firms not disclosing management earnings forecasts was 7,287. Test against a two-sided alternative the null hypothesis that the central locations of the popula-

FIGURE 13.7
PHStat Output for Study
Hours Example

Level of Significance	0.05
Population 1 Sample	
Sample Size	10
Sum of Ranks	93.5
Population 2 Sample	
Sample Size	12
Sum of Ranks	159.5

Total Sample Size n	22
$T1$ Test Statistic	93.5
$T1$ Mean	115
Standard Error of $T1$	15.16575
Z Test Statistic	**-1.41767**

Two-Tailed Test	
Lower Critical Value	-1.95996
Upper Critical Value	1.959961
p-value	0.156288
Do not reject the null hypothesis	

PHStat Instructions

1. Open file Hours
2. Click on PHStat
3. Select Two-Sample Tests
4. Select Wilcoxon Rank Sum Test
5. Complete the dialog box

Comment

We find the same
p-value = 0.156288

tion distributions of earnings variabilities are the same for these two types of firms. Show that the results are the same with both the Mann-Whitney U Test and the Wilcoxon Rank Sum Test (reference 5).

SOLUTION

Since we have $n_1 = 80$, $n_2 = 80$ and $R_1 = 7{,}287$ the calculated value of the Mann-Whitney statistic is

$$U = n_1 n_2 + \frac{n_1(n_1 + 1)}{2} - R_1 = (80)(80) + \frac{(80)(81)}{2} - 7{,}287 = 2{,}353$$

Under the null hypothesis, the Mann-Whitney statistic has mean

$$\mu_U = \frac{n_1 n_2}{2} = \frac{(80)(80)}{2} = 3{,}200$$

and variance

$$\sigma_U^2 = \frac{n_1 n_2 (n_1 + n_2 + 1)}{12} = \frac{(80)(80)(161)}{12} = 85{,}867$$

Here, we have

$$Z = \frac{2{,}353 - 3{,}200}{\sqrt{85{,}867}} = -2.89$$

From the Standard Normal Distribution table, we see that the value of $a/2$ corresponding to a Z value of 2.89 is 0.0019, so a is 0.0038. Hence, the null hypothesis can be rejected at all levels higher than 0.38%.

The Wilcoxon Rank Sum Test is found using Equations 13.19 through 13.21. The mean of T is

$$E(T) = \frac{n_1(n_1 + n_2 + 1)}{2} = \frac{80(161)}{2} = 6{,}440$$

The variance of T is the same as the variance of U (Equation 13.14 is the same as Equation 13.20). Thus, by Equation 13.21,

$$Z = \frac{T - \mu_T}{\sigma_T} = \frac{7,287 - 6,440}{\sqrt{85,867}} = 2.89$$

and again the null hypothesis can be rejected at all levels higher than 0.38%. The results are the same by use of either the Mann-Whitney U Test or the Wilcoxon Rank Sum Test. These data, then, present very strong evidence against the hypothesis that the central locations of the distributions of population variabilities in earnings growth rates are the same for firms that give management earnings forecasts as for those that do not.

Now, if we had been given the actual data rather than just the ranks, we could have carried out a test of the null hypothesis using the methods of Chapter 9. However, using the Mann-Whitney test, we have found that the null hypothesis can be rejected *without the assumption of population normality*.

EXERCISES

13.16 A corporation interviews both marketing and finance majors for general management positions. A random sample of 10 marketing majors and an independent random sample of 14 finance majors were subjected to intensive interviewing and testing by a team of the corporation's senior managers. The candidates were then ranked from 1 (most suitable for employment) to 24, as shown in the accompanying table. Test the null hypothesis that, overall, the corporation's senior management has no preference between marketing and finance majors against the alternative that finance majors are preferred.

1. finance	9. marketing	17. marketing
2. finance	10. marketing	18. marketing
3. marketing	11. finance	19. finance
4. finance	12. finance	20. finance
5. finance	13. marketing	21. finance
6. marketing	14. finance	22. marketing
7. finance	15. finance	23. marketing
8. marketing	16. finance	24. finance

13.17 A random sample of 15 male students and an independent random sample of 15 female students were asked to write essays at the conclusion of a writing course. These essays were then ranked from 1 (best) to 30 (worst) by a professor. The following rankings resulted.

MALE:	26	24	15	16	8	29	12	6	18
	11	13	19	10	28	7			
FEMALE:	22	2	17	25	14	21	5	30	3
	9	4	1	27	23	20			

Test the null hypothesis that in the aggregate the two genders are equally ranked, against a two-sided alternative.

13.18 A newsletter rates mutual funds. Independent random samples of 10 funds with the highest rating and 10 funds with the lowest rating were chosen. The following figures are percentage rates of return achieved by these 20 funds in the next year.

HIGHEST RATED:	8.1	12.7	13.9	2.3	16.1	5.4	7.3
	9.8	14.3	4.1				
LOWEST RATED:	3.5	14.0	11.1	4.7	6.2	13.3	7.0
	7.3	4.6	10.0				

Test the null hypothesis of no difference between the central locations of population distributions of rates of return against the alternative that the highest rated funds tended to achieve higher rates of return than the lowest rated funds.

13.19 A random sample of 50 students was asked what salary the college should be prepared to pay to attract the right individual to coach the football team. An independent random sample of 50 faculty members was asked the same question. The 100 salary figures were then pooled and ranked in order (with rank 1 assigned to the lowest salary). The sum of the ranks for faculty members was 2,024. Test the null hypothesis that there is no difference between the central locations of the distributions of salary proposals of students and faculty members against the alternative that in the aggregate, students would propose a higher salary to attract a football coach.

13.20 The time taken in days from year-end for a random sample of 120 Australian companies with clean audit reports to release a preliminary profit report was compared with the time taken for an independent random sample of 86 companies whose reports had a "subject to" qualification. The times taken for the 206 compa-

nies were pooled and ranked with shortest time assigned rank 1. The sum of the ranks for companies with a "subject to" qualification was 9,686. Test the null hypothesis that the central locations of the two population distributions are identical against the alternative that companies with "subject to" qualifications tend to take longer to produce their preliminary profit reports (reference 9).

13.21 Starting salaries of M.B.A. graduates from two leading business schools were compared. Independent random samples of 30 students from each school were taken, and the 60 starting salaries were pooled and ranked. The sum of the ranks for students from one of these schools was 1,243. Test the null hypothesis that the central locations of the population distributions are identical.

13.5 SPEARMAN RANK CORRELATION

The sample correlation coefficient can be seriously affected by odd extreme observations. Moreover, tests based on it rely for their validity on an assumption of normality. A measure of correlation that is not susceptible to serious influence by extreme values and on which valid tests can be based for very general population distributions is obtained through the use of ranks. The resulting test will then be nonparametric.

SPEARMAN RANK CORRELATION

Suppose that a random sample $(x_1, y_1),...,(x_n, y_n)$ of n pairs of observations is taken. If the x_i and y_i are each ranked in ascending order and the sample correlation of these ranks is calculated, the resulting coefficient is called the **Spearman rank correlation coefficient**. If there are no tied ranks, an equivalent formula for computing this coefficient is

$$r_s = 1 - \frac{6 \sum_{i=1}^{n} d_i^2}{n(n^2 - 1)} \tag{13.22}$$

where the d_i are the differences of the ranked pairs.

The following tests of the null hypothesis H_0 of no association in the population have significance level α:

i. To test against the alternative of positive association, the decision rule is

$$\text{Reject } H_0 \text{ if } r_s > r_{s,\alpha} \tag{13.23}$$

ii. To test against the alternative of negative association, the decision rule is

$$\text{Reject } H_0 \text{ if } r_s < -r_{s,\alpha} \tag{13.24}$$

iii. To Test against the two-sided alternative of some association, the decision rule is

$$\text{Reject } H_0 \text{ if } r_s < -r_{s,\alpha/2} \quad \text{or} \quad r_s > r_{s,\alpha/2} \tag{13.25}$$

EXAMPLE 13.8

CRUISE INDUSTRY PROMOTION (SPEARMAN RANK CORRELATION)

To promote the cruise industry in Florida, suppose that James Thorne of the Cruise Emporium of Ormond Beach, ran an advertisement in 17 tourism magazines. Readers were invited to write for additional brochures and literature. The two variables to be related are

X: Cost of advertising and circulation (in thousands of dollars)
Y: Return-on-inquiry cost

where the latter is defined as

Y = (Estimated revenue from inquiries – Cost of advertisement) ÷ Cost of advertisement

Table 13.5 lists the ranks of these two variables for the 17 magazine advertisements. Calculate Spearman rank correlation coefficient and test for association between the variables.

SOLUTION

Since there are no ties in the ranks, we use Equation 13.22 and obtain

$$r_s = 1 - \frac{6\sum_{i=1}^{n} d_i^2}{n(n^2 - 1)} = 1 - \frac{6(1{,}168)}{17[(17)^2 - 1]} = -0.431$$

Since there are 17 pairs of observations, the cutoff points (see table in Appendix) for 10%-level and 5%-level tests are, respectively

$$r_{s,0.05} = 0.412 \qquad \text{and} \qquad r_{s,0.025} = 0.49$$

TABLE 13.5
Rank Correlation Calculations for Cruise Example

MAGAZINE	RANK (x_i)	RANK (y_i)	d_i = RANK(x_i) – RANK(y_i)	d_i^2
1	14	2	12	144
2	8	4	4	16
3	1	16	−15	225
4	16	1	15	225
5	17	5	12	144
6	13	6	7	49
7	15	8	7	49
8	2	11	−9	81
9	7	9	−2	4
10	3	13	−10	100
11	6	12	−6	36
12	9	17	−8	64
13	5	3	2	4
14	4	7	−3	9
15	11	14	−3	9
16	12	15	−3	9
17	10	10	0	0
				Sum 1,168

The null hypothesis of no association can be rejected against the two-sided alternative, according to the decision rule, at the 10% significance level but not at the 5% level. Our conclusions are not based on the assumption of population normality.

If there are no ties in the ranks, then to calculate Spearman rank correlation with either Minitab or Excel is straightforward. First delete any rows that contain missing values. Both Minitab and Excel can be used to rank the data. Once the data is in rank order, then in Minitab follow the command sequence

```
STAT > BASIC STATISTICS > CORRELATION
```

to find the correlation coefficient of the rank data. In Excel, you can obtain the correlation coefficient several ways: (1) Under the Statistical Function category, select Statistical and the function name CORREL; (2) Use Correlation under the Data Analysis ToolPak add-in; or (3) in PHStat, select Regression followed by Simple Linear Regression....

EXERCISES

13.22 Students in an e-business technology course were given a written final examination as well as a project to complete as part of their final grade. For a random sample of 10 students, the scores on both the exam and the project are

Exam	81	62	74	78	93	69	72	83	90	84
Project	76	71	69	76	87	62	80	75	92	79

(a) Find the Spearman rank correlation coefficient.
(b) Test for association.

13.23 The accompanying table shows, for a random sample of 20 long-term growth mutual funds, percentage return over a period of 12 months and total assets (in millions of dollars).

RETURN	ASSETS	RETURN	ASSETS	RETURN	ASSETS
29.3	300	16.0	421	12.9	75
27.6	70	15.5	99	11.3	610
23.7	3,004	15.2	756	9.9	264
22.3	161	15.0	730	7.9	27
22.0	827	14.4	436	6.7	71
19.6	295	14.0	143	3.3	719
17.6	29	13.7	117		

(a) Calculate Spearman rank correlation coefficient.
(b) Carry out a nonparametric test of the null hypothesis of no association in the population against a two-sided alternative.
(c) Discuss the advantages of a nonparametric test for these data.

SUMMARY

The nonparametric tests discussed in this chapter represent a very small subset of the nonparametric procedures in current use. We will meet some other distribution-free tests in later chapters.

It is instructive to compare the tests of this chapter with those of Chapter 9, where we considered the problem of testing the equality of two population means, *assuming the population distributions to be normal*. The tests developed in this chapter can be regarded also as tests of this null hypothesis, but assuming only that the two population distribu-

tions have the same shape. This brings out the major advantage of nonparametric methods. They are appropriate under a wide range of assumptions about the underlying population distributions.

Some advantages of nonparametric tests include:

(a) *Fewer population assumptions*
Normality is not required. These nonparametric tests are appropriate under a wide range of assumptions about underlying population distributions.

(b) *Computationally more straightforward*
Nonparametric tests can be carried out quite rapidly. This is particularly true of the sign test.

(c) *Nominal or ordinal data can be tested*
For example, if all that was known in a product comparison study was which product is preferred, the sign test would be immediately applicable. In many practical situations, data are available only in the form of ranks, leading naturally to such procedures as the Wilcoxon test or the Mann-Whitney test.

(d) *Less influenced by outliers*
Just as the mean is greatly susceptible to influence by extreme outlying observations, so are inferences based on the *t* tests of Chapter 9. By contrast, tests based on ranks give far less weight to odd outlying sample values.

One disadvantage of nonparametric tests is that under the assumption of normality in the population nonparametric procedures are *less powerful*. For normally distributed populations, the parametric tests of Chapter 9 are more powerful than tests based on rankings, since the latter discard some of the information in the data. That is, the parametric tests have better ability to detect departures from the null hypothesis. However, at least in samples of moderate size, tests such as the Wilcoxon and Mann-Whitney are only a little less powerful than the competing *t* tests when the population distributions are normal. For this reason, together with their broader applicability, these nonparametric tests are very popular. Moreover, when the population distribution differs markedly from the normal, nonparametric tests can have much more power than the corresponding normal-theory tests. Computer software has also enhanced the use of the nonparametric tests.

Since nonparametric methods are rather difficult to extend to problems that involve complex model building, the traditional procedures of Chapter 9, whose development is far more straightforward, remain in the mainstream of statistical analysis.

KEY WORDS

Mann-Whitney *U* Test, 543
  Minitab, 547
  normal approximation, 544
  statistic, 544
Sign Test, 532
  Minitab, 536
  normal approximation, 535
  paired samples, 533

PHStat, 536
p-value, 533
  population median, 536
Spearman Rank Correlation, 551
  coefficient, 551
  tests, 551
Wilcoxon Rank Sum Test, 547

PHStat, 548
  statistic, 548
Wilcoxon Signed Rank Test, 539
  Minitab, 540
  normal approximation, 541
  statistic, 540
  paired samples, 539

CHAPTER EXERCISES AND APPLICATIONS

13.24 What does it mean to say that a test is nonparametric? What are the relative advantages of such tests?

13.25 Construct a realistic example of a statistical problem in the business area where you would prefer the use of a nonparametric test to the alternative parametric test.

13.26 In a random sample of twelve analysts, seven believed that automobile sales in the United States were likely to be significantly higher next year than in the present year, two believed that sales would be significantly lower, and the others anticipated that next year's sales would be roughly the same as those in the current year. What can you conclude from these data?

13.27 In a random sample of sixteen exchange rate analysts, eight believed that the Japanese yen would be an excellent investment this year, five believed that it would be a poor investment, and three had no strong opinion on the question. What conclusions can be drawn from these data?

13.28 Of a random sample of 100 college students, 35 expected to achieve a higher standard of living than their parents, 43 expected a lower standard of living, and 22 expected about the same standard of living as their parents. Do these data present strong evidence that, for the population of students, more expect a lower standard of living, compared with their parents, than expect a higher standard of living?

13.29 Of a random sample of 120 business school professors, 48 believed students' analytical skills had improved over the last decade, 35 believed these skills had deteriorated, and 37 saw no discernible change. Evaluate the strength of the sample evidence suggesting that, for all business school professors, more believe that analytical skills have improved than believe that these skills have deteriorated.

13.30 A random sample of 10 corporate analysts was asked to rate, on a scale from 1 (very poor) to 10 (very high), the prospects for their own corporations and for the economy at large in the current year. The results obtained are shown in the accompanying table. Using the Wilcoxon test, discuss the proposition that in the aggregate, corporate analysts are more optimistic about the prospect for their own companies than for the economy at large.

ANALYST	OWN CORPORATION	ECONOMY AT LARGE	ANALYST	OWN CORPORATION	ECONOMY AT LARGE
1	8	8	6	6	9
2	7	5	7	7	7
3	6	7	8	5	2
4	5	4	9	4	6
5	8	4	10	9	6

13.31 Nine pairs of hypothetical profiles were constructed for corporate employees applying for admission to an executive MBA program. Within each pair, these profiles were identical, except that one candidate was male and the other female. For interviews for employment of these graduates, evaluations on a scale of 1 (low) to 10 (high) were made of the candidates' suitability for employment. The results are shown in the accompanying table. Analyze these data using the Wilcoxon test.

INTERVIEW	MALE	FEMALE	INTERVIEW	MALE	FEMALE
1	8	8	6	9	9
2	9	10	7	5	3
3	7	5	8	4	5
4	4	7	9	6	2
5	8	8			

REFERENCES

1. Brandbury, M.E., "The Incentives for Voluntary Audit Committee Formation," *Journal of Accounting and Public Policy*, 9 (1990), 19–36.
2. Brickley, F.H. Dark and M.S. Weisbach, "An Agency Perspective on Franchising," *Financial Management*, 20 (1991), no. 1, 27–35.
3. Hettmansperger, T.P. and S.J. Sheather, "Confidence Intervals Based on Interpolated Order Statistics," *Statistics and Probability Letters* 4 (1986): 75–79.
4. Irvine, Paul and James Rosenfeld, "Raising Capital Using Monthly Income Preferred Stock: Market Reaction and Implications for Capital Structure Theory," *Financial Management* 29 (2000): 5–20.
5. Jaggi, B. and P. Grier, "A comparative analysis of forecast disclosing and nondisclosing firms," *Financial Management*, 9, no. 2 (1980): 38–43.
6. Lehman, E.L., *Nonparametrics: Statistical Methods Based on Ranks.* (San Francisco, CA: Holden-Day 1975).
7. Minitab User's Guide 2: Data Analysis and Quality Tools (State College, PA: Minitab, Inc. 1997).
8. Meyers, M.D. L.A. Gordon and M.M. Hamer, "Postauditing Capital Assets and Firm Performance: an Empirical Investigation," *Managerial and Decision Economics*, 12 (1991), 317–327.
9. Whittred, G.P., "Audit Qualification and the Timeliness of Corporate Annual Reports," *Accounting Review*, 55 (1980), 563–577.

GOODNESS-OF-FIT TESTS AND CONTINGENCY TABLES

INTRODUCTION

In this chapter, certain tests that are based on the chi-square distribution are discussed. A test of the hypothesis that data are generated by a *fully specified* probability distribution is considered first. This technique is often used by market researchers to determine if products are equally preferred by potential customers or to check if the market shares for several brands of a product have changed over a given period of time.

Next, we test the hypothesis that data are generated by some distribution, such as the binomial, the Poisson, or the normal, without assuming the parameters of that distribution to be known. In these circumstances, the available data can be used to estimate the unknown population parameters. A goodness-of-fit test is used when population parameters are estimated.

The chi-square test can be extended to deal with a problem in which a sample is taken from a population, each of whose members can be uniquely cross classified according to a pair of attributes. The hypothesis to be tested is of no association in the population between possessions of these attributes. Business professionals use this procedure frequently. For larger contingency tables, it is convenient to use a software package to determine the test statistic and *p*-value.

14.1   GOODNESS-OF-FIT TESTS: SPECIFIED PROBABILITIES

The most straightforward test of this type is illustrated with a study that observed a random sample of thirty-three subjects purchasing a soft drink. Of these subjects, eight selected Brand A, ten selected Brand B, and the remainder selected Brand C. This information is displayed in Table 14.1, which lists the numbers of sample members in each of three possible categories.

More generally, consider a random sample of n observations that can be classified according to K categories. If the numbers of observations falling into each category are O_1, O_2, ..., O_K, the setup is as shown in Table 14.2.

The sample data are to be used to test a null hypothesis specifying the probabilities that an observation falls in each of the categories. In the example of thirty-three subjects purchasing a soft drink, the null hypothesis (H_0) might be that a randomly chosen subject is equally likely to select any of the three different varieties. This null hypothesis, then, specifies that the probability is one-third that a sample observation falls into each of the three categories. To test this hypothesis, it is natural to compare the sample numbers *observed* with what would be *expected* if the null hypothesis were true. Given a total of thirty-three sample observations, the expected number of subjects in each category under the null hypothesis would be $(33)(1/3) = 11$. This information is summarized in Table 14.3.

In the general case of K categories, suppose that the null hypothesis specifies π_1, π_2, ..., π_K for the probabilities that an observation falls into the categories. Assume that these possibilities are mutually exclusive and collectively exhaustive—that is, each sample observation must belong to one of the categories and cannot belong to more than one. In this case, the hypothesized probabilities must sum to 1, that is

$$\pi_1 + \pi_2 + \cdots + \pi_K = 1$$

TABLE 14.1
Brand Selection

CATEGORY (BRANDS)	A	B	C	TOTAL
NUMBER OF SUBJECTS	8	10	15	33

TABLE 14.2
Classification on n Observations into K Categories

CATEGORY	1	2	...	K	TOTAL
NUMBER OF OBSERVATIONS	O_1	O_2	...	O_K	n

Then, if there are n sample observations, the expected numbers in each category, under the null hypothesis, will be

$$E_i = n\pi_i \quad (i = 1, 2, \ldots, K)$$

This is shown in Table 14.4.

The null hypothesis about the population specifies the probabilities that a sample observation will fall into each possible category. The sample observations are to be used to check this hypothesis. If the sample values observed in each category are very close to those expected if the null hypothesis were true, this fact would lend support to that hypothesis. In such circumstances the data provide a close *fit* to the assumed population distribution of probabilities. Tests of the null hypothesis are based on an assessment of the closeness of this fit and are generally referred to as **goodness-of-fit-tests**.

Now, in order to test the null hypothesis, it is natural to look at the magnitudes of the discrepancies between what is observed and what is expected. The larger these discrepancies in absolute value, the more suspicious we are of the null hypothesis. The random variable in Equation 14.1 is known as the chi-square random variable.

THE CHI-SQUARE RANDOM VARIABLE

A random sample of n observations each of which can be classified into exactly one of K categories is selected. Denote the observed numbers in each category by $O_1, O_2, \ldots, O_K$. If a null hypothesis (H_0) specifies probabilities $\pi_1, \pi_2, \ldots, \pi_K$ for an observation falling into each of these categories, the expected numbers in the categories, under H_0 would be

$$E_i = n\pi_i \quad (i = 1, 2, \ldots, K)$$

If the null hypothesis is true and the sample size is large enough so that the expected values are at least five, then the random variable associated with

$$\chi^2 = \sum_{i=1}^{K} \frac{(O_i - E_i)^2}{E_i} \tag{14.1}$$

has, to a good approximation, a **chi-square distribution** with $(K - 1)$ degrees of freedom.

Intuitively, the number of degrees of freedom follows from the fact that the O_i must sum to n. Hence, if the number of sample members n and the numbers of observations falling in any $(K - 1)$ of the categories is known, then the numbers in the Kth category are also known. The null hypothesis will be rejected when the observed numbers differ substantially from the expected numbers—that is, for unusually large values of the statistic in Equation 14.1. The appropriate goodness-of-fit test follows.

TABLE 14.3
Observed and Expected Number of Purchases for Three Brands of Soft Drink

CATEGORY (BRANDS)	A	B	C	TOTAL
OBSERVED NUMBER OF SUBJECTS	8	10	15	33
PROBABILITY (UNDER H_0)	1/3	1/3	1/3	1
EXPECTED NUMBER OF SUBJECTS (UNDER H_0)	11	11	11	33

TABLE 14.4
Observed and Expected
Numbers for n Observations
and K Categories

CATEGORY	1	2	...	K	TOTAL
OBSERVED NUMBER	O_1	O_2	...	O_K	n
PROBABILITY (UNDER H_0)	π_1	π_2	...	π_K	1
EXPECTED NUMBER (UNDER H_0)	$E_1 = n_1\pi_1$	$E_2 = n\pi_2$	...	$E_K = n\pi_K$	n

A GOODNESS-OF-FIT TEST

A **goodness-of-fit test**, of significance level α, of H_0 against the alternative that the specified probabilities are not correct is based on the decision rule

$$\text{Reject } H_0 \text{ if } \sum_{i=1}^{k} \frac{(O_i - E_i)^2}{E_i} > \chi^2_{K-1,\alpha}$$

where $\chi^2_{K-1,\alpha}$ is the number for which

$$P(\chi^2_{K-1} > \chi^2_{K-1,\alpha}) = \alpha$$

and the random variable χ^2_{K-1} follows a chi-square distribution with $(K-1)$ degrees of freedom

To illustrate this test, consider again the data of Table 14.3, on brand selection. The null hypothesis is that the probabilities are the same for the three categories. The test of this hypothesis is based on

$$\chi^2 = \sum_{i-1}^{3} \frac{(O_i - E_i)^2}{E_i} = \frac{(8-11)^2}{11} + \frac{(10-11)^2}{11} + \frac{(15-11)^2}{11} = 2.364$$

There are $K = 3$ categories, so the degrees of freedom associated with the chi-square distribution are $K - 1 = 2$. From the chi-square table in the Appendix,

$$\chi^2_{2,0.10} = 4.61$$

Therefore, according to our decision rule the null hypothesis cannot be rejected at the 10% significance level. These data do not contain strong evidence against the hypothesis that a randomly chosen subject is equally likely to select any of the three soft drink brands.

EXAMPLE 14.1

GAS COMPANY (CHI-SQUARE)

A gas company has determined from past experience that at the end of winter, 80% of its accounts are fully paid, 10% are 1 month in arrears, 6% are 2 months in arrears, and 4% are more than 2 months in arrears. At the end of this winter, the company checked a random sample of 400 of its accounts, finding 287 to be fully paid, 49 to be 1 month in arrears, 30 to be 2 months in arrears, and 34 to be more than 2 months in arrears. Do these data suggest that the pattern of previous years is not being followed this winter?

SOLUTION

Under the null hypothesis that the proportions in the present winter conform to the historical record, the respective probabilities for the four categories are 0.8, 0.1, 0.06, and 0.04. Under that hypothesis, the expected numbers of accounts in each category, for a random sample of 400 accounts, would be

$$400(0.8) = 320 \quad 400(0.1) = 40 \quad 400(0.06) = 24 \quad 400(0.04) = 16$$

The observed and expected numbers are:

NUMBERS OF MONTHS IN ARREARS	0	1	2	MORE THAN 2	TOTAL
OBSERVED NUMBER	287	49	30	34	400
PROBABILITY (UNDER H_0)	0.80	0.10	0.06	0.04	1
EXPECTED NUMBER (UNDER H_0)	320	40	24	16	400

The test of the null hypothesis (H_0) is based on

$$\chi^2 = \sum_{i-1}^{4} \frac{(O_i - E_i)^2}{E_i} = \frac{(287-320)^2}{320} + \frac{(49-40)^2}{40} + \frac{(30-24)^2}{24} + \frac{(34-16)^2}{16} = 27.178$$

Here there are $K = 4$ categories, so the degrees of freedom are $K - 1 = 3$. From the Appendix,

$$\chi^2_{3,0.005} = 12.84$$

Since 27.178 is much bigger than 12.84, the null hypothesis is very clearly rejected, even at the 0.5% significance level. Certainly these data provide considerable evidence to suspect that the pattern of payments of gas bills this year differs from the historical norm. Inspection of the numbers in the table shows that more accounts are in arrears over a longer time period than is usually the case.

A word of caution is in order. The figures used in calculating the test statistic in Equation 14.1 must be the *observed* and *expected numbers* in each category. It is not correct, for example, to use instead the percentages of sample members in each category.

EXERCISES

14.1 A professor is planning to use a new book for a financial accounting course and is considering three possibilities: *Financial Accounting made Easy, Financial Accounting Without Tears,* and *Financial Accounting for Profit and Pleasure.* He contacted a random sample of sixty students who had already taken his course and asked each to review the three books, indicating a first preference. The results obtained are shown in the table. Test the null hypothesis that for this population, first preferences are evenly distributed over the three books.

BOOK	MADE EASY	WITHOUT TEARS	PROFIT AND PLEASURE
Number of first preferences	17	25	18

14.2 A random sample of seventy-five mutual funds whose performance ranked in the top 20% of all funds in 1998–2000 was selected. Their performance was observed over the next three years. In this later period,

suppose that thirteen of the sample funds ranked in the top 20% of all funds, twenty in the second 20%, eighteen in the third 20%, eleven in the fourth 20%, and the remainder in the bottom 20%. Test the null hypothesis that a randomly chosen top 20% fund from 1998–2000 is equally likely to fall into each of the five possible performance categories over the following three years.

14.3 An insurance company in Chattanooga, TN, wanted to determine the importance of price as a factor in choosing a hospital in that region. A random sample of 450 consumers were asked to select "not important," "important," or "very important" as an answer. Respective numbers selecting these answers were 142, 175, and 133. Test the null hypothesis that a randomly chosen consumer is equally likely to select each of these three answers.

14.4 Production records indicate that in normal operation for a certain electronic component 93% have no faults, 5% have one fault, and 2% have more than one fault. For a random sample of 500 of these components from a week's output, 458 were found to have no faults, thirty to have one fault, and twelve to have more than one fault. Test at the 5% level the null hypothesis that the quality of the output from this week conforms to the usual pattern.

14.5 A charity solicits donations by telephone. It has been found that 60% of all calls result in a refusal to donate; 30% result in a request for more information through the mail, with a promise to at least consider donating; and 10% generate an immediate credit card donation. For a random sample of 100 calls made in the current week, sixty-five resulted in a refusal to donate, thirty-one in a request for more information through the mail, and four in an immediate credit card donation. Test at the 10%-level the null hypothesis that the usual pattern of outcomes is being followed in the current week.

14.6 A campus administrator has found that 60% of all students view courses as very useful, 20% as somewhat useful, and 20% as worthless. Of a random sample of 100 students taking business courses, 68 found the course in question very useful, 18 somewhat useful, and 14 worthless. Test the null hypothesis that the population distribution for business courses is the same as that for all courses.

14.7 Several types of yogurt are sold in a small general store in New England. From a past study of customer selections, the owner knows that 20% of the customers ordered flavor A; 35% flavor B; 18% flavor C; 12% flavor D, and the remainder flavor E. Now the owner who thinks that the customer preferences have changed, randomly samples 80 customers and finds that 12 prefer A, 16 prefer B, 30 prefer C, 7 prefer E, and the remainder

prefer D. Determine if the customer's preferences have changed from the last study.

14.8 In a recent market survey, five different soft drinks were tested to determine if consumers have a preference for any of the soft drinks. Each person was asked to indicate his favorite drink. The results were: drink A: 20; drink B: 25; drink C: 28; drink D: 15; and drink E: 27. Is there a preference for any of these soft drinks?

14.9 A team of marketing research students was asked to determine the best liked pizza by students enrolled in their college. Two years ago a similar study was conducted, and it was found that 40% of all students at this college preferred Bellini's pizza, 25% chose Anthony's as the best, 20% selected Ferrara's Pizza, and the rest selected Marie's Pizza. To see if preferences have changed, 180 students were randomly selected and asked to indicate their pizza preferences. The results were that 40 selected Ferrara's as their favorite; 32 students chose Marie's, 80 students preferred Bellini's, and the remainder selected Anthony's. Do the data indicate that the preferences today differ from the last study?

14.10 A random sample of statistics professors was asked to complete a survey including questions on curriculum content, computer integration, and software preferences. Of the 250 responses, 100 professors indicated that they preferred software package M; 80 preferred software package E, while the remainder were evenly split between preference for software package S and software package P. Do the data indicate that professors have a preference for any of these software packages?

14.2 GOODNESS-OF-FIT TESTS: POPULATION PARAMETERS UNKNOWN

In Section 14.1 the hypothesis concerned data that are generated by a *fully specified* probability distribution. The null hypothesis in this test specifies the probability that a sample observation will fall in any category. However, it often is required to test the hypothesis that data are generated by some distribution, such as the binomial, the Poisson, or the normal, without assuming the parameters of that distribution to be known. In these circumstances, Section 14.1 is not applicable, but the available data can be used to estimate the unknown population parameters. The goodness-of-fit test, when population parameters are estimated, is stated below.

GOODNESS-OF-FIT TESTS WHEN POPULATION PARAMETERS ARE ESTIMATED

Suppose that a null hypothesis specifies category probabilities that depend on the estimation (from the data) of m unknown population parameters. The appropriate **goodness-of-fit test of the null hypothesis when population parameters are estimated** is precisely as in Section 14.1, except that the number of degrees of freedom for the chi-square random variable is

$$\text{Degrees of Freedom} = (K - m - 1) \tag{14.2}$$

where K is the number of categories.

Consider a test to determine if data is generated by the Poisson distribution. One procedure for attempting to resolve questions of disputed authorship is to count the number of occurrences of particular words in blocks of text. These can be compared with results from passages whose authorship is known; often this comparison can be achieved through the assumption that the number of occurrences follows a Poisson distribution. An example of this type of research involves the study of *The Federalist Papers* (reference 10).

EXAMPLE 14.2

FEDERALIST PAPERS (CHI-SQUARE)

For a sample of 262 blocks of text (each approximately 200 words in length) from *The Federalist Papers* (reference 10), the mean number of occurrences of the word *may* was 0.66. Table 14.5 shows the observed frequencies of occurrence of this word in the 262 sampled blocks of text. Test the null hypothesis that the population distribution of occurrences is Poisson, without assuming prior knowledge of the mean of this distribution.

TABLE 14.5
Occurrences of the Word *may* in 262 Blocks of Text in *The Federalist Papers*

NUMBER OF OCCURRENCES	0	1	2	3 OR MORE
OBSERVED FREQUENCY	156	63	29	14

SOLUTION

Recall that if the Poisson distribution is appropriate, the probability of x occurrences is

$$P(x) = \frac{e^{-\lambda}\lambda^x}{x!}$$

where λ is the mean number of occurrences. Although this population mean is unknown, it can be estimated by the sample mean 0.66. It is then possible, by substituting 0.66 for λ, to estimate the probability for any number of occurrences under the null hypothesis that the population distribution is Poisson. For example, the probability of two occurrences is

$$P(2) = \frac{e^{-0.66}(0.66)^2}{2!}$$
$$= \frac{(0.5169)(0.66)^2}{2} = 0.1126$$

Similarly, the probabilities for zero and one occurrence can be found, so the probability of three or more occurrences is

$$P(X \geq 3) = 1 - P(0) - P(1) - P(2)$$

These probabilities are shown in the second row of Table 14.6.

Then, exactly as before, the expected frequencies under the null hypothesis are obtained from

$$E_i = n\pi_i \quad (i = 1, 2, \ldots, K)$$

Thus, for example, the expected frequency of two occurrences of the word *may* in 262 blocks of text is $(262)(0.1126) = 29.5$. Since the variable itself is an integer, it is best not to round these expected values to integer values. The bottom row of Table 14.6 shows these expected frequencies. The test statistic is then

$$\chi^2 = \sum_{i=1}^{4} \frac{(O_i - E_i)^2}{E_i} = \frac{(156 - 135.4)^2}{135.4} + \frac{(63 - 89.4)^2}{89.4} + \frac{(29 - 29.5)^2}{29.5} + \frac{(14 - 7.7)^2}{7.7} = 16.08$$

TABLE 14.6
Observed and Expected
Frequencies for *The Federalist Papers*

NUMBER OF OCCURRENCES	0	1	2	3 OR MORE	TOTAL
OBSERVED FREQUENCIES	156	63	29	14	262
PROBABILITIES	0.5169	0.3412	0.1126	0.0293	1
EXPECTED FREQUENCIES UNDER H_0	135.4	89.4	29.5	7.7	262

Since there are four categories and one parameter has been estimated, the approximate number of degrees of freedom for the test is 2. From the chi-square distribution table,

$$\chi^2_{2,0.005} = 10.60$$

Thus, the null hypothesis that the population distribution is Poisson can be rejected at the 0.5% significance level. The evidence in the data against that hypothesis is, then, very strong indeed.

To solve Example 14.2 using Excel see the Appendix to this chapter.

A Test of Normality

The **normal distribution** plays an important role in statistics, and many practical procedures rely for their validity, or for particular optimality properties, on an assumption that sample data are from a normal distribution. In Chapter 2, we discussed the normal probability (quantile) plot to check for evidence of nonnormality. Also, in Chapter 8 (Figure 8.2 and Figure 8.11) we visually tested for evidence of nonnormality by determining if the dots in the normal quantile plots were "close" to the straight line. Next consider a test of the normality assumption through an adaptation of the chi-square procedure. This test is both easy to carry out and likely to be more powerful.

Suppose that we have a sample $X_1, X_2, \ldots, X_n$ of n observations from a population. Our approach is based on checking whether these data reflect two characteristics of the normal distribution. The first characteristic is symmetry about the mean. Using sample information, **skewness** of a population is estimated by

$$\text{Skewness} = \frac{\sum_{i=1}^{n} (x_i - \bar{x})^3 / n}{s^2}$$

where $\bar{x}$ and s are the sample mean and sample standard deviation, respectively. The important part of this expression is the numerator; the denominator serves the purpose of standardization, making units of measurement irrelevant. Positive skewness will result if a distribution is skewed to the right, since average cubed discrepancies about the mean would be positive. Skewness will be negative for distributions skewed to the left and 0 for distributions, such as the normal, that are symmetric about their mean.

Since there are different symmetric distributions, a further characteristic is required to distinguish a normal distribution. In computing the sample variance, squared discrepancies about the mean are used, while skewness is based on cubed discrepancies about the mean. The next logical step is to look at fourth powers of these discrepancies, leading to the sample **kurtosis**:

$$\text{Kurtosis} = \frac{\sum_{i=1}^{n} (x_i - \bar{x})^4 / n}{s^2}$$

Kurtosis provides a measure of the weight in the tails of a probability density function. It is known that for the normal distribution, the population kurtosis is 3.

Sample skewness and kurtosis can be computed from data using these formulas. Skewness and kurtosis are also included in the standard output of most statistical software packages. However, alternative formulas may be used in the software packages to find these values. A test that takes into account both skewness and kurtosis is called the *Bowman-Shelton test statistic* for normality and is given in Equation 14.3.

BOWMAN-SHELTON TEST FOR NORMALITY

The **Bowman-Shelton Test for Normality** is based on the closeness to 0 of the sample skewness and the closeness to 3 of the sample kurtosis. The test statistic is

$$B = n \left[\frac{(\text{Skewness})^2}{6} + \frac{(\text{Kurtosis} - 3)^2}{24} \right] \qquad (14.3)$$

It is known that as the number of sample observations becomes very large, this statistic has, under the null hypothesis that the population distribution is normal, a chi-square distribution with 2 degrees of freedom. The null hypothesis is, of course, rejected for large values of the test statistic.

Unfortunately, the chi-square approximation to the distribution of the Bowman-Shelton test statistic, B, is close only for very large sample sizes. Table 14.7 shows significance points appropriate for a range of sample sizes for tests at the 5% and 10% levels. The recommended procedure, then, is to calculate the statistic, B, in Equation 14.3 and reject the null hypothesis of normality if the test statistic exceeds the appropriate value tabulated in Table 14.7.

TABLE 14.7
Significance points of the Bowman-Shelton Statistic (reference 1)

SAMPLE SIZE N	10% POINT	5% POINT	SAMPLE SIZE N	10% POINT	5% POINT
20	2.13	3.26	200	3.48	4.43
30	2.49	3.71	250	3.54	4.51
40	2.70	3.99	300	3.68	4.60
50	2.90	4.26	400	3.76	4.74
75	3.09	4.27	500	3.91	4.82
100	3.14	4.29	800	4.32	5.46
125	3.31	4.34	∞	4.61	5.99
150	3.43	4.39			

EXAMPLE 14.3

RATES OF RETURN (NORMALITY TEST)

Suppose that a random sample of 300 daily rates of return on a citrus futures contract had skewness 0.0305 and kurtosis 3.08. Test the null hypothesis that the true distribution for these rates of return is normal.

SOLUTION

We find the Bowman-Shelton statistic, B:

$$B = 300 \left[\frac{(0.0305)^2}{6} + \frac{(0.08)^2}{24} \right] = 0.1265$$

Comparison of this result with the significance points in Table 14.7 certainly provides little ground to think that population distribution is not normal.

Numerous other tests for normality exist, including the Kolmogorov-Smirnov Test, the Anderson-Darling Test, and the Ryan-Joiner Test. These procedures, which are not included here, are available using software such as Minitab.

EXERCISES

14.11 The number of times a machine broke down each week was observed over a period of 100 weeks, giving the results shown in the accompanying table. It was found that the average number of breakdowns per week over this period was 2.1. Test the null hypothesis that the population distribution of breakdown is Poisson.

NUMBER OF BREAKDOWNS	0	1	2	3	4	5 OR MORE
NUMBER OF WEEKS		10	24	32	23	6	5

14.12 In a period of 100 minutes, there were a total of 190 arrivals at a highway toll booth. The accompanying table shows the frequency of arrivals per minute over this period. Test the null hypothesis that the population distribution is Poisson.

NUMBER OF ARRIVALS IN MINUTES	0	1	2	3	4 OR MORE
OBSERVED FREQUENCY		10	26	35	24	5

14.13 A random sample of 50 students was asked to estimate how much money they spent on textbooks in a year. The sample skewness of these amounts was found to be 0.83 and the sample kurtosis was 3.98. Test at the 10%-level the null hypothesis that the population distribution of amounts spent is normal.

14.14 A random sample of 100 measurements of the resistance of electronic components produced in a period of one week was taken. The sample skewness was 0.63 and the sample kurtosis was 3.85. Test the null hypothesis that the population distribution is normal.

14.15 Use the Bowman-Shelton test to determine if the amounts spent on groceries for a random sample of customers at Bishop's Supermarket given in Example 2.10 follow a normal distribution.

14.16 A random sample of 125 monthly balances for holders of a particular credit card indicated that the sample skewness was 0.55 and the sample kurtosis was 2.77. Test the null hypothesis that the population distribution is normal.

14.3 CONTINGENCY TABLES

Suppose that a sample is taken from a population, each of whose members can be uniquely cross classified according to a pair of attributes, A and B. The hypothesis to be tested is of no association or dependence in the population between possession of attribute A and attribute B. For example, a travel agency may want to know if there is any relationship between clients' gender and the method clients use to make an airline reservation. An accounting firm may want to examine the relationship between the age of people and the type of income tax return filed by these individuals. Or perhaps, in a medical study, a pharmaceutical company may want to know if the success of a drug used to control cholesterol is dependent on a person's weight. A marketing research company may test if a customer's choice of cereal is in some way dependent on the color of the cereal box. Perhaps, there is an association between political affiliation and support for a particular amendment that is to appear on the next election's ballot.

Assume that there are r categories for A and c categories for B, so a total of rc cross-classifications is possible. The number of sample observations belonging to both the ith category of A and the jth category of B will be denoted O_{ij} as shown in Table 14.8. This tabulation is called an $r \times c$ **contingency table**. For convenience, row and column totals were added to Table 14.8, denoted respectively $R_1, R_2, \ldots, R_r$ and $C_1, C_2, \ldots, C_c$.

To test the null hypothesis of no association between attributes A and B, we ask how many observations we would expect to find in each cross-classification if that hypothesis were true. This question becomes meaningful when the row and column totals are *fixed*. Consider, then, the joint classification corresponding to the ith row and jth column of the table. There are a total of C_j observations in the jth column, and given no association, we would expect these to be distributed among the rows in proportion to the total number of observations in each row. Thus, we would expect a proportion R_i/n of these C_j observations to be in the ith row. Hence, the estimated expected number of observations in the cross-classifications are

$$E_{ij} = \frac{R_i C_j}{n} \quad \text{for } (i = 1, 2, \ldots, r; \; j = 1, 2, \ldots, c)$$

Our test of the null hypothesis of no association is based on the magnitudes of the discrepancies between the observed numbers and those that would be expected if that hypothesis were true. The random variable given in Equation 14.4 is a generalization of that introduced in Section 14.1.

CHI-SQUARE RANDOM VARIABLE FOR CONTINGENCY TABLES

It can be shown that under the null hypothesis the random variable associated with

$$\chi^2 = \sum_{i=1}^{r} \sum_{i=1}^{c} \frac{(O_{ij} - E_{ij})^2}{E_{ij}} \tag{14.4}$$

has, to a good approximation, a chi-square distribution with $(r-1)(c-1)$ degrees of freedom. The approximation works well if each of the estimated expected numbers E_{ij} is at least 5. Sometimes adjacent classes can be combined in order to meet this assumption.

TABLE 14.8
Cross-Classification of n Observations in an $r \times c$ Contingency Table

ATTRIBUTE A	ATTRIBUTE B				TOTALS
	1	2	...	c	
1	O_{11}	O_{12}	...	O_{1c}	R_1
2	O_{21}	O_{22}	...	O_{2c}	R_2
⋮	⋮	⋮	...	⋮	⋮
r	O_{r1}	O_{r2}	...	O_{rc}	R_r
Totals	C_1	C_2	...	C_c	n

The double summation in Equation 14.4 implies that summation extends over all rc cells of the table. The number of degrees of freedom follows from regarding the row and column totals as fixed. If these are known and the $(r-1)(c-1)$ entries corresponding to the first $(r-1)$ rows and $(c-1)$ columns are also known, the remaining entries in the table can be deduced. Clearly, the null hypothesis of no association will be rejected for large absolute discrepancies between observed and expected numbers—that is, for high values of the statistic in Equation 14.4. The test procedure is summarized as follows.

A TEST OF ASSOCIATION IN CONTINGENCY TABLES

Suppose that a sample of n observations is cross classified according to two attributes in an $r \times c$ contingency table. Denote by O_{ij} the number of observations in the cell that is in the ith row and jth column. If the null hypothesis is

H_0: No association exists between the two attributes in the population

the estimated expected number of observations in this cell, under H_0, is

$$E_{ij} = \frac{R_i C_j}{n} \tag{14.5}$$

where R_i and C_j are the corresponding row and column totals. **A test of association** at a significance level α is based on the following decision rule:

$$\text{Reject } H_0 \text{ if } = \sum_{i=1}^{r} \sum_{j=1}^{c} \frac{(O_{ij} - E_{ij})^2}{E_{ij}} > \chi^2_{(r-1)(c-1), \alpha}$$

EXAMPLE 14.4

AMERICAN TRAVELER SURVEY (TEST OF ASSOCIATION)

The 1999 American Traveler Survey (*Travel Weekly*, October 25, 1999) conducted by Plog Research Inc. provides information based on a random sample of 10,536 U.S. adults (18 years or older) concerning their business and leisure travel habits, use of technology, travel spending patterns, and a comparison of the travel habits of travel agent users with those who do not use agents (reference 6). Suppose that in a similar study a travel agent randomly sampled individuals in her target market to determine if there is any association between the respondents' gender and the methods used by respondents to make airline reservations for their last leisure trip, whether domestic or international. Table 14.9 shows the numbers of observations in each of the six possible cross-classifications. For convenience, row and column totals are also given in the table. Test the null hypothesis of no association between these attributes. In this case, that there is no association between subjects' gender and method used to make airline reservations.

SOLUTION

The null hypothesis that is to be tested would imply that, in the population, the proportion of airline reservations made by the client using a travel agent, booked by the client on the Internet, or made by the client calling an airline's toll-free number would be the same for male as for female subjects. To test the null hypothesis of no association between the attributes, we again ask how many observations we would *expect* to find in each cross-classification if that hypothesis were true.

For example, if there were no association between gender and method used to make an airline reservation in Table 14.9, we would expect, since 363 of 513 reservations were made

TABLE 14.9
Air Flight Reservations by
Gender and Booking Method

RESERVATION METHOD	FEMALE	MALE	TOTAL
Used a Travel Agent	256	74	330
Booked on the Internet	41	42	83
Airline's Toll-Free Number	66	34	100
Totals	**363**	**150**	**513**

by women, a proportion 363/513 of the 330 reservations made by use of a travel agent to be made by females; that is

$$E_{11} = \frac{(330)(363)}{513} = 233.5$$

The other expected numbers are calculated in the same way and are shown in Table 14.10 alongside the corresponding observed numbers.

The test of the null hypothesis of no association is based on the magnitudes of the discrepancies between the observed numbers and those that would be expected if that hypothesis were true. Extending Equation 14.1 to include each of the six cross-classifications gives the following value of the chi-square test statistic:

$$\chi^2 = \frac{(256 - 233.5)^2}{233.5} + \frac{(74 - 96.5)^2}{96.5} + \frac{(41 - 58.7)^2}{58.7} + \frac{(42 - 24.3)^2}{24.3}$$
$$+ \frac{(66 - 70.8)^2}{70.8} + \frac{(34 - 29.2)^2}{29.2} = 26.8$$

The degrees of freedom is $(r-1)(c-1)$. Here there are $r = 3$ rows and $c = 2$ columns in the table, so the appropriate number of degrees of freedom is

$$(r-1)(c-1) = (3-1)(2-1) = 2$$

From the Appendix, we find

$$\chi^2_{2,0.005} = 10.60$$

Therefore, the null hypothesis of no association is very clearly rejected, even at the 0.5% level. The evidence against this hypothesis is overwhelming.

TABLE 14.10
Observed (and Expected)
Numbers in Each Cross-
Classification for
Reservations

RESERVATION METHOD	FEMALE	MALE	TOTAL
Used a Travel Agent	256 (233.5)	74 (96.5)	330
Booked on the Internet	41 (58.7)	42 (24.3)	83
Airline's Toll-Free Number	66 (70.8)	34 (29.2)	100
Totals	**363**	**150**	**513**

It should be noted, as was the case for the goodness-of-fit tests of earlier sections, that the figures used in calculating the statistic must be the *actual numbers* observed and not, for example, percentages of the total.

Computer Applications

Various software packages are used by professional research organizations for the types of procedures discussed in this chapter. Example 14.5 illustrates Microsoft Excel PHStat. Minitab can also be used for cross-classifications and chi-square tests. Although not included in this text, SPSS (Statistical Package for the Social Sciences) is an excellent package for chi-square analysis.

EXAMPLE 14.5

INCOME TAX RETURNS (PHStat)

There are several forms that people can use to file their federal income tax returns. One standard method is the 1040 form. Some people use other forms such as the telefile process. Others simply file for an extension (to extend the deadline beyond April 15). Suppose that in a particular locality a study of 200 randomly selected people filing returns was conducted. The filer's age was an important variable in this study. Proportional to the age demographics of the area, the study included 50 people under 25 years of age, 90 people between the ages of 25 and 45, and the remainder were over 45 years of age. Of those under the age of 25 years, 35 used a 1040 form, 8 used another form, and the remainder filed for an extension. Two-thirds of the people in the age category from 25 to 45 years of age use the 1040 form, 20 used a different form, and the remainder filed for an extension. Seventy-five percent of the people in the over 45 age category used the 1040 form, 4 people filed for an extension and the remainder used a different process. Determine if there is any association between a person's age and the method used to file income tax returns.

SOLUTION

Using Microsoft Excel PHStat, we can readily find the expected values for each of the nine categories, the chi-square test-statistic, and the p-value. First, generate a generic 3×3 contingency table by the command sequence:

```
PHSTAT > MULTIPLE-SAMPLE TESTS > CHI-SQUARE TEST...
```

In the dialog box, enter the level of significance, the number of rows, and the number of columns for the desired contingency table. You have the option to include a title. After completing this dialog box, a generic 3×3 contingency table appears. As you enter the observed frequencies, the notation #DIV/0! for each expected frequency is replaced by the actual value of the expected frequency. Label the rows and columns. Your completed contingency table should look like Figure 14.1 on page 571. Notice that the values for the chi-square test, the degrees of freedom and the p-value are also given.

The large p-value suggests that the data is not sufficient to suggest that there is an association between one's age and the method used to file their last federal income tax return.

Minitab can also be used to test for a relationship between two variables. Example 14.6 illustrates this software for a university library study.

EXAMPLE 14.6

LIBRARY STUDY: RANK VERSUS VARIETY (MINITAB)

As part of an exploratory study, a team of students conducted a survey on their college campus. Students were asked to complete a brief survey concerning their college library. Should the library hours be extended? Is it easy to locate books in the library? Are there sufficient databases available for research? Is the technology current? The results are contained in the data file **Library** (reference 13). Is there any association between students' class rank

FIGURE 14.1
Observed and Expected
Frequencies for Example 14.5

Observed Frequencies				
		Returns		
Age	**1040**	**Other**	**Extension**	**Total**
Under 25	35	8	7	50
25 to 45	60	20	10	90
Over 45	45	11	4	60
Total	140	39	21	200

Expected Frequencies				
		Returns		
Age	**1040**	**Other**	**Extension**	**Total**
Under 25	35	9.75	5.25	50
25 to 45	63	17.55	9.45	90
Over 45	42	11.7	6.3	60
Total	140	39	21	200

Data	
Level of Significance	0.05
Number of Rows	3
Number of Columns	3
Degrees of Freedom	4

Results	
Critical Value	9.487728
Chi-Square Test Statistic	2.510175
p-Value	0.642815
Do not reject the null hypothesis	

*Expected frequency assumption
is met.*

(1: first year; 2: sophomore; 3: junior; 4: senior) and the response to the question, "Does the library have an adequate variety of books? (1: yes; 2: no)"

Library

SOLUTION

From the data file **Library**, you see that a total of 355 students responded to this question. Figure 14.2 shows the cross-classification of the responses and the Minitab output.

FIGURE 14.2
Minitab Output for Class
Rank versus Adequate Variety

Tabulated Statistics: Class Rank, Adequate Variety

```
Rows: Class        Columns: Adequate
      Rank                  Variety

          Yes        No      All

  1        73        71      144
         54.76     89.24   144.00

  2        26        76      102
         38.79     63.21   102.00

  3        19        47       66
         25.10     40.90    66.00

  4        17        26       43
         16.35     26.65    43.00

All       135       220      355
        135.00    220.00   355.00

Chi-Square = 19.040, DF = 3, P-Value = 0.000
```

Minitab Instructions

1. Click on Stat
2. Select Tables
3. Select Cross Tabulation...
4. Indicate the row and column variables
5. Check Chi-Square analysis
6. Select Above and expected count

Each of the expected values is greater than five. If this assumption were not valid, a warning message would appear in the Minitab output and adjacent classes could be combined. The small p-value indicates rejection of the null hypothesis of no association.

Although the use of the chi-square test for association may indicate that there is a relationship between two variables, this procedure does not indicate the direction or strength of the relationship.

EXERCISES

14.17 Do commercial-free cable programs promote better citizenship among our school-aged children (*USA Today*, October 30, 2000)? (see reference 7.) Many teachers and administrators believe that the use of commercial-free cable programs can enhance a student's interest in the democratic process in the years prior to the voting age. Other educators think that television is the enemy of education. Suppose that in a study in Texas, a random sample of 150 high school history teachers were asked, "Would you like to use commercial-free cable programs in your classroom?" The following contingency table gives the teachers' response to this question as well as the teacher's opinion concerning whether or not such programming enhances citizenship.

	USE COMMERCIAL-FREE CABLE PROGRAMS?	
Effect	*Yes*	*No*
Promotes better citizenship	78	25
Doesn't promote better citizenship	37	10

(a) Is there a relationship between the teacher's responses to these two questions?
(b) Check your result with PHStat.

14.18 University administrators have collected the following information concerning student grade point average and the school of the student's major.

SCHOOL	GPA < 3.0	GPA 3.0 OR HIGHER
Arts & Sciences	50	35
Business	45	30
Music	15	25

(a) Determine if there is any association between GPA and major.
(b) Verify results with PHStat.

14.19 Should all college students be required to own a laptop computer? Although this policy does exist at many universities, the added expense for students at small private schools should be considered. One business school recently surveyed its students to determine their reaction to this possible policy. The responses are given in the table below along with the students' major.

	OWN A LAPTOP?	
Major	*Yes*	*No*
Accounting	68	42
Finance	40	15
Management	60	50
Marketing	30	25

(a) Do the data indicate that there is an association between one's major and the response to this question?
(b) Find and interpret the output from PHStat.

14.20 How do customers first hear about a new product? A random sample of 200 users of a new product was surveyed to determine the answer to this question. Other demographic data such as age was also collected. The respondents included 50 people under the age of 21 years, 90 people between the age of 21 and 35, and the remainder were over 35 years of age. Of those under 21 years old, 60% heard about the product from a friend, and the remainder saw an advertisement in the local paper. One-third of the people in the age category from 21 to 35 years, saw the advertisement in the local paper. The other two-thirds heard about it from a friend. In the age category over 35 years, only 30% heard about it from a friend, while the remainder saw the local newspaper advertisement. Set up the contingency table for the variables age and method of learning about the product. Is there an association between the consumer's age and the method that the individual heard about the new product?

14.21 Following a presidential debate, people were asked how they might vote in the forth coming election. Is there any association between one's gender and choice of presidential candidate?

	GENDER	
Candidate Preference	*Male*	*Female*
Candidate A	150	130
Candidate B	100	120

SUMMARY

In this chapter you studied some of the applications of the chi-square distribution. Goodness-of-fit tests were used to test the hypothesis that data are generated by a fully specified probability distribution. This technique is often used by market researchers to determine if products are equally preferred by potential customers or to check if the market shares for several brands of a product have changed over a given period of time.

In addition, the goodness-of-fit procedure was used to determine if data is generated by some distribution, such as the binominal, the Poisson or normal distribution, without assuming knowledge of the parameters of that distribution. The Bowman-Shelton test for normality was introduced. Other normality tests can be performed with various statistical software packages.

Finally, tests of association between two variables were considered. For larger contingency tables, it is convenient to use a software package to determine the test statistic and p-value.

KEY WORDS

Bowman-Shelton Test for Normality, 565
chi-square random variable, 559
goodness-of-fit tests, 560

specified probabilities, 558
unknown parameters, 562
poisson distribution, 563
normal distribution, 564

kurtosis, 565
skewness, 564
test of association, 568

CHAPTER EXERCISES AND APPLICATIONS

14.22 Suppose that a random sample of firms with impaired assets were classified according to whether discretionary write-downs of these assets were taken and also according to whether there was evidence of subsequent merger or acquisition activity. Using the data in the accompanying table, test the null hypothesis of no association between these attributes.

	MERGER OR ACQUISITION ACTIVITY?	
Write-Down	Yes	No
Yes	32	48
No	25	57

14.23 A manufacturer of a certain product has three factories located across the United States. There are three major causes of defects in this product, which we will identify as A, B, and C. During a recent week the reported occurrences of product defects in the three factories were as follows:

Factory 1:	A, 15;	B, 25;	C, 23
Factory 2:	A, 10;	B, 12;	C, 21
Factory 3:	A, 32;	B, 28;	C, 44

Based on these frequencies, can we conclude that the defect patterns in the different factories are the same?

14.24 The human resources department is attempting to determine if an employee's undergraduate major influences the performance of this employee. The majors considered are business, economics, mathematics, and all others. Personnel ratings are grouped as excellent, strong, and average. The classifications are based on employees with two to four years of experience, as follows:

Business major:
excellent, 21;   strong, 18;   average, 10;

Economics major:
excellent, 19;   strong, 15;   average, 5;

Mathematics major:
excellent, 10;   strong, 5;   average, 5;

Other major:
excellent, 5;   strong, 15;   average, 13

Do these data indicate that there is a difference in ratings based on undergraduate major?

14.25 A random sample of people from three different job classifications labeled A, B, and C were asked to indicate their preferences for three brands of camping lanterns: Big Star, Lone Star, and Bright Star. The preferences were as follows:

Group A:
Big Star, 54;   Lone Star, 67;   Bright Star, 39

Group B:
Big Star, 23;   Lone Star, 13;   Bright Star, 44

Group C:
Big Star, 69;   Lone Star, 53;   Bright Star, 59

Do these data indicate that there is a difference in ratings for the three different groups?

14.26 A liberal arts college was interested in determining if there were different graduate school patterns for students with undergraduate majors in history and economics. They surveyed a random sample of recent graduates and found that a large number obtained graduate degrees in business, law, and theology. The frequency of persons in the various combinations is shown below. Based on these results, is there evidence that undergraduate economics and history majors pursue different graduate school programs?

	GRADUATE STUDIES		
Undergraduate	*Business*	*Law*	*Theology*
Economics	30	20	10
History	6	34	20

14.27 Suppose that you have collected market survey data for gender and product purchase. Perform a chi-square test to determine if there is a different probability of purchase among men and women. Include in your answer the expected cell values under the null hypothesis.

	GENDER	
Decision	*Male*	*Female*
Purchase	150	150
No Purchase	50	250

14.28 Sally Smith is a long-time political campaign manager from Chicago. In the primary election there are four candidates. She wishes to determine if voter preference is different over the four major districts. A random sample survey results in the candidate preference frequencies by district shown in the contingency table. Perform an appropriate statistical test to determine if candidate preference is related to the district.

	CANDIDATES FOR PRIMARY ELECTION				
District	*A*	*B*	*C*	*D*	*Total*
1	52	34	80	34	200
2	33	15	78	24	150
3	66	54	141	39	300

14.29 A manufacturer of household appliances wanted to determine if there was a relationship between family size and the size of washing machine purchased. They were preparing guidelines for sales personnel and wanted to know if the sales staff should make specific recommendations to customers. A random sample of 300 families was asked about family size and size of washing machine. For the 40 families with one or two people, 25 had an 8-pound washer, 10 had a 10-pound washer, and five had a 12-pound washer. The 140 families with three or four people included 37 with the 8-pound, 62 with the 10-pound, and 41 with the 12-pound. For the remaining 120 families with five or more people, eight had an 8-pound washer, 53 had a 10-pound, and 59 had a 12-pound. Based on these results, what

can be concluded about family size and size of washer? Construct a two-way table, state the hypothesis, compute the statistics, and state your conclusion.

14.30 The gear-cutting department in a large manufacturing firm produces high-quality gears. The number produced per hour by a single machinist is 1, 2, or 3, as shown in the table. Company management is interested in determining the effect of worker experience on the number of units produced per hour. Worker experience is classified in three subgroups: less than one year, two to five years, and more than five years. Use the data in the table to determine if experience and the number of parts produced per hour are independent.

	UNITS PRODUCED/HOUR			
Experience	*1*	*2*	*3*	*Total*
≤ 1 year	10	30	10	50
2-5 years	10	20	20	50
≥ 5 years	10	10	30	50
Total	30	60	60	150

14.31 Agnes Larson has been working on a plan for new store locations as part of her regional expansion. In one city proposed for expansion there are three possible locations: north, east, or west. From past experience she knows that the three major profit centers in her stores are tools, lumber, and paint. In selecting a location, the demand patterns in the different parts of the city were important. She commissioned a sampling study of the city, which resulted a two-way table for the variables "residential location" versus "product purchased." This table was prepared by the market research department using data obtained from the random sample of households in the three major residential areas of the city. Each residential area had a separate phone number prefix, and the last four digits were chosen using a computer random number generator. Is there a difference in the demand patterns for the three major items among the different areas of the city?

	PRODUCT DEMAND		
Area	*Tools*	*Lumber*	*Paint*
East	100	50	50
North	50	95	45
West	65	70	75

14.32 The Speedi-Flex delivery service is conducting a study of its delivery operations. As part of this study they collected data on package type by originating source for one day's operation for one district office in the southeast. These data are shown in the table. The major originating sources were identified as (1) small cities (towns), (2) central business districts (CBDs), (3) light manufacturing districts (factory), or (4) suburban residential communities (suburbs). Size and rate with three major categories classify the items handled. Overnight envelopes must weigh less than 3 pounds and have a fixed charge of $12 anywhere in the United States. Small packages weigh less than 10 pounds and have dimension restrictions. Large packages can weigh up to 75 pounds and have the lowest rate per pound and the longest delivery time.

| | PACKAGE SIZE (LB) | | | |
Package Source	≤ 3	4-10	11-75	Total
Towns	40	40	20	100
CBDs	119	63	18	200
Factory	18	71	111	200
Suburbs	69	64	17	150

(a) Are there any differences in the patterns of packages originated at the various locations?

(b) Which two combinations have the largest percentage deviation from a uniform pattern?

14.33 A travel agent randomly sampled individuals in her target market and asked, "Did you use a travel agent to book your last airline flight?" By cross-referencing the answers to this question with the responses to the rest of the questionnaire, the agent obtained data such as that in the following contingency table:

| DID YOU USE A TRAVEL AGENT TO BOOK YOUR LAST FLIGHT? | | |
Age	Yes	No
Under 30	15	30
30 to 39	20	42
40 to 49	47	42
50 to 59	36	50
60 or older	45	20

Determine if there is an association between one's age and whether the respondent used a travel agent to make reservations for their last flight.

14.34 When the law was passed to give the same legal status to e-signatures as to handwritten signatures, nearly 60% of small-business owners thought that digital signatures would not help them do business online (*USA Today*, October 30, 2000, reference 14). Suppose that the following data were obtained in a similar study of small-business owners classified by the number of years that the company has existed and the CEO's opinion on the effectiveness of e-signatures to increase business.

| WILL DIGITAL SIGNATURES HAVE A POSITIVE EFFECT ON YOUR BUSINESS? | | | |
Age of Company	Yes	No	Uncertain
Less than 5 years	80	68	10
5 to 10 years	60	90	15
More than 10 years	72	63	12

Is there any relationship between the age of the company and the owner's opinion concerning the effectiveness of e-signatures?

14.35 The American Society for Quality (ASQ) offers its members exclusive recruiting tools available online. "Only members seeking to hire quality professionals can post jobs to these free bulletins and only members have access to these jobs online" (*On Q*, Fall 2000, reference 2). Suppose that a random sample of companies were surveyed and asked to indicate if they had used an Internet career service site to search for prospective employees. The companies were also asked questions concerning the posting fee for use of such a site. Is there a relationship between use of such a site and the management's opinion on the posting fee?

| HAVE YOU USED AN INTERNET CAREER SERVICE SITE? | | |
Posting Fee	Yes	No
Fee is too high	36	50
Fee is about right	82	28

14.36 *Business Florida* is the official guide to business growth and development in Florida. It is published annually by Enterprise Florida Inc., the Florida Economic Development Council, Inc., and *Florida Trend* magazine. *In Business Florida 2001* (reference 12), ten reasons are given to encourage a company to select Florida as "a site for business development and expansion." Suppose that in a follow-up study a random sample of businesses that located in Florida within the last three years are surveyed. Does the data in the following contingency table show any relationship between the primary reason for the company's move to Florida and the industry type?

| | INDUSTRY TYPE | | |
Primary Reason	Manufacturing	Retail	Tourism
Emerging Technology	53	25	10
Tax Credits	67	36	20
Labor Force	30	40	33

14.37 Should large retailers offer banking services? Retail giants, such as Nordstrom and Federated Department Stores (corporate parent of Macy's and Bloomingdale's) began offering various banking services by the end of year 2000 (*Forbes*, July 3, 2000, reference 3). Some incentives to attract customers included longer grace periods for late payments, reduced fees for such services as wire transfers, and auto or home improvement loans. Small community banks may be concerned about their future if more retailers enter the world of banking. Suppose that a market research company conducted a national survey for one retailer that is considering offering banking services to its customers. The respondents were asked to indicate the provider (bank, retail store, other) that they most likely would use for certain banking services (assuming that rate is not a factor). Is there a relationship between these two variables?

Service	PROVIDER		
	Bank	Retail Store	Other
Checking Account	100	45	10
Savings Account	85	25	45
Home Mortgage	30	10	80

14.38 Many easy-weight-loss products are just gimmicks that attract people to the hope of a fast way to a slimmer body. Diet-industry groups, health professionals, and federal officials warn that deceptive advertising can lure consumers into danger (reference 4). Suppose that a random sample of residents in one community were asked if they had ever tried a quick-weight-reduction product. Then they were asked if they thought that there should be stricter advertising controls to prohibit deceptive weight-loss advertising.

Advertising	USED A QUICK WEIGHT LOSS PRODUCT?	
	Yes	No
Stricter controls needed	85	40
Stricter controls not needed	25	64

Are respondents' views on advertising controls dependent on whether or not the respondent had ever used a quick weight loss product?

14.39 "Rattled by the trembling stock market, online enterprises began what will no doubt be a long run of layoffs" (*Forbes* July 3, 2000, reference 5). Although the economy is new, apparently the same old downsizing is taking place among dot-com companies. These e-companies claim that firings are necessary to increase profits and save costs. Suppose that the following contingency table shows the number of layoffs in three dot-com companies and the months of service by the those employees that were laid off. Is there any relationship between theses two variables?

Age	DOT-COM COMPANY		
	A	B	C
Less than 6 months	23	40	12
6 months to 1 year	15	21	12
More than one year	12	9	6

14.40 Some marketing research studies indicate the "positive impact of store brand penetration on store profitability as measured by market share" (*Journal of Marketing Research*, August 2000, reference 8). Two years ago, the manager of a local supermarket that sells three national brands (Brands A, B, and C) and one store brand (Brand D) of orange juice found that Brands A and C were equally preferred; 33% preferred Brand B, and 27% preferred the store Brand, D. Now, the manager thinks that there has been a change in customer preferences and that the preference for store brand orange juice has increased and perhaps will positively contribute to increased profits. The results from a recent random sample of shoppers indicate the following preferences.

FAVORITE BRAND	A	B	C	D (STORE BRAND)
Number	56	70	28	126

Has there been a change in customer's preferences from the study two years ago?

14.41 By late Fall 2000, customers who wanted wireless Internet service could choose from four basic categories of hardware: Palm handhelds and their offspring that use the Palm operating system; Pocket PCs; Web-enabled phones; and mobile e-mail devices (reference 11). If the data below are taken from a survey of wireless Internet service users, does satisfaction depend upon the hardware category selected?

Hardware Category	ARE YOU SATISFIED WITH YOUR PURCHASE?	
	Yes	No
Palm handhelds	128	40
Pocket PCs	45	15
Web-enabled phones	30	8
Mobile e-mail devices	30	6

14.42 💿 As part of an exploratory market study, a team of students asked 356 students on their college campus to answer a brief survey concerning their college library (reference 13). Students were asked if library hours should be extended.

(**a**) Use Microsoft Excel PHStat to test for any relationship between students' responses to this question and their class standing. The data is in a file named **Library**.

(**b**) What recommendations would you suggest to the library staff?

14.43 💿 Can a student easily find books in the college library? This question was also included in the college library survey (reference 13).

(**a**) Use Microsoft Excel PHStat with the data file **Library** to test for any relationship between students' responses to this question and their class standing.

(**b**) What recommendations would you suggest to the library staff?

14.44 💿 The Institutional Research Office (IRO) at a major university annually conducts surveys of freshmen, sophomores, and juniors to determine levels of satisfaction with student services, facilities and policies of the university. Seniors are surveyed separately in the Senior Survey. Suppose that the Director of the IRO at one university provides university administrators/faculty/staff with analyzes of trends, comparisons, and other output useful for purpose of continuous improvement.

The 2002 Student Satisfaction Survey, conducted in the spring of 2002 from mid-March to early May, was mailed to a random sample of 600 students (200 freshmen, 200 sophomores and 200 juniors). The response rate was 248 or 42.5% (after adjusting for undeliverable or unclaimed surveys). Demographic information included respondent's school or college of major, age, and gender. Suppose that selected data collected from the 2002 Student Satisfaction Survey are included in the data file IRO. Students were asked to indicate if they were satisfied, neutral, or dissatisfied with online registration, the university bookstore, food service, student accounts/billing office, student financial planning, the work-study program, and various other service providers on campus. From the data, numerous relationships can be investigated. Analyze the data, select and test several possible relationships, and write a summary of findings to be submitted to the university president. Include in your report discussion of any relationship between a student's satisfaction with library hours and the student's class standing; a student's satisfaction level with faculty advising, availability of internships, online registration, and overseas programs with the student's major; student's satisfaction with campus Public Safety office. Your report can be enhanced by descriptive measures, graphs, and estimations.

14.45 A recent study of computer usage (*New York Times*, January 22, 2001, reference 9) found that "children ages 2 to 5 averaged 27 minutes a day at the computer, while children 6 to 11 spent 49 minutes a day, and those 12 to 17 averaged 63 minutes a day." Most schools are now wired to the Internet, but how these computers are used in the classroom varies. According to Jay Becker, a professor at the University of California at Irvine, "schools serving poor children were more likely to emphasize word processing and other simple tasks while those serving more affluent students taught computer skills to promote problem-solving and a deeper understanding of an area of study, " (Ibid.). Suppose that a team of educational researchers under the direction of Dr. Joy Haugaard conducted a survey to test this hypothesis. The study involved 225 schools from both poorer communities and from more affluent districts. The following table gives their responses to the question, "Concerning computer usage, is your school more likely to emphasize basic tasks such as word processing or computer skills involving problem-solving?"

| | ECONOMIC STATUS | |
Content Emphasis	*Poor Community*	*Affluent Community*
Basic Tasks (Word Processing)	75	40
Computer Skills (Problem Solving)	30	80

Do the data from this study agree with Becker's conclusions?

APPENDIX

To solve Example 14.2 by the use of Excel, follow the Excel Instructions in Figure 14.3. Poisson Probabilities could also be obtained with PHStat following the command sequence

```
PHSTAT > PROBABILITY AND PROB. DISTRIBUTIONS > POISSON...
```

FIGURE 14.3
Excel Output To Test if Population Distribution is Poisson

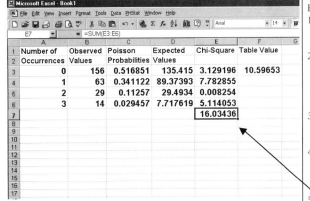

Excel Instructions
1. Type number of occurrences and observed frequencies in Columns A and B;
2. Column C: Poisson Probabilities are found by =POISSON(X,0.66, FALSE) for the x values in Column A where FALSE indicates that you do not want cumulative values
3. Column D: Expected Values are n = 262 times each Poisson Probability
4. Column E: Chi-Square Entries are =((B3-D3)^2/D3) Total of Column E is the Chi-Square Test Statistic = 16.03436
5. Column F: Table Value =CHIINV (0.005,2)

REFERENCES

1. Bera, A.K. and C. M. Jarque. "An Efficient Large-sample Test for Normality of Observations and Regression Residuals." *Working Papers in Economics and Econometrics* 40, Australian National University (1981).

2. "Career Services Program Updated." *On Q*, Fall 2000, Vol. XV, No. 4, Milwaukee, WI: American Society for Quality.

3. Coolidge, Carrie. "Socks and Bonds." *Forbes*, July 3, 2000, p. 62.

4. "Dieter Hunger for Gimmicks." *New York Times* article appearing in *Orlando Sentinel*, Sunday, October 29, 2000, p. A11.

5. Godwin, Jennifer. "New Economy, Same Old Downsizing." *Forbes*, July 3, 2000, p. 60.

6. Jamison, Jane. "Survey Highlights Agents' Strength." *Travel Weekly*, October 25, 1999. pp. 10–47.

7. Keveney, Bill. "Classroom TV Brings Election to Students: Commercial-free Cable Programs Promote Citizenship." *USA Today*, Monday, October 30, 2000, p. 4D.

8. Lal, Rajiv and Marcel Corstjensrajiv Lal. "Building Store Loyalty Through Store Brands." *Journal of Marketing Research*, August 2000, Vol. 37, i3 p. 281.

9. Lewin, Tamara. "Children's Computer Use Grows, but Gap Persist, Study Says." *The New York Times*, January 22, 2001, p. A11.

10. Mosteller, F. and D.L. Wallace. *Interference and Disputed Authorship: The Federalist* © 1964, Addison-Wesley, Reading, Mass., Tables 2.3 and 2.4. Reprinted with permission.

11. Nadeau, Michael. "Cut the Cord." Access: America's Guide to the Internet. *Orlando Sentinel*, Special Magazine Supplement, October 29, 2000, pp. 12–14. (or www.accessmagazine.com).

12. Shepherd, Gary. "10 Reasons Why Your Business Belongs in Florida." *Business Trend's Business Florida 2001*, the official publication of Enterprise Florida (Orlando) and The Florida Economic Development Council (Tallahassee). See (www.businessflorida.com.)

13. Thorne, J. Renee, et al. "University Library Study" unpublished paper. Data available in data file **library**.

14. *USA Today* Snapshot, "Sign Here Please, " Monday, October 30, 2000, p.1B. Source: www.office.com.

C HAPTER 15

ANALYSIS OF VARIANCE

INTRODUCTION

In modern business applications of statistical analysis there are a number of situations that require comparisons of processes at more than two levels. For example, the manager of Integrated Circuits Inc., would like to determine if any of five different processes for assembling components results in higher productivity per hour and in fewer defective components. Analyses to answer these questions come under the general heading of experimental design. An important tool for organizing and analyzing the data from this experiment is called *analysis of variance*, the subject of this chapter. The experiment might also be extended to a design that includes the question of which of four sources of raw materials leads to the highest productivity in combination with the different manufacturing processes. This question could be answered by using two-way analysis of variance. In another example, the president of Prairie Flower Cereal is interested in comparing product sales per week of four different brands over three different stores. Again we have a problem design that can be analyzed using analysis of variance.

15.1 COMPARISON OF SEVERAL POPULATION MEANS

In Section 9.6 we saw how to test the hypothesis of equality of two population means. In fact, two distinct tests were developed, the appropriate test depending on the experimental design—the mechanism employed in the generation of sample observations. Specifically, our tests assume either paired observations or independent random samples. This distinction is important, and to clarify it, we pause to consider a simple illustration. Suppose that it is our objective to compare the fuel consumption recorded for two different makes of automobile, A-cars and B-cars. We could randomly select 10 people to drive these cars over a specified distance, each driver being assigned to a car of each type, so that any particular driver will drive both an A-car and a B-car. The 20 resulting fuel consumption figures obtained will consist of 10 pairs, each pair corresponding to a single driver. This is the matched pairs design, and its attraction lies in its ability to produce a comparison between the quantities of interest (in this case, fuel consumption for the two types of car) while making allowance for the possible importance of an additional relevant factor (individual driver differences). Thus, if a significant difference between the performance of A-cars and B-cars is found, we have some assurance that this is not a result of differences in driver behavior. An alternative design would be to take 20 drivers and randomly assign 10 of them to A-cars and 10 to B-cars (though, in fact, there is no need to have equal numbers of trials for each type of car). The 20 resulting fuel consumption figures would then constitute a pair of independent random samples of 10 observations each on A-cars and B-cars.

For these two types of design, we discussed in Section 9.6 appropriate procedures for testing the null hypothesis of equality of a pair of population means. In this chapter, our aim is to extend these procedures to the development of tests for the equality of several population means. Suppose, for example, that our study included a third make of automobile, the C-car. The null hypothesis of interest would then be that the population mean fuel consumption is the same for all three makes of car. We will see how tests for such hypotheses can be constructed, beginning with the case where independent random samples are taken. In Section 15.4, the extension of the test based on matched pairs will be discussed.

TABLE 15.1
Fuel Consumption Figures
from Three Independent
Random Samples, in Miles
per Gallon

	A-CARS	B-CARS	C-CARS
	22.2	24.6	22.7
	19.9	23.1	21.9
	20.3	22.0	23.2
	21.4	23.5	24.1
	21.2	23.6	22.1
	21.0	22.1	23.4
	20.3	23.5	–
Sums	146.3	162.4	137.4

Suppose that of twenty drivers, seven are randomly assigned to A-cars, seven to B-cars, and six to C-cars. Using the data in Table 15.1, we computed:

$$\text{Sample mean for A-cars} = \frac{146.3}{7} = 20.9$$

$$\text{Sample mean for B-cars} = \frac{162.4}{7} = 23.2$$

$$\text{Sample mean for C-cars} = \frac{137.4}{6} = 22.917$$

Naturally, these sample means are not all the same. As always, however, when testing hypotheses, we are interested in the likelihood of such differences arising by chance if in fact the null hypothesis were true. If it is concluded that such discrepancies would be very unlikely to arise by chance, considerable skepticism about the truth of the null hypothesis would arise.

To clarify the issues involved, consider Figure 15.1, which depicts two hypothetical sets of data. The sample means in part (a) of the figure are precisely the same as those in part (b). The crucial difference is that in the former, the observations are tightly clustered about their respective sample means, while in the latter, there is much greater dispersion. Visual inspection of part (a) suggests very strongly the conjecture that the data in fact arise from three populations with different means. Looking at part (b) of the figure, by contrast, we would not be terribly surprised to learn that this data came from a common population.

FIGURE 15.1
Two Sets of Sample Fuel
Consumption Data on Three
Makes of Automobile

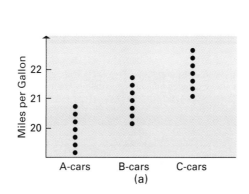

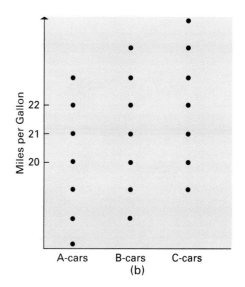

This illustration serves to point out the very essence of the test for equality of population means. The critical factor is the *variability* involved in the data. If the variability *around* the sample means is small compared with the variability *among* the sample means, as in Figure 15.1(a), we would be inclined to doubt the null hypothesis that the population means are equal. If, as in Figure 15.1(b), the variability around the sample means is large compared with the variability among them, the evidence against the null hypothesis is rather weak. This being the case, it seems reasonable to expect that an appropriate test will be based on assessments of variation. This is indeed the case, and for this reason the general technique employed is referred to as the analysis of variance.

15.2　ONE-WAY ANALYSIS OF VARIANCE

The problem introduced in Section 15.1 can be treated quite generally. Suppose that we want to compare the means of K populations, *each of which is assumed to have the same variance*. Independent random samples of $n_1, n_2, \ldots, n_K$ observations are taken from these populations. We will use the symbol x_{ij} to denote the jth observation in the ith population. Then using the format of Table 15.1, we can display the sample data as in Table 15.2.

The procedure for testing the equality of population means in this setup is called one-way analysis of variance, a terminology that will become clearer when we discuss other analysis of variance models.

> ### THE FRAMEWORK FOR ONE-WAY ANALYSIS OF VARIANCE
> Suppose that we have independent random samples of $n_1, n_2, \ldots, n_K$ observations from K populations. If the population means are denoted $\mu_1, \mu_2, \ldots, \mu_K$, the one-way analysis of variance framework is designed to test the null hypothesis
>
> $$H_0 : \mu_1 = \mu_2 = \cdots = \mu_K$$
> $$H_1 : \mu_i \neq \mu_j \quad \text{For at least one pair } \mu_i, \mu_j$$

In this section, we will develop a test of the null hypothesis that the K population means are equal, given independent random samples from those populations. The obvious first step is to calculate the sample means for the K groups of observations. These sample means will be denoted $\bar{x}_1, \bar{x}_2, \ldots, \bar{x}_K$. Formally, then

$$\bar{x}_i = \frac{\sum\limits_{j=1}^{n_i} x_{ij}}{n_i} \quad (i = 1, 2, \ldots, K)$$

where n_i denotes the number of sample observations in group i. In this notation, we have already found for the data of Table 15.1

$$\bar{x}_1 = 20.9 \qquad \bar{x}_2 = 23.2 \qquad \bar{x}_3 = 22.917$$

Now, the null hypothesis of interest specifies that the K populations have a common mean. A logical step, then, is to form an estimate of that common mean from the sample

TABLE 15.2
Sample Observations from
Independent Random
Samples of K Populations

POPULATION			
1	**2**	**...**	**K**
x_{11}	x_{21}	...	x_{K1}
x_{12}	x_{22}	...	x_{K2}
.	.		.
.	.		.
.	.		.
x_{1n_1}	x_{2n_2}		x_{Kn_K}
		...	

observations. This is just the sum of all of the sample values, divided by their total number. If we let n denote the total number of sample observations, then

$$n = \sum_{i=1}^{K} n_i$$

so in our example, $n = 20$. The overall mean of the sample observations can then be expressed as

$$\bar{\bar{x}} = \frac{\displaystyle\sum_{i=1}^{K}\sum_{j=1}^{n_i} x_{ij}}{n}$$

where the double summation notation indicates that we sum over all observations within each group and over all groups—that is, we sum all of the available observations. An equivalent expression is

$$\bar{x} = \frac{\displaystyle\sum_{i=1}^{K} n_i \bar{x}_i}{n}$$

For the fuel consumption data of Table 15.1, the overall mean is

$$\bar{x} = \frac{(7)(20.9) + (7)(23.2) + (6)(22.917)}{20} = 22.31$$

Hence, if in fact the population mean fuel consumption is the same for A-cars, B-cars, and C-cars, we estimate that common mean to be 22.305 miles per gallon.

As indicated in Section 15.1, the test of equality of population means is based on a comparison of two types of variability exhibited by the sample members. The first is variability about the individual sample means within the K groups of observations. It is convenient to refer to this as *within-groups variability*. Second, we are interested in the variability among the K group means. This is called *between-groups variability*. We now seek measures, based on the sample data, of these two types of variability.

To begin, consider variability within groups. To measure variability in the first group, we calculate the sum of squares deviations of the observations about their sample mean $\bar{x}_1$, that is

$$SS_1 = \sum_{j=1}^{n_1} (x_{1j} - \bar{x}_1)^2$$

Similarly, for the second group, whose sample mean is $\bar{x}_2$, we calculate

$$SS_2 = \sum_{j=1}^{n_2} (x_{2j} - \bar{x}_2)^2$$

and so on. The total within-groups variability, denoted SSW, is then the sum of this sum of squares over all K groups, that is

$$SSW = SS_1 + SS_2 + \cdots + SS_K$$

or

$$SSW = \sum_{i=1}^{K} \sum_{j=1}^{n_i} (x_{ij} - \bar{x}_i)^2$$

For the data on fuel consumption, we have

$$
\begin{aligned}
SS_1 &= (22.2 - 20.9)^2 + (19.9 - 20.9)^2 + \cdots + (20.3 - 20.9)^2 = 3.76 \\
SS_2 &= (24.6 - 23.2)^2 + (23.1 - 23.2)^2 + \cdots + (23.5 - 23.2)^2 = 4.96 \\
SS_3 &= (22.7 - 22.917)^2 + (21.9 - 22.917)^2 + \cdots + (23.4 - 22.917)^2 = 3.528
\end{aligned}
$$

The within-group sum of squares is therefore

$$SSW = SS_1 + SS_2 + SS_3 = 3.76 + 4.96 + 3.528 = 12.248$$

Next, we need a measure of variability between groups. A natural measure is based on the discrepancies between the individual group means and the overall mean. In fact, as before, these discrepancies are squared, giving

$$(\bar{x}_1 - \bar{x})^2, (\bar{x}_2 - \bar{x})^2, \ldots, (\bar{x}_K - \bar{x})^2$$

In computing the total between-group sum of squares, SSG, we weight each squared discrepancy by the number of sample observations in the corresponding group (so that most weight is given to the squared discrepancies in groups with most observations), giving

$$SSG = \sum_{i=1}^{K} n_i (\bar{x}_i - \bar{x})^2$$

Thus, for our fuel consumption data

$$
\begin{aligned}
SSG &= (7)(20.9 - 22.305)^2 + (7)(23.2 - 22.305)^2 + (6)(22.917 - 22.305)^2 \\
&= 21.67
\end{aligned}
$$

Another sum of squares is often calculated. This is the sum of squared discrepancies of *all* the sample observations about their *overall* mean. This is called the *total sum of squares* and is expressed as

$$SST = \sum_{i=1}^{K} \sum_{j=1}^{n_i} (x_{ij} - \bar{x})^2$$

In fact, we show in the Appendix to this chapter that the total sum of squares is the sum of the within-group and between-group sum of squares, that is

$$SST = SSW + SSG$$

Hence, for the fuel consumption data, we have

$$SST = 12.248 + 21.67 = 33.918$$

SUM OF SQUARES DECOMPOSITION FOR ONE-WAY ANALYSIS OF VARIANCE

Suppose that we have independent random samples of $n_1, n_2, ..., n_K$ observations from K populations. Denote by $\bar{x}_1, \bar{x}_2, ..., \bar{x}_K$ the K group sample means and by $\bar{x}$ the overall sample mean. We define the following **sum of squares:**

$$\text{WITHIN-GROUPS: } SSW = \sum_{i=1}^{K} \sum_{j=1}^{n_i} (x_{ij} - \bar{x}_i)^2 \tag{15.1}$$

$$\text{BETWEEN-GROUPS: } SSG = \sum_{i=1}^{K} n_i(\bar{x}_i - \bar{x})^2 \tag{15.2}$$

$$\text{TOTAL: } SST = \sum_{i=1}^{K} \sum_{j=1}^{n_i} (x_{ij} - \bar{x})^2 \tag{15.3}$$

Where x_{ij} denotes the jth sample observation in the ith group.
  Then

$$SST = SSW + SSG \tag{15.4}$$

The decomposition of the total sum of squares into the sum of two components—within-groups and between-groups sum of squares—provides the basis for the analysis of variance test of equality of group population means. We can view this decomposition as expressing the total variability of all the sample observations about their overall mean as the sum of variability within groups and variability between groups. Schematically, this is shown in Figure 15.2.

FIGURE 15.2
Sum of Squares
Decomposition for One-way
Analysis of Variance

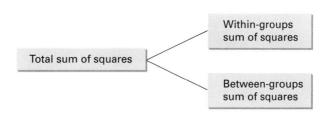

Our test of the equality of population means is based on the assumption that the K populations have a common variance. If the null hypothesis that the population means are all the same is true, each of the sums of squares, SSW and SSG, can be used as the basis for an estimate of the common population variance. To obtain these estimates, the sums of squares must be divided by the appropriate number of degrees of freedom.

First, we show in the chapter Appendix that an unbiased estimator of the population variance results if SSW is divided by $(n - K)$. The resulting estimate is called the *within-groups mean square*, denoted MSW, so that

$$MSW = \frac{SSW}{n - K}$$

For our data, we have

$$MSW = \frac{12.248}{20 - 3} = .72047$$

If the population means are equal, another unbiased estimator of the population variance is obtained by dividing SSG by $(K - 1)$, also shown in the chapter Appendix. The resulting quantity is called the *between-groups mean square*, denoted MSG, and hence

$$MSG = \frac{SSG}{K - 1}$$

For the fuel consumption data

$$MSG = \frac{21.67}{3 - 1} = 10.835$$

When the population means are *not* equal, the between-groups mean square does *not* provide an unbiased estimate of the common population variance. Rather, the expected value of the corresponding random variable exceeds the common population variance, as it also carries information about the squared differences of the true population means.

If the null hypothesis were true, we would now be in possession of two unbiased estimates of the same quantity, the common population variance. It would be reasonable to expect these estimates to be quite close to each other. The greater the discrepancy between these two estimates, all else being equal, the stronger would be our suspicion that the null hypothesis is not true. The test of the null hypothesis is based on the ratio of mean squares (see chapter Appendix)

$$F = \frac{MSG}{MSW}$$

If this ratio is quite close to 1, there would be little cause to doubt the null hypothesis of equality of population means. However, if the variability between groups is large compared to the variability within groups, we would, as already noted, suspect the null hypothesis to be false. This is the case where a value considerably larger than 1 arises for the F-ratio. The null hypothesis is rejected for large values of this ratio.

A formal test follows from the fact that if the null hypothesis of equality of population means is true, the random variable follows the F distribution (discussed in Section 9.8) with numerator degrees of freedom $(K - 1)$ and denominator degrees of freedom $(n - K)$, assuming the population distributions to be normal.

HYPOTHESIS TEST FOR ONE-WAY ANALYSIS OF VARIANCE

Suppose that we have independent random samples of $n_1, n_2, \ldots, n_K$ observations from K populations. Denote by n the total sample size, so that

$$n = n_1 + n_2 + \cdots + n_K$$

We define the **mean squares** as follows:

$$\text{WITHIN-GROUPS: } MSW = \frac{SSW}{n - K} \qquad (15.5)$$

$$\text{BETWEEN-GROUPS: } MSG = \frac{SSG}{K - 1} \qquad (15.6)$$

The null hypothesis to be tested is that the K population means are equal, that is

$$H_0: \mu_1 = \mu_2 = \cdots = \mu_K$$

We make the following additional assumptions:

i. The population variances are equal.
ii. The population distributions are normal.

A test of significance level α is provided by the decision rule

$$\text{Reject } H_0 \text{ if } \frac{MSG}{MSW} > F_{K-1,n-K,\alpha} \qquad (15.7)$$

where $F_{K-1,n-K,\alpha}$ is the number for which

$$P(F_{K-1,n-K} > F_{K-1,n-K,\alpha}) = \alpha$$

and the random variable $F_{K-1,n-K}$ follows an F distribution with numerator degrees of freedom $(K - 1)$ and denominator degrees of freedom $(n - K)$.

The p-value for this test is the smallest significance value that would allow us to reject the null hypothesis.

For the fuel consumption data, we find

$$\frac{MSG}{MSW} = \frac{10.7748}{.7165} = 15.04$$

The numerator and denominator degrees of freedom are, respectively, $(K - 1) = 2$ and $(n - K) = 17$. Thus, for a 1%-level test, from the Appendix, we have

$$F_{2,17,.01} = 6.11$$

Hence, these data allow us to reject, at the 1% significance level, the null hypothesis that population mean fuel consumption is the same for all three types of automobile.

The computations involved in carrying out this test are very conveniently summarized in a **one-way analysis of variance table.** The general form of the table is set out in Table 15.3. For the fuel consumption data, the analysis of variance is set out in Table 15.4. Note

TABLE 15.3
General Format of One-way
Analysis of Variance Table

SOURCE VARIATION	SUM OF SQUARES	DEGREES OF FREEDOM	MEAN SQUARES	F RATIO
Between groups	SSG	$K-1$	$MSG = \dfrac{SSG}{K-1}$	$\dfrac{MSG}{MSW}$
Within groups	SSW	$n-K$	$MSW = \dfrac{SSW}{n-K}$	
Total	SST	$n-1$		

TABLE 15.4
One-way Analysis of Variance
Table for Fuel Consumption
Data

SOURCE OF VARIATION	SUM OF SQUARES	DEGREES OF FREEDOM	MEAN SQUARES	F RATIO
Between groups	21.67	2	10.835	15.04
Within groups	12.248	17	0.72047	
Total	33.918	19		

that in some expositions, the within-groups sum of squares is referred to as the *error sum of squares*.

EXAMPLE 15.1

READING DIFFICULTY OF MAGAZINES (ONE-WAY ANALYSIS OF VARIANCE)

The *fog index* is used to measure the reading difficulty of a written text: The higher the value of the index, the more difficult the reading level. We want to know if the reading difficulty index is different for the three magazines, *Scientific American, Fortune,* and *New Yorker.*

SOLUTION

Independent random samples of six advertisements were taken from *Scientific American, Fortune,* and *New Yorker* magazines, and the fog indices for the eighteen advertisements were measured, as recorded in Table 15.5 (reference 2).

TABLE 15.5
Fog Index of Reading
Difficulty for Three
Magazines

SCIENTIFIC AMERICAN	FORTUNE	NEW YORKER
15.75	12.63	9.27
11.55	11.46	8.28
11.16	10.77	8.15
9.92	9.93	6.37
9.23	9.87	6.37
8.20	9.42	5.66

From these data we can derive the analysis of variance table using a statistical program such as Minitab. Once the data is entered in the spreadsheet, from the Stat menu, choose **ANOVA > One-way (Unstacked)**, as shown in Figure 15.3.

After selecting one-way analysis (unstacked) from the Minitab menu, the entry box shown in Figure 15.4 will be displayed.

To test the null hypothesis that the population mean fog indices are the same, the computed F ratio in the analysis of variance table must be compared with tabulated values of the F distribution with (2, 15) degrees of freedom. From the Appendix, we find

$$F_{2,15,.01} = 6.36$$

FIGURE 15.3
Minitab Menu for One-way
Analysis of Variance

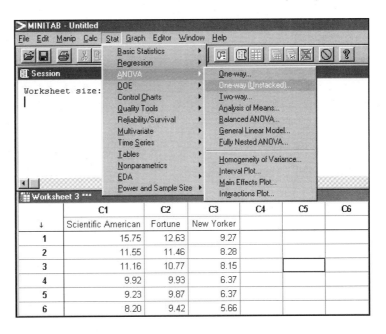

FIGURE 15.4
Minitab Input Box for One-way Analysis of Variance

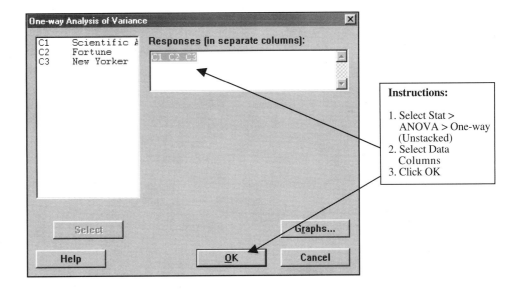

INTERPRETATION

Thus, the null hypothesis of equality of the three population mean fog indices is rejected at the 1% significance level. Note also that the computed *p*-value as found in Figure 15.5 is 0.007. We have strong evidence that the reading difficulty is different, with the *New Yorker* having the lowest index. Note that the Minitab output provides a graphical display of subgroup means and their confidence intervals. This output provides a visual display of the differences between subgroup means, noting in this case that the *New Yorker* differs substantially from *Scientific American* and *Fortune*.

FIGURE 15.5
Minitab One-way Analysis of
Variance for Reading
Difficulty in *Scientific
American, Fortune,* and
New Yorker

One-way Analysis of Variance

```
Analysis of Variance
Source      DF        SS        MS        F        P
Factor       2     48.53     24.26     6.97    0.007
Error       15     52.22      3.48
Total       17    100.75
                                  Individual 95% CIs For Mean
                                  Based on Pooled StDev
Level        N      Mean     StDev    --+---------+---------+---------+----
C1           6    10.968     2.647                     (-------*-------)
C2           6    10.680     1.202                   (-------*-------)
C3           6     7.350     1.412     (-------*-------)
                                      --+---------+---------+---------+----
Pooled StDev =     1.866               6.0       8.0      10.0      12.0
```

This analysis can also be performed by using the Excel command sequence

```
TOOLS > DATA ANALYSIS > ANOVA: SINGLE FACTOR
```

This will provide the input menu screen shown in Figure 15.6. The data for this analysis has been placed in rows A, B, and C in the Excel spreadsheet. Figure 15.7 presents the Excel Output for this problem. Interpretation of this output would result in the same conclusions. However, the Excel output does not include the graphical comparison of subgroup means and their confidence intervals.

FIGURE 15.6
Excel Input Box for One-Way
Analysis of Variance

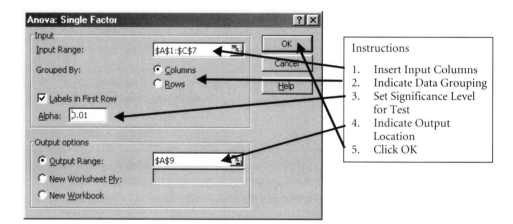

FIGURE 15.7
Excel One-way Analysis
of Variance for Reading
Difficulty in *Scientific
American, Fortune,* and
New Yorker

	A	B	C	D	E	F	G
1	SCIENTIFIC AMERICAN	FORTUNE	NEW YORKER				
2	15.75	12.63	9.27				
3	11.55	11.46	8.28				
4	11.16	10.77	8.15				
5	9.92	9.93	6.37				
6	9.23	9.87	6.37				
7	8.2	9.42	5.66				
8							
9	Anova: Single Factor						
10							
11	SUMMARY						
12	Groups	Count	Sum	Average	Variance		
13	SCIENTIFIC AMERICAN	6	65.81	10.968	7.005		
14	FORTUNE	6	64.08	10.680	1.445		
15	NEW YORKER	6	44.1	7.350	1.994		
16							
17	ANOVA						
18	Source of Variation	SS	df	MS	F	P-value	F crit
19	Between Groups	48.529	2	24.264	6.970	0.007	6.359
20	Within Groups	52.217	15	3.481			
21							
22	Total	100.746	17				

Sheet4 \ Sheet1 \ Sheet2 \ Sheet3 /

Population Model for One-way Analysis of Variance

It is instructive to view the one-way analysis of variance model in a different light. Let the random variable X_{ij} denote the jth observation from the ith population, and let μ_i stand for the mean of this population. Then, X_{ij} can be viewed as the sum of two parts—its mean and a random variable ε_{ij} having mean 0. Therefore, we can write

$$X_{ij} = \mu_i + \varepsilon_{ij}$$

Now, because independent random samples are taken, the random variables ε_{ij} will be uncorrelated with one another. Moreover, given our assumption that the population variances are all the same, it follows that the ε_{ij} all have the same variances. Hence, these random variables satisfy the standard assumptions (see Section 11.3) imposed on the error terms of a multiple regression model. This equation can be viewed as such a model, with unknown parameters $\mu_1, \mu_2,\ldots, \mu_K$. The null hypothesis of interest is

$$H_0: \quad \mu_1 = \mu_2 = \cdots = \mu_K$$

A test on these parameters is facilitated by the further assumption of normality.

The model can be written in a slightly different manner. Let μ denote the overall mean of the K combined populations and G_i the discrepancy between the population mean for the ith group and this overall mean, so that

INTERPRETATION

$$G_i = \mu_i - \mu \qquad \text{or} \qquad \mu_i = \mu + G_i$$

Substituting into the original equation gives

$$X_{ij} = \mu + G_i + \varepsilon_{ij}$$

so that an observation is made up of the sum of an overall mean μ, a group-specific term G_i, and a random error ε_{ij}. Then our null hypothesis is that every population mean μ_i is the same as the overall mean, or

$$H_0: \ G_1 = G_2 = \cdots = G_K = 0$$

This population model and some of the assumptions are illustrated in Figure 15.8. For each type of car, actual fuel consumption recorded in any trial can be represented by a normally distributed random variable. The population means of fuel consumption, μ_1, μ_2, and μ_3, for A-cars, B-cars, and C-cars, respectively, determine the centers of these distributions. According to our assumption, these population distributions must have the same variance. Figure 15.8 also shows the mean μ of the three combined populations and the differences G_i between the individual populations means and the overall mean. Finally, for B-cars, we have marked by a dot the jth sample observation. The random variable ε_{2j} is then the difference between the observed value as the sum of three parts—the overall mean μ, the difference G_2 between the population mean fuel consumption for B-cars and the overall mean, and the discrepancy (due to sampling variability) of the observed value and the mean of the population from which it is drawn.

FIGURE 15.8
Illustration of the Population
Model for the One-way
Analysis of Variance

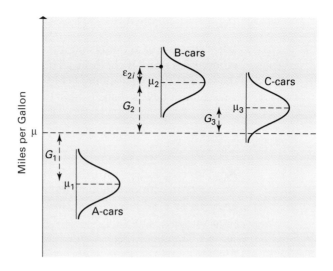

EXERCISES

15.1 A manufacturer of cereal is considering three alternative box colors—red, yellow, and blue. To check whether such consideration has any effect on sales, sixteen stores of approximately equal size are chosen. Red boxes are sent to six of these stores, yellow boxes to five others, and blue boxes to the remaining five. After a few days, a check is made on the number of sales in each store. The results (in tens of boxes) shown in the table were obtained.

RED	YELLOW	BLUE
43	52	61
52	37	29
59	38	38
76	64	53
61	74	79
81		

(a) Calculate the within-groups, between-groups, and total sum of squares.

(b) Complete the analysis of variance table, and test the null hypothesis that the population mean sales levels are the same for all three box colors.

15.2 An instructor has a class of twenty-three students. At the beginning of the semester, each student is randomly assigned to one of four teaching assistants—Smiley, Haydon, Alleline, or Bland. The students are encouraged to meet with their assigned teaching assistant to discuss difficult course material. At the end of the semester, a common examination is administered. The scores obtained by students working with these teaching assistants are shown in the accompanying table.

SMILEY	HAYDON	ALLELINE	BLAND
72	78	80	79
69	93	68	70
84	79	59	61
76	97	75	74
64	88	82	85
	81	68	63

(a) Calculate the within-groups, between-groups, and total sum of squares.

(b) Complete the analysis of variance table, and test the null hypothesis of equality of population mean scores for the teaching assistants.

15.3 Three suppliers provide parts in shipments of 500 units. Random samples of six shipments from each of the three suppliers were carefully checked, and the numbers of parts not conforming to standards were recorded. These numbers are listed in the table.

SUPPLIER A	SUPPLIER B	SUPPLIER C
28	22	33
37	27	29
34	29	39
29	20	33
31	18	37
33	30	38

(a) Set out the analysis of variance table for these data.
(b) Test the null hypothesis that the population mean numbers of parts per shipments not conforming to standards are the same for all three suppliers.

15.4 A corporation is trying to decide which of three makes of automobile to order for its fleet—domestic, Japanese, or European. Five cars of each type were ordered, and after 10,000 miles of driving, the operating cost per mile of each was assessed. The accompanying results in cents per mile were obtained.

DOMESTIC	JAPANESE	EUROPEAN
18.0	20.1	19.3
17.6	15.6	17.4
15.4	16.1	15.1
19.1	15.3	18.6
16.9	15.4	16.1

(a) Set out the analysis of variance table for these data.
(b) Test the null hypothesis that the population mean operating costs per mile are the same for these three types of car.

15.5 Random samples of seven freshmen, seven sophomores, and seven juniors taking a business statistics class were drawn. The accompanying table shows scores on the final examination.

FRESHMEN	SOPHOMORES	JUNIORS
82	71	64
93	62	73
61	85	87
74	94	91
69	78	56
70	66	78
53	71	87

(a) Set out the analysis of variance table.
(b) Test the null hypothesis that the three population mean scores are equal.

15.6 Samples of four salespeople from each of four regions were asked to predict percentage increases in sales volume for their territories in the next twelve months. The predictions are shown in the accompanying table.

WEST	MIDWEST	SOUTH	EAST
6.8	7.2	4.2	9.0
4.2	6.6	4.8	8.0
5.4	5.8	5.8	7.2
5.0	7.0	4.6	7.6

(a) Set out the analysis of variance table.
(b) Test the null hypothesis that the four population mean predictions are equal.

15.7 Independent random samples of six assistant professors, four associate professors, and five full professors were asked to estimate the amount of time outside the classroom spent on teaching responsibilities in the last week. Results, in hours, are shown in the accompanying table.

ASSISTANT	ASSOCIATE	FULL
7	15	11
12	12	7
11	15	6
15	8	9
9		7
14		

(a) Set out the analysis of variance table.
(b) Test the null hypothesis that the three population mean times are equal.

15.8 Two tutoring services offer crash courses in preparation for the C.P.A. exam. To check on the effectiveness of these services, fifteen students were chosen. Five students were randomly assigned to service A, five were assigned to service B, and the remaining five took no crash course. Their scores on the examination, expressed as percentages, are given in the table.

SERVICE A COURSE	SERVICE B COURSE	NO COURSE
79	74	72
74	69	71
92	87	81
67	81	61
85	64	63

(a) Set out the analysis of variance table.
(b) Test the null hypothesis that the three population mean scores are the same.

15.9 In the study of Example 15.1, independent random samples of six advertisements from *True Confessions, People Weekly*, and *Newsweek* were taken. The fog indices for these advertisements are given in the accompanying table. Test the null hypothesis that the population mean fog indices are the same for advertisements in these three magazines.

TRUE CONFESSIONS	PEOPLE WEEKLY	NEWSWEEK
12.89	9.50	10.21
12.69	8.60	9.66
11.15	8.59	7.67
9.52	6.50	5.12
9.12	4.79	4.88
7.04	4.29	3.12

15.10 For the one-way analysis of variance model, we write the jth observation from the ith group as

$$X_{ij} = \mu + G_i + \varepsilon_{ij}$$

where μ is the overall mean, G_i is the effect specific to the ith group, and ε_{ij} is a random error for the jth observation from the ith group. Consider the data of Example 15.1.

(a) Estimate μ.

(b) Estimate G_i for each of the three magazines.

(c) Estimate ε_{32}, the error term corresponding to the second observation (8.28) for *New Yorker*.

15.11 Use the model for the one-way analysis of variance for the data of Exercise 11.9.

(a) Estimate μ.

(b) Estimate G_i for each of the three magazines.

(c) Estimate ε_{13}, the error term corresponding to the third observation (11.15) for *True Confessions*.

15.3   THE KRUSKAL-WALLIS TEST

As we have already noted, the one-way analysis of variance test of Section 15.2 generalizes to the multipopulation case for the *t* test comparing two population means when independent random samples are available. The test is based on an assumption that the underlying population distributions are normal. In Section 13.3, we introduced the Mann-Whitney test, a nonparametric test that is valid for the comparison of the central locations of two populations based on independent random samples, even when the population distributions are not normal. It is also possible to develop a nonparametric alternative to the one-way analysis of variance test. This is known as the **Kruskal-Wallis test**, employed when an investigator has strong grounds for suspecting that the parent population distributions may be markedly different from the normal.

Like the majority of the nonparametric tests we have already encountered, the Kruskal-Wallis test is based on the *ranks* of the sample observations. We will illustrate the computation of the test statistic by reference to the fuel consumption data of Table 15.1. The sample values are all pooled together and ranked in ascending order, as in Table 15.6, using the average of adjacent ranks in the case of ties.

The test is based on the sums of the ranks $R_1, R_2, \ldots, R_K$, for the K samples. In the fuel consumption example

$$R_1 = 32 \quad R_2 = 101.5 \quad R_3 = 76.5$$

TABLE 15.6
Fuel Consumption Figures (in Miles per Gallon) and Ranks from Three Independent Random Samples

A-CARS	RANK	B-CARS	RANK	C-CARS	RANK
22.2	11	24.6	20	22.7	12
19.9	1	23.1	13	21.9	7
20.3	2.5	22.0	8	23.2	14
21.4	6	23.5	16.5	24.1	19
21.2	5	23.6	18	22.1	9.5
21.0	4	22.1	9.5	23.4	15
20.3	2.5	23.5	16.5		
Rank sums	32		101.5		76.5

Now, the null hypothesis to be tested is that the three population means are the same. We would be suspicious of that hypothesis if there were substantial differences among the average ranks for the K samples. In fact, our test is based on the statistic where n_i are the sample sizes in the K groups and n is the total number of sample observations. Define W as

$$W = \frac{12}{n(n+1)} \sum_{i=1}^{K} \frac{R_i^2}{n_i} - 3(n+1)$$

The null hypothesis would be in doubt if a large value for W were observed. The basis for the test follows from the fact that unless the sample sizes are very small, the random variable corresponding to the test statistic has, under the null hypothesis, a distribution that is well approximated by the χ^2 distribution with $(K-1)$ degrees of freedom.

THE KRUSKAL-WALLIS TEST

Suppose that we have independent random samples of $n_1, n_2, \ldots, n_K$ observations from K populations. Let

$$n = n_1 + n_2 + \cdots + n_K$$

denote the total number of sample observations. Denote by $R_1, R_2, \ldots, R_K$ the sums of ranks for the K samples when the sample observations are pooled together and ranked in ascending order. The test of the null hypothesis, H_0, of equality of the population means is based on the statistic

$$W = \frac{12}{n(n+1)} \sum_{i=1}^{K} \frac{R_i^2}{n_i} - 3(n+1) \tag{15.8}$$

A test of significance level α is given by the decision rule

$$\text{Reject } H_0 \text{ if } W > \chi^2_{K-1,\alpha} \tag{15.9}$$

Where $\chi^2_{K-1,\alpha}$ is the number that is exceeded with probability α by a χ^2 random variable with $(K-1)$ degrees of freedom.

This test procedure is approximately valid provided that the sample contains at least five observations from each population.

For our fuel consumption data, we find

$$W = \frac{12}{(20)(21)} \left[\frac{(32)^2}{7} + \frac{(101.5)^2}{7} + \frac{(76.5)^2}{6} \right] - (3)(21) = 11.10$$

Here, we have $(K-1) = 2$ degrees of freedom, so for a .5% significance level test, we find from the Appendix.

$$\chi^2_{2,.005} = 10.60$$

Hence, the null hypothesis that the population mean fuel consumption is the same for the three types of automobiles can be rejected even at the .5% significance level. Of course, we also rejected this hypothesis using the analysis of variance test of Section 15.2. However, here we have been able to do so without imposing the assumption of normality of the population distributions.

EXAMPLE 15.2

IMPORTANCE OF BRAND NAMES (KRUSKAL-WALLIS TEST)

A research study was designed to determine if women from different occupational subgroups assign different levels of importance to brand names when purchasing soft drinks.

SOLUTION

Independent random samples of 101 clerical, 112 administrative, and 96 professional women were asked to rate, on a scale from 1 to 7, the importance they attached to brand name when purchasing soft drinks. The value of the Kruskal-Wallis statistic for this study was reported as 25.22. Test the null hypothesis that the population mean ratings are the same for these three subgroups.

The calculated test statistic is

$$W = 25.22$$

Since there are $K = 3$ groups, we have for a .5%-level test

$$\chi^2_{K-1,\alpha} = \chi^2_{2,.005} = 10.60$$

Thus, the null hypothesis that the three population mean ratings are the same is very clearly rejected on the evidence of this sample, even at the .5% level of significance. We have strong evidence that women from different occupational subgroups assign different levels of importance to brand names.

EXERCISES

15.12 For the data of Exercise 15.1, use the Kruskal-Wallis test of the null hypothesis that the population mean sales levels are identical for three can colors.

15.13 Using the data of Exercise 15.2, perform a Kruskal-Wallis test of the null hypothesis that the population mean test scores are the same for students assigned to the four teaching assistants.

15.14 Using the data of Exercise 15.3, carry out a test of the null hypothesis of equality of the three population mean numbers of parts per shipment not conforming to standards without assuming normality of population distributions.

15.15 For the data of Exercise 15.4, test the null hypothesis that the population mean operating costs per mile are the same for all three types of automobile, without assuming normal population distributions.

15.16 Using the data of Exercise 15.5, carry out a nonparametric test of the null hypothesis of equality of population mean examination scores for freshmen, sophomores, and juniors.

15.17 Based on the data of Exercise 15.6, use the Kruskal-Wallis method to test the null hypothesis of equality of population mean sales growth predictions for the four regions.

15.18 Refer to Exercise 15.7. Without assuming normal population distributions, test the null hypothesis that the population mean times spent on teaching responsibilities are the same for assistant, associate, and full professors.

15.19 Based on the data of Exercise 15.8, perform the Kruskal-Wallis test of the null hypothesis of equal population mean scores on the C.P.A. exam for students using no tutoring services A and B.

15.20 Independent random samples of 101 college sophomores, 112 college juniors, and 96 college seniors were asked to rate, on a scale from 1 to 7, the importance attached to brand name when purchasing a car. The value of the Kruskal-Wallis statistic obtained was .17.
  (a) What null hypothesis can be tested using this information?
  (b) Carry out this test.

15.4 TWO-WAY ANALYSIS OF VARIANCE: ONE OBSERVATION PER CELL, RANDOMIZED BLOCKS

Although our primary interest lies in the analysis of one particular feature of an experiment, we may suspect that a second factor could exert an important influence on the outcome. In the earliest sections of this chapter, we discussed an experiment in which the objective was to compare the fuel consumption of three types of automobile. Data were collected from three independent random samples of trials and analyzed through a one-way analysis of variance. It was assumed that the variability in the sample data was due to two causes—genuine differences between the performance characteristics of these three types of car, and random variation. In fact, we might suspect that part of the observed random variability could be explained by differences in driver habits. Now, if this last factor could be isolated, the amount of random variability in the experiment would be reduced accordingly. This might in turn make it easier to detect differences in the performance of the automobiles. In other words, by designing an experiment to account for differences in driver characteristics, we hope to achieve a more powerful test of the null hypothesis that population mean fuel consumption is the same for all types of automobiles.

In fact, it is quite straightforward to design an experiment in such a way that the influence of a second factor of this kind can be taken into account. Suppose, once again, that we have three makes of automobile (say, α-cars, β-cars, and γ-cars) whose fuel economies we wish to compare. We will consider an experiment in which six trials are to be run with each type of car. If these trials are conducted using six drivers, each of whom drives a car of all three types, it will be possible, since every car will have been tested by every driver, to extract from the results information about driver variability as well as information about differences among the three types of car. The additional variable—in this case, drivers—is sometimes called a *blocking variable*. The experiment is said to be arranged in *blocks*; in our example, there would be six blocks, one for each driver.

This kind of blocked design can be used to obtain information about two factors simultaneously. For example, suppose that we want to compare fuel economy obtained not only by different types of automobile but also by different types of drivers. In particular, we may be interested in the effect of driver age on fuel economy. To do this, drivers can be subdivided into age categories. We might use the following six age classes (in years):

1. 25 and under
2. 26–35
3. 36–45
4. 46–55
5. 56–65
6. Over 65

Then, we can arrange our experiment so that an automobile from each group is driven by a driver from each age class. In this way, in addition to testing the hypothesis that population mean fuel consumption is the same for each automobile type, we can also test the hypothesis that population mean fuel consumption is the same for each age class.

In fact, whether a car of each type is driven by each of six drivers or a car of each type is driven by a driver from each of six age classes, the procedure for testing equality of population mean fuel consumption for the automobile types is the same. In this section, we will use the latter design for purposes of illustration.

Table 15.7 gives results for an experiment involving three automobile types and six driver age classes. The comparison of automobile types is the main focus of interest, and driver ages are used as a blocking variable.

This kind of design is called a **randomized blocks design**. The randomization arises because we randomly select one driver from the first age class to drive an α-car, one driver from the second age class to drive an α-car, and so on. This procedure is repeated for each other driver classes and for each of the cars. If possible, the trials should be carried out in random order rather than block by block.

Suppose that we have K groups and that there are H blocks. We will use x_{ij} to denote the sample observation corresponding to the ith group and the jth block. Thus, the sample data may be set out as in Table 15.8. Notice that the format here is simply an extension of the experimental form used for the paired observations test of Section 9.6, where we had only two groups to allow us to test the equality of several mean populations.

TABLE 15.7
Sample Observations on Fuel
Consumption Recorded for
Three Types of Automobile
Driven by Six Drivers

DRIVER CLASSES	AUTOMOBILES			
	α-*Cars*	β-*Cars*	γ-*Cars*	*Sums*
1	25.1	23.9	26.0	75.0
2	24.7	23.7	25.4	73.8
3	26.0	24.4	25.8	76.2
4	24.3	23.3	24.4	72.0
5	23.9	23.6	24.2	71.7
6	24.2	24.5	25.4	74.1
	148.2	143.4	151.2	442.8

To develop a test of the hypothesis that the population means are the same for all K groups, we require the sample means for these groups. For the mean of the ith group, we use the notation $\bar{x}_{i\bullet}$, so

$$\bar{x}_{i\bullet} = \frac{\sum\limits_{j=1}^{H} x_{ij}}{H} \qquad (i = 1, 2, ..., K)$$

From Table 15.7, we obtain

$$\bar{x}_{1\bullet} = \frac{148.2}{6} = 24.7 \qquad \bar{x}_{2\bullet} = \frac{143.4}{6} = 23.9 \qquad \bar{x}_{3\bullet} = \frac{151.2}{6} = 25.2$$

We are also interested in the differences in the population block means. Hence, we require the sample means for the H blocks. We use $\bar{x}_{\bullet j}$ to denote the sample mean for the jth block, so

$$\bar{x}_{\bullet j} = \frac{\sum\limits_{i=1}^{K} x_{ij}}{K} \qquad (j = 1, 2, ..., H)$$

For the fuel consumption data of Table 15.7, we have

$$\bar{x}_{\bullet 1} = \frac{75.0}{3} = 25.0 \qquad \bar{x}_{\bullet 2} = \frac{73.8}{3} = 24.6 \qquad \bar{x}_{\bullet 3} = \frac{76.2}{3} = 25.4$$

$$\bar{x}_{\bullet 4} = \frac{72.0}{3} = 24.0 \qquad \bar{x}_{\bullet 5} = \frac{71.7}{3} = 23.9 \qquad \bar{x}_{\bullet 6} = \frac{74.1}{3} = 24.7$$

Finally, we require the overall mean of the sample observations. If n denotes the total number of observations, then

$$n = HK$$

TABLE 15.8
Sample Observation on K
Groups and H Blocks

BLOCK	GROUP			
	1	*2*	...	*K*
1	x_{11}	x_{21}	...	x_{K1}
2	x_{12}	x_{22}	...	x_{K2}
.	.	.		.
.	.	.		.
.	.	.		.
H	x_{1H}	x_{2H}	...	x_{KH}

and the sample mean observation is

$$\bar{x} = \frac{\sum_{i=1}^{K}\sum_{j=1}^{H} x_{ij}}{n} = \frac{\sum_{i=1}^{K} \bar{x}_{i\bullet}}{K} = \frac{\sum_{j=1}^{H} x_{\bullet j}}{H}$$

For the data of Table 15.7

$$\bar{x} = \frac{442.8}{18} = 24.6$$

Before proceeding to consider the form of an appropriate test for the hypothesis of interest, it is useful to examine the population model that is implicitly being assumed. Let the random variable X_{ij} correspond to the observation for the ith group and jth block. This value is then regarded as the sum of the following four components:

1. An "overall" mean, μ
2. A parameter G_i, which is specific to the ith group and measures the discrepancy between the mean for that group and the overall mean
3. A parameter B_j, which is specific to the jth block and measures the discrepancy between the mean for that block and the overall mean
4. A random variable ε_{ij}, which represents experimental error, or that part of the observation not explained by either the overall mean or the group or block membership

We can therefore write

$$X_{ij} = \mu + G_i + B_j + \varepsilon_{ij}$$

The error term ε_{ij} is taken to obey the standard assumptions of the multiple regression model. In particular, then, we assume independence and equality of variances.

We can now write this as

$$X_{ij} - \mu = G_i + B_j + \varepsilon_{ij}$$

Now, given sample data, the overall mean μ is estimated by the overall sample mean $\bar{x}$, so an estimate of the left-hand side is provided by $(x_{ij} - \bar{x})$. The difference G_i between the population mean for the ith group and the overall population mean is estimated by the corresponding difference in sample means, $(\bar{x}_{i\bullet} - \bar{x})$. Similarly, B_j is estimated by $(\bar{x}_{\bullet j} - \bar{x})$. Finally, by subtraction, we estimate the error term by

$$(x_{ij} - \bar{x}) - (\bar{x}_{i\bullet} - \bar{x}) - (\bar{x}_{\bullet j} - \bar{x}) = x_{ij} - \bar{x}_{i\bullet} - \bar{x}_{\bullet j} + \bar{x}$$

Thus, we have for the sample members

$$(x_{ij} - \bar{x}) = (\bar{x}_{i\bullet} - \bar{x}) - (\bar{x}_{\bullet j} - \bar{x}) + (x_{ij} - \bar{x}_{i\bullet} - \bar{x}_{\bullet j} + \bar{x})$$

To illustrate, consider the fuel consumption recorded by a driver from the third class with an α-car. From Table 15.7

$$x_{13} = 26.0$$

The term on the left-hand side is

$$x_{13} - \bar{x} = 26.0 - 24.6 = 1.4$$

For the group (automobile) effect, we have

$$\bar{x}_{1\bullet} - \bar{x} = 24.7 - 24.6 = .1$$

(Notice that this term will result whenever the α-car is driven.) For the block (driver) effect, we have

$$\bar{x}_{\bullet 3} - \bar{x} = 25.4 - 24.6 = .8$$

Finally, the error term is

$$x_{13} - \bar{x}_{1\bullet} - \bar{x}_{\bullet 3} + \bar{x} = 26.0 - 24.7 - 25.4 + 24.6 = .5$$

Thus, we have for this observation

$$1.4 = .1 + .8 + .5$$

We can interpret this equation as follows: When a driver from the third age class tested the α-car, she consumed 1.4 miles per gallon more than the average for all cars and drivers. Of this amount, it is estimated that .1 is due to the automobile, .8 to the driver age class, and the remaining .5 mile per gallon to other factors, which we put down to chance variability or experimental error.

Now, if both sides are squared and summed over all n sample observations, it can be shown that the result is

$$\sum_{i=1}^{K} \sum_{j=1}^{H} (x_{ij} - \bar{x})^2 = H \sum_{i=1}^{K} (\bar{x}_{i\bullet} - \bar{x})^2 + K \sum_{j=1}^{H} (\bar{x}_{\bullet j} - \bar{x})^2 + \sum_{i=1}^{K} \sum_{j=1}^{H} (x_{ij} - \bar{x}_{i\bullet} - \bar{x}_{\bullet j} + \bar{x})^2$$

This equation expresses the total sample variability of the observations about their overall mean as the sum of variabilities due to differences among groups, differences among blocks, and error, respectively. It is on these sums of squares decomposition that the analysis of experiments of this type is based. The analysis is called two-way analysis of variance since the data are categorized in two ways, according to groups and blocks.

We illustrate this important sum of squares decomposition in Figure 15.9. Notice, by contrast with the decomposition for the one-way analysis of variance, that the total sum of squares of the sample observations about their overall mean is here broken down into *three* components. We summarize the components in Equations 15.10 to 15.14; the extra components arise because of our ability to extract from the data information about differences among blocks.

For the fuel consumption data of Table 15.7, we find

$$SST = (25.1 - 24.6)^2 + (24.7 - 24.6)^2 + \cdots + (25.4 - 24.6)^2 = 11.88$$
$$SSG = 6[(24.7 - 24.6)^2 + (23.9 - 24.6)^2 + (25.2 - 24.6)^2] = 5.16$$
$$SSB = 3[(25.0 - 24.6)^2 + (24.6 - 24.6)^2 + \cdots + (24.7 - 24.6)^2] = 4.98$$

and so, by subtraction

$$SSE = SST - SSG - SSB = 11.88 - 5.16 - 4.98 = 1.74$$

FIGURE 15.9
Sum of Squares
Decomposition for Two-way
Analysis of Variance with One
Observation per Cell

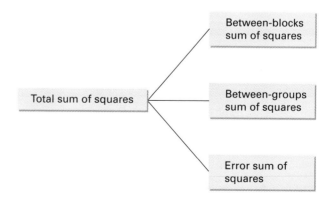

SUM OF SQUARES DECOMPOSITION FOR TWO-WAY ANALYSIS OF VARIANCE

Suppose that we have a sample of observations with x_{ij} denoting the observation in the ith group and jth block. Suppose that there are K groups and H blocks, for a total of

$$n = KH$$

observations. Denote the group sample means by $\bar{x}_{i\bullet}(i = 1, 2, ..., K)$, the block sample means by $\bar{x}_{\bullet j}(j = 1, 2, ..., H)$ and the overall sample mean by $\bar{x}$.

We define the following sum of squares:

$$\text{TOTAL: } SST = \sum_{i=1}^{K} \sum_{j=1}^{H} (x_{ij} - \bar{x})^2 \tag{15.10}$$

$$\text{BETWEEN-GROUPS: } SSG = H \sum_{i=1}^{K} (\bar{x}_{i\bullet} - \bar{x})^2 \tag{15.11}$$

$$\text{BETWEEN-BLOCKS: } SSB = K \sum_{j=1}^{H} (\bar{x}_{\bullet j} - \bar{x})^2 \tag{15.12}$$

$$\text{ERROR: } SSE = \sum_{i=1}^{K} \sum_{j=1}^{H} (x_{ij} - \bar{x}_{i\bullet} - \bar{x}_{\bullet j} + \bar{x})^2 \tag{15.13}$$

Then

$$SST = SSG + SSB + SSE \tag{15.14}$$

From this point, the tests associated with the two-way analysis of variance proceed in a similar fashion to the one-way analysis of Section 15.2. First, the mean squares are obtained by dividing each sum of squares by the appropriate number of degrees of freedom. For the total sum of squares, the degrees of freedom are 1 less than the total number of observations, that is $(n - 1)$. For the sum of squares between groups, the degrees of freedom are 1 less than the number of groups, or $(K - 1)$. Similarly, for the sum of squares between blocks, the number of degrees of freedom is $(H - 1)$. Hence, by subtraction, the degrees of freedom associated with the sum of squared errors are

$$(n - 1) - (K - 1) - (H - 1) = n - K - H + 1$$
$$= KH - K - H + 1$$
$$= (K - 1)(H - 1)$$

The null hypothesis that the population group means are equal can then be tested through the ratio of the mean square for groups to the mean square error as shown in Equations 15.18 and 15.19. Very often, a blocking variable is included in the analysis simply to reduce variability due to experimental error. However, sometimes the hypothesis that the block population means are equal is also of interest. This can be tested through the ratio of the mean square for blocks to the mean square error. As in the case of the one-way analysis of variance, the relevant standard for comparison is obtained from a tail probability of the F distribution.

For the fuel consumption data, the mean squares are

$$MSG = \frac{SSG}{K - 1} = \frac{5.16}{2} = 2.58$$

$$MSB = \frac{SSB}{H - 1} = \frac{4.98}{5} = .996$$

$$MSE = \frac{SSE}{(K - 1)(H - 1)} = \frac{1.74}{10} = .174$$

To test the null hypothesis that the population mean fuel consumption is the same for all three types of automobile, we require

$$\frac{MSG}{MSE} = \frac{2.58}{.174} = 14.83$$

For a 1%-level test, we have from the Appendix

$$F_{K-1,(K-1)(H-1),\alpha} = F_{2,10,.01} = 7.56$$

HYPOTHESIS TESTS FOR TWO-WAY ANALYSIS OF VARIANCE

Suppose that we have a sample observation for each group-block combination in a design containing K groups and H blocks.

$$x_{ij} = \mu + G_i + B_j + E_{ij}$$

where G_i is the group effect and B_j is the block effect.
   Define the following mean squares:

$$\text{BETWEEN-GROUPS:} \quad MSG = \frac{SSG}{K - 1} \qquad \text{(15.15)}$$

$$\text{BETWEEN-BLOCKS:} \quad MSB = \frac{SSB}{H - 1} \qquad \text{(15.16)}$$

$$\text{ERROR:} \quad MSE = \frac{SSE}{(K - 1)(H - 1)} \qquad \text{(15.17)}$$

We assume that the error terms ε_{ij} in the model (15.4.1) are independent of one another and have the same variance. It is further assumed that these errors are normally distributed. Then:
   A test of significance level α of the null hypothesis H_0 that the K population group means are all the same is provided by the decision rule

$$\text{Reject } H_0 \text{ if } \frac{MSG}{MSE} > F_{K-1,(K-1)(H-1),\alpha} \qquad \text{(15.18)}$$

A test of significance level α of the null hypothesis H_0 that the H population block means are all the same is provided by the decision rule

$$\text{Reject } H_0 \text{ if } \frac{MSB}{MSE} > F_{H-1,(K-1)(H-1),\alpha} \qquad \text{(15.19)}$$

Here, $F_{v_1,v_2,\alpha}$ is the number exceeded with probability α by a random variable following an F distribution with numerator degrees of freedom v_1 and denominator degrees of freedom v_2.

TABLE 15.9
General Format of Two-way
Analysis of Variance Table

SOURCE OF VARIATION	SUMS OF SQUARES	DEGREES OF FREEDOM	MEAN SQUARES	F RATIO
Between-groups	SSG	$K - 1$	$MSG = \dfrac{SSG}{K-1}$	$\dfrac{MSG}{MSE}$
Between-blocks	SSB	$H - 1$	$MSB = \dfrac{SSB}{H-1}$	$\dfrac{MSB}{MSE}$
Error	SSE	$(K-1)(H-1)$	$MSE = \dfrac{SSE}{(K-1)(H-1)}$	
Total	SST	$n - 1$		

Therefore, on the evidence of these data, the hypothesis of equal mean population performances for the three types of automobile is clearly rejected at the 1% significance level.

In this particular example, the null hypothesis of equality of the population block means is the hypothesis that population values of mean fuel consumption are the same for each driver age class. The test is based on

$$\frac{MSB}{MSE} = \frac{.996}{.174} = 5.72$$

For a 1%-level test, we have, from the Appendix

$$F_{H-1,(K-1)(H-1),\alpha} = F_{5,10,.01} = 5.64$$

Hence, the null hypothesis of equal population means for the six driver age classes is also rejected at the 1% significance level.

Once again, it is very convenient to summarize the computations in tabular form. The general setup for the **two-way analysis of variance table** is shown in Table 15.9. For the fuel consumption data, this analysis of variance is set out in Figure 15.11. The numbers of degrees of freedom are determined by the numbers of groups and blocks. The mean squares are obtained by dividing the sum of squares by their associated degrees of freedom. The mean square error is then the denominator in the calculation of the two F ratios on which our test are based.

EXAMPLE 15.3

AUTOMOBILE FUEL CONSUMPTION (TWO-WAY ANALYSIS OF VARIANCE)

We wish to determine if there is strong evidence to conclude that there is a difference in automobile fuel consumption for different cars used for different drivers.

SOLUTION

The gas mileage data from Table 15.7 can be arranged in the Minitab spreadsheet shown in Figure 15.10 and entered into Minitab to derive the analysis of variance table. This arrangement allows the variables to be designated as response, row factor, and column factor.

Once the data is entered in the spreadsheet, from the Stat menu, choose **ANOVA > Two-way**. After selecting two-way analysis from the Minitab menu, the dialogue box shown in Figure 15.11 will be displayed. Figure 15.11 also shows the Minitab output including the various sums of squares and F ratios. Using Minitab, you can compute the various statistics that would be used to conduct the analysis of variance procedure.

FIGURE 15.10
Minitab Data for Two-way
Analysis of Variance: Gas
Mileage

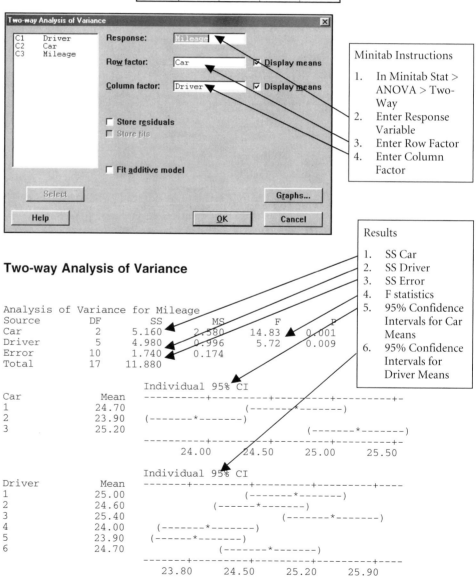

FIGURE 15.11
Minitab Dialog Box for Two-
Way Analysis of Variance

Minitab Instructions

1. In Minitab Stat >
   ANOVA > Two-
   Way
2. Enter Response
   Variable
3. Enter Row Factor
4. Enter Column
   Factor

Results

1. SS Car
2. SS Driver
3. SS Error
4. F statistics
5. 95% Confidence
   Intervals for Car
   Means
6. 95% Confidence
   Intervals for
   Driver Means

Two-way Analysis of Variance

```
Analysis of Variance for Mileage
Source    DF      SS        MS       F       P
Car        2     5.160    2.580    14.83   0.001
Driver     5     4.980    0.996     5.72   0.009
Error     10     1.740    0.174
Total     17    11.880

                      Individual 95% CI
Car        Mean   ---------+---------+---------+---------+-
1          24.70                   (-------*-------)
2          23.90      (-------*-------)
3          25.20                           (-------*-------)
                  ---------+---------+---------+---------+-
                      24.00     24.50     25.00     25.50

                      Individual 95% CI
Driver     Mean   -------+---------+---------+---------+----
1          25.00                 (-------*-------)
2          24.60            (------*-------)
3          25.40                      (-------*-------)
4          24.00       (-------*-------)
5          23.90      (------*-------)
6          24.70              (-------*-------)
                  -------+---------+---------+---------+----
                      23.80     24.50     25.20     25.90
```

EXERCISES

15.21 Four financial analysts were asked to predict earnings growth over the coming year for five oil companies. Their forecasts, as projected percentage increases in earnings, are given in the accompanying table.

OIL COMPANY	ANALYST			
	A	*B*	*C*	*D*
1	8	12	7	13
2	9	9	8	12
3	12	10	9	10
4	11	10	10	12
5	9	8	10	14

(a) Set out the two-way analysis of variance table.
(b) Test the null hypothesis that the population mean growth forecasts are the same for all oil companies.

15.22 An agricultural experiment designed to assess differences in yields of corn for four different varieties, using three different fertilizers, produced the results (in bushels per acre) shown in the table.

FERTILIZER	VARIETY			
	A	*B*	*C*	*D*
1	86	88	77	84
2	92	91	81	93
3	75	80	83	79

(a) Set out the two-way analysis of variance table.
(b) Test the null hypothesis that the population mean yields are identical for all four varieties of corn.
(c) Test the null hypothesis that population mean yields are the same for all three brands of fertilizer.

15.23 A company has test-marketed three new types of soup in selected stores over a period of 1 year. The table records sales achieved (in thousands of dollars) for each of the three soups in each quarter of the year.

QUARTER	SOUP		
	A	*B*	*C*
1	47	57	65
2	63	63	76
3	79	67	54
4	52	50	49

(a) Set out the two-way analysis of variance table.
(b) Test the null hypothesis that population mean sales are the same for all three types of soup.

15.24 A diet soda manufacturer wants to compare the effects on sales of three can colors—red, yellow, and blue. Four regions are selected for the test, and three stores are randomly chosen from each region, each to display one color of cans. The accompanying table shows sales (in tens of cans) at the end of the experimental period.

REGION	CAN COLOR		
	Red	*Yellow*	*Blue*
East	47	52	60
South	56	54	52
Midwest	49	63	55
West	41	44	48

(a) Set out the appropriate analysis of variance table.
(b) Test the null hypothesis that population mean sales are the same for each can color.

15.25 An instructor in an economics class is considering three different texts. She is also considering three types of examinations—multiple choice, essays, and a mix of multiple choice and essays. During the year she teaches nine sections of the course, and randomly assigns a text-examination type combination of each section. At the end of the course, she obtained students evaluations for each section. These ratings are shown in the accompanying table.

EXAMINATION	TEXT		
	A	*B*	*C*
Multiple Choice	4.8	5.3	4.9
Essays	4.6	5.0	4.3
Mix	4.6	5.1	4.8

(a) Set out the analysis of variance table.
(b) Test the null hypothesis of equality of population mean ratings for the three texts.
(c) Test the null hypothesis of equality of population mean ratings for the three examination types.

15.26 We introduced for the two-way analysis of variance the population model

$$X_{ij} - \mu = G_i + \beta_j + \varepsilon_{ij}$$

For the data of Exercise 18.24, obtain sample estimates for each term on the right-hand side of this equation for the East region—red can combination.

15.27 For the data of Exercise 18.25, obtain sample estimates for each term on the right-hand side of the equation used in the previous exercise for the text C—multiple choice combination.

15.28 Four real estate agents were asked to appraise the values of ten houses in a particular neighborhood. The appraisals were expressed in thousands of dollars, with the results shown in the table.

SOURCE OF VARIATION	SUM OF SQUARES
Between agents	268
Between houses	1, 152
Error	2, 352

(a) Complete the analysis of variance table.
(b) Test the null hypothesis that mean assessments are the same for these four real estate agents.

15.29 Four brands of fertilizer were evaluated. Each brand was applied to each six plots of land containing soils of different types. Percentage increases in corn yields were then measured for the twenty-four brand-soil type combinations. The results obtained are summarized in the accompanying table.

SOURCE OF VARIATION	SUM OF SQUARES
Between fertilizers	135.6
Between soil types	81.7
Error	111.3

(a) Complete the analysis of variance table.
(b) Test the null hypothesis that mean yield increases are the same for the four fertilizers.

(c) Test the null hypothesis that mean yield increases are the same for the six soil types.

15.30 Three television pilot shows for potential situation comedy series were shown to audiences in four regions of the country—the East, the South, the Midwest, and the West Coast. Based on audience reactions, a score (on a scale from 0 to 100) was obtained for each show. The sums of squares between groups (shows) and between blocks (regions) were found to be

$$SSG = 95.2 \qquad \text{and} \qquad SSB = 69.5$$

and the error sum of squares was

$$SSE = 79.3$$

Set out the analysis of variance table, and test the null hypothesis that the population mean scores for audience reactions are the same for all three shows.

15.31 Suppose that in the two-way analysis of variance setup with one observation per cell, there are just two groups. Show in this case, the F ratio for testing the equality of the group population means is precisely the square of the test statistic discussed in Section 9.6 for testing equality of population means, given a sample of matched pairs. Hence, deduce that the two tests are equivalent in this particular case.

15.5 TWO-WAY ANALYSIS OF VARIANCE: MORE THAN ONE OBSERVATION PER CELL

In the two-way analysis of variance layout of Section 15.4, we can view the tabulated raw data (as in Tables 15.6 and 15.7) as being broken down into cells, where each cell refers to a particular group-block combination. Thus, for example, the results obtained when a driver from the fourth age class drives a β-car constitute a single cell. A feature of the design analyzed in Section 15.4 is that each cell contains just a single sample observation. Thus, a driver from the fourth age class tests a β-car only once.

In this section, we consider the possibility of replicating the experiment, so that, for example, β-cars would be driven by more than one driver from the fourth age class. The data resulting from such a design would then involve more than just a single observation per cell. There are two major advantages in extending the sample in this way. First, the more sample data that are available, the more precise will be the resulting estimates and the more surely will we be able to distinguish differences among the population means. Second, a design with more than one observation per cell allows the isolation of a further source of variability—the **interaction** between groups and blocks. Such interactions occur when differences in group effects are not distributed uniformly across blocks. For example, drivers who achieve better than average fuel consumption figures may be considerably more successful in getting better fuel economy than other drivers when driving an α-car than when driving a β-car. Thus, this better than average performance is not uniformly spread over all types of cars but rather is more manifest in some types than others. This possibility of

TABLE 15.10
Sample Observations on Fuel Consumption Recorded for Three Types of Automobile Driven by Five Drivers; Three Observations per Cell

DRIVER CLASSES	AUTOMOBILES								
	X-Cars			Y-Cars			Z-Cars		
1	25.0	25.4	25.2	24.0	24.4	23.9	25.9	25.8	25.4
2	24.8	24.8	24.5	23.5	23.8	23.8	25.2	25.0	25.4
3	26.1	26.3	26.2	24.6	24.9	24.9	25.7	25.9	25.5
4	24.1	24.4	24.4	23.9	24.0	23.8	24.0	23.6	23.5
5	24.0	23.6	24.1	24.4	24.4	24.1	25.1	25.2	25.3

driver-car interaction can be taken into account in an analysis based on more than one observation per cell.

To illustrate the kind of data that can be analyzed, Table 15.10 contains results on fuel consumption recorded for drivers from five age classes with three types of automobile: X-cars, Y-cars, and Z-cars. The three observations in each cell refer to independent trials by drivers from a given age class with automobiles of a particular type.

To denote the individual sample observations, we require a triple subscript, so x_{ijl} will denote the lth observation in the ijth cell, that is, the lth observation in the cell corresponding to the ith group and the jth block. As before, we will let K denote the number of groups and H the number of blocks. We denote by L the number of observations per cell. Hence, in the example of Table 15.10, $K = 3$, $H = 5$, and $L = 3$. This notation is illustrated in Table 15.11.

Based on the results of an experiment of this type, there are three null hypotheses that can be tested: no difference between group means, no difference between block means, and no group-block interaction. In order to carry out these tests, we will again calculate various sample means, defined and calculated as follows.

i. Group Means
The mean of *all* the sample observations in the ith group is denoted $\bar{x}_{i\bullet\bullet}$, so

$$\bar{x}_{i\bullet\bullet} = \frac{\sum_{j=1}^{H} \sum_{l=1}^{L} x_{ijl}}{HL}$$

From Table 15.10, we find

$$\bar{x}_{1\bullet\bullet} = \frac{25.0 + 25.4 + \cdots + 23.6 + 24.1}{15} = 24.86$$

$$\bar{x}_{2\bullet\bullet} = \frac{24.0 + 24.4 + \cdots + 24.4 + 24.1}{15} = 24.16$$

$$\bar{x}_{3\bullet\bullet} = \frac{25.9 + 25.8 + \cdots + 25.2 + 25.3}{15} = 25.10$$

TABLE 15.11
Sample Observations on K Groups and H Blocks; L Observations per Cell

BLOCK	GROUP			
	1	2	...	K
1	$x_{111}x_{112}\cdots x_{11L}$	$x_{211}x_{212}\cdots x_{21L}$	...	$x_{K11}x_{K12}\cdots x_{K1L}$
2	$x_{121}x_{122}\cdots x_{12L}$	$x_{221}x_{222}\cdots x_{22L}$		$x_{K21}x_{K22}\cdots x_{K2L}$
.	.	.		.
.	.	.		.
.	.	.		.
H	$x_{1H1}x_{1H2}\cdots x_{1HL}$	$x_{2H1}x_{2H2}\cdots x_{2HL}$	...	$x_{KH1}x_{KH2}\cdots x_{KHL}$

ii. Block Means

The mean for all the sample observations in the jth block is denoted $\bar{x}_{\bullet j \bullet}$, so

$$\bar{x}_{\bullet j \bullet} = \frac{\sum_{i=1}^{K} \sum_{l=1}^{L} x_{ijl}}{KL}$$

For the data of Table 15.10, we have

$$\bar{x}_{\bullet 1 \bullet} = \frac{25.0 + 25.4 + \cdots + 25.8 + 25.4}{9} = 25.00$$

$$\bar{x}_{\bullet 2 \bullet} = \frac{24.8 + 24.8 + \cdots + 25.0 + 25.4}{9} = 24.53$$

$$\bar{x}_{\bullet 3 \bullet} = \frac{26.1 + 26.3 + \cdots + 25.9 + 25.5}{9} = 25.57$$

$$\bar{x}_{\bullet 4 \bullet} = \frac{24.1 + 24.4 + \cdots + 23.6 + 23.5}{9} = 23.97$$

$$\bar{x}_{\bullet 5 \bullet} = \frac{24.0 + 23.6 + \cdots + 25.2 + 25.3}{9} = 24.47$$

iii. Cell Means

To check the possibility of group-block interactions, it is necessary to calculate the sample mean for each cell. Let $\bar{x}_{ij\bullet}$ denote the sample mean for the (i, j)th cell. Then

$$\bar{x}_{ij\bullet} = \frac{\sum_{l=1}^{L} x_{ijl}}{L}$$

Hence we find, for the data of Table 15.10

$$\bar{x}_{11\bullet} = \frac{25.0 + 25.4 + 25.2}{3} = 25.2$$

$$\bar{x}_{12\bullet} = \frac{24.8 + 24.8 + 24.5}{3} = 24.7$$

and similarly

		$\bar{x}_{13\bullet} = 26.2$	$\bar{x}_{14\bullet} = 24.3$	$\bar{x}_{15\bullet} = 23.9$
$\bar{x}_{21\bullet} = 24.1$	$\bar{x}_{22\bullet} = 23.7$	$\bar{x}_{23\bullet} = 24.8$	$\bar{x}_{24\bullet} = 23.9$	$\bar{x}_{25\bullet} = 24.3$
$\bar{x}_{31\bullet} = 25.7$	$\bar{x}_{32\bullet} = 25.2$	$\bar{x}_{33\bullet} = 25.7$	$\bar{x}_{34\bullet} = 23.7$	$\bar{x}_{35\bullet} = 25.2$

iv. Overall Mean

We denote the mean of all the sample observations by $\bar{x}$, so

$$\bar{x} = \frac{\sum_{i=1}^{K} \sum_{j=1}^{H} \sum_{l=1}^{L} x_{ijl}}{KHL}$$

For our data, this quantity is simplest to calculate as the average of the three group sample means, giving

$$\bar{x} = \frac{24.86 + 24.16 + 25.10}{3} = 24.71$$

Now, to get a feeling for the analysis, it is convenient to think in terms of the assumed population model. Let X_{ijl} denote the random variable corresponding to the lth observation in the ijth cell. Then, the model assumed in our analysis is

$$X_{ijl} = \mu + G_i + B_j + I_{ij} + \varepsilon_{ijl}$$

The first three terms on the right-hand side are precisely the same as those in the model without replication. As before, they represent an overall mean, a group–specific factor, and a block-specific factor. The next term I_{ij} represents the effect of being in the ijth cell, given that the overall, group, and block effects are already accounted for. If there were no group-block interaction, this term would be 0. Its presence in the model allows us to test for interaction. Finally, the error term ε_{ijl} is a random variable representing experimental error.

We will rewrite the model in deviation form

$$X_{ijl} - \mu = G_i + B_j + I_{ij} + \varepsilon_{ijl}$$

It is shown that the total sum of squares can be decomposed as the sum of four terms, representing variability due to groups, blocks, interaction between groups and blocks, and error.

Without providing detailed derivations, the decomposition is shown in Equations 15.20 to 15.25 on which the tests are based.

DEFINITION 15.7 TWO-WAY ANALYSIS OF VARIANCE: SEVERAL OBSERVATIONS PER CELL

Suppose that we have a sample of observation on K groups and H blocks, with L observations per cell. Let x_{ijl} denote the lth observation in the cell for the ith group and jth block. Let $\bar{x}$ denote the overall sample mean, $\bar{x}_{i\bullet\bullet}$ the group sample means, $\bar{x}_{\bullet j\bullet}$ the block sample means, and $\bar{x}_{ij\bullet}$ the cell sample means.

Then, we define the following sums of squares and associated degrees of freedom:

	SUMS OF SQUARES	DEGREES OF FREEDOM	
TOTAL:	$SST = \sum_i \sum_j \sum_l (x_{ijl} - \bar{x})^2$	$KHL - 1$	(15.20)
BETWEEN-GROUPS:	$SSG = HL \sum_{i=1}^{K} (\bar{x}_{i\bullet\bullet} - \bar{x})^2$	$K - 1$	(15.21)
BETWEEN-BLOCKS:	$SSB = KL \sum_{j=1}^{H} (\bar{x}_{\bullet j\bullet} - \bar{x})^2$	$H - 1$	(15.22)
INTERACTION:	$SSI = L \sum_{i=1}^{K} \sum_{j=1}^{H} (\bar{x}_{ij\bullet} - \bar{x}_{i\bullet\bullet} - \bar{x}_{\bullet j\bullet} + \bar{x})^2$	$(K-1)(H-1)$	(15.23)
ERROR:	$SSE = \sum_i \sum_j \sum_l (x_{ijl} - \bar{x}_{ij\bullet})^2$	$KH(L-1)$	(15.24)

Then

$$SST = SSG + SSB + SSI + SSE \qquad (15.25)$$

Division of the component sums of squares by their corresponding degrees of freedom yields the mean squares *MSG, MSB, MSI,* and *MSE.*

Tests of the hypotheses of no effects for groups, blocks, and interaction are based on the respective *F* ratios

$$\frac{MSG}{MSE} \qquad \frac{MSB}{MSE} \qquad \frac{MSI}{MSE}$$

The tests are carried out with reference to the *F* distributions with the corresponding numerator and denominator degrees of freedom. Their validity rests on the assumption that the ε_{ijl} behave as a random sample from a normal distribution.

Figure 15.12 depicts the decomposition of the total sum of squares of the sample observations about their overall mean as the sum of four components. It differs from Figure 15.9 in that, as the experiment is replicated, we are now able to isolate an interaction sum of squares.

As before, the calculations involved can be conveniently summarized in an analysis of variance table. The general form of the table when there are *L* observations per cell in a two-way analysis of variance is shown in Table 15.12.

In fact, formulas that are computationally simpler exist for the calculation of the various sums of squares. Nevertheless, the arithmetic involved is still rather tedious and should be performed using a computer. We will not go into further detail here, but will simply report in Figure 15.13 the results of the calculations for our data. In practice, analysis of variance computations are typically carried out using a statistical computer package such as Minitab. Thus, considerations of arithmetic complexity rarely impose any constraint on practical analyses.

The degrees of freedom in Figure 15.13 follow from the fact that for these data, we have

$$K = 3 \qquad H = 5 \qquad L = 3$$

The mean squares are obtained by dividing the sums of squares by their associated degrees of freedom. Finally, the *F* ratios follow from dividing, in turn, each of the first three mean squares by the error mean square.

Using the material in Figure 15.13, we can test the three null hypotheses of interest. First, we test the null hypothesis of no interaction between drivers and automobile type. This test is based on the calculated *F* ratio 21.35 and the *p*-value of 0.000. Since the numer-

FIGURE 15.12
Sum of Squares Decomposition for a Two-way Analysis of Variance with More than one Observation per Cell

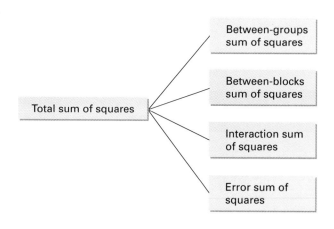

TABLE 15.12
General Format of the Two-way Analysis of Variance Table with L Observations per Cell

SOURCE OF VARIATION	SUM OF SQUARES	DEGREES OF FREEDOM	MEAN SQUARES	F RATIOS
Between-groups	SSG	$K - 1$	$MSG = \dfrac{SSG}{K - 1}$	$\dfrac{MSG}{MSE}$
Between-blocks	SSB	$H - 1$	$MSB = \dfrac{SSB}{H - 1}$	$\dfrac{MSB}{MSE}$
Interaction	SSI	$(K - 1)(H - 1)$	$MSI = \dfrac{SSI}{(K - 1)(H - 1)}$	$\dfrac{MSI}{MSE}$
Error	SSE	$KH(L - 1)$	$MSE = \dfrac{SSE}{KH(L - 1)}$	
Total	SST	$KHL - 1$		

ator and denominator degrees of freedom are 8 and 30, respectively, we have, from the Appendix

$$F_{8,30,.01} = 3.17$$

The null hypothesis of no interaction between car and driver type is very clearly rejected at the 1% level of significance.

Next, we test the null hypothesis that the population mean fuel consumption is the same for X-cars, Y-cars, and Z-cars. The test is based on the calculated F ratio 92.46. From the Appendix, we find for 1%-level test with numerator and denominator degrees of freedom 2 and 30, respectively.

$$F_{2,30,.01} = 5.39$$

Hence, the null hypothesis of equality of the population means for automobile types is overwhelmingly rejected at the 1% significance level.

FIGURE 15.13
Minitab Analysis of Variance Output for Fuel Consumption Data of Table 15.10

Two-way Analysis of Variance

```
Analysis of Variance for Mileage
Source          DF        SS         MS         F        P
Car              2     7.1560     3.5780     92.53    0.000
Driver           4    13.1480     3.2870     85.01    0.000
Interaction      8     6.6040     0.8255     21.35    0.000
Error           30     1.1600     0.0387
Total           44    28.0680
                              Individual 95% CI
Car           Mean    ---------+---------+---------+---------+--
1            24.860                                 (---*--)
2            24.160       (--*---)
3            25.100                                     (---*--)
                      ---------+---------+---------+---------+--
                         24.300     24.600     24.900     25.200
                              Individual 95% CI
Driver        Mean    ----+---------+---------+---------+-------
1            25.000                            (--*--)
2            24.533                  (--*-)
3            25.567                                  (-*--)
4            23.967       (-*--)
5            24.467               (-*--)
                      ----+---------+---------+---------+-------
                        24.000     24.500     25.000     25.500
```

Finally, we test the null hypothesis that the population mean fuel consumption is the same for all five-driver age classes. From Figure 15.13, the test is based on the calculated F ratio 84.96. Hence, the numerator and denominator degrees of freedom are 4 and 30, so for a 1%-level test

$$F_{4, 30, .01} = 4.02$$

The null hypothesis of equality of population means for these driver age classes is very clearly rejected at the 1% significance level.

INTERPRETATION

The evidence of our data points very firmly to the following three conclusions:

1. Average fuel consumption is not the same for X-cars, Y-cars, and Z-cars.
2. The average performance levels are not the same for all driver classes.
3. The differences in driver performance are not spread evenly over all three types of automobile. Rather, compared with other drivers, a driver from a particular age class is likely to do relatively better in one automobile type than in another.

So far in this section, we have assumed that the number of observations in each cell is the same. However, this restriction is not necessary and may, on occasion, be inconvenient for an investigator. In fact, the formulas for the computation of sums of squares can be modified to allow for unequal cell contents. We will not be concerned here with the technical details of the calculation of appropriate sums of squares. Generally an investigator will have available a computer package for this purpose. Rather, our interest lies in the analysis of the results.

EXAMPLE 15.4

WORKER SATISFACTION LEVEL (TWO-WAY ANALYSIS OF VARIANCE)

A study (reference 1) was designed to compare the satisfaction levels of introverted and extroverted workers performing stimulating and nonstimulating tasks. For the purpose of this study, there are two worker types and two task types, giving four combinations. The sample mean satisfaction levels reported by workers in these four combinations were as follows:

Introverted worker, nonstimulating task (16 observations):	2.78
Extroverted worker, nonstimulating task (15 observations):	1.85
Introverted worker, stimulating task (17 observations):	3.87
Extroverted worker, stimulating task (19 observations):	4.12

The following table shows the calculated sums of squares and associated degrees of freedom. Complete the analysis of variance table, and analyze the results of this experiment.

SOURCE OF VARIATION	SUMS OF SQUARES	DEGREES OF FREEDOM
Task	62.04	1
Worker type	.06	1
Interaction	1.85	1
Error	23.31	63
Total	87.26	66

SOLUTION:

Once again, the mean squares are obtained from division of the sums of squares by their associated degrees of freedom. The *F* ratios then follow from division of the task, worker type, and interaction mean squares by the error mean square. The analysis of variance table may now be completed as shown.

SOURCE OF VARIATION	SUMS OF SQUARES	DEGREES OF FREEDOM	MEAN SQUARES	*F* RATIOS
Task	62.04	1	62.04	167.68
Worker type	.06	1	.06	.16
Interaction	1.85	1	1.85	5.00
Error	23.31	63	.37	
Total	87.26	66		

INTERPRETATION

The analysis of variance table can be used as the basis for testing three null hypotheses. For the null hypothesis of equal mean population satisfaction levels with the two types of task, the calculated *F* ratio is 167.68. We have numerator degrees of freedom 1 and denominator degrees of freedom 63, so from the Appendix, for a 1%-level test

$$F_{1,63,.01} = 7.07$$

Hence, the null hypothesis of equal population mean satisfaction levels for stimulating and nonstimulating tasks is very clearly rejected. This result is not surprising. We would naturally expect workers to be more satisfied when performing stimulating rather than nonstimulating tasks.

Next, we test the null hypothesis that the population mean satisfaction levels are the same for introverted and extroverted workers. Here, the calculated *F* ratio is .16. Again, the degrees of freedom are 1 and 63, so for a 5%-level test

$$F_{1,63,.05} = 4.00$$

The null hypothesis of equal mean levels of satisfaction for introverted and extroverted workers cannot be rejected at the 5% level of significance.

In many studies, the interaction term is not, in itself, of any great importance. The main reason for including it in the analysis is to "soak up" some of the variability in the data, rendering any differences between population means easier to detect. However, in this particular study, the interaction is of major interest. The null hypothesis of no interaction between task and worker type in determining worker satisfaction levels is tested through the calculated *F* ratio 5.00. Once again, the numerator and denominator degrees of freedom are 1 and 63, respectively. Hence, comparison with the tabulated values of the *F* distribution reveals that the null hypothesis of no interaction can be rejected at the 5% level but not at the 1% level of significance.

EXERCISES

15.32 Suppose that scores given by judges to competitors in the ski jumping events of the Winter Olympics were analyzed. For the men's ski jumping competition, suppose there were twenty-two contestants and nine judges. Each judge in seven subevents assessed each contestant. The scores given can thus be treated in the framework of a two-way analysis of variance with 198 contestant-judge cells, seven observations per cell. The sums of squares are given in the table.

SOURCE OF VARIATION	SUMS OF SQUARES
Between contestants	364.50
Between judges	.81
Interaction	4.94
Error	1,069.94

(a) Complete the analysis of variance table.

(b) Carry out the associated F tests, and interpret your findings.

15.33 Refer to Exercise 15.32. Twelve pairs were entered in the ice-dancing competition. Once again, there were nine judges, and contestants were assessed in seven subevents. The sums of squares between groups (pairs of contestants) and between blocks (judges) were found to be

$$SSG = 60.10 \quad \text{and} \quad SSB = 1.65$$

while the interaction and error sums of squares were

$$SSI = 3.35 \quad \text{and} \quad SSE = 31.61$$

Analyze these results, and verbally interpret the conclusions.

15.34 A psychologist is working with three types of aptitude tests that may be given to prospective management trainees. In deciding how to structure the testing process, an important issue is the possibility of interaction between test takers and test type. If there were no interaction, only one type of test would be needed. Three tests of each type are given to members of each of four groups of subject type. These were distinguished by ratings of poor, fair, good, and excellent in preliminary interviews. The scores obtained are listed in the following table.

SUBJECT TYPE	TEST TYPE								
	Profile Fit			*Mindbender*			*Psych Out*		
Poor	65	68	62	69	71	67	75	75	78
Fair	74	79	76	72	69	69	70	69	65
Good	64	72	65	68	73	75	78	82	80
Excellent	83	82	84	78	78	75	76	77	75

(a) Set up the analysis of variance table.

(b) Test the null hypothesis of no interaction between subject type and test type.

15.35 Random samples of two freshman, two sophomores, two juniors, and two seniors each from four dormitories were asked to rate on a scale from 1 (poor) to 10 (excellent) the quality of dormitory environment for studying. The results are shown in the table.

YEAR	DORMITORY							
	A		*B*		*C*		*D*	
Freshman	7	5	8	6	9	8	9	9
Sophomore	6	8	5	5	7	8	8	9
Junior	5	4	7	6	6	7	7	8
Senior	7	4	6	8	7	5	6	7

(a) Set up the analysis of variance table.

(b) Test the null hypothesis that the population mean ratings are the same for the four dormitories.

(c) Test the null hypothesis that the population mean ratings are the same for the four student years.

(d) Test the null hypothesis of no interaction between student year and dormitory ratings.

15.36 In some experiments with several observations per cell, the analyst is prepared to assume that there is no interaction between groups and blocks. Any apparent interaction found is then attributed to random error. When such an assumption is made, the analysis is carried out in the usual way, except that what were previously the interaction and error sums of squares are added together to form a new error sum of squares. Similarly, the corresponding degrees of freedom are also added. If the assumption of no interaction is correct, this approach has the advantage of providing more error degrees of freedom and hence more powerful tests of the equality of group and block means. For the study of Exercise 15.35, suppose that we now make the assumption of no interaction between dormitories and student years.

(a) State, in words, what is implied by this assumption.

(b) Given this assumption, set up the new analysis of variance table.

(c) Test the null hypothesis that the mean ratings are the same for all dormitories.

(d) Test the null hypothesis that the mean ratings are the same for all four-student years.

15.37 Refer to Exercise 15.22. Having carried out the experiment to compare mean yields per acre of four varieties of corn and three brands of fertilizer, an agricultural researcher suggested that there might be some interaction between variety and fertilizer. To check this possibility, another set of trials was carried out, producing the yields in the table.

FERILIZER	VARIETY			
	A	*B*	*C*	*D*
1	80	88	73	88
2	94	91	79	93
3	81	78	83	83

(a) What would be implied by an interaction between variety and fertilizer?

(b) Combine the data from the two sets of trials and set up an analysis of variance table.

(c) Test the null hypothesis that the mean yield is the same for all four varieties of corn.

(d) Test the null hypothesis that the mean yield is the same for all three brands of fertilizer.

(e) Test the null hypothesis of no interaction between variety of corn and brand of fertilizer.

15.38 Refer to Exercise 15.24. Suppose that a second store for each region–can color combination is added to the study, yielding the results shown in the following table. Combining these results with those of Exercise 15.24, carry out the analysis of variance calculations and discuss your findings.

REGION	CAN COLOR		
	Red	*Yellow*	*Blue*
East	45	50	54
South	49	51	58
Midwest	43	60	50
West	38	49	44

15.39 Having carried out the study of Exercise 15.25, the instructor decided to replicate the study the following year. The results obtained are shown in the table. Combining these results with those of Exercise 15.25, carry out the analysis of variance calculations and discuss your findings.

EXAMINATION	TEXT		
	A	*B*	*C*
Multiple Choice	4.7	5.1	4.8
Essays	4.4	4.6	4.0
Mix	4.5	5.3	4.9

SUMMARY

In this chapter we developed the basic components of the analysis of variance procedure. Analysis of variance provides a way to determine if one or more discrete level factors influence an outcome measurement. These procedures are a fundamental background for experimental design—widely used by industry to determine best practices for maximizing productivity and minimizing defects. One-way analysis of variance provides a method for comparing the means of three or more processes simultaneously. We also included the Kruskal-Wallis test as a useful nonparametric procedure for comparing three or more groups using ranked data. Two-way analysis of variance considers the effect of two different multiple-level factors on an outcome measurement. We can consider the effect of each factor by itself, and by using multiple cell observations we can also consider the interaction between specific combinations of factor levels. Analysis of variance procedures provides a complement to multiple regression procedures. Similar objectives can also be achieved by using dummy variable procedures as discussed in Chapter 12.

KEY WORDS

hypothesis test for one-way analysis of variance, 587
hypothesis tests for two-way analysis of variance, 602
interaction, 606
kruskal-wallis test, 595

one-way analysis of variance, 582
randomized blocks design, 597
sum of squares decomposition for one-way analysis of variance, 585

sum of squares decomposition for two-way analysis of variance, 601
two-way analysis of variance: several observations per cell, 609

CHAPTER EXERCISES AND APPLICATIONS

15.40 Carefully distinguish between the one-way analysis of variance framework and the two-way analysis of variance framework. Give examples different from those discussed in the text and exercises of business problems for which each might be appropriate.

15.41 Carefully explain what is meant by the interaction effect in the two-way analysis of variance with more than one observation per cell. Give examples of this effect in business-related problems.

15.42 Consider a study to assess the readability of financial report messages. The technique for assessing the effectiveness of the written message uses a standard procedure. Financial reports were given to independent random samples from three groups—certified public accountants, chartered financial analysts, and commercial bank loan officer trainees. The procedure was then administered, and the scores for the sample members were recorded. The null hypothesis of interest is that the population mean scores for the three groups are identical. Test this hypothesis given the information in the accompanying table.

SOURCE OF VARIATION	SUMS OF SQUARES	DEGREES OF FREEDOM
Between groups	5,165	2
Within groups	120,802	1,005
Total	125,967	1,007

15.43 In an experiment designed to assess aids to the success of interviews of graduate students carried out by faculty mentors, interviewers were randomly assigned to one of three interview modes—feedback, feedback and goal setting, and control. For the feedback mode, interviewers had the opportunity to examine and discuss their graduate students reactions to previous interviews. In the feedback-and-goal-setting mode, faculty mentors were encouraged to set goals for the forthcoming interview. For the control group, interviews were carried out in the usual way, without feedback or goal setting. After the interviews were completed, the satisfaction levels of the graduate students with the interviews were assessed. For the 45 people in the feedback group, the mean satisfaction level was 13.98. The 49 people in the feedback-and-goal-setting group had a mean satisfaction level of 15.12, while the 41 control group members had a mean satisfaction level of 13.07. The F ratio computed from the data was 4.12.
(**a**) Set out the complete analysis of variance table.
(**b**) Test the null hypothesis that the population mean satisfaction levels are the same for all three types of interview.

15.44 A study classified each of 134 lawyers into one of four groups, based on observation and an interview. The 62 lawyers in group A were categorized as having high levels of stimulation and support and average levels of public spirit. The 52 lawyers in group B had low stimulation, average support, and high public spirit. Group C contained 7 lawyers, with average stimulation, low support, and low public spirit. The 13 lawyers in group D were assessed as low on all three criteria. Salary levels for these four groups were compared. The sample means were 7.87 for group A, 7.47 for group B, 5.14 for group C, and 3.69 for group D. The F ratio calculated from these data was 25.60.
(**a**) Set out the complete analysis of variance table.
(**b**) Test the null hypothesis that the population mean salaries are the same for lawyers in these four groups.

15.45 In a study to estimate the effects of smoking on routine health risk, employees were classed as continuous smokers, recent ex-smokers, long-term ex-smokers, and those who never smoked. Samples of 96, 34, 86, and 206 members of these groups were taken. Sample mean numbers of medical contacts per month were found to be 2.15, 2.21, 1.47, and 1.69, respectively. The F ratio calculated from these data was 2.56.
(**a**) Set out the complete analysis of variance table.
(**b**) Test the null hypothesis of equality of the four population mean health risk rates.

15.46 Lower Michigan has had restrictions on price advertising for wine. However, for a period, these restrictions were lifted. Data were collected on total wine sales over three periods of time—under restricted price advertising, with restrictions lifted, and after the reimposition of restrictions. The accompanying table shows sums of squares and degrees of freedom. Assuming that the usual requirements for the analysis of variance are met—in particular that sample observations are independent of one another—test the null hypothesis of equality of mean sales in these three time periods.

SOURCE OF VARIATION	SUMS OF SQUARES	DEGREES OF FREEDOM
Between groups	11,438.3028	2
Within groups	109,200.0000	15
Total	120,638.3028	17

15.47 Independent random samples of the selling prices of houses in four districts were taken. The selling prices (in thousands of dollars) are shown in the accompanying table. Test the null hypothesis that population mean selling prices are the same in all four districts.

DISTRICT A	DISTRICT B	DISTRICT C	DISTRICT D
73	85	97	61
63	59	86	67
89	84	76	84
75	70	78	67
70	80	76	69

15.48 For the data of Exercise 15.47, use the Kruskal-Wallis test to test the null hypothesis that the population mean selling prices of houses are the same in the four districts.

15.49 A study was aimed at assessing class schedule satisfaction levels, on a scale from 1 (very dissatisfied) to 7 (very satisfied), of non-tenured who were either job-sharers, full-time, or part-time. For a sample of 25 job-sharers, the mean satisfaction level was 6.60; for a sample of 24 full-time faculty, the mean satisfaction level was 5.37; for a sample of 20 part-time faculty, the mean satisfaction level was 5.20. The F ratio calculated from these data was 6.62.
(**a**) Set out the complete analysis of variance table.
(**b**) Test the null hypothesis of equality of the three population mean satisfaction levels.

15.50 Consider the one-way analysis of variance setup.
(**a**) Show that the within-groups sum of squares can be written

$$SSW = \sum_{i=1}^{K} \sum_{j=1}^{n_i} x_{ij}^2 - \sum_{i=1}^{K} n_i \bar{x}_i^2$$

(**b**) Show that the between-groups sum of squares can be written

$$SSG = \sum_{i=1}^{K} n_i \bar{x}_i^2 - n\bar{x}^2$$

(**c**) Show that the total sum of squares can be written

$$SST = \sum_{i=1}^{K} \sum_{j=1}^{n_i} x_{ij}^2 - n\bar{x}^2$$

15.51 Consider the two-way analysis of variance setup, with one observation per cell.

(**a**) Show that the between-groups sum of squares can be written

$$SSG = H \sum_{i=1}^{K} \bar{x}_{i\bullet}^2 - n\bar{x}^2$$

(**b**) Show that the between-blocks sum of squares can be written

$$SSB = K \sum_{j=1}^{H} \bar{x}_{\bullet j}^2 - n\bar{x}^2$$

(**c**) Show that the total sum of squares can be written

$$SST = \sum_{i=1}^{K} \sum_{j=1}^{H} x_{ij}^2 - n\bar{x}^2$$

(**d**) Show that the error sum of squares can be written

$$SSE = \sum_{i=1}^{K} \sum_{j=1}^{H} x_{ij}^2 - H \sum_{i=1}^{K} \bar{x}_{i\bullet}^2 - K \sum_{j=1}^{H} \bar{x}_{\bullet j}^2 + n\bar{x}^2$$

15.52 Information on consumer satisfactions of three price groupings for beer: high, medium, low—were obtained from a random sample of 125 consumers. The sums of squares for these satisfaction measures are given in the accompanying table. Complete the analysis of variance table, and test the null hypothesis that the population mean satisfaction levels are the same for all three price groupings.

SOURCE OF VARIATION	SUMS OF SQUARES
Between consumers	37,571.5
Between brands	32,987.3
Error	55,710.7

15.53 Three real estate agents were each asked to assess the values of five houses in a neighborhood. The results, in thousands of dollars, are set out in the table. Set out the analysis of variance table, and test the null hypothesis that population mean valuations are the same for the three real estate agents.

HOUSE	AGENT		
	A	*B*	*C*
1	210	218	226
2	192	190	198
3	183	187	185
4	227	223	237
5	242	240	237

15.54 Students were classified according to three parental income groups and also according to three possible score ranges in the SAT examination. One student was chosen randomly from each of the nine cross-classifications, and the grade point average of each sample member at the end of the sophomore year was recorded. The results are shown in the accompanying table.

SAT SCORE	INCOME GROUP		
	High	*Moderate*	*Low*
Very high	3.7	3.6	3.6
High	3.4	3.5	3.2
Moderate	2.9	2.8	3.0

(**a**) Set out the analysis of variance table.
(**b**) Test the null hypothesis that the population mean grade point averages are the same for all three income groups.
(**c**) Test the null hypothesis that the population mean grade point averages are the same for all three SAT score groups.

15.55 For the two-way analysis of variance model with one observation per cell, write the observation from the ith group and jth block as

$$X_{ij} = \mu + G_i + B_j + \varepsilon_{ij}$$

Refer to Exercise 15.53 and consider the observation on agent B and house 1 ($x_{21} = 218$).
(**a**) Estimate μ.
(**b**) Estimate, and interpret, G_2.
(**c**) Estimate, and interpret, B_1.
(**d**) Estimate ε_{21}.

15.56 Refer to Exercise 15.54 and consider the observation on moderate-income group and high SAT score ($x_{22} = 3.5$).
(**a**) Estimate μ.
(**b**) Estimate and interpret, G_2.
(**c**) Estimate and interpret, B_1.
(**d**) Estimate ε_{21}.

15.57 Consider the two-way analysis of variance setup, with L observations per cell.
(**a**) Show that the between-groups sum of squares can be written

$$SSG = HL \sum_{i=1}^{K} \bar{x}_{i\bullet\bullet}^2 - HKL\bar{x}^2$$

(**b**) Show that the between-blocks sum of squares can be written

$$SSB = KL\sum_{j=1}^{H} \bar{x}_{\bullet j \bullet}^2 - HKL\bar{x}^2$$

(**c**) Show that the error sum of squares can be written

$$SSE = \sum_{i=1}^{K}\sum_{j=1}^{H}\sum_{l=1}^{L} x_{ijl}^2 - L\sum_{i=1}^{K}\sum_{j=1}^{H} \bar{x}_{ij\bullet}^2$$

(**d**) Show that the total sum of squares can be written

$$SST = \sum_{i=1}^{K}\sum_{j=1}^{H}\sum_{l=1}^{L} x_{ijl}^2 - HKL\bar{x}^2$$

(**e**) Show that the interaction sum of squares can be written

$$SSI = L\sum_{i=1}^{K}\sum_{j=1}^{H} \bar{x}_{ij\bullet}^2 - HL\sum_{i=1}^{K} \bar{x}_{i\bullet\bullet}^2 - KL\sum_{j=1}^{H} \bar{x}_{\bullet j\bullet}^2 + HKL\bar{x}^2$$

15.58 Purchasing agents were given information about a cellular phone system and asked to assess its quality. The information given was identical except for two factors—price and country of origin. For price, there were three possibilities: $150, $80, or no price given. For country or origin, there were also three possibilities: United States, Tawain, or no country given. Parts of the analysis of variance table for the quality assessments of the purchasing agents is shown here. Complete the analysis of variance table and provide a full analysis of these data.

SOURCE OF VARIATION	SUMS OF SQUARES	DEGREES OF FREEDOM
Between prices	.178	2
Between countries	4.365	2
Interaction	1.262	4
Error	93.330	99

15.59 In the study of Exercise 15.58, information on the dictation system was also shown to M.B.A. students. Part of the analysis of variance table for their quality assessments is shown here. Complete the analysis of variance table and provide a full analysis of these data.

SOURCE OF VARIATION	SUMS OF SQUARES	DEGREES OF FREEDOM
Between prices	.042	2
Between countries	15.319	2
Interaction	2.235	4
Error	70.414	50

15.60 Having carried out the study of Exercise 15.54, the investigator decided to take an independent random sample of one student from each of the nine income–SAT score categories. The grade point averages found are given in the accompanying table.

SAT SCORE	INCOME GROUP		
Very high	3.9	3.7	3.8
High	3.2	3.6	3.4
Moderate	2.7	3.0	2.8

(**a**) Set out the analysis of variance table.
(**b**) Test the null hypothesis that the population mean grade point averages are the same for all three income groups.
(**c**) Test the null hypothesis that the population mean grade point averages are the same for all three SAT score groups.
(**d**) Test the null hypothesis of no interaction between income group and SAT score.

15.61 An experiment was carried out to test the effects on yields of five varieties of corn and five types of fertilizer. For each variety–fertilizer combination, six plots were used and the yields recorded, with the results shown in the table.

FERTILIZER VARIETY										
	A		B		C		D		E	
1	75	77	74	67	93	90	79	83	72	77
	79	83	73	65	87	82	87	88	79	83
	85	78	79	80	86	88	86	90	78	86
2	80	72	71	69	84	88	77	82	70	75
	76	73	75	62	90	79	84	87	80	80
	70	74	77	63	83	80	82	83	74	81
3	85	87	76	73	88	94	81	86	77	83
	80	79	77	70	89	86	90	90	87	79
	87	80	83	80	89	93	87	88	86	88
4	80	79	74	77	86	87	80	77	79	85
	82	77	69	78	90	85	90	84	88	80
	85	80	74	76	83	88	80	88	87	82
5	75	79	75	80	92	88	82	78	80	87
	86	82	84	80	89	94	85	86	90	83
	79	83	72	77	86	90	82	89	86	83

(**a**) Test the null hypothesis that the population mean yields are the same for all five varieties of corn.
(**b**) Test the null hypothesis that the population mean yields are the same for all five brands of fertilizer.
(**c**) Test the null hypothesis of no interaction between variety and fertilizer.

APPENDIX

TOTAL SUM OF SQUARES

$$SST = \sum_{i=1}^{K} \sum_{j=1}^{n_i} \left(x_{ij} - \bar{x}\right)^2$$

$$= \sum_{i=1}^{K} \sum_{j=1}^{n_i} \left(x_{ij} - \bar{x}_i + \bar{x}_i - \bar{x}\right)^2$$

$$= \sum_{i=1}^{K} \sum_{j=1}^{n_i} \left(x_{ij} - \bar{x}_i\right)^2 + \sum_{i=1}^{K} \sum_{j=1}^{n_i} \left(\bar{x}_i - \bar{x}\right)^2 + 2 \sum_{i=1}^{K} \left(\bar{x}_i - \bar{x}\right) \sum_{j=1}^{n_i} \left(x_{ij} - \bar{x}_i\right)$$

$$= \sum_{i=1}^{K} \sum_{j=1}^{n_i} \left(x_{ij} - \bar{x}_i\right)^2 + \sum_{i=1}^{K} n_i \left(\bar{x}_i - \bar{x}\right)^2$$

$$SST = SSW + SSG$$

Note: $$\sum_{j=1}^{n_i} \left(x_{ij} - \bar{x}_i\right) = 0$$

WITHIN-GROUPS MEAN SQUARE (MSW)

For each Subgroup i

$$\sigma^2 = E\left[\frac{\sum_{j=1}^{n_i} \left(x_{ij} - \mu_i\right)^2}{n_i}\right]$$

$$= E\left[\frac{\sum_{j=1}^{n_i} \left(x_{ij} - \bar{x}_i + \bar{x}_i - \mu_i\right)^2}{n_i}\right]$$

$$= E\left[\frac{\sum_{j=1}^{n_i} \left(x_{ij} - \bar{x}_i\right)^2}{n_i}\right] + \frac{\sigma^2}{n_i}$$

$$\frac{(n_i - 1)\sigma^2}{n_i} = E\left[\frac{\sum_{j=1}^{n_i} \left(x_{ij} - \bar{x}_i\right)^2}{n_i}\right]$$

$$\hat{\sigma}^2 = \frac{\sum_{j=1}^{n_i} \left(x_{ij} - \bar{x}_i\right)^2}{n_i - 1}$$

Summing over K subgroups

$$\hat{\sigma}^2 = \frac{\sum_{i=1}^{K} \sum_{j=1}^{n_i} \left(x_{ij} - \bar{x}_i\right)^2}{n - K} = \frac{SSW}{n - K}$$

$$\hat{\sigma}^2 = MSW$$

BETWEEN-GROUPS MEAN SQUARE (MSG)

$$\mu_i = \mu \quad i = 1, \ldots, K$$

then

$$\hat{\sigma}^2 = E\left[\frac{\sum_{i=1}^{K}\sum_{j=1}^{n_i}\left(x_{ij} - \bar{x}\right)^2}{n-1}\right]$$

$$= E\left[\frac{\sum_{i=1}^{K}\sum_{j=1}^{n_i}\left(x_{ij} - \bar{x}_i + \bar{x}_i - \bar{x}\right)^2}{n-1}\right]$$

$$= E\left[\frac{\sum_{i=1}^{K}\sum_{j=1}^{n_i}\left(x_{ij} - \bar{x}_i\right)^2}{n-1} + \frac{\sum_{i=1}^{K}\sum_{j=1}^{n_i}\left(\bar{x}_i - \bar{x}\right)^2}{n-1}\right]$$

$$= \frac{\left(n-K\right)\hat{\sigma}^2}{n-1} + \frac{\sum_{i=1}^{K}n_i\left(\bar{x}_i - \bar{x}\right)^2}{n-1}$$

$$\frac{\left(K-1\right)\hat{\sigma}^2}{n-1} = \frac{\sum_{i=1}^{K}n_i\left(\bar{x}_i - \bar{x}\right)^2}{n-1}$$

$$\hat{\sigma}^2 = \frac{\sum_{i=1}^{K}n_i\left(\bar{x}_i - \bar{x}\right)^2}{K-1}$$

$$\hat{\sigma}^2 = MSG = \frac{SSG}{K-1}$$

RATIO OF MEAN SQUARES

If

$$H_0\colon \; \mu_1 = \mu_2 = \cdots \mu_K$$

is true, then *MSG*—with $K - 1$ degrees of freedom—is an estimator of σ^2 from 15-C and

$$\chi^2_{K-1} = \frac{\left(K-1\right)MSG}{\sigma^2}$$

In addition, *MSW* with $n - K$ degrees is an estimator of σ^2 from 15-B and therefore

$$\chi^2_{n-K} = \frac{\left(n-K\right)MSW}{\sigma^2}$$

Thus

$$F_{K-1,n-K} = \frac{\dfrac{\chi^2_{K-1}}{K-1}}{\dfrac{\chi^2_{n-K}}{n-K}} = \frac{MSG}{MSW}$$

REFERENCES

1. Kim, J.S., "Relationships of Personality of Perceptual and Behavioral Responses in Stimulating and Nonstimulating Tasks." *Academy of Management Journal, 23,* (1980), 307–319.

2. Shuptrine, F.K. and D.D. McVicker, "Readability Levels of Magazine Advertisements." *Journal of Advertising Research, 21,* no. 5 (1981), 45–50.

INTRODUCTION TO QUALITY

INTRODUCTION

In this chapter, statistical procedures that are both quite straightforward and far from new are introduced. Historically called *statistical process control* or *statistical quality control,* these procedures are now included with other process improvement techniques in the study of management and quality control. Originally, many process improvement applications were applied by manufacturing to monitor production processes. Benefits were soon realized, and the principles of quality were adopted by educational institutions, health care facilities, government agencies, the legal environment, the entertainment industry, tourism, transportation, and many other service-oriented as well as profit and nonprofit agencies. Delivery companies and airlines monitor on-time arrival of packages and planes; restaurants monitor food quality, preparation time, and service; hotels and hospitals are concerned about customer satisfaction. Businesses and organizations have customers, and customers demand high-quality goods and services. Quality is essential in all arenas, with applications to all segments of society. Since quality is fundamental in the global community, continuous and never-ending improvement of processes, products, and services is of paramount significance.

16.1   THE IMPORTANCE OF QUALITY

What do the following companies have in common: Nokia Mobile Phones, Europe & Africa (Finland); Inland Revenue, Account Office Cumbernauld (UK, Scotland); Burton-Apta Refractory Manufacturing Ltd (Hungary); STMicroelectronics, Inc. (Carrollton, TX); BI (Minneapolis, MN); The Ritz-Carlton Hotel Company, L.L.C. (Atlanta, GA); Sunny Fresh Foods (Monticello, MN); Motorola, Inc. (Schaumburg, IL); Texas Nameplate Company, Inc. (Dallas, TX); Solectron Corporation (Milpitas, CA); Xerox Business Services (Rochester, NY); Wainwright Industries, Inc. (St. Peters, MO), Operations Management International, Inc. (with offices in 29 states, Brazil, Canada, Egypt, Israel, Malaysia, New Zealand, Philippines, and Thailand)? Some are manufacturing companies; others are service organizations. Some are large companies; others are small. Some are American firms; others are European. But the common thread is that each of these companies (and this is only a partial list) has received a prestigious award for demonstrating excellence in quality management and continuous improvement. For example, in September 2000 at the European Foundation for Quality Management (EFQM) Forum in Istanbul, Nokia Mobile Phones, Inland Revenue, and Burton-Apta Refractory joined the list of Europe's most outstanding organizations from both the public and private sectors that have won the European Quality Prize. The European Foundation has given this award for Quality Management since 1992 (for more information see their web site at www.efqm.org). The other companies mentioned are only a few of the winners of the Malcolm Baldrige National Quality Award, America's premier award for performance excellence and quality achievement, given since 1988. Individual states and corporations give numerous other quality awards. Quality and continuous improvement are of global importance.

Consider the manufacturing industry. Clearly, the goal is not simply to inspect a finished product. By then, it may be that little can be done other than to discard or rework rejects, leading to considerable waste. Instead, it is essential to monitor a production process *at each stage* where intermediate output required to meet verifiable standards is produced. The aim is to ensure quality at each stage of the production process, so that time and money are not wasted in continuing to work on substandard products. In continuous process improvement, then, each stage of production is viewed as generating output whose quality should be assessed.

In the U.S. manufacturing industry, statistical quality control methods did not come into widespread use until the 1980s—a decade that witnessed an explosion of interest in these techniques. Yet, as has been indicated, statistical quality control methods are certainly not new. Neither are they at all difficult to understand or implement. Indeed, the basic methods—the ones most commonly used today—are nothing more than fairly routine applications of the statistical techniques discussed in early chapters of this book. Although they were neglected in the United States for many years, the early development of statistical control methods is due to an American, Walter A. Shewhart, who in the 1920s advocated the approaches that underlie the methodology that has now achieved wide acceptance. In fact, broad application of Shewhart's ideas in the private manufacturing sector was first achieved in postwar Japan.

Quality control was at the heart of Japan's rise to become a world economic leader. This development owed much to the influence of another American statistician, **W. Edwards Deming**, a former colleague of Shewhart. Two of Deming's important concepts (references 2, 3, 11) are:

1. Quality results from a careful study of the entire production process and direct action by management to correct all of the small problems that contribute to defects.
2. Data need to be collected regularly and analyzed by appropriate statistical procedures to ensure that the process has a stable operation with minimum variance. Whenever deviations from standard are identified, they need to be corrected immediately.

In addition to the work of W. Edwards Deming, the efforts of Joseph Juran (reference 7 and 8), Philip Crosby, Armand V. Feigenbaum, Kaoru Ishikawa and many others contributed to modern quality thinking. Despite their differences, Deming, Juran and Crosby agreed that commitment from top management is an absolute necessity; that responsibility for quality belongs to management, not the workers; and that improvement is continuous and never-ending (reference 5). Together their activities led to an important change in the philosophy of quality control. Traditional quality control practice emphasized inspection of final product units—either all units or a random sample. By this inspection defective units would be identified, removed, and either repaired or scrapped. Critical of this approach, Deming said, "Inspection with the aim of finding the bad ones and throwing them out is too late, ineffective, and costly. In the first place, you can't find the bad ones, not all of them. Second, it costs too much. Quality comes not from inspection but from improvement of the process" (reference 11). If only end inspection is used, workers at earlier stages in the production process may be tempted to be less concerned with the product's quality. Deming insisted that quality was the responsibility of everyone in the organization and that management had to organize the process to ensure uniformly high standards. The old method of *detection* of errors needed to be replaced by the philosophy of *prevention* of errors (references 2, 11).

Subsequently, much attention was paid to quality improvement in Japanese manufacturing, and a number of refinements and modifications of the original methods were developed and implemented. For example, **Genichi Taguchi**, a Japanese engineer, described the cost of variation in monetary terms in what is often referred to as the Taguchi loss function (references 4, 8, 9). His view of quality, based on economic implications of not meeting target specifications, was concerned about product design. The Taguchi premise is to "design the product to achieve high quality despite the variation that will occur on the production line (reference 5)."

By the end of the 1970s, U.S. industry was facing, as never before, intense foreign competition for domestic markets. Imports of manufactured goods grew dramatically, while many American industries failed to achieve comparable success in foreign markets. The consequences of this development were profound. At the macroeconomic level, the United States suffered trade deficits for some time. At the microeconomic level, whole industries declined, while others were forced to make rapid, and sometimes painful, adjustments to meet the competition. In these circumstances it is not surprising that American eyes turned toward their most successful competitor—the Japanese. There are, of course, many differences between Japanese and American social and economic organizations. A full discussion of these differences, in an attempt to explain the relative success of Japanese industry, would take us far beyond the scope of this book. For our purposes, it is sufficient to note that many Japanese products available in the American market came to acquire an enviable reputation for quality. It is the recognition by much of America's industry of the need to meet this challenge that explains the rapid growth in the implementation of statistical methods in the United States since the 1980s.

Some of the benefits of these methods should be obvious:

1. *Increased productivity.* If substandard parts resulting from process defects are detected early and corrected, then much wastage of time and material can be avoided. The implementation of successful statistical process control can lead to the production of greater volume and higher product quality without increased cost or worker effort.
2. *Increased sales.* A deserved reputation for product quality is a huge asset in the competitive marketplace. Such a reputation is generally hard-won, but in many industries its absence can prove fatal.
3. *Increased profits.* The net effect of reduced unit costs of production and increased sales is, of course, felt in the corporate bottom line. Quality control methods are now in widespread use because they are profitable.

Variation

Quality begins with a complete analysis of the system and process used to produce goods or services. In Chapter 1 a system was defined as a number of components that are logically and sometimes physically linked together for some purpose, and that a process is a set of activities operating on a system that transforms inputs to outputs. The objective is to identify all of the factors that contribute to the production of the final product and hence contribute to product quality. Problems that result in product defects must be identified and corrected. "Every process has *input* to which the process adds *value* to produce output.... Outcome indicators measure the output of the process and are fed back into the process for process adjustment and/or removal of defects that inhibit the achievement of the customer requirements" (reference 6). This general process model is illustrated in Figure 16.1 (reference 6).

From input to output, management will use statistical thinking (see Chapter 1) to monitor and improve the process. Notice in Figure 16.1 that management must first know that input meets or exceeds quality standards, or the old problem "garbage in/garbage out" takes place. For example, automobile manufacturers require suppliers of input, such as rubber molding for doors, to meet specified standards. The space program and airplane manufacturers require suppliers of parts, such as welded metal bellows, to certify the quality standards of their products. Throughout the process stage, statistical methods are used to monitor and correct defects. Necessary adjustments will be made to the process. Constant feedback contributes to continued process and product/service improvement.

One of the fundamental principles of statistical thinking is that *variation exists in all processes* (see Chapter 1). It is important to understand variation in order to predict the

FIGURE 16.1
General Process Model

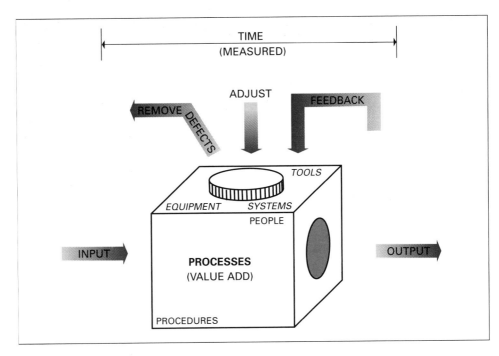

future performance of the process. To begin a study of statistical tools that are used for process improvement, first consider two causes of process variation: common causes and assignable causes.

COMMON AND ASSIGNABLE CAUSES OF VARIATION

Common causes of variation (also called random or uncontrollable causes) are those causes that are random in occurrence and are inherent in all processes. Management, not the workers, are responsible for these causes. **Assignable causes of variation** (also called special causes) are the result of external sources, that is, sources that are outside the system. These causes can and must be detected, and corrective action must be taken to remove them from the process. Failing to do so will increase variation and lower quality.

From the general process model of Figure 16.1, defects resulting from assignable causes are removed and necessary adjustments are made to the process. Examples of common causes include unpleasant working conditions (too hot or too cold) or random human error. Some examples of assignable causes are a defective batch of raw materials, operator errors, or machine-setting errors. Assignable causes must be removed; random causes will always be inherent in a process. Only when all assignable causes are removed is a process stable.

STABLE PROCESS

A process is **stable** (in-control) if all assignable causes are removed; thus, variation results only from common causes.

Although the importance of product quality has been discussed, it is not yet clear where statistical methods enter the picture. They do so because the typical quality control procedure, once implemented, must necessarily involve *sampling* and *statistical analysis*. The aim is to monitor an operational production process. Almost inevitably, it will not be feasible to measure the characteristics of every item produced. Instead, relatively small samples of items are drawn from time to time and measurements taken, so that progress over time can be charted and any changes can be noted and investigated. The important point is that inference about the behavior of the process will be based on statistical evidence. In addition, since product measurements are made on the shop floor—and ideally, judgments should be made fairly quickly—it is desirable that relatively simple methods, such as control charts, be used.

A control chart is a time plot of a process characteristic, such as *central tendency* or *variation*. There are several types of control charts, whose applicability depends on the type of data available and the variables to be monitored. In this chapter, four of the most common control charts are introduced. These are the $\overline{X}$-chart (for averages), the s-chart (for variation), the p-chart (for proportion of nonconforming items) and the c-chart (for the number of occurrences of some event, such as imperfections). A discussion of the R-chart (for ranges) is included in the Appendix to this chapter. All control charts have a center line (CL), a lower control limit (LCL), and an upper control limit (UCL). Measurements taken at periodic intervals are plotted on control charts and examined for patterns that suggest a potential problem resulting from assignable causes.

The importance of statistical ideas in quality control lies in the understanding of *variability* and *chance*. The production process that manufactures *identical* items has not been invented—and never will be. It is inevitable, in practice, that there will be some variability in item characteristics. Therefore, in looking for changes in production characteristics over time, it is important not to be misled by mere chance variability.

EXERCISES

16.1 Select one of the 50 states in the United States that gives a quality award. Write a short essay including the name of the award, the criteria that is used to grant this award, the date that the award was established, the types of organizations that are eligible to receive this award, and a brief synopsis of a recent recipient of that state's award. Why do you think that organization received this particular award? Include references and Web site addresses.

16.2 Select a European or Asian quality award. Write a short essay including the name of the award, the criteria that is used to grant this award, the date that the award was

established, the types of organizations that are eligible to receive this award, and a brief synopsis of a recent recipient of this award. What were the quality initiatives of this particular recipient that were recognized by this award? Include references and Web site addresses.

16.3 Discuss Deming's 14 points for quality organizations (references 2, 11).

16.4 Check at least three of the Web sites listed at the end of this chapter. Discuss the type of information available at these Web sites.

16.5 Search the Web and discuss at least five other Web sites pertinent to quality.

16.2   CONTROL CHARTS FOR MEANS AND STANDARD DEVIATIONS

Consider now a production process that yields an output whose characteristic of interest can be measured on a continuum. It is desired to set up a quality control scheme for that process. This can be achieved by taking, over time, a sequence of small samples of output. Often, samples of four or five observations are taken, and, to establish a reasonable record of performance, it is desirable to have twenty or more samples. The frequency of sample observations over time depends on the characteristics of the production process. Management will be interested in both the average performance of the process and the variability in performance. Too much variability would indicate that many substandard items are being produced, even if the average performance is adequate.

In this section the sample means and standard deviations are used to track process performance. These quantities are plotted on control charts. Control limits are set to help understand the fluctuations over time of the sample mean and sample standard deviation. Before proceeding, however, it should be noted that while use of the mean is quite standard, in some applications the range rather than the standard deviation is used to assess variability. Presumably, the attraction of this option is that the range—that is, the difference between the largest and smallest sample observation—is more easily calculated on the shop floor where control exercises are implemented on-the-job. However, this may no longer be the case given the wide availability of electronic calculators, which routinely compute sample means and sample standard deviations, requiring only the input of the sample observations. Details of control chart construction when the range is used instead of the standard deviation are discussed in the chapter Appendix. The principles of control chart construction and interpretation are essentially the same whichever measure of variability is used, though the details differ somewhat.

Three measures used in the development of control charts for means and standard deviations are the overall mean, the average sample standard deviation, and the process standard deviation.

OVERALL MEAN, AVERAGE SAMPLE STANDARD DEVIATION, PROCESS STANDARD DEVIATION

A sequence of K samples, each of n observations, is taken over time on a measurable characteristic of the output of a production process. The sample means denoted $\overline{X}_i$ for $i = 1, 2, \ldots, K$ can be graphed on an $\overline{X}$-chart. The **average of these sample means** is the **overall mean** of all the sample observations

$$\overline{\overline{X}} = \sum_{i=1}^{K} \overline{X}_i / K \tag{16.1}$$

The sample standard deviations denoted s_i for $i = 1, 2, \ldots, K$ can be graphed on an s-chart. The **average sample standard deviation** is

$$\overline{s} = \sum_{i=1}^{K} s_i / K \tag{16.2}$$

The **process standard deviation**, σ, is the standard deviation of the population from which the samples were drawn, and it must be estimated from sample data.

An Estimate of the Process Standard Deviation

As a step toward setting control limits in both the $\overline{X}$-chart and s-chart, it is necessary to estimate the process standard deviation, σ. One possibility would be to base this estimate on the overall sample standard deviation of all the observations. However, in applied quality control work it is more usual to base an estimate of σ on $\overline{s}$, the average sample standard deviation. Whichever estimate is used, recall that the sample standard deviation is a biased estimator of the population standard deviation. It is desirable to attempt to correct for this bias. In fact, when it is known that the population distribution is normal, it is possible to find an expression for the expected value of the sample standard deviation. If the sample standard deviation s_i is based on n observations, it can be shown that

$$E(s_i) = c_4 \sigma$$

where c_4 is a number that can be computed as a function of the sample size n. It follows immediately that

$$E(\overline{s}) = c_4 \sigma$$

and hence that an unbiased estimate of the process standard deviation is given by $\hat{\sigma} = \bar{s}/c_4$. Of course, the population distribution may not be exactly normal. Nevertheless, it is felt that this correction is worth making and that it will usually reduce the bias inherent in the sample standard deviation as an estimator of the corresponding population quantity.

ESTIMATE OF PROCESS STANDARD DEVIATION BASED ON S

An **estimate of process standard deviation**, $\hat{\sigma}$, is

$$\hat{\sigma} = \bar{s}/c_4 \qquad (16.3)$$

where $\bar{s}$ is the average sample standard deviation, and the control chart factor, c_4, which depends on the sample size n, can be found in Table 16.1 or the Factors for Control Charts table in the Appendix. If the population distribution is normal, the estimator is unbiased.

Table 16.1 lists values of c_4 corresponding to sample sizes ranging from two to ten. Also shown in that table are factors for other control charts that will be discussed throughout this chapter. A more complete table of factors is in the appendix. In practical quality control work, tables of control chart factors are available and routinely used.

The following example, based on the data file **Signal**, will be referred to throughout this chapter.

TABLE 16.1
Factors for Control Charts

N	C_4	A_3	B_3	B_4
2	.789	2.66	0	3.27
3	.886	1.95	0	2.57
4	.921	1.63	0	2.27
5	.940	1.43	0	2.09
6	.952	1.29	0.03	1.97
7	.959	1.18	0.12	1.88
8	.965	1.10	0.18	1.82
9	.969	1.03	0.24	1.76
10	.973	0.98	0.28	1.72

EXAMPLE 16.1

TIMING SIGNAL EMITTED BY AN ELECTRONIC COMPONENT
$(\bar{\bar{X}}, \bar{s}, \hat{\sigma})$

Signal

The duration, in milliseconds, for a timing signal emitted by an electronic component for a sequence of twenty samples, each of five observations, is listed in Table 16.2 and contained in the data file **Signal**. Find the overall mean, the average sample standard deviation, and an estimate of the process standard deviation.

SOLUTION

Table 16.2 includes the sample mean and sample standard deviation for each observation period. The overall sample mean, which is simply the average of all 100 sample observations, is

$$\bar{\bar{X}} = \frac{(298.2 + 300.6 + \cdots + 300.4)}{20} = 299.9$$

The average of the sample standard deviations is

$$\bar{s} = \frac{(2.77 + 2.51 + \cdots + 3.21)}{20} = 4.48$$

TABLE 16.2
Duration, in Milliseconds, of
Timing Signal Emitted by an
Electronic Component

SAMPLE NUMBER						SAMPLE MEAN	SAMPLE ST. DEV.
1	297	296	297	303	298	298.2	2.77
2	301	301	300	304	297	300.6	2.51
3	297	306	296	302	304	301.0	4.36
4	296	302	299	298	309	300.8	5.07
5	305	304	293	309	293	300.8	7.36
6	298	294	303	306	305	301.2	5.07
7	297	304	299	298	306	300.8	3.96
8	292	292	307	295	300	297.8	6.38
9	295	297	307	304	306	301.8	5.45
10	296	297	309	297	305	300.8	5.85
11	299	301	290	298	297	297.0	4.18
12	303	307	296	298	294	299.6	5.32
13	301	292	313	302	307	303.0	7.78
14	299	298	300	301	295	298.6	2.30
15	299	299	306	303	298	301.0	3.39
16	301	303	297	298	304	300.6	3.05
17	300	296	301	300	304	300.2	2.86
18	295	293	300	299	289	295.2	4.49
19	298	298	306	297	295	298.8	4.21
20	296	303	300	304	299	300.4	3.21

From Table 16.1 with $n = 5$ observations,

$$c_4 = 0.940$$

Therefore, an estimate of the process standard deviation is found to be:

$$\hat{\sigma} = \frac{\bar{s}}{c_4} = \frac{4.48}{0.940} = 4.77$$

Control Charts for Means

Table 16.2 listed mean durations for timing signals for a sequence of twenty samples of five observations each taken over time. In quality control work, for ease of interpretation, such information is invariably graphed on a time plot, such as an $\overline{X}$-chart or an s-chart. First, statistical procedures to obtain control charts are studied, and then an interpretation of charts for indications of process instability is considered.

For production management, it is important to look for signals of deterioration in quality. One possible indication of such a problem would be a sample mean that deviates substantially from the "usual" performance. For example, from Table 16.2 the mean for the eighteenth sample is 295.2, a value somewhat lower than the previous ones. Is this the kind of result that one might reasonably expect through sampling variability? In quality control, this judgment is made through comparison with control limits drawn on the control charts.

To determine control limits for $\overline{X}$-charts, it is assumed that the process has been operating at a constant level of performance over the whole observation period and that all sample observations can be viewed as having been drawn from the same normal distribution. The mean of that distribution is estimated by the overall mean, $\overline{\overline{X}}$, of all sample observations, and the standard deviation is estimated by $\hat{\sigma}$ as given in Equation 16.3.

Consider now a single sample of five observations, viewing them as having been drawn from a normal distribution with mean $\overline{\overline{X}}$ and standard deviation $\hat{\sigma}$. The sampling distribution of this sample mean is normal, with mean $\overline{\overline{X}}$ and standard error $\hat{\sigma}/\sqrt{n} = \hat{\sigma}/\sqrt{5}$. This result is used as the basis for setting control limits.

When a problem is indicated, some investigative action needs to be taken. This may involve the interruption and thorough investigation of the production process, which can be quite costly. Naturally, it is undesirable that this should occur frequently when, in fact, the process is functioning satisfactorily. To guard against the occurrence of too many "false signals" of this sort, it is usual in quality control work to set control limits of three standard errors on either side of the mean of the sampling distribution. (These are sometimes called 3σ limits.) Then, if the distribution of the sample statistic—here the sample mean—is normal, the probability of a value outside the 3σ limits is

$$P(Z > 3) + P(Z < -3) = 2(0.0014) = 0.0028$$

where Z is a standard normal random variable. Thus, if limits are set in this way, under the assumptions stated the probability of a false signal for any particular sample is less than three in one thousand. Of course, typically these assumptions will not be absolutely true, so this figure is only approximate. Nevertheless, it should provide a reasonable guide, and the use of 3σ limits is very common.

Returning now to the construction of control charts for sample means, the sampling distribution is centered on the overall mean $\overline{\overline{X}}$, and this *center line* is drawn on the chart. Then, if three-standard error limits are to be used, the control limits are

$$\overline{\overline{X}} \pm 3\,\hat{\sigma}/\sqrt{n} = \overline{\overline{X}} \pm 3\,\overline{s}/(c_4\,\sqrt{n}) = \overline{\overline{X}} \pm A_3\overline{s} \quad \text{where} \quad A_3 = \frac{3}{c_4\sqrt{n}}$$

$\overline{X}$-CHART

The $\overline{X}$**-chart** is a time plot of the sequence of sample means. The **center line** is

$$CL_{\overline{X}} = \overline{\overline{X}} \tag{16.4}$$

In addition, there are three-standard error control limits. The **lower control limit** is

$$LCL_{\overline{X}} = \overline{\overline{X}} - A_3\overline{s} \tag{16.5}$$

and the **upper control limit** is

$$UCL_{\overline{X}} = \overline{\overline{X}} + A_3\overline{s} \tag{16.6}$$

where certain values of A_3 are given in Table 16.1 or the Control Chart Constants Table in the Appendix.

EXAMPLE 16.2

TIMING SIGNAL CONTROL CHART FOR MEANS ($\overline{X}$-CHART)

Signal

Construct the $\overline{X}$-chart for the timing signal example with the data file **Signal**.

SOLUTION

Referring to Table 16.1 and to previous calculations, with a sample size of five

$$\overline{\overline{X}} = 299.9 \qquad \overline{s} = 4.48 \qquad A_3 = 1.$$

The center line is

$$CL_{\overline{X}} = \overline{\overline{X}} = 299.9$$

FIGURE 16.2
$\overline{X}$-Chart for Timing Signal
Example

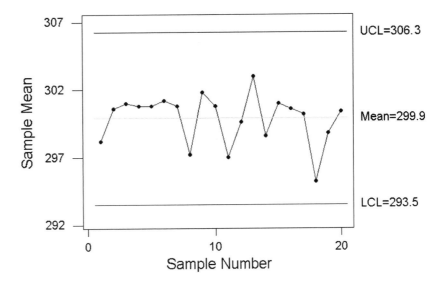

The lower control limit is

$$LCL_{\overline{X}} = \overline{\overline{X}} - A_3\overline{s} = 299.9 - (1.43)(4.48) = 293.5$$

and the upper control limit is

$$UCL_{\overline{X}} = \overline{\overline{X}} + A_3\overline{s} = 299.9 + (1.43)(4.48) = 306.3$$

Each of the individual sample means, $\overline{X}_i$, are now plotted on the $\overline{X}$-chart in Figure 16.2.

Control Charts for Standard Deviations

To assess the progress of process variability over time, the standard deviations can also be plotted on a control chart called an *s*-chart. The center line on this chart is the average sample standard deviation, $\overline{s}$, and it is usual to set three-standard error limits.

S-CHART

The *s*-chart is a time plot of the sequence of sample standard deviations. The **center line** on an *s*-chart is

$$CL_s = \overline{s} \qquad (16.7)$$

For three-standard error limits, the **lower control limit** is

$$LCL_s = B_3\overline{s} \qquad (16.8)$$

and the **upper control limit** is

$$UCL_s = B_4\overline{s} \qquad (16.9)$$

where values for the control chart constants B_3 and B_4 are shown in Table 16.1.

For samples of size $n \leq 5$, subtracting three standard errors from $\overline{s}$ gives a negative number. Obviously, standard deviations cannot be negative, so the lower limit is taken to be 0. In practice, there will rarely be concern about too little variability, so the lower limit is usually not of much interest.

EXAMPLE 16.3

TIMING SIGNAL CONTROL CHART FOR STANDARD DEVIATIONS (S-CHART)

Signal

Use the data file **Signal** to find the s-chart for the timing signal example.

SOLUTION

To construct the s-chart for the data in the file **Signal** (Table 16.2), it follows that

$$\bar{s} = 4.48 \qquad B_3 = 0 \qquad B_4 = 2.09$$

Therefore, the three lines on our chart are

$$CL_s = 4.48 \qquad LCL_s = 0 \qquad UCL_s = (2.09)(4.48) = 9.36$$

Next, plot each of the individual standard deviations, s_i, on a control chart with center line, $CL_s = 4.48$, lower control limit, $LCL_s = 0$, and upper control limit, $UCL_s = 9.36$. The s-chart will look like Figure 16.3 which was obtained with Minitab.

FIGURE 16.3

s-Chart for Timing Signal Example

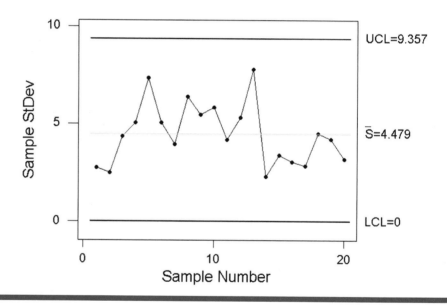

Interpretation of Control Charts

Having developed initial control charts to monitor average performance and variability in performance, some further analysis and interpretation is necessary. Experience and judgment along with an understanding of control chart patterns lead to improvements. A brief discussion of some issues that might be involved is included. The central issue is an assessment of the performance of the process over the observation period.

If a process is stable, the points on a control chart will fluctuate randomly between the upper and lower control limits and there will be no nonrandom pattern of points. Essentially, at this stage, the analyst is looking for a pattern of data points distributed more or less randomly around the center line and generally well within the control limits. From this perspective, Figures 16.2 and 16.3 look quite reasonable. In those circumstances, the process under study appears to be *in control*, meaning that its performance characteristics appear to be quite stable. Statistical quality control can be viewed as a means of determining whether a process is in control, as an aid to keeping the process in control, and as a mechanism for inducing reduced variability in product quality.

If a process is not stable, it is possible that the data is unreliable or that a process subject to serious operating problems generated the data. Such data will not provide us with a reliable indication of what can be expected when the process is operating normally. Assignable causes that contribute to process instability are brought to management's attention through various control chart patterns. Thus, interpretation of control charts begins with understanding various patterns that indicate an *out-of-control* situation.

There are several patterns of control chart data points that indicate that a process might be out of control. Only three tests that check for this possibility are included here. For additional tests and more extensive study see the reference section of this chapter.

OUT OF CONTROL PATTERNS

Certain patterns of data points in a control chart indicate that a process might be **out-of control**. Three of these patterns are:

1. A value outside the control limits (one point more than 3 sigmas from center line)
2. Trend in sample statistics (six points in a row, all increasing or decreasing)
3. Too many points on one side of the center line (nine points in a row on same side of center line)

---

1. **A Value Outside the Control Limits**

   Consider Figure 16.4A. Most of the sample statistics (in this particular illustration, the sample means) are well within the control limits. However, for sample 7, the statistic is outside these limits; that is, the sample mean is greater than the mean plus 3 sigma, which is the Upper Control Limit, 308.5. With three-standard error limits this would be an extremely unusual occurrence for a process that is in control. What exists is a phenomenon that requires investigation. The analyst needs to do some detective work, seeking the cause of this extreme value. It will likely emerge that this is not a mere chance variability, but arose from some peculiar assignable cause. It is wise to check first if that assignable cause is merely that the value of an observation had been incorrectly recorded.

2. **Trend in Sample Statistics (six points in a row, all increasing or decreasing)**

   Figure 16.4B is clearly one of nonrandomness. The sample statistics do not appear to be randomly dispersed around the center line. Rather, there is a tendency for them to increase over time, with the last eight points all increasing in value. This increasing variability is cause for concern, even though no sample value has fallen outside the control limits. Perhaps the cause is deteriorating machinery.

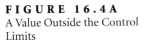

FIGURE 16.4A
A Value Outside the Control Limits

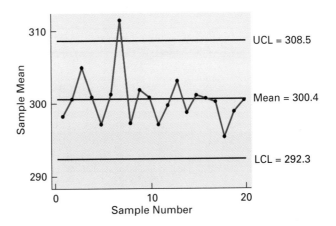

FIGURE 16.4B
Trend in Sample Standard
Deviations

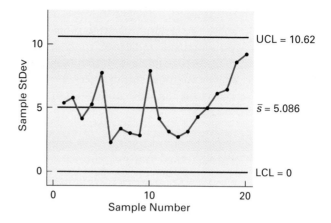

3. **Too Many Points on One Side of Center Line (nine points in a row on same side of center line)**

In Figure 16.4C nine consecutive points (representing sample standard deviations) fall below the center line. Investigation for assignable causes may reveal a potential problem area.

Only when there is some assurance that a production process is in control is it reasonable to proceed. Look back to Figure 16.2 and Figure 16.3 for the Signal data to see if there are indications of out-of control patterns. There seems to be no great cause for concern. None of the sample means is outside the control limits, and indeed the great majority of the sample means are well within those limits. Earlier we questioned if the mean of sample eighteen, 295.2, was a signal of concern. Apparently, there is no cause for alarm. Similarly, there does not seem to be cause for undue concern for process variability as indicated by the s-chart in Figure 16.3. The observed sample standard deviations are generally well below the upper control limit. There is some suggestion of increased variability in the central portion of the observation period, for which it might perhaps be worthwhile seeking an explanation in order to learn more about the production process. Neither of the two control charts for the data file Signal suggests that assignable causes are present in the system.

The next section considers determining if a stable process meets design specifications.

FIGURE 16.4C
Too Many Points on the Same
Side of the Center Line

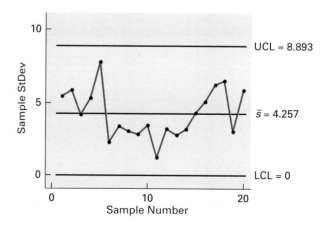

EXERCISES

16.6 The production process for an electronic component has been monitored, and the strength of electrical emission of the components has been measured. Results are available for a sequence of thirty samples, each of seven observations. The overall mean of the sample observations was 192.6, and the average sample standard deviation was 5.42.

(a) Use an unbiased estimator to find an estimate of the process standard deviation.

(b) Find the center line and lower and upper control limits for an $\overline{X}$-chart.

(c) Find the center line and lower and upper control limits for an s-chart.

16.7 Measures are taken on the resistance, in ohms, of an electrical component. A sequence of twenty-five samples, each of six observations, was drawn. The overall mean of the sample observations was 93.2 and the average sample standard deviation was 3.67.

(a) Use an unbiased estimator to find an estimate of the process standard deviation.

(b) Find the center line and lower and upper control limits for an $\overline{X}$-chart.

(c) Find the center line and lower and upper control limits for an s-chart.

16.8 Weights of samples of canned fruit were measured. A sequence of sixteen samples, each of eight observations, was taken. The overall mean of the sample observations was 19.86 ounces, and the average sample standard was 1.23 ounces.

(a) Use an unbiased estimator to find an estimate of the process standard deviation.

(b) Find the center line and lower and upper control limits for an $\overline{X}$-chart.

(c) Find the center line and lower and upper control limits for an s-chart.

16.9 Recall Example 2.1. Jennie Bishop, the operations manager at a suntan lotion manufacturing plant, wants to be sure that the filling process for a new product, SunProtector, is operating properly. Currently, the company is testing the weights of 8-oz. (237-mL) bottles of SunProtector. Measurements were taken of the weights of the 8-oz. bottles. A sequence of 25 samples, each of five observations, was taken. The overall mean of the sample observations was 230.5 mL, and the average sample standard deviation was 1.75 mL.

(a) Use an unbiased estimator to find an estimate of the process standard deviation.

(b) Find the center line and lower and upper control limits for an $\overline{X}$-chart.

(c) Find the center line and lower and upper control limits for an s-chart.

16.10 🌐 The accompanying table shows sample means and standard deviations for a sequence of thirty samples of eight observations each on a quality characteristic of a product. The data file is simply **Exercise 16-10**.

SAMPLE	$\overline{X}$	s	SAMPLE	$\overline{X}$	s	SAMPLE	$\overline{X}$	s
1	148.2	2.26	11	156.0	4.79	21	148.7	6.28
2	146.4	4.37	12	150.4	3.92	22	149.7	8.92
3	149.9	7.93	13	148.7	8.31	23	151.3	6.20
4	152.8	6.79	14	151.1	7.29	24	150.8	7.39
5	148.7	5.31	15	147.2	3.80	25	147.2	6.97
6	150.6	3.17	16	152.9	4.87	26	141.9	9.68
7	151.5	6.15	17	150.7	3.88	27	152.7	4.28
8	149.2	4.71	18	147.2	8.93	28	148.6	6.51
9	153.9	5.82	19	149.4	6.85	29	150.2	7.29
10	150.6	4.98	20	154.3	7.29	30	148.6	4.73

(a) Find the overall mean of the sample observations.

(b) Find the average sample standard deviation.

(c) Use an unbiased estimator to find an estimate of the process standard deviation.

(d) Find the center line and lower and upper control limits for an $\overline{X}$-chart.

(e) Draw the $\overline{X}$-chart and discuss its features.

(f) Find the center line and lower and upper control limits for an s-chart.

(g) Draw the s-chart and discuss its features.

16.11 🌐 The accompanying table shows sample means and standard deviations for a sequence of twenty samples of six observations each on content weights of cans of vegetables, in ounces. The data file is called **Exercise 16-11**.

SAMPLE	$\overline{X}$	s	SAMPLE	$\overline{X}$	s	SAMPLE	$\overline{X}$	s
1	20.2	1.9	8	21.0	2.3	15	20.7	1.9
2	18.9	2.7	9	20.6	1.4	16	19.3	2.2
3	19.6	1.7	10	19.1	2.7	17	19.9	3.1
4	20.8	2.3	11	18.8	2.9	18	18.8	2.9
5	19.4	1.2	12	19.3	1.1	19	19.6	2.2
6	19.8	2.1	13	19.8	1.3	20	20.1	1.1
7	20.9	1.6	14	20.2	1.2			

(a) Find the overall mean of the sample observations.

(b) Find the average sample standard deviation.

(c) Use an unbiased estimator to find an estimate of the process standard deviation.

(d) Find the center line and lower and upper control limits for an $\overline{X}$-chart.

(e) Draw the $\overline{X}$-chart and discuss its features.

(f) Find the center line and lower and upper control limits for an s-chart.

(g) Draw the s-chart and discuss its features.

16.3   PROCESS CAPABILITY

Section 16.2 concerned the use of control charts, aided by control limits, to judge whether a process was in control—that is, whether its performance was stable. However, this information is insufficient to assess whether the process is performing adequately to the standards for which it was designed. After all, a consistent performance could be consistently mediocre, or even consistently poor. Before proceeding further with a quality control or quality improvement program, it is important to determine whether the production process is operating to required specifications. If a process is currently in control, is it *capable* of meeting these specifications? This judgment is formed on the basis of data generated by a process that appears to be in control. Therefore, if the sample record includes extreme observations due to assignable causes, these problems should be corrected before assessing *process capability*. More seriously, when it appears that things have been going wrong over the sample observation period, as for example in cases such as those illustrated in Figure 16.3B and Figure 16.3C, corrective action may need to be taken by the engineers. Only when an in-control mode has been established is it possible to go on to assess process capability.

A common problem, approached through the analysis of sample means and sample standard deviations, is considered in this section. Typically, management will set a range for the values of some characteristic of process output, bounded by lower and upper **specification limits.** In the case of the duration of a timing signal emitted by an electronic component, management may have set a range of tolerable values running from 280 to 320 milliseconds, in order to assure that the product performs at a quality level. A process capable of meeting these specifications is one that is very likely to produce output in this range.

For a process that is in control, it is natural to base an assessment of capability on all the sample observations, and, in particular, on estimates of the process mean and standard deviation based on these observations. For the timing signal data, the estimates are

$$\overline{\overline{X}} = 299.9 \qquad \hat{\sigma} = 4.77$$

Then, if the process distribution is assumed to be normal, approximately 99.72% of all output should fall within three standard deviations of the mean. It is common, then, in quality control work to calculate the interval $\overline{\overline{X}} \pm 3\hat{\sigma}$. In our example,

$$(\overline{\overline{X}} - 3\hat{\sigma}, \overline{\overline{X}} + 3\hat{\sigma}) = (285.6, 314.2)$$

These are the limits within which the process will normally perform. The width of this interval

$$6\hat{\sigma} = (6)(4.77) = 28.6$$

is sometimes called the **natural tolerance** of the process. It provides a measure of the variability in product specifications that can be expected.

Having used the sample data to assess what a production process actually can do, it is only necessary to compare this finding with management specifications of what the process ought to do. What is required is that the interval, $\overline{\overline{X}} \pm 3\hat{\sigma}$, lies between, and preferably comfortably between, the lower and upper specification limits. The timing signal data appear quite satisfactory from this point of view. The interval from 285.6 to 314.2 is comfortably between 280 and 320 milliseconds. It appears that the process is capable of meeting these specifications. Notice here that the overall sample mean of 299.9 is very near the center, 300 milliseconds, of the tolerance range. In such circumstances, the performance interval is said to be *centered* in the tolerance range. Such centering will often occur and will frequently be desirable. It is not, however, necessary for a performance interval to be centered in the tolerance range in order for the process to be capable of meeting standards.

More formal measures of process capability are the capability index and the C_{pk} index. You will find, as the authors have, that in companies dedicated to process improvement, employees are knowledgeable about these measures of process capability and understand their significance.

MEASURES OF PROCESS CAPABILITY

Assume that management sets lower (L) and upper (U) tolerance limits for process performance. Process capability is judged by the extent to which $\overline{\overline{X}} \pm 3\hat{\sigma}$ lies between these limits.

1. **Capability Index.** This measure is appropriate when the sample data are **centered** between the tolerance limits, i.e. $\overline{\overline{X}} \approx (L + U)/2$. The index is

$$C_p = \frac{U - L}{6\hat{\sigma}} \tag{16.10}$$

A satisfactory value of this index is usually taken to be one that is at least 1.33. [This implies that the **natural tolerance** of the process should be no more than 75% of $(U - L)$, the width of the range of acceptable values.]

2. **C_{pk} Index.** When the sample data are not centered between the tolerance limits, it is necessary to allow for the fact that the process is operating closer to one tolerance limit than the other. The resulting measure, called the C_{pk} index, is

$$C_{pk} = \text{Min}\left[\frac{U - \overline{\overline{X}}}{3\hat{\sigma}}, \frac{\overline{\overline{X}} - L}{3\hat{\sigma}}\right] \tag{16.11}$$

Again, this is taken to be satisfactory if its value is at least 1.33.

EXAMPLE 16.4

TIMING SIGNAL CAPABILITY (CAPABILITY INDICES)

Signal

Consider again the case of the duration of a timing signal emitted by an electronic component and suppose that management set a range of tolerable values running from 280 to 320 milliseconds. Determine if the production process for the timing signal example stored in the data file **Signal** (Table 16.2) is capable of meeting specifications? Use the capability measures given in Equations 16.10 and 16.11.

SOLUTION

For the timing signal data,

$$\overline{\overline{X}} = 299.9 \qquad \hat{\sigma} = 4.77 \qquad L = 280 \qquad U = 320$$

Hence, the capability index is

$$C_p = \frac{U - L}{6\hat{\sigma}} = \frac{320 - 280}{6(4.77)} = 1.398$$

The C_{pk} index is

$$C_{pk} = \text{Min}\left[\frac{U - \overline{\overline{X}}}{3\hat{\sigma}}, \frac{\overline{\overline{X}} - L}{3\hat{\sigma}}\right] = \text{Min}(1.405, 1.391) = 1.391$$

In this particular case, since the sample data are, for all practical purposes, centered, the two indices are virtually identical. Both comfortably exceed 1.33 indicating that the production process is capable of meeting the specifications.

Once process capability has been assessed, either the process is not capable of meeting the specifications or the process is capable of meeting the set of performance standards. Suppose that the process is found to be incapable of meeting the specifications. This type of problem must be turned over to management for further analysis and correction. It is not a problem for shop-floor production workers who may be able to point to the problem but are unlikely to be equipped to solve it. Perhaps capital equipment is inadequate for the job, possibly through deterioration. Perhaps the performance standards that have been set are overly and unnecessarily optimistic. Whatever the case, continued operation and analysis of the process in its current state is of little value.

The happier outcome is that the production process will be found to be capable of meeting the set performance standards. In that case, the quality control process can be continued. The production process should be regularly monitored, and control charts constructed. From time to time, as the process evolves, it is desirable to recompute control limits for these charts. Periodic checks of process capability should also be made. Quality control is not merely a passive activity. Neither is it only a mechanism for detecting problems, though it is certainly valuable for this purpose. The goal of a quality control exercise is improvement in quality, which can be viewed as a reduction in the natural tolerance of the process. These gains can arise from the greater awareness and understanding of good quality and its sources when production workers are involved in the collection and interpretation of data for quality control studies.

EXERCISES

16.12 Refer to Exercise 16.6. Management has specified that the strength of electrical emission of components produced by this process should be between 170 and 215.
- **(a)** Compute the interval $\overline{\overline{X}} \pm 3\hat{\sigma}$ and comment on your finding.
- **(b)** Find the capability index C_p and discuss the result.
- **(c)** Find the C_{pk} index and discuss the result.

16.13 Refer to Exercise 16.7. Management has specified that the resistance of components produced by this process should be between 85 and 100 ohms.
- **(a)** Compute the interval $\overline{\overline{X}} \pm 3\hat{\sigma}$ and comment on your finding.
- **(b)** Find the capability index C_p and discuss the result.
- **(c)** Find the C_{pk} index and discuss the result.

16.14 Refer to Exercise 16.8. Management has specified that the weights of canned fruit should be between 18 and 22 ounces.

- **(a)** Compute the interval $\overline{\overline{X}} \pm 3\hat{\sigma}$ and comment on the result.
- **(b)** Find and discuss the capability index C_p.
- **(c)** Find and discuss the C_{pk} index.

16.15 Refer to Exercise 16.10. Management has specified that the values of the quality characteristics for this process should be between 130 and 170.
- **(a)** Compute the interval $\overline{\overline{X}} \pm 3\hat{\sigma}$ and comment on your finding.
- **(b)** Find the capability index C_p and discuss the result.
- **(c)** Find the C_{pk} index and discuss the result.

16.16 Refer to Exercise 16.11. Management has determined that contents weights should be between 16 and 24 ounces.
- **(a)** Compute the interval $\overline{\overline{X}} \pm 3\hat{\sigma}$ and comment on your finding.
- **(b)** Find the capability index C_p and discuss the result.
- **(c)** Find the C_{pk} index and discuss the result.

16.4   CONTROL CHART FOR PROPORTIONS

Rather than analyzing numerical data that measures some characteristic of a product, consider now situations where individual product items will be judged to have conformed or not to have conformed to specifications. Again, a sequence of samples is taken over time to assess product quality, and the results are plotted on a control chart. It is important to distinguish between the terms *defect* and *defective*.

DEFECT AND DEFECTIVE

"A **defect** is a single nonconforming quality characteristic of an item. An item may have several defects. The term **defective** refers to items having one or more defects" (reference 5).

Our interest is the proportion of **nonconforming**, or **defective**, items in each sample. Obviously, it is desirable that this proportion be as small as possible, and any increasing trend over time should cause concern. The *p*-chart is used to monitor the proportion of *defective* items. In the next section the *c*-chart that is used to monitor for *defects* is discussed.

One important difference in the development of control charts for proportions, compared with the charts of Section 16.2, is that here much larger sample sizes are necessary. This is so because any competently engineered production process is not going to generate a large proportion of nonconforming items. Therefore, to get a reasonable assessment of this measure of quality, a relatively large sample is essential. For many applications, samples of between fifty and two hundred items each are recommended, though often larger samples are needed. A rule of thumb often employed in practice is that the average number of nonconforming items per sample should be at least five or six. So, for example, if it is expected that around 1% of all items will fail to conform to standards, then samples of at least 500 to 600 are required. One consequence of the need for large samples is that it may be desirable to take samples of unequal sizes. For example, it may be necessary to inspect the entire output of a day, or of a work shift, to generate sufficient observations. Typically, these numbers will not remain constant over time. For convenience, attention is here restricted to the case of equal sample sizes, though extension to the case of unequal sample sizes is quite straightforward.

A further important issue in the development of control charts for proportions of nonconforming items concerns the element of subjective judgment inherent in the generation of the data. Nonconformity to standards will be judged by inspectors, and, given the element of subjectivity that is involved, it is likely that different inspectors will not generate consistent results. In consequence, extra variability or the appearance of lack of control in the charts could result from inspector differences. It is important to be aware of this possibility in interpreting control charts for proportions. At the outset, when data are to be generated by more than one inspector, it is necessary to be as specific as possible in setting out the standards for nonconformity.

The average of sample proportions is given in Equation 16.12.

AVERAGE OF SAMPLE PROPORTIONS

A sequence of *K* samples, each of *n* observations, is taken over time, and the proportions of sample members **not conforming** to standards are determined. These sample proportions denoted p_i for $i = 1, 2, \ldots, K$ can be plotted on a *p*-chart. If the samples are of the same size, the **average of the sample proportions** is the **overall proportion of nonconforming** items. This is

$$\bar{p} = \sum_{i=1}^{K} \frac{p_i}{K} \qquad (16.12)$$

If the process has been operating consistently over the whole observation period, each of the samples can be viewed as having been drawn from a common population. The proportion of nonconforming items in that population is estimated by the average of the sample proportions, $\bar{p}$. Thus, recalling our discussion earlier in this book on the sampling distribution of sample proportions, the individual sample proportions p_i have sampling distribution with mean estimated by $\bar{p}$ and standard error given by

$$\hat{\sigma}_p = \sqrt{\frac{\bar{p}(1-\bar{p})}{n}}$$

As with other applications in quality control, standard practice here is to set three-standard error limits on the control charts.

---

p-CHART

The ***p*-chart** is a time plot of the sequence of sample proportions of nonconforming items with center line given by $CL_p = \bar{p}$. The lower and upper control limits are:

$$LCL_p = \bar{p} - 3\sqrt{\frac{\bar{p}(1-\bar{p})}{n}} \quad \text{and} \quad UCL_p = \bar{p} + 3\sqrt{\frac{\bar{p}(1-\bar{p})}{n}} \qquad \textbf{(16.13)}$$

The formula for the lower control limit given in Equation 16.13 can give a negative value, which is of course an impossible value for a proportion. In that case, the lower control limit is set at 0. In any case, breach of the lower limit will typically not cause concern. It may imply that the process is more reliable. However, another possibility might be poor performance by inspectors in detecting nonconforming items.

EXAMPLE 16.5

NONCONFORMING ELECTRONIC COMPONENTS (*P*-CHART)

Electronic Component

Twenty samples, each of 200 observations taken over time, of an electronic component are taken. For each sample, the numbers and proportions of sampled components not conforming to standards are recorded in Table 16.3 and stored in the data file **Electronic Component**. Construct the *p*-chart for this data.

SOLUTION

The average of these sample proportions is

$$\bar{p} = (0.090 + 0.075 + \cdots + 0.090)/20 = 0.096$$

The *p*-chart for the data of Table 16.3 is shown in Figure 16.5. The center line on the chart is

$$CL_p = \bar{p} = 0.096$$

TABLE 16.3
Nonconforming Items in Samples of 200 Electronic Components

SAMPLE NUMBER	NUMBER NONCONFORMING	P	SAMPLE NUMBER	NUMBER NONCONFORMING	P
1	18	.090	11	19	.095
2	15	.075	12	26	.130
3	23	.115	13	11	.155
4	9	.045	14	28	.140
5	17	.085	15	22	.110
6	29	.145	16	14	.070
7	11	.055	17	25	.125
8	21	.105	18	17	.085
9	25	.125	19	23	.115
10	14	.070	20	18	.090

FIGURE 16.5

p-Chart for Electronic Components Data of Table 16.3

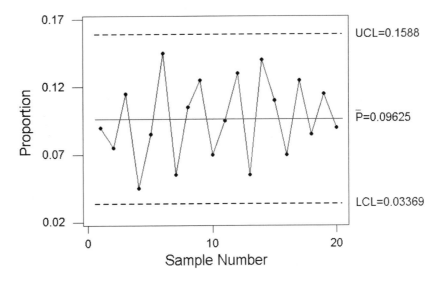

The lower control limit is

$$LCL_p = \bar{p} - 3\sqrt{\frac{\bar{p}(1-\bar{p})}{n}} = 0.096 - 3\sqrt{\frac{(0.096)(0.904)}{200}} = 0.096 - 0.062 = 0.034$$

and the upper control limit is

$$UCL_p = \bar{p} + 3\sqrt{\frac{\bar{p}(1-\bar{p})}{n}} = 0.096 + 3\sqrt{\frac{(0.096)(0.904)}{200}} = 0.096 + 0.062 = 0.158$$

Looking at Figure 16.5, it can be seen that all the sample proportions lie between the control limits and that the great majority are well within these limits. There is a suggestion of moderately high variability in quality, which might warrant further investigation. However, it would not be unreasonable to conclude from the chart that the process is in control. In that case, under current operating conditions, about 9.6% of all items produced will fail to conform to standards.

Interpretation of *p*-charts is similar to that of the charts of Section 16.2. Sample values that lie outside the control limits are further investigated, and if assignable causes for extreme values are found, these are eliminated and the control limits recalculated. A particular concern would be the appearance of an upward trend over time in a *p*-chart. This would suggest the possibility of an increasing proportion of nonconforming items—that is, deterioration in quality. Once it has been established that a process is in control, the limits can be used to evaluate further data. However, as with other control charts, it is good practice to compute the control limits periodically to account for improved performance as the quality exercise proceeds.

Of course, the analysis of nonconformities in this way may reveal that uncomfortably many substandard items are being produced. In that case, further analysis may be desirable and possible through Pareto diagrams. In Chapter 2 you learned that this type of graph is essentially a bar chart, isolating the individual causes of nonconformity. The various individual problems with the substandard items are listed, and the number of items in each category is calculated. The bar charts may be organized to display either the raw numbers of products with different types of defects or the total costs of correcting these defects. From these charts, management should be able to form a quick visual impression of where effort needs to be concentrated to achieve the greatest reduction in the nonconformities rate or in the cost of reworking nonconforming items. In this manner, the quality control exercise will have made a valuable contribution to trouble-shooting.

EXERCISES

16.17 In the study of an automotive component, 30 samples, each of 250 observations, were taken. The average of the sample proportions of nonconforming items was .056. Find the center line and lower and upper control limits for a p-chart.

16.18 In the study of an aircraft part, the manufacturer took 25 samples, each of 500 observations. The average of the sample proportions of nonconforming items was .016. Find the center line and lower and upper control limits for a p-chart.

16.19   The accompanying table shows proportions of nonconforming items in a sequence of 30 samples, each of 200 observations. The data file is **Exercise 16-19.**

SAMPLE NUMBER	p	SAMPLE NUMBER	p	SAMPLE NUMBER	p
1	.125	11	.135	21	.105
2	.140	12	.170	22	.135
3	.090	13	.105	23	.140
4	.085	14	.095	24	.085
5	.175	15	.130	25	.145
6	.160	16	.145	26	.175
7	.130	17	.155	27	.105
8	.135	18	.090	28	.130
9	.095	19	.125	29	.085
10	.115	20	.145	30	.090

(a) Find the center line and lower and upper control limits for a p-chart.
(b) Draw the p-chart and discuss its features.

16.20   Proportions of nonconforming items in a sequence of 20 samples, each of 500 observations, are given in the next table. The data file is called **Exercise 16-20.**

SAMPLE NUMBER	p	SAMPLE NUMBER	p	SAMPLE NUMBER	p
1	.048	8	.052	15	.068
2	.062	9	.032	16	.036
3	.056	10	.038	17	.030
4	.060	11	.048	18	.064
5	.038	12	.042	19	.056
6	.042	13	.076	20	.048
7	.066	14	.058		

(a) Find the center line and lower and upper control limits for a p-chart.
(b) Draw the p-chart and discuss its features.

16.21   The number of nonconforming items in a sequence of 25 samples, each of 250 observations, is given as follows. The data file is **Exercise 16-21.**

SAMPLE NUMBER	NUMBER NON-CONFORMING	SAMPLE NUMBER	NUMBER NON-CONFORMING	SAMPLE NUMBER	NUMBER NON-CONFORMING
1	23	10	15	18	26
2	15	11	25	19	12
3	18	12	17	20	16
4	12	13	11	21	23
5	28	14	25	21	20
6	22	15	19	23	16
7	21	16	23	24	15
8	19	17	21	25	22
9	36				

(a) Find the average of the sample proportions.
(b) Find the center line and lower and upper control limits for a p-chart.
(c) Draw the p-chart and discuss its features.

16.5   CONTROL CHARTS FOR NUMBER OF OCCURRENCES

Recall that the Poisson distribution can often be useful in representing the *number of occurrences* of an event. A common application in quality control is to inspect a finished item and to count the number of defects, or imperfections, of a particular type. If items are inspected over time, and *counts* of number of imperfections per item are recorded, this information can be presented in a control chart. This is called a *c-chart.*

As with the other control charts studied in this chapter, here are some general notations used for control charts for number of occurrences.

SAMPLE MEAN NUMBER OF OCCURRENCES

A sequence of K items is inspected over time. For each item, the number of occurrences of some event, such as an imperfection, is recorded. These *numbers of occurrences* are denoted c_i for $i = 1, 2, \ldots, K$. The **sample mean number of occurrences** is then

$$\bar{c} = \sum_{i=1}^{K} \frac{c_i}{K} \tag{16.14}$$

The sample mean number of occurrences, $\bar{c}$, provides an estimate of the population mean. Moreover, if the distribution of the number of occurrences is Poisson, the standard deviation of the distribution is the square root of the mean:

$$\hat{\sigma}_c = \sqrt{\bar{c}}$$

A control chart for the number of occurrences can be constructed in the usual way.

C-CHART

The **c-chart** is a time plot of the number of occurrences of an event. The center line is

$$CL_c = \bar{c} \tag{16.15}$$

For three-standard error limits, the lower control limit is

$$\begin{aligned} LCL_c &= \bar{c} - 3\sqrt{\bar{c}} & \text{if } \bar{c} > 9 \\ LCL_c &= 0 & \text{if } \bar{c} \leq 9 \end{aligned} \tag{16.16}$$

and the upper control limit is

$$UCL_c = \bar{c} + 3\sqrt{\bar{c}} \tag{16.17}$$

EXAMPLE 16.6

C-CHART FOR TEXTILE MANUFACTURER (*C*-CHART)

A manufacturer of textiles produces bolts of cloth. Periodically, a bolt is carefully inspected, and the number of imperfections is recorded. Table 16.4 shows a sequence of 20 such results, recorded over time. In situations such as this, it is convenient to have the same inspector examine each item. Then, any apparent trends that appear will not be due to differences in standards applied by, or experience of, different inspectors. Construct the *c*-chart. The data is found in the data file **Cloth**.

TABLE 16.4
Number of Imperfections in Bolts of Cloth

CLOTH BOLT	NUMBER OF IMPERFECTIONS	CLOTH BOLT	NUMBER OF IMPERFECTIONS	CLOTH BOLT	NUMBER OF IMPERFECTIONS
1	8	8	2	15	1
2	8	9	3	16	7
3	6	10	10	17	9
4	8	11	7	18	11
5	9	12	6	19	9
6	5	13	8	20	6
7	7	14	2		

FIGURE 16.6
c-Chart for Textile
Manufacturer

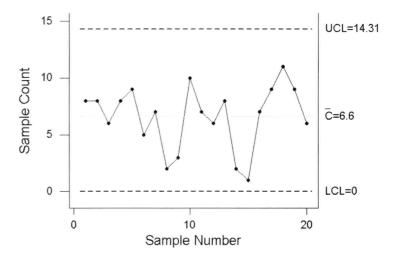

SOLUTION

In this example, the average number of imperfections per bolt of cloth is $\bar{c} = (8 + 8 + \cdots + 6)/20 = 6.6$.

This provides a natural estimate of the population mean number of imperfections per bolt. The standard deviation of the number of occurrences is estimated by

$$\sqrt{\bar{c}} = \sqrt{6.6} = 2.569$$

Since $\bar{c}$ is less than nine, the lower control limit is $LCL_c = 0$.

The upper control limit is $UCL_c = \bar{c} + 3\sqrt{\bar{c}} = 6.6 + 3\sqrt{6.6} = 14.3$.
Figure 16.6 shows the control chart for the data of Table 16.4.

Inspection of this *c*-chart suggests no cause for concern. The observations are all well below the upper control limit, and there is no evidence of an increasing number of imperfections over time. It appears, then, that the production process is in control.

Cloth

EXERCISES

16.22 A process produces rolls of coated paper. A sequence of 20 rolls were inspected over time and the numbers of imperfections were recorded. The results are shown in the accompanying table and stored in the data file **Paper**.

ROLL	NUMBER OF IMPERFECTIONS	ROLL	NUMBER OF IMPERFECTIONS	ROLL	NUMBER OF IMPERFECTIONS
1	1	8	6	15	2
2	7	9	4	16	6
3	5	10	8	17	8
4	6	11	6	18	12
5	9	12	5	19	5
6	4	13	6	20	4
7	1	14	7		

(a) Find the sample mean number of imperfections per roll.

(b) Find the center line and lower and upper limits for a *c*-chart.

(c) Draw the *c*-chart and discuss its features.

16.23 A newspaper reader has very carefully read her local paper for 20 weeks. For each Wednesday's edition she has counted the number of typographical and/or spelling errors. The results are shown in the accompanying table and stored in the data file **Newspaper**.

WEEK	ERRORS	WEEK	ERRORS	WEEK	ERRORS
1	12	8	21	15	7
2	19	9	14	16	18
3	8	10	7	17	12
4	11	11	13	18	13
5	15	12	19	19	13
6	17	13	11	20	20
7	11	14	10		

(a) Find the sample mean number of errors for these 20 Wednesdays.
(b) Find the center line and lower and upper control limits for a *c*-chart.
(c) Draw the *c*-chart and discuss its features.

16.24 A process manufactures raisin scones. Periodically, a scone is inspected and the number of raisins it contains is counted. The accompanying table shows results for 15 scones. Stored in data file **Raisins**.

SCONES	RAISINS	SCONES	RAISINS	SCONES	RAISINS
1	18	6	16	11	15
2	15	7	13	12	9
3	22	8	18	13	10
4	14	9	14	14	7
5	17	10	12	15	8

(a) Find the sample mean number of raisins per scone.
(b) Find the center line and lower and upper limits for a *c*-chart.
(c) Draw the *c*-chart and discuss its features.

16.6 COMPUTER APPLICATIONS

Now that you understand the basic structure of control charts, consider how statistical software packages are used to facilitate finding control limits and testing for out-of control patterns. For the purposes of this chapter, the authors found Minitab to be more satisfactory and user-friendly than Excel (for Excel, see reference 13). Therefore, comments are restricted to this software package. Minitab is useful to obtain $\overline{X}$-charts, *s*-charts, *p*-charts and *c*-charts, as well as for process indices, such as C_p and C_{pk}.

Minitab Output for Xbar and *s*-Charts

The $\overline{X}$-chart is written as Xbar chart in Minitab. Both it and the *s*-chart for the timing signal example (Example 16.1) using the data file **Signal** are easily found with Minitab. Minitab instructions are given in Figure 16.7. The Minitab output given in Figure 16.8 is similar to Figure 16.2 and Figure 16.3 with the inclusion of the three-sigma limit lines chosen under Options.

Minitab Output for Capability Analysis (Normal)

Remember that a process must be stable before you consider process capability. Recall from Example 16.4 that the capability index is

$$C_p = \frac{U - L}{6\hat{\sigma}} = \frac{320 - 280}{6(4.77)} = 1.398$$

FIGURE 16.7
Minitab Dialog Box for Xbar Chart and *s*-Chart

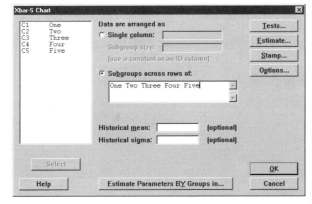

Minitab Instructions

1. Open file Signal
2. Click on Stat
3. Select Control Charts
4. Select Xbar-S...
5. Complete dialog box as shown entering data columns in "Subgroups across rows of..."
6. Select Tests...
7. Choose desired tests for assignable (special) causes; the first three tests were discussed in this chapter
8. Select Options to add title or sigma limits

FIGURE 16.8

$\overline{X}$- and *s*-Chart for Timing
Signal Example

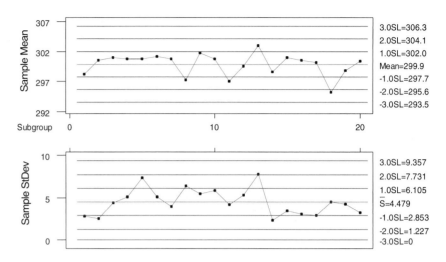

Timing Signal Example

and the C_{pk} index is

$$C_{pk} = \text{Min}\left[\frac{U - \overline{\overline{X}}}{3\hat{\sigma}}, \frac{\overline{\overline{X}} - L}{3\hat{\sigma}}\right] = \text{Min}(1.405, 1.391) = 1.391$$

The Minitab output in Figure 16.9 includes a graph, values for C_p and C_{pk}, and other results beyond the scope of this text.

Minitab Output for Capability Sixpack (Normal)

A nice feature of Minitab is the selection "Capability Sixpack (Normal)" rather than "Quality Analysis (Normal)" in step 4 of the Minitab Instructions box for Figure 16.9. Since a process must be stable before capability is considered, this option includes both control charts and normality checks along with the capability indices. Minitab output included with Capability Sixpack (Normal) are the $\overline{X}$-chart, the *R*-chart, plot of last 20 subgroups, capability histogram and normal probability plot, and the capability plot that includes values for C_p and C_{pk}. The only drawback to this feature is that the *R*-chart (see Appendix to

FIGURE 16.9

Capability Analysis (Normal)
for Timing Signal Example

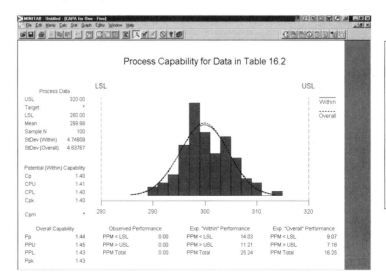

FIGURE 16.10
Capability Sixpack (Normal)
for Timing Signal Example

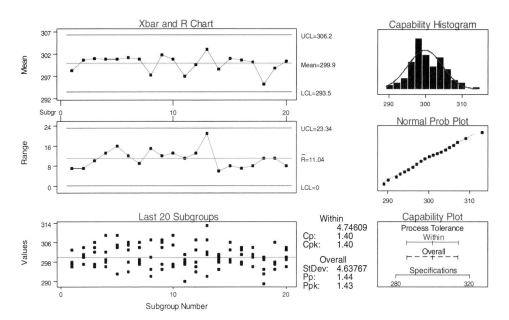

FIGURE 16.10
Capability Sixpack (Normal)
for Timing Signal Example

this chapter) and not the *s*-chart is given to test process variation. The Minitab output selection Capability Sixpack (Normal) for the timing signal example (data file Signal) is given in Figure 16.10.

Minitab Output for *p*-Charts

Simply complete a dialog box, such as the Minitab dialog box illustrated in Figure 16.11 for the example of nonconforming electronic components (Example 16.5).

The *p*-chart obtained with Minitab was given in Figure 16.5 and simply repeated here as Figure 16.12 with the inclusion of the three-sigma limit lines.

Minitab for *c*-Charts

With Minitab *c*-charts are so easily constructed that our remarks are quite limited. Enter the data, say in C1; click on **Stat**; select **control charts**; select **C….** The only information requested in the dialog box is the column location of the data. As with *p*-charts, tests for assignable causes, titles, sigma limits, and so forth can be selected.

FIGURE 16.11
Minitab Dialog Box for *p*-Charts

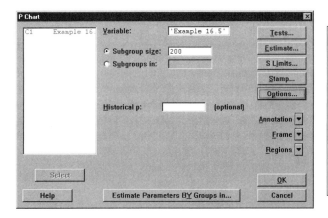

Minitab Instructions

1. Open file Electronic Component
2. Click on Stat
3. Select Control Charts
4. Select P…
5. Enter Variable location (C1 for Example 16.5)
6. Enter Subgroup size (200 for Example 16.5); or if sample sizes vary, corresponding sample sizes should be in C2. Then select "Subgroups in" and enter C2.
7. Tests, Options, Estimates, Annotations are optional

FIGURE 16.12
Minitab Output for *p*-Chart
for Electronic Component
Example

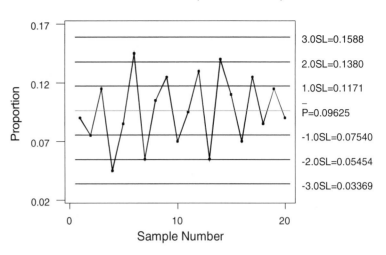

Electronics Component Example

EXERCISES

16.25 A manufacturer of precision bolts is required to produce bolts for a luxury automobile that have a mean strength of 60,000 psi. Every fifteen minutes, the strength of four bolts is tested. The data for a three-hour period is contained in the data file **Bolts**. Find the $\overline{X}$-chart and *s*-charts using Minitab.

16.26 Refer to the data file **Bolts** in Exercise 16.25. Find the process capability indices using Minitab with LCL = 58,5000 and UCL = 61,5000.
(a) Capability Analysis (Normal)
(b) Capability Sixpack (Normal)

16.27 Construct and interpret the *p*-chart using Minitab or some other software package for the data in Exercise 16.21.

16.28 Find the *c*-chart using Minitab or some other software package for:
(a) the data in Exercise 16.22
(b) the data in Exercise 16.23
(c) the data in Exercises 16.24

SUMMARY

The statistical control charts in this chapter provide information necessary for an informed discussion of current quality performance. These methods are not at all difficult to understand, and the emphasis on charts renders interpretation of the data relatively straightforward. This is important, as it allows access to information to a wide range of employees without their need to understand high-powered statistical concepts. Indeed, an understanding of *variability* and its causes should get one far along the road to a capacity for intelligent interpretation of the data. No process will yield perfectly identical pieces of output. There will inevitably be some *natural variability,* attributed to chance. An important element of quality control is the recognition of patterns of measurements that are unlikely to reflect natural variability, but rather signal some structural cause that requires investigation.

This chapter is merely an introduction to selected statistical procedures employed in continuous process improvement. In no way are control charts the only tools available. Essential to a process improvement program are flow charts, Ishikawa diagrams (commonly called fishbone diagrams or cause-and-effect diagrams), Pareto diagrams (Chapter 2), scatter plots (Chapter 3), and other techniques beyond the purpose of this book. For additional study, see the reference list and selected Web sites for information concerning quality philosophies, quality awards, on-line workshops, quality books, and organizations such as the Deming Institute or the Juran Institute.

Throughout this chapter, Minitab was used for its simplicity and accuracy. Other statistical software packages are available.

KEY WORDS

CHAPTER EXERCISES AND APPLICATIONS

16.29 Distinguish between each of the following pairs of terms.

  (a) A process is *in control,* and a process is *capable* of performing to specifications.

  (b) *Natural variability* and *assignable causes.*

16.30 In quality control work it is usual to employ three-standard error limits in constructing the charts. Explain the rationale behind, and the implications of, this choice.

16.31 🌐 Sample means and standard deviations for a sequence of twenty-five samples of five observations on a quality characteristic of a product are given in the following table and stored in the data file **Exercise 16-31**.

SAMPLE	$\overline{X}$	s	SAMPLE	$\overline{X}$	s	SAMPLE	$\overline{X}$	s
1	120.3	2.6	8	120.7	1.4	15	120.9	1.9
2	119.5	1.8	9	120.9	2.2	16	119.2	3.1
3	118.4	2.2	10	118.7	2.8	17	119.9	2.2
4	120.9	1.7	11	119.2	2.4	18	118.7	2.6
5	119.3	1.2	12	118.9	1.4	19	120.6	1.4
6	119.7	2.3	13	119.9	1.2	20	119.4	1.9
7	121.1	1.9	14	120.3	1.5			

  (a) Find the overall mean of the sample observations.

  (b) Find the average sample standard deviation.

  (c) Use an unbiased estimator to find an estimate of the process standard deviation.

  (d) Find the center line and lower and upper control limits for an $\overline{X}$-chart.

  (e) Draw the $\overline{X}$-chart and discuss its features.

  (f) Find the center line and lower and upper control limits for an s-chart.

  (g) Draw the s-chart and discuss its features.

  (h) Management has specified that the values of the quality characteristic for this process should be between 115 and 125.

    (i) Compute the interval $\overline{\overline{X}} \pm 3\hat{\sigma}$ and comment on your finding.

    (ii) Find the capability index C_p and discuss the result.

    (iii) Find the C_{pk} index and discuss the result.

16.32 🌐 The accompanying table shows sample means and standard deviations for a sequence of twenty-five samples of eight observations on a quality characteristic of a product. The data are stored in the data file **Exercise 16-32**.

SAMPLE	$\overline{X}$	s	SAMPLE	$\overline{X}$	s	SAMPLE	$\overline{X}$	s
1	347.9	2.37	10	356.1	4.82	18	349.8	6.27
2	349.8	4.26	11	348.7	3.90	19	350.7	5.92
3	346.5	7.81	12	352.1	8.61	20	352.3	9.64
4	352.7	5.62	13	353.6	7.59	21	347.1	3.68
5	350.4	3.17	14	349.1	6.28	22	342.8	6.52
6	348.6	6.09	15	347.4	3.87	23	348.7	7.13
7	351.7	5.27	16	354.3	8.21	24	354.1	4.36
8	353.8	4.31	17	350.5	4.19	25	352.3	5.19
9	349.4	4.97						

  (a) Find the overall mean of the sample observations.

  (b) Find the average sample standard deviation.

  (c) Use an unbiased estimator to find an estimate of the process standard deviation.

  (d) Find the center line and lower and upper control limits for an $\overline{X}$-chart

  (e) Draw the $\overline{X}$-chart and discuss its features.

  (f) Find the center line and lower and upper control limits for an s-chart.

  (g) Draw the s-chart and discuss its features.

  (h) Management has specified that the values of the quality characteristic for this process should be between 325 and 375.

    (i) Compute the interval $\overline{\overline{X}} \pm 3\hat{\sigma}$ and comment on your findings.

    (ii) Find the capability index C_p and discuss the result.

    (iii) Find the C_{pk} index and discuss the result.

  (i) Use Minitab to answer parts (a) through (h).

16.33 🌐 The accompanying table shows proportions of nonconforming items in a sequence of 20 samples, each of 500 observations. The data are stored in the data file **Exercise 16-33**.

SAMPLE NUMBER	p	SAMPLE NUMBER	p	NUMBER SAMPLE	p
1	.078	8	.080	15	.094
2	.062	9	.068	16	.066
3	.048	10	.076	17	.070
4	.086	11	.064	18	.088
5	.092	12	.068	19	.062
6	.074	13	.058	20	.054
7	.076	14	.082		

(a) Find the average of the sample proportions.
(b) Find the center line and lower and upper control limits for a p-chart.
(c) Draw the p-chart and discuss its features.
(d) Use Minitab to develop the p-chart.

16.34 A department store customer complaints department has recorded the number of complaints received over a period of 18 weeks. The results are shown in the accompanying table and stored in the data file **Complaints**.

WEEK	COMPLAINTS	WEEK	COMPLAINTS	WEEK	COMPLAINTS
1	15	7	20	13	22
2	10	8	11	14	15
3	17	9	15	15	9
4	19	10	15	16	16
5	14	11	19	17	17
6	12	12	10	18	14

(a) Find the sample mean number of complaints per week.
(b) Find the center line and lower and upper limits for a c-chart.
(c) Draw the c-chart and discuss its features.
(d) Use Minitab to draw the c-chart.

16.35 The accompanying table shows sample observations for a sequence of sixteen samples, each of four observations, on a quality characteristic of a product. The data are stored in the data file **Exercise 16-35**.

SAMPLE NUMBER				
1	340	346	351	338
2	332	348	330	344
3	339	343	339	347
4	342	338	346	338
5	350	340	345	347
6	344	332	347	351
7	336	348	362	331
8	345	342	349	330
9	356	342	348	329
10	337	361	332	344
11	353	329	323	360
12	348	367	323	320
13	370	354	358	340
14	368	328	339	347
15	366	328	343	351
16	330	323	364	339

(a) Find the sixteen sample means and sample standard deviations.
(b) Find the overall mean of the sample observations.
(c) Find the average sample standard deviation.
(d) Use an unbiased estimator to find an estimate of the process standard deviation.
(e) Find the center line and lower and upper control limits for an $\overline{X}$-chart.
(f) Draw the $\overline{X}$-chart and discuss its features.
(g) Find the center line and lower and upper control limits for an s-chart.
(h) Draw the s-chart and discuss its features.
(i) Use Minitab or some other software to construct the $\overline{X}$-chart and the s-chart.

16.36 Determine if each of the following causes is most likely to be a common cause or an assignable cause.
(a) Poor lighting
(b) High humidity
(c) Substitute operator
(d) Incorrect machine setting
(e) Data entered incorrectly

16.37 A consumer product that has flourished in the last few years is bottled natural spring water. Ann Thorne is the CEO of a company that sells natural spring water. She has requested a report of the filling process of the 24-oz. (710-mL) bottles to be sure that they are being properly filled. To check if the process needs to be adjusted, John Cadariu who monitors the process, randomly samples and weighs five bottles every fifteen minutes for a five-hour period. The data are contained in the data file **Bottles**.
(a) Find the $\overline{X}$-chart and s-chart for this problem.
(b) Test for assignable causes and determine if the process is stable.
(c) If the lower specification limit is 685 and the upper specification limit is 730 mL, determine the process capability.

16.38 Prairie Flower Cereal Inc. is a small but growing producer of hot and ready-to-eat breakfast cereals. The company was started in 1910 by Gordon Thorson, a successful grain farmer (reference 1). You have been asked to test the cereal-packing process of 18-oz. (510-gram) boxes of sugar-coated wheat cereal. Two machines are used for the packaging process. Twenty samples of five boxes each are randomly sampled and weighed. The data is contained in the file **Sugar Coated Wheat**. The lower and upper specification limits have been set at 500 grams and 525 grams respectively.

(a) Determine if the packaging process is in control for Machine 1.

(b) Determine if the packaging process is in control for Machine 2.

(c) Is Machine 1 capable of meeting the specification limits?

(d) Is Machine 2 capable of meeting the specification limits?

(e) What recommendations would you suggest to Prairie Flower Cereal Inc. concerning the packaging process of sugar-coated wheat cereal?

16.39 🌐 Another product packaged by Prairie Flower Cereal Inc. is Apple Cinnamon Cereal. To test the packaging process of 40-oz (1134-gram) boxes of this cereal, twenty-three samples of six boxes each are randomly sampled and weighed. The lower and upper specifica-

tion limits have been set at 1120 grams and 1150 grams respectively. The data are contained in the data file **Granola**.

(a) Is the packaging process stable?

(b) If the process is stable, determine the capability of the process to meet the given specifications.

16.40 🌐 Al Fiedler, plant manager at LDS Vacuum Products, Altamonte Springs, FL, applies statistical thinking in his workplace. As a major supplier to automobile manufacturers, LDS wants to be sure that the leak rate (in cubic centimeters per second) of transmission oil coolers (TOC) meets the established specification limits. Random samples of TOCs are tested, and the leak rates are recorded in the data file **Toc**. Test if the leak rate process is stable. Subgroup size is five.

APPENDIX

Prior to the availability of statistical software, R-charts for ranges rather than s-charts for standard deviations were used more frequently to examine process variability. This was so, since workers on the floor found it easier to compute the difference between the largest and the smallest sample values rather than to calculate sample standard deviations. If the R-chart showed process stability, then the $\overline{X}$-chart based on sample ranges was examined. A discussion of the R-chart is included here for completeness.

R-Chart

The center line and the control limits for the R-chart are found by Equations 16.18 and 16.19.

R-CHART

The ***R*-chart** is a time plot of the sequence of ranges with center line

$$CL_R = \overline{R} \tag{16.18}$$

and control limits

$$LCL_R = D_3\overline{R} \qquad\qquad UCL_R = D_4\overline{R} \tag{16.19}$$

where factors D_3 and D_4 are given in the Factors for Control Charts table in the Appendix. Selected control chart factors appear in Table 16.5.

TABLE 16.5
Selected Factors for Control Charts

n	D_2	A_2	D_3	D_4
2	1.128	1.88	0	3.27
3	1.693	1.02	0	2.57
4	2.059	0.73	0	2.28
5	2.326	0.58	0	2.11
6	2.534	0.48	0	2.00
7	2.704	0.42	0.08	1.92
8	2.847	0.37	0.14	1.86
9	2.970	0.34	0.18	1.82
10	3.078	0.31	0.22	1.78

TABLE 16.6
Sample Ranges for Timing
Signal Device

SAMPLE NUMBER	R	SAMPLE NUMBER	R	SAMPLE NUMBER	R
1	7	8	15	15	8
2	7	9	12	16	7
3	10	10	13	17	8
4	13	11	11	18	11
5	16	12	13	19	11
6	12	13	21	20	8
7	9	14	6		

Next, find the R-chart for the Timing Signal Example 16.1. Sample ranges are given in Table 16.6. The average sample range is then

$$\overline{R} = (7 + 7 + \cdots + 8)/20 = 10.9$$

Using Equations 16.18 and 16.19, the center line of the R-chart is

$$CL_R = \overline{R} = 10.9$$

and the control limits are

$$LCL_R = D_3\overline{R} = 0(10.9) = 0 \quad \text{and} \quad UCL_R = D_4\overline{R} = (2.11)(10.9) = 23$$

Plot the individual sample ranges on the R-chart, or use Minitab, and obtain Figure 16.13.

FIGURE 16.13
Range Chart for Timing
Signal Example

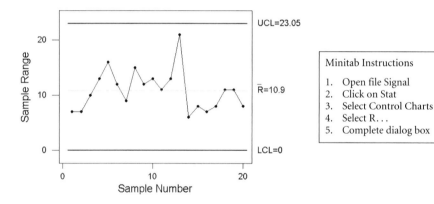

Minitab Instructions
1. Open file Signal
2. Click on Stat
3. Select Control Charts
4. Select R...
5. Complete dialog box

$\overline{X}$ -Chart and R-Charts

Since inspection of the R-chart does not suggest concern, the $\overline{X}$ -chart based on ranges is now developed.

$\overline{X}$-CHART BASED ON RANGES

The $\overline{X}$ **-chart based on ranges** is a time plot of the sequence of means with center line

$$CL_{\overline{X}} = \overline{\overline{X}} \tag{16.20}$$

and control limits

$$LCL_{\overline{X}} = \overline{\overline{X}} - A_2\overline{R} \quad \text{and} \quad UCL_{\overline{X}} = \overline{\overline{X}} + A_2\overline{R} \tag{16.21}$$

where A_2 is found in the Factors for Control Charts table. Selected values of A_2 are given in Table 16.5. It can be shown that,

$$A_2 = \frac{3}{d_2\sqrt{n}} \tag{16.22}$$

FIGURE 16.14
$\overline{X}$-Chart and R-Chart for
Timing Signal Example 16.1

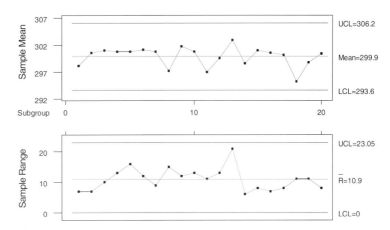

XBar-R Charts for Timing Signal Example

In Example 16.1, the overall mean was found to be $\overline{\overline{X}} = 299.9$ and with $n = 5$ from Table 16.5 the value of the constant A_2 is 0.58. The control limits are then,

$$LCL_{\overline{X}} = \overline{\overline{X}} - A_2\overline{R} = 299.9 - (0.58)(10.9) = 293.6$$

and

$$UCL_{\overline{X}} = \overline{\overline{X}} + A_2\overline{R} = 299.9 + (0.58)(10.9) = 306.2$$

Plot the individual sample means on a control chart, or use Minitab, to obtain both the $\overline{X}$-chart and the R-chart together (see Figure 16.14).

Estimate Process Standard Deviation Based on Ranges

Although individual sample standard deviations are not computed when using ranges, it is still useful to estimate the process standard deviation.

ESTIMATED PROCESS STANDARD DEVIATION BASED ON RANGES

An **estimate of the process standard deviation based on ranges** is

$$\hat{\sigma} = \overline{R}/d_2 \tag{16.23}$$

where d_2 is found in the Factors for Control Charts table in the book Appendix or in Table 16.5.

In the timing signal example, the estimated process standard deviation is therefore

$$\hat{\sigma} = \overline{R}/d_2 = 10.9/2.326 = 4.69$$

Now the process capability calculations of C_p and C_{pk} given in Equations 16.10 and 16.11 can be carried out using this estimate of the process standard deviation.

REFERENCES

1. Carlson, William L., *Cases in Managerial Data Analysis.* (San Francisco: Duxbury Press, 1997).

2. Deming, W. Edwards, *Out of the Crisis.* (Cambridge, MA: MIT Center for Advanced Engineering Study, 1986).

3. Deming, W. Edwards, *The New Economics for Business, Industry, and Government*. (Cambridge, MA: MIT Center for Advanced Engineering Study, 1993).

4. Evans, James R., *Production/Operations Management: Quality, Performance, and Value,* 5th edition. (Minneapolis/St. Paul, MN: West Publishing Company, 1997).

5. Evans, James R. and William M. Lindsay, *The Management and Control of Quality,* 4th edition. (Cincinnati, OH: Southwestern College Publishing, 1999).

6. Fiedler, Alfred W., LDS Vacuum Products Study: Delphi Leak Detector #1. (Altamonte Springs, FL: 2000 LDS Vacuum Products).

7. Juran, Joseph M., *Juran on Quality by Design*. (New York: The Free Press, Revised 1995).

8. Juran, Joseph M. and A. Blanton Godfrey, *Juran's Quality Handbook*, 5th edition. (New York: McGraw Hill, 1999).

9. Taguchi, Genichi, *Introduction to Quality Engineering*. (Tokyo: Asian Productivity Organization, 1986).

10. Tague, Nancy, *The Quality Toolbox*. (Milwaukee, WI: ASQ Quality Press, 1995).

11. Walton, Mary, *The Deming Management Method*. (New York: The Putnam Publishing Group, 1986).

12. Wise, Stephen A. and Douglas C. Fair, *Innovative Control Charting: Practical SPC Solutions for Today's Manufacturing Environment*. (Milwaukee, WI: ASQ Quality Press, 1997).

13. Zimmerman, Steven M. and Marjorie L. Icenogle, *Statistical Quality Control Using Excel*. (Milwaukee, WI: ASQ Quality Press, 1999).

Selected Current Web Addresses of Interest:

WEB ADDRESS	ORGANIZATION
www.asq.org	American Society for Quality (ASQ)
www.deming.org	W. Edwards Deming Institute
www.efqm.org	European Foundation for Quality Management
www.nist.gov	National Institute of Standards and Technology
www.juran.com	Juran Institute
www.nokia.com	Nokia
www.philipcrosby.com	Philip Crosby Associates II, Inc.
www.qualitypress.asq.org	ASQ On-Line Bookstore

C H A P T E R 17

TIME SERIES ANALYSIS AND FORECASTING

INTRODUCTION

In this chapter, we will develop procedures for analyzing data sets that contain measurements over time for various variables. Examples of time series data include monthly product sales and interest rates, quarterly corporate earnings and aggregate consumption, and daily closing prices for shares of common stock.

> ## TIME SERIES
> A time series is a set of measurements, ordered over time, on a particular quantity of interest. In a time series the sequence of the observations is important, in contrast to cross section data for which the sequence of observations is not important.

Time series data typically possess special characteristics—associated with the sequence of the observations—that necessitate the development of special statistical analysis methods. Virtually all of the procedures of data analysis and inference that we have developed are based on the assumption of random samples—in particular that the observations errors are independent. Only very rarely will the assumption of independence be realistic for time series data. For example, consider a series of monthly sales for a manufactured product and note possible reasons for lack of independence. If sales were higher than average last month then it is reasonable to expect that high sales will continue because the strong underlying economic and business conditions are not likely to change abruptly. Thus we can expect similarity in sales during adjacent months. We also note that sales of many products have a seasonal pattern—shorts and swimsuits have higher sales in spring and early summer compared to winter. Many retail sales have peaks during the fourth quarter because of Christmas gift purchases. These and many other examples establish the case for lack of independence.

The lack of independence between time series observations lead to serious problems if conventional statistical procedures—which assume independence—are used with time series data. We saw the problem in Section 12.8 when examining the problems of using conventional regression procedures when the errors were correlated between observations. The independence assumption is crucial, and other serious problems can occur if conventional procedures are used when the observations are dependent. In this chapter we will focus on examining time-series-analysis procedures that apply to a single time series.

We have considered the negative aspect of the kinds of dependency patterns likely to occur in time series data. These are real problems and require special procedures. However, this dependency can also be exploited to produce lower variance forecasts of future time series values. For example if there is a correlation between adjacent month errors in a retail series, then that correlation can be used to provide a better forecast for the next month, compared to a forecast based on a random sample. We will develop procedures based on the assumption that past patterns of relationship between measurements in a time series will continue into the future and can be used for forecasting—this is rather like arguing that we can in fact learn from a study of past history.

In the next section we will develop index numbers, which are used in a number of economic writings. The time-series-analysis procedures contained in subsequent sections do not require a knowledge of index numbers. They are included here to provide a complete presentation of topics related to time-series analysis.

17.1   INDEX NUMBERS

Our discussion begins with the development of index numbers. To motivate our discussion consider the question, What changes have occurred in the price of automobiles built in the United States in the past 10 years? It almost goes without saying that their prices have risen, but how can this price rise be described quantitatively? On the surface this question may not seem very difficult to answer. As a first step one could collect price information about these automobiles in each of the past 10 years and graph them using a time plot.

However, thinking about the problem carefully may lead to a number of questions. First we note that automobiles are not homogeneous and thus we need to be more specific in our definition of the particular type of automobile. There are clearly a wide range of prices and quality, and the change in average price of all automobiles sold may merely reflect a change in the pattern of purchase—Do sales consist of more higher-priced automobiles? In the latter case the average price would increase because we have more higher-priced cars. Other changes in the market mix could result in other movements of the mean. Table 17.1 provides a simple hypothetical example of a market with only a low-priced and a high-priced automobile. Note that the average price decreased but that this was the result of more low-priced cars and fewer high-priced cars in the mix. This is not a particularly useful way to compare the price of automobiles over two different years.

Another possible solution is to compute the average price of a single car of each type as shown in Table 17.2. This procedure is also flawed because we have a market in which subcompact cars are considerably more popular than luxury cars. The price of single cars is the same over the two years, while the price of luxury cars doubles. As a result the average based on a single car of each type is considerably higher in the second year. But this does not provide an accurate picture because it gives equal weights to each car type, when in fact subcompact cars are purchased much more frequently.

These examples demonstrate that to form a reliable picture of the overall price pattern over time, it is necessary to take carefully into account the quantities purchased in each time period. We will see how appropriate weighted averages can be formed.

Another similar confusion occurs if consumers purchase more cars with optional extra equipment in the second year compared to the first. In that case consumers are implicitly purchasing higher-quality cars compared to the previous year. We could possibly look at only prices for cars without any extra equipment in order to obtain a valid comparison.

Difficulties also occur because of technological improvements. It is not surprising to note that present cars have higher fuel efficiency and last longer than cars produced in the 1970s and 1980s. Thus price increases might be highly influenced by changes in quality. Accounting for changes in quality is of major importance and should not be ignored in judging price comparisons, but techniques for analyzing the effect of quality changes is beyond the scope of our work here.

TABLE 17.1
Hypothetical Data on
Automobile Prices and Sales

| YEAR | SUBCOMPACT CARS | | LUXURY CARS | | ALL CARS |
	Price (thousand dollars)	Number Sold (thousands)	Price (thousand dollars)	Number Sold (thousands)	Average Price (thousand dollars)
1	10	5	30	15	25.0
2	11	15	33	5	16.5

TABLE 17.2
Hypothetical Data on
Automobile Prices and Sales:
Equal Weighting

YEAR	SUBCOMPACT CARS		LUXURY CARS		ALL CARS
	Price (thousand dollars)	*Number Sold (thousands)*	*Price (thousand dollars)*	*Number Sold (thousands)*	*Average Price of a Single Car of Each Type (thousand dollars)*
1	10	100	24	1	17
2	10	100	48	1	29

We have used examples of a single product to illustrate the problem, but such comparisons are typically only of interest to those directly related to purchasing and selling that product. Thus we will direct our concern to comparing the price changes of individual products with those of other products.

The index number problem examined next is directed toward comparing the movement of prices for a group of commodities. For example, the price of common stock in each company whose shares are traded on the New York Stock Exchange will change over a one-month period. We would like to produce a measure of the aggregate change in prices. Index numbers are designed to solve such problems.

Price Index for a Single Item

We begin our discussion of index numbers with a simple case. Figure 17.1 is an Excel spreadsheet that shows the computation of a price index for Ford Motor Company stock over a 12-week period. The second column contains the actual stock price. Interpreting these numbers is a bit confusing, but this task can be simplified by computing a price index with the first-week price being the base period. In the third column we see the computed price index. Thus for the second week the price index is

$$100\left(\frac{19.875}{20.25}\right) = 98.1$$

based on the second-week price of 19.875. The percentages calculated in this fashion are called index numbers of price. The choice of the base period is arbitrary. We could have chosen any other week as our base and expressed all prices as a percentage of the price for that week.

The advantage of using index numbers here lies in the greater ease of interpretation of the numbers. We see immediately from Figure 17.1, for instance, that the price of Ford Motor Company stock was 13.6% higher in week 12 than in week 1.

FIGURE 17.1
Prices and Price Index for
Ford Motor Company Stock
Over 12 Weeks

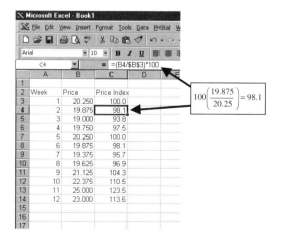

CALCULATING PRICE INDICES FOR A SINGLE ITEM

Suppose that we have a series of observations over time on the price of a single item. To form a price index, one time period is chosen as a base, and the price for every period is expressed as a percentage of the base period price. Thus, if p_0 denotes the price in the base period and p_1 the price in a second period, the price index for this second period is

$$100\left(\frac{p_1}{p_0}\right)$$

An Unweighted Aggregate Price Index

Next we will consider how to represent aggregate price movements for a group of items. Figure 17.2 is an Excel spreadsheet that shows the prices paid to U.S. farmers, in dollars per bushel, for wheat, corn, and soybeans over 10 crop years. The table also shows one way of achieving an aggregate price index for these crops. We compute the average price for each year and then use that average to construct an index for the average, using the first year as a base.

The resulting unweighted aggregate index of prices is easy to calculate as shown in Figure 17.2. It expresses the average price in each year as a percentage of the average price in the base year. However, no account is taken of the differences in quantities produced of these crops. The computation equation in Figure 17.2 indicates division of the sums of prices. This is, of course, the same as dividing by the averages of these prices. The averages would result from dividing the sums in the numerator and the denominator by 3.

AN UNWEIGHTED PRICE INDEX

Suppose that we have a series of observations over time on the prices of a group of K items. As before, one time is chosen as a base.

The **unweighted aggregate index of prices** is obtained by calculating the average price of these items in each time period and calculating an index for these average prices. That is, the average price in every period is expressed as a percentage of the average price in the base period. Let p_{0i} denote the price of the ith item in the base period and p_{1i} the price of this item in a second period. The unweighted aggregate index of prices for this second period is

$$100\left(\frac{\sum_{i=1}^{K} p_{1i}}{\sum_{i=1}^{K} p_{0i}}\right)$$

FIGURE 17.2
Prices per Bushel of Three Crops in 10 Years: Unweighted Aggregate Index of Prices

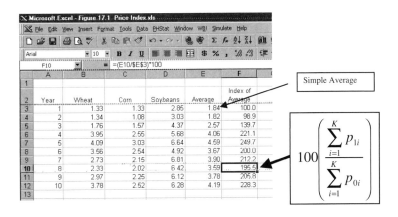

A Weighted Aggregate Price Index

In general we would like to weight the individual prices by some measures of the quantity sold. One possibility is to use average quantities over some or all of the time periods in question. In many cases quantities are expensive to obtain and instead the indices are based on quantities in a single time period. When these quantities are from the base period the resulting index is called *Laspeyres price index*.

The Laspeyres index, in effect, compares the total cost of purchasing the base-period quantities in the base period with what would have been the total cost of purchasing these same quantities in other periods. To illustrate, consider using the crop price data from Figure 17.2 with the additional information that production in year 1 was 1,352 million bushels of wheat, 4,152 million bushels of corn, and 1,127 million bushels of soybeans. Hence, the cost, in millions of dollars, of the year 1 total output was

$$(1,352)(1.33) + (4,152)(1.33) + (1,127)(2.85) = 10,532$$

In Year 2, at the prices then prevailing, the total cost of purchasing the base-year quantities would have been

$$(1,352)(1.34) + (4,152)(1.08) + (1,127)(3.03) = 9,711$$

The Laspeyres price index for year 2 is therefore

$$100\left(\frac{9,711}{10,532}\right) = 92.2$$

Figure 17.3 shows the complete index, calculated in this way, for these data.

THE LASPEYRES PRICE INDEX

Suppose that we have a group of K commodities for which price information is available over a period of time. One period is selected as the base for an index. The **Laspeyres price index** in any period is the total cost of purchasing the quantities traded in the base period at prices in the period of interest, expressed as a percentage of the total cost of purchasing these same quantities in the base period.

Let P_{oi} denote the price and q_{0i} the quantity purchased of the ith item in the base period. If p_{1i} is the price of the ith item in a second period, the Laspeyres price index for the period is

$$100\left(\frac{\displaystyle\sum_{i=1}^{K} q_{0i}p_{1i}}{\displaystyle\sum_{i=1}^{K} q_{0i}P_{0i}}\right)$$

Comparison of the formula for the Laspeyres price index with that for the unweighted aggregate index of prices is instructive. The difference is that in forming the Laspeyres index, the price of each item is weighted by the quantity traded in the base period.

We see that the Laspeyres price index uses quantity information from only the base period. This is valuable when it is difficult to obtain that information for every year. This could be a disadvantage if the base period quantities were not representative of the time series being considered. Thus the Laspeyres index could become outdated. One way around this problem is to construct a moving Laspeyres price index, in which the base period is changed from time to time through the acquisition of quantity information for new base periods. Many published national price indices, such as the Consumer Price Index, are constructed in essentially this way.

FIGURE 17.3
Laspeyres Price Index for
Three Crops

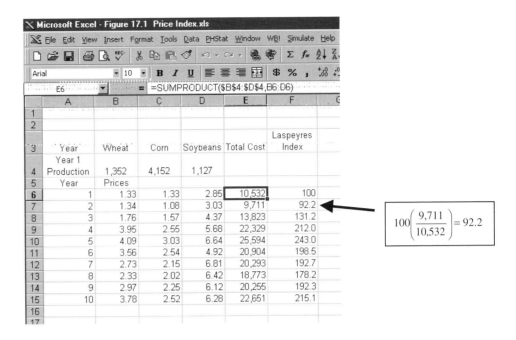

A Weighted Aggregate Quantity Index

Price indices provide a representation of the changes over time in aggregate prices of a group of commodities. We might also want a picture of the evolution of overall quantities traded. Again, any reasonable approach to this problem is likely to result in a weighted quantity index, since we would presumably want to give more weight to a change in the quantity purchased of a very expensive item than to a change by the same amount in purchases of an inexpensive item. One procedure for achieving this is through the *Laspeyres quantity index*, which we will illustrate for the quantities produced of wheat, corn, and soybeans given in Figure 17.4.

The Laspeyres quantity index weights the individual quantities by the base period prices. The price weights are 1.33, 1.33, and 2.85 for wheat, corn, and soybeans, resulting in a total value for year 1 on 10,532 million dollars. To obtain a quantity index for year 2, we compare this with the total value of year 2 production, had year 1 prices prevailed; that is,

$$(1{,}618)(1.33) + (5{,}641)(1.33) + (1{,}176)(2.85) = 13{,}006$$

FIGURE 17.4
Production, in Millions of
Bushels, and Quantity Index

The Laspeyres quantity index for year 2 is therefore

$$100\left(\frac{13{,}006}{10{,}532}\right) = 123.5$$

Figure 17.4 shows the quantities produced and the quantity index for a 10-year period.

THE LASPEYRES QUANTITY INDEX

We have quantity data for a set of items collected over a set of K years. One period is selected as a base period. The **Laspeyres quantity index** in any period is then the total cost of the quantities traded in that period, based on the base-period prices, expressed as a percentage of the total cost of the base-period quantities.

Let q_{0i} and p_{0i} denote the quantity and price of the ith item in the base period and q_{1i} the quantity of that item in the period of interest. The Laspeyres quantity index for that period is then

$$100\left(\frac{\displaystyle\sum_{i=1}^{K} q_{1i}p_{0i}}{\displaystyle\sum_{i=1}^{K} q_{0i}p_{0i}}\right)$$

Change in Base Period

Officially published series of index numbers are updated at various times by bringing forward the base period. In these circumstances, the value of the original index at the new base point is typically given. As an illustration, note the calculation in column F in Figure 17.5, showing the price indices for wheat, corn, and soybeans. Column F shows the price index for crop years 1 through 6, using year 1 as a base beginning with row 14 of Column F. Column H gives the Laspeyres price index for years 6 through 10, using year 6 as the base. These indices are plotted in Figure 17.6, where the discontinuity in year 6 is obvious.

Examining Figure 17.6, it is difficult to obtain a clear understanding of the price patterns over the entire time period. Thus we would prefer to examine a **spliced price index** that has year six as the base year. In the original index based on year 1, the index for year six

FIGURE 17.5
Aggregate Laspeyres Price
Indices Using Different Base
Years

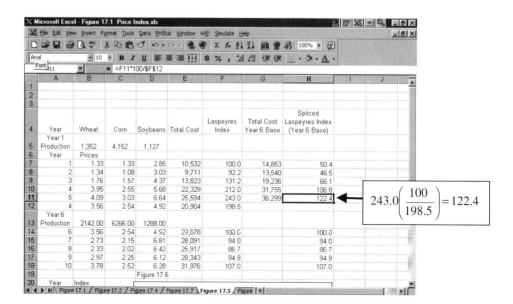

FIGURE 17.6
Time Plots of Laspeyres
Aggregate Price Indices With
Years 1 – 6 (Base Year 1) and
Years 6 –10 (Base Year 6)

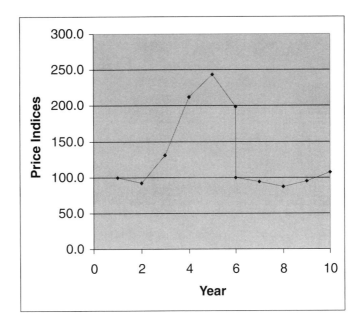

was 198.5 as seen in Figure 17.5. To transform the year 6 index, based on year 1, to a year 6 index based on year 6, we divide by 198.5 and multiply by 100. Similarly, all of the other indices based on year 1 can be converted to a year 6 base by dividing by 198.5 and multiplying by 100. For example, the new index for year 5 is

$$243.0\left(\frac{100}{198.5}\right) = 122.4$$

The spliced index obtained using a year 6 base is plotted in Figure 17.7. This graph presents a clearer picture of the pattern of price variation over the 10-year period.

FIGURE 17.7
Spliced Aggregate Lespeyres
Price Index for Wheat, Corn,
and Soybeans (Year 6 =100)

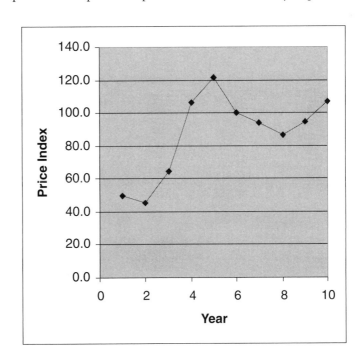

EXERCISES

17.1 Universities incur many costs in their operation, including the cost of energy, books, laboratory and other equipment, stationary, and labor. Suppose that you are asked to show how price levels faced by your university have changed over the past 10 years. What difficulties would you expect to encounter, and how would you attempt to proceed?

17.2 Note: the following problems should be completed using Excel. The accompanying table shows the price per share of stock in Bank of New York, Inc. for 12 weeks.

WEEK	PRICE	WEEK	PRICE	WEEK	PRICE
1	35	5	35	9	34 6/8
2	35 7/8	6	34 7/8	10	35 2/8
3	34 6/8	7	35	11	38 6/8
4	34 3/8	8	34 6/8	12	37 1/8

(a) Form a price index with week 1 as the base.
(b) Form a price index with week 4 as the base.

17.3 A restaurant offers three "specials"—steak, seafood, and chicken. Their average prices (in dollars) for the 12 months of last year are shown in the table.

MONTH	STEAK	SEAFOOD	CHICKEN
January	7.12	6.45	5.39
February	7.41	6.40	5.21
March	7.45	6.25	5.25
April	7.70	6.60	5.40
May	7.72	6.70	5.45
June	7.75	6.85	5.60
July	8.10	6.90	5.54
August	8.15	6.84	5.70
September	8.20	6.96	5.72
October	8.30	7.10	5.69
November	8.45	7.10	5.85
December	8.65	7.14	6.21

The following base table shows numbers of orders of these specials in each month. Take January as the base.

MONTH	STEAK	SEAFOOD	CHICKEN
January	123	169	243
February	110	160	251
March	115	181	265

MONTH	STEAK	SEAFOOD	CHICKEN
April	101	152	231
May	118	140	263
June	100	128	237
July	92	129	221
August	87	130	204
September	123	164	293
October	131	169	301
November	136	176	327
December	149	193	351

(a) Find the unweighted aggregate price index.
(b) Find the Laspeyres price index.
(c) Find the Laspeyres quantity index.

17.4 The accompanying table shows hourly wage rates over six years for three types of employees in a small company.

YEAR	MANUAL	CLERICAL	SUPERVISORY
1	10.60	8.40	16.40
2	11.10	8.70	17.50
3	11.80	9.10	17.90
4	11.90	9.20	18.80
5	12.30	9.60	19.00
6	12.50	9.70	19.30

Take year 1 as base. In that year there were 72 manual employees, 23 clerical employees, and 10 supervisory employees.
(a) Find the unweighted index of hourly wage rates.
(b) Find the Laspeyres index for hourly wage rates.

17.5 The accompanying table shows a price index for a group of commodities over six years. Obtain a spliced index with year 4 as base.

YEAR	1	2	3	4	5	6
BASE YEAR 1	100	108.4	114.3	120.2		
BASE YEAR 2				100	103.5	107.8

17.6 Explain why it is useful to develop a price index for a group of products—for example, an index of energy prices. What are the advantages of a *weighted* index of prices?

17.2   A NONPARAMETRIC TEST FOR RANDOMNESS

The first step in our process of analyzing time series data will be to consider a test for randomness in time series. We will develop the *runs test*, which is a nonparametric test that is particularly easy to perform.

To demonstrate the test, we will first look at a series of 16 daily observations on an index of the volume of shares traded on the New York Stock Exchange. The data are shown in Table 17.3 and graphed in Figure 17.8. A line has been drawn on this figure at the median. For an even number of observations, the median is the average of the middle pair, when the observations are arranged in ascending order. Here, that is

$$\text{Median} = \frac{107 + 108}{2} = 107.5$$

If this series was random, then the volume traded on one day would be independent of the volume traded on any other day. In particular, a high-volume day would be no more likely to be followed by another high-volume day than would any other day. The runs test developed here separates the observations into a subgroup above the median and a subgroup below the median, as shown in Figure 17.8 with the median at 107.5. Then letting a + denote observations above the median and a − denote observations below the median we find the following pattern over the sequential days

$$- - - - + + - - + - + + + + + -$$

This sequence consists of a run of four "−", followed by a run of two "+", a run of two "−", a run of one "+", a run of one "−", a run of five "+", and finally a run of one "−". In total there are therefore $R = 7$ runs.

TABLE 17.3
Index of Volume of Shares Traded

DAY	VOLUME	DAY	VOLUME	DAY	VOLUME	DAY	VOLUME
1	98	5	113	9	114	13	109
2	93	6	111	10	107	14	108
3	82	7	104	11	111	15	128
4	103	8	103	12	109	16	92

FIGURE 17.8
Index of Volume of Shares Traded versus Day

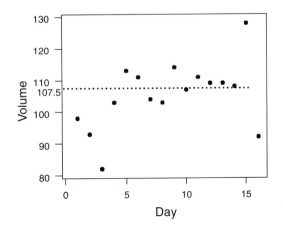

If, as might be suspected here, there was a positive association between adjacent observations in time, we would expect to find relatively few runs. In our example, we ask how likely it is to observe seven or fewer runs if the series is truly random. This requires knowledge of the distribution of the number of runs when the null hypothesis of randomness is true. The cumulative distribution is tablulated in Table 11 of the Appendix. From that table we see that for $n = 16$ observations, the probability under the null hypothesis of finding 7 or fewer runs is 0.214. Therefore, the null hypothesis of randomness can only be rejected against the alternative of positive association between adjacent observations at the 21.4% significance level. This is not small enough to reasonably reject the null hypothesis, nor is it large enough to provide strong support in favor of the null hypothesis. We have merely failed to find strong evidence to reject it. Test of randomness based on small samples such as this have quite low power.

THE RUNS TEST

Suppose we have a time series of n observations. Denote observations above the median with "+" signs and observations below the median with "−" signs. Use these signs to define the sequence of observations in the series. Let R denote the number of runs in the sequence. The null hypothesis is that the series is a set of random variables. The table in the Appendix gives the smallest significance level against which this null hypothesis can be rejected against the alternative of positive association between adjacent observations, as a function of R and n.

If the alternative is the two-sided hypothesis on nonrandomness, the significance level must be doubled if it is less than 0.5. Alternatively, if the significance level, α, read from the table is bigger than 0.5, the appropriate significance level for the test against the two-sided alternative is $2(1 - \alpha)$.

For time series with $n > 20$, the distribution of the number of runs under the null hypothesis can be approximated by a normal distribution. It can be shown that under the null hypothesis

$$Z = \frac{R - \dfrac{n}{2} - 1}{\sqrt{\dfrac{n^2 - 2n}{4(n - 1)}}}$$

has a standard normal distribution. This result provides a test for randomness.

THE RUNS TEST: LARGE SAMPLES

Given that we have a time series with n observations, $n > 20$, define the number of runs, R, as the number of sequences above or below the median. We want to test the null hypothesis

H_0: The series is random

The following tests have significance level α:

i. If the alternative hypothesis is positive association between adjacent observations, the decision rule is

$$\text{Reject } H_0 \text{ if } Z = \frac{R - \dfrac{n}{2} - 1}{\sqrt{\dfrac{n^2 - 2n}{4(n - 1)}}} < -z_\alpha \tag{17.1}$$

ii. If the alternative is two-sided, of nonrandomness, the decision rule is

$$\text{Reject } H_0 \text{ if } Z = \frac{R - \dfrac{n}{2} - 1}{\sqrt{\dfrac{n^2 - 2n}{4(n-1)}}} < -z_{\alpha/2} \quad \text{or} \quad Z = \frac{R - \dfrac{n}{2} - 1}{\sqrt{\dfrac{n^2 - 2n}{4(n-1)}}} > z_{\alpha/2} \quad \textbf{(17.2)}$$

EXAMPLE 17.1

ANALYSIS OF SALES DATA
(RUNS TEST)

Pinkham Sales Data

You have been asked to determine if the 30 years of annual sales follows a random walk.

SOLUTION

The data for this study are stored in a data file named **Pinkham Sales Data,** stored on the data disk. Figure 17.9 is a time series plot of the data with the median drawn on the graph. Examination of the plot suggests that the observations are not independent since they appear to follow a pattern. The runs-test statistics can be computed using Minitab by using the command sequence

```
STAT > NONPARAMETRICS > RUNS TEST
```

Figure 17.10 shows the data-entry screen for this example and the resulting computer output. From this analysis we see that the series has eight runs and that the null hypothesis of a random time series is rejected with p-value = 0.0030.

We could also use the number of runs and the test statistic to compute the Z value for the test as

$$Z = \frac{R - \dfrac{n}{2} - 1}{\sqrt{\dfrac{n^2 - 2n}{4(n-1)}}} = \frac{8 - 15 - 1}{\sqrt{\dfrac{900 - 60}{116}}} = -2.97$$

and the resulting p-value for a two-tailed test is 0.0030, from the table in the Appendix. Thus we see the evidence in favor of a nonrandom series is quite overwhelming.

FIGURE 17.9
Lydia Pinkham Sales Data
over Time

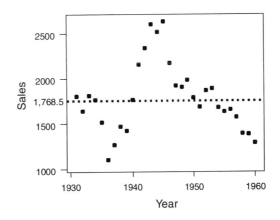

FIGURE 17.10
Minitab Runs Test for
Pinkham Sales Data

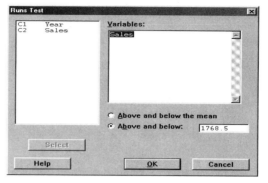

```
Sales

    K =  1768.5000

    The observed number of runs =    8
    The expected number of runs =   16.0000
    15 Observations above K    15 below
                The test is significant at   0.0030
```

EXERCISES

17.7   The data file, **Exchange Rate**, shows an index of the value of the U.S. dollar against trading partners' currencies over 12 consecutive months. Use the runs test to test this series for randomness.

17.8   The data file **Inventory Sales** shows the inventory-sales ratio for manufacturing and trade in the United States over a period of 12 years. Test this series for randomness using the runs test.

17.9   The data file **Stock Market Index** shows annual returns on a stock market index over 14 years. Test for randomness using the runs test.

17.10   The data file **Gold Price** shows the year-end price of gold (in dollars) over 14 consecutive years. Use the runs test to test this series for randomness.

17.3   COMPONENTS OF A TIME SERIES

In the following Sections 17.3 through 17.5 we will develop some descriptive procedures for analyzing time series data. The series of interest will be denoted by $X_1, X_2, \ldots, X_n$, and at time t the series value is X_t.

A standard model for the behavior of time series identifies various components of the series. Traditionally four components are considered as being represented at least in part in most time series. The components are

1. Trend Component
2. Seasonality Component
3. Cyclical Component
4. Irregular Component

Many time series exhibit a tendency to grow or decrease rather steadily over long periods of time, indicating a trend component. For example, measures of national wealth such as Gross Domestic Product have typically grown over time. Trends often hold up over time and when they do this provides an important component for developing forecasts. Figure 17.11 shows the time series for quarterly domestic product for over 50 years, from the data file **Macro2000** contained on the data disk. This pattern clearly shows a strong upward trend component that is stronger in some periods than in others. This time plot reveals a

Macro 2000

FIGURE 17.11
Gross Domestic Product By
Time Indicating a Trend

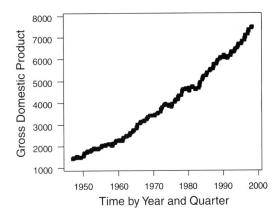

major trend component that is important for initial analysis and is usually followed by more sophisticated analyses, as we will show in future sections.

Another important component is the seasonal pattern: Figure 17.12 shows quarterly earnings per share of a corporation. The fourth quarter earnings are substantially higher and the second quarter earnings are somewhat higher compared to the other periods. Note how this pattern continues to repeat over the four-quarter cycle representing each year. In addition to the seasonality component there is also a noticeable upward trend in earnings per share. Our treatment of seasonality depends on our objectives. For example, if it were important to forecast each quarter as precisely as possible then we would include a seasonality component in our model. In Section 12.3, for instance, we showed how dummy variables can be used to estimate a seasonal component in a time series. Thus if we anticipate that the seasonality pattern will continue, then the seasonal component estimation must be an important component of our forecasting model.

For some other purposes seasonality can be a nuisance. In many applications, the analyst requires an assessment of overall movements in a time series, uncontaminated by the influence of seasonal factors. For instance, suppose that we have just received the most recent fourth-quarter earnings figures of the corporation in Figure 17.12. We already know that these will very likely be a good deal higher than those of the previous quarter. What we would like to do is assess how much of this increase in earnings is due to purely seasonal factors and how much represents real underlying growth. In other words, we would like to produce a time series free from seasonal influence. Such a series is said to be seasonally adjusted. We will say a little more about seasonal adjustment in Section 17.6.

FIGURE 17.12
Quarterly Earnings per Share
of a Corporation

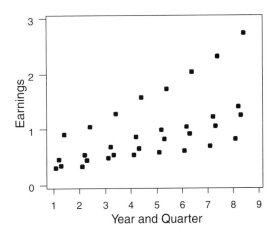

Seasonal patterns in a time series constitute one form of regular, oscillatory behavior. In addition, many business and economic time series exhibit oscillatory or cyclical patterns not related to seasonal behavior. For example, many economic series follow business cycle patterns of upswings and downswings. In Figure 17.9 we saw a cyclical pattern for Lydia Pinkham sales data. We see a decrease in sales to a trough in 1936 followed by an upswing to a peak in the mid-1940s, and thereafter a steady decline. This pattern is a common business cycle time series, and we can describe historical behavior by cyclical movements. However, we are not suggesting that there is sufficient regularity in such historical patterns to allow the reliable prediction of future peaks and troughs. Indeed, the available evidence suggests that this is not the case.

We have discussed three sources of variability in a time series. If we could characterize time series primarily in terms of trend, seasonal, and cyclical components then the series would vary smoothly over time and forecasts could be made by using these components. However, actual data do not behave in that way. In addition to the major components the series will exhibit irregular components, induced by a multitude of factors influencing the behavior of any actual series and whose pattern looks rather unpredictable on the basis of past experience. These patterns can be thought of as similar to the random error term in a regression model. In all of the components examples that we have plotted so far we can see the irregular component clearly on top of the structural components.

TIME SERIES COMPONENTS ANALYSIS

A time series can be described by models based on the following components:

T_t Trend Component

S_t Seasonal Component

C_t Cyclical Component

I_t Irregular Component

Using these components we can define a time series as the sum of its components or an additive model

$$X_t = T_t + S_t + C_t + I_t$$

Alternatively, in other circumstances we might define a time series as the product of its components or a multiplicative model — often represented as a logarithmic additive model

$$X_t = T_t S_t C_t I_t$$

We do not have to restrict ourselves to just these two structural forms. For example, in some cases we might have a combination of additive and multiplicative forms.

Much of the early work in time series analysis concentrated on the isolation of the individual components from a series. Thus at any point in time the series value could be expressed as a function of the components. Often this approach was achieved by the use of moving averages, as we will discuss in the next two sections. This approach has been replaced in large part by more modern approaches. An exception is the problem of seasonal adjustment, which requires the extraction of the seasonal component from the series, that we will discuss in Section 17.6.

The more modern approach to time series analysis involves the construction of a formal model, in which various components are either explicitly or implicitly present, to describe the behavior of a data series. In model building , there are two possible treatments of series components. One is to regard them as being fixed over time, so that a trend might be represented by a straight line. This approach is often valuable in the analysis of physical data but is far less appropriate in business and economic applications, where experience suggests that any apparently fixed regularities are all too often illusory on closer examination. To illustrate the point, suppose that we consider the Lydia Pinkham data for the years 1936 through 1943 only. We see in Figure 17.9 that over this period, there appears to be a steady, fixed upward trend. However, had this "trend" been projected forward a few years from 1943, the resulting forecasts of future sales would have been highly inaccurate. It is only when we look at the picture in future years that we see just how inappropriate a fixed-trend model would have been.

For business and economic data, another treatment of the regular components of a time series is preferable. Rather than regarding them as being fixed for all time, it is generally more sensible to think of them as steadily evolving over time. Thus, we need not be committed to fixed trend or seasonal patterns but can allow the possibility that these components change with time. Models of this sort will be considered after we have looked at moving averages.

EXERCISES

17.11 The data file **Housing Starts** shows private housing units started per thousand of population in the United States over a period of 24 years.
(a) Use the large-sample variant of the runs test to test this series for randomness.
(b) Draw a time plot of this series and comment on the components of the series revealed by this plot.

17.12 The data file **Earnings per Share** shows earnings per share of a corporation over a period of 28 years.
(a) Use the large-sample variant of the runs test to test this series for randomness.
(b) Draw a time plot of this series and comment on the components of the series revealed by this plot.

17.4   MOVING AVERAGES

The irregular component in some time series may be so large that it obscures any underlying regularities, thus rendering difficult any visual interpretation of the time plot. In these circumstances, the actual plot will appear rather jagged, and we may want to smooth it to achieve a clearer picture. We can reduce this problem by using a moving average.

We can smooth using the method of moving averages, based on the idea that any large irregular component at any point in time will exert a smaller effect if we average the point with its immediate neighbors. The simplest procedure we can use is a simple centered $(2m + 1)$-point moving average. That is, we would replace each observation X_t by the average of itself and its neighbors so

$$X_t^* = \frac{1}{2m + 1} \sum_{j=-m}^{m} X_{t+j}$$
$$= \frac{X_{t-m} + X_{t-m+1} + \cdots + X_t + \cdots + X_{t+m-1} + X_{t+m}}{2m + 1}$$

For example, if we set m at 2, the 5-point moving average is

$$X_t^* = \frac{X_{t-2} + X_{t-1} + X_t + X_{t+1} + X_{t+2}}{5}$$

since the first observation is X_1, the first moving average term would be

$$X_3^* = \frac{X_1 + X_2 + X_3 + X_4 + X_5}{5}$$

This is the average of the first five observations. For the Lydia Pinkham sales data of Example 17.1 we have for 1933

$$X_3^* = \frac{1{,}806 + 1{,}644 + 1{,}814 + 1{,}770 + 1{,}518}{5} = 1{,}710.4$$

Similarly, X_4^* is the average of the second through the sixth observations, and so on. Table 17.4 gives the original and smoothed series. Notice that for centered moving averages we lose the first and last m observations. Thus while the original series runs from 1931 through 1960 the smoothed series goes from 1933 through 1958.

SIMPLE CENTERED (2*M* + 1)-POINT MOVING AVERAGES

Let $X_1, X_2, X_3, \ldots, X_n$ be *n* observations on a time series of interest. A smoothed series can be obtained by using a simple centered (2*m* + 1)-point moving average

$$X_t^* = \frac{1}{2m+1} \sum_{j=-m}^{m} X_{t+j} \qquad (t = m+1,\ m+2, \ldots, n-m) \qquad (17.3)$$

A moving average can be generated using Minitab as shown in Figure 17.13. We see both the original series and the smoothed series—the 5-Point Moving Average Series—plotted versus time. As we can see the moving average series is indeed smoother than the original series. Thus the moving average series has removed the underlying irregular component from the series to reveal better the structural components.

The kind of moving average discussed in this section is just one of many that might have been used. It is often deemed desirable to use a weighted average, in which most weight is given to the central observation, with weights for other values decreasing as their distance from the central observation increases. For example we might use a weighted average such as

$$X_t^* = \frac{X_{t-2} + 2X_{t-1} + 4X_t + 2X_{t+1} + X_{t+2}}{10}$$

TABLE 17.4
Annual Sales of Lydia Pinkham with the Simple Centered 5-Point Moving Average

YEAR	SALES	AVER1	YEAR	SALES	AVER1
1931	1806*		1946	2177	2232.4
1932	1644*		1947	1920	2125.6
1933	1814	1710.4	1948	1910	1955.6
1934	1770	1569.8	1949	1984	1858
1935	1518	1494.2	1950	1787	1847.2
1936	1103	1426	1951	1689	1844.4
1937	1266	1356.6	1952	1866	1784.4
1938	1473	1406.4	1953	1896	1753.6
1939	1423	1618	1954	1684	1747.2
1940	1767	1832	1955	1633	1687.8
1941	2161	2057.8	1956	1657	1586.6
1942	2336	2276.8	1957	1569	1527.2
1943	2602	2450.8	1958	1390	1458.4
1944	2518	2454	1959	1387*	
1945	2637	2370.8	1960	1289*	

FIGURE 17.13
Simple Centered 5-Point
Moving Average of Lydia
Pinkham Sales Data

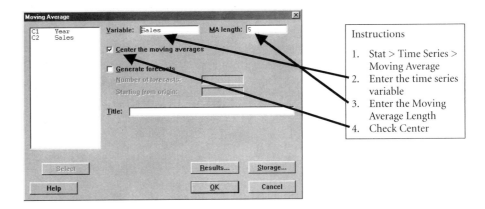

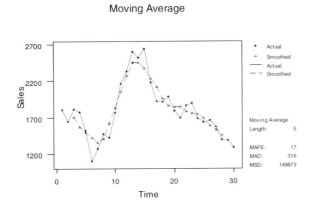

In any event, the objective in using moving averages remains the smoothing out of the irregular component in order to allow us to form a clearer picture of the underlying irregularities in a time series. The technique is perhaps of most value for descriptive purposes, in the production of graphs such as Figure 17.13.

Extraction of the Seasonal Component Through Moving Averages

We now move to develop a procedure for using moving averages to extract seasonal components from business and economic series. Seasonal components can be a nuisance, and the analyst may want to remove it from the series to obtain a keener appreciation of the behavior of other components. Recall also that in Section 12.2 we showed how dummy variables could be used to estimate and control seasonal effects.

Consider a quarterly time series with a seasonal component. Our strategy to remove seasonality will be to produce four period moving averages so that the various seasonal values are brought together in a single seasonal moving average. For example, using the earnings per share data in Table 17.5 the first member of the series would be

$$\frac{0.300 + 0.460 + 0.345 + 0.910}{4} = 0.50375$$

and the second member would be

$$\frac{0.460 + 0.345 + 0.910 + 0.330}{4} = 0.51125$$

The complete series is shown in Table 17.5.

TABLE 17.5
Actual Earnings per Share of a Corporation and Centered 4-Point Moving Average

YEAR QUARTER	EARNINGS	4-POINT MOVING AVERAGES	CENTERED 4-POINT MOVING AVERAGES
1.1	0.3	*	*
1.2	0.46	*	*
1.3	0.345	0.50375	0.5075
1.4	0.91	0.51125	0.5219
2.1	0.33	0.53250	0.5444
2.2	0.545	0.55625	0.5725
2.3	0.44	0.58875	0.6094
2.4	1.04	0.63000	0.6469
3.1	0.495	0.66375	0.6769
3.2	0.68	0.69000	0.7206
3.3	0.545	0.75125	0.7581
3.4	1.285	0.76500	0.7888
4.1	0.55	0.81250	0.8269
4.2	0.87	0.84125	0.8781
4.3	0.66	0.91500	0.9200
4.4	1.58	0.92500	0.9400
5.1	0.59	0.95500	0.9763
5.2	0.99	0.99750	1.0163
5.3	0.83	1.03500	1.0375
5.4	1.73	1.04000	1.0475
6.1	0.61	1.05500	1.0663
6.2	1.05	1.07750	1.1163
6.3	0.92	1.15500	1.1663
6.4	2.04	1.17750	1.2000
7.1	0.7	1.22250	1.2400
7.2	1.23	1.25750	1.2925
7.3	1.06	1.32750	1.3425
7.4	2.32	1.35750	1.3800
8.1	0.82	1.40250	1.4263
8.2	1.41	1.45000	1.5013
8.3	1.25	1.55250	*
8.4	2.73	*	*

This new series of moving averages should be free from seasonality, but there is still a problem. The location in time of the members of the series of moving averages does not correspond precisely with that of the members of the original series. The first term is the average of the first four observations and thus we might regard it as being centered between the second and third observations

$$X_{2.5}^* = \frac{X_1 + X_2 + X_3 + X_4}{4}$$

and similarly, the second term could be written as

$$X_{3.5}^* = \frac{X_2 + X_3 + X_4 + X_5}{4}$$

This problem can be overcome by centering our series of 4-point moving averages. This can be done by calculating the averages of adjacent pairs, which for the first value is

$$X_3^* = \frac{X_{2.5}^* + X_{3.5}^*}{2} = \frac{0.50375 + 0.51125}{2} = 0.5075$$

This value is the centered moving average corresponding to the third observation of the original series. The remainder of the series of centered moving averages is in the final column of Table 17.5. Note again that this procedure results in the loss of two observations from each end of the series.

The series of centered moving averages is plotted in Figure 17.14 along with the original series. Clearly the seasonality component has been removed. In addition, because we have used moving averages the irregular component has also been smoothed. The resulting picture thus allows us to judge the nonseasonal regularities in the data. We see that the smoothed series is dominated by an upward trend. Closer examination reveals steady earnings growth in the early part of the series, a central portion of rather slower growth, and resumption in the last part of the period of a pattern similar to the early one.

A SIMPLE MOVING AVERAGE PROCEDURE FOR SEASONAL ADJUSTMENT

Let X_t ($t = 1, 2, \ldots, n$) be a seasonal time series of period s ($s = 4$ for quarterly data and $s = 12$ for monthly data). A centered s-point moving average series, X_t^*, is obtained through the following steps, where it is assumed that s is even:

i. Form the s-point moving averages

$$X_{t+.5}^* = \frac{\sum\limits_{j=-(s/2)+1}^{s/2} X_{t+j}}{s} \qquad \left(t = \frac{s}{2}, \frac{s}{2}+1, \ldots, n - \frac{s}{2} \right) \qquad (17.4)$$

ii. Form the centered s-point moving averages

$$X_t^* = \frac{X_{t-.5}^* + X_{t+.5}^*}{2} \qquad \left(t = \frac{s}{2}+1, \frac{s}{2}+2, \ldots, n - \frac{s}{2} \right) \qquad (17.5)$$

FIGURE 17.14
Centered 4-Point Moving Averages and Original Series for Earnings per Share of a Corporation

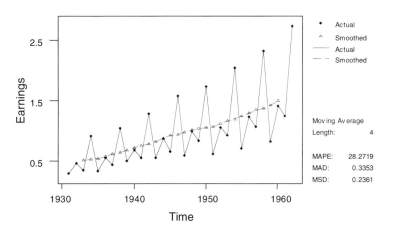

We have seen that the series of centered s-point moving averages can be a useful tool for gaining descriptive insight into the structure of a time series. Since it is largely free from seasonality and embodies a smoothing of the irregular component, it is well suited for the identification of a trend and/or cyclical component. This series of moving averages also forms the basis for many practical seasonal adjustment procedures. The specific procedure depends on a number of factors, including the amount of stability one assumes in the seasonal pattern and whether seasonality is viewed as additive or multiplicative. In the later case we often take logarithms of the data.

Next we will discuss a seasonal adjustment approach that is based on the implicit assumption of a stable seasonal pattern over time. The procedure is known as the seasonal index method. We assume that for any month or quarter, in each year, the effect of seasonality is to increase or decrease the series by the same percentage.

We will illustrate the seasonal index method using the corporate earnings data. The seasonally adjusted series is computed in Table 17.6. The first two columns contain the original series and the centered 4-point moving average. To assess the influence of seasonality, we express the original series as a percentage of the 4-point moving average series. Thus, for example, for the third quarter of year 1, we have

$$100 \left(\frac{X_3}{X_3^*} \right) = 100 \left(\frac{0.345}{0.5075} \right) = 67.98$$

These percentages are also entered into Table 17.7, where the calculation of the seasonal indices is shown. To assess the effect of seasonality in the first quarter, we find the median of the seven percentages for that quarter. This is the fourth value when they are arranged in ascending order; that is, 60.43. In a similar way we find the median of X_t as a percentage of X_t^* for each of the other quarters.

To obtain seasonal indices we also adjust the indices so that their average is 100. In Table 17.7 we see that the four medians sum only to 395.88. We can obtain the final indices—that have a mean of 100—by multiplying each median by (400/395.88). For the first quarter we have

$$\text{Seasonal Index} = 60.43 \left(\frac{400}{395.88} \right) = 61.06$$

We interpret this figure as estimating that the effect of seasonality is to lower first quarter earnings to 61.06% of what they would have been in the absence of seasonal factors.

The seasonal indicies, from the last row of Table 17.7, are entered in the fifth column of Table 17.6. Notice that the same index is used for any particular quarter in every year. Finally, we obtain our seasonally adjusted value as

$$\text{Adjusted value} = \text{Original value} \left(\frac{100}{\text{Seasonal Index}} \right)$$

For example, for the third quarter of year 1, the seasonally adjusted value is

$$0.345 \left(\frac{100}{72.95} \right) = 0.4729$$

TABLE 17.6
Seasonal Adjustment of Earnings per Share of a Corporation by the Seasonal Index Method

YEAR QUARTER	X_t	X_t^*	$100\left(\dfrac{X_t}{X_t^*}\right)$	SEASONAL INDEX	ADJUSTED SERIES
1.1	0.300*			61.06	0.4913
1.2	0.460*			96.15	0.4784
1.3	0.345	0.5075	67.98	72.95	0.4729
1.4	0.910	0.5219	174.37	169.84	0.5358
2.1	0.330	0.5444	60.62	61.06	0.5405
2.2	0.545	0.5725	95.20	96.15	0.5668
2.3	0.440	0.6094	72.20	72.95	0.6032
2.4	1.040	0.6469	160.77	169.84	0.6123
3.1	0.495	0.6769	73.13	61.06	0.8107
3.2	0.680	0.7206	94.36	96.15	0.7072
3.3	0.545	0.7581	71.89	72.95	0.7471
3.4	1.285	0.7888	162.92	169.84	0.7566
4.1	0.550	0.8269	66.52	61.06	0.9008
4.2	0.870	0.8781	99.07	96.15	0.9048
4.3	0.660	0.9200	71.74	72.95	0.9047
4.4	1.580	0.9400	168.09	169.84	0.9303
5.1	0.590	0.9763	60.44	61.06	0.9663
5.2	0.990	1.0163	97.42	96.15	1.0296
5.3	0.830	1.0375	80.00	72.95	1.1378
5.4	1.730	1.0475	165.16	169.84	1.0186
6.1	0.610	1.0663	57.21	61.06	0.9990
6.2	1.050	1.1163	94.06	96.15	1.0920
6.3	0.920	1.1663	78.89	72.95	1.2611
6.4	2.040	1.2000	170.00	169.84	1.2011
7.1	0.700	1.2400	56.45	61.06	1.1464
7.2	1.230	1.2925	95.16	96.15	1.2793
7.3	1.060	1.3425	78.96	72.95	1.4531
7.4	2.320	1.3800	168.12	169.84	1.3660
8.1	0.820	1.4263	57.49	61.06	1.3429
8.2	1.410	1.5013	93.92	96.15	1.4665
8.3	1.250*			72.95	1.7135
8.4	2.730*			169.84	1.6074

TABLE 17.7
Calculation of Seasonal Indices for Earnings per Share Data of a Corporation

YEAR	QUARTER 1	QUARTER 2	QUARTER 3	QUARTER 4	SUMS
1			67.98	174.36	
2	60.62	95.20	72.20	160.77	
3	73.13	94.37	71.89	162.91	
4	66.51	99.08	71.74	168.09	
5	60.43	97.41	80.00	165.16	
6	57.21	94.06	78.88	170.00	
7	56.45	95.16	78.96	168.12	
8	57.49	93.92			
Median	60.43	95.16	72.20	168.09	395.88
Seasonal Index	61.06	96.15	72.95	169.84	400

FIGURE 17.15
Seasonally Adjusted Earnings
per Share of a Corporation

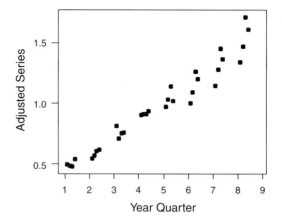

The complete seasonally adjusted series obtained in this way is given in the final column of Table 17.6 and graphed in Figure 17.15. Notice that there is a suggestion of a little remaining seasonality in the latter part of the period. This suggests that a more elaborate approach, allowing for changing seasonal patterns may be desirable.

The seasonal index method presented here provides one simple solution to the index problem. Many important time series, such as gross domestic product and its components, employment and unemployment, prices, and wages, have strong seasonal components. Generally, data on such quantities are published by government agencies in both unadjusted and adjusted form. Although they are more complex than the method described here, official adjustment procedures are typically based on moving averages. The seasonal adjustment procedure most commonly employed in official U.S. government publications is the Census X-11 method. It differs from the seasonal index method in allowing for a steadily evolving seasonal pattern over time. It can be shown that in its additive version, X-11, estimates the seasonal component of a monthly time series, to a close approximation by

$$S_t = \frac{Z_{t-36} + 2Z_{t-24} + 3Z_{t-12} + 3Z_t + 3Z_{t+12} + 2Z_{t+24} + Z_{t+36}}{15}$$

where

$$Z_t = X_t - X_t^*$$

with X_t the original value of the series at time t and X_t^* the corresponding centered 12-point moving average. Of course, if such a procedure is used, some special treatment is needed for values toward the end of the series, as the expression for the seasonal factor will involve values in the time series that have not yet occurred. A possible way of accomplishing this is to replace unknown future values of a series in the moving average by forecasts based on the available data.

EXERCISES

17.13 ⊙ The data file **Quarterly Earnings 17.13** shows quarterly sales of a corporation over a period of six years.
(**a**) Draw a time plot of this series, and discuss its features.

(**b**) Use the seasonal index method to seasonally adjust this series. Graph the seasonally adjusted series and discuss its features.

17.14 ⊙ The data file **Quarterly Sales** shows quarterly sales of a corporation over a period of six years.

(a) Draw a time plot of this series, and discuss its features.

(b) Use the seasonal index method to seasonally adjust this series. Graph the seasonally adjusted series and discuss its features.

17.15 Compute a simple centered 3-point moving average series for the gold price data of Exercise 17.10. Plot the smoothed series and discuss the resulting graph.

17.16 Compute simple centered 5-point moving averages for the housing starts data of Exercise 17.11. Draw a time plot of the smoothed series and comment on your results.

17.17 Compute a simple centered 7-point moving average series for the corporate earnings data of Exercise 17.12. Based on a time plot of the smoothed series, what can be said about its regular components?

17.18 Let

$$X_t^* = \frac{1}{2m+1} \sum_{j=-m}^{m} X_{t+j}$$

be a simple centered $(2m+1)$-point moving average. Show that

$$X_{t+1}^* = X_t^* \frac{X_{t+m+1} - X_{t-m}}{2m+1}$$

How might this result be used in the efficient computation of series of centered moving averages?

17.19 The data file **Quarterly Earnings 17.19** shows earnings per share of a corporation over a period of seven years.

(a) Draw a time plot of these data. Does your graph suggest the presence of a strong seasonal component in this earnings series?

(b) Using the seasonal index method, obtain a seasonally adjusted earnings series. Graph this series, and comment on its behavior.

17.20 (a) Show that the centered s-point moving average series of Section 17.6 can be written

$$X_t^* = \frac{X_{t-(s/2)} + 2\left(X_{t-(s/2)+1} + \cdots + X_{t+(s/2)-1}\right) + X_{t+(s/2)}}{2s}$$

(b) Show that

$$X_{t+1}^* = X_t^* + \frac{X_{t+(s/2)+1} + X_{t+(s/2)} - X_{t-(s/2)+1} - X_{t-(s/2)}}{2s}$$

Discuss the computational advantages of this formula in the seasonal adjustment of monthly time series.

17.21 The data file **Monthly Sales** shows monthly product sales over a period of three years. Use the seasonal index method to obtain a seasonally adjusted series.

17.5   EXPONENTIAL SMOOTHING

We now examine some procedures for using the current and past values of a time series to forecast future values of the series. This easily stated problem can be very difficult to resolve satisfactorily. A vast array of forecasting methods are in common use, and to a great extent, the eventual choice will be problem-specific, depending on the resources and objectives of the analyst and the nature of the available data.

Our aim is to use the available observations $X_1, X_2,\ldots, X_t$, on a series to predict the unknown future values $X_{t+1}, X_{t+2},\ldots$. Forecasting is of crucial importance in the business environment as a rational basis for decision making. For example, monthly product sales are predicted as a basis for inventory control policy. Forecasts of future earnings are used when making investment decisions.

In this section we will introduce a forecasting method known as **simple exponential smoothing** that performs quite effectively in a number of forecasting applications. In addition, it forms the basis for some more elaborate forecasting methods. Exponential smoothing is appropriate when the series is nonseasonal and has no consistent upward or downward trend.

In the absence of trend and seasonality, the objective is to estimate the current level of the time series and then use this estimate to forecast future values. Our position is that we are standing at time t, looking back on the series of observations $X_t, X_{t-1}, X_{t-2},\ldots$, and we want to form an assessment of the current level of the series. As a prelude, we will consider two extreme possibilities. First, we might simply use the most recent observation to forecast all future observations. In some cases such as prices in speculative markets this may be the best we can do, but the result is not very successful. However, in many series with irregular components we would likely want to use a number of previous observations in the series. This would identify any patterns that might exist in the time series and avoid using only a random fluctuation as the basis of our forecast.

At the opposite extreme, we might use the average of all past values as our estimate of the current level. A moment's reflection will suggest that often this would not be useful, because all past values would be treated equally. Thus, for example, if we tried to predict future sales by this procedure we would be assigning equal importance to sales many years ago and to recent sales. It seems reasonable that more recent experience should have a greater impact on our forecast.

Simple exponential smoothing allows a compromise between these extremes, providing a forecast based on a weighted average of current and past values. In forming this average, most weight is given to the most recent observation, rather less to the immediately preceding value, less to the one before that, and so on. We estimate the level at the current time t by

$$\hat{X}_t = (1 - \alpha)X_t + \alpha(1 - \alpha)X_{t-1} + \alpha^2(1 - \alpha)X_{t-2} + \cdots$$

where α is a number between 0 and 1. For example with $\alpha = 0.5$ the forecast of future observations is

$$\hat{X}_t = .5X_t + .25X_{t-1} + .125X_{t-2} + \cdots$$

so that a weighted average, with declining weights, is applied to current and past observations in computing the forecasts.

From this model we see that the forecast of the series at any time t is estimated by

$$\hat{X}_t = (1 - \alpha)X_t + \alpha(1 - \alpha)X_{t-1} + \alpha^2(1 - \alpha)X_{t-2} + \cdots$$

and, similarly, the level at the previous time period $(t - 1)$, would be estimated by

$$\hat{X}_{t-1} = (1 - \alpha)X_{t-1} + \alpha(1 - \alpha)X_{t-2} + \alpha^2(1 - \alpha)X_{t-3} + \cdots$$

Multiplying through by α we have

$$\alpha\hat{X}_{t-1} = \alpha(1 - \alpha)X_{t-1} + \alpha^2(1 - \alpha)X_{t-2} + \alpha^3(1 - \alpha)X_{t-3} + \cdots$$

Hence, on subtracting these two equations we obtain

$$\hat{X}_t - \alpha\hat{X}_{t-1} = (1 - \alpha)X_t$$

And by simple manipulation we have the equation for computing the simple exponential smoothing forecast

$$\hat{X}_t = \alpha\hat{X}_{t-1} + (1 - \alpha)X_t \quad \text{for } 0 < \alpha < 1$$

This provides a convenient recursive algorithm for calculating forecasts. The forecast value, $\hat{X}_t$, at time t is a weighted average of the previous period forecast $\hat{X}_{t-1}$ and the latest observation X_t. The weights given to each depend on the choice of α, which is defined as the smoothing constant. Note that a large value of α gives greater weight to $\hat{X}_{t-1}$, which is based on the past history of the series, and less weight to X_t which represents the most recent data.

We can illustrate the procedure using the Lydia Pinkham sales data with a value of $\alpha = 0.4$. The process begins by setting the first element of the series

$$\hat{X}_1 = X_1 = 1{,}806$$

the second value in the forecast would be

$$\hat{X}_2 = .4\hat{X}_1 + .6X_2$$
$$= (.4)(1,806) + (.6)(1,644) = 1,708.8$$

And this process continues through the series so that

$$\hat{X}_3 = .4\hat{X}_2 + .6X_3$$
$$= (.4)(1,708.8) + (.6)(1,814) = 1,771.9$$

FORECASTING THROUGH SIMPLE EXPONENTIAL SMOOTHING

Let X_1, X_2,..., X_n be a set of observations on a nonseasonal time series with no consistent upward or downward trend. The **simple exponential smoothing method of forecasting** then proceeds as follows:

i. Obtain the smoothed series $\hat{X}_t$, as

$$\hat{X}_1 = X_1$$

$$\hat{X}_t = \alpha \hat{X}_{t-1} + (1-\alpha)X_t \qquad (0 < \alpha < 1; t = 2,3,\ldots,n) \qquad (17.6)$$

where α is a smoothing constant whose value is fixed between 0 and 1.

ii. Standing at time n, we obtain forecasts of future values, X_{n+h}, of the series by

$$\hat{X}_{n+h} = \hat{X}_n \qquad (h = 1, 2, 3 \ldots)$$

So far, we have said little about the choice of the smoothing constant, α, in practical applications. In applications this choice may be based on either subjective or objective grounds. One possibility is to rely on experience or judgement. For instance, an analyst who wants to predict product demand may have had considerable experience in working with data on similar product lines and may use that experience to select an appropriate α. Visual inspection of a graph of the available data can also be useful in suggesting an appropriate value for the smoothing constant. If the series appears to contain a substantial irregular element, we would not want to give too much weight to the most recent observation alone, since it might not indicate what we expect in the future. This would suggest a relatively high value for the smoothing constant. But if the series is rather smooth we would use a lower value for α in order to give more weight to the most recent observation.

A more objective approach is to try several different values and see which would have been most successful in predicting historical movements in the time series. We might, for example, compute the smoothed series at values of α of 0.2, 0.4, 0.6, and 0.8 and choose the value that provides the best forecast in the historical series. We would compute the error for each forecast

$$e_t = X_t - \hat{X}_{t-1}$$

One possibility is to compute, for each trial value of α, the sum of squared forecast errors

$$SS = \sum_{t=2}^{n} e_t^2 = \sum_{t=2}^{n} \left(X_t - \hat{X}_{t-1}\right)^2$$

FIGURE 17.16
Simple Exponential
Smoothing for Pinkham Sales
Data ($\alpha = 0.1$)

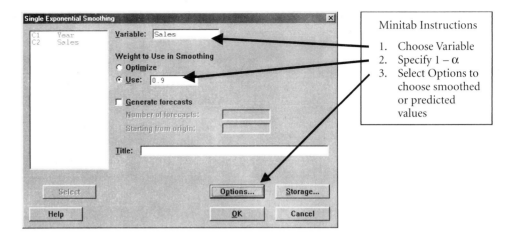

The value of α that minimizes the sum of squared forecast errors will be used for future predictions. Simple exponential smoothing can be performed using Minitab as shown in Figure 17.16. Note that the Minitab algorithm uses $1 - \alpha$ instead of α as its parameter. To access the procedure we use the Minitab command sequence

```
STAT > TIME SERIES > SINGLE EXPONENTIAL SMOOTHING
```

Figure 17.17 shows a plot of the original and smoothed series using $\alpha = 0.1$, which was established by trying different values and finding the value that provided a satisfactory fit. The reported MSD in Figure 17.17 is the sum of squared forecast errors, SS, divided by the number of observations, n.

Whatever value of the smoothing constant is used, Equation 17.6 can be regarded as an updating mechanism. At time $(t - 1)$, the level of the series is estimated by $\hat{X}_{t-1}$. Then, in the next period the new observation X_t is used to update this estimate, so that the new estimate of level is a weighted average of the previous estimate and the new observation.

FIGURE 17.17
Lydia Pinkham Sales Data
with Original and Simple
Exponential Smoothing
Values

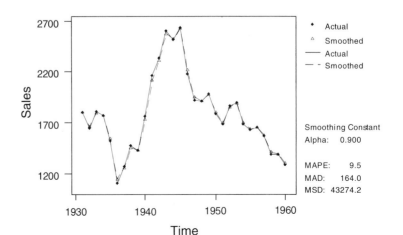

The Holt-Winters Exponential Smoothing Forecasting Model

Many business forecasting procedures are based on extensions of simple exponential smoothing. The Holt-Winters Exponential Smoothing procedure allows for trend, and possibly also seasonality, in a time series.

First we consider a nonseasonal time series. We want to estimate not only the current level of the series but also the trend—regarded as the difference between the current level and the preceding level.

We denote the observed value as X_t and $\hat{X}_t$ as the estimate of the level. The trend estimate is represented as T_t. The principle behind the estimation of these two quantities is much the same as in the simple exponential smoothing algorithm. The two estimating equations are

$$\hat{X}_t = \alpha\left(\hat{X}_{t-1} + T_{t-1}\right) + \left(1 - \alpha\right)X_t \qquad \left(0 < \alpha < 1\right)$$

$$T_t = \beta T_{t-1} + (1 - \beta)(\hat{X}_t - \hat{X}_{t-1}) \qquad (0 < \beta < 1)$$

where α and β are smoothing constants whose values are set between 0 and 1.

Comparable to simple exponential smoothing the Holt-Winters procedure uses these equations to update previous estimates using a new observation. The estimate of level, $\hat{X}_{t-1}$, made at time $(t - 1)$, taken in conjunction with the trend estimate, T_{t-1}, suggests for time t a level $(\hat{X}_{t-1} + T_{t-1})$. This estimate is modified, in light of the new observation, X_t, to obtain an updated estimate of level, $\hat{X}_t$, using the given equation.

Similarly, trend at time $(t - 1)$ is estimated as T_{t-1}. However, once the new observation X_t is available, an estimate of trend is suggested as the difference between the two most recent estimates of level. The trend estimate at time t is then the weighted average as given.

We begin the computations by setting

$$T_2 = X_2 - X_1 \qquad \text{and} \qquad \hat{X}_2 = X_2$$

Then the above equations are applied in turn for $t = 3, 4, \ldots, n$. We will demonstrate these calculations in Example 17.2. The entire procedure is summarized in the box.

FORECASTING WITH THE HOLT-WINTERS METHOD: NONSEASONAL SERIES

Let $X_1, X_2, \ldots, X_n$ be a set of observations on a nonseasonal time series. The **Holt-Winters method** of forecasting proceeds as follows

i. Obtain estimates of level $\hat{X}_t$ and trend T_t as

$$\hat{X}_t = X_2 \qquad\qquad T_2 = X_2 - X_1$$

$$\hat{X}_t = \alpha(\hat{X}_{t-1} + T_{t-1}) + (1 - \alpha)X_t \qquad (0 < \alpha < 1; t = 3, 4\ldots, n)$$

$$T_t = \beta T_{t-1} + (1 - \beta)(\hat{X}_t - \hat{X}_{t-1}) \ (0 < \beta < 1; t = 3, 4, \ldots, n) \qquad \textbf{(17.7)}$$

where α and β are smoothing constants whose values are fixed between 0 and 1.

ii. Standing at time n, we obtain forecasts of future values, X_{n+h}, of the series by

$$\hat{X}_{n+h} = \hat{X}_n + hT_n \qquad\qquad \textbf{(17.8)}$$

EXAMPLE 17.2

FORECASTING CONSUMER CREDIT (HOLT-WINTERS EXPONENTIAL SMOOTHING)

You are asked to obtain a forecast for outstanding consumer credit using Holt-Winters exponential smoothing procedure.

SOLUTION

The calculations that follow use the consumer credit data in Table 17.8, which also includes the calculations for the Holt-Winters procedure.

The initial estimates of level and trend in year 2, are

$$\hat{X}_2 = X_2 = 155$$

and

$$T_2 = X_2 - X_1 = 155 - 133 = 22$$

This smoothing application will use $\alpha = 0.3$ and $\beta = 0.4$ and the equations

$$\hat{X}_t = 0.3(\hat{X}_{t-1} + T_{t-1}) + 0.7 X_t$$
$$T_t = 0.4 T_{t-1} + 0.6(\hat{X}_t - \hat{X}_{t-1})$$

Then for $t = 3$

$$\hat{X}_3 = 0.3(\hat{X}_2 + T_2) + 0.7 X_3$$
$$= (0.3)(155 + 22) + (0.7)(165)$$
$$= 168.6$$

and in addition

$$T_3 = 0.4 T_2 + 0.6(\hat{X}_3 - \hat{X}_2)$$
$$= (0.4)(22) + (0.6)(168.6 - 155)$$
$$= 16.96$$

Then for $t = 4$

$$\hat{X}_4 = 0.3(\hat{X}_3 + T_3) + 0.7 X_4$$
$$= (0.3)(168.6 + 16.96) + (0.7)(171)$$
$$= 175.4$$

and in addition

$$T_4 = 0.4 T_3 + 0.6(\hat{X}_4 - \hat{X}_3)$$
$$= (0.4)(16.96) + (0.6)(175.4 - 168.6)$$
$$= 10.84$$

TABLE 17.8
Holt-Winters Calculations for Consumer Credit Outstanding ($\alpha = .3$, $\beta = .4$)

t	X_t	$\hat{X}_t$	T_t
1	133		
2	155	155	22
3	165	169	17
4	171	175	11
5	194	192	14
6	231	223	25
7	274	266	36
8	312	309	40
9	313	324	25
10	333	338	18
11	343	347	13

The remaining calculations continue in the same way, setting in turn $t = 5, 6, \ldots, 11$. The results of these calculations are shown in Table 17.8.

Now let us use these level and trend estimates to forecast future observations. Given a series $X_1, X_2, \ldots, X_n$, the most recent level and trend estimates are $\hat{X}_t$ and T_n, respectively. In the production of forecasts, it is assumed that this latest trend will continue from the most recent level. Thus we forecast using the relationships

$$\hat{X}_{n+1} = \hat{X}_n + T_n$$

and the following one as

$$\hat{X}_{n+2} = \hat{X}_n + 2 T_n$$

and in general for h periods ahead

$$\hat{X}_{n+h} = \hat{X}_n + hT_n$$

From Table 17.8 the most recent level and trend estimates are

$$\hat{X}_{11} = 347 \qquad T_{11} = 13$$

Then the forecasts for the next three periods are

$$\hat{X}_{12} = 347 + 13 = 360$$
$$\hat{X}_{13} = 347 + (2)(13) = 373$$
$$\hat{X}_{14} = 347 + (3)(13) = 386$$

The Holt-Winters procedure can be computed in Minitab using the command sequence

```
STAT > TIME SERIES > DOUBLE EXPONENTIAL SMOOTHING
```

Figure 17.18 shows how to initiate the procedure in Minitab and Figure 17.19 presents the time series graph and the forecasts. The Minitab procedure differs slightly from the procedure just described. First the Level and Trend entries are equal to

$$\text{Level} = 1 - \alpha$$
$$\text{Trend} = 1 - \beta$$

In addition Minitab computes an estimate for the first period using the following procedure:

1. Minitab fits a linear regression model to time series data (y variable) versus time (x variable).
2. The constant from this regression is the initial estimate of the level component, the slope coefficient is the initial estimate of the trend component.

As a result the values calculated by the Minitab program will differ slightly from those in Table 17.8. The comparable values computed by the Minitab procedure are shown in Table 17.9. The Minitab procedures will generally provide slightly better forecasts compared to the more simplified procedure we have shown. For other statistical packages, check the

FIGURE 17.18
Implementing Holt-Winter Time Series Forecasts

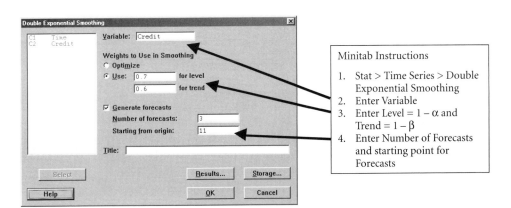

Minitab Instructions

1. Stat > Time Series > Double Exponential Smoothing
2. Enter Variable
3. Enter Level = $1 - \alpha$ and Trend = $1 - \beta$
4. Enter Number of Forecasts and starting point for Forecasts

FIGURE 17.19
Consumer Credit
Outstanding Observed and
Forecasts

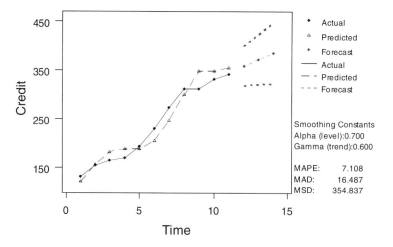

Double Exponential Smoothing for Credit

TABLE 17.9
Minitab Calculations for
Consumer Credit
Outstanding ($\alpha = 0.3$,
$\beta = 0.4$)

TIME	OBSERVED CONSUMER CREDIT	LEVEL EXPECTED VALUE	TREND	FORECASTS
1	133	130	28	
2	155	156	27	
3	165	170	19	
4	171	177	12	
5	194	192	14	
6	231	224	24	
7	274	266	35	
8	312	309	40	
9	313	324	25	
10	333	338	18	
11	343	347	13	
12				360
13				373
14				385

specific computational algorithms to ensure that you understand what is being computed. Usually this can be done by clicking the Help option.

Forecasting Seasonal Time Series

We will now examine an extension of the Holt-Winters method that allows for seasonality. In most practical problems, the seasonal factor is taken to be multiplicative, so that, for example, in dealing with monthly sales figures, we might think of January in terms of a proportion of average monthly sales. As before, the trend component is assumed to be additive.

Similar to the nonseasonal case, we will use X_t, $\hat{X}_t$, and T_t to denote, respectively, the observed value and level and trend estimates at time t. The seasonal factor will be denoted F_t, so if the time series contains s periods per year the seasonal factor for the corresponding period in the previous year will be F_{t-s}.

In the Holt-Winters model, the estimates of level, trend, and the seasonal factor are updated by the following three equations:

$$\hat{X}_t = \alpha(\hat{X}_{t-1} + T_{t-1}) + (1-\alpha)\frac{X_t}{F_{t-s}} \quad (0 < \alpha < 1)$$

$$T_t = \beta T_{t-1} + (1-\beta)(\hat{X}_t - \hat{X}_{t-1}) \quad (0 < \beta < 1)$$

$$F_t = \gamma F_{t-s} + (1-\gamma)\frac{X_t}{\hat{X}_t} \quad (0 < \gamma < 1)$$

where α, β, and γ are smoothing constants with values between 0 and 1.

The term, $\left(\hat{X}_{t-1} + T_{t-1}\right)$ is an estimate of the level at time, formed at the previous time period $t-1$. This estimate is then updated when X_t becomes available. But we also remove the influence of seasonality by deflating it by the latest available estimate, F_{t-s}, of the seasonal factor for that period. The updating equation for trend; T_t, is the same as used previously.

Finally, the seasonal factor, F_t, is estimated using the third equation. The most recent estimate of the factor, available from the previous year, is F_{t-s}. However, dividing the new observation X_t by the level estimate $\hat{X}_t$ suggests a seasonal factor $X_t / \hat{X}_t$. The new estimate of the seasonal factor is then a weighted average of these two quantities.

FORECASTING WITH THE HOLT-WINTERS METHOD: SEASONAL SERIES

Let $X_1, X_2, \ldots, X_t$ be a set of observations on a seasonal time series of period s (with $s = 4$ for quarterly data and $s = 12$ for monthly data). The **Holt-Winters method** of forecasting uses a set of recursive estimates from the historical series. These estimates utilize a level factor, α, a trend factor, β, and a multiplicative seasonal factor, γ. The recursive estimates are based on the following equations

$$\hat{X}_t = \alpha(\hat{X}_{t-1} + T_{t-1}) + (1-\alpha)\frac{X_t}{F_{t-s}} \quad (0 < \alpha < 1)$$

$$T_t = \beta T_{t-1} + (1-\beta)(\hat{X}_t - \hat{X}_{t-1}) \quad (0 < \beta < 1) \qquad \textbf{(17.9)}$$

$$F_t = \gamma F_{t-s} + (1-\gamma)\frac{X_t}{\hat{X}_t} \quad (0 < \gamma < 1)$$

Where $\hat{X}_t$ is the smoothed level of the series, T_t is the smoothed trend of the series, and F_t is the smoothed seasonal adjustment for the series. The computational details are tedious and best left to a computer. We have demonstrated the algorithm used by Minitab, but numerous quality statistical packages have similar procedures. These computer procedures may differ in the way they handle the generation of factors for the initial periods of an observed time series, and thus you should consult the documentation for the package to determine the exact procedure used. Minitab uses a dummy variable regression procedure to obtain estimates for the initial periods.

After the initial procedures generates the level, trend, and seasonal factors from a historical series we can use the results to forecast future values at, h, time periods ahead from the last observation X_n in the historical series. The forecast equation is

$$\hat{X}_{t+h} = (\hat{X}_t + hT_t)F_{t+h-s} \qquad \textbf{(17.10)}$$

We note that the seasonal factor, F, is the one generated for the most recent seasonal time period.

The procedure that we have developed here can be implemented using the Minitab procedure labeled "Winters" smoothing forecast. Specifically the method described here uses the

FIGURE 17.20
Minitab Procedure for Holt-Winters Forecast of Corporate Earnings per Share

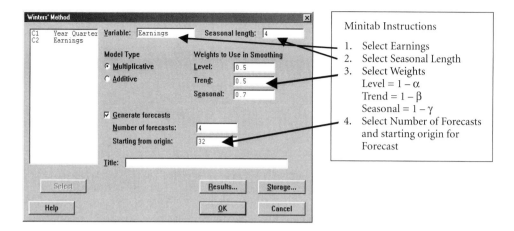

"multiplicative" option. The Winters method employs a level component, a trend component, and a seasonal component at each period. It uses three weights, or smoothing parameters, to update the components at each period. Initial values for the level and trend components are obtained from a linear regression on time. Initial values for the seasonal component are obtained from a dummy-variable regression using detrended data. The Winters method smoothing equations for the multiplicative model are those previously used.

This procedure will be demonstrated using the corporate earnings per share in Minitab as shown in Figure 17.20. A plot of observed and fitted values along with forecasts for the next four periods are shown in Figure 17.21. Forecasts are obtained by using the most recent trend and level estimates and then adjusting for the particular seasonal factor. Given a season containing s time periods the forecast for one period ahead would be

$$\hat{X}_{t+1} = (\hat{X}_n + T_t)F_{t+1-s}$$

Our example data contains 32 time periods and a seasonal factor $s = 4$ indicating quarterly data. Thus to forecast the next observation beyond the end of the series we would use

$$\hat{X}_{33} = (\hat{X}_{32} + T_{32})F_{29}$$

FIGURE 17.21
History and Forecast of Corporate Earnings Using Holt-Winters Method

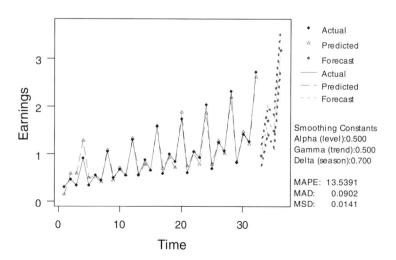

Winters' Multiplicative Model for Earnings

This forecast would be for the first quarter; thus we would use the most recent first quarter seasonal factor and that is F_{29}. In general, if we are forecasting h periods into the future we would obtain the forecast as

$$\hat{X}_{n+h} = (\hat{X}_n + hT_n)F_{n+h-s}$$

The Minitab command for computing the factor and the forecast is

```
STAT > TIME SERIES > WINTERS METHOD
```

The forecast here uses a level factor, $\alpha = 0.5$, a trend, $\beta = 0.5$, and a seasonal factor, $\gamma = 0.3$.

Finally, in Table 17.10 we show the detailed results of the computation of trend, level, and seasonal factor for each period.

TABLE 17.10
Computational Results: Minitab Application of Holt-Winters Smoothing Procedure

YEAR QUARTER	CORPORATE EARNINGS	SMOOTHED VALUE	LEVEL ESTIMATE	TREND ESTIMATE	SEASONAL ESTIMATE	FORECAST
1.1	0.300	0.043	0.387	0.242	0.713	
1.2	0.460	0.360	0.562	0.208	0.851	
1.3	0.345	0.433	0.609	0.128	0.628	
1.4	0.910	1.055	0.631	0.075	1.529	
2.1	0.330	0.450	0.584	0.014	0.609	
2.2	0.545	0.498	0.619	0.024	0.872	
2.3	0.440	0.389	0.672	0.039	0.646	
2.4	1.040	1.028	0.696	0.031	1.505	
3.1	0.495	0.424	0.770	0.053	0.633	
3.2	0.680	0.671	0.801	0.042	0.856	
3.3	0.545	0.518	0.843	0.042	0.646	
3.4	1.285	1.269	0.869	0.034	1.486	
4.1	0.550	0.550	0.886	0.025	0.624	
4.2	0.870	0.758	0.964	0.052	0.888	
4.3	0.660	0.623	1.019	0.053	0.648	
4.4	1.580	1.514	1.067	0.051	1.482	
5.1	0.590	0.666	1.032	0.008	0.588	
5.2	0.990	0.916	1.077	0.026	0.910	
5.3	0.830	0.697	1.193	0.071	0.681	
5.4	1.730	1.767	1.215	0.047	1.441	
6.1	0.610	0.714	1.150	−0.009	0.548	
6.2	1.050	1.047	1.147	−0.006	0.914	
6.3	0.920	0.782	1.246	0.046	0.721	
6.4	2.040	1.795	1.354	0.077	1.487	
7.1	0.700	0.741	1.355	0.039	0.526	
7.2	1.230	1.238	1.370	0.027	0.902	
7.3	1.060	0.988	1.433	0.045	0.734	
7.4	2.320	2.131	1.519	0.066	1.515	
8.1	0.820	0.799	1.572	0.059	0.523	
8.2	1.410	1.419	1.597	0.042	0.889	
8.3	1.250	1.172	1.671	0.058	0.744	
8.4	2.730	2.531	1.765	0.076	1.537	
9.1						0.963
9.2						1.705
9.3						1.48
9.4						3.18

The actual forecasts obtained through the Holt-Winters approach will depend on the specific values chosen for the smoothing constants. As in our earlier discussion of exponential smoothing, this choice could be based on either subjective or objective criteria. The analyst's experience with similar data sets might suggest suitable values of the smoothing constants. Alternatively, several different sets of possible values could be tried on the available historical data, and the set that would have yielded the best forecasts for that data would be used to generate the forecasts. This strategy is easy to implement by using a statistical computer package, such as the example we demonstrated using Minitab.

EXERCISES

17.22 Based on the data of Exercise 17.8, use the method of simple exponential smoothing to obtain forecasts of inventory-sales ratio over the next four years. Use a smoothing constant of $\alpha = .4$. Graph the observed time series and the forecasts.

17.23 Use the method of simple exponential smoothing, with a smoothing constant of $\alpha = .3$, to obtain forecasts of the price of gold in the next five years, based on the data of Exercise 17.10.

17.24 Using the data of Exercise 17.11, employ the method of simple exponential smoothing, with smoothing constant $\alpha = .5$, to predict housing starts in the next three years.

17.25 ◉ The data file **Earnings per Share 17.25** shows earnings per share of a corporation over a period of 18 years.
  (a) Using smoothing constants $\alpha = .2, .4, .6,$ and $.8$, find forecasts based on simple exponential smoothing.
  (b) Which of the forecasts would you choose to use?

17.26 (a) If forecasts are based on simple exponential smoothing, with $\hat{X}_t$ denoting the smoothed value of the series at time t, show that the error made in forecasting X_t, standing at time $(t - 1)$, can be written

$$e_t = X_t - \hat{X}_{t-1}$$

  (b) Hence, show that we can write $\hat{X}_t = X_t - \alpha e_t$ from which we see that the most recent observation and the most recent forecast error are used to compute the next forecast.

17.27 Suppose that in the simple exponential smoothing method, the smoothing constant α is set equal to 1. What forecasts will result?

17.28 Comment on the following statement: "We know that all business and economic time series exhibit variability

through time. Yet if simple exponential smoothing is used, the same forecast results for all future values of the time series. Since we know that all future values will not be the same, this is absurd."

17.29 ◉ The data file **Industrial Production Canada** shows an index of industrial production for Canada over a period of 15 years. Use the Holt-Winters procedure, with smoothing constants $\alpha = .3$ and $\beta = .5$, to obtain forecasts over the next 5 years.

17.30 ◉ The data file **Hourly Earnings** shows manufacturing hourly earnings in the United States over 24 months. Use the Holt-Winters procedure, with smoothing constants $\alpha = .3$ and $\beta = .4$, to obtain forecasts for the next 3 months.

17.31 ◉ The data file **Food Prices** shows an index of food prices, seasonally adjusted, over a period of 14 months in the United States. Use the Holt-Winters method with smoothing constants $\alpha = .5$ and $\beta = .5$ to obtain forecasts for the next 3 months.

17.32 ◉ The data file **Profit Margins** shows percentage profit margins of a corporation over a period of 11 years. Obtain forecasts for the next 2 years, using the Holt-Winters method with smoothing constants $\alpha = .6$ and $\beta = .6$.

17.33 Use the Holt-Winters seasonal method to obtain forecasts of sales up to eight quarters ahead, based on the data of Exercise 17.13. Employ smoothing constants $\alpha = .6, \beta = .5,$ and $\gamma = .4$. Graph the data and the forecasts.

17.34 Use the Holt-Winters seasonal method to obtain forecasts of sales up to eight quarters ahead, based on the data of Exercise 17.14. Employ smoothing constants $\alpha = .5, \beta = .4,$ and $\gamma = .3$. Graph the data and the forecasts.

17.6 AUTOREGRESSIVE MODELS

In this section we present a different approach to time series forecasting. This approach involves using the available data to estimate parameters of a model of the process that might have generated the time series. In this section we will consider one widely used procedure, *autoregressive models*, that is based on the model building approach.

In Section 12.3 we introduced the use of lagged dependent variables in multiple regression models and that approach is the basis of the models we will discuss here. Essentially, the idea is to regard a time series as a series of random variables. For practical purposes, we might often be prepared to assume that these random variables all have the same means and variances. However, we cannot assume that they are independent of each other. Certainly if we consider a series of product sales it is very likely that sales in adjacent periods are correlated with each other. Correlation patterns such as those between adjacent periods are sometimes referred to as *autocorrelation*.

In principle, any number of autocorrelation patterns are possible. However, some are considerably more likely to arise than others. A particularly attractive possibility arises when we think of a fairly strong correlation between adjacent observations in time, a less strong correlation between observations two time periods apart, a weaker correlation yet between values three time periods apart, and so on. A very simple autocorrelation pattern of this sort arises when the correlation between adjacent values is some number, say ϕ_1, that between values two time periods apart is, ϕ_1^2, that between values three time periods apart is, ϕ_1^3, and so on. Thus if we let X_t denote the value of the series at time t, we have under this model of autocorrelation

$$\text{Corr}(X_t, X_{t-j}) = \phi_1^j \qquad (j = 1, 2, 3, \ldots)$$

This autocorrelation structure gives rise to a time series model of the form

$$X_t = \gamma + \phi_1 X_{t-1} + \varepsilon_t$$

where γ and ϕ_1 are fixed parameters and the random variables ε_t have means 0 and fixed variances for all t and are not correlated with each other. The purpose of the parameter γ is to allow for the possibility that the series X_t has some mean other than 0. Otherwise, this is the model we used in Section 12.7 to represent autocorrelation in the error terms of a regression equation. It is called a *first-order autoregressive model*.

The first-order autoregressive model expresses the current value, X_t, of a series in terms of the previous value, X_{t-1}, and a nonautocorrelated random variable ε_t. Since the random variable ε_t is not autocorrelated, it is unpredictable. For series generated by the first-order autoregressive model, forecasts of future values depend only on the most recent value of the series. However, in many applications, we would want to use more than this one observation as a basis for forecasting. An obvious extension of the model would be to make the current value of the series dependent on the two most recent observations. Thus we could use a model

$$X_t = \gamma + \phi_1 X_{t-1} + \phi_2 X_{t-2} + \varepsilon_t$$

where γ, ϕ_1, and ϕ_2 are fixed parameters. This is called a *second-order autoregressive model*.

More generally, for any positive integer p, the current value of the series can be made (linearly) dependent on the p previous values through the autoregressive model of order p

$$X_t = \gamma + \phi_1 X_{t-1} + \phi_2 X_{t-2} + \cdots + \phi_p X_{t-p} + \varepsilon_t$$

where γ, ϕ_1, $\phi_2, \ldots, \phi_p$ are fixed parameters. This equation depicts the general autoregressive model. In the remainder of this section we will consider the fitting of such models and their use in forecasting future values.

Suppose that we have a series of observations $X_1, X_2, \ldots, X_n$. We want to use these to estimate the unknown parameters γ, ϕ_1, $\phi_2, \ldots, \phi_p$ for which the sum of squared discrepancies

$$SS = \sum_{t=p+1}^{n} (X_t - \gamma - \phi_1 X_{t-1} - \phi_2 X_{t-2} - \cdots - \phi_p X_{t-p})^2$$

is smallest. Hence, the estimation can be carried out using a multiple regression program. We will demonstrate, in Example 17.3, this procedure for the Lydia Pinkham Sales data.

AUTOREGRESSIVE MODELS AND THEIR ESTIMATION

Let X_t $(t = 1, 2, \ldots, n)$ be a time series. A model that can often be used effectively to represent that series is the autoregressive model of order p:

$$X_t = \gamma + \phi_1 X_{t-1} + \phi_2 X_{t-2} + \cdots + \phi_p X_{t-p} + \varepsilon_t \tag{17.11}$$

where $\gamma, \phi_1, \phi_2, \ldots, \phi_p$ are fixed parameters and the ε_t are random variables that have means 0 and constant variance and are uncorrelated with one another.

The parameters of the autoregressive model are estimated through a least squares algorithm, as the values of $\gamma, \phi_1, \phi_2, \ldots, \phi_p$ for which the sum of squares

$$SS = \sum_{t=p+1}^{n} (X_t - \gamma - \phi_1 X_{t-1} - \phi_2 X_{t-2} - \cdots - \phi_p X_{t-p})^2 \tag{17.12}$$

is a minimum.

EXAMPLE 17.3

FORECASTING SALES DATA (AUTOREGRESSIVE MODEL)

Pinkham Sales Data

You have been asked to develop an autoregressive model to forecast the Lydia **Pinkham Sales Data**.

SOLUTION

To use an autoregressive model to generate forecasts of future values it is necessary to fix a value for p, the order of the autoregression. In making this choice we must choose p large enough to account for all of the important autocorrelation behavior of the series. But in addition we do not want p to be so large that we are including irrelevant parameters, and as a result having inefficient estimation of the important parameters. In general parsimonious—simple but sufficient to accomplish the objective—models are preferred for good time series forecasting.

One possibility is to fix the value of p arbitrarily, perhaps on the basis of past experience with similar data sets. An alternative approach is to set some maximal order, K, of the autoregression and fit in turn models of order $p = K, K - 1, K - 2, \ldots$. For each value of p, the null hypothesis that the final autoregression parameter, ϕ_p, of the model is 0 is tested against a two-sided alternative. The procedure terminates when we find a value of p for which this null hypothesis is not rejected. Our aim, then, is to test the null hypothesis

$$H_0 : \phi_p = 0$$

against the alternative

$$H_1 : \phi_p \neq 0$$

In Chapter 10 we developed procedures for testing the null hypothesis H_0. Basically we know that the ratio of the coefficient estimate divided by the estimated coefficient standard deviation follows a student t distribution. The Minitab and PHSTAT regression output—and the regression output from any statistical package—includes that Student's t calculation and in addition the probability of the null hypothesis being true—the p-value for the null hypothesis—given the computed Student's t.

FORECASTING FROM ESTIMATED AUTOREGRESSIVE MODELS

Suppose that we have observations $X_1, X_2, \ldots, X_t$ from a time series and that an autoregressive model of order p has been fitted to these data. Write the estimated model as

$$X_t = \hat{\gamma} + \hat{\phi}_1 X_{t-1} + \hat{\phi}_2 X_{t-2} + \cdots + \hat{\phi}_p X_{t-p} + \varepsilon_t \qquad (17.13)$$

Standing at time n, we obtain forecasts of future values of the series from

$$\hat{X}_{t+h} = \hat{\gamma} + \hat{\phi}_1 \hat{X}_{t+h-1} + \hat{\phi}_2 \hat{X}_{t+h-2} + \cdots + \hat{\phi}_p \hat{X}_{t+h-p} \qquad (h = 1, 2, 3, \ldots) \quad (17.14)$$

where for $j > 0$, $\hat{X}_{n+j}$ is the forecast of X_{t+j} standing at time n and for $j \leq 0$, $\hat{X}_{t+j}$ is simply the observed value of X_{t+j}.

Figure 17.22 presents abbreviated copies of Minitab regression output for autoregressive models using the Lydia Pinkam sales data with $p = 1, 2, 3, 4$. The lag variables were created by the procedure

```
STAT > TIME SERIES > LAG
```

FIGURE 17.22
Autoregressive Models for the
Lydia Pinkham Sales Data

Regression with p = 1

```
Sales = 193 + 0.883 Salelag1
29 cases used 1 cases contain missing values
```

Predictor	Coef	StDev	T	P
Constant	193.3	189.0	1.02	0.316
Salelag1	0.8831	0.1024	8.62	0.000

S = 207.0   R-Sq = 73.4%   R-Sq(adj) = 72.4%

Regression with p = 2

```
Sales = 314 + 1.18 Salelag1 - 0.358 Salelag2
28 cases used 2 cases contain missing values
```

Predictor	Coef	StDev	T	P
Constant	313.7	192.5	1.63	0.116
Salelag1	1.1801	0.1870	6.31	0.000
Salelag2	-0.3578	0.1914	-1.87	0.073

S = 199.6   R-Sq = 76.9%   R-Sq(adj) = 75.1%

Regression with p = 3

```
Sales = 322 + 1.19 Salelag1 - 0.317 Salelag2 - 0.057 Salslag3
27 cases used 3 cases contain missing values
```

Predictor	Coef	StDev	T	P
Constant	322.3	215.7	1.49	0.149
Salelag1	1.1881	0.2065	5.75	0.000
Salelag2	-0.3168	0.3081	-1.03	0.315
Salslag3	-0.0574	0.2098	-0.27	0.787

S = 203.0   R-Sq = 78.1%   R-Sq(adj) = 75.2%

Regression with p = 4

```
Sales = 446 + 1.19 Salelag1 - 0.439 Salelag2 + 0.286 Salslag3 - 0.291
Salelag4
26 cases used 4 cases contain missing values
```

Predictor	Coef	StDev	T	P
Constant	446.2	232.8	1.92	0.069
Salelag1	1.1937	0.2108	5.66	0.000
Salelag2	-0.4391	0.3238	-1.36	0.190
Salslag3	0.2859	0.3174	0.90	0.378
Salelag4	-0.2914	0.2101	-1.39	0.180

S = 202.6   R-Sq = 80.1%   R-Sq(adj) = 76.3%

We will apply this approach for the Pinkham sales data, using a 10% significance level for our tests. Using the results in Figure 17.22 we begin with the regression with $p = 4$. We find that the coefficient of X_{t-4} has a student t statistic of -1.39 and a p-value of 0.180. Thus we cannot reject the null hypothesis that the coefficient is 0, and we move on to the regression with $p = 3$. Here we see that the coefficient of X_{t-3} has a Student's t statistic of equal to -0.27 and a p-value of 0.787. Again we cannot reject the null hypothesis that this coefficient is 0. For the regression model with $p = 2$ we see that the coefficient of X_{t-2} has a Student's t statistic of -1.87 and a p-value of 0.073. Thus we can reject the null hypothesis that the coefficient of X_{t-2} is 0. Our chosen model then is the one with two lagged values, $p = 2$. The final equation is

$$\hat{X}_t = 313.7 + 1.1801X_{t-1} - 0.3578X_{t-2}$$

Now that we have the model we want to apply it to obtain forecasts for the Lydia Pinkham sales data. We will begin by noting that the last two values in the data series are

$$X_{29} = 1{,}387 \qquad \text{and} \qquad X_{30} = 1{,}289$$

We can now predict the next value X_{31} as

$$
\begin{aligned}
\hat{X}_{31} &= 313.68 + 1.180X_{30} - 0.358X_{29} \\
&= 313.68 + (1.180)(1{,}289) - (0.358)(1{,}387) = 1{,}338.2
\end{aligned}
$$

We recognize that the predicted value of the error term ε_t is 0. Now we can forecast the next value in the series following the same procedure, except that we must use the forecast value for X_{31}, that is $\hat{X}_t$

$$
\begin{aligned}
\hat{X}_{32} &= 313.68 + 1.180\hat{X}_{31} - 0.358X_{30} \\
&= 313.68 + (1.180)(1{,}338.2) - (0.358)(1{,}289) = 1{,}431.249
\end{aligned}
$$

These calculations can be performed directly by Minitab—or any other good statistical package—and the results are shown in Figure 17.23.

FIGURE 17.23
Predicted Values from Autoregressive Model for Pinkham Sales Data

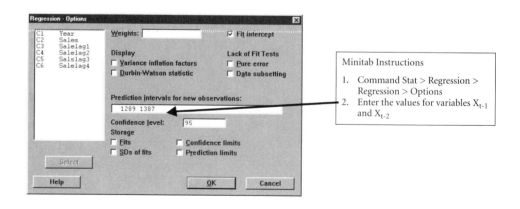

Minitab Instructions

1. Command Stat > Regression > Regression > Options
2. Enter the values for variables X_{t-1} and X_{t-2}

```
Sales = 314 + 1.18 Salelag1 - 0.358 Salelag2

28 cases used 2 cases contain missing values

Predictor        Coef       StDev          T        P
Constant        313.7       192.5       1.63    0.116
Salelag1       1.1801      0.1870       6.31    0.000
Salelag2      -0.3578      0.1914      -1.87    0.073

S = 199.6      R-Sq = 76.9%     R-Sq(adj) = 75.1%

Predicted Values

    Fit  StDev Fit        95.0% CI             95.0% PI
 1338.2       63.5   ( 1207.7,  1469.4)   (  907.1,  1770.1)
```

FIGURE 17.24
Sales of Lydia Pinkham and
Forecasts Based on a Fitted
Second-Order Autoregressive
Model

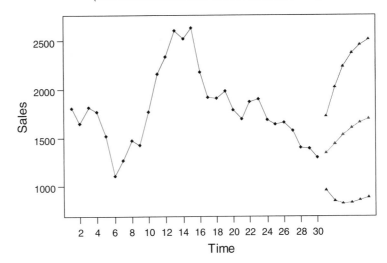

Time Series Plot for Sales

(with forecasts and their 95% confidence limits)

We can continue with this process and obtain predictions for as many future periods as we would like. The sales time series and the forecasts for six periods is shown in Figure 17.24.

EXERCISES

17.35 Using the data of Table 17.10, estimate a first-order autoregressive model for the index of volume of shares traded. Use the fitted model to obtain forecasts for the next four days.

17.36 The data file **Trading Volume** shows the volume of transactions (in hundreds of thousands) in shares of a corporation over a period of 12 weeks. Using these data, estimate a first-order autoregressive model, and use the fitted model to obtain forecasts of volume for the next 3 weeks.

17.37 Using the data file **Housing Starts** of Exercise 17.11 on housing starts, estimate autoregressive models of orders 1 through 4. Use the method of Section 17.6 for testing that the order of the autoregression is $(p - 1)$ against the alternative that the order is p, with a significance level of 10%. Select one of these models, and calculate forecasts of housing starts for the next five years. Draw a time plot showing the original observations together with the forecasts. Would different forecasts result if a significance level of 5% were used for the tests of autoregressive order?

17.38 From the data file **Earnings per Share** of Exercise 17.12 on corporate earning per share, fit autoregressive models of orders 1 through 4. Use the procedure of Section 17.6 for testing that the order of the autoregression is $(p - 1)$ against the alternative that the true order is p, with 10% significance level. Choose one of these models, and compute forecasts of earnings per share for the next five years. Draw a graph showing the original data along with these forecasts. Would the results differ if 5% significance levels were used for the tests?

17.39 Refer to the data file **Earnings per Share 17.25** of Exercise 17.25 on corporate earnings per share. Fit autoregressive models of orders 1, 2, and 3. Use the procedure of Section 17.6 to test the hypothesis that the order of the autoregression is $(p - 1)$ against the alternative that it is p, at 10% significance level, and thereby select a value for autoregressive order. Use the selected model to generate earnings-per-share forecasts up to four years ahead. Draw a time plot of the observations and forecasts. Would different results be obtained with 5%-level significance tests?

17.40 In Section 17.6, Figure 17.21, fitted autoregressive models of orders 1 through 4 are given for annual sales data. We then selected a model by testing the null hypothesis of autoregression of order $(p - 1)$ against the alternative of autoregression of order p, at the 10% significance level. Repeat this procedure, but testing at the 5% significance level.
(a) What autoregressive model is now selected?
(b) Obtain forecasts of sales for the next three years, based on this selected model.

17.41 For a certain product, it was found that annual sales volume could be well described by a third-order autoregressive model. The estimated model obtained was

$$X_t = 202 + 1.10 X_{t-1} - .48 X_{t-2} + .17 X_{t-3} + \varepsilon_t$$

For 1993, 1994, and 1995, sales were 867, 923, and 951, respectively. Calculate sales forecasts for the years 1996 through 1998.

17.42 For many time series, particularly prices in speculative markets, the *random walk* model has been found to give a good representation of actual data. This model is written

$$X_t = X_{t-1} + \varepsilon_t$$

Show that if this model is appropriate, forecasts of X_{n+h}, standing at time n, are given by

$$\hat{X}_{n+h} = X_n \qquad (h = 1, 2, 3 \ldots)$$

17.43 Refer to the data file **Hourly Earnings** of Exercise 17.30, showing earnings over 24 months. Denote the observations X_t ($t = 1, 2, \ldots, 24$). Now, form the series of first differences

$$Z_t = X_t - X_{t-1} \qquad (t = 2, 3, \ldots, 24)$$

Fit autoregressive models of orders 1 through 4 to the series Z_t. Using the approach of Section 17.6 for testing that the autoregressive order is $(p - 1)$ against the alternative of order p, with a 10% significance level, select one of these models. Using the selected model, find forecasts for Z_t, $t = 25, 26, 27$. Hence, obtain forecasts of earnings for the next three months.

17.7   AUTOREGRESSIVE INTEGRATED MOVING AVERAGE MODELS

In this section, we will briefly introduce an approach to time series forecasting that is widely used in business applications. The models to be discussed include as special cases the autoregressive models discussed in Section 17.6.

In a classic book, George Box and Gwilyn Jenkins introduced a methodology sufficiently versatile to provide a moderately skillful user with good results for a wide range of forecasting problems that occur in practice.[1] The essence of the Box-Jenkins approach is the contemplation of a very broad class of models from which forecasts can be derived, together with a methodology for picking, on the basis of the characteristics of the available data, a suitable model for any forecasting problem.

The general class of models is the class of autoregressive integrated moving average (ARIMA) models. These are rather natural extensions of the autoregressive models of Section 17.6. Moreover, the simple exponential smoothing and Holt-Winters predictors of Section 17.5 can be derived from specific members of this general class, as can many other widely used forecasting algorithms. The models and the Box-Jenkins time series analysis techniques can be generalized to allow for seasonality and also to deal with related time series so that future values of one series can be predicted from information not only on its own past but also on the past of other relevant series. This last possibility allows an approach to forecasting that generalizes the regression procedures discussed in Chapters 10 through 12.

It is not possible in the space available to provide a full discussion of the Box-Jenkins methodology.[2] In essence, it involves three stages:

1. Based on summary statistics that are readily calculated from the available data, the analyst selects a specific model that might be appropriate from the general class. This is not simply a matter of automatically following a set of rules but rather requires a certain amount of judgment and experience. However, one is not forever committed to the model chosen at this stage but can abandon it in favor of some alternative at a later stage of the analysis if that appears desirable.

[1] G. E. P. Box and G. M. Jenkins, *Time Series Analysis, Forecasting, and Control.* (San Francisco: Holden-Day, 1970).
[2] For an introduction to this methodology, see P. Newbold and T. Bos, *Introductory Business Forecasting*, 2nd edition. (Cincinnati, OH: South-Western, 1994).

2. The specific model chosen will almost invariably have some unknown coefficients. These must be estimated from the available data using efficient statistical techniques, such as least squares.

3. Finally, checks are applied to determine whether the estimated model provides an adequate representation of the available time series data. Any inadequacies revealed at this stage may suggest some alternative specification, and the process of model selection, coefficient estimation, and model checking is iterated until a satisfactory model is found.

The Box-Jenkins approach to forecasting has the great advantage of flexibility—a wide range of predictors is available, and choice among them is based on data evidence. Moreover, when this approach to forecasting has been compared with other methods, using actual economic and business time series, it has usually been found to perform very well. Thus, the procedure can be said to have survived the acid test: In practice, it works!

In concluding this brief discussion, note that computer programs for performing a time series analysis through the fitting to data of autoregressive integrated moving average models are widely available—including a set of procedures in Minitab. However, the method does have a drawback compared with other simpler procedures discussed in earlier sections of this chapter. Because flexibility is allowed in choosing an appropriate model from the general class, the Box-Jenkins approach is more costly in terms of skilled worker time than methods that force a single model structure onto every time series.

SUMMARY

This chapter has provided an introduction to the analysis of time series data. Initially we developed index numbers to provide a standardized measure of change over time. Then the remainder of the chapter developed a number of useful procedures for forecasting time series data.

Index numbers provide a consistent basis over time to represent prices, quantities, and other important measures. Simple index numbers provide a measure of change with respect to a fixed time period. Weighted index numbers, such as the Lespeyres index, assume a constant "market basket" proportion of goods and indicate how price changes for individual goods influences the overall price of the market basket.

Time series forecasting began with a discussion of major time series components, trend, cyclical, seasonal, and irregular. From there we developed a series of applied forecasting tools that have been shown to be effective in forecasting.

Various versions of weighted moving average models and exponential models were developed. We saw how particular variations of these procedures can be used to control and estimate the effect of the major components.

Autoregressive models were introduced to illustrate the stochastic modeling approach to time series forecasting. In that approach we estimate parameters of a model that might have generated the time series. One approach is to use autoregressive models in which a measure at time t is modeled as a linear function of past observations plus a random error term. Model development involves model specification, estimation and then testing the model to determine its effectiveness for forecasting. Finally we presented an overview discussion of Autoregressive Integrated Moving Average (ARIMA) models. These provide the base for a wide range of model specifications, depending on the perceived structure of the process.

KEY WORDS

CHAPTER EXERCISES AND APPLICATIONS

17.44 ✪ Refer to Exercise 17.30 and the data file **Hourly Earnings** which shows monthly hourly earnings in manufacturing.
  (**a**) Obtain an index with month 1 as base.
  (**b**) Obtain an index with month 5 as base.

17.45 ✪ A library purchases both books and journals. The accompanying table and data file **Library Purchases** shows the average prices (in dollars) paid for each and the quantities purchased over a period of six years. Use year 1 as base.

YEAR	BOOKS		JOURNALS	
	PRICE	*QUANTITY*	*PRICE*	*QUANTITY*
1	20.4	694	30.1	155
2	22.3	723	33.4	159
3	23.3	687	36.0	160
4	24.6	731	39.8	163
5	27.0	742	45.7	160
6	29.2	748	50.7	155

  (**a**) Find the unweighted aggregate index of prices.
  (**b**) Find the Laspeyres price index.
  (**c**) Find the Laspeyres quantity index.

17.46 Explain the statement that a time series can be viewed as being made up of a number of components. Provide examples of business and economic time series for which you would expect particular components to be important.

17.47 In many business applications, forecasts for future values of time series, such as sales and earnings, are made exclusively on the basis of past information on the time series in question. What features of time series behavior are exploited in the production of such forecasts?

17.48 A manager in charge of inventory control requires sales forecasts for several products, on a monthly basis, over the next six months. This manager has available monthly sales records over the past four years for each of these products. He decides to use, as forecasts for each of the next six months, the average monthly sales over the previous four years. Do you think this is a good strategy? Provide reasons.

17.49 What is meant by the seasonal adjustment of a time series? Explain why government agencies expend a large amount of effort on the seasonal adjustment of economic time series.

17.50 ✪ The data file **US Industrial Production** shows an index of U.S. industrial production over 14 years.
  (**a**) Test this series for randomness using the runs test.

  (**b**) Draw a time plot of these data, and discuss the features revealed by the graph.
  (**c**) Compute the series of simple centered 3-point moving averages. Graph this smoothed series, and discuss its behavior.

17.51 ✪ The data file **Product Sales** shows 24 annual observations on sales of a product.
  (**a**) Use the large-sample variant of the runs test to test this series for randomness.
  (**b**) Draw a time plot of the data and discuss the characteristics of the series shown by this graph.
  (**c**) Compute the series of simple centered 5-point moving averages. Graph this smoothed series, and discuss its behavior.

17.52 ✪ The data file **Quarterly Earnings 17.53** shows quarterly earnings per share of a corporation over seven years.
  (**a**) Draw a time plot of these data. Does this graph suggest the presence of a strong seasonal component?
  (**b**) Use the seasonal index method to obtain a seasonally adjusted series.

17.53 ✪ The data file **Price Index** shows 15 monthly values on the price index of a commodity.
  (**a**) Calculate the series of simple centered 3-point moving averages.
  (**b**) Draw a time plot of the smoothed series and comment on its characteristics.

17.54 ✪ Refer to Exercise 17.52 and the data file **Product Sales**. Use simple exponential smoothing, with smoothing constant $\alpha = .5$, to obtain forecasts of sales for the next three years.

17.55 ✪ Refer to Exercise 17.54 and the data file **Price Index**. Use the Holt-Winters method, with smoothing constants $\alpha = .3$ and $\beta = .4$, to obtain forecasts of the price index for the next four months.

17.56 ✪ Refer to Exercise 17.52 and the data file **Quarterly Earnings 17.53**. Use the Holt-Winters seasonal method, with smoothing constants $\alpha = .4$, $\beta = .4$, and $\gamma = .2$, to obtain forecasts of this earnings-per-share series for the next four quarters.

17.57 ✪ Using the data file **Product Sales** of Exercise 17.54, estimate autoregressive models of orders 1 through 4 for product sales. Using the procedure of Section 17.6 for testing that the autoregressive order is $(p - 1)$ against the alternative that the order is p, with a significance level of 10%, choose one of these models. Compute forecasts for the next three years from the chosen model.

REFERENCE

1. Granger, C.W. and P. Newbold, *Forecasting Economic Time Series*, 2nd ed. (Orlando, FL: Academic Press, 1986).

C HAPTER 18

ADDITIONAL TOPICS IN SAMPLING

INTRODUCTION

Much of statistical inference is concerned with problems of making statements about a population on the basis of information from a sample. In our discussions to this point, two important topics have been treated rather cursorily. First, very little has been said about how one would actually go about selecting the sample members. Second, it has generally been assumed that the number of population members is very large compared with the number of sample members. The problem of a researcher who wants to discover something about a population that is not necessarily large is considered in this chapter. The investigator intends to collect information on only a subset of the population members and requires guidance as to how to proceed.

18.1   BASIC STEPS OF A SAMPLING STUDY

Market researchers often survey human populations to elicit information about product preferences. Auditors typically select a sample of a corporation's accounts receivable. Inferences are made about the corresponding population based on these samples. Personnel directors often require information on employees' attitudes toward proposed new production methods and find it convenient to sample the labor force. Of course, the use of sampling methods is extremely widespread, extending well beyond the field of business. Perhaps the best-known examples are the regular survey of voter preferences prior to elections. The information gathered is of interest not only to the general public but also to advisers of candidates who are trying to determine where their efforts should be most heavily concentrated. Such surveys of voters have escalated to the point where voter opinions are sought on all aspects of public policy, and the professional pollster has become an important figure in the politician's entourage.

Before asking how a sample should be taken from a population, you might ask, "Why sample at all?" The alternative is to attempt to obtain information from every population member. This would be referred to as a *census* rather than a sample. There are several good reasons why a sample is often preferred to a census. First, in many applications, taking a complete census would be enormously expensive, frequently prohibitively so. Second, information is often required fairly quickly; a full census, even when financially feasible, may take so long to complete that the value of the results is seriously diminished. Another reason to sample is that with modern statistical methods it is generally possible to obtain results of the desired level of precision through sampling. Any time and money expended on producing numbers whose apparent precision exceeds the investigator's needs could be better spent elsewhere. Moreover, if a relatively small sample is taken, the gains derived through extra effort in securing accurate information from the sample members could well outweigh the benefits of having information from a larger group, which, because of time and cost constraints, may be less reliable. A fourth factor to consider is that some sampling is destructive and the items tested are destroyed in the study. Such would be the case for testing the lifetime of light bulbs, the mileage of a particular brand of automobile tires, or the breaking strength of glass tubing. Taken together, these factors—cost, time, precision, and destructive nature —dictate a preference for a sample rather than a census, on many occasions.

Suppose now that information about a population is required and that the decision has been made to take a sample. It is convenient to think of a sampling study as involving the following six steps, each aimed at producing the answer to a single question. These steps are set out in Figure 18.1.

FIGURE 18.1
Steps in a Sampling Study

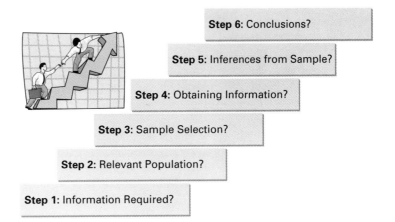

1. Step 1: What information is required?
2. Step 2: What is the relevant population, and is a listing of it available?
3. Step 3: How should the sample members be selected?
4. Step 4: How should information be obtained from the sample members?
5. Step 5: How should sample information be used to make inferences about the population?
6. Step 6: What conclusions can be drawn about the population?

Each of these steps is discussed with reference to a market research problem. Suppose that a publisher intends to bring out a new business statistics text and wants information on the current state of the market. Valuable information might include the number of students enrolled in business statistics courses, the market penetration of existing texts, and instructors' views as to which topics are the most important for their courses. Assume that the publisher decides to gather data from a sample of college campuses.

1. What Information is Required?

The answer to this question provides both the motivation and the starting point for the study. If the necessary information is either already available or impossible to obtain, there is no point in carrying out the survey. However straightforward though the question seems, a rather delicate balance is often needed at this stage. The investigator may have in mind just a single requirement, or there may be several topics of interest. But given that a survey is to be carried out, with all its costs, it is usually worthwhile asking whether further potentially useful information can be gleaned from the study at minimal additional expense. For the publisher of the business statistics text, the most useful questions concern the size of the market, the standing of competitors, and the topics that instructors view as most important. Given that sample members are to be contacted to elicit this information, it may be worthwhile to ask some additional questions. These may include whether the course is one or two semesters long, whether it is optional or compulsory, the department of the instructor, the procedure for textbook adoption, and the length of time the current text has been in use. Once having started along this road, you may be tempted to allow the list of questions to grow dramatically, because this would not generally increase greatly the cost of carrying out the study. However, there *is* a potential penalty. Respondents are more likely to cooperate in a study that asks relatively few questions and consequently takes up little of their time. Thus, it is important for the investigator to strike a balance whereby questions on central issues are asked (for if an important omission is discovered, it may prove too costly to repeat the whole exercise) and the number of questions asked remains tolerable to potential respondents.

2. What is the Relevant Population, and is a Listing of it Available?

It seems rather trivial to point out that if inferences are to be made about a particular population, then that is the population that must be sampled. Nevertheless, dubious conclusions have often been reached following an otherwise perfectly respectable analysis of survey data precisely because this elementary point has been ignored. Many publications invite the opinions of their readers on particular questions. It would, however, be dangerous to generalize their responses to a wider population. The population studied here is simply the readership of the publication, and this readership is likely to be unrepresentative of the public at large. In many practical studies, the *real* population of interest may be impossible to define. For example, an organization attempting to predict the result of a presidential election is really interested in only people who will, in fact, vote. Although this is the relevant population, its members are not easy to distinguish. One possibility, of course, is to ask a sample member if he or she intends to vote. However, it is well known that the proportion answering such a question in the affirmative is higher than the proportion that does eventually vote. Another possibility is to ask whether the respondent voted in the previous election, but this too is far from completely satisfactory.

The textbook publisher is likely to regard the relevant population as all instructors (or, perhaps, all colleges) teaching business statistics courses. The population is quite easy to identify, and, as a result of earlier marketing activities, the publisher will almost certainly have a fairly accurate listing of its members.

3. How Should the Sample Members be Selected?

Much of the remainder of this chapter will be devoted to answering this question. Put succinctly, there is no unique way to go about providing the "best " sampling scheme. The appropriate choice will generally depend on the problem at hand and on the resources of the investigator. The notion of *simple random sampling,* in which each potential sample of n members has an equal chance of being chosen, was previously introduced. Indeed, all of the data-analytic tools introduced to this point have been based on an assumption that the sample was chosen in such a fashion. There are, however, many circumstances in which alternative sampling schemes might be preferred. Suppose that our publisher is concerned about differences in the treatment of business statistics courses between 2-year and 4-year colleges. It would be important that the sample contain enough colleges of each type to allow reliable conclusions about both to be drawn. However, simple random sampling by no means guarantees attainment of this objective. It is entirely possible, for example, that the sample chosen will contain a preponderance of 4-year colleges. To guard against this possibility, one can draw separate simple random samples of 2-year and 4-year colleges from their respective populations. This is an example of *stratified sampling,* which will be discussed in more detail in Section 18.4. Another matter to be decided at this stage is the number of sample members. Essentially, the choice here depends on the degree of accuracy required and also on the costs involved. This question is addressed in Section 18.5.

4. How Should Information be Obtained from the Sample Members?

This is an extremely important question, the subject of much research. Broadly speaking, two important issues are involved. First, the investigator will want to obtain answers from as high a proportion as possible of the sample members. If the number not responding is high, it will be difficult to be sure that those who do respond are representative of the population at large. For instance, professors failing to supply information to the textbook publisher may be those most heavily involved in research, consulting, or other activities, and their preferences about texts could well differ from those of their colleagues. Recall that the number of questions asked in a survey could affect the response rate. The manner in which sample members are contacted is also influential. Frequently, questionnaires are mailed to those selected for the sample, and it often happens that the proportion responding is disappointingly low. Many researchers attempt to improve the response rate by including a cover letter, explaining the purposes of the study and politely soliciting help. An assurance of anonymity may also be valuable. The inclusion of a postpaid envelope for returning the questionnaire is generally worthwhile, and some modest monetary inducement or gift might be promised. Nevertheless, there will almost inevitably be a proportion of nonrespondents, and it is good practice to institute a follow-up inquiry to try to learn something about them. More expensive contact methods, such as telephone calls or home visits by interviewers, are likely to achieve a higher level of response. However, such methods can be costly in terms of time as well as money, and the decision on how to collect information must depend on the investigator's resources and the extent to which nonresponse is thought to be a serious potential problem.

The textbook publisher may decide to mail questionnaires to sample members. This would be inexpensive, so a relatively large initial sample could be drawn. The hope must be that the proportion of nonrespondents is not too high and that the responses obtained are reasonably representative. If it is feared that nonresponse will induce substantial bias should a mail questionnaire be used, a smaller initial sample might be drawn and a greater effort made to contact individual sample members. A feasible strategy might be to ask the company's representatives, who regularly visit campuses, to carry out interviews with the sample members on their next visits. Such a procedure should ensure quite a high response rate. Its major difficulty would be the time taken before all the interviews were completed rather than the additional costs, which would be quite low.

The second point is to obtain answers that are as accurate and as honest as possible. Nothing is to be gained from a highly sophisticated statistical analysis of basically unreliable information. There is an art in designing questions, whether asked through mail survey or by interviewer, in such a way as to extract honest and accurate replies. It is important that the questions be phrased as clearly and unambiguously as possible, so that subjects understand what is being asked. Also, it is well known that the wording of the questions or the tone of an interviewer can bias respondents toward providing particular answers. Interviewers should in no way convey the impression of having strong views on the subject at hand or of wanting a particular answer. It is also important not to "lead the witness"— questions should be phrased as neutrally as possible. As an extreme example, consider the following two methods of asking essentially the same question:

(a) Which three topics do you regard as most important in your business statistics course?
(b) Do you agree that modern methods of quality management, because of their overwhelming importance in the business world, must now be considered one of the most important topics in any business statistics course?

Of course, no one interested in an accurate picture of instructors' opinions would ask the second question. However, much less clearly biased wording than this has been found to make an appreciable difference to subjects' replies.

As an illustration of this point, Opinion Research Corporation of Princeton, NJ, annually surveys public attitudes toward government. Concerned about the influence of question wording, the organization asked the same question in two ways in one such survey. Respondents were asked what programs might best be sacrificed in the event of a severe budget squeeze. Among the list of candidates was "Aid to the needy." This item was selected for cutbacks by only 7% of all respondents. Two months later, when the same question was asked, the description "Aid to the needy" was replaced by "Public welfare." This time the item was chosen for cuts by 39% of respondents!

5. How Should Sample Information be Used to Make Inferences About the Population?

The greater part of this book has been devoted to providing answers to just this question. In subsequent sections of this chapter, methods of inference for particular sampling designs are discussed. The chief purpose of the present section is to note the importance of other aspects of a statistical sampling study.

6. What Conclusions Can be Drawn about the Population?

Finally, we come full circle and ask what can be said about the population under study as a result of a statistical investigation. Has the study produced clear answers to the questions that motivated it? Have additional important questions emerged in the course of the study? The investigator at this stage has the task of summarizing and presenting the information gathered. This may involve point or interval estimates, tabular summaries, or graphical presentation of results. What is the best estimate of the number of students enrolled in business statistics courses, and can confidence bands be put around this estimate? Which are the most popular texts at present? What topics do instructors consider most important? Are there significant differences between the 2-year and 4-year college markets? At this stage, the task is to report the findings of the study and to decide how to proceed. It may be that the analysis will suggest the desirability of gathering further information.

It often happens that important unanticipated issues arise during the course of a survey, and the investigator is stimulated to further study the population. It is for this reason that our publisher asks an open-ended question, such as, "Our Company is planning to bring to market a new business statistics text. Are there any features that you would particularly welcome in such a book?" Assume further that when the questionnaires are returned, an appreciable number mention the possibility of simultaneously marketing a large database containing data on real business problems. Students could get "hands-on" experience in course topics by analyzing these data. Before going to the expense of producing this software, the publisher might find it worthwhile to take another sample in order to assess the chances for success of this venture.

EXERCISES

18.1 Suppose that you want to conduct a study to determine the views of business majors on your campus as to whether statistics should be a required course. Discuss the steps that you would take in setting up this study, the problems you might expect to encounter, and techniques you might employ to overcome the problems.

18.2 A campus administrator is interested in the views of residence hall students concerning various university services (such as registration, food service, or health service). You have been approached to carry out a survey. Suggest how you might proceed following the six steps of a sampling study.

18.3 The manager of a campus clothing store is considering introducing some additional brand name items and wants to assess possible student demand for them. You have been asked to design a survey to elicit this information. Discuss, in detail, how you would proceed.

18.4 A financial services corporation is considering the possibility of introducing three new types of mutual funds. It is believed that, at least initially, most support for these is likely to come from its current customers. The corporation would like to assess the degree of interest these customers have in the proposed new products, preferably learning also relevant characteristics of those people likely to be most interested. You are commissioned to design a study, with a limited budget. How would you proceed?

18.5 Insurance company executives, aware of substantial increases in certain types of insurance premiums in the last few years, have become concerned about the public image of their industry and the possibility of political repercussions. It has been decided to mount a public relations campaign to educate the public about the reasons for the cost increases. However, there is considerable uncertainty both about the areas in which people have the strongest concerns and the extent to which the factors underlying the price increases for insurance policies are understood. Describe how you could set up a study to obtain relevant information. Follow the basic steps of a sampling plan.

18.2   SAMPLING AND NONSAMPLING ERRORS

When a sample is taken from a population, the value of any population parameter, such as the mean or proportion, will not be able to be known *precisely*. Any point estimate will inevitably be in error. Recall that one source of error, called **sampling error**, results from the fact that information is available on only a subset of all the population members. Given certain assumptions, statistical theory allows us to characterize the nature of the sampling error and to make well-defined probabilistic statements about population parameters, such as the confidence intervals discussed in Chapter 8. In subsequent sections of this chapter, methods of statistical inference for various important sampling schemes are discussed. However, it is important to recognize first the potential for another source of error, which cannot be analyzed in such an elegant or clear-cut fashion.

In practical analyses, there is the possibility of an error unconnected with the kind of sampling procedure used. Indeed, such errors could just as well arise if a complete census of the population were taken. These are referred to as **nonsampling errors**. In any particular survey, the potential for nonsampling error exists at a number of places. Examples include the following:

1. *The population actually sampled is not the relevant one*. A celebrated instance of this sort occurred in 1936, when *Literary Digest* magazine confidently predicted that Alfred Landon would win the presidential election over Franklin Roosevelt. In the event, Roosevelt won by a very comfortable margin. This erroneous forecast resulted from the fact that the members of the *Digest's* sample had been taken from telephone directories and other listings, such as magazine subscription lists and automobile registrations. These sources considerably underrepresented the poor, who were predominantly Democrats. To make an inference about a population (in this case, the U.S. electorate), it is important to sample that population and not some subgroup of it, however convenient the latter course might appear.

2. *Survey subjects may give inaccurate or dishonest answers*. This could happen because questions are phrased in a manner that is difficult to understand or in a way that appears to make a particular answer seem more palatable or more desirable. Also, many questions that one might want to ask are so sensitive that it would be foolhardy to expect uniformly honest responses. Suppose, for example, that a plant manager wants to assess the annual losses to the company caused by employee thefts. In principle, a random sample of employees could be selected and sample members asked, "What have you stolen from this plant in the past 12 months?" This is clearly not the most reliable means of obtaining the required information!

3. *Nonresponse to survey questions.* Survey subjects may not respond at all or they may not respond to certain questions. If this is substantial, it can induce additional sampling and nonsampling errors. The sampling error arises because the achieved sample size will be smaller than that intended. Nonsampling error possibly occurs because, in effect, the population being sampled is not the population of interest. The results obtained can be regarded as a random sample *from the population that is willing to respond*. These people may differ in important

ways from the larger population. If this is so, a bias will be induced in the resulting estimates.

There is no general procedure for identifying and analyzing nonsampling errors. But they could be important. The main prescription is that the investigator takes care in such matters as identifying the relevant population, designing the questionnaire, and dealing with nonresponse in order to minimize its significance. In the remainder of this chapter, it will be assumed that such care has been taken, and our discussion will center on the treatment of sampling errors.

EXERCISES

18.6 Refer to the study of Exercise 18.2.
  (a) Within the sampling framework you have designed, do you see the potential for nonsampling errors? If so, what steps would you take to minimize their magnitude?
  (b) Is nonresponse likely to be a serious issue in this study? If so, what might be done about it?
18.7 Refer to the study of Exercise 18.3.
  (a) Discuss likely sources of nonsampling errors, and indicate how these could be minimized.
  (b) Would you expect nonresponse to be a serious problem in carrying out this study? If so, how might the problem be alleviated?

18.8 For the study of Exercise 18.5, discuss the potential for nonsampling errors and nonresponse. Indicate how you would go about minimizing these problems.
18.9 One approach to nonresponse of a particular kind is the *recall method*. A survey of households is conducted by having interviewers call on a Thursday evening. Households where no one was home are called again the following Thursday evening. This process can be continued so those households that could not be reached at the first two attempts are recontacted on the next Thursday evening. What might be the value of information obtained in this fashion?

18.3   SIMPLE RANDOM SAMPLING

In the rest of this chapter, consideration is given to problems where a sample of *n* individuals or objects is to be drawn from a population containing a total of *N* members. In practical applications, many schemes have been employed for the selection of such samples. The bulk of our discussions will concentrate on *probability sampling* methods—procedures where some mechanism involving *chance* is used to determine the sample members and the probability of any particular sample being drawn is known. Because of its importance the concept of simple random sampling and how to select a simple random sample from a finite population are again emphasized.

> **SIMPLE RANDOM SAMPLING**
> Suppose that it is required to select a sample of *n* objects from a population of *N* objects. A **simple random sampling** procedure is one in which every possible sample of *n* objects is equally likely to be chosen.

Suppose that our population contains 1,000 individuals, numbered 1 through 1,000, and that a simple random sample of 100 population members is required. Minitab can easily generate a simple random sample. The first step in Minitab is to create a column with numbers from 1 to 1,000. This is straightforward by making patterned data as illustrated in Figure 18.2.

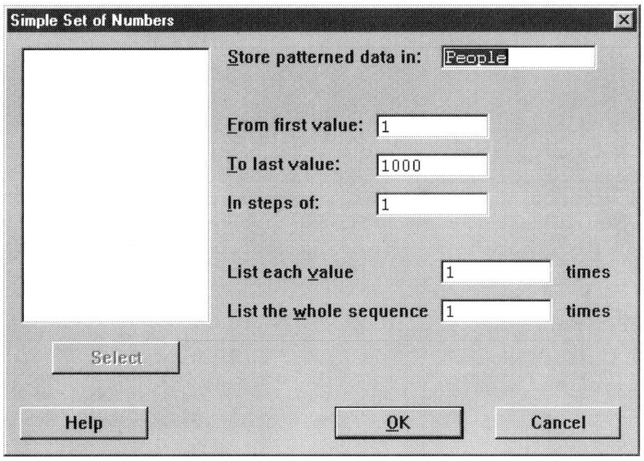

FIGURE 18.2
Minitab Dialog Box to Make Patterned Data

Minitab Instructions

1. Click on Calc
2. Select Make Patterned Data
3. Select Simple Set of Numbers
4. Complete dialog box indicating:
   a) where to store data (this can be a column name, like "People," or a column number, "C1")
   b) first and last values; for a population of 1,000, these are "1" and "1,000" respectively.
   c) steps of "1"
   d) each value listed only one time;
   e) list sequence only one time

The result is a column of numbers from 1 to 1,000 stored in column C1 called "People." Next, randomly sample 100 numbers from this column. To do so, follow the Minitab instructions accompanying Figure 18.3.

A partial list of the 100 random numbers that we generated includes people numbered:

$$457 \qquad 229 \qquad 843 \qquad 460 \qquad 918 \qquad 311$$

We will consider only *sampling without replacement* where any number drawn that has already been obtained is ignored, and the process continues until 100 *different* numbers have been obtained. The alternative, *sampling with replacement,* which allows the possibility of an individual being included in the sample more than once, will not be discussed here, and therefore, it is not selected in the dialog box in Figure 18.3.

Systematic sampling is a statistical sampling procedure often used as an alternative to random sampling.

SYSTEMATIC SAMPLING

Suppose that the population list is arranged in some fashion unconnected with the subject of interest. **Systematic sampling** involves the selection of every jth item in the population, where j is the ratio of the population size N to the desired sample size, n; that is, $j = \dfrac{N}{n}$. Randomly select a number from 1 to j to obtain the first item to be included in your systematic sample.

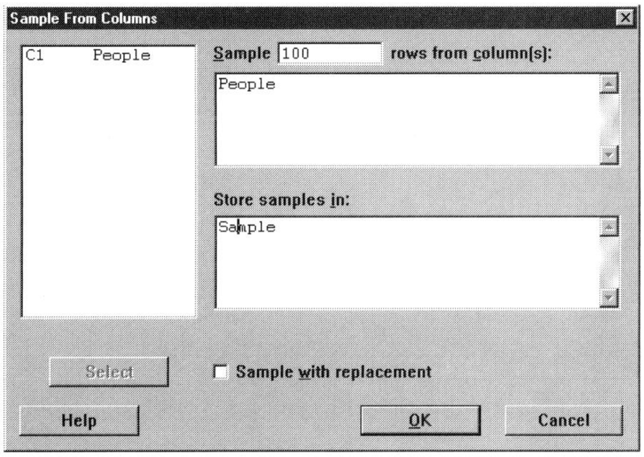

FIGURE 18.3
Minitab Dialog Box for Random Data Selection

Minitab Instructions

1. Click on Calc
2. Select Random Data
3. Select Sample From Columns...
4. Enter sample size (here, it is 100) in the edit box for Sample rows from columns(s):
5. Enter Column containing population (here, it is People)
6. Complete edit box for Store samples in: with name or column number desired (here it is Sample)
7. Click OK. A simple random sample of numbers will appear in column C2.

Suppose that a sample size of 100 is desired and that the population consists of 5,000 names in alphabetical order. Then $j = 50$. Randomly select a number from 1 to 50. If your number is 20, select it and every fiftieth number giving the systematic sample of elements numbered 20, 70, 120, 170, and so forth until all 100 items are selected. A systematic sample is analyzed in the same fashion as a simple random sample on the grounds that, relative to the subject of inquiry, the population listing is already in random order. The danger is that there could be some subtle, unsuspected link between the ordering of the population and the subject under study. If this were so, bias would be induced if systematic sampling were employed. Systematic samples provide a good representation of the population if there is no cyclical variation in the population.

Analysis of Results from Simple Random Sampling

The material in this section extends the confidence intervals estimations developed in Chapter 8. However, here cases where the number of sample members is not a negligible proportion of the number of population members is considered. As a result, the **finite population correction factor** $(N - n)/N$ is used. It will be assumed that the sample is sufficiently large that recourse to the central limit theorem is appropriate.

ESTIMATION OF THE POPULATION MEAN, SIMPLE RANDOM SAMPLE

Let $X_1, X_2, \ldots, X_n$ denote the values observed from a simple random sample of size n, taken from a population of N member with mean μ.

i.   The sample mean is an unbiased estimator of the population mean, μ. The point estimate is:

$$\overline{X} = \frac{1}{n} \sum_{i=1}^{n} X_i$$

ii. An unbiased estimation procedure for the variance of the sample mean yields the point estimate

$$\hat{\sigma}_{\overline{X}}^2 = \frac{s^2}{n} \frac{N - n}{N} \tag{18.1}$$

iii. Provided the sample size is large, $100(1 - \alpha)\%$ confidence intervals for the population mean are given by

$$\overline{X} - Z_{\alpha/2} \hat{\sigma}_{\overline{X}} < \mu < \overline{X} + Z_{\alpha/2} \hat{\sigma}_{\overline{X}} \tag{18.2}$$

EXAMPLE 18.1

MORTGAGES (CONFIDENCE INTERVAL)

In a particular city, 1,118 mortgages were taken out last year. A random sample of 60 of these had mean amount $87,300 and standard deviation $19,200. Estimate the mean amount of all mortgages taken out in this city last year, and find a 95% confidence interval.

SOLUTION

Denote the population mean by μ. It is known that

$$N = 1{,}118; \quad n = 60; \quad \overline{X} = \$87{,}300; \text{ and } s = 19{,}200$$

To obtain interval estimates, use Equation 18.1,

$$\hat{\sigma}_{\overline{X}}^2 = \frac{s^2}{n} \frac{(N - n)}{N} = \frac{(19{,}200)^2}{60} \frac{1{,}058}{1{,}118} = 5{,}814{,}268$$

and take the square root to obtain the estimated standard error,

$$\hat{\sigma}_{\overline{X}} = 2{,}411$$

Hence, the 95% confidence interval for the mean amount of all mortgages taken out in this city last year is

$$\$87{,}300 - (1.96)(2{,}411) < \mu < \$87{,}300 + (1.96)(2{,}411)$$

or

$$\$82{,}574 < \mu < \$92{,}026$$

That is, the interval runs from $82,574 to $92,026.

Frequently, interest centers on the population total rather than the mean. For example, the publisher of a business statistics text will want an estimate of the total number of students taking business statistics courses in all U.S. colleges. Inference about the population total is straightforward. The relevant results follow from the fact that, in our notation, population total = $N\mu$.

ESTIMATION OF THE POPULATION TOTAL, SIMPLE RANDOM SAMPLE

Suppose a simple random sample of size n from a population of size N is selected and that the quantity to be estimated is the population total $N\mu$.

i.   An unbiased estimation procedure for the population total $N\mu$ yields the point estimate $N\overline{X}$.

ii. An unbiased estimation procedure for the variance of our estimator of the population total yields the point estimate

$$N^2 \hat{\sigma}_{\overline{X}}^2 = \frac{s^2}{n} N(N - n) \tag{18.3}$$

iii. Provided the sample size is large, a $100(1 - \alpha)$% confidence interval for the population total are obtained from

$$N\overline{X} - Z_{\alpha/2} N\hat{\sigma}_{\overline{X}} < N\mu < N\overline{X} + Z_{\alpha/2} N\hat{\sigma}_{\overline{X}} \tag{18.4}$$

EXAMPLE 18.2

ENROLLMENT IN BUSINESS STATISTICS COURSES (CONFIDENCE INTERVAL)

Suppose that there are 1,395 colleges in the United States. From a simple random sample of 400 of these schools, it was found that the sample mean enrollment during the past year in business statistics courses was 320.8 students, and the sample standard deviation was found to be 149.7 students. Estimate the total number of students enrolled in business statistics courses in the year, and find a 99% confidence interval.

SOLUTION

If the population mean is μ, an estimate of $N\mu$ includes

$$N = 1{,}395 \quad n = 400 \quad \overline{X} = 320.8 \quad s = 149.7$$

Our point estimate for the total is

$$N\overline{X} = (1{,}395)(320.8) = 447{,}516$$

It is estimated that a total of 447,516 students are enrolled in business statistics courses. To obtain interval estimates, Equation 18.3 is used to obtain the variance of the estimator,

$$N^2 \hat{\sigma}_{\bar{X}}^2 = \frac{s^2}{n} N(N-n) = \frac{(149.7)^2}{400}(1{,}395)(995) = 77{,}764{,}413$$

Taking the square root yields

$$N\hat{\sigma}_{\bar{X}} = 8{,}818.4$$

Hence, the 99% confidence interval for the population total is found by Equation 18.4, with $Z_{\alpha/2} = 2.58$

$$N\bar{X} - Z_{\alpha/2} N\hat{\sigma}_{\bar{X}} < N\mu < N\bar{X} + Z_{\alpha/2} N\hat{\sigma}_{\bar{X}}$$

or

$$447{,}516 - (2.58)(8{,}818.4) < N\mu < 447{,}516 + (2.58)(8{,}818.4)$$

or

$$447{,}516 \pm 22{,}751$$
$$424{,}765 < N\mu < 470{,}267$$

Thus, our interval runs from 424,765 to 470,267 students.

Finally, consider the case where it is required to estimate the *proportion* π of individuals in the population possessing some specific characteristic. Inference about this proportion should be based on the hypergeometric distribution when the number of sample members is not very small compared to the number of population members. Again assume that the sample size is large enough to allow the central limit theorem to be invoked.

ESTIMATION OF THE POPULATION PROPORTION, SIMPLE RANDOM SAMPLE

Let p be the proportion possessing a particular characteristic in a random sample of n observations from a population, a proportion, π, of whose members possess that characteristic.

i.   The sample proportion, p, is an unbiased estimator of the population proportion, π.
ii. An unbiased estimation procedure for the variance of our estimator of the population proportion yields the point estimate

$$\hat{\sigma}_p^2 = \frac{p(1-p)}{n-1} \times \frac{(N-n)}{N} \tag{18.5}$$

iii. Provided the sample size is large, $100(1-\alpha)\%$ confidence intervals for the population proportion are given by

$$p - Z_{\alpha/2}\hat{\sigma}_p < \pi < p + Z_{\alpha/2}\hat{\sigma}_p \tag{18.6}$$

EXAMPLE 18.3

TWO SEMESTERS OF BUSINESS STATISTICS CONFIDENCE INTERVAL)

From a simple random sample of 400 of the 1,395 colleges in our population, it was found that business statistics was a two-semester course in 141 of the sampled colleges. Estimate the proportion of all colleges for which the course is two semesters long, and find a 90% confidence interval.

SOLUTION

To estimate the population proportion, π, given

$$N = 1{,}395 \qquad n = 400 \qquad p = \frac{141}{400} = 0.3525$$

our point estimate of π is simply $p = 0.3525$. That is, the course is two semesters long in approximately 35.25% of all colleges. To calculate interval estimates, the variance of our estimate is found by Equation 18.5,

$$\hat{\sigma}_p^2 = \frac{p(1-p)}{n-1} \times \frac{(N-n)}{N} = \frac{(0.3525)(0.6475)}{399} \times \frac{995}{1{,}395} = 0.0004080$$

so

$$\hat{\sigma}_p = 0.0202$$

For a 90% confidence interval, $Z_{\alpha/2} = Z_{0.05} = 1.645$. The 90% confidence interval is found by Equation 18.6,

$$p - Z_{\alpha/2}\hat{\sigma}_p < \pi < p + Z_{\alpha/2}\hat{\sigma}_p$$

or

$$0.3525 - (1.645)(0.0202) < \pi < 0.3525 + (1.645)(0.0202)$$

or

$$0.3193 < \pi < 0.3857$$

Thus, the 90% confidence interval for the percentage of all colleges in which business statistics is a two-semester course runs from 31.93% to 38.57%.

EXERCISES

18.10 Consult today's *Wall Street Journal* to obtain a list of all stocks traded on the New York Stock Exchange. Use Minitab to obtain a simple random sample of 20 of these stocks. For your sample, find the mean percentage increase in price over the past week.

18.11 Obtain from your local newspaper a list of all houses advertised for sale in your city. Use Minitab to obtain a simple random sample of 15 advertisements, and find the sample mean of the advertised prices.

18.12 A campus has 12,723 students. From a complete list of these students you want a random sample of 100. Explain how to use Minitab to obtain such a random sample.

18.13 Take a random sample of 50 pages from this book and estimate the proportion of all pages that contain Figures.

18.14 A firm employs 189 junior accountants. In a random sample of 50 of these, the mean number of hours overtime billed in a particular week was 9.7, and the sample standard deviation was 6.2 hours. Find a 95% confidence interval for the mean number of hours overtime billed per junior accountant in this firm that week.

18.15 An auditor, examining a total of 820 accounts receivable of a corporation, took a random sample of 60 of them. The sample mean was $127.43, and the sample standard deviation was $43.27.

(a) Using an unbiased estimation procedure, find an estimate of the population mean.

(b) Using an unbiased estimation procedure, find an estimate of the variance of the sample mean.

(c) Find a 90% confidence interval for the population mean.

(d) A statistician found, for the population mean, a confidence interval running from $117.43 to $137.43. What is the probability content of this interval?

18.16 On a particular day, a consumer advice bureau received 125 calls. For a random sample of 40 of these calls, it was found that mean time taken in providing the requested advice was 7.28 minutes, and the sample standard deviation was 5.32 minutes. Find a 99% confidence interval for the mean time taken per call.

18.17 State whether each of the following statements is true or false:

(a) For a given number of population members and a given sample variance, the larger the number of sample members, the wider is a 95% confidence interval for the population mean.

(b) For a given number of population members and a given number of sample members, the larger the sample variance, the wider is a 95% confidence interval for the population mean.

(c) For a given number of sample members and a given sample variance, the larger the number of population members, the wider is a 95% confidence interval for the population mean. Justify your answer.

(d) For a given number of population members, a given number of sample members, and a given sample variance, a 95% confidence interval for the population mean is wider that a 90% confidence interval for the population mean.

18.18 Show that our estimate of the variance of the sample mean can be written

$$\hat{\sigma}_{\bar{X}}^2 = s^2 \left(\frac{1}{n} - \frac{1}{N} \right)$$

18.19 Using the data of Exercise 18.14, find a 99% confidence interval for the total number of hours overtime billed by junior accountants in the firm during the week of interest.

18.20 Using the data of Exercise 18.15, find a 95% confidence interval for the total amount of these 820 accounts receivable.

18.21 Use the data of Exercise 18.16, find a 90% confidence interval for the total amount of time taken in answering these 125 calls.

18.22 A senior manager, responsible for a group of 120 junior executives, is interested in the total amount of time per week spent by these people in internal meetings. A random sample of 35 of these executives was asked to keep diary records during the next week. When the results were analyzed, it was found that these sample members spent a total of 143 hours in internal meetings. The sample standard deviation was 3.1 hours. Find a 90% confidence interval for the total number of hours spent in internal meetings by all 120 junior executives in the week.

18.23 A simple random sample of 400 from a total 1,395 colleges in the United States contained 39 colleges that use the text *Statistics Made Difficult and Boring*. Find a 95% confidence interval for the proportion of all colleges using this text.

18.24 A business school dean is contemplating proposing a change in the requirements for graduation. At present, business majors are required to take one science course, chosen from a list of possible courses. The proposal is that this be replaced by the requirement that a course in ecology be taken. The business school has 420 students. Of a random sample of 100 of them, 56 expressed opposition to this proposal. Find a 90% confidence interval for the proportion of all the school's students opposed to the proposed change in requirements.

18.25 In a college dormitory, 257 of the residents are freshmen. Of a random sample of 120 of them, 37 indicated strong interest in living in the dormitory next year. Find a 95% confidence interval for the proportion of freshmen in this dormitory with a strong interest in living there next year.

18.26 A class has 420 students. The final examination is optional—taking it can raise, but not lower, a student's grade. Of a random sample of 80 students, 31 indicated that they would take the final examination. Find a 90% confidence interval for the total number of students in this class intending to take the final examination.

18.4   STRATIFIED SAMPLING

Suppose that you decide to investigate the views of students on your campus concerning some sensitive topic, and the framing of appropriately worded questions could be difficult. It is likely that you would want to ask several questions of every sample member and so, given limited resources, would be able to take only a fairly small sample. You would presumably select a simple random sample of, say, 100 students from a list of all students on campus. Suppose, however, that on closer inspection of the records of the sample members, you find that only two of them are business majors, though the population proportion of business majors is far higher than this. Your problem at this stage is twofold. First, you may well be interested in comparing the views of business majors with those of the rest of the student population. This is hardly feasible given their minimal representation in your sample. Second, you may suspect that the views of business majors on this question will differ from those of their fellow students. If that were the case, you would worry about the reliability of inference based on a sample in which this group is seriously underrepresented.

You could perhaps console yourself with the thought that since you have taken a random sample, any estimators derived in the usual way will be unbiased, and the resulting inference, in the statistical sense, will be strictly valid. However, a little reflection should convince you that this is scant consolation indeed! All that unbiasedness promises is that if the sampling procedure is repeated a very large number of times and the estimator calculated, its average will be equal to the corresponding population value. But, in fact, you are *not* going to repeat the sampling procedure a large number of times. You have to base your conclusions on *just a single sample*, and the fact that business majors could have been overrepresented in other samples you might have drawn, so that things "average out" in the long run, is not terribly useful.

There is a second tempting possibility, one that is in many ways preferable to proceeding with the original sample. You could simply discard the original sample, and take another. If the constitution of the sample achieved at the second attempt looks more representative of the population at large, you may well be better off to proceed with it. The difficulty now is that the sampling procedure you have adopted—the population is to be sampled until you achieve a sample you like the looks of—is very difficult to formalize, and consequently, the sample results are very hard to analyze with any statistical validity. This is no longer simple random sampling, and the procedures of Section 18.3 are therefore not strictly valid.

Fortunately, a third alternative sampling scheme exists to afford protection against just this type of problem. If it is suspected at the outset that particular identifiable characteristics of population members are germane to the subject of inquiry, or if particular subgroups of the population are of special interest to the investigator, it is not necessary (and probably not desirable) to be content with simple random sampling as a means of selecting the sample members. Instead the population can be broken down into subgroups, or *strata*, and a simple random sample taken from each stratum. The only requirement is that each individual member of the population be identifiable as belonging to one, and only one, of the strata.

STRATIFIED RANDOM SAMPLING

Suppose that a population of N individuals can be subdivided into K mutually exclusive and collectively exhaustive groups, or strata. **Stratified random sampling** is the selection of independent simple random samples from each stratum of the population. If the K strata in the population contain $N_1, N_2, \ldots, N_K$ members, then

$$N_1 + N_2 + \cdots + N_K = N$$

There is no need to take the same number of sample members from every stratum. Denote the numbers in the sample by $n_1, n_2, \ldots, n_K$. Then the total number of sample members is

$$n_1 + n_2 + \cdots + n_K = n$$

The population of students whose views are to be canvassed could be divided into two strata—business majors and nonbusiness majors. Less straightforward stratification is also possible. Suppose that on some other topic, you believe that a student's gender and class year (senior, junior, sophomore, or freshman) are both potentially relevant. In that case, to satisfy the requirement that the strata be mutually exclusive and collectively exhaustive, eight strata—senior women, senior men, and so on—are needed.

Later in this section the question of how to allocate the sampling effort among the strata is considered. An attractive possibility, often employed in practice, is *proportional allocation*: the proportion of sample members from any stratum is the same as the proportion of population members in that stratum.

Analysis of Results from Stratified Random Sampling

The analysis of the results of a stratified random sample is relatively straightforward. Let μ_1, $\mu_2, \ldots, \mu_K$ denote the population means in the K strata and $\overline{X}_1, \overline{X}_2, \ldots, \overline{X}_K$ the corresponding sample means. Consider a particular stratum, say the jth stratum. Then, since a simple random sample has been taken in this stratum, the stratum sample mean is an unbiased estimator of the population mean μ_j. Also, from an unbiased estimation procedure for the variance of the stratum sample mean, the point estimate is

$$\hat{\sigma}^2_{\overline{x}_j} = \frac{s_j^2}{n_j} \times \frac{(N_j - n_j)}{N_j}$$

where s_j^2 is the sample variance in the jth stratum. Inference about individual strata can therefore be made in the same way as in Section 18.3.

Generally, inferences about the overall population mean μ are of interest where

$$\mu = \frac{N_1\mu_1 + N_2\mu_2 + \cdots + N_K\mu_K}{N} = \frac{1}{N}\sum_{j=1}^{K} N_j\mu_j$$

A natural point estimate is provided by

$$\overline{X}_{st} = \frac{1}{N}\sum_{j=1}^{K} N_j\overline{X}_j$$

An unbiased estimator of the variance of the estimator of μ follows from the fact that the samples in each stratum are independent of one another, and the point estimate is given by

$$\hat{\sigma}^2_{\overline{X}_{st}} = \frac{1}{N^2}\sum_{j=1}^{K} N_j^2\hat{\sigma}^2_{\overline{X}_j}$$

Inferences about the overall population mean can be based on these results.

ESTIMATION OF THE POPULATION MEAN, STRATIFIED RANDOM SAMPLE

Suppose that random samples of n_j individuals are taken from strata containing N_j individuals ($j = 1, 2, \ldots, K$). Let

$$\sum_{j=1}^{K} N_j = N \qquad \text{and} \qquad \sum_{j=1}^{K} n_j = n$$

Denote the sample means and variances in the strata by $\overline{X}_j$ and s_j^2 ($j = 1, 2, \ldots, K$) and the overall population mean by μ.

i. An unbiased estimation procedure for the overall population mean μ yields the point estimate

$$\overline{X}_{st} = \frac{1}{N} \sum_{j=1}^{K} N_j \overline{X}_j \qquad (18.7)$$

ii. An unbiased estimation procedure for the variance of our estimator of the overall population mean yields the point estimate

$$\hat{\sigma}^2_{\overline{X}_{st}} = \frac{1}{N^2} \sum_{j=1}^{K} N_j^2 \hat{\sigma}^2_{\overline{X}_j} \qquad (18.8)$$

where

$$\hat{\sigma}^2_{\overline{x}_j} = \frac{s_j^2}{n_j} \times \frac{(N_j - n_j)}{N_j} \qquad (18.9)$$

iii. Provided the sample size is large, $100(1 - \alpha)\%$ **confidence intervals for the population mean for stratified random samples** are obtained from

$$\overline{X}_{st} - Z_{\alpha/2}\hat{\sigma}_{\overline{X}_{st}} < \mu < \overline{X}_{st} + Z_{\alpha/2}\hat{\sigma}_{\overline{X}_{st}} \qquad (18.10)$$

EXAMPLE 18.4

RESTAURANT CHAIN (ESTIMATION)

A restaurant chain has 60 restaurants in Illinois, 50 in Indiana, and 45 in Ohio. Management is considering adding a new item to the menus. To test the likely demand for this item, it was introduced on the menus of random samples of 12 restaurants in Illinois, 10 in Indiana, and 9 in Ohio. Using the subscripts 1, 2, and 3 to denote Illinois, Indiana, and Ohio, respectively, the sample means and standard deviations for numbers of orders received for this item per restaurant in the three states in a week were

$$\begin{array}{ll} \overline{X}_1 = 21.2 & s_1 = 12.8 \\ \overline{X}_2 = 13.3 & s_2 = 11.4 \\ \overline{X}_3 = 26.1 & s_3 = 9.2 \end{array}$$

Estimate the mean number of weekly orders per restaurant, μ, for all restaurants in this chain.

SOLUTION

It is known that

$$\begin{array}{llll} N_1 = 60 & N_2 = 50 & N_3 = 45 & N = 155 \\ n_1 = 12 & n_2 = 10 & n_3 = 9 & n = 31 \end{array}$$

Our estimate of the population mean is

$$\overline{X}_{st} = \frac{1}{N} \sum_{j=1}^{K} N_j \overline{X}_j = \frac{(60)(21.2) + (50)(13.3) + (45)(26.1)}{155} = 20.1$$

Thus, the estimated mean number of weekly orders per restaurant is 20.1.

The next step is to calculate the quantities

$$\hat{\sigma}^2_{\bar{X}_1} = \frac{s_1^2}{n_1} \times \frac{(N_1 - n_1)}{N_1} = \frac{(12.8)^2}{12} \times \frac{48}{60} = 10.923$$

$$\hat{\sigma}^2_{\bar{X}_2} = \frac{s_2^2}{n_2} \times \frac{(N_2 - n_2)}{N_2} = \frac{(11.4)^2}{10} \times \frac{40}{50} = 10.397$$

$$\hat{\sigma}^2_{\bar{X}_3} = \frac{s_3^2}{n_3} \times \frac{(N_3 - n_3)}{N_3} = \frac{(9.2)^2}{9} \times \frac{36}{45} = 7.524$$

Together with the individual stratum sample means, these quantities can be used to compute confidence intervals for the population means of the three strata, exactly as in Example 18.1 (although in this case the sample sizes are too small for comfort). Our concentration is on the overall population mean. To obtain confidence intervals for this quantity,

$$\hat{\sigma}^2_{\bar{X}_{st}} = \frac{1}{N^2} \sum_{j=1}^{K} N_j^2 \hat{\sigma}^2_{\bar{X}_j}$$

$$= \frac{(60)^2(10.923) + (50)^2(10.397) + (45)^2(7.524)}{(155)^2} = 3.353$$

and on taking the square root

$$\hat{\sigma}_{\bar{X}_{st}} = 1.83$$

Thus, the 95% confidence interval for the mean number of orders per restaurant received in a week is

$$20.1 - (1.96)(1.83) < \mu < 20.1 + (1.96)(1.83)$$

or

$$16.5 < \mu < 23.7$$

The 95% confidence interval runs from 16.5 to 23.7 orders per restaurant.

Since the population total is the product of the population mean and the number of population members, these procedures can readily be modified to allow its estimation, as described next.

ESTIMATION OF THE POPULATION TOTAL, STRATIFIED RANDOM SAMPLE

Suppose that random samples of n_j individuals from strata containing N_j individuals ($j = 1, 2,\ldots, K$) are selected and that the quantity to be estimated is the population total, $N\mu$.

i. An unbiased estimation procedure for $N\mu$ leads to the point estimate

$$N\bar{X}_{st} = \sum_{j=1}^{K} N_j \bar{X}_j \qquad \text{(18.11)}$$

ii. An unbiased estimation procedure for the variance of our estimator of the population total yields the estimate

$$N^2 \hat{\sigma}^2_{\bar{X}_{st}} = \sum_{j=1}^{K} N_j^2 \hat{\sigma}^2_{\bar{X}_j} \qquad \text{(18.12)}$$

iii. Provided the sample size is large, $100(1 - \alpha)\%$ **confidence intervals for the population total for stratified random sample** are obtained from

$$N\overline{X}_{st} - Z_{\alpha/2}N\hat{\sigma}_{\overline{X}_{st}} < N\mu < N\overline{X}_{st} + Z_{\alpha/2}N\hat{\sigma}_{\overline{X}_{st}} \qquad (18.13)$$

EXAMPLE 18.5

TOTAL ANNUAL ENROLLMENT IN BUSINESS STATISTICS (ESTIMATION)

Of the 1,395 colleges in the United States, 364 have 2-year programs and 1,031 are 4-year schools. A simple random sample of forty 2-year schools and an independent simple random sample of sixty 4-year schools were taken. The sample means and standard deviations of numbers of students enrolled in the past year in business statistics courses are given in the table. Estimate the total annual enrollment in business statistics courses.

	2-YEAR SCHOOLS	4-YEAR SCHOOLS
Mean	154.3	411.8
Standard Deviation	87.3	219.9

SOLUTION

It is known that

$$N_1 = 364 \qquad n_1 = 40 \qquad \overline{X}_1 = 154.3 \qquad s_1 = 87.3$$
$$N_2 = 1{,}031 \qquad n_2 = 60 \qquad \overline{X}_2 = 411.8 \qquad s_2 = 219.9$$

Our estimate of the population total is

$$N\overline{X}_{st} = \sum_{j=1}^{K} N_j \overline{X}_j = (364)(154.3) + (1{,}031)(411.8) = 480{,}731$$

Next,

$$\hat{\sigma}^2_{\overline{X}_1} = \frac{s_1^2}{n_1} \times \frac{(N_1 - n_1)}{N_1} = \frac{(87.3)^2}{40} \times \frac{324}{364} = 169.59$$

$$\hat{\sigma}^2_{\overline{X}_2} = \frac{s_2^2}{n_2} \times \frac{(N_2 - n_2)}{N_2} = \frac{(219.9)^2}{60} \times \frac{971}{1{,}031} = 759.03$$

Finally,

$$N^2\hat{\sigma}^2_{\overline{X}_{st}} = \sum_{j=1}^{K} N_j^2 \hat{\sigma}^2_{\overline{X}_{st}} = (364)^2(169.59) + (1{,}031)^2(759.03) = 829{,}289{,}284$$

and, on taking the square root,

$$N\hat{\sigma}_{\overline{X}_{st}} = 28{,}797$$

For a 95% confidence interval, $Z_{\alpha/2} = Z_{0.025} = 1.96$
The required 95% interval is therefore

$$480{,}731 - (1.96)(28{,}797) < N\mu < 480{,}731 + (1.96)(28{,}797)$$

or

$$424{,}289 < N\mu < 537{,}173$$

Thus, our 95% confidence interval runs from 424,289 to 537,173 students enrolled.

Next, consider the problem of estimating a population proportion based on a stratified random sample. Let π_1, π_2, ..., π_K be the population proportions in the K strata and p_1, p_2,..., p_K the corresponding sample proportions. If π denotes the overall population proportion, its estimate is based on the fact that

$$\pi = \frac{N_1\pi_1 + N_2\pi_2 + \cdots + N_K\pi_K}{N} = \frac{1}{N}\sum_{j=1}^{K} N_j\pi_j$$

The procedures to estimate the population proportion from a stratified random sample follow.

ESTIMATION OF THE POPULATION PROPORTION, STRATIFIED RANDOM SAMPLE

Suppose that random samples of n_j individuals from strata containing N_j individuals ($j = 1, 2,..., K$) are obtained. Let π_j be the population proportion and p_j the sample proportion, in the jth stratum, of those possessing a particular characteristic. If π is the overall population proportion:

i.   An unbiased estimation procedure for π yields

$$p_{st} = \frac{1}{N}\sum_{j=1}^{K} N_j p_j \tag{18.14}$$

ii. An unbiased estimation procedure for the variance of our estimator of the overall population proportion is

$$\hat{\sigma}^2_{p_{st}} = \frac{1}{N^2}\sum_{j=1}^{K} N_j^2 \hat{\sigma}^2_{p_j} \tag{18.15}$$

where

$$\hat{\sigma}^2_{p_j} = \frac{p_j(1-p_j)}{n_j - 1} \times \frac{(N_j - n_j)}{N_j} \tag{18.16}$$

is the estimate of the variance of the sample proportion in the jth stratum.

iii. Provided the sample size is large, $100(1 - \alpha)\%$ **confidence intervals for the population proportion for stratified random samples** are obtained from

$$p_{st} - Z_{\alpha/2}\hat{\sigma}_{p_{st}} < \pi < p_{st} + Z_{\alpha/2}\hat{\sigma}_{p_{st}} \tag{18.17}$$

EXAMPLE 18.6

STATISTICS TAUGHT IN ECONOMICS DEPARTMENTS (ESTIMATION)

In the study of Example 18.5, suppose that it was found that business statistics was taught by members of the economics department in seven of the 2-year colleges and thirteen of the 4-year colleges in the sample. Estimate the proportion of all colleges in which this course is taught in the economics department.

SOLUTION

It is known that

$$N_1 = 364 \qquad n_1 = 40 \qquad p_1 = \frac{7}{40} = 0.175$$

$$N_2 = 1,031 \qquad n_2 = 60 \qquad p_2 = \frac{13}{60} = 0.217$$

Our estimate of the population proportion is

$$p_{st} = \frac{1}{N} \sum_{j=1}^{K} N_j p_j = \frac{(364)(0.175) + (1,031)(0.217)}{1,395} = 0.206$$

Thus, it is estimated that in 20.6% of all colleges, the economics department teaches the course.

Next

$$\hat{\sigma}_{p_1}^2 = \frac{p_1(1 - p_1)}{n_1 - 1} \times \frac{(N_1 - n_1)}{N_1} = \frac{(0.175)(0.825)}{39} \times \frac{324}{364} = 0.003295$$

$$\hat{\sigma}_{p_2}^2 = \frac{p_2(1 - p_2)}{n_2 - 1} \times \frac{(N_2 - n_2)}{N_2} = \frac{(0.217)(0.783)}{59} \times \frac{971}{1,031} = 0.002712$$

Together with the individual stratum sample proportions, these values can be used to calculate confidence intervals for the two stratum population proportions, exactly as in Example 18.3. Here, focus is given to interval estimation for the overall population proportion, for which

$$\hat{\sigma}_{p_{st}}^2 = \frac{1}{N^2} \sum_{j=1}^{K} N_j^2 \hat{\sigma}_{p_j}^2 = \frac{(364)^2(0.003295) + (1,031)^2(0.002712)}{(1,395)^2} = 0.001706$$

so taking the square root yields

$$\hat{\sigma}_{p_{st}} = 0.0413$$

For a 90% confidence level,

$$Z_{\alpha/2} = Z_{0.05} = 1.645$$

and the 90% confidence interval for the population proportion from a stratified random sample is

$$(0.206) - (1.645)(0.0413) < \pi < (0.206) + (1.645)(0.0413)$$
$$0.138 < \pi < 0.274$$

This interval runs from 13.8% to 27.4% of all colleges.

Allocation of Sample Effort Among Strata

The question of the allocation of the sample effort among the various strata remains to be discussed. Assuming that a total of n sample members is to be selected, how many of these sample observations should be allocated to each stratum? In fact, the survey in question may have multiple objectives, meaning that no clear-cut answer is available. Nevertheless, it is possible to specify criteria for choice that the investigator might keep in mind. If little or nothing is known beforehand about the population and if there are no strong requirements for the production of information about sparsely populated individual strata, a natural choice is *proportional allocation*.

PROPORTIONAL ALLOCATION: SAMPLE SIZE

The proportion of sample members in any stratum is the same as the proportion of population members in that stratum. Thus, for the jth stratum,

$$\frac{n_j}{n} = \frac{N_j}{N} \tag{18.18}$$

so that the **sample size for the jth stratum using proportional allocation** is

$$n_j = \frac{N_j}{N} \times n \tag{18.19}$$

This intuitively reasonable allocation mechanism is frequently employed and generally provides a satisfactory analysis. Notice that proportional allocation was used in Example 18.4. A total of $N = 155$ restaurants were divided into three strata (Illinois, Indiana, and Ohio). A sample of $n = 31$ was selected with $n_1 = \dfrac{60}{155} \times 31 = 12$ $n_2 = \dfrac{50}{155} \times 31 = 10$ and $n_3 = \dfrac{45}{155} \times 31 = 9$.

Sometimes strict adherence to proportional allocation will produce relatively few observations in strata in which the investigator is particularly interested. In that case, inference about the population parameters of these particular strata could be quite imprecise. In these circumstances, one might prefer to allocate more observations to such strata than is dictated by proportional allocation. In Examples 18.5 and 18.6, 364 of the 1,395 colleges are 2-year schools, and a sample of 100 observations is to be taken. If proportional allocation had been used, the number of 2-year schools in the sample would have been

$$n_1 = \frac{N_1}{N} \times n = \frac{364}{1,395} \times 100 = 26$$

Since the publisher was particularly interested in acquiring information about this market, it was thought that a sample of only twenty-six observations would be inadequate. For this reason, forty of the 100 sample observations were allocated to this stratum.

If the sole objective of a survey is to estimate as precisely as possible an overall population parameter, such as the mean, total, or proportion, and if enough is known about the population, it is possible to derive an *optimal allocation*.

OPTIMAL ALLOCATION: SAMPLE SIZE FOR jTH STRATUM, OVERALL POPULATION MEAN OR TOTAL

If it is required to estimate an overall population mean or total and if the population variances in the individual strata are denoted, σ_j^2, it can be shown that the most precise estimators are obtained with optimal allocation. The **sample size for the jth stratum using optimal allocation** is:

$$n_j = \frac{N_j \sigma_j}{\displaystyle\sum_{i=1}^{K} N_i \sigma_i} \times n \tag{18.20}$$

This formula is intuitively plausible. Compared with proportional allocation, it allocates relatively more sample effort to strata in which the population variance is highest.

That is to say, a larger sample size is required where the greater population variability exists. Thus, in Example 18.4, where proportional allocation was used, if the differences observed in the sample standard deviations correctly reflect differences in the population quantities, it would have been preferable to take fewer observations in the third stratum and more in the first.

An immediate objection arises to the use of Equation 18.20. It requires knowledge of the population standard deviations, σ_j, whereas very often one will not even have worthwhile estimates of these values before the sample is taken. This point is considered in the final section of the chapter.

Now consider the sample size required under optimal allocation for a population proportion.

OPTIMAL ALLOCATION: SAMPLE SIZE FOR _j_TH STRATUM, POPULATION PROPORTION

For estimating the overall population proportion, estimators with the smallest possible variance are obtained by optimal allocation. **The sample size for the _j_th stratum for population proportion using optimal allocation is,**

$$n_j = \frac{N_j \sqrt{\pi_j(1 - \pi_j)}}{\displaystyle\sum_{i=1}^{K} N_i \sqrt{\pi_i(1 - \pi_i)}} \times n \tag{18.21}$$

Compared with the proportional allocation, this formula allocates more sample observations to strata in which the true population proportions are closest to 0.5, for if a proportion is close to 0 or 1, this can be learned with a fair amount of assurance from a relatively small sample. The difficulty in using Equation 18.21 is that it involves the unknown proportions π_j for ($j = 1, 2, \ldots, K$), the very quantities that the survey is designed to estimate.

Nevertheless, sometimes prior knowledge about the population can provide at least a rough idea as to which strata have proportions closest to 0.5. In Example 18.6, the sample proportions suggest that the number of 2-year colleges in the sample should have been less than the number resulting from proportional allocation. The same conclusion also holds for this study when one compares the sample standard deviations of Example 18.5 with Equation 18.20. In spite of this, it was decided that *more*, rather than fewer, 2-year colleges should be included in the sample. The reason for this decision was that, in this particular study, the publisher was eager to obtain reliable information about both the 2-year and 4-year college markets.

This illustration serves as an example of an important point. Although the division of sample effort suggested by Equation 18.20 and Equation 18.21 is often referred to as the *optimum allocation*, it is optimal only with regard to the narrow criterion of efficient estimation of overall population parameters. Frequently, surveys have broader objectives than this, in which case it may well be reasonable to depart from the optimum allocation.

EXERCISES

18.27 A small town contains a total of 1,800 households. The town is divided into three districts, containing 820, 540, and 440 households, respectively. A stratified random sample of 300 households contains 120, 90, and 90 households, respectively, from these three districts. Sample members were asked to estimate their total energy bills for the winter months. The respective sample means were $290, $352, and $427, and the respective sample standard deviations were $47, $61, and $93.

(a) Use an unbiased estimation procedure to estimate the mean winter energy bill for all households in this town.

(b) Use an unbiased estimation procedure to find an estimate of the variance of the estimator of part (a).

(c) Find a 95% confidence interval for the population mean winter energy bill for households in this town.

18.28 A college has 152 assistant professors, 127 associate professors, and 208 full professors. The college administration is investigating the amount of time these faculty members spend in meetings in a semester. Random samples of 40 assistant professors, 40 associate professors, and 50 full professors were asked to keep records of time spent in meetings during a semester. The sample means were 27.6 hours for assistant professors, 39.2 hours for associate professors, and 43.3 hours for full professors. The sample standard deviations were 7.1 hours for assistant professors, 9.9 hours for associate professors, and 12.3 hours for full professors.

(a) Find a 90% confidence interval for the mean time spent in meetings by full professors in this college in the semester.

(b) Using an unbiased estimation procedure, estimate the mean time spent in meetings by all faculty members in this college in the semester.

(c) Find 90% and 95% confidence intervals for the mean time spent in meetings by all faculty members in this college in the semester.

18.29 A local bus company is planning a new route to serve four housing subdivisions. Random samples of households are taken from each subdivision and sample members are asked to rate on a scale from 1 (strongly opposed) to 5 (strongly in favor) their reaction to the proposed service. The results are summarized in the accompany table.

	SUBDIVISION 1	SUBDIVISION 2	SUBDIVISION 3	SUBDIVISION 4
N_i	240	190	350	280
n_i	40	40	40	40
$\overline{X}_i$	2.5	3.6	3.9	2.8
s_i	0.8	0.9	1.2	0.7

(a) Find a 90% confidence interval for the mean reaction of households in subdivision 1.

(b) Using an unbiased estimation procedure, estimate the mean reaction of all households to be served by the new route.

(c) Find 90% and 95% confidence intervals for the mean reaction of all households to be served by the new route.

18.30 In a stratified random sample of students on a small campus, sample members were asked to rate, on a scale from 1 (poor) to 5 (excellent), opportunities for extracurricular activities. The results are shown in the accompanying table.

	Freshmen and Sophomores	Juniors and Seniors
N_i	632	529
n_i	50	50
$\overline{X}_i$	3.12	3.37
s_i	1.04	0.86

(a) Find a 95% confidence interval for the mean rating that would be given by all freshmen and sophomores on this campus.

(b) Find a 95% confidence interval for the mean rating that would be given by all juniors and seniors on this campus.

(c) Find a 95% confidence interval for the mean rating that would be given by all undergraduate students on this campus.

18.31 Refer to Exercise 18.28.

(a) Find a 90% confidence interval for the total amount of time spent in meetings by all full professors in this college in the semester.

(b) Find a 90% confidence interval for the total amount of time spent in meetings by all faculty members in this college in the semester.

18.32 A company has three divisions, and auditors are attempting to estimate the total amounts of the company's accounts receivable. Random samples of these accounts were taken for each of the three divisions, yielding the results shown in the table.

	DIVISION 1	DIVISION 2	DIVISION 3
N_i	120	150	180
n_i	40	45	50
$\overline{X}_i$	$237	$198	$131
s_i	$93	$64	$47

(a) Using an unbiased estimation procedure, find a point estimate of the total value of all accounts receivable for this company.

(b) Find a 95% confidence interval for the total value of all accounts receivable for this company.

18.33 Of the 1,395 colleges in the United States, 364 have 2-year schools. In a random sample of 40 two-year schools, it was found that the text *Statistics Can Be Fun* was used in 10 of the schools. In an independent random sample of 60 4-year schools, this text was used by 8 of the sample members.

(a) Find an estimate of the proportion of all colleges using this text, using an unbiased estimation procedure.

(b) Find a 95% confidence interval for the proportion of all colleges using this text.

18.34 A consulting company has developed a short course on modern business forecasting methods for corporate executives. The first course was attended by 150 executives. From the information they supplied, it was concluded that the technical skills of 100 course members were more than adequate to follow the course material, while those of the remaining 50 were judged barely adequate. After the completion of the course, questionnaires were sent to independent random samples of 25 people from each of these two groups in order to obtain feedback that could lead to improved presentation in subsequent courses. Six of the most skilled and 14 of the less skilled group indicated that they believed the course had been too theoretical.

(a) Find an estimate of the proportion of all course members with this opinion, using an unbiased estimation procedure.

(b) Find 90% and 95% confidence intervals for this population proportion.

18.35 A college has 152 assistant professors, 127 associate professors, and 208 full professors. A journalist with the student newspaper was interested in whether faculty members were actually in their offices during posted office hours. She decided to investigate samples of 40 assistant professors, 40 associate professors, and 50 full professors. Student volunteers were sent to knock on the doors of these sample members during their posted office hours. It was found that 31 of the assistant professors, 29 of the associate professors, and 34 of the full professors were actually in their offices at these times.

(a) Using an unbiased estimation procedure, find a point estimate of the proportion of all faculty members who are in their offices during posted office hours.

(b) Find 90% and 95% confidence intervals for the proportion of all faculty members who are in their offices during posted office hours.

18.36 Refer to Exercise 18.28. If a total sample of 130 faculty members is to be taken, determine how many of these should be full professors under each of the following schemes:

(a) Proportional allocation.

(b) Optimum allocation, assuming the stratum population standard deviations are the same as the corresponding sample values.

18.37 Refer to the data of Exercise 18.29. If a total sample of 160 households is to be taken, determine how many of these should be from subdivision 1 under each of the following schemes:

(a) Proportional allocation.

(b) Optimum allocation, assuming the stratum population standard deviations are the same as the corresponding sample values.

18.38 Refer to the data of Exercise 18.30. If a total sample of 100 students is to be taken, determine how many of these should be freshmen and sophomores under each of the following schemes:

(a) Proportional allocation.

(b) Optimum allocation, assuming the stratum population standard deviations are the same as the corresponding sample values.

18.39 Refer to the data of Exercise 18.32. If a total sample of 135 accounts receivable is to be taken, determine how many of these should be from Division 1 under each of the following schemes:

(a) Proportional allocation.

(b) Optimum allocation, assuming the stratum population standard deviations are the same as the corresponding sample values.

18.40 Refer to the data of Example 18.5. If a total sample of 100 colleges is to be taken, determine how many of these should be 4-year schools under each of the following schemes:

(a) Proportional allocation.

(b) Optimum allocation, assuming the stratum population standard deviations are the same as the corresponding sample values.

18.5 DETERMINING SAMPLE SIZE

An important aspect of the planning of any survey involves the determination of an appropriate number of sample members. Several factors may be relevant. If the procedure for contacting sample members is thought likely to lead to a high rate of nonresponse, this eventuality should be taken into account. In many instances, the resources available to the investigator, in terms of time and money, will place constraints on what can be achieved. In this section, however, we abstract from such considerations and relate sample size to the variances of the estimators of population parameters and consequently to the widths of resulting confidence intervals.

Sample Sizes for Simple Random Sampling: Estimation of Population Mean or Total

Consider the problem of estimating the population mean from a simple random sample of n observations. If the random variable $\overline{X}$ denotes the sample mean, it is known from Chapter 7 that the variance of this random variable is

$$\text{Var}(\overline{X}) = \sigma_{\overline{X}}^2 = \frac{\sigma^2}{n} \times \frac{(N-n)}{(N-1)}$$

If the population variance σ^2 is known, by solving the equation $\text{Var}(\overline{X})$ you can determine the sample size n that is needed to achieve any specified value $\sigma_{\overline{X}}^2$ for the variance of the sample mean. Similar procedures are available if the quantity of interest is the population total.

SAMPLE SIZE: POPULATION MEAN OR TOTAL, SIMPLE RANDOM SAMPLING

Consider estimating the mean of a population of N members, which has variance σ^2. If the desired variance, $\sigma_{\overline{X}}^2$, of the sample mean is specified, **the required sample size to estimate population mean through simple random sampling** is

$$n = \frac{N\sigma^2}{(N-1)\sigma_{\overline{X}}^2 + \sigma^2} \tag{18.22}$$

i. Often, it is more convenient to specify directly the width of confidence intervals for the population mean rather than $\sigma_{\overline{X}}^2$. This is easily accomplished since, for example, a 95% confidence interval for the population mean will extend an approximate amount $1.96\sigma_{\overline{x}}$ on each side of the sample mean, $\overline{X}$.

ii. If the object of interest is the **population total**, the variance of the sample estimator of this quantity is $N^2\sigma_{\overline{X}}^2$ and that a 95% confidence interval for it extends an approximate amount of $1.96N\,\sigma_{\overline{X}}$ on each side of $N\overline{X}$.

An obvious difficulty with the practical use of Equation 18.22 is that it involves the population variance σ^2, which will typically be unknown. However, an investigator will often have a rough idea of the value of this quantity. Sometimes the population variance can be estimated from a preliminary sample of the population.

EXAMPLE 18.7

MORTGAGES (SAMPLE SIZE)

As in Example 18.1, suppose that in a city last year 1,118 mortgages were taken out and that a simple random sample is to be taken in order to estimate the mean amount of these mortgages. From previous experience of such populations, it is estimated that the population standard deviation is approximately $20,000. A 95% confidence interval for the population mean must extend an amount $4,000 on each side of the sample mean. How many sample observations are needed to achieve this objective?

SOLUTION

First,

$$N = 1{,}118 \qquad \sigma = 20{,}000 \qquad 1.96\sigma_{\overline{x}} = 4{,}000$$

The required sample size is then,

$$n = \frac{N\sigma^2}{(N-1)\sigma_{\overline{X}}^2 + \sigma^2} = \frac{(1{,}118)(20{,}000)^2}{(1{,}117)(2{,}041)^2 + (20{,}000)^2} = 88.5$$

Thus, a simple random sample of 89 observations should suffice to meet our objective.

Sample Sizes for Simple Random Sampling: Estimation of Population Proportion

Consider simple random sampling for the estimation of a population proportion π. Recall from earlier in the text that

$$\operatorname{Var}(p_X) = \sigma^2_{p_X} = \frac{\pi(1-\pi)}{n} \times \frac{(N-n)}{(N-1)}$$

Solving for n leads to the sample size given in Equation 18.23 and Equation 18.24.

SAMPLE SIZE: POPULATION PROPORTION, SIMPLE RANDOM SAMPLING

Consider estimation of the proportion π of individuals in a population of size N who possess a certain attribute. If the desired variance, $\sigma^2_{p_X}$, of the sample proportion is specified, the required sample size to estimate the population proportion through simple random sampling is:

$$n = \frac{N\pi(1-\pi)}{(N-1)\sigma^2_{p_X} + \pi(1-\pi)} \tag{18.23}$$

The largest possible value for this expression, whatever the value of π, is

$$n_{max} = \frac{0.25N}{(N-1)\sigma^2_{p_X} + 0.25} \tag{18.24}$$

A 95% confidence interval for the population proportion will extend an approximate amount $1.96\sigma_{p_X}$ on each side of the sample proportion.

EXAMPLE 18.8

CAMPUS SURVEY (SAMPLE SIZE)

As in Example 18.3, suppose that a simple random sample of the 1,395 U.S. colleges is taken to estimate the proportion in which the business statistics course is two semesters long. It is desired that whatever the true proportion, a 95% confidence interval extends no further than 0.04 on each side of the sample proportion. How many sample observations should be taken?

SOLUTION
From the problem,

$$1.96\sigma_{p_X} = 0.04$$

or

$$\sigma_{p_X} = 0.0204$$

The sample size needed is then,

$$n_{max} = \frac{0.25N}{(N-1)\sigma^2_{p_X} + 0.25} = \frac{(0.25)(1{,}395)}{(1{,}394)(0.0204)^2 + 0.25} = 420.1$$

Hence, a sample of 421 observations is needed.

Sample Sizes for Stratified Random Sampling with Specified Degree of Precision

It is also possible to derive formulas for the sample size needed to yield a specified degree of precision when stratified random sampling is employed.

VARIANCE OF ESTIMATOR OF POPULATION MEAN, STRATIFIED SAMPLING

Let the random variable $\overline{X}_{st}$ denote the **estimator of the population mean from stratified sampling** and $\overline{X}_j$ ($j = 1, 2, \ldots, K$) the sample means for the individual strata. It then follows, since

$$\overline{X}_{st} = \frac{1}{N} \sum_{j=1}^{K} N_j \overline{X}_j \tag{18.25}$$

that the **variance of** $\overline{X}_{st}$ is

$$\mathrm{Var}(\overline{X}_{st}) = \sigma^2_{\overline{X}_{st}} = \frac{1}{N^2} \sum_{j=1}^{K} N_j^2 \, \mathrm{Var}(\overline{X}_j) = \frac{1}{N^2} \sum_{j=1}^{K} N_j^2 \frac{\sigma_j^2}{n_j} \times \frac{(N_j - n_j)}{N_j - 1} \tag{18.26}$$

where the σ_j^2 are the population variances for the K strata.

Now, for any choice of $n_1, n_2, \ldots, n_K$, the variance of $\overline{X}_{st}$ given in Equation 18.26 can be used to derive the corresponding variance of the estimator of the population mean. However, the actual total sample size, n, required to achieve a particular value for this variance will depend on the manner in which the sample observations are allocated among the strata. In Section 18.4 two frequently used procedures, proportional allocation and optimum allocation, were discussed. In either case, by substituting for n_j in Equation 18.26 you can solve the resulting equation and obtain the sample size n. The results are given in Equations 18.27 and 18.28.

TOTAL SAMPLE SIZE TO ESTIMATE OVERALL MEAN (STRATUM POPULATION VARIANCES SPECIFIED), STRATIFIED RANDOM SAMPLING

Suppose that a population of N members is subdivided in K strata containing $N_1, N_2, \ldots, N_K$ members. Let σ_j^2 denote the population variance in the jth stratum, and suppose that an **estimate the overall population mean** is desired. If the desired variance, $\sigma^2_{\overline{X}_{st}}$, of the sample estimator is specified, the required total sample size, n, is as follows:

i. **Proportional allocation:**

$$n = \frac{\displaystyle\sum_{j=1}^{K} N_j \sigma_j^2}{N \sigma^2_{\overline{X}_{st}} + \dfrac{1}{N} \displaystyle\sum_{j=1}^{K} N_j \sigma_j^2} \tag{18.27}$$

ii. **Optimal allocation:**

$$n = \frac{\dfrac{1}{N} \left(\displaystyle\sum_{j=1}^{K} N_j \sigma_j \right)^2}{N \sigma^2_{\overline{X}_{st}} + \dfrac{1}{N} \displaystyle\sum_{j=1}^{K} N_j \sigma_j^2} \tag{18.28}$$

EXAMPLE 18.9

RESTAURANT IN THREE STATES (SAMPLE SIZE)

As in Example 18.4, take a stratified random sample to estimate the mean number of orders per restaurant of a new food item when the numbers of restaurants in the three states are

$$N_1 = 60 \qquad N_2 = 50 \qquad N_3 = 45$$

Suppose also that the experience of the restaurant chain suggests that the population standard deviations for the three states are likely to be approximately

$$\sigma_1 = 13 \qquad \sigma_2 = 11 \qquad \sigma_3 = 9$$

If a 95% confidence interval is required for the population mean extending an amount three orders per restaurant on each side of the sample point estimate, how many sample observations, in total are needed?

SOLUTION

Note that

$$1.96\sigma_{\bar{X}_{st}} = 3, \qquad \text{so} \qquad \sigma_{\bar{X}_{st}} = 1.53$$

$$\sum_{j=1}^{K} N_j \sigma_j^2 = (60)(13)^2 + (50)(11)^2 + (45)(9)^2 = 19{,}835$$

and that

$$\frac{1}{N}\left(\sum_{j=1}^{K} N_j \sigma_j\right)^2 = \frac{[(60)(13) + (50)(11) + (45)(9)]^2}{155} = 19{,}421$$

For **proportional allocation**, the sample size needed is

$$n = \frac{\displaystyle\sum_{j=1}^{K} N_j \sigma_j^2}{N\sigma_{\bar{X}_{st}}^2 + \dfrac{1}{N}\displaystyle\sum_{j=1}^{K} N_j \sigma_j^2} = \frac{19{,}835}{(155)(1.53)^2 + 19{,}835/155} = 40.4$$

Thus, a sample of 41 observations will suffice to produce the required level of precision.

If **optimal allocation** is to be used, the sample size needed is

$$n = \frac{\dfrac{1}{N}\left(\displaystyle\sum_{j=1}^{K} N_j \sigma_j\right)^2}{N\sigma_{\bar{X}_{st}}^2 + \dfrac{1}{N}\displaystyle\sum_{j=1}^{K} N_j \sigma_j^2} = \frac{19{,}421}{(155)(1.53)^2 + 19{,}835/155} = 39.6$$

so the same degree of reliability can be obtained with 40 observations if this method of allocation is used. In this particular case, since the population standard deviations are quite close, this represents only a very small savings compared with proportional allocation.

EXERCISES

18.41 The mean amount of the 812 mortgages taken out in a city in the past year must be estimated. Based on previous experience, a real estate broker knows that the population standard deviation is likely to be about $20,000. If a 95% confidence interval for the population mean is to extend $2,000 on each side of the sample mean, how many sample observations are needed if a simple random sample is taken?

18.42 An automobile dealer has an inventory of 400 used cars. To estimate the mean mileage of this inventory, he intends to take a simple random sample of used cars. Previous studies suggest that the population standard deviation is 10,000 miles. It is required that a 90% confidence interval for the population mean extends 2,000 miles on each side of its sample estimate. How large a sample size is necessary to satisfy this requirement?

18.43 A country club wants to poll a random sample of its 320 members to estimate the proportion likely to attend an early-season function. The number of sample observations should be sufficiently large to ensure that a 99% confidence interval for the population extends at most .05 on each side of the sample proportion. How large a sample is necessary?

18.44 An instructor in a class of 417 students is considering the possibility of a take-home final examination. She wants to take a random sample of class members to estimate the proportion who prefer this form of examination. If it is required that a 90% confidence interval for the population proportion extends at most .04 on each side of the sample proportion, how large a sample is needed?

18.45 An auditor wants to estimate the mean value of a corporation's accounts receivable. The population is divided into four strata, containing 500, 400, 300, and 200 accounts, respectively. On the basis of past experience, it is estimated that the standard deviations of values in these strata will be $150, $200, $300, and $400, respectively. If a 90% confidence interval for the overall population mean is to extend $25 on each side of the sample estimate, determine the total sample size needed under both proportional allocation and optimal allocation.

18.46 Mean household income must be estimated for a town that can be divided into three districts. The relevant information is shown in the table.

DISTRICT	POPULATION SIZE	ESTIMATED STANDARD DEVIATION ($)
1	1,150	4,000
2	2,120	6,000
3	930	8,000

If a 95% confidence interval for the population mean, extending $500 on each side of the sample estimate, is required, determine how many sample observations in total are needed under proportional allocation and optimal allocation.

18.6   OTHER SAMPLING METHODS

Simple random sampling and stratified random sampling have been discussed briefly. These are not the only procedures used for choosing a sample. Some alternative methods are discussed in this section.

Cluster Sampling

Suppose that an investigator wants to survey a population spread over a wide geographical area, such as a large city or a state. If either a simple random sample or a stratified random sample is to be used, two immediate problems will arise. First, in order to draw the sample, the investigator will need a reasonably accurate listing of the population members. Such a list may not be available or could perhaps be obtained only at a prohibitively high cost. Second, even if the investigator does possess a list of the population, the resulting sample members will almost inevitably be thinly spread over a large area. In that case, contacting each individual sample member by interviewers will be quite costly. Of course, if a mail questionnaire is to be used, this latter problem does not arise. However, this means of contact may lead to an unacceptably high rate of nonresponse, leading the investigator to prefer personal interviews.

Faced with the dilemma of either not having a reliable population listing or wanting to set up personal interviews with sample members when budget resources are tight, the investigator may use an alternative sampling procedure known as *cluster sampling*. This approach is attractive when a population can conveniently be subdivided into relatively small, geographically compact units called *clusters*. For example, a city might be subdivided into political wards or residential blocks. This can generally be achieved even when a complete listing of residents or households is unavailable.

In cluster sampling, a simple random sample of clusters is selected from the population, and every individual in each of the sampled clusters is contacted; that is, a complete census is carried out in each of the chosen clusters. In the following equations, procedures for deriving valid inferences about the population mean and proportion from the results of a cluster sample are given.

ESTIMATORS FOR CLUSTER SAMPLING

A population is subdivided into M clusters and a simple random sample of m of these clusters is selected and information is obtained from every member of the sampled clusters. Let $n_1, n_2, \ldots, n_m$ denote the numbers of population members in the m sampled clusters. Denote the means of these clusters by $\overline{X}_1, \overline{X}_2, \ldots, \overline{X}_m$ and the proportions of cluster members possessing an attribute of interest by $\pi_1, \pi_2, \ldots, \pi_m$. The objective is to estimate the overall population mean μ and proportion π.

i.   Unbiased estimation procedures give

$$\overline{X}_c = \frac{\sum_{i=1}^{m} n_i \overline{X}_i}{\sum_{i=1}^{m} n_i} \tag{18.29}$$

and

$$p_c = \frac{\sum_{i=1}^{m} n_i \pi_i}{\sum_{i=1}^{m} n_i} \tag{18.30}$$

ii.   Estimates of the variance of these estimators, following from unbiased estimation procedures, are

$$\hat{\sigma}_{\overline{X}_c}^2 = \frac{M - m}{Mm\bar{n}^2} \left(\frac{\sum_{i=1}^{m} n_i^2 (\overline{X}_i - \overline{X}_c)^2}{m - 1} \right) \tag{18.31}$$

and

$$\hat{\sigma}_{p_c}^2 = \frac{M - m}{Mm\bar{n}^2} \left(\frac{\sum_{i=1}^{m} n_i^2 (\pi_i - p_c)^2}{m - 1} \right) \tag{18.32}$$

where $\bar{n} = \dfrac{\sum_{i=1}^{m} n_i}{m}$ is the average number of individuals in the sampled clusters.

Based on these estimators, the confidence intervals with cluster sampling follow.

ESTIMATION OF POPULATION MEAN, CLUSTER SAMPLING

Provided the sample size is large, a $100(1 - \alpha)\%$ **confidence intervals for the population mean using cluster sampling** is

$$\overline{X}_c - Z_{\alpha/2}\hat{\sigma}_{\overline{X}_c} < \mu < \overline{X}_c + Z_{\alpha/2}\hat{\sigma}_{\overline{X}_c} \tag{18.33}$$

Similarly, confidence intervals for the population proportion based on cluster sampling are established.

ESTIMATION OF POPULATION PROPORTION, CLUSTER SAMPLING

Provided the sample size is large, a $100(1 - \alpha)\%$ **confidence intervals for the population proportion using cluster sampling** is

$$p_c - Z_{\alpha/2}\hat{\sigma}_{p_c} < \pi < p_c + Z_{\alpha/2}\hat{\sigma}_{p_c} \tag{18.34}$$

Notice that inferences can be made with relatively little prior information about the population. All that is required is a breakdown into identifiable clusters. It is not necessary to know the total number of population members. It is sufficient to know the numbers in each of the *sampled* clusters, and these can be determined during the course of the survey, since a full census is taken in each cluster in the sample. In addition, since sample members will be geographically close to one another within clusters, their contact by interviewers is relatively inexpensive.

EXAMPLE 18.10

CLUSTER SAMPLING FOR FAMILY INCOMES (ESTIMATION)

Income Clusters

A simple random sample of 20 blocks is taken from a residential area containing a total of 1,100 blocks. Each household in the sampled blocks is then contacted, and information is obtained about family incomes. The mean annual incomes and the proportion of families with incomes below $15,000 per year in the sampled blocks are contained in the data file **Income Clusters**. For this residential area, estimate the mean family income and the proportion of families with incomes below $15,000 per year.

SOLUTION

It is known that

$$m = 20 \quad \text{and} \quad M = 1,000$$

The total number of households in the sample is

$$\sum_{i=1}^{m} n_i = (23 + 31 + \cdots + 41) = 607$$

To obtain point estimates,

$$\sum_{i=1}^{m} n_i \overline{X}_i = (23)(26{,}283) + (31)(19{,}197) + \cdots + (41)(16{,}493) = 15{,}848{,}158$$

and

$$\sum_{i=1}^{m} n_i \pi_i = (23)(0.1304) + (31)(0.4516) + \cdots + (41)(0.3659) = 153$$

Our point estimates are therefore

$$\overline{X}_c = \frac{\sum n_i \overline{X}_i}{\sum n_i} = \frac{15{,}848{,}158}{607} = 26{,}109$$

$$P_c = \frac{\sum n_i \pi_i}{\sum n_i} = \frac{153}{607} = 0.2521$$

Thus, on the basis of this sample evidence, it is estimated that for this residential area, mean annual household income is \$26,109 and 25.21% of households have income below \$15,000 per year.

To obtain interval estimates of the population mean, the average cluster size is needed where

$$\overline{n} = \frac{\sum n_i}{m} = \frac{607}{20} = 30.35$$

Also

$$\frac{\sum_{i=1}^{m} n_i^2 (\overline{X}_i - \overline{X}_c)^2}{m-1} = \frac{(23)^2 (26{,}283 - 26{,}109)^2 + \cdots + (41)^2 (16{,}493 - 26{,}109)^2}{19} = 69{,}270{,}551{,}000$$

so

$$\sigma_{\overline{X}_c}^2 = \frac{M-m}{Mm\overline{n}^2} \times \frac{\sum n_i^2 (\overline{X}_i - \overline{X}_c)^2}{m-1} = \frac{(980)(69{,}270{,}551{,}000)}{(1{,}000)(20)(30.35)^2} = 3{,}684{,}914$$

and taking the square root

$$\hat{\sigma}_{\overline{X}} = 1{,}920$$

A 95% confidence interval for the population mean is

$$26{,}109 - (1.96)(1{,}920) < \mu < 26{,}109 + (1.96)(1{,}920)$$

or

$$22{,}346 < \mu < 29{,}872$$

A 95% confidence interval for the mean income of all families in this area therefore runs from \$22,346 to \$29,872.

To obtain interval estimates for the population proportion,

$$\frac{\sum_{i=i}^{m} n_i^2(\pi_i - p_i)^2}{m-1} = \frac{(23)^2(0.1304 - 0.02521)^2 + \cdots + (41)^2(0.3659 - 0.2521)^2}{19} = 38.1547$$

Then,

$$\hat{\sigma}_{p_c}^2 = \frac{M-m}{Mm\bar{n}^2}\left(\frac{\sum_{i=1}^{m} n_i^2(\pi_i - p_c)^2}{m-1}\right)$$

$$= \frac{(980)(38.1547)}{(1,000)(20)(30.35)^2} = 0.0020297$$

and taking the square root,

$$\hat{\sigma}_{p_c} = 0.0451$$

The 95% confidence interval for the population proportion is

$$0.2521 - (1.96)(0.0451) < \pi < 0.2521 + (1.96)(0.0451)$$

or

$$0.164 < \pi < 0.340$$

Our 95% confidence interval for the percentage of households with annual incomes below $15,000 runs from 16.4% to 34.0%.

Cluster sampling has a superficial resemblance to stratified sampling. In both, the population is first divided into subgroups. However, the similarity is rather illusory. In stratified random sampling, a sample is taken from *every stratum* of the population, in an attempt to ensure that important segments of the population are given due weight. By contrast, in cluster sampling, a random sample of *clusters* is taken, so that some clusters will have no members in the sample. Since, within clusters, population members will probably be fairly homogeneous, the danger is that important subgroups of the population may be either not represented at all or grossly underrepresented in the final sample. In consequence, while the great advantage of cluster sampling lies in its convenience, this convenience may well be at the cost of additional imprecision in the sample estimates. A further distinction between cluster sampling and stratified sampling is that in the former, a *complete census* of cluster members is taken, while in the latter, a *random sample* of stratum members is drawn. This difference, however, is not essential. Indeed, on occasions, an investigator may draw a random sample of cluster members rather than take a full census.

Two-Phase Sampling

In many investigations, the population is not surveyed at a single step. Rather, it is often convenient to carry out an initial pilot study in which a relatively small proportion of the sample members are contacted. The results obtained are then analyzed prior to conducting the bulk of the survey. The chief disadvantage of such a procedure is that it can be quite time-consuming. However, this factor may be outweighed by several advantages. One important benefit is that the investigator is able, at modest cost, to try out the proposed questionnaire in order to ensure that the various questions can be thoroughly understood. The pilot study may also suggest additional questions whose potential importance had previously been overlooked. Moreover, this study should also provide an estimate of the likely rate of nonresponse. Should this prove unacceptably high, some modification in the method of soliciting responses might appear desirable.

Conducting a survey in two stages, beginning with a pilot study, is known as **two-phase sampling.** This approach has two further advantages. First, if stratified random sampling is employed, the pilot study can be used to provide estimates of the individual stratum variances. These, in turn, can be employed to estimate the optimum allocation of the sample among the various strata. Second, the results of the pilot study can be used to estimate the number of observations needed to obtain estimators of population parameters with a specified level of precision. The following examples serve to illustrate these points. Consider a straightforward situation in which a simple random sample is to be used to estimate a population mean. At the outset, relatively little is known about this population, so an initial pilot survey is to be carried out to get some idea of the sample size required.

EXAMPLE 18.11

MEAN VALUE OF ACCOUNTS RECEIVABLE (SAMPLE SIZE)

An auditor wishes to estimate the mean value of accounts receivable in a total population of 1,120 accounts. He wants to produce a 95% confidence interval for the population mean extending approximately $4 on each side of the sample mean. To begin, he takes a simple random sample of 100 accounts, finding a sample standard deviation of $30.27. How many more accounts should be sampled?

SOLUTION

From Section 18.5, the sample size needed was found to be

$$n = \frac{N\sigma^2}{(N-1)\sigma_{\bar{X}}^2 + \sigma^2}$$

where $N = 1{,}120$ is the number of population members in this case. In order for the 95% confidence interval to be the required width,

$$1.96\sigma_{\bar{X}} = 4$$

so that, $\sigma_{\bar{X}}$, the standard deviation of the sample mean, must be

$$\sigma_{\bar{X}} = \frac{4}{1.96} = 2.04$$

The population standard deviation, σ, is unknown. However, as a result of the initial study of 100 accounts receivable, it is estimated to be 30.27. The total number of sample observations needed is therefore:

$$n = \frac{N\sigma^2}{(N-1)\sigma_{\bar{X}}^2 + \sigma^2} = \frac{(1{,}120)(30.27)^2}{(1{,}119)(2.04)^2 + (30.27)^2} = 184.1$$

Since 100 observations have already been taken, an additional 85 will suffice to satisfy the auditor's objective.

EXAMPLE 18.12

INCOME (SAMPLE SIZE)

An investigator intends to take a stratified random sample to estimate mean family income in a town where the numbers in the three stratum districts are

$$N_1 = 1{,}150 \qquad N_2 = 2{,}120 \qquad N_3 = 930$$

To begin, the investigator conducts a pilot study, sampling 30 households from each district, obtaining the sample standard deviations $3,657, $6,481, and $8,403, respectively. Suppose that the objective is to obtain, with as small size as possible, a 95% confidence interval for the population mean extending $500 one each side of the sample estimate. How many additional observations should be taken in each district?

SOLUTION

The requirement that a specified degree of precision be obtained with as few sample observations as possible implies that optimal allocation must be used. Recall from Equation 18.20, that the numbers n_1, n_2, n_3 to be sampled in the three strata are as follows:

$$n_j = \frac{N_j \sigma_j}{\sum\limits_{i=1}^{K} N_i \sigma_i} \times n \qquad (j = 1, 2, 3)$$

where the σ_i are the stratum population standard deviations. Using our sample estimates in place of these quantities,

$$n_1 = \frac{(1,150)(3,657)}{(1,150)(3,657) + (2,120)(6,481) + (930)(8,403)} \times n = 0.163n$$

$$n_2 = \frac{(2,120)(6,481)}{(1,150)(3,657) + (2,120)(6,481) + (930)(8,403)} \times n = 0.533n$$

$$n_3 = \frac{(930)(8,403)}{(1,150)(3,657) + (2,120)(6,481) + (930)(8,403)} \times n = 0.303n$$

The properties of the total sample to be allocated to each stratum under the optimal scheme are now specified. It remains to determine the total number n of sample observations.

Nonprobabilistic Sampling Methods

Various sampling schemes for which it is possible to specify the probability that any particular sample will be drawn from the population have been considered. Because of this feature of the sampling methods, valid statistical inferences based on the sample results can be made. Otherwise, the derivation of unbiased point estimates and confidence intervals with specified probability content could not be achieved with strict statistical validity.

Nevertheless, in many practical applications, **nonprobabilistic methods** are used for selecting sample members, primarily as a matter of convenience. For example, suppose that you want to assess the reactions of students on your campus to some issue of topical interest. One possibility would be to ask all your friends how they feel about it. This group would not constitute a random sample from the population of all students. Accordingly, if you proceed to analyze the data as if they were obtained from a random sample, the resulting inference would lack proper statistical validity.

A more sophisticated version of the approach just described, called **quota sampling,** is commonly used by polling organizations. Interviewers are assigned to a particular locale and instructed to contact specified numbers of people of certain age, race, and gender characteristics. These assigned quotas represent what are thought to be appropriate proportions for the population at large. However, once the quotas are determined, interviewers are granted flexibility in the choice of sample members. Their choice is typically not random. Quota sampling can, and often does, produce quite accurate estimates of population parameters. The drawback is that since the sample is not chosen using probabilistic methods, there is no valid way of determining the reliability of the resulting estimates.

EXERCISES

18.47 A market research organization wants to estimate the mean amounts of time in a week that television sets are in use in households in a city that contains 65 precincts. A simple random sample of 10 precincts was selected, and every household in each sampled precinct was questioned. The following results were obtained.

SAMPLED PRECINCT	NUMBER OF HOUSEHOLDS	MEAN TIME TELEVISION IN USE(HOURS)
1	28	29.6
2	35	18.4
3	18	32.7
4	52	26.3
5	41	22.4
6	38	31.6
7	36	19.7
8	30	23.8
9	23	25.4
10	42	24.1

(a) Find a point estimate of the population mean amount of time that televisions are in use in this city.
(b) Find a 90% confidence interval for the population mean.

18.48 A union executive wants to estimate the mean value of bonus payments made to a corporation's clerical employees in the first month of a new plan. This corporation has fifty-two subdivisions, and a simple random sample of eight of these is taken. Information is then obtained from the payroll records of every clerical worker in each of the sampled subdivisions. The results obtained are shown in the table.

SAMPLED SUBDIVISION	NUMBER OF CLERICAL EMPLOYEES	MEAN BONUS (DOLLARS)
1	69	83
2	75	64
3	41	42
4	36	108
5	59	136
6	82	102
7	64	95
8	71	98

(a) Find a point estimate of the population mean bonus per clerical employee for this month.
(b) Find a 99% confidence interval for the population mean.

18.49 In the survey of Exercise 18.47, the households were asked if they had cable television. The numbers having cable are given in the accompanying table.

PRECINCT	1	2	3	4	5	6	7	8	9	10
Number	12	11	10	29	15	13	20	14	9	26

(a) Find a point estimate of the proportion of all households in the city having cable television.
(b) Find a 90% confidence interval for this population proportion.

18.50 In the survey of Exercise 18.48, the clerical employees in the eight sampled subdivisions were asked if they were satisfied with the operation of the bonus plan. The results obtained are listed in the table.

SUBDIVISION	1	2	3	4	5	6	7	8
Number	24	25	11	21	35	44	30	34

(a) Find a point estimate of the proportion of all clerical employees satisfied with the bonus plan.
(b) Find a 95% confidence interval for this population proportion.

18.51 A city is divided into 50 geographical subdivisions. It was required to estimate the proportion of households in the city interested in a new lawn-care service. A random sample of three subdivisions contained 611, 521, and 734 households, respectively. The numbers expressing interest in the service were 128, 131, and 172, respectively. Find a 90% confidence interval for the proportion of all households in this city interested in the lawn-care service.

18.52 A bank holds 720 delinquent mortgages in residential properties. It is required to estimate the mean current appraised value of these properties. Initially, a random sample of 20 was appraised, and a sample standard deviation of $37,600 was found. If the bank requires a 90% confidence interval for the population mean extending $5,000 on each side of the sample mean, how many more properties must be appraised?

18.53 A college has 3,200 undergraduate students and 800 graduate students. Interest is in the amount of money spent in a year on textbooks by these students. Initially, simple random samples of 30 undergraduate students and 30 graduate students were taken. The sample standard deviations for amounts spent were $40 and $58, respectively. It is required that a 90% confidence interval for the overall population mean extends $5 on each side of the sample point estimate. Estimate the smallest total number of additional sample observations needed to achieve this goal.

18.54 A corporation has a fleet of 480 company cars—100 compact, 180 midsize, and 200 full-size. To estimate the overall mean annual repair costs for these cars, a preliminary random sample of 10 cars of each type is selected. The sample standard deviations for repair costs were $105 for compacts, $162 for midsize, and $183 for full-size cars. It is required that a 95% confidence interval for the overall population mean annual repair cost per car extend $20 on each side of the sample point estimate. Estimate the smallest total number of additional sample observations that must be taken.

SUMMARY

This chapter concentrated on the problem of a researcher who wants to discover something about a population that is not necessarily large. The investigator intends to collect information on only a subset of the population members and requires guidance as to how to proceed. First, the necessary steps in a sampling plan must be considered. Then, sampling and non-sampling errors must be distinguished; equations to estimate a population mean, population total, and population proportion for simple random sampling as well as for stratified sampling must be determined; the sample size to estimate a population mean, population total, and population proportion using simple random sampling or stratified sampling if the desired variance of the sample mean is specified must be determined; cluster sampling and established equations to determine confidence intervals for a population mean and a population proportion, if the sample size is large, should be considered. A brief mention of two-phase sampling and non-probabilistic sampling methods was included.

Since much of statistics is concerned with problems of making statements about a population on the basis of sample information, it is to our benefit to understand the material in this chapter. For more detailed discussions of survey sampling designs, see the reference section at the end of this chapter.

KEY WORDS

cluster sampling, 728
estimation, 708
   population mean, random, 708
   population mean, stratified, 714
   population mean, cluster, 730
   population total, random, 709
   population total, stratified, 716
   population proportion, random, 710
   population proportion, stratified, 718
   population proportion, cluster, 730

finite population correction factor, 708
nonprobabilistic methods, 734
nonsampling error, 705
optimal allocation, 720
proportional allocation, 720
quota sampling, 734
sample size, 721
   optimal allocation, 720
   population mean, random, 724
   population mean, stratified, 726

population proportion, random, 725
   proportional allocation, 720
sampling study, 700
sampling error, 705
simple random sampling, 706
stratified random sampling, 713
systematic sampling, 707
two-phase sampling, 732

CHAPTER EXERCISES AND APPLICATIONS

18.55 You have been asked to design and carry out a survey in your city on the effectiveness of a radio advertising campaign aimed at promoting a new movie.
(**a**) Outline how you would proceed.
(**b**) Discuss the possibilities for nonsampling errors and means for minimizing their importance.
(**c**) To what extent would you expect nonresponse to be a problem in this survey?

18.56 Based on a random sample of 10 members of your class, estimate the average amount of money per semester spent by class members on textbooks.

18.57 Carefully explain the distinction between stratified random sampling and cluster sampling. Provide illustra-tions of sampling problems where each of these tech-niques might be useful.

18.58 A test was taken by 90 students. A random sample of 10 scores found the following results:

   93   71   62   75   81   63   87   59   84   72

(**a**) Find a 90% confidence interval for the population mean score.
(**b**) Without doing the calculations, state whether a 95% confidence interval for the population mean would be wider than or narrower than the interval found in part (a).

18.59 A corporation has 272 accounts receivable in a particu-lar category. A random sample of 50 of them was taken.

The sample mean was $492.36 and the sample standard deviation was $149.92.

(a) Find a 99% confidence interval for the population mean value of these accounts receivable.

(b) Find a 95% confidence interval for the total value of these accounts receivable.

(c) Without doing the calculations, state whether a 90% confidence interval for the population total would be wider than or narrower than the interval found in part (b).

18.60 The U.S. Senate has 100 members. Information was obtained from the individuals responsible for managing correspondence in 61 senators' offices. Of these, 38 specified a minimum number of letters that must be received on an issue before a form letter in response is created.

(a) Assume these observations constitute a random sample from the population, and find a 90% confidence interval for the proportion of all senators' offices with this policy.

(b) In fact, information was *not* obtained from a random sample of senate offices. Questionnaires were sent to *all* one hundred offices, but only 61 responded. How does this information influence your view of the answer to part (a)? (reference 2)

18.61 A corporation employs 148 sales representatives. A random sample of sixty of them was taken, and it was found that for 36 of the sample members, volume of orders taken this month was higher than for the same month last year. Find a 95% confidence interval for the population proportion of sales representatives with a higher volume of orders.

18.62 A company has three subdivisions, employing a total of 970 managers. Independent random samples of managers were taken from each subdivision, and the number of years with the company was determined for each sample member. The results are summarized in the accompanying table.

	SUBDIVISION 1	SUBDIVISION 2	SUBDIVISION 3
N_i	352	287	331
n_i	30	20	30
$\overline{X}_i$	9.2	12.3	13.5
s_i	4.9	6.4	7.6

(a) Find a 99% confidence interval for the mean number of years with the company for managers in subdivision 1.

(b) Find a 99% confidence interval for the mean number of years with the company for all managers.

18.63 Of the 300 pages in a particular book, 180 pages are primarily nontechnical, while the remainder is technical. Independent random samples of technical and nontechnical pages were taken, and the numbers of errors per page were recorded. The results are summarized in the table.

	TECHNICAL	NONTECHNICAL
N_i	120	180
n_i	20	20
$\overline{X}_i$	1.6	0.74
s_i	0.98	0.56

(a) Find a 95% confidence interval for the mean number of errors per page in this book.

(b) Find a 99% confidence interval for the total number of errors in the book.

18.64 In the analysis of Exercise 18.63, it was found that nine of the sampled technical pages and 15 of the sampled nontechnical pages, contained no errors. Find a 90% confidence interval for the proportion of all pages in this book that have no errors.

18.65 Refer to the data of Exercise 18.62. If a total of 80 managers were sampled, determine how many sample members would be from subdivision 1 under each of the following schemes:

(a) Proportional allocation.

(b) Optimum allocation, assuming that the stratum population standard deviations are the same as the corresponding sample quantities.

18.66 Refer to the data of Exercise 18.63. If a total of 40 pages are to be sampled, determine how many sampled pages would be technical under each of the following schemes:

(a) Proportional allocation.

(b) Optimum allocation, assuming that the stratum population standard deviations are the same as the corresponding sample quantities.

18.67 You intend to sample the students in your university to assess their views on the adequacy of space in the library. You decide to use a stratified sample by year—freshmen, sophomore, and so forth. Discuss the factors you would take into account in deciding how many sample observations to take in each stratum.

18.68 An automobile dealer has an inventory of 328 used cars. The mean mileage of these vehicles is to be estimated. Previous experience suggests that the population standard deviation is likely to be about 12,000 miles. If a 90% confidence interval for the population mean is to extend 2,000 miles on each side of the sample mean, how large a sample is required if simple random sampling is employed?

18.69 A simple random sample is to be taken of 527 business majors in a college to estimate the proportion favoring greater emphasis on business ethics in the curriculum. How many observations are necessary to ensure that a 95% confidence interval for the population proportion extends at most .06 on each side of the sample proportion?

18.70 A market research group takes a random sample of eight of a city's fifty precincts. Every household in each sampled precinct is questioned as to whether it has a central air-conditioning system and also on its summer monthly electricity costs. The results are found in the data file **Electricity Costs**.

(a) Find a 95% confidence interval for the population mean summer monthly electricity costs.

(b) Find a 95% confidence interval for the population proportion of households with central air conditioning.

18.71 Suppose that you were asked by your state office of elections to assist in resolving an election dispute between two candidates (or perhaps, you were asked to be a statistical expert in a lawsuit concerning the outcome of a close election, such as the 2000 United States Presidential election). Many questions arise. Should all ballots in the state be recounted? Should only ballots in certain counties be recounted? If only certain ballots are recounted, which ballots? These and other similar questions were asked during the 2000 United States Presidential election. Discuss the advantages and disadvantages of various sampling designs that might be used to select ballots to be recounted.

REFERENCES

1. Cochran, W.G., *Sampling Techniques,* 3rd edition. (New York: Wiley, 1977).

2. Culnan, M. J., "Processing Unstructured Organizational Transactions: Mail Handling in the U.S. Senate," *Organizational Science,* 3 (1992), 117–37.

3. Deming, W. E., *Sample Design in Business Research.* (New York: Wiley, 1960).

4. Hogg, Robert and Allen T. Craig, *Introduction to Mathematical Statistics,* 4th edition. (New York: Macmillan, 1977).

5. Kish, Leslie, *Survey Sampling.* (New York: Wiley, 1965).

6. Levy, Paul S. and Stanley Lemeshow, *Sampling of Populations: Methods and Applications.* (New York: Wiley, 1991).

7. *Minitab for Windows Version 13* (State College, PA: Minitab, Inc., 2000).

8. Schaeffer, Richard L., William Mendenhall, and Lyman Ott, *Elementary Survey Sampling,* 5th edition. (Belmont, CA: Duxbury Press, 1996).

C H A P T E R 19

STATISTICAL
DECISION
THEORY

INTRODUCTION

The topic of this chapter could be characterized as capturing the essence of management problems in any organization. Indeed, the applicability of the subject matter extends further, touching many aspects of our everyday lives. Situations in which an individual, a group, or a corporation has available several alternative feasible courses of action will be considered. The decision as to which course to follow must be made in a world in which there is uncertainty about the future behavior of the factors that will determine the consequences stemming from the action taken. In this chapter, four criteria for decision making are discussed. The maximin criterion and the minimax regret criterion are nonprobabilistic decision-making criteria. That is, these decision criteria "do not take into account the probability associated with the outcomes for each alternative; they merely focus on the dollar value of the outcomes" (reference 4). Two decision-making criteria that include information about the chances of each outcome's occurrence are the expected monetary value criterion and the expected utility criterion.

19.1   DECISION MAKING UNDER UNCERTAINTY

We are all constrained to operate in an environment whose future direction is uncertain. For example, you may consider attending a baseball game but are doubtful because of the possibility of rain. If you *knew* that it was not going to rain, you would go to the game; if you were *certain* that heavy rain was going to fall for several hours, you would not go. But you are unable to predict the weather with complete assurance, and your decision must be made while contemplating an uncertain future. As another example, at some stage during your final year in college, you will have to decide what to do upon graduation. It is possible that you will have offers of employment from several sources. Graduate school, too, may be a possibility. The decision as to initial career direction is clearly an important one. Certainly you will have acquired information about the alternatives. You will know what starting salaries are on offer, and you will have learned something about the business operations of your future potential employers and how you might fit into these operations.

However, one really does not have a very clear picture of where one will be in a year or two if a particular offer is accepted. This important decision, then, is made in the face of uncertainty about the future.

In the business world, circumstances of this type often arise, as the following examples illustrate:

1. In a recession, a company must decide whether to lay off employees. If the downturn in business activity is to be short-lived, it may be preferable to retain these workers, who might be difficult to replace when demand improves. If the recession is to be prolonged, however, their retention would be costly. Unfortunately, the art of economic forecasting has not reached the stage where it is possible to predict with great certainty the length or severity of a recession.

2. An investor may believe that interest rates are currently at a peak. In that case, long-term bonds would appear to be very attractive. However, it is impossible to be sure about the future direction of interest rates, and if they were to continue to rise, the decision to tie up funds in long-term bonds would have been suboptimal.

3. Contractors are often required to submit bids for a program of work. The decision to be made is the level at which the bid should be pitched. Two areas of uncertainty may be relevant here. First, the contractor will not know how low a bid will be nec-

essary in order to secure the work. Second, the contractor can't be sure precisely how much it will cost to fulfill the contract. Again, in spite of this uncertainty, some decision must be made.

4. The cost of drilling exploratory offshore oil wells is enormous, and in spite of excellent geological advice, oil companies will not know, before a well is drilled, whether commercially viable quantities of oil will be discovered. The decision as to whether and where to drill in a particular field is one that must be made in an uncertain environment.

Our objective is to study methods for attacking decision-making problems of the type just described. A decision maker is faced with a finite number, K, of possible *actions*, which will be labeled a_1, a_2,..., a_K. At the time a particular action must be selected, the decision maker is uncertain about the future of some factor that will determine the consequences of the chosen action. It is assumed that a finite number, H, of possible *states of nature*, can characterize the possibilities for this factor. These will be denoted s_1, s_2,..., s_H. Finally, it is assumed that the decision maker is able to specify the monetary reward, or *payoffs*, for each action–state of nature combination. Let M_{ij} represent the payoff for action a_i in the event of the occurrence of state of nature s_j. Actions, states of nature, monetary payoffs, and payoff tables are part of the general framework for any decision-making problem.

FRAMEWORK FOR A DECISION PROBLEM

i. Decision maker has available K possible courses of **action**: a_1, a_2,..., a_K. Actions are sometimes called alternatives.

ii. There are H possible uncertain **states of nature**: s_1, s_2,..., s_H. States of nature are the possible outcomes over which the decision maker has no control. Sometimes states of nature are called events.

iii. For each possible action–state of nature combination, there is an associated outcome representing either profit or loss, called the monetary **payoff**, M_{ij}, that corresponds to action a_i and state of nature s_j. The table of all such outcomes for a decision problem is called a **payoff table**.

The general form of a payoff table is shown in Table 19.1.

When a decision maker is faced with alternative courses of action, the appropriate choice will depend to a considerable extent on the objectives. It is possible to describe various lines of attack that have been employed in the solution of business decision-making problems. However, it must be kept in mind that each individual problem has its own special features and that the objectives of decision makers may vary considerably and indeed be rather complex. A situation of this sort arises when one contemplates the position of a middle manager in a large corporation. In practice, this manager's objectives may differ

TABLE 19.1
Payoff Table for a Decision Problem with K Possible Actions and H Possible States of Nature

ACTIONS	STATES OF NATURE			
a_i / s_j	s_1	s_2	...	s_H
a_1	M_{11}	M_{12}	...	M_{1H}
a_2	M_{21}	M_{22}	...	M_{2H}
.	.	.		.
.	.	.		.
.	.	.		.
a_K	M_{K1}	M_{K2}	...	M_{KH}

somewhat from those of the corporation. In making decisions, the manager is very likely to be conscious of his or her own position as well as the overall good of the corporation.

In spite of the individual nature of decision-making problems, it may be possible to eliminate some actions from further consideration under any circumstances.

ADMISSIBLE AND INADMISSIBLE ACTIONS

If the payoff for action a_i is at least as high as that for a_j, whatever the state of nature, and if the payoff for a_i is higher than that for a_j for at least one state of nature, then action a_i is said to *dominate* action a_j. Any action that is dominated in this way is said to be **inadmissible**. Inadmissible actions are removed from the list of possibilities prior to further analysis of a decision-making problem. Any action that is not dominated by some other action and is therefore not inadmissible is said to be **admissible**.

(The following example is used throughout this chapter).

EXAMPLE 19.1

CELLULAR PHONE MANUFACTURER (ADMISSIBLE ACTIONS)

Consider a manufacturer planning to introduce a new cellular phone. The manufacturer has available four alternative production processes, denoted A, B, C, and D, ranging in scope from a relatively minor modification of existing facilities to a quite major extension of the plant. The decision as to which course of action to follow must be made at a time when the eventual demand for the product will be unknown. For convenience, this potential demand is characterized as either "low," "moderate," or "high." It will also be assumed that the manufacturer is able to calculate, for each production process, the profit over the lifetime of the investment for each of the three levels of demand. Table 19.2 shows these profit levels (in dollars) for each production process-level of demand combination. Determine if there are any inadmissible actions.

SOLUTION

In this example, there are four possible actions corresponding to the four possible production process adoptions and three possible states of nature, corresponding to the three possible levels of demand for the product.

Referring to Table 19.2, consider production process D. The payoff from this process will be precisely the same as that from process C if there is a low level of demand and lower than that from process C if the level of demand were to be either moderate or high. It therefore makes no sense to choose option D, since there is another available choice through which the payoffs can be no lower and could be higher. Since action C is necessarily at least as rewarding as and possibly more rewarding than action D, then action C is said to *dominate* action D. Since production process D is dominated by another available alternative, production process C, production process D is said to be *inadmissible*. This action should be removed from further consideration, as it would be suboptimal to adopt it. Accordingly, this possibility will be dropped from further consideration, and in our subsequent analysis of this problem, only the possibility of adoption of processes A, B, or C is considered.

TABLE 19.2
Estimated Profits of a Cellular Phone Manufacturer for Different Process-Demand Combinations

ACTIONS	STATES OF NATURE		
Production Process	*Low Demand*	*Moderate Demand*	*High Demand*
A	70,000	120,000	200,000
B	80,000	120,000	180,000
C	100,000	125,000	160,000
D	100,000	120,000	150,000

The decision-making problem as outlined is essentially discrete in character. That is to say, there are only a finite number of available alternatives and a finite number of possible states of nature. However, many practical problems are continuous. The state of nature, for instance, may be more appropriately measured on a continuum than depicted by a number of discrete possibilities. In the cellular phone manufacturer example, it may be possible to anticipate a range of potential demand levels, rather than simply to specify three levels. Also, in some problems the available actions are most appropriately represented by a continuum. This would be the case, for example, when a contractor must decide on the level at which to bid for a contract. The remainder of this chapter focuses on the discrete case. The *principles* involved in the analysis of the continuous case are no different. However, the details of that analysis are based on calculus and will not be considered further here.

EXERCISES

19.1 An investor is considering three alternatives—a certificate of deposit, a low-risk stock fund, and a high-risk stock fund—for a $20,000 investment. She considers three possible states of nature:

s_1: Strong stock market

s_2: Moderate stock market

s_3: Weak stock market

The payoff table (in dollars) is as follows:

ACTIONS	STATES OF NATURE		
Possible Investment Alternatives	s_1	s_2	s_3
Certificate of Deposit	1,200	1,200	1,200
Low-risk Stock Fund	4,300	1,200	−600
High-risk Stock Fund	6,600	800	−1,500

Are any of these actions inadmissible?

19.2 A manufacturer of deodorant is about to expand production capacity to make a new product. Four alternative production processes are available. The accompanying table shows estimated profits, in dollars, for these processes for each of three possible demand levels for the product.

ACTIONS	STATES OF NATURE		
Production Process	Low Demand	Moderate Demand	High Demand
A	100,000	350,000	900,000
B	150,000	400,000	700,000
C	250,000	400,000	600,000
D	250,000	400,000	550,000

Are any of these actions inadmissible?

19.2 SOLUTIONS NOT INVOLVING SPECIFICATION OF PROBABILITIES: MAXIMIN CRITERION, MINIMAX REGRET CRITERION

Before deciding which production process to employ, our manufacturer of cellular phones is likely to ask, "What are the chances of each of these levels of demand actually materializing?" The bulk of this chapter discusses solutions to a decision-making problem that require the specification of outcome probabilities for the various states of nature. However, in this section, two choice criteria that are not based on such probabilities and in fact have no probabilistic content are presented. Rather, these approaches (and others of the same type) depend only on the structure of the payoff table.

The two procedures considered in this section are called the *maximin criterion* and the *minimax regret criterion*. Each criterion is discussed in relation to the payoff table for the cellular phone manufacturer in Example 19.1, with the inadmissible strategy of choosing production process D ignored. The manufacturer must therefore select from among three available actions, faced with three possible states of nature.

TABLE 19.3
Maximin Criterion Output
for Example 19.1

ACTIONS	STATES OF NATURE			MINIMUM PAYOFF
Production Process	*Low Demand*	*Moderate Demand*	*High Demand*	*Minimum Payoff For Each Process*
A	70,000	120,000	200,000	70,000
B	80,000	120,000	180,000	80,000
C	100,000	125,000	160,000	**100,000 (Maximum)**

Maximin Criterion

Consider the worst possible outcome for each action, whatever state of nature materializes. This *worst outcome* is simply the smallest payoff that could conceivably result. The **maximin criterion** selects the action for which the minimum payoff is highest—that is, we *maximize* the *minimum* payoff.

CELLULAR MANUFACTURER EXAMPLE: MAXIMIN CRITERION SELECTS PROCESS C

For the cellular phone manufacturer's problem, the smallest payoff, whatever production process is used, in fact occurs at the low level of demand. Clearly, as set out in Table 19.3, the maximum value of these minimum payoffs is $100,000, which will occur if production process C is used. Thus, maximin criterion selects this action.

Since the maximum value of the minimum payoffs for each production process is $100,000, it follows that production process C is selected as the course of action under the maximin criterion.

EXAMPLE 19.2

INVESTMENT OPPORTUNITY
(MAXIMIN)

An investor wishes to choose between investing $10,000 for one year at an assured interest rate of 12% and investing the same amount over that period in a portfolio of common stocks. If the fixed-interest choice is made, the investor will be assured of a payoff of $1,200. If the portfolio of stocks is chosen, the return will depend on the performance of the market over the year. If the market is buoyant, a profit of $2,500 is expected; if the market is steady, the expected profit is $500, while for a depressed market, a loss of $1,000 is expected. Set up the payoff table for this investor, and find the maximin choice of action.

SOLUTION

Table 19.4 shows the payoffs (in dollars), with a negative payoff indicating a loss. The minimum payoff for the fixed-interest investment is $1,200, as this will occur whatever happens in the stock market. The minimum payoff from the stock portfolio is a loss of $1,000, or −$1,000, which occurs when the market is depressed. Since the largest minimum payoff arises from the fixed-interest investment, it follows that fixed interest is selected as the course of action under the Maximin Criterion.

TABLE 19.4
Maximin Criterion Output
for Example 19.2

ACTIONS	STATES OF NATURE			MINIMUM PAYOFF
Investment Options	*Buoyant State*	*Steady State*	*Depressed State*	*Minimum Payoff For Each Investment Option*
Fixed Interest	1,200	1,200	1,200	**1,200 (Maximum)**
Stock Portfolio	2,500	500	−1,000	−1,000

From these illustrations, the general form of the decision rule based on the maximin criterion is clear. The objective of the maximin criterion is to *maximize* the *minimum* payoff.

DECISION RULE BASED ON MAXIMIN CRITERION

Suppose that a decision maker has to choose from K admissible actions $a_1, a_2, \ldots, a_K$, given H possible states of nature $s_1, s_2, \ldots, s_H$. Let M_{ij} denote the payoff corresponding to the ith action and jth state of nature. For each action, seek the smallest possible payoff. For the action a_1, for example, this is the smallest of $M_{11, 12}, \ldots M_{1H}$. Let us denote this minimum M_1^* where

$$M_1^* = \text{Min}(M_{11}, M_{12}, \ldots M_{1H})$$

More generally, the smallest possible payoff for action a_i is given by

$$M_i^* = (M_{i1}, M_{i2}, \ldots M_{iH})$$

The **maximin criterion** then selects the action a_i for which the corresponding M_i^* is largest (that is, the action for which the minimum payoff is highest).

The positive feature of the maximin criterion for decision making is that it produces the largest possible payoff that can be *guaranteed*. If production process C is used, the cellular phone manufacturer is *assured* a payoff of at least $100,000, whatever the level of demand turns out to be. Similarly, for the investor of Example 19.2, the choice of fixed interest makes a *certain* profit of $1,200. In neither example can any available alternative action *guarantee* as much.

However, it is precisely within this guarantee that reservations about the maximin criterion arise, because one must often pay a price for such a guarantee. The price here lies in the forgoing of opportunities to receive a larger payoff, through the choice of some other action, *however unlikely* the worst-case situation seems to be. Thus, for example, the cellular phone manufacturer may be virtually certain that a high level of demand will result, in which case production process C would be a poor choice, since it yields the lowest payoff at this demand level.

The maximin criterion, then, can be thought of as providing a very cautious strategy for choosing among alternative actions. Such a strategy may, in certain circumstances, be appropriate, but only an extreme pessimist would use it invariably. For this reason, it is sometimes called the *criterion of pessimism.* "Maximin is often used in situations where the planner feels he or she cannot afford to be wrong. (Defense planning might be an example, as would investing your life savings). The planner chooses a decision that does as well as possible in the worst possible (most pessimistic) case" (reference 1).

Minimax Regret Criterion

The decision maker wanting to use the *minimax regret criterion* must imagine being in the position where a choice of action has been made and one of the states of nature has occurred. He or she can look back on the choice made either with satisfaction or with disappointment because, as things turned out, some alternative action would have been preferable. The decision maker then determines the *regret,* or *opportunity loss,* of not making the best decision for a given state of nature and established a regret table.

REGRET OR OPPORTUNITY LOSS TABLE

Suppose that a payoff table is arranged as a rectangular array, with rows corresponding to actions and columns to states of nature. If each payoff in the table is subtracted from the largest payoff *in its column*, the resulting array is called a **regret table**, or **opportunity loss table.**

By considering the difference between the actual monetary payoff that occurs for a decision and the optimal payoff for the same state of nature, the decision maker can select the action that *minimizes* the *maximum* loss or regret.

DECISION RULE BASED ON MINIMAX REGRET CRITERION

Given the regret table, the action dictated by the **minimax regret criterion** is found as follows:

i. For each row (action), find the maximum regret.
ii. Choose the action corresponding to the *minimum* of these *maximum* regrets.

The **minimax regret criterion** selects the action for which the maximum regret is smallest; that is, the minimax regret criterion produces the smallest possible opportunity loss that can be guaranteed.

Consider again the cellular phone manufacturer in Example 19.1. It will be shown that Process B is selected by the minimax regret criterion. Suppose that the level of demand for the new product turns out to be low. In that case, the best choice of action would have been production process C, yielding a payoff of $100,000. Had this choice been made, the manufacturer would have had 0 regret. Had process A been chosen, the resulting profit would have been only $70,000. The extent of the manufacturer's regret, in this eventuality, is the difference between the best payoff that could have been obtained ($100,000) and that resulting from what turned out to be an inferior choice of action. Thus, the regret would be $100,000 − $70,000 = $30,000. Similarly, given low demand, if process B had been chosen, the regret would be

$$\$100,000 - \$80,000 = \$20,000$$

Continuing in this way, the regrets involved for moderate and high levels of demand are calculated. In each case, the regret is 0 for what would have turned out to be the best choice of action (process C for moderate demand and process A for high demand). These regrets, or opportunity losses of not making the best decision for a given state of nature, are given in Table 19.5, with the largest amount of regret for a given process included in the last column.

   Clearly, the minimax regret criterion selects production process B since the maximum regret for this process is the smallest of the three processes A, B, and C.

Computer for Opportunity Loss Tables

It is straightforward to use Excel to select the course of action based on either the maximin criterion or the minimax regret criterion. Simply set up an Excel sheet and use the Excel functions Min and Max. Try this for the cellular phone manufacturer in Example 19.1 or the investor in Example 19.2.

   What action would the investor in Example 19.2 choose if the minimax regret criterion were followed? Once again, 0 regret follows from the action that would, in the event, have proved the better alternative. Although the regret table for this example is easily established, illustrated in Figure 19.1 is the use of PHStat to obtain the opportunity loss table to provide you a means to obtain such tables for more complex decision-making problems.

TABLE 19.5
Minimax Regret Criterion Output for Example 19.1

ACTIONS	STATES OF NATURE			REGRETS
Production Process	*Low Demand*	*Moderate Demand*	*High Demand*	*Maximum Regret For Each Process*
A	30,000	5,000	0	30,000
B	20,000	5,000	20,000	**20,000 (Minimum)**
C	0	0	40,000	40,000

FIGURE 19.1
PHStat Output for Example
19.2

Payoff Table:

	Fixed Interest	Stock Portfolio
Buoyant State	1,200	2,500
Steady State	1,200	500
Depressed State	1,200	-1,000

Opportunity Loss Table:

	Optimum Action	Optimum Profit	Alternatives Interest	Portfolio
Buoyant State	Portfolio	2500	1300	0
Steady State	Interest	1200	0	700
Depressed State	Interest	1200	0	2200

PHStat Instructions

1. Click on PHStat
2. Select Decision-Making
3. Select Opportunity Loss...
4. Complete dialog box with Number of Events (states of nature) and Number of Alternative Actions
5. Complete the Payoff Table (notice that rows are states of nature and columns are actions)

INTERPRETATION

Since the rows and columns are reversed, you need to select the maximum value for each column representing an action. From the alternative action column for fixed interest, the maximum is $1300; from the alternative action column for stock portfolio, the maximum is $2200. The minimax regret criterion selects the fixed-interest investment which has the minimum regret of $1300.

Neither the maximin criterion nor the minimax regret criterion allows the decision maker to inject personal views as to the likelihood of occurrence of states of nature into the decision-making process. Since most practical business problems occur in an environment with which the decision maker is at least moderately familiar, this represents a waste of expertise. The probabilities associated with the outcomes for each alternative action are considered in the next section.

EXERCISES

19.3 Consider again Exercise 19.11 where an investor is considering three alternatives—a certificate of deposit, a low-risk stock fund, and a high-risk stock fund—for a $20,000 investment. She considers three possible states of nature:

s_1: Strong stock market
s_2: Moderate stock market
s_3: Weak stock market

The payoff table (in dollars) is as follows:

ACTIONS Possible Investment Alternatives	STATES OF NATURE		
	S_1	S_2	S_3
Certificate of Deposit	1,200	1,200	1,200
Low-risk Stock Fund	4,300	1,200	-600
High-risk Stock Fund	6,600	800	-1,500

(a) Which action is selected by the maximin criterion?
(b) Which action is selected by the minimax regret criterion?

19.4 Consider the manufacturer of deodorant in Exercise 19.2, who is about to expand production capacity to make a new product. Four alternative production processes are available. The accompanying table shows estimated profits, in dollars, for these processes for each of three possible demand levels for the product.

ACTIONS Production Process	STATES OF NATURE		
	Low Demand	Moderate Demand	High Demand
A	100,000	350,000	900,000
B	150,000	400,000	700,000
C	250,000	400,000	600,000
D	250,000	400,000	550,000

(a) Which action is chosen by the maximin criterion?
(b) Which action is chosen by the minimax regret criterion?

19.5 Another criterion for selecting a decision is the *maximax criterion*, sometimes known as the *criterion of optimism*. This criterion chooses the action with the largest possible payoff.
(a) What action would be chosen by the cellular phone manufacturer, with the payoffs of Table 19.2, according to this criterion?
(b) The investor of Example 19.2 according to this criterion would choose what action?

19.6 The cellular phone manufacturer has three admissible actions—processes A, B, and C. When these are considered together, process B is chosen by the minimax regret criterion. Suppose now that a fourth admissible alternative, production process E, is available. Estimated payoffs for this action are $60,000 under low demand, $115,000 for moderate demand, and $220,000 for high demand. Show that when production processes A, B, C, and E are considered together, process A is chosen by the minimax regret criterion. Thus, while adding process E to the available actions does not result in the selection of that process, it does lead to the choice of a different action than would otherwise have been the case. Comment on the intuitive appeal of the minimax regret criterion in light of this example.

19.7 Consider a decision problem with two possible actions and two states of nature.

   (a) Give an example of a payoff table where both actions are admissible and the same action is chosen by both the maximin criterion and the minimax regret criterion.

   (b) Give an example of a payoff table according to which different actions are chosen by the maximin criterion and the minimax regret criterion.

19.8 Consider a decision problem with two admissible actions and two possible states of nature. Formulate a description of the form that the payoff table must take in order that the same action be chosen by the maximin criterion and by the minimax regret criterion.

19.9 The prospective operator of a shoe store has the opportunity to locate in an established and successful shopping center. Alternatively, at lower cost, he can locate in a new center, whose development has recently been completed. If the new center turns out to be very successful, it is expected that annual store profits from location in it would be $130,000. If the center is only moderately successful, annual profits would be $60,000. If the new center is unsuccessful, an annual loss of $10,000 would be expected. The profits to be expected from location in the established center will also depend to some extent on the degree of success of the new center, as potential customers may be drawn to it. If the new center were to be unsuccessful, annual profit for the shoe store located in the established center would be expected to be $90,000. However, if the new center were moderately successful, this expected profit would be $70,000, while it would be $30,000 if the new center turned out to be very successful.

   (a) Set up the payoff table for the decision-making problem of this shoe store operator.

   (b) Which action is chosen by the maximin criterion?

   (c) Which action is chosen by the minimax regret criterion?

19.3   EXPECTED MONETARY VALUE; TREEPLAN

An important ingredient in the analysis of many business decision-making problems is likely to be the decision maker's assessment of the chances that various states of nature relevant in the determination of the eventual payoff will occur. The criteria discussed in Section 19.2 do not allow the incorporation of this kind of assessment into the decision-making process. However, a manager will almost invariably have a good feeling for the environment in which the decision is to be made and will want this expertise to be taken into account before deciding on a course of action. The discussion in this section assumes that a *probability* of occurrence can be attached to each state of nature, and it will be shown how these probabilities are employed in arriving at an eventual decision.

In general, when there are H possible states of nature, a probability must be attached to each. These probabilities are denoted by $\pi_1, \pi_2, ..., \pi_H$ so that probability π_j corresponds to state of nature s_j. The general set-up for this decision-making problem is shown in Table

TABLE 19.6
Payoffs with State-of-Nature Probabilities

ACTIONS	STATES OF NATURE			
$a_i \Big/ s_i$	$s_1 (\pi_1)$	$s_2 (\pi_2)$	$\cdots$	$s_H (\pi_H)$
a_1	M_{11}	M_{12}	$\cdots$	M_{1H}
a_2	M_{21}	M_{22}	$\cdots$	M_{2H}
$\vdots$	$\vdots$	$\vdots$	$\vdots$	$\vdots$
a_K	M_{K1}	M_{K2}	$\cdots$	M_{KH}

19.6. Since one, and only one, of the states of nature must occur, these probabilities necessarily sum to 1, so that

$$\sum_{j=1}^{H} \pi_j = 1$$

When choosing an action, the decision maker will see each particular choice as having a specific probability of receiving the associated payoff and will therefore be able to calculate the *expected payoff* arising from each action. The expected payoff for this action is then the sum of the individual payoffs, weighted by their associated probabilities. These expected payoffs are often called the **expected monetary values** of the actions.

EXPECTED MONETARY VALUE (EMV) CRITERION

Suppose that a decision maker has K possible actions, $a_1, a_2, \ldots, a_K$ and is faced with H states of nature. Let M_{ij} denote the payoff corresponding to the ith action and jth state and π_j the probability of occurrence of the jth state of nature, with $\sum_{j=1}^{H} \pi_j = 1$. The **expected monetary value of action** a_i, **EMV(a_i)**, is

$$EMV(a_i) = \pi_1 M_{i1} + \pi_2 M_{i2} + \cdots + \pi_H M_{iH} = \sum_{j=1}^{H} \pi_j M_{ij} \qquad (19.1)$$

The **Expected Monetary Value Criterion** adopts the action with the largest expected monetary value; that is, given a choice among alternative actions, the **EMV** Criterion dictates the choice of the action for which the EMV is highest.

Let's return to the Cellular Phone Manufacturer and calculate the EMV for each of the production processes. The cellular phone manufacturer will presumably have some experience of the market for his product and, on the basis of that experience, will be able to form a view as to the likelihood of occurrence of low, moderate, or high demand. Suppose that the cellular phone manufacturer knows that of all previous new introductions of this type of product, 10% have had low demand, 50% moderate demand, and 40% high demand. In the absence of any further information, it is then reasonable to postulate, for this particular market introduction, the following probabilities for the states of nature:

$$\pi_1 = P(s_1) = \text{Probability of low demand} = 0.1$$
$$\pi_2 = P(s_2) = \text{Probability of moderate demand} = 0.5$$
$$\pi_3 = P(s_3) = \text{Probability of high demand} = 0.4$$

Since one, and only one, of the states of nature must occur, these probabilities necessarily sum to 1; that is, the states of nature are mutually exclusive and collectively exhaustive. These probabilities are added to the payoff table (Table 19.2) giving Table 19.7.

TABLE 19.7
Payoffs and State-of-Nature Probabilities for Cellular Phone Manufacturer, Example 19.1

ACTIONS	STATES OF NATURE		
	Low Demand	*Moderate Demand*	*High Demand*
Production Process	*($\pi = 0.10$)*	*($\pi = 0.50$)*	*($\pi = 0.40$)*
A	70,000	120,000	200,000
B	80,000	120,000	180,000
C	100,000	125,000	160,000

If the cellular phone manufacturer adopts production process A, he will receive a payoff of $70,000 with probability 0.1, $120,000 with probability 0.5, and $200,000 with probability 0.4. For the cellular phone manufacturer, the expected monetary values for the three admissible actions are as follows:

EMV(Process A) = (0.1)(70,000) + (0.5)(120,000) + (0.4)(200,000) = $147,000
EMV(Process B) = (0.1)(80,000) + (0.5)(120,000) + (0.4)(180,000) = $140,000
EMV(Process C) = (0.1)(100,000) + (0.5)(125,000) + (0.4)(160,000) = $136,500

The cellular phone manufacturer would choose production process A. It is interesting to note that neither the maximin criterion nor the minimax regret criterion led to this particular choice. However, the information that a high level of demand appears much more likely than a low level has been added. This renders process A to be a relatively attractive option.

Computers for EMV

As with the maximin criterion or the minimax regret criterion, it is quite straightforward to use Excel to determine the expected monetary value of each production process. Simply set up a spreadsheet and use the multiplication function.

Also it is quite easy to use PHStat to select the course of action based on the expected monetary value criterion. Simply complete the probabilities and payoff table, remembering that rows are states of nature and columns are actions. The instructions in Figure 19.2 are similar to those given in the PHStat instructions box for Figure 19.1. The only difference is to select "Expected Monetary Value …" rather than "Opportunity Loss Table…."

INTERPRETATION

Since the Expected Monetary Value for Production Process A ($147,000) is the largest EMV for the three possible actions, the EMV criterion selects process A.

FIGURE 19.2
PHStat Output for Expected Monetary Value

Probabilities & Payoff Table:

	P	A	B	C
Low Demand	0.1	70,000	80,000	100,000
Moderate Demand	0.5	120,000	120,000	125,000
High Demand	0.4	200,000	180,000	160,000

Statistics	A	B	C
Expected Monetary Value	147000	140000	136500

PHStat Instructions

1. Click on PHStat
2. Select Decision-Making
3. Select Expected Monetary Value...
4. Complete dialog box
5. Complete probabilities and payoff table

Decision Trees

The analysis of a decision problem by means of the expected monetary value criterion can be conveniently set out diagrammatically through a mechanism called a **decision tree**. When faced with analyzing decisions under risk, the tree diagram is a graphical device that forces the decision maker "to examine all possible outcomes, including unfavorable ones. He or she is also forced to make decisions in a logical, sequential manner (reference 4)." Decision trees are especially helpful when a sequence of decisions must be made. All decision trees contain:

☐ **Decision (or action) nodes**. These squares indicate that a decision must be made and are sometimes called square nodes.

○ **Event (state of nature) nodes**. These circular junctions, from which emerge *branches*, represent a possible state of nature, to which the associated probability is attached. These nodes are sometimes called circular nodes.

| **Terminal nodes.** A vertical bar represents the end of the decision–event branch. Originally, a triangle was used to designate this point. Sometimes no designation is given.

After carefully defining a problem, the decision maker draws the decision tree, assigns probabilities to the possible events (states of nature), and estimates the payoffs for each possible decision–event combination (every combination of action and state of nature). Now the decision maker is ready to find the optimal decision. This is called "solving the tree" (reference 1). To solve a decision tree, one must work backwards (called *folding back* the tree). Compute the expected monetary value (EMV) for each state of nature by starting at the far right of the decision tree and working back to decision nodes on the left.

A tree diagram for the cellular phone manufacturer is given in Figure 19.3. The following steps were taken to choose the action with the largest EMV:

1. Beginning at the left-hand side of the figure, branches emerge from the **decision node** (square junction) representing the three possible actions: Process A, Process B, or Process C. Next, come **event nodes** (circular junctions), from which emerge branches, each representing a possible state of nature (level of demand).

2. The *associated probability* to each state-of nature (low, moderate, or high) is attached.

3. The *payoffs* corresponding to each action–state of nature combination are inserted at the far right of the tree.

4. The computations proceed from *right to left*, beginning with these payoffs. For each circular junction, the sum of the probability times the payoff for the emerging branches is found. This provides the *EMV for each action.*

5. The *optimal decision* has the highest EMV and is indicated at the far left square junction. Process A is therefore chosen by the expected monetary value criterion. This choice of action results in an expected monetary value, or expected profit, of $147,000 for the cellular phone manufacturer.

FIGURE 19.3
Decision Tree for Cellular Phone Manufacturer (*Action with Maximum EMV)

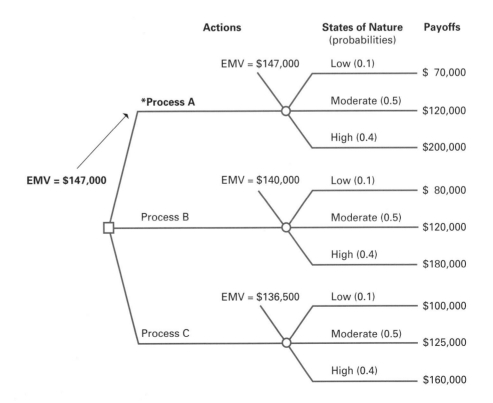

Using TreePlan to Solve a Decision Tree

Developed by Michael Middleton (reference 3) and included with this text, TreePlan is an Excel add-in that can be used to draw decision trees. The EMVs will be computed giving the optimal decision. Check the website http://www.treeplan.com for both documentation and details to continue use of this add-in beyond this course (reference 5).

EXAMPLE 19.3

INVESTMENT OPPORTUNITY (EMV CRITERION)

The investor in Example 19.2 needed to decide between a fixed-interest-rate investment and a portfolio of stocks. Let us assume that this investor is, in fact, very optimistic about the future course of the stock market, believing the probability of a buoyant market is 0.6, while the probability is 0.2 for each of the other two states. The payoffs and state-of-nature probabilities are therefore those given in the accompanying table:

ACTIONS	STATES OF NATURE		
Investment	*Buoyant State* $(\pi = 0.60)$	*Steady State* $(\pi = 0.20)$	*Depressed State* $(\pi = 0.20)$
Fixed Interest	1,200	1,200	1,200
Stock Portfolio	2,500	500	−1,000

Which investment should be chosen according to the expected monetary value criterion?

SOLUTION

Since a payoff of $1,200 will result from the fixed-interest investment, whatever happens in the stock market, the expected monetary value of this investment is $1,200. The EMV for the stock portfolio is

$$\text{EMV(Stock Portfolio)} = (0.6)(2,500) + (0.2)(500) + (0.2)(-1,000) = \$1,400$$

Since this is the higher expected monetary value, the investor would choose the *portfolio of common stocks*, according to the expected monetary value criterion.

Now let's solve this example with TreePlan. Once TreePlan is installed, the simplest way to access TreePlan is to open a new Excel spreadsheet and hit Ctrl-t (the tree will begin wherever the cursor appears. Be sure to leave enough space for the decision table and the tree). Click on "New Tree" and the default tree with 2 decision nodes in Figure 19.4 will appear. The completed decision tree is Figure 19.5.

FIGURE 19.4
Beginning TreePlan

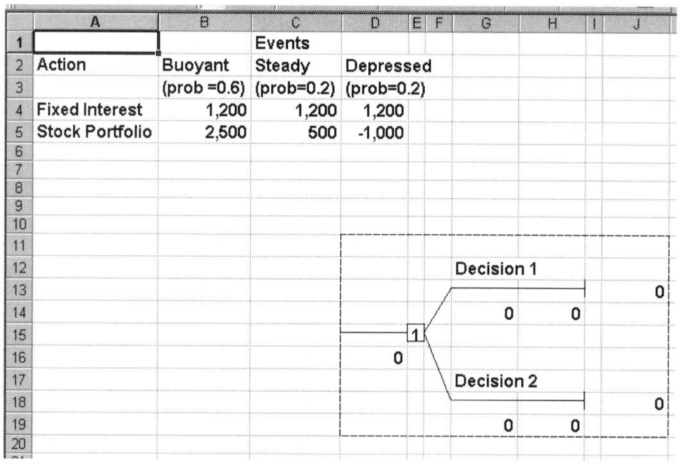

TreePlan Instructions

1. Add branches for the events by placing the cursor to the right of each terminal node and click Ctrl-t again
2. Label branches
3. Add probabilities
4. Replace the "0" in the far right with the Payoffs

FIGURE 19.5
Decision Tree for Example
19.3 using TreePlan; Optimal
Decision: Select the Stock
Portfolio

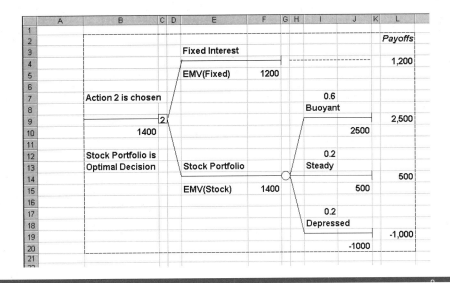

A problem that requires a *sequence* of decisions is considered next.

EXAMPLE 19.4

DRUG MANUFACTURER (EMV CRITERION)

A drug manufacturer holds the patent rights to a new formula for lowering cholesterol levels. The manufacturer is able to sell the patent for $50,000 or to proceed with intensive tests of the drug's efficacy. The cost of carrying out these tests is $10,000. If the drug is found to be ineffective, it will not be marketed, and the cost of the tests is written off as a loss. In the past, tests of drugs of this type have shown 60% to be effective and 40% ineffective.

If the tests should now reveal the drug to be effective, the manufacturer again has two options available. He can sell the patent rights and test results for $120,000, or he can market the drug himself. If the drug is marketed, it is estimated that profits on sales (exclusive of the cost of the tests) will amount to $180,000 if the sales campaign is highly successful but only $90,000 if it is just moderately successful. It is estimated that these two levels of market penetration are equally likely. According to the expected monetary value criterion, how should the drug manufacturer proceed?

SOLUTION

It is best to attack this problem through the construction of a decision tree. The completed tree is shown in Figure 19.6. The manufacturer may decide either to sell the patent, in which case there is nothing further to be done, or to retain it and carry out tests on the drug's efficacy. There are two possible states of nature—the drug is either effective (with probability 0.6) or ineffective (with probability 0.4). In the latter case, the story ends. However, if the drug proves to be effective, a second decision must be made—whether to market it or to sell the patent rights and test results. If the former option is adopted, then the level of marketing success determines the eventual outcome, which could be either moderate or high (each with probability 0.5).

Next, the payoffs resulting from all action–state of nature combinations are considered. Begin at the bottom of the decision tree. If the manufacturer's original decision is to sell the patent, he receives $50,000. If the patent is kept but the drug turns out to be ineffective, the manufacturer sustains a loss of $10,000, the cost of carrying out the tests. This is shown as a negative payoff in that amount. If the drug is found to be effective and the patent and test results are then sold, the manufacturer receives $120,000, from which must be subtracted the cost of the tests, leaving a payoff of $110,000. Finally, if the drug is mar-

FIGURE 19.6
Decision Tree for Example
19.4; Optimal Decision:
Retain Patent and If Test
Shows Drug to Be Effective,
Then Market the Drug
(EMV = $71,000)

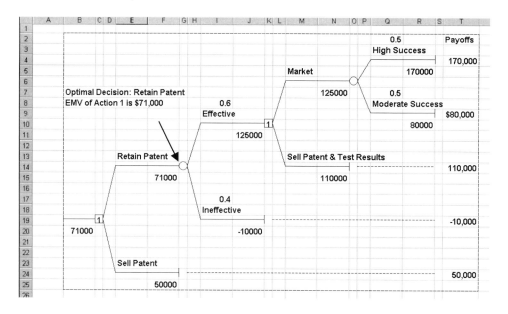

keted, the payoffs for moderate and high success are, respectively, $90,000 and $180,000, less the cost of the tests, leaving $80,000 and $170,000, respectively.

Having reached this point, the decision problem is solved by working backward from right to left along the tree. This is necessary because the appropriate action at the first decision point cannot be determined until the expected monetary value of the best available option at the second decision point is found.

Therefore, begin by supposing that initially the patent was retained and that the tests proved the drug to be effective. If the patent and test results are sold, then a profit of $110,000 will result. The expected monetary value from marketing the drug is

$$EMV = (0.5)(170,000) + (0.5)(80,000) = \$125,000$$

Since this exceeds $110,000, the better option at this stage, by the expected monetary value criterion, is to market the drug. This amount is therefore entered at the square junction of the second decision point and is treated as the payoff that results if the manufacturer's initial decision is to retain the patent and the tests indicate that the drug is effective. Hence, for the initial decision, the payoff table with state-of-nature probabilities is as shown here. The expected monetary value of selling the patent is the assured $50,000, while the expected monetary value of retaining it is $(0.6)(125,000) + (0.4)(-10,000) = \$71,000$. Then, by the expected monetary value criterion, the patent should be retained.

ACTIONS	STATES OF NATURE	
Actions	*Effective Drug ($\pi = 0.60$)*	*Ineffective Drug ($\pi = 0.40$)*
Retain Patent	125,000	−10,000
Sell Patent	50,000	50,000

If the objective is the maximization of expected monetary value (that is, expected profit), then the manufacturer should retain the patent. However, if the tests prove the drug to be effective, then the manufacturer should market it. This strategy yields an expected profit of $71,000.

By use of TreePlan, the same result appears in Figure 19.6.

Sensitivity Analysis

For the cellular phone manufacturer, production process A was selected by the expected monetary value criterion. This decision was based on estimated payoffs for each action–state of nature combination and on estimated probabilities of occurrence for the states of nature. However, often a decision maker will be uncertain about such estimates, so it is useful to ask under what range of specifications of a decision problem a particular action will be optimal under the expected monetary value criterion. **Sensitivity analysis** seeks to answer such questions, the most straightforward case being where a single problem specification is allowed to vary while all other specifications are held fixed.

To illustrate, suppose that the cellular phone manufacturer agrees with the assessment that the probability of high demand is 0.4 but is less sure of the assessments for the other two states of nature. Let p denote the probability of low demand, so that the probability of moderate demand must be $(0.6 - p)$. According to the expected monetary value criterion, under what range of values of p would the adoption of process A be optimal? Using the payoffs of Table 19.7, the expected monetary values are

$$EMV(A) = (p)(70{,}000) + (.6 - p)(120{,}000) + (0.4)(200{,}000) = 152{,}000 - 50{,}000p$$
$$EMV(B) = (p)(80{,}000) + (.6 - p)(120{,}000) + (0.4)(180{,}000) = 144{,}000 - 40{,}000p$$
$$EMV(C) = (p)(100{,}000) + (.6 - p)(125{,}000) + (0.4)(160{,}000) = 139{,}000 - 25{,}000p$$

Choice of process A will remain optimal provided the associated EMV is higher than that of each of the other two processes. Thus, for process A to be preferred to process B, it must follow that

$$152{,}000 - 50{,}000p \geq 144{,}000 - 40{,}000p$$

or

$$8{,}000 \geq 10{,}000p$$

so

$$p \leq 0.8$$

This must be so, since, by our assumptions, the probability of low demand cannot exceed 0.6. Similarly, for process A to be preferred to process C, then

$$152{,}000 - 50{,}000p \geq 139{,}000 - 25{,}000p$$

or

$$13{,}000 \geq 25{,}000p$$

so

$$p \leq .52$$

If the payoffs are as postulated in Table 19.7 and the probability of high demand is 0.4, then production process A is the best choice under the expected monetary value criterion provided that the probability of low demand does not exceed 0.52.

Now suppose that the cellular phone manufacturer is uncertain about the estimated payoff of $200,000 for process A under high demand. Consider under what range of payoffs process A will be the optimal choice, when all other problem specifications are kept at their initial levels, given in Table 19.7. If M is the payoff for process A under high demand, then the expected monetary value for this process is

$$EMV(A) = (0.1)(70{,}000) + (0.5)(120{,}000) + 0.4M = 67{,}000 + 0.4M$$

The expected monetary values for processes B and C are, as before, $140,000 and $136,500. Therefore, process A will be the best choice according to the expected monetary value criterion, provided that

$$67,000 + 0.4M \geq 140,000$$

or

$$0.4M \geq 73,000$$

or

$$M \geq 182,500$$

If all other specifications are as originally given in Table 19.7, then production process A will be selected by the expected monetary value criterion, provided that the payoff for process A under high demand is at least $182,500.

EXERCISES

19.10 A student already has offers of employment. She must now decide whether to visit another potential employer for further interviews. She views the time and effort of doing so as a cost of $500, which will be incurred whether or not she takes a job with this employer. If the employer offers a position preferable to her other alternatives, this would be viewed as a benefit worth $5,000 (from which the $500 cost must be subtracted). Otherwise her time and effort would have been wasted.
   (a) Set up the payoff table for the student's decision-making problem.
   (b) Suppose the student believes that the probability is .05 that she would be offered a position preferable to her other alternatives by this employer. According to the expected monetary value criterion, should she visit this potential employer?

19.11 A manager has to choose between two actions, a_1 and a_2. There are two possible states of nature, s_1 and s_2. The payoffs are shown in the accompanying table. If the manager believes that each state of nature is equally likely to occur, which action should be chosen according to the expected monetary value criterion?

ACTIONS	STATES OF NATURE	
	S_1	S_2
a_1	72,000	51,000
a_2	78,000	47,000

19.12 The investor of Exercise 19.1 believes that the probability of a strong stock market is 0.2, the probability of a moderate stock market is 0.5, and the probability of a weak stock market is 0.3.
   (a) Which action should be chosen according to the expected monetary value criterion?
   (b) Draw the decision tree for the investor's problem.

19.13 The deodorant manufacturer in Exercise 19.2 knows that historically 30% of new products of this type have met high demand, 40% moderate demand, and 30% low demand.
   (a) According to the expected monetary value criterion, which production process should be used?
   (b) Draw the decision tree for this manufacturer's problem.

19.14 Consider a decision problem with two admissible actions and two possible states of nature, each of which is equally likely to occur.
   (a) Determine whether each of the following statements is true or false for such problems:
      (i)   The action chosen by the expected monetary value criterion will always be the same as the action chosen by the maximin criterion.
      (ii) The action chosen by the expected monetary value criterion will always be the same as the action chosen by the minimax regret criterion.
      (iii) The action chosen by the expected monetary value criterion will always be that for which the average possible payoff is higher.

(b) Would your answer to statement (iii) in part (a) be the same if the two states of nature were not equally likely to occur?

19.15 A decision problem has K possible actions and H possible states of nature. If one of these actions is inadmissible, show that it cannot be chosen by the expected monetary value criterion.

19.16 The shoe store operator of Exercise 19.9 believe that the probability is 0.4 that the new shopping center will be very successful, 0.4 that it will be moderately successful, and 0.2 that it will be unsuccessful.

(a) According to the expected monetary value criterion, where should the shoe store be located?

(b) Draw the decision tree.

19.17 Refer to the decision-making problem in Exercises 19.1 and 19.12. This investor is comfortable with the assessment of a probability of 0.2 for a strong market. However, she is less sure of the probability assessments for the other two states of nature. Under what range of probabilities for a weak stock market does the expected monetary value criterion give the choice of action found in Exercise 19.12?

19.18 Refer to the problem of the deodorant manufacturer of Exercises 19.2 and 19.13.

(a) The manufacturer is comfortable with an assessment that the probability of low demand is 0.3, but is less secure about the probabilities for the other two demand levels. Under what range of probabilities for moderate demand will the expected monetary value criterion yield the choice of action found in Exercise 19.13?

(b) Take the remaining problem specifications to be as given in Exercises 19.2 and 19.13. Under what range of profits for high demand when process A is used will the expected monetary value criterion give the choice of action found in Exercise 19.13?

19.19 Refer to the problem of the shoe store operator of Exercises 19.9 and 19.16.

(a) The shoe store operator is happy with the assessment that the probability is 0.2 that the new shopping center will be unsuccessful but is less sure about the probability assessments for the other two states of nature. Under what range of probabilities that the new shopping center will be very successful will the expected monetary value criterion lead to the choice of action found in Exercise 19.16?

(b) Assuming that the other problem specifications are as in Exercises 19.9 and 19.16, under what range of profit levels for location in the new center if it turns out to be very successful will the expected monetary value criterion lead to the choice of action found in Exercise 19.16?

19.20 A manufacturer receives regular contracts for large consignments of parts for the automobile industry. This manufacturer's production process is such that when it is operating correctly, 10% of all parts produced do not meet industry specifications. However, the production process is prone to a particular malfunction, whose presence can be checked at the beginning of a production run. When the process is operated with this malfunction, 30% of the parts produced fail to meet industry specifications. The manufacturer supplies parts under a contract that will yield a profit of $20,000 if only 10% of the parts are defective and a profit of $12,000 if 30% of the parts are defective. The cost of checking for the malfunction is $1,000, and if it turns out that repair is needed, this costs a further $2,000. If incurred, these costs must be subtracted from the profit of the contract. Historically, it has been found that the production process functions correctly 80% of the time. The manufacturer must decide whether to check the process at the beginning of a production run.

(a) According to the expected monetary value criterion, what is the optimal decision?

(b) Draw the decision tree.

(c) Suppose that the proportion of occasions on which the production process operates correctly is unknown. Under what range of values for this proportion would the decision selected in part (a) be optimal, according to the expected monetary value criterion?

19.21 A contractor has to decide whether to submit a bid for a construction project. It will cost $16,000 to prepare the bid. This cost would be incurred whether or not the bid was accepted. The contractor intends to bid at a level that will produce a $110,000 profit (less the cost of preparing the bid). The contractor knows that 20% of bids prepared in this way have been successful.

(a) Set up the payoff table.

(b) Should a bid be prepared and submitted, according to the expected monetary value criterion?

(c) Under what range of probabilities that the bid will be successful should a bid be prepared and submitted, according to the expected monetary value criterion?

19.22 On Thursday evening, the manager of a small branch of a car rental agency finds that he has available six cars for rental on the following day. However, he is able to request delivery of additional cars at a cost of $20 each from the regional depot. Each car that is rented produces an expected profit of $40. (The cost of delivery of the car must be subtracted from this profit.) Each potential customer requesting a car when none is available is counted a $10 loss in goodwill. On reviewing his records for previous Fridays, the manager finds that the number of cars requested have ranged from six to ten; the percentages are shown in the accompanying table. The manager must decide how many cars, if any, to order from the regional depot.

NUMBER OF REQUESTS	6	7	8	9	10
PERCENT		10	30	30	20	10

(a) Set up the payoff table
(b) If the expected monetary value criterion is used, how many cars should be ordered?

19.23 A contractor has decided to place a bid for a project. Bids are to be set in multiples of $20,000. It is estimated that the probability that a bid of $240,000 will secure the contract is .2, the probability that a bid of $220,000 will be successful is .6, and the probability that a bid of $200,000 will be accepted is .8. It is thought that any bid under $200,000 is certain to succeed and any bid over $240,000 is certain to fail. If the manufacturer wins the contract, he must solve a design problem with two possible choices at this stage. He can hire outside consultants, who will guarantee a satisfactory solution, for a price of $80,000. Alternatively, he can invest $30,000 of his own resources in an attempt to solve the problem internally; if this effort fails, he must then engage the consultants. It is estimated that the probability of success-fully solving the problem internally is .6. Once this problem has been solved, the additional cost of fulfilling the contract is $140,000.
(a) Potentially, this contractor has two decisions to make. What are they?
(b) Draw the decision tree.
(c) What is the optimal course of action, according to the expected monetary value criterion?

19.24 Consider a decision problem with two actions, a_1 and a_2, and two states of nature, s_1 and s_2. Let M_{ij} denote the payoff corresponding to action a_i and state of nature s_j. Assume that the probability of occurrence of state of nature s_1 is p, so the probability of state s_2 is $(1 - p)$.
(a) Show that action a_1 is selected by the EMV criterion if

$$p(M_{11} - M_{21}) > (1 - p)(M_{22} - M_{12})$$

(b) Hence, show that if a_1 is an admissible action, there is some probability, p, for which it will be chosen. However, if a_1 is not admissible, it cannot be chosen, whatever the value of p.

19.4 SAMPLE INFORMATION: BAYESIAN ANALYSIS AND VALUE

Decisions made in the business world can often involve considerable amounts of money, and the cost of making a suboptimal choice may turn out to be substantial. This being the case, it could well pay the decision maker to make an effort to obtain as much relevant information as possible before the decision is made. In particular, he or she will want to become as thoroughly informed as possible about the chances of occurrence of the various states of nature that determine the eventual payoff.

This feature of any careful analysis of a decision problem has not been apparent in our discussion so far. The cellular phone manufacturer, in Section 19.3, assessed the probabilities of low, moderate, and high levels of demand for a new cellular phone as 0.1, 0.5, and 0.4, respectively. However, this assessment reflected no more than the historical proportions achieved by previous products. In practice, he might well want to carry out some market research on the prospects for the new product. Given such research, these initial or *prior probabilities* may be modified, yielding new probabilities, called *posterior probabilities*, for the three demand levels. The information (in this case, the market research results) leading to the modification of probabilities for the states of nature will be referred to as *sample information*.

Use of Bayes' Theorem

In an earlier chapter the mechanism for modifying prior probabilities to produce posterior probabilities was given. This is accomplished through **Bayes' theorem**, which, for convenience, is restated in the framework of our decision-making problem.

> ## BAYES' THEOREM
>
> Let $s_1, s_2, \ldots, s_H$ be H mutually exclusive and collectively exhaustive events, corresponding to the H states of nature of a decision problem. Let A be some other event. Denote the conditional probability that s_i will occur, given that A occurs, by $P(s_i|A)$., and the probability of A, given s_i, by $P(A|s_i)$. **Bayes' Theorem** states that the conditional probability of s_i given A, can be expressed as
>
> $$P(s_i|A) = \frac{P(A|s_i)P(s_i)}{P(A)}$$
>
> $$= \frac{P(A|s_i)P(s_i)}{P(A|s_1)P(s_1) + P(A|s_2)P(s_2) + \cdots + P(A|s_H)P(s_H)} \tag{19.2}$$
>
> In the terminology of this section, $P(s_i)$ is the **prior probability** of s_i and is modified to the **posterior probability**, $P(s_i|A)$., given the **sample information** that event A has occurred.

Now, suppose that the cellular phone manufacturer hires a market research organization to predict the level of demand for his new product. Of course, there will be a fee for this service. Later in this chapter the question of whether the return merits the cost involved is discussed. The organization provides a rating of "poor," "fair," or "good," on the basis of its research. A review of the market research company's records reveals the quality of its past predictions in this field. Table 19.8 shows, for each level of demand outcome, the proportion of poor, fair, and good assessments. For example, on 10% of occasions that demand was high, the assessment was "poor." Thus, in the notation of conditional probability, denoting low, moderate, and high demand levels by s_1, s_2, and s_3, respectively, it follows that

$$P(\text{Poor }|s_1) = 0.6 \qquad P(\text{Poor }|s_2) = 0.3 \qquad P(\text{Poor }|s_3) = 0.1$$

(It is only a coincidence that the sum of $P(\text{Poor}|s_1) = 0.6$, $P(\text{Poor}|s_2) = 0.3$, and $P(\text{Poor}|s_3) = 0.1$ is 1.0. These conditional probabilities do not have to sum to 1. Take "fair" for example, notice that the sum of $P(\text{Fair}|s_1) = 0.2$, $P(\text{Fair}|s_2) = 0.4$, and $P(\text{Fair}|s_3) = 0.2$ is only 0.8 and not 1.0).

Suppose now that the market research firm is consulted and produces an assessment of "poor" for the prospects of the cellular phone. Given this new information, the prior probabilities

$$P(s_1) = 0.1 \qquad P(s_2) = 0.5 \qquad P(s_3) = 0.4$$

for the three demand levels can be modified using Bayes' theorem. For a low level of demand, the posterior probability is

$$P(s_1|\text{Poor}) = \frac{P(\text{Poor}|s_1)P(s_1)}{P(\text{Poor}|s_1)P(s_1) + P(\text{Poor}|s_2)P(s_2) + P(\text{Poor}|s_3)P(s_3)}$$

$$= \frac{(0.6)(0.1)}{(0.6)(0.1) + (0.3)(0.5) + (0.1)(0.4)} = \frac{0.06}{0.25} = 0.24$$

TABLE 19.8
Proportion of Assessments of Each Type Provided by Market Research Organization for Cellular Phones Achieving Given Levels of Demand

ACTIONS	STATES OF NATURE		
Assessment	*Low Demand (s_1)*	*Moderate Demand (s_2)*	*High Demand (s_3)*
POOR	0.6	0.3	0.1
FAIR	0.2	0.4	0.2
GOOD	0.2	0.3	0.7

Similarly, for the other two demand levels, the posterior probabilities are

$$P(s_2 | \text{Poor}) = \frac{(0.3)(0.5)}{0.25} = 0.6$$

$$P(s_3 | \text{Poor}) = \frac{(0.1)(0.4)}{0.25} = 0.16$$

The posterior probabilities can then be employed to calculate the expected monetary values. Table 19.9 shows the payoffs (without the fee of the organization), together with the posterior probabilities for the three demand levels. This is simply a modification of Table 19.7, with the posterior probabilities replacing the prior probabilities of that table.

The expected monetary values for the three production processes can be found in precisely the same manner as before. These are as follows:

EMV(Process A) = (0.24)(70,000) + (0.60)(120,000) + (0.16)(200,000 = $120,800
EMV(Process B) = (0.24)(80,000) + (0.60)(120,000) + (0.16)(180,000) = $120,000
EMV(Process C) = (0.24)(100,000) + (0.60)(125,000) + (0.16)(160,000) = $124,000

If the assessment of market prospects is "poor," then according to the expected monetary value criterion production process C should be used. The market research group's assessment has rendered low demand much more likely and high demand considerably less likely than was previously the case. This shift in the view of market prospects is sufficient to induce the cellular phone manufacturer to switch preference from process A (based on the prior probabilities) to process C.

Following the same line of argument, one can determine the decisions that would be made if the prospects for the cellular phone market success were rated either "fair" or "good." Again, the posterior probabilities for the three levels of demand can be obtained through Bayes' theorem. For a "fair" assessment, these are

$$P(s_1 | \text{Fair}) = \frac{1}{15} \qquad P(s_2 | \text{Fair}) = \frac{10}{15} \qquad P(s_3 | \text{Fair}) = \frac{4}{15}$$

For a "good" assessment

$$P(s_1 | \text{Good}) = \frac{2}{45} \qquad P(s_2 | \text{Good}) = \frac{15}{45} \qquad P(s_3 | \text{Good}) = \frac{28}{45}$$

Using these posterior probabilities, the expected monetary values of each of the production processes for each given assessment can be determined. Table 19.10 contains these quantities.

As has been shown previously, if the assessment is "poor," then process C is preferred by the expected monetary value criterion. If any other assessment is made, then production process A would be chosen according to this criterion.

TABLE 19.9
Payoffs for Cellular Phone Manufacturer and Posterior Probabilities for States of Nature, Given an Assessment of "Poor" by Market Research Organization

ACTIONS	STATES OF NATURE		
Production Process	*Low Demand* ($\pi = 0.24$) *	*Moderate Demand* ($\pi = 0.60$)	*High Demand* ($\pi = 0.16$)
A	70,000	120,000	200,000
B	80,000	120,000	180,000
C	100,000	125,000	160,000
	*Posterior Probabilities		

TABLE 19.10
EMVs for Cellular Phone
Manufacturer for Three
Possible Assessments by
Market Research Firm

ACTIONS	STATES OF NATURE		
Production Process	*Poor Assessment*	*Fair Assessment*	*Good Assessment*
A	120,800	138,000	167,556
B	120,000	133,333	155,556
C	124,600	132,667	145,667

Recall that for the cellular phone manufacturer's problem when the prior probabilities for levels of demand were used, then the optimal decision according to the expected monetary value criterion was to use process A. It can be the case (if an assessment of "poor" is obtained) that a different decision will be made when these prior probabilities are modified by sample information. Hence, it turns out that consulting the market research organization could be valuable for the manufacturer. Of course, if the choice of process A had proved optimal, whatever the assessment, the sample information could not possibly be of value.

EXAMPLE 19.5

DRUG MANUFACTURER REVISITED (EXPECTED MONETARY VALUE)

In Example 19.4, a drug manufacturer had to decide whether to sell the patent for a cholesterol lowering formula before subjecting the drug to thorough testing. (Subsequently, if the patent was retained and the drug found to be effective, a second decision—to market the drug or to sell the patent and test results—also had to be made.) For the initial decision, the two states of nature were s_1: Drug is effective; and s_2: Drug is ineffective. The associated prior probabilities, formed on the basis of previous experience, are

$$P(s_1) = 0.6 \qquad \text{and} \qquad P(s_2) = 0.4$$

The drug manufacturer has the option of carrying out, at modest cost, an initial test before the first decision is made. The test is not infallible. For drugs that have subsequently proved effective, the preliminary test result was positive on 60% of occasions and negative on the remainder. For ineffective drugs, a positive preliminary test result was obtained 30% of the time, the other results being negative. Given the results of the preliminary test, how should the drug manufacturer proceed? Assume that it is still possible to sell the patent for $50,000 if the preliminary test result is negative.

SOLUTION

First, notice that if the patent is retained and the exhaustive tests prove the drug to be effective, then in the absence of any sample information on market conditions, the optimal decision at this stage, as in Example 19.4, is to market the drug. The information provided by the preliminary test is irrelevant in that particular decision. However, it could conceivably influence the initial decision as to whether to sell the patent. Accordingly, only this decision is considered.

The conditional probabilities of the sample outcomes, given the states of nature, are

$$P(\text{Positive} \,|\, s_1) = 0.6 \qquad P(\text{Negative} \,|\, s_1) = 0.4$$
$$P(\text{Positive} \,|\, s_2) = 0.3 \qquad P(\text{Negative} \,|\, s_2) = 0.7$$

If the result of the preliminary test is positive, then the posterior probability for the state s_1 (Effective), given this information, is

$$P(s_1 | \text{Positive}) = \frac{P(\text{Positive} \,|\, s_1) P(s_1)}{P(\text{Positive} \,|\, s_1) P(s_1) + P(\text{Positive} \,|\, s_2) P(s_2)} = \frac{(0.6)(0.6)}{(0.6)(0.6) + (0.3)(0.4)} = 0.75$$

Further, since the two posterior probabilities must sum to 1, then $P(s_2|\text{Positive}) = 0.25$. The accompanying payoff table is the same as in Example 19.4, with these posterior probabilities added.

ACTIONS	STATES OF NATURE	
Actions	*Effective Drug ($\pi = 0.75$)**	*Ineffective Drug ($\pi = 0.25$)*
Retain Patent	125,000	−10,000
Sell Patent	50,000	50,000
	*Posterior Probabilities	

The expected monetary value, if the patent is sold, is $50,000, while if the patent is retained, the expected monetary value is

$$(0.75)(125{,}000) + (0.25)(-10{,}000) = \$91{,}250$$

Therefore, if the initial test result is positive, the patent should be retained, according to this criterion.

Next, consider the case where the preliminary test result is negative. The posterior probability for the state s_1 is, by Bayes' theorem

$$P(s_1|\text{Negative}) = \frac{P(\text{Negative}|s_1)P(s_1)}{P(\text{Negative}|s_1)P(s_1) + P(\text{Negative}|s_2)P(s_2)} = \frac{(0.4)(0.6)}{(0.4)(0.6) + (0.7)(0.4)} = 0.4615$$

Hence, the posterior probability for the state s_2 is

$$P(s_2|\text{Negative}) = 0.5385$$

Once more, if the patent is sold, the expected monetary value is the $50,000 that will be received. If the patent is retained, the expected monetary value of this decision is

$$(0.4615)(125{,}000) + (0.5385)(-10{,}000) = \$52{,}302.50$$

Thus, even if the preliminary test result is negative, the optimal decision, by the expected monetary value criterion, is to retain the patent.

In this particular example, then, whatever the sample information, the chosen action is the same. The manufacturer should retain the patent in the event of either result emerging from the preliminary test. Since the sample information cannot possibly affect the decision, there is, of course, no point in gathering it. In fact, since performing the preliminary test will not be costless, it will be suboptimal to do so. Thus, according to the expected monetary value criterion, the drug manufacturer should retain the patent, and if the thorough tests prove the drug to be effective, then the manufacturer should market it. The preliminary test should not be carried out.

The Value of Sample Information

It has been shown how sample information can be incorporated into the decision-making process. The potential value of such information lies, of course, in its provision of a better feel for the chances of occurrence of the relevant states of nature. This, in turn, can provide firmer ground on which to base a decision. This section shows how a *monetary* value can be attached to the sample information. This is important, since there will typically be some cost involved in obtaining the sample information, and the decision maker will want to know whether the expected benefits exceed this cost.

Example 19.5 illustrates a situation where the same action was optimal, whatever the sample result. In such a case, the sample information clearly has no value, since the same action would have been taken without it. This is a general rule: If the sample information cannot affect the choice of action, then it has value 0.

Accordingly the remainder of this section concerns only circumstances in which the sample result can affect the choice of action. Our example of the cellular phone manufacturer planning to introduce a new product is such a case. This manufacturer has to choose from three production processes and is faced with three states of nature, representing different levels of demand for the product. Section 19.3 showed that in the absence of sample information and using only the prior probabilities that process A with an expected monetary value of $147,000 is selected.

Now, in practice, having obtained sample information, the decision maker will typically not know which state of nature will occur but will have more firmly grounded probabilistic assessments for these states. However, before discussing the value of sample information in this general framework, it is useful to consider the extreme case where **perfect information** is obtainable—that is, the case where the decision maker is able to gain information that will tell *with certainty* which state will occur. What is the value to the decision maker of having such perfect information?

EXPECTED VALUE OF PERFECT INFORMATION, EVPI

Suppose that a decision maker has to choose from among K possible actions, in the face of H states of nature, s_1, $s_2, \ldots, s_H$. **Perfect information** corresponds to knowledge of which state of nature will arise. The expected value of perfect information is obtained as follows:

i. Determine which action will be chosen if only the prior probabilities $P(s_1)$, $P(s_2), \ldots, P(s_H)$ are used.

ii. For each possible state of nature, s_i, find the difference, W_i, between the payoff for the best choice of action, if it were known that state would arise, and the payoff for the action chosen if only the prior probabilities are used. This is the **value of perfect information**, when it is known that s_i will occur.

iii. The **expected value of perfect information, EVPI,** is then

$$\text{EVPI} = P(s_1)W_1 + P(s_2)W_2 + \cdots + P(s_H)W_H \qquad (19.3)$$

Let's return again to the cellular phone manufacturer and calculate the EVPI. In the context of this manufacturer, perfect information corresponds to knowledge of which of the three possible demand levels will actually result. In the absence of any sample information and on the basis of the prior probabilities only, process A will be chosen. However, referring to Table 19.7, if the level of demand would be low, then the best choice would be process C. Since this has a payoff that exceeds by $30,000 that of process A, the value of knowing that demand would be low is $30,000. Similarly, if it were known that moderate demand would result, process C would again be chosen. Here, the payoff from the best available choice exceeds that of process A by $5,000, which is, accordingly, the value of knowing that demand will be moderate. If it were known that high demand would occur, then process A would be chosen. Thus, this particular knowledge is of no value, since the same decision would have been made without it. The value of perfect information depends on the information. Using the prior probabilities of the various states of nature, the expected value of perfect information is found.

For the cellular phone manufacturer, the prior probabilities are 0.1 for low, 0.5 for moderate, and 0.4 for high demand. It therefore follows that to this manufacturer, the value of perfect information is $30,000 with probability 0.1, $5,000 with probability 0.5, and $0 with probability 0.4. The expected value of perfect information is, accordingly

$$\text{EVPI} = (0.1)(30,000) + (0.5)(5,000) + (0.4)(0) = \$5,500$$

This dollar amount, then, represents the expected value to the cellular phone manufacturer of knowing what level of demand will result.

PHStat for EVPI

For more complex problems, software such as PHStat could be used to obtain EVPI. First, obtain the opportunity loss table. For the cellular phone manufacturer, the opportunity losses were previously recorded in Table 19.5. Recall, that PHStat could also be used to obtain these values. Next, enter these regrets into the Expected Opportunity Loss dialog box. The EVPI will automatically be given. The PHStat output for the EVPI for Example 19.1 is given in Figure 19.7.

INTERPRETATION

Although perfect information will not be available typically, the calculation of the expected value of perfect information can be useful. Since, of course, no sample information can be better than perfect, its expected value cannot be higher than that of the expected value of perfect information. Thus, the expected value of perfect information provides an *upper limit* for the expected value of any sample information. For example, if the cellular phone manufacturer is offered information at a cost of $6,000, it is not necessary to inquire further about the quality of this information. It should not be purchased, however reliable, according to the expected monetary value criterion, since its expected value cannot be more than $5,500.

Consider now the more general problem of assessing the value of sample information that is not necessarily perfect. Again, consider the decision-making problem of the cellular phone manufacturer, who has the option of obtaining an assessment from a market research organization of the prospects for the new cellular phone. These prospects will be rated either "poor," "fair," or "good." In Section 19.4 it was shown that in the last two of the three eventualities, process A will still be chosen. Thus, if a "fair" or "good" rating is obtained, the initial choice of action will remain unchanged, and nothing will have been gained from consulting the market research company.

However if the prospects are rated "poor," then Table 19.10 shows that the optimal choice is process C. This optimal choice would yield an expected monetary value of $124,600, whereas process A, which otherwise would have been used, gives an expected monetary value of $120,800. The difference in these amounts, $3,800, represents the gain from the sample information *if the assessment is "poor."* The gains from the sample information are $0 for ratings of "good" or "fair" and $3,800 for a rating of "poor."

We now need to know how likely these gains are to materialize, so in our example, we must find the probability of a "poor" assessment. In general, if A denotes a piece of sample information, and $s_1, s_2, ..., s_H$ the H possible states of nature, then

$$P(A) = P(A|s_1)P(s_1) + P(A|s_2)P(s_2) + \cdots + P(A|s_H)P(s_H)$$

FIGURE 19.7
PHStat Output for EVPI for Example 19.1

Expected Opportunity Loss Analysis

Probabilities & Opportunity Losses:

	P	A	B	C
Low Demand	0.1	30,000	20,000	0
Moderate Demand	0.5	5,000	5,000	0
High Demand	0.4	0	20,000	40,000

	A	B	C
Expected Opportunity Loss	5500	12500	16000

EVPI

For the cellular phone example, with s_1, s_2, s_3 denoting low, moderate, and high levels of demand, then

$$P(s_1) = 0.1 \qquad P(s_2) = 0.5 \qquad P(s_3) = 0.4$$
$$P(\text{Poor}|s_1) = 0.6 \qquad P(\text{Poor}|s_2) = 0.3 \qquad P(\text{Poor}|s_3) = 0.1$$

Therefore, the probability of a "poor" assessment is

$$P(\text{Poor}) = P(\text{Poor}|s_1)(P(s_1) + P(\text{Poor}|s_2)P(s_2) + P(\text{Poor}|s_3)P(s_3)$$
$$= (0.6)(0.1) + (0.3)(0.5) + (0.1)(0.4) = 0.25$$

In the same way, using the conditional probabilities of Table 19.8, the probabilities for the other two assessments are

$$P(\text{Fair}) = 0.30 \qquad P(\text{Good}) = 0.45$$

Thus the value of the sample information is $3,800 with probability 0.25, $0 with probability 0.30, and $0 with probability 0.45. It therefore follows that the **expected value of the sample information is**

$$\text{EVSI} = (0.25)(3,800) + (0.30)(0) + (0.45)(0) = \$950$$

This dollar amount, then, represents the expected value of the sample information to the decision maker. In terms of the expected monetary value criterion, this sample information will be worth acquiring if its cost is less than its expected value. The **expected net value of sample information** is the difference between its expected value and its cost.

Suppose that the market research group charges a fee of $750 for its assessment. The expected net value of this assessment to the cellular phone manufacturer is then $950 − 750 = \$200$. Thus, the manufacturer's expected payoff will be $200 higher if the sample information is purchased than if it is not. This amount represents the expected worth of having that information, taking into account its cost. In this case, the manufacturer's optimal strategy is to purchase the market research report and then use production process A if the assessment is either "good" or "fair" and process C if the assessment is "poor." The EMV of this strategy is $147,200, that is, the $147,000 that would result from no sample information plus the expected net value of the sample information.

The general framework for obtaining the expected value of sample information is given in the box that follows.

EXPECTED VALUE OF SAMPLE INFORMATION, EVSI

Suppose that a decision maker has to choose from K possible actions in the face of H states of nature $s_1, s_2, \ldots, s_H$. The decision maker may obtain sample information. Let there be M possible sample results, $A_1, A_2, \ldots, A_M$.
   The expected value of sample information is obtained as follows:

i.   Determine which action would be chosen if only the prior probabilities were used.
ii. Determine the probabilities of obtaining each sample result:

$$P(A_i) = P(A_i|s_1)P(s_1) + P(A_i|s_2)P(s_2) + \cdots + P(A_i|s_H)P(s_H)$$

iii. For each possible sample result A_i, find the difference, V_i, between the expected monetary value for the optimal action and that for the action chosen if only prior probabilities are used. This is the **value of the sample information,** given that A_i was observed.
iv. The **expected value of sample information, EVSI**, is then:

$$\text{EVSI} = P(A_1)V_1 + P(A_2)(V_2) + \cdots + P(A_M)V_M \qquad \textbf{(19.4)}$$

Value of Sample Information Viewed By Means of Decision Trees

The expected value of sample information can be computed in an alternative (but equivalent) manner, which is arithmetically slightly more cumbersome but does provide a convenient way of representing the problem in terms of a sequence of decisions through the construction of a decision tree. The first decision to make is whether to obtain the sample information. Next, it is necessary to decide which of the alternative actions should be followed.

To illustrate, consider again the problem of the cellular phone manufacturer. Figure 19.8 shows the decision trees following from the three possible market research appraisals. These trees have the same general structure as Figure 19.3. The essential difference is that the probabilities associated with the three states of nature are the appropriate *posterior probabilities,* given the specific sample information. These posterior probabilities were found in Section 19.4. The payoffs are now weighted by the posterior probabilities, yielding the expected monetary value of each action, given each possible sample result. These are the expected monetary values shown in Table 19.10. Finally, at the left of each part of Figure 19.8 is the highest possible expected monetary value for each sample outcome.

This information is transferred to the right of Figure 19.9 on page 768, in which the decision whether to purchase the market research study is analyzed. If this information is not bought, then the bottom part of the figure shows an expected monetary value of $147,000. This results from using the prior probabilities and is taken from Figure 19.3.

Turning now to the upper part of Figure 19.9 the expected monetary value that results will depend on the sample outcome. The probabilities are 0.25 for "poor," 0.30 for "fair," and 0.45 for "good." Thus, since $124,600 can be expected with probability 0.25, $138,000 with probability 0.30, and $167,556 with probability 0.45, the expected payoff if the sample information is purchased is

$$(0.25)(124,600) + (0.30)(138,000) + (0.45)(167,556) = \$147,950$$

FIGURE 19.8
Decision Trees for the Cellular Phone Manufacturer, Given the Market Research Organization Assessments of (a) "poor," (b) "fair," (c) "good" (*Action with Maximum EMV)

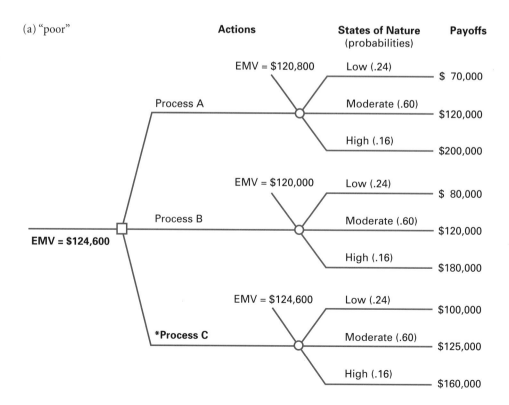

(b) "fair"

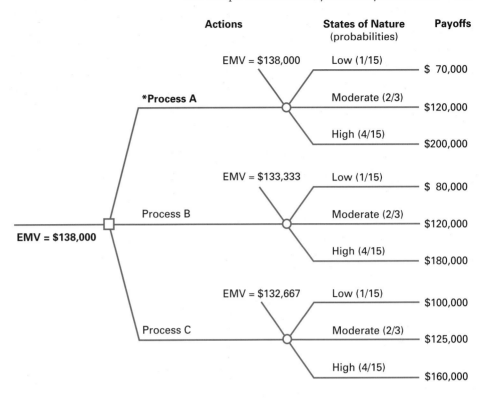

(c) "good"

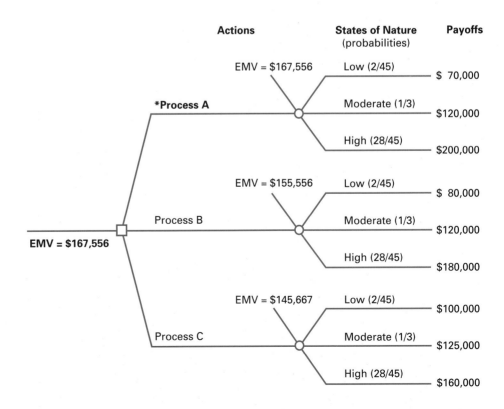

FIGURE 19.9
Cellular Phone
Manufacturer's Decision
to Purchase the Services
of the Market Research
Organization (*Action with
Maximum EMV)

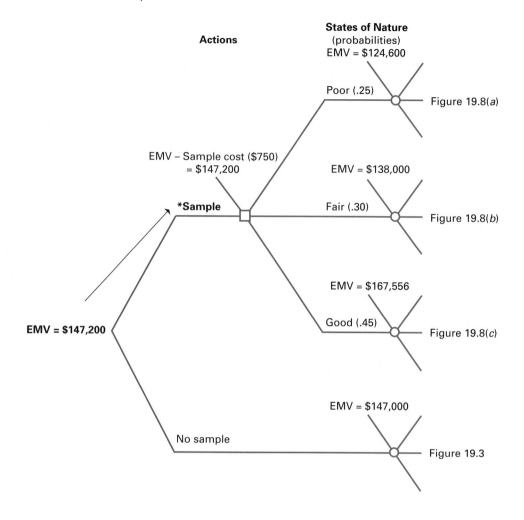

Actions

States of Nature
(probabilities)
EMV = $124,600

Poor (.25) — Figure 19.8(*a*)

EMV – Sample cost ($750)
= $147,200

EMV = $138,000

***Sample**

Fair (.30) — Figure 19.8(*b*)

EMV = $167,556

EMV = $147,200

Good (.45) — Figure 19.8(*c*)

EMV = $147,000

No sample — Figure 19.3

INTERPRETATION

However, it is necessary to subtract from this amount the $750 cost of the sample information, leaving $147,200. Since this is more than the expected payoff when no sample information is obtained, the best strategy, according to the expected monetary value criterion, is to purchase the services of the market research group. The optimal decision has, as indicated at the left of Figure 19.9, an expected monetary value of $147,200.

EXERCISES

19.25 A manufacturer must decide whether to mount, at a cost of $100,000, an advertising campaign for a product whose sales have been rather flat. It is estimated that a highly successful campaign would add $400,000 (from which the campaign's costs must be subtracted) to profits, a moderately successful campaign would add $100,000, but an unsuccessful campaign would add nothing. Historically, 40% of all similar campaigns have been very successful, 30% moderately successful, and

the remainder unsuccessful. This manufacturer consults a media consultant for a judgment on the potential effectiveness of the campaign. This consultant's record is such that she has reported favorably on 80% of campaigns that turned out to be highly successful, 40% of those that were moderately successful, and 10% of unsuccessful campaigns.

(a) Find the prior probabilities for the three states of nature.

(b) In the absence of any report from media consultant, should this advertising campaign be mounted, according to the EMV criterion?

(c) Find the posterior probabilities for the three states of nature, given that the media consultant reports favorably.

(d) Given a favorable report from the consultant, should the advertising campaign be mounted, according to the EMV criterion.

(e) Find the posterior probabilities for the three states of nature, given that the media consultant does not report favorably.

(f) If the consultant's report is not favorable, should the advertising campaign be mounted, according to the EMV criterion.

19.26 Refer to Exercise 19.2. The deodorant manufacturer has four possible production processes from which to choose, depending on the view that is taken of future demand levels. On the basis of past experience, the prior probabilities are 0.3 for high demand, 0.4 for moderate demand, and 0.3 for low demand. The accompanying table shows proportions of "poor," "fair," and "good" assessments for prospects provided by a market research group for similar products that have achieved these demand levels.

ACTIONS	STATES OF NATURE		
Assessment	Low Demand	Moderate Demand	High Demand
POOR	0.5	0.3	0.1
FAIR	0.3	0.4	0.2
GOOD	0.2	0.3	0.7

(a) If the market research group is not consulted, which action should be chosen according to the EMV criterion?

(b) Find the posterior probabilities of the three demand levels, given an assessment of "poor."

(c) Which action should be chosen according to the EMV criterion, given an assessment of "poor"?

(d) Find the posterior probabilities of the three demand levels, given an assessment of "fair."

(e) Which action should be chosen according to the EMV criterion, given an assessment of "fair."

(f) Find the posterior probabilities of the three demand levels, given an assessment of "good."

(g) Which action should be chosen according to the EMV criterion, given an assessment of "good"?

19.27 The shoe store operator of Exercise 19.9 has available two courses of action. His decision is based on his view of the likely level of success of the new shopping center. Historically, 40% of new centers of this type have been very successful, 40% moderately successful, and 20% unsuccessful. A consulting group sells assessments of the prospects of this type of shopping center. The table given here shows the proportion of "good," "fair," and "poor" assessments, given the particular outcome actually resulting.

ACTIONS	STATES OF NATURE (SUCCESS LEVEL)		
Assessment	Very Successful	Moderately Successful	Unsuccessful
GOOD	0.6	0.3	0.2
FAIR	0.3	0.4	0.3
POOR	0.1	0.3	0.5

(a) What are the prior probabilities for the three states of nature?

(b) If the shoe store operator does not seek advice from the consulting group, what action should he take, according to the EMV criterion?

(c) What are the posterior probabilities of the three states of nature, given an assessment of "good"?

(d) According to the EMV criterion, given an assessment of "good," what course of action should the shoe store operator adopt?

(e) What are the posterior probabilities of the three states of nature, given an assessment of "fair"?

(f) According to the EMV criterion, given an assessment of "fair," which action should be chosen?

(g) What are the posterior probabilities of the three states of nature, given an assessment of "poor"?

(h) If the EMV criterion is followed, which action should be chosen, given a forecast of "poor"?

19.28 Consider the drug manufacturer of Example 19.5, who had to decide whether to sell the patent for a pain relief formula before subjecting the drug to thorough testing. In the example, we saw that whatever the result of a certain preliminary test of the drug's efficacy, the optimal decision was to retain the patent. Subsequently, this manufacturer developed a superior preliminary test, which again could be carried out at modest cost. For drugs that subsequently proved effective, this new test gave a positive result 80% of the time, while a positive result was obtained for only 10% of the drugs that proved to be ineffective.

(a) Find the posterior probabilities of the two states of nature, given a positive result from this new preliminary test.

(b) According to the EMV criterion, should the patent be sold if the new test result is positive?

(c) Find the posterior probabilities of the two states of nature, given a negative result from the new preliminary test.

(d) According to the EMV criterion, should the patent be sold if the new test result is negative?

19.29 In Exercise 19.20, a supplier of parts to the automobile industry had to decide whether to check the production process for a certain malfunction before starting a production run. The two states of nature were

s_1:   Repair not needed (10% of all parts produced fail to meet specifications)

s_2:   Repair needed (30% of all parts produced fail to meet specifications)

The prior probabilities, derived from the historical record for this production process, are

$$P(s_1) = 0.8 \qquad \text{and} \qquad P(s_2) = 0.2$$

The manufacturer can, before beginning a full production run, produce a single part and check whether it meets specifications, basing a decision on whether to check the production process on the resulting sample information.

(a) If the single part checked meets specifications, what are the posterior probabilities of the states of nature?

(b) If the single part checked meets specifications, should the production process be checked according to the EMV criterion?

(c) If the single part checked does not meet specifications, what are the posterior probabilities of the states of nature?

(d) If the single part checked does not meet specifications, should the production process be checked according to the EMV criterion?

19.30 Continuing Exercise 19.29, suppose now that before making a decision on whether to check the production process, *two* parts are made and examined.

(a) If, in fact, repair is not needed, what are the probabilities that both parts, just one part, or neither part will fail to meet specifications?

(b) Compute the same probabilities, as in part (a), given that repair of the production process is in fact needed.

(c) Compute the posterior probabilities of the states of nature and determine the optimal action under the expected monetary value criterion, given each of the following circumstances:

(i)   Both parts fail to meet specifications.

(ii) Just one part fails to meet specifications.

(iii) Neither part fails to meet specifications.

19.31 The Watts New Lightbulb Corporation ships large consignments of light bulbs to big industrial users. When the production process is functioning correctly (which is 90% of the time), 10% of all bulbs produced are defective. However, the process is susceptible to an occasional malfunction, leading to a defective rate of 20%. The Watts New Lightbulb Corporation counts the cost, in terms of goodwill, of a shipment with the higher defective rate to an industrial user as $5,000. If a consignment is suspected to contain this larger proportion of defectives, it can instead be sold to a chain of discount stores, though this involves a reduction of $600 in

profits, whether or not the consignment does indeed contain a large proportion of defective bulbs. Decisions by this company are made through the EMV criterion.

(a) A consignment is produced. In the absence of any further information, should it be shipped to an industrial user or to the discount chain?

(b) Suppose that a single bulb from the consignment is checked. Determine where the consignment should be shipped under each of the following circumstances:

(i)   This bulb is defective.

(ii) This bulb is not defective.

(c) Suppose that two bulbs from the consignment are checked. Determine where the consignment should be shipped for each of the following situations:

(i)   Both bulbs are defective.

(ii) Just one bulb is defective.

(iii) Neither bulb is defective.

(d) Without doing the calculations, indicate how the decision problem could be attacked if 100 bulbs were checked prior to shipping the consignment.

19.32 Refer to the problem of the investor of Exercise 19.1.

(a) Explain what is meant by "perfect information" in the context of this investor's problem.

(b) The prior probabilities are 0.2 for a strong stock market, 0.5 for a moderate stock market, and 0.3 for a weak stock market. What is the expected value of perfect information to this investor?

19.33 For the deodorant manufacturer of Exercise 19.2, the prior probabilities are 0.3 for high demand, 0.4 for moderate demand, and 0.3 for low demand. Find the EVPI to this manufacturer.

19.34 For the shoe store operator of Exercise 19.9, the prior probabilities are 0.4 that the new shopping center will be very successful, 0.4 that it will be moderately successful, and 0.2 that it will be unsuccessful. What is the expected value of perfect information to this shoe store operator?

19.35 The manufacturer of automobile parts of Exercise 19.20 must decide whether to check the production process before beginning a full production run. Given that the production process functions correctly 80% of the time, what is the value of perfect information to this manufacturer?

19.36 Before showing how to find the expected value of sample information, we discussed separately the determination of the expected value of perfect information. In fact, this was not necessary because perfect information is just a special kind of sample information. Given the general procedure for finding the expected value of sample information, show how to specialize this to the case of perfect information.

19.37 Refer to Exercise 19.25. The manufacturer is considering an advertising campaign and first seeks the advice of a media consultant.

(a) What is the expected value to the manufacturer of the media consultant's advice?

(b) The media consultant charges a fee of $5,000. What is the expected net value of the consultant's advice?

(c) This manufacturer faces a two-stage decision problem. First, he must decide whether to purchase advice from the media consultant. Next, he must decide whether to mount the advertising campaign. Draw the complete decision tree, and indicate how the manufacturer should proceed.

19.38 Refer to Exercise 19.26. Find the largest fee the deodorant manufacturer should pay to the market research group, according to the expected monetary value criterion.

19.39 Refer to Exercise 19.27. Find the expected value to the shoe store operator of an assessment of the shopping center's prospects provided by the consulting group.

19.40 Refer to Exercise 19.28. Before deciding whether to sell the patent of a new pain relief formula, the drug manufacturer carries out the new preliminary test. Find the expected value to the manufacturer of the test result.

19.41 Refer to Exercise 19.29. The supplier of automobile parts is able to produce and examine a single part before deciding whether to check the production process. What is the EVSI?

19.42 Consider the Watts New Lightbulb Corporation of Exercise 19.31. The corporation can check one or more light bulbs before deciding whether to ship a consignment to an industrial user or to a discount chain.

(a) What is the expected value to the corporation of checking a single light bulb?

(b) What is the expected value to the corporation of checking two light bulbs?

(c) What is the difference between expected values of checking two bulbs and one bulb?

(d) If the first bulb checked turns out to be defective, what is the expected value of checking the second?

(e) If the first bulb checked turns out not to be defective, what is the expected value of checking the second?

19.5   ALLOWING FOR RISK: UTILITY ANALYSIS

The expected monetary value criterion provides a framework for decision making that has wide practical applicability. That is to say, in many instances, an individual or corporation will believe that the action offering the highest expected monetary value is the preferred course. However, this is not invariably the case, as the following examples illustrate.

1. Many individuals purchase term life insurance through which, for a relatively modest outlay, the insured person's estate is generously compensated in the event of death during the term of the policy. Now, insurance companies are able to calculate the death probability of an individual of any given age during a specified period of time. Accordingly, their rates are set in such a way that the price of a policy exceeds the amount of money that is expected to be paid out. The amount of this excess covers the insurance company's costs and provides, on the average, a margin of profit. It then follows that for the person insured, the expected payoff from the life insurance policy is less than its cost. Therefore, if everyone based decisions on the expected monetary value criterion, term life insurance would not be purchased. Nevertheless, many people do buy this form of insurance, demonstrating a willingness to sacrifice something in expected returns for the assurance that the heirs will be provided a financial cushion in the event of death.

2. Suppose that an investor is considering purchasing shares in one or more of a group of corporations, whose prospects he regards as bright. In principle, it is possible to postulate the various states of nature that will influence the returns from investment in each of these corporations. In this way, the expected monetary value of an investment of a fixed amount in each corporation could be determined. According to the expected monetary value criterion, the investor should then put all of his available capital into the corporation for which the expected monetary value is highest. In fact, a great many investors in the stock market do not follow such a strategy. Rather, they spread their cash over a portfolio of stocks. The abandonment of the option of "putting all one's eggs in a single basket," while leading to a lower

expected return, provides a hedge against the possibility of losing a good deal of money if the single stock with the highest expected return happens to perform badly. In opting for a portfolio of stocks, the investor is asserting a willingness to sacrifice something in expected monetary value for a smaller chance of a large financial loss.

In each of these examples, the decision maker has exhibited a preference for a criterion of choice other than expected monetary value, and in each circumstance this preference seems to be extremely reasonable. The two examples involve a common ingredient, in addition to expected returns. In both cases, the decision maker wants to take *risk* into account. The purchaser of term life insurance is prepared to accept a negative expected return as the price to be paid for the chance of a large positive return in the event of death. In doing so, he is expressing a **preference for risk** (of course, he is guarding against the risk that his family will be financially ill-prepared for his death). By contrast, the investor who, in spreading his investment over a portfolio of stocks, accepts a lower expected return in order to reduce the chances of a large loss is expressing an **aversion to risk**.

The expected monetary value criterion is inappropriate for decision makers who either prefer or are averse to risk. Fortunately, it is not too difficult to modify this criterion to handle situations in which risk is a relevant factor. Essentially, the idea is to replace the monetary payoffs by quantities that reflect not only the dollar amounts to be received but also the decision maker's attitude to risk.

The Concept of Utility

Example 19.3 considered the problem of an investor choosing between a guaranteed fixed-interest investment and a portfolio of stocks. The former yielded a payoff of $1,200, while gains of $2,500 and $500 resulted for the latter if the stock market were to be buoyant or steady, but a loss of $1,000 resulted if it were to be depressed. This investor believed that the respective probabilities for these three states of nature were 0.6, 0.2, and 0.2. In that event, the expected monetary value from choosing the stock portfolio was $1,400, exceeding by $200 that of the fixed-interest investment. At this juncture, we need to inquire whether this higher expected return merits the risk of losing $1,000, as would occur if the market were depressed. A very wealthy investor, who could quite comfortably sustain such a loss, would almost certainly decide that it did. However, the position of a relatively poor person, to whom a loss of $1,000 would be quite disastrous, may well be different. For such an investor, the payoffs must be replaced by some other quantities that more adequately reflect the calamitous nature of a loss of $1,000. These quantities must measure the value, or *utility*, to the investor of a loss of $1,000 as compared with, for example, gains of $500 or $2,500.

The early works of researchers such as Von Neumann and Morgenstern (reference 6) enhanced the concept of utility, which even today plays a central role in economics. Utility analysis provides the basis for the solution of decision-making problems in the presence of risk preference or aversion. To employ it, only fairly mild and usually quite reasonable assumptions are needed. Suppose that an individual is faced with several possible payoffs, which may or may not be monetary. It is assumed that the individual can rank in order (possibly with ties) the utility, or satisfaction, that would be derived from each. Thus, if payoff A is preferred to B and B is preferred to C, A must be preferred to C.

Also assume that if payoff A is preferred to B and B is preferred to C, then there exists a gamble, which offers A with probability π and C with probability $(1 - \pi)$, such that the decision maker will be indifferent between taking this gamble and receiving B with certainty. Given these and certain other, generally innocuous assumptions whose details need not detain us, it is possible to show that the rational decision maker will choose the action for which expected utility is highest. Consequently, the decision problem is analyzed precisely as in the preceding sections, *but with utilities instead of payoffs*. That is to say, a utility table rather than a payoff table is constructed and then the state-of-nature probabilities to compare expected utilities are employed.

Now consider how the utilities corresponding to the various payoffs are determined. The possible payoffs for our investor are −$1,000, $500, $1,200, and $2,500. The first step is to obtain a utilities function.

OBTAINING A UTILITY FUNCTION

Suppose that a decision maker may receive several alternative payoffs. The transformation from payoffs to **utilities** is obtained as follows:

i. The units in which utility is measured are arbitrary. Accordingly, a scale can be fixed in any convenient fashion. Let *L* be the lowest and *H* the highest of all the payoffs. Assign utility 0 to payoff *L* and utility 100 to payoff *H*.

ii. Let *I* be any payoff between *L* and *H*. Determine the probability π such that the decision maker is indifferent between the following alternatives:

    (a) Receive payoff *I* with certainty
    (b) Receive payoff *H* with probability π and payoff *L* with probability $(1 - \pi)$.

iii. The utility to the decision maker of payoff *I* is then 100 π . The curve relating utility to payoff is called a **utility function.**

The first step is straightforward and simply provides us with a convenient metric for measuring utility. The choice of the numbers 0 and 100 to represent the utilities of the lowest and highest payoffs is entirely arbitrary. Any other pair of numbers could equally well be used, as long as the utility of the highest payoff is greater than that of the lowest, without affecting the remaining analysis.

As a practical matter, the second step is the most difficult, partly because it presupposes that the decision maker can manipulate probabilities in a coherent way. In practice, the probability must be determined by trial and error, through the asking of questions such as, "Would you prefer to receive *I* with certainty or a gamble in which you could obtain *H* with probability 0.9 and *L* with probability 0.1?" Or perhaps, the question, "Would you prefer to receive *I* with certainty or a gamble in which you could obtain *H* with probability 0.8 and *L* with probability 0.2?" This process is continued until the point of indifference is reached.

The logic of the final step is quite straightforward. Since *H* has utility 100 and *L* has utility 0, the *expected utility* if *H* is obtained with probability π and *L* with probability $(1 - \pi)$ is

$$100\pi + 0(1 - \pi) = 100\pi$$

Since the decision maker is indifferent between this gamble and receiving *I* with certainty, the utility 100 π is associated with the payoff *I*.

Return now to our investor. At the first step, we attach utility 0 to the lowest payoff, −$1,000, and utility 100 to the highest, $2,500.

It remains to determine the utilities for the immediate payoffs, $500 and $1,200. This is achieved by posing to the decision maker a series of questions, such as, " Would you prefer to receive $500 with certainty or a gamble in which you could obtain a gain of $2,500 with probability π and a loss of $1,000 with probability $(1 - \pi)$?" Different values of the probability π are tried until the value at which the decision maker is indifferent between the two alternatives is found. This process is repeated for the payoff of $1,200.

Suppose that the investor is indifferent between a payoff of $500 and this gamble with $\pi = 0.6$ and between a payoff of $1,200 and the gamble with $\pi = 0.8$. The utilities for the intermediate payoffs are then

Payoff $500   Utility $= (100)(0.6) = 60$
Payoff $1,200   Utility $= (100)(0.8) = 80$

The four utilities for this investor are plotted against the corresponding payoffs as points in Figure 19.10. A curve is drawn through these points to indicate the general shape of this investor's utility function. The shape of this curve is interesting, since it characterizes the investor's attitude to risk. As must be the case, utility increases as the payoff increases. However, notice that the *rate of increase* of utility is highest at the lowest payoffs and decreases as payoff increases. This implies a distaste for the lowest payoffs that is more than commensurate with their monetary amounts, indicating *aversion* to risk. This aversion can be seen from the investor's attitude to the gambles offered. For example, the investor is indifferent between a sure payoff of $500 and a gamble in which $2,500 might be won with probability 0.6 and $1,000 lost with probability 0.4. The expected monetary value of this gamble is

$$(0.6)(2,500) + (0.4)(-1,000) = \$1,100$$

which considerably exceeds the equally preferred sure payoff of $500. The amount of this difference provides a measure of the extent of the aversion to risk.

The shape of Figure 19.10 is typical of risk aversion.

Friedman and Savage suggested, "an important class of reactions of individuals to risk can be rationalized by a rather simple extension of orthodox utility analysis" (reference 2). They developed graphs of utility functions similar to the three types of utility functions shown in Figure 19.11. The function in part (a) of the figure, where utility increases at a *decreasing* rate as payoff increases, has the same shape as Figure 19.10, once again reflecting an *aversion* to risk. In part (b) of the figure, utility increases at an *increasing* rate as the payoffs become higher. This implies a taste for the highest payoffs that is more than commensurate with the monetary amounts involved, thus showing *preference* for risk. Finally, part (c) of Figure 19.11 shows the intermediate case with utility increasing at a *constant* rate for all payoffs. In this case, the monetary values of the payoffs provide a true measure of their utility to the decision maker, who thus demonstrates **indifference to risk**.

The three curves of Figure 19.11 characterize aversion for, preference for, and indifference to risk. However, it is not necessarily the case that a decision-maker will exhibit just one of these attitudes over the whole range of possible payoffs.

FIGURE 19.10
Utility Function for an
Investor

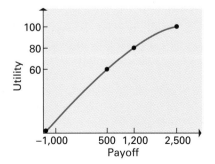

FIGURE 19.11
Utility functions; (a) Risk Aversion; (b) Preference for Risk; (c) Indifference to Risk

(a) Risk Aversion   (b) Preference for Risk   (c) Indifference to Risk

Figure 19.12 illustrates a more complex situation. Here, for payoffs in the range between M_1 and M_2, the utility function has the shape of Figure 19.11(a), indicating aversion to risk in this payoff range. However, for payoffs of monetary amounts between M_2 and M_3, this utility function has the shape of Figure 19.11(b). Hence, for this range of payoffs, the decision maker exhibits a preference for risk. Finally, in the range of highest payoffs, between M_3 and M_4, the position is once again reversed, the decision maker being averse to risk in this region. Such a utility function can arise in practical problems (Figure 19.11c). For example, an investor may well be averse to sustaining a substantial loss, while being prepared to accept some risk to obtain a fairly high positive return rather than a modest one. However, if a satisfactorily high return can be achieved at modest risk, the investor may be reluctant to risk much more for the possibility of an even higher return.

Expected Utility Criterion for Decision Making

Having determined the appropriate utilities, it remains only to solve the decision-making problem by finding that course of action with the highest expected utility. These expected utilities are obtained in the usual manner, employing the probabilities of the states of nature, as given in Equation 19.5.

FIGURE 19.12
Utility Function Showing Aversion to Risk for Payoffs Between M_1 and M_2 and Between M_3 and M_4 and Preference for Risk Between Payoffs M_2 and M_3.

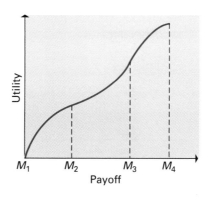

THE EXPECTED UTILITY CRITERION

Suppose that a decision maker has K possible actions, $a_1, a_2, \ldots, a_K$ and is faced with H states of nature. Let U_{ij} denote the utility corresponding to the ith action and jth state and π_j the probability of occurrence of the jth state of nature. Then the **expected utility**, $EU(a_i)$, of the action a_i is

$$EU(a_i) = \pi_1 U_{i1} + \pi_2 U_{i2} + \cdots + \pi_H U_{iH} = \sum_{j=1}^{H} \pi_j U_{ij} \qquad (19.5)$$

Given a choice between alternative actions, the **expected utility criterion** dictates the choice of the action for which expected utility is highest. Under generally reasonable assumptions, it can be shown that the rational decision maker should adopt this criterion.

   If the decision maker is indifferent to risk, the expected utility criterion and the expected monetary value criterion are equivalent.

Table 19.11 shows the utilities and state-of-nature probabilities for our investor. If the fixed-interest investment is chosen, a utility of 80 is assured, whichever state of nature prevails. For the portfolio of stocks, the expected utility is

$$(0.6)(100) + (0.2)(60) + (0.2)(0) = 0.72$$

Since this is less than 80, this investor should elect to make the fixed-interest investment, according to the expected utility criterion.

   In Example 19.3, investment in the portfolio of stocks was selected by the expected monetary value criterion. However, the incorporation into the analysis of another factor—the extent of this investor's aversion to risk—leads to the conclusion that the fixed-interest option is the better choice. This example serves to illustrate that on occasion, when risk is an important factor, the expected monetary value criterion is inadequate for solving decision-making problems.

   The expected utility criterion is the most generally applicable and intellectually defensible of the criteria introduced for attacking decision-making problems.

   Its chief drawback arises from the difficulty of eliciting information about which gambles are regarded as equally attractive as particular assured payoffs. This type of information is essential in the determination of utilities. For a wide range of problems where indifference to risk can safely be assumed, the expected monetary value criterion remains applicable. This would typically be the case, for example, in a small proportion of the corporation's total turnover. If, however (as may be the case in the development of a new commercial airliner, for example), possible losses from a project could threaten a corporation with insolvency, the utilities should appropriately reflect an aversion to risk. A company may attempt to spread this risk by forming partnerships with other firms in the industry or with possible customers.

TABLE 19.11
Utilities and State-of-Nature Probabilities for an Investor

ACTIONS	STATES OF THE MARKET		
Investment	*Buoyant State* ($\pi = 0.60$)	*Steady State* ($\pi = 0.20$)	*Depressed State* ($\pi = 0.20$)
Fixed Interest	80	80	80
Stock Portfolio	100	60	0

EXERCISES

19.43 A decision maker faces a problem in which the possible payoffs (in dollars) are:

1,000   3,000   6,000   9,000   10,000   12,000

Utility 0 is assigned to a payoff of $1,000 and utility 100 to a payoff of $12,000. This decision maker is indifferent to risk for payoffs in this range.

(a) Find the utilities for the four intermediate payoffs.

(b) For each intermediate payoff, I, find the probability π such that the decision maker is indifferent between receiving I with certainty and a wager in which $12,000 is received with probability π and $1,000 with probability $(1 - \pi)$.

19.44 The shoe store operator of Exercise 19.9 has six possible payoffs (in dollars):

−10,000   30,000   60,000   70,000   90,000   130,000

Assign utility 0 to a loss of $10,000 and utility 100 to a profit of $130,000. For each intermediate payoff I, the probabilities p such that the shoe store operator is indifferent between receiving I with certainty and a gamble in which $130,000 would be gained with probability π and $10,000 lost with probability $(1 - \pi)$ are shown in the accompanying table.

PAYOFF	30,000	60,000	70,000	90,000
π	0.35	0.60	0.70	0.85

(a) What are the utilities for the intermediate payoffs?

(b) Suppose that the probabilities that the new shopping center will be very successful, moderately successful, and unsuccessful are 0.4, 0.4, and 0.2, respectively. Which action should be taken if expected utility is to be maximized?

19.45 The shoe store operator of Exercise 19.44 is unsure what value π to attach to indifference between receiving $30,000 with certainty and a gamble in which $130,000 would be gained with probability p and $10,000 lost with probability $(1 - \pi)$. Assuming that the remaining problem specifications are as in Exercise 19.44, under what range of values for this probability will the expected utility criterion yield the same choice of action?

19.46 Consider the contractor of Exercise 19.21. In fact, this contractor is indifferent between submitting and not submitting a bid. What does this imply about the contractor's utility function?

SUMMARY

This chapter is intended as an introduction to decision analysis. All of us must live and work in an environment whose future is uncertain. Corporate decision making is no exception. The framework of a decision problem was considered, various criteria to select an optimal action were studied, the value of sample information was discussed, and situations where the decision maker may be more interested in taking into account risk rather than maximizing expected monetary values were examined. In the latter situation, a utility function was considered. Four criteria for decision making were considered in this chapter: maximin, minimax regret, expected monetary value, and expected utility. PHStat was used to obtain the opportunity loss tables, the expected monetary values, and the expected value of perfect information. TreePlan was used to obtain decision trees.

KEY WORDS

action, 741
admissible action, 742
aversion to risk, 772
Bayes' Theorem, 759
decision nodes, 750
decision trees, 750
EMV, 749
event nodes, 750
EVPI, 763
EVSI, 765
expected monetary value, 749
expected monetary value criterion, 749

expected net value of sample
   information, 765
expected utility criterion, 776
expected value of perfect information,
   763
expected value of sample information,
   765
inadmissible action, 742
indifference to risk, 774
maximin criterion, 744
minimax regret criterion, 746
opportunity loss table, 745

payoff table, 741
perfect information, 763
preference for risk, 772
regret table, 745
sensitivity analysis, 755
states of nature, 741
terminal nodes, 750
treeplan, 748
utility function, 773
value of perfect information, 763
value of sample information, 765

CHAPTER EXERCISES AND APPLICATIONS

19.47 A consultant is considering submitting detailed bids for two possible contracts. The bid for the first contract costs $100 to prepare, while that for the second contract costs $150 to prepare. If the bid for the first contract is accepted and the work is carried out, a profit of $800 will result. If the bid for the second contract is accepted and the work is carried out, a profit of $1,200 will result. Any costs of bid preparation must be subtracted from these profits. The consultant can, if he wishes, submit bids for both contracts. He does not, however, have the resources to carry out both pieces of work simultaneously. If a bid is submitted and accepted and the consultant is then unable to carry out the work, he counts this as a cost of $200 in lost goodwill. For the decision-making process, there are four possible states of nature:

> s_1: Both bids rejected
>
> s_2: Bid for the first contract accepted, bid for the second contract rejected
>
> s_3: Bid for the second contract accepted, bid for the first contract rejected
>
> s_4: Both bids accepted

(a) The consultant has four possible courses of action. What are they?

(b) Set out the payoff table for this consultant's decision-making problem.

(c) Which action is chosen by the maximin criterion?

(d) Which action is chosen by the minimax regret criterion?

19.48 Refer to Exercise 19.47. The consultant believes that the probability is 0.7 that a bid for the first contract would be accepted and 0.4 that a bid for the second contract would be accepted. He also believes that the acceptance of one bid is independent of acceptance of the other.

(a) What are the probabilities for the four states of nature?

(b) According to the expected monetary value criterion, which action should the consultant adopt, and what is the expected monetary value of this action?

(c) Draw the decision tree for the consultant's problem.

(d) What is the expected value of perfect information to this consultant?

(e) The consultant is offered "inside information" on the prospects of the bid for the first contract. This information is entirely reliable, in the sense that it would allow him to know for sure whether the bid would be accepted. However, no further information is available on the prospects of the bid for the second contract. What is the expected value of this "inside information"?

19.49 Refer to Exercises 19.47 and 19.48. There are nine possible payoffs for this consultant, as follows (in dollars):

$$-250 \quad -150 \quad -100 \quad 0 \quad 550 \quad 700 \quad 750 \quad 950 \quad 1,050$$

A utility of 0 is assigned to a loss of $250 and a utility of 100 to a profit of $1,050. For each intermediate payoff I, the probabilities p such that the consultant is indifferent between payoff I with certainty and a gamble in which $1,050 is gained with probability p and $250 lost with probability $(1 - p)$ are shown in the accompanying table. According to the expected utility criterion, which action should the consultant choose, and what is the expected utility of this action?

PAYOFF	−150	−100	0	550	700	750	950
π	.05	.10	.20	.65	.70	.75	.85

REFERENCES

1. Eppen, G.D., F.J. Gould, et al., *Introductory Management Science: Decision Modeling with Spreadsheets*, 5th edition. (Upper Saddle River, NJ: Prentice Hall, 1998).

2. Friedman, Milton and L. J. Savage, "The Utility Analysis of Choices Involving Risk." *The Journal of Political Economy*, LVI (1948): 279–304.

3. Middleton, Michael. Professor, University of San Francisco. http://www.usaf.edu/~middleton.

4. Render, Barry and Ralph M. Stair, Jr., *Quantitative Analysis for Management*, 7th edition. (Upper Saddle River, NJ: Prentice Hall, 2000).

5. "TreePlan Documentation." Available from Web site: http://www.treeplan.com.

6. Von Neumann, John and Oskar Morgenstern, *The Theory of Games and Economic Behavior*, 3rd edition. (Princeton, NJ: Princeton University Press, 1953).

TABLE 1 Cumulative Distribution Function of the Standard Normal Distribution

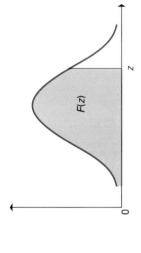

z	F(z)	z	F(z)	z	F(z)	z	F(z)	z	F(z)	z	F(z)
.00	.5000	.31	.6217	.61	.7291	.91	.8186	1.21	.8869	1.51	.9345
.01	.5040	.32	.6255	.62	.7324	.92	.8212	1.22	.8888	1.52	.9357
.02	.5080	.33	.6293	.63	.7357	.93	.8238	1.23	.8907	1.53	.9370
.03	.5120	.34	.6331	.64	.7389	.94	.8264	1.24	.8925	1.54	.9382
.04	.5160	.35	.6368	.65	.7422	.95	.8289	1.25	.8944	1.55	.9394
.05	.5199										
.06	.5239	.36	.6406	.66	.7454	.96	.8315	1.26	.8962	1.56	.9406
.07	.5279	.37	.6443	.67	.7486	.97	.8340	1.27	.8980	1.57	.9418
.08	.5319	.38	.6480	.68	.7517	.98	.8365	1.28	.8997	1.58	.9429
.09	.5359	.39	.6517	.69	.7549	.99	.8389	1.29	.9015	1.59	.9441
.10	.5398	.40	.6554	.70	.7580	1.00	.8413	1.30	.9032	1.60	.9452
.11	.5438	.41	.6591	.71	.7611	1.01	.8438	1.31	.9049	1.61	.9463
.12	.5478	.42	.6628	.72	.7642	1.02	.8461	1.32	.9066	1.62	.9474
.13	.5517	.43	.6664	.73	.7673	1.03	.8485	1.33	.9082	1.63	.9484
.14	.5557	.44	.6700	.74	.7704	1.04	.8508	1.34	.9099	1.64	.9495
.15	.5596	.45	.6736	.75	.7734	1.05	.8531	1.35	.9115	1.65	.9505
.16	.5636	.46	.6772	.76	.7764	1.06	.8554	1.36	.9131	1.66	.9515
.17	.5675	.47	.6803	.77	.7794	1.07	.8577	1.37	.9147	.167	.9525
.18	.5714	.48	.6844	.78	.7823	1.08	.8599	1.38	.9162	1.68	.9535
.19	.5753	.49	.6879	.79	.7852	1.09	.8621	1.39	.9177	1.69	.9545
.20	.5793	.50	.6915	.80	.7881	1.10	.8643	1.40	.9192	1.70	.9554
.21	.5832	.51	.6950	.81	.7910	1.11	.8665	1.41	.9207	1.71	.9564
.22	.5871	.52	.6985	.82	.7939	1.12	.8686	1.42	.9222	1.72	.9573
.23	.5910	.53	.7019	.83	.7967	1.13	.8708	1.43	.9236	1.73	.9582
.24	.5948	.54	.7054	.84	.7995	1.14	.8729	1.44	.9251	1.74	.9591
.25	.5987	.55	.7088	.85	.8023	1.15	.8749	1.45	.9265	1.75	.9599
.26	.6026	.56	.7123	.86	.8051	1.16	.8770	1.46	.9279	1.76	.9608
.27	.6064	.57	.7157	.87	.8078	1.17	.8790	1.47	.9292	1.77	.9616
.28	.6103	.58	.7190	.88	.8106	1.18	.8810	1.48	.9306	1.78	.9625
.29	.6141	.59	.7224	.89	.8133	1.19	.8830	1.49	.9319	1.79	.9633
.30	.6179	.60	.7257	.90	.8159	1.20	.8849	1.50	.9332	1.80	.9641

z	F(z)	z	F(z)	z	F(z)	z	F(z)	z	F(z)	z	F(z)
1.81	.9649	2.21	.9864	2.61	.9955	3.01	.9987	3.41	.9997	3.81	.9999
1.82	.9656	2.22	.9868	2.62	.9956	3.02	.9987	3.42	.9997	3.82	.9999
1.83	.9664	2.23	.9871	2.63	.9957	3.03	.9988	3.43	.9997	3.83	.9999
1.84	.9671	2.24	.9875	2.64	.9959	3.04	.9988	3.44	.9997	3.84	.9999
1.85	.9678	2.25	.9878	2.65	.9960	3.05	.9989	3.45	.9997	3.85	.9999
1.86	.9686	2.26	.9881	2.66	.9961	3.06	.9989	3.46	.9997	3.86	.9999
1.87	.9693	2.27	.9884	2.67	.9962	3.07	.9989	3.47	.9997	3.87	.9999
1.88	.9699	2.28	.9887	2.68	.9963	3.08	.9990	3.48	.9997	3.88	.9999
1.89	.9706	2.29	.9890	2.69	.9964	3.09	.9990	3.49	.9998	3.89	1.0000
1.90	.9713	2.30	.9893	2.70	.9965	3.10	.9990	3.50	.9998	3.90	1.0000
1.91	.9719	2.31	.9896	2.71	.9966	3.11	.9991	3.51	.9998	3.91	1.0000
1.92	.9726	2.32	.9898	2.72	.9967	3.12	.9991	3.52	.9998	3.92	1.0000
1.93	.9732	2.33	.9901	2.73	.9968	3.13	.9991	3.53	.9998	3.93	1.0000
1.94	.9738	2.34	.9904	2.74	.9969	3.14	.9992	3.54	.9998	3.94	1.0000
1.95	.9744	2.35	.9906	2.75	.9970	3.15	.9992	3.55	.9998	3.95	1.0000
1.96	.9750	2.36	.9909	2.76	.9971	3.16	.9992	3.56	.9998	3.96	1.0000
1.97	.9756	2.37	.9911	2.77	.9972	3.17	.9992	3.57	.9998	3.97	1.0000
1.98	.9761	2.38	.9913	2.78	.9973	3.18	.9993	3.58	.9998	3.98	1.0000
1.99	.9767	2.39	.9916	2.79	.9974	3.19	.9993	3.59	.9998	3.99	1.0000
2.00	.9772	2.40	.9918	2.80	.9974	3.20	.9993	3.60	.9998		
2.01	.9778	2.41	.9920	2.81	.9975	3.21	.9993	3.61	.9998		
2.02	.9783	2.42	.9922	2.82	.9976	3.22	.9994	3.62	.9999		
2.03	.9788	2.43	.9925	2.83	.9977	3.23	.9994	3.63	.9999		
2.04	.9793	2.44	.9927	2.84	.9977	3.24	.9994	3.64	.9999		
2.05	.9798	2.45	.9929	2.85	.9978	3.25	.9994	3.65	.9999		
2.06	.9803	2.46	.9931	2.86	.9979	3.26	.9994	3.66	.9999		
2.07	.9808	2.47	.9932	2.87	.9979	3.27	.9995	3.67	.9999		
2.08	.9812	2.48	.9934	2.88	.9980	3.28	.9995	3.68	.9999		
2.09	.9817	2.49	.9936	2.89	.9981	3.29	.9995	3.69	.9999		
2.10	.9821	2.50	.9938	2.90	.9981	3.30	.9995	3.70	.9999		
2.11	.9826	2.51	.9940	2.91	.9982	3.31	.9995	3.71	.9999		
2.12	.0830	2.52	.9941	2.92	.9982	3.32	.9996	3.72	.9999		
2.13	.9834	2.53	.9943	2.93	.9983	3.33	.9996	3.73	.9999		
2.14	.9838	2.54	.9945	2.94	.9984	3.34	.9996	3.74	.9999		
2.15	.9842	2.55	.9946	2.95	.9984	3.35	.9996	3.75	.9999		
2.16	.9846	2.56	.9948	2.96	.9985	3.36	.9996	3.76	.9999		
2.17	.9850	2.57	.9949	2.97	.9985	3.37	.9996	3.77	.9999		
2.18	.9854	2.58	.9951	2.98	.9986	3.38	.9996	3.78	.9999		
2.19	.9857	2.59	.9952	2.99	.9986	3.39	.9997	3.79	.9999		
2.20	.9861	2.60	.9953	3.00	.9986	3.40	.9997	3.80	.9999		

TABLE 2   Probability Function of the Binomial Distribution
The table shows the probability of x successes in n independent trials, each with probability of success π. For example, the probability of four successes in eight independent trials, each with probability of success .35, is .1875.

n	x	.05	.10	.15	.20	.25	.30	.35	.40	.45	.50
							π				
1	0	.9500	.9000	.8500	.8000	.7500	.7000	.6500	.6000	.5500	.5000
	1	.0500	.1000	.1500	.2000	.2500	.3000	.3500	.4000	.4500	.5000
2	0	.9025	.8100	.7225	.6400	.5625	.4900	.4225	.3600	.3025	.2500
	1	.0950	.1800	.2550	.3200	.3750	.4200	.4550	.4800	.4950	.5000
	2	.0025	.0100	.0225	.0400	.0625	.0900	.1225	.1600	.2025	.2500
3	0	.8574	.7290	.6141	.5120	.4219	.3430	.2746	.2160	.1664	.1250
	1	.1354	.2430	.3251	.3840	.4219	.4410	.4436	.4320	.4084	.3750
	2	.0071	.0270	.0574	.0960	.1406	.1890	.2389	.2880	.3341	.3750
	3	.0001	.0010	.0034	.0080	.0156	.0270	.0429	.0640	.0911	.1250
4	0	.8145	.6561	.5220	.4096	.3164	.2401	.1785	.1296	.0915	.0625
	1	.1715	.2916	.3685	.4096	.4219	.4116	.3845	.3456	.2995	.2500
	2	.0135	.0486	.0975	.1536	.2109	.2646	.3105	.3456	.3675	.3750
	3	.0005	.0036	.0115	.0256	.0469	.0756	.1115	.1536	.2005	.2500
	4	.0000	.0001	.0005	.0016	.0039	.0081	.0150	.0256	.0410	.0625
5	0	.7738	.5905	.4437	.3277	.2373	.1681	.1160	.0778	.0503	.0312
	1	.2036	.3280	.3915	.4096	.3955	.3602	.3124	.2592	.2059	.1562
	2	.0214	.0729	.1382	.2048	.2637	.3087	.3364	.3456	.3369	.3125
	3	.0011	.0081	.0244	.0512	.0879	.1323	.1811	.2304	.2757	.3125
	4	.0000	.0004	.0022	.0064	.0146	.0284	.0488	.0768	.1128	.1562
	5	.0000	.0000	.0001	.0003	.0010	.0024	.0053	.0102	.0185	.0312
6	0	.7351	.5314	.3771	.2621	.1780	.1176	.0754	.0467	.0277	.0156
	1	.2321	.3543	.3993	.3932	.3560	.3025	.2437	.1866	.1359	.0938
	2	.0305	.0984	.1762	.2458	.2966	.3241	.3280	.3110	.2780	.2344
	3	.0021	.0146	.0415	.0819	.1318	.1852	.2355	.2765	.3032	.3125
	4	.0001	.0012	.0055	.0154	.0330	.0595	.0951	.1382	.1861	.2344
	5	.0000	.0001	.0004	.0015	.0044	.0102	.0205	.0369	.0609	.0938
	6	.0000	.0000	.0000	.0001	.0002	.0007	.0018	.0041	.0083	.0156
7	0	.6983	.4783	.3206	.2097	.1335	.0824	.0490	.0280	.0152	.0078
	1	.2573	.3720	.3960	.3670	.3115	.2471	.1848	.1306	.0872	.0547
	2	.0406	.1240	.2097	.2753	.3115	.3177	.2985	.2613	.2140	.1641
	3	.0036	.0230	.0617	.1147	.1730	.2269	.2679	.2903	.2918	.2734
	4	.0002	.0026	.0109	.0287	.0577	.0972	.1442	.1935	.2388	.2734
	5	.0000	.0002	.0012	.0043	.0115	.0250	.0466	.0774	.1172	.1641
	6	.0000	.0000	.0001	.0004	.0013	.0036	.0084	.0172	.0320	.0547
	7	.0000	.0000	.0000	.0000	.0001	.0002	.0006	.0016	.0037	.0078
8	0	.6634	.4305	.2725	.1678	.1001	.0576	.0319	.0168	.0084	.0039
	1	.2793	.3826	.3847	.3355	.2670	.1977	.1373	.0896	.0548	.0312
	2	.0515	.1488	.2376	.2936	.3115	.2965	.2587	.2090	.1569	.1094
	3	.0054	.0331	.0839	.1468	.2076	.2541	.2786	.2787	.2568	.2188
	4	.0004	.0046	.0185	.0459	.0865	.1361	.1875	.2322	.2627	.2734
	5	.0000	.0004	.0026	.0092	.0231	.0467	.0808	.1239	.1719	.2188
	6	.0000	.0000	.0002	.0011	.0038	.0100	.0217	.0413	.0703	.1094
	7	.0000	.0000	.0000	.0001	.0004	.0012	.0033	.0079	.0164	.0312
	8	.0000	.0000	.0000	.0000	.0000	.0001	.0002	.0007	.0017	.0039
9	0	.6302	.3874	.2316	.1342	.0751	.0404	.0207	.0101	.0046	.0020
	1	.2985	.3874	.3679	.3020	.2253	.1556	.1004	.0605	.0339	.0176

TABLE 2   Probability Function of the Binomial Distribution (cont.)

n	x	.05	.10	.15	.20	.25	.30	.35	.40	.45	.50
						π					
	2	.0629	.1722	.2597	.3020	.3003	.2668	.2162	.1612	.1110	.0703
	3	.0077	.0446	.1069	.1762	.2336	.2668	.2716	.2508	.2119	.1641
	4	.0006	.0074	.0283	.0661	.1168	.1715	.2194	.2508	.2600	.2461
	5	.0000	.0008	.0050	.0165	.0389	.0735	.1181	.1672	.2128	.2461
	6	.0000	.0001	.0006	.0028	.0087	.0210	.0424	.0743	.1160	.1641
	7	.0000	.0000	.0000	.0003	.0012	.0039	.0098	.0212	.0407	.0703
	8	.0000	.0000	.0000	.0000	.0001	.0004	.0013	.0035	.0083	.0176
	9	.0000	.0000	.0000	.0000	.0000	.0000	.0001	.0003	.0008	.0020
10	0	.5987	.3487	.1969	.1074	.0563	.0282	.0135	.0060	.0025	.0010
	1	.3151	.3874	.3474	.2684	.1877	.1211	.0725	.0403	.0207	.0098
	2	.0746	.1937	.2759	.3020	.2816	.2335	.1757	.1209	.0763	.0439
	3	.0105	.0574	.1298	.2013	.2503	.2668	.2522	.2150	.1665	.1172
	4	.0010	.0112	.0401	.0881	.1460	.2001	.2377	.2508	.2384	.2051
	5	.0001	.0015	.0085	.0264	.0584	.1029	.1536	.2007	.2340	.2461
	6	.0000	.0001	.0012	.0055	.0162	.0368	.0689	.1115	.1596	.2051
	7	.0000	.0000	.0001	.0008	.0031	.0090	.0212	.0425	.0746	.1172
	8	.0000	.0000	.0000	.0001	.0004	.0014	.0043	.0106	.0226	.0439
	9	.0000	.0000	.0000	.0000	.0000	.0001	.0004	.0016	.0042	.0098
	10	.0000	.0000	.0000	.0000	.0000	.0000	.0000	.0001	.0003	.0010
11	0	.5688	.3138	.1673	.0859	.0422	.0198	.0088	.0036	.0014	.0005
	1	.3293	.3835	.3248	.2362	.1549	.0932	.0518	.0266	.0125	.0054
	2	.0867	.2131	.2866	.2953	.2581	.1998	.1395	.0887	.0513	.0269
	3	.0137	.0710	.1517	.2215	.2581	.2568	.2254	.1774	.1259	.0806
	4	.0014	.0158	.0536	.1107	.1721	.2201	.2428	.2365	.2060	.1611
	5	.0001	.0025	.0132	.0388	.0803	.1321	.1830	.2207	.2360	.2256
	6	.0000	.0003	.0023	.0097	.0268	.0566	.0985	.1471	.1931	.2256
	7	.0000	.0000	.0003	.0017	.0064	.0173	.0379	.0701	.1128	.1611
	8	.0000	.0000	.0000	.0002	.0011	.0037	.0102	.0234	.0462	.0806
	9	.0000	.0000	.0000	.0000	.0001	.0005	.0018	.0052	.0126	.0269
	10	.0000	.0000	.0000	.0000	.0000	.0000	.0002	.0007	.0021	.0054
	11	.0000	.0000	.0000	.0000	.0000	.0000	.0000	.0000	.0002	.0005
12	0	.5404	.2824	.1422	.0687	.0317	.0138	.0057	.0022	.0008	.0002
	1	.3413	.3766	.3012	.2062	.1267	.0712	.0368	.0174	.0075	.0029
	2	.0988	.2301	.2924	.2835	.2323	.1678	.1088	.0639	.0339	.0161
	3	.0173	.0852	.1720	.2362	.2581	.2397	.1954	.1419	.0923	.0537
	4	.0021	.0213	.0683	.1329	.1936	.2311	.2367	.2128	.1700	.1208
	5	.0002	.0038	.0193	.0532	.1032	.1585	.2039	.2270	.2225	.1934
	6	.0000	.0005	.0040	.0155	.0401	.0792	.1281	.1766	.2124	.2256
	7	.0000	.0000	.0006	.0033	.0015	.0291	.0591	.1009	.1489	.1934
	8	.0000	.0000	.0001	.0005	.0024	.0078	.0199	.0420	.0762	.1208
	9	.0000	.0000	.0000	.0001	.0004	.0015	.0048	.0125	.0277	.0537
	10	.0000	.0000	.0000	.0000	.0000	.0002	.0008	.0025	.0068	.0161
	11	.0000	.0000	.0000	.0000	.0000	.0000	.0001	.0003	.0010	.0029
	12	.0000	.0000	.0000	.0000	.0000	.0000	.0000	.0000	.0001	.0002
13	0	.5133	.2542	.1209	.0550	.0238	.0097	.0037	.0013	.0004	.0001
	1	.3512	.3672	.2774	.1787	.1029	.0540	.0259	.0113	.0045	.0016
	2	.1109	.2448	.2937	.2680	.2059	.1388	.0836	.0453	.0220	.0095
	3	.0214	.0997	.1900	.2457	.2517	.2181	.1651	.1107	.0660	.0349
	4	.0028	.0277	.0838	.1535	.2097	.2337	.2222	.1845	.1350	.0873
	5	.0003	.0055	.0266	.0691	.1258	.1803	.2154	.2214	.1989	.1571
	6	.0000	.0008	.0063	.0230	.0559	.1030	.1546	.1968	.2169	.2095
	7	.0000	.0001	.0011	.0058	.0186	.0442	.0833	.1312	.1775	.2095

TABLE 2   Probability Function of the Binomial Distribution (cont.)

n	x	π									
		.05	.10	.15	.20	.25	.30	.35	.40	.45	.50
	8	.0000	.0000	.0001	.0011	.0047	.0142	.0336	.0656	.1089	.1571
	9	.0000	.0000	.0000	.0001	.0009	.0034	.0101	.0243	.0495	.0873
	10	.0000	.0000	.0000	.0000	.0001	.0006	.0022	.0065	.0162	.0349
	11	.0000	.0000	.0000	.0000	.0000	.0001	.0003	.0012	.0036	.0095
	12	.0000	.0000	.0000	.0000	.0000	.0000	.0000	.0001	.0005	.0016
	13	.0000	.0000	.0000	.0000	.0000	.0000	.0000	.0000	.0000	.0001
14	0	.4877	.2288	.1028	.0440	.0178	.0068	.0024	.0008	.0002	.0001
	1	.3593	.3559	.2539	.1539	.0832	.0407	.0181	.0073	.0027	.0009
	2	.1229	.2570	.2912	.2501	.1802	.1134	.0634	.0317	.0141	.0056
	3	.0259	.1142	.2056	.2501	.2402	.1943	.1366	.0845	.0462	.0222
	4	.0037	.0348	.0998	.1720	.2202	.2290	.2022	.1549	.1040	.0611
	5	.0004	.0078	.0352	.0860	.1468	.1963	.2178	.2066	.1701	.1222
	6	.0000	.0013	.0093	.0322	.0734	.1262	.1759	.2066	.2088	.1833
	7	.0000	.0002	.0019	.0092	.0280	.0618	.1082	.1574	.1952	.2095
	8	.0000	.0000	.0003	.0020	.0082	.0232	.0510	.0918	.1398	.1833
	9	.0000	.0000	.0000	.0003	.0018	.0066	.0183	.0408	.0762	.1222
	10	.0000	.0000	.0000	.0000	.0003	.0014	.0049	.0136	.0312	.0611
	11	.0000	.0000	.0000	.0000	.0000	.0002	.0010	.0033	.0093	.0222
	12	.0000	.0000	.0000	.0000	.0000	.0000	.0001	.0005	.0019	.0056
	13	.0000	.0000	.0000	.0000	.0000	.0000	.0000	.0001	.0002	.0009
	14	.0000	.0000	.0000	.0000	.0000	.0000	.0000	.0000	.0000	.0001
15	0	.4633	.2059	.0874	.0352	.0134	.0047	.0016	.0005	.0001	.0000
	1	.3658	.3432	.2312	.1319	.0668	.0305	.0126	.0047	.0016	.0005
	2	.1348	.2669	.2856	.2309	.1559	.0916	.0476	.0219	.0090	.0032
	3	.0307	.1285	.2184	.2501	.2252	.1700	.1110	.0634	.0318	.0139
	4	.0049	.0428	.1156	.1876	.2252	.2186	.1792	.1268	.0780	.0417
	5	.0006	.0105	.0449	.1032	.1651	.2061	.2123	.1859	.1404	.0916
	6	.0000	.0019	.0132	.0430	.0917	.1472	.1906	.2066	.1914	.1527
	7	.0000	.0003	.0030	.0138	.0393	.0811	.1319	.1771	.2013	.1964
	8	.0000	.0000	.0005	.0035	.0131	.0348	.0710	.1181	.1647	.1964
	9	.0000	.0000	.0001	.0007	.0034	.0116	.0298	.0612	.1048	.1527
	10	.0000	.0000	.0000	.0001	.0007	.0030	.0096	.0245	.0515	.0916
	11	.0000	.0000	.0000	.0000	.0001	.0006	.0024	.0074	.0191	.0417
	12	.0000	.0000	.0000	.0000	.0000	.0001	.0004	.0016	.0052	.0139
	13	.0000	.0000	.0000	.0000	.0000	.0000	.0001	.0003	.0010	.0032
	14	.0000	.0000	.0000	.0000	.0000	.0000	.0000	.0000	.0001	.0005
	15	.0000	.0000	.0000	.0000	.0000	.0000	.0000	.0000	.0000	.0000
16	0	.4401	.1853	.0743	.0281	.0100	.0033	.0010	.0003	.0001	.0000
	1	.3706	.3294	.2097	.1126	.0535	.0228	.0087	.0030	.0009	.0002
	2	.1463	.2745	.2775	.2111	.1336	.0732	.0353	.0150	.0056	.0018
	3	.0359	.1423	.2285	.2463	.2079	.1465	.0888	.0468	.0215	.0085
	4	.0061	.0514	.1311	.2001	.2552	.2040	.1553	.1014	.0572	.0278
	5	.0008	.0137	.0555	.1201	.1802	.2099	.2008	.1623	.1123	.0667
	6	.0001	.0028	.0180	.0550	.1101	.1649	.1982	.1983	.1684	.1222
	7	.0000	.0004	.0045	.0197	.0524	.1010	.1524	.1889	.1969	.1746
	8	.0000	.0001	.0009	.0055	.0197	.0487	.0923	.1417	.1812	.1964
	9	.0000	.0000	.0001	.0012	.0058	.0185	.0442	.0840	.1318	.1746
	10	.0000	.0000	.0000	.0002	.0014	.0056	.0167	.0392	.0755	.1222
	11	.0000	.0000	.0000	.0000	.0002	.0013	.0049	.0142	.0337	.0667
	12	.0000	.0000	.0000	.0000	.0000	.0002	.0011	.0040	.0115	.0278
	13	.0000	.0000	.0000	.0000	.0000	.0000	.0002	.0008	.0029	.0085
	14	.0000	.0000	.0000	.0000	.0000	.0000	.0000	.0001	.0005	.0018
	15	.0000	.0000	.0000	.0000	.0000	.0000	.0000	.0000	.0001	.0002

TABLE 2   Probability Function of the Binomial Distribution (cont.)

n	x	.05	.10	.15	.20	.25	.30	.35	.40	.45	.50
	16	.0000	.0000	.0000	.0000	.0000	.0000	.0000	.0000	.0000	.0000
17	0	.4181	.1668	.0631	.0225	.0075	.0023	.0007	.0002	.0000	.0000
	1	.3741	.3150	.1893	.0957	.0426	.0169	.0060	.0019	.0005	.0001
	2	.1575	.2800	.2673	.1914	.1136	.0581	.0260	.0102	.0035	.0010
	3	.0415	.1556	.2359	.2393	.1893	.1245	.0701	.0341	.0144	.0052
	4	.0076	.0605	.1457	.2093	.2209	.1868	.1320	.0796	.0411	.0182
	5	.0010	.0175	.0068	.1361	.1914	.2081	.1849	.1379	.0875	.0472
	6	.0001	.0039	.0236	.0680	.1276	.1784	.1991	.1839	.1432	.0944
	7	.0000	.0007	.0065	.0267	.0668	.1201	.1685	.1927	.1841	.1484
	8	.0000	.0001	.0014	.0084	.0279	.0644	.1134	.1606	.1883	.1855
	9	.0000	.0000	.0003	.0021	.0093	.0276	.0611	.1070	.1540	.1855
	10	.0000	.0000	.0000	.0004	.0025	.0095	.0263	.0571	.1008	.1484
	11	.0000	.0000	.0000	.0001	.0005	.0026	.0090	.0242	.0525	.0944
	12	.0000	.0000	.0000	.0000	.0001	.0006	.0024	.0081	.0215	.0472
	13	.0000	.0000	.0000	.0000	.0000	.0001	.0005	.0021	.0068	.0182
	14	.0000	.0000	.0000	.0000	.0000	.0000	.0001	.0004	.0016	.0052
	15	.0000	.0000	.0000	.0000	.0000	.0000	.0000	.0001	.0003	.0010
	16	.0000	.0000	.0000	.0000	.0000	.0000	.0000	.0000	.0000	.0001
	17	.0000	.0000	.0000	.0000	.0000	.0000	.0000	.0000	.0000	.0000
18	0	.3972	.1501	.0536	.0180	.0056	.0016	.0004	.0001	.0000	.0000
	1	.3763	.3002	.1704	.0811	.0338	.0126	.0042	.0012	.0003	.0001
	2	.1683	.2835	.2556	.1723	.0958	.0458	.0190	.0069	.0022	.0006
	3	.0473	.1680	.2406	.2297	.1704	.1046	.0547	.0246	.0095	.0031
	4	.0093	.0700	.1592	.2153	.2130	.1681	.1104	.0614	.0291	.0117
	5	.0014	.0218	.0787	.1507	.1988	.2017	.1664	.1146	.0666	.0327
	6	.0002	.0052	.0301	.0816	.1436	.1873	.1941	.1655	.1181	.0708
	7	.0000	.0010	.0091	.0350	.0820	.1376	.1792	.1892	.1657	.1214
	8	.0000	.0002	.0022	.0120	.0376	.0811	.1327	.1734	.1864	.1669
	9	.0000	.0000	.0004	.0033	.0139	.0386	.0794	.1284	.1694	.1855
	10	.0000	.0000	.0001	.0008	.0042	.0149	.0385	.0771	.1248	.1669
	11	.0000	.0000	.0000	.0001	.0010	.0046	.0151	.0374	.0742	.1214
	12	.0000	.0000	.0000	.0000	.0002	.0012	.0047	.0145	.0354	.0708
	13	.0000	.0000	.0000	.0000	.0000	.0002	.0012	.0044	.0134	.0327
	14	.0000	.0000	.0000	.0000	.0000	.0000	.0002	.0011	.0039	.0117
	15	.0000	.0000	.0000	.0000	.0000	.0000	.0000	.0002	.0009	.0031
	16	.0000	.0000	.0000	.0000	.0000	.0000	.0000	.0000	.0001	.0006
	17	.0000	.0000	.0000	.0000	.0000	.0000	.0000	.0000	.0000	.0001
	18	.0000	.0000	.0000	.0000	.0000	.0000	.0000	.0000	.0000	.0000
19	0	.3774	.1351	.0456	.0144	.0042	.0011	.0003	.0001	.0000	.0000
	1	.3774	.2852	.1529	.0685	.0268	.0093	.0029	.0008	.0002	.0000
	2	.1787	.2852	.2428	.1540	.0803	.0358	.0138	.0046	.0013	.0003
	3	.0533	.1796	.2428	.2182	.1517	.0869	.0422	.0175	.0062	.0018
	4	.0112	.0798	.1714	.2182	.2023	.1419	.0909	.0467	.0203	.0074
	5	.0018	.0266	.0907	.1636	.2023	.1916	.1468	.0933	.0497	.0222
	6	.0002	.0069	.0374	.0955	.1574	.1916	.1844	.1451	.0949	.0518
	7	.0000	.0014	.0122	.0443	.0974	.1525	.1844	.1797	.1443	.0961
	8	.0000	.0002	.0032	.0166	.0487	.0981	.1489	.1797	.1771	.1442
	9	.0000	.0000	.0007	.0051	.0198	.0514	.0980	.1464	.1771	.1762
	10	.0000	.0000	.0001	.0013	.0066	.0220	.0528	.0976	.1449	.1762
	11	.0000	.0000	.0000	.0003	.0018	.0077	.0233	.0532	.0970	.1442
	12	.0000	.0000	.0000	.0000	.0004	.0022	.0083	.0237	.0529	.0961
	13	.0000	.0000	.0000	.0000	.0001	.0005	.0024	.0085	.0233	.0518
	14	.0000	.0000	.0000	.0000	.0000	.0001	.0006	.0024	.0082	.0222

TABLE 2   Probability Function of the Binomial Distribution (cont.)

n	x	π									
		.05	.10	.15	.20	.25	.30	.35	.40	.45	.50
	15	.0000	.0000	.0000	.0000	.0000	.0000	.0001	.0005	.0022	.0074
	16	.0000	.0000	.0000	.0000	.0000	.0000	.0000	.0001	.0005	.0018
	17	.0000	.0000	.0000	.0000	.0000	.0000	.0000	.0000	.0001	.0003
	18	.0000	.0000	.0000	.0000	.0000	.0000	.0000	.0000	.0000	.0000
	19	.0000	.0000	.0000	.0000	.0000	.0000	.0000	.0000	.0000	.0000
20	0	.3585	.1216	.0388	.0115	.0032	.0008	.0002	.0000	.0000	.0000
	1	.3774	.2702	.1368	.0576	.0211	.0068	.0020	.0005	.0001	.0000
	2	.1887	.2852	.2293	.1369	.0669	.0278	.0100	.0031	.0008	.0002
	3	.0596	.1901	.2428	.2054	.1339	.0716	.0323	.0123	.0040	.0011
	4	.0133	.0898	.1821	.2182	.1897	.1304	.0738	.0350	.0139	.0046
	5	.0022	.0319	.1028	.1746	.2023	.1789	.1272	.0746	.0365	.0148
	6	.0003	.0089	.0454	.1091	.1686	.1916	.1712	.1244	.0746	.0370
	7	.0000	.0020	.0160	.0545	.1124	.1643	.1844	.1659	.1221	.0739
	8	.0000	.0004	.0046	.0222	.0609	.1144	.1614	.1797	.1623	.1201
	9	.0000	.0001	.0011	.0074	.0271	.0654	.1158	.1597	.1771	.1602
	10	.0000	.0000	.0002	.0020	.0099	.0308	.0686	.1171	.1593	.1762
	11	.0000	.0000	.0000	.0005	.0030	.0120	.0336	.0710	.1185	.1602
	12	.0000	.0000	.0000	.0001	.0008	.0039	.0136	.0355	.0727	.1201
	13	.0000	.0000	.0000	.0000	.0002	.0010	.0045	.0146	.0366	.0739
	14	.0000	.0000	.0000	.0000	.0000	.0002	.0012	.0049	.0150	.0370
	15	.0000	.0000	.0000	.0000	.0000	.0000	.0003	.0013	.0049	.0148
	16	.0000	.0000	.0000	.0000	.0000	.0000	.0000	.0003	.0013	.0046
	17	.0000	.0000	.0000	.0000	.0000	.0000	.0000	.0000	.0002	.0011
	18	.0000	.0000	.0000	.0000	.0000	.0000	.0000	.0000	.0000	.0002
	19	.0000	.0000	.0000	.0000	.0000	.0000	.0000	.0000	.0000	.0000
	20	.0000	.0000	.0000	.0000	.0000	.0000	.0000	.0000	.0000	.0000

Reproduced with permission from National Bureau of Standards, *Tables of the Binomial Probability Distribution*, United States Department of Commerce (1950).

TABLE 3 Cumulative Binomial Probabilities

The table shows the probability of x or fewer successes in n independent trials each with probability of success π. For example, the probability of two or less successes in four independent trials, each with probability of success 0.35 is 0.874.

n	x	π									
		.05	.10	.15	.20	.25	.30	.35	.40	.45	.500
2	0	.902	.81	.722	.64	.562	.49	.422	.36	.302	.25
	1	.998	.99	.978	.96	.937	.91	.877	.84	.797	.75
	2	1.00	1.00	1.00	1.00	1.00	1.00	1.00	1.00	1.00	1.00
3	0	.857	.729	.614	.512	.422	.343	.275	.216	.166	.125
	1	.993	.972	.939	.896	.844	.784	.718	.648	.575	.500
	2	1.00	.999	.997	.992	.984	.973	.957	.936	.909	.875
	3	1.00	1.00	1.00	1.00	1.00	1.00	1.00	1.00	1.00	1.000
4	0	.815	.656	.522	.41	.316	.24	.179	.13	.092	.062
	1	.986	.948	.89	.819	.738	.652	.563	.475	.391	.312
	2	1.00	.996	.988	.973	.949	.916	.874	.821	.759	.687
	3	1.00	1.00	.999	.998	.996	.992	.985	.974	.959	.937
	4	1.00	1.00	1.00	1.00	1.00	1.00	1.00	1.00	1.00	1.000
5	0	.774	.59	.444	.328	.237	.168	.116	.078	.05	.031
	1	.977	.919	.835	.737	.633	.528	.428	.337	.256	.187
	2	.999	.991	.973	.942	.896	.837	.765	.683	.593	.500
	3	1.00	1.00	.998	.993	.984	.969	.946	.913	.869	.812
	4	1.00	1.00	1.00	1.00	.999	.998	.995	.99	.982	.969
	5	1.00	1.00	1.00	1.00	1.00	1.00	1.00	1.00	1.00	1.000
6	0	.735	.531	.377	.262	.178	.118	.075	.047	.028	.016
	1	.967	.886	.776	.655	.534	.42	.319	.233	.164	.109
	2	.998	.984	.953	.901	.831	.744	.647	.544	.442	.344
	3	1.00	.999	.994	.983	.962	.93	.883	.821	.745	.656
	4	1.00	1.00	1.00	.998	.995	.989	.978	.959	.931	.891
	5	1.00	1.00	1.00	1.00	1.00	.999	.998	.996	.992	.984
	6	1.00	1.00	1.00	1.00	1.00	1.00	1.00	1.00	1.00	1.000
7	0	.698	.478	.321	.21	.133	.082	.049	.028	.015	.008
	1	.956	.85	.717	.577	.445	.329	.234	.159	.102	.062
	2	.996	.974	.926	.852	.756	.647	.532	.42	.316	.227
	3	1.00	.997	.988	.967	.929	.874	.80	.71	.608	.500
	4	1.00	1.00	.999	.995	.987	.971	.944	.904	.847	.773
	5	1.00	1.00	1.00	1.00	.999	.996	.991	.981	.964	.937
	6	1.00	1.00	1.00	1.00	1.00	1.00	.999	.998	.996	.992
	7	1.00	1.00	1.00	1.00	1.00	1.00	1.00	1.00	1.00	1.000
8	0	.663	.43	.272	.168	.10	.058	.032	.017	.008	.004
	1	.943	.813	.657	.503	.367	.255	.169	.106	.063	.035
	2	.994	.962	.895	.797	.679	.552	.428	.315	.22	.145
	3	1.00	.995	.979	.944	.886	.806	.706	.594	.477	.363
	4	1.00	1.00	.997	.99	.973	.942	.894	.826	.74	.637
	5	1.00	1.00	1.00	.999	.996	.989	.975	.95	.912	.855
	6	1.00	1.00	1.00	1.00	1.00	.999	.996	.991	.982	.965
	7	1.00	1.00	1.00	1.00	1.00	1.00	1.00	.999	.998	.996
	8	1.00	1.00	1.00	1.00	1.00	1.00	1.00	1.00	1.00	1.000
9	0	.63	.387	.232	.134	.075	.04	.021	.01	.005	.002
	1	.929	.775	.599	.436	.30	.196	.121	.071	.039	.020
	2	.992	.947	.859	.738	.601	.463	.337	.232	.15	.090
	3	.999	.992	.966	.914	.834	.73	.609	.483	.361	.254
	4	1.00	.999	.994	.98	.951	.901	.828	.733	.621	.500

TABLE 3   Cumulative Binomial Probabilities (cont.)

n	x					π					
		.05	**.10**	**.15**	**.20**	**.25**	**.30**	**.35**	**.40**	**.45**	**.500**
	5	1.00	1.00	.999	.997	.99	.975	.946	.901	.834	.746
	6	1.00	1.00	1.00	1.00	.999	.996	.989	.975	.95	.910
	7	1.00	1.00	1.00	1.00	1.00	1.00	.999	.996	.991	.980
	8	1.00	1.00	1.00	1.00	1.00	1.00	1.00	1.00	.999	.998
	9	1.00	1.00	1.00	1.00	1.00	1.00	1.00	1.00	1.00	1.000
10	0	.599	.349	.197	.107	.056	.028	.013	.006	.003	.001
	1	.914	.736	.544	.376	.244	.149	.086	.046	.023	.011
	2	.988	.93	.82	.678	.526	.383	.262	.167	.10	.055
	3	.999	.987	.95	.879	.776	.65	.514	.382	.266	.172
	4	1.00	.998	.99	.967	.922	.85	.751	.633	.504	.377
	5	1.00	1.00	.999	.994	.98	.953	.905	.834	.738	.623
	6	1.00	1.00	1.00	.999	.996	.989	.974	.945	.898	.828
	7	1.00	1.00	1.00	1.00	1.00	.998	.995	.988	.973	.945
	8	1.00	1.00	1.00	1.00	1.00	1.00	.999	.998	.995	.989
	9	1.00	1.00	1.00	1.00	1.00	1.00	1.00	1.00	1.00	.999
	10	1.00	1.00	1.00	1.00	1.00	1.00	1.00	1.00	1.00	1.000
11	0	.569	.314	.167	.086	.042	.02	.009	.004	.001	.000
	1	.898	.697	.492	.322	.197	.113	.061	.03	.014	.006
	2	.985	.91	.779	.617	.455	.313	.20	.119	.065	.033
	3	.998	.981	.931	.839	.713	.57	.426	.296	.191	.113
	4	1.00	.997	.984	.95	.885	.79	.668	.533	.397	.274
	5	1.00	1.00	.997	.988	.966	.922	.851	.753	.633	.500
	6	1.00	1.00	1.00	.998	.992	.978	.95	.901	.826	.726
	7	1.00	1.00	1.00	1.00	.999	.996	.988	.971	.939	.887
	8	1.00	1.00	1.00	1.00	1.00	.999	.998	.994	.985	.967
	9	1.00	1.00	1.00	1.00	1.00	1.00	1.00	.999	.998	.994
	10	1.00	1.00	1.00	1.00	1.00	1.00	1.00	1.00	1.00	1.000
	11	1.00	1.00	1.00	1.00	1.00	1.00	1.00	1.00	1.00	1.000
12	0	.54	.282	.142	.069	.032	.014	.006	.002	.001	.000
	1	.882	.659	.443	.275	.158	.085	.042	.02	.008	.003
	2	.98	.889	.736	.558	.391	.253	.151	.083	.042	.019
	3	.998	.974	.908	.795	.649	.493	.347	.225	.134	.073
	4	1.00	.996	.976	.927	.842	.724	.583	.438	.304	.194
	5	1.00	.999	.995	.981	.946	.882	.787	.665	.527	.387
	6	1.00	1.00	.999	.996	.986	.961	.915	.842	.739	.613
	7	1.00	1.00	1.00	.999	.997	.991	.974	.943	.888	.806
	8	1.00	1.00	1.00	1.00	1.00	.998	.994	.985	.964	.927
	9	1.00	1.00	1.00	1.00	1.00	1.00	.999	.997	.992	.981
	10	1.00	1.00	1.00	1.00	1.00	1.00	1.00	1.00	.999	.997
	11	1.00	1.00	1.00	1.00	1.00	1.00	1.00	1.00	1.00	1.000
	12	1.00	1.00	1.00	1.00	1.00	1.00	1.00	1.00	1.00	1.000
13	0	.513	.254	.121	.055	.024	.01	.004	.001	.00	.000
	1	.865	.621	.398	.234	.127	.064	.03	.013	.005	.002
	2	.975	.866	.692	.502	.333	.202	.113	.058	.027	.011
	3	.997	.966	.882	.747	.584	.421	.278	.169	.093	.046
	4	1.00	.994	.966	.901	.794	.654	.501	.353	.228	.133
	5	1.00	.999	.992	.97	.92	.835	.716	.574	.427	.291
	6	1.00	1.00	.999	.993	.976	.938	.871	.771	.644	.50
	7	1.00	1.00	1.00	.999	.994	.982	.954	.902	.821	.709
	8	1.00	1.00	1.00	1.00	.999	.996	.987	.968	.93	.867
	9	1.00	1.00	1.00	1.00	1.00	.999	.997	.992	.98	.954
	10	1.00	1.00	1.00	1.00	1.00	1.00	1.00	.999	.996	.989

TABLE 3   Cumulative Binomial Probabilities (cont.)

n	x	.05	.10	.15	.20	.25	.30	.35	.40	.45	.500
						π					
	11	1.00	1.00	1.00	1.00	1.00	1.00	1.00	1.00	.999	.998
	12	1.00	1.00	1.00	1.00	1.00	1.00	1.00	1.00	1.00	1.000
14	0	.488	.229	.103	.044	.018	.007	.002	.001	.00	.000
	1	.847	.585	.357	.198	.101	.047	.021	.008	.003	.001
	2	.97	.842	.648	.448	.281	.161	.084	.04	.017	.006
	3	.996	.956	.853	.698	.521	.355	.22	.124	.063	.029
	4	1.00	.991	.953	.87	.742	.584	.423	.279	.167	.090
	5	1.00	.999	.988	.956	.888	.781	.641	.486	.337	.212
	6	1.00	1.00	.998	.988	.962	.907	.816	.692	.546	.395
	7	1.00	1.00	1.00	.998	.99	.969	.925	.85	.741	.605
	8	1.00	1.00	1.00	1.00	.998	.992	.976	.942	.881	.788
	9	1.00	1.00	1.00	1.00	1.00	.998	.994	.982	.957	.910
	10	1.00	1.00	1.00	1.00	1.00	1.00	.999	.996	.989	.971
	11	1.00	1.00	1.00	1.00	1.00	1.00	1.00	.999	.998	.994
	12	1.00	1.00	1.00	1.00	1.00	1.00	1.00	1.00	1.00	.999
	13	1.00	1.00	1.00	1.00	1.00	1.00	1.00	1.00	1.00	1.000
15	0	.463	.206	.087	.035	.013	.005	.002	.00	.00	.000
	1	.829	.549	.319	.167	.08	.035	.014	.005	.002	.000
	2	.964	.816	.604	.398	.236	.127	.062	.027	.011	.004
	3	.995	.944	.823	.648	.461	.297	.173	.091	.042	.018
	4	.999	.987	.938	.836	.686	.515	.352	.217	.12	.059
	5	1.00	.998	.983	.939	.852	.722	.564	.403	.261	.151
	6	1.00	1.00	.996	.982	.943	.869	.755	.61	.452	.304
	7	1.00	1.00	.999	.996	.983	.95	.887	.787	.654	.500
	8	1.00	1.00	1.00	.999	.996	.985	.958	.905	.818	.696
	9	1.00	1.00	1.00	1.00	.999	.996	.988	.966	.923	.849
	10	1.00	1.00	1.00	1.00	1.00	.999	.997	.991	.975	.941
	11	1.00	1.00	1.00	1.00	1.00	1.00	1.00	.998	.994	.982
	12	1.00	1.00	1.00	1.00	1.00	1.00	1.00	1.00	.999	.996
	13	1.00	1.00	1.00	1.00	1.00	1.00	1.00	1.00	1.00	1.000
16	0	.44	.185	.074	.028	.01	.003	.001	.00	.00	.000
	1	.811	.515	.284	.141	.063	.026	.01	.003	.001	.000
	2	.957	.789	.561	.352	.197	.099	.045	.018	.007	.002
	3	.993	.932	.79	.598	.405	.246	.134	.065	.028	.011
	4	.999	.983	.921	.798	.63	.45	.289	.167	.085	.038
	5	1.00	.997	.976	.918	.81	.66	.49	.329	.198	.105
	6	1.00	.999	.994	.973	.92	.825	.688	.527	.366	.227
	7	1.00	1.00	.999	.993	.973	.926	.841	.716	.563	.402
	8	1.00	1.00	1.00	.999	.993	.974	.933	.858	.744	.598
	9	1.00	1.00	1.00	1.00	.998	.993	.977	.942	.876	.773
	10	1.00	1.00	1.00	1.00	1.00	.998	.994	.981	.951	.895
	11	1.00	1.00	1.00	1.00	1.00	1.00	.999	.995	.985	.962
	12	1.00	1.00	1.00	1.00	1.00	1.00	1.00	.999	.997	.989
	13	1.00	1.00	1.00	1.00	1.00	1.00	1.00	1.00	.999	.998
	14	1.00	1.00	1.00	1.00	1.00	1.00	1.00	1.00	1.00	1.000
17	0	.418	.167	.063	.023	.008	.002	.001	.00	.00	.000
	1	.792	.482	.252	.118	.05	.019	.007	.002	.001	.000
	2	.95	.762	.52	.31	.164	.077	.033	.012	.004	.001
	3	.991	.917	.756	.549	.353	.202	.103	.046	.018	.006
	4	.999	.978	.901	.758	.574	.389	.235	.126	.06	.025
	5	1.00	.995	.968	.894	.765	.597	.42	.264	.147	.072
	6	1.00	.999	.992	.962	.893	.775	.619	.448	.29	.166

TABLE 3   Cumulative Binomial Probabilities (cont.)

n	x	.05	.10	.15	.20	.25	.30	.35	.40	.45	.500
						π					
	7	1.00	1.00	.998	.989	.96	.895	.787	.641	.474	.315
	8	1.00	1.00	1.00	.997	.988	.96	.901	.801	.663	.500
	9	1.00	1.00	1.00	1.00	.997	.987	.962	.908	.817	.685
	10	1.00	1.00	1.00	1.00	.999	.997	.988	.965	.917	.834
	11	1.00	1.00	1.00	1.00	1.00	.999	.997	.989	.97	.928
	12	1.00	1.00	1.00	1.00	1.00	1.00	.999	.997	.991	.975
	13	1.00	1.00	1.00	1.00	1.00	1.00	1.00	1.00	.998	.994
	14	1.00	1.00	1.00	1.00	1.00	1.00	1.00	1.00	1.00	.999
	15	1.00	1.00	1.00	1.00	1.00	1.00	1.00	1.00	1.00	1.00
18	0	.397	.15	.054	.018	.006	.002	.00	.00	.00	.000
	1	.774	.45	.224	.099	.039	.014	.005	.001	.00	.000
	2	.942	.734	.48	.271	.135	.06	.024	.008	.003	.001
	3	.989	.902	.72	.501	.306	.165	.078	.033	.012	.004
	4	.998	.972	.879	.716	.519	.333	.189	.094	.041	.015
	5	1.00	.994	.958	.867	.717	.534	.355	.209	.108	.048
	6	1.00	.999	.988	.949	.861	.722	.549	.374	.226	.119
	7	1.00	1.00	.997	.984	.943	.859	.728	.563	.391	.240
	8	1.00	1.00	.999	.996	.981	.94	.861	.737	.578	.407
	9	1.00	1.00	1.00	.999	.995	.979	.94	.865	.747	.593
	10	1.00	1.00	1.00	1.00	.999	.994	.979	.942	.872	.760
	11	1.00	1.00	1.00	1.00	1.00	.999	.994	.98	.946	.881
	12	1.00	1.00	1.00	1.00	1.00	1.00	.999	.994	.982	.952
	13	1.00	1.00	1.00	1.00	1.00	1.00	1.00	.999	.995	.985
	14	1.00	1.00	1.00	1.00	1.00	1.00	1.00	1.00	.999	.996
	15	1.00	1.00	1.00	1.00	1.00	1.00	1.00	1.00	1.00	.999
	16	1.00	1.00	1.00	1.00	1.00	1.00	1.00	1.00	1.00	1.000
19	0	.377	.135	.046	.014	.004	.001	.00	.00	.00	.000
	1	.755	.42	.198	.083	.031	.01	.003	.001	.00	.000
	2	.933	.705	.441	.237	.111	.046	.017	.005	.002	.000
	3	.987	.885	.684	.455	.263	.133	.059	.023	.008	.002
	4	.998	.965	.856	.673	.465	.282	.15	.07	.028	.010
	5	1.00	.991	.946	.837	.668	.474	.297	.163	.078	.032
	6	1.00	.998	.984	.932	.825	.666	.481	.308	.173	.084
	7	1.00	1.00	.996	.977	.923	.818	.666	.488	.317	.180
	8	1.00	1.00	.999	.993	.971	.916	.815	.667	.494	.324
	9	1.00	1.00	1.00	.998	.991	.967	.913	.814	.671	.500
	10	1.00	1.00	1.00	1.00	.998	.989	.965	.912	.816	.676
	11	1.00	1.00	1.00	1.00	1.00	.997	.989	.965	.913	.820
	12	1.00	1.00	1.00	1.00	1.00	.999	.997	.988	.966	.916
	13	1.00	1.00	1.00	1.00	1.00	1.00	.999	.997	.989	.968
	14	1.00	1.00	1.00	1.00	1.00	1.00	1.00	.999	.997	.990
	15	1.00	1.00	1.00	1.00	1.00	1.00	1.00	1.00	.999	.998
	16	1.00	1.00	1.00	1.00	1.00	1.00	1.00	1.00	1.00	1.000
20	0	.358	.122	.039	.012	.003	.001	.00	.00	.00	.000
	1	.736	.392	.176	.069	.024	.008	.002	.001	.00	.000
	2	.925	.677	.405	.206	.091	.035	.012	.004	.001	.000
	3	.984	.867	.648	.411	.225	.107	.044	.016	.005	.001
	4	.997	.957	.83	.63	.415	.238	.118	.051	.019	.006
	5	1.00	.989	.933	.804	.617	.416	.245	.126	.055	.021
	6	1.00	.998	.978	.913	.786	.608	.417	.25	.13	.058
	7	1.00	1.00	.994	.968	.898	.772	.601	.416	.252	.132
	8	1.00	1.00	.999	.99	.959	.887	.762	.596	.414	.252
	9	1.00	1.00	1.00	.997	.986	.952	.878	.755	.591	.412

TABLE 3 Cumulative Binomial Probabilities (cont.)

n	x	π									
		.05	.10	.15	.20	.25	.30	.35	.40	.45	.500
	10	1.00	1.00	1.00	.999	.996	.983	.947	.872	.751	.588
	11	1.00	1.00	1.00	1.00	.999	.995	.98	.943	.869	.748
	12	1.00	1.00	1.00	1.00	1.00	.999	.994	.979	.942	.868
	13	1.00	1.00	1.00	1.00	1.00	1.00	.998	.994	.979	.942
	14	1.00	1.00	1.00	1.00	1.00	1.00	1.00	.998	.994	.979
	15	1.00	1.00	1.00	1.00	1.00	1.00	1.00	1.00	.998	.994
	16	1.00	1.00	1.00	1.00	1.00	1.00	1.00	1.00	1.00	.999
	17	1.00	1.00	1.00	1.00	1.00	1.00	1.00	1.00	1.00	1.000

TABLE 4   Values of $e^{-\lambda}$

λ	$e^{-\lambda}$	λ	$e^{-\lambda}$	λ	$e^{-\lambda}$	λ	$e^{-\lambda}$
0.00	1.000000	2.60	.074274	5.10	.006097	7.60	.000501
0.10	.904837	2.70	.067206	5.20	.005517	7.70	.000453
0.20	.818731	2.80	.060810	5.30	.004992	7.80	.000410
0.30	.740818	2.90	.055023	5.40	.004517	7.90	.000371
0.40	.670320	3.00	.049787	5.50	.004087	8.00	.000336
0.50	.606531	3.10	.045049	5.60	.003698	8.10	.000304
0.60	.548812	3.20	.040762	5.70	.003346	8.20	.000275
0.70	.496585	3.30	.036883	5.80	.003028	8.30	.000249
0.80	.449329	3.40	.033373	5.90	.002739	8.40	.000225
0.90	.406570	3.50	.030197	6.00	.002479	8.50	.000204
1.00	.367879	3.60	.027324	6.10	.002243	8.60	.000184
1.10	.332871	3.70	.024724	6.20	.002029	8.70	.000167
1.20	.301194	3.80	.022371	6.30	.001836	8.80	.000151
1.30	.272532	3.90	.020242	6.40	.001661	8.90	.000136
1.40	.246597	4.00	.018316	6.50	.001503	9.00	.000123
1.50	.223130	4.10	.016573	6.60	.001360	9.10	.000112
1.60	.201897	4.20	.014996	6.70	.001231	9.20	.000101
1.70	.182684	4.30	.013569	6.80	.001114	9.30	.000091
1.80	.165299	4.40	.012277	6.90	.001008	9.40	.000083
1.90	.149569	4.50	.011109	7.00	.000912	9.50	.000075
2.00	.135335	4.60	.010052	7.10	.000825	9.60	.000068
2.10	.122456	4.70	.009095	7.20	.000747	9.70	.000061
2.20	.110803	4.80	.008230	7.30	.000676	9.80	.000056
2.30	.100259	4.90	.007447	7.40	.000611	9.90	.000050
2.40	.090718	5.00	.006738	7.50	.000553	10.00	.000045
2.50	.082085						

TABLE 5   Individual Poisson Probabilities

MEAN ARRIVAL RATE λ

	0.1	0.2	0.3	0.4	0.5	0.6	0.7	0.8	0.9	1.0
0	.9048	.8187	.7408	.6703	.6065	.5488	.4966	.4493	.4066	.3679
1	.0905	.1637	.2222	.2681	.3033	.3293	.3476	.3595	.3659	.3679
2	.0045	.0164	.0333	.0536	.0758	.0988	.1217	.1438	.1647	.1839
3	.0002	.0011	.0033	.0072	.0126	.0198	.0284	.0383	.0494	.0613
4	.0	.0001	.0003	.0007	.0016	.0030	.0050	.0077	.0111	.0153
5	.0	.0	.0	.0001	.0002	.0004	.0007	.0012	.0020	.0031
6	.0	.0	.0	.0	.0	.0	.0001	.0002	.0003	.0005
7	.0	.0	.0	.0	.0	.0	.0	.0	.0	.0001

MEAN ARRIVAL RATE λ

	1.1	1.2	1.3	1.4	1.5	1.6	1.7	1.8	1.9	2.0
0	.3329	.3012	.2725	.2466	.2231	.2019	.1827	.1653	.1496	.1353
1	.3662	.3614	.3543	.3452	.3347	.3230	.3106	.2975	.2842	.2707
2	.2014	.2169	.2303	.2417	.2510	.2584	.2640	.2678	.2700	.2707
3	.0738	.0867	.0998	.1128	.1255	.1378	.1496	.1607	.1710	.1804
4	.0203	.0260	.0324	.0395	.0471	.0551	.0636	.0723	.0812	.0902
5	.0045	.0062	.0084	.0111	.0141	.0176	.0216	.0260	.0309	.0361
6	.0008	.0012	.0018	.0026	.0035	.0047	.0061	.0078	.0098	.0120
7	.0001	.0002	.0003	.0005	.0008	.0011	.0015	.0020	.0027	.0034
8	.0	.0	.0001	.0001	.0001	.0002	.0003	.0005	.0006	.0009
9	.0	.0	.0	.0	.0	.0	.0001	.0001	.0001	.0002

MEAN ARRIVAL RATE λ

	2.1	2.2	2.3	2.4	2.5	2.6	2.7	2.8	2.9	3.0
0	.1225	.1108	.1003	.0907	.0821	.0743	.0672	.0608	.0550	.0498
1	.2572	.2438	.2306	.2177	.2052	.1931	.1815	.1703	.1596	.1494
2	.2700	.2681	.2652	.2613	.2565	.2510	.2450	.2384	.2314	.2240
3	.1890	.1966	.2033	.2090	.2138	.2176	.2205	.2225	.2237	.2240
4	.0992	.1082	.1169	.1254	.1336	.1414	.1488	.1557	.1622	.1680
5	.0417	.0476	.0538	.0602	.0668	.0735	.0804	.0872	.0940	.1008
6	.0146	.0174	.0206	.0241	.0278	.0319	.0362	.0407	.0455	.0504
7	.0044	.0055	.0068	.0083	.0099	.0118	.0139	.0163	.0188	.0216
8	.0011	.0015	.0019	.0025	.0031	.0038	.0047	.0057	.0068	.0081
9	.0003	.0004	.0005	.0007	.0009	.0011	.0014	.0018	.0022	.0027
10	.0001	.0001	.0001	.0002	.0002	.0003	.0004	.0005	.0006	.0008
11	.0	.0	.0	.0	.0	.0001	.0001	.0001	.0002	.0002
12	.0	.0	.0	.0	.0	.0	.0	.0	.0	.0001

MEAN ARRIVAL RATE λ

	3.1	3.2	3.3	3.4	3.5	3.6	3.7	3.8	3.9	4.0
0	.0450	.0408	.0369	.0334	.0302	.0273	.0247	.0224	.0202	.0183
1	.1397	.1304	.1217	.1135	.1057	.0984	.0915	.0850	.0789	.0733
2	.2165	.2087	.2008	.1929	.1850	.1771	.1692	.1615	.1539	.1465
3	.2237	.2226	.2209	.2186	.2158	.2125	.2087	.2046	.2001	.1954
4	.1733	.1781	.1823	.1858	.1888	.1912	.1931	.1944	.1951	.1954
5	.1075	.1140	.1203	.1264	.1322	.1377	.1429	.1477	.1522	.1563
6	.0555	.0608	.0662	.0716	.0771	.0826	.0881	.0936	.0989	.1042
7	.0246	.0278	.0312	.0348	.0385	.0425	.0466	.0508	.0551	.0595
8	.0095	.0111	.0129	.0148	.0169	.0191	.0215	.0241	.0269	.0298
9	.0033	.0040	.0047	.0056	.0066	.0076	.0089	.0102	.0116	.0132

TABLE 5   Individual Poisson Probabilities (cont.)

	MEAN ARRIVAL RATE λ									
	3.1	3.2	3.3	3.4	3.5	3.6	3.7	3.8	3.9	4.0
10	.0010	.0013	.0016	.0019	.0023	.0028	.0033	.0039	.0045	.0053
11	.0003	.0004	.0005	.0006	.0007	.0009	.0011	.0013	.0016	.0019
12	.0001	.0001	.0001	.0002	.0002	.0003	.0003	.0004	.0005	.0006
13	.0	.0	.0	.0	.0001	.0001	.0001	.0001	.0002	.0002
14	.0	.0	.0	.0	.0	.0	.0	.0	.0	.0001

	MEAN ARRIVAL RATE λ									
	4.1	4.2	4.3	4.4	4.5	4.6	4.7	4.8	4.9	5.0
0	.0166	.0150	.0136	.0123	.0111	.0101	.0091	.0082	.0074	.0067
1	.0679	.0630	.0583	.0540	.0500	.0462	.0427	.0395	.0365	.0337
2	.1393	.1323	.1254	.1188	.1125	.1063	.1005	.0948	.0894	.0842
3	.1904	.1852	.1798	.1743	.1687	.1631	.1574	.1517	.1460	.1404
4	.1951	.1944	.1933	.1917	.1898	.1875	.1849	.1820	.1789	.1755
5	.1600	.1633	.1662	.1687	.1708	.1725	.1738	.1747	.1753	.1755
6	.1093	.1143	.1191	.1237	.1281	.1323	.1362	.1398	.1432	.1462
7	.0640	.0686	.0732	.0778	.0824	.0869	.0914	.0959	.1002	.1044
8	.0328	.0360	.0393	.0428	.0463	.0500	.0537	.0575	.0614	.0653
9	.0150	.0168	.0188	.0209	.0232	.0255	.0281	.0307	.0334	.0363
10	.0061	.0071	.0081	.0092	.0104	.0118	.0132	.0147	.0164	.0181
11	.0023	.0027	.0032	.0037	.0043	.0049	.0056	.0064	.0073	.0082
12	.0008	.0009	.0011	.0013	.0016	.0019	.0022	.0026	.0030	.0034
13	.0002	.0003	.0004	.0005	.0006	.0007	.0008	.0009	.0011	.0013
14	.0001	.0001	.0001	.0001	.0002	.0002	.0003	.0003	.0004	.0005

	MEAN ARRIVAL RATE λ									
	5.1	5.2	5.3	5.4	5.5	5.6	5.7	5.8	5.9	6.0
0	.0061	.0055	.0050	.0045	.0041	.0037	.0033	.0030	.0027	.0025
1	.0311	.0287	.0265	.0244	.0225	.0207	.0191	.0176	.0162	.0149
2	.0793	.0746	.0701	.0659	.0618	.0580	.0544	.0509	.0477	.0446
3	.1348	.1293	.1239	.1185	.1133	.1082	.1033	.0985	.0938	.0892
4	.1719	.1681	.1641	.1600	.1558	.1515	.1472	.1428	.1383	.1339
5	.1753	.1748	.1740	.1728	.1714	.1697	.1678	.1656	.1632	.1606
6	.1490	.1515	.1537	.1555	.1571	.1584	.1594	.1601	.1605	.1606
7	.1086	.1125	.1163	.1200	.1234	.1267	.1298	.1326	.1353	.1377
8	.0692	.0731	.0771	.0810	.0849	.0887	.0925	.0962	.0998	.1033
9	.0392	.0423	.0454	.0486	.0519	.0552	.0586	.0620	.0654	.0688
10	.0200	.0220	.0241	.0262	.0285	.0309	.0334	.0359	.0386	.0413
11	.0093	.0104	.0116	.0129	.0143	.0157	.0173	.0190	.0207	.0225
12	.0039	.0045	.0051	.0058	.0065	.0073	.0082	.0092	.0102	.0113
13	.0015	.0018	.0021	.0024	.0028	.0032	.0036	.0041	.0046	.0052
14	.0006	.0007	.0008	.0009	.0011	.0013	.0015	.0017	.0019	.0022

	MEAN ARRIVAL RATE λ									
	6.1	6.2	6.3	6.4	6.5	6.6	6.7	6.8	6.9	7.0
0	.0022	.0020	.0018	.0017	.0015	.0014	.0012	.0011	.0010	.0009
1	.0137	.0126	.0116	.0106	.0098	.0090	.0082	.0076	.0070	.0064
2	.0417	.0390	.0364	.0340	.0318	.0296	.0276	.0258	.0240	.0223
3	.0848	.0806	.0765	.0726	.0688	.0652	.0617	.0584	.0552	.0521
4	.1294	.1249	.1205	.1162	.1118	.1076	.1034	.0992	.0952	.0912
5	.1579	.1549	.1519	.1487	.1454	.1420	.1385	.1349	.1314	.1277

TABLE 5   Individual Poisson Probabilities (cont.)

	MEAN ARRIVAL RATE λ									
	6.1	**6.2**	**6.3**	**6.4**	**6.5**	**6.6**	**6.7**	**6.8**	**6.9**	**7.0**
6	.1605	.1601	.1595	.1586	.1575	.1562	.1546	.1529	.1511	.1490
7	.1399	.1418	.1435	.1450	.1462	.1472	.1480	.1486	.1489	.1490
8	.1066	.1099	.1130	.1160	.1188	.1215	.1240	.1263	.1284	.1304
9	.0723	.0757	.0791	.0825	.0858	.0891	.0923	.0954	.0985	.1014
10	.0441	.0469	.0498	.0528	.0558	.0588	.0618	.0649	.0679	.0710
11	.0244	.0265	.0285	.0307	.0330	.0353	.0377	.0401	.0426	.0452
12	.0124	.0137	.0150	.0164	.0179	.0194	.0210	.0227	.0245	.0263
13	.0058	.0065	.0073	.0081	.0089	.0099	.0108	.0119	.0130	.0142
14	.0025	.0029	.0033	.0037	.0041	.0046	.0052	.0058	.0064	.0071

	MEAN ARRIVAL RATE λ									
	7.1	**7.2**	**7.3**	**7.4**	**7.5**	**7.6**	**7.7**	**7.8**	**7.9**	**8.0**
0	.0008	.0007	.0007	.0006	.0006	.0005	.0005	.0004	.0004	.0003
1	.0059	.0054	.0049	.0045	.0041	.0038	.0035	.0032	.0029	.0027
2	.0208	.0194	.0180	.0167	.0156	.0145	.0134	.0125	.0116	.0107
3	.0492	.0464	.0438	.0413	.0389	.0366	.0345	.0324	.0305	.0286
4	.0874	.0836	.0799	.0764	.0729	.0696	.0663	.0632	.0602	.0573
5	.1241	.1204	.1167	.1130	.1094	.1057	.1021	.0986	.0951	.0916
6	.1468	.1445	.1420	.1394	.1367	.1339	.1311	.1282	.1252	.1221
7	.1489	.1486	.1481	.1474	.1465	.1454	.1442	.1428	.1413	.1396
8	.1321	.1337	.1351	.1363	.1373	.1381	.1388	.1392	.1395	.1396
9	.1042	.1070	.1096	.1121	.1144	.1167	.1187	.1207	.1224	.1241
10	.0740	.0770	.08	.0829	.0858	.0887	.0914	.0941	.0967	.0993
11	.0478	.0504	.0531	.0558	.0585	.0613	.0640	.0667	.0695	.0722
12	.0283	.0303	.0323	.0344	.0366	.0388	.0411	.0434	.0457	.0481
13	.0154	.0168	.0181	.0196	.0211	.0227	.0243	.0260	.0278	.0296
14	.0078	.0086	.0095	.0104	.0113	.0123	.0134	.0145	.0157	.0169
15	.0037	.0041	.0046	.0051	.0057	.0062	.0069	.0075	.0083	.0090
16	.0016	.0019	.0021	.0024	.0026	.0030	.0033	.0037	.0041	.0045
17	.0007	.0008	.0009	.0010	.0012	.0013	.0015	.0017	.0019	.0021
18	.0003	.0003	.0004	.0004	.0005	.0006	.0006	.0007	.0008	.0009
19	.0001	.0001	.0001	.0002	.0002	.0002	.0003	.0003	.0003	.0004

	MEAN ARRIVAL RATE λ									
	8.1	**8.2**	**8.3**	**8.4**	**8.5**	**8.6**	**8.7**	**8.8**	**8.9**	**9.0**
0	.0003	.0003	.0002	.0002	.0002	.0002	.0002	.0002	.0001	.0001
1	.0025	.0023	.0021	.0019	.0017	.0016	.0014	.0013	.0012	.0011
2	.01	.0092	.0086	.0079	.0074	.0068	.0063	.0058	.0054	.0050
3	.0269	.0252	.0237	.0222	.0208	.0195	.0183	.0171	.0160	.0150
4	.0544	.0517	.0491	.0466	.0443	.0420	.0398	.0377	.0357	.0337
5	.0882	.0849	.0816	.0784	.0752	.0722	.0692	.0663	.0635	.0607
6	.1191	.1160	.1128	.1097	.1066	.1034	.1003	.0972	.0941	.0911
7	.1378	.1358	.1338	.1317	.1294	.1271	.1247	.1222	.1197	.1171
8	.1395	.1392	.1388	.1382	.1375	.1366	.1356	.1344	.1332	.1318
9	.1256	.1269	.1280	.1290	.1299	.1306	.1311	.1315	.1317	.1318
10	.1017	.1040	.1063	.1084	.1104	.1123	.1140	.1157	.1172	.1186
11	.0749	.0776	.0802	.0828	.0853	.0878	.0902	.0925	.0948	.0970
12	.0505	.0530	.0555	.0579	.0604	.0629	.0654	.0679	.0703	.0728
13	.0315	.0334	.0354	.0374	.0395	.0416	.0438	.0459	.0481	.0504
14	.0182	.0196	.0210	.0225	.0240	.0256	.0272	.0289	.0306	.0324
15	.0098	.0107	.0116	.0126	.0136	.0147	.0158	.0169	.0182	.0194
16	.0050	.0055	.0060	.0066	.0072	.0079	.0086	.0093	.0101	.0109

TABLE 5 Individual Poisson Probabilities (cont.)

	MEAN ARRIVAL RATE λ									
	8.1	8.2	8.3	8.4	8.5	8.6	8.7	8.8	8.9	9.0
17	.0024	.0026	.0029	.0033	.0036	.0040	.0044	.0048	.0053	.0058
18	.0011	.0012	.0014	.0015	.0017	.0019	.0021	.0024	.0026	.0029
19	.0005	.0005	.0006	.0007	.0008	.0009	.0010	.0011	.0012	.0014

	MEAN ARRIVAL RATE λ									
	9.1	9.2	9.3	9.4	9.5	9.6	9.7	9.8	9.9	10.0
0	.0001	.0001	.0001	.0001	.0001	.0001	.0001	.0001	.0001	.0000
1	.0010	.0009	.0009	.0008	.0007	.0007	.0006	.0005	.0005	.0005
2	.0046	.0043	.0040	.0037	.0034	.0031	.0029	.0027	.0025	.0023
3	.0140	.0131	.0123	.0115	.0107	.01	.0093	.0087	.0081	.0076
4	.0319	.0302	.0285	.0269	.0254	.0240	.0226	.0213	.0201	.0189
5	.0581	.0555	.0530	.0506	.0483	.0460	.0439	.0418	.0398	.0378
6	.0881	.0851	.0822	.0793	.0764	.0736	.0709	.0682	.0656	.0631
7	.1145	.1118	.1091	.1064	.1037	.1010	.0982	.0955	.0928	.0901
8	.1302	.1286	.1269	.1251	.1232	.1212	.1191	.1170	.1148	.1126
9	.1317	.1315	.1311	.1306	.13	.1293	.1284	.1274	.1263	.1251
10	.1198	.1210	.1219	.1228	.1235	.1241	.1245	.1249	.1250	.1251
11	.0991	.1012	.1031	.1049	.1067	.1083	.1098	.1112	.1125	.1137
12	.0752	.0776	.0799	.0822	.0844	.0866	.0888	.0908	.0928	.0948
13	.0526	.0549	.0572	.0594	.0617	.0640	.0662	.0685	.0707	.0729
14	.0342	.0361	.0380	.0399	.0419	.0439	.0459	.0479	.05	.0521
15	.0208	.0221	.0235	.0250	.0265	.0281	.0297	.0313	.0330	.0347
16	.0118	.0127	.0137	.0147	.0157	.0168	.0180	.0192	.0204	.0217
17	.0063	.0069	.0075	.0081	.0088	.0095	.0103	.0111	.0119	.0128
18	.0032	.0035	.0039	.0042	.0046	.0051	.0055	.0060	.0065	.0071
19	.0015	.0017	.0019	.0021	.0023	.0026	.0028	.0031	.0034	.0037

	MEAN ARRIVAL RATE λ									
	10.1	10.2	10.3	10.4	10.5	10.6	10.7	10.8	10.9	11.0
0	.00	.00	.00	.00	.00	.00	.00	.00	.00	.0000
1	.0004	.0004	.0003	.0003	.0003	.0003	.0002	.0002	.0002	.0002
2	.0021	.0019	.0018	.0016	.0015	.0014	.0013	.0012	.0011	.0010
3	.0071	.0066	.0061	.0057	.0053	.0049	.0046	.0043	.0040	.0037
4	.0178	.0168	.0158	.0148	.0139	.0131	.0123	.0116	.0109	.0102
5	.0360	.0342	.0325	.0309	.0293	.0278	.0264	.0250	.0237	.0224
6	.0606	.0581	.0558	.0535	.0513	.0491	.0470	.0450	.0430	.0411
7	.0874	.0847	.0821	.0795	.0769	.0743	.0718	.0694	.0669	.0646
8	.1103	.1080	.1057	.1033	.1009	.0985	.0961	.0936	.0912	.0888
9	.1238	.1224	.1209	.1194	.1177	.1160	.1142	.1124	.1105	.1085
10	.1250	.1249	.1246	.1241	.1236	.1230	.1222	.1214	.1204	.1194
11	.1148	.1158	.1166	.1174	.1180	.1185	.1189	.1192	.1193	.1194
12	.0966	.0984	.1001	.1017	.1032	.1047	.1060	.1072	.1084	.1094
13	.0751	.0772	.0793	.0814	.0834	.0853	.0872	.0891	.0909	.0926
14	.0542	.0563	.0584	.0604	.0625	.0646	.0667	.0687	.0708	.0728
15	.0365	.0383	.0401	.0419	.0438	.0457	.0476	.0495	.0514	.0534
16	.0230	.0244	.0258	.0272	.0287	.0303	.0318	.0334	.0350	.0367
17	.0137	.0146	.0156	.0167	.0177	.0189	.0200	.0212	.0225	.0237
18	.0077	.0083	.0089	.0096	.004	.0111	.0119	.0127	.0136	.0145
19	.0041	.0045	.0048	.0053	.0057	.0062	.0067	.0072	.0078	.0084
20	.0021	.0023	.0025	.0027	.0030	.0033	.0036	.0039	.0043	.0046

TABLE 5 Individual Poisson Probabilities (cont.)

				MEAN ARRIVAL RATE λ						
	11.1	**11.2**	**11.3**	**11.4**	**11.5**	**11.6**	**11.7**	**11.8**	**11.9**	**12.0**
0	.0000	.0000	.0000	.0000	.0000	.0000	.0000	.0000	.0000	.0000
1	.0002	.0002	.0001	.0001	.0001	.0001	.0001	.0001	.0001	.0001
2	.0009	.0009	.0009	.0008	.0007	.0007	.0006	.0006	.0005	.0004
3	.0034	.0032	.0030	.0028	.0026	.0024	.0022	.0021	.0019	.0018
4	.0096	.0090	.0084	.0079	.0074	.0069	.0065	.0061	.0057	.0053
5	.0212	.0201	.0190	.0180	.0170	.0160	.0152	.0143	.0135	.0127
6	.0393	.0375	.0358	.0341	.0325	.0310	.0295	.0281	.0268	.0255
7	.0623	.0600	.0578	.0556	.0535	.0514	.0494	.0474	.0455	.0437
8	.0864	.0840	.0816	.0792	.0769	.0745	.0722	.0700	.0677	.0655
9	.1065	.1045	.1024	.1003	.0982	.0961	.0939	.0917	.0895	.0874
10	.1182	.1170	.1157	.1144	.1129	.1114	.1099	.1082	.1066	.1048
11	.1193	.1192	.1189	.1185	.1181	.1175	.1169	.1161	.1153	.1144
12	.1104	.1112	.1120	.1126	.1131	.1136	.1139	.1142	.1143	.1144
13	.0942	.0958	.0973	.0987	.1001	.1014	.1025	.1036	.1046	.1056
14	.0747	.0767	.0786	.0804	.0822	.0840	.0857	.0874	.0889	.0905
15	.0553	.0572	.0592	.0611	.0630	.0649	.0668	.0687	.0706	.0724
16	.0384	.0401	.0418	.0435	.0453	.0471	.0489	.0507	.0525	.0543
17	.0250	.0264	.0278	.0292	.0306	.0321	.0336	.0352	.0367	.0383
18	.0154	.0164	.0174	.0185	.0196	.0207	.0219	.0231	.0243	.0255
19	.0090	.0097	.0104	.0111	.0119	.0126	.0135	.0143	.0152	.0161
20	.0050	.0054	.0059	.0063	.0068	.0073	.0079	.0084	.0091	.0097

				MEAN ARRIVAL RATE λ						
	12.1	**12.2**	**12.3**	**12.4**	**12.5**	**12.6**	**12.7**	**12.8**	**12.9**	**13.0**
4	.0050	.0046	.0043	.0041	.0038	.0035	.0033	.0031	.0029	.0027
5	.0120	.0113	.0107	.0101	.0095	.0089	.0084	.0079	.0074	.0070
6	.0242	.0230	.0219	.0208	.0197	.0187	.0178	.0169	.0160	.0152
7	.0419	.0402	.0385	.0368	.0353	.0337	.0323	.0308	.0295	.0281
8	.0634	.0612	.0591	.0571	.0551	.0531	.0512	.0493	.0475	.0457
9	.0852	.0830	.0808	.0787	.0765	.0744	.0723	.0702	.0681	.0661
10	.1031	.1013	.0994	.0975	.0956	.0937	.0918	.0898	.0878	.0859
11	.1134	.1123	.1112	.1100	.1087	.1074	.1060	.1045	.1030	.1015
12	.1143	.1142	.1139	.1136	.1132	.1127	.1121	.1115	.1107	.1099
13	.1064	.1072	.1078	.1084	.1089	.1093	.1096	.1098	.1099	.1099
14	.0920	.0934	.0947	.0960	.0972	.0983	.0994	.1004	.1013	.1021
15	.0742	.0759	.0777	.0794	.0810	.0826	.0841	.0856	.0871	.0885
16	.0561	.0579	.0597	.0615	.0633	.0650	.0668	.0685	.0702	.0719
17	.0399	.0416	.0432	.0449	.0465	.0482	.0499	.0516	.0533	.0550
18	.0268	.0282	.0295	.0309	.0323	.0337	.0352	.0367	.0382	.0397
19	.0171	.0181	.0191	.0202	.0213	.0224	.0235	.0247	.0259	.0272
20	.0103	.0110	.0118	.0125	.0133	.0141	.0149	.0158	.0167	.0177

				MEAN ARRIVAL RATE λ						
	13.1	**13.2**	**13.3**	**13.4**	**13.5**	**13.6**	**13.7**	**13.8**	**13.9**	**14.0**
5	.0066	.0062	.0058	.0055	.0051	.0048	.0045	.0042	.0040	.0037
6	.0144	.0136	.0129	.0122	.0115	.0109	.0103	.0097	.0092	.0087
7	.0269	.0256	.0245	.0233	.0222	.0212	.0202	.0192	.0183	.0174
8	.0440	.0423	.0407	.0391	.0375	.0360	.0345	.0331	.0318	.0304
9	.0640	.0620	.0601	.0582	.0563	.0544	.0526	.0508	.0491	.0473
10	.0839	.0819	.0799	.0779	.0760	.0740	.0720	.0701	.0682	.0663
11	.0999	.0983	.0966	.0949	.0932	.0915	.0897	.0880	.0862	.0844

TABLE 5   Individual Poisson Probabilities (cont.)

	MEAN ARRIVAL RATE λ									
	13.1	**13.2**	**13.3**	**13.4**	**13.5**	**13.6**	**13.7**	**13.8**	**13.9**	**14.0**
12	.1091	.1081	.1071	.1060	.1049	.1037	.1024	.1011	.0998	.0984
13	.1099	.1098	.1096	.1093	.1089	.1085	.1080	.1074	.1067	.1060
14	.1028	.1035	.1041	.1046	.1050	.1054	.1056	.1058	.1060	.1060
15	.0898	.0911	.0923	.0934	.0945	.0955	.0965	.0974	.0982	.0989
16	.0735	.0751	.0767	.0783	.0798	.0812	.0826	.0840	.0853	.0866
17	.0567	.0583	.0600	.0617	.0633	.0650	.0666	.0682	.0697	.0713
18	.0412	.0428	.0443	.0459	.0475	.0491	.0507	.0523	.0539	.0554
19	.0284	.0297	.0310	.0324	.0337	.0351	.0365	.0380	.0394	.0409
20	.0186	.0196	.0206	.0217	.0228	.0239	.0250	.0262	.0274	.0286

	MEAN ARRIVAL RATE λ									
	14.1	**14.2**	**14.3**	**14.4**	**14.5**	**14.6**	**14.7**	**14.8**	**14.9**	**15.0**
6	.0082	.0078	.0073	.0069	.0065	.0061	.0058	.0055	.0051	.0048
7	.0165	.0157	.0149	.0142	.0135	.0128	.0122	.0115	.0109	.0104
8	.0292	.0279	.0267	.0256	.0244	.0234	.0223	.0213	.0204	.0194
9	.0457	.0440	.0424	.0409	.0394	.0379	.0365	.0351	.0337	.0324
10	.0644	.0625	.0607	.0589	.0571	.0553	.0536	.0519	.0502	.0486
11	.0825	.0807	.0789	.0771	.0753	.0735	.0716	.0698	.0681	.0663
12	.0970	.0955	.0940	.0925	.0910	.0894	.0878	.0861	.0845	.0829
13	.1052	.1043	.1034	.1025	.1014	.1004	.0992	.0981	.0969	.0956
14	.1060	.1058	.1057	.1054	.1051	.1047	.1042	.1037	.1031	.1024
15	.0996	.1002	.1007	.1012	.1016	.1019	.1021	.1023	.1024	.1024
16	.0878	.0889	.0900	.0911	.0920	.0930	.0938	.0946	.0954	.0960
17	.0728	.0743	.0757	.0771	.0785	.0798	.0811	.0824	.0836	.0847
18	.0570	.0586	.0602	.0617	.0632	.0648	.0663	.0677	.0692	.0706
19	.0423	.0438	.0453	.0468	.0483	.0498	.0513	.0528	.0543	.0557
20	.0298	.0311	.0324	.0337	.0350	.0363	.0377	.0390	.0404	.0418
21	.0200	.0210	.0220	.0231	.0242	.0253	.0264	.0275	.0287	.0299
22	.0128	.0136	.0143	.0151	.0159	.0168	.0176	.0185	.0194	.0204
23	.0079	.0084	.0089	.0095	.0100	.0106	.0113	.0119	.0126	.0133
24	.0046	.0050	.0053	.0057	.0061	.0065	.0069	.0073	.0078	.0083

	MEAN ARRIVAL RATE λ									
	15.1	**15.2**	**15.3**	**15.4**	**15.5**	**15.6**	**15.7**	**15.8**	**15.9**	**16.0**
7	.0098	.0093	.0088	.0084	.0079	.0075	.0071	.0067	.0063	.0060
8	.0186	.0177	.0169	.0161	.0153	.0146	.0139	.0132	.0126	.0120
9	.0311	.0299	.0287	.0275	.0264	.0253	.0243	.0232	.0223	.0213
10	.0470	.0454	.0439	.0424	.0409	.0395	.0381	.0367	.0354	.0341
11	.0645	.0628	.0611	.0594	.0577	.0560	.0544	.0527	.0512	.0496
12	.0812	.0795	.0778	.0762	.0745	.0728	.0711	.0695	.0678	.0661
13	.0943	.0930	.0916	.0902	.0888	.0874	.0859	.0844	.0829	.0814
14	.1017	.1010	.1001	.0993	.0983	.0974	.0963	.0953	.0942	.0930
15	.1024	.1023	.1021	.1019	.1016	.1012	.1008	.1003	.0998	.0992
16	.0966	.0972	.0977	.0981	.0984	.0987	.0989	.0991	.0992	.0992
17	.0858	.0869	.0879	.0888	.0897	.0906	.0914	.0921	.0928	.0934
18	.0720	.0734	.0747	.0760	.0773	.0785	.0797	.0808	.0819	.0830
19	.0572	.0587	.0602	.0616	.0630	.0645	.0659	.0672	.0686	.0699
20	.0432	.0446	.0460	.0474	.0489	.0503	.0517	.0531	.0545	.0559
21	.0311	.0323	.0335	.0348	.0361	.0373	.0386	.0400	.0413	.0426
22	.0213	.0223	.0233	.0244	.0254	.0265	.0276	.0287	.0298	.0310
23	.0140	.0147	.0155	.0163	.0171	.0180	.0188	.0197	.0206	.0216
24	.0088	.0093	.0099	.0105	.0111	.0117	.0123	.0130	.0137	.0144
25	.0053	.0057	.0061	.0064	.0069	.0073	.0077	.0082	.0087	.0092

TABLE 5   Individual Poisson Probabilities (cont.)

	MEAN ARRIVAL RATE λ									
	16.1	**16.2**	**16.3**	**16.4**	**16.5**	**16.6**	**16.7**	**16.8**	**16.9**	**17.0**
7	.0057	.0054	.0051	.0048	.0045	.0043	.0040	.0038	.0036	.0034
8	.0114	.0108	.0103	.0098	.0093	.0088	.0084	.0080	.0076	.0072
9	.0204	.0195	.0187	.0178	.0171	.0163	.0156	.0149	.0142	.0135
10	.0328	.0316	.0304	.0293	.0281	.0270	.0260	.0250	.0240	.0230
11	.0481	.0466	.0451	.0436	.0422	.0408	.0394	.0381	.0368	.0355
12	.0645	.0628	.0612	.0596	.0580	.0565	.0549	.0534	.0518	.0504
13	.0799	.0783	.0768	.0752	.0736	.0721	.0705	.0690	.0674	.0658
14	.0918	.0906	.0894	.0881	.0868	.0855	.0841	.0828	.0814	.0800
15	.0986	.0979	.0971	.0963	.0955	.0946	.0937	.0927	.0917	.0906
16	.0992	.0991	.0989	.0987	.0985	.0981	.0978	.0973	.0968	.0963
17	.0939	.0944	.0949	.0952	.0956	.0958	.0960	.0962	.0963	.0963
18	.0840	.0850	.0859	.0868	.0876	.0884	.0891	.0898	.0904	.0909
19	.0712	.0725	.0737	.0749	.0761	.0772	.0783	.0794	.0804	.0814
20	.0573	.0587	.0601	.0614	.0628	.0641	.0654	.0667	.0679	.0692
21	.0439	.0453	.0466	.0480	.0493	.0507	.0520	.0533	.0547	.0560
22	.0322	.0333	.0345	.0358	.0370	.0382	.0395	.0407	.0420	.0433
23	.0225	.0235	.0245	.0255	.0265	.0276	.0287	.0297	.0309	.0320
24	.0151	.0159	.0166	.0174	.0182	.0191	.0199	.0208	.0217	.0226
25	.0097	.0103	.0108	.0114	.0120	.0127	.0133	.0140	.0147	.0154

	MEAN ARRIVAL RATE λ									
	17.1	**17.2**	**17.3**	**17.4**	**17.5**	**17.6**	**17.7**	**17.8**	**17.9**	**18.0**
8	.0068	.0064	.0061	.0058	.0055	.0052	.0049	.0046	.0044	.0042
9	.0129	.0123	.0117	.0112	.0107	.0101	.0097	.0092	.0088	.0083
10	.0221	.0212	.0203	.0195	.0186	.0179	.0171	.0164	.0157	.0150
11	.0343	.0331	.0319	.0308	.0297	.0286	.0275	.0265	.0255	.0245
12	.0489	.0474	.0460	.0446	.0432	.0419	.0406	.0393	.0380	.0368
13	.0643	.0628	.0612	.0597	.0582	.0567	.0553	.0538	.0524	.0509
14	.0785	.0771	.0757	.0742	.0728	.0713	.0699	.0684	.0669	.0655
15	.0895	.0884	.0873	.0861	.0849	.0837	.0824	.0812	.0799	.0786
16	.0957	.0951	.0944	.0936	.0929	.0920	.0912	.0903	.0894	.0884
17	.0963	.0962	.0960	.0958	.0956	.0953	.0949	.0945	.0941	.0936
18	.0914	.0919	.0923	.0926	.0929	.0932	.0934	.0935	.0936	.0936
19	.0823	.0832	.0840	.0848	.0856	.0863	.0870	.0876	.0882	.0887
20	.0704	.0715	.0727	.0738	.0749	.0760	.0770	.0780	.0789	.0798
21	.0573	.0586	.0599	.0612	.0624	.0637	.0649	.0661	.0673	.0684
22	.0445	.0458	.0471	.0484	.0496	.0509	.0522	.0535	.0547	.0560
23	.0331	.0343	.0354	.0366	.0378	.0390	.0402	.0414	.0426	.0438
24	.0236	.0246	.0255	.0265	.0275	.0286	.0296	.0307	.0318	.0328
25	.0161	.0169	.0177	.0185	.0193	.0201	.0210	.0218	.0227	.0237

	MEAN ARRIVAL RATE λ									
	18.1	**18.2**	**18.3**	**18.4**	**18.5**	**18.6**	**18.7**	**18.8**	**18.9**	**19.0**
9	.0079	.0075	.0072	.0068	.0065	.0061	.0058	.0055	.0053	.0050
10	.0143	.0137	.0131	.0125	.0120	.0114	.0109	.0104	.0099	.0095
11	.0236	.0227	.0218	.0209	.0201	.0193	.0185	.0178	.0171	.0164
12	.0356	.0344	.0332	.0321	.0310	.0299	.0289	.0278	.0269	.0259
13	.0495	.0481	.0468	.0454	.0441	.0428	.0415	.0403	.0390	.0378
14	.0640	.0626	.0611	.0597	.0583	.0569	.0555	.0541	.0527	.0514
15	.0773	.0759	.0746	.0732	.0719	.0705	.0692	.0678	.0664	.0650
16	.0874	.0864	.0853	.0842	.0831	.0820	.0808	.0796	.0785	.0772
17	.0931	.0925	.0918	.0912	.0904	.0897	.0889	.0881	.0872	.0863
18	.0936	.0935	.0934	.0932	.0930	.0927	.0924	.0920	.0916	.0911

TABLE 5 Individual Poisson Probabilities (cont.)

	MEAN ARRIVAL RATE λ									
	18.1	**18.2**	**18.3**	**18.4**	**18.5**	**18.6**	**18.7**	**18.8**	**18.9**	**19.0**
19	.0891	.0896	.0899	.0902	.0905	.0907	.0909	.0910	.0911	.0911
20	.0807	.0815	.0823	.0830	.0837	.0844	.0850	.0856	.0861	.0866
21	.0695	.0706	.0717	.0727	.0738	.0747	.0757	.0766	.0775	.0783
22	.0572	.0584	.0596	.0608	.0620	.0632	.0643	.0655	.0666	.0676
23	.0450	.0462	.0475	.0487	.0499	.0511	.0523	.0535	.0547	.0559
24	.0340	.0351	.0362	.0373	.0385	.0396	.0408	.0419	.0431	.0442
25	.0246	.0255	.0265	.0275	.0285	.0295	.0305	.0315	.0326	.0336

	MEAN ARRIVAL RATE λ									
	19.1	**19.2**	**19.3**	**19.4**	**19.5**	**19.6**	**19.7**	**19.8**	**19.9**	**20.0**
10	.0090	.0086	.0082	.0078	.0074	.0071	.0067	.0064	.0061	.0058
11	.0157	.0150	.0144	.0138	.0132	.0126	.0121	.0116	.0111	.0106
12	.0249	.0240	.0231	.0223	.0214	.0206	.0198	.0191	.0183	.0176
13	.0367	.0355	.0344	.0333	.0322	.0311	.0301	.0291	.0281	.0271
14	.0500	.0487	.0474	.0461	.0448	.0436	.0423	.0411	.0399	.0387
15	.0637	.0623	.0610	.0596	.0582	.0569	.0556	.0543	.0529	.0516
16	.0760	.0748	.0735	.0723	.0710	.0697	.0684	.0671	.0659	.0646
17	.0854	.0844	.0835	.0825	.0814	.0804	.0793	.0782	.0771	.0760
18	.0906	.0901	.0895	.0889	.0882	.0875	.0868	.0860	.0852	.0844
19	.0911	.0910	.0909	.0907	.0905	.0903	.0900	.0896	.0893	.0888
20	.0870	.0874	.0877	.0880	.0883	.0885	.0886	.0887	.0888	.0888
21	.0791	.0799	.0806	.0813	.0820	.0826	.0831	.0837	.0842	.0846
22	.0687	.0697	.0707	.0717	.0727	.0736	.0745	.0753	.0761	.0769
23	.0570	.0582	.0594	.0605	.0616	.0627	.0638	.0648	.0659	.0669
24	.0454	.0466	.0477	.0489	.0500	.0512	.0523	.0535	.0546	.0557
25	.0347	.0358	.0368	.0379	.0390	.0401	.0412	.0424	.0435	.0446

	MEAN ARRIVAL RATE λ									
	20.1	**20.2**	**20.3**	**20.4**	**20.5**	**20.6**	**20.7**	**20.8**	**20.9**	**21.0**
10	.0055	.0053	.0050	.0048	.0045	.0043	.0041	.0039	.0037	.0035
11	.0101	.0097	.0092	.0088	.0084	.0080	.0077	.0073	.0070	.0067
12	.0169	.0163	.0156	.0150	.0144	.0138	.0132	.0127	.0122	.0116
13	.0262	.0253	.0244	.0235	.0227	.0219	.0211	.0203	.0195	.0188
14	.0376	.0365	.0353	.0343	.0332	.0322	.0311	.0301	.0292	.0282
15	.0504	.0491	.0478	.0466	.0454	.0442	.0430	.0418	.0406	.0395
16	.0633	.0620	.0607	.0594	.0581	.0569	.0556	.0543	.0531	.0518
17	.0748	.0736	.0725	.0713	.0701	.0689	.0677	.0665	.0653	.0640
18	.0835	.0826	.0817	.0808	.0798	.0789	.0778	.0768	.0758	.0747
19	.0884	.0879	.0873	.0868	.0861	.0855	.0848	.0841	.0834	.0826
20	.0888	.0887	.0886	.0885	.0883	.0881	.0878	.0875	.0871	.0867
21	.0850	.0854	.0857	.0860	.0862	.0864	.0865	.0866	.0867	.0867
22	.0777	.0784	.0791	.0797	.0803	.0809	.0814	.0819	.0824	.0828
23	.0679	.0688	.0698	.0707	.0716	.0724	.0733	.0741	.0748	.0756
24	.0568	.0579	.0590	.0601	.0611	.0622	.0632	.0642	.0652	.0661
25	.0457	.0468	.0479	.0490	.0501	.0512	.0523	.0534	.0545	.0555

TABLE 6   Cumulative Poisson Probabilities

	MEAN ARRIVAL RATE λ									
	0.1	0.2	0.3	0.4	0.5	0.6	0.7	0.8	0.9	1.0
0	.9048	.8187	.7408	.6703	.6065	.5488	.4966	.4493	.4066	.3679
1	.9953	.9825	.9631	.9384	.9098	.8781	.8442	.8088	.7725	.7358
2	.9998	.9989	.9964	.9921	.9856	.9769	.9659	.9526	.9371	.9197
3	1.0000	.9999	.9997	.9992	.9982	.9966	.9942	.9909	.9865	.9810
4	1.0000	1.0000	1.0000	.9999	.9998	.9996	.9992	.9986	.9977	.9963
5	1.0000	1.0000	1.0000	1.0000	1.0000	1.0000	.9999	.9998	.9997	.9994
6	1.0000	1.0000	1.0000	1.0000	1.0000	1.0000	1.0000	1.0000	1.0000	.9999
7	1.0000	1.0000	1.0000	1.0000	1.0000	1.0000	1.0000	1.0000	1.0000	1.0000

	MEAN ARRIVAL RATE λ									
	1.1	1.2	1.3	1.4	1.5	1.6	1.7	1.8	1.9	2.0
0	.3329	.3012	.2725	.2466	.2231	.2019	.1827	.1653	.1496	.1353
1	.6990	.6626	.6268	.5918	.5578	.5249	.4932	.4628	.4337	.4060
2	.9004	.8795	.8571	.8335	.8088	.7834	.7572	.7306	.7037	.6767
3	.9743	.9662	.9569	.9463	.9344	.9212	.9068	.8913	.8747	.8571
4	.9946	.9923	.9893	.9857	.9814	.9763	.9704	.9636	.9559	.9473
5	.9990	.9985	.9978	.9968	.9955	.9940	.9920	.9896	.9868	.9834
6	.9999	.9997	.9996	.9994	.9991	.9987	.9981	.9974	.9966	.9955
7	1.0000	1.0000	.9999	.9999	.9998	.9997	.9996	.9994	.9992	.9989
8	1.0000	1.0000	1.0000	1.0000	1.0000	1.0000	.9999	.9999	.9998	.9998
9	1.0000	1.0000	1.0000	1.0000	1.0000	1.0000	1.0000	1.0000	1.0000	1.0000

	MEAN ARRIVAL RATE λ									
	2.1	2.2	2.3	2.4	2.5	2.6	2.7	2.8	2.9	3.0
0	.1225	.1108	.1003	.0907	.0821	.0743	.0672	.0608	.0550	.0498
1	.3796	.3546	.3309	.3084	.2873	.2674	.2487	.2311	.2146	.1991
2	.6496	.6227	.5960	.5697	.5438	.5184	.4936	.4695	.4460	.4232
3	.8386	.8194	.7993	.7787	.7576	.7360	.7141	.6919	.6696	.6472
4	.9379	.9275	.9162	.9041	.8912	.8774	.8629	.8477	.8318	.8153
5	.9796	.9751	.9700	.9643	.9580	.9510	.9433	.9349	.9258	.9161
6	.9941	.9925	.9906	.9884	.9858	.9828	.9794	.9756	.9713	.9665
7	.9985	.9980	.9974	.9967	.9958	.9947	.9934	.9919	.9901	.9881
8	.9997	.9995	.9994	.9991	.9989	.9985	.9981	.9976	.9969	.9962
9	.9999	.9999	.9999	.9998	.9997	.9996	.9995	.9993	.9991	.9989
10	1.0000	1.0000	1.0000	1.0000	.9999	.9999	.9999	.9998	.9998	.9997
11	1.0000	1.0000	1.0000	1.0000	1.0000	1.0000	1.0000	1.0000	.9999	.9999
12	1.0000	1.0000	1.0000	1.0000	1.0000	1.0000	1.0000	1.0000	1.0000	1.0000

	MEAN ARRIVAL RATE λ									
	3.1	3.2	3.3	3.4	3.5	3.6	3.7	3.8	3.9	4.0
0	.0450	.0408	.0369	.0334	.0302	.0273	.0247	.0224	.0202	.0183
1	.1847	.1712	.1586	.1468	.1359	.1257	.1162	.1074	.0992	.0916
2	.4012	.3799	.3594	.3397	.3208	.3027	.2854	.2689	.2531	.2381
3	.6248	.6025	.5803	.5584	.5366	.5152	.4942	.4735	.4532	.4335
4	.7982	.7806	.7626	.7442	.7254	.7064	.6872	.6678	.6484	.6288
5	.9057	.8946	.8829	.8705	.8576	.8441	.8301	.8156	.8006	.7851
6	.9612	.9554	.9490	.9421	.9347	.9267	.9182	.9091	.8995	.8893
7	.9858	.9832	.9802	.9769	.9733	.9692	.9648	.9599	.9546	.9489
8	.9953	.9943	.9931	.9917	.9901	.9883	.9863	.9840	.9815	.9786
9	.9986	.9982	.9978	.9973	.9967	.9960	.9952	.9942	.9931	.9919

TABLE 6 Cumulative Poisson Probabilities (cont.)

	MEAN ARRIVAL RATE λ									
	3.1	**3.2**	**3.3**	**3.4**	**3.5**	**3.6**	**3.7**	**3.8**	**3.9**	**4.0**
10	.9996	.9995	.9994	.9992	.9990	.9987	.9984	.9981	.9977	.9972
11	.9999	.9999	.9998	.9998	.9997	.9996	.9995	.9994	.9993	.9991
12	1.0000	1.0000	1.0000	.9999	.9999	.9999	.9999	.9998	.9998	.9997
13	1.0000	1.0000	1.0000	1.0000	1.0000	1.0000	1.0000	1.0000	.9999	.9999
14	1.0000	1.0000	1.0000	1.0000	1.0000	1.0000	1.0000	1.0000	1.0000	1.0000

	MEAN ARRIVAL RATE λ									
	4.1	**4.2**	**4.3**	**4.4**	**4.5**	**4.6**	**4.7**	**4.8**	**4.9**	**5.0**
0	.0166	.0150	.0136	.0123	.0111	.0101	.0091	.0082	.0074	.0067
1	.0845	.0780	.0719	.0663	.0611	.0563	.0518	.0477	.0439	.0404
2	.2238	.2102	.1974	.1851	.1736	.1626	.1523	.1425	.1333	.1247
3	.4142	.3954	.3772	.3594	.3423	.3257	.3097	.2942	.2793	.2650
4	.6093	.5898	.5704	.5512	.5321	.5132	.4946	.4763	.4582	.4405
5	.7693	.7531	.7367	.7199	.7029	.6858	.6684	.6510	.6335	.6160
6	.8786	.8675	.8558	.8436	.8311	.8180	.8046	.7908	.7767	.7622
7	.9427	.9361	.9290	.9214	.9134	.9049	.8960	.8867	.8769	.8666
8	.9755	.9721	.9683	.9642	.9597	.9549	.9497	.9442	.9382	.9319
9	.9905	.9889	.9871	.9851	.9829	.9805	.9778	.9749	.9717	.9682
10	.9966	.9959	.9952	.9943	.9933	.9922	.9910	.9896	.9880	.9863
11	.9989	.9986	.9983	.9980	.9976	.9971	.9966	.9960	.9953	.9945
12	.9997	.9996	.9995	.9993	.9992	.9990	.9988	.9986	.9983	.9980
13	.9999	.9999	.9998	.9998	.9997	.9997	.9996	.9995	.9994	.9993
14	1.0000	1.0000	1.0000	.9999	.9999	.9999	.9999	.9999	.9998	.9998

	MEAN ARRIVAL RATE λ									
	5.1	**5.2**	**5.3**	**5.4**	**5.5**	**5.6**	**5.7**	**5.8**	**5.9**	**6.0**
0	.0061	.0055	.0050	.0045	.0041	.0037	.0033	.0030	.0027	.0025
1	.0372	.0342	.0314	.0289	.0266	.0244	.0224	.0206	.0189	.0174
2	.1165	.1088	.1016	.0948	.0884	.0824	.0768	.0715	.0666	.0620
3	.2513	.2381	.2254	.2133	.2017	.1906	.1800	.1700	.1604	.1512
4	.4231	.4061	.3895	.3733	.3575	.3422	.3272	.3127	.2987	.2851
5	.5984	.5809	.5635	.5461	.5289	.5119	.4950	.4783	.4619	.4457
6	.7474	.7324	.7171	.7017	.6860	.6703	.6544	.6384	.6224	.6063
7	.8560	.8449	.8335	.8217	.8095	.7970	.7841	.7710	.7576	.7440
8	.9252	.9181	.9106	.9027	.8944	.8857	.8766	.8672	.8574	.8472
9	.9644	.9603	.9559	.9512	.9462	.9409	.9352	.9292	.9228	.9161
10	.9844	.9823	.9800	.9775	.9747	.9718	.9686	.9651	.9614	.9574
11	.9937	.9927	.9916	.9904	.9890	.9875	.9859	.9841	.9821	.9799
12	.9976	.9972	.9967	.9962	.9955	.9949	.9941	.9932	.9922	.9912
13	.9992	.9990	.9988	.9986	.9983	.9980	.9977	.9973	.9969	.9964
14	.9997	.9997	.9996	.9995	.9994	.9993	.9991	.9990	.9988	.9986

	MEAN ARRIVAL RATE λ									
	6.1	**6.2**	**6.3**	**6.4**	**6.5**	**6.6**	**6.7**	**6.8**	**6.9**	**7.0**
0	.0022	.0020	.0018	.0017	.0015	.0014	.0012	.0011	.0010	.0009
1	.0159	.0146	.0134	.0123	.0113	.0103	.0095	.0087	.0080	.0073
2	.0577	.0536	.0498	.0463	.0430	.0400	.0371	.0344	.0320	.0296
3	.1425	.1342	.1264	.1189	.1118	.1052	.0988	.0928	.0871	.0818
4	.2719	.2592	.2469	.2351	.2237	.2127	.2022	.1920	.1823	.1730
5	.4298	.4141	.3988	.3837	.3690	.3547	.3406	.3270	.3137	.3007
6	.5902	.5742	.5582	.5423	.5265	.5108	.4953	.4799	.4647	.4497

TABLE 6 Cumulative Poisson Probabilities (cont.)

	MEAN ARRIVAL RATE λ									
	6.1	**6.2**	**6.3**	**6.4**	**6.5**	**6.6**	**6.7**	**6.8**	**6.9**	**7.0**
7	.7301	.7160	.7017	.6873	.6728	.6581	.6433	.6285	.6136	.5987
8	.8367	.8259	.8148	.8033	.7916	.7796	.7673	.7548	.7420	.7291
9	.9090	.9016	.8939	.8858	.8774	.8686	.8596	.8502	.8405	.8305
10	.9531	.9486	.9437	.9386	.9332	.9274	.9214	.9151	.9084	.9015
11	.9776	.9750	.9723	.9693	.9661	.9627	.9591	.9552	.9510	.9467
12	.9900	.9887	.9873	.9857	.9840	.9821	.9801	.9779	.9755	.9730
13	.9958	.9952	.9945	.9937	.9929	.9920	.9909	.9898	.9885	.9872
14	.9984	.9981	.9978	.9974	.9970	.9966	.9961	.9956	.9950	.9943

	MEAN ARRIVAL RATE λ									
	7.1	**7.2**	**7.3**	**7.4**	**7.5**	**7.6**	**7.7**	**7.8**	**7.9**	**8.0**
0	.0008	.0007	.0007	.0006	.0006	.0005	.0005	.0004	.0004	.0003
1	.0067	.0061	.0056	.0051	.0047	.0043	.0039	.0036	.0033	.0030
2	.0275	.0255	.0236	.0219	.0203	.0188	.0174	.0161	.0149	.0138
3	.0767	.0719	.0674	.0632	.0591	.0554	.0518	.0485	.0453	.0424
4	.1641	.1555	.1473	.1395	.1321	.1249	.1181	.1117	.1055	.0996
5	.2881	.2759	.2640	.2526	.2414	.2307	.2203	.2103	.2006	.1912
6	.4349	.4204	.4060	.3920	.3782	.3646	.3514	.3384	.3257	.3134
7	.5838	.5689	.5541	.5393	.5246	.5100	.4956	.4812	.4670	.4530
8	.7160	.7027	.6892	.6757	.6620	.6482	.6343	.6204	.6065	.5925
9	.8202	.8096	.7988	.7877	.7764	.7649	.7531	.7411	.7290	.7166
10	.8942	.8867	.8788	.8707	.8622	.8535	.8445	.8352	.8257	.8159
11	.9420	.9371	.9319	.9265	.9208	.9148	.9085	.9020	.8952	.8881
12	.9703	.9673	.9642	.9609	.9573	.9536	.9496	.9454	.9409	.9362
13	.9857	.9841	.9824	.9805	.9784	.9762	.9739	.9714	.9687	.9658
14	.9935	.9927	.9918	.9908	.9897	.9886	.9873	.9859	.9844	.9827
15	.9972	.9969	.9964	.9959	.9954	.9948	.9941	.9934	.9926	.9918
16	.9989	.9987	.9985	.9983	.9980	.9978	.9974	.9971	.9967	.9963
17	.9996	.9995	.9994	.9993	.9992	.9991	.9989	.9988	.9986	.9984
18	.9998	.9998	.9998	.9997	.9997	.9996	.9996	.9995	.9994	.9993
19	.9999	.9999	.9999	.9999	.9999	.9999	.9998	.9998	.9998	.9997
20	1.0000	1.0000	1.0000	1.0000	1.0000	1.0000	.9999	.9999	.9999	.9999

	MEAN ARRIVAL RATE λ									
	8.1	**8.2**	**8.3**	**8.4**	**8.5**	**8.6**	**8.7**	**8.8**	**8.9**	**9.0**
0	.0003	.0003	.0002	.0002	.0002	.0002	.0002	.0002	.0001	.0001
1	.0028	.0025	.0023	.0021	.0019	.0018	.0016	.0015	.0014	.0012
2	.0127	.0118	.0109	.0100	.0093	.0086	.0079	.0073	.0068	.0062
3	.0396	.0370	.0346	.0323	.0301	.0281	.0262	.0244	.0228	.0212
4	.0940	.0887	.0837	.0789	.0744	.0701	.0660	.0621	.0584	.0550
5	.1822	.1736	.1653	.1573	.1496	.1422	.1352	.1284	.1219	.1157
6	.3013	.2896	.2781	.2670	.2562	.2457	.2355	.2256	.2160	.2068
7	.4391	.4254	.4119	.3987	.3856	.3728	.3602	.3478	.3357	.3239
8	.5786	.5647	.5507	.5369	.5231	.5094	.4958	.4823	.4689	.4557
9	.7041	.6915	.6788	.6659	.6530	.6400	.6269	.6137	.6006	.5874
10	.8058	.7955	.7850	.7743	.7634	.7522	.7409	.7294	.7178	.7060
11	.8807	.8731	.8652	.8571	.8487	.8400	.8311	.8220	.8126	.8030
12	.9313	.9261	.9207	.9150	.9091	.9029	.8965	.8898	.8829	.8758
13	.9628	.9595	.9561	.9524	.9486	.9445	.9403	.9358	.9311	.9261
14	.9810	.9791	.9771	.9749	.9726	.9701	.9675	.9647	.9617	.9585
15	.9908	.9898	.9887	.9875	.9862	.9848	.9832	.9816	.9798	.9780
16	.9958	.9953	.9947	.9941	.9934	.9926	.9918	.9909	.9899	.9889

TABLE 6   Cumulative Poisson Probabilities (cont.)

	MEAN ARRIVAL RATE λ									
	8.1	**8.2**	**8.3**	**8.4**	**8.5**	**8.6**	**8.7**	**8.8**	**8.9**	**9.0**
17	.9982	.9979	.9977	.9973	.9970	.9966	.9962	.9957	.9952	.9947
18	.9992	.9991	.9990	.9989	.9987	.9985	.9983	.9981	.9978	.9976
19	.9997	.9997	.9996	.9995	.9995	.9994	.9993	.9992	.9991	.9989
20	.9999	.9999	.9998	.9998	.9998	.9998	.9997	.9997	.9996	.9996

	MEAN ARRIVAL RATE λ									
	9.1	**9.2**	**9.3**	**9.4**	**9.5**	**9.6**	**9.7**	**9.8**	**9.9**	**10.0**
0	.0001	.0001	.0001	.0001	.0001	.0001	.0001	.0001	.0001	.0000
1	.0011	.0010	.0009	.0009	.0008	.0007	.0007	.0006	.0005	.0005
2	.0058	.0053	.0049	.0045	.0042	.0038	.0035	.0033	.0030	.0028
3	.0198	.0184	.0172	.0160	.0149	.0138	.0129	.0120	.0111	.0103
4	.0517	.0486	.0456	.0429	.0403	.0378	.0355	.0333	.0312	.0293
5	.1098	.1041	.0986	.0935	.0885	.0838	.0793	.0750	.0710	.0671
6	.1978	.1892	.1808	.1727	.1649	.1574	.1502	.1433	.1366	.1301
7	.3123	.3010	.2900	.2792	.2687	.2584	.2485	.2388	.2294	.2202
8	.4426	.4296	.4168	.4042	.3918	.3796	.3676	.3558	.3442	.3328
9	.5742	.5611	.5479	.5349	.5218	.5089	.4960	.4832	.4705	.4579
10	.6941	.6820	.6699	.6576	.6453	.6329	.6205	.6080	.5955	.5830
11	.7932	.7832	.7730	.7626	.7520	.7412	.7303	.7193	.7081	.6968
12	.8684	.8607	.8529	.8448	.8364	.8279	.8191	.8101	.8009	.7916
13	.9210	.9156	.9100	.9042	.8981	.8919	.8853	.8786	.8716	.8645
14	.9552	.9517	.9480	.9441	.9400	.9357	.9312	.9265	.9216	.9165
15	.9760	.9738	.9715	.9691	.9665	.9638	.9609	.9579	.9546	.9513
16	.9878	.9865	.9852	.9838	.9823	.9806	.9789	.9770	.9751	.9730
17	.9941	.9934	.9927	.9919	.9911	.9902	.9892	.9881	.9870	.9857
18	.9973	.9969	.9966	.9962	.9957	.9952	.9947	.9941	.9935	.9928
19	.9988	.9986	.9985	.9983	.9980	.9978	.9975	.9972	.9969	.9965
20	.9995	.9994	.9993	.9992	.9991	.9990	.9989	.9987	.9986	.9984

	MEAN ARRIVAL RATE λ									
	10.1	**10.2**	**10.3**	**10.4**	**10.5**	**10.6**	**10.7**	**10.8**	**10.9**	**11.0**
0	.0000	.0000	.0000	.0000	.0000	.0000	.0000	.0000	.0000	.0000
1	.0005	.0004	.0004	.0003	.0003	.0003	.0003	.0002	.0002	.0002
2	.0026	.0023	.0022	.0020	.0018	.0017	.0016	.0014	.0013	.0012
3	.0096	.0089	.0083	.0077	.0071	.0066	.0062	.0057	.0053	.0049
4	.0274	.0257	.0241	.0225	.0211	.0197	.0185	.0173	.0162	.0151
5	.0634	.0599	.0566	.0534	.0504	.0475	.0448	.0423	.0398	.0375
6	.1240	.1180	.1123	.1069	.1016	.0966	.0918	.0872	.0828	.0786
7	.2113	.2027	.1944	.1863	.1785	.1710	.1636	.1566	.1498	.1432
8	.3217	.3108	.3001	.2896	.2794	.2694	.2597	.2502	.2410	.2320
9	.4455	.4332	.4210	.4090	.3971	.3854	.3739	.3626	.3515	.3405
10	.5705	.5580	.5456	.5331	.5207	.5084	.4961	.4840	.4719	.4599
11	.6853	.6738	.6622	.6505	.6387	.6269	.6150	.6031	.5912	.5793
12	.7820	.7722	.7623	.7522	.7420	.7316	.7210	.7104	.6996	.6887
13	.8571	.8494	.8416	.8336	.8253	.8169	.8083	.7995	.7905	.7813
14	.9112	.9057	.9	.8940	.8879	.8815	.8750	.8682	.8612	.8540
15	.9477	.9440	.9400	.9359	.9317	.9272	.9225	.9177	.9126	.9074
16	.9707	.9684	.9658	.9632	.9604	.9574	.9543	.9511	.9477	.9441
17	.9844	.9830	.9815	.9799	.9781	.9763	.9744	.9723	.9701	.9678
18	.9921	.9913	.9904	.9895	.9885	.9874	.9863	.9850	.9837	.9823
19	.9962	.9957	.9953	.9948	.9942	.9936	.9930	.9923	.9915	.9907
20	.9982	.9980	.9978	.9975	.9972	.9969	.9966	.9962	.9958	.9953

TABLE 6 Cumulative Poisson Probabilities (cont.)

	MEAN ARRIVAL RATE λ									
	11.1	**11.2**	**11.3**	**11.4**	**11.5**	**11.6**	**11.7**	**11.8**	**11.9**	**12.0**
0	.0000	.0000	.0000	.0000	.0000	.0000	.0000	.0000	.0000	.0000
1	.0002	.0002	.0002	.0001	.0001	.0001	.0001	.0001	.0001	.0001
2	.0011	.0010	.0009	.0009	.0008	.0007	.0007	.0006	.0006	.0005
3	.0046	.0042	.0039	.0036	.0034	.0031	.0029	.0027	.0025	.0023
4	.0141	.0132	.0123	.0115	.0107	.0100	.0094	.0087	.0081	.0076
5	.0353	.0333	.0313	.0295	.0277	.0261	.0245	.0230	.0217	.0203
6	.0746	.0708	.0671	.0636	.0603	.0571	.0541	.0512	.0484	.0458
7	.1369	.1307	.1249	.1192	.1137	.1085	.1035	.0986	.0940	.0895
8	.2232	.2147	.2064	.1984	.1906	.1830	.1757	.1686	.1617	.1550
9	.3298	.3192	.3089	.2987	.2888	.2791	.2696	.2603	.2512	.2424
10	.4480	.4362	.4246	.4131	.4017	.3905	.3794	.3685	.3578	.3472
11	.5673	.5554	.5435	.5316	.5198	.5080	.4963	.4847	.4731	.4616
12	.6777	.6666	.6555	.6442	.6329	.6216	.6102	.5988	.5874	.5760
13	.7719	.7624	.7528	.7430	.7330	.7230	.7128	.7025	.6920	.6815
14	.8467	.8391	.8313	.8234	.8153	.8069	.7985	.7898	.7810	.7720
15	.9020	.8963	.8905	.8845	.8783	.8719	.8653	.8585	.8516	.8444
16	.9403	.9364	.9323	.9280	.9236	.9190	.9142	.9092	.9040	.8987
17	.9654	.9628	.9601	.9572	.9542	.9511	.9478	.9444	.9408	.9370
18	.9808	.9792	.9775	.9757	.9738	.9718	.9697	.9674	.9651	.9626
19	.9898	.9889	.9879	.9868	.9857	.9845	.9832	.9818	.9803	.9787
20	.9948	.9943	.9938	.9932	.9925	.9918	.9910	.9902	.9893	.9884

	MEAN ARRIVAL RATE λ									
	12.1	**12.2**	**12.3**	**12.4**	**12.5**	**12.6**	**12.7**	**12.8**	**12.9**	**13.0**
5	.0191	.0179	.0168	.0158	.0148	.0139	.0130	.0122	.0115	.0107
6	.0433	.0410	.0387	.0366	.0346	.0326	.0308	.0291	.0274	.0259
7	.0852	.0811	.0772	.0734	.0698	.0664	.0631	.0599	.0569	.0540
8	.1486	.1424	.1363	.1305	.1249	.1195	.1143	.1093	.1044	.0998
9	.2338	.2254	.2172	.2092	.2014	.1939	.1866	.1794	.1725	.1658
10	.3368	.3266	.3166	.3067	.2971	.2876	.2783	.2693	.2604	.2517
11	.4502	.4389	.4278	.4167	.4058	.3950	.3843	.3738	.3634	.3532
12	.5645	.5531	.5417	.5303	.5190	.5077	.4964	.4853	.4741	.4631
13	.6709	.6603	.6495	.6387	.6278	.6169	.6060	.5950	.5840	.5730
14	.7629	.7536	.7442	.7347	.7250	.7153	.7054	.6954	.6853	.6751
15	.8371	.8296	.8219	.8140	.8060	.7978	.7895	.7810	.7724	.7636
16	.8932	.8875	.8816	.8755	.8693	.8629	.8563	.8495	.8426	.8355
17	.9331	.9290	.9248	.9204	.9158	.9111	.9062	.9011	.8959	.8905
18	.9600	.9572	.9543	.9513	.9481	.9448	.9414	.9378	.9341	.9302
19	.9771	.9753	.9734	.9715	.9694	.9672	.9649	.9625	.9600	.9573
20	.9874	.9863	.9852	.9840	.9827	.9813	.9799	.9783	.9767	.9750
21	.9934	.9927	.9921	.9914	.9906	.9898	.9889	.9880	.9870	.9859
22	.9966	.9963	.9959	.9955	.9951	.9946	.9941	.9936	.9930	.9924
23	.9984	.9982	.9980	.9978	.9975	.9973	.9970	.9967	.9964	.9960

	MEAN ARRIVAL RATE λ									
	13.1	**13.2**	**13.3**	**13.4**	**13.5**	**13.6**	**13.7**	**13.8**	**13.9**	**14.0**
5	.0101	.0094	.0088	.0083	.0077	.0072	.0068	.0063	.0059	.0055
6	.0244	.0230	.0217	.0204	.0193	.0181	.0171	.0161	.0151	.0142
7	.0513	.0487	.0461	.0438	.0415	.0393	.0372	.0353	.0334	.0316
8	.0953	.0910	.0868	.0828	.0790	.0753	.0718	.0684	.0652	.0621
9	.1593	.1530	.1469	.1410	.1353	.1297	.1244	.1192	.1142	.1094
10	.2432	.2349	.2268	.2189	.2112	.2037	.1964	.1893	.1824	.1757

TABLE 6   Cumulative Poisson Probabilities (cont.)

	MEAN ARRIVAL RATE λ									
	13.1	**13.2**	**13.3**	**13.4**	**13.5**	**13.6**	**13.7**	**13.8**	**13.9**	**14.0**
11	.3431	.3332	.3234	.3139	.3045	.2952	.2862	.2773	.2686	.2600
12	.4522	.4413	.4305	.4199	.4093	.3989	.3886	.3784	.3684	.3585
13	.5621	.5511	.5401	.5292	.5182	.5074	.4966	.4858	.4751	.4644
14	.6649	.6546	.6442	.6338	.6233	.6128	.6022	.5916	.5810	.5704
15	.7547	.7456	.7365	.7272	.7178	.7083	.6987	.6890	.6792	.6694
16	.8282	.8208	.8132	.8054	.7975	.7895	.7813	.7730	.7645	.7559
17	.8849	.8791	.8732	.8671	.8609	.8545	.8479	.8411	.8343	.8272
18	.9261	.9219	.9176	.9130	.9084	.9035	.8986	.8934	.8881	.8826
19	.9546	.9516	.9486	.9454	.9421	.9387	.9351	.9314	.9275	.9235
20	.9732	.9713	.9692	.9671	.9649	.9626	.9601	.9576	.9549	.9521
21	.9848	.9836	.9823	.9810	.9796	.9780	.9765	.9748	.9730	.9712
22	.9917	.9910	.9902	.9894	.9885	.9876	.9866	.9856	.9845	.9833
23	.9956	.9952	.9948	.9943	.9938	.9933	.9927	.9921	.9914	.9907

	MEAN ARRIVAL RATE λ									
	14.1	**14.2**	**14.3**	**14.4**	**14.5**	**14.6**	**14.7**	**14.8**	**14.9**	**15.0**
6	.0134	.0126	.0118	.0111	.0105	.0098	.0092	.0087	.0081	.0076
7	.0299	.0283	.0268	.0253	.0239	.0226	.0214	.0202	.0191	.0180
8	.0591	.0562	.0535	.0509	.0484	.0460	.0437	.0415	.0394	.0374
9	.1047	.1003	.0959	.0918	.0878	.0839	.0802	.0766	.0732	.0699
10	.1691	.1628	.1566	.1507	.1449	.1392	.1338	.1285	.1234	.1185
11	.2517	.2435	.2355	.2277	.2201	.2127	.2054	.1984	.1915	.1848
12	.3487	.3391	.3296	.3203	.3111	.3021	.2932	.2845	.2760	.2676
13	.4539	.4434	.4330	.4227	.4125	.4024	.3925	.3826	.3728	.3632
14	.5598	.5492	.5387	.5281	.5176	.5071	.4967	.4863	.4759	.4657
15	.6594	.6494	.6394	.6293	.6192	.6090	.5988	.5886	.5783	.5681
16	.7472	.7384	.7294	.7204	.7112	.7020	.6926	.6832	.6737	.6641
17	.8200	.8126	.8051	.7975	.7897	.7818	.7737	.7656	.7573	.7489
18	.8770	.8712	.8653	.8592	.8530	.8466	.8400	.8333	.8265	.8195
19	.9193	.9150	.9106	.9060	.9012	.8963	.8913	.8861	.8807	.8752
20	.9492	.9461	.9430	.9396	.9362	.9326	.9289	.9251	.9211	.9170
21	.9692	.9671	.9650	.9627	.9604	.9579	.9553	.9526	.9498	.9469
22	.9820	.9807	.9793	.9779	.9763	.9747	.9729	.9711	.9692	.9673
23	.9899	.9891	.9882	.9873	.9863	.9853	.9842	.9831	.9818	.9805
24	.9945	.9941	.9935	.9930	.9924	.9918	.9911	.9904	.9896	.9888
25	.9971	.9969	.9966	.9963	.9959	.9956	.9952	.9947	.9943	.9938

	MEAN ARRIVAL RATE λ									
	15.1	**15.2**	**15.3**	**15.4**	**15.5**	**15.6**	**15.7**	**15.8**	**15.9**	**16.0**
7	.0170	.0160	.0151	.0143	.0135	.0127	.0120	.0113	.0106	.0100
8	.0355	.0337	.0320	.0304	.0288	.0273	.0259	.0245	.0232	.0220
9	.0667	.0636	.0607	.0579	.0552	.0526	.0501	.0478	.0455	.0433
10	.1137	.1091	.1046	.1003	.0961	.0921	.0882	.0845	.0809	.0774
11	.1782	.1718	.1657	.1596	.1538	.1481	.1426	.1372	.1320	.1270
12	.2594	.2514	.2435	.2358	.2283	.2209	.2137	.2067	.1998	.1931
13	.3537	.3444	.3351	.3260	.3171	.3083	.2996	.2911	.2827	.2745
14	.4554	.4453	.4353	.4253	.4154	.4056	.3959	.3864	.3769	.3675
15	.5578	.5476	.5374	.5272	.5170	.5069	.4968	.4867	.4767	.4667
16	.6545	.6448	.6351	.6253	.6154	.6056	.5957	.5858	.5759	.5660
17	.7403	.7317	.7230	.7141	.7052	.6962	.6871	.6779	.6687	.6593
18	.8123	.8051	.7977	.7901	.7825	.7747	.7668	.7587	.7506	.7423
19	.8696	.8638	.8578	.8517	.8455	.8391	.8326	.8260	.8192	.8122

TABLE 6 Cumulative Poisson Probabilities (cont.)

	MEAN ARRIVAL RATE λ									
	15.1	**15.2**	**15.3**	**15.4**	**15.5**	**15.6**	**15.7**	**15.8**	**15.9**	**16.0**
20	.9128	.9084	.9039	.8992	.8944	.8894	.8843	.8791	.8737	.8682
21	.9438	.9407	.9374	.9340	.9304	.9268	.9230	.9190	.9150	.9108
22	.9652	.9630	.9607	.9583	.9558	.9532	.9505	.9477	.9448	.9418
23	.9792	.9777	.9762	.9746	.9730	.9712	.9694	.9674	.9654	.9633
24	.9880	.9871	.9861	.9851	.9840	.9829	.9817	.9804	.9791	.9777
25	.9933	.9928	.9922	.9915	.9909	.9902	.9894	.9886	.9878	.9869

	MEAN ARRIVAL RATE λ									
	16.1	**16.2**	**16.3**	**16.4**	**16.5**	**16.6**	**16.7**	**16.8**	**16.9**	**17.0**
8	.0208	.0197	.0186	.0176	.0167	.0158	.0149	.0141	.0133	.0126
9	.0412	.0392	.0373	.0355	.0337	.0321	.0305	.0290	.0275	.0261
10	.0740	.0708	.0677	.0647	.0619	.0591	.0565	.0539	.0515	.0491
11	.1221	.1174	.1128	.1084	.1041	.0999	.0959	.0920	.0883	.0847
12	.1866	.1802	.1740	.1680	.1621	.1564	.1508	.1454	.1401	.1350
13	.2664	.2585	.2508	.2432	.2357	.2285	.2213	.2144	.2075	.2009
14	.3583	.3492	.3402	.3313	.3225	.3139	.3054	.2971	.2889	.2808
15	.4569	.4470	.4373	.4276	.4180	.4085	.3991	.3898	.3806	.3715
16	.5560	.5461	.5362	.5263	.5165	.5067	.4969	.4871	.4774	.4677
17	.6500	.6406	.6311	.6216	.6120	.6025	.5929	.5833	.5737	.5640
18	.7340	.7255	.7170	.7084	.6996	.6908	.6820	.6730	.6640	.6550
19	.8052	.7980	.7907	.7833	.7757	.7681	.7603	.7524	.7444	.7363
20	.8625	.8567	.8508	.8447	.8385	.8321	.8257	.8191	.8123	.8055
21	.9064	.9020	.8974	.8927	.8878	.8828	.8777	.8724	.8670	.8615
22	.9386	.9353	.9319	.9284	.9248	.9210	.9171	.9131	.9090	.9047
23	.9611	.9588	.9564	.9539	.9513	.9486	.9458	.9429	.9398	.9367
24	.9762	.9747	.9730	.9713	.9696	.9677	.9657	.9637	.9616	.9594
25	.9859	.9849	.9839	.9828	.9816	.9804	.9791	.9777	.9763	.9748
26	.9920	.9913	.9907	.9900	.9892	.9884	.9876	.9867	.9858	.9848

	MEAN ARRIVAL RATE λ									
	17.1	**17.2**	**17.3**	**17.4**	**17.5**	**17.6**	**17.7**	**17.8**	**17.9**	**18.0**
8	.0119	.0112	.0106	.0100	.0095	.0089	.0084	.0079	.0075	.0071
9	.0248	.0235	.0223	.0212	.0201	.0191	.0181	.0171	.0162	.0154
10	.0469	.0447	.0426	.0406	.0387	.0369	.0352	.0335	.0319	.0304
11	.0812	.0778	.0746	.0714	.0684	.0655	.0627	.0600	.0574	.0549
12	.1301	.1252	.1206	.1160	.1116	.1074	.1033	.0993	.0954	.0917
13	.1944	.1880	.1818	.1758	.1699	.1641	.1585	.1531	.1478	.1426
14	.2729	.2651	.2575	.2500	.2426	.2354	.2284	.2215	.2147	.2081
15	.3624	.3535	.3448	.3361	.3275	.3191	.3108	.3026	.2946	.2867
16	.4581	.4486	.4391	.4297	.4204	.4112	.4020	.3929	.3839	.3751
17	.5544	.5448	.5352	.5256	.5160	.5065	.4969	.4875	.4780	.4686
18	.6458	.6367	.6275	.6182	.6089	.5996	.5903	.5810	.5716	.5622
19	.7281	.7199	.7115	.7031	.6945	.6859	.6773	.6685	.6598	.6509
20	.7985	.7914	.7842	.7769	.7694	.7619	.7542	.7465	.7387	.7307
21	.8558	.8500	.8441	.8380	.8319	.8255	.8191	.8126	.8059	.7991
22	.9003	.8958	.8912	.8864	.8815	.8765	.8713	.8660	.8606	.8551
23	.9334	.9301	.9266	.9230	.9193	.9154	.9115	.9074	.9032	.8989
24	.9570	.9546	.9521	.9495	.9468	.9440	.9411	.9381	.9350	.9317
25	.9732	.9715	.9698	.9680	.9661	.9641	.9621	.9599	.9577	.9554
26	.9838	.9827	.9816	.9804	.9791	.9778	.9764	.9749	.9734	.9718
27	.9905	.9898	.9891	.9883	.9875	.9866	.9857	.9848	.9837	.9827

TABLE 6   Cumulative Poisson Probabilities (cont.)

	MEAN ARRIVAL RATE λ									
	18.1	18.2	18.3	18.4	18.5	18.6	18.7	18.8	18.9	19.0
9	.0146	.0138	.0131	.0124	.0117	.0111	.0105	.0099	.0094	.0089
10	.0289	.0275	.0262	.0249	.0237	.0225	.0214	.0203	.0193	.0183
11	.0525	.0502	.0479	.0458	.0438	.0418	.0399	.0381	.0363	.0347
12	.0881	.0846	.0812	.0779	.0748	.0717	.0688	.0659	.0632	.0606
13	.1376	.1327	.1279	.1233	.1189	.1145	.1103	.1062	.1022	.0984
14	.2016	.1953	.1891	.1830	.1771	.1714	.1658	.1603	.1550	.1497
15	.2789	.2712	.2637	.2563	.2490	.2419	.2349	.2281	.2214	.2148
16	.3663	.3576	.3490	.3405	.3321	.3239	.3157	.3077	.2998	.2920
17	.4593	.4500	.4408	.4317	.4226	.4136	.4047	.3958	.3870	.3784
18	.5529	.5435	.5342	.5249	.5156	.5063	.4970	.4878	.4786	.4695
19	.6420	.6331	.6241	.6151	.6061	.5970	.5879	.5788	.5697	.5606
20	.7227	.7146	.7064	.6981	.6898	.6814	.6729	.6644	.6558	.6472
21	.7922	.7852	.7781	.7709	.7636	.7561	.7486	.7410	.7333	.7255
22	.8494	.8436	.8377	.8317	.8256	.8193	.8129	.8065	.7998	.7931
23	.8944	.8899	.8852	.8804	.8755	.8704	.8652	.8600	.8545	.8490
24	.9284	.9249	.9214	.9177	.9139	.9100	.9060	.9019	.8976	.8933
25	.9530	.9505	.9479	.9452	.9424	.9395	.9365	.9334	.9302	.9269
26	.9701	.9683	.9665	.9646	.9626	.9606	.9584	.9562	.9539	.9514
27	.9816	.9804	.9792	.9779	.9765	.9751	.9736	.9720	.9704	.9687

	MEAN ARRIVAL RATE λ									
	19.1	19.2	19.3	19.4	19.5	19.6	19.7	19.8	19.9	20.0
10	.0174	.0165	.0157	.0149	.0141	.0134	.0127	.0120	.0114	.0108
11	.0331	.0315	.0301	.0287	.0273	.0260	.0248	.0236	.0225	.0214
12	.0580	.0556	.0532	.0509	.0488	.0467	.0446	.0427	.0408	.0390
13	.0947	.0911	.0876	.0842	.0809	.0778	.0747	.0717	.0689	.0661
14	.1447	.1397	.1349	.1303	.1257	.1213	.1170	.1128	.1088	.1049
15	.2084	.2021	.1959	.1899	.1840	.1782	.1726	.1671	.1617	.1565
16	.2844	.2768	.2694	.2621	.2550	.2479	.2410	.2342	.2276	.2211
17	.3698	.3613	.3529	.3446	.3364	.3283	.3203	.3124	.3047	.2970
18	.4604	.4514	.4424	.4335	.4246	.4158	.4071	.3985	.3899	.3814
19	.5515	.5424	.5333	.5242	.5151	.5061	.4971	.4881	.4792	.4703
20	.6385	.6298	.6210	.6122	.6034	.5946	.5857	.5769	.5680	.5591
21	.7176	.7097	.7016	.6935	.6854	.6772	.6689	.6605	.6521	.6437
22	.7863	.7794	.7724	.7653	.7580	.7507	.7433	.7358	.7283	.7206
23	.8434	.8376	.8317	.8257	.8196	.8134	.8071	.8007	.7941	.7875
24	.8888	.8842	.8795	.8746	.8697	.8646	.8594	.8541	.8487	.8432
25	.9235	.9199	.9163	.9126	.9087	.9048	.9007	.8965	.8922	.8878
26	.9489	.9463	.9437	.9409	.9380	.9350	.9319	.9288	.9255	.9221
27	.9670	.9651	.9632	.9612	.9591	.9570	.9547	.9524	.9500	.9475

	MEAN ARRIVAL RATE λ									
	20.1	20.2	20.3	20.4	20.5	20.6	20.7	20.8	20.9	21.0
10	.0102	.0097	.0092	.0087	.0082	.0078	.0074	.0070	.0066	.0063
11	.0204	.0194	.0184	.0175	.0167	.0158	.0150	.0143	.0136	.0129
12	.0373	.0356	.0340	.0325	.0310	.0296	.0283	.0270	.0257	.0245
13	.0635	.0609	.0584	.0560	.0537	.0515	.0493	.0473	.0453	.0434
14	.1010	.0973	.0938	.0903	.0869	.0836	.0805	.0774	.0744	.0716
15	.1514	.1464	.1416	.1369	.1323	.1278	.1234	.1192	.1151	.1111
16	.2147	.2084	.2023	.1963	.1904	.1847	.1790	.1735	.1682	.1629
17	.2895	.2821	.2748	.2676	.2605	.2536	.2467	.2400	.2334	.2270
18	.3730	.3647	.3565	.3484	.3403	.3324	.3246	.3168	.3092	.3017

TABLE 6 Cumulative Poisson Probabilities (cont.)

	MEAN ARRIVAL RATE λ									
	20.1	**20.2**	**20.3**	**20.4**	**20.5**	**20.6**	**20.7**	**20.8**	**20.9**	**21.0**
19	.4614	.4526	.4438	.4351	.4265	.4179	.4094	.4009	.3926	.3843
20	.5502	.5413	.5325	.5236	.5148	.5059	.4972	.4884	.4797	.4710
21	.6352	.6267	.6181	.6096	.6010	.5923	.5837	.5750	.5664	.5577
22	.7129	.7051	.6972	.6893	.6813	.6732	.6651	.6569	.6487	.6405
23	.7808	.7739	.7670	.7600	.7528	.7456	.7384	.7310	.7235	.7160
24	.8376	.8319	.8260	.8201	.8140	.8078	.8016	.7952	.7887	.7822
25	.8833	.8787	.8739	.8691	.8641	.8591	.8539	.8486	.8432	.8377
26	.9186	.9150	.9114	.9076	.9037	.8997	.8955	.8913	.8870	.8826
27	.9449	.9423	.9395	.9366	.9337	.9306	.9275	.9242	.9209	.9175

	MEAN ARRIVAL RATE λ									
	21.1	**21.2**	**21.3**	**21.4**	**21.5**	**21.6**	**21.7**	**21.8**	**21.9**	**22.0**
11	.0123	.0116	.0110	.0105	.0099	.0094	.0090	.0085	.0080	.0076
12	.0234	.0223	.0213	.0203	.0193	.0184	.0175	.0167	.0159	.0151
13	.0415	.0397	.0380	.0364	.0348	.0333	.0318	.0304	.0291	.0278
14	.0688	.0661	.0635	.0610	.0586	.0563	.0540	.0518	.0497	.0477
15	.1072	.1034	.0997	.0962	.0927	.0893	.0861	.0829	.0799	.0769
16	.1578	.1528	.1479	.1432	.1385	.1340	.1296	.1253	.1211	.1170
17	.2206	.2144	.2083	.2023	.1965	.1907	.1851	.1796	.1743	.1690
18	.2943	.2870	.2798	.2727	.2657	.2588	.2521	.2454	.2389	.2325
19	.3760	.3679	.3599	.3519	.3440	.3362	.3285	.3209	.3134	.3060
20	.4623	.4537	.4452	.4367	.4282	.4198	.4115	.4032	.3950	.3869
21	.5490	.5403	.5317	.5230	.5144	.5058	.4972	.4887	.4801	.4716
22	.6322	.6238	.6155	.6071	.5987	.5902	.5818	.5733	.5648	.5564
23	.7084	.7008	.6930	.6853	.6774	.6695	.6616	.6536	.6455	.6374
24	.7755	.7687	.7619	.7550	.7480	.7409	.7337	.7264	.7191	.7117
25	.8321	.8264	.8206	.8146	.8086	.8025	.7963	.7900	.7836	.7771
26	.8780	.8734	.8686	.8638	.8588	.8537	.8486	.8433	.8379	.8324
27	.9139	.9103	.9065	.9027	.8988	.8947	.8906	.8863	.8820	.8775

TABLE 7   Cutoff Points of the Chi-Square Distribution Function

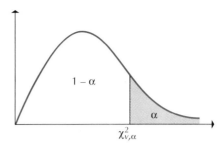

For selected probabilities α, the table shows the values $\chi^2_{v,\alpha}$ such that $\alpha = P(\chi^2_v > \chi^2_{v,\alpha})$, where χ^2_v is a chi-square random variable with v degrees of freedom. For example, the probability is .100 that a chi-square random variable with 10 degrees of freedom is greater than 15.99.

v	α									
	.995	.990	.975	.950	.900	.100	.050	.025	.010	.005
1	0.0^4393	0.0^3157	0.0^3982	0.0^2393	0.0158	2.71	3.84	5.02	6.63	7.88
2	0.0100	0.0201	0.0506	0.103	0.211	4.61	5.99	7.38	9.21	10.60
3	0.072	0.115	0.216	0.352	0.584	6.25	7.81	9.35	11.34	12.84
4	0.207	0.297	0.484	0.711	1.064	7.78	9.49	11.14	13.28	14.86
5	0.412	0.554	0.831	1.145	1.61	9.24	11.07	12.83	15.09	16.75
6	0.676	0.872	1.24	1.64	2.20	10.64	12.59	14.45	16.81	18.55
7	0.989	1.24	1.69	2.17	2.83	12.02	14.07	16.01	18.48	20.28
8	1.34	1.65	2.18	2.73	3.49	13.36	15.51	17.53	20.09	21.96
9	1.73	2.09	2.70	3.33	4.17	14.68	16.92	19.02	21.67	23.59
10	2.16	2.56	3.25	3.94	4.87	15.99	18.31	20.48	23.21	25.19
11	2.60	3.05	3.82	4.57	5.58	17.28	19.68	21.92	24.73	26.76
12	3.07	3.57	4.40	5.23	6.30	18.55	21.03	23.34	26.22	28.30
13	3.57	4.11	5.01	5.89	7.04	19.81	22.36	24.74	27.69	29.82
14	4.07	4.66	5.63	6.57	7.79	21.06	23.68	26.12	29.14	31.32
15	4.60	5.23	6.26	7.26	8.55	22.31	25.00	27.49	30.58	32.80
16	5.14	5.81	6.91	7.96	9.31	23.54	26.30	28.85	32.00	34.27
17	5.70	6.41	7.56	8.67	10.09	24.77	27.59	30.19	33.41	35.72
18	6.26	7.01	8.23	9.39	10.86	25.99	28.87	31.53	34.81	37.16
19	6.84	7.63	8.91	10.12	11.65	27.20	30.14	32.85	36.19	38.58
20	7.43	8.26	9.59	10.85	12.44	28.41	31.41	34.17	37.57	40.00
21	8.03	8.90	10.28	11.59	13.24	29.62	32.67	35.48	38.93	41.40
22	8.64	9.54	10.98	12.34	14.04	30.81	33.92	36.78	40.29	42.80
23	9.26	10.20	11.69	13.09	14.85	32.01	35.17	38.08	41.64	44.18
24	9.89	10.86	12.40	13.85	15.66	33.20	36.42	39.36	42.98	45.56
25	10.52	11.52	13.12	14.61	16.47	34.38	37.65	40.65	44.31	46.93
26	11.16	12.20	13.84	15.38	17.29	35.56	38.89	41.92	45.64	48.29
27	11.81	12.88	14.57	16.15	18.11	36.74	40.11	43.19	46.96	49.64
28	12.46	13.56	15.31	16.93	18.94	37.92	41.34	44.46	48.28	50.99
29	13.12	14.26	16.05	17.71	19.77	39.09	42.56	45.72	49.59	52.34
30	13.79	14.95	16.79	18.49	20.60	40.26	43.77	46.98	50.89	53.67
40	20.71	22.16	24.43	26.51	29.05	51.81	55.76	59.34	63.69	66.77
50	27.99	29.71	32.36	34.76	37.69	63.17	67.50	71.42	76.15	79.49
60	35.53	37.48	40.48	43.19	46.46	74.40	79.08	83.30	88.38	91.95
70	43.28	45.44	48.76	51.74	55.33	85.53	90.53	95.02	100.4	104.2
80	51.17	53.54	57.15	60.39	64.28	96.58	101.9	106.6	112.3	116.3
90	59.20	61.75	65.65	69.13	73.29	107.6	113.1	118.1	124.1	128.3
100	67.33	70.06	74.22	77.93	82.36	118.5	124.3	129.6	135.8	140.2

Reproduced with permission from C. M. Thompson, "Tables of percentage points of the chi-square distribution," *Biometrika*, 32 (1941).

TABLE 8   Cutoff Points for the Student's *t* Distribution

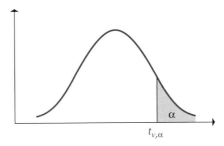

For selected probabilities, α, the table shows the values $t_{v,\alpha}$ such that $P(t_v > t_\alpha) = \alpha$, where t_v is a Student's *t* random variable with v degrees of freedom. For example, the probability is .10 that a Student's *t* random variable with 10 degrees of freedom exceeds 1.372.

v	α				
	0.100	**0.050**	**0.025**	**0.010**	**0.005**
1	3.078	6.314	12.706	31.821	63.657
2	1.886	2.920	4.303	6.965	9.925
3	1.638	2.353	3.182	4.541	5.841
4	1.533	2.132	2.776	3.747	4.604
5	1.476	2.015	2.571	3.365	4.032
6	1.440	1.943	2.447	3.143	3.707
7	1.415	1.895	2.365	2.998	3.499
8	1.397	1.860	2.306	2.896	3.355
9	1.383	1.833	2.262	2.821	3.250
10	1.372	1.812	2.228	2.764	3.169
11	1.363	1.796	2.201	2.718	3.106
12	1.356	1.782	2.179	2.681	3.055
13	1.350	1.771	2.160	2.650	3.012
14	1.345	1.761	2.145	2.624	2.977
15	1.341	1.753	2.131	2.602	2.947
16	1.337	1.746	2.120	2.583	2.921
17	1.333	1.740	2.110	2.567	2.898
18	1.330	1.734	2.101	2.552	2.878
19	1.328	1.729	2.093	2.539	2.861
20	1.325	1.725	2.086	2.528	2.845
21	1.323	1.721	2.080	2.518	2.831
22	1.321	1.717	2.074	2.508	2.819
23	1.319	1.714	2.069	2.500	2.807
24	1.318	1.711	2.064	2.492	2.797
25	1.316	1.708	2.060	2.485	2.787
26	1.315	1.706	2.056	2.479	2.779
27	1.314	1.703	2.052	2.473	2.771
28	1.313	1.701	2.048	2.467	2.763
29	1.311	1.699	2.045	2.462	2.756
30	1.310	1.697	2.042	2.457	2.750
40	1.303	1.684	2.021	2.423	2.704
60	1.296	1.671	2.000	2.390	2.660
∞	1.282	1.645	1.960	2.326	2.576

TABLE 9 Cutoff Points for the F Distribution

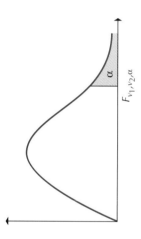

For probabilities $\alpha = 0.5$ and $\alpha = .01$, the tables show the values $F_{\nu_1,\nu_2,\alpha}$ such that $P(F_{\nu_1,\nu_2} > F_{\nu_1,\nu_2,\alpha}) = \alpha$, where F_{ν_1,ν_2} is an F random variable, with numerator degrees of freedom ν_1 and denominator degrees of freedom ν_2. For example, the probability is .05 that an $F_{3,7}$ random variable exceeds 4.35.

$\alpha = .05$

DENOMINATOR ν_2	NUMERATOR ν_1																		
	1	2	3	4	5	6	7	8	9	10	12	15	20	24	30	40	60	120	∞
1	161.4	199.5	215.7	224.6	230.2	234.0	236.8	238.9	240.5	241.9	243.9	245.9	248.0	249.1	250.1	251.1	252.2	253.3	254.3
2	18.51	19.00	19.16	19.25	19.30	19.33	19.35	19.37	19.38	19.40	19.41	19.43	19.45	19.45	19.46	19.47	19.48	19.49	19.50
3	10.13	9.55	9.28	9.12	9.01	8.94	8.89	8.85	8.81	8.79	8.74	8.70	8.66	8.64	8.62	8.59	8.57	8.55	8.53
4	7.71	6.94	6.59	6.39	6.26	6.16	6.09	6.04	6.00	5.96	5.91	5.86	5.80	5.77	5.75	5.72	5.69	5.66	5.63
5	6.61	5.79	5.41	5.19	5.05	4.95	4.88	4.82	4.77	4.74	4.68	4.62	4.56	4.53	4.50	4.46	4.43	4.40	4.36
6	5.99	5.14	4.76	4.53	4.39	4.28	4.21	4.15	4.10	4.06	4.00	3.94	3.87	3.84	3.81	3.77	3.74	3.70	3.67
7	5.59	4.74	4.35	4.12	3.97	3.87	3.79	3.73	3.68	3.64	3.57	3.51	3.44	3.41	3.38	3.34	3.30	3.27	3.23
8	5.32	4.46	4.07	3.84	3.69	3.58	3.50	3.44	3.39	3.35	3.28	3.22	3.15	3.12	3.08	3.04	3.01	2.97	2.93
9	5.12	4.26	3.86	3.63	3.48	3.37	3.29	3.23	3.18	3.14	3.07	3.01	2.94	2.90	2.86	2.83	2.79	2.75	2.71
10	4.96	4.10	3.71	3.48	3.33	3.22	3.14	3.07	3.02	2.98	2.91	2.85	2.77	2.74	2.70	2.66	2.62	2.58	2.54
11	4.84	3.98	3.59	3.36	3.20	3.09	3.01	2.95	2.90	2.85	2.79	2.72	2.65	2.61	2.57	2.53	2.49	2.45	2.40
12	4.75	3.89	3.49	3.26	3.11	3.00	2.91	2.85	2.80	2.75	2.69	2.62	2.54	2.51	2.47	2.43	2.38	2.34	2.30
13	4.67	3.81	3.41	3.18	3.03	2.92	2.83	2.77	2.71	2.67	2.60	2.53	2.46	2.42	2.38	2.34	2.30	2.25	2.21
14	4.60	3.74	3.34	3.11	2.96	2.85	2.76	2.70	2.65	2.60	2.53	2.46	2.39	2.35	2.31	2.27	2.22	2.18	2.13
15	4.54	3.68	3.29	3.06	2.90	2.79	2.71	2.64	2.59	2.54	2.48	2.40	2.33	2.29	2.25	2.20	2.16	2.11	2.07
16	4.49	3.63	3.24	3.01	2.85	2.74	2.66	2.59	2.54	2.49	2.42	2.35	2.28	2.24	2.19	2.15	2.11	2.06	2.01
17	4.45	3.59	3.20	2.96	2.81	2.70	2.62	2.55	2.49	2.45	2.38	2.31	2.23	2.19	2.15	2.10	2.06	2.01	1.96
18	4.41	3.55	3.16	2.93	2.77	2.66	2.58	2.51	2.46	2.41	2.34	2.27	2.19	2.15	2.11	2.06	2.02	1.97	1.92
19	4.38	3.52	3.13	2.90	2.74	2.63	2.54	2.48	2.42	2.38	2.31	2.23	2.16	2.11	2.07	2.03	1.98	1.93	1.88
20	4.35	3.49	3.10	2.87	2.71	2.60	2.51	2.45	2.39	2.35	2.28	2.20	2.12	2.08	2.04	1.99	1.95	1.90	1.84
21	4.32	3.47	3.07	2.84	2.68	2.57	2.49	2.42	2.37	2.32	2.25	2.18	2.10	2.05	2.01	1.96	1.92	1.87	1.81
22	4.30	3.44	3.05	2.82	2.66	2.55	2.46	2.40	2.34	2.30	2.23	2.15	2.07	2.03	1.98	1.94	1.89	1.84	1.78
23	4.28	3.42	3.03	2.80	2.64	2.53	2.44	2.37	2.32	2.27	2.20	2.13	2.05	2.01	1.96	1.91	1.86	1.81	1.76
24	4.26	3.40	3.01	2.78	2.62	2.51	2.42	2.36	2.30	2.25	2.18	2.11	2.03	1.98	1.94	1.89	1.84	1.79	1.73
25	4.24	3.39	2.99	2.76	2.60	2.49	2.40	2.34	2.28	2.24	2.16	2.09	2.01	1.96	1.92	1.87	1.82	1.77	1.71
26	4.23	3.37	2.98	2.74	2.59	2.47	2.39	2.32	2.27	2.22	2.15	2.07	1.99	1.95	1.90	1.85	1.80	1.75	1.69
27	4.21	3.35	2.96	2.73	2.57	2.46	2.37	2.31	2.25	2.20	2.13	2.06	1.97	1.93	1.88	1.84	1.79	1.73	1.67
28	4.20	3.34	2.95	2.71	2.56	2.45	2.36	2.29	2.24	2.19	2.12	2.04	1.96	1.91	1.87	1.82	1.77	1.71	1.65
29	4.18	3.33	2.93	2.70	2.55	2.43	2.35	2.28	2.22	2.18	2.10	2.03	1.94	1.90	1.85	1.81	1.75	1.70	1.64

ν_2	1	2	3	4	5	6	7	8	9	10	12	15	20	24	30	40	60	120	∞
30	4.17	3.32	2.92	2.69	2.53	2.42	2.33	2.27	2.21	2.16	2.09	2.01	1.93	1.89	1.84	1.79	1.74	1.58	1.62
40	4.08	3.23	2.84	2.61	2.45	2.34	2.25	2.18	2.12	2.08	2.00	1.92	1.84	1.79	1.74	1.69	1.64	1.58	1.51
60	4.00	3.15	2.76	2.53	2.37	2.25	2.17	2.10	2.04	1.99	1.92	1.84	1.75	1.70	1.65	1.59	1.53	1.47	1.39
120	3.92	3.07	2.68	2.45	2.29	2.17	2.09	2.02	1.96	1.91	1.83	1.75	1.66	1.61	1.55	1.50	1.43	1.35	1.25
∞	3.84	3.00	2.60	2.37	2.21	2.10	2.01	1.94	1.88	1.83	1.75	1.67	1.57	1.52	1.46	1.39	1.32	1.22	1.00

DENOMINATOR ν_2

$\alpha = .01$

NUMERATOR ν_1

ν_2	1	2	3	4	5	6	7	8	9	10	12	15	20	24	30	40	60	120	∞
1	4052	4999.5	5403	5625	5764	5859	5928	5982	6022	6056	6106	6157	6209	6235	6261	6287	6313	6339	6366
2	98.50	99.00	99.17	99.25	99.30	99.33	99.36	99.37	99.39	99.40	99.42	99.43	99.45	99.46	99.47	99.47	99.48	99.48	99.50
3	34.12	30.82	29.46	28.71	28.24	27.91	27.67	27.49	27.35	27.23	27.05	26.87	26.69	26.60	26.50	26.41	26.32	26.22	26.13
4	21.20	18.00	16.69	15.98	15.52	15.21	14.98	14.80	14.66	14.55	14.37	14.20	14.02	13.93	13.84	13.75	13.65	13.56	13.46
5	16.26	13.27	12.06	11.39	10.97	10.67	10.46	10.29	10.16	10.05	9.89	9.72	9.55	9.47	9.38	9.29	9.20	9.11	9.02
6	13.75	10.92	9.78	9.15	8.75	8.47	8.26	8.10	7.98	7.87	7.72	7.56	7.40	7.31	7.23	7.14	7.06	6.97	6.88
7	12.25	9.55	8.45	7.85	7.46	7.19	6.99	6.84	6.72	6.62	6.47	6.31	6.16	6.07	5.99	5.91	5.82	5.74	5.65
8	11.26	8.65	7.59	7.01	6.63	6.37	6.18	6.03	5.91	5.81	5.67	5.52	5.36	5.28	5.20	5.12	5.03	4.95	4.86
9	10.56	8.02	6.99	6.42	6.06	5.80	5.61	5.47	5.35	5.26	5.11	4.96	4.81	4.73	4.65	4.57	4.48	4.40	4.31
10	10.04	7.56	6.55	5.99	5.64	5.39	5.30	5.06	4.94	4.85	4.71	4.56	4.41	4.33	4.25	4.17	4.08	4.00	3.91
11	9.65	7.21	6.22	5.67	5.32	5.07	4.89	4.74	4.63	4.54	4.40	4.25	4.10	4.02	3.94	3.86	3.78	3.69	3.60
12	9.33	6.93	5.95	5.41	5.06	4.82	4.64	4.50	4.39	4.30	4.16	4.01	3.86	3.78	3.70	3.62	3.54	3.45	3.36
13	9.07	6.70	5.74	5.21	4.86	4.62	4.44	4.30	4.19	4.10	3.96	3.82	3.66	3.59	3.51	3.43	3.34	3.25	3.17
14	8.86	6.51	5.56	5.04	4.69	4.46	4.28	4.14	4.03	3.94	3.80	3.66	3.51	3.43	3.35	3.27	3.18	3.09	3.00
15	8.68	6.36	5.42	4.89	4.56	4.32	4.14	4.00	3.89	3.80	3.67	3.52	3.37	3.29	3.21	3.13	3.05	2.96	2.87
16	8.53	6.23	5.29	4.77	4.44	4.20	4.03	3.89	3.78	3.69	3.55	3.41	3.26	3.18	3.10	3.02	2.93	2.84	2.75
17	8.40	6.11	5.18	4.67	4.34	4.10	3.93	3.79	3.68	3.59	3.46	3.31	3.16	3.08	3.00	2.92	2.83	2.75	2.65
18	8.29	6.01	5.09	4.58	4.25	4.01	3.84	3.71	3.60	3.51	3.37	3.23	3.08	3.00	2.92	2.84	2.75	2.66	2.57
19	8.18	5.93	5.01	4.50	4.17	3.94	3.77	3.63	3.52	3.43	3.30	3.15	3.00	2.92	2.84	2.76	2.67	2.58	2.49
20	8.10	5.85	4.94	4.43	4.10	3.87	3.70	3.56	3.46	3.37	3.23	3.09	2.94	2.86	2.78	2.69	2.61	2.52	2.42
21	8.02	5.78	4.87	4.37	4.04	3.81	3.64	3.51	3.40	3.31	3.17	3.03	2.88	2.80	2.72	2.64	2.55	2.46	2.36
22	7.95	5.72	4.82	4.31	3.99	3.76	3.59	3.45	3.35	3.26	3.12	2.98	2.83	2.75	2.67	2.58	2.50	2.40	2.31
23	7.88	5.66	4.76	4.26	3.94	3.71	3.54	3.41	3.30	3.21	3.07	2.93	2.78	2.70	2.62	2.54	2.45	2.35	2.26
24	7.82	5.61	4.72	4.22	3.90	3.67	3.50	3.36	3.26	3.17	3.03	2.89	2.74	2.66	2.58	2.49	2.40	2.31	2.21
25	7.77	5.57	4.68	4.18	3.85	3.63	3.46	3.32	3.22	3.13	2.99	2.85	2.70	2.62	2.54	2.45	2.36	2.27	2.17
26	7.72	5.53	4.64	4.14	3.82	3.59	3.42	3.29	3.18	3.09	2.96	2.81	2.66	2.58	2.50	2.42	2.33	2.23	2.13
27	7.68	5.49	4.60	4.11	3.78	3.56	3.39	3.26	3.15	3.06	2.93	2.78	2.63	2.55	2.47	2.38	2.29	2.20	2.10
28	7.64	5.45	4.57	4.07	3.75	3.53	3.36	3.23	3.12	3.03	2.90	2.75	2.60	2.52	2.44	2.35	2.26	2.17	2.06
29	7.60	5.42	4.54	4.04	3.73	3.50	3.33	3.20	3.09	3.00	2.87	2.73	2.57	2.49	2.41	2.33	2.23	2.14	2.03
30	7.56	5.39	4.51	4.02	3.70	3.47	3.30	3.17	3.07	2.98	2.84	2.70	2.55	2.47	2.39	2.30	2.21	2.11	2.01
40	7.31	5.18	4.31	3.83	3.51	3.29	3.12	2.99	2.89	2.80	2.66	2.52	2.37	2.29	2.20	2.11	2.02	1.92	1.80
60	7.08	4.98	4.13	3.65	3.34	3.12	2.95	2.82	2.72	2.63	2.50	2.35	2.20	2.12	2.03	1.94	1.84	1.73	1.60
120	6.85	4.79	3.95	3.48	3.17	2.96	2.79	2.66	2.56	2.47	2.34	2.19	2.03	1.95	1.86	1.76	1.66	1.53	1.38
∞	6.63	4.61	3.78	3.32	3.02	2.80	2.64	2.51	2.41	2.32	2.18	2.04	1.88	1.79	1.70	1.59	1.47	1.32	1.00

TABLE 10 Cutoff Points for the Distribution of the Wilcoxon Test Statistic

For sample size n, the table shows, for selected probabilities α, the numbers T_α such that $P(T \leq T_\alpha) = \alpha$, where the distribution of the random variable T is that of the Wilcoxon test statistic under the null hypothesis.

n	α				
	.005	.010	.025	.050	.100
4	0	0	0	0	1
5	0	0	0	1	3
6	0	0	1	3	4
7	0	1	3	4	6
8	1	2	4	6	9
9	2	4	6	9	11
10	4	6	9	11	15
11	6	8	11	14	18
12	8	10	14	18	22
13	10	13	18	22	27
14	13	16	22	26	32
15	16	20	26	31	37
16	20	24	30	36	43
17	24	28	35	42	49
18	28	33	41	48	56
19	33	38	47	54	63
20	38	44	53	61	70

Reproduced with permission from R. L. McCormack, "Extended tables of the Wilcoxon matched pairs signed rank statistics," *Journal of the American Statistical Association, 60* (1965).

TABLE 11   Cutoff Points for the Distribution of Spearman Rank
Correlation Coefficient

For sample size n, the table shows, for selected probabilities α, the numbers $r_{s,\alpha}$ such that $P(r_s > r_{s,\alpha}) = \alpha$, where the distribution of the random variable r_s is that of Spearman rank correlation coefficient under the null hypothesis of no association.

n	α			
	.050	.025	.010	.005
5	.900	—	—	—
6	.829	.886	.943	—
7	.714	.786	.893	—
8	.643	.738	.833	.881
9	.600	.683	.783	.833
10	.564	.648	.745	.794
11	.523	.623	.736	.818
12	.497	.591	.703	.780
13	.475	.566	.673	.745
14	.457	.545	.646	.716
15	.441	.525	.623	.689
16	.425	.507	.601	.666
17	.412	.490	.582	.645
18	.399	.476	.564	.625
19	.388	.462	.549	.608
20	.377	.450	.534	.591
21	.368	.438	.521	.576
22	.359	.428	.508	.562
23	.351	.418	.496	.549
24	.343	.409	.485	.537
25	.336	.400	.475	.526
26	.329	.392	.465	.515
27	.323	.385	.456	.505
28	.317	.377	.448	.496
29	.311	.370	.440	.487
30	.305	.364	.432	.478

Reproduced with permission from E. G. Olds, "Distribution of sums of squares of rank differences for small samples," *Annals of Mathematical Statistics*, 9 (1938).

TABLE 12   Cutoff Points for the Distribution of the Durbin-Watson Test Statistic

Let d_α be the number such that $P(d < d_\alpha) = \alpha$, where the random variable d has the distribution of the Durbin-Watson statistic under the null hypothesis of no autocorrelation in the regression errors. For probabilities $\alpha = .05$ and $\alpha = .01$, the tables show, for numbers of independent variables, K, values d_L and d_U such that $d_L \le d_\alpha \le d_U$, for numbers n of observations.

	$\alpha = .05$									
	K									
	1		2		3		4		5	
n	d_L	d_U	d_L	d_U	d_L	d_U	d_L	d_U	d_L	d_U
15	1.08	1.36	0.95	1.54	0.82	1.75	0.69	1.97	0.56	2.21
16	1.10	1.37	0.98	1.54	0.86	1.73	0.74	1.93	0.62	2.15
17	1.13	1.38	1.02	1.54	0.90	1.71	0.78	1.90	0.67	2.10
18	1.16	1.39	1.05	1.53	0.93	1.69	1.82	1.87	0.71	2.06
19	1.18	1.40	1.08	1.53	0.97	1.68	0.86	1.85	0.75	2.02
20	1.20	1.41	1.10	1.54	1.00	1.68	0.90	1.83	0.79	1.99
21	1.22	1.42	1.13	1.54	1.03	1.67	0.93	1.81	0.83	1.96
22	1.24	1.43	1.15	1.54	1.05	1.66	0.96	1.80	0.86	1.94
23	1.26	1.44	1.17	1.54	1.08	1.66	0.99	1.79	0.90	1.92
24	1.27	1.45	1.19	1.55	1.10	1.66	1.01	1.78	0.93	1.90
25	1.29	1.45	1.21	1.55	1.12	1.66	1.04	1.77	0.95	1.89
26	1.30	1.46	1.22	1.55	1.14	1.65	1.06	1.76	0.98	1.88
27	1.32	1.47	1.24	1.56	1.16	1.65	1.08	1.76	1.01	1.86
28	1.33	1.48	1.26	1.56	1.18	1.65	1.10	1.75	1.03	1.85
29	1.34	1.48	1.27	1.56	1.20	1.65	1.12	1.74	1.05	1.84
30	1.35	1.49	1.28	1.57	1.21	1.65	1.14	1.74	1.07	1.83
31	1.36	1.50	1.30	1.57	1.23	1.65	1.16	1.74	1.09	1.83
32	1.37	1.50	1.31	1.57	1.24	1.65	1.18	1.73	1.11	1.82
33	1.38	1.51	1.32	1.58	1.26	1.65	1.19	1.73	1.13	1.81
34	1.39	1.51	1.33	1.58	1.27	1.65	1.21	1.73	1.15	1.81
35	1.40	1.52	1.34	1.58	1.28	1.65	1.22	1.73	1.16	1.80
36	1.41	1.52	1.35	1.59	1.29	1.65	1.24	1.73	1.18	1.80
37	1.42	1.53	1.36	1.59	1.31	1.66	1.25	1.72	1.19	1.80
38	1.43	1.54	1.37	1.59	1.32	1.66	1.26	1.72	1.21	1.79
39	1.43	1.54	1.38	1.60	1.33	1.66	1.27	1.72	1.22	1.79
40	1.44	1.54	1.39	1.60	1.34	1.66	1.29	1.72	1.23	1.79
45	1.48	1.57	1.43	1.62	1.38	1.67	1.34	1.72	1.29	1.78
50	1.50	1.59	1.46	1.63	1.42	1.67	1.38	1.72	1.34	1.77
55	1.53	1.60	1.49	1.64	1.45	1.68	1.41	1.72	1.38	1.77
60	1.55	1.62	1.51	1.65	1.48	1.69	1.44	1.73	1.41	1.77
65	1.57	1.63	1.54	1.66	1.50	1.70	1.47	1.73	1.44	1.77
70	1.58	1.64	1.55	1.67	1.52	1.70	1.49	1.74	1.46	1.77
75	1.60	1.65	1.57	1.68	1.54	1.71	1.51	1.74	1.49	1.77
80	1.61	1.66	1.59	1.69	1.56	1.72	1.53	1.74	1.51	1.77
85	1.62	1.67	1.60	1.70	1.57	1.72	1.55	1.75	1.52	1.77
90	1.63	1.68	1.61	1.70	1.59	1.73	1.57	1.75	1.54	1.78
95	1.64	1.69	1.62	1.71	1.60	1.73	1.58	1.75	1.56	1.78
100	1.65	1.69	1.63	1.72	1.61	1.74	1.59	1.76	1.57	1.78

TABLE 12   Cutoff Points for the Distribution of the Durbin-Watson Test Statistic (cont.)

	\alpha = .01									
n	K									
	1		2		3		4		5	
	d_L	d_U	d_L	d_U	d_L	d_U	d_L	d_U	d_L	d_U
15	0.81	1.07	0.70	1.25	0.59	1.46	0.49	1.70	0.39	1.96
16	0.84	1.09	0.74	1.25	0.63	1.44	0.53	1.66	0.44	1.90
17	0.87	1.10	0.77	1.25	0.67	1.43	0.57	1.63	0.48	1.85
18	0.90	1.12	0.80	1.26	0.71	1.42	0.61	1.60	0.52	1.80
19	0.93	1.13	0.83	1.26	0.74	1.41	0.65	1.58	0.56	1.77
20	0.95	1.15	0.86	1.27	0.77	1.41	0.68	1.57	0.60	1.74
21	0.97	1.16	0.89	1.27	0.80	1.41	0.72	1.55	0.63	1.71
22	1.00	1.17	0.91	1.28	0.83	1.40	0.75	1.54	0.66	1.69
23	1.02	1.19	0.94	1.29	0.86	1.40	0.77	1.53	0.70	1.67
24	1.04	1.20	0.96	1.30	0.88	1.41	0.80	1.53	0.72	1.66
25	1.05	1.21	0.98	1.30	0.90	1.41	0.83	1.52	0.75	1.65
26	1.07	1.22	1.00	1.31	0.93	1.41	0.85	1.52	0.78	1.64
27	1.09	1.23	1.02	1.32	0.95	1.41	0.88	1.51	0.81	1.63
28	1.10	1.24	1.04	1.32	0.97	1.41	0.90	1.51	0.83	1.62
29	1.12	1.25	1.05	1.33	0.99	1.42	0.92	1.51	0.85	1.61
30	1.13	1.26	1.07	1.34	1.01	1.42	0.94	1.51	0.88	1.61
31	1.15	1.27	1.08	1.34	1.02	1.42	0.96	1.51	0.90	1.60
32	1.16	1.28	1.10	1.35	1.04	1.43	0.98	1.51	0.92	1.60
33	1.17	1.29	1.11	1.36	1.05	1.43	1.00	1.51	0.94	1.59
34	1.18	1.30	1.13	1.36	1.07	1.43	1.01	1.51	0.95	1.59
35	1.19	1.31	1.14	1.37	1.08	1.44	1.03	1.51	0.97	1.59
36	1.21	1.32	1.15	1.38	1.10	1.44	1.04	1.51	0.99	1.59
37	1.22	1.32	1.16	1.38	1.11	1.45	1.06	1.51	1.00	1.59
38	1.23	1.33	1.18	1.39	1.12	1.45	1.07	1.52	1.02	1.58
39	1.24	1.34	1.19	1.39	1.14	1.45	1.09	1.52	1.03	1.58
40	1.25	1.34	1.20	1.40	1.15	1.46	1.10	1.52	1.05	1.58
45	1.29	1.38	1.24	1.42	1.20	1.48	1.16	1.53	1.11	1.58
50	1.32	1.40	1.28	1.45	1.24	1.49	1.20	1.54	1.16	1.59
55	1.36	1.43	1.32	1.47	1.28	1.51	1.25	1.55	1.21	1.59
60	1.38	1.45	1.35	1.48	1.32	1.52	1.28	1.56	1.25	1.60
65	1.41	1.47	1.38	1.50	1.35	1.53	1.31	1.57	1.28	1.61
70	1.43	1.49	1.40	1.52	1.37	1.55	1.34	1.58	1.31	1.61
75	1.45	1.50	1.42	1.53	1.39	1.56	1.37	1.59	1.34	1.62
80	1.47	1.52	1.44	1.54	1.42	1.57	1.39	1.60	1.36	1.62
85	1.48	1.53	1.46	1.55	1.43	1.58	1.41	1.60	1.39	1.63
90	1.50	1.54	1.47	1.56	1.45	1.59	1.43	1.61	1.41	1.64
95	1.51	1.55	1.49	1.57	1.47	1.60	1.45	1.62	1.42	1.64
100	1.52	1.56	1.50	1.58	1.48	1.60	1.46	1.63	1.44	1.65

Reproduced with permission from J. Durbin and G. S. Watson, "Testing for serial correlation in least squares regression, II," *Biometrika*, *38* (1951).

TABLE 13   Factors for Control Charts

	x-CHARTS				s-CHARTS				R-CHARTS					
n	A	A_2	A_3	c_4	B_3	B_4	B_5	B_6	d_2	d_3	D_1	D_2	D_3	D_4
2	2.121	1.880	2.659	0.7979	0	3.267	0	2.606	1.128	0.853	0	3.686	0	3.267
3	1.732	1.023	1.954	0.8862	0	2.568	0	2.276	1.693	0.888	0	4.358	0	2.574
4	1.500	0.729	1.628	0.9213	0	2.266	0	2.088	2.059	0.880	0	4.698	0	2.282
5	1.342	0.577	1.427	0.9400	0	2.089	0	1.964	2.326	0.864	0	4.918	0	2.114
6	1.225	0.483	1.287	0.9515	0.030	1.970	0.029	1.874	2.534	0.848	0	5.078	0	2.004
7	1.134	0.419	1.182	0.9594	0.118	1.882	0.113	1.806	2.704	0.833	0.204	5.204	0.076	1.924
8	1.061	0.373	1.099	0.9650	0.185	1.815	0.179	1.751	2.847	0.820	0.388	5.306	0.136	1.864
9	1.000	0.337	1.032	0.969	0.239	1.761	0.232	1.707	2.970	0.808	0.547	5.393	0.184	1.816
10	0.949	0.308	0.975	0.9727	0.284	1.716	0.276	1.669	3.078	0.797	0.687	5.469	0.223	1.777
11	0.905	0.285	0.927	0.9754	0.321	1.679	0.313	1.637	3.173	0.787	0.811	5.535	0.256	1.744
12	0.866	0.266	0.886	0.9776	0.354	1.646	0.346	1.610	3.258	0.778	0.922	5.594	0.283	1.717
13	0.832	0.249	0.850	0.9794	0.382	1.618	0.374	1.585	3.336	0.770	1.025	5.647	0.307	1.693
14	0.802	0.235	0.817	0.9810	0.406	1.594	0.399	1.563	3.407	0.763	1.118	5.696	0.328	1.672
15	0.775	0.223	0.789	0.9823	0.428	1.572	0.421	1.544	3.472	0.756	1.203	5.741	0.347	1.653
16	0.750	0.212	0.763	0.9835	0.448	1.552	0.440	1.526	3.532	0.750	1.282	5.782	0.363	1.637
17	0.728	0.203	0.739	0.9845	0.466	1.534	0.458	1.511	3.588	0.744	1.356	5.820	0.378	1.622
18	0.707	0.194	0.718	0.9854	0.482	1.518	0.475	1.496	3.640	0.739	1.424	5.856	0.391	1.608
19	0.688	0.187	0.698	0.9862	0.497	1.503	0.490	1.483	3.689	0.734	1.487	5.891	0.403	1.597
20	0.671	0.180	0.680	0.9869	0.510	1.490	0.504	1.470	3.735	0.729	1.549	5.921	0.415	1.585
21	0.655	0.173	0.663	0.9876	0.523	1.477	0.516	1.459	3.778	0.724	1.605	5.951	0.425	1.575
22	0.640	0.167	0.647	0.9882	0.534	1.466	0.528	1.448	3.819	0.720	1.659	5.979	0.434	1.566
23	0.626	0.162	0.633	0.9887	0.545	1.455	0.539	1.438	3.858	0.716	1.710	6.006	0.443	1.557
24	0.612	0.157	0.619	0.9892	0.555	1.445	0.549	1.429	3.895	0.712	1.759	6.031	0.451	1.548
25	0.600	0.153	0.606	0.9896	0.565	1.435	0.559	1.420	3.931	0.708	1.806	6.056	0.459	1.541

Source: Adapted from Table 27 of ASTM STP 15D ASTM *Manual on Presentation of Data and Control Chart Analysis.* ©1976 American Society for Testing and Materials, Philadelphia, PA.

TABLE 14 Cumulative Distribution Function of the Runs Test Statistic

For a given number n of observations, the table shows the probability, for a random time series, that the number of runs will not exceed K.

n	\multicolumn{19}{c	}{K}
	2	3	4	5	6	7	8	9	10	11	12	13	14	15	16	17	18	19	20
6	.100	.300	.700	.900	1.000														
8	.029	.114	.371	.629	.886	.971	1.000												
10	.008	.040	.167	.357	.643	.833	.960	.992	1.000										
12	.002	.013	.067	.175	.392	.608	.825	.933	.987	.998	1.000								
14	.001	.004	.025	.078	.209	.383	.617	.791	.922	.975	.996	.999	1.000						
16	.000	.001	.009	.032	.100	.214	.405	.595	.786	.900	.968	.991	.999	1.000					
18	.000	.000	.003	.012	.044	.109	.238	.399	.601	.762	.891	.956	.988	.997	1.000	1.000	1.000		
20	.000	.000	.001	.004	.019	.051	.128	.242	.414	.586	.758	.872	.949	.981	.996	.999	1.000	1.000	1.000

Reproduced with permission from F. Swed and C. Eisenhart, "Tables for testing randomness of grouping in a sequence of alternatives," *Annals of Mathematical Statistics, 14* (1943).

CHAPTER 2

2. (a) Categorical; ordinal (b) Categorical; nominal
   (c) Numerical; discrete
4. (a) Categorical; nominal (b) Categorical; nominal
   (c) Numerical; quantitative measurement (continuous)
6. Answers will vary. One possiblility is to use five classes with width of ten.

(a) If the first class is 50 less than 60, the following results:

CLASSES	FREQUENCY
50 < 60	4
60 < 70	7
70 < 80	10
80 < 90	11
90<100	8

(b) The cumulative frequency distribution is:

SCORES	CUMULATIVE FREQUENCY
< 60	4 or 10.00%
< 70	11 or 27.50%
< 80	21 or 52.50%
< 90	32 or 80.00%
<100	40 or 100.00%

(c)

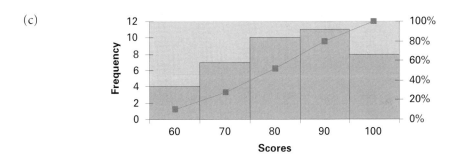

(d) Stem Unit = 10

5	4669
6	0226788
7	0033357899
8	11233566899
9	00133458

8. (a)

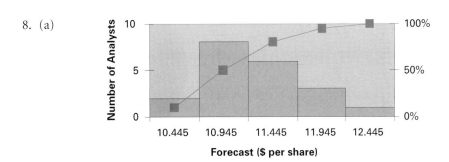

(b), (c), (d)

FREQUENCY	RELATIVE FREQ.	CUMULATIVE FREQ.	CUMULATIVE %
2	0.1	2	10.00%
8	0.4	10	50.00%
6	0.3	16	80.00%
3	0.15	19	95.00%
1	0.05	20	100.00%

10. (a)

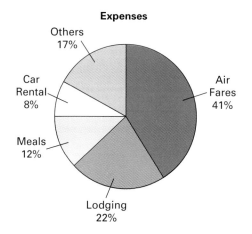

11. (b)

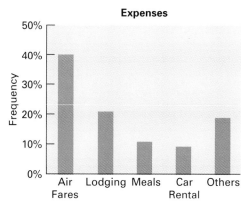

12. (a) Pie chart

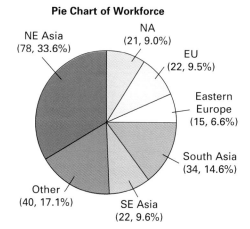

(b) Bar chart

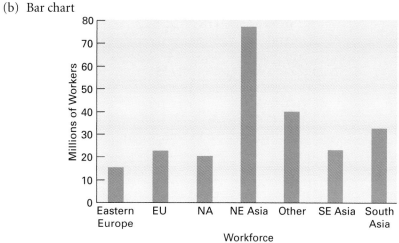

14.

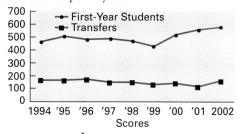

16. The University should determine factors that contribute to the increase in the number of transfer students over the last couple of years.

18.

Defect	A	C	D	B	E	G	Others
Count	17	13	3	2	2	2	1
Percent	42.5	32.5	7.5	5.0	5.0	5.0	2.5
Cum%	42.5	75.0	82.5	87.5	92.5	97.5	100.0

20. (a) Mean = 11.4
    (b) Median = (11 + 13)/2 = 12
22. (a) Mean = 3.35
    (b) Sample Median = 3.4
24. (a) Sample Median = 17.55
    (b) Sample Mean = 19.9083
26. (a) 5.53248
    (b) 12.87 years to double at the given growth rate
28. (a) Range = 0.54; Variance = 0.01049; Standard Deviation = 0.1024
    (b)

Five-number Summary	
Minimum	3.57
First Quartile	3.74
Median	3.79
Third Quartile	3.87
Maximum	4.11

(c) IQR = 3.87 − 3.74 = 0.13; Excluding the top and bottom 25% of the values, the IQR states that the middle 50% of the bottles have a weight between 3.74 and 3.87.

(d) Coefficient of Variation = $\dfrac{s}{\overline{X}} = \dfrac{0.1024}{3.8079} = 0.0269$

(e)

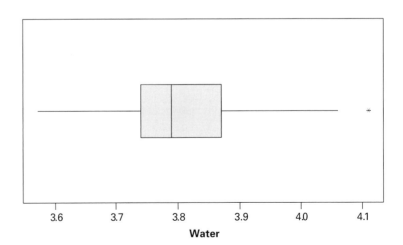

Boxplot of Water

30. (a) S = 3.86959
32. (a) Sample mean = 9.36
    (b) Sample variance = 20.9067, standard deviation = 4.572

34. (a)

Pie Chart of Internet Usage: Males

Do Not Use Internet (58.0%)

Internet User (42.0%)

Pie Chart of Internet Usage: Females

Do Not Use Internet (65.0%)

Internet User (35.0%)

(b)

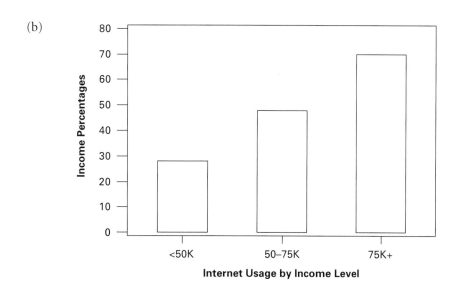

Internet Usage by Income Level

36.

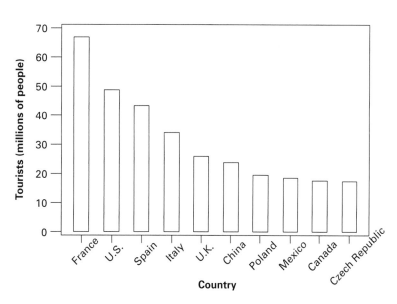

38. (a)

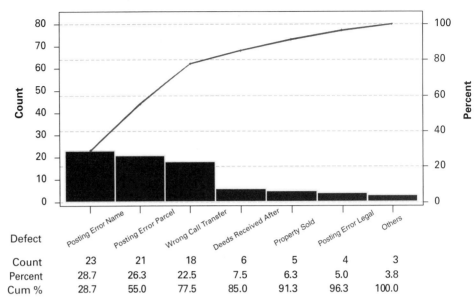

Pareto Chart for Defects

Defect	Posting Error Name	Posting Error Parcel	Wrong Call Transfer	Deeds Received After	Property Sold	Posting Error Legal	Others
Count	23	21	18	6	5	4	3
Percent	28.7	26.3	22.5	7.5	6.3	5.0	3.8
Cum %	28.7	55.0	77.5	85.0	91.3	96.3	100.0

(b) Recommendations should include a discussion of the data entry process. The data entry was being made by individuals with no knowledge of the data. Training of the data entry personnel should be a major recommendation. Increasing the size of the monitors used by the data entry staff could also reduce the number of errors.

CHAPTER 3

2. Scatter plot
4. Scatter plot
6. (a) 0.00008527   (b) 0.147
8. (a) 1069   (b) 0.989
   (c) Number of workers and number of tables change in the same direction.
10. (a) −5.5   (b) −.776
    (c) Higher prices are associated with faster delivery time.
12. (a) $Y = 53.7 + 0.134X$ (b) 54.40, 55.71
    (c) Recovery time increases with drug usage; dosage = 0
14. Emphasize; tools, east, paint, north, tools, lumber, west
16. (a) Scatter plot
    (b) 0.679, 0.679
       Revenue = 134517 + 30.7 households
       Revenue = 134517 + 21.9 tons
    (c) 2,900 households revenue = $223,416
       12,600 tons   revenue = $410,326
    (d) M.R. = 21.90 per ton
18. His forecast provides direction for investing based on temperature and the correlation coefficient is reasonable given the observation.
20. (a) Quantity = 268.72 − 18.22 price
    (b) 22.39(5); −31.17(7); −2.96(8); e = 22.28; −31.32; 13.28
    (c) Specific mathematical relationship
22. (a) Scatter plot   (b) $Y = −14.4 + 5.47X$; marginal value = 5.47

24. (a) Scatter plot   (b) Production = 1506 + .999 export
    (c) Marginal value = 0.999
26. (a) 0.408   (b) Pounds of grits = 14851 + 0.0506 production
    (c) 0.0506 pounds of grits
28. (a) Scatter plot
    (b) Health = $-37.65 + 0.099$ Income
        Retail Sales = 2127 + 0.278 Income
        Energy = 92.15 + 0.0262 Income
30. (a) Scatter plot   (b) 0.137   (c) GDP growth = 5.18 + 0.0259 defense
    (d) Very little if any effect   (e) Defense expenditures reduce GDP growth
    (f) Not substantially
32. Scatter plots

CHAPTER 4

2. (a) $(\underline{A} \cap B)$ is the event that the Dow-Jones average rises on both days which is O_1.
       $(A \cap B)$ is the event that the Dow-Jones average does not rise on the first day but it
       rises on the second day which is O_3. The union between these two will be the events
       $O_1 O_3$ which by definition is event B: the Dow-Jones average rises on the second day.
   (b) Since $(A \cap B)$ is the event the Dow-Jones average does not rise on the first day but
       rises on the second day which is O_3 and because A is the event that the Dow-Jones
       average rises on the first day, then the union will be the event that either the Dow-
       Jones average does not rise on the first day but rises on the second day or the Dow-
       Jones average rises on the first day or both. This is the definition of $A \cup \overline{B}$.
4. (a) $P(A) = .68$ (b) $P(B) = .73$ (c) $P(\overline{A}) = .32$ (d) $P(A \cap B) = .41$
   (e) $P(A \cup B) = 1.0$
6. (a) $P(A) = 0.5$ (b) $P(B) = 0.25$ (c) $P(A \cap B) = 0.25$
   (d) $P(A \cup B) = 0.5 + 0.25 - 0.25 = P(A)$ of 0.5
8. (a) $P(A) = .86$ (b) $P(B) = .91$ (c) $P(\overline{A}) = .14$
   (d) $P(A \cup B) = .86 + .91 - .77 = 1.00$ (e) $P(A \cap B) = .39 + .23 + .15 = .77$
   (f) Check if $P(A \cap B) = 0$. Because $P(A \cap B) = .77 \neq 0$, A and B are not mutually exclusive.
   (g) Yes, because $P(A \cup B) = 1$, A and B are collectively exhaustive.
10. The probability of the intersection between two independent events is equal to the prod-
    uct of the individual probabilities. Therefore, the probability of both Superior Packaging
    and Intense Media campaign = $(1/3)(1/3) = 1/9$
12. $P_2^{50} = 2,450$
14. If A is the event "no graduate student is selected," then the number of combinations of 3
    chosen from 6 is $C_3^6 = 6!/3! \, 3! = 20$ and the number of combinations of 0 objects chosen
    from 2 is $C_0^2 = 2!/0! \, 2! = 2$. $P(A) = 2/20 = .10$
16. (a) Number of arrangements = 24
    (b) $C_1^4 = 4$. The probability of one assignment is ¼
18. (a) $P_2^7 = 42$ (b) $P_1^6 = 6$ (c) $P_1^6 = 6$
    (d) Probability of being chosen as the heroine = 6 chances out of 42 = 1/7.
    (e) Since being chosen as the heroine or as the best friend are mutually exclusive, then
        $P(A \cup B) = P(A) + P(B) - P(A \cap B) = 1/7 + 1/7 - 0 = 2/7$.
20. (a) $C_2^6 = 6!/2! \, 4! = 15$, $C_2^4 = 4!/2! \, 2! = 6$. Because the selections are independent, there
        are $(15)(6) = 90$ different sets of funds from which to choose.
    (b) P(no U.S. fund underperforms) = 10/15. P(no foreign fund underperforms) = 3/6,
        P(at least one fund underperforms) = $1 - P$(no fund underperforms) = $1 -$
        $(10/15)(3/6) = 2/3$
22. $P(A \cup B) = .35$

24. (a) $P(4 \text{ misses}) = (.95)^4 = .8145$
    (b) $P(\text{donation}) = .10$; $P(4 \text{ misses}) = (.9)^4 = .6561$
26. Probability that the player will be eligible is $(.98)(.85) = .833$.
28. $P(B) = .01/.08 = .125$
30. $P(B|A) = [(.4)(.05)]/.15 = .1333$
32. $P(A \cup B) = .0331$. Therefore, the probability of getting either the high-tech stocks or the airline stocks picked correctly is relatively small.
34. (a) $P(A \cap B) = .12$ (b) $P(A|B) = .06$ (c) $P(A \cup B) = .78$
    (d) $.12 \neq .2$, therefore, the two events are dependent events
36. $P(C|(A \cap B) = .125$
38. (a) $P(PH) = .3$ (b) $P(H) = .38$ (c) $P(PH|H) = .6053$
    (d) $P(H|PH) = .7667$ (e) $P(L|PH) = .0333$
40. (a) $P(D) = .1$ (b) $P(B) = .35$ (c) $P(D|B) = .1429$ (d) $P(B|D) = .5$
    (e) No, since $P(G \cap B)$ which is $.3 \neq P(G)P(B)$ which is $.315$.
    (f) $P(G|A) = .27/.29 = .931$, $P(G|B) = .3/.35 = .857$ $P(G|C) = .33/.36 = .917$. Therefore, subcontractor A is the most reliable
42. (a) $P(M) = .77$ (b) $P(L) = .19$ (c) $P(L|S) = .2609$
    (d) $P(M|S) = .7901$
44. (a) $P(J) = .082$ (b) $P(W|J) = .6585$
46. (a) $P(HC \cap WS) = .1428$ (b) $P(HC \cup WS) = .4972$
    (c) $P(HC|WS) = .6491$
48. (a) $P(H|F) = .571$ (b) $P(L|U) = .5184$
    (c) $P(L|N \cup F) = .2129$ (d) $P(N \cup F|L) = .5236$
50. (a) $P(E|SE) = .8485$, $P(3E|SE) = .6109$ (b) $P(\text{at least } 1E|SE) = .9965$
52. (a) E_1 = Stock performs much better than the market average.
        A = Stock is rated a "Buy"
        $P(E_1|A) = .444$
54. (a) True   (b) False   (c) True   (d) True   (e) True
    (f) True   (g) False
56. Bayes' theorem
58. Definitions: *joint, marginal, and conditional probability*
60. $P(A \cup B) = P(A) + P(B)[1 - P(A|B)]$
62. (a) $P(\text{thick}) = 8/19$ (b) $P(\text{thin}) = 12/19$
    (c) $P(\text{thick} \cap \text{thin}) = .2526$
64. (a) $(HM \cap S) = .125$ (b) $P(S|HM) = .3571$
    (c) $P(\overline{HM} \cup \overline{S}) = .875$ (d)   No (e)   No (f)   No
66. (a) $(M \cap HS) = .48$ (b) $P(G) = .11$ (c) $P(M|G) = .7273$
    (d) No   (e) $P(F|\overline{G}) = .191$
68. (a) 1,820   (b) .089
70. (a) $P(C \cap T) = .075$ (b) $P(T|C) = .1429$ (c) $10!90!/100!$
72. .2581
74. .6364
76. (a) .4526   (b) .6632   (c) .9406   (d) No
78. (a) .58   (b) .6034   (c) .3966

CHAPTER 5

2. Discrete
4. Total sales, advertising expenditures, competitor's sales
6. (a) 0.55   (b) 0.45   (c) 0.75   (d) 0.55
8. (c) $\mu = 1.25$ (d) $\sigma^2 = 1.1675$

10. (c) 0.70   (d) 0.8556   (e) $\mu = 49.9, \sigma^2 = 1.3964$

12. (a) 0.81, 0.18, 0.01   (b) $\dfrac{153}{190}, \dfrac{36}{190}, \dfrac{1}{190}$ (c) $\mu = 0.2, \sigma^2 = 0.18$

(d) $\mu = 0.2, \sigma^2 = 0.1705$

14. 1.3125   1.50

16. $E[x] = 3.29$ $\sigma = 1.1515$

18. $\mu = 1.82$ $\sigma = 1.0137$

20. (a) .7351   (b) .2321   (c) .0328

22. (a) .9891   (b) .5798

24. (a) .000011   (b) .3771   (c) .2235

26. .032

28. (a) 7.5, 2.525   (b) $1,875, $631

30. $\mu = 2.0$ and $\sigma^2 = 1.2$

32. (a) .81   (b) .28   (c) .06

34. .916

36. .38

38. .262

40. (a) .267   (b) .264

42. (a) .171   (b) .219

44. .758

46. .83

48. (a) .53   (b) $P(310) = 9/19, P(410) = 7/19, P(510) = 3/19$
    (c) $P(015) = 1/8, P(115) = 5/12, P(215) = 11/24$ (d) .109   (e) no

50. (a) $P(0,0) = .54, P(0,1) = .30, P(1,0) = .01, P(1,1) = .01\ P(1,1) = .15$
    (b) $P(0,2) = 1/16, P(1,1) = 15/16$ (c) .078

52. Because of independence, the joint probabilities are the products of the marginal proba-
    bilities, so $P(0,0) = .0216$, and so on.

54. 28.4, 4.54

56. (a) 0.25   (b) 3.2   (c) 1.03   (d) $2,059

58. (a) 2.25   (b) 1.249   (c) 3.25, 1.30

60. (a) $P(0)$ .0001, $P(1)$ .0041, $P(2)$ .0571, $P(3)$ .3231, $P(4)$ .6156
    (b) 3.55   (c) 0.6225

62. (a) 0.767   (b) 0.2765   (c) 2.4, 1.2   (d) 7.2, 3.6

64. (a) 0.71021   (b) 0.27648   (c) .432, 0.48

66. 0.16202

68. 0.98696

CHAPTER 6

2. (b) $F(x) = .25x$, for $0 \le x \le 4$
   (c) .25
   (d) .25

4. (a) .2   (b) Between .4 and .6

6. $26.4 million, $1 million

8. $54,000, $14,400

10. (a) .52   (b) −.67   (c) −.84   (d) −0.25

12. (a) 0.9772   (b) 0.6826   (c) 1,328

14. (a) 0.1401   (b) 0.0455   (c) 0.493

16. (a) 0.5762   (b) 458,000   (c) [402,598]

18. 16.152

20. (a) 0.1587   (b) 0.2426   (c) 502.6
22. 0.9332, 0.9082, supplier A better
24. (a) 0.2266   (b) 0.2266   (c) graph   (d) 100.6
26. (a) 0.3413   (b) 0.0122   (c) smaller   (d) 174.4
28. (a) 0.0475   (b) 0.3372
30. 0.0207
32. (a) 0.2743   (b) 0.392
34. 0.2148 $E[x] = 8.2137$ 0.0436
36. .3012
38. (a) $e^{-3\lambda}$ (b) $e^{-6\lambda}$ (c) $e^{-3\lambda}$
40. $1,000, $134.16 (assuming year-to-year independence)
42. If $\alpha = 0$ Var(R) = $1,100,000\sigma^2$
44. 600, 35.8
46. (a) The cumulative density function provides information about the probability that the variable will be less than a specific value (x).
    (b) The probability density function shows the relative frequencies of a random variable for each value of the random variable.
    (c) The mean of a continuous random variable is a measure of location of a random variable. This is the expected value of the random variable.
    (d) The standard deviation shows how far on average the values in the distribution lie from the mean.
    (e) The covariance is a measure of how two variables vary together. It is the average of the deviation products of the two variables.
48. (a) The area under the normal curve can be found through integral calculus; however, the calculation requires approximation techniques. The tables provide a simplified method of determining the probabilities.
    (b) All normal probability distributions with any mean and any variance can all be converted into the 'standard normal' distribution with a mean of zero and a standard deviation of 1. Thus, only one table is necessary once the conversion is done.
    (c) There are examples of variables that occur in the real world that can be approximated by the normal probability distribution, and it has properties that allow for convenient calculations of probabilities.
50. (a) 1/6   (b) 2/3   (c) $1,333.33
    (d) Let B denote the bid (in thousands of dollars). Then the expected profit is $(B - 10)(20 - B)/12$ thousand dollars. Choose B to maximize this, giving $B = $15,000.
52. (c) .75
54. (a) $768.50   (b) $100.05   (c) %165, $34.50
58. (a) .3085   (b) .6826   (c) 79.6   (d) 53.3 to 66.7 minutes
    (e) .2731
60. (a) .7888   (b) .0062   (c) .0306   (d) 17.9 to 22.1 minutes
    (e) 19--21   (f) 21–23
62. 23.58%
64. Almost 1.0
66. (a) .16   (b) .135   (c) .393   (d) .050
68. (a) .7745   (b) 137.28   (c) .1587   (d) .0062

CHAPTER 7

2. Use binomial $\pi = 0.40$
   (a) $\eta = 5$ (b) $\eta = 10$
4. (a) 92   (b) 3.24   (c) 1.8   (d) 0.2877

6. (a) 0.3085, 0.1587, 0.0228
8. (a) 20   (b) 0.3085   (c) 0.9332
10. (a) 0.3   (b) 0.1587   (c) 0.0228   (d) 0.905   (e) 0.762
12. (a) 0.3085   (b) 0.2266   (c) 0.6826   (d) Lower, lower, lower
14. (a) $\eta = 40$ (b) Larger   (c) Larger
16. (a) 47/12   (b) 47/120   (c) 47/120
18. (a) 26,859.689   (b) 0.1762   (c) 0.7704   (d) 0.4147
20. (a) 0.9207   (b) 0.9207   (d) 0.1586
22. (a) 0.75   (b) 0.001875   (c) 0.0433   (d) 0.1251
24. (a) 0.0324   (b) 0.0618   (c) 0.1762   (d) 0.6476
26. (a) 0.0285   (b) 0.0025   (c) 0.6111   (d) 0.41–0.43
28. (a) 0.0274   (b) 0.7673   (c) 0.29–0.31
30. $\eta = 1068$
32. 0.04802   0.0708
34. 0.05065   0.1611
36. (a) 0.05038   (b) 0.1814   (c) 0.6785
38. .0201
40. (a) 0.1187   (b) 0.0118
42. (a) 0.0428   (b) 0.0004
44. $\sigma^2 = \dfrac{47}{12}$ mean of $S^2 = 4.7$
46. (a) 1.6311   (b) 2.1133   (c) b Interval smaller
48. (a) 0.4155   (b) 0.5073   (c) 0.3427   1.9927
50. 0.5438
52. (a) 15   (b) (41,39) . . . (33,38)   (c) 4.533 . . . 2.667
54. 3/15, 9/15, 3/15, 3/6
56. (a) .1587   (b) 53.6   (c) 14.4337   (d) 4.4121
58. (a) 0.8413   (b) 1,704   (c) 487.825
60. (a) 0.0228   (b) 91.57   (c) 17.525
62. (a) 2.5701   (b) 0.468   (c) 0.882
64. (a) 0.0228   (b) 0.6826   (c) Larger a, smaller b
66. 0.0618
68. (a) 0.0003   (b) ≈ 0
70. 0.0559

CHAPTER 8

2. (a) No evidence of nonnormality exists. Check the Normal Probability Plot in Minitab
    (b) 101.375   (c) 25.2121   (d) 0.375
4. (a) $E(\overline{X}) = \dfrac{1}{2} E(X_1) + \dfrac{1}{2} E(X_2) = \dfrac{\mu}{2} + \dfrac{\mu}{2} = \mu$

    $E(Y) = \dfrac{1}{4} E(X_1) + \dfrac{3}{4} E(X_2) = \dfrac{\mu}{4} + \dfrac{3\mu}{4} = \mu$

    $E(Z) = \dfrac{1}{3} E(X_1) + \dfrac{2}{3} E(X_2) = \dfrac{\mu}{3} + \dfrac{2\mu}{3} = \mu$

6. (a) No evidence of nonnormality exists. Check the Normal Probability Plot in Minitab
    (b) 0.0515   (c) 9.557192E-6
8. (a) $2.7236 < \mu < 3.0764$
    (b) Since $Z_{\alpha/2} = 1$, the confidence level is 68.26%.
10. (a) $174.076 < \mu < 201.724$
    (b) Since $Z_{\alpha/2} = 2.05$, the confidence level is 95.96%.

12. (a) 519.379 up to 522.517   (b) Narrower

14. 64.24%

16. Margin of Error $= t_{\alpha/2} \dfrac{s}{\sqrt{n}} = t_{(0.025,6)} \dfrac{s}{\sqrt{7}} = 2.447 \dfrac{6.3957}{\sqrt{7}} = 5.9152$

18. $\$41,104.28 < \mu < \$44,375.72$

20. .3369 up to .4215

22. $0.900 - 0.879 = 0.021 = Z_{\alpha/2} \sqrt{\dfrac{(0.879)(0.121)}{600}} = Z_{\alpha/2}(0.0133)$

   Thus, $Z_{\alpha/2} = 1.58$ and the confidence level is 88.58%

24. Using PHStat, the result is:

Sample Proportion	0.705263158
Z Value	-2.57583451
Standard Error of the Proportion	0.046776854
Interval Half Width	0.120489435

CONFIDENCE INTERVAL	
Interval Lower Limit	0.584773723
Interval Upper Limit	0.825752593

26. $n = 198$, $p = 98/198 = 0.4949$. $Z = 1.41$ and the confidence level is 84.14%.

28. With PHStat

Sample Proportion	0.1626
Z Value	-2.3263
Standard Error of the Proportion	0.0235
Interval Half Width	0.00547

CONFIDENCE INTERVAL	
Interval Lower Limit	0.1079
Interval Upper Limit	0.2173

30. $\dfrac{49(.000478)^2}{70.222} < \sigma^2 < \dfrac{49(.000478)^2}{31.555}$ or $1.59\text{E-}7 < \sigma^2 < 3.55\text{E-}7$

32. $\dfrac{(19)(6.62)}{32.85} < \sigma^2 < \dfrac{(19)(6.62)}{8.91}$ or $3.83 < \sigma^2 < 14.12$

   Similar values are found with PHStat,

Degrees of Freedom	19
Sum of Squares	125.78
Single Tail Area	0.025
Lower Chi-Square Value	8.9065
Upper Chi-Square Value	32.852

RESULTS	
Interval Lower Limit for Variance	3.8285
Interval Upper Limit for Variance	14.122

Assumption: Population from which sample was drawn has an approximate normal distribution.

34. (a) $\dfrac{(14)(2.36)^2}{26.12} < \sigma^2 < \dfrac{(14)(2.36)^2}{5.63}$ or $2.99 < \sigma^2 < 13.85$

From PHStat, similar results.

Interval Lower Limit for Variance	2.9854
Interval Upper Limit for Variance	13.853

Assumption: Population from which sample was drawn has an approximate normal distribution.

(b) Wider

36. Let X = Without Passive Solar; Y = With Passive Solar; Using Equation 8.8, we find

$37.3 \pm (1.833) \dfrac{17.6575}{\sqrt{10}}$ or $27.06 < \mu_X - \mu_Y < 47.54$

38. -5.286 up to 8.306

40. -3270.41 up to 1388.41

42. -9.1207 up to -1.5193

44. -6.2971 up to 2.8971

46. $-.2521$ up to $.0289$

48. Width $= 0.10 - 0.04 = 0.06$; thus, Bound $= 0.03$. Using Equation 8.20,

$0.03 = Z_{\alpha/2} \sqrt{\dfrac{(0.61)(0.39)}{100} + \dfrac{(0.54)(0.46)}{100}} = Z_{\alpha/2}(0.0697)$

$Z_{\alpha/2} = 0.03/0.0697 = 0.43$. This gives a 33.28% confidence level.

50. (a) $n = 423$ (b) $n = 601$ (c) Using $Z = 2.33$, $n = 543$

52. $n = 752$

54.

Standard Error of the Mean	3
Degrees of Freedom	15
t Value	2.131450856
Interval Half Width	6.394352567

CONFIDENCE INTERVAL	
Interval Lower Limit	143.61
Interval Upper Limit	156.39

It is recommended that he stock 157 gallons.

56. Using PHStat,

DATA	
Sample Standard Deviation	24.43925414
Sample Mean	136.22
Sample Size	50
Confidence Level	95%
Standard Error of the Mean	3.456232466
Degrees of Freedom	49
t Value	2.009574018
Interval Half Width	6.945554964

CONFIDENCE INTERVAL	
Interval Lower Limit	129.27
Interval Upper Limit	143.17

58. $(0.62 - 0.57) \pm 1.96 \sqrt{\dfrac{(0.62)(0.38)}{225} + \dfrac{(0.57)(0.43)}{210}}$ or $-.04136$ up to $.14295$

60. 6.0553 up to 13.9447

62. (a) $X = 3.375$ and $s^2 = 0.4993$ (b) $p = 3/8 = 0.375$

CHAPTER 9

2. $H_0 : T_B \le T_G$ $H_1 : T_B > T_G$ Bush with more votes
4. $H_0 : \mu_A \le \mu_B$ $H_1 : \mu_A > \mu_B$ Higher mean after the change
6. Test statistic is -1.8; reject H_0 at 10% level.
8. Test statistic is -3.33; reject H_0 at levels above 0.04%.
10. .0008
12. .0004
14. (a) No   (b) Yes
16. Test statistic is 1.741; fail to reject H_0 at 5% level.
18. Test statistic is -3.189; reject H_0 at 5% level.
20. Test statistic is 1.79; p-value $= 0.0367$; reject H_0.
22. $Z = -1.2649$; p-value $= 0.2076$; fail to reject H_0.
24. $Z = 0.8485$; p-value $= 0.1977$
26. $Z = -1.8676$; p-value $= 0.0307$; reject H_0.
28. (a) $s^2 = 5.1556$ (b)   test statistic is 20.6224; reject H_0 at the 5% level.
30. $x^2 = 26.4556$; fail to reject at 5% level
32. $t = 2.239$; reject H_0 at levels in excess of 3%
34. $t = 2.0417$; p-value $= 0.043$
36. $Z = 12.96$; reject H_0
38. $t = -1.90$; p-value $= 0.0616$
40. $t = 1.275$; fail to reject at 10% level
42. $Z = -1.466$; fail to reject at 5% level
44. $Z = -8.216$; reject H_0
46. $Z = -18.44$; reject H_0
48. $F = 7.095$; reject H_0 at 5% level
50. $F = 1.57$; fail to reject at 5% level
52. Power $= 0.3897$
54. $\beta = 0.8599$
56. Power $= 0.985$
58. (a) 0.0082   (b) 0.1151   (c) 0.6554
64. (a) False   (b) True   (c) True   (d) False   (e) False
     (f) True   (g) False
66. (a) Test statistic is -1.02; fail to reject H_0 at 5% level.
     (b) Test statistic is 154.19; fail to reject H_0 at 5% level.
68. (a) 0.0228   (b) 0.0014   (c) (i) smaller (ii) smaller
     (d) (i) smaller (ii) larger
70. Test statistic $= -.39$; p-value $= 0.6966$
72. Test statistic is 2.36; reject H_0 at 5% level
74. Test statistic is 2.217; reject H_0 at 10% level
76. Test statistic $= 1.76$; p-value $=.0784$
78. Test statistic is $-.37$; fail to reject H_0 at 10% level
80. Test statistic is 3.33; reject H_0 at 5% level

82. Test statistic is -2.30; p-value $= 0.0107$

84. (a) Test statistic is -1.20; fail to reject H_0 at 5% level
    (b) Test statistic is 0.93; fail to reject H_0 at 5% level

86. Test statistic is -1.19; fail to reject H_0 at 1% level

88. Test statistic $= -1.65$; p-value $= .0495$

90. No

92. $H_0 : \mu \le 100$ $H_1 : \mu > 100$ $\overline{X} = 101.19$ fail to reject H_0

96. $H_0 : W \le 3000$; $H_1 : W > 3000$, $\overline{X} = 3{,}050 > 3{,}041$ reject H_0

98. $H_0 : \mu \le 40$; $H_1 : \mu > 40$, $\overline{X} = 49.73 > 42.86$ reject H_0

CHAPTER 10

2. (a) $-.4066$
   (b) Test statistic is -1.476; fail to reject H_0 at 10% level.

4. Sample correlation is .057; test statistic .22 fail to reject H_0.

6. Test statistic is 2.073; reject at 2.5% level.

8. The estimated model provides the best coefficients for the population model given the sample data.

10. The constant represents an adjustment for the estimated model and not the number sold when the price is zero.

12. (a) $\hat{y} = 644.5 - 42.58x$ (b) -42.58

14. (a) $\hat{y} = 1.89 + 0.0896x$ (b) 0.0906%

16. $\hat{y} = -0.23 + 1.08x$

18. $\hat{y} = 2.88 + 0.51x$

22. $\beta = -2.03$ $R^2 = 0.1653$ $r = -.4066$

24. (a) $\hat{y} = 0.0449 - .2243x$
    (b) $SST = 1.1$ $SSR = 0.713$ $SSE = 0.387$
    (c) $R^2 = .648$

26. (a) $\hat{y} = -11.5 + 0.402x$ (c) $R^2 = .60$ (d) $r = 0.77$

28. (a) 162.4   (b) 41.19   (c) $-55.2 < \beta_1 < 30.0$

30. (a) $S_e^2 = 0.4124$ (b) $S_b^2 = 0.000299$
    (c) 95% Interval $0.05382 < \beta_1 < 0.1254$

32. $\hat{y} = 135.69 - 5.9x$, $S_b^2 = 0.3316$

34. (a) $\hat{y} = 97.2 - 58.4x$ (b) $-67.3 < \beta < -49.5$ (c) No

36. Test statistic is 3.002; reject at 2.5% level

40. Test statistic is 0.48; fail to reject H_0 at 10% level

42. (a) 440   (b) $404 < y_{n+1} < 476$, $423 < y_{n+1} < 457$

44. $-.35 < y_{n+1} < .44$, $-.07 < y_{n+1} < .16$

46. $10.1 < y_{n+1} < 23.2$, $7.8 < y_{n+1} < 25.4$

52. $T = 3.232$; reject H_0 at 1% level

54. $T = 2.522$; reject H_0 at 2% level

56. $\hat{y} = 76.75 + 0.425x$

58. (a) $\hat{y} = -8.5 + 9.03x$ (c) $R^2 = 0.4194$

60. (a) $R^2 = 0.3092$ (b) $s_e^2 = 10.21$ $S_{b_1}^2 = 0.1776$ $t = 19.93$

62. (a) $r = 0.8485$ (b) $t = 6.8031$ (c) 0.0691

64. (b) Econ GPA $= 1.48 + 0.0293$ satverb; Econ GPA $= 1.36 + 0.0705$ Acteng

66. (a) Deaths $= 0.283 - 0.184$ propurb; deaths $= -0.671 + 0.145$ ruspeed

68. (a) Retsal84 $= 2127 + 0.278$ perinc84
    (b) Decrease by 278
    (c) At $1000 above the mean, 5814 ± 203.6

CHAPTER 11

2. All else being equal, an increase of one unit in change in equity purchases leads to expected increase of .057 unit in change in stock price. All else being equal, an increase of one unit in change in equity sales leads to expected decrease of .065 unit in change in stock price.

4. (a) All else being equal, one extra meal per week leads to extra expected weight gain of .653 pound; one extra hour exercise per week leads to extra expected weight loss of 1.345 pounds; one extra beer per week leads to extra expected weight gain of .613 pound.

   (b) No

6. (a) salesmw2 = –647,363 + 19,895 priclec2 + 2.35 numcust2

   (b) salesmw2 = –410,202 + 2.20 numcust2

   (c) salesmw2 = 2,312,260 – 165,275 priclec2 + 56.1 degrday2

   (d) salesmw2 = 293,949 + 326 Yd872 + 58.4 degrday2

8. (a) horspwr = 23.5 + 0.0154 weight + 0.157 displace

   (b) horspwr = 16.7 + 0.0163 weight + 0.105 displace + 2.57 cylinder

   (c) horspwr = 93.6 + 0.00203 weight + 0.165 displace – 1.24 milpgal

   (d) horspwr = 98.1 – 0.00032 weight + 0.175 displace – 1.32 milpgal + 0.000138 price

10. (a) .456; 45.6% of variability in milk consumption in the sample is explained by its linear relation with the independent variables.

    (b) .416

    (c) .675 = sample correlation between observed and predicted values of milk consumption.

12. (a) Y profit = 1.55 – 0.000120 X_2 offices

    (b) X_1 revenue = –0.078 + 0.000543 X_2 offices

    (c) Y profit = 1.33 – 0.169 X_1 revenue

    (d) X_2 offices = 957 + 1631 X_1 revenue

    (e) Using the residuals obtained from a, b: r = .6731

    (f) Using the residuals obtained from c, d: r = –.8562

14. (a) Test statistic is 2.261; can reject H_0 at 2.5% level, but not at 1% level.

    (b) $.54 < \beta_2 < 1.74$, $.42 < \beta_2 < 1.86$, $.17 < \beta_2 < 2.11$

16. (a) Test statistic is –.428; cannot reject H_0 at 20% level.

    (b) Test statistic is 13.06; reject H_0 at 1% level.

18. (a) All else being equal, an extra $1 in mean per capita personal income leads to an expected extra $.04 of net revenue per capita from the lottery.

    (b) $.2359 < \beta_2 < 1.5185$

    (c) Test statistic is –1.383; can reject H_0 at 10% level, but not at 5% level.

20. (a) $.18 < \beta_1 < .22$

    (b) Test statistic is –1.19; cannot reject H_0 at 10% level.

22. (a) $.0173 < \beta_5 < .0817$

    (b) Test statistic is .617; cannot reject H_0 at 20% level.

    (c) Test statistic is 2.108; can reject H_0 at 5% level, but not at 2% level.

24. (a) Test statistic is 82.0; can reject H_0 at 1% level.

26. (a) Test statistic is 11.31; can reject H_0 at 1% level.

28. Test statistic is 6.24; can reject H_0 at 1% level.

30. Test statistic is 217; can reject H_0 at 1% level.

34. 10.6 pounds

36. 794,000 worker hours

38. Average cost versus number of units produced.

42. (a) A 1% increase in median income leads to an expected .68% increase in store size.

    (b) Test statistic is 8.83; can reject H_0 at .51% level.

44. Log $y_t = -4.07 + 1.3593 \log x_{1_t} + 0.1009 \log x_{2_t}$

    $R^2 = 0.997$

48. (a) All else being equal, expected selling price is higher by \$3,219 if house has a fireplace.

    (b) All else being equal, expected selling price is higher by \$2,005 if house has brick siding.

    (c) $1,363 < \beta_4 < 5,075$

    (d) Test statistic is 2,611; can reject H_0 at .5% level.

50. $b_0 = 6.512$ $b_1 = 3.502$ $b_2 = 0.491$ $b_3 = 10.327$

    $R^2 = 0.356$ $F_{3,46} = 8.48$

52. $y_i = 1.9968 + 0.0099x_i + 0.0763x_{2_i} - 0.1365x_{3_i} + 0.0636x_{4_i} + 0.1379x_{5_i}$

    $R^2 = 0.2646$

54. $F = 25.62$; reject H_0

60. $Y = 2.9694 - 0.0045x_1 + 0.2188x_2$; $Y = -6.54 + 0.0268x_1 - 0.000015x_1$

62. $Y = -1158.37 + 0.252x_1, -19.56x_2$

64. Given the assumptions the estimators are the most efficient linear unbiased estimators.

66. (a) False   (b) False   (c) True   (d) False   (e) True

68. This could occur with high multicollinearity.

70. (b) $R^2 = .766$ (c) C.I. $3.816 \pm 1.67(2.063)$ (d) $t = -0.29$; cannot reject H_0

74. $F = 5.804$; reject H_0 at 1% level.

76. (a) $0.0974 \pm 2.819(0.0215)$ (b) $t = 1.789$ (c) $R^2 = 0.9175$

    (d) $F = 122.33$ (e) $R = 0.9579$

78. (a) $t = -2.737$ (b) $t = -0.119$ (c) 17%   (d) $R = 0.4123$

86. Retsal85 = $3054 - 86.3$ Unemp84 + 0.254 perinc 84

    (b) Reduce sales by \$254.

    (c) No.

CHAPTER 12

4. (a) For any observation, the values of the dummy variables sum to one. Since the equation has an intercept term, there is perfect multicollinearity.

   (b) β_3 measures the expected difference between demand in the first and fourth quarters, all else being equal.

6. $y_t = 1751.62 + 0.3673x_{1_t} + 0.0533y_{t-1}$

   $t = 0.2619$; fail to reject.

8. $y_t = 1.65 + 0.228x_{1_t} + 0.95y_{t-1}$

   $R^2 = 0.959$

10. $y_t = 21,262 + 0.485x_{1_t} + 0.192y_{t-1}$

    $R^2 = 0.937$

12. Log $Y_t = 0.405 + 0.373 \log x_{t-1} + 0.558y_{t-1}$

    $R^2 = 0.996$

16. The multiple regression coefficient estimators are a function of the correlations between the x variables.

18. Likely to lead to serious specification bias

20. $e^2 = -63,310.41 + 13.75y$

    $nR^2 = 1.5299$; fail to reject.

22. $e^2 = 20.34 - .201y$ $nR^2 = 0.161$; fail to reject.

26. Fail to reject H_0 at 5% level.

28. $d = 1.72$; fail to reject H_0 at 1% level; test is inconclusive at 5% level.

30. Nothing beyond the appearance of a serious problem of autocorrelated errors

32. $D = .85$. Can reject hypothesis of no autocorrelation in the errors at 1% level. Serious specification error can lead to the appearance of autocorrelated errors.

36. The statement is not valid. The combination of single variable effects does not provide the combined effect of variables.

38. (a) Test statistic is 1.179; do not reject H_0 at 10% level.
    (b) Test statistic is .495; do not reject H_0 at 10% level
    (c) Muticollinearity.

40. Nothing has been learned because x_5 and x_6 are perfectly collinear.

42. (a) All else being equal, a 1% increase in value of new orders leads to an expected decrease of .82% in number of failures.
    (b) Reject this hypothesis at 1% level; autocorrelation in errors.
    (c) No   (d) .755

44. (a) $0.35 < \beta < .471$
    (b) $.253 increase in current period, further $.138 increase next period, $.075 increase two periods ahead, and so on. Total expected increase of $.557.
    (c) Test statistic is .56; cannot reject H_0 at usual levels.

46. $\text{Log } y_t = -2.14 + .9095 \log x_{1t} + 0.1945 x_{2t}$
    $d = 1.66$

48. $\text{Log } y_t = 0.4352 - 0.101 \log x_{1t} + 0.2365 \log x_{2t} + 0.6658 \log y_{t-1}$
    $d = 2.22$; reject H_0

50. $\text{Log } y_t = 2.72 - 0.0252 \log x_{2t} + 0.315 \log x_{2t} + 0.379 \log x_{3t}$
    $d = 1.73$
    H_0 : accepted at 1% and 5% levels.

52. (a) $\partial = 0.11$; reject H_0; positive autocorrelation
    (b) $h = 2.518$; do not reject H_0; no autocorrelation

CHAPTER 13

2. $n = 9$, $P(X \geq 8) = .0196$

4. $n = 57$, $S = 39$, $z = 2.65$, p-value $= .0040$

6. $n = 49$, $S = 29$, $z = 1.14$, p-value $= .2542$

8. $n = 9$, $T = 7.0$, $T_{.05} = 9$, p-value $= .038$

10. $T = 281$, $\mu_T = 410$, $\sigma_T^2 = 5535$, $z = -1.73$, p-value $= .0418$

12. $T = 1502$, $\mu_T = 1620$, $\sigma_T^2 = 43{,}470$, $z = -.57$, p-value $= .5686$

14. $R_1 = 137$, $n_1 = 10$, $n_2 = 10$,
    $U = 18$, $\mu_U = 50$, $\sigma_U^2 = 175$, $z = -2.42$, p-value $= .0078$

16. $R_1 = 171$, $n_1 = 14$, $n_2 = 10$, $U = 74$, $\mu_U = 70$, $\sigma_U^2 = 291.667$
    $z = .234$, p-value $= .4090$

18. $R_1 = 113.5$, $n_1 = 10$, $n_2 = 10$,
    $U = 41.5$, $\mu_U = 50$, $\sigma_U^2 = 175$, $z = -.64$, p-value $= .2611$

20. $R_1(\text{subject to}) = 9686$, $n_1 = 86$, $n_2 = 120$
    $U = 4375$, $\mu_U = 5160$, $\sigma_U^2 = 178{,}020$, $z = -1.8605$, p-value $= .0314$

22. (a) Spearman rank correlation $= .717$
    (b) $n = 10$, $r_{s,0.025} = .648$, $r_{s,0.01} = .745$

24. Less restrictive assumptions, less weight is placed on outliers.

26. $n = 9$, $P(2 \geq X \geq 7) = .1798$

28. $n = 78$, $z = -.79$, p-value $= .2148$

30. $n = 8$, $T = 11$, $T_{.10} = 9$

CHAPTER 14

2. $\chi^2 = 3.8667$, $\chi^2_{(4,.1)} = 7.78$. Therefore, fail to reject H_0 at the 10% level.

4. $\chi^2 = 1.505$, $\chi^2_{(2,.05)} = 5.99$. Therefore, do not reject H_0 at the 5% level.

6. $\chi^2 = 3.067$, $\chi^2_{(2,.10)} = 4.61$. Therefore, do not reject H_0 at the 10% level.

8. $\chi^2 = 5.1304$, $\chi^2_{(4,.10)} = 7.78$. Therefore, do not reject H_0 at the 10% level.

10. $\chi^2 = 51.6$, $\chi^2_{(3,.005)} = 12.84$. Therefore, reject H_0 at the .5% level.

12. $\chi^2 = 11.52$, $\chi^2_{(3,.01)} = 11.34$ $\chi^2_{(3,.005)} = 12.84$. Therefore, reject H_0 at the 1% level but not at the .5% level.

14. $B = 9.625$. Therefore, reject H_0 at the 5% level.

16. $B = 6.578$. Therefore, reject H_0 at the 5% level.

18. $\chi^2 = 6.209$, $\chi^2_{(2,.05)} = 5.99$. Therefore, reject H_0 at the 5% level.

20. (a) Contingency table:

	METHOD OF LEARNING ABOUT PRODUCT		
AGE	FRIEND	AD	COL. TOTAL
<21	30	20	50
21–35	60	30	90
35+	18	42	60
Row total	108	92	200

(b) $\chi^2 = 20.451$, $\chi^2_{(2,.005)} = 10.6$. Therefore, reject H_0 at the .5% level.

22. $\chi^2 = 1.607$, $\chi^2_{(1,.10)} = 2.71$. Therefore, do not reject H_0 at the 10% level.

24. $\chi^2 = 13.648$, $\chi^2_{(6,.05)} = 12.59$. Therefore, reject H_0 at the 5% level.

26. $\chi^2 = 22.963$, $\chi^2_{(2,.005)} = 10.60$. Therefore, reject H_0 at the .5% level.

28. $\chi^2 = 9.478$, $\chi^2_{(6,.10)} = 10.64$. Therefore, do not reject H_0 at the 10% level.

30. $\chi^2 = 20.000$, $\chi^2_{(4,.005)} = 14.86$. Therefore, reject H_0 at the .5% level.

32. $\chi^2 = 179.594$, $\chi^2_{(6,.005)} = 18.55$. Therefore, reject H_0 at the .5% level.

34. $\chi^2 = 8.222$, $\chi^2_{(4,.05)} = 9.49$. Therefore, do not reject H_0 at the 5% level.

36. $\chi^2 = 25.210$, $\chi^2_{(4,.005)} = 14.86$. Therefore, reject H_0 at the .5% level.

38. $\chi^2 = 33.148$, $\chi^2_{(1,.005)} = 7.88$. Therefore, reject H_0 at the .5% level.

40. $\chi^2 = 24.697$, $\chi^2_{(3,.005)} = 12.84$. Therefore, reject H_0 at the .5% level.

42. $\chi^2 = 9.2499$, $\chi^2_{(3,.05)} = 7.81$. Therefore, reject H_0 at the 5% level.

CHAPTER 15

2. (a) SSW = 1,342.0; SSG = 836.6; SST = 2,178.6

SOURCE	SS	DF	MS	F RATIO
Between Groups	836.6	3	278.867	3.95
Within Groups	1,342.0	19	70.632	
Total	2,178.6	22		

(b) H_0 is rejected at the 5% level but not at the 1% level.

4. (a)

SOURCE	SS	DF	MS	F RATIO
Between Groups	2.433	2	1.2165	0.40
Within Groups	36.100	12	3.0083	
Total	38.533	14		

(b) H_0 is not rejected at the 5% level.

6. (a)

SOURCE	SS	DF	MS	F RATIO
Between Groups	23.24	3	7.747	11.80
Within Groups	7.88	12	.657	
Total	31.12	15		

(b) H_0 is rejected at the 1% level.

8. (a)

SOURCE	SS	DF	MS	F RATIO
Between Groups	240.93	2	120.465	1.50
Within Groups	966.40	12	80.533	
Total	1,207.33	14		

(b) H_0 is not rejected at the 5% level.

10. (a) 9.666   (b) 1.302; 1.014; -2.316 (c) 2.316

12. Test statistic is 1.22; H_0 is not rejected at the 10% level.

14. Test statistic is 9.38; reject H_0 at the 1% level, but not at the .5% level.

16. Test statistic is .74; cannot reject H_0 at the 10% level.

18. Test statistic is 5.245; reject H_0 at the 10% level, but not at the 5% level.

20. (a) Equality of the centers at the population distributions
    (c) H_0 is not rejected at the 10% level.

22. (a)

SOURCE	SS	DF	MS	F RATIO
Fertilizers	200.67	2	100.335	4.56
Varieties	62.25	3	20.750	.94
Error	132.00	6	22.000	
Total	394.92	11		

(b) H_0 is not rejected at the 5% level.

24. (a)

SOURCE	SS	DF	MS	F RATIO
Regions	230.92	3	76.97	3.22
Colors	74.00	2	37.00	1.55
Error	143.33	6	23.89	
Total	448.25	11		

(b) H_0 is not rejected at the 5% level.

26. $G_1 = -3.5$, $B_2 = 1.25$, $\varepsilon_1 = -2.5$
28. (a)

SOURCE	SS	DF	MS	F RATIO
Agents	268	3	89.333	1.03
Houses	1,152	9	128.000	1.47
Error	2,352	27	87.111	
Total	3,772	39		

(b) H_0 is not rejected at the 5% level.

30. (a)

SOURCE	SS	DF	MS	F RATIO
Shows	95.2	2	47.6000	3.60
Regions	69.5	3	23.167	1.75
Error	79.3	6	13.217	
Total	244.0	11		

(b) H_0 is not rejected at the 5% level.

32. (a)

SOURCE	SS	DF	MS	F RATIO
Contestants	364.50	21	17.3571	19.27
Judges	.81	8	.1012	.11
Interaction	4.94	168	.0294	.03
Error	1,069.94	1,188	.9006	
Total	1,440.19	1,385		

(b) Null hypothesis of no difference between contestants is rejected at 1% level; the other two null hypotheses are not rejected at the 5% level.

34. (a)

SOURCE	SS	DF	MS	F RATIO
Subject Types	389.00	3	129.667	21.22
Test Types	57.56	2	28.78	4.71
Interaction	586.00	6	15.98	2.61
Error	146.67	24	6.111	
Total	1,179.23	35		

(b) H_0 is rejected at the 1% level.

36. (a) There is no interaction between student year and dormitory.
    (b)

SOURCE	SS	DF	MS	F RATIO
Dormitory	20.3438	3	6.7813	4.9453
Year	10.5938	3	3.5313	2.5752
Error	34.2813	25	1.3713	
Total	65.2189	31		

(c) Mean ratings are the same for all four dormitories.
   $F_{3,25,0.01} = 4.68 < 4.9453$ reject H_0 at the 1% level.
(d) Mean rating is the same for all four student years.
   $F_{3,25,0.05} = 2.99 > 2.5752$ fail to reject H_0 at the 5% level.

38.

SOURCE	SS	DF	MS	F RATIO
Can Color	243.2500	2	121.625	11.3140
Region	354.0000	3	118.000	10.9767
Interaction	189.7500	6	31.6250	2.9419
Error	129.0000	12	10.7500	
Total	916.000	23		

40. One-way ANOVA examines the effect of a single factor. Two-way ANOVA recognizes situations in which more than one factor may be significant.

42.

SOURCE	SS	DF	MS	F RATIO
Between Groups	5,165	2	2,578	21.45
Within Groups	120,802	1,005	120.2	
Total	125,967	1,007		

H_0 is rejected at the 1% level.

44. (a)

SOURCE	SS	DF	MS	F RATIO
Between Groups	221.34	3	73.780	25.60
Within Groups	374.66	130	2.882	
Total	596.00	133		

H_0 is rejected at the 1% level.

46.

SOURCE	SS	DF	MS	F RATIO
Between Groups	11,438.3028	2	5,716.15	.79
Within Groups	109,200.0000	15	7,280.0000	
Total	120,638.3028	17		

H_0 is not rejected at the 5% level.

48. Test statistic is 5.05; H_0 is not rejected at the 10% level.

52.

SOURCE	SS	DF	MS	F RATIO
Consumers	37,571.5	124	302.966	1.35
Brands	32,987.3	2	16,493.65	73.43
Error	55,701.7	248	224.64	
Total	126,269.5	374		

H_0 is rejected at the 1% level.

54. (a)

SOURCE	SS	DF	MS	F RATIO
SAT Scores	.82667	2	.41333	24.79
Incomes	.00667	2	.00333	.20
Error	.06667	4	.01667	
Total	.9001	8		

(b) H_0 is not rejected at the 5% level.
(c) H_0 is rejected at the 1% level.

56. (a) 3.3   (b) 0   (c) .0667   (d) .1333

58.

SOURCE	SS	DF	MS	F RATIO
Prices	.178	2	.0890	.09
Countries	4.365	2	2.1825	2.32
Interaction	1.262	4	.3155	.33
Error	93.330	99	.9427	
Total	99.135	107		

None of the three null hypotheses is rejected at the 5% level.

60. (a)

SOURCE	SS	DF	MS	F RATIO
SAT Scores	2.20111	2	1.10056	66.03
Incomes	.01778	2	.00889	.53
Interaction	.10223	4	.02556	1.53
Error	.15000	9	.01667	
Total	2.47112	17		

(b) H_0 is not rejected at the 5% level.
(c) H_0 is rejected at the 1% level.
(d) H_0 is not rejected at the 5% level.

CHAPTER 16

2. Various answers
4. Various answers
6. (a) $\hat{\sigma} = 5.6517$
   (b) CL = 192.6, LCL = 186.2044, UCL = 198.9956
   (c) CL = 5.42, LCL = .6504, UCL = 10.1896
8. (a) $\hat{\sigma} = 1.2746$
   (b) CL = 19.86, LCL = 18.507, UCL = 21.213
   (c) CL = 1.23, LCL = .2214, UCL = 2.2386
10. (a) $\bar{\bar{x}} = 149.98$ (b) $\bar{s} = 5.989$ (c) $\hat{\sigma} = 6.2062$
    (d) CL = 149.98, LCL = 143.3921, UCL = 156.5679
    (e) The $\bar{X}$ chart shows a process where the level is under statistical control.
    (f) CL = 5.989, LCL = 1.078, UCL = 10.9

12. (a) 175.6449, 209.5551. These values lie within the tolerance limits.
  (b) $C_p = 1.327$. The process is not capable since $C_p < 1.33$.
  (c) $C_{pk} = 1.321$. The process is not capable since $C_{pk} < 1.33$.

14. (a) 16.0362, 23.6838. These limits are beyond the tolerances set by management.
  (b) $C_p = .523$. The process is not capable since $C_p < 1.33$.
  (c) $C_{pk} = .486$. The process is not capable since $C_{pk} < 1.33$.

16. (a) 13.5691, 26.1109. These limits are beyond the tolerances set by management.
  (b) $C_p = .638$. The process is not capable since $C_p < 1.33$.
  (c) $C_{pk} = .612$. The process is not capable since $C_{pk} < 1.33$.

18. CL = .016, LCL = 0, UCL = .0328

20. (a) $\bar{p} = .051$, CL = .051, LCL = .0215, UCL = .0805
  (b) p-chart. No evidence that the process is out of statistical control.

22. (a) $\bar{c} = 5.6$ (b) CL = 5.6, LCL = 0, UCL = 12.70
  (c) c chart. No evidence of a process that is out of statistical control.

24. (a) $\bar{c} = 208/15 = 13.8667$ (b) CL = 13.8667, LCL = 2.6953, UCL = 25.0381
  (c) No evidence of a process going out of control; keep monitoring the process.

26. (a) Meaningless, process is not stable   (b) Meaningless, process is not stable

28. (a) See Exercise 16.22   (b) See Exercise 16.23   (c) See Exercise 16.24

30. There are two types of errors that can be made, 1) identifying a special or assignable cause of variation when there is none and 2) ignoring a special cause by assuming that it is due to natural variability. The use of the three sigma limits as control limits was set by Shewhart as an appropriate balance between the two.

32. (a) $\bar{\bar{x}} = 350.416$ (b) $\bar{s} = 5.602$ (c) $\hat{\sigma} = 5.8052$
  (d) CL = 350.416, LCL = 344.2538, UCL = 356.5782
  (f) CL = 5.602, LCL = 1.0084, UCL = 10.1956
  (h) i) 333.0004, 367.8316
     ii) $C_p = 1.435$. Therefore, the process is capable.
     iii) $C_{pk} = 1.412$. Therefore, the process is capable.

34. (a) $\bar{c} = 15$ (b) CL = 15, LCL = 3.381, UCL = 26.619
  (c) No evidence that the process is out of control

36. (a) Common cause—affects all workers within the process
  (b) Common cause—affects all workers within the process
  (c) Assignable cause   (d) Assignable cause   (e) Assignable cause

38. (a) Machine 1 – X bar – s chart: Machine 1 shows no evidence of being "out of statistical control."
  (b) Machine 2 – X bar – s chart: Likewise, Machine 2 shows no evidence of being "out of statistical control."
  (c) Machine 1 – capability analysis: $C_p = .44$; $C_{pk} = .14$
  (d) Machine 2 – capability analysis: $C_p = .80$; $C_{pk} = .72$
  (e) Neither machine is capable of meeting specifications. Note that Machine 1 has greater variability than Machine 2.

40. X bar chart for TOC data: All data points are within the control limits. No pattern analysis rule has been violated.

CHAPTER 17

2. (a) 100, 102.5, 99.3, 98.2, 100.0, 99.6, 100.0, 99.3, 99.3, 100.7, 110.7, 106.1
  (b) 101.8, 104.4, 101.1, 100, 101.8, 101.5, 101.8, 101.1, 101.1, 102.6, 112.7, 108.0

4. (a) 100, 105.4, 109.6, 112.7, 115.5, 117.2
  (b) 100, 104.8, 110.5, 112.1, 115.7, 117.5

6. A price index for energy is helpful in that it allows us to say something about price movements over time for a group of commodities, namely, energy prices. A weighted index of prices allows one to compare the cost of a group of products across periods.

8. $R = 7$; H_0 is rejected only at high significance levels.

10. $R = 5$; H_0 is rejected against one-sided alternative at 10% level, $p = 0.0951$.

12. (a) $R = 7$; test statistic is -3.08; H_0 is rejected, $p = 0.0021$.

16. Values for years 3 and 4 are 7.8 and 7.7.

22. All forecasts are 1.36.

24. All forecasts are 5.2.

28. Simple exponential smoothing is appropriate for only nonseasonal and nontrend series. Given these conditions the forecast estimates are not absurd, but will differ from observed values.

30. Forecast for years 25–27, 11.20, 11.19, 11.19

32. 6.6, 6.3

34. $\hat{x}_n = 304.11$ $T_n = 2.61$ forecast 7:1, 367.88, 8:4, 299.64

36. $X_t = 18.515 - .032x_{t-1} + a_t$; 17.9, 17.9, 17.9

38. Fail to reject H_0 at 10% level.

40. (a) Order 1   (b) 1,331, 1,369, 1,402

42. $\hat{X}_{n+1} = X_n, \hat{X}_{n+2} = X_n, \hat{X}_{n+n} = X_n$.

44. (a) $I_2 = 100.85$ (b) $I_2 = 96.56$

46. Values of a time series can be made up of trend, seasonal, cyclical and random components. For example, total retail sales in the U.S. tend to have a seasonal component with much larger retail sales in the November/December months than others due to gift buying for the holiday season. Strong trend components tend to exist in total personal income in the U.S. since the factors that influence income change slowly over time. Unemployment rates in the U.S. show strong cyclical behavior due to the ups and downs of the business cycle.

48. This will very likely not be a successful strategy since the manager could use the trend and seasonal patterns that exist in the monthly data to generate more accurate forecasts.

54. All forecasts are 520.89

56. Forecasts are 0.638, 0.494, 0.424, 0.417

58. $\hat{X}_{n+1} = .021 + 1.74(13.147) - .74(13.217) = 13.116$
$\hat{X}_{n+2} = 13.114, \hat{X}_{n+3} = 13.133, \hat{X}_{n+4} = 13.168$

CHAPTER 18

2. Answers should refer to steps outlined in Figure 18.1.

6. Answers should deal with issues such as (a) the identification of the correct population, (b) selection (nonresponse) bias, (c) response bias

10. Within Minitab, go to Calc → Make Patterned Data . . . in order to generate a simple set of numbers of size "n". Then use Calc → Random Data . . . Sample from Columns . . . in order to generate a simple random sample of size "n".

14. $\bar{x} = 9.7, s = 6.2, \hat{\sigma}_{\bar{x}} = .7519, 8.2262$ up to 11.1738

16. $\hat{\sigma}_{\bar{x}} = .6936, 5.4904$ up to 9.0696 using $z = 2.58$

18. $\hat{\sigma}_{\bar{x}}^2 = \dfrac{(s)^2}{n} \dfrac{N-n}{N} = \dfrac{s^2}{n}\left[1 - \dfrac{n}{N}\right] = s^2\left[\dfrac{1}{n} - \dfrac{1}{N}\right]$

20. 95% confidence interval: $95{,}849.2706 < N\mu < 113{,}135.9294$

22. $\bar{x} = 4.0857$, 90% confidence interval: $403.2307 < N\mu < 577.3407$

24. $p = .56, \sigma_p = .0435$, 90% confidence interval: .4884 up to .6316

26. $p = .3875, \sigma_p = .0493$, 90% confidence interval: .3064 up to .4686
$128.688 < Np < 196.812$ or between 129 and 197 students

28. (a) $\bar{x}_3 = 43.3$, $\hat{\sigma}^2_{\bar{x}_3} = 2.2984$, 90% confidence interval: 40.806 up to 45.794

    (b) $\bar{x}_{st} = 37.3306$

    (c) $\hat{\sigma}^2_{\bar{x}_1} = .9286$, $\hat{\sigma}^2_{\bar{x}_2} = 1.6785$, $\hat{\sigma}^2_{\bar{x}_{st}} = .6239$

        90% confidence interval: 36.0313 up to 38.6299

        95% confidence interval: 35.7825 up to 38.8787

30. (a) $\hat{\sigma}^2_{\bar{x}_1} = .0199$; 2.8435 up to 3.3965

    (b) $\hat{\sigma}^2_{\bar{x}_2} = .0134$; 3.1431 up to 3.5969

    (c) $\hat{\sigma}^2_{\bar{x}_{st}} = .0087$; $\bar{x}_{st} = 3.2339$, 3.0513 up to 3.4166

32. (a) $N\bar{x}_{st} = 81720$

    (b) $\hat{\sigma}^2_{\bar{x}_1} = 144.15$, $\hat{\sigma}^2_{\bar{x}_2} = 63.7156$, $\hat{\sigma}^2_{\bar{x}_3} = 31.9078$

        $\hat{\sigma}^2_{\bar{x}_{st}} = 22.4354$, 95% confidence interval:

        $77542.3153 < N\mu < 85897.6847$

34. (a) $p_{st} = .3467$

    (b) $\hat{\sigma}^2_{p_1} = .0057$, $\hat{\sigma}^2_{p_2} = .0051$, $\hat{\sigma}^2_{st} = .0031$

        90% confidence interval: .2550 up to .4383,

        95% confidence interval: .2375 up to .4559

36. (a) $n_3 = 55.52(56)$ (b) $n_3 = 67.95(68)$

38. (a) $n_1 = 54.43(55)$ (b) $n_1 = 59.09(60)$

40. (a) $n_2 = 73.91(74)$ (b) $n_2 = 87.71(88)$

44. $\sigma_p = .0243$, $n = 210.33(211)$

46. (a) $\sigma_{\bar{x}} = 255.1020$, $\Sigma N_j \sigma_j^2 = 15424 \times 10^7$, $n = 497.47(498)$

        $\Sigma N_j \sigma_j = 24760000$, $n = 470.78(471)$

48. (a) $\bar{x}_c = 91.6761$

    (b) $\hat{\sigma}^2_{\bar{x}_c} = 66.409$, 99% confidence interval: 70.692 up to 112.6602

50. (a) $p_c = .4507$

    (b) $\hat{\sigma}^2_{p_c} = .0013$, 95% confidence interval: .38 up to .5214

52. $\sigma_{\bar{x}} = 3039.5$, $n = 126.34(127)$. Additional sample observations needed = 107.

54. $\sigma_{\bar{x}} = 10.2$, $n = 159.35(160)$. Additional sample observations needed = 130.

56. Discussion question—various answers

58. (a) $\bar{x} = 74.7$, $s = 11.44$, $\hat{\sigma}^2_{\bar{x}} = 11.633$

        90% confidence interval: 69.089 up to 80.311

    (b) Wider

60. (a) $p = .623$, $\hat{\sigma}_p = .0015$, 90% confidence interval: .559 up to .687

    (b) If the sample information is not random, conclusions may be biased

62. (a) $\bar{x}_{st} = 11.5845$, $\hat{\sigma}^2_{\bar{x}_1} = .7321$, $\hat{\sigma}^2_{\bar{x}_2} = 1.9053$, $\hat{\sigma}^2_{\bar{x}_3} = 1.7508$,

        $\hat{\sigma}^2_{\bar{x}_{st}} = .4671$, 99% confidence interval for subdivision 1: 6.997 up to 11.403

    (b) 99% confidence interval for all managers: 9.8247 up to 13.3444

64. $p_1 = .45$, $p_2 = .75$, $p_{st} = .63$, $\hat{\sigma}^2_{p_1} = .0109$, $\hat{\sigma}^2_{p_2} = .0088$

    $\hat{\sigma}^2_{p_{st}} = .0049$, 90% confidence interval: .5147 up to .7453

66. (a) $n_1 = 16$

    (b) $n_1 = 21.54(22)$

68. $\sigma_{\bar{x}} = 1215.8$, $n = 75.28(76)$

70. (a) $\bar{x}_c = 62.7607$, $\hat{\sigma}^2_c = 23.1736$

        95% confidence interval: 53.3255 up to 72.1959

    (b) $p_c = .55$, $\hat{\sigma}_c = .0038$, 95% confidence interval: .4292 up to .6708

CHAPTER 19

2. *D* is dominated by *C*. Hence *D* is inadmissible.

4. (a)

	LOW	MODERATE	HIGH	MINIMUM
A	100,000	350,000	900,000	100,000
B	150,000	400,000	700,000	150,000
C	250,000	400,000	600,000	250,000

Maximin criterion selects *C*.

(b)

	LOW	MODERATE	HIGH	MAX. REGRET
A	150,000	50,000	0	150,000
B	100,000	0	200,000	200,000
C	0	0	300,000	300,000

Minimax regret criterion selects *A*.

6.

	MAX. REGRET
A	30,000
B	40,000
C	60,000
D	Inadmissible
E	40,000

Minimax regret criterion selects *A*.

8. Let us assume that we have a situation with two states of nature and two actions. Let both actions be admissible. The payoff matrix is:

	S_1	S_2
a_1	M_{11}	M_{12}
a_2	M_{21}	M_{22}

Then action a_1 will be chosen by both maximin and minimax regret criteria if for:
$M_{11} > M_{21}$ and $M_{12} < M_{22}$ $(M_{11} - M_{21}) > (M_{22} - M_{12})$.

10. (a)

	OFFERED BETTER POSITION	NOT OFFERED BETTER POSITION
Interview	4500	−500
Don't Interview	0	0

(b) EMV(Interview) = $(0.05)(4500) + (0.95)(-500) = -250$
EMV(Don't Interview) = 0
Optimal Action: Don't Interview

12. (a) EMV(CD) = 1200
    EMV(Low-risk stock fund) = $(0.2)(4300) + (0.5)(1200) + (0.3)(-600) = 1280$
    EMV(High-risk stock fund) = $(0.2)(6600) + (0.5)(800) + (0.3)(-1500) = 1270$
    Optimal Action: Low-risk stock fund

14. (a) (i) False   (ii) True   (iii) True
    (b) No

16. (a) EMV(New) = $(0.4)(130,000) + (0.4)(60,000) + (0.2)(-10,000) = 74,000$
    EMV(Old) = $(0.4)(30,000) + (0.4)(70,000) + (0.2)(90,000) = 58,000$
    Optimal Action: New Center

18. (a) EMV(A) = $30,000 + 350,000p + 900,000(0.7 - p) = 660,000 - 550,000p$
    EMV(B) = $45,000 + 400,000p + 700,000(0.7 - p) = 535,000 - 300,000p$
    EMV(C) = $75,000 + 400,000p + 600,000(0.7 - p) = 495,000 - 200,000p$
    EMV(D) = $75,000 + 400,000p + 550,000(0.7 - p) = 460,000 - 150,000p$
    EMV(A) = $660 - 550p > 535 - 300p =$ EMV(B) if $p < 0.5$
    EMV(A) = $660 - 550p > 495 - 200p =$ EMV(C) if $p < 0.471$
    EMV(A) = $660 - 550p > 460 - 150p =$ EMV(D) if $p < 0.5$
    For $p < 0.471$, the EMV criterion chooses A.
    (b) EMV(A) = $170,000 + 0.3a > 415,000 =$ EMV(B) > EMV(C) > EMV(D) when A > 816,667

20. (a) EMV(check) = $0.8(20,000 - 1,000) + 0.2(20,000 - 1,000 - 2,000) = 18,600$
    EMV(not check) = $0.8(20,000) + 0.2(12,000) = 18,400$
    Optimal action: check the process
    (b) EMV(check) = $19,000p + 17,000(1 - p) > 20,000p + 12,000(1 - p)$ when $p < 5/6$

22. (a)

EXTRA ORDERING	DEMAND				
	6	7	8	9	10
0	0	-10	-20	-30	-40
1	-20	20	10	0	-10
2	-40	0	40	30	20
3	-60	-20	20	60	50
4	-80	-40	0	40	80

(b)

EXTRA ORDERING	DEMAND					EMV
	6	7	8	9	10	
0	0(0.1)	-10(0.3)	-20(0.3)	-30(0.2)	-40(0.1)	-19
1	-20(0.1)	20(0.3)	10(0.3)	0(0.2)	-10(0.1)	6
2	-40(0.1)	0(0.3)	40(0.3)	30(0.2)	20(0.1)	16
3	-60(0.1)	-20(0.3)	20(0.3)	60(0.2)	50(0.1)	11
4	-80(0.1)	-40(0.3)	0(0.3)	40(0.2)	80(0.1)	-4

Optimal Action: Order 2 extra cars.

24. (a) Action a_1 is taken if $M_{11}p + M_{12}(1 - p) > M_{21}p + M_{22}(1 - p)$ or if $p(M_{11} - M_{21}) > (1 - p)(M_{22} - M_{12})$
    (b) Action a_1 inadmissible implies that a_1 will be chosen only if $p > 1$.
    In short, for (a) to be true both payoffs of a_1 cannot be less than the corresponding payoffs of a_2.

26. (a) Optimal action: A (see Question 13)

(b) $P(L \mid P) = \dfrac{(0.5)(0.3)}{(0.5)(0.3) + (0.3)(0.4) + (0.1)(0.3)} = \dfrac{0.15}{0.30} = 0.5$

$P(M \mid P) = \dfrac{0.12}{0.3} = 0.4$

$P(H \mid P) = \dfrac{0.03}{0.3} = 0.1$

(c) EMV(A) = 280,000, EMV(B) = 305,000, EMV(C) = 345,000
Optimal action: C

(d) $P(L \mid F) = \dfrac{(0.3)(0.3)}{(0.3)(0.3) + (0.4)(0.4) + (0.2)(0.3)} = \dfrac{0.09}{0.31} = 0.2903$

$P(M \mid F) = 0.5161$
$P(H \mid F) = 0.1935$

(e) EMV(A) = 383,815 EMV(B) = 385,435 EMV(C) = 395,115
Optimal action: C

(f) $P(L \mid G) = 0.1538$; $P(M \mid G) = 0.3077$; $P(H \mid G) = 0.5385$

(g) EMV(A) = 607,692, EMV(B) = 523,077, EMV(C) = 484,615
Optimal action: A

28. (a) $P(E \mid P) = 12/13 = 0.9231$, $P(\text{not } E \mid P) = 1/13 = 0.0769$
(b) EMV(S) = 50,000, EMV(R) = 114,615
Optimal action: Retain
(c) $P(E \mid N) = 0.25$, $P(\text{not } E \mid N) = 0.75$
(d) EMV(S) = 50,000, EMV(R) = 23,750
Optimal action: Sell
(e) Yes

30. (a) $P(2 \mid 10\%) = 0.01$, $P(1 \mid 10\%) = 0.18$, $P(0 \mid 10\%) = 0.81$
(b) $P(2 \mid 30\%) = 0.09$, $P(1 \mid 30\%) = 0.42$, $P(0 \mid 30\%) = 0.49$
(c)

PROB. OF STATES GIVEN	10% DEF	30% DEF
(i) 2 def	0.308	0.692
(ii) 1 def	0.632	0.368
(iii) 0 def	0.869	0.131

EMV OF ACTIONS GIVEN	CHECK	NOT CHECK
(i) 2 def	17,616	14,464
(ii) 1 def	18,264	17,056
(iii) 0 def	18,737	18,952

32. (b) Optimal action: Low-risk stock fund (see Question 19.12).
EVPI = 0.2(6600 − 4300) + 0.5(0) + 0.3(1200 − (−600)) = 1000

34. Optimal action: New center.
EVPI = 0.4(0) + 0.4(70,000 − 60,000) + 0.2(90,000 − (−10,000)) = 24,000

36. The expected value of sample information is $\sum_{i=1}^{M} P(A_i)V_i$ where $P(A_i) = \sum_{j=1}^{H} P(A_i \mid s_j)$.
For perfect information, $P(A_i \mid s_j) = 0$ for $i \neq j$ and $P(A_i \mid s_j) = 1$ for $i = j$, thus $P(A_i) = P(s_i)$.

38. EVSI = 0.3(345,000 − 280,000) + 0.31(395,115 − 383,815) + 0.39(0) = 23,003

40. Optimal action: Retain the patent.
EVSI = 0.42(0) + 0.52(50,000 − 23,750) = 13,650

42. (a) $\text{EVSI} = 0.11(-600 - (-910)) + 0.89(0) = 34.1$
    (b) $\text{EVSI} = 0.013(-600 - (-1540)) + 0.194(-600 - (-825)) + 0.793(0) = 55.87$
    (c) Difference $= 21.77$
    (d) None
    (e) 24.75

44. (a)

Payoff	$-10,000$	30,000	60,000	70,000	90,000	130,000
Utility	0	35	60	70	85	100

    (b) $\text{EU(New)} = 0.4(100) + 0.4(60) + 0.2(0) = 64$
        $\text{EU(Old)} = 0.4(35) + 0.4(70) + 0.2(85) = 59$
        Optimal action: New center.

46. $94,000p - 16,000(1 - p) = 0 \Rightarrow p = 16/110$

Payoff	$-160,000$	0	94,000
Utility	0	160/110	100

    $\text{Slope } (-16,000, 0) = \dfrac{160/110}{16,000} = 0.00009$

    $\text{Slope } (0, 94,000) = \dfrac{100 - 160/100}{94,000} = 0.00105$

    Contractor has a preference for risk.

48. (a) $P(s_1) = (0.3)(0.6) = 0.18$, $P(s_2) = 0.42$, $P(s_3) = 0.12$, $P(s_4) = 0.28$
    (b) $\text{EMV}(a_1) = 460$, $\text{EMV}(a_2) = 330$, $\text{EMV}(a_3) = 0$, $\text{EMV}(a_4) = 510$
        Optimal action: a_4
    (d) $\text{EVPI} = 0.18(250) + 0.42(150) + 0.12(100) + 0.28(300) = 204$
    (e) 79

LICENSE AGREEMENT AND LIMITED WARRANTY

READ THIS LICENSE CAREFULLY BEFORE USING THIS PACKAGE. BY USING THIS PACKAGE, YOU ARE AGREEING TO THE TERMS AND CONDITIONS OF THIS LICENSE. IF YOU DO NOT AGREE, DO NOT USE THE PACKAGE. PROMPTLY RETURN THE UNUSED PACKAGE AND ALL ACCOMPANYING ITEMS TO THE PLACE YOU OBTAINED. **THESE TERMS APPLY TO ALL LICENSED SOFTWARE ON THE DISK EXCEPT THAT THE TERMS FOR USE OF ANY SHAREWARE OR FREEWARE ON THE DISKETTES ARE AS SET FORTH IN THE ELECTRONIC LICENSE LOCATED ON THE DISK:**

1. GRANT OF LICENSE and OWNERSHIP: The enclosed computer programs and data ("Software") are licensed, not sold, to you by Prentice-Hall, Inc. ("We" or the "Company") in consideration of your purchase or adoption of the accompanying Company textbooks and/or other materials, and your agreement to these terms. We reserve any rights not granted to you. You own only the disk(s) but we and/or licensors own the Software itself. This license allows you to install, use and display the enclosed copy of the Software on individual computers in the computer lab designated for use by any students of a course requiring the accompanying Company textbook and only for as long as such textbook is a required text for such course, at a single campus or branch or geographic location of an educational institution, for academic use only, so long as you comply with the terms of this Agreement.

2. RESTRICTIONS: You may <u>not</u> transfer or distribute the Software or documentation to anyone else. You may <u>not</u> copy the documentation or the Software. You may *not* reverse engineer, disassemble, decompile, modify, adapt, translate, or create derivative works based on the Software or the Documentation. You may be held legally responsible for any copying or copyright infringement which is caused by your failure to abide by the terms of these restrictions.

3. TERMINATION: This license is effective until terminated. This license will terminate automatically without notice from the Company if you fail to comply with any provisions or limitations of this license. Upon termination, you shall destroy the Documentation and all copies of the Software. All provisions of this Agreement as to limitation and disclaimer of warranties, limitation of liability, remedies or damages, and our ownership rights shall survive termination.

4. LIMITED WARRANTY AND DISCLAIMER OF WARRANTY: Company warrants that for a period of 60 days from the date you purchase this Software (or purchase or adopt the accompanying textbook), the Software, when properly installed and used in accordance with the Documentation, will operate in substantial conformity with the description of the Software set forth in the Documentation, and that for a period of 30 days the disk(s) on which the Software is delivered shall be free from defects in materials and workmanship under normal use. The Company does <u>not</u> warrant that the Software will meet your requirements or that the operation of the Software will be uninterrupted or error-free. Your only remedy and the Company's only obligation under these limited warranties is, at the Company's option, return of the disk for a refund of any amounts paid for it by you or replacement of the disk. THIS LIMITED WARRANTY IS THE ONLY WARRANTY PROVIDED BY THE COMPANY AND ITS LICENSORS, AND THE COMPANY AND ITS LICENSORS DISCLAIM ALL OTHER WARRANTIES, EXPRESS OR IMPLIED, INCLUDING WITHOUT LIMITATION, THE IMPLIED WARRANTIES OF MERCHANTABILITY AND FITNESS FOR A PARTICULAR PURPOSE. THE COMPANY DOES NOT WARRANT, GUARANTEE OR MAKE ANY REPRESENTATION REGARDING THE ACCURACY, RELIABILITY, CURRENTNESS, USE, OR RESULTS OF USE, OF THE SOFTWARE.

5. LIMITATION OF REMEDIES AND DAMAGES: IN NO EVENT, SHALL THE COMPANY OR ITS EMPLOYEES, AGENTS, LICENSORS, OR CONTRACTORS BE LIABLE FOR ANY INCIDENTAL, INDIRECT, SPECIAL, OR CONSEQUENTIAL DAMAGES ARISING OUT OF OR IN CONNECTION WITH THIS LICENSE OR THE SOFTWARE, INCLUDING FOR LOSS OF USE, LOSS OF DATA, LOSS OF INCOME OR PROFIT, OR OTHER LOSSES, SUSTAINED AS A RESULT OF INJURY TO ANY PERSON, OR LOSS OF OR DAMAGE TO PROPERTY, OR CLAIMS OF THIRD PARTIES, EVEN IF THE COMPANY OR AN AUTHORIZED REPRESENTATIVE OF THE COMPANY HAS BEEN ADVISED OF THE POSSIBILITY OF SUCH DAMAGES. IN NO EVENT SHALL THE LIABILITY OF THE COMPANY FOR DAMAGES WITH RESPECT TO THE SOFTWARE EXCEED THE AMOUNTS ACTUALLY PAID BY YOU, IF ANY, FOR THE SOFTWARE OR THE ACCOMPANYING TEXTBOOK. SOME JURISDICTIONS DO NOT ALLOW THE LIMITATION OF LIABILITY IN CERTAIN CIRCUMSTANCES, THE ABOVE LIMITATIONS MAY NOT ALWAYS APPLY.

6. GENERAL: THIS AGREEMENT SHALL BE CONSTRUED IN ACCORDANCE WITH THE LAWS OF THE UNITED STATES OF AMERICA AND THE STATE OF NEW YORK, APPLICABLE TO CONTRACTS MADE IN NEW YORK, AND SHALL BENEFIT THE COMPANY, ITS AFFILIATES AND ASSIGNEES. This Agreement is the complete and exclusive statement of the agreement between you and the Company and supersedes all proposals, prior agreements, oral or written, and any other communications between you and the company or any of its representatives relating to the subject matter. If you are a U.S. Government user, this Software is licensed with "restricted rights" as set forth in subparagraphs (a)-(d) of the Commercial Computer-Restricted Rights clause at FAR 52.227-19 or in subparagraphs (c)(1)(ii) of the Rights in Technical Data and Computer Software clause at DFARS 252.227-7013, and similar clauses, as applicable.

Should you have any questions concerning this agreement or if you wish to contact the Company for any reason, please contact in writing: Director, Media Production

Pearson Education

1 Lake Street

Upper Saddle River, NJ 07458